EIGHTH EDITION

Programming iOS 11

Matt Neuburg

Beijing · Boston · Farnham · Sebastopol · Tokyo

Programming iOS 11, Eighth Edition

by Matt Neuburg

Copyright © 2018 Matt Neuburg. All rights reserved.

Printed in the United States of America.

Published by O'Reilly Media, Inc., 1005 Gravenstein Highway North, Sebastopol, CA 95472.

O'Reilly books may be purchased for educational, business, or sales promotional use. Online editions are also available for most titles (*http://oreilly.com/safari*). For more information, contact our corporate/institutional sales department: 800-998-9938 or *corporate@oreilly.com*.

Editor: Rachel Roumeliotis		**Cover Designer:** Randy Comer
Production Editor: Kristen Brown		**Interior Designer:** David Futato
Proofreader: O'Reilly Production Services		**Illustrator:** Matt Neuburg
Indexer: Matt Neuburg		

May 2011:	First Edition
March 2012:	Second Edition
March 2013:	Third Edition
December 2013:	Fourth Edition
December 2014:	Fifth Edition
November 2015:	Sixth Edition
November 2016:	Seventh Edition
November 2017:	Eighth Edition

Revision History for the Eighth Edition:

2017-12-06:   First release

See *http://oreilly.com/catalog/errata.csp?isbn=9781491999226* for release details.

The O'Reilly logo is a registered trademark of O'Reilly Media, Inc. *Programming iOS 11*, the cover image of a kingbird, and related trade dress are trademarks of O'Reilly Media, Inc.

Many of the designations used by manufacturers and sellers to distinguish their products are claimed as trademarks. Where those designations appear in this book, and O'Reilly Media, Inc., was aware of a trademark claim, the designations have been printed in caps or initial caps.

While the publisher and the author have used good faith efforts to ensure that the information and instructions contained in this work are accurate, the publisher and the author disclaim all responsibility for errors or omissions, including without limitation responsibility for damages resulting from the use of or reliance on this work. Use of the information and instructions contained in this work is at your own risk. If any code samples or other technology this work contains or describes is subject to open source licenses or the intellectual property rights of others, it is your responsibility to ensure that your use thereof complies with such licenses and/or rights.

978-1-491-99922-6

[LSI]

Table of Contents

Part II. Interface

Part III.   Some Frameworks

Preface

Aut lego vel scribo; doceo scrutorve sophian.
—Sedulius Scottus

On June 2, 2014, Apple's WWDC keynote address ended with a shocking announcement: "We have a new programming language." This came as a huge surprise to the developer community, which was accustomed to Objective-C, warts and all, and doubted that Apple could ever possibly relieve them from the weight of its venerable legacy. The developer community, it appeared, had been wrong.

Having picked themselves up off the floor, developers immediately began to consider this new language — Swift — studying it, critiquing it, and deciding whether to use it. My own first move was to translate all my existing iOS apps into Swift; this was enough to convince me that Swift deserved to be, and probably would be, adopted by new students of iOS programming, and that my books, therefore, should henceforth assume that readers are using Swift.

Therefore, Swift is the programming language used throughout this book. Still, the reader may also need some awareness of Objective-C (including C). The Foundation and Cocoa APIs, the built-in commands with which your code must interact in order to make anything happen on an iOS device, are still written in C and Objective-C. In order to interact with them, you might have to know what those languages would expect.

The Scope of This Book

Programming iOS 11 is actually the second of a pair with my other book, *iOS 11 Programming Fundamentals with Swift*; it picks up exactly where the other book leaves off. They complement and supplement one another. The two-book architecture should, I believe, render the size and scope of each book tractable for readers. Together, they provide a complete grounding in the knowledge needed to begin writing iOS apps; thus, when you *do* start writing iOS apps, you'll have a solid and rigorous understanding of what you are doing and where you are heading. If writing an iOS program is like building a house of bricks, *iOS 11 Programming Fundamentals with Swift* teaches you what a brick is and how to handle it, while *Programming iOS 11* hands you some actual bricks and tells you how to assemble them.

Like Homer's *Iliad*, *Programming iOS 11* begins in the middle of the story, with the reader jumping with all four feet into views and view controllers. Discussion of the Swift programming language, as well as the Xcode IDE (including the nature of nibs, outlets, and actions, and the mechanics of nib loading), plus the fundamental conventions, classes, and architectures of the Cocoa Touch framework (including delegation, the responder chain, key–value coding, key–value observing, memory management, and so on), has been relegated to *iOS 11 Programming Fundamentals with Swift*.

So if something appears to be missing from this book, that's why! If you start reading *Programming iOS 11* and wonder about such unexplained matters as Swift language basics, the UIApplicationMain function, the nib-loading mechanism, Cocoa patterns of delegation and notification, and retain cycles, wonder no longer — I don't explain them here because I have already explained them in *iOS 11 Programming Fundamentals with Swift*. If you're not sufficiently conversant with those topics, I'd suggest that you might want to read that book first; you will then be completely ready for this one.

Here's a summary of the major sections of *Programming iOS 11*:

- Part I describes views, the fundamental units of an iOS app's interface. Views are what the user can see and touch in an iOS app. To make something appear before the user's eyes, you need a view. To let the user interact with your app, you need a view. This part of the book explains how views are created, arranged, drawn, layered, animated, and touched.

- Part II starts by discussing view controllers. Perhaps the most important aspect of iOS programming, view controllers enable views to come and go coherently within the interface, thus allowing a single-windowed app running on what may be a tiny screen to contain multiple screens of material. View controllers are used to manage interface and to respond to user actions; most of your app's code will be in a view controller. This part of the book talks about how view controllers work, and the major built-in types of view controller that iOS gives you. It also describes every kind of view provided by the Cocoa framework — the primary building blocks with which you'll construct an app's interface.

- Part III surveys the most commonly used frameworks provided by iOS. These are clumps of code, sometimes with built-in interface, that are not part of your app by default, but are there for the asking if you need them, allowing you to work with such things as sound, video, user libraries, maps, and the device's sensors.

- Part IV wraps up the book with some miscellaneous but significant topics: files, networking, threading, and how to implement undo.

- Appendix A summarizes the basic lifetime event messages sent to your app delegate.
- Appendix B catalogs some useful Swift utility functions that I've written. My example code takes advantage of these functions, but they aren't built into iOS, so you should keep an eye on this appendix, consulting it whenever a mysterious method name appears.
- Appendix C is an excursus discussing an often misunderstood aspect of iOS programming: asynchronous code.

Someone who has read this book (and is conversant with the material in *iOS 11 Programming Fundamentals with Swift*) will, I believe, be capable of writing a real-life iOS app, with a clear understanding of what he or she is doing and where the app is going as it grows and develops. The book itself doesn't show how to write any particularly interesting iOS apps; but it is backed by dozens of example projects that you can download from my GitHub site, *http://github.com/mattneub/Programming-iOS-Book-Examples*, and it constantly uses my own real apps and real programming situations to illustrate and motivate its explanations.

This book is also intended to prepare you for your own further explorations. Certain chapters, especially in Parts III and IV, introduce a topic, providing an initial basic survey of its concepts, its capabilities, and its documentation, along with some code examples; but the topic itself may be far more extensive than that. Your feet, nevertheless, will now be set firmly on the path, and you will know enough that you can now proceed on your own whenever the need or interest arises. In Part IV, for example, I peek at Core Data, and demonstrate its use in code, but a true study of Core Data would require an entire book of its own (and such books exist); so, having opened the door, I quickly close it again, lest this book suddenly double in size.

Indeed, there is *always* more to learn about iOS. iOS is vast! It is all too easy to find areas of iOS that have had to be ruled outside the scope of this book, and are not mentioned at all. For example:

OpenGL
An open source C library for drawing, including 3D drawing, that takes full advantage of graphics hardware. This is often the most efficient way to draw, especially when animation is involved. iOS incorporates a simplified version of OpenGL called OpenGL ES. Open GL interface configuration, texture loading, shading, and calculation are simplified by the GLKit framework. The Metal and Metal Kit and Model I/O classes allow you to increase efficiency and performance.

Sprite Kit
Sprite Kit provides a built-in framework for designing 2D animated games.

Scene Kit

Ported from macOS, this framework makes it much easier to create 3D games and interactive graphics.

Accelerate

Certain computation-intensive processes will benefit from the vector-based Accelerate framework.

Game Kit

The Game Kit framework covers three areas that can enhance your user's game experience: wireless or Bluetooth communication directly between devices (peer-to-peer); voice communication across an existing network connection; and Game Center, which facilitates these and many other aspects of interplayer communication, such as posting and viewing high scores and setting up competitions. Users can even make screencasts of their own game play for sharing with one another.

Printing

See the "Printing" chapter of the *Drawing and Printing Guide for iOS*.

Security

This book does not discuss security topics such as keychains, certificates, and encryption. See the *Security Overview* and the Security framework.

Accessibility

VoiceOver assists visually impaired users by describing the interface aloud. To participate, views must be configured to describe themselves usefully. Built-in views already do this to a large extent, and you can extend this functionality. See the *Accessibility Programming Guide for iOS*.

Telephone

The Core Telephony framework lets your app get information about a particular cellular carrier and call. Call Kit allows VoIP apps to integrate with the built-in Phone app.

Pass Kit

The Pass Kit framework allows creation of downloadable passes to go into the user's Wallet app.

Health Kit

The Health Kit framework lets your app obtain, store, share, and present data and statistics related to body activity and exercise.

Externalities

The user can attach an external accessory to the device, either directly via USB or wirelessly via Bluetooth. Your app can communicate with such an accessory. See *External Accessory Programming Topics*. The Home Kit framework lets the user communicate with devices in the physical world, such as light switches and door locks. This book also doesn't discuss iBeacon or near field communication (the Core NFC framework, new in iOS 11).

Handoff
Handoff permits your app to post to the user's iCloud account a record of what the user is doing, so that the user can switch to another copy of your app on another device and resume doing the same thing. See the *Handoff Programming Guide.*

Spotlight
The user's Spotlight search results can include data supplied by your app. See the *App Search Programming Guide.*

Siri Kit
The SiriKit framework lets you configure your app so that the user can talk to the device to tell it what to do.

Augmented Reality
New in iOS 11, certain devices can impose drawn objects into the world viewed live through the device's camera by means of the ARKit framework.

Machine Learning
New in iOS 11, the Core ML framework embraces image analysis (the Vision framework) as well as decision trees (Gameplay Kit) and language analysis (NSLinguisticTagger).

Versions

This book is geared to Swift 4, iOS 11, and Xcode 9. In general, only very minimal attention is given to earlier versions of iOS and Xcode. It is not my intention to embrace in this book any detailed knowledge about earlier versions of the software, which is, after all, readily and compendiously available in my earlier books.

A word about method names. I generally give method names in Swift, in the style of a function reference — that is, the name plus parentheses containing the parameter labels followed by colon. Now and then, if a method is already under discussion and there is no ambiguity, I'll use the bare name. In a few places, where the Objective-C language is explicitly under discussion, I use Objective-C method names.

Please bear in mind that Apple continues to make adjustments to the Swift language and to the way the Objective-C APIs are bridged to it. I have tried to keep my code up-to-date right up to the moment when the manuscript left my hands; but if, at some future time, a new version of Xcode is released along with a new version of Swift, some of the code in this book might be slightly incorrect. Please make allowances, and be prepared to compensate.

Screenshots of Xcode were taken using Xcode 9 under macOS 10.12 Sierra. I have *not* upgraded my machine to macOS 10.13 High Sierra, because at the time of this writing it was too new to be trusted with mission-critical work. If you are braver than I am and running High Sierra, your interface may naturally look very slightly different from the screenshots, but this difference will be minimal and shouldn't cause any confusion.

Acknowledgments

My thanks go first and foremost to the people at O'Reilly Media who have made writing a book so delightfully easy: Rachel Roumeliotis, Sarah Schneider, Kristen Brown, Dan Fauxsmith, Adam Witwer, and Sanders Kleinfeld come particularly to mind. And let's not forget my first and long-standing editor, Brian Jepson, whose influence is present throughout.

As in the past, I have been greatly aided by some fantastic software, whose excellences I have appreciated at every moment of the process of writing this book. I should like to mention, in particular:

- git (*http://git-scm.com*)
- SourceTree (*http://www.sourcetreeapp.com*)
- TextMate (*http://macromates.com*)
- AsciiDoc (*http://www.methods.co.nz/asciidoc*)
- Asciidoctor (*http://asciidoctor.org*)
- BBEdit (*http://barebones.com/products/bbedit/*)
- EasyFind (*http://www.devontechnologies.com/products/freeware.html*)
- Snapz Pro X (*http://www.ambrosiasw.com*)
- GraphicConverter (*http://www.lemkesoft.com*)
- OmniGraffle (*http://www.omnigroup.com*)
- GoodReader (*http://www.goodreader.com*)

The book was typed and edited entirely on my faithful Unicomp Model M keyboard (*http://pckeyboard.com*), without which I could never have done so much writing over so long a period so painlessly. For more about my physical work environment, see *http://matt.neuburg.usesthis.com*.

From the Programming iOS 4 Preface

A programming framework has a kind of personality, an overall flavor that provides an insight into the goals and mindset of those who created it. When I first encountered Cocoa Touch, my assessment of its personality was: "Wow, the people who wrote this are really clever!" On the one hand, the number of built-in interface objects was severely and deliberately limited; on the other hand, the power and flexibility of some of those objects, especially such things as UITableView, was greatly enhanced over their OS X counterparts. Even more important, Apple created a particularly brilliant way (UIViewController) to help the programmer make entire blocks of interface come and go and supplant one another in a controlled, hierarchical manner, thus allowing that tiny iPhone display to unfold virtually into multiple interface worlds within a single app without the user becoming lost or confused.

The popularity of the iPhone, with its largely free or very inexpensive apps, and the subsequent popularity of the iPad, have brought and will continue to bring into the fold many new programmers who see programming for these devices as worthwhile and doable, even though they may not have felt the same way about OS X. Apple's own annual WWDC developer conventions have reflected this trend, with their emphasis shifted from OS X to iOS instruction.

The widespread eagerness to program iOS, however, though delightful on the one hand, has also fostered a certain tendency to try to run without first learning to walk. iOS gives the programmer mighty powers that can seem as limitless as imagination itself, but it also has fundamentals. I often see questions online from programmers who are evidently deep into the creation of some interesting app, but who are stymied in a way that reveals quite clearly that they are unfamiliar with the basics of the very world in which they are so happily cavorting.

It is this state of affairs that has motivated me to write this book, which is intended to ground the reader in the fundamentals of iOS. I love Cocoa and have long wished to write about it, but it is iOS and its popularity that has given me a proximate excuse to do so. Here I have attempted to marshal and expound, in what I hope is a pedagogically helpful and instructive yet ruthlessly Euclidean and logical order, the principles and elements on which sound iOS programming rests. My hope, as with my previous books, is that you will both read this book cover to cover (learning something new often enough to keep you turning the pages) and keep it by you as a handy reference.

This book is not intended to disparage Apple's own documentation and example projects. They are wonderful resources and have become more wonderful as time goes on. I have depended heavily on them in the preparation of this book. But I also find that they don't fulfill the same function as a reasoned, ordered presentation of the facts. The online documentation must make assumptions as to how much you already know; it can't guarantee that you'll approach it in a given order. And online documentation is more suitable to reference than to instruction. A fully written example, no matter how well commented, is difficult to follow; it demonstrates, but it does not teach.

A book, on the other hand, has numbered chapters and sequential pages; I can assume you know views before you know view controllers for the simple reason that Part I precedes Part II. And along with facts, I also bring to the table a degree of experience, which I try to communicate to you. Throughout this book you'll find me referring to "common beginner mistakes"; in most cases, these are mistakes that I have made myself, in addition to seeing others make them. I try to tell you what the pitfalls are because I assume that, in the course of things, you will otherwise fall into them just as naturally as I did as I was learning. You'll also see me construct many examples piece by piece or extract and explain just one tiny portion of a larger app. It is not a massive finished program that teaches programming, but an exposition of the thought process that developed that program. It is this thought process, more than anything else, that I hope you will gain from reading this book.

Conventions Used in This Book

The following typographical conventions are used in this book:

Italic
> Indicates new terms, URLs, email addresses, filenames, and file extensions.

`Constant width`
> Used for program listings, as well as within paragraphs to refer to program elements such as variable or function names, databases, data types, environment variables, statements, and keywords.

`Constant width bold`
> Shows commands or other text that should be typed literally by the user.

`Constant width italic`
> Shows text that should be replaced with user-supplied values or by values determined by context.

This element signifies a tip or suggestion.

This element signifies a general note.

This element indicates a warning or caution.

Using Code Examples

Supplemental material (code examples, exercises, etc.) is available for download at *https://github.com/mattneub/Programming-iOS-Book-Examples*.

This book is here to help you get your job done. In general, if example code is offered with this book, you may use it in your programs and documentation. You do not need to contact us for permission unless you're reproducing a significant portion of the code. For example, writing a program that uses several chunks of code from this book does not require permission. Selling or distributing a CD-ROM of examples from O'Reilly books does require permission. Answering a question by citing this book and quoting example code does not require permission. Incorporating a significant amount of example code from this book into your product's documentation does require permission.

We appreciate, but do not require, attribution. An attribution usually includes the title, author, publisher, and ISBN. For example: "*Programming iOS 11* by Matt Neuburg (O'Reilly). Copyright 2018 Matt Neuburg, 978-1-491-99922-6."

If you feel your use of code examples falls outside fair use or the permission given above, feel free to contact us at *permissions@oreilly.com*.

O'Reilly Safari

 Safari (formerly Safari Books Online) is membership-based training and reference platform for enterprise, government, educators, and individuals.

Members have access to thousands of books, training videos, Learning Paths, interactive tutorials, and curated playlists from over 250 publishers, including O'Reilly Media, Harvard Business Review, Prentice Hall Professional, Addison-Wesley Professional, Microsoft Press, Sams, Que, Peachpit Press, Adobe, Focal Press, Cisco Press, John Wiley & Sons, Syngress, Morgan Kaufmann, IBM Redbooks, Packt, Adobe Press, FT Press, Apress, Manning, New Riders, McGraw-Hill, Jones & Bartlett, and Course Technology, among others.

For more information, please visit *http://oreilly.com/safari*.

How to Contact Us

Please address comments and questions concerning this book to the publisher:

O'Reilly Media, Inc.
1005 Gravenstein Highway North
Sebastopol, CA 95472

800-998-9938 (in the United States or Canada)
707-829-0515 (international or local)
707-829-0104 (fax)

We have a web page for this book, where we list errata, examples, and any additional information. You can access this page at *http://bit.ly/programming_iOS11*.

To comment or ask technical questions about this book, send email to *bookquestions@oreilly.com*.

For more information about our books, courses, conferences, and news, see our website at *http://www.oreilly.com*.

Find us on Facebook: *http://facebook.com/oreilly*

Follow us on Twitter: *http://twitter.com/oreillymedia*

Watch us on YouTube: *http://www.youtube.com/oreillymedia*

PART I

Views

Views are what your user sees on the screen and interacts with by touching the screen. The book begins by explaining how they work.

- Chapter 1 discusses views in their most general aspect — their hierarchy, visibility, position, and layout.
- Chapter 2 is about drawing. A view knows how to draw itself; this chapter explains how to tell a view what you want it to draw.
- Chapter 3 explains about layers. The drawing power of a view comes ultimately from its layer.
- Chapter 4 talks about animation, which you'll use to enliven your app's interface.
- Chapter 5 explains how your app senses and responds to the user touching the screen.

CHAPTER 1

Views

A *view* (an object whose class is UIView or a subclass of UIView) knows how to draw itself into a rectangular area of the interface. Your app has a visible interface thanks to views; everything the user sees is ultimately because of a view. Creating and configuring a view can be extremely simple: "Set it and forget it." For example, you can configure a UIButton in the nib editor; when the app runs, the button appears, and works properly. But you can also manipulate views in powerful ways, in real time. Your code can do some or all of the view's drawing of itself (Chapter 2); it can make the view appear and disappear, move, resize itself, and display many other physical changes, possibly with animation (Chapter 4).

A view is also a responder (UIView is a subclass of UIResponder). This means that a view is subject to user interactions, such as taps and swipes. Thus, views are the basis not only of the interface that the user sees, but also of the interface that the user touches (Chapter 5). Organizing your views so that the correct view reacts to a given touch allows you to allocate your code neatly and efficiently.

The *view hierarchy* is the chief mode of view organization. A view can have subviews; a subview has exactly one immediate superview. Thus there is a tree of views. This hierarchy allows views to come and go together. If a view is removed from the interface, its subviews are removed; if a view is hidden (made invisible), its subviews are hidden; if a view is moved, its subviews move with it; and other changes in a view are likewise shared with its subviews. The view hierarchy is also the basis of, though it is not identical to, the responder chain.

A view may come from a nib, or you can create it in code. On balance, neither approach is to be preferred over the other; it depends on your needs and inclinations and on the overall architecture of your app.

The Window and Root View

The top of the view hierarchy is the app's window. It is an instance of UIWindow (or your own subclass thereof), which is a UIView subclass. Your app should have *exactly one main window*. It is created at launch time and is never destroyed or replaced. It forms the background to, and is the ultimate superview of, all your other visible views. Other views are visible by virtue of being subviews, at some depth, of your app's window.

 If your app can display views on an external screen, you'll create an additional UIWindow to contain those views; but in this book I'll assume there is just one screen, the device's own screen, and just one window.

How an App Launches

How does your app, at launch time, come to have a main window, and how does that window come to be populated and displayed? If your app uses a main storyboard, it all happens automatically. Your app consists, ultimately, of a single call to the UIApplicationMain function. (Unlike an Objective-C project, a typical Swift project doesn't make this call explicitly, in code; it is called for you, behind the scenes.) Here are some of the first things this call does:

1. UIApplicationMain instantiates UIApplication and retains this instance, to serve as the shared application instance, which your code can later refer to as UIApplication.shared. It then instantiates the app delegate class. (It knows which class is the app delegate because it is marked @UIApplicationMain.) It retains the app delegate instance and assigns it as the application instance's delegate.

2. UIApplicationMain looks to see whether your app uses a main storyboard. It knows whether you are using a main storyboard, and what its name is, by looking at the *Info.plist* key "Main storyboard file base name" (UIMainStoryboardFile). (You can easily edit this key, if necessary, by editing the target and, in the General pane, changing the Main Interface value in the Deployment Info section. By default, a new iOS project has a main storyboard called *Main.storyboard*, and the Main Interface value is Main. You will rarely have reason to change this.)

3. If your app uses a main storyboard, UIApplicationMain instantiates UIWindow and assigns the window instance to the app delegate's window property, which retains it, thus ensuring that the window will persist for the lifetime of the app. It also *sizes* the window so that it will initially fill the device's screen. This is ensured by setting the window's frame to the screen's bounds. (I'll explain later in this chapter what "frame" and "bounds" are.)

4. If your app uses a main storyboard, UIApplicationMain instantiates that story-board's initial view controller. (I'll talk more about that in Chapter 6.) It then assigns this view controller instance to the window's rootViewController property, which retains it. When a view controller becomes the main window's root-ViewController, its main view (its view) is made the one and only immediate subview of your main window — the main window's *root view*. All other views in your main window will be subviews of the root view.

   Thus, the root view is the highest object in the view hierarchy that the user will usually see. There might be just a chance, under certain circumstances, that the user will catch a glimpse of the window, behind the root view; for this reason, you may want to assign the main window a reasonable backgroundColor. In general you'll have no reason to change anything else about the window itself.

5. UIApplicationMain calls the app delegate's application(_:didFinishLaunching-WithOptions:).

6. Your app's interface is not visible until the window, which contains it, is made the app's key window. Therefore, if your app uses a main storyboard, UIApplication-Main calls the window's instance method makeKeyAndVisible.

Launching Without a Main Storyboard

It is also possible to write an app that lacks a main storyboard, or that has a main storyboard but, under certain circumstances, effectively ignores it at launch time by overriding the automatic UIApplicationMain behavior. Such an app simply does in code — typically, in application(_:didFinishLaunchingWithOptions:) — every-thing that UIApplicationMain does automatically if the app has a main storyboard (see Appendix B for a full implementation):

1. Instantiate UIWindow and assign it as the app delegate's window property. With a little clever coding, we can avoid doing this if UIApplicationMain did it already:

   ```
   self.window = self.window ?? UIWindow()
   ```

2. Instantiate a view controller, configure it as needed, and assign it as the window's rootViewController property. If UIApplicationMain already assigned a root view controller, this view controller replaces it.

3. Call makeKeyAndVisible on the window, to show it. This does no harm even if there is a main storyboard, as UIApplicationMain will not subsequently repeat this call.

For example, imagine something like a login screen that appears at launch if the user has not logged in, but doesn't appear on subsequent launches once the user *has* logged in. In step 2, we would look (probably in UserDefaults) to see if the user has logged in. If not, we set the `rootViewController` to our login screen's view controller. Otherwise, we do nothing, leaving the storyboard's initial view controller as the `rootViewController`.

Subclassing UIWindow

Another possible variation is to subclass UIWindow. That is uncommon nowadays, though it can be a way of intervening in hit-testing (Chapter 5) or the target–action mechanism (Chapter 12). To make an instance of your UIWindow subclass your app's main window, you would need to prevent `UIApplicationMain` from assigning a plain vanilla UIWindow instance as your app delegate's `window`. The rule is that, after `UIApplicationMain` has instantiated the app delegate, it asks the app delegate instance for the value of its `window` property. If that value is `nil`, `UIApplicationMain` instantiates UIWindow and assigns that instance to the app delegate's `window` property. If that value is *not* `nil`, `UIApplicationMain` leaves it alone. Therefore, to make your app's main window be an instance of your UIWindow subclass, all you have to do is assign that instance as the default value for the app delegate's `window` property:

```
@UIApplicationMain
class AppDelegate : UIResponder, UIApplicationDelegate {
    var window : UIWindow? = MyWindow()
    // ...
}
```

Referring to the Window

Once the app is running, there are various ways for your code to refer to the window:

- If a UIView is in the interface, it automatically has a reference to the window through its own `window` property. Your code will probably be running in a view controller with a main view, so `self.view.window` is usually the best way to refer to the window.

  You can also use a UIView's `window` property as a way of asking whether it is ultimately embedded in the window; if it isn't, its `window` property is `nil`. A UIView whose `window` property is `nil` cannot be visible to the user.

- The app delegate instance maintains a reference to the window through its `window` property. You can get a reference to the app delegate from elsewhere through the shared application's `delegate` property, and through it you can refer to the window:

  ```
  let w = UIApplication.shared.delegate!.window!!
  ```

If you prefer something less generic (and requiring less extreme unwrapping of Optionals), cast the `delegate` explicitly to your app delegate class:

```
let w = (UIApplication.shared.delegate as! AppDelegate).window!
```

- The shared application maintains a reference to the window through its `key-Window` property:

```
let w = UIApplication.shared.keyWindow!
```

That reference, however, is slightly volatile, because the system can create temporary windows and interpose them as the application's key window.

Experimenting with Views

In the course of this and subsequent chapters, you may want to experiment with views in a project of your own. If you start your project with the Single View app template, it gives you the simplest possible app — a main storyboard containing one scene consisting of one view controller instance along with its main view. As I described in the preceding section, when the app runs, that view controller will become the app's main window's `rootViewController`, and its main view will become the window's root view. Thus, if you can get *your* views to become subviews of that view controller's main view, they will be present in the app's interface when it launches.

In the nib editor, you can drag a view from the Object library into the main view as a subview, and it will be instantiated in the interface when the app runs. However, my initial examples will all create views and add them to the interface *in code*. So where should that code go? View controllers aren't formally explained until Chapter 6, so you'll just have to believe me when I tell you the answer: The simplest place is the view controller's `viewDidLoad` method, which is provided as a stub by the project template code.

The `viewDidLoad` method has a reference to the view controller's main view as `self.view`. In my code examples, whenever I say `self.view`, you can assume we're in a view controller and that `self.view` is this view controller's main view. For example:

```
override func viewDidLoad() {
    super.viewDidLoad() // this is template code
    let v = UIView(frame:CGRect(x:100, y:100, width:50, height:50))
    v.backgroundColor = .red // small red square
    self.view.addSubview(v) // add it to main view
}
```

Try it! Make a new project from the Single View app template, and make the View-Controller class's `viewDidLoad` look like that. Run the app. You will actually *see* the small red square in the running app's interface.

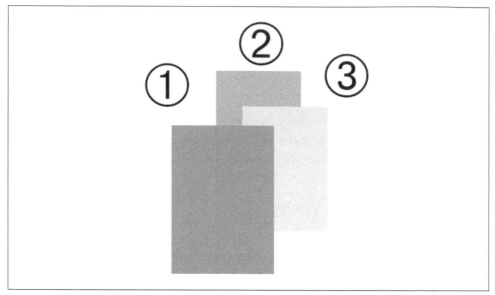

Figure 1-1. Overlapping views

Subview and Superview

Once upon a time, and not so very long ago, a view owned precisely its own rectangular area. No part of any view that was not a subview of this view could appear inside it, because when this view redrew its rectangle, it would erase the overlapping portion of the other view. No part of any subview of this view could appear outside it, because the view took responsibility for its own rectangle and no more.

Those rules, however, were gradually relaxed, and starting in OS X 10.5, Apple introduced an entirely new architecture for view drawing that lifted those restrictions completely. iOS view drawing is based on this revised architecture. In iOS, some or all of a subview can appear outside its superview, and a view can overlap another view and can be drawn partially or totally in front of it without being its subview.

For example, Figure 1-1 shows three overlapping views. All three views have a background color, so each is completely represented by a colored rectangle. You have no way of knowing, from this visual representation, exactly how the views are related within the view hierarchy. In actual fact, View 1 is a sibling view of View 2 (they are both direct subviews of the root view), and View 3 is a subview of View 2.

When views are created in the nib, you can examine the view hierarchy in the nib editor's document outline to learn their actual relationship (Figure 1-2). When views are created in code, you know their hierarchical relationship because you created that hierarchy. But the visible interface doesn't tell you, because view overlapping is so flexible.

Figure 1-2. A view hierarchy as displayed in the nib editor

Nevertheless, a view's position within the view hierarchy is extremely significant. For one thing, the view hierarchy dictates the *order* in which views are drawn. Sibling subviews of the same superview have a definite order: one is drawn before the other, so if they overlap, it will appear to be behind its sibling. Similarly, a superview is drawn before its subviews, so if they overlap it, it will appear to be behind them.

You can see this illustrated in Figure 1-1. View 3 is a subview of View 2 and is drawn on top of it. View 1 is a sibling of View 2, but it is a later sibling, so it is drawn on top of View 2 and on top of View 3. View 1 *cannot* appear behind View 3 but in front of View 2, because those two views are subview and superview and are drawn together — both are drawn either before or after View 1, depending on the ordering of the siblings.

This layering order can be governed in the nib editor by arranging the views in the document outline. (If you click in the canvas, you may be able to use the menu items of the Editor → Arrange menu instead — Send to Front, Send to Back, Send Forward, Send Backward.) In code, there are methods for arranging the sibling order of views, which we'll come to in a moment.

Here are some other effects of the view hierarchy:

- If a view is removed from or moved within its superview, its subviews go with it.
- A view's degree of transparency is inherited by its subviews.
- A view can optionally limit the drawing of its subviews so that any parts of them outside the view are not shown. This is called *clipping* and is set with the view's `clipsToBounds` property.
- A superview *owns* its subviews, in the memory-management sense, much as an array owns its elements; it retains them and is responsible for releasing a subview when that subview ceases to be its subview (it is removed from the collection of this view's subviews) or when it itself goes out of existence.
- If a view's size is changed, its subviews can be resized automatically (and I'll have much more to say about that later in this chapter).

A UIView has a `superview` property (a UIView) and a `subviews` property (an array of UIView objects, in back-to-front order), allowing you to trace the view hierarchy in code. There is also a method `isDescendant(of:)` letting you check whether one view is a subview of another at any depth.

If you need a reference to a particular view, you will probably arrange it beforehand as a property, perhaps through an outlet. Alternatively, a view can have a numeric tag (its `tag` property), and can then be referred to by sending any view higher up the view hierarchy the `viewWithTag(_:)` message. Seeing that all tags of interest are unique within their region of the hierarchy is up to you.

Manipulating the view hierarchy in code is easy. This is part of what gives iOS apps their dynamic quality, and it compensates for the fact that there is basically just a single window. It is perfectly reasonable for your code to rip an entire hierarchy of views out of the superview and substitute another, right before the user's very eyes! You can do this directly; you can combine it with animation (Chapter 4); you can govern it through view controllers (Chapter 6).

The method `addSubview(_:)` makes one view a subview of another; `removeFromSuperview` takes a subview out of its superview's view hierarchy. In both cases, if the superview is part of the visible interface, the subview will appear or disappear; and of course this view may itself have subviews that accompany it. Just remember that removing a subview from its superview releases it; if you intend to reuse that subview later on, you will need to retain it first. This is often taken care of by assignment to a property.

Events inform a view of these dynamic changes. To respond to these events requires subclassing. Then you'll be able to override any of these methods:

- `willRemoveSubview(_:)`, `didAddSubview(_:)`
- `willMove(toSuperview:)`, `didMoveToSuperview`
- `willMove(toWindow:)`, `didMoveToWindow`

When `addSubview(_:)` is called, the view is placed last among its superview's subviews; thus it is drawn last, meaning that it appears frontmost. That might not be what you want. A view's subviews are indexed, starting at 0, which is rearmost, and there are methods for inserting a subview at a given index, or below (behind) or above (in front of) a specific view; for swapping two sibling views by index; and for moving a subview all the way to the front or back among its siblings:

- `insertSubview(at:)`
- `insertSubview(belowSubview:)`, `insertSubview(aboveSubview:)`
- `exchangeSubview(at:withSubviewAt:)`
- `bringSubview(toFront:)`, `sendSubview(toBack:)`

Oddly, there is no command for removing all of a view's subviews at once. However, a view's `subviews` array is an immutable copy of the internal list of subviews, so it is legal to cycle through it and remove each subview one at a time:

```
myView.subviews.forEach {$0.removeFromSuperview()}
```

Visibility and Opacity

A view can be made invisible by setting its `isHidden` property to `true`, and visible again by setting it to `false`. Hiding a view takes it (and its subviews, of course) out of the visible interface without the overhead of actually removing it from the view hierarchy. A hidden view does not (normally) receive touch events, so to the user it really is as if the view weren't there. But it is there, so it can still be manipulated in code.

A view can be assigned a background color through its `backgroundColor` property. A color is a UIColor. A view whose background color is `nil` (the default) has a transparent background. If such a view does no additional drawing of its own, it will be invisible! Such a view is perfectly reasonable, however; you might create one just so that it can act as a convenient superview to other views, making them behave together.

A view can be made partially or completely transparent through its `alpha` property: 1.0 means opaque, 0.0 means transparent, and a value may be anywhere between them, inclusive. A view's `alpha` property value affects both the apparent transparency of its background color and the apparent transparency of its contents. For example, if a view displays an image and has a background color and its `alpha` is less than 1, the background color will seep through the image (and whatever is behind the view will seep through both). Moreover, a view's `alpha` property affects the apparent transparency of its subviews! If a superview has an `alpha` of `0.5`, none of its subviews can have an *apparent* opacity of more than `0.5`, because whatever `alpha` value they have will be drawn relative to `0.5`. A view that is completely transparent (or very close to it) is like a view whose `isHidden` is `true`: it is invisible, along with its subviews, and cannot (normally) be touched.

(Just to make matters more complicated, colors have an alpha value as well. So, for example, a view can have an `alpha` of `1.0` but still have a transparent background because its `backgroundColor` has an alpha less than `1.0`.)

A view's `isOpaque` property, on the other hand, is a horse of a different color; changing it has no effect on the view's appearance. Rather, this property is a hint to the drawing system. If a view completely fills its bounds with ultimately opaque material and its `alpha` is `1.0`, so that the view has no effective transparency, then it can be drawn more efficiently (with less drag on performance) if you inform the drawing system of this fact by setting its `isOpaque` to `true`. Otherwise, you should set its isOpaque to `false`. The `isOpaque` value is *not* changed for you when you set a view's `backgroundColor` or `alpha`! Setting it correctly is entirely up to you; the default, perhaps surprisingly, is `true`.

Frame

A view's `frame` property, a CGRect, is the position of its rectangle within its superview, *in the superview's coordinate system*. By default, the superview's coordinate system will have the origin at its top left, with the x-coordinate growing positively rightward and the y-coordinate growing positively downward.

Setting a view's frame to a different CGRect value repositions the view, or resizes it, or both. If the view is visible, this change will be visibly reflected in the interface. On the other hand, you can also set a view's frame when the view is not visible — for example, when you create the view in code. In that case, the frame describes where the view *will* be positioned within its superview when it is given a superview. UIView's designated initializer is `init(frame:)`, and you'll often assign a frame this way, especially because the default frame might otherwise be `CGRect.zero`, which is rarely what you want.

 Forgetting to assign a view a frame when creating it in code, and then wondering why it isn't appearing when added to a superview, is a common beginner mistake. A view with a zero-size frame is effectively invisible. If a view has a standard size that you want it to adopt, especially in relation to its contents (like a UIButton in relation to its title), an alternative is to call its `sizeToFit` method.

We are now in a position to generate programmatically the interface displayed in Figure 1-1 (for the CGRect initializer with no argument labels, see Appendix B):

```
let v1 = UIView(frame:CGRect(113, 111, 132, 194))
v1.backgroundColor = UIColor(red: 1, green: 0.4, blue: 1, alpha: 1)
let v2 = UIView(frame:CGRect(41, 56, 132, 194))
v2.backgroundColor = UIColor(red: 0.5, green: 1, blue: 0, alpha: 1)
let v3 = UIView(frame:CGRect(43, 197, 160, 230))
v3.backgroundColor = UIColor(red: 1, green: 0, blue: 0, alpha: 1)
self.view.addSubview(v1)
v1.addSubview(v2)
self.view.addSubview(v3)
```

In that code, we determined the layering order of `v1` and `v3` (the middle and left views, which are siblings) by the order in which we inserted them into the view hierarchy with `addSubview(_:)`.

Figure 1-3. A subview inset from its superview

Bounds and Center

Suppose we have a superview and a subview, and the subview is to appear inset by 10 points, as in Figure 1-3. CGRect methods like insetBy(dx:dy:) make it easy to derive one rectangle as an inset from another. But *what* rectangle should we inset from? Not the superview's frame; the frame represents a view's position within *its* superview, and in that superview's coordinates. What we're after is a CGRect describing our superview's rectangle in its *own* coordinates, because those are the coordinates in which the subview's frame is to be expressed. The CGRect that describes a view's rectangle in its own coordinates is the view's bounds property.

So, the code to generate Figure 1-3 looks like this:

Figure 1-4. A subview exactly covering its superview

```
let v1 = UIView(frame:CGRect(113, 111, 132, 194))
v1.backgroundColor = UIColor(red: 1, green: 0.4, blue: 1, alpha: 1)
let v2 = UIView(frame:v1.bounds.insetBy(dx: 10, dy: 10))
v2.backgroundColor = UIColor(red: 0.5, green: 1, blue: 0, alpha: 1)
self.view.addSubview(v1)
v1.addSubview(v2)
```

You'll very often use a view's bounds in this way. When you need coordinates for positioning content inside a view, whether drawing manually or placing a subview, you'll refer to the view's bounds.

If you change a view's bounds *size*, you change its *frame*. The change in the view's frame takes place around its *center*, which remains unchanged. So, for example:

```
let v1 = UIView(frame:CGRect(113, 111, 132, 194))
v1.backgroundColor = UIColor(red: 1, green: 0.4, blue: 1, alpha: 1)
let v2 = UIView(frame:v1.bounds.insetBy(dx: 10, dy: 10))
v2.backgroundColor = UIColor(red: 0.5, green: 1, blue: 0, alpha: 1)
self.view.addSubview(v1)
v1.addSubview(v2)
v2.bounds.size.height += 20
v2.bounds.size.width += 20
```

What appears is a single rectangle; the subview completely and exactly covers its superview, its frame being the same as the superview's bounds. The call to `insetBy` started with the superview's bounds and shaved 10 points off the left, right, top, and bottom to set the subview's frame (Figure 1-3). But then we added 20 points to the subview's bounds height and width, and thus added 20 points to the subview's frame height and width as well (Figure 1-4). The subview's center didn't move, so we effectively put the 10 points back onto the left, right, top, and bottom of the subview's frame.

If you change a view's bounds *origin*, you move the *origin of its internal coordinate system*. When you create a UIView, its bounds coordinate system's zero point (0.0,0.0) is at its top left. Because a subview is positioned in its superview with respect to its superview's coordinate system, a change in the bounds origin of the

Figure 1-5. The superview's bounds origin has been shifted

superview will change the apparent position of a subview. To illustrate, we start once again with our subview inset evenly within its superview, and then change the bounds origin of the superview:

```
let v1 = UIView(frame:CGRect(113, 111, 132, 194))
v1.backgroundColor = UIColor(red: 1, green: 0.4, blue: 1, alpha: 1)
let v2 = UIView(frame:v1.bounds.insetBy(dx: 10, dy: 10))
v2.backgroundColor = UIColor(red: 0.5, green: 1, blue: 0, alpha: 1)
self.view.addSubview(v1)
v1.addSubview(v2)
v1.bounds.origin.x += 10
v1.bounds.origin.y += 10
```

Nothing happens to the superview's size or position. But the subview has moved up and to the left so that it is flush with its superview's top-left corner (Figure 1-5). Basically, what we've done is to say to the superview, "Instead of calling the point at your upper left (0.0,0.0), call that point (10.0,10.0)." Because the subview's frame origin is itself at (10.0,10.0), the subview now touches the superview's top-left corner. The effect of changing a view's bounds origin may seem directionally backward — we increased the superview's origin in the positive direction, but the subview moved in the negative direction — but think of it this way: a view's bounds origin point coincides with its frame's top left.

We have seen that changing a view's bounds size affects its frame size. The converse is also true: changing a view's frame size affects its bounds size. What is *not* affected by changing a view's bounds size is the view's center. This property, like the frame property, represents a subview's position within its superview, in the superview's coordinates; in particular, it is the position within the superview of the subview's bounds center, the point derived from the bounds like this:

```
let c = CGPoint(theView.bounds.midX, theView.bounds.midY)
```

A view's center is thus a single point establishing the positional relationship between the view's bounds and its superview's bounds.

Changing a view's bounds does not change its center; changing a view's center does not change its bounds. Thus, a view's bounds and center are orthogonal (independent), and completely describe the view's size and its position within its superview. The view's frame is therefore superfluous! In fact, the frame property is merely a convenient expression of the center and bounds values. In most cases, this won't matter to you; you'll use the frame property anyway. When you first create a view from scratch, the designated initializer is init(frame:). You can change the frame, and the bounds size and center will change to match. You can change the bounds size or the center, and the frame will change to match. Nevertheless, the proper and most reliable way to position and size a view within its superview is to use its bounds and center, not its frame; there are some situations in which the frame is meaningless (or will at least behave very oddly), but the bounds and center will always work.

We have seen that every view has its own coordinate system, expressed by its bounds, and that a view's coordinate system has a clear relationship to its superview's coordinate system, expressed by its center. This is true of every view in a window, so it is possible to convert between the coordinates of any two views in the same window. Convenience methods are supplied to perform this conversion both for a CGPoint and for a CGRect:

- convert(_:to:)
- convert(_:from:)

The first parameter is either a CGPoint or a CGRect. The second parameter is a UIView; if the second parameter is nil, it is taken to be the window. The recipient is another UIView; the CGPoint or CGRect is being converted between its coordinates and the second view's coordinates.

For example, if v1 is the superview of v2, then to center v2 within v1 you could say:

```
v2.center = v1.convert(v1.center, from:v1.superview)
```

 When setting a view's position by setting its center, if the height or width of the view is not an integer (or, on a single-resolution screen, not an even integer), the view can end up *misaligned*: its point values in one or both dimensions are located between the screen pixels. This can cause the view to be displayed incorrectly; for example, if the view contains text, the text may be blurry. You can detect this situation in the Simulator by checking Debug → Color Misaligned Images. A simple solution is to set the view's frame to its own integral.

Window Coordinates and Screen Coordinates

The device screen has no frame, but it has bounds. The main window has no superview, but its frame is set with respect to the screen's bounds:

```
let w = UIWindow(frame: UIScreen.main.bounds)
```

In iOS 9 and later, you can omit the `frame` parameter, as a shortcut; the effect is exactly the same:

```
let w = UIWindow()
```

The window thus starts out life filling the screen, and generally continues to fill the screen, and so, for the most part, *window coordinates are screen coordinates*. (I'll discuss a possible exception in Chapter 9.)

In iOS 7 and before, the screen's coordinates were invariant. iOS 8 introduced a major change: when the app rotates to compensate for the rotation of the device, the screen (and with it, the window) is what rotates. Thus there is a transposition of the size components of the screen's bounds, and a corresponding transposition of the size components of the window's bounds: in portrait orientation, the size is taller than wide, but in landscape orientation, the size is wider than tall.

The screen therefore reports its coordinates through two different properties; their values are typed as UICoordinateSpace, a protocol (also adopted by UIView) that provides a bounds property:

UIScreen's `coordinateSpace` *property*
> This coordinate space *rotates*. Its bounds height and width are transposed when the app rotates to compensate for a change in the orientation of the device; its origin is at the top left of the *app*.

UIScreen's `fixedCoordinateSpace` *property*
> This coordinate space is *invariant*. Its bounds origin is at the top left of the *physical device*, regardless of how the device itself is held. (A good way to think of this is with respect to the Home button, which is at the bottom of the physical device.)

To help you convert between coordinate spaces, UICoordinateSpace provides methods parallel to the coordinate-conversion methods I listed in the previous section:

- `convert(_:from:)`
- `convert(_:to:)`

The first parameter is either a CGPoint or a CGRect. The second parameter is a UICoordinateSpace, which might be a UIView or the UIScreen; so is the recipient.

So, for example, suppose we have a UIView v in our interface, and we wish to learn its position in fixed device coordinates. We could do it like this:

```
let screen = UIScreen.main.fixedCoordinateSpace
let r = v.superview!.convert(v.frame, to: screen)
```

Imagine that we have a subview of our main view, at the exact top left corner of the main view. When the device and the app are in portrait orientation, the subview's top left is at {0,0} in window coordinates and in screen `fixedCoordinateSpace` coordinates. When the device is rotated left into landscape orientation, and if the app rotates to compensate, the window rotates, so the subview is *still* at the top left from the user's point of view, and is *still* at the top left in window coordinates. But in screen `fixedCoordinateSpace` coordinates, the subview's top left x-coordinate will have a large positive value, because the origin is now at the lower left and its x grows positively upward.

Occasions where you need such information, however, will be rare. Indeed, my experience is that it is rare even to worry about window coordinates. All of your app's visible action takes place within your root view controller's main view, and the bounds of that view, which are adjusted for you automatically when the app rotates to compensate for a change in device orientation, are probably the highest coordinate system that will interest you.

Transform

A view's `transform` property alters how the view is drawn — it may, for example, change the view's apparent size and orientation — without affecting its bounds and center. A transformed view continues to behave correctly: a rotated button, for example, is still a button, and can be tapped in its apparent location and orientation.

A transform value is a CGAffineTransform, which is a struct representing six of the nine values of a 3×3 transformation matrix (the other three values are constants, so there's no need to represent them in the struct). You may have forgotten your high-school linear algebra, so you may not recall what a transformation matrix is. For the details, which are quite simple really, see the "Transforms" chapter of Apple's *Quartz 2D Programming Guide*, especially the section called "The Math Behind the Matrices." But you don't really need to know those details, because initializers are provided for creating three of the basic types of transform: rotation, scaling, and translation (i.e., changing the view's apparent position). A fourth basic transform type, skewing or shearing, has no initializer.

By default, a view's transformation matrix is CGAffineTransform.identity, the identity transform. It has no visible effect, so you're unaware of it. Any transform that you do apply takes place around the view's center, which is held constant.

Here's some code to illustrate use of a transform:

```
let v1 = UIView(frame:CGRect(113, 111, 132, 194))
v1.backgroundColor = UIColor(red: 1, green: 0.4, blue: 1, alpha: 1)
let v2 = UIView(frame:v1.bounds.insetBy(dx: 10, dy: 10))
v2.backgroundColor = UIColor(red: 0.5, green: 1, blue: 0, alpha: 1)
```

Figure 1-6. A rotation transform

```
self.view.addSubview(v1)
v1.addSubview(v2)
v1.transform = CGAffineTransform(rotationAngle: 45 * .pi/180)
print(v1.frame)
```

The `transform` property of the view `v1` is set to a rotation transform. The result (Figure 1-6) is that the view appears to be rocked 45 degrees clockwise. (I think in degrees, but Core Graphics thinks in radians, so my code has to convert.) Observe that the view's `center` property is unaffected, so that the rotation seems to have occurred around the view's center. Moreover, the view's `bounds` property is unaffected; the internal coordinate system is unchanged, so the subview is drawn in the same place relative to its superview. The view's `frame`, however, is now useless, as no mere rectangle can describe the region of the superview apparently occupied by the view; the frame's actual value, roughly (`63.7,92.7,230.5,230.5`), describes the minimal bounding rectangle surrounding the view's apparent position. The rule is that if a view's `transform` is not the identity transform, you should not set its `frame`; also, automatic resizing of a subview, discussed later in this chapter, requires that the superview's transform be the identity transform.

Suppose, instead of a rotation transform, we apply a scale transform, like this:

```
v1.transform = CGAffineTransform(scaleX:1.8, y:1)
```

The `bounds` property of the view `v1` is still unaffected, so the subview is still drawn in the same place relative to its superview; this means that the two views seem to have stretched horizontally together (Figure 1-7). No bounds or centers were harmed by the application of this transform!

Methods are provided for transforming an existing transform. This operation is not commutative; that is, order matters. (That high school math is starting to come back to you now, isn't it?) If you start with a transform that translates a view to the right and then apply a rotation of 45 degrees, the rotated view appears to the right of its original position; on the other hand, if you start with a transform that rotates a view

Figure 1-7. A scale transform

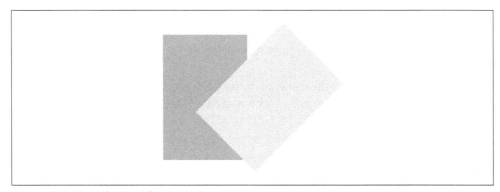

Figure 1-8. Translation, then rotation

45 degrees and then apply a translation to the right, the meaning of "right" has changed, so the rotated view appears 45 degrees down from its original position. To demonstrate the difference, I'll start with a subview that exactly overlaps its superview:

```
let v1 = UIView(frame:CGRect(20, 111, 132, 194))
v1.backgroundColor = UIColor(red: 1, green: 0.4, blue: 1, alpha: 1)
let v2 = UIView(frame:v1.bounds)
v2.backgroundColor = UIColor(red: 0.5, green: 1, blue: 0, alpha: 1)
self.view.addSubview(v1)
v1.addSubview(v2)
```

Then I'll apply two successive transforms to the subview, leaving the superview to show where the subview was originally. In this example, I translate and then rotate (Figure 1-8):

```
v2.transform =
    CGAffineTransform(translationX:100, y:0).rotated(by: 45 * .pi/180)
```

In this example, I rotate and then translate (Figure 1-9):

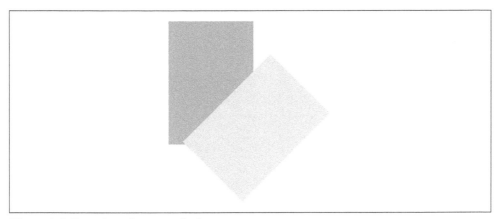

Figure 1-9. Rotation, then translation

```
v2.transform =
    CGAffineTransform(rotationAngle: 45 * .pi/180).translatedBy(x: 100, y: 0)
```

The concatenating method concatenates two transform matrices using matrix multiplication. Again, this operation is not commutative. The order is the *opposite* of the order when chaining transforms. Thus, this code gives the same result as the previous example (Figure 1-9):

```
let r = CGAffineTransform(rotationAngle: 45 * .pi/180)
let t = CGAffineTransform(translationX:100, y:0)
v2.transform = t.concatenating(r) // not r.concatenating(t)
```

To remove a transform from a combination of transforms, apply its inverse. The inverted method lets you obtain the inverse of a given affine transform. Again, order matters. In this example, I rotate the subview and shift it to its "right," and then remove the rotation (Figure 1-10):

```
let r = CGAffineTransform(rotationAngle: 45 * .pi/180)
let t = CGAffineTransform(translationX:100, y:0)
v2.transform = t.concatenating(r)
v2.transform = r.inverted().concatenating(v2.transform)
```

Finally, as there is no initializer for creating a skew (shear) transform, I'll illustrate by creating one manually, without further explanation (Figure 1-11):

```
v1.transform = CGAffineTransform(a:1, b:0, c:-0.2, d:1, tx:0, ty:0)
```

Transforms are useful particularly as temporary visual indicators. For example, you might call attention to a view by applying a transform that scales it up slightly, and then applying the identity transform to restore it to its original size, and animating those changes (Chapter 4).

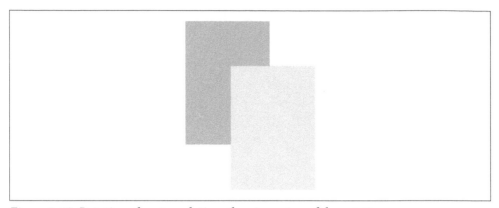

Figure 1-10. Rotation, then translation, then inversion of the rotation

Figure 1-11. Skew (shear)

App Rotation

In iOS 7 and before, the `transform` property lay at the heart of an iOS app's ability to rotate its interface: the window's frame and bounds were invariant, locked to the screen, and an app's interface rotated to compensate for a change in device orientation by applying a rotation transform to the root view, so that its origin moved to what the user now saw as the top left of the view.

In iOS 8 and later, as I've already mentioned, this is no longer the case. The screen's coordinate space is effectively rotated, but a coordinate space doesn't have a `transform` property. You can work out what has happened, if you really want to, by comparing the screen's `coordinateSpace` with its `fixedCoordinateSpace`, but none of the views in the story — neither the window, nor the root view, nor any of its sub-views — receives a rotation transform when the app's interface rotates.

Instead, you are expected to concentrate on the *dimensions* of the window, the root view, and so forth. This might mean their absolute dimensions, but it will often mean their dimensions as embodied in a set of *size classes* which are vended by a view's `traitCollection` property as a UITraitCollection object. I'll discuss trait collections and size classes further in the next section.

You can thus treat app rotation as effectively nothing more than a change in the interface's *proportions*: when the app rotates, the long dimension (of the root view, the window, and the screen's coordinate space bounds) becomes its short dimension and *vice versa*. This, after all, is what your interface needs to take into account in order to keep working when the app rotates.

Consider, for example, a subview of the root view, located at the bottom right of the screen when the device is in portrait orientation. If the root view's bounds width and bounds height are effectively transposed, then that poor old subview will now be outside the bounds height, and therefore off the screen — unless your app responds in some way to this change to reposition it. Such a response is called *layout*, a subject that will occupy most of the rest of this chapter. The point, however, is that what you're responding *to* is just a change in the window's proportions; the fact that this change stems from rotation of the app's interface is all but irrelevant.

Trait Collections and Size Classes

Every view in the interface, from the window on down, as well as any view controller whose view is part of the interface, inherits from the environment the value of its `traitCollection` property, which it has by virtue of implementing the UITraitEnvironment protocol. The `traitCollection` is a UITraitCollection, a value class. UITraitCollection was introduced in iOS 8; it has grown since then, and is now freighted with a considerable number of properties describing the environment. In addition to its `displayScale` (the screen resolution) and `userInterfaceIdiom` (the general device type, iPhone or iPad), a trait collection now also reports such things as the device's force touch capability and display gamut. But just two properties in particular concern us with regard to views in general:

`horizontalSizeClass`
`verticalSizeClass`
> A UIUserInterfaceSizeClass value, either `.regular` or `.compact`.

These are called *size classes*. The size classes, in combination, have the following meanings when, as will usually be the case, your app occupies the entire screen:

Both the horizontal and vertical size classes are `.regular`
> We're running on an iPad.

The horizontal size class is `.compact` *and the vertical size class is* `.regular`
> We're running on an iPhone with the app in portrait orientation.

The horizontal size class is `.regular` *and the vertical size class is* `.compact`
  We're running on an iPhone 6/7/8 Plus with the app in landscape orientation.

Both the horizontal and vertical size classes are `.compact`
  We're running on an iPhone (except an iPhone 6/7/8 Plus) with the app in landscape orientation.

(I'll explain in Chapter 9 how your app might *not* occupy the entire screen due to iPad multitasking.)

The size class trait collection properties can change while the app is running. In particular, the size classes on an iPhone reflect the orientation of the app — which can change as the app rotates in response to a change in the orientation of the device. Therefore, both at app launch time and if the trait collection changes while the app is running, the `traitCollectionDidChange(_:)` message is propagated down the hierarchy of UITraitEnvironments (meaning primarily, for our purposes, view controllers and views); the old trait collection (if any) is provided as the parameter, and the new trait collection can be retrieved as `self.traitCollection`.

It is possible to construct a trait collection yourself. (In the next chapter, I'll give an example of why that might be useful.) Oddly, though, you can't set any trait collection properties directly; instead, you form a trait collection through an initializer that determines just *one* property, and if you want to add further property settings, you have to combine trait collections by calling `init(traitsFrom:)` with an array of trait collections. For example:

```
let tcdisp = UITraitCollection(displayScale: UIScreen.main.scale)
let tcphone = UITraitCollection(userInterfaceIdiom: .phone)
let tcreg = UITraitCollection(verticalSizeClass: .regular)
let tc1 = UITraitCollection(traitsFrom: [tcdisp, tcphone, tcreg])
```

The `init(traitsFrom:)` array works like inheritance: an *ordered intersection* is performed. If two trait collections are combined, and they both set the same property, the winner is the trait collection that appears later in the array or further down the inheritance hierarchy. If one sets a property and the other doesn't, the one that sets the property wins. Thus, if you create a trait collection, the value for any unspecified property will be inherited if the trait collection finds itself in the inheritance hierarchy.

To compare trait collections, call `containsTraits(in:)`. This returns `true` if the value of every *specified* property of the parameter trait collection matches that of this trait collection.

 You cannot insert a trait collection directly into the inheritance hierarchy simply by setting a view's trait collection; `traitCollection` isn't a settable property. Instead, you'll use a special `overrideTraitCollection` property or method; I'll give an example in Chapter 6.

Layout

We have seen that a subview moves when its superview's bounds *origin* is changed. But what happens to a subview when its superview's bounds (or frame) *size* is changed?

Of its own accord, nothing happens. The subview's bounds and center haven't changed, and the superview's bounds origin hasn't moved, so the subview stays in the same position relative to the top left of its superview. In real life, however, that often won't be what you want. You'll want subviews to be resized and repositioned when their superview's bounds size is changed. This is called *layout*.

Here are some ways in which a superview might be resized dynamically:

- Your app might compensate for the user rotating the device 90 degrees by rotating itself so that its top moves to the new top of the screen, matching its new orientation — and, as a consequence, transposing the width and height values of its bounds.

- An iPhone app might launch on screens with different aspect ratios: for example, the screen of the iPhone 5s is relatively shorter than the screen of later iPhone models, and the app's interface may need to adapt to this difference.

- A universal app might launch on an iPad or on an iPhone. The app's interface may need to adapt to the size of the screen on which it finds itself running.

- A view instantiated from a nib, such as a view controller's main view or a table view cell, might be resized to fit the interface into which it is placed.

- A view might respond to a change in its surrounding views. For example, when a navigation bar is shown or hidden dynamically, the remaining interface might shrink or grow to compensate, filling the available space.

- The user might alter the width of your app's window on an iPad, as part of the iPad multitasking interface.

In any of those situations, and others, layout will probably be needed. Subviews of the view whose size has changed will need to shift, change size, redistribute themselves, or compensate in other ways so that the interface still looks good and remains usable.

Layout is performed in three primary ways:

Manual layout
> The superview is sent the `layoutSubviews` message whenever it is resized; so, to lay out subviews manually, provide your own subclass and override `layout-Subviews`. Clearly this could turn out to be a lot of work, but it means you can do anything you like.

Autoresizing

>   Autoresizing is the oldest way of performing layout automatically. When its superview is resized, a subview will respond in accordance with the rules prescribed by its own `autoresizingMask` property value.

Autolayout

>   Autolayout depends on the *constraints* of views. A constraint (an instance of NSLayoutConstraint) is a full-fledged object with numeric values describing some aspect of the size or position of a view, often in terms of some other view; it is much more sophisticated, descriptive, and powerful than the `autoresizing-Mask`. Multiple constraints can apply to an individual view, and they can describe a relationship between *any* two views (not just a subview and its superview). Autolayout is implemented behind the scenes in `layoutSubviews`; in effect, constraints allow you to write sophisticated `layoutSubviews` functionality without code.

Your layout strategy can involve any combination of these. The need for manual layout is rare, but it's there if you need it. Autoresizing is used by default. Autolayout may be regarded as an opt-in alternative to autoresizing, but in real life, if you're doing layout at all, you generally *will* opt in. Autolayout can be used for whatever areas of your interface you find appropriate; a view that uses autolayout can live side by side with a view that uses autoresizing.

The default layout behavior for a view depends on how it was created:

In code

>   A view that your code creates and adds to the interface, by default, uses autoresizing, not autolayout. This means that if you want such a view to use autolayout, you must deliberately suppress its use of autoresizing, as I'll explain later in this chapter.

In a nib file

>   All new *.storyboard* and *.xib* files opt in to autolayout. To see this, select the file in the Project navigator, show the File inspector, and examine the "Use Auto Layout" checkbox. This means that their views are ready for autolayout. But a view in the nib editor can still use autoresizing, even with "Use Auto Layout" checked, as I'll explain later.

Autoresizing

Autoresizing is a matter of conceptually assigning a subview "springs and struts." A spring can stretch; a strut can't. Springs and struts can be assigned internally or externally, horizontally or vertically. Thus you can specify (using internal springs and struts) whether and how the view can be resized, and (using external springs and struts) whether and how the view can be repositioned. For example:

- Imagine a subview that is centered in its superview and is to stay centered, but is to resize itself as the superview is resized. It would have struts externally and springs internally.

- Imagine a subview that is centered in its superview and is to stay centered, and is *not* to resize itself as the superview is resized. It would have springs externally and struts internally.

- Imagine an OK button that is to stay in the lower right of its superview. It would have struts internally, struts externally to its right and bottom, and springs externally to its top and left.

- Imagine a text field that is to stay at the top of its superview. It is to widen as the superview widens. It would have struts externally, but a spring to its bottom; internally it would have a vertical strut and a horizontal spring.

In code, a combination of springs and struts is set through a view's `autoresizing-Mask` property, which is a bitmask so that you can combine options. The options (UIViewAutoresizing) represent springs; whatever isn't specified is a strut. The default is the empty set, apparently meaning all struts — but of course it can't really be *all* struts, because if the superview is resized, *something* needs to change; in reality, an empty `autoresizingMask` is the same as `.flexibleRightMargin` together with `.flexibleBottomMargin`.

In debugging, when you log a UIView to the console, its `autoresizingMask` is reported using the word "autoresize" and a list of the springs. The margins are LM, RM, TM, and BM; the internal dimensions are W and H. For example, `autoresize = LM+TM` means that what's flexible is the left and top margins; `autoresize = W+BM` means that what's flexible is the width and the bottom margin.

To demonstrate autoresizing, I'll start with a view and two subviews, one stretched across the top, the other confined to the lower right (Figure 1-12):

```
let v1 = UIView(frame:CGRect(100, 111, 132, 194))
v1.backgroundColor = UIColor(red: 1, green: 0.4, blue: 1, alpha: 1)
let v2 = UIView(frame:CGRect(0, 0, 132, 10))
v2.backgroundColor = UIColor(red: 0.5, green: 1, blue: 0, alpha: 1)
let v1b = v1.bounds
let v3 = UIView(frame:CGRect(v1b.width-20, v1b.height-20, 20, 20))
v3.backgroundColor = UIColor(red: 1, green: 0, blue: 0, alpha: 1)
self.view.addSubview(v1)
v1.addSubview(v2)
v1.addSubview(v3)
```

To that example, I'll add code applying springs and struts to the two subviews to make them behave like the text field and the OK button I was hypothesizing earlier:

```
v2.autoresizingMask = .flexibleWidth
v3.autoresizingMask = [.flexibleTopMargin, .flexibleLeftMargin]
```

Figure 1-12. Before autoresizing

Figure 1-13. After autoresizing

Now I'll resize the superview, thus bringing autoresizing into play; as you can see (Figure 1-13), the subviews remain pinned in their correct relative positions:

```
v1.bounds.size.width += 40
v1.bounds.size.height -= 50
```

If autoresizing isn't sophisticated enough to achieve what you want, you have two choices:

- Combine it with manual layout in `layoutSubviews`. Autoresizing happens before `layoutSubviews` is called, so your `layoutSubviews` code is free to come marching in and tidy up whatever autoresizing didn't get quite right.

- Use autolayout. This is actually the same solution, because autolayout is in fact a way of injecting functionality into `layoutSubviews`. But using autolayout is a lot easier than writing your own `layoutSubviews` code!

Autolayout and Constraints

Autolayout is an opt-in technology, at the level of each individual view. You can use autoresizing and autolayout in different areas of the same interface — even for different subviews of the same view. One sibling view can use autolayout while another sibling view does not, and a superview can use autolayout while some or all of its subviews do not.

However, autolayout is implemented through the superview chain, so if a view uses autolayout, then automatically so do all its superviews; and if (as will almost certainly be the case) one of those views is the main view of a view controller, that view controller receives autolayout-related events.

But *how* does a view opt in to using autolayout? Simply put: by becoming involved with a constraint. Constraints are your way of telling the autolayout engine that you want it to perform layout on this view, as well as how you want the view laid out.

An autolayout constraint, or simply *constraint*, is an NSLayoutConstraint instance, and describes either the absolute width or height of a view or a relationship between an attribute of one view and an attribute of another view. In the latter case, the attributes don't have to be the same attribute, and the two views don't have to be siblings (subviews of the same superview) or parent and child (superview and subview) — the only requirement is that they share a common ancestor (a superview somewhere up the view hierarchy).

Here are the chief properties of an NSLayoutConstraint:

firstItem, firstAttribute, secondItem, secondAttribute
> The two views and their respective attributes involved in this constraint. If the constraint is describing a view's absolute height or width, the second view will be nil and the second attribute will be .notAnAttribute. Aside from that, the possible attribute values are (NSLayoutAttribute`):
>
> - .width, .height
> - .top, .bottom
> - .left, .right, .leading, .trailing
> - .centerX, .centerY
> - .firstBaseline, .lastBaseline
>
> .firstBaseline applies primarily to multiline labels, and is some distance down from the top of the label (Chapter 10); .lastBaseline is some distance up from the bottom of the label.
>
> The meanings of the other attributes are intuitively obvious, except that you might wonder what .leading and .trailing mean: they are the international equivalent of .left and .right, automatically reversing their meaning on systems for which your app is localized and whose language is written right-to-left. Starting in iOS 9, the *entire* interface is automatically reversed on such systems — but that will work properly only if you've used .leading and .trailing constraints throughout.

`multiplier, constant`

These numbers will be applied to the second attribute's value to determine the first attribute's value. The `multiplier` is multiplied by the second attribute's value; the `constant` is added to that product. The first attribute is set to the result. (The name *constant* is a very poor choice, as this value isn't constant; have the Apple folks never heard the term *addend*?) Basically, you're writing an equation $a_1 = ma_2 + c$, where a_1 and a_2 are the two attributes, and m and c are the multiplier and the constant. Thus, in the degenerate case where the first attribute's value is to equal the second attribute's value, the multiplier will be 1 and the constant will be 0. If you're describing a view's width or height absolutely, the multiplier will be 1 and the constant will be the width or height value.

`relation`

How the two attribute values are to be related to one another, as modified by the `multiplier` and the `constant`. This is the operator that goes in the spot where I put the equal sign in the equation in the preceding paragraph. Possible values are (NSLayoutRelation):

- `.equal`
- `.lessThanOrEqual`
- `.greaterThanOrEqual`

`priority`

Priority values range from 1000 (required) down to 1, and certain standard behaviors have standard priorities. Constraints can have different priorities, determining the order in which they are applied. New in iOS 11, a priority is not a number but a struct (UILayoutPriority) wrapping the numeric value as its `raw-Value`, initializable with `init(rawValue:)`.

A constraint belongs to a view. A view can have many constraints: a UIView has a `constraints` property, along with these instance methods:

- `addConstraint(_:)`, `addConstraints(_:)`
- `removeConstraint(_:)`, `removeConstraints(_:)`

The question then is *which* view a given constraint will belong to. The answer is: the view that is closest up the view hierarchy from both views involved in the constraint. If possible, it should *be* one of those views. Thus, for example, if the constraint dictates a view's absolute width, it belongs to that view; if it sets the top of a view in relation to the top of its superview, it belongs to that superview; if it aligns the tops of two sibling views, it belongs to their common superview.

However, you'll probably never call any of those methods. Starting in iOS 8, instead of adding a constraint to a particular view explicitly, you can *activate* the constraint using the NSLayoutConstraint class method `activate(_:)`, which takes an array of constraints. The activated constraints are *added to the correct view automatically*, relieving you from having to determine what view that would be. There is also a method `deactivate(_:)`, which removes constraints from their view. Also, a constraint has an `isActive` property; you can set it to activate or deactivate a single constraint, plus it tells you whether a given constraint is part of the interface at this moment.

NSLayoutConstraint properties are read-only, except for `priority`, `constant`, and `isActive`. If you want to change anything else about an existing constraint, you must remove the constraint and add a new one.

 Once you are using explicit constraints to position and size a view, *do not set its frame* (or bounds and center) subsequently; use constraints alone. Otherwise, when `layoutSubviews` is called, the view will jump back to where its constraints position it. (However, you may set a view's frame from *within* an implementation of `layoutSubviews`, and it is perfectly normal to do so.)

Autoresizing Constraints

The mechanism whereby individual views can opt in to autolayout can suddenly involve other views in autolayout, even though those other views were not using autolayout previously. Therefore, there needs to be a way, when such a view becomes involved in autolayout, to generate constraints for it — constraints that will determine that view's position and size identically to how its `frame` and `autoresizingMask` were determining them. The autolayout engine takes care of this for you: it reads the view's `frame` and `autoresizingMask` settings and translates them into *implicit* constraints (of class NSAutoresizingMaskLayoutConstraint). The autolayout engine treats a view in this special way only if it has its `translatesAutoresizingMaskInto-Constraints` property set to `true` — which happens to be the default.

I'll construct an example in two stages. In the first stage, I add to my interface, in code, a UILabel that *doesn't* use autolayout. I'll decide that this view's position is to be somewhere near the top right of the screen. To keep it in position near the top right, its `autoresizingMask` will be [`.flexibleLeftMargin`, `.flexibleBottomMargin`]:

```
let lab1 = UILabel(frame:CGRect(270,20,42,22))
lab1.autoresizingMask = [.flexibleLeftMargin, .flexibleBottomMargin]
lab1.text = "Hello"
self.view.addSubview(lab1)
```

If we now rotate the device (or Simulator window), and the app rotates to compensate, the label stays correctly positioned near the top right corner by autoresizing.

Now, however, I'll add a second label that *does* use autolayout — and in particular, I'll attach it by a constraint to the first label (the meaning of this code will be made clear in subsequent sections; just accept it for now):

```
let lab2 = UILabel()
lab2.translatesAutoresizingMaskIntoConstraints = false
lab2.text = "Howdy"
self.view.addSubview(lab2)
NSLayoutConstraint.activate([
    lab2.topAnchor.constraint(
        equalTo: lab1.bottomAnchor, constant: 20),
    lab2.trailingAnchor.constraint(
        equalTo: self.view.trailingAnchor, constant: -20)
])
```

This causes the first label to be involved in autolayout. Therefore, the first label magically acquires four automatically generated implicit constraints of class NSAutoresizingMaskLayoutConstraint, such as to give the label the same size and position, and the same *behavior* when its superview is resized, that it had when it was configured by its `frame` and `autoresizingMask`:

```
<NSAutoresizingMaskLayoutConstraint:0x6000002818b0 h=&-- v=--&
    UILabel:0x7f9d3820bf80'Hello'.midX == UIView:0x7f9d383079d0.width-29>
<NSAutoresizingMaskLayoutConstraint:0x60000009fe50 h=&-- v=--&
    UILabel:0x7f9d3820bf80'Hello'.midY == 31>
<NSAutoresizingMaskLayoutConstraint:0x60000009fef0 h=&-- v=--&
    UILabel:0x7f9d3820bf80'Hello'.width == 42>
<NSAutoresizingMaskLayoutConstraint:0x6000002821c0 h=&-- v=--&
    UILabel:0x7f9d3820bf80'Hello'.height == 22>
```

It is important to bear in mind, however, that within this helpful automatic behavior lurks a trap. Suppose a view has acquired automatically generated implicit constraints, and suppose you then proceed to attach *further constraints* to this view, explicitly setting its position or size. There will then almost certainly be a *conflict* between your explicit constraints and the implicit constraints. The solution is to set the view's `translatesAutoresizingMaskIntoConstraints` property to `false`, so that the implicit constraints are not generated and the view's *only* constraints are your explicit constraints.

In a nib with "Use Auto Layout" checked, there is no difficulty in this regard. The nib editor itself will switch a view's `translatesAutoresizingMaskIntoConstraints` property to `false` as soon as you add constraints that would cause a problem. The trouble is most likely to arise when you create a view *in code* and then position or size that view with constraints, *forgetting* that you also need to set its `translatesAutoresizingMaskIntoConstraints` property to `false`. If that happens, you'll get a conflict between constraints. (To be honest, I usually *do* forget, and am reminded only when I *do* get a conflict between constraints.)

Creating Constraints in Code

We are now ready to write some code that creates constraints! I'll start by using the NSLayoutConstraint initializer:

- `init(item:attribute:relatedBy:toItem:attribute:multiplier:constant:)`

This initializer sets every property of the constraint, as I described them a moment ago — except the `priority`, which defaults to `.required` (1000) and can be set later if necessary.

I'll generate the same views and subviews and layout behavior as in Figures 1-12 and 1-13, but using constraints. First, I'll create the views and add them to the interface. Observe that I don't bother to assign the subviews v2 and v3 explicit frames as I create them, because constraints will take care of positioning them. Also, I remember (for once) to set their `translatesAutoresizingMaskIntoConstraints` properties to `false`, so that they won't sprout additional implicit NSAutoresizingMaskLayout-Constraints:

```
let v1 = UIView(frame:CGRect(100, 111, 132, 194))
v1.backgroundColor = UIColor(red: 1, green: 0.4, blue: 1, alpha: 1)
let v2 = UIView()
v2.backgroundColor = UIColor(red: 0.5, green: 1, blue: 0, alpha: 1)
let v3 = UIView()
v3.backgroundColor = UIColor(red: 1, green: 0, blue: 0, alpha: 1)
self.view.addSubview(v1)
v1.addSubview(v2)
v1.addSubview(v3)
v2.translatesAutoresizingMaskIntoConstraints = false
v3.translatesAutoresizingMaskIntoConstraints = false
```

Now here come the constraints:

```
v1.addConstraint(
    NSLayoutConstraint(item: v2,
        attribute: .leading,
        relatedBy: .equal,
        toItem: v1,
        attribute: .leading,
        multiplier: 1, constant: 0)
)
v1.addConstraint(
    NSLayoutConstraint(item: v2,
        attribute: .trailing,
        relatedBy: .equal,
        toItem: v1,
        attribute: .trailing,
        multiplier: 1, constant: 0)
)
v1.addConstraint(
```

```
            NSLayoutConstraint(item: v2,
                attribute: .top,
                relatedBy: .equal,
                toItem: v1,
                attribute: .top,
                multiplier: 1, constant: 0)
        )
        v2.addConstraint(
            NSLayoutConstraint(item: v2,
                attribute: .height,
                relatedBy: .equal,
                toItem: nil,
                attribute: .notAnAttribute,
                multiplier: 1, constant: 10)
        )
        v3.addConstraint(
            NSLayoutConstraint(item: v3,
                attribute: .width,
                relatedBy: .equal,
                toItem: nil,
                attribute: .notAnAttribute,
                multiplier: 1, constant: 20)
        )
        v3.addConstraint(
            NSLayoutConstraint(item: v3,
                attribute: .height,
                relatedBy: .equal,
                toItem: nil,
                attribute: .notAnAttribute,
                multiplier: 1, constant: 20)
        )
        v1.addConstraint(
            NSLayoutConstraint(item: v3,
                attribute: .trailing,
                relatedBy: .equal,
                toItem: v1,
                attribute: .trailing,
                multiplier: 1, constant: 0)
        )
        v1.addConstraint(
            NSLayoutConstraint(item: v3,
                attribute: .bottom,
                relatedBy: .equal,
                toItem: v1,
                attribute: .bottom,
                multiplier: 1, constant: 0)
        )
```

Now, I know what you're thinking. You're thinking: "What are you, nuts? That is a boatload of code!" (Except that you probably used another four-letter word instead of "boat.") But that's something of an illusion. I'd argue that what we're doing here is actually *simpler* than the code with which we created Figure 1-12 using explicit frames and autoresizing.

After all, we merely create eight constraints in eight simple commands. (I've broken each command into multiple *lines*, but that's mere formatting.) They're verbose, but they are the same command repeated with different parameters, so creating them is simple. Moreover, our eight constraints determine the *position, size, and layout behavior* of our two subviews, so we're getting a lot of bang for our buck.

Even more telling, these constraints are a far clearer expression of what's supposed to happen than setting a frame and `autoresizingMask`. The position of our subviews is described once and for all, both as they will initially appear and as they will appear if their superview is resized. And it is described meaningfully; we don't have to use arbitrary math. Recall what we had to say before:

```
let v1b = v1.bounds
let v3 = UIView(frame:CGRect(v1b.width-20, v1b.height-20, 20, 20))
```

That business of subtracting the view's height and width from its superview's bounds height and width in order to position the view is confusing and error-prone. With constraints, we can speak the truth directly; our constraints say, plainly and simply, "v3 is 20 points wide and 20 points high and *flush with the bottom-right corner* of v1."

In addition, constraints can express things that autoresizing can't. For example, instead of applying an absolute height to v2, we could require that its height be exactly one-tenth of v1's height, regardless of how v1 is resized. To do that without autolayout, you'd have to implement `layoutSubviews` and enforce it manually, in code.

Anchor notation

The `NSLayoutConstraint(item:...)` initializer is rather verbose, but it has the virtue of singularity: one method can create any constraint. There's another way to do everything I just did, making exactly the same eight constraints and adding them to the same views, using a much more compact notation that takes the opposite approach: it concentrates on brevity but sacrifices singularity. Instead of focusing on the constraint, the compact notation focuses on the *attributes* to which the constraint relates. These attributes are expressed as *anchor* properties of a UIView:

- `widthAnchor`, `heightAnchor`
- `topAnchor`, `bottomAnchor`
- `leftAnchor`, `rightAnchor`, `leadingAnchor`, `trailingAnchor`
- `centerXAnchor`, `centerYAnchor`
- `firstBaselineAnchor`, `lastBaselineAnchor`

The anchor values are instances of NSLayoutAnchor subclasses. The constraint-forming methods are anchor instance methods, and there are a lot of legal combinations, with your choice depending on how much information you need to express. You can provide another anchor, another anchor and a constant, another anchor and a multiplier, another anchor and both a constant and a multiplier, or a constant alone (for an absolute width or height constraint). If the constant is omitted, it is 0; if the multiplier is omitted, it is 1. And in every case, there are three possible relations:

- `constraint(equalTo:)`
- `constraint(greaterThanOrEqualTo:)`
- `constraint(lessThanOrEqualTo:)`
- `constraint(equalTo:constant:)`
- `constraint(greaterThanOrEqualTo:constant:)`
- `constraint(lessThanOrEqualTo:constant:)`
- `constraint(equalTo:multiplier:)`
- `constraint(greaterThanOrEqualTo:multiplier:)`
- `constraint(lessThanOrEqualTo:multiplier:)`
- `constraint(equalTo:multiplier:constant:)`
- `constraint(greaterThanOrEqualTo:multiplier:constant:)`
- `constraint(lessThanOrEqualTo:multiplier:constant:)`
- `constraint(equalToConstant:)`
- `constraint(greaterThanOrEqualToConstant:)`
- `constraint(lessThanOrEqualToConstant:)`

In iOS 10, a method was added that generates, not a constraint, but a new width or height anchor expressing the distance between two anchors; the idea is that you could then set a view's width or height anchor to equal it:

- `anchorWithOffset(to:)`

New in iOS 11, additional methods create a constraint based on a `constant` value provided by the runtime. This is helpful for getting the standard spacing between views, and is especially valuable when connecting text baselines vertically, because the system spacing will change according to the text size:

- `constraintEqualToSystemSpacing(after:multiplier:)`
- `constraintGreaterThanOrEqualToSystemSpacing(after:multiplier:)`

- constraintLessThanOrEqualToSystemSpacing(after:multiplier:)
- constraintEqualToSystemSpacing(below:multiplier:)
- constraintGreaterThanOrEqualToSystemSpacing(below:multiplier:)
- constraintLessThanOrEqualToSystemSpacing(below:multiplier:)

All of that may sound very elaborate when I describe it, but when you see it in action, you will appreciate immediately the benefit of this compact notation: it's easy to write (especially thanks to Xcode's code completion), easy to read, and easy to maintain. The anchor notation is particularly convenient in connection with `activate(_:)`, as we don't have to worry about specifying what view each constraint should be added to.

Here we generate exactly the same constraints as in the preceding example:

```
NSLayoutConstraint.activate([
    v2.leadingAnchor.constraint(equalTo:v1.leadingAnchor),
    v2.trailingAnchor.constraint(equalTo:v1.trailingAnchor),
    v2.topAnchor.constraint(equalTo:v1.topAnchor),
    v2.heightAnchor.constraint(equalToConstant:10),
    v3.widthAnchor.constraint(equalToConstant:20),
    v3.heightAnchor.constraint(equalToConstant:20),
    v3.trailingAnchor.constraint(equalTo:v1.trailingAnchor),
    v3.bottomAnchor.constraint(equalTo:v1.bottomAnchor)
])
```

That's eight constraints in eight lines of code — plus the surrounding `activate` call to put those constraints into our interface. It isn't strictly necessary to activate all one's constraints at once, but it's best to try to do so.

Visual format notation

Another way to abbreviate your creation of constraints is to use a text-based shorthand called a *visual format*. This has the advantage of allowing you to describe multiple constraints simultaneously, and is appropriate particularly when you're arranging a series of views horizontally or vertically. I'll start with a simple example:

```
"V:|[v2(10)]"
```

In that expression, `V:` means that the vertical dimension is under discussion; the alternative is `H:`, which is also the default (so you can omit it). A view's name appears in square brackets, and a pipe (`|`) signifies the superview, so we're portraying v2's top edge as butting up against its superview's top edge. Numeric dimensions appear in parentheses, and a numeric dimension accompanying a view's name sets that dimension of that view, so we're also setting v2's height to 10.

To use a visual format, you have to provide a dictionary that maps the string name of each view mentioned by the visual format string to the actual view. For example, the dictionary accompanying the preceding expression might be ["v2":v2].

Here is yet another way of expressing of the preceding example, generating exactly the same eight constraints using four commands instead of eight, thanks to the visual format shorthand:

```
let d = ["v2":v2,"v3":v3]
NSLayoutConstraint.activate([
    NSLayoutConstraint.constraints(withVisualFormat:
        "H:|[v2]|", metrics: nil, views: d),
    NSLayoutConstraint.constraints(withVisualFormat:
        "V:|[v2(10)]", metrics: nil, views: d),
    NSLayoutConstraint.constraints(withVisualFormat:
        "H:[v3(20)]|", metrics: nil, views: d),
    NSLayoutConstraint.constraints(withVisualFormat:
        "V:[v3(20)]|", metrics: nil, views: d)
].flatMap{$0})
```

(The constraints(withVisualFormat:...) class method yields an array of constraints, so my literal array is an array of arrays of constraints. But activate(_:) expects an array of constraints, so I flatten my literal array.)

The visual format syntax shows itself to best advantage when multiple views are laid out in relation to one another along the same dimension; in that situation, you get a lot of bang for your buck (many constraints generated by one visual format string). The syntax, however, is somewhat limited in what constraints it can readily express; it conceals the number and exact nature of the constraints that it produces; and personally I find it easier to make a mistake with the visual format syntax than with the explicit expression of each individual constraint. Still, you'll want to become familiar with the visual format syntax, not least because console messages describing a constraint sometimes use it.

Here are some further things to know when generating constraints with the visual format syntax:

- The metrics: parameter is a dictionary with numeric values. This lets you use a name in the visual format string where a numeric value needs to go.

- The options: parameter, omitted in the preceding example, is a bitmask (NSLayoutFormatOptions) chiefly allowing you to specify alignments (which are applied to all the views mentioned in the visual format string).

- To specify the distance between two successive views, use hyphens surrounding the numeric value, like this: "[v1]-20-[v2]". The numeric value may optionally be surrounded by parentheses.

- A numeric value in parentheses may be preceded by an equality or inequality operator, and may be followed by an at sign with a priority. Multiple numeric values, separated by comma, may appear in parentheses together. For example: "[v1(>=20@400,<=30)]".

For formal details of the visual format syntax, see the "Visual Format Syntax" chapter of Apple's *Auto Layout Guide*.

Constraints as Objects

The examples so far have involved creating constraints and adding them directly to the interface — and then forgetting about them. But it is frequently useful to form constraints and keep them on hand for future use, typically in a property. A common use case is where you intend, at some future time, to change the interface in some radical way, such as by inserting or removing a view; you'll probably find it convenient to keep multiple sets of constraints on hand, each set being appropriate to a particular configuration of the interface. It is then trivial to swap constraints out of and into the interface along with views that they affect.

In this example, we create within our main view (`self.view`) three views, v1, v2, and v3, which are red, yellow, and blue rectangles respectively. For some reason, we will later want to remove the yellow view (v2) dynamically as the app runs, moving the blue view to where the yellow view was; and then, still later, we will want to insert the yellow view once again (Figure 1-14). So we have two alternating view configurations.

To prepare for this, we create *two* sets of constraints, one describing the positions of v1, v2, and v3 when all three are present, the other describing the positions of v1 and v3 when v2 is absent. For purposes of maintaining these sets of constraints, we have already prepared two properties, `constraintsWith` and `constraintsWithout`, initialized as empty arrays of NSLayoutConstraint. We will also need a strong reference to v2, so that it doesn't vanish when we remove it from the interface:

```
var v2 : UIView!
var constraintsWith = [NSLayoutConstraint]()
var constraintsWithout = [NSLayoutConstraint]()
```

Here's the code for creating the views:

```
let v1 = UIView()
v1.backgroundColor = .red
v1.translatesAutoresizingMaskIntoConstraints = false
let v2 = UIView()
v2.backgroundColor = .yellow
v2.translatesAutoresizingMaskIntoConstraints = false
let v3 = UIView()
v3.backgroundColor = .blue
v3.translatesAutoresizingMaskIntoConstraints = false
```

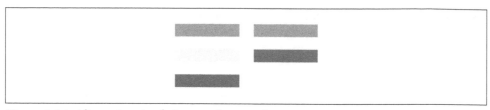

Figure 1-14. Alternate sets of views and constraints

```
self.view.addSubview(v1)
self.view.addSubview(v2)
self.view.addSubview(v3)
self.v2 = v2 // retain
```

Now we create the constraints and combine them into two groups:

```
// construct constraints
let c1 = NSLayoutConstraint.constraints(withVisualFormat:
    "H:|-(20)-[v(100)]", metrics: nil, views: ["v":v1])
let c2 = NSLayoutConstraint.constraints(withVisualFormat:
    "H:|-(20)-[v(100)]", metrics: nil, views: ["v":v2])
let c3 = NSLayoutConstraint.constraints(withVisualFormat:
    "H:|-(20)-[v(100)]", metrics: nil, views: ["v":v3])
let c4 = NSLayoutConstraint.constraints(withVisualFormat:
    "V:|-(100)-[v(20)]", metrics: nil, views: ["v":v1])
let c5with = NSLayoutConstraint.constraints(withVisualFormat:
    "V:[v1]-(20)-[v2(20)]-(20)-[v3(20)]", metrics: nil,
    views: ["v1":v1, "v2":v2, "v3":v3])
let c5without = NSLayoutConstraint.constraints(withVisualFormat:
    "V:[v1]-(20)-[v3(20)]", metrics: nil, views: ["v1":v1, "v3":v3])
// first set of constraints
self.constraintsWith.append(contentsOf:c1)
self.constraintsWith.append(contentsOf:c2)
self.constraintsWith.append(contentsOf:c3)
self.constraintsWith.append(contentsOf:c4)
self.constraintsWith.append(contentsOf:c5with)
// second set of constraints
self.constraintsWithout.append(contentsOf:c1)
self.constraintsWithout.append(contentsOf:c3)
self.constraintsWithout.append(contentsOf:c4)
self.constraintsWithout.append(contentsOf:c5without)
```

Finally, we apply our constraints. We start with v2 present, so it is the first set of constraints that we initially make active:

```
// apply first set
NSLayoutConstraint.activate(self.constraintsWith)
```

All that preparation may seem extraordinarily elaborate, but the result is that when the time comes to swap v2 out of or into the interface, swapping the appropriate constraints is trivial:

```
if self.v2.superview != nil {
    self.v2.removeFromSuperview()
    NSLayoutConstraint.deactivate(self.constraintsWith)
    NSLayoutConstraint.activate(self.constraintsWithout)
} else {
    self.view.addSubview(v2)
    NSLayoutConstraint.deactivate(self.constraintsWithout)
    NSLayoutConstraint.activate(self.constraintsWith)
}
```

In that code, I deactivated the old constraints before activating the new ones. Always proceed in that order; activating the new constraints with the old constraints still in force will cause a conflict (as I'll explain later in this chapter) and will break the example (because the same constraints appear in both groups).

Margins and Guides

So far, I've been assuming that the anchor points of your constraints represent the edges and centers of views. For example:

```
let c = v2.leadingAnchor.constraint(equalTo:v1.leadingAnchor)
```

Sometimes, however, you want a view to vend a set of secondary edges, with respect to which other views can be positioned. For example, you might want subviews to keep a minimum distance from the edge of their superview, and the superview should be able to dictate what that minimum distance is.

This notion of secondary edges is expressed in two different ways:

Edge insets

A view vends secondary edges as a UIEdgeInsets, a struct consisting of four floats representing inset values starting at the top and proceeding counterclockwise — top, left, bottom, right. This is useful when you need to interface with the secondary edges as numeric values — to set them, for example, or to perform manual layout.

Layout guides

The UILayoutGuide class (introduced in iOS 9) represents secondary edges as a kind of pseudoview. It has a frame (its `layoutFrame`) with respect to the view that vends it, but its important properties are its anchors, which are the same as for a view. This, obviously, is useful for autolayout.

Safe area

An important set of secondary edges you'll encounter when programming iOS 11 is the *safe area*. This is a feature of a UIView, but it is imposed by the UIViewController that manages this view. One reason a safe area is needed is that the top and bottom of the interface are often occupied by a bar (status bar, navigation bar, toolbar, tab bar —

see Chapter 12). Your layout of subviews will typically occupy the region *between* these bars. But that's not easy, because:

- A view controller's main view will typically extend vertically to the edges of the window *behind* those bars.
- The bars can come and go dynamically, and can change their heights. For example, by default, in an iPhone app, the status bar will be present when the app is portrait orientation, but will vanish when the app is in landscape orientation; similarly, a navigation bar is taller when the app is in portrait orientation than when the app is in landscape orientation.

Therefore, you need something else, other than the *literal* top and bottom of a view controller's main view, to which to anchor the vertical constraints that position its subviews — something that will *move* dynamically to reflect the current location of the bars. Otherwise, an interface that looks right under some circumstances will look wrong in others.

Consider, for instance, a view whose top is literally constrained to the top of the view controller's main view, which is its superview:

```
let arr = NSLayoutConstraint.constraints(withVisualFormat:
    "V:|-0-[v]", metrics: nil, views: ["v":v])
```

When the app is in landscape orientation, with the status bar removed by default, this view will be right up against the top of the screen, which is fine. But in portrait orientation, this view will *still* be right up against the top of the screen — which might look bad, because the status bar reappears and overlaps it. If this view is a label, for example, the status bar is now overlapping its text.

To solve this problem, a UIViewController imposes the safe area on its main view, describing the region of the main view that is overlapped by the status bar and other bars. The top of the safe area matches the bottom of the lowest top bar, or the top of the main view if there is no top bar; the bottom of the safe area matches the top of the bottom bar, or the bottom of the main view if there is no bottom bar. The safe area changes as the situation changes — when the top or bottom bar changes its height, or vanishes entirely.

In real life, you'll be most concerned to position subviews of a view controller's main view with respect to the main view's safe area. Your views constrained to the main view's safe area will avoid being overlapped by bars, and will move to track the edges of the main view's visible area. Moreover, when a view performs layout, it imposes the safe area on its own subviews, describing the region of each subview that is overlapped by its own safe area. Thus, *every* view "knows" where the bars are.

To retrieve a view's safe area as edge insets, fetch its `safeAreaInsets`. To retrieve a view's safe area as a layout guide, fetch its `safeAreaLayoutGuide`. You can learn that a subclassed view's safe area has changed by overriding `safeAreaInsetsDidChange`, or that a view controller's main view's safe area has changed by overriding the view controller's `viewSafeAreaInsetsDidChange`; in real life, however, using autolayout, you probably won't need that information — you'll just allow views pinned to a safe area layout guide to move as the safe area changes.

In this example, `v` is a view controller's main view, and `v1` is its subview; we construct a constraint between the top of `v1` and the top of the main view's safe area:

```
let c = v1.topAnchor.constraint(equalTo: v.safeAreaLayoutGuide.topAnchor)
```

The safe area is new in iOS 11. Earlier systems used two objects, the so-called "top layout guide" and "bottom layout guide," which were actually invisible views injected by the view controller as subviews of its main views. The Xcode 9 nib editor provides access to a view controller's main view's safe area so that you can make constraints to it (as I'll explain later in this chapter); if you have an older project, you can transition to using the safe area in the nib editor by checking Use Safe Area Layout Guides in the File inspector.

A view controller can inset even further the safe area it imposes on its main view; set its `additionalSafeAreaInsets`. This, as the name implies, is added to the automatic safe area. For example, if you set a view controller's `additionalSafeAreaInsets` to a UIEdgeInsets with a top of 50, and if the status bar is showing and there is no other top bar, the default safe area top would be 20, so now it's 70. The `additionalSafe-AreaInsets` is helpful if your main view has material at its edge that must always remain visible.

The safe area permits effects that were difficult to achieve in previous systems, such as centering a view vertically within the visible region between the top and bottom bars.

 The safe area insets are of increased importance on a device without a bezel, such as the iPhone X, where they help keep your views away from the rounded corners of the screen, and prevent them from being interfered with by the sensors and the home indicator, both in portrait and in landscape.

Margins

A view also has margins of its own. Unlike the safe area, which propagates down the view hierarchy from the view controller, you are free to set an individual view's margins. Once again, the idea is that a subview might be positioned with respect to its superview's margins, especially through an autolayout constraint. By default, a view has a margin of 8 on all four edges.

A view's margins are available as a UILayoutGuide through the UIView `layout-MarginsGuide` property. Here's a constraint between a subview's leading edge and its superview's leading margin:

```
let c = v.leadingAnchor.constraint(equalTo:
    self.view.layoutMarginsGuide.leadingAnchor)
```

In visual format syntax, a view pinned to its superview's edge using a single hyphen, with no explicit distance value, is interpreted as a constraint to the superview's margin:

```
let arr = NSLayoutConstraint.constraints(withVisualFormat:
    "H:|-[v]", metrics: nil, views: ["v":v])
```

The layoutMarginsGuide property is read-only. To allow you to set a view's margins, a UIView has a layoutMargins property, a writable UIEdgeInsets. New in iOS 11, however, Apple would prefer that you set the directionalLayoutMargins property instead; this has the feature that when your interface is reversed in a right-to-left system language for which your app is localized, its leading and trailing values behave correctly (the left-to-right leading value becomes the right-to-left leading value). It is expressed as an NSDirectionalEdgeInsets struct (also new in iOS 11), whose properties are top, leading, bottom, and trailing.

Optionally, a view's layout margins can propagate down to its subview, in the following sense: a subview that overlaps its superview's margin may acquire the amount of overlap as a minimum margin of its own. To switch on this option, set the subview's preservesSuperviewLayoutMargins to true. For example, suppose we set the superview's directionalLayoutMargins to an NSDirectionalEdgeInsets with a leading value of 40. And suppose the subview is pinned 10 points from the superview's leading edge, so that it overlaps the superview's leading margin by 30 points. Then, if the subview's preservesSuperviewLayoutMargins is true, the subview's leading margin is 30.

New in iOS 11, a view's margin values are treated as insets *from the safe area*. For example, suppose a view's top margin is 8. And suppose this view underlaps the entire status bar, and thus has acquired a safe area top of 20. Then its *effective* top margin value is 28 — meaning that a subview whose top is pinned exactly to this view's top margin will appear 28 points below this view's top. If you don't like that behavior (perhaps because you have code from iOS 10 that predates the existence of the safe area), you can switch it off by setting the view's insetsLayoutMarginsFromSafeArea property to false; now a top margin value of 8 means an effective top margin value of 8.

In iOS 10 and before, a view controller imposed margins on its main view, and these could not be changed; you could set the main view's margins, but this would have no effect. New in iOS 11, this policy has been softened. The view controller now has a systemMinimumLayoutMargins property; it imposes these margins on its main view as a minimum, meaning that you can increase the main view's margins beyond these limits, but an attempt to decrease a margin below them will fail silently. You can evade even that restriction, however, by setting the view controller's viewRespects-

`SystemMinimumLayoutMargins` property to `false`. The `systemMinimumLayout-Margins` default value is a top and bottom margin of 0 and side margins of 16 on a smaller device, with side margins of 20 on a larger device.

A second set of margins, a UIView's `readableContentGuide` (a UILayoutGuide), which you cannot change, was introduced in iOS 9. The basic idea is that a subview consisting of text should not be allowed to grow as wide as an iPad in landscape, because that's too wide to read easily, especially if the text is small. By constraining such a subview horizontally to its superview's `readableContentGuide`, you ensure that that won't happen.

Custom layout guides

You can add your own custom UILayoutGuide objects to a view, for whatever purpose you like. They constitute a view's `layoutGuides` array, and are managed by calling `addLayoutGuide(_:)` or `removeLayoutGuide(_:)`. Each custom layout guide object must be configured entirely using constraints.

Why would you want to do that? Well, you can constrain a view to a UILayoutGuide, by means of its anchors. Thus, since a UILayoutGuide is configured by constraints, and since other views can be constrained to it, it can participate in layout exactly as if it were a subview — but it is *not* a subview, and therefore it avoids all the overhead and complexity that a UIView would have.

For example, consider the question of how to distribute views equally within their superview. This is easy to arrange initially, but it is not obvious how to design evenly spaced views that will remain evenly spaced when their superview is resized. The problem is that constraints describe relationships between *views*, not between *constraints*; there is no way to constrain the spacing constraints between views to remain equal *to one another* automatically as the superview is resized.

You can, on the other hand, constrain the heights or widths of *views* to remain equal to one another. The traditional solution, therefore, is to resort to spacer views with their `isHidden` set to `true`. But spacer views are views; hidden or not, they add overhead with respect to drawing, memory, touch detection, and more. Custom UILayoutGuides solve the problem; they can serve the same purpose as spacer views, but they are *not* views.

I'll demonstrate. Suppose I have four views that are to remain equally distributed vertically. I constrain their left and right edges, their heights, and the top of the first view and the bottom of the last view. This leaves open the question of how we will determine the vertical position of the two middle views; they must move in such a way that they are always equidistant from their vertical neighbors (Figure 1-15).

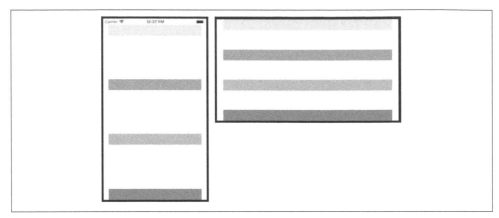

Figure 1-15. Equal distribution

To solve the problem, I introduce three UILayoutGuide objects between my real views. A custom UILayoutGuide object is added to a UIView, so I'll add mine to the superview of my four real views:

```
let guides = [UILayoutGuide(), UILayoutGuide(), UILayoutGuide()]
for guide in guides {
    self.view.addLayoutGuide(guide)
}
```

I then involve my three layout guides in the layout. Remember, they must be configured entirely using constraints (the three layout guides are referenced through my guides array, and the four views are referenced through another array, views):

```
NSLayoutConstraint.activate([
    // guide left is arbitrary, let's say superview margin ❶
    guides[0].leadingAnchor.constraint(equalTo:self.view.leadingAnchor),
    guides[1].leadingAnchor.constraint(equalTo:self.view.leadingAnchor),
    guides[2].leadingAnchor.constraint(equalTo:self.view.leadingAnchor),
    // guide widths are arbitrary, let's say 10
    guides[0].widthAnchor.constraint(equalToConstant:10),
    guides[1].widthAnchor.constraint(equalToConstant:10),
    guides[2].widthAnchor.constraint(equalToConstant:10),
    // bottom of each view is top of following guide ❷
    views[0].bottomAnchor.constraint(equalTo:guides[0].topAnchor),
    views[1].bottomAnchor.constraint(equalTo:guides[1].topAnchor),
    views[2].bottomAnchor.constraint(equalTo:guides[2].topAnchor),
    // top of each view is bottom of preceding guide
    views[1].topAnchor.constraint(equalTo:guides[0].bottomAnchor),
    views[2].topAnchor.constraint(equalTo:guides[1].bottomAnchor),
    views[3].topAnchor.constraint(equalTo:guides[2].bottomAnchor),
    // guide heights are equal! ❸
    guides[1].heightAnchor.constraint(equalTo:guides[0].heightAnchor),
    guides[2].heightAnchor.constraint(equalTo:guides[0].heightAnchor),
])
```

❶ I constrain the leading edges of the layout guides (arbitrarily, to the leading edge of their superview) and their widths (arbitrarily).

❷ I constrain each layout guide to the bottom of the view above it and the top of the view below it.

❸ Finally, our whole purpose is to distribute our views *equally*, so the heights of our layout guides must be *equal to one another*.

In that code, I clearly could have (and should have) generated each group of constraints as a loop, thus making this approach suitable for any number of distributed views; I have deliberately unrolled those loops for the sake of the example.

In real life, you are unlikely to use this technique directly, because you will use a UIStackView instead, and let the UIStackView generate all of that code — as I will explain a little later.

Unfortunately, a custom UILayoutGuide can be created and configured only in code. If you want to configure a layout entirely in the nib editor, and if this configuration requires the use of spacer views and cannot be constructed by a UIStackView, you'll have to use spacer views — you cannot replace them with UILayoutGuide objects, because there are no UILayoutGuide objects in the nib editor.

Intrinsic Content Size and Alignment Rects

Some built-in interface objects, when using autolayout, have an inherent size in one or both dimensions. For example:

- A UIButton, by default, has a standard height, and its width is determined by its title.
- A UIImageView, by default, adopts the size of the image it is displaying.
- A UILabel, by default, if it consists of multiple lines and if its width is constrained, adopts a height sufficient to display all of its text.

This inherent size is the object's *intrinsic content size*. The intrinsic content size is used to generate constraints implicitly (of class NSContentSizeLayoutConstraint).

A change in the characteristics or content of a built-in interface object — a button's title, an image view's image, a label's text or font, and so forth — may thus cause its intrinsic content size to change. This, in turn, may alter your layout. You will want to configure your autolayout constraints so that your interface responds gracefully to such changes.

You do not have to supply explicit constraints configuring a dimension of a view whose intrinsic content size configures that dimension. But you might! And when you do, the tendency of an interface object to size itself to its intrinsic content size must not be allowed to conflict with its tendency to obey your explicit constraints. Therefore, the constraints generated from a view's intrinsic content size have a lowered priority, and come into force only if no constraint of a higher priority prevents them. The following methods allow you to access these priorities (the parameter is a UILayoutConstraintAxis, either .horizontal or .vertical):

contentHuggingPriority(for:)
> A view's resistance to growing larger than its intrinsic size in this dimension. In effect, there is an inequality constraint saying that the view's size in this dimension should be less than or equal to its intrinsic size. The default priority is usually .defaultLow (250), though some interface classes will default to a higher value if initialized in a nib.

contentCompressionResistancePriority(for:)
> A view's resistance to shrinking smaller than its intrinsic size in this dimension. In effect, there is an inequality constraint saying that the view's size in this dimension should be greater than or equal to its intrinsic size. The default priority is usually .defaultHigh (750).

Those methods are getters; there are corresponding setters. Situations where you would need to change the priorities of these tendencies are few, but they do exist. For example, here are visual formats configuring two horizontally adjacent labels (lab1 and lab2) to be pinned to the superview and to one another:

```
"V:|-20-[lab1]"
"V:|-20-[lab2]"
"H:|-20-[lab1]"
"H:[lab2]-20-|"
"H:[lab1(>=100)]-(>=20)-[lab2(>=100)]"
```

The inequalities ensure that as the superview becomes narrower or the text of the labels becomes longer, a reasonable amount of text will remain visible in both labels. At the same time, one label will be squeezed down to 100 points width, while the other label will be allowed to grow to fill the remaining horizontal space. The question is: which label is which? You need to answer that question. To do so, it suffices to raise the compression resistance priority of one of the labels by a single point above that of the other (see Appendix B for an extension allowing a number to be added to a UILayoutPriority):

```
let p = lab2.contentCompressionResistancePriority(for: .horizontal)
lab1.setContentCompressionResistancePriority(p+1, for: .horizontal)
```

You can supply an intrinsic size in your own custom UIView subclass by overriding intrinsicContentSize. Obviously you should do this only if your view's size depends on its contents. If you need the runtime to ask for your intrinsicContent-

---

Size again, because that size has changed and the view needs to be laid out afresh, it's up to you to call your view's `invalidateIntrinsicContentSize` method.

Another question with which your custom UIView subclass might be concerned is what it should mean for another view to be aligned with it. It might mean aligned with your view's frame edges, but then again it might not. A possible example is a view that draws, internally, a rectangle with a shadow; you probably want to align things with that drawn rectangle, not with the outside of the shadow. To determine this, you can override your view's `alignmentRectInsets` property (or, more elaborately, its `alignmentRect(forFrame:)` and `frame(forAlignmentRect:)` methods).

 Be careful with changing a view's `alignmentRectInsets`, as you are effectively changing where the view's edges are for purposes of *all* constraints involving those edges. For example, if a view's alignment rect has a left inset of 30, then *all* constraints involving that view's `.leading` attribute or `leadingAnchor` are reckoned from that inset.

By the same token, you may want to be able to align your custom UIView with another view by their baselines. The assumption here is that your view has a subview containing text and, therefore, possessing a baseline. Your custom view will return that subview in its implementation of `forFirstBaselineLayout` or `forLastBaselineLayout`.

Stack Views

A stack view (UIStackView), introduced in iOS 9, is a view whose primary task is to generate constraints for some or all of its subviews. These are its *arranged subviews*. In particular, a stack view solves the problem of providing constraints when subviews are to be configured linearly in a horizontal row or a vertical column. In practice, it turns out that many layouts can be expressed as an arrangement, possibly nested, of simple rows and columns of subviews. Thus, you are likely to resort to stack views to make your layout easier to construct and maintain.

You can supply a stack view with arranged subviews by calling its initializer `init(arrangedSubviews:)`. The arranged subviews become the stack view's `arrangedSubviews` read-only property. You can also manage the arranged subviews with these methods:

- `addArrangedSubview(_:)`
- `insertArrangedSubview(_:at:)`
- `removeArrangedSubview(_:)`

The `arrangedSubviews` array is different from, but is a subset of, the stack view's `subviews`. It's fine for the stack view to have subviews that are *not* arranged (and which you'll have to provide with constraints yourself), but if you set a view as an arranged subview and it is not already a subview, the stack view will adopt it as a subview at that moment.

The *order* of the arrangedSubviews is independent of the order of the subviews; the subviews order, you remember, determines the order in which the subviews are drawn, but the arrangedSubviews order determines how the stack view will *position* those subviews.

Using its properties, you configure the stack view to tell it *how* it should arrange its arranged subviews:

axis
> Which way should the arranged subviews be arranged? Your choices are (UILayoutConstraintAxis):
>
> * .horizontal
> * .vertical

alignment
> This describes how the arranged subviews should be laid out with respect to the *other* dimension. Your choices are (UIStackViewAlignment):
>
> * .fill
> * .leading (or .top)
> * .center
> * .trailing (or .bottom)
> * .firstBaseline or .lastBaseline (if the axis is .horizontal)
>
> If the axis is .vertical, you can still involve the subviews' baselines in their spacing by setting the stack view's isBaselineRelativeArrangement to true.

distribution
> How should the arranged subviews be positioned along the axis? This is why you are here! You're using a stack view in the first place because you want this positioning performed for you. Your choices are (UIStackViewDistribution):
>
> .fill
>> The arranged subviews can have real size constraints or intrinsic content sizes along the arranged dimension. Using those sizes, the arranged subviews will fill the stack view from end to end. But there must be at least *one* view *without* a real size constraint, so that it can be resized to fill the space not taken up by the other views. If more than one view lacks a real size constraint, one must have a lowered content hugging (if stretching) or

compression resistance (if squeezing) so that the stack view knows which view to resize.

.fillEqually

The arranged subviews will be made the same size in the arranged dimension, so as to fill the stack view. No view may have a real size constraint along the arranged dimension.

.fillProportionally

All arranged subviews *must* have an intrinsic content size and *no* real size constraint along the arranged dimension. The views will then fill the stack view, sized according to the *ratio* of their intrinsic content sizes.

.equalSpacing

The arranged subviews can have real size constraints or intrinsic content sizes along the arranged dimension. Using those sizes, the arranged subviews will fill the stack view from end to end with equal space between each adjacent pair.

.equalCentering

The arranged subviews can have real size constraints or intrinsic content sizes along the arranged dimension. Using those sizes, the arranged subviews will fill the stack view from end to end with equal distance between the centers of each adjacent pair.

The stack view's spacing property determines the spacing (or minimum spacing) between all the views; new in iOS 11, you can set the spacing for individual views by calling setCustomSpacing(_:after:).

isLayoutMarginsRelativeArrangement

If true, the stack view's internal layoutMargins are involved in the positioning of its arranged subviews. If false (the default), the stack view's literal edges are used.

 Do *not* manually add constraints positioning an arranged subview! Adding those constraints is precisely the job of the stack view. Your constraints will conflict with the constraints created by the stack view. On the other hand, you *must* constrain the stack view *itself* (unless the stack view is itself an arranged view of a containing stack view).

To illustrate, I'll rewrite the equal distribution code from earlier in this chapter (Figure 1-15). I have four views, with height constraints. I want to distribute them vertically in my main view. This time, I'll have a stack view do all the work for me:

```
// give the stack view arranged subviews
let sv = UIStackView(arrangedSubviews: views)
// configure the stack view
sv.axis = .vertical
sv.alignment = .fill
sv.distribution = .equalSpacing
// constrain the stack view
sv.translatesAutoresizingMaskIntoConstraints = false
self.view.addSubview(sv)
let marg = self.view.layoutMarginsGuide
let safe = self.view.safeAreaLayoutGuide
NSLayoutConstraint.activate([
    sv.topAnchor.constraint(equalTo:safe.topAnchor),
    sv.leadingAnchor.constraint(equalTo:marg.leadingAnchor),
    sv.trailingAnchor.constraint(equalTo:marg.trailingAnchor),
    sv.bottomAnchor.constraint(equalTo:self.view.bottomAnchor),
])
```

Inspecting the resulting constraints, you can see that the stack view is doing for us effectively just what we did earlier (generating UILayoutGuide objects and using them as spacers). But letting the stack view do it is a lot easier!

Another nice feature of UIStackView is that it responds intelligently to changes. For example, having configured things with the preceding code, if we were subsequently to make one of our arranged subviews invisible (by setting its isHidden to true), the stack view would respond by distributing the remaining subviews evenly, as if the hidden subview didn't exist. Similarly, we can change properties of the stack view itself in real time. Such flexibility can be very useful for making whole areas of your interface come and go and rearrange themselves at will.

Internationalization

Your app's entire interface and its behavior are reversed when the app runs on a system for which the app is localized and whose language is right-to-left. Wherever you use leading and trailing constraints instead of left and right constraints, or if your constraints are generated by stack views or are constructed using the visual format language, your app's layout will participate in this reversal more or less automatically.

There may, however, be exceptions. Apple gives the example of a horizontal row of transport controls that mimic the buttons on a CD player: you wouldn't want the Rewind button and the Fast Forward button to be reversed just because the user's language reads right-to-left. Therefore, a UIView is endowed with a semanticContent-Attribute property stating whether it should be flipped; the default is .unspecified, but a value of .playback or .spatial will prevent flipping, and you can also force an absolute direction with .forceLeftToRight or .forceRightToLeft. This property can also be set in the nib editor (using the Semantic pop-up menu in the Attributes inspector).

Interface directionality is a trait, a trait collection's `.layoutDirection`; and a UIView has an `effectiveUserInterfaceLayoutDirection` property that reports the direction that it will use to lay out its contents, and which you can consult if you are constructing a view's subviews in code.

 You can test your app's right-to-left behavior easily by changing the scheme's Run option Application Language to Right to Left Pseudolanguage.

Mistakes with Constraints

Creating constraints manually, as I've been doing so far in this chapter, is an invitation to make a mistake. Your totality of constraints constitute instructions for view layout, and it is all too easy, as soon as more than one or two views are involved, to generate faulty instructions. You can (and will) make two major kinds of mistake with constraints:

Conflict
You have applied constraints that can't be satisfied simultaneously. This will be reported in the console (at great length).

Underdetermination (ambiguity)
A view uses autolayout, but you haven't supplied sufficient information to determine its size and position. This is a far more insidious problem, because nothing bad may seem to happen. If you're lucky, the view will at least fail to appear, or will appear in an undesirable place, alerting you to the problem.

Only `.required` constraints (priority 1000) can contribute to a conflict, as the runtime is free to ignore lower-priority constraints that it can't satisfy. Constraints with different priorities do not conflict with one another. Nonrequired constraints with the same priority can contribute to ambiguity.

Under normal circumstances, layout isn't performed until your code finishes running — and even then only if needed. Ambiguous layout isn't ambiguous until layout actually takes place; it is perfectly reasonable to cause an ambiguous layout temporarily, provided you resolve the ambiguity before `layoutSubviews` is called. On the other hand, a conflicting constraint conflicts the instant it is added. That's why, when deactivating and then activating constraints in code, you should deactivate first and activate second, and not the other way around.

Let's start by generating a conflict. In this example, we return to our small red square in the lower right corner of a big magenta square (Figure 1-12) and append a contradictory constraint:

```
let d = ["v2":v2,"v3":v3]
NSLayoutConstraint.activate([
    NSLayoutConstraint.constraints(withVisualFormat:
        "H:|[v2]|", metrics: nil, views: d),
    NSLayoutConstraint.constraints(withVisualFormat:
        "V:|[v2(10)]", metrics: nil, views: d),
    NSLayoutConstraint.constraints(withVisualFormat:
        "H:[v3(20)]|", metrics: nil, views: d),
    NSLayoutConstraint.constraints(withVisualFormat:
        "V:[v3(20)]|", metrics: nil, views: d),
    NSLayoutConstraint.constraints(withVisualFormat:
        "V:[v3(10)]|", metrics: nil, views: d) // *
].flatMap{$0})
```

The height of v3 can't be both 10 and 20. The runtime reports the conflict, and tells you which constraints are causing it:

```
Unable to simultaneously satisfy constraints. Probably at least one of the
constraints in the following list is one you don't want...

<NSLayoutConstraint:0x60008b6d0 UIView:0x7ff45e803.height == + 20 (active)>,
<NSLayoutConstraint:0x60008bae0 UIView:0x7ff45e803.height == + 10 (active)>
```

 You can assign a constraint (or a UILayoutGuide) an identifier string; this can make it easier to determine which constraint in a conflict report is which.

Now we'll generate an ambiguity. Here, we neglect to give our small red square a height:

```
let d = ["v2":v2,"v3":v3]
NSLayoutConstraint.activate([
    NSLayoutConstraint.constraints(withVisualFormat:
        "H:|[v2]|", metrics: nil, views: d),
    NSLayoutConstraint.constraints(withVisualFormat:
        "V:|[v2(10)]", metrics: nil, views: d),
    NSLayoutConstraint.constraints(withVisualFormat:
        "H:[v3(20)]|", metrics: nil, views: d)
].flatMap{$0})
```

No console message alerts us to our mistake. Fortunately, however, v3 fails to appear in the interface, so we know something's wrong. *If your views fail to appear, suspect ambiguity.* In a less fortunate case, the view might appear, but (if we're lucky) in the wrong place. In a truly unfortunate case, the view might appear in the right place, but not consistently.

Suspecting ambiguity is one thing; tracking it down and proving it is another. Fortunately, the *view debugger* will report ambiguity instantly (Figure 1-16). With the app running, choose Debug → View Debugging → Capture View Hierarchy, or click the Debug View Hierarchy button in the debug toolbar. The exclamation mark in the Debug navigator, at the left, is telling us that this view (which does not appear in the

Figure 1-16. View debugging

canvas) has ambiguous layout; moreover, the Issue navigator, in the Runtime pane, tells us more explicitly, in words: "Height and vertical position are ambiguous for UIView."

Another useful trick is to pause in the debugger and give the following mystical command in the console:

```
(lldb) expr -l objc++ -O -- [[UIWindow keyWindow] _autolayoutTrace]
```

The result is a graphical tree describing the view hierarchy and marking any ambiguously laid out views:

```
UIWindow:0x7fe8d0d9dbd0
|   •UIView:0x7fe8d0c2bf00
|   |   +UIView:0x7fe8d0c2c290
|   |   |   *UIView:0x7fe8d0c2c7e0
|   |   |   *UIView:0x7fe8d0c2c9e0- AMBIGUOUS LAYOUT
```

UIView also has a hasAmbiguousLayout property; I find it useful to set up a utility method that lets me check a view and all its subviews at any depth for ambiguity:

```
extension NSLayoutConstraint {
    class func reportAmbiguity (_ v:UIView?) {
        var v = v
        if v == nil {
            v = UIApplication.shared.keyWindow
        }
        for vv in v!.subviews {
            print("\(vv) \(vv.hasAmbiguousLayout)")
            if vv.subviews.count > 0 {
                self.reportAmbiguity(vv)
            }
        }
    }
}
```

You can call that method in your code, or while paused in the debugger:

```
(lldb) expr NSLayoutConstraint.reportAmbiguity(nil)
```

To get a full list of the constraints responsible for positioning a particular view within its superview, log the results of calling the UIView instance method `constraints-AffectingLayout(for:)`. The parameter is an axis (UILayoutConstraintAxis), either `.horizontal` or `.vertical`. These constraints do not necessarily belong to this view (and the output doesn't tell you what view they do belong to). If a view doesn't participate in autolayout, the result will be an empty array. Again, a utility method can come in handy:

```
extension NSLayoutConstraint {
    class func listConstraints (_ v:UIView?) {
        var v = v
        if v == nil {
            v = UIApplication.shared.keyWindow
        }
        for vv in v!.subviews {
            let arr1 = vv.constraintsAffectingLayout(for:.horizontal)
            let arr2 = vv.constraintsAffectingLayout(for:.vertical)
            NSLog("\n\n%@\nH: %@\nV:%@", vv, arr1, arr2);
            if vv.subviews.count > 0 {
                self.listConstraints(vv)
            }
        }
    }
}
```

And here's how to call it from the debugger:

```
(lldb) expr NSLayoutConstraint.listConstraints(nil)
```

UILayoutGuide responds to `hasAmbiguousLayout` and `constraintsAffecting-Layout(for:)` as well.

Given the notions of conflict and ambiguity, it is easier to understand what priorities are for. Imagine that all constraints have been placed in boxes, where each box is a priority value, in descending order. Now pretend that we are the runtime, performing layout in obedience to these constraints. How do we proceed?

The first box (`.required`, 1000) contains all the required constraints, so we obey them first. (If they conflict, that's bad, and we report this in the log.) If there still isn't enough information to perform unambiguous layout given the required priorities alone, we pull the constraints out of the next box and try to obey them. If we can, consistently with what we've already done, fine; if we can't, or if ambiguity remains, we look in the *next* box — and so on. For a box after the first, we don't care about obeying exactly the constraints it contains; if an ambiguity remains, we can use a lower-priority constraint value to give us something to aim at, resolving the ambiguity, without fully obeying the lower-priority constraint's desires. For example, an inequality is an ambiguity, because an infinite number of values will satisfy it; a lower-priority equality can tell us what value to prefer, resolving the ambiguity, but there's no conflict even if we can't fully achieve that preferred value.

Configuring Layout in the Nib

The focus of the discussion so far has been on configuring layout in code. This, however, will often be unnecessary; instead, you'll set up your layout in the nib, using the nib editor. It would not be strictly true to say that you can do absolutely anything in the nib that you could do in code, but the nib editor is certainly a remarkably powerful way of configuring layout (and where it falls short, you can always supplement it with some code in addition).

In the File inspector when a *.storyboard* or *.xib* file is selected, you can make three major choices related to layout, by way of checkboxes. The default is that these checkboxes are *checked*, and I recommend that you leave them that way:

Use Auto Layout
> If unchecked, no constraints can be created in the nib editor; layout for your views must be configured entirely using autoresizing.

Use Trait Variations
> If checked, various settings in the nib editor, such as the value of a constraint's constant, can be made to depend upon the environment's size classes at runtime ("Trait Collections and Size Classes" on page 23); moreover, the modern repertoire of segues, such as popover and detail segues, springs to life.

Use Safe Area Layout Guides
> If unchecked, the top layout guide and bottom layout guide (invisible views imposed on its main view by a view controller) are displayed, and you can construct constraints to them. If checked, the iOS 11 safe area is used instead. The nib's safe area is backward compatible to systems before iOS 11; it will be translated into the top layout guide and bottom layout guide on those systems.

Autoresizing in the Nib

When you drag a view from the Object library into the canvas, it uses autoresizing by default, and will continue to do so unless you involve it in autolayout by adding a constraint that affects it.

When editing a view that uses autoresizing, you can assign it springs and struts in the Size inspector. A solid line externally represents a strut; a solid line internally represents a spring. A helpful animation shows you the effect on your view's position and size as its superview is resized.

Figure 1-17. Creating a constraint by Control-dragging

Creating a Constraint

The nib editor provides two primary ways to create a constraint:

Control-drag
> Control-drag from one view to another. A HUD (heads-up display) appears, listing constraints that you can create (Figure 1-17). Either view can be in the canvas or in the document outline. To create an internal width or height constraint, Control-drag from a view to itself.
>
> When you Control-drag within the canvas, the direction of the drag is used to winnow the options presented in the HUD; for example, if you Control-drag horizontally within a view in the canvas, the HUD lists Width but not Height.
>
> While viewing the HUD, you might want to toggle the Option key to see some alternatives; for example, this might make the difference between an edge or safe area constraint and a margin-based constraint. Holding the Shift key lets you create multiple constraints simultaneously.

Layout bar buttons
> Click the Align or Add New Constraints button at the right end of the layout bar below the canvas. These buttons summon little popover dialogs where you can choose multiple constraints to create (possibly for multiple views, if that's what you've selected beforehand) and provide them with numeric values (Figure 1-18). Constraints are not actually added until you click Add Constraints at the bottom.

To set a view's layout margins explicitly, switch to the Size inspector and change the Layout Margins pop-up menu to Fixed (or better, new in Xcode 9, to Language Directional). To make a view's layout margins behave as `readableContentGuide` margins, check Follow Readable Width.

A view controller's main view's safe area is displayed automatically in the document outline, so you can Control-drag to it to create a constraint. If you need to see any other view's safe area, switch to the Size inspector and check Safe Area Layout Guide.

Figure 1-18. Creating constraints from the layout bar

 A constraint that you create in the nib does not have to be perfect immediately upon creation! You will subsequently be able to edit the constraint and configure it further, as I'll explain in the next section.

If you create constraints and then move or resize a view affected by those constraints, the constraints are *not* automatically changed. This means that the constraints no longer match the way the view is portrayed; if the constraints were to position the view, they wouldn't put it where you've put it. The nib editor will alert you to this situation (a Misplaced Views issue), and can readily resolve it for you, but it won't do so unless you explicitly ask it to.

Viewing and Editing Constraints

Constraints in the nib are full-fledged objects. They can be selected, edited, and deleted. Moreover, you can create an outlet to a constraint (and there are reasons why you might want to do so).

Constraints in the nib are visible in three places (Figure 1-19):

In the document outline

Constraints are listed in a special category, "Constraints," under the view to which they belong. (You'll have a much easier time distinguishing these constraints if you give your views meaningful labels!)

In the canvas

Constraints appear graphically as dimension lines when you select a view that they affect (unless you uncheck Editor → Canvas → Show Constraints).

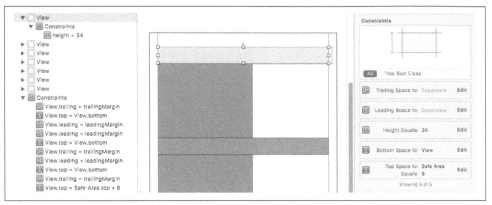

Figure 1-19. A view's constraints displayed in the nib

In the Size inspector

> When a view affected by constraints is selected, the Size inspector lists those constraints, along with a grid that displays the view's constraints graphically. Clicking a constraint in the grid filters the constraints listed below it.

When you select a constraint in the document outline or the canvas, you can view and edit its values in the Attributes or Size inspector. The inspector gives you access to almost all of a constraint's features: the anchors involved in the constraint (the First Item and Second Item pop-up menus), the relation between them, the constant and multiplier, and the priority. You can also set the identifier here (useful when debugging, as I mentioned earlier).

The First Item and Second Item pop-up menus may list alternative constraint types; thus, for example, a width constraint may be changed to a height constraint. New in Xcode 9, these pop-up menus may also list alternative *objects* to constrain to, such as other sibling views, the superview, and the safe area. Also, these pop-up menus may have a "Relative to margin" option, which you can check or uncheck to toggle between an edge-based and a margin-based constraint. Thus, if you accidentally created the wrong constraint, or if you weren't quite able to specify the desired constraint at creation time, editing will usually permit you to fix things. For example, when you constrain a subview to the view controller's main view, the HUD offers no way to constrain to the main view's edge; but if you hold Option and constrain to the main view's margin, you can then uncheck "Relative to margin" in the pop-up menu.

For simple editing of a constraint's constant, relation, priority, and multiplier, double-click the constraint in the canvas to summon a little popover dialog. When a constraint is listed in a view's Size inspector, double-click it to edit it in its own inspector, or click its Edit button to summon the little popover dialog.

A view's Size inspector also provides access to its content hugging and content compression resistance priority settings. Beneath these, there's an Intrinsic Size pop-up menu. The idea here is that your custom view might have an intrinsic size, but the nib editor doesn't know this, so it will report an ambiguity when you fail to provide (say) a width constraint that you know isn't actually needed; choose Placeholder to supply an intrinsic size and relieve the nib editor's worries.

In a constraint's Attributes or Size inspector, there is a Placeholder checkbox ("Remove at build time"). If you check this checkbox, the constraint you're editing *won't* be instantiated when the nib is loaded: in effect, you are deliberately generating ambiguous layout when the views and constraints are instantiated from the nib. You might do this because you want to simulate your layout in the nib editor, but you intend to provide a different constraint in code; perhaps you weren't quite able to describe this constraint in the nib, or the constraint depends upon circumstances that won't be known until runtime.

Problems with Nib Constraints

I've already said that generating constraints manually, in code, is error-prone. But it isn't error-prone in the nib editor! The nib editor *knows* whether it contains problematic constraints. If a view is affected by any constraints, the Xcode nib editor will permit them to be ambiguous or conflicting, but it will also complain helpfully. You should pay attention to such complaints! The nib editor will bring the situation to your attention in various places:

Canvas
Constraints drawn in the canvas when you select a view that they affect use color coding to express their status:

Satisfactory constraints
Drawn in blue.

Problematic constraints
Drawn in red.

Misplacement constraints
Drawn in orange; these constraints are valid, but they are inconsistent with the frame you have imposed upon the view. I'll discuss misplaced views in the next paragraph.

Document outline
If there are layout issues, the document outline displays a right arrow in a red or orange circle. Click it to see a detailed list of the issues (Figure 1-20). Hover the mouse over a title to see an Info button which you can click to learn more about

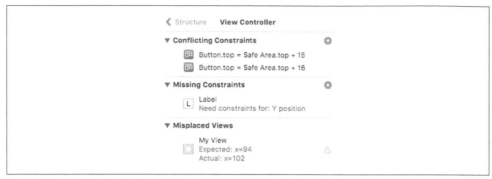

Figure 1-20. Layout issues in the document outline

the nature of this issue. The icons at the right are buttons: click one for a list of things the nib editor is offering to do to fix the issue for you. The chief issues are:

Conflicting Constraints
 A conflict between constraints.

Missing Constraints
 Ambiguous layout.

Misplaced Views
 If you manually change the frame of a view that is affected by constraints (including its intrinsic size), then the canvas may be displaying that view differently from how it would really appear if the current constraints were obeyed. A Misplaced Views situation is also described in the canvas:

 - The constraints in the canvas, drawn in orange, display the numeric *difference* between their values and the view's frame.

 - A dotted outline in the canvas may show where the view *would* be drawn if the existing constraints were obeyed.

 You can turn off ambiguity checking for a particular view; use the Ambiguity pop-up menu in the view's Size inspector. This means you can omit a needed constraint and *not* be notified by the nib editor that there's a problem. You will need to generate the missing constraint in code, obviously, or you'll have ambiguous layout.

Having warned you of problems with your layout, the nib editor also provides tools to fix them.

The Update Frames button in the layout bar (or Editor → Update Frames) changes the way the selected views or all views are drawn in the canvas, to show how things would really appear in the running app under the constraints as they stand. Alternatively, if you have resized a view with intrinsic size constraints, such as a button or a label, and you want it to resume the size it would have according to those intrinsic size constraints, select the view and choose Editor → Size to Fit Content.

 Be careful with Update Frames: if constraints are ambiguous, *this can cause a view to disappear.*

The Resolve Auto Layout Issues button in the layout bar (or the Editor → Resolve Auto Layout Issues hierarchical menu) proposes large-scale moves involving all the constraints affecting either selected views or all views:

Update Constraint Constants
Choose this menu item to change numerically all the existing constraints affecting a view to match the way the canvas is currently drawing the view's frame.

Add Missing Constraints
Create new constraints so that the view has sufficient constraints to describe its frame unambiguously. The added constraints correspond to the way the canvas is currently drawing the view's frame.

This command may not do what you ultimately want; you should regard it as a starting point. After all, the nib editor can't read your mind! For example, it doesn't know whether you think a certain view's width should be determined by an internal width constraint or by pinning it to the left and right of its superview; and it may generate alignment constraints with other views that you never intended.

Reset to Suggested Constraints
This is as if you chose Clear Constraints followed by Add Missing Constraints: it removes all constraints affecting the view, and replaces them with a complete set of automatically generated constraints describing the way the canvas is currently drawing the view's frame.

Clear Constraints
Removes all constraints affecting the view.

Varying the Screen Size

The purpose of constraints will usually be to design a layout that responds to the possibility of the app launching on devices of different sizes, and perhaps subsequently being rotated. Imagining how this is going to work in real life is not always easy, and you may doubt that you are getting the constraints right as you configure them in the nib editor. Have no fear: Xcode is here to help.

There's a View As button at the lower left of the canvas. Click it to reveal (if they are not already showing) buttons representing a variety of device types and orientations. Click a button, and the canvas's main views are resized accordingly.

When that happens, the layout dictated by your constraints is obeyed immediately. Thus, you can try out the effect of your constraints under different screen sizes right there in the canvas.

 This feature works only if the view controller's Simulated Size pop-up menu in the Size inspector says Fixed. If it says Freeform, the view won't be resized when you click a device type or orientation button.

Conditional Interface Design

The View As button at the lower left of the canvas states the *size classes* (see "Trait Collections and Size Classes" on page 23) for the currently chosen device and orientation, using a notation like this: wR hC. The w and h stand for "width" and "height," corresponding to the trait collection's .horizontalSizeClass and .verticalSize-Class respectively; the R and C stand for .regular and .compact.

The reason you're being given this information is that you might want the configuration of your constraints and views in the nib editor to be *conditional* upon the size classes that are in effect *at runtime*. You can arrange in the nib editor for your app's interface to detect the traitCollectionDidChange notification and respond to it. Thus, for example:

- You can design directly into your interface a complex rearrangement of the interface when an iPhone app rotates to compensate for a change in device orientation.

- A single *.storyboard* or *.xib* file can be used to design the interface of a universal app, even though the iPad interface and the iPhone interface may be quite different from one another.

The idea when constructing a conditional interface is that you design *first* for the most general case. When you've done that, and when you want to do something *different* for a *particular* size class situation, you'll describe that difference in the Attributes or Size inspector, or design that difference in the canvas:

In the Attributes or Size inspector
Look for a Plus symbol to the left of a value in the Attributes or Size inspector. This is a value that you can vary conditionally, depending on the environment's size class at runtime. The Plus symbol is a button! Click it to see a popover from which you can choose a specialized size class combination. When you do, that value now appears *twice*: once for the general case, and once for the specialized

case which is marked using wR hC notation. You can now provide different values for those two cases.

In the canvas

Click the Vary for Traits button, to the right of the device types buttons. Two checkboxes appear, allowing you to specify that you want to match the width or height size class (or both) of the current size class. Any designing you now do in the canvas will be applied only to that width or height size class (or both), also modifying the Attributes or Size inspector as needed.

I'll illustrate these approaches with a little tutorial. You'll need to have an example project on hand; make sure it's a Universal app.

Size classes in the inspectors

Suppose we have a button in the canvas, and we want this button to have a yellow background *on iPad only*. (This is improbable but dramatic.) You can configure this directly in the Attributes inspector, as follows:

1. Select the button in the interface.

2. Switch to the Attributes inspector, and locate the Background pop-up menu in the View section of the inspector.

3. Click the Plus button to bring up a popover with pop-up menus for specifying size classes. An iPad has width (horizontal) size class Regular and height (vertical) size class Regular), so change the first two pop-up menus so that they both say Regular. Click Add Variation.

4. A second Background pop-up menu has appeared, marked wR hR. Change it to yellow (or any desired color).

The button now has a colored background on iPad but not on iPhone. To see that this is true, without running the app on different device types, use the View As button and the device buttons at the lower left of the canvas to switch between different screen sizes. When you click an iPad button, the button in the canvas has a yellow background. When you click an iPhone button, the button in the canvas has its default clear background.

Now that you know what the Plus button means, look over the Attributes and Size inspectors. Anything with a Plus button can be varied in accordance with the size class environment. For example, a button's text can be a different font and size; this makes sense because you might want the text to be larger on an iPad. A button's Hidden checkbox can be different for different size classes, so that the button is invisible on some device types (new in Xcode 9). And at the bottom of the Attributes inspector is the Installed checkbox; unchecking this for a particular size class combination causes the button to be entirely absent from the interface.

Size classes in the canvas

Suppose your interface has a button pinned by its top and left to the top *left* of its superview. And suppose that, on iPad devices only, you want this button to be pinned by its right to the top *right* of its superview. (Again, this is improbable but dramatic.) That means the leading constraint will exist only on iPhone devices, to be replaced by a trailing constraint on iPad devices. The constraints are different objects. The way to configure different objects for different size classes is to use the Vary for Traits button, as follows:

1. Among the device type buttons, click one of the iPhone buttons (furthest to the right). Configure the button so that it's pinned by its top and left to the top left of the main view.

2. Among the device type buttons, click one of the iPad buttons (furthest to the left). The size classes are now listed as wR hR.

3. Click Vary for Traits. In the little popover that appears, check *both* boxes: we want the change we are about to make to apply only when *both* the width size class *and* the height size class match our *current* size class (they should *both* be .regular). The entire layout bar becomes blue, to signify that we are operating in a special conditional design mode.

4. Make the desired change: Select the button in the interface; select the left constraint; delete the left constraint; slide the button to the right of the interface; Control-drag from the button to the right and create a new trailing constraint. If necessary, click the Update Frames button to make the orange Misplaced Views warning symbol go away.

5. Click Done Varying. The layout bar ceases to be blue.

We've created a conditional constraint. To see that this is true, click an iPhone device button and then click an iPad device button. As you do, the button in the interface jumps between the left and right sides of the interface. Its position depends upon the device type!

The inspectors for this button accord with the change we've just made. To see that this is true, click the button, select the trailing or leading constraint (depending on the device type), and look in the Attributes or Size inspector. The constraint has two Installed checkboxes, one for the general case and one for wR hR. Only one of these checkboxes is checked; the constraint is present in one case but not the other.

 In the document outline, a constraint or view that is not installed for the current set of size classes is listed with a faded icon.

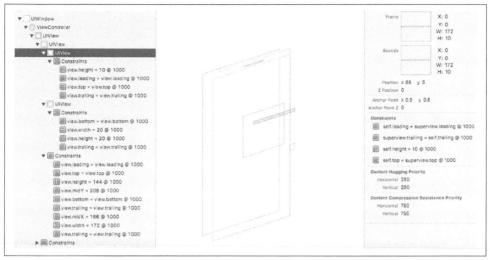

Figure 1-21. View debugging (again)

Xcode View Features

This section summarizes some miscellaneous view-related features of Xcode that are worth knowing about.

View Debugger

To enter the view debugger, choose Debug → View Debugging → Capture View Hierarchy, or click the Debug View Hierarchy button in the debug bar. The result is that your app's current view hierarchy is analyzed and displayed (Figure 1-21):

- On the left, in the Debug navigator, the views and their constraints are listed hierarchically. (New in Xcode 9, view controllers are also listed as part of the hierarchy.)

- In the center, in the canvas, the views and their constraints are displayed graphically. The window starts out facing front, much as if you were looking at the screen with the app running; but if you swipe sideways a little in the canvas, the window rotates and its subviews are displayed in front of it, in layers. You can adjust your perspective in various ways; for example:

  - The slider at the lower left changes the distance between the layers.

  - The double-slider at the lower right lets you eliminate the display of views from the front or back of the layering order (or both).

  - You can double-click a view to focus on it, eliminating its superviews from the display. Double-click outside the view to exit focus mode.

- You can switch to wireframe mode.
- You can display constraints for the currently selected view.

- On the right, the Object inspector and the Size inspector tell you details about the currently selected object (view or constraint).

When a view is selected in the Debug navigator or in the canvas, the Size inspector lists its bounds and all the constraints that determine those bounds. This, along with the layered graphical display of your views and constraints in the canvas, can help you ferret out the cause of any constraint-related difficulties.

Previewing Your Interface

When you're displaying the nib editor in Xcode, show the assistant pane. Its Tracking menu (the first component in its jump bar) includes the Preview option. Choose it to see a preview of the currently selected view controller's view (or, in a *.xib* file, the top-level view).

At the lower left, the Plus button lets you add previews for different devices and device sizes; you can thus compare your interface on different devices *simultaneously*. At the bottom of each preview, a Rotate button lets you toggle its orientation. The previews take account of constraints and conditional interface.

At the lower right, a language pop-up menu lets you switch your app's text (buttons and labels) to another language for which you have localized your app, or to an artificial "double-length" language.

Designable Views and Inspectable Properties

Your custom view can be drawn correctly in the nib editor canvas and preview *even if it is configured in code.* To take advantage of this feature, you need a UIView subclass declared @IBDesignable.

If an instance of this UIView subclass appears in the nib editor, then its self-configuration methods, such as willMove(toSuperview:), will be compiled and run as the nib editor prepares to portray your view. In addition, your view can implement the special method prepareForInterfaceBuilder to perform visual configurations aimed specifically at how it will be portrayed in the nib editor. In this way, you can even portray in the nib editor a feature that your view will adopt *later* in the life of the app. For example, if your view contains a UILabel that is created and configured empty but will eventually contain text, you could implement prepareForInterface-Builder to give the label some sample text to be displayed in the nib editor.

In Figure 1-22, I refactor a familiar example. Our view subclass gives itself a magenta background, along with two subviews, one across the top and the other at the lower

Figure 1-22. A designable view

right — all designed in code. The nib contains an instance of this view subclass. When the app runs, willMove(toSuperview:) will be called, the code will run, and the subviews will be present. But because willMove(toSuperview:) is also called by the nib editor, the subviews are displayed in the nib editor as well:

```
@IBDesignable class MyView: UIView {
    func configure() {
        self.backgroundColor = UIColor(red: 1, green: 0.4, blue: 1, alpha: 1)
        let v2 = UIView()
        v2.backgroundColor = UIColor(red: 0.5, green: 1, blue: 0, alpha: 1)
        let v3 = UIView()
        v3.backgroundColor = UIColor(red: 1, green: 0, blue: 0, alpha: 1)
        v2.translatesAutoresizingMaskIntoConstraints = false
        v3.translatesAutoresizingMaskIntoConstraints = false
        self.addSubview(v2)
        self.addSubview(v3)
        NSLayoutConstraint.activate([
            v2.leftAnchor.constraint(equalTo:self.leftAnchor),
            v2.rightAnchor.constraint(equalTo:self.rightAnchor),
            v2.topAnchor.constraint(equalTo:self.topAnchor),
            v2.heightAnchor.constraint(equalToConstant:20),
            v3.widthAnchor.constraint(equalToConstant:20),
            v3.heightAnchor.constraint(equalTo:v3.widthAnchor),
            v3.rightAnchor.constraint(equalTo:self.rightAnchor),
            v3.bottomAnchor.constraint(equalTo:self.bottomAnchor),
```

```
    ])
}
override func willMove(toSuperview newSuperview: UIView!) {
    self.configure()
}
}
```

In addition, you can configure custom view properties directly in the nib editor. If your UIView subclass has a property whose value type is understood by the nib editor, and if this property is declared @IBInspectable, then if an instance of this UIView subclass appears in the nib, that property will get a field of its own at the top of the view's Attributes inspector. Thus, when a custom UIView subclass is to be instantiated from the nib, its custom properties can be set in the nib editor rather than having to be set in code. (This feature is actually a convenient equivalent of setting a nib object's User Defined Runtime Attributes in the Identity inspector.)

Inspectable property types are: Bool, number, String, CGRect, CGPoint, CGSize, NSRange, UIColor, or UIImage. For classes (UIColor and UIImage), the property type can be an Optional. You can assign a default value in code; the Attributes inspector won't portray this value as the default, but you can tell it to use the default by leaving the field empty (or, if you've entered a value, by deleting that value).

@IBDesignable and @IBInspectable are unrelated, but the former is aware of the latter. Thus, you can use an inspectable property to change the nib editor's display of your interface.

In this example, we use @IBDesignable and @IBInspectable to work around an annoying limitation of the nib editor. A UIView can draw its own border automatically, by setting its layer's borderWidth (Chapter 3). But this can be configured only in code. There's nothing in a view's Attributes inspector that lets you set a layer's border-Width, and special layer configurations are not normally portrayed in the canvas. @IBDesignable and @IBInspectable to the rescue:

```
@IBDesignable class MyButton : UIButton {
    @IBInspectable var borderWidth : Int {
        set {
            self.layer.borderWidth = CGFloat(newValue)
        }
        get {
            return Int(self.layer.borderWidth)
        }
    }
}
```

The result is that, in nib editor, our button's Attributes inspector has a Border Width custom property, and when we change the Border Width property setting, the button is redrawn with that border width (Figure 1-23). Moreover, we are setting this

Figure 1-23. A designable view with an inspectable property

property in the nib, so when the app runs and the nib loads, the button really does have that border width in the running app.

 A view's `@IBInspectable` property won't be displayed in the Attributes inspector unless its type is declared explicitly.

Layout Events

This section summarizes the chief UIView events related to layout. These are events that you can receive and respond to by overriding them in your UIView subclass. You might want to do this in situations where layout is complex — for example, when you need to supplement autoresizing or autolayout with manual layout in code, or when your layout configuration needs to change in response to changing conditions.

 These UIView events are not the same as the layout-related events you can receive and respond to in a UIViewController. I'll discuss those in Chapter 6.

`updateConstraints`

If your interface involves autolayout and constraints, then `updateConstraints` is propagated *up* the hierarchy, starting at the deepest subview, when the runtime thinks your code might need an opportunity to configure your constraints. For example, this happens at launch time. It also happens the first time the app rotates, but only for the view at the top of the hierarchy (if the constraints of other views have not changed).

You might override `updateConstraints` in a UIView subclass if your subclass is capable of altering its own constraints and you need a signal that now is the time to do so. You must finish up by calling `super` or the app will crash (with a helpful error message).

You should never call `updateConstraints` directly. To trigger an immediate call to `updateConstraints`, send a view the `updateConstraintsIfNeeded` message. To force `updateConstraints` to be sent to a particular view, send it the `setNeeds-UpdateConstraints` message.

If a view isn't involved with constraints, `updateConstraints` may not be called for it. Thus, if you wanted to add constraints to this view in its `update-Constraints` at launch time, you are thwarted. To get `updateConstraints` to be called for this view at launch time, override the class method `requires-ConstraintBasedLayout` to return `true`.

`traitCollectionDidChange(_:)`

At launch time, and if the environment's trait collection changes thereafter, the `traitCollectionDidChange(_:)` message is propagated *down* the hierarchy of UITraitEnvironments. The incoming parameter is the *old* trait collection; to get the new trait collection, ask for `self.traitCollection`.

Thus, if your interface needs to respond to a change in the trait collection — by changing constraints, adding or removing subviews, or what have you — an override of `traitCollectionDidChange` is the place to do it. For example, earlier in this chapter I showed some code for swapping a view into or out of the interface together with the entire set of constraints laying out that interface. But I left open the matter of the conditions under which we wanted such swapping to occur; `traitCollectionDidChange` might be an appropriate moment. A typical implementation would examine the new trait collection and respond depending on its horizontal or vertical size class.

`layoutSubviews`

The `layoutSubviews` message is the moment when layout itself takes place. It is propagated *down* the hierarchy, starting at the top (typically the root view) and working down to the deepest subview. Layout can be triggered even if the trait collection didn't change; for example, perhaps a constraint was changed, or the text of a label was changed, or a superview's size changed.

You can override `layoutSubviews` in a UIView subclass in order to take a hand in the layout process. If you're not using autolayout, `layoutSubviews` does nothing by default; `layoutSubviews` is your opportunity to perform manual layout after autoresizing has taken place. If you are using autolayout, you must call `super` or the app will crash (with a helpful error message).

You should never call `layoutSubviews` directly; to trigger an immediate call to `layoutSubviews`, send a view the `layoutIfNeeded` message (which may cause layout of the entire view tree, not only below but also above this view), or send `setNeedsLayout` to trigger a call to `layoutSubviews` later on, after your code finishes running, when layout would normally take place.

When you're using autolayout, what happens in `layoutSubviews`? The runtime examines all the constraints affecting this view's subviews, works out values for their center and bounds, and assigns those views those center and bounds values. In other words, `layoutSubviews` performs manual layout! The constraints are merely instructions attached to the views; `layoutSubviews` reads them and responds accordingly, sizing and positioning views in the good old-fashioned way, by setting their frames, bounds, and centers.

Knowing this, you might override `layoutSubviews` when you're using autolayout, in order to tweak the outcome. A typical structure is: first you call `super`, causing all the subviews to adopt their new frames; then you examine those frames; if you don't like the outcome, you can change things; and finally you call `super` *again*, to get a new layout outcome. As I mentioned earlier, setting a view's frame (or bounds or center) explicitly in `layoutSubviews` is perfectly fine, even if this view uses autolayout; that, after all, is what the autolayout engine itself is doing. Keep in mind, however, that you must *cooperate* with the autolayout engine. Do not call `setNeedsUpdateConstraints` — that moment has passed — and do not stray beyond the subviews *of this view*. (Disobeying those rules can cause your app to hang.)

A change to the safe area or to a view's layout margins can trigger layout. In that case, `layoutMarginsDidChange` and `safeAreaInsetsDidChange` are generally called before `layoutSubviews`, but you probably should not be doing anything in those methods that relies on things happening in any particular order.

It is possible to *simulate* layout of a view in accordance with its constraints and those of its subviews. This is useful for discovering ahead of time what a view's size would be if layout were performed at this moment. Send the view the `systemLayoutSize-Fitting(_:)` message. The system will attempt to reach or at least approach the size you specify, at a very low priority; mostly likely you'll specify either `UILayoutFitting-CompressedSize` or `UILayoutFittingExpandedSize`, depending on whether what you're after is the smallest or largest size the view can legally attain. I'll show an example in Chapter 7.

CHAPTER 2

Drawing

The views illustrated in Chapter 1 were mostly colored rectangles; they had a `backgroundColor` and no more. But that's not what a real iOS program looks like. Everything the user sees is a UIView, and what the user sees is a lot more than a bunch of colored rectangles. That's because the views that the user sees have *content*. They contain *drawing*.

Many UIView subclasses, such as a UIButton or a UILabel, know how to draw themselves. Sooner or later, you're also going to want to do some drawing of your own. You can prepare your drawing as an image file beforehand. You can draw an image as your app runs, in code. You can display an image in a UIView subclass that knows how to show an image, such as a UIImageView or a UIButton. A pure UIView is all about drawing, and it leaves that drawing largely up to you; your code determines what the view draws, and hence what it looks like in your interface.

This chapter discusses the mechanics of drawing. Don't be afraid to write drawing code of your own! It isn't difficult, and it's often the best way to make your app look the way you want it to. (For how to draw text, see Chapter 10.)

Images and Image Views

The basic general UIKit image class is UIImage. UIImage can read a stored file, so if an image does not need to be created dynamically, but has already been created before your app runs, then drawing may be as simple as providing an image file as a resource in your app's bundle. The system knows how to work with many standard image file types, such as TIFF, JPEG, GIF, and PNG; when an image file is to be included in your app bundle, iOS has a special affinity for PNG files, and you should prefer them whenever possible. You can also obtain image data in some other way, such as by downloading it, and transform this into a UIImage.

(The converse operation, saving image data as an image file, is discussed in Chapter 22.)

 Starting in iOS 11, users with appropriate hardware will capture photos in the new HEIC format. Naturally, the system knows how to work with this format as well.

Image Files

A pre-existing image file in your app's bundle can be obtained through the UIImage initializer `init(named:)`, which takes a string and returns a UIImage wrapped in an Optional, in case the image doesn't exist. This method looks in two places for the image:

Asset catalog
> We look in the asset catalog for an image set with the supplied name. The name is case-sensitive.

Top level of app bundle
> We look at the top level of the app's bundle for an image file with the supplied name. The name is case-sensitive and should include the file extension; if it doesn't include a file extension, *.png* is assumed.

When calling `init(named:)`, an asset catalog is searched before the top level of the app's bundle. If there are multiple asset catalogs, they are all searched, but the search order is indeterminate, so avoid multiple image sets with the same name.

A nice thing about `init(named:)` is that the image data may be cached in memory, and if you ask for the same image by calling `init(named:)` again later, the cached data may be supplied immediately. Alternatively, you can read an image file from anywhere in your app's bundle directly and without caching, using `init(contentsOfFile:)`, which expects a pathname string; you can get a reference to your app's bundle with `Bundle.main`, and Bundle then provides instance methods for getting the pathname of a file within the bundle, such as `path(forResource:ofType:)`.

 Typing a literal string image name into your code is an invitation to make a mistake. Xcode has a solution. In a context where a UIImage is expected, start typing the image's name (*not* in quotes) and ask for code completion; known image names will appear. Choose one, and a thumbnail of the image appears in your code. Under the hood, this is a call to `#imageLiteral(resourceName:)`, which behaves like `init(named:)`; it takes a literal string, but the compiler supplies the string and *won't* make a mistake. Moreover, the result isn't an Optional, so there's no need to unwrap it.

Methods that specify a resource in the app bundle, such as `init(named:)` and `path(forResource:ofType:)`, respond to special suffixes in the name of an actual resource file:

High-resolution variants

On a device with a double-resolution screen, when an image is obtained by name from the app bundle, a file with the same name extended by `@2x`, if there is one, will be used automatically, with the resulting UIImage marked as double-resolution by assigning it a `scale` property value of `2.0`. Similarly, if there is a file with the same name extended by `@3x`, it will be used on the triple-resolution screen of the iPhone 6/7/8 Plus or iPhone X, with a `scale` property value of `3.0`.

In this way, your app can contain different versions of an image file for different resolutions. Thanks to the `scale` property, a high-resolution version of an image has the same dimensions as the single-resolution image. Thus, on a high-resolution screen, your code continues to work without change, but your images look sharper.

Device type variants

A file with the same name extended by `~ipad` will automatically be used if the app is running natively on an iPad. You can use this in a universal app to supply different images automatically depending on whether the app runs on an iPhone (or iPod touch), on the one hand, or on an iPad, on the other. (This is true not just for images but for *any* resource obtained by name from the bundle. See Apple's *Resource Programming Guide*.)

One of the great benefits of an asset catalog, though, is that you can forget all about those name suffix conventions! An asset catalog knows when to use an alternate image within an image set, not from its name, but from its place in the catalog. Put the single-, double-, and triple-resolution alternatives into the slots marked "1x," "2x," and "3x" respectively. For a distinct iPad version of an image, check iPhone and iPad in the Attributes inspector for the image set; separate slots for those device types will appear in the asset catalog.

Alternatively, your image in the asset catalog can be a vector PDF. Switch the Scales pop-up menu to Single Scale and put the image into the single slot. It will be resized automatically for all three resolutions, and because it's a vector image, the resizing will be sharp. (New in Xcode 9 and iOS 11, you can check Preserve Vector Data for this image; when you do, it will be resized sharply for *any* size, both when scaled automatically by a UIImageView or other interface item, and when your code redraws the image at a different size.)

An asset catalog can also distinguish between versions of an image intended for different size class situations. (See the discussion of size classes and trait collections in Chapter 1.) In the Attributes inspector for your image set, use the Width Class and

Height Class pop-up menus to specify which size class possibilities you want slots for. Thus, for example, if we're on an iPhone with the app rotated to landscape orientation, and if there's both an Any Height and a Compact Height alternative in the image set, the Compact Height version is used. These features are live as the app runs; if the app rotates from landscape to portrait, and there's both an Any height and a Compact height alternative in the image set, the Compact Height version is *replaced* with the Any Height version in your interface, there and then, automatically.

How does an asset catalog perform this magic? When an image is obtained from an asset catalog through `init(named:)`, its `imageAsset` property is a UIImageAsset that effectively points back into the asset catalog at the image set that it came from. Each image in the image set has a trait collection associated with it (its `traitCollection`). By calling `image(with:)` and supplying a trait collection, you can ask an image's `imageAsset` for the image from the same image set appropriate to that trait collection. A built-in interface object that displays an image is automatically trait collection–aware; it receives the `traitCollectionDidChange(_:)` message and responds accordingly.

To demonstrate how this works under the hood, we can build a custom UIView with an `image` property that behaves the same way:

```
class MyView: UIView {
    var image : UIImage!
    override func traitCollectionDidChange(_: UITraitCollection?) {
        self.setNeedsDisplay() // causes draw(_:) to be called
    }
    override func draw(_ rect: CGRect) {
        if var im = self.image {
            if let asset = self.image.imageAsset {
                im = asset.image(with:self.traitCollection)
            }
            im.draw(at:.zero)
        }
    }
}
```

It is also possible to associate images as trait-based alternatives for one another *without* using an asset catalog. You might do this, for example, because you have constructed the images themselves in code, or obtained them over the network while the app is running. The technique is to instantiate a UIImageAsset and then associate each image with a different trait collection by *registering* it with this same UIImageAsset. For example:

```
let tcreg = UITraitCollection(verticalSizeClass: .regular)
let tccom = UITraitCollection(verticalSizeClass: .compact)
let moods = UIImageAsset()
let frowney = UIImage(named:"frowney")!
let smiley = UIImage(named:"smiley")!
moods.register(frowney, with: tcreg)
moods.register(smiley, with: tccom)
```

The amazing thing is that if we now display either `frowney` or `smiley` in a UIImage-View, we automatically see the image associated with the environment's current vertical size class, and it automatically switches to the other image when the app changes orientation on an iPhone. Moreover, this works even though I didn't keep any persistent reference to `frowney`, `smiley`, or the UIImageAsset! (The reason is that the images are cached by the system and they maintain a strong reference to the UIImage-Asset with which they are registered.)

 An image set in an asset catalog can make numerous further distinctions based on a device's processor type, wide color capabilities, and more. Moreover, these distinctions are used not only by the runtime when the app runs, but also by the App Store when thinning your app for a specific target device. For this and other reasons, asset catalogs should be regarded as preferable over keeping your images at the top level of the app bundle.

Image Views

Many built-in Cocoa interface objects will accept a UIImage as part of how they draw themselves; for example, a UIButton can display an image, and a UINavigationBar or a UITabBar can have a background image. I'll discuss those in Chapter 12. But when you simply want an image to appear in your interface, you'll probably hand it to an image view — a UIImageView — which has the most knowledge and flexibility with regard to displaying images and is intended for this purpose.

The nib editor supplies some shortcuts in this regard: the Attributes inspector of an interface object that can have an image will have a pop-up menu listing known images in your project, and such images are also listed in the Media library (Command-Option-Control-4). Media library images can often be dragged onto an interface object such as a button in the canvas to assign them; and if you drag a Media library image into a plain view, the image is transformed into a UIImageView displaying that image.

A UIImageView can actually have *two* images, one assigned to its `image` property and the other assigned to its `highlightedImage` property; the value of the UIImageView's `isHighlighted` property dictates which of the two is displayed at any given moment. A UIImageView does not automatically highlight itself merely because the user taps it, the way a button does. However, there are certain situations where a UIImageView will respond to the highlighting of its surroundings; for example, within a table view cell, a UIImageView will show its highlighted image when the cell is highlighted (Chapter 8).

A UIImageView is a UIView, so it can have a background color in addition to its image, it can have an alpha (transparency) value, and so forth (see Chapter 1). An image may have areas that are transparent, and a UIImageView will respect this; thus an image of any shape can appear. A UIImageView without a background color is invisible except for its image, so the image simply appears in the interface, without the user being aware that it resides in a rectangular host. A UIImageView without an image and without a background color is invisible, so you could start with an empty UIImageView in the place where you will later need an image and subsequently assign the image in code. You can assign a new image to substitute one image for another, or set the image view's `image` property to `nil` to remove it.

How a UIImageView draws its image depends upon the setting of its `contentMode` property (UIViewContentMode). (This property is inherited from UIView; I'll discuss its more general purpose later in this chapter.) For example, `.scaleToFill` means the image's width and height are set to the width and height of the view, thus filling the view completely even if this alters the image's aspect ratio; `.center` means the image is drawn centered in the view without altering its size. The best way to get a feel for the meanings of the various `contentMode` settings is to assign a UIImageView a small image in the nib editor and then, in the Attributes inspector, change the Mode pop-up menu, and see where and how the image draws itself.

You should also pay attention to a UIImageView's `clipsToBounds` property; if it is `false`, its image, even if it is larger than the image view and even if it is not scaled down by the `contentMode`, may be displayed in its entirety, extending beyond the image view itself.

 By default, the `clipsToBounds` of a UIImageView created in the nib editor is `false`. This is unlikely to be what you want!

When creating a UIImageView in code, you can take advantage of a convenience initializer, `init(image:)`. The default `contentMode` is `.scaleToFill`, but the image is not initially scaled; rather, *the view itself is sized to match the image.* You will still probably need to position the UIImageView correctly in its superview. In this example, I'll put a picture of the planet Mars in the center of the app's interface (Figure 2-1; for the CGRect `center` property, see Appendix B):

```
let iv = UIImageView(image:UIImage(named:"Mars"))
self.view.addSubview(iv)
iv.center = iv.superview!.bounds.center
iv.frame = iv.frame.integral
```

Figure 2-1. Mars appears in my interface

What happens to the size of an existing UIImageView when you assign an image to it depends on whether the image view is using autolayout. If it isn't, the image view's size doesn't change. But under autolayout, the size of the new image becomes the image view's new `intrinsicContentSize`, so the image view will adopt the image's size unless other constraints prevent.

 New in iOS 11, if an image view's `adjustsImageSizeForAccessibilityContent-SizeCategory` is `true`, the image view will scale itself up from the image's intrinsic content size if the user switches to an accessibility text size (see Chapter 10). You can set this property in the nib editor (Adjusts Image Size in the Attributes inspector).

An image view automatically acquires its `alignmentRectInsets` from its image's `alignmentRectInsets`. Thus, if you're going to be aligning the image view to some other object using autolayout, you can attach appropriate `alignmentRectInsets` to the image that the image view will display, and the image view will do the right thing. To do so, derive a new image by calling the original image's `withAlignmentRect-Insets(_:)` method. You can also set an image's `alignmentRectInsets` in the asset catalog (use the four Alignment fields).

Resizable Images

Certain places in the interface require an image that can be coherently resized to any desired proportions. For example, a custom image that serves as the track of a slider or progress view (Chapter 12) must be able to fill a space of any length. And there can frequently be other situations where you want to fill a background by tiling or stretching an existing image. Such an image is called a *resizable image*.

To make a resizable image, start with a normal image and call its `resizable-Image(withCapInsets:resizingMode:)` method. The `capInsets:` argument is a UIEdgeInsets, whose components represent distances inward from the edges of the image. In a context larger than the image, a resizable image can behave in one of two ways, depending on the `resizingMode:` value (UIImageResizingMode):

Figure 2-2. Tiling the entire image of Mars

Figure 2-3. Tiling the interior of Mars

`.tile`

The interior rectangle of the inset area is tiled (repeated) in the interior; each edge is formed by tiling the corresponding edge rectangle outside the inset area. The four corner rectangles outside the inset area are drawn unchanged.

`.stretch`

The interior rectangle of the inset area is stretched *once* to fill the interior; each edge is formed by stretching the corresponding edge rectangle outside the inset area *once*. The four corner rectangles outside the inset area are drawn unchanged.

In these examples, assume that `self.iv` is a UIImageView with absolute height and width (so that it won't adopt the size of its image) and with a `contentMode` of `.scaleToFill` (so that the image will exhibit resizing behavior). First, I'll illustrate tiling an entire image (Figure 2-2); note that the `capInsets:` is `UIEdgeInsets.zero`:

```
let mars = UIImage(named:"Mars")!
let marsTiled = mars.resizableImage(withCapInsets:.zero, resizingMode: .tile)
self.iv.image = marsTiled
```

Now we'll tile the interior of the image, changing the `capInsets:` argument from the previous code (Figure 2-3):

```
let marsTiled = mars.resizableImage(withCapInsets:
    UIEdgeInsetsMake(
        mars.size.height / 4.0,
        mars.size.width / 4.0,
        mars.size.height / 4.0,
        mars.size.width / 4.0
    ), resizingMode: .tile)
```

Figure 2-4. Stretching the interior of Mars

Figure 2-5. Stretching a few pixels at the interior of Mars

Next, I'll illustrate stretching. We'll start by changing just the `resizingMode:` from the previous code (Figure 2-4):

```
let marsTiled = mars.resizableImage(withCapInsets:
    UIEdgeInsetsMake(
        mars.size.height / 4.0,
        mars.size.width / 4.0,
        mars.size.height / 4.0,
        mars.size.width / 4.0
    ), resizingMode: .stretch)
```

A common stretching strategy is to make almost half the original image serve as a cap inset, leaving just a tiny rectangle in the center that must stretch to fill the entire interior of the resulting image (Figure 2-5):

```
let marsTiled = mars.resizableImage(withCapInsets:
    UIEdgeInsetsMake(
        mars.size.height / 2.0 - 1,
        mars.size.width / 2.0 - 1,
        mars.size.height / 2.0 - 1,
        mars.size.width / 2.0 - 1
    ), resizingMode: .stretch)
```

You should also experiment with different scaling `contentMode` settings. In the preceding example, if the image view's `contentMode` is `.scaleAspectFill`, and if the image view's `clipsToBounds` is `true`, we get a sort of gradient effect, because the top and bottom of the stretched image are outside the image view and aren't drawn (Figure 2-6).

Alternatively, you can configure a resizable image without code, in the project's asset catalog. It is often the case that a particular image will be used in your app chiefly as a resizable image, and always with the same `capInsets:` and `resizingMode:`, so it makes sense to configure this image once rather than having to repeat the same code.

Figure 2-6. Mars, stretched and clipped

Figure 2-7. Mars, sliced in the asset catalog

Figure 2-8. Mars, sliced and stretched

To configure an image in an asset catalog as a resizable image, select the image and, in the Slicing section of the Attributes inspector, change the Slices pop-up menu to Horizontal, Vertical, or Horizontal and Vertical. When you do this, additional interface appears. You can specify the `resizingMode` with the Center pop-up menu. You can work numerically, or click Show Slicing at the lower right of the canvas and work graphically. The graphical editor is zoomable, so zoom in to work comfortably.

This feature is actually even more powerful than `resizableImage(withCap-Insets:resizingMode:)`. It lets you specify the end caps *separately* from the tiled or stretched region, with the rest of the image being sliced out. In Figure 2-7, for example, the dark areas at the top left, top right, bottom left, and bottom right will be drawn as is. The narrow bands will be stretched, and the small rectangle at the top center will be stretched to fill most of the interior. But the rest of the image, the large central area covered by a sort of gauze curtain, will be omitted entirely. The result is shown in Figure 2-8.

Figure 2-9. One image in two rendering modes

Transparency Masks

Several places in an iOS app's interface want to treat an image as a *transparency mask*, also known as a *template*. This means that the image color values are ignored, and only the transparency (alpha) values of each pixel matter. The image shown on the screen is formed by combining the image's transparency values with a single tint color. Such, for example, is the default behavior of a tab bar item's image.

The way an image will be treated is a property of the image, its `renderingMode`. This property is read-only; to change it, start with an image and generate a new image with a different rendering mode, by calling its `withRenderingMode(_:)` method. The rendering mode values (UIImageRenderingMode) are:

- `.automatic`

- `.alwaysOriginal`

- `.alwaysTemplate`

The default is `.automatic`, which means that the image is drawn normally everywhere except in certain limited contexts, where it is used as a transparency mask. With the other two rendering mode values, you can *force* an image to be drawn normally, even in a context that would usually treat it as a transparency mask, or you can *force* an image to be treated as a transparency mask, even in a context that would otherwise treat it normally.

To accompany this feature, iOS gives every UIView a `tintColor`, which will be used to tint any template images it contains. Moreover, this `tintColor` by default is inherited down the view hierarchy, and indeed throughout the entire app, starting with the window (Chapter 1). Thus, assigning your app's main window a tint color is probably one of the few changes you'll make to the window; otherwise, your app adopts the system's blue tint color. (Alternatively, if you're using a main storyboard, set the Global Tint color in its File inspector.) Individual views can be assigned their own tint color, which is inherited by their subviews. Figure 2-9 shows two buttons displaying the same background image, one in normal rendering mode, the other in template rendering mode, in an app whose window tint color is red. (I'll say more about template images and `tintColor` in Chapter 12.)

An asset catalog can assign an image a rendering mode. Select the image set in the asset catalog, and use the Render As pop-up menu in the Attributes inspector to set the rendering mode to Default (`.automatic`), Original Image (`.alwaysOriginal`), or Template Image (`.alwaysTemplate`). This is an excellent approach whenever you have an image that you will use primarily in a specific rendering mode, because it saves you from having to remember to set that rendering mode in code every time you fetch the image. Instead, any time you call `init(named:)`, this image arrives with the rendering mode already set.

Reversible Images

Starting in iOS 9, the entire interface is automatically reversed when your app runs on a system for which your app is localized if the system language is right-to-left. In general, this probably won't affect your images. The runtime assumes that you *don't* want images to be reversed when the interface is reversed, so its default behavior is to leave them alone.

Nevertheless, you *might* want an image reversed when the interface is reversed. For example, suppose you've drawn an arrow pointing in the direction from which new interface will arrive when the user taps a button. If the button pushes a view controller onto a navigation interface, that direction is from the right on a left-to-right system, but from the left on a right-to-left system. This image has directional meaning within the app's own interface; it needs to flip horizontally when the interface is reversed.

To make this possible, call the image's `imageFlippedForRightToLeftLayout-Direction` method and use the resulting image in your interface. On a left-to-right system, the normal image will be used; on a right-to-left system, a reversed version of the image will be created and used automatically. You can override this behavior, even if the image is reversible, for a particular UIView displaying the image, such as a UIImageView, by setting that view's `semanticContentAttribute` to prevent mirroring.

You can make the same determination for an image in the asset catalog using the Direction pop-up menu (choose one of the Mirrors options). Moreover, the layout direction (as I mentioned in Chapter 1) is a trait. This means that, just as you can have pairs of images to be used on iPhone or iPad, or triples of images to be used on single-, double-, or triple-resolution screens, you can have pairs of images to be used under left-to-right or right-to-left layout. The easy way to configure such pairs is to choose Both in the asset catalog's Direction pop-up menu; now there are left-to-right and right-to-left image slots where you can place your images. Alternatively, you can register the paired images with a UIImageAsset in code, as I demonstrated earlier in this chapter.

You can also force an image to be flipped horizontally without regard to layout direction or semantic content attribute by calling its `withHorizontallyFlipped-Orientation` method.

Graphics Contexts

Instead of plopping an existing image file directly into your interface, you may want to create some drawing yourself, in code. To do so, you will need a *graphics context*.

A graphics context is basically a place you can draw. Conversely, you can't draw in code unless you've got a graphics context. There are several ways in which you might obtain a graphics context; these are the most common:

You create an image context
: In iOS 9 and before, this was done by calling `UIGraphicsBeginImageContext-WithOptions`. Starting in iOS 10, you should use a UIGraphicsImageRenderer. I'll go into detail later.

Cocoa creates the graphics context
: You subclass UIView and implement `draw(_:)`. At the time your `draw(_:)` implementation is called, Cocoa has already created a graphics context and is asking you to draw into it, right now; whatever you draw is what the UIView will display.

Cocoa passes you a graphics context
: You subclass CALayer and implement `draw(in:)`, or else you give a CALayer a delegate and implement the delegate's `draw(_:in:)`. The `in:` parameter is a graphics context. (Layers are discussed in Chapter 3.)

Moreover, at any given moment there either is or is not a *current graphics context*:

- When you create an image context, that image context automatically becomes the current graphics context.
- When UIView's `draw(_:)` is called, the UIView's drawing context is already the current graphics context.
- When CALayer's `draw(in:)` or its delegate's `draw(_:in:)` is called, the `in:` parameter is a graphics context, but it is *not* the current context. It's up to you to make it current if you need to.

What beginners find most confusing about drawing is that there are two sets of tools for drawing, which take different attitudes toward the context in which they will draw. One set needs a current context; the other just needs a context:

UIKit

Various Cocoa classes know how to draw themselves; these include UIImage, NSString (for drawing text), UIBezierPath (for drawing shapes), and UIColor. Some of these classes provide convenience methods with limited abilities; others are extremely powerful. In many cases, UIKit will be all you'll need.

With UIKit, you can draw *only into the current context*. If there's already a current context, you just draw. But with CALayer, where you are handed a context as a parameter, if you want to use the UIKit convenience methods, you'll have to make that context the current context; you do this by calling `UIGraphicsPush‐Context` (and be sure to restore things with `UIGraphicsPopContext` later).

Core Graphics

This is the full drawing API. Core Graphics, often referred to as Quartz, or Quartz 2D, is the drawing system that underlies all iOS drawing; UIKit drawing is built on top of it. It is low-level and consists of C functions (though in Swift these are mostly "renamified" to look like method calls). There are a lot of them! This chapter will familiarize you with the fundamentals; for complete information, you'll want to study Apple's *Quartz 2D Programming Guide*.

With Core Graphics, you must *specify a graphics context* (a CGContext) to draw into, explicitly, for each bit of your drawing. With CALayer, you are handed the context as a parameter, and that's the graphics context you want to draw into. But if there is already a current context, you have no reference to a context; to use Core Graphics, you need to get such a reference. You call `UIGraphicsGetCurrent‐Context` to obtain it.

 You don't have to use UIKit or Core Graphics *exclusively*. On the contrary, you can intermingle UIKit calls and Core Graphics calls in the same chunk of code to operate on the same graphics context. They merely represent two different ways of telling a graphics context what to do.

So we have two sets of tools and three ways in which a context might be supplied; that makes six ways of drawing. I'll now demonstrate all six of them! Without worrying just yet about the actual drawing commands, focus your attention on how the context is specified and on whether we're using UIKit or Core Graphics. First, I'll draw a blue circle by implementing a UIView subclass's `draw(_:)`, using UIKit to draw into the current context, which Cocoa has already prepared for me:

```
override func draw(_ rect: CGRect) {
    let p = UIBezierPath(ovalIn: CGRect(0,0,100,100))
    UIColor.blue.setFill()
    p.fill()
}
```

Now I'll do the same thing with Core Graphics; this will require that I first get a reference to the current context:

```
override func draw(_ rect: CGRect) {
    let con = UIGraphicsGetCurrentContext()!
    con.addEllipse(in:CGRect(0,0,100,100))
    con.setFillColor(UIColor.blue.cgColor)
    con.fillPath()
}
```

Next, I'll implement a CALayer delegate's draw(_:in:). In this case, we're handed a reference to a context, but it isn't the current context. So I have to make it the current context in order to use UIKit (and I must remember to stop making it the current context when I'm done drawing):

```
override func draw(_ layer: CALayer, in con: CGContext) {
    UIGraphicsPushContext(con)
    let p = UIBezierPath(ovalIn: CGRect(0,0,100,100))
    UIColor.blue.setFill()
    p.fill()
    UIGraphicsPopContext()
}
```

To use Core Graphics in a CALayer delegate's draw(_:in:), I simply keep referring to the context I was handed:

```
override func draw(_ layer: CALayer, in con: CGContext) {
    con.addEllipse(in:CGRect(0,0,100,100))
    con.setFillColor(UIColor.blue.cgColor)
    con.fillPath()
}
```

Finally, I'll make a UIImage of a blue circle. We can do this at any time (we don't need to wait for some particular method to be called) and in any class (we don't need to be in a UIView subclass). The old way of doing this, in iOS 9 and before, was as follows:

1. You call UIGraphicsBeginImageContextWithOptions. It creates an image context and makes it the current context.

2. You draw, thus generating the image.

3. You call UIGraphicsGetImageFromCurrentImageContext to extract an actual UIImage from the image context.

4. You call UIGraphicsEndImageContext to dismiss the context.

The desired image is the result of step 3, and now you can display it in your interface, draw it into some other graphics context, save it as a file, or whatever you like.

Starting in iOS 10, UIGraphicsBeginImageContextWithOptions is superseded by UIGraphicsImageRenderer (though you can still use the old way if you want to). The reason for this change is that the old way assumed you wanted an sRGB image with 8-bit color pixels, whereas the introduction of the iPad Pro 9.7-inch and iPhone 7 makes that assumption wrong: they can display "wide color," meaning that you probably want a P3 image with 16-bit color pixels. UIGraphicsImageRenderer knows how to make such an image, and will do so by default if we're running on a "wide color" device.

Another nice thing about UIGraphicsImageRenderer is that its `image` method takes a function containing your drawing commands and returns the image. Thus there is no need for the step-by-step imperative style of programming required by `UIGraphics-BeginImageContextWithOptions`, where after drawing you had to remember to fetch the image and dismiss the context yourself. Moreover, UIGraphicsImageRenderer doesn't have to be torn down after use; if you know that you're going to be drawing multiple images with the same size and format, you can keep a reference to the renderer and call its `image` method again.

So now, I'll draw my image using UIKit:

```
let r = UIGraphicsImageRenderer(size:CGSize(100,100))
let im = r.image { _ in
    let p = UIBezierPath(ovalIn: CGRect(0,0,100,100))
    UIColor.blue.setFill()
    p.fill()
}
// im is the blue circle image, do something with it here ...
```

And here's the same thing using Core Graphics:

```
let r = UIGraphicsImageRenderer(size:CGSize(100,100))
let im = r.image { _ in
    let con = UIGraphicsGetCurrentContext()!
    con.addEllipse(in:CGRect(0,0,100,100))
    con.setFillColor(UIColor.blue.cgColor)
    con.fillPath()
}
// im is the blue circle image, do something with it here ...
```

(Instead of calling `image`, you can call UIGraphicsImageRenderer methods that generate JPEG or PNG image data, suitable for saving as an image file.)

In those examples, we're calling UIGraphicsImageRenderer's `init(size:)` and accepting its default configuration, which is usually what's wanted. To configure its image context further, call the UIGraphicsImageRendererFormat class method `default`, configure the format through its properties, and pass it to UIGraphicsImage-Renderer's `init(size:format:)`. Those properties are:

opaque
By default, `false`; the image context is transparent. If `true`, the image context is opaque and has a black background, and the resulting image has no transparency.

scale

By default, the same as the scale of the main screen, `UIScreen.main.scale`. This means that the resolution of the resulting image will be correct for the device we're running on.

prefersExtendedRange

By default, `true` only if we're running on a device that supports "wide color."

 New in iOS 11, you can call a UIGraphicsImageRendererFormat initializer, `init(for:)`, which takes a UITraitCollection; typically, this will be `self.trait‑ Collection`, and the `scale` and `prefersExtendedRange` properties of the renderer will be set from the current environment.

You may also be wondering about the parameter that arrives into the UIGraphics‑ImageRenderer's `image` function (which is ignored in the preceding examples). It's a UIGraphicsImageRendererContext. This provides access to the configuring UIGraphicsImageRendererFormat (its `format`). It also lets you obtain the graphics context (its `cgContext`); you can alternatively get this by calling `UIGraphicsGet‑ CurrentContext`, and the preceding code does so, for consistency with the other ways of drawing. In addition, the UIGraphicsImageRendererContext can hand you a copy of the image as drawn up to this point (its `currentImage`); also, it implements a few basic drawing commands of its own.

UIImage Drawing

A UIImage provides methods for drawing itself into the current context. We know how to obtain a UIImage, and we know how to obtain a graphics context and make it the current context, so we can experiment with these methods.

Here, I'll make a UIImage consisting of two pictures of Mars side by side (Figure 2-10):

```
let mars = UIImage(named:"Mars")!
let sz = mars.size
let r = UIGraphicsImageRenderer(size:CGSize(sz.width*2, sz.height))
let im = r.image { _ in
    mars.draw(at:CGPoint(0,0))
    mars.draw(at:CGPoint(sz.width,0))
}
```

Observe that image scaling works perfectly in that example. If we have multiple resolution versions of our original Mars image, the correct one for the current device is used, and is assigned the correct `scale` value. The image context that we are drawing into also has the correct `scale` by default. And the resulting image has the correct `scale` as well. Thus, this same code produces an image that looks correct on the current device, whatever its screen resolution may be.

Figure 2-10. Two images of Mars combined side by side

Figure 2-11. Two images of Mars in different sizes, composited

Additional UIImage methods let you scale an image into a desired rectangle as you draw, and specify the compositing (blend) mode whereby the image should combine with whatever is already present. To illustrate, I'll create an image showing Mars centered in another image of Mars that's twice as large, using the `.multiply` blend mode (Figure 2-11):

```
let mars = UIImage(named:"Mars")!
let sz = mars.size
let r = UIGraphicsImageRenderer(size:CGSize(sz.width*2, sz.height*2))
let im = r.image { _ in
    mars.draw(in:CGRect(0,0,sz.width*2,sz.height*2))
    mars.draw(in:CGRect(sz.width/2.0, sz.height/2.0, sz.width, sz.height),
        blendMode: .multiply, alpha: 1.0)
}
```

 New in Xcode 9 and iOS 11, a PDF vector image in the asset catalog for which you have checked Preserve Vector Data will scale sharply when you call `draw(in:)`.

Sometimes, you may want to extract a smaller region of the original image — effectively *cropping* the image as you draw it. Unfortunately, there is no UIImage drawing method for specifying the source rectangle. You can work around this by creating a smaller graphics context and positioning the image drawing so that the desired region falls into it. For example, to obtain an image of the right half of Mars, you can make a graphics context half the width of the `mars` image, and then draw `mars` shifted left, so that only its right half intersects the graphics context. There is no harm in doing this,

Figure 2-12. Half the original image of Mars

and it's a perfectly standard strategy; the left half of mars simply isn't drawn (Figure 2-12):

```
let mars = UIImage(named:"Mars")!
let sz = mars.size
let r = UIGraphicsImageRenderer(size:CGSize(sz.width/2.0, sz.height))
let im = r.image { _ in
    mars.draw(at:CGPoint(-sz.width/2.0,0))
}
```

CGImage Drawing

The Core Graphics version of UIImage is CGImage. In essence, a UIImage is (usually) a wrapper for a CGImage: the UIImage is bitmap image data plus scale, orientation, and other information, whereas the CGImage is the bare bitmap image data alone. The two are easily converted to one another: a UIImage has a cgImage property that accesses its Quartz image data, and you can make a UIImage from a CGImage using init(cgImage:) or its more configurable sibling, init(cgImage:scale:orientation:).

A CGImage lets you create a new image cropped from a rectangular region of the original image, which you can't do with UIImage. (A CGImage has other powers a UIImage doesn't have; for example, you can apply an image mask to a CGImage.) I'll demonstrate by splitting the image of Mars in half and drawing the two halves separately (Figure 2-13):

```
let mars = UIImage(named:"Mars")!
// extract each half as CGImage
let marsCG = mars.cgImage!
let sz = mars.size
let marsLeft = marsCG.cropping(to:
    CGRect(0,0,sz.width/2.0,sz.height))!
let marsRight = marsCG.cropping(to:
    CGRect(sz.width/2.0,0,sz.width/2.0,sz.height))!
let r = UIGraphicsImageRenderer(size: CGSize(sz.width*1.5, sz.height))
let im = r.image { ctx in
    let con = ctx.cgContext
    con.draw(marsLeft, in:
```

Figure 2-13. Image of Mars split in half (and flipped)

```
        CGRect(0,0,sz.width/2.0,sz.height))
    con.draw(marsRight, in:
        CGRect(sz.width,0,sz.width/2.0,sz.height))
}
```

But there's a problem with that example: the drawing is upside-down! It isn't rotated; it's mirrored top to bottom, or, to use the technical term, *flipped*. This phenomenon can arise when you create a CGImage and then draw it, and is due to a mismatch in the native coordinate systems of the source and target contexts.

There are various ways of compensating for this mismatch between the coordinate systems. One is to draw the CGImage into an intermediate UIImage and extract *another* CGImage from that. Example 2-1 presents a utility function for doing this.

Example 2-1. Utility for flipping an image drawing

```
func flip (_ im: CGImage) -> CGImage {
    let sz = CGSize(CGFloat(im.width), CGFloat(im.height))
    let r = UIGraphicsImageRenderer(size:sz)
    return r.image { ctx in
        ctx.cgContext.draw(im, in: CGRect(0, 0, sz.width, sz.height))
    }.cgImage!
}
```

Armed with the utility function from Example 2-1, we can fix our CGImage drawing calls in the previous example so that they draw the halves of Mars the right way up:

```
    con.draw(flip(marsLeft!), in:
        CGRect(0,0,sz.width/2.0,sz.height))
    con.draw(flip(marsRight!), in:
        CGRect(sz.width,0,sz.width/2.0,sz.height))
```

However, we've *still* got a problem: on a high-resolution device, if there is a high-resolution variant of our image file, the drawing comes out all wrong. The reason is that we are obtaining our initial Mars image using UIImage's init(named:), which returns a UIImage that compensates for the increased size of a high-resolution image by setting its own scale property to match. But a CGImage doesn't have a scale property, and knows nothing of the fact that the image dimensions are increased! Therefore, on a high-resolution device, the CGImage that we extract from our Mars

UIImage as `mars.cgImage` is larger (in each dimension) than `mars.size`, and all our calculations after that are wrong.

It would be best, therefore, is to wrap each CGImage in a UIImage and draw the UIImage *instead* of the CGImage. The UIImage can be formed in such a way as to compensate for scale: call `init(cgImage:scale:orientation:)`. Moreover, by drawing a UIImage instead of a CGImage, we avoid the flipping problem! So here's an approach that deals with both flipping and scale, with no need for the `flip` utility:

```
let mars = UIImage(named:"Mars")!
let sz = mars.size
let marsCG = mars.cgImage!
let szCG = CGSize(CGFloat(marsCG.width), CGFloat(marsCG.height))
let marsLeft =
    marsCG.cropping(to:
        CGRect(0,0,szCG.width/2.0,szCG.height))
let marsRight =
    marsCG.cropping(to:
        CGRect(szCG.width/2.0,0,szCG.width/2.0,szCG.height))
let r = UIGraphicsImageRenderer(size:CGSize(sz.width*1.5, sz.height))
let im = r.image { _ in
    UIImage(cgImage: marsLeft!,
        scale: mars.scale,
        orientation: mars.imageOrientation).draw(at:CGPoint(0,0))
    UIImage(cgImage: marsRight!,
        scale: mars.scale,
        orientation: mars.imageOrientation).draw(at:CGPoint(sz.width,0))
}
```

 Yet another solution to flipping is to apply a transform to the graphics context before drawing the CGImage, effectively flipping the context's internal coordinate system. This is elegant, but can be confusing if there are other transforms in play. I'll talk more about graphics context transforms later in this chapter.

Snapshots

An entire view — anything from a single button to your whole interface, complete with its contained hierarchy of views — can be drawn into the current graphics context by calling the UIView instance method `drawHierarchy(in:afterScreen-Updates:)`. (This method is much faster than the CALayer method `render(in:)`; nevertheless, the latter does still come in handy, as I'll show in Chapter 5.) The result is a *snapshot* of the original view: it looks like the original view, but it's basically just a bitmap image of it, a lightweight visual duplicate.

An even faster way to obtain a snapshot of a view is to use the UIView (or UIScreen) instance method `snapshotView(afterScreenUpdates:)`. The result is a UIView, not a UIImage; it's rather like a UIImageView that knows how to draw only one image, namely the snapshot. Such a snapshot view will typically be used as is, but you can enlarge its bounds and the snapshot image will stretch. If you want the stretched snapshot to behave like a resizable image, call `resizableSnapshotView(from:after-ScreenUpdates:withCapInsets:)` instead. It is perfectly reasonable to make a snapshot view from a snapshot view.

Snapshots are useful because of the dynamic nature of the iOS interface. For example, you might place a snapshot of a view in your interface in front of the real view to hide what's happening, or use it during an animation to present the illusion of a view moving when in fact it's just a snapshot.

Here's an example from one of my apps. It's a card game, and its `views` portray cards. I want to animate the removal of all those cards from the board, flying away to an offscreen point. But I don't want to animate the views themselves! They need to stay put, to portray future cards. So I make a snapshot view of each of the card views; I then make the card views invisible, put the snapshot views in their place, and animate the snapshot views. This code will mean more to you after you've read Chapter 4, but the strategy is evident:

```
for v in views {
    let snapshot = v.snapshotView(afterScreenUpdates: false)!
    let snap = MySnapBehavior(item:snapshot, snapto:CGPoint(
        x: self.anim.referenceView!.bounds.midX,
        y: -self.anim.referenceView!.bounds.height)
    )
    self.snaps.append(snapshot) // keep a list so we can remove them later
    snapshot.frame = v.frame
    v.isHidden = true
    self.anim.referenceView!.addSubview(snapshot)
    self.anim.addBehavior(snap)
}
```

CIFilter and CIImage

The "CI" in CIFilter and CIImage stands for Core Image, a technology for transforming images through mathematical filters. Core Image started life on the desktop (macOS), and when it was originally migrated into iOS 5, some of the filters available on the desktop were not available in iOS (presumably because they were too intensive mathematically for a mobile device). Over the years, however, more and more macOS filters were added to the iOS repertoire, and now the two have complete parity: *all* macOS filters are available in iOS, and the two platforms have nearly identical APIs.

A filter is a CIFilter. The 200 available filters fall naturally into several broad categories:

Patterns and gradients
These filters create CIImages that can then be combined with other CIImages, such as a single color, a checkerboard, stripes, or a gradient.

Compositing
These filters combine one image with another, using compositing blend modes familiar from image processing programs.

Color
These filters adjust or otherwise modify the colors of an image. Thus you can alter an image's saturation, hue, brightness, contrast, gamma and white point, exposure, shadows and highlights, and so on.

Geometric
These filters perform basic geometric transformations on an image, such as scaling, rotation, and cropping.

Transformation
These filters distort, blur, or stylize an image.

Transition
These filters provide a frame of a transition between one image and another; by asking for frames in sequence, you can animate the transition (I'll demonstrate in Chapter 4).

Special purpose
These filters perform highly specialized operations such as face detection and generation of barcodes.

The basic use of a CIFilter is quite simple:

- You specify what filter you want by supplying its string name; to learn what these names are, consult Apple's *Core Image Filter Reference*, or call the CIFilter class method `filterNames(inCategories:)` with a `nil` argument.

- Each filter has a small number of keys and values that determine its behavior (as if a filter were a kind of dictionary). You can learn about these keys entirely in code, but typically you'll consult the documentation. For each key that you're interested in, you supply a key–value pair. In supplying values, a number must be wrapped up as an NSNumber (Swift will take care of this for you), and there are a few supporting classes such as CIVector (like CGPoint and CGRect combined) and CIColor, whose use is easy to grasp.

Among a CIFilter's keys may be the input image or images on which the filter is to operate; such an image must be a CIImage. You can obtain this CIImage from a CGImage with `init(cgImage:)` or from a UIImage with `init(image:)`.

 Do not attempt, as a shortcut, to obtain a CIImage directly from a UIImage through the UIImage's `ciImage` property. This property does *not* transform a UIImage into a CIImage! It merely points to the CIImage that *already* backs the UIImage, if the UIImage *is* backed by a CIImage; but your images are *not* backed by a CIImage, but rather by a CGImage. I'll explain where a CIImage-backed UIImage comes from in just a moment.

Alternatively, you can obtain a CIImage as the output of a filter — which means that *filters can be chained together.*

There are three ways to describe and use a filter:

- Create the filter with CIFilter's `init(name:)`. Now append the keys and values by calling `setValue(_:forKey:)` repeatedly, or by calling `setValuesForKeys(_:)` with a dictionary. Obtain the output CIImage as the filter's `outputImage`.
- Create the filter and supply the keys and values in a single move, by calling CIFilter's `init(name:withInputParameters:)`. Obtain the output CIImage as the filter's `outputImage`.
- If a CIFilter requires an input image and you already have a CIImage to fulfill this role, specify the filter and supply the keys and values, *and receive the output CIImage as a result*, all in a single move, by calling the CIImage instance method `applyingFilter(_:parameters:)`.

As you build a chain of filters, nothing actually happens. The only calculation-intensive move comes at the very end, when you transform the final CIImage in the chain into a bitmap drawing. This is called *rendering* the image. There are two main ways to do this:

With a CIContext
Create a CIContext by calling `init()` or `init(options:)`, and then call its `createCGImage(_:from:)`, handing it the final CIImage as the first argument. This renders the image. The only mildly tricky thing here is that a CIImage

doesn't have a frame or bounds; it has an extent. You will often use this as the second argument to createCGImage(_:from:). The final output CGImage is ready for any purpose, such as for display in your app, for transformation into a UIImage, or for use in further drawing.

With a UIImage

Create a UIImage wrapping the final CIImage by calling init(ciImage:) or init(ciImage:scale:orientation:). You then *draw* the UIImage into some graphics context. At the moment of drawing, the image is rendered. (Apple claims that you can simply hand a UIImage created by calling init(ciImage:) to a UIImageView, as its image, and that the UIImageView will render the image. In my experience, this is *not true*. You must draw the image *explicitly* in order to render it.)

 Rendering a CIImage in either of these ways is slow and expensive. With the first approach, the expense comes at the moment when you create the CIContext; wherever possible, you should create your CIContext once, beforehand — preferably, once per app — and reuse it each time you render. With the second approach, the expense comes at the moment of drawing the UIImage. Other ways of rendering a CIImage, involving things like GLKView or CAEAGLLayer, which are not discussed in this book, have the advantage of being very fast and suitable for animated or rapid rendering.

To illustrate, I'll start with an ordinary photo of myself (it's true I'm wearing a motorcycle helmet, but it's still ordinary) and create a circular vignette effect (Figure 2-14). We derive from the image of me (moi) a CIImage (moici). We use a CIFilter (grad) to form a radial gradient between the default colors of white and black. Then we use a second CIFilter that treats the radial gradient as a mask for blending between the photo of me and a default clear background: where the radial gradient is white (everything inside the gradient's inner radius) we see just me, and where the radial gradient is black (everything outside the gradient's outer radius) we see just the clear color, with a gradation in between, so that the image fades away in the circular band between the gradient's radii. The code illustrates two different ways of configuring a CIFilter:

```
let moi = UIImage(named:"Moi")!
let moici = CIImage(image:moi)!
let moiextent = moici.extent
let center = CIVector(x: moiextent.width/2.0, y: moiextent.height/2.0)
let smallerDimension = min(moiextent.width, moiextent.height)
let largerDimension = max(moiextent.width, moiextent.height)
// first filter
let grad = CIFilter(name: "CIRadialGradient")!
grad.setValue(center, forKey:"inputCenter")
grad.setValue(smallerDimension/2.0 * 0.85, forKey:"inputRadius0")
grad.setValue(largerDimension/2.0, forKey:"inputRadius1")
```

Figure 2-14. A photo of me, vignetted

```
let gradimage = grad.outputImage!
// second filter
let blendimage = moici.applyingFilter("CIBlendWithMask",
    parameters: [ "inputMaskImage":gradimage ])
```

We now have the final CIImage in the chain (`blendimage`); remember, the processor has not yet performed any rendering. Now, however, we want to generate the final bitmap and display it. Let's say we're going to display it as the `image` of a UIImage-View `self.iv`. We can do it in two different ways. We can create a CGImage by passing the CIImage through a CIContext; in this code, I have prepared this CIContext beforehand as a property, `self.context`, by calling `CIContext()`:

```
let moicg = self.context.createCGImage(blendimage, from: moiextent)!
self.iv.image = UIImage(cgImage: moicg)
```

Alternatively, we can capture our final CIImage as a UIImage and then draw with it in order to generate the bitmap output of the filter chain:

```
let r = UIGraphicsImageRenderer(size:moiextent.size)
self.iv.image = r.image { _ in
    UIImage(ciImage: blendimage).draw(in:moiextent)
}
```

A filter chain can be encapsulated into a single custom filter by subclassing CIFilter. Your subclass just needs to override the `outputImage` property (and possibly other methods such as `setDefaults`), with additional properties to make it key–value coding compliant for any input keys. Here's our vignette filter as a simple CIFilter subclass with two input keys; `inputImage` is the image to be vignetted, and `inputPercentage` is a percentage (between 0 and 1) adjusting the gradient's inner radius:

```
class MyVignetteFilter : CIFilter {
    @objc var inputImage : CIImage?
    @objc var inputPercentage : NSNumber? = 1.0
    override var outputImage : CIImage? {
        return self.makeOutputImage()
    }
```

```
private func makeOutputImage () -> CIImage? {
    guard let inputImage = self.inputImage else {return nil}
    guard let inputPercentage = self.inputPercentage else {return nil}
    let extent = inputImage.extent
    let grad = CIFilter(name: "CIRadialGradient")!
    let center = CIVector(x: extent.width/2.0, y: extent.height/2.0)
    let smallerDimension = min(extent.width, extent.height)
    let largerDimension = max(extent.width, extent.height)
    grad.setValue(center, forKey:"inputCenter")
    grad.setValue(smallerDimension/2.0 * (inputPercentage as! CGFloat),
        forKey:"inputRadius0")
    grad.setValue(largerDimension/2.0, forKey:"inputRadius1")
    let blend = CIFilter(name: "CIBlendWithMask")!
    blend.setValue(inputImage, forKey: "inputImage")
    blend.setValue(grad.outputImage, forKey: "inputMaskImage")
    return blend.outputImage
}
}
```

And here's how to use our CIFilter subclass and display its output in a UIImageView:

```
let vig = MyVignetteFilter()
let moici = CIImage(image: UIImage(named:"Moi")!)!
vig.setValuesForKeys([
    "inputImage":moici,
    "inputPercentage":0.7
])
let outim = vig.outputImage!
let outimcg = self.context.createCGImage(outim, from: outim.extent)!
self.iv.image = UIImage(cgImage: outimcg)
```

Blur and Vibrancy Views

Certain views on iOS, such as navigation bars and the control center, are translucent and display a blurred rendition of what's behind them. To help you imitate this effect, iOS provides the UIVisualEffectView class. You can place other views in front of a UIVisualEffectView, but any subviews should be placed inside its contentView. To tint what's seen through a UIVisualEffectView, set the backgroundColor of its contentView.

To use a UIVisualEffectView, create it with init(effect:); the effect: argument will be an instance of a UIVisualEffect subclass:

UIBlurEffect

> To initialize a UIBlurEffect, call init(style:); the styles (UIBlurEffectStyle) are .dark, .light, and .extraLight. (.extraLight is suitable particularly for pieces of interface that function like a navigation bar or toolbar.) For example:

```
let fuzzy = UIVisualEffectView(effect:(UIBlurEffect(style:.light)))
```

Figure 2-15. A blurred background and a vibrant label

UIVibrancyEffect

To initialize a UIVibrancyEffect, call `init(blurEffect:)`. Vibrancy tints a view so as to make it harmonize with the blurred colors underneath it. The intention here is that the vibrancy effect view should sit in front of a blur effect view, typically in its `contentView`, adding vibrancy to a single UIView that's inside its *own* `contentView`; you tell the vibrancy effect what the underlying blur effect is, so that they harmonize. You can fetch a visual effect view's blur effect as its `effect` property, but that's a UIVisualEffect — the superclass — so you'll have to cast down to a UIBlurEffect in order to hand it to `init(blurEffect:)`.

Here's an example of a blur effect view covering and blurring the interface (`self.view`), and containing a UILabel wrapped in a vibrancy effect view (Figure 2-15):

```
let blur = UIVisualEffectView(effect: UIBlurEffect(style: .extraLight))
blur.frame = self.view.bounds
blur.autoresizingMask = [.flexibleWidth, .flexibleHeight]
let vib = UIVisualEffectView(effect: UIVibrancyEffect(
    blurEffect: blur.effect as! UIBlurEffect))
let lab = UILabel()
lab.text = "Hello, world!"
lab.sizeToFit()
vib.frame = lab.frame
vib.contentView.addSubview(lab)
vib.center = CGPoint(blur.bounds.midX, blur.bounds.midY)
vib.autoresizingMask = [.flexibleTopMargin, .flexibleBottomMargin,
    .flexibleLeftMargin, .flexibleRightMargin]
blur.contentView.addSubview(vib)
self.view.addSubview(blur)
```

Apple seems to think that vibrancy makes a view more legible in conjunction with the underlying blur, but I'm not persuaded. The vibrant view's color is made to harmonize with the blurred color behind it, but harmony implies similarity, which can make the vibrant view *less* legible. You'll have to experiment. With the particular interface I'm blurring, the vibrant label in Figure 2-15 looks okay with a `.dark` or `.extraLight` blur effect view, but is hard to see with a `.light` blur effect view.

There are a lot of useful additional notes, well worth consulting, in the headers. For example, the *UIVibrancyEffect.h* header points out that an image displayed in an image view needs to be a template image in order to receive the benefit of a vibrancy effect view.

Observe that both a blur effect view and a blur effect view with an embedded vibrancy effect view are available as built-in objects in the nib editor.

Drawing a UIView

The examples of drawing so far in this chapter have mostly produced UIImage objects, suitable for display by a UIImageView or any other interface object that knows how to display an image. But, as I've already explained, a UIView *itself* provides a graphics context; whatever you draw into that graphics context *will appear directly in that view*. The technique here is to subclass UIView and implement the subclass's draw(_:) method.

So, for example, let's say we have a UIView subclass called MyView. You would then instantiate this class and get the instance into the view hierarchy. One way to do this would be to drag a UIView into a view in the nib editor and set its class to MyView in the Identity Inspector; another would be to run code that creates the MyView instance and puts it into the interface.

The result is that, from time to time, or whenever you send it the setNeedsDisplay message, MyView's draw(_:) will be called. This is your subclass, so you get to write the code that runs at that moment. Whatever you draw will appear inside the MyView instance. There will usually be no need to call super, since UIView's own implementation of draw(_:) does nothing. At the time that draw(_:) is called, the current graphics context has already been set to the view's own graphics context. You can use Core Graphics functions or UIKit convenience methods to draw into that context. I gave some basic examples earlier in this chapter ("Graphics Contexts" on page 87).

The need to draw in real time, on demand, surprises some beginners, who worry that drawing may be a time-consuming operation. This can indeed be a reasonable consideration, and where the same drawing will be used in many places in your interface, it may well make sense to construct a UIImage instead, once, and then reuse that UIImage by drawing it in a view's draw(_:). In general, however, you should not optimize prematurely. The code for a drawing operation may appear verbose and yet be extremely fast. Moreover, the iOS drawing system is efficient; it doesn't call draw(_:) unless it has to (or is told to, through a call to setNeedsDisplay), and once a view has drawn itself, the result is cached so that the cached drawing can be reused instead of repeating the drawing operation from scratch. (Apple refers to this cached drawing as the view's *bitmap backing store*.) You can readily satisfy yourself of this fact with some caveman debugging, logging in your draw(_:) implementation; you may be amazed to discover that your custom UIView's draw(_:) code is called only once in the entire lifetime of the app! In fact, moving code to draw(_:) is commonly a way to *increase* efficiency. This is because it is more efficient for the drawing engine to render directly onto the screen than for it to render offscreen and then copy those pixels onto the screen.

Here are three important caveats with regard to UIView's `draw(_:)` method:

- Don't call `draw(_:)` yourself. If a view needs updating and you want its `draw(_:)` called, send the view the `setNeedsDisplay` message. This will cause `draw(_:)` to be called at the next proper moment.

- Don't override `draw(_:)` unless you are assured that this is legal. For example, it is not legal to override `draw(_:)` in a subclass of UIImageView; you cannot combine your drawing with that of the UIImageView.

- Don't do anything in `draw(_:)` except draw. That sort of thing is a common beginner mistake. Other configuration, such as setting the view's background color, or giving it subviews or sublayers, should be performed elsewhere, such as its initializer override.

Where drawing is extensive and can be compartmentalized into sections, you may be able to gain some additional efficiency by paying attention to the parameter passed into `draw(_:)`. This parameter is a CGRect designating the region of the view's bounds that needs refreshing. Normally, this is the view's entire bounds; but if you call `setNeedsDisplay(_:)`, which takes a CGRect parameter, it will be the CGRect that you passed in as argument. You could respond by drawing only what goes into those bounds; but even if you don't, your drawing will be clipped to those bounds, so, while you may not spend less time drawing, the system will draw more efficiently.

When a custom UIView subclass has a `draw(_:)` implementation and you create an instance of this subclass in code, you may be surprised (and annoyed) to find that the view has a black background! This is a source of considerable confusion among beginners. The black background arises when two things are true:

- The view's `backgroundColor` is `nil`.
- The view's `isOpaque` is `true`.

Unfortunately, when creating a UIView in code, both those things *are* true by default! So if you don't want the black background, you must do something about at least one of them. If this view isn't going to be opaque, then, this being your own UIView subclass, you might implement its `init(frame:)` (the designated initializer) to have the view set its own `isOpaque` to `false`:

```
class MyView : UIView {
    override init(frame: CGRect) {
        super.init(frame:frame)
        self.isOpaque = false
    }
    // ...
}
```

With a UIView created in the nib, on the other hand, the black background problem doesn't arise. This is because such a UIView's `backgroundColor` is not `nil`. The nib assigns it *some* actual background color, even if that color is `UIColor.clear`.

Graphics Context Commands

Whenever you draw, you are giving commands to the graphics context into which you are drawing. This is true regardless of whether you use UIKit methods or Core Graphics functions. Thus, learning to draw is really a matter of understanding how a graphics context works. That's what this section is about.

Under the hood, Core Graphics commands to a graphics context are global C functions with names like `CGContextSetFillColor`; but Swift "renamification" recasts them as if a CGContext were a genuine object representing the graphics context. The Core Graphics functions thus appear as methods sent to the CGContext. Moreover, thanks to Swift overloading, multiple functions are collapsed into a single command. Thus, for example, `CGContextSetFillColor` and `CGContextSetFillColorWithColor` and `CGContextSetRGBFillColor` and `CGContextSetGrayFillColor` all become `setFillColor`.

Graphics Context Settings

As you draw in a graphics context, the drawing obeys the context's current settings. Thus, the procedure is always to configure the context's settings first, and then draw. For example, to draw a red line followed by a blue line, you would first set the context's line color to red, and then draw the first line; then you'd set the context's line color to blue, and then draw the second line. To the eye, it appears that the redness and blueness are properties of the individual lines, but in fact, at the time you draw each line, line color is a feature of the entire graphics context.

A graphics context thus has, at every moment, a *state*, which is the sum total of all its settings; the way a piece of drawing looks is the result of what the graphics context's state was at the moment that piece of drawing was performed. To help you manipulate entire states, the graphics context provides a *stack* for holding states. Every time you call `saveGState`, the context pushes the entire current state onto the stack; every time you call `restoreGState`, the context retrieves the state from the top of the stack (the state that was most recently pushed) and sets itself to that state.

Thus, a common pattern is:

1. Call `saveGState`.
2. Manipulate the context's settings, thus changing its state.
3. Draw.
4. Call `restoreGState` to restore the state and the settings to what they were before you manipulated them.

You do not have to do this before *every* manipulation of a context's settings, however, because settings don't necessarily conflict with one another or with past settings. You can set the context's line color to red and then later to blue without any difficulty. But in certain situations you do want your manipulation of settings to be undoable, and I'll point out several such situations later in this chapter.

Many of the settings that constitute a graphics context's state, and that determine the behavior and appearance of drawing performed at that moment, are similar to those of any drawing application. Here are some of them, along with some of the commands that determine them (and some UIKit properties and methods that call them):

Line thickness and dash style
> `setLineWidth(_:)`, `setLineDash(phase:lengths:)` (and UIBezierPath line-Width, `setLineDash(_:count:phase:)`)

Line end-cap style and join style
> `setLineCap(_:)`, `setLineJoin(_:)`, `setMiterLimit(_:)` (and UIBezierPath lineCapStyle, lineJoinStyle, miterLimit)

Line color or pattern
> `setStrokeColor(_:)`, `setStrokePattern(_:colorComponents:)` (and UIColor setStroke)

Fill color or pattern
> `setFillColor(_:)`, `setFillPattern(_:colorComponents:)` (and UIColor set-Fill)

Shadow
> `setShadow(offset:blur:color:)`

Overall transparency and compositing
> `setAlpha(_:)`, `setBlendMode(_:)`

Anti-aliasing
> `setShouldAntialias(_:)`

Additional settings include:

Clipping area
    Drawing outside the clipping area is not physically drawn.

Transform (or "CTM," for "current transform matrix")
    Changes how points that you specify in subsequent drawing commands are mapped onto the physical space of the canvas.

Many of these settings will be illustrated by examples later in this chapter.

Paths and Shapes

By issuing a series of instructions for moving an imaginary pen, you construct a *path*, tracing it out from point to point. You must first tell the pen where to position itself, setting the current point; after that, you issue a series of commands telling it how to trace out each subsequent piece of the path. Each additional piece of the path starts at the current point; its end becomes the new current point.

Note that a path, in and of itself, does *not* constitute drawing! First you provide a path; *then* you draw. Drawing can mean stroking the path or filling the path, or both. Again, this should be a familiar notion from certain drawing applications.

Here are some path-drawing commands you're likely to give:

Position the current point
    move(to:)

Trace a line
    addLine(to:), addLines(between:)

Trace a rectangle
    addRect(_:), addRects(_:)

Trace an ellipse or circle
    addEllipse(in:)

Trace an arc
    addArc(tangent1End:tangent2End:radius:)

Trace a Bezier curve with one or two control points
    addQuadCurve(to:control:), addCurveTo(to:control1:control2:)

Close the current path
    closePath. This appends a line from the last point of the path to the first point. There's no need to do this if you're about to fill the path, since it's done for you.

Stroke or fill the current path
    strokePath, fillPath(using:), drawPath. Stroking or filling the current path *clears the path*. Use drawPath if you want both to fill and to stroke the path in a

single command, because if you merely stroke it first with `strokePath`, the path is cleared and you can no longer fill it.

There are also some convenience functions that create a path from a CGRect or similar and stroke or fill it all in a single move:

- `stroke(_:)`, `strokeLineSegments(between:)`
- `fill(_:)`
- `strokeEllipse(in:)`
- `fillEllipse(in:)`

A path can be compound, meaning that it consists of multiple independent pieces. For example, a single path might consist of two separate closed shapes: a rectangle and a circle. When you call `move(to:)` in the middle of constructing a path (that is, after tracing out a path and without clearing it by filling or stroking it), you pick up the imaginary pen and move it to a new location without tracing a segment, thus preparing to start an independent piece of the same path. If you're worried, as you begin to trace out a path, that there might be an existing path and that your new path might be seen as a compound part of that existing path, you can call `beginPath` to specify that this is a different path; many of Apple's examples do this, but in practice I usually do not find it necessary.

To illustrate the typical use of path-drawing commands, I'll generate the up-pointing arrow shown in Figure 2-16. This might not be the best way to create the arrow, and I'm deliberately avoiding use of the convenience functions, but it's clear and shows a nice basic variety of typical commands:

```
// obtain the current graphics context
let con = UIGraphicsGetCurrentContext()!
// draw a black (by default) vertical line, the shaft of the arrow
con.move(to:CGPoint(100, 100))
con.addLine(to:CGPoint(100, 19))
con.setLineWidth(20)
con.strokePath()
// draw a red triangle, the point of the arrow
con.setFillColor(UIColor.red.cgColor)
con.move(to:CGPoint(80, 25))
con.addLine(to:CGPoint(100, 0))
con.addLine(to:CGPoint(120, 25))
con.fillPath()
// snip a triangle out of the shaft by drawing in Clear blend mode
con.move(to:CGPoint(90, 101))
con.addLine(to:CGPoint(100, 90))
con.addLine(to:CGPoint(110, 101))
con.setBlendMode(.clear)
con.fillPath()
```

Figure 2-16. A simple path drawing

If a path needs to be reused or shared, you can encapsulate it as a CGPath. Like CGContext, CGPath and its mutable partner CGMutablePath are treated as class types under "renamification," and the global C functions that manipulate them are treated as methods. You can copy the graphics context's current path using the CGContext `path` method, or you can create a new CGMutablePath and construct the path using various functions, such as `move(to:transform:)` and `add-Line(to:transform:)`, that parallel the CGContext path-construction functions. Also, there are ways to create a path based on simple geometry or on an existing path:

- `init(rect:transform:)`
- `init(ellipseIn:transform:)`
- `init(roundedRect:cornerWidth:cornerHeight:transform:)`
- `init(strokingWithWidth:lineCap:lineJoin:miterLimit:transform:)`
- `copy(dashingWithPhase:lengths:transform:)`
- `copy(using:)` (takes a pointer to a CGAffineTransform)

The UIKit class UIBezierPath is actually a wrapper for CGPath; the wrapped path is its `cgPath` property. It provides methods parallel to the CGContext and CGPath functions for constructing a path, such as:

- `init(rect:)`
- `init(ovalIn:)`
- `init(roundedRect:cornerRadius:)`
- `move(to:)`
- `addLine(to:)`
- `addArc(withCenter:radius:startAngle:endAngle:clockwise:)`
- `addQuadCurve(to:controlPoint:)`
- `addCurve(to:controlPoint1:controlPoint2:)`
- `close`

When you call the UIBezierPath instance methods `fill` or `stroke` or `fill(with:alpha:)` or `stroke(with:alpha:)`, the current graphics context settings are saved, the wrapped CGPath is made the current graphics context's path and stroked or filled, and the current graphics context settings are restored.

Thus, using UIBezierPath together with UIColor, we could rewrite our arrow-drawing routine entirely with UIKit methods:

```
let p = UIBezierPath()
// shaft
p.move(to:CGPoint(100,100))
p.addLine(to:CGPoint(100, 19))
p.lineWidth = 20
p.stroke()
// point
UIColor.red.set()
p.removeAllPoints()
p.move(to:CGPoint(80,25))
p.addLine(to:CGPoint(100, 0))
p.addLine(to:CGPoint(120, 25))
p.fill()
// snip
p.removeAllPoints()
p.move(to:CGPoint(90,101))
p.addLine(to:CGPoint(100, 90))
p.addLine(to:CGPoint(110, 101))
p.fill(with:.clear, alpha:1.0)
```

There's no savings of code here over calling Core Graphics functions, so your choice of Core Graphics or UIKit is a matter of taste.

Clipping

A path can be used to mask out areas, protecting them from future drawing. This is called *clipping*. By default, a graphics context's clipping region is the entire graphics context: you can draw anywhere within the context.

The clipping area is a feature of the context as a whole, and any new clipping area is applied by intersecting it with the existing clipping area. To restore your clipping area to the default, call `resetClip`.

To illustrate, I'll rewrite the code that generated our original arrow (Figure 2-16) to use clipping instead of a blend mode to "punch out" the triangular notch in the tail of the arrow. This is a little tricky, because what we want to clip to is not the region inside the triangle but the region outside it. To express this, we'll use a compound path consisting of more than one closed area — the triangle, and the drawing area as a whole (which we can obtain as the context's `boundingBoxOfClipPath`).

Both when filling a compound path and when using it to express a clipping region, the system follows one of two rules:

Winding rule
> The fill or clipping area is denoted by an alternation in the direction (clockwise or counterclockwise) of the path demarcating each region.

Even-odd rule (EO)
> The fill or clipping area is denoted by a simple count of the paths demarcating each region.

Our situation is extremely simple, so it's easier to use the even-odd rule:

```
// obtain the current graphics context
let con = UIGraphicsGetCurrentContext()!
// punch triangular hole in context clipping region
con.move(to:CGPoint(90, 100))
con.addLine(to:CGPoint(100, 90))
con.addLine(to:CGPoint(110, 100))
con.closePath()
con.addRect(con.boundingBoxOfClipPath)
con.clip(using:.evenOdd)
// draw the vertical line
con.move(to:CGPoint(100, 100))
con.addLine(to:CGPoint(100, 19))
con.setLineWidth(20)
con.strokePath()
// draw the red triangle, the point of the arrow
con.setFillColor(UIColor.red.cgColor)
con.move(to:CGPoint(80, 25))
con.addLine(to:CGPoint(100, 0))
con.addLine(to:CGPoint(120, 25))
con.fillPath()
```

The UIBezierPath clipping commands are `usesEvenOddFillRule` and `addClip`.

Gradients

Gradients can range from the simple to the complex. A simple gradient (which is all I'll describe here) is determined by a color at one endpoint along with a color at the other endpoint, plus (optionally) colors at intermediate points; the gradient is then painted either linearly between two points or radially between two circles. You can't use a gradient as a path's fill color, but you can restrict a gradient to a path's shape by clipping, which will sometimes be good enough.

To illustrate, I'll redraw our arrow, using a linear gradient as the "shaft" of the arrow (Figure 2-17):

```
// obtain the current graphics context
let con = UIGraphicsGetCurrentContext()!
// punch triangular hole in context clipping region
con.move(to:CGPoint(10, 100))
con.addLine(to:CGPoint(20, 90))
con.addLine(to:CGPoint(30, 100))
con.closePath()
con.addRect(con.boundingBoxOfClipPath)
con.clip(using: .evenOdd)
// draw the vertical line, add its shape to the clipping region
con.move(to:CGPoint(20, 100))
con.addLine(to:CGPoint(20, 19))
con.setLineWidth(20)
con.replacePathWithStrokedPath()
con.clip()
// draw the gradient
let locs : [CGFloat] = [ 0.0, 0.5, 1.0 ]
let colors : [CGFloat] = [
    0.8, 0.4, // starting color, transparent light gray
    0.1, 0.5, // intermediate color, darker less transparent gray
    0.8, 0.4, // ending color, transparent light gray
]
let sp = CGColorSpaceCreateDeviceGray()
let grad = CGGradient(
    colorSpace:sp, colorComponents: colors, locations: locs, count: 3)!
con.drawLinearGradient(grad,
    start: CGPoint(89,0), end: CGPoint(111,0), options:[])
con.resetClip() // done clipping
// draw the red triangle, the point of the arrow
con.setFillColor(UIColor.red.cgColor)
con.move(to:CGPoint(80, 25))
con.addLine(to:CGPoint(100, 0))
con.addLine(to:CGPoint(120, 25))
con.fillPath()
```

The call to replacePathWithStrokedPath pretends to stroke the current path, using the current line width and other line-related context state settings, but then creates a new path representing the outside of that stroked path. Thus, instead of a thick line we have a rectangular region that we can use as the clip region.

We then create the gradient and paint it. The procedure is verbose but simple; everything is boilerplate. We describe the gradient as an array of locations on the continuum between one endpoint (0.0) and the other endpoint (1.0), along with the color

Figure 2-17. Drawing with a gradient

components of the colors corresponding to each location; in this case, I want the gradient to be lighter at the edges and darker in the middle, so I use three locations, with the dark one at 0.5. We must also supply a color space; this will tell the gradient how to interpret our color components. Finally, we create the gradient and paint it into place.

(There are also gradient CIFilters, as I demonstrated earlier in this chapter; for yet another way to create a simple gradient, see the discussion of CAGradientLayer in the next chapter.)

Colors and Patterns

A color is a CGColor. CGColor is not difficult to work with, and can be converted to and from a UIColor through UIColor's init(cgColor:) and its cgColor property.

A pattern is also a kind of color. You can create a pattern color and stroke or fill with it. The simplest way is to draw a minimal tile of the pattern into a UIImage and create the color by calling UIColor's init(patternImage:). To illustrate, I'll create a pattern of horizontal stripes and use it to paint the point of the arrow instead of a solid red color (Figure 2-18):

```
// create the pattern image tile
let r = UIGraphicsImageRenderer(size:CGSize(4,4))
let stripes = r.image { ctx in
    let imcon = ctx.cgContext
    imcon.setFillColor(UIColor.red.cgColor)
    imcon.fill(CGRect(0,0,4,4))
    imcon.setFillColor(UIColor.blue.cgColor)
    imcon.fill(CGRect(0,0,4,2))
}
// paint the point of the arrow with it
let stripesPattern = UIColor(patternImage:stripes)
stripesPattern.setFill()
let p = UIBezierPath()
p.move(to:CGPoint(80,25))
p.addLine(to:CGPoint(100,0))
p.addLine(to:CGPoint(120,25))
p.fill()
```

Figure 2-18. A patterned fill

The Core Graphics equivalent, CGPattern, is considerably more powerful, but also much more elaborate:

```
con.saveGState()
let sp2 = CGColorSpace(patternBaseSpace:nil)!
con.setFillColorSpace(sp2)
let drawStripes : CGPatternDrawPatternCallback = { _, con in
    con.setFillColor(UIColor.red.cgColor)
    con.fill(CGRect(0,0,4,4))
    con.setFillColor(UIColor.blue.cgColor)
    con.fill(CGRect(0,0,4,2))
}
var callbacks = CGPatternCallbacks(
    version: 0, drawPattern: drawStripes, releaseInfo: nil)
let patt = CGPattern(info:nil, bounds: CGRect(0,0,4,4),
    matrix: .identity,
    xStep: 4, yStep: 4,
    tiling: .constantSpacingMinimalDistortion,
    isColored: true, callbacks: &callbacks)!
var alph : CGFloat = 1.0
con.setFillPattern(patt, colorComponents: &alph)
con.move(to:CGPoint(80, 25))
con.addLine(to:CGPoint(100, 0))
con.addLine(to:CGPoint(120, 25))
con.fillPath()
con.restoreGState()
```

To understand that code, it helps to read it backward. Everything revolves around the creation of patt using the CGPattern initializer. A pattern is a drawing in a rectangular "cell"; we have to state both the size of the cell (bounds:) and the spacing between origin points of cells (xStep:, yStep:). In this case, the cell is 4×4, and every cell exactly touches its neighbors both horizontally and vertically. We have to supply a transform to be applied to the cell (matrix:); in this case, we're not doing anything with this transform, so we supply the identity transform. We supply a tiling rule (tiling:). We have to state whether this is a color pattern or a stencil pattern; it's a color pattern, so isColored: is true. And we have to supply a pointer to a callback function that actually draws the pattern into its cell (callbacks:).

Except that that's *not* what we have to supply as the callbacks: argument. What we actually have to supply here is a pointer to a CGPatternCallbacks struct. This struct consists of a version: whose value is fixed at 0, along with pointers to *two* functions, the drawPattern: to draw the pattern into its cell, and the releaseInfo: called when the pattern is released. We're not specifying the second function, however; it is for memory management, and we don't need it in this simple example.

As you can see, the actual pattern-drawing function (drawStripes) is very simple. The only tricky issue is that it must agree with the CGPattern as to the size of a cell, or the pattern won't come out the way you expect. We know in this case that the cell is 4×4. So we fill it with red, and then fill its lower half with blue. When these cells are tiled touching each other horizontally and vertically, we get the stripes that you see in Figure 2-18.

Having generated the CGPattern, we call the context's setFillPattern; instead of setting a fill color, we're setting a fill pattern, to be used the next time we fill a path (in this case, the triangular arrowhead). The colorComponents: parameter is a pointer to a CGFloat, so we have to set up the CGFloat itself beforehand.

The only thing left to explain is the first three lines of that code. It turns out that before you can call setFillPattern with a colored pattern, you have to set the context's fill color space to a pattern color space. If you neglect to do this, you'll get an error when you call setFillPattern. This means that the code as presented has left the graphics context in an undesirable state, with its fill color space set to a pattern color space. This would cause trouble if we were later to try to set the fill color to a normal color. The solution is to wrap the code in calls to saveGState and restore-GState.

You may have observed in Figure 2-18 that the stripes do not fit neatly inside the triangle of the arrowhead: the bottommost stripe is something like half a blue stripe. This is because a pattern is positioned not with respect to the shape you are filling (or stroking), but with respect to the graphics context as a whole. We could shift the pattern position by calling setPatternPhase before drawing.

Graphics Context Transforms

Just as a UIView can have a transform, so can a graphics context. However, applying a transform to a graphics context has no effect on the drawing that's already in it; like other graphics context settings, it affects only the drawing that takes place after it is applied, altering the way the coordinates you provide are mapped onto the graphics context's area. A graphics context's transform is called its CTM, for "current transform matrix."

It is quite usual to take full advantage of a graphics context's CTM to save yourself from performing even simple calculations. You can multiply the current transform by any CGAffineTransform using concatCTM; there are also convenience functions for applying a translate, scale, or rotate transform to the current transform.

The base transform for a graphics context is already set for you when you obtain the context; that's how the system is able to map context drawing coordinates onto screen coordinates. Whatever transforms you apply are applied to the current transform, so the base transform remains in effect and drawing continues to work. You can return to the base transform after applying your own transforms by wrapping your code in calls to saveGState and restoreGState.

For example, we have hitherto been drawing our upward-pointing arrow with code that knows how to place that arrow at only one location: the top left of its rectangle is hard-coded at (80,0). This is silly. It makes the code hard to understand, as well as inflexible and difficult to reuse. Surely the sensible thing would be to draw the arrow at (0,0), by subtracting 80 from all the x-values in our existing code. Now it is easy to draw the arrow at *any* position, simply by applying a translate transform beforehand, mapping (0,0) to the desired top-left corner of the arrow. So, to draw it at (80,0), we would say:

```
con.translateBy(x:80, y:0)
// now draw the arrow at (0,0)
```

A rotate transform is particularly useful, allowing you to draw in a rotated orientation without any nasty trigonometry. However, it's a bit tricky because the point around which the rotation takes place is the origin. This is rarely what you want, so you have to apply a translate transform first, to map the origin to the point around which you really want to rotate. But then, after rotating, in order to figure out where to draw, you will probably have to reverse your translate transform.

To illustrate, here's code to draw our arrow repeatedly at several angles, pivoting around the end of its tail (Figure 2-19). Since the arrow will be drawn multiple times, I'll start by encapsulating the drawing of the arrow as a UIImage. This is not merely to reduce repetition and make drawing more efficient; it's also because we want the entire arrow to pivot, including the pattern stripes, and this is the simplest way to achieve that:

```
lazy var arrow : UIImage = {
    let r = UIGraphicsImageRenderer(size:CGSize(40,100))
    return r.image { _ in
        self.arrowImage()
    }
}()
func arrowImage () {
    // obtain the current graphics context
    let con = UIGraphicsGetCurrentContext()!
    // draw the arrow into the graphics context
    // draw it at (0,0)! adjust all x-values by subtracting 80
    // ... actual code omitted ...
}
```

In our draw(_:) implementation, we draw the arrow image multiple times:

Figure 2-19. Drawing rotated

Figure 2-20. Drawing with a shadow

```
override func draw(_ rect: CGRect) {
    let con = UIGraphicsGetCurrentContext()!
    self.arrow.draw(at:CGPoint(0,0))
    for _ in 0..<3 {
        con.translateBy(x: 20, y: 100)
        con.rotate(by: 30 * .pi/180.0)
        con.translateBy(x: -20, y: -100)
        self.arrow.draw(at:CGPoint(0,0))
    }
}
```

Shadows

To add a shadow to a drawing, give the context a shadow value before drawing. The shadow position is expressed as a CGSize, where the positive direction for both values indicates down and to the right. The blur value is an open-ended positive number; Apple doesn't explain how the scale works, but experimentation shows that 12 is nice and blurry, 99 is so blurry as to be shapeless, and higher values become problematic.

Figure 2-20 shows the result of the same code that generated Figure 2-19, except that before we start drawing the arrow repeatedly, we give the context a shadow:

```
let con = UIGraphicsGetCurrentContext()!
con.setShadow(offset: CGSize(7, 7), blur: 12)
self.arrow.draw(at:CGPoint(0,0))
// ... and so on
```

It may not be evident from Figure 2-20, but we are adding a shadow each time we draw. Thus the arrows are able to cast shadows on one another. Suppose, however, that we want all the arrows to cast a single shadow collectively. The way to achieve this is with a *transparency layer*; this is basically a subcontext that accumulates all drawing and then adds the shadow. Our code for drawing the shadowed arrows now looks like this:

```
let con = UIGraphicsGetCurrentContext()!
con.setShadow(offset: CGSize(7, 7), blur: 12)
con.beginTransparencyLayer(auxiliaryInfo: nil)
self.arrow.draw(at:CGPoint(0,0))
for _ in 0..<3 {
    con.translateBy(x: 20, y: 100)
    con.rotate(by: 30 * .pi/180.0)
    con.translateBy(x: -20, y: -100)
    self.arrow.draw(at:CGPoint(0,0))
}
con.endTransparencyLayer()
```

Erasing

The CGContext `clear(_:)` function erases all existing drawing in a CGRect; combined with clipping, it can erase an area of any shape. The result can "punch a hole" through all existing drawing.

The behavior of `clear(_:)` depends on whether the context is transparent or opaque. This is particularly obvious and intuitive when drawing into an image context. If the image context is transparent, `clear(_:)` erases to transparent; otherwise it erases to black.

When drawing directly into a view, if the view's background color is `nil` or a color with even a tiny bit of transparency, the result of `clear(_:)` will appear to be transparent, punching a hole right through the view including its background color; if the background color is completely opaque, the result of `clear(_:)` will be black. This is because the view's background color determines whether the view's graphics context is transparent or opaque; thus, this is essentially the same behavior that I described in the preceding paragraph.

Figure 2-21 illustrates; the blue square on the left has been partly cut away to black, while the blue square on the right has been partly cut away to transparency. Yet these are instances of the same UIView subclass, drawn with exactly the same code! The UIView subclass's `draw(_:)` looks like this:

```
let con = UIGraphicsGetCurrentContext()!
con.setFillColor(UIColor.blue.cgColor)
con.fill(rect)
con.clear(CGRect(0,0,30,30))
```

The difference between the views in Figure 2-21 is that the `backgroundColor` of the first view is solid red with an alpha of 1, while the `backgroundColor` of the second view is solid red with an alpha of 0.99. This difference is imperceptible to the eye

Figure 2-21. The very strange behavior of the clear function

(not to mention that the red color never appears, as it is covered with a blue fill), but it completely changes the effect of clear(_:).

Points and Pixels

A point is a dimensionless location described by an x-coordinate and a y-coordinate. When you draw in a graphics context, you specify the points at which to draw, and this works regardless of the device's resolution, because Core Graphics maps your drawing nicely onto the physical output using the base CTM and anti-aliasing. Therefore, throughout this chapter I've concerned myself with graphics context points, disregarding their relationship to screen pixels.

However, pixels do exist. A pixel is a physical, integral, dimensioned unit of display in the real world. Whole-numbered points effectively lie between pixels, and this can matter if you're fussy, especially on a single-resolution device. For example, if a vertical path with whole-number coordinates is stroked with a line width of 1, half the line falls on each side of the path, and the drawn line on the screen of a single-resolution device will seem to be 2 pixels wide (because the device can't illuminate half a pixel).

You may sometimes encounter the suggestion that if this effect is objectionable, you should try shifting the line's position by 0.5, to center it in its pixels. This advice may appear to work, but it makes some simpleminded assumptions. A more sophisticated approach is to obtain the UIView's contentScaleFactor property. You can divide by this value to convert from pixels to points. Consider also that the most accurate way to draw a vertical or horizontal line is not to stroke a path but to fill a rectangle. So this UIView subclass code will draw a perfect 1-pixel-wide vertical line on any device (con is the current graphics context):

```
con.fill(CGRect(100,0,1.0/self.contentScaleFactor,100))
```

Content Mode

A view that draws something within itself, as opposed to merely having a background color and subviews (as in the previous chapter), has *content*. This means that its contentMode property becomes important whenever the view is resized. As I mentioned earlier, the drawing system will avoid asking a view to redraw itself from

Figure 2-22. Automatic stretching of content

scratch if possible; instead, it will use the cached result of the previous drawing operation (the bitmap backing store). So, if the view is resized, the system may simply stretch or shrink or reposition the cached drawing, if your `contentMode` setting instructs it to do so.

It's a little tricky to illustrate this point when the view's content is coming from `draw(_:)`, because I have to arrange for the view to obtain its content (from `draw(_:)`) and then cause it to be resized without also causing it to be redrawn (that is, without `draw(_:)` being called *again*). As the app starts up, I'll create an instance of a UIView subclass, MyView, that knows how to draw our arrow; then I'll use delayed performance to resize the instance after the window has shown and the interface has been initially displayed (for my `delay` function, see Appendix B):

```
delay(0.1) {
    mv.bounds.size.height *= 2 // mv is the MyView instance
}
```

We double the height of the view without causing `draw(_:)` to be called. The result is that the view's drawing appears at double its correct height. For example, if our view's `draw(_:)` code is the same as the code that generated Figure 2-17, we get Figure 2-22.

Sooner or later, however, `draw(_:)` will be called, and the drawing will be refreshed in accordance with our code. Our code doesn't say to draw the arrow at a height that is relative to the height of the view's bounds; it draws the arrow at a fixed height. Thus, the arrow will snap back to its original size.

A view's `contentMode` property should therefore usually be in agreement with how the view draws itself. Our `draw(_:)` code dictates the size and position of the arrow relative to the view's bounds origin, its top left; so we could set its `contentMode` to `.topLeft`. Alternatively, we could set it to `.redraw`; this will cause automatic scaling of the cached content to be turned off — instead, when the view is resized, its `setNeedsDisplay` method will be called, ultimately triggering `draw(_:)` to redraw the content.

CHAPTER 3

Layers

The tale told in Chapters 1 and 2 of how a UIView works and how it draws itself is only half the story. A UIView has a partner called its *layer*, a CALayer. A UIView does not actually draw itself onto the screen; it draws itself into its layer, and it is the layer that is portrayed on the screen. As I've already mentioned, a view is not redrawn frequently; instead, its drawing is cached, and the cached version of the drawing (the bitmap backing store) is used where possible. The cached version is, in fact, the layer. What I spoke of in Chapter 2 as the view's graphics context is actually the layer's graphics context.

This might seem to be a mere implementation detail, but layers are important and interesting. To understand layers is to understand views more deeply; layers extend the power of views. In particular:

Layers have properties that affect drawing

> Layers have drawing-related properties beyond those of a UIView. Because a layer is the recipient and presenter of a view's drawing, you can modify how a view is drawn on the screen by accessing the layer's properties. In other words, by reaching down to the level of its layer, you can make a view do things you can't do through UIView methods alone.

Layers can be combined within a single view

> A UIView's partner layer can contain additional layers. Since the purpose of layers is to draw, portraying visible material on the screen, this allows a UIView's drawing to be composed of multiple distinct pieces. This can make drawing easier, with the constituents of a drawing being treated as objects.

Figure 3-1. A compass, composed of layers

Layers are the basis of animation

Animation allows you to add clarity, emphasis, and just plain coolness to your interface. Layers are made to be animated; the "CA" in "CALayer" stands for "Core Animation." Animation is the subject of Chapter 4.

For example, suppose we want to add a compass indicator to our app's interface. Figure 3-1 portrays a simple version of such a compass. It takes advantage of the arrow that we figured out how to draw in Chapter 2; the arrow is drawn into a layer of its own. The other parts of the compass are layers too: the circle is a layer, and each of the cardinal point letters is a layer. The drawing is thus easy to composite in code (and later in this chapter, that's exactly what we'll do); even more intriguing, the pieces can be repositioned and animated separately, so it's easy to rotate the arrow without moving the circle (and in Chapter 4, that's exactly what we'll do).

The documentation discusses layers chiefly in connection with animation (in particular, in the *Core Animation Programming Guide*). This categorization gives the impression that layers are of interest only if you intend to animate. That's misleading. Layers are the basis of animation, but they are also the basis of view drawing, and are useful and important even if you don't use them for animation.

View and Layer

A UIView instance has an accompanying CALayer instance, accessible as the view's `layer` property. This layer has a special status: it is partnered with this view to embody all of the view's drawing. The layer has no corresponding `view` property, but the view is the layer's `delegate` (adopting CALayerDelegate). The documentation sometimes speaks of this layer as the view's *underlying layer*.

By default, when a UIView is instantiated, its layer is an instance of CALayer. If you subclass UIView and you want your subclass's underlying layer to be an instance of a

CALayer subclass (built-in or your own), implement the UIView subclass's `layer-Class` class property to return that CALayer subclass.

That, for example, is how the compass in Figure 3-1 is created. We have a UIView subclass, CompassView, and a CALayer subclass, CompassLayer. Here is Compass-View's implementation:

```
class CompassView : UIView {
    override class var layerClass : AnyClass {
        return CompassLayer.self
    }
}
```

Thus, when CompassView is instantiated, its underlying layer is a CompassLayer. In this example, there is no drawing in CompassView; its job — in this case, its *only* job — is to give CompassLayer a place in the visible interface, because a layer cannot appear without a view.

Because every view has an underlying layer, there is a tight integration between the two. The layer portrays all the view's drawing; if the view draws, it does so by contributing to the layer's drawing. The view is the layer's delegate. And the view's properties are often merely a convenience for accessing the layer's properties. For example, when you set the view's `backgroundColor`, you are really setting the layer's `backgroundColor`, and if you set the layer's `backgroundColor` directly, the view's `backgroundColor` is set to match. Similarly, the view's `frame` is really the layer's `frame` and *vice versa*.

 A CALayer's `delegate` property is settable (to an instance of any class adopting CALayerDelegate), but a UIView and its underlying layer have a special relationship. A UIView *must* be the delegate of its underlying layer; moreover, it must *not* be the delegate of any *other* layer. *Don't do anything to mess this up.* If you do, drawing will stop working correctly.

The view draws into its layer, and the layer caches that drawing; the layer can then be manipulated, changing the view's appearance, without necessarily asking the view to redraw itself. This is a source of great efficiency in the drawing system. It also explains such phenomena as the content stretching that we encountered in the last section of Chapter 2: when the view's bounds size changes, the drawing system, by default, simply stretches or repositions the cached layer image, until such time as the view is told to draw freshly, replacing the layer's content.

Layers and Sublayers

A layer can have sublayers, and a layer has at most one superlayer. Thus there is a tree of layers. This is similar and parallel to the tree of views (Chapter 1). In fact, so tight is the integration between a view and its underlying layer that these hierarchies are

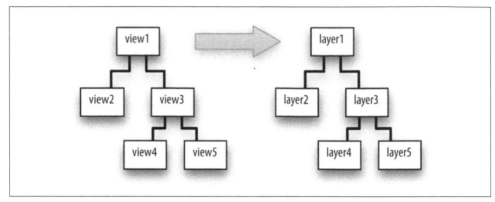

Figure 3-2. A hierarchy of views and the hierarchy of layers underlying it

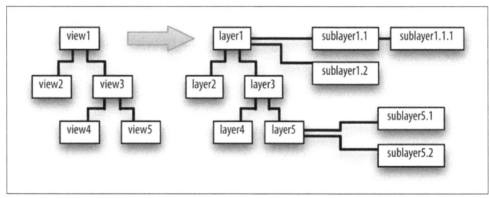

Figure 3-3. Layers that have sublayers of their own

effectively the *same* hierarchy. Given a view and its underlying layer, that layer's superlayer is the view's superview's underlying layer, and that layer has as sublayers all the underlying layers of all the view's subviews. Indeed, because the layers are how the views actually get drawn, one might say that the view hierarchy really *is* a layer hierarchy (Figure 3-2).

At the same time, the layer hierarchy can go *beyond* the view hierarchy. A view has exactly one underlying layer, but a layer can have sublayers that are *not the underlying layers of any view*. So the hierarchy of layers that underlie views exactly matches the hierarchy of views, but the total layer tree may be a superset of that hierarchy. In Figure 3-3, we see the same view-and-layer hierarchy as in Figure 3-2, but two of the layers have additional sublayers that are theirs alone (that is, sublayers that are not any view's underlying layers).

From a visual standpoint, there may be nothing to distinguish a hierarchy of views from a hierarchy of layers. For example, in Chapter 1 we drew three overlapping

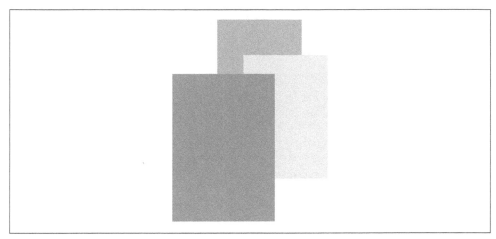

Figure 3-4. Overlapping layers

rectangles using a hierarchy of views (Figure 1-1). This code gives exactly the same visible display by manipulating layers (Figure 3-4):

```
let lay1 = CALayer()
lay1.backgroundColor = UIColor(red: 1, green: 0.4, blue: 1, alpha: 1).cgColor
lay1.frame = CGRect(113, 111, 132, 194)
self.view.layer.addSublayer(lay1)
let lay2 = CALayer()
lay2.backgroundColor = UIColor(red: 0.5, green: 1, blue: 0, alpha: 1).cgColor
lay2.frame = CGRect(41, 56, 132, 194)
lay1.addSublayer(lay2)
let lay3 = CALayer()
lay3.backgroundColor = UIColor(red: 1, green: 0, blue: 0, alpha: 1).cgColor
lay3.frame = CGRect(43, 197, 160, 230)
self.view.layer.addSublayer(lay3)
```

A view's subview's underlying layer is a sublayer of that view's underlying layer, just like any other sublayers of that view's underlying layer. Therefore, it can be positioned anywhere among them in the drawing order. The fact that a view can be interspersed among the sublayers of its superview's underlying layer is surprising to beginners. For example, let's construct Figure 3-4 again, but between adding lay2 and lay3 to the interface, we'll add a subview:

```
// ...
lay1.addSublayer(lay2)
let iv = UIImageView(image:UIImage(named:"smiley"))
self.view.addSubview(iv)
iv.frame.origin = CGPoint(180,180)
let lay3 = CALayer() // the red rectangle
// ...
```

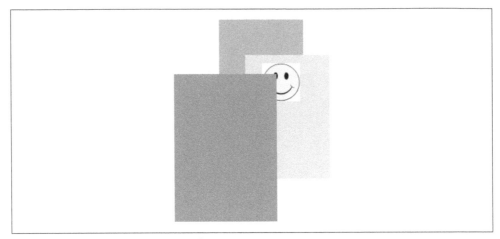

Figure 3-5. Overlapping layers and a view

The result is Figure 3-5. The smiley face was added to the interface before the red (left and frontmost) rectangle, so it appears behind that rectangle. By reversing the order in which the red rectangle (lay3) and the smiley face (iv) are added to the interface, the smiley face can be made to appear in front of that rectangle. The smiley face is a *view*, whereas the rectangle is just a *layer*; so they are not siblings as views, since the rectangle is not a view. But the smiley face is both a view and its layer; as layers, the smiley face and the rectangle *are* siblings, since they have the same superlayer, so either one can be made to appear in front of the other.

Whether a layer displays regions of its sublayers that lie outside that layer's own bounds depends upon the value of its `masksToBounds` property. This is parallel to a view's `clipsToBounds` property, and indeed, for a layer that is its view's underlying layer, they are the same thing. In Figures 3-4 and 3-5, the layers all have `clipsToBounds` set to `false` (the default); that's why the right layer is visible beyond the bounds of the middle layer, which is its superlayer.

Like a UIView, a CALayer has an `isHidden` property that can be set to take it and its sublayers out of the visible interface without actually removing it from its superlayer.

Manipulating the Layer Hierarchy

Layers come with a full set of methods for reading and manipulating the layer hierarchy, parallel to the methods for reading and manipulating the view hierarchy. A layer has a `superlayer` property and a `sublayers` property, along with these methods:

- `addSublayer(_:)`
- `insertSublayer(_:at:)`

- insertSublayer(_:below:), insertSublayer(_:above:)
- replaceSublayer(_:with:)
- removeFromSuperlayer

Unlike a view's subviews property, a layer's sublayers property is writable; thus, you can give a layer multiple sublayers in a single move, by assigning to its sublayers property. To remove all of a layer's sublayers, set its sublayers property to nil.

Although a layer's sublayers have an order, reflected in the sublayers order and regulated with the methods I've just mentioned, this is not necessarily the same as their back-to-front drawing order. By default, it is, but a layer also has a zPosition property, a CGFloat, and this also determines drawing order. The rule is that all sublayers with the same zPosition are drawn in the order they are listed among their sublayers siblings, but lower zPosition siblings are drawn before higher zPosition siblings. (The default zPosition is 0.0.)

Sometimes, the zPosition property is a more convenient way of dictating drawing order than sibling order is. For example, if layers represent playing cards laid out in a solitaire game, it will likely be a lot easier and more flexible to determine how the cards overlap by setting their zPosition than by rearranging their sibling order.

Moreover, a subview's layer is itself just a layer, so you can rearrange the drawing order of subviews by setting the zPosition of their underlying layers! In our code constructing Figure 3-5, if we assign the image view's underlying layer a zPosition of 1, it is drawn in front of the red (left) rectangle:

```
self.view.addSubview(iv)
iv.layer.zPosition = 1
```

Methods are also provided for converting between the coordinate systems of layers within the same layer hierarchy; the first parameter can be a CGPoint or a CGRect:

- convert(_:from:)
- convert(_:to:)

Positioning a Sublayer

Layer coordinate systems and positioning are similar to those of views. A layer's own internal coordinate system is expressed by its bounds, just like a view; its size is its bounds size, and its bounds origin is the internal coordinate at its top left.

However, a sublayer's position within its superlayer is not described by its center, like a view; a layer does not have a center. Instead, a sublayer's position within its superlayer is defined by a combination of *two* properties:

position

A point expressed in the superlayer's coordinate system.

anchorPoint

Where the position point is located, with respect to the layer's own bounds. It is a CGPoint describing a fraction (or multiple) of the layer's own bounds width and bounds height. Thus, for example, (0.0,0.0) is the top left of the layer's bounds, and (1.0,1.0) is the bottom right of the layer's bounds.

Here's an analogy; I didn't make it up, but it's pretty apt. Think of the sublayer as pinned to its superlayer; then you have to say both where the pin passes through the sublayer (the anchorPoint) and where it passes through the superlayer (the position).

If the anchorPoint is (0.5,0.5) (the default), the position property works like a view's center property. A view's center is thus a special case of a layer's position. This is quite typical of the relationship between view properties and layer properties; the view properties are often a simpler — but less powerful — version of the layer properties.

A layer's position and anchorPoint are orthogonal (independent); changing one does not change the other. Therefore, changing either of them without changing the other changes where the layer is drawn within its superlayer.

For example, in Figure 3-1, the most important point in the circle is its center; all the other objects need to be positioned with respect to it. Therefore, they all have the same position: the center of the circle. But they differ in their anchorPoint. For example, the arrow's anchorPoint is (0.5,0.8), the middle of the shaft, near the tail. On the other hand, the anchorPoint of a cardinal point letter is (0.5,3.0), well outside the letter's bounds, so as to place the letter near the edge of the circle.

A layer's frame is a purely derived property. When you get the frame, it is calculated from the bounds size along with the position and anchorPoint. When you set the frame, you set the bounds size and position. In general, you should regard the frame as a convenient façade and no more. Nevertheless, it is convenient! For example, to position a sublayer so that it exactly overlaps its superlayer, you can just set the sublayer's frame to the superlayer's bounds.

 A layer created in code (as opposed to a view's underlying layer) has a frame and bounds of CGRect.zero and will not be visible on the screen even when you add it to a superlayer that is on the screen. Be sure to give your layer a nonzero width and height if you want to be able to see it! Creating a layer and adding it to a superlayer and then wondering why it isn't appearing in the interface is a common beginner error.

CAScrollLayer

If you're going to be moving a layer's bounds origin as a way of repositioning its sublayers *en masse*, you might like to make the layer a CAScrollLayer, a CALayer subclass that provides convenience methods for this sort of thing. (Despite the name, a CAScrollLayer provides no scrolling interface; the user can't scroll it by dragging, for example.) By default, a CAScrollLayer's masksToBounds property is true; thus, the CAScrollLayer acts like a window through which you see can only what is within its bounds. (You can set its masksToBounds to false, but this would be an odd thing to do, as it somewhat defeats the purpose.)

To move the CAScrollLayer's bounds, you can talk either to it or to a sublayer (at any depth):

Talking to the CAScrollLayer

scroll(to:)
> Takes a CGPoint or a CGRect. If a CGPoint, changes the CAScrollLayer's bounds origin to that point. If a CGRect, changes the CAScrollLayer's bounds origin minimally so that the given portion of the bounds rect is visible.

Talking to a sublayer

scroll(_:)
> Changes the CAScrollLayer's bounds origin so that the given point *of the sublayer* is at the top left of the CAScrollLayer.

scrollRectToVisible(_:)
> Changes the CAScrollLayer's bounds origin so that the given rect *of the sublayer's bounds* is within the CAScrollLayer's bounds area. You can also ask the sublayer for its visibleRect, the part of this sublayer now within the CAScrollLayer's bounds.

Layout of Sublayers

The view hierarchy is actually a layer hierarchy (Figure 3-2). The positioning of a view within its superview is actually the positioning of its layer within its superlayer (the superview's layer). A view can be repositioned and resized automatically in accordance with its autoresizingMask or through autolayout based on its constraints. Thus, there is automatic layout for layers *if they are the underlying layers of views*. Otherwise, there is *no* automatic layout for layers in iOS. The only option for layout of layers that are not the underlying layers of views is manual layout that you perform in code.

When a layer needs layout, either because its bounds have changed or because you called `setNeedsLayout`, you can respond in either of two ways:

- The layer's `layoutSublayers` method is called; to respond, override `layout-Sublayers` in your CALayer subclass.
- Alternatively, implement `layoutSublayers(of:)` in the layer's delegate. (Remember, if the layer is a view's underlying layer, the view is its delegate.)

For your layer to do effective manual layout of its sublayers, you'll probably need a way to identify or refer to the sublayers. There is no layer equivalent of `viewWith-Tag(_:)`, so such identification and reference is entirely up to you. A CALayer does have a `name` property that you might misuse for your own purposes. Key–value coding can also be helpful here; layers implement key–value coding in a special way, discussed at the end of this chapter.

For a view's underlying layer, `layoutSublayers` or `layoutSublayers(of:)` is called after the view's `layoutSubviews`. Under autolayout, you must call `super` or else autolayout will break. Moreover, these methods may be called more than once during the course of autolayout; if you're looking for an automatically generated signal that it's time to do manual layout of sublayers, a view layout event might be a better choice (see "Layout Events" on page 71).

Drawing in a Layer

The simplest way to make something appear in a layer is through its `contents` property. This is parallel to the `image` in a UIImageView (Chapter 2). It is expected to be a CGImage (or `nil`, signifying no image). So, for example, here's how we might modify the code that generated Figure 3-5 in such a way as to generate the smiley face as a layer rather than a view:

```
let lay4 = CALayer()
let im = UIImage(named:"smiley")!
lay4.frame = CGRect(origin:CGPoint(180,180), size:im.size)
lay4.contents = im.cgImage
self.view.layer.addSublayer(lay4)
```

 Unfortunately, the CALayer `contents` property is typed as Any (wrapped in an Optional). That means you can assign *anything* to it. Setting a layer's `contents` to a UIImage, rather than a CGImage, will *fail silently* — the image doesn't appear, but there is no error either. This is absolutely maddening, and I wish I had a nickel for every time I've done it and then wasted hours figuring out why my layer isn't appearing.

There are also four methods that can be implemented to provide or draw a layer's content on demand, similar to a UIView's `draw(_:)`. A layer is very conservative about calling these methods (and you must not call any of them directly). When a layer *does* call these methods, I will say that the layer *redisplays itself*. Here is how a layer can be caused to redisplay itself:

- If the layer's needsDisplayOnBoundsChange property is false (the default), then the only way to cause the layer to redisplay itself is by calling setNeedsDisplay (or setNeedsDisplay(_:), specifying a CGRect). Even this might not cause the layer to redisplay itself right away; if that's crucial, then you will also call display-IfNeeded.
- If the layer's needsDisplayOnBoundsChange property is true, then the layer will also redisplay itself when the layer's bounds change (rather like a view's .redraw content mode).

Here are the four methods that can be called when a layer redisplays itself; pick one to implement (don't try to combine them, you'll just confuse things):

display *in a subclass*
> Your CALayer subclass can override display. There's no graphics context at this point, so display is pretty much limited to setting the contents image.

display(_:) *in the delegate*
> You can set the CALayer's delegate property and implement display(_:) in the delegate. As with CALayer's display, there's no graphics context, so you'll just be setting the contents image.

draw(in:) *in a subclass*
> Your CALayer subclass can override draw(in:). The parameter is a graphics context into which you can draw directly; it is *not* automatically made the current context.

draw(_:in:) *in the delegate*
> You can set the CALayer's delegate property and implement draw(_:in:). The second parameter is a graphics context into which you can draw directly; it is *not* automatically made the current context.

Assigning a layer a contents image and drawing directly into the layer are, in effect, mutually exclusive. So:

- If a layer's contents is assigned an image, this image is shown immediately and replaces whatever drawing may have been displayed in the layer.
- If a layer redisplays itself and draw(in:) or draw(_:in:) draws into the layer, the drawing replaces whatever image may have been displayed in the layer.

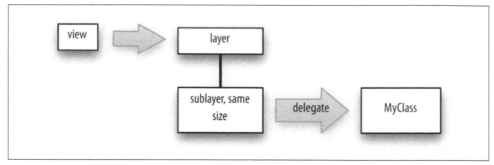

Figure 3-6. A view and a layer delegate that draws into it

- If a layer redisplays itself and none of the four methods provides any content, the layer will be empty.

If a layer is a view's underlying layer, you usually won't use any of the four methods to draw into the layer: you'll use the view's draw(_:). However, you *can* use these methods if you really want to. In that case, you will probably want to implement draw(_:) anyway, leaving that implementation empty. The reason is that this causes the layer to redisplay itself at appropriate moments. When a view is sent setNeedsDisplay — including when the view first appears — the view's underlying layer is also sent set-NeedsDisplay, *unless the view has no draw(_:) implementation* (because in that case, it is assumed that the view never needs redrawing). So, if you're drawing a view entirely by drawing to its underlying layer directly, and if you want the underlying layer to be redisplayed automatically when the view is told to redraw itself, you should implement draw(_:) to do nothing. (This technique has no effect on sublayers of the underlying layer.)

Thus, these are legitimate (but unusual) techniques for drawing into a view:

- The view subclass implements an empty draw(_:), along with either display-Layer: or draw(_:in:).
- The view subclass implements an empty draw(_:) plus layerClass, to give the view a custom layer subclass — and the custom layer subclass implements either display or draw(in:).

Remember, you *must not* set the delegate property of a view's underlying layer! The view is its delegate and must remain its delegate. A useful architecture for drawing into a layer through a delegate of your choosing is to treat a view as a *layer-hosting* view: the view and its underlying layer do nothing except to serve as a host to a sublayer of the view's underlying layer, which is where the drawing occurs (Figure 3-6).

Drawing-Related Layer Properties

A layer has a scale, its contentsScale, which maps point distances in the layer's graphics context to pixel distances on the device. A layer that's managed by Cocoa, if it has contents, will adjust its contentsScale automatically as needed; for example, if a view implements draw(_:), then on a device with a double-resolution screen its underlying layer is assigned a contentsScale of 2. A layer that you are creating and managing yourself, however, has no such automatic behavior; it's up to you, if you plan to draw into the layer, to set its contentsScale appropriately. Content drawn into a layer with a contentsScale of 1 may appear pixellated or fuzzy on a high-resolution screen. And when you're starting with a UIImage and assigning its CGImage as a layer's contents, if there's a mismatch between the UIImage's scale and the layer's contentsScale, then the image may be displayed at the wrong size.

Three further layer properties strongly affect what the layer displays:

backgroundColor
> Equivalent to a view's backgroundColor (and if this layer is a view's underlying layer, it *is* the view's backgroundColor). Changing the backgroundColor takes effect immediately. Think of the backgroundColor as separate from the layer's own drawing, and as painted *behind* the layer's own drawing.

opacity
> Affects the overall apparent transparency of the layer. It is equivalent to a view's alpha (and if this layer is a view's underlying layer, it *is* the view's alpha). It affects the apparent transparency of the layer's sublayers as well. It affects the apparent transparency of the background color and the apparent transparency of the layer's content separately (just as with a view's alpha). Changing the opacity property takes effect immediately.

isOpaque
> Determines whether the layer's graphics context is opaque. An opaque graphics context is black; you can draw on top of that blackness, but the blackness is still there. A nonopaque graphics context is clear; where no drawing is, it is completely transparent. Changing the isOpaque property has no effect until the layer redisplays itself. A view's underlying layer's isOpaque property is independent of the view's isOpaque property; they are unrelated and do entirely different things.

If a layer is the underlying layer of a view that implements draw(_:), then setting the view's backgroundColor changes the layer's isOpaque: the latter becomes true if the new background color is opaque (alpha component of 1), and false otherwise. That's the reason behind the strange behavior of CGContext's clear(_:) method, described in Chapter 2.

When drawing directly into a *layer*, the behavior of clear(_:) differs from what was described in Chapter 2 for drawing into a *view*: instead of punching a hole through the background color, it effectively paints with the layer's background color. This can have curious side effects, and I regard it as deeply weird.

Content Resizing and Positioning

A layer's content is stored (cached) as a bitmap which is then treated like an image:

- If the content came from setting the layer's contents property to an image, the cached content is that image; its size is the point size of the CGImage we started with.

- If the content came from drawing directly into the layer's graphics context (draw(in:), draw(_:in:)), the cached content is the layer's entire graphics context; its size is the point size of the layer itself at the time the drawing was performed.

The layer's content is then drawn in relation to the layer's bounds in accordance with various layer properties, which cause the cached content to be resized, repositioned, cropped, and so on, as it is displayed. The properties are:

contentsGravity

This property, a string, is parallel to a UIView's contentMode property, and describes how the content should be positioned or stretched in relation to the bounds. For example, kCAGravityCenter means the content is centered in the bounds without resizing; kCAGravityResize (the default) means the content is sized to fit the bounds, even if this means distorting its aspect; and so forth.

 For historical reasons, the terms bottom and top in the names of the contents-Gravity settings have the opposite of their expected meanings.

contentsRect

A CGRect expressing the proportion of the content that is to be displayed. The default is (0.0,0.0,1.0,1.0), meaning the entire content is displayed. The specified part of the content is sized and positioned in relation to the bounds in accordance with the contentsGravity. Thus, for example, by setting the contentsRect, you can scale up part of the content to fill the bounds, or slide part of a larger image into view without redrawing or changing the contents image.

You can also use the contentsRect to scale down the content, by specifying a larger contentsRect such as (-0.5,-0.5,1.5,1.5); but any content pixels that touch the edge of the contentsRect will then be extended outward to the edge of the layer (to prevent this, make sure that the outermost pixels of the content are all empty).

contentsCenter

A CGRect, structured like contentsRect, expressing the central region of nine rectangular regions of the contentsRect that are variously allowed to stretch if the contentsGravity calls for stretching. The central region (the actual value of the contentsCenter) stretches in both directions. Of the other eight regions (inferred from the value you provide), the four corner regions don't stretch, and the four side regions stretch in one direction. (This should remind you of how a resizable image stretches! See Chapter 2.)

If a layer's content comes from drawing directly into its graphics context, then the layer's contentsGravity, of itself, has no effect, because the size of the graphics context, by definition, fits the size of the layer exactly; there is nothing to stretch or reposition. But the contentsGravity *will* have an effect on such a layer if its contentsRect is not (0.0,0.0,1.0,1.0), because now we're specifying a rectangle of some *other* size; the contentsGravity describes how to fit that rectangle into the layer.

Again, if a layer's content comes from drawing directly into its graphics context, then when the layer is resized, if the layer is asked to display itself again, the drawing is performed again, and once more the layer's content fits the size of the layer exactly. But if the layer's bounds are resized when needsDisplayOnBoundsChange is false, then the layer does *not* redisplay itself, so its cached content no longer fits the layer, and the contentsGravity matters.

By a judicious combination of settings, you can get the layer to perform some clever drawing for you that might be difficult to perform directly. For example, Figure 3-7 shows the result of the following settings:

```
arrow.needsDisplayOnBoundsChange = false
arrow.contentsCenter = CGRect(0.0, 0.4, 1.0, 0.6)
arrow.contentsGravity = kCAGravityResizeAspect
arrow.bounds = arrow.bounds.insetBy(dx: -20, dy: -20)
```

Because needsDisplayOnBoundsChange is false, the content is not redisplayed when the arrow's bounds are increased; instead, the cached content is used. The contents-Gravity setting tells us to resize proportionally; therefore, the arrow is both longer and wider than in Figure 3-1, but not in such a way as to distort its proportions. However, notice that although the triangular arrowhead is wider, it is not longer; the increase in length is due entirely to the stretching of the arrow's shaft. That's because the contentsCenter region is within the shaft.

A layer's masksToBounds property has the same effect on its content that it has on its sublayers. If it is false, the whole content is displayed, even if that content (after

Figure 3-7. One way of resizing the compass arrow

taking account of the `contentsGravity` and `contentsRect`) is larger then the layer. If it is `true`, only the part of the content within the layer's bounds will be displayed.

 The value of a layer's bounds origin does not affect where its content is drawn. It affects only where its sublayers are drawn.

Layers that Draw Themselves

A few built-in CALayer subclasses provide some basic but helpful self-drawing ability:

CATextLayer

A CATextLayer has a `string` property, which can be an NSString or NSAttributedString, along with other text formatting properties, somewhat like a simplified UILabel; it draws its `string`. The default text color, the `foreground-Color` property, is white, which is unlikely to be what you want. The text is different from the `contents` and is mutually exclusive with it: either the contents image or the text will be drawn, but not both, so in general you should not give a CATextLayer any contents image. In Figures 3-1 and 3-7, the cardinal point letters are CATextLayer instances.

CAShapeLayer

A CAShapeLayer has a `path` property, which is a CGPath. It fills or strokes this path, or both, depending on its `fillColor` and `strokeColor` values, and displays the result; the default is a `fillColor` of black and no `strokeColor`. It has properties for line thickness, dash style, end-cap style, and join style, similar to a graphics context; it also has the remarkable ability to draw only part of its path (`strokeStart` and `strokeEnd`), making it very easy, for example, to draw an arc of an ellipse. A CAShapeLayer may also have `contents`; the shape is displayed on top of the contents image, but there is no property permitting you to specify a

Figure 3-8. A gradient drawn behind the compass

compositing mode. In Figures 3-1 and 3-7, the background circle is a CAShape-Layer instance, stroked with gray and filled with a lighter, slightly transparent gray.

CAGradientLayer

A CAGradientLayer covers its background with a simple linear gradient; thus, it's an easy way to draw a gradient in your interface (and if you need something more elaborate you can always draw with Core Graphics instead). The gradient is defined much as in the Core Graphics gradient example in Chapter 2, an array of locations and an array of corresponding colors, along with a start and end point. To clip the gradient's shape, you can add a mask to the CAGradientLayer (masks are discussed later in this chapter). A CAGradientLayer's contents are not displayed.

Figure 3-8 shows our compass drawn with an extra CAGradientLayer behind it.

Transforms

The way a layer is drawn on the screen can be modified though a transform. This is not surprising, because a view can have a transform (see Chapter 1), and a view is drawn on the screen by its layer. But a layer's transform is more powerful than a view's transform; you can use it to accomplish things that you can't accomplish with a view's transform alone.

Affine Transforms

In the simplest case, when a transform is two-dimensional, you can access a layer's transform through the affineTransform method (and the corresponding setter, set-AffineTransform(_:)). The value is a CGAffineTransform, familiar from Chapters 1 and 2. The transform is applied around the anchorPoint. (Thus, the anchorPoint has a second purpose that I didn't tell you about when discussing it earlier.)

You now know everything needed to understand the code that generated Figure 3-8, so here it is. In this code, self is the CompassLayer; it does no drawing of its own, but merely assembles and configures its sublayers. The four cardinal point letters are each drawn by a CATextLayer; they are drawn at the same coordinates, but they have different rotation transforms, and are anchored so that their rotation is centered at the center of the circle. To generate the arrow, CompassLayer adopts CALayerDelegate, makes itself the arrow layer's delegate, and calls setNeedsDisplay on the arrow layer; this causes draw(_:in:) to be called in CompassLayer (that code is just the same code we developed for drawing the arrow in Chapter 2, and is not repeated here). The arrow layer is positioned by an anchorPoint pinning its tail to the center of the circle, and rotated around that pin by a transform:

```
// the gradient
let g = CAGradientLayer()
g.contentsScale = UIScreen.main.scale
g.frame = self.bounds
g.colors = [
    UIColor.black.cgColor,
    UIColor.red.cgColor
]
g.locations = [0.0,1.0]
self.addSublayer(g)
// the circle
let circle = CAShapeLayer()
circle.contentsScale = UIScreen.main.scale
circle.lineWidth = 2.0
circle.fillColor = UIColor(red:0.9, green:0.95, blue:0.93, alpha:0.9).cgColor
circle.strokeColor = UIColor.gray.cgColor
let p = CGMutablePath()
p.addEllipse(in: self.bounds.insetBy(dx: 3, dy: 3))
circle.path = p
self.addSublayer(circle)
circle.bounds = self.bounds
circle.position = self.bounds.center
// the four cardinal points
let pts = "NESW"
for (ix,c) in pts.characters.enumerated() {
    let t = CATextLayer()
    t.contentsScale = UIScreen.main.scale
    t.string = String(c)
    t.bounds = CGRect(0,0,40,40)
    t.position = circle.bounds.center
    let vert = circle.bounds.midY / t.bounds.height
    t.anchorPoint = CGPoint(0.5, vert)
    t.alignmentMode = kCAAlignmentCenter
    t.foregroundColor = UIColor.black.cgColor
    t.setAffineTransform(
        CGAffineTransform(rotationAngle:CGFloat(ix) * .pi/2.0))
    circle.addSublayer(t)
}
```

```
// the arrow
let arrow = CALayer()
arrow.contentsScale = UIScreen.main.scale
arrow.bounds = CGRect(0, 0, 40, 100)
arrow.position = self.bounds.center
arrow.anchorPoint = CGPoint(0.5, 0.8)
arrow.delegate = self // we will draw the arrow in the delegate method
arrow.setAffineTransform(CGAffineTransform(rotationAngle:.pi/5.0))
self.addSublayer(arrow)
arrow.setNeedsDisplay() // draw, please
```

3D Transforms

A full-fledged layer transform, the value of the transform property, takes place in three-dimensional space; its description includes a z-axis, perpendicular to both the x-axis and y-axis. (By default, the positive z-axis points out of the screen, toward the viewer's face.) Layers do not magically give you realistic three-dimensional rendering — for that you would use OpenGL, which is beyond the scope of this discussion. Layers are two-dimensional objects, and they are designed for speed and simplicity. Nevertheless, they do operate in three dimensions, quite sufficiently to give a cartoonish but effective sense of reality, especially when performing an animation. We've all seen the screen image flip like turning over a piece of paper to reveal what's on the back; that's a rotation in three dimensions.

A three-dimensional transform takes place around a three-dimensional extension of the anchorPoint, whose z-component is supplied by the anchorPointZ property. Thus, in the reduced default case where anchorPointZ is 0.0, the anchorPoint is sufficient, as we've already seen in using CGAffineTransform.

The transform itself is described mathematically by a struct called a CATransform3D. The Quartz Core *Core Animation Functions* reference page lists the functions for working with these transforms. They are a lot like the CGAffineTransform functions, except they've got a third dimension. For example, a 2D scale transform depends upon two values, the scale on the x-axis and the y-axis; for a 3D scale transform, there's also a z-axis so you have to supply a third parameter.

The rotation 3D transform is a little more complicated. In addition to the angle, you also have to supply three coordinates describing the vector around which the rotation is to take place. Perhaps you've forgotten from your high-school math what a vector is, or perhaps trying to visualize three dimensions boggles your mind, so here's another way to think of it.

Pretend for purposes of discussion that the anchor point is the origin, (0.0,0.0,0.0). Now imagine an arrow emanating from the anchor point; its other end, the pointy end, is described by the three coordinates you provide. Now imagine a plane that intersects the anchor point, perpendicular to the arrow. That is the plane

Figure 3-9. An anchor point plus a vector defines a rotation plane

in which the rotation will take place; a positive angle is a clockwise rotation, as seen from the side of the plane with the arrow (Figure 3-9). In effect, the three coordinates you supply describe (relative to the anchor point) where your eye would have to be to see this rotation as an old-fashioned two-dimensional rotation.

A vector specifies a direction, not a point. Thus it makes no difference on what scale you give the coordinates: (1.0,1.0,1.0) means the same thing as (10.0,10.0,10.0), so you might as well say (1.0,1.0,1.0), sticking to the unit scale; that's called a *normalized* vector.

If the three normalized values are (0.0,0.0,1.0), with all other things being equal, the case is collapsed to a simple CGAffineTransform, because the rotational plane is the screen. If the three normalized values are (0.0,0.0,-1.0), it's a backward CGAffineTransform, so that a positive angle looks counterclockwise (because we are looking at the "back side" of the rotational plane).

A layer can itself be rotated in such a way that its "back" is showing. For example, the following rotation flips a layer around its y-axis:

```
someLayer.transform = CATransform3DMakeRotation(.pi, 0, 1, 0)
```

By default, the layer is considered double-sided, so when it is flipped to show its "back," what's drawn is an appropriately reversed version of the content of the layer (along with its sublayers, which by default are still drawn in front of the layer, but reversed and positioned in accordance with the layer's transformed coordinate system). But if the layer's isDoubleSided property is false, then when it is flipped to show its "back," the layer disappears (along with its sublayers); its "back" is transparent and empty.

Depth

There are two ways to place layers at different nominal depths with respect to their siblings. One is through the z-component of their position, which is the zPosition property. (Thus the zPosition, too, has a second purpose that I didn't tell you about earlier.) The other is to apply a transform that translates the layer's position in the z-direction. These two values, the z-component of a layer's position and the z-component of its translation transform, are related; in some sense, the zPosition is a shorthand for a translation transform in the z-direction. (If you provide both a zPosition and a z-direction translation, you can rapidly confuse yourself.)

In the real world, changing an object's zPosition would make it appear larger or smaller, as it is positioned closer or further away; but this, by default, is not the case in the world of layer drawing. There is no attempt to portray perspective; the layer planes are drawn at their actual size and flattened onto one another, with no illusion of distance. (This is called *orthographic projection*, and is the way blueprints are often drawn to display an object from one side.)

If we want to portray a visual sense of depth using layers, then, we're going to need some additional techniques.

Sublayer transform

Here's a widely used trick for introducing a quality of perspective into the way layers are drawn: make them sublayers of a layer whose sublayerTransform property maps all points onto a "distant" plane. (This is probably just about the only thing the sublayerTransform property is ever used for.) Combined with orthographic projection, the effect is to apply one-point perspective to the drawing, so that things do get perceptibly smaller in the negative z-direction.

For example, let's try applying a sort of "page-turn" rotation to our compass: we'll anchor it at its right side and then rotate it around the y-axis. Here, the sublayer we're rotating (accessed through a property, rotationLayer) is the gradient layer, and the circle and arrow are its sublayers so that they rotate with it:

```
self.rotationLayer.anchorPoint = CGPoint(1,0.5)
self.rotationLayer.position = CGPoint(self.bounds.maxX, self.bounds.midY)
self.rotationLayer.transform = CATransform3DMakeRotation(.pi/4.0, 0, 1, 0)
```

The results are disappointing (Figure 3-10); the compass looks more squashed than rotated. Now, however, we'll also apply the distance-mapping transform. The superlayer here is self:

```
var transform = CATransform3DIdentity
transform.m34 = -1.0/1000.0
self.sublayerTransform = transform
```

Figure 3-10. A disappointing page-turn rotation

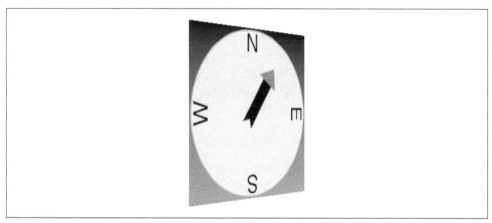

Figure 3-11. A dramatic page-turn rotation

The results (shown in Figure 3-11) are better, and you can experiment with values to replace 1000.0; for example, 500.0 gives an even more exaggerated effect. Also, the zPosition of the rotationLayer will now affect how large it is.

Transform layers

Another way to draw layers with depth is to use CATransformLayer. This CALayer subclass doesn't do any drawing of its own; it is intended solely as a host for other layers. It has the remarkable feature that you can apply a transform to it and it will maintain the depth relationships among its own sublayers. In this example, lay1 is a layer that might be a CATransformLayer:

```
let lay2 = CALayer()
lay2.frame = f // some CGRect
lay2.backgroundColor = UIColor.blue.cgColor
lay1.addSublayer(lay2)
let lay3 = CALayer()
lay3.frame = f.offsetBy(dx: 20, dy: 30)
```

```
lay3.backgroundColor = UIColor.green.cgColor
lay3.zPosition = 10
lay1.addSublayer(lay3)
lay1.transform = CATransform3DMakeRotation(.pi, 0, 1, 0)
```

In that code, the superlayer lay1 has two sublayers, lay2 and lay3. The sublayers are added in that order, so lay3 is drawn in front of lay2. Then lay1 is flipped like a page being turned by setting its transform. If lay1 is a normal CALayer, the sublayer drawing order doesn't change; lay3 is *still* drawn in front of lay2, even after the transform is applied. But if lay1 is a CATransformLayer, lay3 is drawn *behind* lay2 after the transform; they are both sublayers of lay1, so their depth relationship is maintained.

Figure 3-12 shows our page-turn rotation yet again, still with the sublayerTransform applied to self, but this time the only sublayer of self is a CATransformLayer:

```
var transform = CATransform3DIdentity
transform.m34 = -1.0/1000.0
self.sublayerTransform = transform
let master = CATransformLayer()
master.frame = self.bounds
self.addSublayer(master)
self.rotationLayer = master
```

The CATransformLayer, to which the page-turn transform is applied, holds the gradient layer, the circle layer, and the arrow layer. Those three layers are at different depths (using different zPosition settings), and I've tried to emphasize the arrow's separation from the circle by adding a shadow (discussed in the next section):

```
circle.zPosition = 10
arrow.shadowOpacity = 1.0
arrow.shadowRadius = 10
arrow.zPosition = 20
```

You can see from its apparent offset that the circle layer floats in front of the gradient layer, but I wish you could see this page-turn as an animation, which makes the circle jump right out from the gradient as the rotation proceeds.

Even more remarkable, I've added a little white peg sticking through the arrow and running into the circle! It is a CAShapeLayer, rotated to be perpendicular to the CATransformLayer (I'll explain the rotation code later in this chapter):

```
let peg = CAShapeLayer()
peg.contentsScale = UIScreen.main.scale
peg.bounds = CGRect(0,0,3.5,50)
let p2 = CGMutablePath()
p2.addRect(peg.bounds)
peg.path = p2
peg.fillColor = UIColor(red:1.0, green:0.95, blue:1.0, alpha:0.95).cgColor
peg.anchorPoint = CGPoint(0.5,0.5)
peg.position = master.bounds.center
```

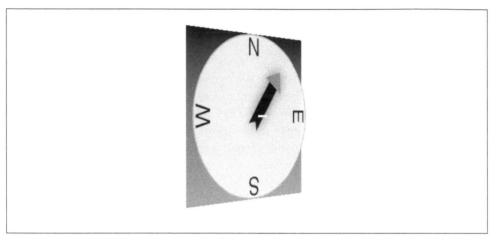

Figure 3-12. Page-turn rotation applied to a CATransformLayer

```
master.addSublayer(peg)
peg.setValue(Float.pi/2, forKeyPath:"transform.rotation.x")
peg.setValue(Float.pi/2, forKeyPath:"transform.rotation.z")
peg.zPosition = 15
```

In that code, the peg runs straight out of the circle toward the viewer, so it is initially seen end-on, and because a layer has no thickness, it is invisible. But as the CATransformLayer pivots in our page-turn rotation, the peg maintains its orientation relative to the circle, and comes into view. In effect, the drawing portrays a 3D model constructed entirely out of layers.

There is, I think, a slight additional gain in realism if the same `sublayerTransform` is applied also to the CATransformLayer, but I have not done so here.

Further Layer Features

A CALayer has many additional properties that affect details of how it is drawn. Since these drawing details can be applied to a UIView's underlying layer, they are effectively view features as well.

Shadows

A CALayer can have a shadow, defined by its `shadowColor`, `shadowOpacity`, `shadow-Radius`, and `shadowOffset` properties. To make the layer draw a shadow, set the `shadowOpacity` to a nonzero value. The shadow is normally based on the shape of the layer's nontransparent region, but deriving this shape can be calculation-intensive (so much so that in early versions of iOS, layer shadows weren't implemented). You can vastly improve performance by defining the shape yourself and assigning this shape as a CGPath to the `shadowPath` property.

If a layer's maskstoBounds is true, no part of its shadow lying outside its bounds is drawn. (This includes the underlying layer of a view whose clipsToBounds is true.) Wondering why the shadow isn't appearing for a layer that masks to its bounds is a common beginner mistake.

Borders and Rounded Corners

A CALayer can have a border (borderWidth, borderColor); the borderWidth is drawn inward from the bounds, potentially covering some of the content unless you compensate.

A CALayer's corners can be rounded, effectively bounding the layer with a rounded rectangle, by giving it a cornerRadius greater than zero. If the layer has a border, the border has rounded corners too. If the layer has a backgroundColor, that background is clipped to the shape of the rounded rectangle. If the layer's masksToBounds is true, the layer's content and its sublayers are clipped by the rounded corners.

New in iOS 11, you can round individual corners of a CALayer rather than having to round all four corners at once. To do so, set the layer's maskedCorners property to a CACornerMask, a bitmask whose values have these simply dreadful names:

- layerMinXMinYCorner
- layerMaxXMinYCorner
- layerMinXMaxYCorner
- layerMaxXMaxYCorner

Even if you set the maskedCorners, you won't see any corner rounding unless you also set the cornerRadius to a nonzero number.

Masks

A CALayer can have a mask. This is itself a layer, whose content must be provided somehow. The transparency of the mask's content in a particular spot becomes (all other things being equal) the transparency of the layer at that spot. The mask's colors (hues) are irrelevant; only transparency matters. To position the mask, pretend it's a sublayer.

For example, Figure 3-13 shows our arrow layer, with the gray circle layer behind it, and a mask applied to the arrow layer. The mask is silly, but it illustrates very well how masks work: it's an ellipse, with an opaque fill and a thick, semitransparent stroke. Here's the code that generates and applies the mask:

Figure 3-13. A layer with a mask

```
let mask = CAShapeLayer()
mask.frame = arrow.bounds
let path = CGMutablePath()
path.addEllipse(in: mask.bounds.insetBy(dx: 10, dy: 10))
mask.strokeColor = UIColor(white:0.0, alpha:0.5).cgColor
mask.lineWidth = 20
mask.path = path
arrow.mask = mask
```

Using a mask, we can do more generally what the `cornerRadius` and `masksToBounds` properties do. For example, here's a utility method that generates a CALayer suitable for use as a rounded rectangle mask:

```
func mask(size sz:CGSize, roundingCorners rad:CGFloat) -> CALayer {
    let rect = CGRect(origin:.zero, size:sz)
    let r = UIGraphicsImageRenderer(bounds:rect)
    let im = r.image { ctx in
        let con = ctx.cgContext
        con.setFillColor(UIColor(white:0, alpha:0).cgColor)
        con.fill(rect)
        con.setFillColor(UIColor(white:0, alpha:1).cgColor)
        let p = UIBezierPath(roundedRect:rect, cornerRadius:rad)
        p.fill()
    }
    let mask = CALayer()
    mask.frame = rect
    mask.contents = im.cgImage
    return mask
}
```

The CALayer returned from that method can be placed as a mask anywhere in a layer by adjusting its frame origin and assigning it as the layer's `mask`. The result is that all of that layer's content drawing and its sublayers (including, if this layer is a view's underlying layer, the view's subviews) are clipped to the rounded rectangle shape; everything outside that shape is not drawn.

A mask can have values between opaque and transparent, and it can be any shape. The transparent region doesn't have to be on the outside of the mask; you can use a mask that's opaque on the outside and transparent on the inside to "punch a hole" in a layer (or a view).

Alternatively, you can apply a mask as a view directly to another view through its mask property, rather than having to drop down to the level of layers. This may be a notational convenience, but it is not functionally distinct from applying the mask view's layer to the view's layer; under the hood, in fact, it *is* applying the mask view's layer to the view's layer.

A mask is like a sublayer, in that there is no built-in mechanism for automatically resizing the mask as the layer is resized. If *you* don't resize the mask when the layer is resized, the mask *won't* be resized. A common beginner mistake is to apply a mask to a view's underlying layer before the view has been fully laid out; when the view *is* laid out, its size changes, but the mask's size doesn't, and now the mask doesn't "fit."

Using a mask view (as opposed to a mask layer) does nothing to help with this problem; a mask view isn't a subview, so it is not subject to autoresizing or autolayout. On the other hand, if you resize a mask view manually, you can do so using view properties. That's very convenient if you're already resizing the view itself manually (for example, using view property animation, as discussed in the next chapter).

Layer Efficiency

By now, you're probably envisioning all sorts of compositing fun, with layers masking sublayers and laid semitransparently over other layers. There's nothing wrong with that, but when an iOS device is asked to shift its drawing from place to place, the movement may stutter because the device lacks the necessary computing power to composite repeatedly and rapidly. This sort of issue is likely to emerge particularly when your code performs an animation (Chapter 4) or when the user is able to animate drawing through touch, as when scrolling a table view (Chapter 8). You may be able to detect these problems by eye, and you can quantify them on a device by using the Core Animation template in Instruments, which shows the frame rate achieved during animation. Also, both the Core Animation template and the Simulator's Debug menu let you summon colored overlays that provide clues as to possible sources of inefficient drawing which can lead to such problems.

Tricks like shadows and rounded corners and masks are easy and fun; but in general, opaque drawing is most efficient. (Nonopaque drawing is what Instruments marks in red as "blended layers.") You may think that for some particular use case you *have* to do nonopaque drawing, but think again, because you might be wrong about that. If a layer will always be shown over a background consisting of a single color, you can give the layer its own background of that same color; when additional layer content is supplied, the visual effect will be the same as if that additional layer content were composited over a transparent background. For example, instead of an image masked to a rounded rectangle (with a layer's cornerRadius or mask property), you could use Core Graphics to clip the drawing of that image to a rounded rectangle shape within the graphics context of an opaque layer whose background color is the same as that of the destination in front of which the drawing will be shown.

Another way to gain some efficiency is by "freezing" the entirety of the layer's drawing as a bitmap. In effect, you're drawing everything in the layer to a secondary cache and using the cache to draw to the screen. Copying from a cache is less efficient than drawing directly to the screen, but this inefficiency may be compensated for, if there's a deep or complex layer tree, by not having to composite that tree every time we render. To do this, set the layer's `shouldRasterize` to `true` and its `rasterizationScale` to some sensible value (probably `UIScreen.main.scale`). You can always turn rasterization off again by setting `shouldRasterize` to `false`, so it's easy to rasterize just before some massive or sluggish rearrangement of the screen and then unrasterize afterward.

In addition, there's a layer property `drawsAsynchronously`. The default is `false`. If set to `true`, the layer's graphics context accumulates drawing commands and obeys them later on a background thread. Thus, your drawing commands run very quickly, because they are not in fact being obeyed at the time you issue them. I haven't had occasion to use this, but presumably there could be situations where it keeps your app responsive when drawing would otherwise be time-consuming.

Layers and Key–Value Coding

All of a layer's properties are accessible through Cocoa key–value coding by way of keys with the same name as the property. Thus, to apply a mask to a layer, instead of saying this:

```
layer.mask = mask
```

we could have said:

```
layer.setValue(mask, forKey: "mask")
```

In addition, CATransform3D and CGAffineTransform values can be expressed through key–value coding and key paths. For example, instead of writing this:

```
self.rotationLayer.transform = CATransform3DMakeRotation(.pi/4.0, 0, 1, 0)
```

we can write this:

```
self.rotationLayer.setValue(.pi/4.0, forKeyPath:"transform.rotation.y")
```

This notation is possible because CATransform3D is key–value coding compliant for a repertoire of keys and key paths. These are not properties, however; a CATransform3D doesn't have a `rotation` property. It doesn't have *any* properties, because it isn't even an object. You cannot say:

```
self.rotationLayer.transform.rotation.y = //... no, sorry
```

The transform key paths you'll use most often are:

- `"rotation.x"`, `"rotation.y"`, `"rotation.z"`
- `"rotation"` (same as `"rotation.z"`)
- `"scale.x"`, `"scale.y"`, `"scale.z"`
- `"translation.x"`, `"translation.y"`, `"translation.z"`
- `"translation"` (two-dimensional, a CGSize)

The Quartz Core framework also injects key–value coding compliance into CGPoint, CGSize, and CGRect, allowing you to use keys and key paths matching their struct component names. For a complete list of KVC compliant classes related to CALayer, along with the keys and key paths they implement, plus rules for how to wrap nonobject values as objects, see "Core Animation Extensions to Key-Value Coding" in Apple's *Core Animation Programming Guide*.

Moreover, you can treat a CALayer as a kind of dictionary, and get and set the value for *any* key. This means you can attach arbitrary information to an individual layer instance and retrieve it later. For example, earlier I mentioned that to apply manual layout to a layer's sublayers, you will need a way of identifying those sublayers. This feature could provide a way of doing that. For example:

```
myLayer1.setValue("manny", forKey:"pepboy")
myLayer2.setValue("moe", forKey:"pepboy")
```

A layer doesn't have a `pepboy` property; the `"pepboy"` key is something I'm attaching to these layers arbitrarily. Now I can identify these layers later by getting the value of their respective `"pepboy"` keys.

Also, CALayer has a `defaultValue(forKey:)` class method; to implement it, you'll need to subclass and override. In the case of keys whose value you want to provide a default for, return that value; otherwise, return the value that comes from calling `super`. Thus, even if a value for a particular key has never been explicitly provided, it can have a non-`nil` value.

The truth is that this feature, though delightful (and I often wish that all classes behaved like this), is not put there solely for your convenience and enjoyment. It's there to serve as the basis for animation, which is the subject of the next chapter.

CHAPTER 4

Animation

Animation is an attribute changing over time. In general, this will usually be a visible attribute of something in the interface. The changing attribute might be positional: something moves or changes size, not jumping abruptly, but sliding smoothly. Other kinds of attribute can animate as well. A view's background color might change from red to green, not switching colors abruptly, but fading from one to the other. A view might change from opaque to transparent, not vanishing abruptly, but fading away.

Without help, most of us would find animation beyond our reach. There are just too many complications — complications of calculation, of timing, of screen refresh, of threading, and many more. Fortunately, help is provided. You don't perform an animation yourself; you describe it, you order it, and it is performed for you. You get *animation on demand.*

Asking for an animation can be as simple as setting a property value; under some circumstances, a single line of code will result in animation:

```
myLayer.backgroundColor = UIColor.red.cgColor // animate to red
```

Animation is easy because Apple wants to facilitate your use of it. Animation isn't just cool and fun; it clarifies that something is changing or responding. It is crucial to the character of the iOS interface.

For example, one of my first apps was based on a macOS game in which the user clicks cards to select them. In the macOS version, a card was highlighted to show it was selected, and the computer would beep to indicate a click on an ineligible card. On iOS, these indications were insufficient: the highlighting felt weak, and you can't use a sound warning in an environment where the user might have the volume turned off or be listening to music. So in the iOS version, animation is the indicator for card selection (a selected card waggles eagerly) and for tapping on an ineligible card (the whole interface shudders, as if to shrug off the tap).

Drawing, Animation, and Threading

Animation is based on an interesting fact about how iOS draws to the screen: drawing doesn't actually take place at the time you give your drawing commands. When you give a command that requires a view to be redrawn, the system remembers your command and marks the view as needing to be redrawn. Later, when all your code has run to completion and the system has, as it were, a free moment, then it redraws all views that need redrawing. Let's call this the *redraw moment*. (I'll explain what the redraw moment really is later in this chapter.)

Animation works the same way, and is part of the same process. When you ask for an animation to be performed, the animation doesn't start happening on the screen until the next redraw moment. (You can force an animation to start immediately, but this is unusual.) Like a movie (especially an old-fashioned animated cartoon), an animation has "frames." An animated value does not change smoothly and continuously; it changes in small, individual increments that give the *illusion* of smooth, continuous change. This illusion works because the device itself undergoes a periodic, rapid, more or less regular screen refresh — a constant succession of redraw moments — and the incremental changes are made to fall between these refreshes. Apple calls the system component responsible for this the *animation server*.

Think of the "animation movie" as being interposed between the user and the "real" screen. While the animation lasts, this movie is superimposed onto the screen. When the animation is finished, the movie is removed, revealing the state of the "real" screen behind it. The user is unaware of all this, because (if you've done things correctly) at the time that it starts, the movie's first frame looks just like the state of the "real" screen at that moment, and at the time that it ends, the movie's last frame looks just like the state of the "real" screen at *that* moment.

So, when you animate a view's movement from position 1 to position 2, you can envision a typical sequence of events like this:

1. You reposition the view. The view is now set to position 2, but there has been no redraw moment, so it is still portrayed at position 1.

2. You order an animation of the view from position 1 to position 2.

3. The rest of your code runs to completion.

4. The redraw moment arrives. If there were no animation, the view would now suddenly be portrayed at position 2. But there *is* an animation, and so the "animation movie" appears. It starts with the view portrayed at position 1, so that is still what the user sees.

5. The animation proceeds, each "frame" portraying the view at intermediate positions between position 1 and position 2. (The documentation describes the animation as now *in-flight*.)

6. The animation ends, portraying the view ending up at position 2.

7. The "animation movie" is removed, revealing the view indeed at position 2 — where you put it in the first step.

Realizing that the "animation movie" is different from what happens to the *real* view is key to configuring an animation correctly. A frequent complaint of beginners is that a position animation is performed as expected, but then, at the end, the view "jumps" to some other position. This happens because you set up the animation but failed to move the view to match its final position in the "animation movie"; when the "movie" is whipped away at the end of the animation, the real situation that's revealed doesn't match the last frame of the "movie," so the view appears to jump.

There isn't really an "animation movie" in front of the screen — but it's a good analogy, and the effect is much the same. In reality, it is not a layer itself that is portrayed on the screen; it's a derived layer called the *presentation layer*. Thus, when you animate the change of a view's position or a layer's position from position 1 to position 2, its nominal position changes immediately; meanwhile, the presentation layer's position remains unchanged until the redraw moment, and then changes over time, and because that's what's actually drawn on the screen, that's what the user sees.

(A layer's presentation layer can be accessed through its `presentation` method — and the layer itself may be accessed through the presentation layer's `model` method. I'll give examples, in this chapter and the next, of situations where accessing the presentation layer is a useful thing to do.)

The animation server operates on an independent thread. You don't have to worry about the details (thank heavens, because multithreading is generally rather tricky and complicated), but you can't ignore it either. Your code runs independently of and possibly simultaneously with the animation — that's what multithreading means — so communication between the animation and your code can require some planning.

Arranging for your code to be notified when an animation ends is a common need. Most of the animation APIs provide a way to set up such a notification. One use of an "animation ended" notification might be to chain animations together: one animation ends and then another begins, in sequence. Another use is to perform some sort of cleanup. A very frequent kind of cleanup has to do with handling of touches: while an animation is in-flight, if your code is not running, the interface by default is responsive to the user's touches, which might cause all kinds of havoc as your views try to respond while the animation is still happening and the screen presentation doesn't match reality. To take care of this, you might turn off your app's responsiveness to touches as you set up an animation and then turn it back on when you're notified that the animation is over.

Since your code can run even after you've set up an animation, or might start running while an animation is in-flight, you need to be careful about setting up conflicting animations. Multiple animations can be set up (and performed) simultaneously, but trying to animate or change a property that's already in the middle of being animated may be an incoherency. You'll want to take care not to let your animations step on each other's feet accidentally.

Outside forces can interrupt your animations. The user might click the Home button to send your app to the background, or an incoming phone call might arrive while an animation is in-flight. The system deals coherently with this situation by simply canceling all in-flight animations when an app is backgrounded; you've already arranged *before* the animation for your views to assume the final states they will have *after* the animation, so no harm is done — when your app resumes, everything is in that final state you arranged beforehand. But if you wanted your app to resume an animation in the middle, where it left off when it was interrupted, that would require some canny coding on your part.

Image View and Image Animation

UIImageView provides a form of animation so simple as to be scarcely deserving of the name; still, sometimes it might be all you need. You supply the UIImageView with an array of UIImages, as the value of its `animationImages` or `highlightedAnimation-Images` property. This array represents the "frames" of a simple cartoon; when you send the `startAnimating` message, the images are displayed in turn, at a frame rate determined by the `animationDuration` property, repeating as many times as specified by the `animationRepeatCount` property (the default is 0, meaning to repeat forever), or until the `stopAnimating` message is received. Before and after the animation, the image view continues displaying its `image` (or `highlightedImage`).

For example, suppose we want an image of Mars to appear out of nowhere and flash three times on the screen. This might seem to require some sort of Timer-based solution, but it's far simpler to use an animating UIImageView:

```
let mars = UIImage(named: "Mars")!
let empty = UIGraphicsImageRenderer(size:mars.size).image {_ in}
let arr = [mars, empty, mars, empty, mars]
let iv = UIImageView(image:empty)
iv.frame.origin = CGPoint(100,100)
self.view.addSubview(iv)
iv.animationImages = arr
iv.animationDuration = 2
iv.animationRepeatCount = 1
iv.startAnimating()
```

You can combine UIImageView animation with other kinds of animation. For example, you could flash the image of Mars while at the same time sliding the UIImage-View rightward, using view animation as described in the next section.

UIImage supplies a form of animation parallel to that of UIImageView: an image can itself be an *animated image*. Just as with UIImageView, this means that you've prepared multiple images that form a sequence serving as the "frames" of a simple cartoon. You can create an animated image with one of these UIImage class methods:

`animatedImage(with:duration:)`
> As with UIImageView's `animationImages`, you supply an array of UIImages. You also supply the duration for the whole animation.

`animatedImageNamed(_:duration:)`
> You supply the name of a single image file, as with `init(named:)`, with no file extension. The runtime appends `"0"` (or, if that fails, `"1"`) to the name you supply and makes *that* image file the first image in the animation sequence. Then it increments the appended number, gathering images and adding them to the sequence (until there are no more, or we reach `"1024"`).

`animatedResizableImageNamed(_:capInsets:resizingMode:duration:)`
> Combines an animated image with a resizable image (Chapter 2).

You do not tell an animated image to start animating, nor are you able to tell it how long you want the animation to repeat. Rather, an animated image is *always animating*, repeating its sequence once every `duration` seconds, so long as it appears in your interface; to control the animation, add the image to your interface or remove it from the interface, possibly exchanging it for a similar image that isn't animated.

An animated image can appear in the interface anywhere a UIImage can appear as a property of some interface object. In this example, I construct a sequence of red circles of different sizes, in code, and build an animated image which I then display in a UIButton:

```
var arr = [UIImage]()
let w : CGFloat = 18
for i in 0 ..< 6 {
    let r = UIGraphicsImageRenderer(size:CGSize(w,w))
    arr += [r.image { ctx in
        let con = ctx.cgContext
        con.setFillColor(UIColor.red.cgColor)
        let ii = CGFloat(i)
        con.addEllipse(in:CGRect(0+ii,0+ii,w-ii*2,w-ii*2))
        con.fillPath()
    }]
}
let im = UIImage.animatedImage(with:arr, duration:0.5)
b.setImage(im, for:.normal) // b is a button in the interface
```

New in iOS 11, the system understands animated GIF images. Unfortunately, it does not understand them so well as to animate them for you! If you want to display an animated GIF in a UIImageView or as an animated UIImage, it is up to you to decompose it into its individual frames. Apple's sample code ("Using Photos framework") supplies an AnimatedImage class that can extract each frame's image data, along with other information such as the animation duration. Using this, you could configure a UIImageView's `animationImages` and `animationDuration`, or display the animation with Apple's AnimatedImageView class from the same sample code.

View Animation

All animation is ultimately layer animation, which I'll discuss later in this chapter. However, for a limited range of properties, you can animate a UIView directly: these are its `alpha`, `bounds`, `center`, `frame`, `transform`, and (if the view doesn't implement `draw(_:)`) its `backgroundColor`. The UIVisualEffectView `effect` property is animatable between `nil` and a UIBlurEffect. New in iOS 11, a view's underlying layer's `cornerRadius` is animatable under view animation as well. You can also animate a UIView's change of contents. This list of animatable features, despite its brevity, will often prove quite sufficient.

A Brief History of View Animation

The view animation API has evolved historically by way of three distinct major stages. Older stages have not been deprecated or removed; all three stages are present simultaneously:

Begin and commit
> Way back at the dawn of iOS time, a view animation was constructed imperatively using a sequence of UIView class methods. To use this API, you call `begin-Animations`, configure the animation, set an animatable property, and *commit* the animation by calling `commitAnimations`. For example:

```
UIView.beginAnimations(nil, context: nil)
UIView.setAnimationDuration(1)
self.v.backgroundColor = .red
UIView.commitAnimations()
```

Block-based animation
> When Objective-C blocks were introduced, the entire operation of configuring a view animation was reduced to a single UIView class method, to which you pass a block in which you set the animatable property. In Swift, an Objective-C block is a function — usually an anonymous function:

```
UIView.animate(withDuration:1) {
    self.v.backgroundColor = .red
}
```

Property animator

iOS 10 introduced a new object — a property animator (UIViewPropertyAnimator). It, too, receives a function:

```
let anim = UIViewPropertyAnimator(duration: 1, curve: .linear) {
    self.v.backgroundColor = .red
}
anim.startAnimation()
```

Although begin-and-commit animation still exists, you're unlikely to use it. Block-based animation completely supersedes it — except in one special situation where you want an animation that repeats a specific number of times (I'll demonstrate later in this chapter).

The property animator does *not* supersede block-based animation; rather, it supplements and expands it. There are certain kinds of animation (repeating animation, autoreversing animation, transition animation) where a property animator can't help you, and you'll go on using block-based animation. But for the bulk of basic view animations, the property animator brings some valuable advantages — a full range of timing curves, multiple completion functions, and the ability to pause, resume, reverse, and interact by touch with a view animation.

Property Animator Basics

The UIViewPropertyAnimator class derives its methods and properties not only from itself but also from its protocol inheritance. It adopts the UIViewImplicitlyAnimating protocol, which itself adopts the UIViewAnimating protocol. (The reason for this division of powers won't arise in this chapter; it has to do with custom view controller transition animations, discussed in Chapter 6.) Here's an overview of UIViewPropertyAnimator's inheritance:

UIViewAnimating protocol

As a UIViewAnimating protocol adopter, UIViewPropertyAnimator can have its animation started with `startAnimation`, paused with `pauseAnimation`, and stopped with `stopAnimation(_:)` plus `finishAnimation(at:)`. Its `state` property reflects its current state (UIViewAnimatingState) — `.inactive`, `.active`, or `.stopped` — and its `isRunning` property distinguishes whether it is `.active` but paused.

UIViewAnimating also provides two settable properties:

- The `fractionComplete` property is essentially the current "frame" of the animation.

- The `isReversed` property dictates whether the animation is running forward or backward.

UIViewImplicitlyAnimating protocol

As a UIViewImplicitlyAnimating protocol adopter, UIViewPropertyAnimator can be given completion functions to be executed when the animation finishes, with `addCompletion(_:)`. It can also be given additional animation functions, with `addAnimations(_:)` or `addAnimations(_:delayFactor:)`; animations defined by multiple animation functions are combined additively (I'll explain later what that means). UIViewImplicitlyAnimating also provides a `continueAnimation(withTimingParameters:durationFactor:)` method that allows a paused animation to be resumed with altered timing and duration; the `durationFactor` is the desired fraction of the animation's original duration, or zero to mean whatever remains of the original duration.

UIViewPropertyAnimator

UIViewPropertyAnimator's own methods consist solely of initializers; I'll explain how to initialize a property animator later, when I talk about timing curves. It has some read-only properties describing how it was configured and started (for example, reporting its animation's `duration`). UIViewPropertyAnimator also provides five settable properties:

- If `isInterruptible` is `true` (the default), the animator can be paused or stopped.

- If `isUserInteractionEnabled` is `true` (the default), animated views can be tapped midflight.

- If `scrubsLinearly` is `true` (the default), then when the animator is paused, the animator's animation curve is temporarily replaced with a linear curve. This property is new in iOS 11.

- If `isManualHitTestingEnabled` is `true`, hit-testing is up to you; the default is `false`, meaning that the animator performs hit-testing on your behalf, which is usually what you want. (See Chapter 5 for more about hit-testing animated views.)

- If `pausesOnCompletion` is `true`, then when the animation finishes, it does not revert to `.inactive`; the default is `false`. This property is new in iOS 11.

As you can see, a property animator comes packed with power for controlling the animation after it starts. You can pause the animation in mid-flight, allow the user to manipulate the animation gesturally, resume the animation, reverse the animation, and much more. I'll illustrate all those features in this and subsequent chapters. In the simplest case, however, you'll just launch the animation and stand back, as I demonstrated earlier:

```
let anim = UIViewPropertyAnimator(duration: 1, curve: .linear) {
    self.v.backgroundColor = .red
}
anim.startAnimation()
```

In that code, the UIViewPropertyAnimator object `anim` is instantiated as a local variable, and we are not retaining it in a persistent property; yet the animation works because the animation server retains it. We *can* keep a persistent reference to the property animator if we're going to need it elsewhere, and I'll give examples later showing how that can be a useful thing to do; but the animation will still work even if we don't.

It will be useful to have a sense for how a property animator's states work. At the moment the property animator is started with `startAnimation`, it transitions through state changes, as follows:

1. The animator starts life in the `.inactive` state.

2. When `startAnimation` is called, the animator immediately enters the `.active` state with `isRunning` set to `false` (paused).

3. The animator then immediately transitions again to the `.active` state with `isRunning` set to `true`.

Nevertheless, the "animation movie" doesn't start running until the next redraw moment. Once the animation is set in motion, it continues to its finish and then runs through those same states in reverse:

1. The running animator was in the `.active` state with `isRunning` set to `true`.

2. When the animation finishes, the animator switches to `.active` with `isRunning` set to `true` (paused).

3. The animator then immediately transitions back to the `.inactive` state.

When the animator finishes and reverts to the `.inactive` state, it jettisons its animations. This means that the animator, if you've retained it, is reusable after finishing only if you supply new animations. New in iOS 11, however, you can overcome that difficulty by setting the animator's `pausesOnCompletion` to `true`; in that case, the third step is omitted — the animation comes to an end without the animator transitioning back to the `.inactive` state. Ultimately stopping the animation is then up to you.

To stop an animator, send it the `stopAnimation(_:)` message. The animator then enters the special `.stopped` state. Typically, you will then call `finishAnimation(at:)`, after which the animator returns to `.inactive`. The `stopAnimation(_:)` parameter is a Bool signifying whether you want to dispense with finishAnimation(at:) and let the runtime clean up for you.

 New in iOS 11, it is a runtime error to let an animator go out of existence while paused (.active but isRunning is false) or stopped (.stopped). Your app will crash unceremoniously if you allow that to happen. If you pause an animator, you *must* call stopAnimation(true), or else call stopAnimation(false) followed by finishAnimation(at:), thus bringing it back to the .inactive state in good order, before the animator goes out of existence.

View Animation Basics

A function in which you order a view animation by setting animatable properties is an *animations function*. Any animatable change made within an animations function will be animated, so we can, for example, animate a change both in the view's color and in its position simultaneously:

```
let anim = UIViewPropertyAnimator(duration: 1, curve: .linear) {
    self.v.backgroundColor = .red
    self.v.center.y += 100
}
anim.startAnimation()
```

You can add an animations function to a property animator after instantiating it; indeed, the init(duration:timingParameters:) initializer actually requires that you do this, as it lacks an animations: parameter. Thus a property animator can end up with multiple animations functions:

```
let anim = UIViewPropertyAnimator(duration: 1,
    timingParameters: UICubicTimingParameters(animationCurve:.linear))
anim.addAnimations {
    self.v.backgroundColor = .red
}
anim.addAnimations {
    self.v.center.y += 100
}
anim.startAnimation()
```

A completion function, which can be added to a property animator with the add-Completion(_:) method, lets us specify what should happen after the animation ends. As with the animation functions, a property animator can be assigned more than one completion function; the completion functions are executed in the order in which they were added:

```
var anim = UIViewPropertyAnimator(duration: 1, curve: .linear) {
    self.v.backgroundColor = .red
    self.v.center.y += 100
}
anim.addCompletion {_ in
```

```
    print("hey")
}
anim.addCompletion {_ in
    print("ho")
}
anim.startAnimation() // animates, finishes, then prints "hey" and "ho"
```

Changes not only to multiple properties but even to multiple views can be combined into a single animations function. In this way, elaborate effects can be combined into a single animation. For example, suppose we want to make one view dissolve into another. We start with the second view present in the view hierarchy, with the same frame as the first view, but with an alpha of 0, so that it is invisible. Then we animate the change of the first view's alpha to 0 and the second view's alpha to 1. Indeed, we can place the second view in the view hierarchy just before the animation starts (invisibly, because its alpha starts at 0) and remove the first view just after the animation ends (invisibly, because its alpha ends at 0):

```
let v2 = UIView()
v2.backgroundColor = .black
v2.alpha = 0
v2.frame = self.v.frame
self.v.superview!.addSubview(v2)
let anim = UIViewPropertyAnimator(duration: 1, curve: .linear) {
    self.v.alpha = 0
    v2.alpha = 1
}
anim.addCompletion { _ in
    self.v.removeFromSuperview()
}
anim.startAnimation()
```

 Another way to remove a view from the view hierarchy with animation is to call the UIView class method perform(_:on:options:animations:completion:) with .delete as its first argument (this is, in fact, the only possible first argument). This causes the view to blur, shrink, and fade, and sends it removeFromSuperview() afterward.

Code that isn't about animatable view properties can appear in an animations function with no problem, and will in fact run immediately when startAnimation is called. But we must be careful to keep any changes to animatable properties that we do *not* want animated out of the animations function. In the preceding example, in setting v2.alpha to 0, I just want to set it right now, instantly; I don't want that change to be animated. So I've put that line *outside* the animations function (and in particular, *before* it).

Sometimes, though, that's not so easy; perhaps, within the animations function, we must call a method that might perform animatable changes. The UIView class method performWithoutAnimation(_:) solves the problem; it goes inside an animations function, but whatever happens in *its* function is *not* animated. In this rather artificial example, the view jumps to its new position and then slowly turns red:

```
let anim = UIViewPropertyAnimator(duration: 1, curve: .linear) {
    self.v.backgroundColor = .red
    UIView.performWithoutAnimation {
        self.v.center.y += 100
    }
}
anim.startAnimation()
```

The material inside an animations function (but not inside a `performWithout-Animation` function) *orders* the animation — that is, it gives instructions for what the animation will be when the redraw moment comes. If you change an animatable view property as part of the animation, you should *not* change that property again afterward; the results can be confusing, because there's a conflict with the animation you've already ordered. This code, for example, is essentially incoherent:

```
let anim = UIViewPropertyAnimator(duration: 2, curve: .linear) {
    self.v.center.y += 100
}
self.v.center.y += 300
anim.startAnimation()
```

What actually happens is that the view *jumps* 300 points down and then *animates* 100 points further down. That's probably not what you intended. After you've ordered an animatable view property to be animated inside an animations function, *don't change that view property's value again* until after the animation is over.

On the other hand, this code, while somewhat odd, nevertheless does a smooth single animation to a position 400 points further down:

```
let anim = UIViewPropertyAnimator(duration: 2, curve: .linear) {
    self.v.center.y += 100
    self.v.center.y += 300
}
anim.startAnimation()
```

That's because basic positional view animations are *additive* by default. This means that the second animation is run simultaneously with the first, and is blended with it.

View Animation Configuration

The details of how you configure a view animation differ depending on whether you're using a property animator or calling a UIView class method. With a property animator, as my examples have already shown, you can construct the animator in several steps before telling it to start animating. With a UIView class method, on the other hand, everything has to be supplied in a single command. The full form of the chief UIView class method for performing view animation is:

- `animate(withDuration:delay:options:animations:completion:)`

There are shortened versions of the same command; for example, you can omit the `delay:` and `options:` parameters, and even the `completion:` parameter. But it's still the same command, and the configuration of the animation is complete at this point.

Animations function

The animations function contains the commands setting animatable view properties. With a block-based UIView class method, this is the `animations:` parameter. With a property animator, the animations function is usually provided as the `animations:` argument when the property animator is instantiated. However, a property animator can have one or more animations functions added after instantiation, by calling `add-Animations(_:)`, as we saw earlier.

Completion function

A completion function contains commands to be executed when the animation finishes. With a UIView class method, the completion function is the `completion:` parameter. It takes one parameter, a Bool reporting whether the animation finished.

A property animator can have multiple completion functions, provided by calling `add-Completion(_:)`. The completion function takes one parameter, a UIViewAnimatingPosition reporting where the animation ended up: `.end`, `.start`, or `.current`. (I'll talk later about what those values mean.) A property animator that is told to stop its animation with `stopAnimation(_:)` does *not* execute its completion functions until it is subsequently told to finish with `finishAnimation(at:)`. The `stopAnimation(_:)` parameter comes into play here:

- If you call `stopAnimation(false)` followed by `finishAnimation(at:)`, the animator's completion functions are then executed.
- If you call `stopAnimation(true)`, or if you call `stopAnimation(false)` but omit to call `finishAnimation(at:)`, the animator's completion functions are *not* executed.

Animation duration

The duration of an animation represents how long it takes (in seconds) to run from start to finish. You can also think of this as the animation's speed. Obviously, if two views are told to move different distances in the same time, the one that must move further must move faster.

Interestingly, a duration of 0 doesn't really mean 0. It means "use the default duration." This fact will be of interest later when we talk about nesting animations. Outside of a nested animation, the default is two-tenths of a second.

With a block-based UIView class method, the animation duration is the `duration:` parameter. With a property animator, it is supplied as the `duration:` parameter when the property animator is initialized.

Animation delay

It is permitted to order the animation along with a delay before the animation goes into action. The default is no delay. A delay is *not* the same as applying the animation using delayed performance; the animation is applied immediately, but when it starts running it spins its wheels, with no visible change, until the delay time has elapsed.

With a block-based UIView class method, this is the `delay:` parameter. To apply a delay to an animation with a property animator, call `startAnimation(afterDelay:)` instead of `startAnimation`.

Animation timing

An animation has a timing curve that maps interpolated values to time. For example, the notion of moving a view downward by 100 points in the course of 1 second can have many meanings. Should we move at a constant rate the whole time? Should we move slowly at first and more quickly later? There are a lot of possibilities.

With a UIView class method, you get a choice of just four timing curves (supplied as part of the `options:` argument, as I'll explain in a moment). But a property animator gives you very broad powers to configure the timing curve the way you want. This is such an important topic that I'll deal with it in a separate section later.

Animation options

In a UIView class method, the `options:` argument is a bitmask combining additional options. Here are some of the chief `options:` values (UIViewAnimationOptions) that you might wish to use:

Timing curve
 When supplied in this way, only four built-in timing curves are available. The term "ease" means that there is a gradual acceleration or deceleration between the animation's central speed and the zero speed at its start or end. Specify one at most:

 - `.curveEaseInOut` (the default)
 - `.curveEaseIn`
 - `.curveEaseOut`

- .curveLinear (constant speed throughout)

.repeat

If included, the animation will repeat indefinitely. There is no way, as part of this command, to specify a certain number of repetitions; you ask either to repeat forever or not at all. This feels like a serious oversight in the design of the block-based animation API; I'll suggest a workaround in a moment.

.autoreverse

If included, the animation will run from start to finish (in the given duration time), and will then run from finish to start (also in the given duration time). The documentation's claim that you can autoreverse only if you also repeat is incorrect; you can use either or both (or neither).

When using .autoreverse, you will want to clean up at the end so that the view is back in its original position when the animation is over. To see what I mean, consider this code:

```
let opts : UIViewAnimationOptions = .autoreverse
let xorig = self.v.center.x
UIView.animate(withDuration:1, delay: 0, options: opts, animations: {
    self.v.center.x += 100
    }, completion: nil
)
```

The view animates 100 points to the right and then animates 100 points back to its original position — and then *jumps* 100 points *back to the right*. The reason is that the last actual value we assigned to the view's center x is 100 points to the right, so when the animation is over and the "animation movie" is whipped away, the view is revealed still sitting 100 points to the right. The solution is to move the view back to its original position in the completion: function:

```
let opts : UIViewAnimationOptions = .autoreverse
let xorig = self.v.center.x
UIView.animate(withDuration:1, delay: 0, options: opts, animations: {
    self.v.center.x += 100
    }, completion: { _ in
        self.v.center.x = xorig
})
```

Working around the inability to specify a finite number of repetitions is tricky. The simplest solution is to resort to a command from the first generation of animation methods:

```
let opts : UIViewAnimationOptions = .autoreverse
let xorig = self.v.center.x
UIView.animate(withDuration:1, delay: 0, options: opts, animations: {
    UIView.setAnimationRepeatCount(3) // *
```

```
        self.v.center.x += 100
    }, completion: { _ in
        self.v.center.x = xorig
    })
```

There are also some options saying what should happen if another animation is already ordered or in-flight (so that we are effectively *nesting* animations):

.overrideInheritedDuration

Prevents inheriting the duration from a surrounding or in-flight animation (the default is to inherit it).

.overrideInheritedCurve

Prevents inheriting the timing curve from a surrounding or in-flight animation (the default is to inherit it).

.beginFromCurrentState

If this animation animates a property already being animated by an animation that is previously ordered or in-flight, then instead of canceling the previous animation (completing the requested change instantly), if that is what would normally happen, this animation will use the presentation layer to decide where to start, and, if possible, will "blend" its animation with the previous animation.

There is little need for .beginFromCurrentState in iOS 8 and later, because simple view animations are additive by default. To illustrate what it means for animations to be additive, let's take advantage of the fact that a property animator allows us to add a second animation that doesn't take effect until some amount of the first animation has elapsed:

```
let anim = UIViewPropertyAnimator(duration: 2, curve: .easeInOut) {
    self.v.center.y += 100
}
anim.addAnimations({
    self.v.center.x += 100
    }, delayFactor: 0.5)
anim.startAnimation()
```

The delayFactor: of 0.5 means that the second animation will start halfway through the duration. So the animated view heads straight downward for 1 second and then smoothly swoops off to the right while continuing down for another second, ending up 100 points down and 100 points to the right of where it started. The two animations might appear to conflict — they are both changing the center of our view, and they have different durations and therefore different speeds — but instead they blend together seamlessly.

An even stronger example is what happens when the two animations directly oppose one another:

```
let yorig = self.v.center.y
let anim = UIViewPropertyAnimator(duration: 2, curve: .easeInOut) {
    self.v.center.y += 100
}
anim.addAnimations({
    self.v.center.y = yorig
    }, delayFactor: 0.5)
anim.startAnimation()
```

That's a smooth autoreversing animation. The animated view starts marching toward a point 100 points down from its original position, but at about the halfway point it smoothly — not abruptly or sharply — slows and reverses itself and returns to its original position.

Timing Curves

A timing curve maps the fraction of the animation's time that has elapsed (the x-axis) against the fraction of the animation's change that has occurred (the y-axis); its endpoints are therefore at (0.0,0.0) and (1.0,1.0), because at the beginning of the animation there has been no elapsed time and no change, and at the end of the animation all the time has elapsed and all the change has occurred. There are two kinds of timing curve: cubic Bézier curves and springing curves.

Cubic timing curves

A cubic Bézier curve is defined by its endpoints, where each endpoint needs only one Bézier control point to define the tangent to the curve. Because the curve's endpoints are known, defining the two control points is sufficient to describe the entire curve. That is, in fact, how it is expressed.

So, for example, the built-in ease-in-out timing function is defined by the two points (0.42, 0.0) and (0.58, 1.0) — this is, it's a Bézier curve with one endpoint at (0.0,0.0), whose control point is (0.42,0.0), and the other endpoint at (1.0,1.0), whose control point is (0.58,1.0) (Figure 4-1).

With a UIView class method, you have a choice of four built-in timing curves; you specify one of them through the options: argument, as I've already explained.

With a property animator, you'll specify a timing curve as part of initialization. That's why, earlier, I postponed telling you how to initialize a property animator — until now! Here are three property animator initializers and how the timing curve is expressed when you call them:

init(duration:curve:animations:)
    The curve: is a built-in timing curve, specified as a UIViewAnimationCurve enum. These are the same built-in timing curves as for a UIView class method:

    • .easeInOut

Figure 4-1. An ease-in-out Bézier curve

- .easeIn
- .easeOut
- .linear

`init(duration:controlPoint1:controlPoint2:animations:)`
The curve is supplied as the two control points that define it.

`init(duration:timingParameters:)`
This is most general form of initializer; the other two are convenience initializers that call it. There's no `animations:` parameter, so you'll have to call `add-Animations` later to supply the animations function. The `timingParameters:` is an object adopting the UITimingCurveProvider protocol, which can be a UICubicTimingParameters instance or a UISpringTimingParameters instance (I'll talk about springing timing curves in a moment). The UICubicTimingParameters initializers are:

`init(animationCurve:)`
The value is one of the four built-in timing curves that I already mentioned, specified as a UIViewAnimationCurve enum.

`init()`
Provides a fifth built-in timing curve, used as the default for many built-in behaviors.

`init(controlPoint1:controlPoint2:)`
Defines the curve by its control points.

For example, here's a cubic timing curve that eases in very slowly and finishes up all in a rush, whipping quickly into place after about two-thirds of the time has elapsed. I call this the "clunk" timing function:

```
anim = UIViewPropertyAnimator(
    duration: 1, timingParameters:
        UICubicTimingParameters(
            controlPoint1:CGPoint(0.9,0.1),
            controlPoint2:CGPoint(0.7,0.9)))
```

Springing timing curves

A springing timing curve is the solution to a physics problem whose initial conditions describe a mass attached to a stretched spring. The animation mimics releasing the spring and letting it rush toward and settle down at the destination value.

Springing timing curves are much more useful and widespread than you might suppose. A springing animation doesn't have to animate a view from place to place, and doesn't have to look particularly springy to be effective. A small initial spring velocity and a high damping gives a normal animation that wouldn't particularly remind anyone of a spring, but that does have a pleasingly rapid beginning and slow ending; many of Apple's own system animations are actually spring animations of that type (consider, for example, the way folders open in the home screen).

To use a springing timing curve with UIView block-based animation, you call a different class method:

- `animate(withDuration:delay:usingSpringWithDamping:initialSpring-Velocity:options:animations:completion:)`

You're supplying two parameters that vary the nature of the initial conditions, and hence the behavior of the animation over time:

Damping ratio
> The `damping:` parameter is a number between `0.0` and `1.0` that describes the amount of final oscillation. A value of `1.0` is *critically damped* and settles directly into place; lower values are *underdamped*. A value of `0.8` just barely overshoots and snaps back to the final value. A value of `0.1` waggles around the final value for a while before settling down.

Initial velocity
> Higher values cause greater overshoot, depending on the damping ratio. For example, with a damping ratio of `0.3`, an initial velocity value of `1` overshoots a little and bounces about twice before settling into place, a value of `10` overshoots a bit further, and a value of `100` overshoots by more than twice the distance.

Normally, you'll probably leave the initial velocity at zero. It is useful particularly when converting from a gesture to an animation — that is, where the user is moving a view and releases it, and you want a springing animation to take over from there, starting out at the same velocity that the user was applying at the moment of release.

With a property animator, once again, you'll supply the timing curve as part of initialization:

`init(duration:dampingRatio:animations:)`
  The `dampingRatio:` argument is the same as the `damping:` in the UIView class method I just described. The initial velocity is zero.

`init(duration:timingParameters:)`
  This is the same initializer I discussed in connection with cubic timing curves. Recall that the `timingParameters:` is a UITimingCurveProvider; this can be a UISpringTimingParameters object, whose initializers are:

`init(dampingRatio:)`
  You supply a damping ratio, and the initial velocity is zero.

`init(dampingRatio:initialVelocity:)`
  The `initialVelocity:` is similar to the `initialSpringVelocity:` in the UIView class method I described a moment ago, except that it is a CGVector. Normally, only the x-component matters, in which case they are effectively the same thing; the y-component is considered only if what's being animated follows a two-dimensional path — for example, if you're changing both components of a view's `center`.

`init(mass:stiffness:damping:initialVelocity:)`
  A slightly different way of looking at the initial conditions. The overall `duration:` value is ignored; the actual duration will be calculated from the other parameters (and this calculated duration can be discovered by reading the resulting property animator's `duration`). The first three parameters are in proportion to one another. A high `mass:` can cause a vast overshoot. A low `stiffness:` or a low `damping:` can result in a long settle-down time. Thus, the mass is usually quite small, while the stiffness and damping are usually quite large.

`init()`
  The default spring animation; it is quite heavily damped, and settles into place in about half a second. The overall `duration:` value is ignored. In terms of the previous initializer, the `mass:` is 3, the `stiffness:` is 1000, the `damping:` is 500, and the `initialVelocity:` is (0,0).

Canceling a View Animation

Once a view animation is in-flight, how can you cancel it? And what should "cancel" mean in the first place? This is one of the key areas where a property animator shows off its special powers.

Canceling a block-based animation

To illustrate the problem, I'll first show what you would have had to do before property animators were invented. Imagine a simple unidirectional positional animation, with a long duration so that we can interrupt it in midflight. To facilitate the explanation, I'll conserve both the view's original position and its final position in properties:

```
self.pOrig = self.v.center
self.pFinal = self.v.center
self.pFinal.x += 100
UIView.animateWithDuration(4, animations: {
    self.v.center = self.pFinal
})
```

Now imagine that we have a button that we can tap during that animation, and that this button is supposed to cancel the animation. How can we do that?

One possibility is to reach down to the CALayer level and call `removeAllAnimations`:

```
self.v.layer.removeAllAnimations()
```

That has the advantage of simplicity, but the effect is jarring: the "animation movie" is whipped away instantly, "jumping" the view to its final position, effectively doing what the system does automatically when the app goes into the background.

So let's try to devise a more subtle form of cancellation: the view should hurry to its final position. This is a case where the additive nature of animations actually gets in our way. We cannot merely impose another animation that moves the view to its final position with a short duration, because this doesn't cancel the existing animation. Therefore, we must remove the first animation manually. We already know how to do that: call `removeAllAnimations`. But we also know that if we do that, the view will jump to its final position; we want it to remain, for the moment, at its current position — meaning *the animation's* current position. But where on earth is that?

To find out, we have to ask the view's *presentation layer* where it currently is. We reposition the view at the location of its presentation layer, and *then* remove the animation, and *then* perform the final "hurry home" animation:

```
self.v.layer.position = self.v.layer.presentation()!.position
self.v.layer.removeAllAnimations()
UIView.animate(withDuration:0.1) {
    self.v.center = self.pFinal
}
```

Another alternative is that cancellation means returning the view to its original position. In that case, animate the view's center to its original position instead of its destination position:

```
self.v.layer.position = self.v.layer.presentation()!.position
self.v.layer.removeAllAnimations()
UIView.animate(withDuration:0.1) {
    self.v.center = self.pOrig
}
```

Yet another possibility is that cancellation means just stopping wherever we happen to be. In that case, omit the final animation:

```
self.v.layer.position = self.v.layer.presentation()!.position
self.v.layer.removeAllAnimations()
```

Canceling a property animator's animation

Now I'll show how do those things with a property animator. We don't have to reach down to the level of the layer. We don't call removeAllAnimations. We don't query the presentation layer. We don't have to memorize the start position or the end position. The property animator does all of that for us!

For the sake of ease and generality, let's hold the animator in an instance property where all of our code can see it. Here's how it is configured:

```
self.anim = UIViewPropertyAnimator(
    duration: 4, timingParameters: UICubicTimingParameters())
self.anim.addAnimations {
    self.v.center.x += 100
}
self.anim.startAnimation()
```

Here's how to cancel the animation by hurrying home to its end:

```
self.anim.pauseAnimation()
self.anim.continueAnimation(withTimingParameters: nil, durationFactor: 0.1)
```

We first *pause* the animation, because otherwise we can't make changes to it. But the animation does not visibly pause, because we resume at once with a modification of the original animation, which is smoothly blended into the existing animation. The short durationFactor: is the "hurry up" part; we want a much shorter duration than the original duration. We don't have to tell the animator where to animate to; in the absence of any other commands, it animates to its original destination. The nil value for the timingParameters: tells the animation to use the existing timing curve.

What about canceling the animation by hurrying home to its beginning? It's exactly the same, except that we reverse the animation:

```
self.anim.scrubsLinearly = false
self.anim.pauseAnimation()
self.anim.isReversed = true
self.anim.continueAnimation(withTimingParameters: nil, durationFactor: 0.1)
```

Again, we don't have to tell the animator where to animate to; it knows where we started, and reversing means to go there. Setting the animator's scrubsLinearly to false prevents a jump to the right before the reversed animation starts. (I regard the need for this in iOS 11 as a bug, because iOS 10 has no such property and no such jump.) The reason is that pausing the animation when scrubsLinearly is true (the default) causes the timing curve to change to .linear, meaning that the view is located further to the right for the amount of already elapsed time.

Using the same technique, we could interrupt the animation and hurry to anywhere we like — by adding another animation function before continuing. Here, for example, cancellation causes us to rush right off the screen:

```
self.anim.pauseAnimation()
self.anim.addAnimations {
    self.v.center = CGPoint(-200,-200)
}
self.anim.continueAnimation(withTimingParameters: nil, durationFactor: 0.1)
```

What about canceling the animation by stopping wherever we are? Just stop the animation:

```
self.anim.stopAnimation(false)
self.anim.finishAnimation(at: .current)
```

Recall that the false argument means: "Please allow me to call finish-Animation(at:)." We want to call finishAnimation(at:) in order to specify where the view should end up when the "animation movie" is removed. By passing in .current, we state that we want the animated view to end up right where it is now. If we were to pass in .start or .end, the view would *jump* to that position (if it weren't there already).

We can now understand the incoming parameter in the completion function! It is the position where we ended up. If the animation finished by proceeding to its end, that parameter is .end. If we reversed the animation and it finished by proceeding back to its start, as in our second cancellation example, that parameter is .start. If we called finishAnimation(at:), it is the at: argument we specified in the call.

Canceling a repeating animation

Finally, suppose that the animation we want to cancel is an infinitely repeating autoreversing animation. It will have to be created with the UIView class method:

```
self.pOrig = self.v.center
let opts : UIViewAnimationOptions = [.autoreverse, .repeat]
UIView.animate(withDuration:1, delay: 0, options: opts, animations: {
    self.v.center.x += 100
})
```

Let's say our idea of cancellation is to have the animated view hurry back to its original position; that is why we have saved the original position as an instance property. This is a situation where the `.beginFromCurrentState` option is useful! That's because a repeating animation is *not* additive with a further animation. It is therefore sufficient simply to impose the "hurry home" animation on top of the existing repeating animation, because it *does* contradict the repeating animation and therefore also cancels it. The `.beginFromCurrentState` option prevents the view from jumping momentarily to the "final" position, 100 points to the right, to which we set it when we initiated the repeating animation:

```
let opts : UIViewAnimationOptions = .beginFromCurrentState
UIView.animate(withDuration:0.1, delay:0, options:opts, animations: {
    self.v.center = self.pOrig
})
```

(In that example, I'm storing the view's original position as a view controller property. If you find that objectionable because it's not a very encapsulated approach, then consider storing it instead in the view's layer, using key–value coding. The implementation is left as an exercise for the reader.)

Frozen View Animation

Another important feature of a property animator is that its animation can be *frozen*. We already know that the animation can be paused — or never even started. A frozen animation is simply left in this state. It can be started or resumed at any time subsequently. Alternatively, instead of starting it, we can keep the animation frozen, but move it to a different "frame" of the animation by setting its `fractionComplete`; in this way, we can control the frozen animation manually.

In this simple example, we have in the interface a slider (a UISlider) and a small red square view. As the user slides the slider from left to right, the red view follows along — and gradually turns green, depending how far the user slides the slider. If the user slides the slider all the way to the right, the view is at the right and is fully green. If the user slides the slider all the way back to the left, the view is at the left and is fully red.

To accomplish this, the property animator is configured with an animation moving it all the way to right and turning it all the way green. But the animation is never started:

```
self.anim = UIViewPropertyAnimator(duration: 1, curve: .easeInOut) {
    self.v.center.x = self.pTarget.x
    self.v.backgroundColor = .green()
}
```

The slider, whenever the user moves it, simply changes the animator's `fraction-Complete` to match its own percentage:

```
self.anim.fractionComplete = CGFloat(slider.value)
```

Apple refers to this technique of manually moving a frozen animation back and forth from frame to frame as *scrubbing*. A common use case is that the user will touch and move the animated view itself. This will come in handy in connection with interactive view controller transitions in Chapter 6.

In that example, I deliberately set the timing curve to `.easeInOut` in order to illustrate the real purpose of the `scrubsLinearly` property, which is new in iOS 11. You would think that a nonlinear timing curve would affect the relationship between the position of the slider and the position of the view: with an `.easeInOut` timing curve, for example, the view would arrive at the far right before the slider does. But that doesn't happen, because a nonrunning animation switches its timing curve to `.linear` *automatically* for as long as it is nonrunning. The purpose of the `scrubs-Linearly` property, whose default property is true, is to allow you to turn *off* that behavior by setting it to false on the rare occasions when this might be desirable.

Custom Animatable View Properties

You can define your own custom view property that can be animated by changing it in an animations function, provided the custom view property itself changes an animatable view property.

For example, imagine a UIView subclass, MyView, which has a Bool `swing` property. All this does is reposition the view: when `swing` is set to `true`, the view's `center` x-coordinate is increased by 100; when `swing` is set to `false`, it is decreased by 100. A view's `center` is animatable, so the `swing` property *itself* can be animatable.

The trick (suggested by an Apple WWDC 2014 video) is to implement MyView's `swing` setter with a zero-duration animation:

```
class MyView : UIView {
    var swing : Bool = false {
        didSet {
            var p = self.center
            p.x = self.swing ? p.x + 100 : p.x - 100
            UIView.animate(withDuration:0) {
                self.center = p
```

```
            }
         }
      }
   }
```

If we now change a MyView's `swing` directly, the view jumps to its new position; there is no animation. But if an animations function changes the `swing` property, the `swing` setter's animation inherits the duration of the surrounding animations function — because such inheritance is, as I mentioned earlier, the default. Thus the change in position is animated, with the specified duration:

```
let anim = UIViewPropertyAnimator(duration: 1, curve: .easeInOut) {
    self.v.swing = !self.v.swing
}
anim.startAnimation()
```

Keyframe View Animation

A view animation can be described as a set of keyframes. This means that, instead of a simple beginning and end point, you specify multiple *stages* in the animation and those stages are joined together for you. This can be useful as a way of chaining animations together, or as a way of defining a complex animation that can't be described as a single change of value.

To create a keyframe animation, you call this UIView class method:

- `animateKeyframes(withDuration:delay:options:animations:completion:)`

It takes an animations function, and inside that function you call this UIView class method multiple times to specify each stage:

- `addKeyframe(withRelativeStartTime:relativeDuration:animations:)`

Each keyframe's start time and duration is between 0 and 1, *relative to the animation as a whole*. (Giving a keyframe's start time and duration in seconds is a common beginner mistake.)

For example, here I'll waggle a view back and forth horizontally while moving it down the screen vertically:

```
var p = self.v.center
let dur = 0.25
var start = 0.0
let dx : CGFloat = 100
let dy : CGFloat = 50
var dir : CGFloat = 1
UIView.animateKeyframes(withDuration:4, delay: 0, animations: {
    UIView.addKeyframe(withRelativeStartTime:start,
        relativeDuration: dur) {
```

```
            p.x += dx*dir; p.y += dy
            self.v.center = p
        }
    start += dur; dir *= -1
    UIView.addKeyframe(withRelativeStartTime:start,
        relativeDuration: dur) {
            p.x += dx*dir; p.y += dy
            self.v.center = p
        }
    start += dur; dir *= -1
    UIView.addKeyframe(withRelativeStartTime:start,
        relativeDuration: dur) {
            p.x += dx*dir; p.y += dy
            self.v.center = p
        }
    start += dur; dir *= -1
    UIView.addKeyframe(withRelativeStartTime:start,
        relativeDuration: dur) {
            p.x += dx*dir; p.y += dy
            self.v.center = p
        }
})
```

In that code, there are four keyframes, evenly spaced: each is 0.25 in duration (one-fourth of the whole animation) and each starts 0.25 later than the previous one (as soon as the previous one ends). In each keyframe, the view's center x-coordinate increases or decreases by 100, alternately, while its center y-coordinate keeps increasing by 50.

The keyframe values are points in space and time; the actual animation interpolates between them. How this interpolation is done depends upon the options: parameter (omitted in the preceding code). Several UIKeyframeAnimationOptions values have names that start with calculationMode; pick one. The default is .calculationMode-Linear. In our example, this means that the path followed by the view is a sharp zig-zag, the view seeming to bounce off invisible walls at the right and left. But if our choice is .calculationModeCubic, our view describes a smooth S-curve, starting at the view's initial position and ending at the last keyframe point, and passing through the three other keyframe points like the maxima and minima of a sine wave.

Because my keyframes are perfectly even, I could achieve the same effects by using .calculationModePaced or .calculationModeCubicPaced, respectively. The paced options ignore the relative start time and relative duration values of the keyframes; you might as well pass 0 for all of them. Instead, they divide up the times and durations evenly, exactly as my code has done.

Finally, .calculationModeDiscrete means that the changed animatable properties don't animate: the animation jumps to each keyframe.

The outer animations function can contain other changes to animatable view properties, as long as they don't conflict with the `addKeyframe` animations; these are animated over the total duration. For example:

```
UIView.animateKeyframes(withDuration:4, delay: 0, animations: {
    self.v.alpha = 0
    // ...
```

The result is that as the view zigzags back and forth down the screen, it also gradually fades away.

It is also legal and meaningful to supply a timing curve as part of the `options:` argument. Unfortunately, the documentation fails to make this clear; and Swift's obsessive-compulsive attitude toward data types resists folding a UIViewAnimation-Options timing curve directly into a value typed as a UIViewKeyframeAnimation-Options. Yet if you don't do it, the default is `.curveEaseInOut`, which may not be what you want. Here's how to combine `.calculationModeLinear` with `.curveLinear`:

```
var opts : UIViewKeyframeAnimationOptions = .calculationModeLinear
let opt2 : UIViewAnimationOptions = .curveLinear
opts.insert(UIViewKeyframeAnimationOptions(rawValue:opt2.rawValue))
```

That's two different senses of `linear`! The first means that the path described by the moving view is a sequence of straight lines. The second means that the moving view's speed along that path is steady.

You might want to pause or reverse a keyframe view animation by way of a property animator. To do so, nest your call to `UIView.animateKeyframes...` inside the property animator's animations function. The property animator's duration and timing curve are then inherited, so this is another way to dictate the keyframe animation's timing.

The power of keyframe animations often goes unappreciated by beginners. Keyframes do not have to be sequential, nor do they all have to involve the same property. Thus, they can be used to coordinate different animations. In this example, our view animates slowly to the right, and changes color suddenly *in the middle* of its movement:

```
let anim = UIViewPropertyAnimator(
    duration: 4, timingParameters: UICubicTimingParameters())
anim.addAnimations {
    UIView.animateKeyframes(withDuration: 0, delay: 0, animations: {
        UIView.addKeyframe(withRelativeStartTime: 0,
            relativeDuration: 1) {
                self.v.center.x += 100
        }
        UIView.addKeyframe(withRelativeStartTime: 0.5,
            relativeDuration: 0.25) {
                self.v.backgroundColor = .red
```

```
        }
    })
}
anim.startAnimation()
```

There are other ways to arrange the same outward effect, to be sure; but this way, the entire animation is placed under the control of a single property animator, and is thus easy to pause, scrub, reverse, and so on.

Transitions

A transition is an animation that emphasizes a view's change of content. Transitions are ordered using one of two UIView class methods:

- transition(with:duration:options:animations:completion:)
- transition(from:to:duration:options:completion:)

The transition animation types are expressed as part of the options: bitmask:

- .transitionFlipFromLeft, .transitionFlipFromRight
- .transitionCurlUp, .transitionCurlDown
- .transitionFlipFromBottom, .transitionFlipFromTop
- .transitionCrossDissolve

Transitioning one view

transition(with:...) takes one UIView parameter, and performs the transition animation on that view. In this example, a UIImageView containing an image of Mars flips over as its image changes to a smiley face; it looks as if the image view were two-sided, with Mars on one side and the smiley face on the other:

```
let opts : UIViewAnimationOptions = .transitionFlipFromLeft
UIView.transition(with:self.iv, duration: 0.8, options: opts, animations: {
    self.iv.image = UIImage(named:"Smiley")
})
```

In that example, I've put the content change inside the animations function. That's conventional but misleading; the truth is that if all that's changing is the content, *nothing* needs to go into the animations function. The change of content can be any-where, before or even after this entire line of code. It's the flip that's being animated. You might use the animations function here to order additional animations, such as a change in a view's center.

You can do the same sort of thing with a custom view that does its own drawing. Let's say that I have a UIView subclass, MyView, that draws either a rectangle or an ellipse depending on the value of its Bool reverse property:

```
class MyView : UIView {
    var reverse = false
    override func draw(_ rect: CGRect) {
        let f = self.bounds.insetBy(dx: 10, dy: 10)
        let con = UIGraphicsGetCurrentContext()!
        if self.reverse {
            con.strokeEllipse(in:f)
        }
        else {
            con.stroke(f)
        }
    }
}
```

This code flips a MyView instance while changing its drawing from a rectangle to an ellipse or *vice versa*:

```
let opts : UIViewAnimationOptions = .transitionFlipFromLeft
self.v.reverse = !self.v.reverse
UIView.transition(with:self.v, duration: 1, options: opts, animations: {
    self.v.setNeedsDisplay()
})
```

By default, if a view has subviews whose layout changes as part of a transition animation, that change in layout is *not* animated: the layout changes directly to its final appearance when the transition ends. If you want to display a subview of the transitioning view being animated as it assumes its final state, use .allowAnimatedContent in the options: bitmask.

Transitioning two views and their superview

transition(from:to:...) takes two UIView parameters; the first view is *replaced* by the second, while *their superview* undergoes the transition animation. There are two possible configurations, depending on the options: you provide:

Remove one subview, add the other
>   If .showHideTransitionViews is *not* one of the options:, then the second subview is not in the view hierarchy when we start; the transition removes the first subview from its superview and adds the second subview to that same superview.

Hide one subview, show the other
>   If .showHideTransitionViews *is* one of the options:, then both subviews are in the view hierarchy when we start; the isHidden of the first is false, the isHidden of the second is true, and the transition reverses those values.

In this example, a label `self.lab` is already in the interface. The animation causes the superview of `self.lab` to flip over, while at the same time a different label, `lab2`, is substituted for the existing label:

```
let lab2 = UILabel(frame:self.lab.frame)
lab2.text = self.lab.text == "Hello" ? "Howdy" : "Hello"
lab2.sizeToFit()
UIView.transition(from:self.lab, to: lab2,
    duration: 0.8, options: .transitionFlipFromLeft) { _ in
        self.lab = lab2
}
```

It's up to you to make sure beforehand that the second view has the desired position, so that it will appear in the right place in its superview.

Implicit Layer Animation

Animating a layer can be as simple as setting a property. A change in what the documentation calls an *animatable property* is *automatically* interpreted as a request to animate that change. In other words, animation of layer property changes is the default! Multiple property changes are considered part of the same animation. This mechanism is called *implicit animation*.

You may be wondering: if implicit animation is the default, why didn't we notice it happening in any of the layer examples in Chapter 3? It's because there are two common situations where implicit layer animation *doesn't* happen:

- Implicit layer animation doesn't operate on a UIView's underlying layer. You can animate a UIView's underlying layer directly, but you must use explicit layer animation (discussed later in this chapter).

- Implicit layer animation doesn't affect a layer as it is being created, configured, and added to the interface. Implicit animation comes into play when you change an animatable property of a layer that is *already* present in the interface.

In Chapter 3 we constructed a compass out of layers. The compass itself is a CompassView that does no drawing of its own; its underlying layer is a Compass-Layer that also does no drawing, serving only as a superlayer for the layers that constitute the drawing. None of the layers that constitute the actual drawing is the underlying layer of a view, so a property change to any of them, once they are established in the interface, is animated automatically.

So, presume that we *have* established all our compass layers in the interface. And suppose we have a reference to the arrow layer (`arrow`). If we rotate the arrow layer simply by changing its `transform` property, *the arrow rotation is animated*:

```
arrow.transform = CATransform3DRotate(arrow.transform, .pi/4.0, 0, 0, 1)
```

CALayer properties listed in the documentation as animatable in this way are anchor-Point and anchorPointZ, backgroundColor, borderColor, borderWidth, bounds, contents, contentsCenter, contentsRect, cornerRadius, isDoubleSided, isHidden, masksToBounds, opacity, position and zPosition, rasterizationScale and shouldRasterize, shadowColor, shadowOffset, shadowOpacity, shadowRadius, and sublayerTransform and transform.

In addition, a CAShapeLayer's path, strokeStart, strokeEnd, fillColor, stroke-Color, lineWidth, lineDashPhase, and miterLimit are animatable; so are a CAText-Layer's fontSize and foregroundColor, and a CAGradientLayer's colors, locations, and endPoint.

Basically, a property is animatable because there's some sensible way to interpolate the intermediate values between one value and another. The nature of the animation attached to each property is therefore generally just what you would intuitively expect. When you change a layer's isHidden property, it fades out of view (or into view). When you change a layer's contents, the old contents are dissolved into the new contents. And so forth.

 A layer's cornerRadius is animatable by explicit layer animation, or by view animation, but not by implicit layer animation.

Animation Transactions

Animation operates with respect to a *transaction* (a CATransaction), which collects all animation requests and hands them over to the animation server in a single batch. Every animation request takes place in the context of some transaction. You can make this explicit by wrapping your animation requests in calls to the CATransaction class methods begin and commit; the result is a *transaction block*. Additionally, there is always an *implicit transaction* surrounding your code, and you can operate on this implicit transaction without any begin and commit.

To modify the characteristics of an implicit animation, you modify the transaction that surrounds it. Typically, you'll use these CATransaction class methods:

setAnimationDuration(_:)
    The duration of the animation.

setAnimationTimingFunction(_:)
    A CAMediaTimingFunction; layer timing functions are discussed in the next section.

setDisableActions(_:)
    Toggles implicit animations for this transaction.

```
setCompletionBlock(_:)
```
A function (taking no parameters) to be called when the animation ends; it is called even if no animation is triggered during this transaction.

CATransaction also implements key–value coding to allow you to set and retrieve a value for an arbitrary key, similar to CALayer.

By nesting transaction blocks, you can apply different animation characteristics to different elements of an animation. You can also use transaction commands outside of any transaction block to modify the implicit transaction. So, in our previous example, we could slow down the animation of the arrow like this:

```
CATransaction.setAnimationDuration(0.8)
arrow.transform = CATransform3DRotate(arrow.transform, .pi/4.0, 0, 0, 1)
```

An important use of transactions is to turn implicit animation *off*. This is valuable because implicit animation is the default, and can be unwanted (and a performance drag). To turn off implicit animation, call `setDisableActions(true)`. There are other ways to turn off implicit animation (discussed later in this chapter), but this is the simplest.

`setCompletionBlock(_:)` is an extraordinarily useful and probably underutilized tool. The transaction's completion function signals the end, not only of the implicit layer property animations you yourself have ordered as part of this transaction, but of *all* animations ordered during this transaction, including Cocoa's own animations. Thus, it's a way to be notified when any and all animations come to an end.

The "redraw moment" that I've spoken of in connection with drawing, layout, layer property settings, and animation is actually the end of the current transaction. Thus, for example:

- You set a view's background color; the displayed color of the background is changed when the transaction ends.
- You call `setNeedsDisplay`; `draw(_:)` is called when the transaction ends.
- You call `setNeedsLayout`; layout happens when the transaction ends.
- You order an animation; the animation starts when the transaction ends.

What's really happening is this. Your code runs within an implicit transaction. Your code comes to an end, and the transaction commits itself. It is then, as part of the transaction commit procedure, that the screen is updated: first layout, then drawing, then obedience to layer property changes, then the start of any animations. The animation server then continues operating on a background thread; it has kept a reference to the transaction, and calls its completion function, if any, when the animations are over.

An explicit transaction block that orders an animation to a layer, if the block is *not preceded by any other changes to the layer*, can cause animation to begin immediately when the CATransaction class method `commit` is called, without waiting for the redraw moment, while your code continues running. In my experience, this can cause trouble (animation delegate messages cannot arrive, and the presentation layer can't be queried properly) and should be avoided.

Media Timing Functions

The CATransaction class method `setAnimationTimingFunction(_:)` takes as its parameter a media timing function (CAMediaTimingFunction). This is the Core Animation way of describing the same cubic Bézier timing curves I discussed earlier.

To specify a built-in timing curve, call the CAMediaTimingFunction initializer `init(name:)` with one of these parameters:

- `kCAMediaTimingFunctionLinear`
- `kCAMediaTimingFunctionEaseIn`
- `kCAMediaTimingFunctionEaseOut`
- `kCAMediaTimingFunctionEaseInEaseOut`
- `kCAMediaTimingFunctionDefault`

To define your own timing curve, supply the coordinates of the two Bézier control points by calling `init(controlPoints:)`. Here we define the "clunk" timing curve and apply it to the rotation of the compass arrow:

```
let clunk = CAMediaTimingFunction(controlPoints: 0.9, 0.1, 0.7, 0.9)
CATransaction.setAnimationTimingFunction(clunk)
arrow.transform = CATransform3DRotate(arrow.transform, .pi/4.0, 0, 0, 1)
```

Core Animation

Core Animation is the fundamental underlying iOS animation technology. Core Animation is *explicit layer animation*, and revolves primarily around the CAAnimation class and its subclasses, which allow you the fullest possible freedom in specifying animations. Among other things:

- Core Animation works even on a view's underlying layer. Thus, Core Animation is the *only* way to apply full-on layer property animation to a view.
- Core Animation allows animations to be grouped into complex combinations.
- Core Animation provides transition animation effects that aren't available otherwise, such as new content "pushing" the previous content out of a layer.

View animation and implicit layer animation are merely convenient façades for Core Animation. Conceivably, you might never program at the level of Core Animation; view animation and implicit layer animation could give you everything you need. Still, you should read this section anyway, if only to learn how animation really works.

 Animating a view's underlying layer with Core Animation is layer animation, not view animation — so you don't get any automatic layout of that view's subviews. This can be a reason for preferring view animation.

CABasicAnimation and Its Inheritance

The simplest way to animate a property with Core Animation is with a CABasicAnimation object. CABasicAnimation derives much of its power through its inheritance, so I'll describe that inheritance along with CABasicAnimation itself. You will readily see that all the property animation features we have met already are embodied in a CABasicAnimation instance.

CAAnimation
  CAAnimation is an abstract class, meaning that you'll only ever use a subclass of it. Some of CAAnimation's powers come from its implementation of the CAMediaTiming protocol.

  delegate
    An adopter of the CAAnimationDelegate protocol. The delegate messages are:

    • `animationDidStart(_:)`

    • `animationDidStop(_:finished:)`

    A CAAnimation instance *retains its delegate*; this is very unusual behavior and can cause trouble if you're not conscious of it (I'm speaking from experience). Alternatively, don't set a delegate; to make your code run after the animation ends, call the CATransaction class method `setCompletion-Block(_:)` before configuring the animation.

  `duration`, `timingFunction`
    The length of the animation, and its timing function (a CAMediaTiming-Function). A duration of 0 (the default) means 0.25 seconds unless overridden by the transaction.

  `autoreverses`, `repeatCount`, `repeatDuration`
    For an infinite `repeatCount`, use `Float.infinity`. The `repeatDuration` property is a different way to govern repetition, specifying how long the

repetition should continue rather than how many repetitions should occur; don't specify both a repeatCount and a repeatDuration.

beginTime
    The delay before the animation starts. To delay an animation with respect to now, call CACurrentMediaTime and add the desired delay in seconds. The delay does not eat into the animation's duration.

timeOffset
    A shift in the animation's overall timing; looked at another way, specifies the starting frame of the "animation movie," which is treated as a loop. For example, consider an animation with a duration of 8 and a time offset of 4: it plays its second half followed by its first half.

CAAnimation, along with all its subclasses, implements key–value coding to allow you to set and retrieve a value for an arbitrary key, similar to CALayer (Chapter 3) and CATransaction.

CAPropertyAnimation
    CAPropertyAnimation is a subclass of CAAnimation. It too is abstract, and adds the following:

keyPath
    The all-important string specifying the CALayer key that is to be animated. Recall from Chapter 3 that CALayer properties are accessible through KVC keys; now we are using those keys! The convenience initializer init(key-Path:) creates the instance and assigns it a keyPath.

isAdditive
    If true, the values supplied by the animation are added to the current presentation layer value.

isCumulative
    If true, a repeating animation starts each repetition where the previous repetition ended rather than jumping back to the start value.

valueFunction
    Converts a simple scalar value that you supply into a transform.

 There is no animatable CALayer key called "frame". To animate a layer's frame using explicit layer animation, if both its position and bounds are to change, you must animate both. Similarly, you cannot use explicit layer animation to animate a layer's affineTransform property, because affineTransform is not a property (it's a pair of convenience methods); you must animate its transform instead. Attempting to form an animation with a key path of "frame" or "affineTransform" is a common beginner error.

CABasicAnimation

CABasicAnimation is a subclass (not abstract!) of CAPropertyAnimation. It adds the following:

`fromValue`, `toValue`

The starting and ending values for the animation. These values must be Objective-C objects, so numbers and structs will have to be wrapped accordingly, using NSNumber and NSValue; fortunately, Swift will automatically take care of this for you. If neither `fromValue` nor `toValue` is provided, the former and current values of the property are used. If just one of them is provided, the other uses the current value of the property.

`byValue`

Expresses one of the endpoint values as a *difference* from the other rather than in absolute terms. So you would supply a `byValue` instead of a `from-Value` or instead of a `toValue`, and the actual `fromValue` or `toValue` would be calculated for you by subtraction or addition with respect to the other value. If you supply *only* a `byValue`, the `fromValue` is the property's current value.

Using a CABasicAnimation

Having constructed and configured a CABasicAnimation, the way you order it to be performed is to *add it to a layer*. This is done with the CALayer instance method `add(_:forKey:)`. (I'll discuss the purpose of the `forKey:` parameter later; it's fine to ignore it and use `nil`, as I do in the examples that follow.)

However, there's a slight twist. A CAAnimation is *merely* an animation; all it does is describe the hoops that the presentation layer is to jump through, the "animation movie" that is to be presented. It has no effect on the layer *itself*. Thus, if you naïvely create a CABasicAnimation and add it to a layer with `add(_:forKey:)`, the animation happens and then the "animation movie" is whipped away to reveal the layer sitting there in exactly the same state as before. It is up to *you* to change the layer to match what the animation will ultimately portray. The converse, of course, is that you *don't* have to change the layer if it *doesn't* change as a result of the animation.

To ensure good results, start by taking a plodding, formulaic approach to the use of CABasicAnimation, like this:

1. Capture the start and end values for the layer property you're going to change, because you're likely to need these values in what follows.

2. Change the layer property to its end value, first calling `setDisable-Actions(true)` if necessary to prevent implicit animation.

3. Construct the explicit animation, using the start and end values you captured earlier, and with its `keyPath` corresponding to the layer property you just changed.

4. Add the explicit animation to the layer.

An explicit animation is *copied* when it is added to a layer. That's why the animation must be configured first and added to the layer later. The copy added to the layer is immutable after that.

Here's how you'd use this approach to animate our compass arrow rotation:

```
// capture the start and end values
let startValue = arrow.transform
let endValue = CATransform3DRotate(startValue, .pi/4.0, 0, 0, 1)
// change the layer, without implicit animation
CATransaction.setDisableActions(true)
arrow.transform = endValue
// construct the explicit animation
let anim = CABasicAnimation(keyPath:#keyPath(CALayer.transform))
anim.duration = 0.8
let clunk = CAMediaTimingFunction(controlPoints:0.9, 0.1, 0.7, 0.9)
anim.timingFunction = clunk
anim.fromValue = startValue
anim.toValue = endValue
// ask for the explicit animation
arrow.add(anim, forKey:nil)
```

Once you're comfortable with the full form, you will find that in many cases it can be condensed. For example, when the `fromValue` and `toValue` are not set, the former and current values of the property are used automatically. (This magic is possible because, at the time the CABasicAnimation is added to the layer, the presentation layer still has the former value of the property, while the layer itself has the new value; thus, the CABasicAnimation is able to retrieve them.) In our example, therefore, there is no need to set the `fromValue` and `toValue`, and no need to capture the start and end values beforehand. Here's the condensed version:

```
CATransaction.setDisableActions(true)
arrow.transform = CATransform3DRotate(arrow.transform, .pi/4.0, 0, 0, 1)
let anim = CABasicAnimation(keyPath:#keyPath(CALayer.transform))
anim.duration = 0.8
let clunk = CAMediaTimingFunction(controlPoints:0.9, 0.1, 0.7, 0.9)
anim.timingFunction = clunk
arrow.add(anim, forKey:nil)
```

As I mentioned earlier, you will omit changing the layer if it doesn't change as a result of the animation. For example, let's make the compass arrow appear to vibrate rapidly, without ultimately changing its current orientation. To do this, we'll waggle it back and forth, using a repeated animation, between slightly clockwise from its current position and slightly counterclockwise from its current position. The "animation movie" neither starts nor stops at the current position of the arrow, but for this animation it doesn't matter, because it all happens so quickly as to appear natural:

```
// capture the start and end values
let nowValue = arrow.transform
let startValue = CATransform3DRotate(nowValue, .pi/40.0, 0, 0, 1)
let endValue = CATransform3DRotate(nowValue, -.pi/40.0, 0, 0, 1)
// construct the explicit animation
let anim = CABasicAnimation(keyPath:#keyPath(CALayer.transform))
anim.duration = 0.05
anim.timingFunction =
    CAMediaTimingFunction(name:kCAMediaTimingFunctionLinear)
anim.repeatCount = 3
anim.autoreverses = true
anim.fromValue = startValue
anim.toValue = endValue
// ask for the explicit animation
arrow.add(anim, forKey:nil)
```

That code, too, can be shortened considerably from its full form. We can eliminate the need to calculate the new rotation values based on the arrow's current transform by setting our animation's isAdditive property to true; this means that the animation's property values are added to the existing property value for us, so that they are relative, not absolute. For a transform, "added" means "matrix-multiplied," so we can describe the waggle without any reference to the arrow's current rotation. Moreover, because our rotation is so simple (around a cardinal axis), we can take advantage of CAPropertyAnimation's valueFunction; the animation's property values can then be simple scalars (in this case, angles), because the valueFunction tells the animation to interpret these as rotations around the z-axis:

```
let anim = CABasicAnimation(keyPath:#keyPath(CALayer.transform))
anim.duration = 0.05
anim.timingFunction =
    CAMediaTimingFunction(name:kCAMediaTimingFunctionLinear)
anim.repeatCount = 3
anim.autoreverses = true
anim.isAdditive = true
anim.valueFunction = CAValueFunction(name:kCAValueFunctionRotateZ)
anim.fromValue = Float.pi/40
anim.toValue = -Float.pi/40
arrow.add(anim, forKey:nil)
```

 Instead of using a valueFunction, we could have set the animation's key path to "transform.rotation.z" to achieve the same effect. However, Apple advises against this, as it can result in mathematical trouble when there is more than one rotation.

Let's return once more to our arrow "clunk" rotation for one final alternative implementation using the isAdditive and valueFunction properties. We set the arrow layer to its final transform at the outset, so when the time comes to configure the animation, its toValue, in isAdditive terms, will be 0; the fromValue will be its current value expressed *negatively*, like this:

```
let rot = CGFloat.pi/4.0
CATransaction.setDisableActions(true)
arrow.transform = CATransform3DRotate(arrow.transform, rot, 0, 0, 1)
// construct animation additively
let anim = CABasicAnimation(keyPath:#keyPath(CALayer.transform))
anim.duration = 0.8
let clunk = CAMediaTimingFunction(controlPoints:0.9, 0.1, 0.7, 0.9)
anim.timingFunction = clunk
anim.fromValue = -rot
anim.toValue = 0
anim.isAdditive = true
anim.valueFunction = CAValueFunction(name:kCAValueFunctionRotateZ)
arrow.add(anim, forKey:nil)
```

That is an interesting way of describing the animation; in effect, it expresses the animation in reverse, regarding the final position as correct and the current position as an aberration to be corrected. It also happens to be how additive view animations are rewritten behind the scenes, and explains their behavior.

 Interesting effects can be achieved by using explicit layer animation, such as a CABasicAnimation, on a CAReplicatorLayer. I'll give an example in Chapter 12.

Springing Animation

Starting in iOS 9, springing animation is exposed at the Core Animation level, through the CASpringAnimation class (a CABasicAnimation subclass). Its properties are the same as the parameters of the fullest form of the UISpringTimingParameters initializer, except that its initialVelocity is a CGFloat, not a CGVector. The duration is ignored, but don't omit it. The actual duration calculated from your specifications can be extracted as the settlingDuration property. For example:

```
CATransaction.setDisableActions(true)
self.v.layer.position.y += 100
let anim = CASpringAnimation(keyPath: #keyPath(CALayer.position))
anim.damping = 0.7
anim.initialVelocity = 20
anim.mass = 0.04
anim.stiffness = 4
anim.duration = 1 // ignored, but you need to supply something
self.v.layer.add(anim, forKey: nil)
```

Keyframe Animation

Keyframe animation (CAKeyframeAnimation) is an alternative to basic animation (CABasicAnimation); they are both subclasses of CAPropertyAnimation, and they are used in similar ways. The difference is that you need to tell the keyframe animation what the keyframes are. In these simplest case, you can just set its `values` array. This tells the animation its starting value, its ending value, and some specific values through which it should pass on the way between them.

Here's a new version of our animation for waggling the compass arrow, expressing it as a keyframe animation. The stages include the start and end states and eight alternating waggles in between, with the degree of waggle becoming progressively smaller:

```
var values = [0.0]
let directions = sequence(first:1) {$0 * -1}
let bases = stride(from: 20, to: 60, by: 5)
for (base, dir) in zip(bases, directions) {
    values.append(Double(dir) * .pi / Double(base))
}
values.append(0.0)
let anim = CAKeyframeAnimation(keyPath:#keyPath(CALayer.transform))
anim.values = values
anim.isAdditive = true
anim.valueFunction = CAValueFunction(name: kCAValueFunctionRotateZ)
arrow.add(anim, forKey:nil)
```

Here are some CAKeyframeAnimation properties:

values
> The array of values that the animation is to adopt, including the starting and ending value.

timingFunctions
> An array of timing functions, one for each stage of the animation (so that this array will be one element shorter than the `values` array).

keyTimes
> An array of times to accompany the array of values, defining when each value should be reached. The times start at 0 and are expressed as increasing fractions of 1, ending at 1.

calculationMode
> Describes how the `values` are treated to create *all* the values through which the animation must pass:
>
> - The default is `kCAAnimationLinear`, a simple straight-line interpolation from value to value.
>
> - `kCAAnimationCubic` constructs a single smooth curve passing through all the values (and additional advanced properties, `tensionValues`, `continuityValues`, and `biasValues`, allow you to refine the curve).

- kCAAnimationPaced and kCAAnimationCubicPaced means the timing functions and key times are ignored, and the velocity is made constant through the whole animation.

- kCAAnimationDiscrete means no interpolation: we jump directly to each value at the corresponding key time.

path

When you're animating a property whose values are pairs of floats (CGPoints), this is an alternative way of describing the values; instead of a values array, which must be interpolated to arrive at the intermediate values along the way, you supply the entire interpolation as a single CGPath. The points used to define the path are the keyframe values, so you can still apply timing functions and key times. If you're animating a position, the rotationMode property lets you ask the animated object to rotate so as to remain perpendicular to the path.

In this example, the values array is a sequence of five images (self.images) to be presented successively and repeatedly in a layer's contents, like the frames in a movie; the effect is similar to image animation, discussed earlier in this chapter:

```
let anim = CAKeyframeAnimation(keyPath:#keyPath(CALayer.contents))
anim.values = self.images.map {$0.cgImage!}
anim.keyTimes = [0.0, 0.25, 0.5, 0.75, 1.0]
anim.calculationMode = kCAAnimationDiscrete
anim.duration = 1.5
anim.repeatCount = .infinity
self.sprite.add(anim, forKey:nil) // sprite is a CALayer
```

Making a Property Animatable

So far, we've been animating built-in animatable properties. If you define your own property on a CALayer subclass, you can easily make that property animatable through a CAPropertyAnimation. For example, here we animate the increase or decrease in a CALayer subclass property called thickness, using essentially the pattern for explicit animation that we've already developed:

```
let lay = self.v.layer as! MyLayer
let cur = lay.thickness
let val : CGFloat = cur == 10 ? 0 : 10
lay.thickness = val
let ba = CABasicAnimation(keyPath:#keyPath(MyLayer.thickness))
ba.fromValue = cur
lay.add(ba, forKey:nil)
```

To make our layer responsive to such a command, it needs a thickness property (obviously), and it must return true from the class method needsDisplay(forKey:) for this property:

```
class MyLayer : CALayer {
    @objc var thickness : CGFloat = 0
    override class func needsDisplay(forKey key: String) -> Bool {
        if key == #keyPath(thickness) {
            return true
        }
        return super.needsDisplay(forKey:key)
    }
}
```

Returning `true` from `needsDisplay(forKey:)` causes this layer to be redisplayed repeatedly as the `thickness` property changes. So if we want to *see* the animation, this layer also needs to draw itself in some way that depends on the `thickness` property. Here, I'll implement the layer's `draw(in:)` to make `thickness` the thickness of the black border around a red rectangle:

```
override func draw(in con: CGContext) {
    let r = self.bounds.insetBy(dx:20, dy:20)
    con.setFillColor(UIColor.red.cgColor)
    con.fill(r)
    con.setLineWidth(self.thickness)
    con.stroke(r)
}
```

At every frame of the animation, `draw(in:)` is called, and because the `thickness` value differs at each step, it appears animated.

We have made MyLayer's `thickness` property animatable when using explicit layer animation, but it would be even cooler to make it animatable when using implicit layer animation (that is, when setting `lay.thickness` directly). Later in this chapter, I'll show how to do that.

 No law says that you *have* to draw in response to animated changes in a layer property. Consider layer animation more abstractly as a way of getting the runtime to calculate and send you timed interpolated value changes! The possibilities are limitless.

Grouped Animations

A grouped animation (CAAnimationGroup) combines multiple animations into one, by means of its `animations` property (an array of animations). By delaying and timing the various component animations, complex effects can be achieved.

A CAAnimationGroup is itself an animation; it is a CAAnimation subclass, so it has a `duration` and other animation features. Think of the CAAnimationGroup as the parent, and its `animations` as its children. Then *the children inherit default property values from their parent*. Thus, for example, if you don't set a child's duration explicitly, it will inherit the parent's duration.

Let's use a grouped animation to construct a sequence where the compass arrow rotates and then waggles. This requires very little modification of code we've already written. We express the first animation in its full form, with explicit fromValue and toValue. We postpone the second animation using its beginTime property; notice that we express this in relative terms, as a number of seconds into the parent's duration, not with respect to CACurrentMediaTime. Finally, we set the overall parent duration to the sum of the child durations, so that it can embrace both of them (failing to do this, and then wondering why some child animations never occur, is a common beginner error):

```
// capture current value, set final value
let rot = .pi/4.0
CATransaction.setDisableActions(true)
let current = arrow.value(forKeyPath:"transform.rotation.z") as! Double
arrow.setValue(current + rot, forKeyPath:"transform.rotation.z")
// first animation (rotate and clunk)
let anim1 = CABasicAnimation(keyPath:#keyPath(CALayer.transform))
anim1.duration = 0.8
let clunk = CAMediaTimingFunction(controlPoints:0.9, 0.1, 0.7, 0.9)
anim1.timingFunction = clunk
anim1.fromValue = current
anim1.toValue = current + rot
anim1.valueFunction = CAValueFunction(name:kCAValueFunctionRotateZ)
// second animation (waggle)
var values = [0.0]
let directions = sequence(first:1) {$0 * -1}
let bases = stride(from: 20, to: 60, by: 5)
for (base, dir) in zip(bases, directions) {
    values.append(Double(dir) * .pi / Double(base))
}
values.append(0.0)
let anim2 = CAKeyframeAnimation(keyPath:#keyPath(CALayer.transform))
anim2.values = values
anim2.duration = 0.25
anim2.isAdditive = true
anim2.beginTime = anim1.duration - 0.1
anim2.valueFunction = CAValueFunction(name: kCAValueFunctionRotateZ)
// group
let group = CAAnimationGroup()
group.animations = [anim1, anim2]
group.duration = anim1.duration + anim2.duration
arrow.add(group, forKey:nil)
```

In that example, I grouped two animations that animated the same property sequentially. Now let's go to the other extreme and group some animations that animate different properties simultaneously. I have a small view (self.v), located near the top-right corner of the screen, whose layer contents are a picture of a sailboat facing to the left. I'll "sail" the boat in a curving path, both down the screen and left and right across the screen, like an extended letter "S" (Figure 4-2). Each time the boat comes

Figure 4-2. A boat and the course she'll sail

to a vertex of the curve, changing direction across the screen, I'll flip the boat so that it faces the way it's about to move. At the same time, I'll constantly rock the boat, so that it always appears to be pitching a little on the waves.

Here's the first animation, the movement of the boat along its curving path. It illustrates the use of a CAKeyframeAnimation with a CGPath; the calculationMode of kCAAnimationPaced ensures an even speed over the whole path. We don't set an explicit duration because we want to adopt the duration of the group:

```
let h : CGFloat = 200
let v : CGFloat = 75
let path = CGMutablePath()
var leftright : CGFloat = 1
var next : CGPoint = self.v.layer.position
var pos : CGPoint
path.move(to:CGPoint(next.x, next.y))
for _ in 0 ..< 4 {
    pos = next
    leftright *= -1
    next = CGPoint(pos.x+h*leftright, pos.y+v)
    path.addCurve(to:CGPoint(next.x, next.y),
        control1: CGPoint(pos.x, pos.y+30),
        control2: CGPoint(next.x, next.y-30))
}
let anim1 = CAKeyframeAnimation(keyPath:#keyPath(CALayer.position))
anim1.path = path
anim1.calculationMode = kCAAnimationPaced
```

Here's the second animation, the reversal of the direction the boat is facing. This is simply a rotation around the y-axis. It's another CAKeyframeAnimation, but we make no attempt at visually animating this reversal: the calculationMode is kCAAnimationDiscrete, so that the boat image reversal is a sudden change, as in our earlier "sprite" example. There is one less value than the number of points in our first animation's path, and the first animation has an even speed, so the reversals take place at each curve apex with no further effort on our part. (If the pacing were more complicated, we could give both the first and the second animation identical keyTimes arrays, to coordinate them.) Once again, we don't set an explicit duration:

```
let revs = [0.0, .pi, 0.0, .pi]
let anim2 = CAKeyframeAnimation(keyPath:#keyPath(CALayer.transform))
anim2.values = revs
anim2.valueFunction = CAValueFunction(name:kCAValueFunctionRotateY)
anim2.calculationMode = kCAAnimationDiscrete
```

Here's the third animation, the rocking of the boat. It has a short duration, and repeats indefinitely:

```
let pitches = [0.0, .pi/60.0, 0.0, -.pi/60.0, 0.0]
let anim3 = CAKeyframeAnimation(keyPath:#keyPath(CALayer.transform))
anim3.values = pitches
anim3.repeatCount = .infinity
anim3.duration = 0.5
anim3.isAdditive = true
anim3.valueFunction = CAValueFunction(name:kCAValueFunctionRotateZ)
```

Finally, we combine the three animations, assigning the group an explicit duration that will be adopted by the first two animations. As we hand the animation over to the layer displaying the boat, we also change the layer's position to match the final position from the first animation, so that the boat won't jump back to its original position afterward:

```
let group = CAAnimationGroup()
group.animations = [anim1, anim2, anim3]
group.duration = 8
self.v.layer.add(group, forKey:nil)
CATransaction.setDisableActions(true)
self.v.layer.position = next
```

Here are some further CAAnimation properties (from the CAMediaTiming protocol) that come into play especially when animations are grouped:

speed

> The ratio between a child's timescale and the parent's timescale. For example, if a parent and child have the same duration, but the child's speed is 1.5, its animation runs one-and-a-half times as fast as the parent.

fillMode

> Suppose the child animation begins after the parent animation, or ends before the parent animation, or both. What should happen to the appearance of the

property being animated, outside the child animation's boundaries? The answer depends on the child's fillMode:

- kCAFillModeRemoved means the child animation is removed, revealing the layer property at its actual current value whenever the child is not running.
- kCAFillModeForwards means the final presentation layer value of the child animation remains afterward.
- kCAFillModeBackwards means the initial presentation layer value of the child animation appears right from the start.
- kCAFillModeBoth combines the previous two.

Freezing an Animation

An animation can be frozen at the level of the layer, with an effect similar to what we did with a property animator earlier. CALayer adopts the CAMediaTiming protocol. Thus, a layer can have a speed. This will affect any animation attached to it. A CALayer with a speed of 2 will play a 10-second animation in 5 seconds. A CALayer with a speed of 0 effectively freezes any animation attached to the layer.

A layer can also have a timeOffset. You can thus change the timeOffset to display any single frame of the layer's animation.

To illustrate freezing an animation at the CALayer level, let's explore the animatable path property of a CAShapeLayer. Consider a layer that can display a rectangle or an ellipse *or any of the intermediate shapes between them*. I can't imagine what the notion of an intermediate shape between a rectangle or an ellipse may mean, let alone how to draw such an intermediate shape; but thanks to frozen animations, I don't have to. Here, I'll construct the CAShapeLayer, add it to the interface, give it an animation from a rectangle to an ellipse, and keep a reference to it as a property:

```
let shape = CAShapeLayer()
shape.frame = v.bounds
v.layer.addSublayer(shape)
shape.fillColor = UIColor.clear.cgColor
shape.strokeColor = UIColor.red.cgColor
let path = CGPath(rect:shape.bounds, transform:nil)
shape.path = path
let path2 = CGPath(ellipseIn:shape.bounds, transform:nil)
let ba = CABasicAnimation(keyPath:#keyPath(CAShapeLayer.path))
ba.duration = 1
ba.fromValue = path
ba.toValue = path2
shape.speed = 0
shape.timeOffset = 0
shape.add(ba, forKey: nil)
self.shape = shape
```

I've added the animation to the layer, but because the layer's speed is 0, no animation takes place; the rectangle is displayed and that's all. As in my earlier example, there's a UISlider in the interface. I'll respond to the user changing the value of the slider by setting the frame of the animation:

```
self.shape.timeOffset = Double(slider.value)
```

Transitions

A layer transition is an animation involving two "copies" of a single layer, in which the second "copy" appears to replace the first. It is described by an instance of CATransition (a CAAnimation subclass), which has these chief properties specifying the animation:

type
> Your choices are:
>
> - kCATransitionFade
> - kCATransitionMoveIn
> - kCATransitionPush
> - kCATransitionReveal

subtype
> If the type is not kCATransitionFade, your choices are:
>
> - kCATransitionFromRight
> - kCATransitionFromLeft
> - kCATransitionFromTop
> - kCATransitionFromBottom

 For historical reasons, the terms bottom and top in the names of the subtype settings have the opposite of their expected meanings.

To understand a layer transition, first implement one without changing anything else about the layer:

```
let t = CATransition()
t.type = kCATransitionPush
t.subtype = kCATransitionFromBottom
t.duration = 2
lay.add(t, forKey: nil)
```

The entire layer exits moving down from its original place while fading away, and another copy of the very same layer enters moving down from above while fading in. If, at the same time, we change something about the layer's contents, then the old

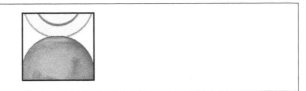

Figure 4-3. A push transition

contents will appear to exit downward while the new contents appear to enter from above:

```
// ... configure the transition as before ...
CATransaction.setDisableActions(true)
lay.contents = UIImage(named: "Smiley")!.cgImage
lay.add(t, forKey: nil)
```

A common device is for the layer that is to be transitioned to be inside a superlayer that is exactly the same size and whose masksToBounds is true. This confines the visible transition to the bounds of the layer itself. Otherwise, the entering and exiting versions of the layer are visible outside the layer. In Figure 4-3, which shows a smiley face pushing an image of Mars out of the layer, I've emphasized this arrangement by giving the superlayer a border as well.

A transition on a superlayer can happen simultaneously with animation of a sublayer. The animation will be seen to occur on the second "copy" of the layer as it moves into position. This is analogous to the .allowAnimatedContent option for a view animation.

Animations List

The method that asks for an explicit animation to happen is CALayer's add(_:for-Key:). To understand how this method actually works (and what the "key" is), you need to know about a layer's *animations list*.

An animation is an object (a CAAnimation) that modifies how a layer is drawn. It does this merely by being attached to the layer; the layer's drawing mechanism does the rest. A layer maintains a list of animations that are currently in force. To add an animation to this list, you call add(_:forKey:). When the time comes to draw itself, the layer looks through its animations list and draws itself in accordance with whatever animations it finds there. (The list of things the layer must do in order to draw itself is sometimes referred to by the documentation as the *render tree*.) The order in which animations were added to the list is the order in which they are applied.

The animations list is maintained in a curious way. The list is not exactly a dictionary, but it behaves somewhat like a dictionary. An animation has a key — the forKey: parameter in add(_:forKey:). If an animation with a certain key is added to the list, and an animation with that key is already in the list, the one that is already in the list is removed. Thus a rule is maintained that *only one animation with a given key* can be in the list at a time — the *exclusivity rule*. This explains why sometimes ordering an animation can cancel an animation already ordered or in-flight: the two animations had the same key, so the first one was removed. (Additive view animations affecting the same property work around this limitation by giving the additional animations a *different key name* — for example, `"position"` and `"position-2"`.)

It is also possible to add an animation with *no key* (the key is `nil`); it is then *not* subject to the exclusivity rule (that is, there can be more than one animation in the list with no key).

The `forKey:` parameter in `add(_:forKey:)` is thus *not a property name*. It *could* be a property name, but it can be any arbitrary value. Its purpose is to enforce the exclusivity rule. It does *not* have any meaning with regard to what property a CAProperty-Animation animates; that is the job of the animation's `keyPath`. (Apple's use of the term "key" in `add(_:forKey:)` is thus unfortunate and misleading; I wish they had named this method `add(_:identifier:)` or something like that.)

However, there *is* a relationship between the "key" in `add(_:forKey:)` and a CAPropertyAnimation's `keyPath`. If a CAPropertyAnimation's `keyPath` is `nil` at the time that it is added to a layer with `add(_:forKey:)`, *that keyPath is set to the forKey: value*. Thus, you can *misuse* the `forKey:` parameter in `add(_:forKey:)` as a way of specifying what `keyPath` an animation animates. (Implicit layer animation crucially depends on this fact.)

 I have seen many prominent but misleading examples that use this technique, apparently in the mistaken belief that the "key" in `add(_:forKey:)` is the way you are *supposed* to specify what property to animate. *This is wrong.* Set the animation's `keyPath` explicitly (as do all my examples); that's what it's for.

You can use the exclusivity rule to your own advantage, to keep your code from stepping on its own feet. Some code of yours might add an animation to the list using a certain key; then later, some other code might come along and correct this, removing that animation and replacing it with another. By using the same key, the second code is easily able to override the first: "You may have been given some other animation with this key, but throw it away; play this one instead."

In some cases, the key you supply is ignored and a different key is substituted. In particular, the key with which a CATransition is added to the list is always `kCATransition` (which happens to be `"transition"`); thus there can be only one transition animation in the list.

You can think of an animation in a layer's animations list as being the "animation movie" I spoke of at the start of this chapter. As long as an animation is in the list, the movie is present, either waiting to be played or actually playing. An animation that has finished playing is, in general, pointless; the animation should now be removed from the list, as its presence serves no purpose and it imposes an extra burden on the render tree. Therefore, an animation has an isRemovedOnCompletion property, which defaults to true: when the "movie" is over, the animation removes itself from the list.

 You may encounter examples that set isRemovedOnCompletion to false and set the animation's fillMode to kCAFillModeForwards or kCAFillModeBoth, as a way of causing the layer to keep the appearance of the last frame of the "animation movie" even after the animation is over, and preventing a property from apparently jumping back to its initial value when the animation ends. *This is wrong.* The correct approach, as I have explained, is to change the property value to match the final frame of the animation. The proper use of kCAFillMode-Forwards is in connection with a child animation within a grouped animation.

You can't access the entire animations list directly. You can access the key names of the animations in the list, with animationKeys; and you can obtain or remove an animation with a certain key, with animation(forKey:) and removeAnimation(for-Key:); but animations with a nil key are inaccessible. You can, however, remove all animations, including animations with a nil key, using removeAllAnimations. When your app is suspended, removeAllAnimations is called on all layers for you; that is why it is possible to suspend an app coherently in the middle of an animation.

If an animation is in-flight when you remove it from the animations list manually, by calling removeAllAnimations or removeAnimation(forKey:), it will stop; however, that doesn't happen until the next redraw moment. You might be able to work around this, if you need an animation to be removed immediately, by wrapping the call in an explicit transaction block.

Actions

For the sake of completeness, I will now explain how implicit animation really works — that is, how implicit animation is turned into explicit animation behind the scenes. The basis of implicit animation is the *action mechanism*. Feel free to skip this section if you don't want to get into the under-the-hood nitty-gritty of implicit animation.

What an Action Is

An *action* is an object that adopts the CAAction protocol. This means simply that it implements run(forKey:object:arguments:). The action object could do *anything* in response to this message. The notion of an action is completely general. The only built-in class that adopts the CAAction protocol is CAAnimation, but in fact the action object doesn't have to be an animation — it doesn't even have to perform an animation.

You would never send `run(forKey:object:arguments:)` to an object directly. Rather, this message is sent to an action object for you, as the basis of implicit animation. The key is the property that was set, and the `object` is the layer whose property was set.

What an animation does when it receives `run(forKey:object:arguments:)` is to assume that the `object:` is a layer, and to add itself to that layer's animations list. Thus, for an animation, receiving the `run(forKey:object:arguments:)` message is like being told: "Play yourself!"

This is where the rule comes into play, which I mentioned earlier, that if an animation's `keyPath` is `nil`, the key by which the animation is assigned to a layer's animations list is used as the `keyPath`. When an animation is sent `run(for-Key:object:arguments:)`, it calls `add(_:forKey:)` to add itself to the layer's animation's list, *using the name of the property as the key*. The animation's `keyPath` for an implicit layer animation is usually `nil`, so the animation's `keyPath` winds up being set to the same key! That is how the property that you set ends up being the property that is animated.

Action Search

When you set a property of a layer, you trigger the *action search*: the layer *searches* for an action object (a CAAction) to which it can send the `run(for-Key:object:arguments:)` message. The procedure by which the layer searches for this object is quite elaborate.

The search for an action object begins when something causes the layer to be sent the `action(forKey:)` message. Three sorts of event can cause this to happen:

- A CALayer property is set — by calling the setter method explicitly, by setting the property itself, or by means of `setValue(_:forKey:)`. All animatable properties, and indeed most (or all) other built-in CALayer properties, will call `action(for-Key:)` in response to being set.

    (Setting a layer's `frame` property sets its `position` and `bounds` and calls `action(forKey:)` for the `"position"` and `"bounds"` keys. Calling a layer's `set-AffineTransform(_:)` method sets its `transform` and calls `action(forKey:)` for the `"transform"` key. You can configure a custom property to call `action(for-Key:)` by designating it as `@NSManaged`, as I'll demonstrate later in this chapter.)

- The layer is sent `setValue(_:forKey:)` with a key that is *not* a property. This is because CALayer's `setValue(_:forUndefinedKey:)`, by default, calls `action(for-Key:)`.

- Various other miscellaneous types of event take place, such as the layer being added to the interface. I'll give some examples later in this chapter.

CATransaction's `setDisableActions(_:)`, with an argument of `true`, prevents the `action(forKey:)` message from being sent. That's how it actually works behind the scenes.

At each stage of the action search, the following rules are obeyed regarding what is returned from that stage of the search:

An action object
> If an action object is produced, that is the end of the search. The action mechanism sends that action object the `run(forKey:object:arguments:)` message; if this an animation, the animation responds by adding itself to the layer's animations list.

`NSNull()`
> If `NSNull()` is produced, that is the end of the search. There will be no implicit animation; `NSNull()` means, "Do nothing and stop searching."

`nil`
> If `nil` is produced, the search continues to the next stage.

The action search proceeds by stages, as follows:

1. The layer's `action(forKey:)` might terminate the search before it even starts. The layer will do this if it is the underlying layer of a view, or if the layer is not part of a window's layer hierarchy. In such a case, there should be no implicit animation, so the whole mechanism is nipped in the bud. (This stage is special in that a returned value of `nil` ends the search and no animation takes place.)

2. If the layer has a delegate that implements `action(for:forKey:)`, that message is sent to the delegate, with this layer as the first parameter and the property name as the key. If an action object or `NSNull()` is returned, the search ends.

3. The layer has a property called `actions`, which is a dictionary. If there is an entry in this dictionary with the given key, that value is used, and the search ends.

4. The layer has a property called `style`, which is a dictionary. If there is an entry in this dictionary with the key `actions`, it is assumed to be a dictionary; if this `actions` dictionary has an entry with the given key, that value is used, and the search ends. Otherwise, if there is an entry in the `style` dictionary called `style`, the same search is performed within it, and so on recursively until either an `actions` entry with the given key is found (the search ends) or there are no more `style` entries (the search continues).

   (If the `style` dictionary sounds profoundly weird, that's because it is profoundly weird. It is actually a special case of a larger, separate mechanism, which is also profoundly weird, having to do not with actions, but with a CALayer's implementation of KVC. When you call `value(forKey:)` on a layer, if the key is undefined by the layer itself, the `style` dictionary is consulted. I have never written or seen code that uses this mechanism for anything.)

5. The layer's class is sent `defaultAction(forKey:)`, with the property name as the key. If an action object or `NSNull()` is returned, the search ends.

6. If the search reaches this last stage, a default animation is supplied, as appropriate. For a property animation, this is a plain vanilla CABasicAnimation.

Hooking Into the Action Search

You can affect the action search at any of its various stages to modify what happens when the search is triggered. This is where the fun begins.

For example, you can turn off implicit animation for some particular property. One way would be to return `nil` from `action(forKey:)` itself, in a CALayer subclass. Here's the code from a CALayer subclass that doesn't animate its `position` property (but does animate its other properties normally):

```
override func action(forKey key: String) -> CAAction? {
    if key == #keyPath(position) {
        return nil
    }
    return super.action(forKey:key)
}
```

For more flexibility, we can take advantage of the fact that a CALayer acts like a dictionary, allowing us to set an arbitrary key's value. We'll embed a switch in our CALayer subclass that we can use to turn implicit `position` animation on and off at will:

```
override func action(forKey key: String) -> CAAction? {
    if key == #keyPath(position) {
        if self.value(forKey:"suppressPositionAnimation") != nil {
            return nil
        }
    }
    return super.action(forKey:key)
}
```

To turn off implicit `position` animation for an instance of this layer, we set its `"suppressPositionAnimation"` key to a non-`nil` value:

```
layer.setValue(true, forKey:"suppressPositionAnimation")
```

Another possibility is to cause some stage of the search to produce an action object of your own. You would then be affecting how implicit animation behaves.

Let's say we want a certain layer's duration for an implicit `position` animation to be 5 seconds. We can achieve this with a minimally configured animation, like this:

```
let ba = CABasicAnimation()
ba.duration = 5
```

The idea now is to situate this animation where it will be produced by the action search for the "position" key. We could, for instance, put it into the layer's actions dictionary:

```
layer.actions = ["position": ba]
```

The only property of this animation that we have set is its duration; that setting, however, is final. Although animation properties that you don't set can be set through CATransaction, in the usual manner for implicit property animation, animation properties that you *do* set can *not* be overridden through CATransaction. Thus, when we set this layer's position, if an implicit animation results, its duration is 5 seconds, even if we try to change it through CATransaction:

```
CATransaction.setAnimationDuration(1.5) // won't work
layer.position = CGPoint(100,100) // animated, takes 5 seconds
```

Storing an animation in the actions dictionary, however, is a somewhat inflexible way to hook into the action search. If we have to write our animation beforehand, we know nothing about the layer's starting and ending values for the changed property. A much more powerful approach is to make our action object a custom CAAction object — because in that case, it will be sent run(forKey:...), and we can construct and run an animation *now*, when we are in direct contact with the layer to be animated. Here's a barebones version of such an object:

```
class MyAction : NSObject, CAAction {
    func run(forKey event: String, object anObject: Any,
        arguments dict: [AnyHashable : Any]?) {
            let anim = CABasicAnimation(keyPath: event)
            anim.duration = 5
            let lay = anObject as! CALayer
            let newP = lay.value(forKey:event)
            let oldP = lay.presentation()!.value(forKey:event)
            lay.add(anim, forKey:nil)
    }
}
```

The idea is that a MyAction instance would then be the action object that we store in the actions dictionary:

```
layer.actions = ["position": MyAction()]
```

Our custom CAAction object, MyAction, doesn't do anything very interesting — but it could. That's the point. As the code demonstrates, we have access to the name of the animated property (event), the old value of that property (from the layer's presentation layer), and the new value of that property (from the layer itself). We are thus free to configure the animation in all sorts of ways. In fact, we can add more than one animation to the layer, or a group animation. We don't even have to add an animation to the layer! We are free to interpret the setting of this property in any way we like.

Here's a modification of our MyAction object that creates and runs a keyframe animation that "waggles" as it goes from the start value to the end value:

```
class MyWagglePositionAction : NSObject, CAAction {
    func run(forKey event: String, object anObject: Any,
        arguments dict: [AnyHashable : Any]?) {
            let lay = anObject as! CALayer
            let newP = lay.value(forKey:event) as! CGPoint
            let oldP = lay.presentation()!.value(forKey:event) as! CGPoint
            let d = sqrt(pow(oldP.x - newP.x, 2) + pow(oldP.y - newP.y, 2))
            let r = Double(d/3.0)
            let theta = Double(atan2(newP.y - oldP.y, newP.x - oldP.x))
            let wag = 10 * .pi/180.0
            let p1 = CGPoint(
                oldP.x + CGFloat(r*cos(theta+wag)),
                oldP.y + CGFloat(r*sin(theta+wag)))
            let p2 = CGPoint(
                oldP.x + CGFloat(r*2*cos(theta-wag)),
                oldP.y + CGFloat(r*2*sin(theta-wag)))
            let anim = CAKeyframeAnimation(keyPath: event)
            anim.values = [oldP,p1,p2,newP]
            anim.calculationMode = kCAAnimationCubic
            lay.add(anim, forKey:nil)
    }
}
```

By adding this CAAction object to a layer's `actions` dictionary under the `"position"` key, we have created a CALayer that waggles when its `position` property is set. Our CAAction doesn't set the animation's `duration`, so our own call to CATransaction's `setAnimationDuration(_:)` works. The power of this mechanism is simply staggering. We can modify *any* layer in this way — even one that doesn't belong to us.

Instead of modifying the layer's `actions` dictionary, we could hook into the action search by setting the layer's delegate to an instance that responds to `action(for:for-Key:)`. This has the advantage of serving as a single locus that can do different things depending on what the layer is and what the key is. Here's an implementation that does exactly what the `actions` dictionary did — it returns an instance of our custom CAAction object, so that setting the layer's position waggles it into place:

```
func action(for layer: CALayer, forKey key: String) -> CAAction? {
    if key == #keyPath(CALayer.position) {
        return MyWagglePositionAction()
    }
}
```

Finally, I'll demonstrate overriding `defaultAction(forKey:)`. This code would go into a CALayer subclass; setting this layer's `contents` will automatically trigger a push transition from the left:

```
override class func defaultAction(forKey key: String) -> CAAction? {
    if key == #keyPath(contents) {
        let tr = CATransition()
        tr.type = kCATransitionPush
        tr.subtype = kCATransitionFromLeft
        return tr
    }
    return super.defaultAction(forKey:key)
}
```

 Both the delegate's `action(for:forKey:)` and the subclass's `defaultAction(for-Key:)` are declared as returning a `CAAction`. Therefore, to return `NSNull()` from your implemention of one of these methods, you'll need to typecast it to `CAAction` to quiet the compiler; you're lying (NSNull does not adopt the CAAction protocol), but it doesn't matter.

Making a Custom Property Implicitly Animatable

Earlier in this chapter, we made a custom layer's `thickness` property animatable through explicit layer animation. Now that we know how implicit layer animation works, we can make our layer's `thickness` property animatable through implicit animation as well. Thus, we will be able to animate our layer's thickness with code like this:

```
let lay = self.v.layer as! MyLayer
let cur = lay.thickness
let val : CGFloat = cur == 10 ? 0 : 10
lay.thickness = val // implicit animation
```

We have already implemented `needsDisplay(forKey:)` to return `true` for the `"thickness"` key, and we have provided an appropriate `draw(in:)` implementation. Now we'll add two further pieces of the puzzle. As we now know, to make our MyLayer class respond to direct setting of a property, we need to hook into the action search and return a CAAction. The obvious place to do this is in the layer itself, at the very start of the action search, in an `action(forKey:)` implementation:

```
override func action(forKey key: String) -> CAAction? {
    if key == #keyPath(thickness) {
        let ba = CABasicAnimation(keyPath: key)
        ba.fromValue = self.presentation()!.value(forKey:key)
        return ba
    }
    return super.action(forKey:key)
}
```

Finally, we must declare MyLayer's `thickness` property `@NSManaged`. Otherwise, `action(forKey:)` won't be called in the first place and the action search will never happen:

```
class MyLayer : CALayer {
    @NSManaged var thickness : CGFloat
    // ...
}
```

 The `@NSManaged` declaration invites Cocoa to generate and dynamically inject getter and setter accessors into our layer class; it is the equivalent of Objective-C's `@dynamic` (and is completely different from Swift's `dynamic`).

Nonproperty Actions

An action search is also triggered when a layer is added to a superlayer (key `kCAOnOrderIn`) and when a layer's sublayers are changed by adding or removing a sublayer (key `"sublayers"`).

 These triggers and their keys are incorrectly described in Apple's documentation (and headers).

In this example, we use our layer's delegate so that when our layer is added to a super-layer, it will "pop" into view:

```
let layer = CALayer()
// ... configure layer here ...
layer.delegate = self
self.view.layer.addSublayer(layer)
```

In the layer's delegate (`self`), we implement the actual animation as a group animation, fading the layer quickly in from an opacity of 0 and at the same time scaling its transform to make it momentarily appear a little larger:

```
func action(for layer: CALayer, forKey key: String) -> CAAction? {
    if key == kCAOnOrderIn {
        let anim1 = CABasicAnimation(keyPath:#keyPath(CALayer.opacity))
        anim1.fromValue = 0.0
        anim1.toValue = layer.opacity
        let anim2 = CABasicAnimation(keyPath:#keyPath(CALayer.transform))
        anim2.toValue = CATransform3DScale(layer.transform, 1.2, 1.2, 1.0)
        anim2.autoreverses = true
        anim2.duration = 0.1
        let group = CAAnimationGroup()
        group.animations = [anim1, anim2]
        group.duration = 0.2
        return group
    }
}
```

The documentation says that when a layer is removed from a superlayer, an action is sought under the key kCAOnOrderOut. This is true but useless, because by the time the action is sought, the layer has already been removed from the superlayer, so returning an animation has no visible effect. A possible workaround is to trigger the animation in some other way (and remove the layer afterward, if desired).

Recall, for example, that an action search is triggered when an arbitrary key is set on a layer. Let's implement the key "farewell" so that it shrinks and fades the layer and then removes it from its superlayer:

```
layer.delegate = self
layer.setValue("", forKey:"farewell")
```

The supplier of the action object — in this case, the layer's delegate — returns the shrink-and-fade animation; it also sets itself as that animation's delegate, and removes the layer when the animation ends:

```
func action(for layer: CALayer, forKey key: String) -> CAAction? {
    if key == "farewell" {
        let anim1 = CABasicAnimation(keyPath:#keyPath(CALayer.opacity))
        anim1.fromValue = layer.opacity
        anim1.toValue = 0.0
        let anim2 = CABasicAnimation(keyPath:#keyPath(CALayer.transform))
        anim2.toValue = CATransform3DScale(layer.transform, 0.1, 0.1, 1.0)
        let group = CAAnimationGroup()
        group.animations = [anim1, anim2]
        group.duration = 0.2
        group.delegate = self
        group.setValue(layer, forKey:"remove")
        layer.opacity = 0
        return group
    }
}
func animationDidStop(_ anim: CAAnimation, finished flag: Bool) {
    if let layer = anim.value(forKey:"remove") as? CALayer {
        layer.removeFromSuperlayer()
    }
}
```

Emitter Layers

Emitter layers (CAEmitterLayer) are, to some extent, on a par with animated images: once you've set up an emitter layer, it just sits there animating all by itself. The nature of this animation is rather narrow: an emitter layer emits particles, which are CAEmitterCell instances. However, by clever setting of the properties of an emitter layer and its emitter cells, you can achieve some astonishing effects. Moreover, the animation is itself animatable using Core Animation.

Here are some useful basic properties of a CAEmitterCell:

contents, contentsRect

These are modeled after the eponymous CALayer properties, although CAEmitterCell is not a CALayer subclass; so, respectively, an image (a CGImage) and a CGRect specifying a region of that image. They define the image that a cell will portray.

birthrate, lifetime

How many cells per second should be emitted, and how many seconds each cell should live before vanishing, respectively.

velocity

The speed at which a cell moves. The unit of measurement is not documented; perhaps it's points per second.

emissionLatitude, emissionLongitude

The angle at which the cell is emitted from the emitter, as a variation from the perpendicular. Longitude is an angle within the plane; latitude is an angle out of the plane.

So, here's code to create a very elementary emitter cell:

```
// make a gray circle image
let r = UIGraphicsImageRenderer(size:CGSize(10,10))
let im = r.image {
    ctx in let con = ctx.cgContext
    con.addEllipse(in:CGRect(0,0,10,10))
    con.setFillColor(UIColor.gray.cgColor)
    con.fillPath()
}
// make a cell with that image
let cell = CAEmitterCell()
cell.contentsScale = UIScreen.main.scale
cell.birthRate = 5
cell.lifetime = 1
cell.velocity = 100
cell.contents = im.cgImage
```

The result is that little gray circles should be emitted slowly and steadily, five per second, each one vanishing in one second. Now we need an emitter layer from which these circles are to be emitted. Here are some basic CAEmitterLayer properties (beyond those it inherits from CALayer); these define an imaginary object, an emitter, that will be producing the emitter cells:

emitterPosition

The point at which the emitter should be located, in superlayer coordinates. You can optionally add a third dimension to this point, emitterZPosition.

emitterSize

The size of the emitter.

Figure 4-4. A really boring emitter layer

emitterShape

> The shape of the emitter. The dimensions of the shape depend on the emitter's size; the cuboid shape depends also on a third size dimension, emitterDepth. Your choices are:
>
> - kCAEmitterLayerPoint
> - kCAEmitterLayerLine
> - kCAEmitterLayerRectangle
> - kCAEmitterLayerCuboid
> - kCAEmitterLayerCircle
> - kCAEmitterLayerSphere

emitterMode

> The region of the shape from which cells should be emitted. Your choices are:
>
> - kCAEmitterLayerPoints
> - kCAEmitterLayerOutline
> - kCAEmitterLayerSurface
> - kCAEmitterLayerVolume

Let's start with the simplest possible case, a single point emitter:

```
let emit = CAEmitterLayer()
emit.emitterPosition = CGPoint(30,100)
emit.emitterShape = kCAEmitterLayerPoint
emit.emitterMode = kCAEmitterLayerPoints
```

We tell the emitter what types of cell to emit by assigning those cells to its emitter-Cells property (an array of CAEmitterCell). We then add the emitter to our interface, and presto, it starts emitting:

```
emit.emitterCells = [cell]
self.view.layer.addSublayer(emit)
```

The result is a constant stream of gray circles emitted from the point (30.0,100.0), each circle marching steadily to the right and vanishing after one second (Figure 4-4).

Now that we've succeeded in creating a boring emitter layer, we can start to vary some parameters. The emissionRange defines a cone in which cells will be emitted; if we increase the `birthRate` and widen the `emissionRange`, we get something that looks like a stream shooting from a water hose:

```
cell.birthRate = 100
cell.lifetime = 1.5
cell.velocity = 100
cell.emissionRange = .pi/5.0
```

In addition, as the cell moves, it can be made to accelerate (or decelerate) in each dimension, using its `xAcceleration`, `yAcceleration`, and `zAcceleration` properties. Here, we turn the stream into a falling cascade, like a waterfall coming from the left:

```
cell.xAcceleration = -40
cell.yAcceleration = 200
```

All aspects of cell behavior can be made to vary randomly, using the following CAEmitterCell properties:

`lifetimeRange`, `velocityRange`

> How much the lifetime and velocity values are allowed to vary randomly for different cells.

`scale`
`scaleRange`, `scaleSpeed`

> The scale alters the size of the cell; the range and speed determine how far and how rapidly this size alteration is allowed to change over the lifetime of each cell.

`color`
`redRange`, `greenRange`, `blueRange`, `alphaRange`
`redSpeed`, `greenSpeed`, `blueSpeed`, `alphaSpeed`

> The color is painted in accordance with the opacity of the cell's contents image; it combines with the image's color, so if we want the color stated here to appear in full purity, our contents image should use only white. The range and speed determine how far and how rapidly each color component is to change.

`spin`
`spinRange`

> The spin is a rotational speed (in radians per second); its range determines how far this speed is allowed to change over the lifetime of each cell.

Here we add some variation so that the circles behave a little more independently of one another. Some live longer than others, some come out of the emitter faster than others. And they all start out a shade of blue, but change to a shade of green about halfway through the stream (Figure 4-5):

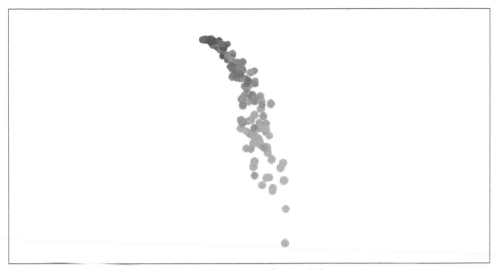

Figure 4-5. An emitter layer that makes a sort of waterfall

```
cell.lifetimeRange = 0.4
cell.velocityRange = 20
cell.scaleRange = 0.2
cell.scaleSpeed = 0.2
cell.color = UIColor.blue.cgColor
cell.greenRange = 0.5
cell.greenSpeed = 0.75
```

Once the emitter layer is in place and animating, you can change its parameters and the parameters of its emitter cells through key–value coding on the emitter layer. You can access the emitter cells through the emitter layer's `"emitterCells"` key path; to specify a cell type, use its `name` property (which you'll have to have assigned earlier) as the next piece of the key path. For example, suppose we've set `cell.name` to `"circle"`; now we'll change the cell's `greenSpeed` so that each cell changes from blue to green much earlier in its lifetime:

```
emit.setValue(3.0, forKeyPath:"emitterCells.circle.greenSpeed")
```

The significance of this is that such changes can themselves be animated! Here, we'll attach to the emitter layer a repeating animation that causes our cell's `greenSpeed` to move slowly back and forth between two values. The result is that the stream varies, over time, between being mostly blue and mostly green:

```
let key = "emitterCells.circle.greenSpeed"
let ba = CABasicAnimation(keyPath:key)
ba.fromValue = -1.0
ba.toValue = 3.0
```

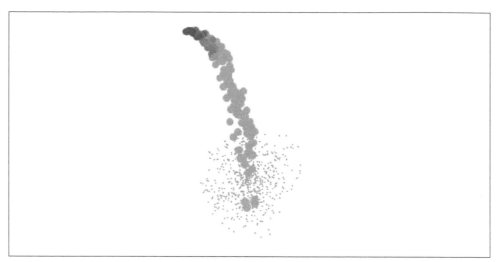

Figure 4-6. The waterfall makes a kind of splash

```
ba.duration = 4
ba.autoreverses = true
ba.repeatCount = .infinity
emit.add(ba, forKey:nil)
```

A CAEmitterCell can itself function as an emitter — that is, it can have cells of its own. Both CAEmitterLayer and CAEmitterCell conform to the CAMediaTiming protocol, and their `beginTime` and `duration` properties can be used to govern their times of operation, much as in a grouped animation. For example, this code causes our existing waterfall to spray tiny droplets in the region of the "nozzle" (the emitter):

```
let cell2 = CAEmitterCell()
cell.emitterCells = [cell2]
cell2.contents = im.cgImage
cell2.emissionRange = .pi
cell2.birthRate = 200
cell2.lifetime = 0.4
cell2.velocity = 200
cell2.scale = 0.2
cell2.beginTime = 0.04
cell2.duration = 0.2
```

But if we change the `beginTime` to be larger (hence later), the tiny droplets happen near the bottom of the cascade. We must also increase the `duration`, or stop setting it altogether, since if the `duration` is less than the `beginTime`, no emission takes place at all (Figure 4-6):

```
cell2.beginTime = 1.4
cell2.duration = 0.4
```

Figure 4-7. Midway through a starburst transition

We can also alter the picture by changing the behavior of the emitter itself. This change turns the emitter into a line, so that our cascade becomes broader (more like Niagara Falls):

```
emit.emitterPosition = CGPoint(100,25)
emit.emitterSize = CGSize(100,100)
emit.emitterShape = kCAEmitterLayerLine
emit.emitterMode = kCAEmitterLayerOutline
cell.emissionLongitude = 3 * .pi/4
```

There's more to know about emitter layers and emitter cells, but at this point you know enough to understand Apple's sample code simulating such things as fire and smoke and pyrotechnics, and you can explore further on your own.

CIFilter Transitions

Core Image filters (Chapter 2) include transitions. You supply two images and a frame time between 0 and 1; the filter supplies the corresponding frame of a one-second animation transitioning from the first image to the second. For example, Figure 4-7 shows the frame at frame time 0.75 for a starburst transition from a solid red image to a photo of me. (You don't see the photo of me, because this transition, by default, "explodes" the first image to white first, and then quickly fades to the second image.)

Animating a Core Image transition filter is up to you. Thus we need a way of rapidly calling the same method repeatedly; in that method, we'll request and draw each frame of the transition. This could be a job for a Timer, but a better way is to use a *display link* (CADisplayLink), a form of timer that's highly efficient, especially when repeated drawing is involved, because it is linked directly to the refreshing of the display (hence the name). The display refresh rate is hardware-dependent, but is typically every sixtieth of a second or faster; UIScreen.maximumFramesPerSecond will tell you the nominal value, and the nominal time between refreshes is the display link's `duration`.

Like a timer, the display link calls a designated method of ours every time it fires. We can slow the rate of calls by setting the display link's `preferredFramesPerSecond`. We can learn the exact time when the display link last fired by querying its `timestamp`, and that's the best way to decide what frame needs displaying now.

In this example, I'll display the animation in a view's layer. We initialize ahead of time, in properties, everything we'll need later to obtain an output image for a given frame of the transition — the CIFilter, the image's `extent`, and the CIContext. We also have a `timestamp` property, which we initialize as well:

```
let moi = CIImage(image:UIImage(named:"moi")!)!
self.moiextent = moi.extent
let col = CIFilter(name:"CIConstantColorGenerator")!
let cicol = CIColor(color:.red)
col.setValue(cicol, forKey:"inputColor")
let colorimage = col.value(forKey:"outputImage") as! CIImage
let tran = CIFilter(name:"CIFlashTransition")!
tran.setValue(colorimage, forKey:"inputImage")
tran.setValue(moi, forKey:"inputTargetImage")
let center = CIVector(x:self.moiextent.width/2.0, y:self.moiextent.height/2.0)
tran.setValue(center, forKey:"inputCenter")
self.tran = tran
self.timestamp = 0.0 // signal that we are starting
self.context = CIContext()
```

We create the display link, setting it to call into our `nextFrame` method, and set it going by adding it to the main run loop, which retains it:

```
let link = CADisplayLink(target:self, selector:#selector(self.nextFrame))
link.add(to:.main, forMode:.defaultRunLoopMode)
```

Our `nextFrame(_:)` method is called with the display link as parameter (`sender`). We store the initial `timestamp` in our property, and use the difference between that and each successive `timestamp` value to calculate our desired frame. We ask the filter for the corresponding image and display it. When the frame value exceeds 1, the animation is over and we invalidate the display link (just like a repeating timer), which releases it from the run loop:

```
let SCALE = 1.0
@objc func nextFrame(_ sender:CADisplayLink) {
    if self.timestamp < 0.01 { // pick up and store first timestamp
        self.timestamp = sender.timestamp
        self.frame = 0.0
    } else { // calculate frame
        self.frame = (sender.timestamp - self.timestamp) * SCALE
    }
    sender.isPaused = true // defend against frame loss
```

```
        self.tran.setValue(self.frame, forKey:"inputTime")
        let moi = self.context.createCGImage(
            tran.outputImage!, from:self.moiextent)
        CATransaction.setDisableActions(true)
        self.v.layer.contents = moi
        if self.frame > 1.0 {
            sender.invalidate()
        }
        sender.isPaused = false
    }
```

I have surrounded the time-consuming calculation and drawing of the image with calls to the display link's `isPaused` property, in case the calculation time exceeds the time between screen refreshes; perhaps this isn't necessary, but it can't hurt. Our animation occupies one second; changing that value is merely a matter of multiplying by a different scale value when we set our `frame` property.

 If you experiment with this code, run on a device, as display links do not work well in the Simulator (or, in the Simulator, try an artificially slow scale such as `0.2`).

UIKit Dynamics

The term *UIKit dynamics* refers to a suite of classes supplying a convenient API for animating views in a manner reminiscent of real-world physical behavior. For example, views can be subjected to gravity, collisions, bouncing, and momentary forces, with effects that would otherwise be difficult to achieve.

UIKit dynamics should not be treated as a game engine. It is deliberately quite cartoony and simple, animating only the position (`center`) and rotation transform of views within a flat two-dimensional space. UIKit dynamics relies on CADisplayLink, and the calculation of each frame takes place on the main thread (not on the animation server's background thread). There's no "animation movie" and no distinct presentation layer; the views really are being repositioned in real time. Thus, UIKit Dynamics is not intended for extended use; it is a way of momentarily emphasizing or clarifying functional transformations of your interface.

The Dynamics Stack

Implementing UIKit dynamics involves configuring a "stack" of three things:

A dynamic animator

A dynamic animator, a UIDynamicAnimator instance, is the ruler of the physics world you are creating. It has a reference view, whose bounds define the coordinate system of the animator's world. A view to be animated must be a subview of the reference view (though it does not have to be within the reference view's bounds). Retaining the animator is up to you, typically with an instance property. It's fine for an animator to sit empty until you need it; an animator whose world is empty (or at rest) is not running, and occupies no processor time.

A behavior

A UIDynamicBehavior is a rule describing how a view should behave. You'll typically use a built-in subclass, such as UIGravityBehavior or UICollisionBehavior. You configure the behavior and add it to the animator; an animator has methods and properties for managing its behaviors, such as addBehavior(_:), behaviors, removeBehavior(_:), and removeAllBehaviors. A behavior's configuration can be changed, and behaviors can be added to and removed from an animator, even while an animation is in progress.

An item

An item is any object that implements the UIDynamicItem protocol. A UIView is such an object! You add a UIView (one that's a subview of your animator's reference view) to a behavior (one that belongs to that animator) — and at that moment, the view comes under the influence of that behavior. If this behavior is one that causes motion, and if no other behaviors prevent, the view will now move (the animator is running).

Some behaviors can accept multiple items, and have methods and properties such as addItem(_:), items, and removeItem(_:). Others can have just one or two items and must be initialized with these from the outset.

A UIDynamicItemGroup is a way of combining multiple items to form a single item. Its only property is its items. You apply behaviors to the resulting grouped item, not to the subitems that it comprises. Those subitems maintain their physical relationship to one another. For purposes of collisions, the boundaries of the individual subitems are respected.

That's sufficient to get started, so let's try it! I'll start by creating my animator and storing it in a property:

```
self.anim = UIDynamicAnimator(referenceView: self.view)
```

Now I'll cause an existing subview of self.view (a UIImageView, self.iv) to drop off the screen, under the influence of gravity. I create a UIGravityBehavior, add it to the animator, and add self.iv to it:

```
let grav = UIGravityBehavior()
self.anim.addBehavior(grav)
grav.addItem(self.iv)
```

As a result, self.iv comes under the influence of gravity and is now animated downward off the screen. (A UIGravityBehavior object has properties configuring the strength and direction of gravity, but I've left them here at their defaults.)

An immediate concern is that our view falls forever. This is a serious waste of memory and processing power. If we no longer need the view after it has left the screen, we should take it out of the influence of UIKit dynamics by removing it from any behaviors to which it belongs (and we can also remove it from its superview). One way to do this is by removing from the animator any behaviors that are no longer needed. In our simple example, where the animator's entire world contains just this one item, it will be sufficient to call removeAllBehaviors.

But how will we know when the view is off the screen? A UIDynamicBehavior can be assigned an action function, which is called repeatedly as the animator drives the animation. I'll configure our gravity behavior's action function to check whether self.iv is still within the bounds of the reference view, by calling the animator's items(in:) method. Actually, items(in:) returns an array of UIDynamicItem, but I want an array of UIView, so I like to have on hand a UIDynamicAnimator extension that will cast down safely:

```
extension UIDynamicAnimator {
    func views(in rect: CGRect) -> [UIView] {
        let nsitems = self.items(in: rect) as NSArray
        return nsitems.flatMap{$0 as? UIView}
    }
}
```

Here's my first attempt:

```
grav.action = {
    let items = self.anim.views(in:self.view.bounds)
    let ix = items.index(of:self.iv)
    if ix == nil {
        self.anim.removeAllBehaviors()
        self.iv.removeFromSuperview()
    }
}
```

This works in the sense that, after the image view leaves the screen, the image view is removed from the window and the animation stops. Unfortunately, there is also a memory leak: neither the image view nor the gravity behavior has been released. One solution is, in grav.action, to set self.anim (the animator property) to nil, thus breaking the retain cycle. This is a perfectly appropriate solution if, as here, we no longer need the animator for anything; a UIDynamicAnimator is a lightweight object and can very reasonably come into existence only for as long as we need to run an animation. Another possibility is to use delayed performance; even a delay of 0 solves the problem, presumably because the behavior's action function is no longer running at the time we remove the behavior:

```
grav.action = {
    let items = self.anim.views(in:self.view.bounds)
    let ix = items.index(of:self.iv)
    if ix == nil {
        delay(0) {
            self.anim.removeAllBehaviors()
            self.iv.removeFromSuperview()
        }
    }
}
```

Now let's add some further behaviors. If falling straight down is too boring, we can add a UIPushBehavior to create a slight rightward impulse to be applied to the view as it begins to fall:

```
let push = UIPushBehavior(items:[self.iv], mode:.instantaneous)
push.pushDirection = CGVector(1,0)
self.anim.addBehavior(push)
```

The view now falls in a parabola to the right. Next, let's add a UICollisionBehavior to make our view strike the "floor" of the screen:

```
let coll = UICollisionBehavior()
coll.collisionMode = .boundaries
coll.collisionDelegate = self
coll.addBoundary(withIdentifier:"floor" as NSString,
    from: CGPoint(0, self.view.bounds.maxY),
    to:CGPoint(self.view.bounds.maxX, self.view.bounds.maxY))
self.anim.addBehavior(coll)
coll.addItem(self.iv)
```

The view now falls in a parabola onto the floor of the screen, bounces a tiny bit, and comes to rest. It would be nice if the view bounced a bit more. Characteristics internal to a dynamic item's physics, such as bounciness (`elasticity`), are configured by assigning it to a UIDynamicItemBehavior:

```
let bounce = UIDynamicItemBehavior()
bounce.elasticity = 0.8
self.anim.addBehavior(bounce)
bounce.addItem(self.iv)
```

Our view now bounces higher; nevertheless, when it hits the floor, it stops moving to the right, so it just bounces repeatedly, less and less, and ends up at rest on the floor. I'd prefer that, after it bounces, it should roll to the right, so that it eventually leaves the screen. Part of the problem here is that, in the mind of the physics engine, our view is *not round*. We can change that (starting in iOS 9). We'll have to subclass our view class (UIImageView), and make sure our view is an instance of this subclass:

```
class MyImageView : UIImageView {
    override var collisionBoundsType: UIDynamicItemCollisionBoundsType {
        return .ellipse
    }
}
```

Our image view now has the ability to roll. If the image view is portraying a circular image, the effect is quite realistic: the image itself appears to roll to the right after it bounces. However, it isn't rolling very fast (because we didn't initially push it very hard). To remedy that, I'll add some rotational velocity as part of the first bounce. A UICollisionBehavior has a delegate to which it sends messages when a collision occurs. I'll make `self` the collision behavior's delegate, and when the delegate message arrives, I'll add rotational velocity to the existing dynamic item bounce behavior, so that our view starts spinning clockwise:

```
func collisionBehavior(_ behavior: UICollisionBehavior,
    beganContactFor item: UIDynamicItem,
    withBoundaryIdentifier identifier: NSCopying?,
    at p: CGPoint) {
        // look for the dynamic item behavior
        let b = self.anim.behaviors
        if let ix = b.index(where:{$0 is UIDynamicItemBehavior}) {
            let bounce = b[ix] as! UIDynamicItemBehavior
            let v = bounce.angularVelocity(for:item)
            if v <= 6 {
                bounce.addAngularVelocity(6, for:item)
            }
        }
}
```

The view now falls in a parabola to the right, strikes the floor, spins clockwise, and bounces off the floor and continues bouncing its way off the right side of the screen.

Custom Behaviors

You will commonly find yourself composing a complex behavior out of a combination of several built-in UIDynamicBehavior subclass instances. For neatness, clarity, maintainability, and reusability, it might make sense to express that combination as a single custom UIDynamicBehavior subclass.

To illustrate, I'll turn the behavior from the previous section into a custom subclass of UIDynamicBehavior. Let's call it MyDropBounceAndRollBehavior. Now we can apply this behavior to our view, `self.iv`, very simply:

```
self.anim.addBehavior(MyDropBounceAndRollBehavior(view:self.iv))
```

All the work is now done by the MyDropBounceAndRollBehavior instance. I've designed it to affect just one view, so its initializer looks like this:

```
    let v : UIView
    init(view v:UIView) {
        self.v = v
        super.init()
    }
```

A UIDynamicBehavior receives a reference to its dynamic animator just before being added to it, by implementing willMove(to:), and can refer to it subsequently as self.dynamicAnimator. To incorporate actual behaviors into itself, our custom UIDynamicBehavior subclass creates and configures them, and calls addChild-Behavior(_:); it can refer to the array of its child behaviors as self.child-Behaviors. When our custom behavior is added to or removed from the dynamic animator, the effect is the same as if its child behaviors themselves were added or removed.

Here is the rest of MyDropBounceAndRollBehavior. Our precautions in the gravity behavior's action block not to cause a retain cycle are simpler than before; it suffices to designate self as an unowned reference and remove self from the animator explicitly:

```
    override func willMove(to anim: UIDynamicAnimator?) {
        guard let anim = anim else { return }
        let sup = self.v.superview!
        let grav = UIGravityBehavior()
        grav.action = { [unowned self] in
            let items = anim.views(in: sup.bounds)
            if items.index(of:self.v) == nil {
                anim.removeBehavior(self)
                self.v.removeFromSuperview()
            }
        }
        self.addChildBehavior(grav)
        grav.addItem(self.v)
        let push = UIPushBehavior(items:[self.v], mode:.instantaneous)
        push.pushDirection = CGVector(1,0)
        self.addChildBehavior(push)
        let coll = UICollisionBehavior()
        coll.collisionMode = .boundaries
        coll.collisionDelegate = self
        coll.addBoundary(withIdentifier:"floor" as NSString,
            from: CGPoint(0, sup.bounds.maxY),
            to:CGPoint(sup.bounds.maxX, sup.bounds.maxY))
        self.addChildBehavior(coll)
        coll.addItem(self.v)
        let bounce = UIDynamicItemBehavior()
        bounce.elasticity = 0.8
        self.addChildBehavior(bounce)
        bounce.addItem(self.v)
    }
    func collisionBehavior(_ behavior: UICollisionBehavior,
```

```
        beganContactFor item: UIDynamicItem,
        withBoundaryIdentifier identifier: NSCopying?,
        at p: CGPoint) {
            // look for the dynamic item behavior
            let b = self.childBehaviors
            if let ix = b.index(where:{$0 is UIDynamicItemBehavior}) {
                let bounce = b[ix] as! UIDynamicItemBehavior
                let v = bounce.angularVelocity(for:item)
                if v <= 6 {
                    bounce.addAngularVelocity(6, for:item)
                }
            }
        }
}
```

Animator and Behaviors

Here are some further UIDynamicAnimator methods and properties:

delegate
> The delegate (UIDynamicAnimatorDelegate) is sent messages dynamicAnimator-
> DidPause(_:) and dynamicAnimatorWillResume(_:). The animator is paused
> when it has nothing to do: it has no dynamic items, or all its dynamic items are at
> rest.

isRunning
> If true, the animator is not paused; some dynamic item is being animated.

elapsedTime
> The total time during which this animator has been running since it first started
> running. The elapsedTime does not increase while the animator is paused, nor is
> it reset. You might use this in a delegate method or action method to decide that
> the animation is over.

updateItem(usingCurrentState:)
> Once a dynamic item has come under the influence of the animator, the anima-
> tor is responsible for positioning that dynamic item. If your code manually
> changes the dynamic item's position or other relevant attributes, call this method
> so that the animator can take account of those changes.

 Starting in iOS 9, you can turn on a display that reveals visually what the animator is doing, showing its attachment lines and so forth; assuming that self.anim
refers to the dynamic animator, you would say:

```
    self.anim.perform(Selector(("setDebugEnabled:")), with:true)
```

The rest of this section surveys the various built-in UIDynamicBehavior subclasses.

UIDynamicItemBehavior

A UIDynamicItemBehavior doesn't apply any force or velocity; instead, it is a way of endowing items with internal physical characteristics that will affect how they respond to other dynamic behaviors. Here are some of them:

density
> Changes the impulse-resisting mass in relation to size. In other words, when we speak of an item's mass, we mean a combination of its size and its density.

elasticity
> The item's tendency to bounce on collision.

friction
> The item's tendency to be slowed by sliding past another item.

isAnchored
> An anchored item is not affected by forces that would make an item move; thus it remains stationary. This can give you something with friction and elasticity off of which you can bounce and slide other items.

resistance, angularResistance, allowsRotation
> The item's tendency to come to rest unless forces are actively applied. allows-Rotation can prevent the item from acquiring any angular velocity at all.

charge
> Meaningful only with respect to magnetic and electric fields, which I'll get to in a moment.

addLinearVelocity(_:for:), linearVelocity(for:)
addAngularVelocity(_:for:), angularVelocity(for:)
> Methods for tweaking linear and angular velocity.

UIGravityBehavior

UIGravityBehavior imposes an acceleration on its dynamic items. By default, this acceleration is downward with a magnitude of 1 (arbitrarily defined as 1000 points per second per second). You can customize gravity by changing its gravity-Direction (a CGVector) or its angle and magnitude.

UIFieldBehavior

UIFieldBehavior is a generalization of UIGravityBehavior. A field affects any of its items for as long as they are within its area of influence, as described by these properties:

position
> The center of the field's effective area of influence, in reference view coordinates. The default position is CGPoint.zero, the reference view's top left corner.

region
> The shape of the field's effective area of influence; a UIRegion. The default is that the region is infinite, but you can limit it to a circle by its radius or to a rectangle by its size. More complex region shapes can be achieved by taking the union, intersection, or difference of two regions, or the inverse of a region.

strength
> The magnitude of the field. It can be negative to reverse the directionality of the field's forces.

falloff
> Defines a change in strength proportional to the distance from the center.

minimumRadius
> Specifies a central circle within which there is no field effect.

direction, smoothness, animationSpeed
> Applicable only to those built-in field types that define them.

The built-in field types are obtained by calling a class factory method:

linearGravityField(direction:)
> Like UIGravityBehavior. Accelerates the item in the direction of a vector that you supply, proportionally to its mass, the length of the vector, and the strength of the field. The vector is the field's direction, and can be changed.

velocityField(direction:)
> Like UIGravityBehavior, but it doesn't apply an acceleration (a force) — instead, it applies a constant velocity.

radialGravityField(position:)
> Like a point-oriented version of UIGravityBehavior. Accelerates the item toward, or pushes it away from, the field's designated central point (its position).

springField
> Behaves as if there were a spring stretching from the item to the center, so that the item oscillates back and forth across the center until it settles there.

electricField
> Behaves like an electric field emanating from the center. The default strength and falloff are both 1. If you set the falloff to 0, then a negatively charged item, all other things being equal, will oscillate endlessly across the center.

`magneticField`

Behaves like a magnetic field emanating from the center. A moving charged item's path is bent away from the center.

`vortexField`

Accelerates the item sideways with respect to the center.

`dragField`

Reduces the item's speed.

`noiseField(smoothness:animationSpeed:)`

Adds random disturbance to the position of the item. The `smoothness` is between 0 (noisy) and 1 (smooth). The `animationSpeed` is how many times per second the field should change randomly. Both can be changed in real time.

`turbulenceField(smoothness:animationSpeed:)`

Like a noise field, but takes the item's velocity into account.

Think of a field as an infinite grid of CGVectors, with the potential to affect the speed and direction (that is, the velocity) of an item within its borders; these CGVectors are interactive, in the sense that at every instant of time the vector applicable to a particular item can be recalculated. You can write a custom field by calling the UIField-Behavior class method `field(evaluationBlock:)` with a function that takes the item's position, velocity, mass, and charge, along with the animator's elapsed time, and returns a CGVector.

In this (silly) example, we create a delayed drag field: for the first quarter second it does nothing, but then it suddenly switches on and applies the brakes to its items, bringing them to a standstill if they don't already have enough velocity to escape the region's boundaries:

```
let b = UIFieldBehavior.field {
    (beh, pt, v, m, c, t) -> CGVector in
    if t > 0.25 {
        return CGVector(-v.dx, -v.dy)
    }
    return CGVector(0,0)
}
```

The evaluation function receives the behavior itself as a parameter, so it can consult the behavior's properties in real time. You can define your own properties by subclassing UIFieldBehavior. If you're going to do that, you might as well also define your own class factory function to configure and return the custom field. To illustrate, I'll turn the hard-coded `0.25` delay from the previous example into an instance property:

```
class MyDelayedFieldBehavior : UIFieldBehavior {
    var delay = 0.0
    class func dragField(delay del:Double) -> Self {
        let f = self.field {
            (beh, pt, v, m, c, t) -> CGVector in
            if t > (beh as! MyDelayedFieldBehavior).delay {
                return CGVector(-v.dx, -v.dy)
            }
            return CGVector(0,0)
        }
        f.delay = del
        return f
    }
}
```

Here's an example of creating and configuring our delayed drag field:

```
let b = MyDelayedFieldBehavior.dragField(delay:0.95)
b.region = UIRegion(size: self.view.bounds.size)
b.position = CGPoint(self.view.bounds.midX, self.view.bounds.midY)
b.addItem(v)
self.anim.addBehavior(b)
```

UIPushBehavior

UIPushBehavior applies a force either instantaneously or continuously (mode), the latter constituting an acceleration. How this force affects an object depends in part upon the object's mass. The effect of a push behavior can be toggled with the active property; an instantaneous push is repeated each time the active property is set to true.

To configure a push behavior, set its pushDirection or its angle and magnitude. In addition, a push may be applied at an offset from the center of an item. This will apply an additional angular acceleration. Thus, in my earlier example, I could have started the view spinning clockwise by means of its initial push, like this:

```
push.setTargetOffsetFromCenter(UIOffsetMake(0,-200), for: self.iv)
```

UICollisionBehavior

UICollisionBehavior watches for collisions either between items belonging to this same behavior or between an item and a boundary (mode). One collision behavior can have multiple items and multiple boundaries. A boundary may be described as a line between two points or as a UIBezierPath, or you can turn the reference view's bounds into boundaries (setTranslatesReferenceBoundsIntoBoundary(with:)). Boundaries that you create can have an identifier. The collisionDelegate (UICollision-BehaviorDelegate) is called when a collision begins and again when it ends.

How a given collision affects the item(s) involved depends on the physical characteristics of the item(s), which may be configured through a UIDynamicItemBehavior.

Starting in iOS 9, a dynamic item, such as a UIView, can have a customized collision boundary, rather than its collision boundary being merely the edges of its frame. You can have a rectangle dictated by the frame, an ellipse dictated by the frame, or a custom shape — a convex counterclockwise simple closed UIBezierPath. The relevant properties, collisionBoundsType and (for a custom shape) collisionBoundingPath, are read-only, so you will have to subclass, as I did in my earlier example.

UISnapBehavior

UISnapBehavior causes one item to snap to one point as if pulled by a spring. Its damping describes how much the item should oscillate as its settles into that point. This is a very simple behavior: the snap occurs immediately when the behavior is added to the animator, and there's no notification when it's over.

Starting in iOS 9, the snap behavior's snapPoint is a settable property. Thus, having performed a snap, you can subsequently change the snapPoint and cause another snap to take place.

UIAttachmentBehavior

UIAttachmentBehavior attaches an item to another item or to a point in the reference view, depending on how you initialize it:

- init(item:attachedTo:)
- init(item:attachedToAnchor:)

The attachment point is, by default, the item's center; to change that, there's a different pair of initializers:

- init(item:offsetFromCenter:attachedTo:offsetFromCenter:)
- init(item:offsetFromCenter:attachedToAnchor:)

The attaching medium's physics are governed by the behavior's length, frequency, and damping. If the frequency is 0 (the default), the attachment is like a bar; otherwise, and especially if the damping is very small, it is like a spring.

If the attachment is to another item, that item might move. If the attachment is to an anchor, you can move the anchorPoint. When that happens, this item moves too, in accordance with the physics of the attaching medium. An anchorPoint is particularly useful for implementing a draggable view within an animator world, as I'll demonstrate in the next chapter.

Starting in iOS 9, there are several more varieties of attachment:

Limit attachment

A limit attachment is created with this class method:

- `limitAttachment(with:offsetFromCenter:attachedTo:offsetFrom-Center:)`

It's like a rope running between two items. Each item can move freely and independently until the `length` is reached, at which point the moving item drags the other item along.

Fixed attachment

A fixed attachment is created with this class method:

- `fixedAttachment(with:attachedTo:attachmentAnchor:)`

It's as if there are two rods; each rod has an item at one end, with the other ends of the rods being welded together at the anchor point. If one item moves, it must remain at a fixed distance from the anchor, and will tend to rotate around it while pulling it along, at the same time making the other item rotate around the anchor.

Pin attachment

A pin attachment is created with this class method:

- `pinAttachment(with:attachedTo:attachmentAnchor:)`

A pin attachment is like a fixed attachment, but instead of the rods being welded together, they are hinged together. Each item is thus free to rotate around the anchor point, at a fixed distance from it, *independently*, subject to the pin attachment's `frictionTorque` which injects resistance into the hinge.

Sliding attachment

A sliding attachment can involve one or two items, and is created with one of these class methods:

- `slidingAttachment(with:attachmentAnchor:axisOfTranslation:)`
- `slidingAttachment(with:attachedTo:attachmentAnchor:axisOf-Translation:)`

Imagine a channel running through the anchor point, its direction defined by the axis of translation (a CGVector). Then an item is attached to a rod whose other end slots into that channel and is free to slide up and down it, but whose angle relative to the channel is fixed by its initial definition (given the item's position, the anchor's position, and the channel axis) and cannot change.

The channel is infinite by default, but you can add end caps that define the limits of sliding. To do so, you specify the attachment's `attachmentRange`; this is a

UIFloatRange, which has a minimum and a maximum. The anchor point is 0, and you are defining the minimum and maximum with respect to that; thus, a float range (-100.0,100.0) provides freedom of movement up to 100 points away from the initial anchor point. It can take some experimentation to discover whether the end cap along a given direction of the channel is the minimum or the maximum.

If there is one item, the anchor is fixed. If there are two items, they can slide independently, and the anchor is free to follow along if one of the items pulls it.

Here's an example of a sliding attachment. We start with a black square and a red square, sitting on the same horizontal, and attached to an anchor midway between them:

```
// first view
let v = UIView(frame:CGRect(0,0,50,50))
v.backgroundColor = .black
self.view.addSubview(v)
// second view
let v2 = UIView(frame:CGRect(200,0,50,50))
v2.backgroundColor = .red
self.view.addSubview(v2)
// sliding attachment
let a = UIAttachmentBehavior.slidingAttachment(with:v,
    attachedTo: v2, attachmentAnchor: CGPoint(125,25),
    axisOfTranslation: CGVector(0,1))
a.attachmentRange = UIFloatRangeMake(-200,200)
self.anim.addBehavior(a)
```

The axis through the anchor point is vertical, and we have permitted a maximum of 200. We now apply a slight vertical downward push to the black square:

```
let p = UIPushBehavior(items: [v], mode: .continuous)
p.pushDirection = CGVector(0,0.05)
self.anim.addBehavior(p)
```

The black square moves slowly downward, absolutely vertical, with its rod sliding down the channel, until its rod hits the maximum end cap at 200. At that point, the anchor breaks free and begins to move, dragging the red square with it, the two of them continuing downward and slowly rotating round their connection of two rods and the channel (Figure 4-8).

Motion Effects

A view can respond in real time to the way the user tilts the device. Typically, the view's response will be to shift its position slightly. This is used in various parts of the interface, to give a sense of the interface's being layered (parallax). When an alert is present, for example, if the user tilts the device, the alert shifts its position; the effect

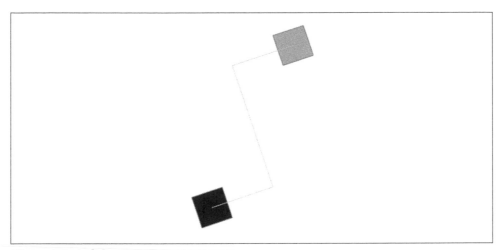

Figure 4-8. A sliding attachment

is subtle, but sufficient to suggest subconsciously that the alert is floating slightly in front of everything else on the screen.

Your own views can behave in the same way. A view will respond to shifts in the position of the device if it has one or more motion effects (UIMotionEffect), provided the user has not turned off motion effects in the device's Accessibility settings. A view's motion effects are managed with methods addMotionEffect(_:) and removeMotion-Effect(_:), and the motionEffects property.

The UIMotionEffect class is abstract. The chief subclass provided is UIInterpolating-MotionEffect. Every UIInterpolatingMotionEffect has a single key path, which uses key–value coding to specify the property of its view that it affects. It also has a type, specifying which axis of the device's tilting (horizontal tilt or vertical tilt) is to affect this property. Finally, it has a maximum and minimum relative value, the furthest distance that the affected property of the view is to be permitted to wander from its actual value as the user tilts the device.

Related motion effects should be combined into a UIMotionEffectGroup (a UIMotionEffect subclass), and the group added to the view. So, for example:

```
let m1 = UIInterpolatingMotionEffect(
    keyPath:"center.x", type:.tiltAlongHorizontalAxis)
m1.maximumRelativeValue = 10.0
m1.minimumRelativeValue = -10.0
let m2 = UIInterpolatingMotionEffect(
    keyPath:"center.y", type:.tiltAlongVerticalAxis)
m2.maximumRelativeValue = 10.0
```

```
m2.minimumRelativeValue = -10.0
let g = UIMotionEffectGroup()
g.motionEffects = [m1,m2]
v.addMotionEffect(g)
```

You can write your own UIMotionEffect subclass by implementing a single method, keyPathsAndRelativeValues(forViewerOffset:), but this will rarely be necessary.

Animation and Autolayout

The interplay between animation and autolayout can be tricky. As part of an animation, you may be changing a view's frame (or bounds, or center). You're really not supposed to do that when you're using autolayout. If you do, an animation may not work correctly. Or, it may appear to work perfectly, because no layout has happened; however, it is entirely possible that layout *will* happen, and that it will be accompanied by undesirable effects. As I explained in Chapter 1, when layout takes place under autolayout, what matters are a view's constraints. If the constraints affecting a view don't resolve to the size and position that the view has at the moment of layout, the view will jump as the constraints are obeyed. This is almost certainly not what you want.

To persuade yourself that this can be a problem, just animate a view's position and then ask for immediate layout, like this:

```
UIView.animateWithDuration(1, animations:{
    self.v.center.x += 100
    }, completion: { _ in
        self.v.superview!.setNeedsLayout()
        self.v.superview!.layoutIfNeeded()
})
```

If we're using autolayout, the view slides to the right and then jumps back to the left. This is bad. It's up to us to keep the constraints synchronized with the reality, so that when layout comes along in the natural course of things, our views don't jump into undesirable states.

One option is to revise the violated constraints to match the new reality. If we've planned far ahead, we may have armed ourselves in advance with a reference to those constraints; in that case, our code can now remove and replace them — or, if the only thing that needs changing is the constant value of a constraint, we can change that value in place. Otherwise, discovering what constraints are now violated, and getting a reference to them, is not at all easy.

Alternatively, instead of performing the animation first and then revising the constraints, we can change the constraints first and then *animate the act of layout*. Again, this assumes that we have a reference to the constraints in question. For example, if we are animating a view (v) 100 points rightward, and if we have a reference (con) to the constraint whose `constant` positions that view horizontally, we would say this:

```
con.constant += 100
UIView.animate(withDuration:1) {
    v.superview!.layoutIfNeeded()
}
```

This technique is not limited to a simple change of `constant`. You can overhaul the constraints quite dramatically and still animate the resulting change of layout. In this example, I animate a view (v) from one side of its superview (`self.view`) to the other by removing its leading constraint and replacing it with a trailing constraint:

```
let c = self.oldConstraint.constant
NSLayoutConstraint.deactivate([self.oldConstraint])
let newConstraint = v.trailingAnchor.constraint(
    equalTo:self.view.layoutMarginsGuide.trailingAnchor, constant:-c)
NSLayoutConstraint.activate([newConstraint])
UIView.animate(withDuration:0.4) {
    v.superview!.layoutIfNeeded()
}
```

Another possibility is to use a snapshot of the original view (Chapter 1). Add the snapshot temporarily to the interface — without using autolayout, and perhaps hiding the original view — and animate the snapshot:

```
let snap = self.v.snapshotView(afterScreenUpdates:false)!
snap.frame = self.v.frame
self.v.superview!.addSubview(snap)
self.v.isHidden = true
UIView.animate(withDuration:1) {
    snap.center.x += 100
}
```

That works because the snapshot view is not under the influence of autolayout, so it stays where we put it even if layout takes place. If, however, we need to remove the snapshot view and reveal the real view, then the real view's constraints will probably still have to be revised.

Still another approach is to animate the view's `transform` instead of the view itself. Back in iOS 6, this triggered spurious layout and caused issues, but that's no longer the case:

```
UIView.animate(withDuration:1) {
    self.v.transform = CGAffineTransform(translationX: 100, y: 0)
}
```

That's extremely robust, but of course it works only if the animation *can* be expressed as a transform, and it leaves open the question of how long we want a transformed view to remain lying around in our interface.

CHAPTER 5

Touches

[Winifred the Woebegone illustrates hit-testing:] Hey nonny nonny, is it you? — Hey nonny nonny nonny no! — Hey nonny nonny, is it you? — Hey nonny nonny nonny no!
—Marshall Barer,
Once Upon a Mattress

A *touch* is an instance of the user putting a finger on the screen. The system and the hardware, working together, know *when* a finger contacts the screen and *where* it is. A finger is fat, but its location is cleverly reduced to a single point.

A UIResponder is a potential recipient of touches. A UIView is a UIResponder, and is thus the *visible* recipient of touches. There are other UIResponder subclasses, but none of them is visible on the screen. The user sees a view by virtue of its underlying layer; the user touches a view by virtue of the fact that it is a UIResponder.

A touch is represented as an object (a UITouch instance) which is bundled up in an envelope (a UIEvent) which the system delivers to your app. It is then up to your app to deliver the envelope to the appropriate UIView. In the vast majority of cases, this will happen automatically the way you expect, and you will respond to a touch by way of the view in which the touch occurred.

In fact, usually you won't concern yourself with UIEvents and UITouches at all. Most built-in interface views deal with these low-level touch reports themselves, and notify your code at a higher level — you hear about functionality and intention rather than raw touches. When a UIButton emits an action message to report a Touch Up Inside control event, it has already performed a reduction of a complex sequence of touches; but what the button reports to you is simply that it was tapped. Similarly, a UIText-Field reports touches on the keyboard as changes in its own text. A UITableView reports that the user selected a cell. A UIScrollView, when dragged, reports that it scrolled; when pinched outward, it reports that it zoomed.

Nevertheless, it is useful to know how to respond to touches directly, so that you can implement your own touchable views, and so that you understand what Cocoa's built-in views are actually doing. In this chapter, I'll start by discussing touch detection and response by views (and other UIResponders) at their lowest level, along with a higher-level, more practical mechanism, gesture recognizers, that categorizes touches into gesture types for you. Then I'll deconstruct the touch-delivery architecture by which touches are reported to your views in the first place.

Touch Events and Views

Imagine a screen that the user is not touching at all: the screen is "finger-free." Now the user touches the screen with one or more fingers. From that moment until the time the screen is once again finger-free, all touches and finger movements together constitute what Apple calls a single *multitouch sequence.*

The system reports to your app, during a given multitouch sequence, every change in finger configuration, so that your app can figure out what the user is doing. Every such report is a UIEvent. In fact, every report having to do with the same multitouch sequence is *the same UIEvent instance*, arriving repeatedly, each time there's a change in finger configuration.

Every UIEvent reporting a change in the user's finger configuration contains one or more UITouch objects. Each UITouch object corresponds to a single finger; conversely, every finger touching the screen is represented in the UIEvent by a UITouch object. Once a UITouch instance has been created to represent a finger that has touched the screen, *the same UITouch instance* is used to represent that finger throughout this multitouch sequence until the finger leaves the screen.

Now, it might sound as if the system, during a multitouch sequence, constantly has to bombard the app with huge numbers of reports. But that's not really true. The system needs to report only *changes* in the finger configuration. For a given UITouch object (representing, remember, a specific finger), only four things can happen. These are called *touch phases*, and are described by a UITouch instance's `phase` property (UITouchPhase):

`.began`
> The finger touched the screen for the first time; this UITouch instance has just been created. This is always the first phase, and arrives only once.

`.moved`
> The finger moved upon the screen.

`.stationary`
> The finger remained on the screen without moving. Why is it necessary to report this? Well, remember, once a UITouch instance has been created, it must be

present every time the UIEvent for this multitouch sequence arrives. So if the UIEvent arrives because something *else* happened (e.g., a new finger touched the screen), we must report what *this* finger has been doing, even if it has been doing nothing.

`.ended`

> The finger left the screen. Like `.began`, this phase arrives only once. The UITouch instance will now be destroyed and will no longer appear in UIEvents for this multitouch sequence.

Those four phases are sufficient to describe everything that a finger can do. Actually, there is one more possible phase:

`.cancelled`

> The system has aborted this multitouch sequence because something interrupted it. What might interrupt a multitouch sequence? There are many possibilities. Perhaps the user clicked the Home button or the screen lock button in the middle of the sequence. A local notification alert may have appeared (Chapter 13); on an iPhone, a call may have come in. And as we shall see, a gesture recognizer recognizing its gesture may also trigger touch cancellation. The point is, if you're dealing with touches yourself, you cannot afford to ignore touch cancellations; they are your opportunity to get things into a coherent state when the sequence is interrupted.

When a UITouch first appears (`.began`), your app works out which UIView it is associated with. (I'll give full details, later in this chapter, as to how it does that.) This view is then set as the touch's `view` property, and *remains* so; from then on, this UITouch is *always* associated with this view (until that finger leaves the screen).

The UITouches that constitute a UIEvent might be associated with different views. Accordingly, one and the same UIEvent is distributed to *all the views of all the UITouches it contains.* Conversely, if a view is sent a UIEvent, it's because that UIEvent contains at least one UITouch whose `view` is this view.

If every UITouch in a UIEvent associated with a certain UIView has the phase `.stationary`, that UIEvent is *not* sent to that UIView. There's no point, because as far as that view is concerned, nothing happened.

 Do not retain a reference to a UITouch or UIEvent object over time; it is mutable and doesn't belong to you. If you want to save touch information, extract and save the information, not the touch itself.

Receiving Touches

A UIResponder, and therefore a UIView, has four methods corresponding to the four UITouch phases that require UIEvent delivery. A UIEvent is delivered to a view by calling one of the four *touch methods*. Here they are:

touchesBegan(_:with:)
> A finger touched the screen, creating a UITouch.

touchesMoved(_:with:)
> A finger previously reported to this view with touchesBegan(_:with:) has moved. (On a device with 3D touch, "moved" might mean a change of pressure rather than location.)

touchesEnded(_:with:)
> A finger previously reported to this view with touchesBegan(_:with:) has left the screen.

touchesCancelled(_:with:)
> We are bailing out on a finger previously reported to this view with touches-Began(_:with:).

The touch methods' parameters are:

The relevant touches
> These are the event's touches whose phase corresponds to the name of the method and (normally) whose view is this view. They arrive as a Set. If there is only one touch in the set, or if any touch in the set will do, you can retrieve it with first (a set is unordered, so *which* element is first is arbitrary).

The event
> This is the UIEvent instance. It contains its touches as a Set, which you can retrieve with the allTouches message. This means *all* the event's touches, including but not necessarily limited to those in the first parameter; there might be touches in a different phase or intended for some other view. You can call touches(for:) to ask for the set of touches associated with a particular view or window.

So, when we say that a certain view *is receiving a touch*, that is a shorthand expression meaning that it is being sent a UIEvent containing this UITouch, over and over, by calling one of its touch methods, corresponding to the phase this touch is in, from the time the touch is created until the time it is destroyed.

A UITouch has some useful methods and properties:

location(in:), previousLocation(in:)
> The current and previous location of this touch with respect to the coordinate system of a given view. The view you'll be interested in will often be `self` or `self.superview`; supply `nil` to get the location with respect to the window. The previous location will be of interest only if the phase is `.moved`.

timestamp
> When the touch last changed. A touch is timestamped when it is created (`.began`) and each time it moves (`.moved`). There can be a delay between the occurrence of a physical touch and the delivery of the corresponding UITouch, so to learn about the timing of touches, consult the timestamp, not the clock.

tapCount
> If two touches are in roughly the same place in quick succession, and the first one is brief, the second one may be characterized as a repeat of the first. They are different touch objects, but the second will be assigned a `tapCount` one larger than the previous one. The default is 1, so if (for example) a touch's `tapCount` is 3, then this is the third tap in quick succession in roughly the same spot.

view
> The view with which this touch is associated.

majorRadius, majorRadiusTolerance
> Respectively, the radius of the touch (approximately half its size) and the uncertainty of that measurement, in points.

A UITouch carries some additional information that may be useful if the touch arrived through an Apple Pencil rather than a finger; for example, it describes how the pencil is oriented.

Here are some additional UIEvent properties:

type
> This will be `UIEventType.touches`. There are other event types, but you're not going to receive any of them this way.

timestamp
> When the event occurred.

Starting in iOS 9, you can reduce the latency between the user's touches and your app's rendering to the screen. On certain devices, the touch detection rate is doubled or even quadrupled, and you can ask for the extra touches. On all devices, a few future touches may be predicted, and you can ask for these. Such features would be useful, for example, in a drawing app.

Restricting Touches

Touch events can be turned off entirely at the application level with UIApplication's `beginIgnoringInteractionEvents`. It is quite common to do this during animations and other lengthy operations during which responding to a touch could cause undesirable results. This call should be balanced by `endIgnoringInteractionEvents`. Pairs can be nested, in which case interactivity won't be restored until the outermost `endIgnoringInteractionEvents` has been reached.

A number of UIView properties also restrict the delivery of touches to particular views:

isUserInteractionEnabled

> If set to `false`, this view (along with its subviews) is excluded from receiving touches. Touches on this view or one of its subviews "fall through" to a view behind it.

alpha

> If set to `0.0` (or extremely close to it), this view (along with its subviews) is excluded from receiving touches. Touches on this view or one of its subviews "fall through" to a view behind it.

isHidden

> If set to `true`, this view (along with its subviews) is excluded from receiving touches. This makes sense, since from the user's standpoint, the view and its subviews are not even present.

isMultipleTouchEnabled

> If set to `false`, this view never receives more than one touch simultaneously; once it receives a touch, it doesn't receive any other touches until that first touch has ended.

isExclusiveTouch

> An `isExclusiveTouch` view receives a touch only if no other views in the same window have touches associated with them; once an `isExclusiveTouch` view has received a touch, then while that touch exists no other view in the same window receives any touches. (This is the only one of these properties that can't be set in the nib editor.)

Interpreting Touches

Thanks to gesture recognizers (discussed later in this chapter), in most cases you won't have to interpret touches at all; you'll let a gesture recognizer do most of that work. Even so, it is beneficial to be conversant with the nature of touch interpretation;

this will help you use, subclass, and create gesture recognizers. Furthermore, not every touch sequence can be codified through a gesture recognizer; sometimes, directly interpreting touches is the best approach.

To figure out what's going on as touches are received by a view, your code must essentially function as a kind of state machine. You'll receive various touch method calls, and your response will partly depend upon what happened previously, so you'll have to record somehow, such as in instance properties, the information that you'll need in order to decide what to do when the next touch method is called. Such an architecture can make writing and maintaining touch-analysis code quite tricky.

To illustrate the business of interpreting touches, we'll start with a view that can be dragged with the user's finger. For simplicity, I'll assume that this view receives only a single touch at a time. (This assumption is easy to enforce by setting the view's isMultipleTouchEnabled to false, which is the default.)

The trick to making a view follow the user's finger is to realize that a view is positioned by its center, which is in superview coordinates, but the user's finger might not be at the center of the view. So at every stage of the drag we must change the view's center by the change in the user's finger position in superview coordinates:

```swift
override func touchesMoved(_ touches: Set<UITouch>, with e: UIEvent?) {
    let t = touches.first!
    let loc = t.location(in:self.superview)
    let oldP = t.previousLocation(in:self.superview)
    let deltaX = loc.x - oldP.x
    let deltaY = loc.y - oldP.y
    var c = self.center
    c.x += deltaX
    c.y += deltaY
    self.center = c
}
```

Next, let's add a restriction that the view can be dragged only vertically or horizontally. All we have to do is hold one coordinate steady; but which coordinate? Everything seems to depend on what the user does initially. So we'll do a one-time test the first time we receive touchesMoved(_:with:). Now we're maintaining two Bool state properties, self.decided and self.horiz:

```swift
override func touchesBegan(_ touches: Set<UITouch>, with e: UIEvent?) {
    self.decided = false
}
override func touchesMoved(_ touches: Set<UITouch>, with e: UIEvent?) {
    let t = touches.first!
    if !self.decided {
        self.decided = true
        let then = t.previousLocation(in:self)
        let now = t.location(in:self)
        let deltaX = abs(then.x - now.x)
```

```
        let deltaY = abs(then.y - now.y)
        self.horiz = deltaX >= deltaY
    }
    let loc = t.location(in:self.superview)
    let oldP = t.previousLocation(in:self.superview)
    let deltaX = loc.x - oldP.x
    let deltaY = loc.y - oldP.y
    var c = self.center
    if self.horiz {
        c.x += deltaX
    } else {
        c.y += deltaY
    }
    self.center = c
}
```

Look at how things are trending. We are maintaining multiple state properties, which we are managing across multiple methods, and we are subdividing a touch method implementation into tests depending on the state of our state machine. Our state machine is very simple, but already our code is becoming difficult to read and to maintain — and things will only become more messy as we try to make our view's behavior more sophisticated.

Another area in which manual touch handling can rapidly prove overwhelming is when it comes to distinguishing between different gestures that the user is to be permitted to perform on a view. Imagine, for example, a view that distinguishes between a finger tapping briefly and a finger remaining down for a longer time. We can't know how long a tap is until it's over, so we must wait until then before deciding; once again, this requires maintaining state in a property (self.time):

```
override func touchesBegan(_ touches: Set<UITouch>, with e: UIEvent?) {
    self.time = touches.first!.timestamp
}
override func touchesEnded(_ touches: Set<UITouch>, with e: UIEvent?) {
    let diff = e!.timestamp - self.time
    if (diff < 0.4) {
        print("short")
    } else {
        print("long")
    }
}
```

A similar challenge is distinguishing between a single tap and a double tap. The UITouch tapCount property already makes this distinction, but that, by itself, is not enough to help us react differently to the two. What we must do, having received a tap whose tapCount is 1, is to use delayed performance in responding to it, so that we wait long enough to give a second tap a chance to arrive. This is unfortunate, because it means that if the user intends a single tap, some time will elapse before anything happens in response to it; however, there's nothing we can readily do about that.

Distributing our various tasks correctly is tricky. We *know* when we have a double tap as early as touchesBegan(_:with:), but we *respond* to the double tap in touches-Ended(_:with:). Therefore, we use a property (self.single) to communicate between the two. We don't start our delayed response to a single tap until touches-Ended(_:with:), because what matters is the time between the taps as a whole, not between the starts of the taps:

```
override func touchesBegan(_ touches: Set<UITouch>, with e: UIEvent?) {
    let ct = touches.first!.tapCount
    switch ct {
    case 2:
        self.single = false
    default: break
    }
}
override func touchesEnded(_ touches: Set<UITouch>, with e: UIEvent?) {
    let ct = touches.first!.tapCount
    switch ct {
    case 1:
        self.single = true
        delay(0.3) {
            if self.single { // no second tap intervened
                print("single tap")
            }
        }
    case 2:
        print("double tap")
    default: break
    }
}
```

As if that code weren't confusing enough, let's now consider combining our detection for a single or double tap with our earlier code for dragging a view horizontally or vertically. This is to be a view that can detect four kinds of gesture: a single tap, a double tap, a horizontal drag, and a vertical drag. We must include the code for all possibilities and make sure they don't interfere with each other. The result is horrifying — a forced join between two already complicated sets of code, along with an additional pair of state properties (self.drag, self.decidedTapOrDrag) to track the decision between the tap gestures on the one hand and the drag gestures on the other:

```
override func touchesBegan(_ touches: Set<UITouch>, with e: UIEvent?) {
    // be undecided
    self.decidedTapOrDrag = false
    // prepare for a tap
    let ct = touches.first!.tapCount
    switch ct {
    case 2:
        self.single = false
        self.decidedTapOrDrag = true
        self.drag = false
```

```
            return
        default: break
        }
        // prepare for a drag
        self.decidedDirection = false
    }
    override func touchesMoved(_ touches: Set<UITouch>, with e: UIEvent?) {
        if self.decidedTapOrDrag && !self.drag {return}
        self.superview!.bringSubview(toFront:self)
        let t = touches.first!
        self.decidedTapOrDrag = true
        self.drag = true
        if !self.decidedDirection {
            self.decidedDirection = true
            let then = t.previousLocation(in:self)
            let now = t.location(in:self)
            let deltaX = abs(then.x - now.x)
            let deltaY = abs(then.y - now.y)
            self.horiz = deltaX >= deltaY
        }
        let loc = t.location(in:self.superview)
        let oldP = t.previousLocation(in:self.superview)
        let deltaX = loc.x - oldP.x
        let deltaY = loc.y - oldP.y
        var c = self.center
        if self.horiz {
            c.x += deltaX
        } else {
            c.y += deltaY
        }
        self.center = c
    }
    override func touchesEnded(_ touches: Set<UITouch>, with e: UIEvent?) {
        if !self.decidedTapOrDrag || !self.drag {
            // end for a tap
            let ct = touches.first!.tapCount
            switch ct {
            case 1:
                self.single = true
                delay(0.3) {
                    if self.single {
                        print("single tap")
                    }
                }
            case 2:
                print("double tap")
            default: break
            }
        }
    }
```

That code seems to work, but it's hard to say whether it covers all possibilities coherently; it's barely legible and the logic borders on the mysterious. This is the kind of situation for which gesture recognizers were devised.

Gesture Recognizers

Writing and maintaining a state machine that interprets touches across a combination of three or four touch methods is hard enough when a view confines itself to expecting only one kind of gesture, such as dragging. It becomes even more involved when a view wants to accept and respond differently to different kinds of gesture. Furthermore, many types of gesture are conventional and standard; it seems insane to require developers to implement independently what is, in effect, a universal vocabulary.

The solution is gesture recognizers, which standardize common gestures and allow the code for different gestures to be separated and encapsulated into different objects. Thanks to gesture recognizers, it is unnecessary to subclass UIView merely in order to implement touch analysis.

Gesture Recognizer Classes

A *gesture recognizer* (a subclass of UIGestureRecognizer) is an object whose job is to detect that a multitouch sequence equates to one particular type of gesture. It is attached to a UIView, which has for this purpose methods addGesture-Recognizer(_:) and removeGestureRecognizer(_:), and a gestureRecognizers property.

A UIGestureRecognizer implements the four touch methods, but it is not a responder (a UIResponder), so it does not participate in the responder chain. If, however, a new touch is going to be delivered to a view, it is also associated with and delivered to that view's gesture recognizers if it has any, *and* to that view's *superview's* gesture recognizers if *it* has any, and so on up the view hierarchy. Thus, the place of a gesture recognizer in the view hierarchy matters, even though it isn't part of the responder chain.

UITouch and UIEvent provide complementary ways of learning how touches and gesture recognizers are associated. UITouch's gestureRecognizers lists the gesture recognizers that are currently handling this touch. UIEvent's touches(for:) can take a gesture recognizer parameter; it then lists the touches that are currently being handled by that gesture recognizer.

Each gesture recognizer maintains its own state as touch events arrive, building up evidence as to what kind of gesture this is. When one of them decides that it has recognized its own particular type of gesture, it emits either a single message (to indicate, for example, that a finger has tapped) or a series of messages (to indicate, for example, that a finger is moving); the distinction here is between a *discrete* and a *continuous* gesture.

What message a gesture recognizer emits, and to what object it sends it, is set through a target–action dispatch table attached to the gesture recognizer; a gesture recognizer is rather like a UIControl in this regard. Indeed, one might say that a gesture recognizer simplifies the touch handling of *any* view to be like that of a control. The difference is that one control may report several different control events, whereas each gesture recognizer reports only one gesture type, with different gestures being reported by different gesture recognizers.

UIGestureRecognizer itself is abstract, providing methods and properties to its subclasses. Among these are:

`init(target:action:)`
    The designated initializer. Each message emitted by a UIGestureRecognizer is a matter of sending the action message to the target. Further target–action pairs may be added with `addTarget(_:action:)` and removed with `removeTarget(_:action:)`.

    Two forms of `action:` selector are possible: either there is no parameter, or there is a single parameter which will be the gesture recognizer. Most commonly, you'll use the second form, so that the target can identify, query, and communicate with the gesture recognizer.

`location(ofTouch:in:)`
    The second parameter is the view whose coordinate system you want to use. The touch is specified by an index number. The `numberOfTouches` property provides a count of current touches; the touches themselves are inaccessible by way of the gesture recognizer.

`isEnabled`
    A convenient way to turn a gesture recognizer off without having to remove it from its view.

`state`, `view`
    I'll discuss state later on. The `view` is the view to which this gesture recognizer is attached.

Built-in UIGestureRecognizer subclasses are provided for six common gesture types: tap, pinch (inward or outward), pan (drag), swipe, rotate, and long press. Each embodies properties and methods likely to be needed for each type of gesture, either in order to configure the gesture recognizer beforehand or in order to query it as to the state of an ongoing gesture:

UITapGestureRecognizer (discrete)

Configuration: `numberOfTapsRequired`, `numberOfTouchesRequired` ("touches" means simultaneous fingers).

UIPinchGestureRecognizer (continuous)

Two fingers moving toward or away from each other. State: `scale`, `velocity`.

UIRotationGestureRecognizer (continuous)

Two fingers moving round a common center. State: `rotation`, `velocity`.

UISwipeGestureRecognizer (discrete)

A straight-line movement in one of the four cardinal directions. Configuration: `direction` (meaning permitted directions, a bitmask), `numberOfTouches-Required`.

UIPanGestureRecognizer (continuous)

Dragging. Configuration: `minimumNumberOfTouches`, `maximumNumberOfTouches`. State: `translation(in:)`, `setTranslation(_:in:)`, `velocity(in:)`; the coordinate system of the specified view is used.

UIScreenEdgePanGestureRecognizer

A UIPanGestureRecognizer subclass. It recognizes a pan gesture that starts at an edge of the screen. It adds a configuration property, `edges`, a UIRectEdge; despite the name (and the documentation), this must be set to a single edge.

UILongPressGestureRecognizer (continuous)

Configuration: `numberOfTapsRequired`, `numberOfTouchesRequired`, `minimum-PressDuration`, `allowableMovement`. The `numberOfTapsRequired` is the count of taps *before* the tap that stays down, so it can be 0 (the default). The `allowable-Movement` setting lets you compensate for the fact that the user's finger is unlikely to remain steady during an extended press; thus we need to provide some limit before deciding that this gesture is, say, a drag, and not a long press after all. On the other hand, once the long press is recognized, the finger is permitted to drag as part of the long press gesture.

UIGestureRecognizer also provides a `location(in:)` method. This is a single point, even if there are multiple touches. The subclasses implement this variously. For example, for UIPanGestureRecognizer, the location is where the touch is if there's a single touch, but it's a sort of midpoint ("centroid") if there are multiple touches.

We already know enough to implement, using a gesture recognizer, a view that responds to a single tap, or a view that responds to a double tap. Here's code (probably from our view controller's `viewDidLoad`) that implements a view (`self.v`) that responds to a single tap by calling our `singleTap` method:

```
let t1 = UITapGestureRecognizer(target:self, action:#selector(singleTap))
self.v.addGestureRecognizer(t1)
```

And here's code that implements a view (`self.v`) that responds to a double tap by calling our `doubleTap` method:

```
let t2 = UITapGestureRecognizer(target:self, action:#selector(doubleTap))
t2.numberOfTapsRequired = 2
self.v.addGestureRecognizer(t2)
```

For a continuous gesture like dragging, we need to know both when the gesture is in progress and when the gesture ends. This brings us to the subject of a gesture recognizer's state.

A gesture recognizer implements a notion of *states* (the `state` property, UIGestureRecognizerState); it passes through these states in a definite progression. The gesture recognizer remains in the `.possible` state until it can make a decision one way or the other as to whether this is in fact the correct gesture. The documentation neatly lays out the possible progressions:

Wrong gesture
> `.possible` → `.failed`. No action message is sent.

Discrete gesture (like a tap), recognized
> `.possible` → `.ended`. One action message is sent, when the state changes to `.ended`.

Continuous gesture (like a drag), recognized
> `.possible` → `.began` → `.changed` (repeatedly) → `.ended`. Action messages are sent once for `.began`, as many times as necessary for `.changed`, and once for `.ended`.

Continuous gesture, recognized but later cancelled
> `.possible` → `.began` → `.changed` (repeatedly) → `.cancelled`. Action messages are sent once for `.began`, as many times as necessary for `.changed`, and once for `.cancelled`.

The same action message arrives at the same target every time, so the action method must differentiate by asking about the gesture recognizer's `state`. The usual implementation involves a switch statement.

To illustrate, we will implement, using a gesture recognizer, a view that lets itself be dragged around in any direction by a single finger. Our maintenance of state is greatly simplified, because a UIPanGestureRecognizer maintains a delta (translation) for us. This delta, available using `translation(in:)`, is reckoned from the touch's initial position. We don't even need to record the view's original `center`, because we can reset the UIPanGestureRecognizer's delta, using `setTranslation(_:in:)`:

```
func viewDidLoad {
    super.viewDidLoad()
    let p = UIPanGestureRecognizer(target:self, action:#selector(dragging))
    self.v.addGestureRecognizer(p)
}
@objc func dragging(_ p : UIPanGestureRecognizer) {
    let v = p.view!
    switch p.state {
    case .began, .changed:
        let delta = p.translation(in:v.superview)
        var c = v.center
        c.x += delta.x; c.y += delta.y
        v.center = c
        p.setTranslation(.zero, in: v.superview)
    default: break
    }
}
```

To illustrate the use of a UIPanGestureRecognizer's velocity(in:), let's imagine a view that the user can drag, but which then springs back to where it was. We can express "springs back" with a spring animation (Chapter 4). All we have to do is add an .ended case to our dragging(_:) method (dest is the original center of our view v):

```
case .ended, .cancelled:
    let anim = UIViewPropertyAnimator(
        duration: 0.4,
        timingParameters: UISpringTimingParameters(
            dampingRatio: 0.6,
            initialVelocity: .zero))
    anim.addAnimations {
        v.center = dest
    }
    anim.startAnimation()
```

That's good, but it would be more realistic if the view had some momentum at the moment the user lets go of it. If the user drags the view quickly away from its home and releases it, the view should keep moving a little in the same direction before springing back into place. That's what the spring animation's initialVelocity: parameter is for! We can easily find out what the view's velocity is, at the moment the user releases it, by asking the gesture recognizer:

```
let vel = p.velocity(in: v.superview!)
```

Unfortunately, we cannot use this value directly as the spring animation's initial-Velocity; there's a type impedance mismatch. The view's velocity is expressed as a CGPoint measured in points per second. But the spring's initialVelocity is expressed as a CGVector measured as a proportion of the distance to be travelled over the course of the animation. Fortunately, the conversion is easy:

```
case .ended, .cancelled:
    let vel = p.velocity(in: v.superview!)
    let c = v.center
    let distx = abs(c.x - dest.x)
    let disty = abs(c.y - dest.y)
    let anim = UIViewPropertyAnimator(
        duration: 0.4,
        timingParameters: UISpringTimingParameters(
            dampingRatio: 0.6,
            initialVelocity: CGVector(vel.x/distx, vel.y/disty)))
    anim.addAnimations {
        v.center = dest
    }
    anim.startAnimation()
```

A pan gesture recognizer can be used also to make a view draggable under the influence of a UIDynamicAnimator (Chapter 4). The strategy here is that the view is attached to one or more anchor points through a UIAttachmentBehavior; as the user drags, we move the anchor point(s), and the view follows. In this example, I set up the whole UIKit dynamics "stack" of objects as the gesture begins, anchoring the view at the point where the touch is; then I move the anchor point to stay with the touch. Instance properties self.anim and self.att store the UIDynamicAnimator and the UIAttachmentBehavior, respectively; self.view is our view's superview, and is the animator's reference view:

```
@IBAction func dragging(_ p: UIPanGestureRecognizer) {
    switch p.state {
    case .began:
        self.anim = UIDynamicAnimator(referenceView:self.view)
        let loc = p.location(ofTouch:0, in:p.view)
        let cen = CGPoint(p.view!.bounds.midX, p.view!.bounds.midY)
        let off = UIOffsetMake(loc.x-cen.x, loc.y-cen.y)
        let anchor = p.location(ofTouch:0, in:self.view)
        let att = UIAttachmentBehavior(item:p.view!,
            offsetFromCenter:off, attachedToAnchor:anchor)
        self.anim.addBehavior(att)
        self.att = att
    case .changed:
        self.att.anchorPoint = p.location(ofTouch:0, in: self.view)
    default:
        self.anim = nil
    }
}
```

The outcome is that the view both moves and rotates in response to dragging, like a plate being pulled about on a table by a single finger.

By adding behaviors to the dynamic animator, we can limit further what the view is permitted to do as it is being dragged by its anchor. For example, imagine a view that can be lifted vertically and dropped, but cannot be moved horizontally. As I demonstrated earlier, you can prevent horizontal dragging through the implementation of your response to touch events (and later in this chapter, I'll show how to do this by subclassing UIPanGestureRecognizer). But the same sort of limitation can imposed by way of the underlying physics of the world in which the view exists — with a sliding attachment, for example.

Gesture Recognizer Conflicts

A view can have more than one gesture recognizer associated with it. This isn't a matter merely of multiple recognizers attached to a single view; as I have said, if a view is touched, not only its own gesture recognizers but also any gesture recognizers attached to views further up the view hierarchy are in play simultaneously. I like to think of a view as surrounded by a *swarm* of gesture recognizers — its own, and those of its superview, and so on. (In reality, it is a touch that has a swarm of gesture recognizers; that's why a UITouch has a `gestureRecognizers` property, in the plural.)

The superview gesture recognizer swarm comes as a surprise to beginners, but it makes sense, because without it, certain gestures would be impossible. Imagine, for example, a pair of views, each of which the user can tap individually, but which the user can also touch simultaneously (one finger on each view) to rotate them together around their mutual centroid. Neither view can detect the rotation *qua* rotation, because neither view receives both touches; only the superview can detect it, so the fact that the views themselves respond to touches must not prevent the superview's gesture recognizer from operating.

The question naturally arises, then, of what happens when multiple gesture recognizers are in play. There is a natural competition between these gesture recognizers, each trying to recognizing the current multitouch sequence as its own appropriate gesture. This is a conflict between gesture recognizers. How will it be resolved?

The rule is simple. In general, by default, once a gesture recognizer succeeds in recognizing its gesture, any *other* gesture recognizers associated with its touches are *forced into the .failed state*, and whatever touches were associated with those gesture recognizers are no longer sent to them; in effect, the first gesture recognizer in a swarm that recognizes its gesture owns the gesture (and its touches) from then on.

In many cases, this "first past the post" behavior, on its own, will correctly eliminate conflicts. For example, we can add both our UITapGestureRecognizer for a single tap and our UIPanGestureRecognizer to a view and everything will just work; dragging works, and single tap works. Thus, "first past the post" is exactly the desired behavior:

```
let t1 = UITapGestureRecognizer(target:self, action:#selector(singleTap))
self.v.addGestureRecognizer(t1)
let p = UIPanGestureRecognizer(target: self, action: #selector(dragging))
self.v.addGestureRecognizer(p)
```

However, you can take a hand in how conflicts are resolved, and sometimes you will need to do so. What happens, for example, if we add a double tap gesture recognizer and a single tap gesture recognizer to the same view? Double tap works, but without preventing the single tap from working: on a double tap, *both* the single tap action method and the double tap action method are called.

If that isn't what we want, we don't have to use delayed performance, as we did earlier. Instead, we can create a *dependency* between one gesture recognizer and another, telling the first to suspend judgement until the second has decided whether this is its gesture. We can do this by sending the first gesture recognizer the `require(toFail:)` message. This method is rather badly named; it doesn't mean "force this other recognizer to fail," but rather, "you can't succeed unless this other recognizer has failed." For example:

```
let t2 = UITapGestureRecognizer(target:self, action:#selector(doubleTap))
t2.numberOfTapsRequired = 2
self.v.addGestureRecognizer(t2)
let t1 = UITapGestureRecognizer(target:self, action:#selector(singleTap))
t1.require(toFail:t2) // *
self.v.addGestureRecognizer(t1)
```

Another conflict that can arise is between a gesture recognizer and a view that already knows how to respond to the same gesture, such as a UIControl. This problem pops up particularly when the gesture recognizer belongs to the UIControl's superview. The UIControl's mere presence does not "block" the superview's gesture recognizer from recognizing a gesture on the UIControl, even if it is a UIControl that responds autonomously to touches. For example, your window's root view might have a UITap-GestureRecognizer attached to it (perhaps because you want to be able to recognize taps on the background); if there is also a UIButton within that view, how is that gesture recognizer to ignore a tap on the button?

The UIView instance method `gestureRecognizerShouldBegin(_:)` solves the problem. It is called automatically; to modify its behavior, use a custom UIView subclass and override it. Its parameter is a gesture recognizer belonging to this view or to a view further up the view hierarchy. That gesture recognizer has recognized its gesture as taking place in this view; but by returning `false`, the view can tell the gesture recognizer to bow out and do nothing, not sending any action messages, and permitting this view to respond to the touch as if the gesture recognizer weren't there.

Thus, for example, a UIButton could return `false` for a single tap UITapGesture-Recognizer; a single tap on the button would then trigger the button's action message and not the gesture recognizer's action message. And in fact a UIButton, by default, *does* return `false` for a single tap UITapGestureRecognizer whose view is not the UIButton itself.

Other built-in controls may also implement `gestureRecognizerShouldBegin(_:)` in such a way as to prevent accidental interaction with a gesture recognizer; the documentation says that a UISlider implements it in such a way that a UISwipeGesture-Recognizer won't prevent the user from sliding the "thumb," and there may be other cases that aren't documented explicitly. Naturally, you can take advantage of this feature in your own UIView subclasses as well.

Yet another way of resolving possible gesture recognizer conflicts is through the gesture recognizer's delegate, or with a gesture recognizer subclass. I'll discuss those in a moment.

Subclassing Gesture Recognizers

To subclass UIGestureRecognizer or a built-in gesture recognizer subclass, you must do the following things:

- Import `UIKit.UIGestureRecognizerSubclass`. This allows you to set a gesture recognizer's `state` property (which is otherwise read-only), and exposes declarations for the methods you may need to override.

- Override any touch methods you need to (as if the gesture recognizer were a UIResponder); if you're subclassing a built-in gesture recognizer subclass, you will almost certainly call `super` so as to take advantage of the built-in behavior. In overriding a touch method, you need to think like a gesture recognizer. As these methods are called, a gesture recognizer is setting its state; you must participate coherently in that process.

To illustrate, we will subclass UIPanGestureRecognizer so as to implement a view that can be moved only horizontally or vertically. Our strategy will be to make *two* UIPan-GestureRecognizer subclasses — one that allows only horizontal movement, and another that allows only vertical movement. They will make their recognition decisions in a mutually exclusive manner, so we can attach an instance of each to our view. This encapsulates the decision-making logic in a gorgeously object-oriented way — a far cry from the spaghetti code we wrote earlier to do this same task.

I will show only the code for the horizontal drag gesture recognizer, because the vertical recognizer is symmetrically identical. We maintain just one property, `self.origLoc`, which we will use once to determine whether the user's initial movement is horizontal. We override `touchesBegan(_:with:)` to set our property with the first touch's location:

```
override func touchesBegan(_ touches: Set<UITouch>, with e: UIEvent) {
    self.origLoc = touches.first!.location(in:self.view!.superview)
    super.touchesBegan(touches, with:e)
}
```

We then override touchesMoved(_:with:); all the recognition logic is here. This method will be called for the first time with the state still at .possible. At that moment, we look to see if the user's movement is more horizontal than vertical. If it isn't, we set the state to .failed. But if it is, we just step back and let the superclass do its thing:

```
override func touchesMoved(_ touches: Set<UITouch>, with e: UIEvent) {
    if self.state == .possible {
        let loc = touches.first!.location(in:self.view!.superview)
        let deltaX = abs(loc.x - self.origLoc.x)
        let deltaY = abs(loc.y - self.origLoc.y)
        if deltaY >= deltaX {
            self.state = .failed
        }
    }
    super.touchesMoved(touches, with:e)
}
```

We now have a view that moves only if the user's initial gesture is horizontal. But that isn't the entirety of what we want; we want a view that, itself, moves horizontally only. To implement this, we'll simply lie to our client about where the user's finger is, by overriding translation(in:):

```
override func translation(in view: UIView?) -> CGPoint {
    var proposedTranslation = super.translation(in:view)
    proposedTranslation.y = 0
    return proposedTranslation
}
```

That example was simple, because we subclassed a fully functional built-in UIGestureRecognizer subclass. If you were to write your own UIGestureRecognizer subclass entirely from scratch, there would be more work to do:

- You should definitely implement all four touch methods. Their job, at a minimum, is to advance the gesture recognizer through the canonical progression of its states. When the first touch arrives at a gesture recognizer, its state will be .possible; you never explicitly set the recognizer's state to .possible yourself. As soon as you know this can't be our gesture, you set the state to .failed. (Apple says that a gesture recognizer should "fail early, fail often.") If the gesture gets past all the failure tests, you set the state instead either to .ended (for a discrete gesture) or to .began (for a continuous gesture); if .began, then you might set it to .changed, and ultimately you must set it to .ended. Don't concern yourself with the sending of action messages; they will be sent automatically at the appropriate moments.

- You should probably implement reset. This is called after you reach the end of the progression of states to notify you that the gesture recognizer's state is about to be set back to `.possible`; it is your chance to return your state machine to its starting configuration (resetting properties, for example).

Keep in mind that your gesture recognizer might stop receiving touches without notice. Just because it gets a `touchesBegan(_:with:)` call for a particular touch doesn't mean it will ever get `touchesEnded(_:with:)` for that touch. If your gesture recognizer fails to recognize its gesture, either because it declares failure or because it is still in the `.possible` state when another gesture recognizer recognizes, it won't get any more touch method calls for any of the touches that were being sent to it. This is why `reset` is so important; it's the one reliable signal that it's time to clean up and get ready to receive the beginning of another possible gesture.

Gesture Recognizer Delegate

A gesture recognizer can have a delegate (UIGestureRecognizerDelegate), which can perform two types of task.

These delegate methods can *block a gesture recognizer's operation*:

`gestureRecognizerShouldBegin(_:)`
> Sent to the delegate before the gesture recognizer passes out of the `.possible` state; return `false` to force the gesture recognizer to proceed to the `.failed` state. (This happens *after* `gestureRecognizerShouldBegin(_:)` has been sent to the view in which the touch took place. That view must not have returned `false`, or we wouldn't have reached this stage.)

`gestureRecognizer(_:shouldReceive:)`
> Sent to the delegate before a touch is sent to the gesture recognizer's `touches-Began(_:with:)` method; return `false` to prevent that touch from ever being sent to the gesture recognizer.

These delegate methods can *mediate gesture recognition conflict*:

`gestureRecognizer(_:shouldRecognizeSimultaneouslyWith:)`
> Sent when a gesture recognizer recognizes its gesture, if this will force the failure of another gesture recognizer, to the delegates of *both* gesture recognizers. Return `true` to prevent that failure, thus allowing both gesture recognizers to operate simultaneously. For example, a view could respond to both a two-fingered pinch and a two-fingered pan, the one applying a scale transform, the other changing the view's center.

`gestureRecognizer(_:shouldRequireFailureOf:)`
`gestureRecognizer(_:shouldBeRequiredToFailBy:)`
> Sent very early in the life of a gesture, when all gesture recognizers in a view's swarm are still in the `.possible` state, to the delegates of *all* of them, pairing the

gesture recognizer whose delegate this is with each of the other gesture recognizers in the swarm. Return true to prioritize between this pair of gesture recognizers, saying that one cannot succeed until the other has first failed. In essence, these delegate methods turn the decision made once and permanently in require(toFail:) into a live decision that can be made freshly every time a gesture occurs.

As an example, we will use delegate messages to combine a UILongPressGestureRecognizer and a UIPanGestureRecognizer, as follows: the user must perform a tap-and-a-half (tap, then tap and hold) to "get the view's attention," which we will indicate by a pulsing animation on the view; then (and only then) the user can drag the view.

The UIPanGestureRecognizer's action method will take care of the drag, as shown earlier in this chapter. The UILongPressGestureRecognizer's action method will take care of starting and stopping the animation:

```
@objc func longPress(_ lp:UILongPressGestureRecognizer) {
    switch lp.state {
    case .began:
        let anim = CABasicAnimation(keyPath: #keyPath(CALayer.transform))
        anim.toValue = CATransform3DMakeScale(1.1, 1.1, 1)
        anim.fromValue = CATransform3DIdentity
        anim.repeatCount = .infinity
        anim.autoreverses = true
        lp.view!.layer.add(anim, forKey:nil)
    case .ended, .cancelled:
        lp.view!.layer.removeAllAnimations()
    default: break
    }
}
```

As we created our gesture recognizers, we kept a reference to the UILongPressGestureRecognizer (self.longPresser), and we made ourself the UIPanGestureRecognizer's delegate. So we will receive delegate messages. If the UIPanGestureRecognizer tries to declare success while the UILongPressGestureRecognizer's state is .failed or still at .possible, we prevent it. If the UILongPressGestureRecognizer succeeds, we permit the UIPanGestureRecognizer to operate as well:

```
func gestureRecognizerShouldBegin(_ g: UIGestureRecognizer) -> Bool {
    switch self.longPresser.state {
    case .possible, .failed:
        return false
    default:
        return true
    }
}
```

```
func gestureRecognizer(_ g: UIGestureRecognizer,
    shouldRecognizeSimultaneouslyWith g2: UIGestureRecognizer) -> Bool {
        return true
}
```

The result is that the view can be dragged only while it is pulsing; in effect, what we've done is to compensate, using delegate methods, for the fact that UIGestureRecognizer has no `require(toSucceed:)` method.

If you are subclassing a gesture recognizer class, you can incorporate delegate-like behavior into the subclass, by overriding the following methods:

- `canPrevent(_:)`
- `canBePrevented(by:)`
- `shouldRequireFailure(of:)`
- `shouldBeRequiredToFail(by:)`

The `prevent` methods are similar to the delegate `shouldBegin` method, and the `fail` methods are similar to the delegate `fail` methods. In this way, you can mediate gesture recognizer conflict at the class level. The built-in gesture recognizer subclasses already do this; that is why, for example, a single tap UITapGestureRecognizer does not, by recognizing its gesture, cause the failure of a double tap UITapGesture-Recognizer.

You can also, in a gesture recognizer subclass, send `ignore(_:for:)` directly to a gesture recognizer (typically, to `self`) to ignore a specific touch of a specific event. This has the same effect as the delegate method `gestureRecognizer(_:shouldReceive:)` returning `false`, blocking all future delivery of that touch to the gesture recognizer. For example, if you're in the middle of an already recognized gesture and a new touch arrives, you might elect to ignore it.

Gesture Recognizers in the Nib

Instead of instantiating a gesture recognizer in code, you can create and configure it in a *.xib* or *.storyboard* file. In the nib editor, drag a gesture recognizer from the Object library onto a view; the gesture recognizer becomes a top-level nib object, and the view's `gestureRecognizers` outlet is connected to the gesture recognizer. (You can add more than one gesture recognizer to a view in the nib: the view's `gesture-Recognizers` property is an array, and its `gestureRecognizers` outlet is an outlet collection.) The gesture recognizer's properties are configurable in the Attributes inspector, and the gesture recognizer has a `delegate` outlet. The gesture recognizer is a full-fledged nib object, so you can make an outlet to it.

To configure a gesture recognizer's target–action pair in the nib editor, treat it like a UIControl's control event. The action method's signature should be marked @IBAction, and it should take a single parameter, which will be a reference to the gesture recognizer. You can form the action in any of the same ways as for a control action, including Control-dragging from the gesture recognizer to your code to create an action method stub. (A gesture recognizer can have multiple target–action pairs, but only one target–action pair can be configured for a gesture recognizer using the nib editor.) A view retains its gesture recognizers, so there will usually be no need for additional memory management on a gesture recognizer instantiated from a nib.

3D Touch Press Gesture

On a device with 3D touch, you can treat pressing as kind of gesture. It isn't formally a gesture; there is, unfortunately, no 3D touch press gesture recognizer. Nevertheless, your code can detect a 3D touch press, responding dynamically to the degree of force being applied.

The simplest way approach is to use the UIPreviewInteraction class. You initialize a UIPreviewInteraction object with the view in which pressing is to be detected, retain the UIPreviewInteraction object, and assign it a delegate (adopting the UIPreviewInteractionDelegate protocol). The delegate is sent these messages, starting when the user begins to apply force within the view:

previewInteractionShouldBegin(_:)
> Optional. Return false to ignore this press gesture. Among other things, this method might query the UIPreviewInteraction's view and location(in:) to decide how to proceed.

previewInteraction(_:didUpdatePreviewTransition:ended:)
> The amount of applied force has changed. The amount of force is reported (in the second parameter) as a value between 0 and 1. When 1 is reached, ended: is also true, and the device vibrates.

previewInteraction(_:didUpdateCommitTransition:ended:)
> Optional. Behaves exactly like the previous method. If implemented, the gesture has two stages, increasing from 0 to 1 and reported by didUpdatePreview, and then increasing from 0 to 1 and reported by didUpdateCommit.

previewInteractionDidCancel(_:)
> The user has backed off the gesture completely, before reaching ended: (or the touch was cancelled for some other reason).

To illustrate, imagine a sort of Whack-a-Mole game where the user is to remove views by pressing each one. (In real life, there would also need to be a way to play the game on a device that lacks 3D touch.) As the user presses, we'll apply a scale transform to the view, increasing its apparent size in proportion to the amount of force, while at the same time fading the view away by decreasing its opacity; if the user reaches a full press, we'll remove the view completely.

We'll implement this in the simplest possible way. The code will all go into the pressable view itself. When the view is added to its superview, it creates and configures the UIPreviewInteraction object, storing it in an instance property (`self.prev`):

```
override func didMoveToSuperview() {
    self.prev = UIPreviewInteraction(view: self)
    self.prev.delegate = self
}
```

As force reports arrive, we'll increase the view's scale transform and decrease its opacity accordingly:

```
func previewInteraction(_ : UIPreviewInteraction,
    didUpdatePreviewTransition prog: CGFloat,
    ended: Bool) {
        let scale = prog + 1
        self.transform = CGAffineTransform(scaleX: scale, y: scale)
        let alph = ((1-prog)*0.6) + 0.3
        self.alpha = alph
        if ended { // device vibrates
            self.removeFromSuperview()
        }
}
```

The view now expands and explodes off the screen with a satisfying pop ("haptic feedback") as the user presses on it. If the user backs off the gesture completely, we'll remove the transform and restore our opacity:

```
func previewInteractionDidCancel(_ : UIPreviewInteraction) {
    self.transform = .identity
    self.alpha = 1
}
```

Instead of applying the transform ourselves, directly, we might use a property animator, taking advantage of its ability to manage a "frozen" animation ("Frozen View Animation" on page 174). Here's a rewrite in which a property animator is used (held in an instance property, `self.anim`):

```
func makeAnimator() {
    self.anim = UIViewPropertyAnimator(duration: 1, curve: .linear) {
        [unowned self] in
        self.alpha = 0.3
        self.transform = CGAffineTransform(scaleX: 2, y: 2)
    }
}
override func didMoveToSuperview() {
    self.prev = UIPreviewInteraction(view: self)
    self.prev.delegate = self
```

```
        self.makeAnimator()
    }
    func previewInteractionDidCancel(_ : UIPreviewInteraction) {
        self.anim.pauseAnimation()
        self.anim.isReversed = true
        self.anim.addCompletion { _ in self.makeAnimator() }
        self.anim.continueAnimation(
            withTimingParameters: nil, durationFactor: 0.01)
    }
    func previewInteraction(_ : UIPreviewInteraction,
        didUpdatePreviewTransition prog: CGFloat,
        ended: Bool) {
            self.anim.fractionComplete = min(max(prog, 0.05), 0.95)
            if ended {
                self.anim.stopAnimation(false)
                self.anim.finishAnimation(at: .end)
                self.removeFromSuperview()
            }
    }
}
```

Touch Delivery

Here's the full standard procedure by which a touch is delivered to views and gesture recognizers:

- Whenever a new touch appears, the application performs hit-testing to determine the view that was touched. This view will be permanently associated with this touch, and is called, appropriately, the *hit-test view*. The logic of ignoring a view (denying it the ability to become the hit-test view) in response to its isUserInteractionEnabled, isHidden, and alpha properties is implemented at this stage.

- Each time the touch situation changes, the application calls its own sendEvent(_:), which in turn calls the window's sendEvent(_:). The window delivers each of an event's touches by calling the appropriate touch method(s), as follows:

  - As a touch first appears, the logic of obedience to isMultipleTouchEnabled and isExclusiveTouch is considered. If permitted by that logic:
    - The touch is delivered to the hit-test view's swarm of gesture recognizers.
    - The touch is delivered to the hit-test view itself.

  - If a gesture is recognized by a gesture recognizer, then for any touch associated with this gesture recognizer:
    - touchesCancelled(_:for:) is sent to the touch's view, and the touch is no longer delivered to its view.

- ○ If the touch was associated with any other gesture recognizer, that gesture recognizer is forced to fail.
  - ▪ If a gesture recognizer fails, either because it declares failure or because it is forced to fail, its touches are no longer delivered to it, but (except as already specified) they continue to be delivered to their view.

The rest of this chapter discusses the details of touch delivery. As you'll see, nearly every bit of the standard procedure can be customized to some extent.

Hit-Testing

Hit-testing is the determination of what view the user touched. View hit-testing uses the UIView instance method hitTest(_:with:), whose first parameter is the CGPoint of interest. It returns either a view (the hit-test view) or nil. The idea is to find the frontmost view containing the touch point. This method uses an elegant recursive algorithm, as follows:

1. A view's hitTest(_:with:) first calls the same method on its own subviews, if it has any, because a subview is considered to be in front of its superview. The subviews are queried in front-to-back order (Chapter 1): thus, if two sibling views overlap, the one in front reports the hit first.

2. If, as a view hit-tests its subviews, any of those subviews responds by returning a view, it stops querying its subviews and immediately returns the view that was returned to it. Thus, the very first view to declare itself the hit-test view percolates all the way to the top of the call chain and *is* the hit-test view.

3. If, on the other hand, a view has no subviews, or if all of its subviews return nil (indicating that neither they nor their subviews was hit), then the view calls point(inside:with:) on itself. If this call reveals that the touch was inside this view, the view returns itself, declaring itself the hit-test view; otherwise it returns nil.

   (No problem arises if a view has a transform, because point(inside:with:) takes the transform into account. That's why a rotated button continues to work correctly.)

It is also up to hitTest(_:with:) to implement the logic of touch restrictions exclusive to a view. If a view's isUserInteractionEnabled is false, or its isHidden is true, or its alpha is close to 0.0, it returns nil without hit-testing any of its subviews and without calling point(inside:with:). Thus these restrictions do not, of themselves, exclude a view from being hit-tested; on the contrary, they operate precisely by affecting a view's hit-test result.

However, hit-testing knows nothing about `isMultipleTouchEnabled` (which involves multiple touches) or `isExclusiveTouch` (which involves multiple views). The logic of obedience to these properties is implemented at a later stage of the story.

Performing Hit-Testing

You can perform hit-testing yourself at any moment where it might prove useful. In calling `hitTest(_:with:)`, supply a point *in the coordinates of the view to which the message is sent*. The second parameter is supposed to be a UIEvent, but it can be `nil` if you have no event.

For example, suppose we have a superview with two UIImageView subviews. We want to detect a tap in either UIImageView, but we want to handle this *at the level of the superview*. We can attach a UITapGestureRecognizer to the superview, but then the gesture recognizer's `view` is the superview, so how will we know which subview, if any, the tap was in?

First, ensure that `isUserInteractionEnabled` is `true` for both UIImageViews. UIImageView is one of the few built-in view classes where this property is `false` by default, and a view whose `isUserInteractionEnabled` is `false` won't normally be the result of a call to `hitTest(_:with:)`. Then, when our gesture recognizer's action method is called, we can perform hit-testing to determine where the tap was:

```
// g is the gesture recognizer
let p = g.location(ofTouch:0, in: g.view)
let v = g.view?.hitTest(p, with: nil)
if let v = v as? UIImageView { // ...
```

Hit-Test Munging

You can override `hitTest(_:with:)` in a view subclass, to alter its results during touch delivery, thus customizing the touch delivery mechanism. I call this *hit-test munging*. Hit-test munging can be used selectively as a way of turning user interaction on or off in an area of the interface. In this way, some unusual effects can be produced.

An important use of hit-test munging is to permit the touching of subviews outside the bounds of their superview. If a view's `clipsToBounds` is `false`, a paradox arises: the user can *see* the regions of its subviews that are outside its bounds, but can't *touch* them. This can be confusing and seems wrong. The solution is for the view to override `hitTest(_:with:)` as follows:

```
override func hitTest(_ point: CGPoint, with e: UIEvent?) -> UIView? {
    if let result = super.hitTest(point, with:e) {
        return result
    }
    for sub in self.subviews.reversed() {
```

```
            let pt = self.convert(point, to:sub)
            if let result = sub.hitTest(pt, with:e) {
                return result
            }
        }
        return nil
    }
```

In this next example, we implement a pass-through view. The idea is that only one object in our interface should be touchable; everything else should behave as if isUserInteractionEnabled were false. In a complex interface, actually cycling through all our subviews and toggling isUserInteractionEnabled is too much trouble. Instead, we place an invisible view in front of the entire interface and use hit-test munging so that only one view behind it (self.passthruView) is touchable:

```
class MyView: UIView {
    weak var passthruView : UIView?
    override func hitTest(_ point: CGPoint, with e: UIEvent?) -> UIView? {
        if let pv = self.passthruView {
            let pt = pv.convert(point, from: self)
            if pv.point(inside: pt, with: e) {
                return nil
            }
        }
        return super.hitTest(point, with: e)
    }
}
```

Hit-Testing For Layers

Layers do *not* receive touches. A touch is reported to a view, not a layer. A layer, except insofar as it is a view's underlying layer and gets touch reporting because of its view, is completely untouchable; from the point of view of touches and touch reporting, it's as if the layer weren't on the screen at all. No matter where a layer may appear to be, a touch falls through the layer, to whatever view is behind it.

Nevertheless, hit-testing for layers is possible. It doesn't happen automatically, as part of sendEvent(_:) or anything else; it's up to you. It's just a convenient way of finding out which layer *would* receive a touch at a point, if layers *did* receive touches. To hit-test layers, call hitTest(_:) on a layer, with a point *in superlayer coordinates*.

In the case of a layer that is a view's underlying layer, you don't need hit-testing. It is the view's drawing; where it appears is where the view is. So a touch in that layer is equivalent to a touch in its view. Indeed, one might say (and it is often said) that this is what views are actually for: to provide layers with touchability.

The only layers on which you'd need special hit-testing, then, would presumably be layers that are not themselves any view's underlying layer, because those are the only ones you don't find out about by normal view hit-testing. However, all layers, including a layer that is its view's underlying layer, are part of the layer hierarchy, and can participate in layer hit-testing. So the most comprehensive way to hit-test layers is to start with the topmost layer, the window's layer. In this example, we subclass UIWindow (see Chapter 1) and override its `hitTest(_:with:)` so as to get layer hit-testing every time there is view hit-testing:

```
override func hitTest(_ point: CGPoint, with e: UIEvent?) -> UIView? {
    let lay = self.layer.hitTest(point)
    // ... possibly do something with that information
    return super.hitTest(point, with:e)
}
```

In that example, `self` is the window, which is a special case. In general, you'll have to convert to superlayer coordinates. In this next example, we return to the Compass-View developed in Chapter 3, in which all the parts of the compass are layers; we want to know whether the user tapped on the arrow layer, and if so, we'll rotate the arrow. For simplicity, we've given the CompassView a UITapGestureRecognizer, and this is its action method, in the CompassView itself. We convert to our superview's coordinates, because these are also our layer's superlayer coordinates:

```
@IBAction func tapped(_ t:UITapGestureRecognizer) {
    let p = t.location(ofTouch:0, in: self.superview)
    let hitLayer = self.layer.hitTest(p)
    let arrow = (self.layer as! CompassLayer).arrow!
    if hitLayer == arrow { // respond to touch
        arrow.transform = CATransform3DRotate(
            arrow.transform, .pi/4.0, 0, 0, 1)
    }
}
```

Layer hit-testing knows nothing of the restrictions on touch delivery; it just reports on every sublayer, even (for example) one whose view has `isUserInteraction-Enabled` set to `false`.

Hit-Testing For Drawings

The preceding example (letting the user tap on the compass arrow) does work, but we might complain that it is reporting a hit on the arrow layer even if the hit misses the *drawing* of the arrow. That's true for view hit-testing as well. A hit is reported if we are within the view or layer as a whole; hit-testing knows nothing of drawing, transparent areas, and so forth.

If you know how the region is drawn and can reproduce the edge of that drawing as a CGPath, you can call `contains(_:using:transform:)` to test whether a point is inside it. So, in our compass layer, we could override `hitTest(_:)` along these lines:

```
override func hitTest(_ p: CGPoint) -> CALayer? {
    var lay = super.hitTest(p)
    if lay == self.arrow {
        let pt = self.arrow.convert(p, from:self.superlayer)
        let path = CGMutablePath()
        path.addRect(CGRect(10,20,20,80))
        path.move(to:CGPoint(0, 25))
        path.addLine(to:CGPoint(20, 0))
        path.addLine(to:CGPoint(40, 25))
        path.closeSubpath()
        if !path.contains(pt, using: .winding) {
            lay = nil
        }
    }
    return lay
}
```

Alternatively, it might be the case that if a pixel of the drawing is transparent, it's out-side the drawn region, so that it suffices to detect whether the pixel tapped is transparent. Unfortunately, there's no built-in way to ask a drawing (or a view, or a layer) for the color of a pixel. Instead, you have to make a *bitmap graphics context* and copy the drawing into it, and then ask the bitmap for the color of a pixel. If you can reproduce the content as an image, and all you care about is transparency, you can make a one-pixel alpha-only bitmap, draw the image in such a way that the pixel you want to test is the pixel drawn into the bitmap, and examine the transparency of the resulting pixel. In this example, im is our UIImage and point is the coordinates of the pixel we want to test:

```
let info = CGImageAlphaInfo.alphaOnly.rawValue
let pixel = UnsafeMutablePointer<UInt8>.allocate(capacity:1)
defer {
    pixel.deinitialize(count: 1)
    pixel.deallocate(capacity:1)
}
pixel[0] = 0
let sp = CGColorSpaceCreateDeviceGray()
let context = CGContext(data: pixel,
    width: 1, height: 1, bitsPerComponent: 8, bytesPerRow: 1,
    space: sp, bitmapInfo: info)!
UIGraphicsPushContext(context)
im.draw(at:CGPoint(-point.x, -point.y))
UIGraphicsPopContext()
let p = pixel[0]
let alpha = Double(p)/255.0
let transparent = alpha < 0.01
```

There may not be a one-to-one relationship between the pixels of the underlying drawing and the points of the drawing as portrayed on the screen — because the drawing is stretched, for example. In many cases, the CALayer method render(in:) can be helpful here. This method allows you to copy a layer's actual drawing into a graphics context of your choice. If that context is an image context (Chapter 2), you can use the resulting image as `im` in the preceding code.

Hit-Testing During Animation

Making a view user-touchable while it is being animated is a tricky business, because the view may not be located where the user sees it. Recall (from Chapter 4) that the animation is just an "animation movie" — what the user sees is the *presentation layer*. The view itself, which the user is trying to touch, is at the location of the *model layer*. If user interaction is allowed during an animation that moves a view from one place to another, and if the user taps where the animated view appears to be, the tap might mysteriously fail because the actual view is elsewhere; conversely, the user might accidentally tap where the view actually is, and the tap will hit the animated view even though it appears to be elsewhere.

For this reason, view animation ordered through a UIView class method, by default, turns off touchability of a view while it is being animated — though you can override that with `.allowUserInteraction` in the `options:` argument. Indeed, it is not uncommon to turn off your entire interface's touchability during animation with UIApplication's `beginIgnoringInteractionEvents`, as I mentioned earlier in this chapter.

Before the advent of the property animator in iOS 10, you could make an animated view touchable if you really wanted to, but it took some work. In particular, you had to *hit-test the presentation layer*. In this simple example, we implement hit-test munging in the view being animated:

```
override func hitTest(_ point: CGPoint, with e: UIEvent?) -> UIView? {
    let pres = self.layer.presentation()!
    let suppt = self.convert(point, to: self.superview!)
    let prespt = self.superview!.layer.convert(suppt, to: pres)
    return super.hitTest(prespt, with: e)
}
```

That works, but the animated view, as Apple puts it in the WWDC 2011 videos, "swallows the touch." For example, suppose the view in motion is a button. Although our hit-test munging makes it possible for the user to tap the button as it is being animated, and although the user sees the button highlight in response, the button's action message is not sent in response to this highlighting if the animation is in-flight when the tap takes place. This behavior seems unfortunate, but it's generally possible to work around it — for instance, with a gesture recognizer.

A property animator makes things far simpler. By default, a property animator's `isUserInteractionEnabled` is `true`. That means the animated view is touchable. As long as you don't also set the property animator's `isManualHitTestingEnabled` to `true`, the property animator will hit-test the animated view's presentation layer for you, so that you don't have to. (If you *do* set `isManualHitTestingEnabled` to `true`, the job of hit-testing is turned back over to you; you might want to do this in complicated situations where the property animator's hit-test munging isn't sufficient.) Moreover, the animated view *doesn't* "swallow the touch." To animate a button that remains tappable while the animation is in-flight, just animate the button:

```
let anim = UIViewPropertyAnimator(duration: 10, curve: .linear) {
    self.button.center = goal
}
anim.startAnimation()
```

By combining the power of a property animator to make its animated view touchable with its power to make its animation interruptible, we can make a view alternate between being animated and being manipulated by the user. To illustrate, I'll extend the preceding example. The view is slowly animating its way toward the `goal` position. But at any time, the user can grab it and drag it around (during which time, the animation is interrupted). As soon as the user releases the view, the animation resumes: the view continues on its way toward the `goal` position.

In order to be draggable, the view has a UIPanGestureRecognizer. The property animator is now retained in an instance property (`self.anim`) so that the action method can access it; we have a method that creates the property animator (you'll see in a moment what the `factor:` parameter is for):

```
func configAnimator(factor:Double = 1) {
    self.anim = UIViewPropertyAnimator(
        duration: 10 * factor, curve: .linear) {
            self.button.center = self.goal
    }
}
```

All the work takes place in the gesture recognizer's action method; as usual, we have a switch statement that tests the gesture recognizer's `state`. In the `.began` case, we interrupt the animation so that dragging can happen:

```
case .began:
    if self.anim.state == .active {
        self.anim.stopAnimation(true)
    }
    fallthrough
```

The `.changed` case is our usual code for making a view draggable:

```
case .changed:
    let delta = p.translation(in:v.superview)
    var c = v.center
    c.x += delta.x; c.y += delta.y
    v.center = c
    p.setTranslation(.zero, in: v.superview)
```

The `.ended` case is the really interesting part. Our aim is to resume animating the view from wherever it now is toward the `goal`. In my opinion, this feels most natural if the *speed* at which the view moves remains the same. Thus, the ratio between durations is the ratio between the distance of the view's *original* position from the `goal` and its *current* distance from the goal:

```
case .ended:
    // how far are we from the goal relative to original distance?
    func pyth(_ pt1:CGPoint, _ pt2:CGPoint) -> CGFloat {
        let x = pt1.x - pt2.x
        let y = pt1.y - pt2.y
        return sqrt(x*x + y*y)
    }
    let origd = pyth(self.oldButtonCenter, self.goal)
    let curd = pyth(v.center, self.goal)
    let factor = curd/origd
    self.configAnimator(factor:Double(factor))
    self.anim.startAnimation()
```

Initial Touch Event Delivery

When the touch situation changes, an event containing all touches is handed to the UIApplication instance by calling its `sendEvent(_:)`, and the UIApplication in turn hands it to the UIWindow by calling *its* `sendEvent(_:)`. The UIWindow then performs the complicated logic of examining, for every touch, the hit-test view and its superviews and their gesture recognizers, and deciding which of them should be sent a touch method call.

You can override `sendEvent(_:)` in a subclass of UIWindow or UIApplication. These are delicate and crucial maneuvers, however, and you wouldn't want to lame your application by interfering with them. Moreover, it is unlikely, nowadays, that you would need to resort to such measures. A typical use case before the advent of gesture recognizers was that you needed to detect touches directed to an object of some built-in interface class in a way that subclassing wouldn't permit.

For example, suppose you want to know when the user swipes a UIWebView; you're not allowed to subclass UIWebView, and in any case it eats the touch. The solution used to be to subclass UIWindow and override `sendEvent(_:)`; you would then work out whether this was a swipe on the UIWebView and respond accordingly, or else call `super`. Now, however, you can attach a UISwipeGestureRecognizer to the UIWebView.

Gesture Recognizer and View

When a touch first appears and is delivered to a gesture recognizer, it is *also* delivered to its hit-test view, the same touch method being called on both.

This is the most reasonable approach, as it means that touch interpretation by a view isn't jettisoned just because gesture recognizers are in the picture. Later on in the multitouch sequence, if all the gesture recognizers in a view's swarm declare failure to recognize their gesture, that view's internal touch interpretation continues as if gesture recognizers had never been invented. Moreover, touches and gestures are two different things; sometimes you want to respond to both. In one of my apps, where the user can tap cards, each card has a single tap gesture recognizer and a double tap gesture recognizer, but it also responds directly to touchesBegan(_:with:) by reducing its own opacity, and to touchesEnded(_:with:) and touches-Cancelled(_:with:) by restoring its opacity. The result is that the user always sees feedback when touching a card, *instantly*, regardless of what the gesture turns out to be.

Later, if a gesture recognizer in a view's swarm recognizes its gesture, that view is sent touchesCancelled(_:with:) for any touches that went to that gesture recognizer and were hit-tested to that view, and subsequently the view *no longer receives those touches*. This behavior can be changed by setting a gesture recognizer's cancels-TouchesInView property to false; if you were to do that for every gesture recognizer in a view's swarm, the view would receive touch events more or less as if no gesture recognizers were in the picture.

If a gesture recognizer happens to be ignoring a touch — because, for example, it was told to do so with ignore(_:for:) — then touchesCancelled(_:with:) *won't* be sent to the view for that touch when that gesture recognizer recognizes its gesture. Thus, a gesture recognizer's ignoring a touch is the same as simply letting it fall through to the view, as if the gesture recognizer weren't there.

Gesture recognizers can also *delay* the delivery of touches to a view, and by default they do. The UIGestureRecognizer property delaysTouchesEnded is true by default, meaning that when a touch reaches .ended and the gesture recognizer's touches-Ended(_:with:) is called, if the gesture recognizer is still allowing touches to be delivered to the view because its state is still .possible, it doesn't deliver this touch until it has resolved the gesture. When it does, either it will recognize the gesture, in which case the view will have touchesCancelled(_:with:) called instead (as already explained), or it will declare failure and *now* the view will have touches-Ended(_:with:) called.

The reason for this behavior is most obvious with a gesture where multiple taps are required. The first tap ends, but this is insufficient for the gesture recognizer to declare success or failure, so it withholds that touch from the view. In this way, the gesture recognizer gets the proper priority. In particular, if there is a second tap, the gesture recognizer should succeed and send touchesCancelled(_:with:) to the view — but it can't do that if the view has already been sent touchesEnded(_:with:).

It is also possible to delay the *entire* suite of touch methods from being called on a view, by setting a gesture recognizer's delaysTouchesBegan property to true. Again, this delay would be until the gesture recognizer can resolve the gesture: either it will recognize it, in which case the view will have touchesCancelled(_:with:) called, or it will declare failure, in which case the view will receive touchesBegan(_:with:) plus any further touch method calls that were withheld — except that it will receive *at most* one touchesMoved(_:with:) call, the last one, because if a lot of these were withheld, to queue them all up and send them all at once now would be simply insane.

When touches are delayed and then delivered, what's delivered is the original touch with the original event, which still have their original timestamps. Because of the delay, these timestamps may differ significantly from now. As I've already said, analysis that is concerned with timing of touches should consult the timestamp, not the clock.

Touch Exclusion Logic

It is up to the UIWindow's sendEvent(_:) to implement the logic of isMultiple-TouchEnabled and isExclusiveTouch:

isMultipleTouchEnabled

> If a new touch is hit-tested to a view whose isMultipleTouchEnabled is false and which already has an existing touch hit-tested to it, then sendEvent(_:) never delivers the new touch to that view. However, that touch *is* delivered to the view's swarm of gesture recognizers; in other words, gesture recognizers are *not* affected by the existence of the isMultipleTouchEnabled property.

isExclusiveTouch

> If there's an isExclusiveTouch view in the window, then sendEvent(_:) must decide whether a particular touch should be delivered, in accordance with the meaning of isExclusiveTouch, which I described earlier. If a touch is not delivered to a view because of isExclusiveTouch restrictions, it is *not* delivered to its swarm of gesture recognizers either; in other words, gesture recognizers *are* affected by the existence of the isExclusiveTouch property.

> For example, suppose you have two views with touch handling, and their common superview has a pinch gesture recognizer. Normally, if you touch both views simultanously and pinch, the pinch gesture recognizer recognizes. But if both views are marked isExclusiveTouch, the pinch gesture recognizer does *not* recognize.

Gesture Recognition Logic

When a gesture recognizer recognizes its gesture, everything changes. As we've already seen, the touches for this gesture recognizer are sent to their hit-test views as a touchesCancelled(_:with:) message, and then no longer arrive at those views (unless the gesture recognizer's cancelsTouchesInView is false). Moreover, all other gesture recognizers pending with regard to these touches are made to fail, and then are no longer sent the touches they were receiving either.

If the very same event would cause more than one gesture recognizer to recognize, there's an algorithm for picking the one that will succeed and make the others fail: a gesture recognizer lower down the view hierarchy (closer to the hit-test view) prevails over one higher up the hierarchy, and a gesture recognizer more recently added to its view prevails over one less recently added.

There are various means for modifying this "first past the post" behavior:

Dependency order
>   Certain methods institute a dependency order, causing a gesture recognizer to be put on hold when it tries to transition from the .possible state to the .began (continuous) or .ended (discrete) state: only if a certain other gesture recognizer fails is this one permitted to perform that transition. Apple says that in a dependency like this, the gesture recognizer that fails first is not sent reset (and won't receive any touches) until the second finishes its state sequence and is sent reset, so that they resume recognizing together. The methods are:
>
>   - require(toFail:) sent to a gesture recognizer
>   - shouldRequireFailure(of:) in a subclass
>   - shouldBeRequiredToFail(by:) in a subclass
>   - gestureRecognizer(_:shouldRequireFailureOf:) in the delegate
>   - gestureRecognizer(_:shouldBeRequiredToFailBy:) in the delegate

The first of those methods sets up a permanent relationship between two gesture recognizers, and cannot be undone; but the others are sent every time a gesture starts in a view whose swarm includes both gesture recognizers, and the result is applied only on this occasion.

The delegate methods work together as follows. For each pair of gesture recognizers in the hit-test view's swarm, the members of that pair are arranged in a fixed order (as I've already described). The first of the pair is sent shouldRequire and then shouldBeRequired, and then the second of the pair is sent should-Require and then shouldBeRequired. But if any of those four methods returns true, the relationship between that pair is settled and we proceed immediately to the next pair.

Success into failure

Certain methods, by returning `false`, turn success into failure; at the moment when the gesture recognizer is about to declare that it recognizes its gesture, transitioning from the `.possible` state to the `.began` (continuous) or `.ended` (discrete) state, it is forced to fail instead:

- UIView's `gestureRecognizerShouldBegin(_:)`
- The delegate's `gestureRecognizerShouldBegin(_:)`

Simultaneous recognition

A gesture recognizer succeeds, but some other gesture recognizer is *not* forced to fail, in accordance with these methods:

- `gestureRecognizer(_:shouldRecognizeSimultaneouslyWith:)`
  in the delegate
- `canPrevent(_:)`
  in a subclass
- `canBePrevented(by:)`
  in a subclass

In the subclass methods, `prevent` means "by succeeding, you force failure upon this other," and `bePrevented` means "by succeeding, this other forces failure on you." They work together as follows. `canPrevent` is called first; if it returns `false`, that's the end of the story for that gesture recognizer, and `canPrevent` is called on the other gesture recognizer. But if `canPrevent` returns `true` when it is first called, the other gesture recognizer is sent `canBePrevented`. If it returns `true`, that's the end of the story; if it returns `false`, the process starts over the other way around, sending `canPrevent` to the second gesture recognizer, and so forth. In this way, conflicting answers are resolved without the device exploding: prevention is regarded as exceptional (even though it is in fact the norm) and will happen only if it is acquiesced to by everyone involved.

PART II

Interface

This part of the book describes view controllers, the major building blocks of an app's interface and functionality, along with the views provided by the Cocoa framework.

- Chapter 6 is about view controllers, the basis of an iOS app's architecture. View controllers manage interface and respond to user actions. Most of your app's code will be in a view controller.

- Chapter 7 is about scroll views, which let the user slide and zoom the interface.

- Chapter 8 explains table views and collection views, which are scroll views for navigating through data.

- Chapter 9 is about popovers, split views, iPad multitasking, and drag and drop.

- Chapter 10 describes how text is presented in an iOS app's interface.

- Chapter 11 explains how to put a web browser inside your app.

- Chapter 12 describes all the remaining built-in UIKit interface objects.

- Chapter 13 is about various forms of modal dialog that can appear in front of an app's interface.

CHAPTER 6

View Controllers

An iOS app's interface is dynamic, and with good reason. The entire interface needs to fit into a single display consisting of a single window, which in the case of the iPhone can be almost forbiddingly tiny. The solution is to introduce, at will, completely new interface — a new view, possibly with an elaborate hierarchy of subviews — replacing or covering the previous interface.

For this to work, regions of interface material — often the entire contents of the screen — must come and go in an agile fashion that is understandable to the user. There will typically be a logical, structural, and functional relationship between the view that was present and the view that replaces or covers it, and this relationship will need to be maintained behind the scenes, in your code, as well as being indicated to the user: multiple views may be pure alternatives or siblings of one another, or one view may be a temporary replacement for another, or views may be like successive pages of a book. Animation is often used to emphasize and clarify these relationships as one view is superseded by another. Navigational interface and a vivid, suggestive gestural vocabulary give the user an ability to control what's seen and an understanding of the possible options: a tab bar whose buttons summon alternate views, a back button or a swipe gesture for returning to a previously visited view, a tap on an interface element to dive deeper into a conceptual world, a Done or Cancel button to escape from a settings screen, and so forth.

In iOS, the management of this dynamic interface is performed through view controllers. A *view controller* is an instance of UIViewController. Actually, a view controller is most likely to be an instance of a UIViewController subclass; the UIViewController class is designed to be subclassed, and you are very unlikely to use a plain vanilla UIViewController object without subclassing it. You might write your own UIViewController subclass; you might use a built-in UIViewController subclass such as UINavigationController or UITabBarController; or you might subclass a built-in UIViewController subclass such as UITableViewController (Chapter 8).

A view controller manages a single view (which can, of course, have subviews); its view property points to the view it manages. This is the view controller's *main view*, or simply its view. A view controller's main view has no explicit pointer to the view controller that manages it, but a view controller is a UIResponder and is in the responder chain just above its view, so it is the view's next responder.

View Controller Responsibilities

A view controller's most important responsibility is its view. A view controller must have a view; it is useless without one. If that view is to be useful, it must somehow *get into the interface*, and hence onto the screen; a view controller is usually responsible for seeing to that, too, but typically *not* the view controller whose view this is; rather, this will be taken care of by some view controller whose view is *already* in the interface. In many cases, this will happen automatically (I'll talk more about that in the next section), but you can participate in the process, and for some view controllers you may have to do the work yourself. A view that comes may also eventually go, and the view controller responsible for putting a view into the interface will then be responsible also for removing it.

A view controller will typically provide *animation* of the interface as a view comes or goes. Built-in view controller subclasses and built-in ways of summoning or removing a view controller and its view come with built-in animations. We are all familiar, for example, with tapping something to make new interface slide in from the side of the screen, and then later tapping a back button to make that interface slide back out again. In cases where you are responsible for getting a view controller's view onto the screen, you are also responsible for providing the animation. And you can take complete charge of the animation even for built-in view controllers.

View controllers, working together, can *save and restore state* automatically. This feature helps you ensure that if your app is terminated in the background and subsequently relaunched, it will quickly resume displaying the same interface that was showing when the user last saw it.

The most powerful view controller is the *top-level view controller*. This might be a fullscreen presented view controller, as I'll explain later in this chapter; but most of the time it will be your app's *root view controller*. This is the view controller managing the *root view*, the view that sits at the top of the view hierarchy, as the one and only direct subview of the main window, acting as the superview for the rest of the app's interface. I described in Chapter 1 how this view controller attains its lofty position: it is assigned to the window's rootViewController property. The window then takes that view controller's main view, gives it the correct frame (resizing it if necessary), and makes it its own subview.

The top-level view controller bears ultimate responsibility for some important decisions about the behavior of your app:

Rotation of the interface
> The user can rotate the device, and you might like the interface to rotate in response, to compensate. The runtime consults the top-level view controller about whether to permit such rotation.

Manipulation of the status bar
> The status bar is actually a secondary window belonging to the runtime. The runtime consults the top-level view controller as to whether the status bar should be present and, if so, whether its text should be light or dark.

Above and beyond all this, view controllers are typically the heart of any app, by virtue of their role in the model–view–controller architecture: view controllers are *controllers* (hence the name). Views give the user something to tap, and display data for the user to see; they are *view*. The data itself is *model*. But the logic of determining, at any given moment, *what* views are shown, *what* data those views display, and *what* the response to the user's gestures should be, is *controller* logic. Typically, that means view controller logic. In any app, view controllers will be the most important controllers — frequently, in fact, the only controllers. View controllers are where you'll put the bulk of the code that actually makes your app do what your app does.

View Controller Hierarchy

There is always one root view controller, along with its view, the root view. There may also be other view controllers, each of which has its own main view. Such view controllers are *subordinate* to the root view controller. In iOS, there are two subordination relationships between view controllers:

Parentage (containment)
> A view controller can *contain* another view controller. The containing view controller is the *parent* of the contained view controller; the contained view controller is a *child* of the containing view controller. A containment relationship between two view controllers is reflected in their views: the child view controller's view, if it is in the interface at all, is a *subview* (at some depth) of the parent view controller's view.

> The parent view controller is responsible for getting a child view controller's view into the interface, by making it a subview of its own view, and (if necessary) for removing it later. Introduction of a view, removal of a view, and replacement of

Figure 6-1. The TidBITS News app

one view with another often involve a parent view controller managing its children and their views.

A familiar example is the navigation interface: the user taps something and new interface slides in from the side, replacing the current interface. Figure 6-1 shows the TidBITS News app displaying a typical iPhone interface, consisting of a list of story headlines and summaries. This interface is managed by a parent view controller (a UINavigationController) with a child view controller whose view is the list of headlines and summaries. If the user taps an entry in the list, the whole list will slide away to one side and the text of that story will slide in from the other side; the parent view controller has acquired an additional child view controller, and has manipulated the views of its children to bring about this animated change of the interface. The parent view controller itself, meanwhile, stays put — and so does its own view, which functions as a stable superview of the child view controllers' views.

Presentation (modal views)

A view controller can *present* another view controller. The first view controller is the *presenting* view controller (not the parent) of the second; the second view controller is the *presented* view controller (not a child) of the first. The second view controller's view replaces or covers, completely or partially, the first view controller's view.

The name of this mechanism, and of the relationship between the view controllers involved, has changed over time. In iOS 4 and before, the presented view controller was called a *modal view controller*, and its view was a *modal view*; there is an analogy here to the desktop, where a window is modal if it sits in front of, and denies the user access to, the rest of the interface until it is explicitly dismissed. The terms *presented view controller* and *presented view* are more recent and more general, but the historical term "modal" still appears in the documentation and in the API.

A presented view controller's view does indeed sometimes look rather like a desktop modal view; for example, it might have a button such as Done or Save for dismissing the view, the implication being that this is a place where the user must make a decision and can do nothing else until the decision is made. However, as I'll explain later, that isn't the only use of a presented view controller.

There is thus a *hierarchy of view controllers*. In a properly constructed iOS app, there should be exactly one root view controller, and it is the *only* nonsubordinate view controller — it has neither a parent view controller nor a presenting view controller. Any other view controller, if its view appears in the interface, *must* be either a child view controller of some parent view controller or a presented view controller of some presenting view controller.

Moreover, there is a clear relationship between the view hierarchy and the view controller hierarchy. Recall that, for a parent view controller and child view controller, the child's view, if present in the interface, must be a subview of the parent's view. Similarly, for a presenting view controller and presented view controller, the presented view controller's view completely replaces, or is coherently interposed in front of, the presenting view controller's view. In this way, the actual views of the interface form a hierarchy dictated by *and parallel to* some portion of the view controller hierarchy: *every* view visible in the interface owes its presence to a view controller's view, either because it *is* a view controller's view, or because it's a subview of a view controller's view.

Automatic Child View Placement

The place of a view controller's view in the view hierarchy will often be automatic. You might never need to put a UIViewController's view into the view hierarchy manually. You'll manipulate view controllers; their hierarchy and their built-in functionality will construct and manage the view hierarchy for you.

For example, in Figure 6-1, we see two interface elements:

- The navigation bar, containing the TidBITS logo.
- The list of stories, which is actually a UITableView.

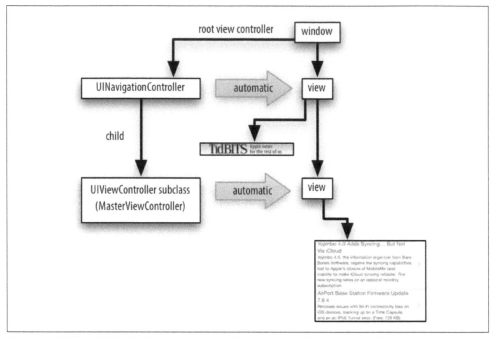

Figure 6-2. The TidBITS News app's initial view controller and view hierarchy

I will describe how all of this comes to appear on the screen through the view controller hierarchy and the view hierarchy (Figure 6-2):

- The app's root view controller is a UINavigationController; the UINavigation-Controller's view is the window's sole immediate subview (the root view). The navigation bar is a subview of that view.

- The UINavigationController contains a second UIViewController — a parent–child relationship. The child is a custom UIViewController subclass (called MasterViewController); *its* view is what occupies the rest of the window, as another subview of the UINavigationController's view. That view is the UITable-View. This architecture means that when the user taps a story listing in the UITableView, the whole table will slide out, to be replaced by the view of a different UIViewController, while the navigation bar stays.

In Figure 6-2, notice the word "automatic" in the two large right-pointing arrows associating a view controller with its view. This is intended to tell you how the view controller's view became part of the view hierarchy. The UINavigationController's view became the window's subview *automatically*, by virtue of the UINavigation-Controller being the window's rootViewController. The MasterViewController's view became the UINavigationController's view's subview *automatically*, by virtue of the MasterViewController being the UINavigationController's child.

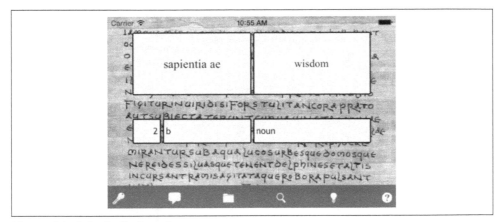

Figure 6-3. A Latin flashcard app

Manual Child View Placement

Sometimes, you'll write your own parent view controller class. In that case, *you* will be doing the kind of work that the UINavigationController was doing in that example, so you will need to put a child view controller's view into the interface *manually*, as a subview (at some depth) of the parent view controller's view.

I'll illustrate with another app of mine (Figure 6-3). The interface displays a flashcard containing information about a Latin word, along with a toolbar (the dark area at the bottom) where the user can tap an icon to choose additional functionality.

Again, I will describe how the interface shown in Figure 6-3 comes to appear on the screen through the view controller hierarchy and the view hierarchy (Figure 6-4). The app actually contains over a thousand of these Latin words, and I want the user to be able to navigate between flashcards to see the next or previous word; there is an excellent built-in view controller for this purpose, the UIPageViewController. However, that's just for the card; the toolbar at the bottom stays there, so the toolbar can't be inside the UIPageViewController's view. Therefore:

- The app's root view controller is my own UIViewController subclass (called RootViewController); its view contains the toolbar, and is also to contain the UIPageViewController's view. My RootViewController's view becomes the window's subview (the root view) *automatically*, by virtue of the RootViewController's being the window's `rootViewController`.

- In order for the UIPageViewController's view to appear in the interface, since it is not the root view controller, it *must* be some view controller's child. There is only one possible parent — my RootViewController. My RootViewController must function as a custom parent view controller, with the UIPageViewController as

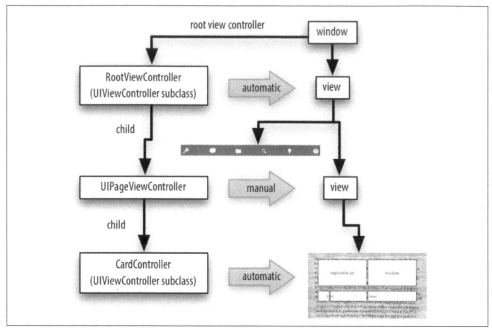

Figure 6-4. The Latin flashcard app's initial view controller and view hierarchy

its child. So I have made that happen, and I have therefore also had to put the UIPageViewController's view *manually* into my RootViewController's view.

- I hand the UIPageViewController an instance of another custom UIView-Controller subclass (called CardController) as its child, and the UIPageView-Controller displays the CardController's view *automatically*.

Presentation View Placement

Here's an example of a presented view controller. My Latin flashcard app has a second mode, where the user is drilled on a subset of the cards in random order; the interface looks very much like the first mode's interface (Figure 6-5), but it behaves completely differently.

To implement this, I have another UIViewController subclass (called DrillView-Controller); it is structured very much like RootViewController. When the user is in drill mode, a DrillViewController is being *presented* by the RootViewController, meaning that the DrillViewController's interface takes over the screen automatically: the DrillViewController's view, with its whole subview hierarchy, including the views of the DrillViewController's children in the view controller hierarchy, replaces the RootViewController's view and *its* whole subview hierarchy (Figure 6-6). The Root-ViewController is still the window's rootViewController, and its hierarchy of child

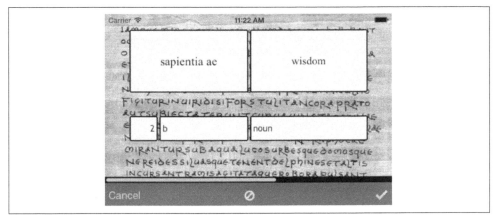

Figure 6-5. The Latin flashcard app, in drill mode

view controllers remains in place, but the corresponding view hierarchy is not in the interface; it will be returned to the interface automatically when we leave drill mode (because the presented DrillViewController is dismissed), and the situation will look like Figure 6-4 once again.

Ensuring a Coherent Hierarchy

For any app that you write, for every moment in the lifetime of that app, you should be able to construct a diagram showing the hierarchy of view controllers and charting how each view controller's view fits into the view hierarchy. The diagram should be similar to mine! The view hierarchy should run in neat parallel with the view controller hierarchy; there should be no crossed wires or orphan views. And every view controller's view should be placed automatically into the view hierarchy, except in the following two situations:

- The view controller is the child of your custom parent view controller. There is a complicated parent–child dance you have to do. See "Container View Controllers" on page 368.

- You're doing a custom transition animation. See "Custom Transition" on page 343.

 What you're really doing by following those rules is ensuring a coherent *responder chain*. The view controller hierarchy is, in fact, a subset of the responder chain.

New in Xcode 9, you can actually *see* the view controller hierarchy as part of the view debugger's display. Figure 6-7 displays the view debugger's outline for the same interface shown in Figure 6-3, and the analysis accords with mine. The window's root view controller is my RootViewController, which has a child UIPageViewController, which

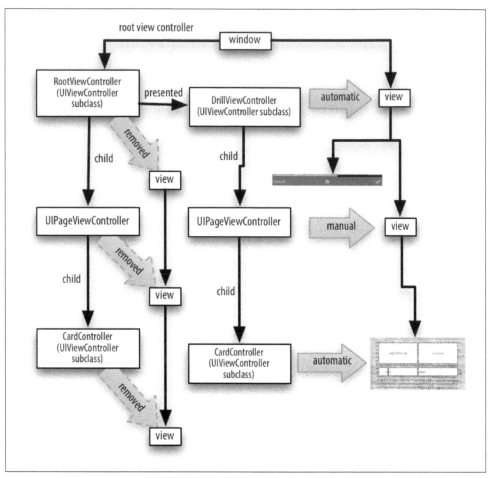

Figure 6-6. The Latin flashcard app's drill mode view controller and view hierarchy

has a child CardController; the window contains the root view controller's view, the root view controller's view contains the toolbar and the UIPageViewController's view, and the page view controller's view contains the CardController's view.

View Controller Creation

A view controller is an instance like any other instance, and it is created like any other instance — by instantiating its class. You might perform this instantiation in code; in that case, you will of course have to initialize the instance properly as you create it. Here's an example from one of my own apps:

```
let llc = LessonListController(terms: self.terms)
let nav = UINavigationController(rootViewController: llc)
```

Figure 6-7. The view debugger displays the view controller hierarchy

In that example, LessonListController is my own UIViewController subclass, so I have called its designated initializer, which I myself have defined; UINavigation-Controller is a built-in UIViewController subclass, and I have used one of its convenience initializers.

Alternatively, a view controller instance might come into existence through the loading of a nib. To make it possible to get a view controller into the nib in the first place, view controllers are included among the object types available through the Object library in the nib editor. For example, a scene in a storyboard contains a view controller; in the built app, that view controller will be stored in a nib, and when the app runs, if that view controller is needed, that nib will be loaded to obtain that view controller instance.

Once a view controller comes into existence, it must be retained so that it will persist. This will happen automatically when the view controller is assigned a place in the view controller hierarchy that I described in the previous section. A view controller assigned as a window's rootViewController is retained by the window. A view controller assigned as another view controller's child is retained by the parent view controller. A presented view controller is retained by the presenting view controller. The parent view controller or presenting view controller then takes ownership, and will release the other view controller in good order when it is no longer needed.

Here's an example, from one of my apps, of view controllers being instantiated and then being retained by being placed into the view controller hierarchy:

```
let llc = LessonListController(terms: self.terms) ❶
let nav = UINavigationController(rootViewController: llc) ❷
self.present(nav, animated: true) ❸
```

That's the same code I showed a moment ago, extended by one line. It comes from a view controller class called RootViewController. Here's how view controller creation and memory management works in those three lines:

❶ I instantiate LessonListController.

❷ I instantiate UINavigationController, and I assign the LessonListController instance to the UINavigationController instance as its child; the navigation controller retains the LessonListController instance and takes ownership of it.

❸ I present the UINavigationController instance on `self`, a RootViewController instance; the RootViewController instance is the presenting view controller, and it retains and takes ownership of the UINavigationController instance as its presented view controller. The RootViewController instance itself is already the window's `rootViewController`, and is retained by the window — and so the view controller hierarchy is safely established.

All of this sounds straightforward, but it is worth dwelling on, because things can go wrong. It is quite possible, if things are mismanaged, for a view controller's view to get into the interface while the view controller itself is allowed to go out of existence. *This must not be permitted.* If such a thing happens, at the very least the view will apparently misbehave, failing to perform its intended functionality, because that functionality is embodied by the view controller, which no longer exists. (I've made this mistake, so I speak from experience here.) If you instantiate a view controller in code, you should immediately ask yourself who will be retaining this view controller.

How a View Controller Obtains Its View

Initially, when it first comes into existence, a view controller *has no view*. A view controller is a small, lightweight object; a view is a relatively heavyweight object, involving interface elements that can occupy a significant amount of memory. Therefore, a view controller postpones obtaining its view until it has to do so, namely, when it is asked for the value of its `view` property. At that moment, if its `view` property is `nil`, the view controller sets about obtaining its view. (We say that a view controller loads its view *lazily*.) Typically, this happens because the time has come to put the view controller's view into the interface.

In working with a newly instantiated view controller, be careful not to refer to its `view` property if you don't need to, since this can trigger the view controller's obtaining its view prematurely. (As usual, I speak from experience here.) To learn whether a view controller has a view without causing it to load its view, consult its `isViewLoaded` property. You can refer to a view controller's view safely, without loading it, as its `viewIfLoaded` (an Optional); you can also cause the view controller to load its view explicitly, rather than as a side effect of mentioning its `view`, by calling `loadViewIfNeeded`.

As soon as a view controller has its view, its `viewDidLoad` method is called. If this view controller is an instance of your own UIViewController subclass, `viewDidLoad` is your opportunity to modify the contents of this view — to populate it with subviews, to tweak the subviews it already has, and so forth — as well as to perform other initializations of the view controller consonant with its acquisition of a view. The view property is now pointing to the view, so it is safe to refer to self.view. Bear in mind, however, that the view may not yet be part of the interface! In fact, it almost certainly is not. (To confirm this, check whether self.view.window is nil.) Thus, for example, you cannot necessarily rely on the *dimensions* of the view at this point to be the dimensions that the view will assume when it becomes visible in the interface. Performing dimension-dependent customizations prematurely in viewDidLoad is a common beginner mistake.

Before viewDidLoad is called, the view controller must *obtain* its view. The question of where and how the view controller will get its view is often crucial. In some cases, to be sure, you won't care about this; in particular, when a view controller is an instance of a built-in UIViewController subclass such as UINavigationController or UITabBarController, its view is out of your hands — you might never even have cause to refer to this view over the entire course of your app's lifetime — and you simply trust that the view controller will somehow generate its view. But when the view controller is an instance of your own subclass of UIViewController, and when you yourself will design or modify its view, it becomes essential to understand the process whereby a view controller gets its view.

This process is not difficult to understand, but it is rather elaborate, because there are multiple possibilities. Most important, this process is *not magic*. Yet it quite possibly causes more confusion to beginners than any other matter connected with iOS programming. Therefore, I will explain it in detail. The more you know about the details of how a view controller gets its view, the deeper and clearer will be your understanding of the entire workings of your app, its view controllers, its *.storyboard* and *.xib* files, and so on.

The main alternatives are as follows:

- The view may be instantiated in the view controller's own code, manually.
- The view may be created as an empty generic view, automatically.
- The view may be loaded from a nib file.

In the rest of this section, I'll demonstrate each of these three ways in which a view controller can obtain its view. For purposes of the demonstration, we'll need a view controller that we instantiate manually (as opposed to a view controller that comes automatically from a storyboard, as explained in the next section). Since I haven't yet described how to do anything with a view controller other than make it the window's rootViewController, this view controller will be the window's rootViewController. If you want to follow along with hands-on experimentation, you can start with a clean project created from the Single View app template. The template includes a storyboard and a UIViewController subclass called ViewController, but we're going to ignore both of those, behaving as if the storyboard didn't exist: we'll create our own UIViewController subclass instance — which I'll call RootViewController — and make it the root view controller (as described in Chapter 1 and Appendix B). When you launch the project, you'll *see* RootViewController's view, thus proving that the view controller has successfully obtained its view.

Manual View

To supply a UIViewController's view manually, in code, override its `loadView` method. Your job here is to obtain an instance of UIView (or a subclass of UIView) — typically by instantiating it directly — and *assign it to `self.view`*. You must *not* call `super` (for reasons that I'll make clear later on).

Let's try it:

1. We need a UIViewController subclass, so choose File → New → File; specify iOS → Source → Cocoa Touch Class. Click Next.

2. Name the class RootViewController, and specify that it is to be a UIView-Controller subclass. Uncheck "Also create XIB file" (if it happens to be checked). Click Next.

3. Confirm that we're saving into the appropriate folder and group, and that these files will be part of the app target. Click Create.

We now have a RootViewController class, and we proceed to edit its code. In *Root-ViewController.swift*, we'll implement `loadView`. To convince ourselves that the example is working correctly, we'll give the view that we create manually an identifiable color, and we'll put some interface inside it, namely a "Hello, World" label:

```
override func loadView() {
    let v = UIView()
    v.backgroundColor = .green
    self.view = v // *
    let label = UILabel()
    v.addSubview(label)
    label.text = "Hello, World!"
    label.autoresizingMask = [
        .flexibleTopMargin,
        .flexibleLeftMargin,
        .flexibleBottomMargin,
        .flexibleRightMargin]
    label.sizeToFit()
    label.center = CGPoint(v.bounds.midX, v.bounds.midY)
    label.frame = label.frame.integral
}
```

The starred line is the key: we made a view and we assigned it to `self.view`. In order to see that that code works, we need to instantiate RootViewController and place that instance into our view controller hierarchy. As I explained a moment ago, we'll do that by making RootViewController the app's root view controller. Edit *App-Delegate.swift* to look like this:

```
import UIKit
@UIApplicationMain
class AppDelegate : UIResponder, UIApplicationDelegate {
    var window : UIWindow?
    func application(_ application: UIApplication,
        didFinishLaunchingWithOptions launchOptions:
        [UIApplicationLaunchOptionsKey : Any]?) -> Bool {
            self.window = self.window ?? UIWindow()
            let theRVC = RootViewController() // *
            self.window!.rootViewController = theRVC // *
            self.window!.backgroundColor = .white
            self.window!.makeKeyAndVisible()
            return true
    }
}
```

Again, the starred lines are the key: we instantiate RootViewController and make that instance the app's root view controller. Build and run the app. Sure enough, there's our green background and our "Hello, world" label!

When we created our view controller's view (`self.view`), we never gave it a reasonable frame. This is because we are relying on someone else to frame the view appropriately. In this case, the "someone else" is the window, which responds to having its `rootViewController` property set to a view controller by framing the view controller's view appropriately as the root view before putting it into the window as a subview. In general, it is the responsibility of whoever puts a view controller's view into the interface to give the view the correct frame — and this will never be the view controller itself (although under some circumstances the view controller can express a preference in this regard). Indeed, the size of a view controller's view may be changed as it is placed into the interface, and you must keep in mind, as you design your view controller's view and its subviews, that this can happen. (That's why, in the preceding code, I used autoresizing to keep the label centered in the view, no matter how the view may be resized.)

Generic Automatic View

We should distinguish between *creating* a view and *populating* it. The preceding example fails to draw this distinction. The lines that create our RootViewController's view are merely these:

```
let v = UIView()
self.view = v
```

Everything else configures and populates the view, turning it green and putting a label into it. A more appropriate place to populate a view controller's view is its view-DidLoad implementation, which, as I've already mentioned, is called after the view exists and can be referred to as self.view. We could therefore rewrite the preceding example like this (just for fun, I'll use autolayout this time):

```
override func loadView() {
    let v = UIView()
    self.view = v
}
override func viewDidLoad() {
    super.viewDidLoad()
    let v = self.view!
    v.backgroundColor = .green
    let label = UILabel()
    v.addSubview(label)
    label.text = "Hello, World!"
    label.translatesAutoresizingMaskIntoConstraints = false
    NSLayoutConstraint.activate([
        label.centerXAnchor.constraint(equalTo:v.centerXAnchor),
        label.centerYAnchor.constraint(equalTo:v.centerYAnchor)
    ])
}
```

But if we're going to do that, we can go even further and remove our implementation of loadView entirely! It turns out that if you *don't* implement loadView, and if no view is supplied in any other way, then UIViewController's default implementation of loadView will do *exactly* what we are doing: it creates a generic UIView object and assigns it to self.view.

If we needed our view controller's view to be a particular UIView subclass, that wouldn't be acceptable; but in this case, our view controller's view *is* a generic UIView object, so it *is* acceptable. Comment out or delete the entire loadView implementation from the preceding code, and build and run the app; our example still works!

View in a Separate Nib

In the preceding examples, we supplied and designed our view controller's view in code. That works, but of course we're missing out on the convenience of configuring and populating the view by designing it graphically in Xcode's nib editor. So now let's see how a view controller can obtain its view, ready-made, from a nib file.

To make this work, the nib file must be properly configured in accordance with the demands of the nib-loading mechanism. The view controller instance will already have been created. It will load the nib, *setting itself as the nib's owner*. The nib itself must be prepared to match this situation. In the nib, the owner object must have same class as the view controller, and its view outlet must point to the view object in the nib. The result is that when the view controller loads the nib, the view instantiated from the nib is assigned to the view controller's `view` property automatically.

Suppose the nib is a *.xib* file. (Storyboards are discussed in the next section.) In a *.xib* file, the owner object is the File's Owner proxy object. Therefore, in a *.xib* file that is to serve as the source of a view controller's view, the following two things must be true:

- The File's Owner proxy object's class must correspond to the class of the view controller whose view this will be. This will also cause the File's Owner to have a `view` outlet.
- The File's Owner proxy object's `view` outlet must be connected to the view.

Let's try it. We can use the example we've already developed, with our RootView-Controller class. Delete the implementation of `loadView` (if you haven't already) and `viewDidLoad` from *RootViewController.swift*, because we want the view to come from a nib and we're going to populate it in the nib. Then:

1. Choose File → New → File and specify iOS → User Interface → View. This will be a *.xib* file containing a UIView object. Click Next.
2. Name the file *MyNib* (meaning *MyNib.xib*). Confirm the appropriate folder and group, and make sure that the file will be part of the app target. Click Create.
3. Edit *MyNib.xib*. Prepare it in the way I described a moment ago:
   a. Select the File's Owner object; in the Identity inspector, set its class to Root-ViewController.
   b. Connect the File's Owner `view` outlet to the View object.
4. Design the view. To make it clear that this is not the same view we were creating previously, perhaps you should give the view a red background color (in the Attributes inspector). Drag a UILabel into the middle of the view and give it some text, such as "Hello, World!"

When our RootViewController instance wants its view, we want it to load the *MyNib* nib. To make it do that, we must associate this nib with our RootViewController instance. Recall these two lines from `application(_:didFinishLaunchingWith-Options:)` in *AppDelegate.swift*:

```
let theRVC = RootViewController()
self.window!.rootViewController = theRVC
```

We're going to change the first of those two lines. A UIViewController has a `nibName` property that tells it what nib, if any, it should load to obtain its view. However, we are not allowed to set the `nibName` property of theRVC (it is read-only). Instead, as we instantiate the view controller, we use the *designated initializer*, `init(nib-Name:bundle:)`, like this:

```
let theRVC = RootViewController(nibName:"MyNib", bundle:nil)
self.window!.rootViewController = theRVC
```

(The `nil` argument to the `bundle:` parameter specifies the main bundle, which is almost always what you want.)

To prove that this works, build and run. The red background appears! Our view controller's view is being obtained by loading it from the nib.

Now I'm going to describe a shortcut, based on the *name* of the nib. It turns out that if the nib name passed to `init(nibName:bundle:)` is `nil`, a nib will be sought automatically *with the same name as the view controller's class*. Moreover, UIViewController's `init()` turns out to be a convenience initializer: it actually calls `init(nibName:bundle:)`, passing `nil` for both arguments. This means, in effect, that we can return to using `init()` to initialize the view controller, provided that the nib file's name *matches the name* of the view controller class.

Let's try it:

1. Rename *MyNib.xib* to *RootViewController.xib*.

2. Change the code that instantiates and initializes our RootViewController back to what it was before:

   ```
   let theRVC = RootViewController()
   self.window!.rootViewController = theRVC
   ```

Build and run. It works!

There's an additional aspect to this shortcut based on the name of the nib. It seems ridiculous that we should end up with a nib that has "Controller" in its name merely because our view controller, as is so often the case, has "Controller" in *its* name. A nib, after all, is not a controller. It turns out that the runtime, in looking for a view controller's corresponding nib, will in fact try stripping "Controller" off the end of the view controller class's name. Thus, we can name our nib file *RootView.xib* instead of *RootViewController.xib*, and it will *still* be properly associated with our RootViewController instance.

When we created our UIViewController subclass, RootViewController, we saw in the Xcode dialog a checkbox offering to create an eponymous *.xib* file at the same time: "Also create XIB file." We deliberately unchecked it. Suppose we had checked it; what would have happened? In that case, Xcode would have created *RootViewController.swift* and *RootViewController.xib*. Moreover, it would have configured *RootViewController.xib* for us: the File's Owner's class would already be set to the view controller's class, RootViewController, and its `view` outlet would already be hooked up to the view. Thus, this view controller and *.xib* file are ready for use together: you instantiate the view controller with a `nil` nib name, and it gets its view from the eponymous nib.

(The *.xib* file created by Xcode in response to checking "Also create XIB file" does *not* have "Controller" stripped off the end of its name. But you can rename it manually later if the default name bothers you.)

Another convention involving the nib name has to do with the rules for loading resources by name generally. The same naming rule that I mentioned in Chapter 2 for an image file extended by the suffix `~ipad` applies to nib files. A nib file named *RootViewController~ipad.xib* will be loaded on an iPad when a nib named `"RootView-Controller"` is sought. This principle can simplify your life when you're writing a universal app, as you can easily use one nib on iPhone and another nib on iPad — though you might not need to do that, since conditional interface design, described in Chapter 1, may permit you to construct an interface differing on iPad and iPhone in a single nib.

Summary

We are now in a position to summarize the sequence whereby a view controller's view is obtained. It turns out that the entire process is driven by `loadView`:

1. When the view controller first decides that it needs its view, `loadView` is *always* called:

   - If we override `loadView`, we supply and set the `view` in code, and we do *not* call `super`. Therefore, the process of seeking a view comes to an end.

   - If we *don't* override `loadView`, UIViewController's built-in default implementation of `loadView` takes over, and performs the rest of the process.

2. UIViewController's default implementation of `loadView` looks for a nib:

   - If the view controller was instantiated with an explicit `nibName:`, a nib with that name is sought, and the process comes to an end. (If there is no such nib, *the app will crash* at launch.)

   - If the view controller was instantiated with a nil `nibName:`, then:

     1. An eponymous nib is sought. If it is found, it is loaded and the process comes to an end.

     2. If the view controller's name ends in "Controller," an eponymous nib without the "Controller" is sought. If it is found, it is loaded and the process comes to an end.

3. If we reach this point, UIViewController's default implementation of `loadView` creates a generic UIView.

How Storyboards Work

By default, a storyboard uses the third approach to supply a view controller with its view: the view is loaded from a nib. To understand how this works, distinguish between what you *see* in a storyboard and what *really* happens. A scene in a storyboard looks like a view controller's view. Actually, if you look more closely at what the scene represents, it is a view controller *and* its view. When the app is built and the storyboard is compiled into a `.storyboardc` bundle, the scene is split into *two nibs*:

View controller nib
> The first nib contains just the view controller.

View nib
> The second nib contains the view, its subviews, and any other top-level objects such as gesture recognizers. The view nib has a special name, such as *01J-lp-oVM-view-Ze5-6b-2t3.nib*. It is correctly configured: its File's Owner class is the view controller's class, with its `view` outlet hooked to the view.

We can thus divide the tale of how storyboards work into two phases, corresponding to how each of those nibs gets loaded.

How a View Controller Nib is Loaded

To instantiate a view controller from a storyboard's view controller nib, we have only to load that nib. The view controller is the nib's sole top-level object. Loading a nib provides a reference to the instances that come from the nib's top-level objects, so now we have a reference to the view controller instance.

Loading a view controller nib from a storyboard starts with a reference to the storyboard. You can get a reference to a storyboard either by calling the UIStoryboard initializer `init(name:bundle:)` or through the `storyboard` property of a view controller that has already been instantiated from that storyboard.

When a view controller instance stored in a storyboard nib is needed, the nib can be loaded and the view controller instantiated in one of four main ways:

Initial view controller
> At most one view controller in the storyboard is designated the storyboard's *initial view controller* (also called its *entry point*). To instantiate that view controller, call the UIStoryboard instance method `instantiateInitialViewController`. The view controller instance is returned.

For an app with main storyboard, that happens automatically at launch time. The main storyboard is designated the app's main storyboard by the *Info.plist* key "Main storyboard file base name" (`UIMainStoryboardFile`). As the app launches, `UIApplicationMain` gets a reference to this storyboard by calling the UIStoryboard initializer `init(name:bundle:)`, instantiates its initial view controller by calling `instantiateInitialViewController`, and makes that instance the window's `rootViewController`.

By identifier
A view controller in a storyboard can be assigned an arbitrary string identifier; this is its Storyboard ID in the Identity inspector. To instantiate that view controller, call the UIStoryboard instance method `instantiateViewController(with-Identifier:)`. The view controller instance is returned.

By relationship
A parent view controller in a storyboard may have immediate children, such as a UINavigationController and its initial child view controller. The nib editor will show a *relationship* connection between them. When the parent is instantiated (the source of the relationship), the initial children (the destination of the relationship) are instantiated automatically at the same time.

By triggered segue
A view controller in a storyboard may be the source of a *segue* whose destination is a *future* child view controller or a *future* presented view controller. When the segue is triggered and performed, it instantiates the destination view controller.

Thus, you can set up your app in such a way that a storyboard is the source of every view controller that your app will ever instantiate. Indeed, by starting with a main storyboard and by configuring relationships and triggered segues in the storyboard, you can arrange that every view controller your app will ever need will be instantiated *automatically*.

I'll go into greater detail about storyboards and segues later in this chapter.

How a View Nib is Loaded

Let's say that, way or another, a view controller has just been instantiated from its storyboard nib — but its view has not. Views are loaded lazily, as we know. Sooner or later, the view controller will probably want its view (typically because it is time to put that view into the interface). How will it get it?

The view nib, as I already mentioned, has been assigned a special name, such as *01J-lp-oVM-view-Ze5-6b-2t3.nib*. It turns out that the view controller, in *its* nib, was handed that same special name, such that when it was instantiated from its *own* nib, its `nibName` property was set to the name of the *view* nib. Thus, when the view controller wants its view, it loads it in the normal way! It has a non-nil nibName, so it looks for a nib by that name — and finds it. The nib is loaded and the view becomes the view controller's view.

That's true for every scene. A storyboard consists ultimately of pairs of nib files, a view controller's nib and its corresponding view nib. As a result, a storyboard has all the memory management advantages of nib files: none of these nib files are loaded until the instances that they contain are needed, and they can be loaded multiple times to give additional instances of the same nib objects. At the same time, you get the convenience of being able to see and edit a lot of your app's interface simultaneously in one place.

The default scene structure is that a view controller in a storyboard scene contains its view — but you don't *have* to use that structure. You can select the view inside a view controller in a storyboard and *delete* it! If you do that, then that view controller won't have a corresponding view nib; instead the view controller will have to obtain its view in one of the *other* ways we've already discussed: by an implementation of loadView in the code of that view controller class, or by loading an eponymous nib file (which you supply as a *.xib* file) — or even, if all of that fails, by creating a generic UIView.

View Resizing

There are several very common ways in which a view controller's view is likely to be resized:

- When it is put into the interface
- When the app rotates
- When the surrounding interface changes; for example, when a navigation bar gets taller or shorter, appears or disappears

As I explained in Chapter 1, if you're designing your view controller's view's interface in the nib editor, you'll almost certainly use layout — most probably, autolayout — possibly along with conditional interface (see "Conditional Interface Design" on page 64), to help your app cope with all this resizing, regardless of the view's size and orientation. If your code also needs to take a hand in responding to a change in the view controller's view size, that code will likely go into the view controller itself. A view controller has properties and receives events connected to the resizing of its view, so that it can respond when such resizing takes place, and can even help dictate the arrangement of the interface if needed. I'll talk later about where you're likely to slot your layout-related code into your view controller.

View Size in the Nib Editor

When you design your interface in the nib editor, every view controller's view has to be displayed at some definite size. That size is up to you. In the nib editor, you can display the view at the size of any actual device. You can also specify an orientation. Using the Simulated Metrics pop-up menus in the Attributes inspector, you can adjust for the presence or absence of interface elements that can affect layout (status bar, top bar, bottom bar).

But no *single* device size, orientation, or metrics can reflect *all* the possible sizes the view may assume when the app runs on different devices, in different orientations, and with different surroundings. If you design the interface *only* for the size you see in the nib editor, you can get a rude surprise when you actually run the app and the view appears at some *other* size! Failing to take account of this possibility is a common beginner mistake.

Be sure to design your app's interface to be coherent at *any* size it may actually assume. You can get a pretty good idea of whether you're doing that successfully, without running on your code on every device type, thanks to the nib editor's ability to switch between displaying different device sizes (using the View As button at the lower left of the canvas), as well as the Preview display in the assistant pane ("Previewing Your Interface" on page 68). If your code also takes a hand in layout, you'll need to run in the Simulator with at least a few different device sizes to see your code at work.

Bars and Underlapping

A view controller's view will often have to adapt to the presence of bars at the top and bottom of the screen:

The status bar is underlapped
> The status bar is transparent, so that the region of a view behind it is visible through it. The root view, and any other fullscreen view, must occupy the *entire window*, including the status bar area, the top of the view being visible behind the transparent status bar. You'll want to design your view so that its top doesn't contain any interface objects that will be overlapped by the status bar.

Top and bottom bars may be underlapped
> The top and bottom bars displayed by a navigation controller (navigation bar, toolbar) or tab bar controller (tab bar) can be translucent. When they are, your view controller's view is, by default, extended *behind* the translucent bar, underlapping it. Again, you'll want to design your view so that this underlapping doesn't conceal any of your view's important interface.

The status bar may be present or absent. Top and bottom bars may be present or absent, and, if present, their height can change. How will your interface cope with such changes? The primary coping mechanism is the view controller's *safe area* (see Chapter 1). The top and bottom of the safe area move automatically at runtime to reflect the view's environment:

Safe area top
> The safe area's top is positioned as follows:
>
> - If there is a status bar and no top bar, at the bottom of the status bar.
> - If there is a top bar, at the bottom of the top bar.
> - If there is no top bar and no status bar, at the top of the view.

Safe area bottom
> The safe area's bottom is positioned as follows:
>
> - If there is a bottom bar, at the top of the bottom bar.
> - If there is no bottom bar, at the bottom of the view.

The easiest way to involve the safe area in your view layout is through autolayout and constraints. A view vends the safe area as its `safeAreaLayoutGuide`. By constraining a view to the `topAnchor` or `bottomAnchor` of the `safeAreaLayoutGuide`, you guarantee that the view will move when the layout guide changes. Typically, the view whose `safeAreaLayoutGuide` you'll be interested in is the view controller's main view. Such constraints are easy to form in the nib editor — they are the default. A view controller's main view will automatically display the safe area, and when you form a constraint from a subview to the main view, the nib editor will offer to configure it with respect to the main view's safe area. (If you need any other view to display its safe area, check Safe Area Layout Guide in the view's Size inspector.)

If you need actual numbers in order to perform layout-related calculations, the distances between the safe area boundaries and the view's edges are reported as the view's `safeAreaInsets`.

The safe area, although it is reported by views, is imposed by the view controller. You wouldn't want to interfere with the workings of the safe area, but you are allowed to augment it. Set your view controller's `additionalSafeAreaInsets` to increase the effective distance between one or more safe area boundaries and view's corresponding edge. In this way you can continue to constrain your views to the safe area while inserting a consistent extra distance between your subviews and the edges of the main view.

Status bar

The default behavior of the status bar is that it is present, except in landscape orientation on an iPhone, where it is absent. The top-level view controller — which is usually the root view controller — gets a say in this behavior; it also determines the look of the status bar when present. Your UIViewController subclass, if the view controller instance is the top-level view controller, can exercise this power by overriding these properties:

preferredStatusBarStyle

> Your choices (UIStatusBarStyle) are .default and .lightContent, meaning dark text and light text, respectively. Use light text for legibility if the view content underlapping the status bar is dark.

prefersStatusBarHidden

> A value of true makes the status bar invisible; a value of false makes the status bar visible, even in landscape orientation on an iPhone.

Your override will be a computed variable with a getter function; your getter can return the result of a call to super to get the default behavior.

Even if your view controller is *not* the top-level view controller, those properties might *still* be consulted be obeyed, if your view controller is the child of a parent that *is* the top-level view controller and delegates the decision-making power to its child, through an override of these properties:

childViewControllerForStatusBarStyle
childViewControllerForStatusBarHidden

> Used to delegate the decision on the status bar style or visibility to a child view controller's preferredStatusBarStyle or prefersStatusBarHidden. For example, a tab bar controller implements these properties to allow *your* view controller to decide the status bar style and visibility when your view controller's view occupies the tab bar controller's view. Thus, your view controller gets to make the decisions even though the tab bar controller is the top-level view controller.

You are not in charge of when these properties are consulted, but you can provide a nudge: if the situation has changed and one of these properties would now give a different answer, call setNeedsStatusBarAppearanceUpdate on your view controller. If this call is inside an animations function, the change in the look of the status bar will be animated with the specified duration. The character of the animation from visible to invisible (and *vice versa*) is set by your view controller's override of preferred-StatusBarUpdateAnimation; the value you return (UIStatusBarAnimation) can be .fade, .slide, or .none.

When you toggle the visibility of the status bar, if there is no other top bar, the top of the safe area will move up or down by 20 points. If your main view has subviews with constraints to the safe area's top anchor, those subviews will move. If this happens when the main view is visible, the user will see this movement as a jump. That is probably not what you want. To prevent it, call `layoutIfNeeded` on your view in the same animations function in which you call `setNeedsStatusBarAppearanceUpdate`; your layout update will then be animated together with the change in status bar visibility. In this example, a button's action method toggles the visibility of the status bar with smooth animation:

```
var hide = false
override var prefersStatusBarHidden : Bool {
    return self.hide
}
@IBAction func doButton(_ sender: Any) {
    self.hide = !self.hide
    UIView.animate(withDuration:0.4) {
        self.setNeedsStatusBarAppearanceUpdate()
        self.view.layoutIfNeeded()
    }
}
```

Extended layout

If your UIViewController's parent is a navigation controller or tab bar controller, you can govern whether its view underlaps a top bar (navigation bar) or bottom bar (toolbar, tab bar) with these UIViewController properties:

edgesForExtendedLayout

> A UIRectEdge. The default is `.all`, meaning that this view controller's view will underlap a translucent top bar or a translucent bottom bar. The other extreme is `.none`, meaning that this view controller's view won't underlap top and bottom bars. Other possibilities are `.top` (underlap translucent top bars only) and `.bottom` (underlap translucent bottom bars only).

extendedLayoutIncludesOpaqueBars

> If `true`, then if `edgesForExtendedLayout` permits underlapping of bars, those bars will be underlapped *even if they are opaque*. The default is `false`, meaning that only translucent bars are underlapped.

Resizing Events

A UIViewController receives events that notify it of pending view size changes (and compare the discussion of related view topics in Chapter 1). The following events are associated primarily with rotation of the interface (as well as with iPad multitasking; see Chapter 9); UIViewController receives them by virtue of adopting the appropriate protocol:

`viewWillTransition(to:with:)` *(UIContentContainer protocol)*

Sent when the app is about to undergo rotation (even if the rotation turns out to be 180 degrees and the size won't actually change) or an iPad multitasking size change. The first parameter is the *new* size (a CGSize). The old size is still available as `self.view.bounds.size`. This event is *not* sent on launch or when your view controller's view is first embedded into the interface. If you override this method, call `super`.

`willTransition(to:with:)` *(UIContentContainer protocol)*

Sent when the app is about to undergo a change in the *trait collection* (because the size classes will change). The first parameter is the *new* trait collection (a UITraitCollection). The old trait collection is still available as `self.trait-Collection`. Common examples are rotation of 90 degrees on an iPhone, or a change between fullscreen and splitscreen on an iPad. This event is *not* sent on launch or when your view controller's view is first embedded into the interface. If you override this method, call `super`.

`traitCollectionDidChange(_:)` *(UITraitEnvironment protocol)*

Sent after the trait collection changes. The parameter is the *old* trait collection; the new trait collection is available as `self.traitCollection`. Sent after the trait collection changes, *including* on launch or when the trait collection is set for the first time (in which case the old trait collection will be `nil`).

(The `with:` parameter in the first two methods is a transition coordinator; I'll describe its use later in this chapter.)

In addition, a UIViewController receives these events related to the layout of its view:

`updateViewConstraints`

The view is about to be told to update its constraints (`updateConstraints`), *including* at application launch. If you override this method, call `super`.

`viewWillLayoutSubviews`
`viewDidLayoutSubviews`

These events surround the moment when the view is sent `layoutSubviews`, *including* at application launch.

In a situation where all these events are sent, the order is:

1. `willTransition(to:with:)` (the trait collection)

2. `viewWillTransition(to:with:)` (the size)

3. `updateViewConstraints`

4. `traitCollectionDidChange(_:)`

5. `viewWillLayoutSubviews`

6. `viewDidLayoutSubviews`

There is no guarantee that any of these events, if sent, will be sent exactly once. Your code should take some care to do nothing if nothing relevant has changed.

 There are many circumstances, such as the showing and hiding of a navigation bar that isn't underlapped, under which your view can be resized *without* `view-WillTransition(to:with:)` being sent. Thus, to detect these changes, you'll have to fall back on layout events such as `viewWillLayoutSubviews`. I regard this as a flaw in the iOS view controller event architecture.

Rotation

Your app can rotate, moving its top to correspond to a different edge of the device's screen. Rotation expresses itself in two ways:

The status bar orientation changes
You can hear about this by way of these app delegate events and notifications:

- `application(_:willChangeStatusBarOrientation:duration:)`
- `.UIApplicationWillChangeStatusBarOrientation` notification
- `application(_:didChangeStatusBarOrientation:)`
- `.UIApplicationDidChangeStatusBarOrientation` notification

The current orientation (which is also the app's current orientation) is available from the UIApplication as its `statusBarOrientation`; the app delegate methods provide the other orientation (the one we are changing to or from, respectively) as the second parameter, and the notifications provide it in the `userInfo` under the `UIApplicationStatusBarOrientationUserInfoKey`. Possible values (UIInterfaceOrientation) are:

- `.portrait`
- `.portraitUpsideDown`
- `.landscapeLeft`
- `.landscapeRight`

Two global convenience functions, `UIInterfaceOrientationIsLandscape` and `UIInterfaceOrientationIsPortrait`, take a UIInterfaceOrientation and return a Bool.

The view controller's view is resized

The view controller receives events related to resizing, described in the preceding section. As I mentioned there, the size needn't be actually about to change; for example, we may be rotating from one landscape orientation to the other.

On the whole, you will probably never concern yourself with the status bar orientation; the resizing events are preferable. The most general way to learn that rotation is taking place is by detecting the size change, through your implementation of view-WillTransition(to:with:). In real life, however, you are quite likely to care only about a 90 degree rotation on an iPhone; in that case, detection of the trait collection change, through willTransition(to:with:), may be sufficient.

There are two complementary uses for rotation:

Compensatory rotation

The app rotates to compensate for the orientation of the device, so that the app appears right way up with respect to how the user is holding the device.

Forced rotation

The app rotates when a particular view appears in the interface, or when the app launches, to indicate that the user needs to rotate the device in order to view the app the right way up. This is typically because the interface has been specifically designed, in view of the fact that the screen is not square, to appear in just one orientation (portrait or landscape).

In the case of the iPhone, no law says that your app has to perform compensatory rotation. Most of my iPhone apps do not do so; indeed, I have no compunction about doing just the opposite, namely forced rotation. My view controller views often look best in just one orientation (either just portrait or just landscape), and they stubbornly stay there regardless of how the user holds the device. A single app may contain view controller views that work best in different orientations; thus, my app forces the user to rotate the device differently depending on what view is being displayed. This is reasonable, because the iPhone is small and easily reoriented with a twist of the user's wrist, and it has a natural right way up. Even iPhone apps that do perform compensatory rotation do not generally rotate to an upside-down orientation, because the user is unlikely to hold the device that way.

On the other hand, Apple thinks of an iPad as having no natural top, and would prefer iPad apps to rotate to at least two opposed orientations (such as portrait with the button on the bottom and portrait with the button on the top), and preferably to all four possible orientations, so that the user isn't restricted in how the device is held.

It's trivial to let your app rotate to two opposed orientations, because once the app is set up to work in one of them, it can work with no change in the other. But allowing a single interface to rotate between two orientations that are 90 degrees apart is trickier, because its dimensions must change — roughly speaking, its height and width are transposed — and this may require a change of layout and might even call for more substantial alterations, such as removal or addition of part of the interface. A good example is the behavior of Apple's Mail app on the iPad: in landscape, the master pane and the detail pane appear side by side, but in portrait, the master pane is removed and must be summoned as a temporary overlay on top of the detail pane (explained in Chapter 9).

Permitting compensatory rotation

By default, when you create an Xcode project, the resulting app will perform compensatory rotation in response to the user's rotation of the device. For an iPhone app, this means that the app can appear with its top at the top of the device or either of the two sides of the device. For an iPad app, this means that the app can assume any orientation.

If the default behavior isn't what you want, it is up to you to change it. There are three levels at which you can make changes:

- The app itself, in its *Info.plist*, may declare once and for all every orientation the interface will ever be permitted to assume. It does this under the "Supported interface orientations" key, `UISupportedInterfaceOrientations` (supplemented, for a universal app, by "Supported interface orientations (iPad)," `UISupported-InterfaceOrientations~ipad`). These keys can be set through checkboxes when you edit the app target, in the General tab.

- The app delegate may implement the `application(_:supportedInterface-OrientationsFor:)` method, returning a bitmask listing every orientation the interface is permitted to assume. This list *overrides* the *Info.plist* settings. Thus, the app delegate can do dynamically what the *Info.plist* can do only statically. `application(_:supportedInterfaceOrientationsFor:)` is called at least once every time the device rotates.

- The top-level view controller — that is, the root view controller, or a view controller presented fullscreen — may override the `supportedInterface-Orientations` property, returning a bitmask listing a set of orientations that *intersects* the set of orientations permitted by the app or the app delegate. The resulting intersection will then be the set of orientations permitted at that moment. This intersection must not be empty; if it is, your app will crash (with a useful message: "Supported orientations has no common orientation with the application"). `supportedInterfaceOrientations` is consulted at least once every time the device rotates.

  The top-level view controller can also override `shouldAutorotate`. This is a Bool, and the default is `true`. `shouldAutorotate` is consulted at least once every time the device rotates; if it returns `false`, the interface will not rotate to compensate at this moment, and `supportedInterfaceOrientations` is not consulted.

 Built-in parent view controllers, when they are the top-level view controller, do *not* automatically consult their children about rotation. If your view controller is a child view controller of a UITabBarController or a UINavigationController, it has no direct say in how the app rotates. Those parent view controllers, however, do consult their *delegates* about rotation, as I'll explain later.

You can call the UIViewController class method `attemptRotationToDevice-Orientation` to prompt the runtime to do immediately what it would do if the user were to rotate the device, namely to walk the three levels I've just described and, if the results permit rotation of the interface to match the current device orientation, to rotate the interface. This would be useful if, say, your view controller had previously returned `false` from `shouldAutorotate`, but is now for some reason prepared to return `true` and wants to be asked again, immediately.

The bitmask you return from `application(_:supportedInterfaceOrientations-For:)` or `supportedInterfaceOrientations` is a UIInterfaceOrientationMask. It may be one of these values, or multiple values combined:

- `.portrait`
- `.landscapeLeft`
- `.landscapeRight`
- `.portraitUpsideDown`
- `.landscape` (a combination of `.left` and `.right`)
- `.all` (a combination of `.portrait`, `.upsideDown`, `.left`, and `.right`)
- `.allButUpsideDown` (a combination of `.portrait`, `.left`, and `.right`)

For example:

```
override var supportedInterfaceOrientations : UIInterfaceOrientationMask {
    return .portrait
}
```

An iPhone would prefer not to permit an app to rotate to `.portraitUpsideDown`. Therefore, if you include `.portraitUpsideDown` under "Supported interface orientations" in the *Info.plist*, it will be ignored. You can work around this, if you really want to, by also including `.portraitUpsideDown` in the top-level view controller's `supportedInterfaceOrientations`.

On iPad, if your app permits all four orientations, and if it doesn't opt out of iPad multitasking (by setting UIRequiresFullScreen in its *Info.plist*), then supported-InterfaceOrientations and shouldAutorotate are never consulted, presumably because the answer is known in advance.

If your code needs to know the current physical orientation of the device (as opposed to the current orientation of the app), it can ask the device:

```
let orientation = UIDevice.current.orientation
```

Possible results (UIDeviceOrientation) are .unknown, .portrait, and so on. Global convenience functions UIDeviceOrientationIsPortrait and UIDeviceOrientation-IsLandscape take a UIDeviceOrientation and return a Bool.

Initial orientation

I've talked about how to determine what orientations your app can support in the course of its lifetime; but what about its initial orientation, the very first orientation your app will assume when it launches?

In general, an app will launch directly into whatever permitted orientation is closest to the device's current orientation at launch time. This behavior, while always the case on iPad, is new in iOS 11 for iPhone apps, and will come as a welcome relief to programmers.

There can be a complication, however, when the orientation in which the device is held would have been legal, but the initial root view controller rules it out. For example, suppose the device is held in portrait, and the *Info.plist* permits all orientations, but the root view controller's supportedInterfaceOrientations is set to return .landscape. Then the app starts to launch into portrait, realizes its mistake, and finishes launching in landscape. On the iPhone, this entails a kind of semirotation: willTransition(to:with:) is sent to report a trait collection change, but there is *no size change*. I regard this behavior as incoherent.

To work around that problem, here's a trick that I use. Let's say that my app needs *eventually* to be able to rotate to portrait, so I need to permit all orientations, but its *initial* root view controller must appear only in landscape — its supportedInterface-Orientations return .landscape. In my *Info.plist*, I permit *only* landscape; that way, my app launches directly into landscape, no matter how the device is oriented. But in my app delegate's application(_:supportedInterfaceOrientationsFor:), I return .all; that way, my app can rotate *subsequently* to portrait if it needs to.

View Controller Manual Layout

A view controller governs its main view, and may well take charge of populating it with subviews and configuring those subviews. What if that involves participating manually in the layout of those subviews? As we have seen, a view controller's view can be resized, both as the view is first put into the interface and later as the app runs and is rotated. Where should your view controller's layout code be placed in order to behave coherently in the face of these potential size changes?

Initial Manual Layout

Let's start with the problem of *initial* layout. There is a natural temptation to perform initial layout-related tasks in `viewDidLoad`. This method is extraordinarily convenient. It is guaranteed to be called exactly once in the life of the view controller; that moment is as early as possible in the life of the view controller; and at that time, the view controller has its view, and if it got that view from a nib, properties connected to outlets from that nib have been set. So this seems like the perfect place for initializations. And so it is — but initialization and layout are not the same thing.

Remember, at the time `viewDidLoad` is called, the view controller's view has been loaded, but it has not yet been inserted into the interface! The view has not yet been fully resized for the first time, and initial layout has not yet taken place. Thus, you cannot do anything here that depends upon knowing the dimensions of the view controller's view or any other nib-loaded view — for the simple reason that you do *not* know them.

Here's an elementary (and artificial) example. Suppose we wish, in code, to create a small black square subview and place it at the top of our view controller's main view, centered horizontally. A naïve attempt might look like this:

```
override func viewDidLoad() {
    super.viewDidLoad()
    let v = UIView(frame:CGRect(0,0,10,10))
    v.backgroundColor = .black
    v.center = CGPoint(self.view.bounds.width/2,5) // bad idea!
    self.view.addSubview(v)
}
```

That code *assumes* that `self.view.bounds.width` at the time `viewDidLoad` is called is the width that our main view will have after it is resized and the user sees it. That might be true, but then again it might not. That code is asking for trouble. You should not be doing layout in `viewDidLoad`. It's too soon. It is a capital mistake to assume that bounds and frame values are valid and final in `viewDidLoad`, and beginners often make this mistake.

However, you can certainly create and insert this black subview in `viewDidLoad` and *configure* it for *future* layout. For example, it is perfectly fine to insert a view and give it autolayout constraints in `viewDidLoad`:

```
let v = UIView()
v.translatesAutoresizingMaskIntoConstraints = false
v.backgroundColor = .black
self.view.addSubview(v)
NSLayoutConstraint.activate([
    v.widthAnchor.constraint(equalToConstant: 10),
    v.heightAnchor.constraint(equalToConstant: 10),
    v.topAnchor.constraint(equalTo: self.view.topAnchor),
    v.centerXAnchor.constraint(equalTo: self.view.centerXAnchor)
])
```

That is *not* a case of doing manual layout in `viewDidLoad`. The constraints are not layout; they are instructions as to how this view should be sized and positioned by the runtime when layout *does* happen, as I explained in Chapter 1. Autoresizing would work fine here too; if you center the black subview horizontally and give it an autoresizing mask that keeps it centered regardless of future changes in the main view's size, all will be well.

But let's say that, for some reason, you can't do that or you don't want to. Let's say you want to govern this view's layout actively and entirely in view controller code. Where should that code go?

Let's start again, with the question of where to put code that positions the black square subview *initially*. We know that the answer isn't `viewDidLoad`, so what is it? The primary layout-related messages we are guaranteed to get in our view controller as the app launches are `traitCollectionDidChange(_:)` and `viewWillLayout-Subviews`. Of these, I prefer `viewWillLayoutSubviews`; after all, its very name means that we are about to perform layout on our subviews, meaning that our main view itself has achieved its initial size.

However, we then face the problem that `viewWillLayoutSubviews` may be called many times over the life of our view controller. Moreover, when it is called, layout is about to happen; we mustn't impinge on that process or do more work than we absolutely have to. A sensible implementation is to use a property flag to make sure we initialize only once; here I'll set an Optional, which will serve both as a flag and as a future reference to this view:

```
weak var blackSquare : UIView?
override func viewWillLayoutSubviews() {
    if self.blackSquare == nil { // both reference and flag
        let v = UIView(frame:CGRect(0,0,10,10))
        v.backgroundColor = .black
        v.center = CGPoint(self.view.bounds.width/2,5)
        self.view.addSubview(v)
        self.blackSquare = v
    }
}
```

Bipartite Manual Layout

Thanks to our implementation of `viewWillLayoutSubviews` in the previous section, the black square will now be horizontally centered at launch time. This brings us to a second problem — how to deal with subsequent rotation. Presume that we want to *keep* the black subview horizontally centered in response to further changes in our main view's size.

For that, we have a choice of two primary events — `willTransition(to:with:)` (the trait collection) and `viewWillTransition(to:with:)` (the size). How to choose between the two methods? The question here is, do you want to respond to rotation on iPhone only, or on both iPhone and iPad? The trouble with the trait collection is that it doesn't change when the iPad rotates. Therefore, if you want to learn about iPad rotation, you will need to be notified of the size change. Let's say this is a universal app, and we want to do layout during rotation on iPad as well as iPhone. So we're going to implement `viewWillTransition(to:with:)`. I call this approach *bipartite manual layout*, because we are implementing `viewWillLayoutSubviews` plus one rotation event.

In `viewWillTransition(to:with:)`, we should not assume, just because we are called, that the size is actually changing; this method is called even on rotations of 180 degrees. So we're going to want to check to make sure that the size *is* changing, and reposition the black subview only if it is.

But here comes another challenge: we should not reposition the black subview immediately, in part because the size change hasn't happened yet, and in part because the subview will then *jump* to its new position, whereas we want to animate the change as part of the rotation animation. With constraint-based layout, the repositioning *is* part of the rotation animation, because layout performed during an animation is itself animated. We want our manual layout to behave like that.

The solution lies in the second parameter of `viewWillTransition(to:with:)`. This is a UIViewControllerTransitionCoordinator, whose job is to perform the rotation animation and to attach to it any animations we care to supply. To supply those animations, we call this method of the coordinator:

`animate(alongsideTransition:completion:)`
> The first parameter is an animations function; the second is an optional completion function to be executed when the rotation is over.

Here's our implementation, making use of the transition coordinator to animate our subview's position change:

```
override func viewWillTransition(to sz: CGSize,
    with coordinator: UIViewControllerTransitionCoordinator) {
        super.viewWillTransition(to:sz, with:coordinator)
        if sz != self.view.bounds.size {
```

```
                coordinator.animate(alongsideTransition:{ _ in
                    self.blackSquare?.center = CGPoint(sz.width/2,5)
                })
            }
        }
```

Tripartite Manual Layout

In that example, our manual layout was distributed over two events, `viewWillLayout-Subviews` and `viewWillTransition(to:with:)` (the size). Sometimes, it is necessary to involve *three* events, implementing `willTransition(to:with:)` (the trait collection) as well. I call this *tripartite manual layout*.

In this next example, I have a large green rectangle that should occupy the left one-third of the interface, but only when we are in landscape orientation (the main view's width is larger than its height) and only when we are in a `.regular` horizontal size class (we might be on an iPad or an iPhone 6/7/8 Plus but not on any other kind of iPhone). This rectangle should come and go in a smooth animated fashion, of course; let's decide to have it appear from, or vanish off to, the left of the interface.

Clearly we have to implement `viewWillTransition(to:with:)` (the size), in order to hear about rotation on an iPad. But we will also need to implement `will-Transition(to:with:)` (the trait collection), in order to know in advance what our horizontal size class is about to be. If there is going to be change of size class, we will hear about the trait collection transition before we hear about the size transition, so we'll store the trait collection information in a property where the size transition method can learn about it.

We're going to have three properties: a lazy UIView property to ensure that we have a green view when we first need one (in real life, this would construct whatever this interface element really is); a Bool flag so that we don't run our initial `viewWill-LayoutSubviews` code more than once; and the upcoming trait collection. And I'll factor my test for whether the green view should appear into a utility function:

```
lazy var greenView : UIView = {
    let v = UIView()
    v.backgroundColor = .green
    return v
}()
var firstTime = true
var nextTraitCollection = UITraitCollection()
func greenViewShouldAppear(size sz: CGSize) -> Bool {
    let tc = self.nextTraitCollection
    if tc.horizontalSizeClass == .regular {
        if sz.width > sz.height {
            return true
```

```
        }
      }
      return false
    }
```

Our implementation of `willTransition(to:with:)` merely keeps `self.nextTrait-Collection` updated:

```
override func willTransition(to newCollection: UITraitCollection,
    with coordinator: UIViewControllerTransitionCoordinator) {
        super.willTransition(to:newCollection, with:coordinator)
        self.nextTraitCollection = newCollection
}
```

Now for our actual manual layout. We need to decide about the green view at launch time, so we implement `viewWillLayoutSubviews`, using our flag to make sure we decide only once. The implementation is simple: either we place the green view into the interface or we don't:

```
override func viewWillLayoutSubviews() {
    if self.firstTime {
        self.firstTime = false
        self.nextTraitCollection = self.traitCollection
        let sz = self.view.bounds.size
        if self.greenViewShouldAppear(size:sz) {
            let v = self.greenView
            v.frame = CGRect(0,0,sz.width/3, sz.height)
            self.view.addSubview(v)
        }
    }
}
```

The implementation of `viewWillTransition(to:with:)` is more complicated. We want to participate in the animation rotation, so the work must be done in a call to `animate(alongsideTransition:completion:)`. Moreover, there are two distinct cases: either we insert the green view off to the left of the interface and animate it rightward onto the scene, or we animate the existing green view leftward off the scene and (in the completion function) remove it from the interface:

```
override func viewWillTransition(to sz: CGSize,
    with coordinator: UIViewControllerTransitionCoordinator) {
        super.viewWillTransition(to:sz, with:coordinator)
        if sz != self.view.bounds.size {
            if self.greenView.window != nil {
                if !self.greenViewShouldAppear(size:sz) {
                    coordinator.animate(alongsideTransition: { _ in
                        let f = self.greenView.frame
                        self.greenView.frame =
                            CGRect(-f.width,0,f.width,f.height)
                    }) { _ in
                        self.greenView.removeFromSuperview()
                    }
```

```
            }
        } else {
            if self.greenViewShouldAppear(size:sz) {
                self.greenView.frame =
                    CGRect(-sz.width/3,0,sz.width/3,sz.height)
                self.view.addSubview(self.greenView)
                coordinator.animate(alongsideTransition: { _ in
                    self.greenView.frame.origin = CGPoint.zero
                })
            }
        }
    }
}
```

This tripartite implementation is complicated, but unfortunately I see no way around it. Things were much simpler in iOS 7 and before, where your view controller received rotation events with `rotate` in their names. In iOS 8, those events were replaced by the `willTransition` events, and there's no change of trait collection when an iPad rotates, so you have to bend over backward to handle all the possibilities coherently.

Presented View Controller

Back when the only iOS device was an iPhone, a presented view controller was called a *modal view controller*. When a modal view controller was presented, the root view controller remained in place, but its view was taken out of the interface and the modal view controller's view was used instead. Thus, this was the simplest way to replace the entire interface with a different interface.

You can see why this configuration is characterized as "modal." The presented view controller's view has, in a sense, blocked access to the "real" view, the root view controller's view. The user is forced to work in the presented view controller's view, until the modal view controller is dismissed — its view is removed and the "real" view is visible again — similar to a modal dialog in a desktop application, where the user can't do anything else but work in the dialog as long as it is present. A presented view controller's view often reinforces this analogy with obvious dismissal buttons with titles like Save, Done, or Cancel.

The color picker view in my Zotz! app is a good example (Figure 6-8); this is an interface that says, "You are now configuring a color, and that's all you can do; change the color or cancel, or you'll be stuck here forever." The user can't get out of this view without tapping Cancel or Done, and the view that the user was previously using is visible as a blur behind this view, waiting for the user to return to it.

Figure 6-5, from my Latin flashcard app, is another example of a presented view. It has a Cancel button, and the user is in a special "mode," performing a drill exercise rather than scrolling through flashcards.

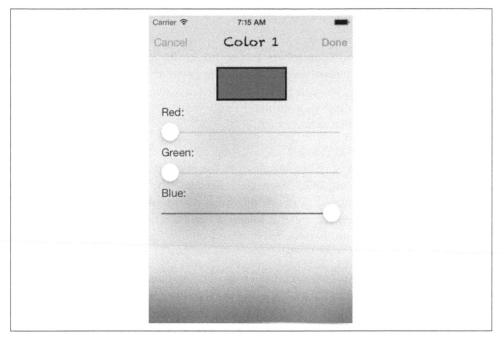

Figure 6-8. A modal view

Nevertheless, the "modal" characterization is not always apt. A presented view controller might be no more than a technique that you, the programmer, have used to alter the interface; it might not feel "modal" at all. A presented view controller's view may have a complex interface; it may have child view controllers; it may present yet *another* view controller; it may take over the interface *permanently*, with the user *never* returning to the interface that it replaced. Furthermore, the range of ways in which a presented view controller's view can be displayed now goes far beyond merely replacing the root view controller's view. For example:

- Instead of replacing the entire interface, a presented view controller's view can replace a *subview* within the existing interface.

- A presented view controller's view may cover the existing interface only *partially*, while the existing interface is never removed.

Presentation and Dismissal

The two key methods for presenting and dismissing a view controller are:

`present(_:animated:completion:)`
    To make a view controller present another view controller, you send the first view controller this message, handing it the second view controller, which you will

probably instantiate for this very purpose. The first view controller is very typically `self`.

We now have two view controllers that stand in the relationship of being one another's `presentingViewController` and `presentedViewController` respectively. The presented view controller is retained, and its view effectively replaces or covers the presenting view controller's view in the interface. (I'll talk later about ways to refine that arrangement.)

`dismiss(animated:completion:)`
>   The "presented" state of affairs described in the previous paragraph persists until the presenting view controller is sent this message. The presented view controller's view is then removed from the interface, the original interface is restored, and the presented view controller is released; it will thereupon typically go out of existence, together with its view, its child view controllers and *their* views, and so on.

As the view of the presented view controller appears, and again when it is dismissed, there's an option for animation to be performed as the transition takes place (the `animated:` argument, a Bool). The `completion:` parameter, which can be `nil`, lets you supply a function to be run after the transition (including the animation) has occurred. I'll talk later about how to govern the nature of the animation.

View controller relationships during presentation

The presenting view controller (the presented view controller's `presentingView-Controller`) is not necessarily the same view controller to which you sent `present(_:animated:completion:)`. It will help if we distinguish *three* roles that view controllers can play in presenting a view controller:

Presented view controller
>   The first argument to `present(_:animated:completion:)`.

Original presenter
>   The view controller to which `present(_:animated:completion:)` was sent. Apple sometimes refers to this view controller as the *source*; "original presenter" is my own term.
>
>   The presented view controller is set as the original presenter's `presentedViewController`.

Presenting view controller
>   The view controller whose view is replaced or covered by the presented view controller's view. By default, it is the view controller that was the top-level view controller prior to the presentation. It might not be the same as the original presenter.

This view controller is set as the presented view controller's `presentingView-Controller`. The presented view controller is set as the presenting view controller's `presentedViewController`. (Thus, the presented view controller might be the `presentedViewController` of two different view controllers.)

The receiver of `dismiss(animated:completion:)` may be *any* of those three objects; the runtime will use the linkages between them to transmit the necessary messages up the chain on your behalf to the `presentingViewController`.

You can test whether a view controller's `presentedViewController` or `presenting-ViewController` is `nil` to learn whether presentation is occurring. For example, a view controller whose `presentingViewController` is `nil` is not a presented view controller at this moment.

A view controller can have at most one `presentedViewController`. If you send `present(_:animated:completion:)` to a view controller whose `presentedView-Controller` isn't `nil`, nothing will happen and the completion function is not called (and you'll get a warning from the runtime). However, a presented view controller can itself present a view controller, so there can be a chain of presented view controllers.

If you send `dismiss(animated:completion:)` to a view controller in the middle of a presentation chain — a view controller that has both a `presentingViewController` and a `presentedViewController` — then its `presentedViewController` is dismissed.

If you send `dismiss(animated:completion:)` to a view controller whose `presented-ViewController` is `nil` and that has no `presentingViewController`, nothing will happen (not even a warning in the console), and the completion function is not called.

Manual view controller presentation

Let's make one view controller present another. We could do this simply by connecting one view controller to another in a storyboard with a modal segue, but I don't want you to do that: a modal segue calls `present(_:animated:completion:)` for you, whereas I want you to call it yourself.

So start with an iPhone project made from the Single View app template. This contains one view controller class, called ViewController. Our first move must be to add a second view controller class, an instance of which will function as the presented view controller:

1. Choose File → New → File and specify iOS → Source → Cocoa Touch Class. Click Next.

2. Name the class SecondViewController, make sure it is a subclass of UIView-Controller, and check the XIB checkbox so that we can design this view controller's view quickly and easily in the nib editor. Click Next.

3. Confirm the folder, group, and app target membership, and click Create.

4. Edit *SecondViewController.xib*, and do something there to make the view distinctive, so that you'll recognize it when it appears; for example, give it a red background color.

5. In *ViewController.swift*, give ViewController an action method that instantiates SecondViewController and presents it:

```
@IBAction func doPresent(_ sender: Any?) {
    let svc = SecondViewController(nibName: nil, bundle: nil)
    self.present(svc, animated:true)
}
```

6. Edit *Main.storyboard* and add a button to the ViewController's main view. Connect that button to ViewController's doPresent.

Run the project. In ViewController's view, tap the button. SecondViewController's view slides into place over ViewController's view.

In our lust for instant gratification, we have neglected to provide a way to dismiss the presented view controller. If you'd like to do that:

1. In *SecondViewController.swift*, give SecondViewController an action method that dismisses SecondViewController:

```
@IBAction func doDismiss(_ sender: Any?) {
    self.presentingViewController?.dismiss(animated:true)
}
```

2. Edit *SecondViewController.xib* and add a button to SecondViewController's view. Connect that button to SecondViewController's doDismiss.

Run the project. You can now alternate between ViewController's view and SecondViewController's view, presenting and dismissing in turn. Go ahead and play for a while with your exciting new app; I'll wait.

Configuring a Presentation

This section describes some configurable aspects of how a view controller's view behaves as the view controller is presented.

Transition style

When a view controller is presented and later when it is dismissed, a simple animation of its view can be performed, according to whether the animated: parameter of the corresponding method is true. There are a few different built-in animation types (*modal transition styles*) to choose from.

 Instead of choosing a simple built-in modal transition style, you can supply your own animation, as I'll explain later in the chapter.

To choose a built-in animation, set the presented view controller's modalTransition-Style property prior to the presentation. This value can be set in code or in the nib editor. Your choices (UIModalTransitionStyle) are:

.coverVertical *(the default)*
> The view slides up from the bottom to cover the presenting view controller's view on presentation and down to reveal it on dismissal. The definition of "bottom" depends on the orientation of the device and the orientations the view controllers support.

.flipHorizontal
> The view flips on the vertical axis as if the two views were the front and back of a piece of paper. The "vertical axis" is the device's long axis, regardless of the app's orientation.

> This transition style provides one of those rare occasions where the user may directly glimpse the window behind the transitioning views. You may want to set the window's background color appropriately.

.crossDissolve
> The views remain stationary, and one fades into the other.

.partialCurl
> The presenting view controller's view curls up like a page in a notepad to reveal the presented view controller's view. In iOS 7 and before, a drawing of a curl covers the top left of the presented view; tapping it dismisses the presented view controller. In iOS 8 and later, the curl drawing is missing, but tapping where it *should* be dismisses the presented view controller anyway! I regard that as a bug; a simple workaround is to avoid .partialCurl entirely.

Presentation style

By default, the presented view controller's view occupies the entire screen, completely replacing that of the presenting view controller. But you can choose from some other built-in options expressing how the presented view controller's view should cover the screen (*modal presentation styles*).

Instead of choosing a simple built-in modal presentation style, you can customize the presentation to place the presented view controller's view anywhere you like, as I'll explain later in this chapter.

To choose a presentation style, set the presented view controller's `modalPresentation-Style` property prior to the presentation. This value can be set in code or in the nib editor. Your choices (UIModalPresentationStyle) are:

`.fullScreen`

> The default. The presenting view controller is the top-level view controller, and its view — meaning the entire interface — is replaced.

`.overFullScreen`

> Similar to `.fullScreen`, but the presenting view controller's view is *not* replaced; instead, it stays where it is, possibly being visible during the transition, and remaining visible behind the presented view controller's view if the latter has some transparency.

`.pageSheet`

> Similar to `.fullScreen`, but in portrait orientation on the iPad it's a little shorter (leaving a gap behind the status bar), and in landscape orientation on the iPad and the iPhone 6/7/8 Plus it's also narrower, with the presenting view controller's view remaining partially visible (and dimmed) behind it. Treated as `.fullScreen` on the iPhone (including the iPhone 6/7/8 Plus in portrait).

`.formSheet`

> Similar to `.pageSheet`, but on the iPad it's even smaller, allowing the user to see more of the presenting view controller's view behind it. As the name implies, this is intended to allow the user to fill out a form (Apple describes this as "gathering structured information from the user"). On the iPhone 6/7/8 Plus in landscape, indistinguishable from `.pageSheet`. Treated as `.fullScreen` on the iPhone (including the iPhone 6/7/8 Plus in portrait).
>
> A `.formSheet` presented view controller, even on an iPad, has a `.compact` horizontal size class.

`.currentContext`

> The presenting view controller can be *any* view controller, such as a child view controller. The presented view controller's view replaces the presenting view controller's view, which may have been occupying only a portion of the screen. I'll explain in a moment how to specify the presenting view controller.

`.overCurrentContext`

> Like `.currentContext`, but the presented view controller's view covers the presenting view controller's view rather than replacing it. Again, this may mean that

the presented view controller's view now covers only a portion of the screen. `.overCurrentContext` will often be a better choice than `.current-Context`, because some subviews don't behave well when automatically removed from their superview and restored later.

Current context presentation

When the presented view controller's `modalPresentationStyle` is `.currentContext` or `.overCurrentContext`, a decision has to be made by the runtime as to what view controller should be the presenting view controller. This will determine what view will be replaced or covered by the presented view controller's view. The decision involves another UIViewController property, `definesPresentationContext` (a Bool), and possibly still *another* UIViewController property, `providesPresentation-ContextTransitionStyle`. Here's how the decision operates:

1. Starting with the original presenter (the view controller to which `present(_:animated:completion:)` was sent), we walk up the chain of parent view controllers, looking for one whose `definesPresentationContext` property is `true`. If we find one, that's the one; it will be the `presentingViewController`, and its view will be replaced or covered by the presented view controller's view.

   (If we *don't* find one, things work as if the presented view controller's `modal-PresentationStyle` had been `.fullScreen`.)

2. If, during the search just described, we find a view controller whose `defines-PresentationContext` property is `true`, we look to see if that view controller's `providesPresentationContextTransitionStyle` property is *also* `true`. If so, *that* view controller's `modalTransitionStyle` is used for this transition animation, rather than the presented view controller's `modalTransitionStyle`.

To illustrate, I need a parent–child view controller arrangement to work with. This chapter hasn't yet discussed any parent view controllers in detail, but the simplest is UITabBarController, which I discuss in the next section, and it's easy to create a working app with a UITabBarController-based interface, so that's the example I'll use:

1. Start with the Tabbed app template. It provides three view controllers — the UITabBarController and two children, FirstViewController and SecondView-Controller.

2. As in the previous example, I want us to create and present the presented view controller manually, rather than letting the storyboard do it automatically; so make a new view controller class with an accompanying *.xib* file, to use as a presented view controller — call it ExtraViewController.

3. In *ExtraViewController.xib*, give the view a distinctive background color, so you'll recognize it when it appears.

4. In the storyboard, put a button in the First View Controller view (First Scene), and connect it to an action method in *FirstViewController.swift* that summons the new view controller as a presented view controller:

```
@IBAction func doPresent(_ sender: Any?) {
    let vc = ExtraViewController(nibName: nil, bundle: nil)
    vc.modalTransitionStyle = .flipHorizontal
    self.present(vc, animated: true)
}
```

Run the project and tap the button. Observe that the presented view controller's view occupies the *entire* interface, covering even the tab bar; it replaces the root view, because the presentation style is .fullScreen. The presenting view controller is the root view controller, which is the UITabBarController.

Now change the code to look like this:

```
@IBAction func doPresent(_ sender: Any?) {
    let vc = ExtraViewController(nibName: nil, bundle: nil)
    vc.modalTransitionStyle = .flipHorizontal
    self.definesPresentationContext = true // *
    vc.modalPresentationStyle = .currentContext // *
    self.present(vc, animated: true)
}
```

Run the project and tap the button. The presented view controller's view replaces only the first view controller's view; the tab bar remains visible. That's because the presented view controller's modalPresentationStyle is .currentContext, and definesPresentationContext is true in FirstViewController. Thus the search for a context stops in FirstViewController, which becomes the presenting view controller — meaning that the presented view replaces FirstViewController's view instead of the root view.

We can also override the presented view controller's transition animation through the modalTransitionStyle property of the presenting view controller:

```
@IBAction func doPresent(_ sender: Any?) {
    let vc = ExtraViewController(nibName: nil, bundle: nil)
    vc.modalTransitionStyle = .flipHorizontal
    self.definesPresentationContext = true
    self.providesPresentationContextTransitionStyle = true // *
    self.modalTransitionStyle = .coverVertical // *
    vc.modalPresentationStyle = .currentContext
    self.present(vc, animated: true)
}
```

Because the presenting view controller's `providesPresentationContextTransition-Style` is `true`, the transition uses the `.coverVertical` animation belonging to the presenting view controller, rather than the `.flipHorizontal` animation of the presented view controller.

Configuration in the nib editor

Most of what I've described so far can be configured in a *.storyboard* or *.xib* file. A view controller's Attributes inspector lets you set its transition style and presentation style, as well as `definesPresentationContext` and `providesPresentationContext-TransitionStyle`.

If you're using a storyboard, you can configure one view controller to present another view controller by connecting them with a Present Modally segue; to do the presentation, you trigger the segue (or give the user a way to trigger it) instead of calling `present(_:animated:completion:)`. The segue's Attributes inspector lets you set the presentation style and transition style (and whether there is to be animation). Dismissal is a little more involved; either you must dismiss the presented view controller in code, by calling `dismiss(animated:completion:)`, or you must use an unwind segue. I'll discuss triggered segues and unwind segues in detail later in this chapter.

Communication with a Presented View Controller

In real life, it is highly probable that the original presenter will have additional information to impart to the presented view controller as the latter is created and presented, and that the presented view controller will want to pass information back to the original presenter as it is dismissed. Knowing how to arrange this exchange of information is very important.

Passing information from the original presenter to the presented view controller is usually easy, because the original presenter typically has a reference to the presented view controller before the latter's view appears in the interface. For example, suppose the presented view controller has a public `data` property. Then the original presenter can easily set this property, especially if the original presenter is the one instantiating the presented view controller in the first place:

```
@IBAction func doPresent(_ sender: Any?) {
    let svc = SecondViewController(nibName: nil, bundle: nil)
    svc.data = "This is very important data!" // *
    self.present(svc, animated:true)
}
```

Indeed, if you're instantiating the presented view controller in code, as we are here, you might even give its class a designated initializer that accepts — and thus requires — this data. In my Latin vocabulary app, for example, I've given DrillViewController a designated initializer `init(terms:)` precisely so that whoever creates it *must* pass it the data it will need to do its job while it exists.

Passing information back from the presented view controller to the original presenter is a more interesting problem. The presented view controller will need to know who the original presenter is, but it doesn't automatically have a reference to it (the original presenter, remember, is not necessarily the same as the `presentingViewController`). Moreover, the presented view controller will need to know the signature of some method, implemented by the original presenter, which it can call in order to hand over the information — and this needs to work regardless of the original presenter's class.

The standard solution is to use delegation, as follows:

1. The presented view controller defines a *protocol* declaring a method that the presented view controller wants to call before it is dismissed.

2. The original presenter conforms to this protocol: it declares adoption of the protocol, and it implements the required method.

3. The presented view controller provides a means whereby it can be handed a reference to an object conforming to this protocol. Think of that reference as the presented view controller's *delegate*. Very often, this will be a property — perhaps called `delegate` — typed as the protocol. (Such a property should probably be weak, since an object usually has no business retaining its delegate.)

4. As the original presenter creates and configures the presented view controller, it hands the presented view controller a reference to itself, in its role as adopter of the protocol, by assigning itself as the presented view controller's delegate.

This sounds elaborate, but with practice you'll find yourself able to implement it very quickly. And you can see why it works: because its delegate is typed as the protocol, the presented view controller is guaranteed that this delegate, if it has one, implements the method declared in the protocol. Thus, the desired communication from the presented view controller to whoever configured and created it is assured.

To illustrate this architecture, suppose that (as in our earlier example) the root view controller, ViewController, presents SecondViewController. Then our code in *SecondViewController.swift* would look like this:

```
protocol SecondViewControllerDelegate : class {
    func accept(data:Any!)
}
class SecondViewController : UIViewController {
    var data : Any?
    weak var delegate : SecondViewControllerDelegate?
```

```
    @IBAction func doDismiss(_ sender: Any?) {
        self.delegate?.accept(data:"Even more important data!")
    }
}
```

It is now ViewController's job to adopt the SecondViewControllerDelegate protocol, and to set itself as the SecondViewController's delegate. If it does so, then when the delegate method is called, ViewController will be handed the data, and it should then dismiss the SecondViewController:

```
class ViewController : UIViewController, SecondViewControllerDelegate {
    @IBAction func doPresent(_ sender: Any?) {
        let svc = SecondViewController(nibName: nil, bundle: nil)
        svc.data = "This is very important data!"
        svc.delegate = self // *
        self.present(svc, animated:true)
    }
    func accept(data:Any!) {
        // do something with data here
        self.dismiss(animated:true)
    }
}
```

That is a perfectly satisfactory implementation, and we could stop at this point. For completeness, I'll just show a variation that I consider slightly better. One might object that too much responsibility rests upon the original presenter (the delegate): it is sent the data and then it must also dismiss the presented view controller. Perhaps the presented view controller should hand back any data and should then dismiss itself (as it did in my earlier example). Even better, the presented view controller should hand back any data *automatically*, regardless of how it is dismissed.

We can arrange that by putting all the responsibility on the presented view controller. In the preceding example, we delete the `self.dismiss` call from ViewController's `accept(data:)`; in SecondViewController, we will implement *both* the task of dismissal *and* the task of handing back the data, *separately*.

To make the latter task automatic, SecondViewController can arrange to hear about its own dismissal by implementing `viewWillDisappear` (discussed later in this chapter), which will then call `accept(data:)` to ensure that the data is handed across. There is more than one reason why `viewWillDisappear` might be called; we can ensure that this really is the moment of our own dismissal by consulting `isBeingDismissed`. Here's how SecondViewController would look now:

```
protocol SecondViewControllerDelegate : class {
    func accept(data:Any!)
}
class SecondViewController : UIViewController {
    var data : Any?
    weak var delegate : SecondViewControllerDelegate?
```

```
@IBAction func doDismiss(_ sender: Any?) {
    self.presentingViewController?.dismiss(animated:true)
}
override func viewWillDisappear(_ animated: Bool) {
    super.viewWillDisappear(animated)
    if self.isBeingDismissed {
        self.delegate?.accept(data:"Even more important data!")
    }
}
```

If you're using a storyboard and a Present Modally segue, things are a bit different. You don't have access to the presented view controller at the moment of creation, and the storyboard will not automatically call a custom initializer on the presented view controller. Instead, in the original presenter (the source of the segue) you typically implement prepare(for:sender:) as a moment when the original presenter and the presented view controller will meet, and the former can hand across any needed data, set itself as delegate, and so forth. If you dismiss the presented view controller automatically by way of an unwind segue, the same is true in reverse: the presented view controller also implements prepare(for:sender:), and this is called on dismissal — so that's when the presented view controller calls the delegate method. I'll give more details later in this chapter.

Adaptive Presentation

When a view controller with a modalPresentationStyle of .pageSheet or .formSheet is about to appear, you get a second opportunity to change its effective modalPresentationStyle, and even to substitute a different view controller, based on the current trait collection environment. This is called *adaptive presentation*. The idea is that your presented view controller might appear one way for certain trait collections and another way for others — for example, on an iPad as opposed to an iPhone.

To implement adaptive presentation, you use a view controller's *presentation controller* (presentationController, a UIPresentationController). Before presenting a view controller, you set its presentation controller's delegate to an object adopting the UIAdaptivePresentationControllerDelegate protocol. Before the presented view controller's view appears, the delegate is sent these messages:

adaptivePresentationStyle(for:traitCollection:)
> The first parameter is the presentation controller, and its presentationStyle is the modalPresentationStyle it proposes to use. Return a different modal presentation style to use instead (or .none if you don't want to change the presentation style).

`presentationController(_:willPresentWithAdaptiveStyle:transition-Coordinator:)`
> Called just before the presentation takes place. If the `adaptiveStyle:` is `.none`, adaptive presentation is *not* going to take place.

`presentationController(_:viewControllerForAdaptivePresentationStyle:)`
> Called only if adaptive presentation *is* going to take place. The first parameter is the presentation controller, and its `presentedViewController` is the view controller it proposes to present. Return a different view controller to present instead (or `nil` to keep the current presented view controller).

What adaptations are you permitted to perform? First, as I've already said, the original `modalPresentationStyle` should be `.pageSheet` or `.formSheet`. It isn't illegal to try to adapt from other presentation styles, but it isn't going to work either. Then the possibilities are as follows:

Adapt sheet to full screen
> You can adapt `.pageSheet` or `.formSheet` to `.fullScreen` or `.overFullScreen`.

Adapt page sheet to form sheet
> You can adapt `.pageSheet` to `.formSheet`. On an iPad, the difference is clearly visible, but on an iPhone 6/7/8 Plus in landscape, the two sheet types are indistinguishable. On an iPhone (including an iPhone 6/7/8 Plus in portrait), the result is something a little unusual and unexpected. It's similar to `.pageSheet` on the iPad in portrait orientation: it is full width, but a little shorter than full height, leaving a gap behind the status bar. (You can also obtain this configuration by adapting `.pageSheet` or `.formSheet` to `.none`.)

For example, here's how to present a view controller as a `.pageSheet` on iPad but as `.overFullScreen` on iPhone:

```
extension ViewController : UIAdaptivePresentationControllerDelegate {
    @IBAction func doPresent(_ sender: Any?) {
        let svc = SecondViewController(nibName: nil, bundle: nil)
        svc.modalPresentationStyle = .pageSheet
        svc.presentationController!.delegate = self // *
        self.present(svc, animated:true)
    }
    func adaptivePresentationStyle(for controller: UIPresentationController,
        traitCollection: UITraitCollection) -> UIModalPresentationStyle {
            if traitCollection.horizontalSizeClass == .compact {
                return .overFullScreen
            }
            return .none // don't adapt
    }
}
```

Now let's extend that example by presenting one view controller on iPad but a different view controller on iPhone; this method won't be called when adaptive-PresentationStyle returns .none, so it affects iPhone only:

```
extension ViewController : UIAdaptivePresentationControllerDelegate {
    func presentationController(_ controller: UIPresentationController,
        viewControllerForAdaptivePresentationStyle: UIModalPresentationStyle)
        -> UIViewController? {
            let newvc = ThirdViewController(nibName: nil, bundle: nil)
            return newvc
    }
}
```

In real life, of course, when substituting a different view controller, you might need to prepare it before returning it (for example, giving it data and setting its delegate). A common scenario is to return the *same* view controller wrapped in a navigation controller; I'll illustrate in Chapter 9.

Presentation, Rotation, and the Status Bar

A fullscreen presented view controller effectively replaces your app's entire interface. Thus, even though it is not the root view controller, it is the *top-level view controller*, and acquires the same mighty powers as if it *were* the root view controller. In particular:

- Its supportedInterfaceOrientations and shouldAutorotate are consulted and honored; this view controller gets to limit your app's legal orientations.

- Its prefersStatusBarHidden and preferredStatusBarStyle are consulted and honored; this view controller gets to dictate the appearance of the status bar.

If a fullscreen presented view controller's supportedInterfaceOrientations do not intersect with the app's current orientation, the app's orientation *will rotate*, as the presented view appears, to an orientation that the presented view controller supports — and the same thing will be true in reverse when the presented view controller is dismissed.

Thus, a presented view controller allows you to *force* the interface to rotate. In fact, a presented view controller is the *only* officially sanctioned way to force the interface to rotate.

Forced rotation is a perfectly reasonable thing to do, especially on the iPhone, where the user can easily rotate the device to compensate for the new orientation of the interface. Some views work better in portrait than landscape, or better in landscape than portrait (especially on the small screen). Forced rotation lets you ensure that each view appears only in the orientation in which it works best.

(On an iPad, forced rotation is unlikely. In fact, if your iPad app permits all four orientations and does not opt out of iPad multitasking, its view controllers' `supportedInterfaceOrientations` are not even consulted, so forced rotation doesn't work.)

The presented view controller's `supportedInterfaceOrientations` bitmask might permit multiple possible orientations. The view controller may then also wish to specify which of those multiple orientations it should have *initially* when it is presented. To do so, override `preferredInterfaceOrientationForPresentation`; this property is consulted before `supportedInterfaceOrientations`, and its value is a single UIInterfaceOrientation (*not* a bitmask).

 Do not attempt to implement forced rotation in a presented view controller whose presentation style is *not* `.fullScreen`. Such a configuration is not supported, and very weird things may happen.

When a view controller is presented, if its presentation style is *not* `.fullScreen`, a question arises of whether its status bar properties (`prefersStatusBarHidden` and `preferredStatusBarStyle`) should be consulted. By default, the answer is no, because this view controller is not the top-level view controller. To make the answer be yes, set this view controller's `modalPresentationCapturesStatusBarAppearance` to `true`.

Tab Bar Controller

A *tab bar* (UITabBar, see also Chapter 12) is a horizontal bar containing items. Each item is a UITabBarItem; it displays, by default, an image and a title. New in iOS 11, a tab bar item is usually displayed with the title *beside* the image, rather than below it as in previous systems; however, on an iPhone in portrait orientation, the title appears below the image. At all times, exactly one of a tab bar's items is selected (highlighted); when the user taps an item, it becomes the selected item.

If there are too many items to fit on a tab bar, the excess items are automatically subsumed into a final More item. When the user taps the More item, a list of the excess items appears, and the user can select one; the user can also be permitted to edit the tab bar, determining which items appear in the tab bar itself and which ones spill over into the More list.

A tab bar is an independent interface object, but it is most commonly used in conjunction with a *tab bar controller* (UITabBarController, a subclass of UIViewController) to form a *tab bar interface*. The tab bar controller displays the tab bar at the bottom of its own view. From the user's standpoint, the tab bar items correspond to views; when the user selects a tab bar item, the corresponding view appears, filling the remainder of the space. The user is thus employing the tab bar to choose an entire area of your app's functionality. In reality, the UITabBarController is a parent view controller; you give it child view controllers, which the tab bar controller then contains, and the views summoned by tapping the tab bar items are the views of those child view controllers.

Familiar examples of a tab bar interface on the iPhone are Apple's Clock app and Music app.

New in iOS 11, a tab bar interface can automatically change the height of its tab bar. By default, the tab bar height is 49 points, as in previous systems. But when the vertical size class is .compact (an iPhone in landscape orientation, except for a 6/7/8 Plus), the tab bar height is reduced to 32, to provide more room to display the main interface.

You can get a reference to the tab bar controller's tab bar through its tabBar property. In general, you won't need this. When using a tab bar interface by way of a UITabBar-Controller, you do not interact (as a programmer) with the tab bar itself; you don't create it or set its delegate. You provide the UITabBarController with children, and it does the rest; when the UITabBarController's view is displayed, there's the tab bar along with the view of the selected item. You can, however, customize the *look* of the tab bar (see Chapter 12 for details).

If a tab bar controller is the top-level view controller, it determines your app's compensatory rotation behavior. To take a hand in that determination without having to subclass UITabBarController, make one of your objects the tab bar controller's delegate (UITabBarControllerDelegate) and implement these methods, as needed:

- tabBarControllerSupportedInterfaceOrientations(_:)
- tabBarControllerPreferredInterfaceOrientationForPresentation(_:)

A top-level tab bar controller also determines your app's status bar appearance. However, a tab bar controller implements childViewControllerForStatusBarStyle and childViewControllerForStatusBarHidden so that the actual decision is relegated to the child view controller whose view is currently being displayed: your preferred-StatusBarStyle and prefersStatusBarHidden are consulted and obeyed.

Tab Bar Items

For each view controller you assign as a tab bar controller's child, you're going to need a *tab bar item*, which will appear as its representative in the tab bar. This tab bar item will be your child view controller's tabBarItem. A tab bar item is a UITabBar-Item; this is a subclass of UIBarItem, an abstract class that provides some of its most important properties, such as title, image, and isEnabled.

There are two ways to make a tab bar item:

By borrowing it from the system

Instantiate UITabBarItem using `init(tabBarSystemItem:tag:)`, and assign the instance to your child view controller's `tabBarItem`. Consult the documentation for the list of available system items. Unfortunately, you can't customize a system tab bar item's title; you must accept the title the system hands you. (You can't work around this restriction by somehow copying a system tab bar item's image.)

By making your own

Instantiate UITabBarItem using `init(title:image:tag:)` and assign the instance to your child view controller's `tabBarItem`. Alternatively, use the view controller's existing `tabBarItem` and set its `image` and `title`. Instead of setting the `title` of the `tabBarItem`, you can set the `title` property of the view controller itself; doing this automatically sets the `title` of its current `tabBarItem` (unless the tab bar item is a system tab bar item), though the converse is not true.

You can add a separate `selectedImage` later, or possibly by initializing with `init(title:image:selectedImage:)`. The `selectedImage` will be displayed in place of the normal image when this tab bar item is selected in the tab bar.

The `image` (and `selectedImage`) for a tab bar item should be a 30×30 PNG. By default, this image will be treated as a transparency mask (a template): the hue of its pixels will be ignored, and the transparency of its pixels will be combined with the tab bar's `tintColor`, which may be inherited from higher up the view hierarchy. However, you can instead display the image as is, and not as a transparency mask, by deriving an image whose rendering mode is `.alwaysOriginal` (see Chapter 2).

New in iOS 11, you have to cope with the possibility that the tab bar item will be displayed within a tab bar whose height has been reduced. The solution is to set its `landscapeImagePhone`, which will be used when the vertical size class is `.compact` — exactly the circumstances under which the tab bar's height is reduced. This image should be a 20×20 PNG.

(Apple recommends that, if possible, you use a PDF vector image instead of a PNG. The reason is that the image will then be automatically resized, with no loss of sharpness, and you won't have to supply a separate `landscapeImagePhone`.)

 As of this writing, the tab bar item's `selectedImage` is not used in a `.compact` vertical size class environment if it also has a separate `landscapeImagePhone`. I regard this as a major bug.

You can also give a tab bar item a badge (see the documentation on the `badgeValue` property). Other ways in which you can customize the look of a tab bar item are discussed in Chapter 12. For example, you can control the font and style of the title, or you can give it an empty title and offset the image.

Configuring a Tab Bar Controller

Basic configuration of a tab bar controller is very simple: just hand it the view controllers that will be its children. To do so, collect those view controllers into an array and set the UITabBarController's `viewControllers` property to that array. The view controllers in the array are now the tab bar controller's child view controllers; the tab bar controller is the `parent` of the view controllers in the array. The tab bar controller is also the `tabBarController` of the view controllers in the array and of all their children; thus a child view controller at any depth can learn that it is contained by a tab bar controller and can get a reference to that tab bar controller. The tab bar controller retains the array, and the array retains the child view controllers.

Here's a simple example from one of my apps, in which I construct and display a tab bar interface in code:

```
func application(_ application: UIApplication,
    didFinishLaunchingWithOptions launchOptions:
    [UIApplicationLaunchOptionsKey : Any]?) -> Bool {
        self.window = self.window ?? UIWindow()
        let vc1 = GameBoardController()
        let sc = SettingsController()
        let vc2 = UINavigationController(rootViewController:sc)
        let tabBarController = UITabBarController()
        tabBarController.viewControllers = [vc1, vc2]
        tabBarController.selectedIndex = 0
        tabBarController.delegate = self
        self.window!.rootViewController = tabBarController
        self.window!.makeKeyAndVisible()
        return true
}
```

The tab bar controller's tab bar will automatically display the `tabBarItem` of each child view controller. The order of the tab bar items is the order of the view controllers in the tab bar controller's `viewControllers` array. Thus, a child view controller will probably want to configure its `tabBarItem` property early in its lifetime, so that the `tabBarItem` is ready by the time the view controller is handed as a child to the tab bar controller. Observe that `viewDidLoad` is *not* early enough! That's because the view controllers (other than the initially selected view controller) have no view when the tab bar controller initially appears. Thus it is common to implement an initializer for this purpose.

Here's an example from the same app as the previous code (in the GameBoardController class):

```
init() {
    super.init(nibName:nil, bundle:nil)
    // tab bar configuration
    self.tabBarItem.image = UIImage(named: "game")
    self.title = "Game"
}
```

If you change the tab bar controller's view controllers array later in its lifetime and you want the corresponding change in the tab bar's display of its items to be animated, call setViewControllers(_:animated:).

Initially, by default, the first child view controller's tab bar item is selected and its view is displayed. To ask the tab bar controller which tab bar item the user has selected, you can couch your query in terms of the child view controller (selectedView-Controller) or by index number in the array (selectedIndex). You can also *set* these properties to switch between displayed child view controllers programmatically. (In fact, it is legal to set a tab bar controller's tab bar's isHidden to true and take charge of switching between children yourself — though if that's your desired architecture, a UIPageViewController might be more appropriate.)

 You can supply a view animation when a tab bar controller's selected tab item changes and one child view controller's view is replaced by another, as I'll explain later in the chapter.

You can also set the UITabBarController's delegate (adopting UITabBarController-Delegate). The delegate gets messages allowing it to prevent a given tab bar item from being selected, and notifying it when a tab bar item is selected and when the user is customizing the tab bar from the More item.

If the tab bar contains few enough items that it doesn't need a More item, there won't be one, and the tab bar won't be user-customizable. If there *is* a More item, you can exclude some tab bar items from being customizable by setting the customizable-ViewControllers property to an array that lacks them; setting this property to nil means that the user can see the More list but can't rearrange the items. Setting the viewControllers property sets the customizableViewControllers property to the same value, so if you're going to set the customizableViewControllers property, do it *after* setting the viewControllers property. The moreNavigationController property can be compared with the selectedViewController property to learn whether the user is currently viewing the More list; apart from this, the More interface is mostly out of your control, but I'll discuss some sneaky ways of customizing it in Chapter 12.

(If you allow the user to rearrange items, you would presumably want to save the new arrangement and restore it the next time the app runs. You might use UserDefaults for this, or you might take advantage of the built-in automatic state saving and restoration facilities, discussed later in this chapter.)

You can configure a UITabBarController in a storyboard. The UITabBarController's contained view controllers can be set directly — there will be a "view controllers" relationship between the tab bar controller and each of its children — and the contained view controllers will be instantiated together with the tab bar controller. Moreover, each contained view controller has a Tab Bar Item; you can select this and set many aspects of the tabBarItem, such as its system item or its title, image, selected image, and tag, directly in the nib editor. (If a view controller in a nib doesn't have a Tab Bar Item and you want to configure this view controller for use in a tab bar interface, drag a Tab Bar Item from the Object library onto the view controller.)

To start a project with a main storyboard that has a UITabBarController as its initial view controller, begin with the Tabbed app template.

Navigation Controller

A *navigation bar* (UINavigationBar, see also Chapter 12) is a horizontal bar displaying a center title and a right button. When the user taps the right button, the navigation bar animates, sliding its interface out to the left and replacing it with a new interface that enters from the right. The new interface displays a back button at the left side, and a new center title — and possibly a new right button. The user can tap the back button to go back to the first interface, which slides in from the left; or, if there's a right button in the second interface, the user can tap it to go further forward to a third interface, which slides in from the right.

The successive interfaces of a navigation bar thus behave like a stack. In fact, a navigation bar does represent an actual stack — an internal stack of *navigation items* (UINavigationItem). It starts out with one navigation item: the *root* or *bottom item* of the stack. Since there is initially just one navigation item, it is also initially the *top item* of the stack (the navigation bar's topItem). The navigation bar's interface is always representing whatever its top item is at that moment. When the user taps a right button, a new navigation item is pushed onto the stack; it becomes the top item, and its interface is seen. When the user taps a back button, the top item is popped off the stack, and what was previously the next item beneath it in the stack — the *back item* (the navigation bar's backItem) — becomes the top item, and its interface is seen.

The state of the stack is thus reflected in the navigation bar's interface. The navigation bar's center title comes automatically from the top item, and its back button comes from the back item. (See Chapter 12 for a complete description.) Thus, the title tells the user what item is current, and the left side is a button telling the user what item we would return to if the user were to tap that button. The animations reinforce this notion of directionality, giving the user a sense of position within a chain of items.

A navigation bar is an independent interface object, but it is most commonly used in conjunction with a *navigation controller* (UINavigationController, a subclass of UIViewController) to form a *navigation interface*. Just as there is a stack of navigation items in the navigation bar, there is a stack of view controllers in the navigation controller. These view controllers are the navigation controller's children, and each navigation item belongs to a view controller — it is a view controller's navigationItem.

The navigation controller performs automatic coordination of the navigation bar and the overall interface. Whenever a view controller comes to the top of the navigation controller's stack, its view is displayed in the interface. At the same time, its navigationItem is automatically pushed onto the top of the navigation bar's stack — and is thus displayed in the navigation bar as its top item. Moreover, the animation in the navigation bar is reinforced by animation of the interface as a whole: by default, a view controller's view slides into the main interface from the side just as its navigation item slides into the navigation bar from the same side.

 You can supply a different view animation when a view controller is pushed onto or popped off of a navigation controller's stack, as I'll explain later in the chapter.

Your code can control the overall navigation, so in real life, the user might push a new view controller not by tapping the right button in the navigation bar, but by tapping something inside the main interface, such as a listing in a table view. (Figure 6-1 is a navigation interface that works this way.) In this situation, your app is deciding in real time, in response to the user's tap, what the next view controller should be; typically, you won't even create the next view controller until the user asks to navigate to it. The navigation interface thus becomes a *master–detail interface*.

Conversely, you might put a view controller inside a navigation controller just to get the convenience of the navigation bar, with its title and buttons, even when no actual navigation is going to take place.

You can get a reference to the navigation controller's navigation bar through its navigationBar property. In general, you won't need this. When using a navigation interface by way of a UINavigationController, you do not interact (as a programmer) with the navigation bar itself; you don't create it or set its delegate. You provide the UINavigationController with children, and it does the rest, handing each child view controller's navigationItem to the navigation bar for display and showing the child view controller's view each time navigation occurs. You can, however, customize the *look* of the navigation bar (see Chapter 12 for details).

A navigation interface may also optionally display a toolbar at the bottom. A toolbar (UIToolbar) is a horizontal view displaying a row of items. As in a navigation bar, a toolbar item may provide information, or it may be something the user can tap. A tapped item is not selected, as in a tab bar; rather, it represents the initiation of an action, like a button. You can get a reference to a UINavigationController's toolbar through its `toolbar` property. The look of the toolbar can be customized (Chapter 12). In a navigation interface, however, the *contents* of the toolbar are determined automatically by the view controller that is currently the top item in the stack: they are its `toolbarItems`.

 A UIToolbar can also be used independently, and often is. It then typically appears at the bottom on an iPhone — Figure 6-3 has a toolbar at the bottom — but often appears at the top on an iPad, where it plays something of the role that the menu bar plays on the desktop. When a toolbar is displayed by a navigation controller, though, it always appears at the bottom.

A familiar example of a navigation interface is Apple's Settings app on the iPhone. The Mail app on the iPhone is a navigation interface that includes a toolbar.

If a navigation controller is the top-level view controller, it determines your app's compensatory rotation behavior. To take a hand in that determination without having to subclass UINavigationController, make one of your objects the navigation controller's delegate (UINavigationControllerDelegate) and implement these methods, as needed:

- `navigationControllerSupportedInterfaceOrientations(_:)`
- `navigationControllerPreferredInterfaceOrientationForPresentation(_:)`

A top-level navigation controller also determines your app's status bar appearance. However, a navigation controller implements `childViewControllerForStatusBarHidden` so that the actual decision is relegated to the child view controller whose view is currently being displayed: your `prefersStatusBarHidden` is consulted and obeyed.

But `preferredStatusBarStyle` is a special case. Your child view controllers can implement `preferredStatusBarStyle`, and the navigation controller's `childViewControllerForStatusBarStyle` defers to its top child view controller — but only if the navigation bar is *hidden*. If the navigation bar is showing, the navigation controller sets the status bar style based on the navigation bar's `barStyle` — to `.default` if the bar style is `.default`, and to `.lightContent` if the bar style is `.black`. So the way for your view controller to set the status bar style, when the navigation bar is showing, is to set the navigation controller's navigation bar style.

Bar Button Items

The items in a UIToolbar or a UINavigationBar are bar button items — UIBarButtonItem, a subclass of UIBarItem. A bar button item comes in one of two broadly different flavors:

Basic bar button item

The bar button item behaves like a simple button.

Custom view

The bar button item has no inherent behavior, but has (and displays) a custom-View.

UIBarItem is not a UIView subclass. A basic bar button item is button-like, but it has no frame, no UIView touch handling, and so forth. A UIBarButtonItem's customView, however, *is* a UIView — indeed, it can be *any* kind of UIView. Thus, a bar button item with a customView can display any sort of view in a toolbar or navigation bar, and that view can have subviews, can implement touch handling, and so on.

Let's start with the basic bar button item (no custom view). A bar button item, like a tab bar item, inherits from UIBarItem the title, image, and isEnabled properties. The title text color, by default, comes from the bar button item's tintColor, which may be inherited from the bar itself or from higher up the view hierarchy. Assigning an image removes the title. The image should usually be quite small; Apple recommends 22×22. By default, it will be treated as a transparency mask (a template): the hue of its pixels will be ignored, and the transparency of its pixels will be combined with the bar button item's tintColor. However, you can instead display the image as is, and not as a transparency mask, by deriving an image whose rendering mode is .alwaysOriginal (see Chapter 2).

A basic bar button item has a style property (UIBarButtonItemStyle); this will usually be .plain. The alternative, .done, causes the title to be bold. You can further refine the title font and style. In addition, a bar button item can have a background image; this will typically be a small, resizable image, and can be used to provide a border. Full details appear in Chapter 12.

A bar button item also has target and action properties. These contribute to its button-like behavior: tapping a bar button item can trigger an action method elsewhere.

There are three ways to make a bar button item:

By borrowing it from the system

Make a UIBarButtonItem with init(barButtonSystemItem:target:action:). Consult the documentation for the list of available system items; they are not the same as for a tab bar item. You can't assign a title or change the image. (But you can change the tint color or assign a background image.)

By making your own basic bar button item

Make a UIBarButtonItem with init(title:style:target:action:) or with init(image:style:target:action:).

An additional initializer, init(image:landscapeImagePhone:style:target:action:), lets you specify a second image for use when the vertical size class is .compact, because the bar's height might be smaller in this situation.

By making a custom view bar button item

Make a UIBarButtonItem with init(customView:), supplying a UIView that the bar button item is to display. The bar button item has no action and target; the UIView itself must somehow implement button behavior if that's what you want. For example, the customView might be a UISegmentedControl, but then it is the UISegmentedControl's target and action that give it button behavior.

New in iOS 11, your custom view can use autolayout internally. Just make sure that you provide sufficient constraints to size the view from the inside out; the runtime will take care of positioning it.

Bar button items in a toolbar are horizontally positioned automatically by the system. You can provide hints to help with this positioning. For example, you can supply an absolute width. Also, you can incorporate spacers into the toolbar; these are created with init(barButtonSystemItem:target:action:), but they have no visible appearance, and cannot be tapped. Place .flexibleSpace system items between the visible items to distribute the visible items equally across the width of the toolbar. There is also a .fixedSpace system item whose width lets you insert a space of defined size.

Navigation Items and Toolbar Items

What appears in a navigation bar (UINavigationBar) depends upon the navigation items (UINavigationItem) in its stack. In a navigation interface, the navigation controller will manage the navigation bar's stack for you; your job is to configure each navigation item by setting properties of the navigationItem of each child view controller. The UINavigationItem properties are as follows (see also Chapter 12):

title
titleView

The title is a string. Setting a view controller's title property sets the title of its navigationItem automatically, and is usually the best approach.

The titleView can be any kind of UIView, and can implement further UIView functionality such as touchability. New in iOS 11, the titleView can use autolayout internally; just be sure to supply sufficient constraints to size the view from the inside out.

In iOS 10 and before, the title or the titleView is displayed in the center of the navigation bar when this navigation item is at the top of the stack; if there is a titleView, it is shown instead of the title. New in iOS 11, the title can be shown at the *bottom* of the navigation bar, in which case both the `title` and the `titleView` can appear; I'll explain more about that in a moment.

prompt

An optional string to appear centered above everything else in the navigation bar. The navigation bar's height will be increased to accommodate it.

rightBarButtonItem *or* rightBarButtonItems

A bar button item or, respectively, an array of bar button items to appear at the right side of the navigation bar; the first item in the array will be rightmost.

backBarButtonItem

When a view controller is pushed on top of this view controller, the navigation bar will display at its left a button pointing to the left, whose title is this view controller's `title`. That button is *this* view controller's navigation item's `backBarButtonItem`. That's right: the back button displayed in the navigation bar belongs, not to the top item (the `navigationItem` of the current view controller), but to the back item (the `navigationItem` of the view controller that is one level down in the stack).

The vast majority of the time, the default behavior is the behavior you'll want, and you'll leave the back button alone. If you wish, though, you can customize the back button by setting a view controller's `navigationItem.backBarButtonItem` so that it contains an image, or a title differing from the view controller's `title`. The best technique is to provide a new UIBarButtonItem whose target and action are nil; the runtime will add a correct target and action, so as to create a working back button. Here's how to create a back button with a custom image instead of a title:

```
let b = UIBarButtonItem(
    image:UIImage(named:"files"), style:.plain, target:nil, action:nil)
self.navigationItem.backBarButtonItem = b
```

A Bool property, `hidesBackButton`, allows the top navigation item to suppress display of the back item's back bar button item. If you set this to `true`, you'll probably want to provide some other means of letting the user navigate back.

The visible indication that the back button *is* a back button is a left-pointing chevron (the *back indicator*) that's separate from the button itself. This chevron can also be customized, but it's a feature of the navigation bar, not the bar button item: set the navigation bar's `backIndicatorImage` and `backIndicator-TransitionMask`. (I'll give an example in Chapter 12.) But if the back button is assigned a background image — not an internal image, as in the example I just gave, but a background image, by calling `setBackButtonBackgroundImage` —

then *the back indicator is removed*; it is up to the background image to point left, if desired.

leftBarButtonItem *or* leftBarButtonItems

A bar button item or, respectively, an array of bar button items to appear at the left side of the navigation bar; the first item in the array will be leftmost. The left-ItemsSupplementBackButton property, if set to true, allows both the back button and one or more left bar button items to appear.

New in iOS 11, a navigation bar can adopt an increased height in order to display the top item's title in a large font *below* the bar button items. This configuration has two great advantages: it very strongly identifies the top item, and it leaves more room in the upper part of the navigation bar to display bar button items (and even a title-View, which is no longer displaced by the title). This is a navigation bar feature, its prefersLargeTitles property. In order to accomodate the possibility that different view controllers will have different preferences in this regard, a navigation item has a largeTitleDisplayMode, which may be one of the following:

.always

The navigation item's title is displayed large if the navigation bar's prefers-LargeTitles is true.

.never

The navigation item's title is *not* displayed large.

.automatic

The navigation item's title display is the same as the title display of the back item — that is, of the navigation item preceding this one in the navigation bar's stack. This is the default. The idea is that all navigation items pushed onto a navigation bar will display their titles in the same way, until a pushed navigation item declares .always or .never.

The navigation controller may grow or shrink its navigation bar to display or hide the large title as the contents of its view are scrolled — yet another reason why a nimble interface based on autolayout and the safe area is crucial.

A view controller's navigation item can have its properties set at any time while being displayed in the navigation bar. This (and not direct manipulation of the navigation bar) is the way to change the navigation bar's contents dynamically. For example, in one of my apps, we play music from the user's library using interface in the navigation bar. The titleView is a progress view (UIProgressView, Chapter 12) that needs updating every second to reflect the playback position in the current song, and the right bar button should be either the system Play button or the system Pause button, depending on whether we are paused or playing. So I have a timer that periodically checks the state of the music player (`self.mp`); observe how we access the progress view and the right bar button by way of `self.navigationItem`:

```
// change the progress view
let prog = self.navigationItem.titleView!.subviews[0] as! UIProgressView
if let item = self.nowPlayingItem {
    let current = self.mp.currentPlaybackTime
    let total = item.playbackDuration
    prog.progress = Float(current / total)
} else {
    prog.progress = 0
}
// change the bar button
let whichButton : UIBarButtonSystemItem? = {
    switch self.mp.currentPlaybackRate {
    case 0..<0.1:
        return .play
    case 0.1...1.0:
        return .pause
    default:
        return nil
    }
}()
if let which = whichButton {
    let bb = UIBarButtonItem(barButtonSystemItem: which,
        target: self, action: #selector(doPlayPause))
    self.navigationItem.rightBarButtonItem = bb
}
```

Each view controller to be pushed onto the navigation controller's stack is responsible also for supplying the items to appear in the navigation interface's toolbar, if there is one. To configure this, set the view controller's `toolbarItems` property to an array of UIBarButtonItem instances. You can change the toolbar items even while the view controller's view and current `toolbarItems` are showing, optionally with animation, by sending `setToolbarItems(_:animated:)` to the view controller.

Configuring a Navigation Controller

You configure a navigation controller by manipulating its stack of view controllers. This stack is the navigation controller's `viewControllers` array property, though you will rarely need to manipulate that property directly.

The view controllers in a navigation controller's `viewControllers` array are the navigation controller's child view controllers; the navigation controller is the `parent` of the view controllers in the array. The navigation controller is also the `navigationController` of the view controllers in the array and of all their children; thus a child view controller at any depth can learn that it is contained by a navigation controller and can get a reference to that navigation controller. The navigation controller retains the array, and the array retains the child view controllers.

The normal way to manipulate a navigation controller's stack is by pushing or popping one view controller at a time. When the navigation controller is instantiated, it is usually initialized with `init(rootViewController:)`; this is a convenience method that assigns the navigation controller a single initial child view controller, the root view controller that goes at the bottom of the stack:

```
let fvc = FirstViewController()
let nav = UINavigationController(rootViewController:fvc)
```

Instead of `init(rootViewController:)`, you might choose to create the navigation controller with `init(navigationBarClass:toolbarClass:)`, in order to set a custom subclass of UINavigationBar or UIToolbar. Typically, this will be in order to customize the appearance of the navigation bar and toolbar; sometimes you'll create, say, a UIToolbar subclass for no other reason than to mark this kind of toolbar as needing a certain appearance. I'll explain about that in Chapter 12. If you use this initializer, you'll have to set the navigation controller's root view controller separately.

You can also set the UINavigationController's delegate (adopting UINavigationControllerDelegate). The delegate receives messages before and after a child view controller's view is shown.

A navigation controller will typically appear on the screen initially containing just its root view controller, and displaying its root view controller's view. There will be no back button, because there is no back item; there is nowhere to go back to. Subsequently, when the user asks to navigate to a new view, you (typically meaning code in the current view controller) obtain the next view controller (typically by creating it) and push it onto the stack by calling `pushViewController(_:animated:)` on the navigation controller. The navigation controller performs the animation, and displays the new view controller's view:

```
let svc = SecondViewController(nibName: nil, bundle: nil)
self.navigationController!.pushViewController(svc, animated: true)
```

The command for going back is `popViewController(animated:)`, but you might never need to call it yourself, as the runtime will call it for you when the user taps the back button to navigate back. When a view controller is popped from the stack, the `viewControllers` array removes and releases the view controller, which is usually permitted to go out of existence at that point.

Alternatively, there's a second way to push a view controller onto the navigation controller's stack, without referring to the navigation controller: `show(_:sender:)`. This UIViewController method lets the caller be agnostic about the current interface situation: it pushes the view controller onto a navigation controller if the view controller to which it is sent is in a navigation interface, but presents it otherwise. I'll talk more about this method in Chapter 9; meanwhile, I'll continue using `pushViewController(_:animated:)` in my examples.

Instead of tapping the back button, the user can go back by dragging a pushed view controller's view from the left edge of the screen. This is actually a way of calling popViewController(animated:), with the difference that the animation is interactive. (Interactive view controller transition animation is the subject of the next section.) The UINavigationController uses a UIScreenEdgePanGestureRecognizer to detect and track the user's gesture. You can obtain a reference to this gesture recognizer as the navigation controller's interactivePopGestureRecognizer; thus you can disable the gesture recognizer and prevent this way of going back, or you can mediate between your own gesture recognizers and this one (see Chapter 5).

You can manipulate the stack more directly if you wish. You can call popViewController(animated:) explicitly; to pop multiple items so as to leave a particular view controller at the top of the stack, call popToViewController(_:animated:), or to pop all the items down to the root view controller, call popToRootViewController(animated:). All of these methods return the popped view controller (or view controllers, as an array), in case you want to do something with them.

To set the entire stack at once, call setViewControllers(_:animated:). You can access the stack through the viewControllers property. Manipulating the stack directly is the only way, for instance, to delete or insert a view controller in the middle of the stack.

The view controller at the top of the stack is the topViewController; the view controller whose view is displayed is the visibleViewController. Those will normally be the same, but they needn't be, as the topViewController might present a view controller, in which case the presented view controller will be the visibleViewController. Other view controllers can be accessed through the viewControllers array by index number. The root view controller is at index 0; if the array's count is c, the back view controller (the one whose navigationItem.backBarButtonItem is currently displayed in the navigation bar) is at index c-2.

The topViewController may need to communicate with the next view controller as the latter is pushed onto the stack, or with the back view controller as it itself is popped off the stack. The problem is parallel to that of communication between an original presenter and a presented view controller, which I discussed earlier in this chapter ("Communication with a Presented View Controller" on page 321), so I won't say more about it here.

A child view controller will probably want to configure its navigationItem early in its lifetime, so as to be ready for display in the navigation bar by the time the view controller is handed as a child to the navigation controller. Apple warns (in the UIViewController class reference, under navigationItem) that loadView and view-DidLoad are not appropriate places to do this, because the circumstances under which the view is needed are not related to the circumstances under which the navigation item is needed. Apple's own code examples routinely violate this warning, but it is probably best to override a view controller initializer for this purpose.

A navigation controller's navigation bar is accessible as its `navigationBar`, and can be hidden and shown with `setNavigationBarHidden(_:animated:)`. (It is possible, though not common, to maintain and manipulate a navigation stack through a navigation controller whose navigation bar never appears.) Its toolbar is accessible as its `toolbar`, and can be hidden and shown with `setToolbarHidden(_:animated:)`.

A view controller also has the power to specify that its ancestor's bottom bar (a navigation controller's toolbar, or a tab bar controller's tab bar) should be hidden as this view controller is pushed onto a navigation controller's stack. To do so, set the view controller's `hidesBottomBarWhenPushed` property to `true`. The trick is that you must do this very early, before the view loads; the view controller's initializer is a good place. The bottom bar remains hidden from the time this view controller is pushed to the time it is popped, even if other view controllers are pushed and popped on top of it in the meantime.

A navigation controller can perform automatic hiding and showing of its navigation bar (and, if normally shown, its toolbar) in response to various situations, as configured by properties:

When tapped

If the navigation controller's `hidesBarsOnTap` is `true`, a tap that falls through the top view controller's view is taken as a signal to toggle bar visibility. The relevant gesture recognizer is the navigation controller's `barHideOnTapGesture-Recognizer`.

When swiped

If the navigation controller's `hidesBarsOnSwipe` is `true`, an upward or downward swipe respectively hides or shows the bars. The relevant gesture recognizer is the navigation controller's `barHideOnSwipeGestureRecognizer`.

In landscape

If the navigation controller's `hidesBarsWhenVerticallyCompact` is `true`, bars are automatically hidden when the app rotates to landscape on the iPhone (and `hidesBarsOnTap` is treated as `true`, so the bars can be shown again by tapping).

When the user is typing

If the navigation controller's `hidesBarsWhenKeyboardAppears` is `true`, bars are automatically hidden when the onscreen keyboard appears (see Chapter 10).

You can configure a UINavigationController, or any view controller that is to serve in a navigation interface, in the nib editor. In the Attributes inspector, use a navigation controller's Bar Visibility and Hide Bars checkboxes to determine the presence of the navigation bar and toolbar. The navigation bar and toolbar are themselves subviews of the navigation controller, and you can configure them with the Attributes inspector as well. New in iOS 11, a navigation bar has a Prefers Large Titles checkbox. A navigation controller's root view controller can be specified; in a storyboard, there will be a "root view controller" relationship between the navigation controller and its root view controller. The root view controller is automatically instantiated together with the navigation controller.

A view controller in the nib editor has a Navigation Item where you can specify its title, its prompt, and the text of its back button. New in iOS 11, a navigation item has a Large Title pop-up menu, where you can set its largeTitleDisplayMode. You can drag Bar Button Items into a view controller's navigation bar in the canvas to set the left buttons and right buttons of its navigationItem. Moreover, the Navigation Item has outlets, one of which permits you to set its titleView. Similarly, you can give a view controller Bar Button Items that will appear in the toolbar. (If a view controller in a nib doesn't have a Navigation Item and you want to configure this view controller for use in a navigation interface, drag a Navigation Item from the Object library onto the view controller.)

To start an iPhone project with a main storyboard that has a UINavigationController as its initial view controller, begin with the Master–Detail app template. Alternatively, start with the Single View app template, remove the existing view controller from the storyboard, and add a Navigation Controller in its place. Unfortunately, the nib editor assumes that the navigation controller's root view controller should be a UITableViewController. If that's not the case, here's a better way: start with the Single View app template, select the existing view controller, and choose Editor → Embed In → Navigation Controller. A view controller to be subsequently pushed onto the navigation stack can be configured in the storyboard as the destination of a push segue; I'll talk more about that later in the chapter.

Custom Transition

You can customize certain built-in transitions between view controller views:

Tab bar controller
> When a tab bar controller changes which of its child view controllers is selected, by default there is no view animation; you can add a custom animation.

Navigation controller
> When a navigation controller pushes or pops a child view controller, by default there is a sideways sliding view animation; you can replace this with a custom animation.

Presented view controller
> When a view controller is presented or dismissed, there is a limited set of built-in view animations; you can supply a custom animation. Moreover, you can

customize the ultimate size and position of the presented view, and how the presenting view is seen behind it; you can also provide ancillary views that remain during the presentation.

Given the extensive animation resources of iOS (see Chapter 4), this is an excellent chance for you to provide your app with variety and distinction. The view of a child view controller pushed onto a navigation controller's stack needn't arrive sliding from the side; it can expand by zooming from the middle of the screen, drop from above and fall into place with a bounce, snap into place like a spring, or whatever else you can dream up. A familiar example is Apple's Calendar app, which transitions from a year to a month, in a navigation controller, by zooming in.

A custom transition animation can optionally be *interactive* — meaning that it is driven in real time by the user's gesture. The user does not merely tap and cause an animation to take place; the user performs an extended gesture and gradually summons the new view to supersede the old one. The user can thus participate in the progress of the transition. A familiar example is the Photos app, which lets the user pinch a photo, in a navigation controller, to pop to the album containing it.

A custom transition animation can optionally be *interruptible*. You can provide a way for the user to pause the animation, possibly interact with the animated view by means of a gesture, and then resume (or cancel) the animation.

Noninteractive Custom Transition Animation

In the base case, you provide a custom animation that is *not* interactive. Configuring your custom animation requires three steps:

1. Before the transition begins, you must have given the view controller in charge of the transition a delegate.
2. As the transition begins, the delegate will be asked for an *animation controller*. You will supply a reference to some object adopting the UIViewControllerAnimatedTransitioning protocol (or `nil` to specify that the default animation, if any, should be used).
3. The animation controller will be sent these messages:

   `transitionDuration(using:)`
   The animation controller must return the duration of the custom animation.

   `animateTransition(using:)`
   The animation controller should perform the animation.

`interruptibleAnimator(using:)`
> Optional; if implemented, the animation controller should return an object adopting the UIViewImplicitlyAnimating protocol, which may be a property animator.

`animationEnded(_:)`
> Optional; if implemented, the animation controller may perform cleanup following the animation.

I like to use a property animator to govern the animation; it will need to be accessible from multiple methods, so it must live in an instance property. I'll type this instance property as an Optional wrapping a UIViewImplicitlyAnimating object:

```
var anim : UIViewImplicitlyAnimating?
```

I then implement all four animation controller methods:

`transitionDuration(using:)`
> We'll return a constant.

`animateTransition(using:)`
> We'll call `interruptibleAnimator(using:)` to obtain the property animator, and we'll tell the property animator to start animating.

`interruptibleAnimator(using:)`
> This is where all the real work happens. We're being asked for the property animator. There is a danger that we will be called multiple times during the animation. So if the property animator already exists in our instance property, we simply return it. If it doesn't exist, we create and configure it and assign it to our instance property, and *then* return it.

`animationEnded(_:)`
> We'll clean up any instance properties; at a minimum, we'll set our property animator instance property to `nil`.

Now let's get down to the nitty-gritty of what `interruptibleAnimator(using:)` actually does to configure the property animator and its animation. In general, a custom transition animation works as follows:

1. The `using:` parameter is an object called the *transition context* (adopting the UIViewControllerContextTransitioning protocol). By querying the transition context, you can obtain:

   - The *container view*, an already existing view within which all the action is to take place.
   - The outgoing and incoming view controllers.

- The outgoing and incoming views. These are probably the main views of the outgoing and incoming view controllers, but you should obtain the views directly from the transition context, just in case they aren't. The outgoing view is already inside the container view.

- The initial `frame` of the outgoing view, and the ultimate `frame` where the incoming view must end up.

2. Having gathered this information, your mission is to *put the incoming view into the container view* and *animate* it in such a way as to end up at its correct ultimate `frame`. You may also animate the outgoing view if you wish.

3. When the animation ends, your completion function *must* call the transition context's `completeTransition` to tell it that the animation is over. In response, the outgoing view is removed automatically, and the animation comes to an end (and our `animationEnded` will be called).

As a simple example, I'll use the transition between two child view controllers of a tab bar controller, when the user taps a different tab bar item. By default, this transition isn't animated; one view just replaces the other. Let's animate the transition.

A possible custom animation is that the new view controller's view should slide in from one side while the old view controller's view should slide out the other side. The direction of the slide should depend on whether the index of the new view controller is greater or less than that of the old view controller. Let's implement that.

Assume that the tab bar controller is our app's root view controller. In that case, all the work can be done in the AppDelegate implementation. The tab bar controller is in charge of the transition, so first step is to give it a delegate. I'll do that in code, in the app delegate's `application(_:didFinishLaunchingWithOptions:)`, making the tab bar controller's delegate be the app delegate itself:

```
(self.window!.rootViewController as! UITabBarController).delegate = self
```

The app delegate, in its role as UITabBarControllerDelegate, will be sent a message whenever the tab bar controller is about to change view controllers. That message is:

- `tabBarController(_:animationControllerForTransitionFrom:to:)`

The second step is to implement that method. We must return an animation controller, namely, some object implementing UIViewControllerAnimatedTransitioning. I'll return `self`:

```
extension AppDelegate : UITabBarControllerDelegate {
    func tabBarController(_ tabBarController: UITabBarController,
        animationControllerForTransitionFrom fromVC: UIViewController,
        to toVC: UIViewController) -> UIViewControllerAnimatedTransitioning? {
            return self
    }
}
```

(There is no particular reason why the animation controller should be self; I'm just using self to keep things simple. The animation controller can be any object — even a dedicated lightweight object instantiated just to govern this transition. There is also no particular reason why the animation controller should be the same object every time this method is called; depending on the circumstances, we could readily provide a different animation controller, or we could return nil to use the default transition — meaning, in this case, no animation.)

The third step is to implement the animation controller (UIViewControllerAnimated-Transitioning). I'll start with stubs for the four methods we're going to write:

```
extension AppDelegate : UIViewControllerAnimatedTransitioning {
    func transitionDuration(using ctx: UIViewControllerContextTransitioning?)
        -> TimeInterval {
            // ...
    }
    func animateTransition(using ctx: UIViewControllerContextTransitioning) {
            // ...
    }
    func interruptibleAnimator(using ctx: UIViewControllerContextTransitioning)
        -> UIViewImplicitlyAnimating {
            // ...
    }
    func animationEnded(_ transitionCompleted: Bool) {
            // ...
    }
}
```

Our transitionDuration must reveal in advance the duration of our animation:

```
func transitionDuration(using ctx: UIViewControllerContextTransitioning?)
    -> TimeInterval {
        return 0.4
}
```

(Again, the value returned needn't be a constant; we could decide on the duration based on the circumstances. But the value returned here *must* be the same as the duration of the animation we'll actually be constructing in interruptibleAnimator.)

Our animateTransition simply calls interruptibleAnimator to obtain the property animator, and tells it to animate:

```
func animateTransition(using ctx: UIViewControllerContextTransitioning) {
    let anim = self.interruptibleAnimator(using: ctx)
    anim.startAnimation()
}
```

The workhorse is `interruptibleAnimator`. If the property animator already exists, we unwrap it and return it, and that's all:

```
func interruptibleAnimator(using ctx: UIViewControllerContextTransitioning)
    -> UIViewImplicitlyAnimating {
        if self.anim != nil {
            return self.anim!
        }
        // ...
}
```

If we haven't returned, we need to form the property animator. First, we thoroughly query the transition context `ctx` to learn all about the parameters of this animation:

```
let vc1 = ctx.viewController(forKey:.from)!
let vc2 = ctx.viewController(forKey:.to)!
let con = ctx.containerView
let r1start = ctx.initialFrame(for:vc1)
let r2end = ctx.finalFrame(for:vc2)
let v1 = ctx.view(forKey:.from)!
let v2 = ctx.view(forKey:.to)!
```

Now we can prepare for our intended animation. In this case, we are sliding the views, so we need to decide the final frame of the outgoing view and the initial frame of the incoming view. We are sliding the views sideways, so those frames should be positioned sideways from the initial frame of the outgoing view and the final frame of the incoming view, which the transition context has just given us. *Which* side they go on depends upon the relative place of these view controllers among the children of the tab bar controller — is this to be a leftward slide or a rightward slide? Since the animation controller is the app delegate, we can get a reference to the tab bar controller the same way we did before:

```
let tbc = self.window!.rootViewController as! UITabBarController
let ix1 = tbc.viewControllers!.index(of:vc1)!
let ix2 = tbc.viewControllers!.index(of:vc2)!
let dir : CGFloat = ix1 < ix2 ? 1 : -1
var r1end = r1start
r1end.origin.x -= r1end.size.width * dir
var r2start = r2end
r2start.origin.x += r2start.size.width * dir
```

Now we're ready to animate! We put the second view controller's view into the container view at its initial frame, and animate our views:

```
v2.frame = r2start
con.addSubview(v2)
let anim = UIViewPropertyAnimator(duration: 0.4, curve: .linear) {
    v1.frame = r1end
    v2.frame = r2end
}
```

We must not neglect to supply the completion function that calls `complete-Transition`:

```
anim.addCompletion { _ in
    ctx.completeTransition(true)
}
```

Our property animator is now formed. We retain it in our `self.anim` property, and we also return it:

```
self.anim = anim
return anim
```

That completes `interruptibleAnimator`. Finally, our `animationEnded` cleans up by destroying the property animator:

```
func animationEnded(_ transitionCompleted: Bool) {
    self.anim = nil
}
```

That's all there is to it. Our example animation wasn't very complex, but an animation needn't be complex to be interesting, significant, and helpful to the user; I use this exact same animation in my own apps, and I think it enlivens and clarifies the transition. And even a more complex animation would be implemented along the same basic lines.

One possibility that I didn't illustrate in my example is that you are free to introduce additional views temporarily into the container view during the course of the animation; you'll probably want to remove them in the completion function. For example, you might make some interface object appear to migrate from one view controller's view into the other (in reality you'd probably use a snapshot view; see Chapter 1).

Interactive Custom Transition Animation

With an interactive custom transition animation, the idea is that we track something the user is doing, typically by means of a gesture recognizer (see Chapter 5), and perform the "frames" of the transition in response.

To make a custom transition animation interactive, you supply, in addition to the animation controller, an *interaction controller*. This is an object adopting the UIView-ControllerInteractiveTransitioning protocol. (This object needn't be the same as the animation controller, but it often is, and in my examples it will be.) The runtime then calls the interaction controller's `startInteractiveTransition(_:)` *instead of* the animation controller's `animateTransition(using:)`.

Configuring your custom animation requires the following steps:

1. Before the transition begins, you must have given the view controller in charge of the transition a delegate.

2. You'll have a gesture recognizer that tracks the interactive gesture. When the gesture recognizer recognizes, it triggers the transition to the new view controller.

3. As the transition begins, the delegate will be asked for an animation controller. You will return a UIViewControllerAnimatedTransitioning object.

4. The delegate will also be asked for an interaction controller. You will return a UIViewControllerInteractiveTransitioning object (or `nil` to prevent the transition from being interactive). This object implements `startInteractiveTransition(_:)`.

5. The gesture recognizer continues by constantly calling `updateInteractiveTransition(_:)` on the transition context, as well as managing the frames of the animation.

6. Sooner or later the gesture will end. At this point, we must decide whether to declare the transition completed or cancelled. A typical approach is to say that if the user performed more than half the full gesture, that constitutes completion; otherwise, it constitutes cancellation. We finish the animation accordingly.

7. The animation is now completed, and its completion function is called. We must call the transition context's `finishInteractiveTransition` or `cancelInteractiveTransition`, and then call its `completeTransition(_:)` with an argument stating whether the transition was finished or cancelled.

8. Our `animationEnded` is called, and we clean up.

(You may be asking: why must we keep talking to our transition context throughout the process, calling `updateInteractiveTransition` throughout the progress of the gesture, and `finishInteractiveTransition` or `cancelInteractiveTransition` at the end? The reason is that the animation might have a component separate from what you're doing — for example, in the case of a navigation controller push or pop transition, the change in the appearance of the navigation bar. The transition context needs to coordinate that animation with the interactive gesture and with your animation. So you need to keep telling it where things are in the course of the interaction.)

As an example, I'll describe how to make an interactive version of the tab bar controller transition animation that we developed in the previous section. The user will be able to drag from the edge of the screen to bring the tab bar controller's adjacent view controller in from the right or from the left.

In the previous section, I cleverly planned ahead for this section. Almost all the code from the previous section can be left as is! I'll build on that code, in such a way that the same custom transition animation can be *either* noninteractive (the user taps a tab bar item) *or* interactive (the user drags from one edge).

I'm going to need two more instance properties, in addition to `self.anim`:

```
var anim : UIViewImplicitlyAnimating?
var interacting = false
var context : UIViewControllerContextTransitioning?
```

The `self.interacting` property will be used as a signal that our transition is to be interactive. The `self.context` property is needed because the gesture recognizer's action method is going to need access to the transition context. (Sharing the transition context through a property may seem ugly, but the elegant alternatives would make the example more complicated, so we'll just do it this way.)

To track the user's gesture, I'll put a pair of UIScreenEdgePanGestureRecognizers into the interface. The gesture recognizers are attached to the tab bar controller's view (tbc.view), as this will remain constant while the views of its view controllers are sliding across the screen. As in the previous section, all the code will go into the app delegate. In `application(_:didFinishLaunchingWithOptions:)`, when I make the app delegate the tab bar controller's delegate, I create the gesture recognizers and make the app delegate *their* delegate as well, so I can dictate which gesture recognizer is applicable to the current situation:

```
let tbc = self.window!.rootViewController as! UITabBarController
tbc.delegate = self
let sep = UIScreenEdgePanGestureRecognizer(target:self, action:#selector(pan))
sep.edges = UIRectEdge.right
tbc.view.addGestureRecognizer(sep)
sep.delegate = self
let sep2 = UIScreenEdgePanGestureRecognizer(target:self, action:#selector(pan))
sep2.edges = UIRectEdge.left
tbc.view.addGestureRecognizer(sep2)
sep2.delegate = self
```

Acting as the delegate of the two gesture recognizers, we prevent either pan gesture recognizer from operating unless there is another child of the tab bar controller available on that side of the current child:

```
extension AppDelegate : UIGestureRecognizerDelegate {
    func gestureRecognizerShouldBegin(_ g: UIGestureRecognizer) -> Bool {
        let tbc = self.window!.rootViewController as! UITabBarController
        var result = false
        if (g as! UIScreenEdgePanGestureRecognizer).edges == .right {
            result = (tbc.selectedIndex < tbc.viewControllers!.count - 1)
        }
        else {
            result = (tbc.selectedIndex > 0)
```

```
        }
        return result
    }
}
```

If the gesture recognizer action method `pan` is called, our interactive transition animation is to take place. I'll break down the discussion according to the gesture recognizer's states. In `.began`, I raise the `self.interacting` flag and trigger the transition by setting the tab bar controller's `selectedIndex`:

```
@objc func pan(_ g:UIScreenEdgePanGestureRecognizer) {
    switch g.state {
    case .began:
        self.interacting = true
        let tbc = self.window!.rootViewController as! UITabBarController
        if g.edges == .right {
            tbc.selectedIndex = tbc.selectedIndex + 1
        } else {
            tbc.selectedIndex = tbc.selectedIndex - 1
        }
    // ...
    }
}
```

The transition begins. We are asked for our animation controller and our transition controller; we will supply a transition controller only if the `self.interacting` flag was raised; if the `self.interacting` flag is *not* raised, the user tapped a tab bar item and we are back in the preceding example:

```
extension AppDelegate: UITabBarControllerDelegate {
    func tabBarController(_ tabBarController: UITabBarController,
        animationControllerForTransitionFrom fromVC: UIViewController,
        to toVC: UIViewController) -> UIViewControllerAnimatedTransitioning? {
            return self
    }
    func tabBarController(_ tabBarController: UITabBarController,
        interactionControllerFor ac: UIViewControllerAnimatedTransitioning)
        -> UIViewControllerInteractiveTransitioning? {
            return self.interacting ? self : nil
    }
}
```

As a UIViewControllerInteractiveTransitioning adopter, our `startInteractiveTransition(_:)` is called instead of `animateTransition(using:)`. However, our `animateTransition(using:)` is still in place, and still does the same job it did in the previous section. So we call it to obtain the property animator, and set the property animator instance property. But we do *not* tell the property animator to animate! We are interactive; that means we intend to manage the "frames" of the animation ourselves. We also set the UIViewControllerContextTransitioning property, so that the gesture recognizer's action method can access it:

```
extension AppDelegate : UIViewControllerInteractiveTransitioning {
    func startInteractiveTransition(_ ctx:UIViewControllerContextTransitioning){
        self.anim = self.interruptibleAnimator(using: ctx)
        self.context = ctx
    }
}
```

The user's gesture proceeds, and we are now back in the gesture recognizer's action method, in the .changed state. We calculate the completed percentage of the gesture, and update both the property animator's "frame" and the transition context:

```
case .changed:
    let v = g.view!
    let delta = g.translation(in:v)
    let percent = abs(delta.x/v.bounds.size.width)
    self.anim?.fractionComplete = percent
    self.context?.updateInteractiveTransition(percent)
```

Ultimately, the user's gesture ends. Our goal now is to "hurry home" to the start of the animation or the end of the animation, depending on how far the user got through the gesture. With a property animator, that's really easy (see "Canceling a View Animation" on page 171):

```
case .ended:
    let anim = self.anim as! UIViewPropertyAnimator
    anim.pauseAnimation()
    if anim.fractionComplete < 0.5 {
        anim.isReversed = true
    }
    anim.continueAnimation(
        withTimingParameters:
        UICubicTimingParameters(animationCurve:.linear),
        durationFactor: 0.2)
```

The animation comes to an end, and the completion function that we gave our property animator in interruptibleAnimator is called. This is the one place in our interruptibleAnimator that needs to be a little different from the preceding example; we must send different messages to the transition context, depending on whether we finished to the end or reversed to the start:

```
anim.addCompletion { finish in
    if finish == .end {
        ctx.finishInteractiveTransition()
        ctx.completeTransition(true)
    } else {
        ctx.cancelInteractiveTransition()
        ctx.completeTransition(false)
    }
}
```

Finally, our animationEnded is called, and we clean up our instance properties:

```
func animationEnded(_ transitionCompleted: Bool) {
    self.interacting = false
    self.context = nil
    self.anim = nil
}
```

Another variation would be to make the custom transition animation interruptible. Again, this is straightforward thanks to the existence of property animators. While a view is in the middle of being animated, the property animator implements touchability of the animated view, and allows you to pause the animation. Thus, the user can be permitted (for example) to grab the animated view in the middle of the animation and move it around with the animation paused, and the animation can then resume when the user lets go of the view (as I demonstrated in "Hit-Testing During Animation" on page 266). You could equally incorporate these features into a custom transition animation.

 You can use a UIPreviewInteraction ("3D Touch Press Gesture" on page 258) to drive a view controller custom transition animation through 3D touch. In that case, the user's press is the gesture, and what advances the interactive custom transition animation is the UIPreviewInteraction and its delegate methods rather than a gesture recognizer and its action method.

Custom Presented View Controller Transition

With a presented view controller transition, you can customize not only the *animation* but also the final *position* of the presented view. Moreover, you can introduce ancillary views which *remain in the scene* while the presented view is presented, and are not removed until after dismissal is complete; for example, if the presented view is smaller than the presenting view and covers it only partially, you might add a dimming view between them, to darken the presenting view (just as a .formSheet presentation does).

There is no existing view to serve as the container view; therefore, when the presentation starts, the runtime constructs the container view and inserts it into the interface, leaving it there for only as long as the view remains presented. In the case of a .full-Screen presentation, the runtime also rips the presenting view out of the interface and inserts it into the container view, because you might want the presenting view to participate in the animation. For other styles of presentation, the container view is in front of the presenting view, which can't be animated and is left in place as the presentation proceeds.

The work of customizing a presentation is distributed between *two* objects: the animation controller (or interaction controller) on the one hand, and a custom presentation controller on the other:

The animation controller

The animation controller should be responsible for only the animation, the movement of the presented view into its final position.

The custom presentation controller

The determination of the presented view's final position is the job of the presentation controller. The presentation controller is also responsible for inserting any extra views, such as a dimming view, into the container view; Apple says that the animation controller animates the content, while the presentation controller animates the "chrome."

This distribution of responsibilities may sound rather elaborate, but in fact the opposite is true: it greatly simplifies things, because if you don't need one kind of customization you can simply omit it. If you supply an animation controller and no custom presentation controller, you dictate the animation, but the presented view will end up wherever the modal presentation style puts it. If you supply a custom presentation controller and no animation controller, a default transition style animation will be performed, but the presented view will end up at the position your custom presentation controller dictates.

Customizing the animation

I'll start with a situation where we don't need to use the presentation controller; all we want to do is customize the animation part of a built-in presentation style. The steps are almost completely parallel to how we customized a tab bar controller animation:

1. Give the presented view controller a delegate. This means that we set the presented view controller's `transitioningDelegate` property to an object adopting the UIViewControllerTransitioningDelegate protocol.

2. The delegate will be asked for an animation controller, and will return an object adopting the UIViewControllerAnimatedTransitioning protocol. Unlike a tab bar controller or navigation controller, a presented view controller's view undergoes *two* animations — the presentation and the dismissal — and therefore the delegate is asked *separately* for controllers:

   - `animationController(forPresented:presenting:source:)`
   - `interactionControllerForPresentation(using:)`
   - `animationController(forDismissed:)`
   - `interactionControllerForDismissal(using:)`

   You are free to customize just one animation, leaving the other at the default by not providing a controller for it.

3. The animation controller will implement its four methods as usual — `transitionDuration`, `animateTransition`, `interruptibleAnimator`, and `animationEnded`.

To illustrate, let's say we're running on an iPad, and we want to present a view using the `.formSheet` presentation style. But instead of using any of the built-in animation types (transition styles), we'll have the presented view appear to grow from the middle of the screen.

The only mildly tricky step is the first one. The problem is that the `transitioning-Delegate` must be set very early in the presented view controller's life — before the presentation begins. But the presented view controller doesn't *exist* before the presentation begins. The most reliable approach, therefore, is for the presented view controller to assign its own delegate in its own initializer:

```
required init?(coder aDecoder: NSCoder) {
    super.init(coder:aDecoder)
    self.transitioningDelegate = self
}
```

The presentation begins, and we're on to the second step. The transitioning delegate (UIViewControllerTransitioningDelegate) is asked for an animation controller; here, I'll have it supply `self` once again, and I'll do this only for the presentation, leaving the dismissal to use the default animation (and I'm not making this example interactive, so I don't implement the `interactionController` methods):

```
func animationController(forPresented presented: UIViewController,
    presenting: UIViewController, source: UIViewController)
    -> UIViewControllerAnimatedTransitioning? {
        return self
}
```

The third step is that the animation controller (UIViewControllerAnimatedTransitioning) is called upon to implement the animation. Our implementations of `transitionDuration`, `animateTransition`, and `animationEnded` are the usual boilerplate, so I'll show only `interruptibleAnimator`, which configures the property animator; observe that we don't care about the `.from` view controller, which remains in place during the presentation (indeed, its view isn't even in the container view):

```
func interruptibleAnimator(using ctx: UIViewControllerContextTransitioning)
    -> UIViewImplicitlyAnimating {
        if self.anim != nil {
            return self.anim!
        }
        let vc2 = ctx.viewController(forKey:.to)
        let con = ctx.containerView
        let r2end = ctx.finalFrame(for:vc2!)
        let v2 = ctx.view(forKey:.to)!
        v2.frame = r2end
```

```
            v2.transform = CGAffineTransform(scaleX: 0.1, y: 0.1)
            v2.alpha = 0
            con.addSubview(v2)
            let anim = UIViewPropertyAnimator(duration: 0.4, curve: .linear) {
                v2.alpha = 1
                v2.transform = .identity
            }
            anim.addCompletion { _ in
                ctx.completeTransition(true)
            }
            self.anim = anim
            return anim
    }
```

If we wish to customize both animation and dismissal using the same animation controller, there is a complication: the roles of the view controllers are reversed in the mind of the transition context. On presentation, the presented view controller is the .to view controller, but on dismissal, it is the .from view controller. For a presentation that isn't .fullScreen, the unused view is nil, so you can distinguish the cases by structuring your code like this:

```
let v1 = ctx.view(forKey:.from)
let v2 = ctx.view(forKey:.to)
if let v2 = v2 { // presenting
    // ...
} else if let v1 = v1 { // dismissing
    // ...
}
```

Customizing the presentation

Now let's involve the presentation controller: we will customize the final frame of the presented view controller's view, and we'll even add some "chrome" to the presentation. This will require some additional steps:

1. In addition to setting a transitioningDelegate, we must set the presented view controller's modalPresentationStyle to .custom.

2. The result of the preceding step is that the delegate (our adopter of UIViewControllerTransitioningDelegate) is sent an additional message:

    • presentationController(forPresented:presenting:source:)

(The source: parameter is what I have termed the "original presenter.") Your mission is to return an instance of a *custom UIPresentationController subclass*. This will then be the presented view controller's presentation controller during the course of this presentation, from the time presentation begins to the time dismissal ends. You must create this instance by calling (directly or indirectly) the designated initializer:

- `init(presentedViewController:presenting:)`

3. By means of appropriate overrides in your UIPresentationController subclass, you participate in the presentation, dictating the presented view's final position (`frameOfPresentedViewInContainerView`) and adding "chrome" to the presentation as desired.

The UIPresentationController has properties pointing to the `presentingViewController` as well the `presentedViewController` and the `presentedView`, plus the `presentationStyle` set by the presented view controller. It also obtains the `containerView`, which it subsequently communicates to the animation controller's transition context. It has some methods and properties that you can override in your subclass; you only need to override the ones that require customization for your particular implementation:

`frameOfPresentedViewInContainerView`
> The final position of the presented view. If there is an animation controller, it will receive this from the transition context's `finalFrame(for:)` method.

`presentationTransitionWillBegin`
`presentationTransitionDidEnd`
`dismissalTransitionWillBegin`
`dismissalTransitionDidEnd`
> Use these events as signals to add or remove "chrome" (extra views) to the container view.

`containerViewWillLayoutSubviews`
`containerViewDidLayoutSubviews`
> Use these layout events as signals to update the "chrome" views if needed.

`shouldRemovePresentersView`
> The default is `false`, except that of course it is `true` for a standard `.fullScreen` presentation, meaning that the presenting view is ripped out of the interface at the end of the presentation transition. You can return `true` for a custom presentation, but it would be rare to do this; even if the presented view completely covers the presenting view, there is no harm in leaving the presenting view in place.

A presentation controller is not a view controller, but UIPresentationController adopts some protocols that UIViewController adopts, and thus gets the same resizing-related messages that a UIViewController gets, as I described earlier in this chapter. It adopts UITraitEnvironment, meaning that it has a `traitCollection` and participates in the trait collection inheritance hierarchy, and receives the `traitCollectionDidChange(_:)` message. It also adopts UIContentContainer, meaning that it receives `willTransition(to:with:)` and `viewWillTransition(to:with:)`.

To illustrate the use of a custom presentation controller, I'll expand the preceding example to implement a custom presentation style that looks like a `.formSheet` *even on an iPhone*. The first step is to set the presentation style to `.custom` at the same time that we set the transitioning delegate:

```
required init?(coder aDecoder: NSCoder) {
    super.init(coder:aDecoder)
    self.transitioningDelegate = self
    self.modalPresentationStyle = .custom // *
}
```

The result (step two) is that this extra UIViewControllerTransitioningDelegate method is called so that we can provide a custom presentation controller:

```
func presentationController(forPresented presented: UIViewController,
    presenting: UIViewController?, source: UIViewController)
    -> UIPresentationController? {
        let pc = MyPresentationController(
            presentedViewController: presented, presenting: presenting)
        return pc
}
```

Everything else happens in our implementation of our UIPresentationController subclass (named MyPresentationController). To make the presentation look like a `.formSheet`, we inset the presented view's frame:

```
override var frameOfPresentedViewInContainerView : CGRect {
    return super.frameOfPresentedViewInContainerView.insetBy(dx:40, dy:40)
}
```

We could actually stop at this point! The presented view now appears in the correct position. However, the presenting view is appearing undimmed behind it. Let's add dimming, by inserting a translucent dimming view into the container view. Note that we are careful to deal with the possibility of subsequent rotation:

```
override func presentationTransitionWillBegin() {
    let con = self.containerView!
    let shadow = UIView(frame:con.bounds)
    shadow.backgroundColor = UIColor(white:0, alpha:0.4)
    con.insertSubview(shadow, at: 0)
    shadow.autoresizingMask = [.flexibleWidth, .flexibleHeight]
}
```

Again, this works perfectly, but now I don't like what happens when the presented view is dismissed: the dimming view vanishes suddenly at the end of the dismissal. I'd rather have the dimming view fade out, and I'd like it to fade out *in coordination with the dismissal animation*. The way to arrange that is through the object vended by the presented view controller's `transitionCoordinator` property. This object is just like the transition coordinator I've already discussed earlier in this chapter in connection with resizing events and rotation: in particular, we can call its `animate(alongside-Transition:completion:)` method to add our own animation:

```
override func dismissalTransitionWillBegin() {
    let con = self.containerView!
    let shadow = con.subviews[0]
    let tc = self.presentedViewController.transitionCoordinator!
    tc.animate(alongsideTransition: { _ in
        shadow.alpha = 0
    })
}
```

Once again, we could stop at this point. But I'd like to add a further refinement. A `.formSheet` view has rounded corners. I'd like to make our presented view look the same way:

```
override var presentedView : UIView? {
    let v = super.presentedView!
    v.layer.cornerRadius = 6
    v.layer.masksToBounds = true
    return v
}
```

Finally, for completeness, it would be nice, during presentation, to dim the appearance of any button titles and other tinted interface elements visible through the dimming view, to emphasize that they are disabled:

```
override func presentationTransitionDidEnd(_ completed: Bool) {
    let vc = self.presentingViewController
    let v = vc.view
    v?.tintAdjustmentMode = .dimmed
}
override func dismissalTransitionDidEnd(_ completed: Bool) {
    let vc = self.presentingViewController
    let v = vc.view
    v?.tintAdjustmentMode = .automatic
}
```

Transition Coordinator

Earlier in this chapter, we encountered resizing-related methods such as `viewWillTransition(to:with:)`, whose second parameter is a UIViewControllerTransitionCoordinator. As I suggested at that time, you can use this transition coordinator to add your own animation to the runtime's animation when the app rotates. It turns out that the view controller itself can obtain its transition coordinator during a view controller transition, through its own `transitionCoordinator` property.

The transition coordinator adopts the UIViewControllerTransitionCoordinatorContext protocol, just like the transition context; indeed, it is a kind of wrapper around the transition context. View controllers can therefore use their `transition-`

Coordinator to find out about the transition they are currently involved in. Moreover, in addition to the methods that it implements by virtue of adopting the UIViewControllerTransitionCoordinatorContext protocol, a transition coordinator implements the following methods:

animate(alongsideTransition:completion:)
> Takes an animations function and a completion function. The animation you supply is incorporated into the transition coordinator's animation. Returns a Bool, informing you in case your commands couldn't be animated. Both functions receive the transition context as a parameter. (See also "View Controller Manual Layout" on page 306, where I discussed this method in connection with rotation.)

A view controller's use of this method will typically be to add animation of its view's internal interface as part of a transition animation. This works equally for a custom animation or a built-in animation; in fact, the point is that the view controller can behave agnostically with regard to how its own view is being animated. In this example, a presented view controller animates part of its interface into place as the animation proceeds (whatever that animation may be):

```
override func viewWillAppear(_ animated: Bool) {
    super.viewWillAppear(animated)
    if let tc = self.transitionCoordinator {
        tc.animate(alongsideTransition:{ _ in
            self.buttonTopConstraint.constant += 200
            self.view.layoutIfNeeded()
        })
    }
}
```

notifyWhenInteractionChanges(_:)
> The parameter is a function to be called; the transition context is the function's parameter. Your function is called whenever the transition changes between being interactive and being noninteractive; this might be because the interactive transition was cancelled. In this example, a navigation controller has pushed a view controller, and now the user is popping it interactively (using the default drag-from-the-left-edge gesture). If the user cancels, the back view controller can hear about it, like this:

```
override func viewWillAppear(_ animated: Bool) {
    super.viewWillAppear(animated)
    let tc = self.transitionCoordinator
    tc?.notifyWhenInteractionChanges { ctx in
        if ctx.isCancelled {
```

```
                    // ...
                }
            }
        }
```

 I have not found any occasion when the child of a tab bar controller has a non-nil transition coordinator — even though you may have given the tab bar controller's transition a custom animation. I regard this as a bug.

Page View Controller

A page view controller (UIPageViewController) is like a book that can be viewed only one page at a time. The user, by a gesture, can navigate in one direction or the other to see the next or the previous page, successively — like turning the pages of a book.

Actually, a page view controller only *seems* to have multiple pages. In effect, it has at any given moment only the one page that the user sees. That page is its child view controller's view. The page view controller navigates to another page by releasing its existing child view controller and replacing it with another. This is a very efficient architecture: it makes no difference whether the page view controller lets the user page through three pages or ten thousand pages, because each page is created in real time, on demand, and exists only as long as the user is looking at it.

The page view controller's children are its `viewControllers`. In general, there will always be at most one of them (though there is a rarely used configuration in which a page view controller can have *two* pages at a time, as I'll explain in a moment). The page view controller is its current child's `parent`.

Preparing a Page View Controller

To create a UIPageViewController in code, use its designated initializer:

- `init(transitionStyle:navigationOrientation:options:)`

Here's what the parameters mean:

`transitionStyle:`
  The animation type during navigation (UIPageViewControllerTransitionStyle). Your choices are:

  - `.pageCurl`
  - `.scroll` (sliding)

`navigationOrientation:`
  The direction of navigation (UIPageViewControllerNavigationOrientation). Your choices are:

- `.horizontal`

- `.vertical`

`options:`
> A dictionary. Possible keys are:

> `UIPageViewControllerOptionSpineLocationKey`
>> If you're using the `.pageCurl` transition style, this is the position of the pivot line around which those page curl transitions rotate. The value (UIPageViewControllerSpineLocation) is one of the following:

>> - `.min` (left or top)

>> - `.mid` (middle; in this configuration there are *two* children, and *two* pages are shown at once)

>> - `.max` (right or bottom)

> `UIPageViewControllerOptionInterPageSpacingKey`
>> If you're using the `.scroll` transition style, this is the spacing between successive pages, visible as a gap during the transition (the default is 0).

You configure the page view controller's initial content by handing it its initial child view controller(s). You do that by calling this method:

- `setViewControllers(_:direction:animated:completion:)`

Here's what the parameters mean:

`viewControllers:`
> An array of one view controller — unless you're using the `.pageCurl` transition style and the `.mid` spine location, in which case it's an array of two view controllers.

`direction:`
> The animation direction (UIPageViewControllerNavigationDirection). This probably won't matter when you're assigning the page view controller its initial content, as you are not likely to want any animation. Possible values are:

> - `.forward`

> - `.backward`

`animated:, completion:`
> A Bool and a completion function.

To allow the user to page through the page view controller, and to supply the page view controller with a new page at that time, you also assign the page view controller a `dataSource`, which should conform to the UIPageViewControllerDataSource protocol. The `dataSource` is told whenever the user starts to change pages, and should respond by immediately providing another view controller whose view will constitute the new page. Typically, the data source will create this view controller on the spot.

Here's a minimal example. Each page in the page view controller is to portray an image of a named Pep Boy. The first question is where the pages will come from. My data model consists of an array (`self.pep`) of the string names of the three Pep Boys:

```
let pep : [String] = ["Manny", "Moe", "Jack"]
```

To match these, I have three eponymous image files (`manny`, `moe`, and `jack`), portraying each Pep Boy. I've also got a UIViewController subclass called Pep, capable of displaying a Pep Boy's image in an image view. I initialize a Pep object with Pep's designated initializer `init(pepBoy:)`, supplying the name of a Pep Boy from the array; the Pep object sets its own boy property:

```
init(pepBoy boy:String) {
    self.boy = boy
    super.init(nibName: nil, bundle: nil)
}
```

Pep's `viewDidLoad` then fetches the corresponding image and assigns it as the image of a UIImageView within its own view:

```
override func viewDidLoad() {
    super.viewDidLoad()
    self.pic.image = UIImage(named:self.boy.lowercased())
}
```

At any given moment, then, our page view controller will have one Pep instance as its child, and thus will portray a Pep Boy. Here's how I create the page view controller itself (in my app delegate):

```
// make a page view controller
let pvc = UIPageViewController(
    transitionStyle: .scroll, navigationOrientation: .horizontal)
// give it an initial page
let page = Pep(pepBoy: self.pep[0])
pvc.setViewControllers([page], direction: .forward, animated: false)
// give it a data source
pvc.dataSource = self
// put its view into the interface
self.window!.rootViewController = pvc
```

The page view controller is a UIViewController, and its view must get into the interface by standard means. You can make the page view controller the window's root‐ViewController, as I do here; you can make it a presented view controller; you can make it a child view controller of a tab bar controller or a navigation controller. If you want the page view controller's view to be a subview of a custom view controller's view, that view controller must be a custom container view controller, as I'll describe later.

Page View Controller Navigation

We now have a page view controller's view in our interface, itself containing and displaying the view of one Pep view controller that is its child. In theory, we have *three* pages, because we have three Pep Boys and their images — but the page view controller knows about only one of them. Just as with a navigation controller, you don't supply (or even create) another page until the moment comes to navigate to it. When that happens, one of these data source methods will be called:

- pageViewController(_:viewControllerAfter:)
- pageViewController(_:viewControllerBefore:)

The job of those methods is to return the requested successive view controller — or nil, to signify that there is no further page in this direction. Your strategy for doing that will depend on how your model maintains the data. My data is an array of unique strings, so all I have to do is find the previous name or the next name in the array:

```
func pageViewController(_ pvc: UIPageViewController,
    viewControllerAfter vc: UIViewController) -> UIViewController? {
        let boy = (vc as! Pep).boy
        let ix = self.pep.index(of:boy)! + 1
        if ix >= self.pep.count {
            return nil
        }
        return Pep(pepBoy: self.pep[ix])
}
func pageViewController(_ pvc: UIPageViewController,
    viewControllerBefore vc: UIViewController) -> UIViewController? {
        let boy = (vc as! Pep).boy
        let ix = self.pep.index(of:boy)! - 1
        if ix < 0 {
            return nil
        }
        return Pep(pepBoy: self.pep[ix])
}
```

We now have a working page view controller! The user, with a sliding gesture, can page through it, one page at a time. When the user reaches the first page or the last page, it is impossible to go further in that direction.

A .scroll style page view controller may cache its view controllers in advance. Thus, you should make no assumptions about *when* these data source methods will be called. If you need to be notified when the user is actually turning the page, use the delegate (which I'll describe later), not the data source.

You can also, at any time, call `setViewControllers` to change programmatically what page is being displayed, possibly with animation. In this way, you can "jump" to a page other than a successive page (something that the user cannot do with a gesture).

Page indicator

If you're using the .scroll transition style, the page view controller can optionally display a page indicator (a UIPageControl, see Chapter 12). The user can look at this to get a sense of what page we're on, and can tap to the left or right of it to navigate. To get the page indicator, you must implement two more data source methods; they are consulted in response to `setViewControllers`. We called that method initially to configure the page view controller; if we never call it again (because the user simply keeps navigating to the next or previous page), these data source methods won't be called again either, because they don't need to be: the page view controller will thenceforth keep track of the current index on its own. Here's my implementation for the Pep Boy example:

```
func presentationCount(for pvc: UIPageViewController) -> Int {
    return self.pep.count
}
func presentationIndex(for pvc: UIPageViewController) -> Int {
    let page = pvc.viewControllers![0] as! Pep
    let boy = page.boy
    return self.pep.index(of:boy)!
}
```

Unfortunately, the page view controller's page indicator by default has white dots and a clear background, so it is invisible in front of a white background. You'll want to customize it to change that. There is no direct access to it, so it's simplest to use the appearance proxy (Chapter 12). For example:

```
let proxy = UIPageControl.appearance()
proxy.pageIndicatorTintColor = UIColor.red.withAlphaComponent(0.6)
proxy.currentPageIndicatorTintColor = .red
proxy.backgroundColor = .yellow
```

Navigation gestures

If you've assigned the page view controller the .pageCurl transition style, the user can navigate by tapping at either edge of the view or by dragging across the view. These gestures are detected through two gesture recognizers, which you can access through the page view controller's `gestureRecognizers` property. The documentation suggests that you might change where the user can tap or drag by attaching them

---

to a different view, and other customizations are possible as well. In this code, I change the behavior of a `.pageCurl` page view controller (pvc) so that the user must double tap to request navigation:

```
for g in pvc.gestureRecognizers {
    if let g = g as? UITapGestureRecognizer {
        g.numberOfTapsRequired = 2
    }
}
```

Of course you are also free to add to the user's stock of gestures for requesting navigation. You can supply any controls or gesture recognizers that make sense for your app, and respond by calling `setViewControllers`. For example, if you're using the `.scroll` transition style, there's no tap gesture recognizer, so the user can't tap at either edge of the page view controller's view to request navigation. Let's change that. I've added invisible views at either edge of my Pep view controller's view, with tap gesture recognizers attached. When the user taps, the tap gesture recognizer fires, and the action method posts a notification whose `object` is the tap gesture recognizer:

```
@IBAction func tap (_ sender: UIGestureRecognizer?) {
    NotificationCenter.default.post(name:.tap, object: sender)
}
```

In the app delegate, I have registered to receive this notification. When it arrives, I use the tap gesture recognizer's view's tag to learn which view was tapped; I then navigate accordingly (pvc is the page view controller):

```
NotificationCenter.default.addObserver(
    forName:.tap, object: nil, queue: .main) { n in
        let g = n.object as! UIGestureRecognizer
        let which = g.view!.tag
        let vc0 = pvc.viewControllers![0]
        guard let vc = (which == 0 ?
            self.pageViewController(pvc, viewControllerBefore: vc0) :
            self.pageViewController(pvc, viewControllerAfter: vc0))
            else {return}
        let dir : UIPageViewControllerNavigationDirection =
            which == 0 ? .reverse : .forward
        UIApplication.shared.beginIgnoringInteractionEvents()
        pvc.setViewControllers([vc], direction: dir, animated: true) {
            _ in
            UIApplication.shared.endIgnoringInteractionEvents()
        }
    }
}
```

In that code, I turn off user interaction when the page animation starts and turn it back on when the animation ends. The reason is that otherwise we can crash (or get into an incoherent state) if the user taps during the animation.

Other Page View Controller Configurations

It is possible to assign a page view controller a delegate (UIPageViewController-Delegate), which gets an event when the user starts turning the page and when the user finishes turning the page, and can change the spine location dynamically in response to a change in device orientation. As with a tab bar controller's delegate or a navigation controller's delegate, a page view controller's delegate also gets messages allowing it to specify the page view controller's app rotation policy, so there's no need to subclass UIPageViewController solely for that purpose.

One further bit of configuration applicable to a `.pageCurl` page view controller is the `isDoubleSided` property. If it is `true`, the next page occupies the back of the previous page. The default is `false`, unless the spine is in the middle, in which case it's `true` and can't be changed. Your only option here, therefore, is to set it to `true` when the spine isn't in the middle, and in that case the back of each page would be a sort of throwaway page, glimpsed by the user during the page curl animation.

A page view controller in a storyboard lets you configure its transition style, navigation orientation, page spacing, spine location, and `isDoubleSided` property. (It also has delegate and data source outlets, but you're not allowed to connect them to other view controllers, because you can't draw an outlet from one scene to another in a storyboard.) It has no child view controller relationship, so you can't set the page view controller's initial child view controller in the storyboard; you'll have to complete the page view controller's initial configuration in code.

Container View Controllers

UITabBarController, UINavigationController, and UIPageViewController are all built-in *parent view controllers*: you hand them a child view controller and they do all the work, retaining that child view controller and putting its view into the interface inside their own view. What if you wanted your own view controller to do the same sort of thing?

You can create your own parent view controller, which can legally manage child view controllers and put their views into the interface. A custom parent view controller of this sort is called a *container view controller*. Your own view controller, behaving as a container view controller, becomes like one of the built-in parent view controllers, except that *you* get to define what it does — what it means for a view controller to be a child of this kind of parent view controller, how many children it has, which of its children's views appear in the interface and where they appear, and so on. A container view controller can also participate actively in the business of trait collection inheritance and view resizing.

An example appears in Figure 6-3 — and the construction of that interface is charted in Figure 6-4. We have a page view controller, but it is not the root view controller, and its view does not occupy the entire interface. How is that achieved?

It's achieved by *following certain rules*. We must *not* simply rip out the page view controller's view and plop it into the interface. We have to behave coherently. Some other view controller (in this case, my RootViewController) must act as a well-behaved container view controller. The page view controller must be made its child, and Root-ViewController is then permitted — as long it follows the rules — to put the page view controller's view into the interface, as a subview of its own view.

Adding and Removing Children

A view controller has a `childViewControllers` array; that's what gives it the power to be a parent. You must not, however, just wantonly populate this array. A child view controller needs to receive certain definite events at particular moments:

- As it becomes a child view controller
- As its view is added to and removed from the interface
- As it ceases to be a child view controller

Therefore, to act as a parent view controller, your UIViewController subclass must fulfill certain responsibilities:

Adding a child
> When a view controller is to *become your view controller's child*, your view controller must do these things, in this order:
>
> 1. Send `addChildViewController(_:)` to itself, with the child as argument. The child is automatically added to your `childViewControllers` array and is retained.
> 2. Get the child view controller's view into the interface (as a subview of your view controller's view), if that's what adding a child view controller means.
> 3. Send `didMove(toParentViewController:)` to the child with your view controller as its argument.

Removing a child
> When a view controller is to *cease being your view controller's child*, your view controller must do these things, in this order:
>
> 1. Send `willMove(toParentViewController:)` to the child with a `nil` argument.
> 2. Remove the child view controller's view from your interface.

3. Send `removeFromParentViewController` to the child. The child is automatically removed from your `childViewControllers` array and is released.

This is a clumsy and rather confusing dance. The underlying reason for it is that a child view controller must always receive `willMove(toParentViewController:)` followed by `didMove(toParentViewController:)` (and your own child view controllers can take advantage of these events however you like). But it turns out that you don't always send both these messages explicitly, because:

- `addChildViewController(_:)` sends `willMove(toParentViewController:)` for you *automatically*.
- `removeFromParentViewController` sends `didMove(toParentViewController:)` for you *automatically*.

Thus, in each case you must send manually the *other* message, the one that adding or removing a child view controller *doesn't* send for you — and of course you must send it so that everything happens in the correct order, as dictated by the rules I just listed.

When you do this dance correctly, the proper parent–child relationship results: the container view controller can refer to its children as its `childViewControllers`, and any child has a reference to the parent as its `parent`. If you don't do it correctly, all sorts of bad things can happen; in a worst-case scenario, the child view controller won't even survive, and its view won't work correctly, because the view controller was never properly retained as part of the view controller hierarchy (see "View Controller Hierarchy" on page 277). So do the dance correctly!

The initial child view controller

Example 6-1 provides a schematic approach for how to obtain an initial child view controller and put its view into the interface, where no child view controller's view was previously. (Alternatively, a storyboard can do this work for you, with no code, as I'll explain later in this chapter.)

Example 6-1. Adding an initial child view controller

```
let vc = // whatever; this is the initial child view controller
self.addChildViewController(vc) // "will" called for us
// insert view into interface between "will" and "did"
self.view.addSubview(vc.view)
vc.view.frame = // whatever, or use constraints
// when we call add, we must call "did" afterward
vc.didMove(toParentViewController: self)
```

In many cases, what I've just described is all you'll need. You have a parent view controller and a child view controller, and they are paired *permanently*, for the lifetime of the parent. That's how Figure 6-3 behaves: RootViewController has a page view controller as its child, and the page view controller's view as its own view's subview, for the entire lifetime of the app.

To illustrate, I'll use the same page view controller that I used in my earlier examples, the one that displays Pep Boys; but this time, its view won't occupy the entire interface. My root view controller will be called RootViewController. I'll create and configure my page view controller as a child of RootViewController, in RootViewController's `viewDidLoad`; note how carefully and correctly I perform the dance:

```
let pep : [String] = ["Manny", "Moe", "Jack"]
override func viewDidLoad() {
    super.viewDidLoad()
    let pvc = UIPageViewController(
        transitionStyle: .scroll, navigationOrientation: .horizontal)
    pvc.dataSource = self
    self.addChildViewController(pvc) // step 1
    self.view.addSubview(pvc.view) // step 2
    // ... configure frame or constraints here ...
    pvc.didMove(toParentViewController: self) // step 3
    let page = Pep(pepBoy: self.pep[0])
    pvc.setViewControllers([page], direction: .forward, animated: false)
}
```

Replacing a child view controller

It is also possible to *replace* one child view controller's view in the interface with another (comparable to how UITabBarController behaves when a different tab bar item is selected). The simplest, most convenient way to do that is with this parent view controller instance method:

- `transition(from:to:duration:options:animations:completion:)`

That method manages the stages in good order, adding the view of one child view controller (`to:`) to the interface before the transition and removing the view of the other child view controller (`from:`) from the interface after the transition, and seeing to it that the child view controllers receive lifetime events (such as `viewWill-Appear(_:)`) at the right moment. Here's what the last three arguments are for:

`options:`
A bitmask (UIViewAnimationOptions) comprising the same possible options that apply to any view transition (see "Transitions" on page 179).

`animations:`
An animations function. This may be used for animating views other than the two views being managed by the transition animation specified in the `options:`

argument; alternatively, if none of the built-in transition animations is suitable, you can animate the transitioning views yourself here (they are both in the interface during this function).

`completion:`

This function will be important if the transition involves the removal or addition of a child view controller. At the time when `transition` is called, both view controllers must be children of the parent view controller; so if you're going to remove one of the view controllers as a child, you'll do it in the completion function. Similarly, if you owe a new child view controller a `didMove(toParentViewController:)` call, you'll use the completion function to fulfill that debt.

Here's an example. To keep things simple, suppose that our view controller has just one child view controller at a time, and displays the view of that child view controller within its own view. So let's say that when our view controller is handed a new child view controller, it substitutes that new child view controller for the old child view controller and replaces the old child view controller's view with the new child view controller's view. Here's code that does that correctly; the view controllers are `fromvc` and `tovc`:

```
// we have already been handed the new view controller
// set up the new view controller's view's frame
tovc.view.frame = // ... whatever
// must have both as children before we can transition between them
self.addChildViewController(tovc) // "will" called for us
// when we call remove, we must call "will" (with nil) beforehand
fromvc.willMove(toParentViewController: nil)
// then perform the transition
self.transition(
    from:fromvc, to:tovc,
    duration:0.4, options:.transitionFlipFromLeft,
    animations:nil) { _ in
        // when we call add, we must call "did" afterward
        tovc.didMove(toParentViewController: self)
        fromvc.removeFromParentViewController() // "did" called for us
}
```

If we're using constraints to position the new child view controller's view, where will we set up those constraints? Before `transition` is too soon, as the new child view controller's view is not yet in the interface. The completion function is too late: if the view is added with no constraints, it will have no initial size or position, so the animation will be performed and then the view will suddenly seem to pop into existence as we provide its constraints. The animations function turns out to be a very good place:

```
// must have both as children before we can transition between them
self.addChildViewController(tovc) // "will" called for us
// when we call remove, we must call "will" (with nil) beforehand
fromvc.willMove(toParentViewController: nil)
```

```
// then perform the transition
self.transition(
    from:fromvc, to:tovc,
    duration:0.4, options:.transitionFlipFromLeft,
    animations: {
        tovc.view.translatesAutoresizingMaskIntoConstraints = false
        // ... configure tovc.view constraints here ...
    }) { _ in
        // when we call add, we must call "did" afterward
        tovc.didMove(toParentViewController: self)
        fromvc.removeFromParentViewController() // "did" called for us
}
```

If the built-in transition animations are unsuitable, you can omit the `options:` argument and provide your own animation in the animations function, at which time both views are in the interface. In this example, I animate a substitute view (an image view showing a snapshot of `tovc.view`) to grow from the top left corner; then I configure the real view's constraints and remove the substitute:

```
// tovc.view.frame is already set
let r = UIGraphicsImageRenderer(size:tovc.view.bounds.size)
let im = r.image { ctx in
    tovc.view.layer.render(in:ctx.cgContext)
}
let iv = UIImageView(image:im)
iv.frame = .zero
self.view.addSubview(iv)
tovc.view.alpha = 0 // hide the real view
// must have both as children before we can transition between them
self.addChildViewController(tovc) // "will" called for us
// when we call remove, we must call "will" (with nil) beforehand
fromvc.willMove(toParentViewController: nil)
// then perform the transition
self.transition(
    from:fromvc, to:tovc,
    duration:0.4, // no options:
    animations: {
        iv.frame = tovc.view.frame // animate bounds change
        // ... configure tovc.view constraints here ...
    }) { _ in
        tovc.view.alpha = 1
        iv.removeFromSuperview()
        // when we call add, we must call "did" afterward
        tovc.didMove(toParentViewController: self)
        fromvc.removeFromParentViewController() // "did" called for us
}
```

Status Bar, Traits, and Resizing

As I've already mentioned, a parent view controller, instead of dictating the status bar appearance through its own implementation of `preferredStatusBarStyle` or

prefersStatusBarHidden, can defer the responsibility to one of its children, by overriding these properties:

- childViewControllerForStatusBarStyle

- childViewControllerForStatusBarHidden

That's what a UITabBarController does, for example. Your custom parent view controller can do the same thing.

A container view controller also participates in trait collection inheritance. In fact,
you might insert a container view controller into your view controller hierarchy for
no other purpose than to engage in such participation. A parent view controller has
the amazing ability to lie to a child view controller about the environment, thanks to
this method:

- setOverrideTraitCollection(_:forChildViewController:)

The first parameter is a UITraitCollection that will be combined with the inherited
trait collection and communicated to the specified child. This is a UIViewController
instance method, so only view controllers have this mighty power. Moreover, you
have to specify a child view controller, so only *parent* view controllers have this
mighty power. (UIPresentationController has a similar power, through its override-
TraitCollection property, allowing it to lie to its presented view controller about the
inherited trait collection.)

Why would you want to lie to a child view controller about its environment? Well,
imagine that we're writing an iPad app, and we have a view controller whose view can
appear either fullscreen or as a small subview of a parent view controller's main view.
The view's interface might need to be different when it appears in the smaller size.
You could configure that difference using size classes (conditional constraints) in the
nib editor, with one interface for a .regular horizontal size class (iPad) and another
interface for a .compact horizontal size class (iPhone). Then, when the view is to
appear in its smaller size, we lie to its view controller and tell it that this *is* an iPhone:

```
let vc = // the view controller we're going to use as a child
self.addChildViewController(vc) // "will" called for us
let tc = UITraitCollection(horizontalSizeClass: .compact)
self.setOverrideTraitCollection(tc, forChildViewController: vc) // heh heh
vc.view.frame = // whatever
self.view.addSubview(vc.view)
vc.didMove(toParentViewController: self)
```

A parent view controller sets the size of a child view controller's view. A child view
controller, however, can express a preference as to what size it would like its view to
be, by setting its own preferredContentSize property. The chief purpose of this
property is to be consulted by a parent view controller when this view controller is its

child. This property is a preference and no more; no law says that the parent must consult the child, or that the parent must obey the child's preference.

If a view controller's `preferredContentSize` is set while it is a child view controller, the runtime automatically communicates this fact to the parent view controller, by calling this UIContentContainer method:

- `preferredContentSizeDidChange(forChildContentContainer:)`

The parent view controller may implement this method to consult the child's `preferredContentSize`, and may change the child's view's size in response if it so chooses.

A parent view controller, as an adopter of the UIContentContainer protocol (along with UIPresentationController), is also responsible for communicating to its children that their sizes are changing and what their new sizes will be. It is the parent view controller's duty to implement this method:

`size(forChildContentContainer:withParentContainerSize:)`
> Should be implemented to return each child view controller's correct size at any moment. Failure to implement this method will cause the child view controller to be handed the wrong size in its implementation of `viewWill-Transition(to:with:)` — it will be given the *parent's* new size rather than its own new size!

If your parent view controller implements `viewWillTransition(to:with:)`, it should call super so that `viewWillTransition(to:with:)` will be passed down to its children. This works even if your implementation is explicitly changing the size of a child view controller, provided you have implemented `size(forChildContent-Container:withParentContainerSize:)` to return the new size.

Peek and Pop

On a device with 3D touch, if the user can trigger a transition to a new view controller, you can permit the user to do a partial press to *preview* the new view controller's view from within the current view controller's view, without actually performing the transition. The user can then either back off the press completely, in which case the preview vanishes, or do a full press, in which case the transition is performed. Apple calls this *peek and pop*.

Apple's own apps use peek and pop extensively. For example, in the Mail app, viewing a mailbox's list of messages, the user can peek at a message's content; in the Calendar app, viewing a month, the user can peek at a day's events; and so on.

The preview during peek and pop is only a preview; the user can't interact with it. In effect, the preview is just a snapshot. However, to give the preview itself some additional functionality, it can be accompanied by menu items, similar to an action sheet (see Chapter 13). The user slides the preview upward to reveal the menu items. The user can then tap a menu item to perform its action, or tap the preview to back out and return to the original view controller.

To implement peek and pop, your source view controller (the one that the user would transition from if the full transition were performed) must register by calling this method:

`registerForPreviewing(with:sourceView:)`

> The first parameter is an object adopting the UIViewControllerPreviewingDelegate protocol (typically `self`). The second parameter is a touchable view within which you want the user to be able to press in order to summon a preview. You can call this method multiple times to register multiple source views.
>
> This method also returns a value, a system-supplied context manager conforming to the UIViewControllerPreviewing protocol. However, for straightforward peek and pop you won't need to capture this object; it will be supplied again in the delegate method calls.

Let's say the user now uses 3D touch to press somewhere on the screen. In order for your UIViewControllerPreviewingDelegate adopter to be called, this press must be within a registered touchable view; if it is within a subview of the registered view, the subview must itself be touchable (because otherwise hit-testing would fail to report the press in the first place). This means it's time to *peek*. The first delegate method is called:

`previewingContext(_:viewControllerForLocation:)`

> The first parameter is the context manager I mentioned a moment ago. The second parameter, the `location:`, is the point where the user is pressing, in `source-View` coordinates; you can examine this to decide whether the press is within an area corresponding to an element for which you want to trigger peek and pop. To prevent peeking, return `nil`. Otherwise:
>
> - Optionally, set the context manager's `sourceRect` to the region, expressed in source view coordinates, that will stay sharp while the rest of the interface blurs to indicate that peeking is about to take place. If you don't do this, the source view itself will be used.
>
> - Instantiate an appropriate destination view controller and return it. The runtime will snapshot the view controller's view and present that snapshot as the preview.

Now let's say the user, while previewing, continues to press harder and reaches full force. This means it's time to *pop*. The second delegate method is called:

`previewingContext(_:commit:)`
> The first parameter is the context manager; the second parameter is the view controller you provided in the previous delegate method. Your job is now to perform the actual transition.
>
> In all likelihood, you will transition to the view controller that arrives as the second parameter. Still, no law requires this; you might implement peek by displaying a subview or simplified interface, using another view controller, and then pop to the real view controller.

Alternatively, you can configure peek and pop in a storyboard, without code. In the nib editor, select a triggered segue emanating from a tappable interface object (an action segue) and check the Peek & Pop checkbox in the Attributes inspector. If you need to add code, similar to the delegate methods, use the pop-up menus to provide custom segues (I'll explain later what custom segues are).

In this artificial example, I have a view controller with three buttons: Manny, Moe, and Jack. My view controller is a container view controller; when the user taps a button, I create the corresponding Pep view controller (whose view contains that Pep boy's image) and make it my view controller's child, displaying its view in my view controller's view:

```
@IBAction func doShowBoy(_ sender : UIButton) {
    let title = sender.title(for: .normal)!
    let pep = Pep(pepBoy: title)
    self.transitionContainerTo(pep)
}
func transitionContainerTo(_ pep:Pep) {
    let oldvc = self.childViewControllers[0]
    pep.view.frame = self.container.bounds
    self.addChildViewController(pep)
    oldvc.willMove(toParentViewController: nil)
    self.transition(
        from: oldvc, to: pep,
        duration: 0.2, options: .transitionCrossDissolve,
        animations: nil) { _ in
            pep.didMove(toParentViewController: self)
            oldvc.removeFromParentViewController()
    }
}
```

Now I want to implement peek and pop for those three buttons. The buttons are subviews of a common superview, `self.buttonSuperview`. I'll register that superview for previewing in my container view controller's `viewDidLoad`:

```
override func viewDidLoad() {
    super.viewDidLoad()
    self.registerForPreviewing(with: self, sourceView: self.buttonSuperview)
}
```

In the first delegate method, I hit-test the press location; if the user is pressing on a button, I set the context manager's sourceRect, instantiate the corresponding Pep view controller, and return it:

```
func previewingContext(_ ctx: UIViewControllerPreviewing,
    viewControllerForLocation loc: CGPoint) -> UIViewController? {
        let sv = ctx.sourceView
        guard let button =
            sv.hitTest(loc, with: nil) as? UIButton else {return nil}
        let title = button.title(for: .normal)!
        let pep = Pep(pepBoy: title)
        ctx.sourceRect = button.convert(button.bounds, to:sv)
        return pep
}
```

In the second delegate method, I perform the transition, exactly as if the user had tapped a button:

```
func previewingContext(_ ctx: UIViewControllerPreviewing,
    commit vc: UIViewController) {
        if let pep = vc as? Pep {
            self.transitionContainerTo(pep)
        }
}
```

Creating menu items to accompany the preview is the job of the *destination* view controller. All it has to do is override the previewActionItems property to supply an array of UIPreviewActionItems. A UIPreviewActionItem can be a UIPreviewAction, which is basically a simple tappable menu item. Alternatively, it can be a UIPreviewActionGroup, consisting of an array of UIPreviewActions; this looks like a menu item, but when the user taps it the menu items vanish and are replaced by the group's menu items, giving in effect a second level of menu hierarchy. A UIPreviewActionItem can have a style: .default, .selected (the menu item has a checkmark), or .destructive (the menu item has a warning red color).

I'll extend the preceding example to demonstrate the use of a UIPreviewActionGroup and the .selected style. My Pep view controller overrides previewActionItems. The user can tap a Colorize menu item to see a secondary menu of three possible colors; tapping one of those will presumably somehow colorize this Pep Boy. The user can also tap a Favorite menu item to make this Pep Boy the favorite (implemented through UserDefaults); if this Pep Boy is *already* the favorite, this menu item has a checkmark:

```
override var previewActionItems: [UIPreviewActionItem] {
    // example of submenu (group)
    let col1 = UIPreviewAction(title:"Blue", style: .default) {
        action, vc in // ...
    }
    let col2 = UIPreviewAction(title:"Green", style: .default) {
        action, vc in // ...
    }
    let col3 = UIPreviewAction(title:"Red", style: .default) {
        action, vc in // ...
    }
    let group = UIPreviewActionGroup(
        title: "Colorize", style: .default, actions: [col1, col2, col3])
    // example of selected style
    let favKey = "favoritePepBoy"
    let style : UIPreviewActionStyle =
        self.boy == UserDefaults.standard.string(forKey:favKey) ?
        .selected : .default
    let fav = UIPreviewAction(title: "Favorite", style: style) {
        action, vc in
        if let pep = vc as? Pep {
            UserDefaults.standard.set(pep.boy, forKey:favKey)
        }
    }
    return [group, fav]
}
```

The function passed to the UIPreviewAction initializer receives as parameters the
UIPreviewAction and the view controller instance (so that you can refer to the view
controller without causing a retain cycle). I take advantage of this in the Favorite
menu item implementation, pulling out the boy instance property string to use as the
value saved into user defaults, thus identifying which Pep Boy is now the favorite.

Storyboards

A storyboard is a way of performing automatically the kind of view controller management I've described throughout this chapter, such as creating a view controller and
transitioning to it. A storyboard doesn't always reduce the amount of code you'll have
to write, but it does clarify the relationships between your view controllers over the
course of your app's lifetime. Instead of having to hunt around in each of your classes
to see which class creates which view controller and when, you can view and manage
the chain of view controller creation graphically in the nib editor. Figure 6-9 shows
the storyboard of a small test app.

A storyboard is a collection of view controller nibs, which are displayed as its scenes.
Each view controller is instantiated from its own nib, as needed, and will then obtain
its view, as needed — typically from a view nib that you've configured in the same
scene by editing the view controller's view. I described this process in detail in "How

Figure 6-9. The storyboard of an app

Storyboards Work" on page 294. As I explained there, a view controller can be instantiated from a storyboard in various ways:

Manual instantiation
> Your code can instantiate a view controller *manually* from a storyboard, by calling one of these methods:
>
> - `instantiateInitialViewController`
> - `instantiateViewController(withIdentifier:)`

Initial view controller
> If your app has a main storyboard, as specified by its *Info.plist*, that storyboard's initial view controller will be instantiated and assigned as the window's `rootView-Controller` *automatically* as the app launches. To specify that a view controller is a storyboard's initial view controller, check the "Is Initial View Controller" checkbox in its Attributes inspector. This will cause any existing initial view controller to lose its initial view controller status. The initial view controller is distinguished graphically in the canvas by an arrow pointing to it from the left, and in the document outline by the presence of the Storyboard Entry Point.

Relationship

Two built-in parent view controllers can specify their children directly in the storyboard, setting their viewControllers array:

- UITabBarController can specify multiple children (its "view controllers").
- UINavigationController can specify its single initial child (its "root view controller").

To add a view controller as a viewControllers child to one of those parent view controller types, Control-drag from the parent view controller to the child view controller; in the little HUD that appears, choose the appropriate listing under Relationship Segue. The result is a *relationship* whose source is the parent and whose destination is the child. The destination view controller will be instantiated *automatically* when the source view controller is instantiated, and will be assigned into its viewControllers array, thus making it a child and retaining it.

Triggered segue

A triggered segue configures a *future* situation, when the segue will be *triggered*. At that time, one view controller that already exists will cause the instantiation of another, bringing the latter into existence *automatically*. Two types of triggered segue are particularly common (their names in the nib editor depend on whether the "Use Trait Variations" checkbox is checked in the File inspector):

Show (formerly Push)

The future view controller will be *pushed* onto the stack of the navigation controller of which the existing view controller is already a child.

The name Show comes from the show(_:sender:) method, which pushes a view controller onto the parent navigation controller if there is one, but behaves adaptively if there is not (I'll talk more about that in Chapter 9). A Show segue from a view controller that is *not* a navigation controller's child will *present* the future view controller rather than pushing it, as there is no navigation stack to push onto. Setting up a Show segue without a navigation controller and then wondering why there is no push is a common beginner mistake.

Present Modally (formerly Modal)

The future view controller will be a *presented* view controller (and the existing view controller will be its original presenter).

Unlike a relationship, a triggered segue does not have to emanate from a view controller (a manual segue). It can emanate from certain kinds of gesture recognizer, or from a tappable view, such as a button or a table view cell, in the first view controller's view; this is a graphical shorthand signifying that the segue should be triggered, bringing the second view controller into existence, when a tap or other gesture occurs (an action segue).

To create a triggered segue, Control-drag from the tappable object in the first view controller, or from the first view controller itself, to the second view controller. In the little HUD that appears, choose the type of segue you want. If you dragged from the view controller, this will be a manual segue; if you dragged from a tappable object, it will be an action segue.

Triggered Segues

A triggered segue is a true segue (as opposed to relationships, which are not really segues at all). The most common types are Show (Push) and Present Modally (Modal). A segue is a full-fledged object, an instance of UIStoryboardSegue, and it can be configured in the nib editor through its Attributes inspector. However, it is not instantiated by the loading of a nib, and it cannot be pointed to by an outlet. Rather, it will be instantiated *when the segue is triggered*, at which time its designated initializer will be called, namely `init(identifier:source:destination:)`.

A segue's `source` and `destination` are the two view controllers between which it runs. The segue is directional, so the source and destination are clearly distinguished. The source view controller is the one that will exist already, before the segue is triggered; the destination view controller will be instantiated together with the segue itself, when the segue is triggered.

A segue's `identifier` is a string. You can set this string for a segue in a storyboard through its Attributes inspector; this can be useful when you want to trigger the segue manually in code (you'll specify it by means of its identifier), or when you have code that can receive a segue as parameter and you need to distinguish which segue this is.

Triggered segue behavior

The default behavior of a segue, when it is triggered, is exactly the behavior of the corresponding manual transition described earlier in this chapter:

Show (Push)
> The segue is going to call `pushViewController(_:animated:)` (if we are in a navigation interface). To set `animated:` to `false`, uncheck the Animates checkbox in the Attributes inspector.

Present Modally (Modal)
> The segue is going to call `present(_:animated:completion:)`. To set `animated:` to `false`, uncheck the Animates checkbox in the Attributes inspector. Other presentation options, such as the modal presentation style and the modal transition style, can be set in the destination view controller's Attributes inspector or in the

segue's Attributes inspector (the segue settings will override the destination view controller settings).

You can further customize a triggered segue's behavior by providing your own UIStoryboardSegue subclass. The key thing is that you must implement your custom segue's perform method, which will be called after the segue is triggered and instantiated, in order to do the actual transition from one view controller to another. You can do this even for a push segue or a modal segue: in the Attributes inspector for the segue, you specify your UIStoryboardSegue subclass, and in that subclass, you call super in your perform implementation.

Let's say, for example, that you want to add a custom transition animation to a modal segue. You can do this by writing a segue class that makes itself the destination controller's transitioning delegate in its perform implementation before calling super:

```
class MyCoolSegue: UIStoryboardSegue {
    override func perform() {
        let dest = self.destination
        dest.modalPresentationStyle = .custom
        dest.transitioningDelegate = self
        super.perform()
    }
}
extension MyCoolSegue: UIViewControllerTransitioningDelegate {
    func animationController(forPresented presented: UIViewController,
        presenting: UIViewController,
        source: UIViewController) -> UIViewControllerAnimatedTransitioning? {
            return self
    }
    // ...
}
extension MyCoolSegue: UIViewControllerAnimatedTransitioning {
    func transitionDuration(using ctx: UIViewControllerContextTransitioning?)
        -> TimeInterval {
            return 0.8
    }
    // ...
}
```

The rest is then exactly as in "Custom Presented View Controller Transition" on page 354. MyCoolSegue is the UIViewControllerTransitioningDelegate, so its animationController(forPresented:...) will be called. MyCoolSegue is the UIViewControllerAnimatedTransitioning object, so its transitionDuration and so forth will be called. In short, we are now off to the races with a custom presented view controller transition, with all the code living inside MyCoolSegue — a pleasant encapsulation of functionality.

You can also create a *completely* custom segue. To do so, in the HUD when you Control-drag to create the segue, ask for a Custom segue, and then, in the Attributes inspector, specify your UIStoryboardSegue subclass. Again, you must override `perform`, but now you *don't* call `super` — the *whole transition* is completely up to you! Your `perform` implementation can access the segue's `identifier`, `source`, and `destination` properties. The `destination` view controller has already been instantiated, but that's all; it is entirely up to your code make this view controller a child view controller or presented view controller and cause its view to appear in the interface.

How a segue is triggered

A triggered segue will be triggered in one of two ways:

Through a user gesture

If a segue emanates from a gesture recognizer or from a tappable view, it becomes an *action segue*, meaning that it will be triggered automatically when the tap or other gesture occurs.

Your source view controller class can prevent an action segue from being triggered. To do so, override this method:

`shouldPerformSegue(withIdentifier:sender:)`

Sent when an action segue is about to be triggered. Returns a Bool (and the default is `true`), so if you don't want this segue triggered on this occasion, return `false`.

In code

If a segue emanates from a view controller as a whole, it is a *manual segue*, and triggering it is up to your code. Send this message to the source view controller:

`performSegue(withIdentifier:sender:)`

Triggers a segue whose source is this view controller. The segue will need an identifier in the storyboard so that you can specify it here! `shouldPerformSegue(withIdentifier:sender:)` will *not* be called, because if you didn't want the segue triggered, you wouldn't have called `performSegue` in the first place.

An action segue with an identifier can be treated as a manual segue: that is, you can trigger it by calling `performSegue`, thus doing in code what the user could have done by tapping.

View controller communication

When a segue is triggered, the destination view controller is instantiated automatically; your code does not instantiate it. This raises a crucial question: how are you going to communicate between the source view controller and the destination view controller? This, you'll remember, was the subject of an earlier section of this chapter

("Communication with a Presented View Controller" on page 321), where I used this code as an example:

```
let svc = SecondViewController(nibName: nil, bundle: nil)
svc.data = "This is very important data!"
svc.delegate = self
self.present(svc, animated:true)
```

In that code, the first view controller creates the second view controller, and therefore has a reference to it at that moment. Thus, it has an opportunity to communicate with it, passing along some data to it, and setting itself as its delegate, before presenting it. With a modal segue, however, the second view controller is instantiated for you, and the segue itself is going to call present(_:animated:completion:). So when and how will the first view controller be able to set svc.data and set itself as svc's delegate?

The answer is that, after a segue has instantiated the destination view controller but before the segue is actually performed, the source view controller is sent prepare(for:sender:). The first parameter is the segue, and the segue has a reference to the destination view controller — so this is the moment when the source view controller and the destination view controller meet! The source view controller can thus perform configurations on the destination view controller, hand it data, and so forth. The source view controller can work out which segue is being triggered by examining the segue's identifier and destination properties, and the sender is the interface object that was tapped to trigger the segue (or, if performSegue(with-Identifier:sender:) was called in code, whatever object was supplied as the sender: argument).

So, for example:

```
override func prepare(for segue: UIStoryboardSegue, sender: Any?) {
    if segue.identifier == "second" {
        let svc = segue.destination as! SecondViewController
        svc.data = "This is very important data!"
        svc.delegate = self
    }
}
```

This solves the communication problem. Unfortunately, it solves it in a clumsy way; prepare(for:sender:) feels like a blunt instrument. The destination arrives typed as a generic UIViewController, and it is up to your code to know its actual type, cast it, and configure it. If more than one segue emanates from a view controller, they are all bottlenecked through the same prepare(for:sender:) implementation, which devolves into an ugly collection of conditions to distinguish them. I regard this aspect of the storyboard architecture as flawed.

Container Views and Embed Segues

The only parent view controllers for which you can create relationship segues specifying their children in a storyboard are the built-in UITabBarController and UINavigationController. That's because the nib editor understands how they work. If you write your own custom container view controller ("Container View Controllers" on page 368), the nib editor doesn't even know that your view controller *is* a container view controller, so it can't be the source of a relationship segue.

Nevertheless, you can perform some initial parent–child configuration of your custom container view controller in a storyboard, if your situation conforms to these assumptions:

- Your parent view controller will have one initial child view controller.
- You want the child view controller's view placed somewhere in the parent view controller's view.

To configure your parent view controller in a storyboard, drag a Container View object from the Object library into the parent view controller's view in the canvas. The result is a view, together with an *embed segue* leading from it to an additional child view controller. You can then specify the child view controller's correct class in its Identity inspector. Alternatively, delete the child view controller, replace it with a different view controller, and Control-drag from the container view to this view controller and, in the HUD, specify an Embed segue.

When an embed segue is triggered, the destination view controller is instantiated and made the source view controller's child, and its view is placed exactly inside the container view as its subview. Thus, the container view is not only a way of generating the embed segue, but also a way of specifying where you want the child view controller's view to go. The entire child-addition dance is performed correctly and automatically for you: addChildViewController(_:) is called, the child's view is put into the interface, and didMove(toParentViewController:) is called.

An embed segue is a triggered segue. It can have an identifier, and the standard messages are sent to the source view controller when the segue is triggered. At the same time, it has this similarity to a relationship: when the source (parent) view controller is instantiated, the runtime wants to trigger the segue automatically, instantiating the child view controller and embedding its view in the container view *now*. If that isn't what you want, override shouldPerformSegue(withIdentifier:sender:) in the parent view controller to return false for this segue, and call performSegue(withIdentifier:sender:) later when you do want the child view controller instantiated.

The parent view controller is sent prepare(for:sender:) before the child's view loads. At this time, the child has not yet been added to the parent's childView-

`Controllers` array. If you allow the segue to be triggered when the parent view controller is instantiated, then by the time the parent's `viewDidLoad` is called, the child's `viewDidLoad` has already been called, the child has already been added to the parent's `childViewControllers`, and the child's view is already inside the parent's view.

If you subsequently want to replace the child view controller's view with another child view controller's view in the interface, you will do so in code, probably by calling `transition(from:to:duration:options:animations:completion:)` as I described earlier in this chapter. If you really want to, you can configure this through a storyboard by using a custom segue.

Storyboard References

When you create a segue in the storyboard (a triggered segue or a relationship), you don't have to Control-drag to a view controller as the destination; instead, you can Control-drag to a *storyboard reference* which you have previously added to the canvas of this storyboard. A storyboard reference is a *placeholder* for a specific view controller. Thus, instead of a large and complicated network of segues running all over your storyboard, possibly crisscrossing in confusing ways, you can effectively *jump* through the storyboard reference to the actual destination view controller.

To specify what view controller a storyboard reference stands for, you need to perform two steps:

1. Select the view controller and, in the Identity inspector, give it a Storyboard ID.
2. Select the storyboard reference and, in the Attributes inspector, enter that same Storyboard ID as its Referenced ID.

But wait — there's more! The referenced view controller doesn't even have to be in the same storyboard as the storyboard reference. You can use a storyboard reference to jump to a view controller in *a different storyboard*. With a storyboard reference that leads into a different storyboard, that storyboard is loaded automatically when needed. This allows you to organize your app's interface into multiple storyboards.

To configure a storyboard reference to refer to a view controller in a different storyboard, use the Storyboard pop-up menu in its Attributes inspector. The rule is that if you specify the Storyboard but not the Referenced ID, the storyboard reference stands for the target storyboard's initial view controller (the one marked as the Storyboard Entry Point in that storyboard's document outline). If you do specify the Referenced ID, then of course the storyboard reference stands for the view controller with that Storyboard ID in the target storyboard. (I find, as a practical matter, that things work best if you always specify *both* the storyboard reference's Storyboard *and* its Referenced ID.)

Unwind Segues

Here's an interesting puzzle: Storyboards and segues would appear to be useful only half the time, because segues are asymmetrical. There is a push segue but no pop segue. There is a present modally segue but no dismiss segue.

The reason, in a nutshell, is that a triggered segue cannot "go back." A triggered segue *instantiates* the destination view controller; it *creates a new view controller instance*. But when dismissing a presented view controller or popping a pushed view controller, we don't need any *new* view controller instances. We want to return, somehow, to an *existing instance* of a view controller.

 Beginners often fail to understand this. They make a triggered segue from view controller A to view controller B, and then try to express the notion "go back" by making *another* triggered segue from view controller B to view controller A. The result is a vicious cycle of segues, with presentation piled on presentation, or push piled on push, one view controller instantiated on top of another on top of another. *Do not construct a cycle of segues*. (Unfortunately, the nib editor doesn't alert you to this mistake.)

The solution is an *unwind segue*. An unwind segue *does* let you express the notion "go back" in a storyboard. Basically, it lets you jump to *any* view controller that is already instantiated further up your view controller hierarchy, destroying the source view controller and any intervening view controllers in good order.

Creating an unwind segue

Before you can create an unwind segue, you must implement an *unwind method* in the class of some view controller represented in the storyboard. This should be a method marked @IBAction as a hint to the storyboard editor, and taking a single parameter, a UIStoryboardSegue. You can call it unwind if you like, but the name doesn't really matter:

```
@IBAction func unwind(_ seg: UIStoryboardSegue) {
    // ...
}
```

Think of this method as a marker, specifying that the view controller in which it appears can be the destination for an unwind segue. It is, in fact, a little more than a marker: it will also be called when the unwind segue is triggered. But its marker functionality is much more important — so much so that, in many cases, you won't give this method any code at all. Its *presence*, and its name, are what matters.

Now you can create an unwind segue. Doing so involves the use of the Exit proxy object that appears in every scene of a storyboard. Control-drag from the view controller you want to go back *from*, or from something like a button in that view controller's view, connecting it to the Exit proxy object *in the same scene* (Figure 6-10). A

Figure 6-10. Creating an unwind segue

little HUD appears, listing all the known unwind methods (similar to how action methods are listed in the HUD when you connect a button to its target). Click the name of the unwind method you want. You have now made an unwind segue, bound to that unwind method.

How an unwind segue works

When the unwind segue is *triggered*, the following steps are performed:

1. If this is an action segue, the source view controller's `shouldPerformSegue(with-Identifier:sender:)` is called — just as for a normal segue. This is your chance to stop the whole process dead at this point by returning `false`.

2. The name of the unwind method to which the unwind segue is bound is *only a name*. The unwind segue's actual destination view controller is *unknown!* Therefore, the runtime now starts walking *up the view controller hierarchy* looking for a destination view controller. Put simply, the first view controller it finds that *implements the unwind method* will, by default, be the destination view controller.

Assume that the destination view controller has been found. (I'll explain *how* it is found in a moment.) Then we proceed to *perform* the segue, as follows:

1. The source view controller's `prepare(for:sender:)` is called with the segue as the first parameter — just as for a normal segue. The two view controllers are now in contact (because the other view controller is the segue's `destination`). This is an opportunity for the source view controller to hand information to the destination view controller before being destroyed! (Thus, an unwind segue is an alternative to delegation as a way of putting one view controller into communication with another: see "Communication with a Presented View Controller" on page 321.)

2. The destination view controller's unwind method is called. Its parameter is the segue. The two view controllers are now in contact *again* (because the other view controller is the segue's `source`). It is perfectly reasonable, as I've already said, for the unwind method body to be empty; the unwind method's real purpose is to mark this view controller as the destination view controller.

3. The segue is actually performed, *destroying* the source controller and any intervening view controllers up to (but not including) the destination view controller, in good order.

Now I'll go back and explain in detail *how* the destination view controller is found, and *how* the segue is actually performed. This is partly out of sheer interest — they are both devilishly clever — and partly in case you need to customize the process. You can skip the discussion if the technical details aren't of interest to you.

 Unwind segues are differently implemented in every version of iOS; they can be quite complicated; and they are sometimes buggy. They are a great time-saver in simple situations, but for anything beyond that, I don't recommend using them; you may be better off popping and dismissing in code.

How the destination view controller is found

The process of locating the destination view controller starts by walking *up* the view controller hierarchy. What do I mean by "up" the hierarchy? Well, every view controller has either a `parent` or a `presentingViewController`, so the next view controller up the hierarchy is that view controller. However, it might also be necessary to walk back *down* the hierarchy, to a child (at some depth) of one of the parents we encounter.

Here's how the walk proceeds:

1. At each step up the view controller hierarchy, the runtime sends this view controller the following event:

   • `allowedChildViewControllersForUnwinding(from:)`

   This view controller's job is to supply an *array of its own direct children*. The array can be empty, but it must be an array. To help form this array, the view controller calls this method:

   • `childViewControllerContaining(_:)`

   This tells the view controller which of its own children is, or is the ultimate parent of, the source view controller. We don't want to go down *that* branch of the view hierarchy; that's the branch we just came *up*. So this view controller *subtracts* that view controller from the array of its own child view controllers, and returns the resulting array.

2. There are two possible kinds of result from the previous step (the value returned from `allowedChildViewControllers...`):

There are children

If the previous step yielded an array with one or more child view controllers in it, the runtime performs step 1 on all of them (stopping if it finds the destination), thus going *down* the view hierarchy.

There are no children

If, on the other hand, the previous step yielded an *empty* array, the runtime asks *this same* view controller the following question:

- `canPerformUnwindSegueAction(_:from:withSender:)`

The default implementation of this method is simply to call `responds(to:)` on `self`, asking whether this view controller contains an implementation of the unwind method we're looking for. The result is a Bool. If it is `true`, we *stop. This is the destination view controller.* If it is `false`, we continue with the search *up* the view controller hierarchy, finding the next view controller and performing step 1 again.

A moment's thought will reveal that the recursive application of this algorithm will eventually arrive at an existing view controller instance with an implementation of the unwind method if there is one. Okay, maybe a moment's thought didn't reveal that to you, so here's an actual example. I'll use the app whose storyboard is pictured in Figure 6-9. Its root view controller is a UITabBarController with two children:

- The first tab bar controller child is a UINavigationController with a root view controller called FirstViewController, which has a push segue to another view controller called PushedViewController.
- The second tab bar controller child is called SecondViewController, which has a modal segue to another view controller called PresentedViewController.

Assume that the user starts in the tab bar controller's first view controller, where she triggers the push segue, thus showing PushedViewController. She then switches to the tab bar controller's second view controller, where she triggers the modal segue, thus showing PresentedViewController. All the view controllers pictured in Figure 6-9 now exist simultaneously.

The unwind method is in FirstViewController, and is called `iAmFirst(_:)`. The corresponding unwind segue, whose action is `"iAmFirst:"`, is triggered from a button in PresentedViewController. The user taps the button in PresentedViewController and thus triggers the `"iAmFirst:"` unwind segue. *What will happen?*

To begin with, PresentedViewController is sent `shouldPerformSegue(with-Identifier:sender:)` and returns `true`, permitting the segue to go forward. The runtime now needs to walk the view controller hierarchy and locate the iAm-First(_:) method. Here's how it does that:

1. We start by walking *up* the view hierarchy. We thus arrive at the original presenter from which PresentedViewController was presented, namely SecondViewController.

   The runtime sends allowedChildViewControllersForUnwinding(from:) to SecondViewController; SecondViewController has no children, so it returns an empty array.

   So the runtime also asks SecondViewController canPerformUnwindSegueAction to find out whether this is the destination — but SecondViewController returns false, so we know this is *not* the destination.

2. We therefore proceed *up* the view hierarchy to SecondViewController's parent, the UITabBarController. The runtime sends the UITabBarController allowed-ChildViewControllersForUnwinding(from:).

   The UITabBarController has two child view controllers, namely the UINavigationController and SecondViewController — but one of them, Second-ViewController, contains the source (as it discovers by calling childView-ControllerContaining(_:)). Therefore, the UITabBarController returns an array containing the *other* child view controller, namely the UINavigation-Controller.

3. The runtime has received an array with a child in it; it therefore proceeds *down* the view hierarchy to that child, the UINavigationController, and asks it the same question: allowedChildViewControllersForUnwinding(from:).

   The navigation controller has two children, namely FirstViewController and PushedViewController, and neither of them is or contains the source, so it returns an array containing *both* of them.

4. The runtime has received an array with two children in it. It therefore notes down that it now has *two* hierarchy branches to explore, and proceeds *down* the hierarchy to explore them:

   a. The runtime starts with PushedViewController, asking it allowedChildView-ControllersForUnwinding(from:). PushedViewController has no children, so the reply is an empty array.

      So the runtime asks PushedViewController canPerformUnwindSegueAction to find out whether this is the destination — but PushedViewController replies false, so we know this is *not* the destination.

   b. So much for *that* branch of the UINavigationController's children; we've reached a dead end. So the runtime proceeds to the *other* branch, namely FirstViewController. The runtime asks FirstViewController allowedChild-

`ViewControllersForUnwinding(from:)`. FirstViewController has no children, so the reply is an empty array.

So the runtime asks `canPerformUnwindSegueAction` to find out whether this is the destination — and FirstViewController replies `true`. We've found the destination view controller!

The destination having been found, the runtime now sends `prepare(for:sender:)` to the source, and then calls the destination's unwind method, `iAmFirst(_:)`. We are now ready to *perform* the segue.

How an unwind segue is performed

The way an unwind segue is performed is just as ingenious as how the destination is found. During the walk in search of the destination view controller, the runtime *remembers* the walk. Thus, it knows where all the presented view controllers are, and it knows where all the parent view controllers are. Thus we have a *path* of presenting view controllers and parent view controllers between the source and the destination. The runtime then proceeds as follows:

- For any presented view controllers on the path, the runtime itself calls `dismiss(animated:completion:)` on the presenting view controller.
- For any parent view controllers on the path, the runtime tells each of them, in turn, to `unwind(for:towardsViewController:)`.

The second parameter of `unwind(for:towardsViewController:)` is the *direct child* of this parent view controller leading down the branch where the destination lives. This child might or might not *be* the destination, but that's no concern of this parent view controller. Its job is merely to *get us onto that branch*, whatever that may mean for this kind of parent view controller. A moment's thought will reveal (don't you wish I'd stop saying that?) that if each parent view controller along the path of parent view controllers does this correctly, we will in fact end up at the destination, releasing in good order all intervening view controllers that need to be released. This procedure is called *incremental unwind*.

Let's try it! The unwind procedure for our example runs as follows:

1. The runtime sends `dismiss(animated:completion:)` to the root view controller, namely the UITabBarController. Thus, PresentedViewController is destroyed in good order.

2. The runtime sends `unwind(for:towardsViewController:)` to the UITabBarController. The second parameter is the tab bar controller's first child, the UINavigationController. The UITabBarController therefore changes its `selectedViewController` to be the UINavigationController.

3. The runtime sends unwind(for:towardsViewController:) to the UINavigation-Controller. The second parameter is the FirstViewController. The navigation controller therefore pops its stack down to the FirstViewController. Thus, Push-edViewController is destroyed in good order, and we are back at the FirstView-Controller — which is exactly what was supposed to happen.

Unwind segue customization

Knowing how an unwind segue works, you can see how to intervene in and customize the process:

- In a custom view controller that contains an implementation of the unwind method, you might implement canPerformUnwindSegueAction(_:from:with-Sender:) to return `false` instead of `true` so that it doesn't become the destination on this occasion.

- In a custom parent view controller, you might implement allowedChildView-ControllersForUnwinding(from:). In all probability, your implementation will consist simply of listing your childViewControllers, calling childView-ControllerContaining(_:) to find out which of your children is or contains the source, subtracting that child from the array, and returning the array — just as the built-in parent view controllers do.

- In a custom parent view controller, you might implement unwind(for:towards-ViewController:). The second parameter is one of your current children; you will do whatever it means for this parent view controller to make this the currently displayed child.

In allowedChildViewControllersForUnwinding(from:) and childViewController-Containing(_:), the parameter is not a UIStoryboardSegue. It's an instance of a special value class called a UIStoryboardUnwindSegueSource, which has no other job than to communicate, in these two methods, the essential information about the unwind segue needed to make a decision. It has a `source`, a `sender`, and an unwind-Action (the Selector specified when forming the unwind segue).

 Do *not* override childViewControllerContaining(_:). It knows more than you do; you wouldn't want to interfere with its operation.

View Controller Lifetime Events

As views come and go, driven by view controllers and the actions of the user, events arrive that give your view controller the opportunity to respond to the various stages of its own existence and the management of its view. By overriding these methods, your UIViewController subclass can perform appropriate tasks at appropriate moments. Here's a list:

`viewDidLoad`

> The view controller has obtained its view (as explained earlier in this chapter); if that involved loading a nib, outlets have been hooked up. This does *not* mean that the view is in the interface or that it has been given its correct size. You should call `super` in your implementation, just in case a superclass has work to do in *its* implementation.

`willTransition(to:with:)`
`viewWillTransition(to:with:)`
`traitCollectionDidChange(_:)`

> The view controller's view is being resized or the trait environment is changing, or both (as explained earlier in this chapter). Your implementation of the first two methods should call `super`.

`updateViewConstraints`
`viewWillLayoutSubviews`
`viewDidLayoutSubviews`

> The view is receiving `updateConstraints` and `layoutSubviews` events (as explained in Chapter 1). Your implementation of `updateViewConstraints` should call `super`.

`willMove(toParentViewController:)`
`didMove(toParentViewController:)`

> The view controller is being added or removed as a child of another view controller (as explained earlier in this chapter).

`viewWillAppear(_:)`
`viewDidAppear(_:)`
`viewWillDisappear(_:)`
`viewDidDisappear(_:)`

> The view is being added to or removed from the interface. This includes being supplanted by another view controller's view or being restored through the removal of another view controller's view. A view that has appeared is in the window; it is part of your app's active view hierarchy. A view that has disappeared is not in the window; its `window` is `nil`. You should call `super` in your override of any of these four methods; if you forget to do so, things may go wrong in subtle ways.

To distinguish more precisely *why* your view is appearing or disappearing, consult any of these properties of the view controller:

- `isBeingPresented`

- isBeingDismissed

- isMovingToParentViewController

- isMovingFromParentViewController

To get a sense for when these events are useful, it helps to examine some situations in which they normally occur. Take, for example, a UIViewController being pushed onto the stack of a navigation controller. It receives, in this order, the following messages:

1. willMove(toParentViewController:)

2. viewWillAppear(_:)

3. updateViewConstraints

4. traitCollectionDidChange(_:)

5. viewWillLayoutSubviews

6. viewDidLayoutSubviews

7. viewDidAppear(_:)

8. didMove(toParentViewController:)

When this same UIViewController is popped off the stack of the navigation controller, it receives, in this order, the following messages:

1. willMove(toParentViewController:) (with parameter nil)

2. viewWillDisappear(_:)

3. viewDidDisappear(_:)

4. didMove(toParentViewController:) (with parameter nil)

Disappearance, as I mentioned a moment ago, can happen because another view controller's view supplants this view controller's view. For example, consider a UIView-Controller functioning as the top (and visible) view controller of a navigation controller. When another view controller is pushed on top of it, the first view controller gets these messages:

1. viewWillDisappear(_:)

2. viewDidDisappear(_:)

3. didMove(toParentViewController:)

The converse is also true. For example, when a view controller is popped from a navigation controller, the view controller that was below it in the stack (the back view controller) receives these messages:

1. `viewWillAppear(_:)`
2. `viewDidAppear`
3. `didMove(toParentViewController:)`

Incoherencies in View Controller Events

Unfortunately, the exact sequence of events and the number of times they will be called for any given view controller transition situation sometimes seems nondeterministic or incoherent. For example:

- Sometimes `didMove(toParentViewController:)` arrives without a corresponding `willMove(toParentViewController:)`.
- Sometimes `didMove(toParentViewController:)` arrives even though this view controller was previously the child of this parent and remains the child of this parent.
- Sometimes the layout events arrive more than once for the same view controller for the same transition.
- Sometimes `viewWillAppear(_:)` arrives without a corresponding `viewDid-Appear(_:)`; similarly, sometimes `viewWillDisappear(_:)` arrives without a corresponding `viewDidDisappear(_:)`. A case in point is when an interactive transition animation begins and is cancelled.

I regard all such behaviors as bugs, but Apple clearly does not. The best advice I can offer is that you should try to structure your code in such a way that incoherencies of this sort don't matter.

Appear and Disappear Events

The `appear` and `disappear` events are particularly appropriate for making sure that a view reflects the model or some form of saved state each time it appears. (A common beginner mistake is to use `viewDidLoad` instead, forgetting that `viewDidLoad` is called only once in the view controller's lifetime.)

Changes to the interface performed in `viewDidAppear(_:)` or `viewWill-Disappear(_:)` may be visible to the user as they occur! If that's not what you want, use the other member of the pair. For example, in a certain view containing a long scrollable text, I want the scroll position to be the same when the user returns to this view as it was when the user left it, so I save the scroll position in `viewWill-Disappear(_:)` and restore it in `viewWillAppear(_:)` — not `viewDidAppear(_:)`, where the user might see the scroll position jump.

These methods are useful also when something must be true exactly so long as a view is in the interface. For example, a repeating Timer that must be running while a view is present can be started in the view controller's `viewDidAppear(_:)` and stopped in its `viewWillDisappear(_:)`. (This architecture also allows you to avoid the retain cycle that could result if you waited to invalidate the timer in a `deinit` that might otherwise never arrive.)

The `appear` events are not layout events! Don't make any assumptions about whether your views have achieved their correct size just because the view is appearing — even if those assumptions seem to be correct. To respond when layout is taking place, implement layout events.

A view does not disappear if a presented view controller's view merely covers it rather than supplanting it. For example, a view controller that presents another view controller using the `.formSheet` presentation style gets no lifetime events during presentation and dismissal.

A view does not disappear merely because the app is backgrounded and suspended. Once suspended, your app might be killed. So you cannot rely on `viewWillDisappear(_:)` or `viewDidDisappear(_:)` alone for saving data that the app will need the next time it launches. If you are to cover every case, you may need to ensure that your data-saving code also runs in response to an application lifetime event such as `applicationWillResignActive` or `applicationDidEnterBackground` (see Appendix A).

Event Forwarding to a Child View Controller

A custom container view controller must effectively send `willMove(toParentView-Controller:)` and `didMove(toParentViewController:)` to its children manually, and it will do this correctly if you do the dance correctly when your view controller acquires or loses a child view controller (see "Container View Controllers" on page 368).

A custom container view controller must forward resizing events to its children. This will happen automatically if you call `super` in your implementation of the `will-Transition` methods. Conversely, if you implement these methods, failure to call `super` may prevent them from being forwarded correctly to the child view controller.

The `appear` and `disappear` events are normally passed along automatically. However, you can take charge by overriding this property:

`shouldAutomaticallyForwardAppearanceMethods`
> If you override this property to return `false`, you are responsible for seeing that the four `appear` and `disappear` methods are called on your view controller's children. You do *not* do this by calling these methods directly. The reason is that you

have no access to the correct moment for sending them. Instead, you call these two methods on your child view controller:

- beginAppearanceTransition(_:animated:); the first parameter is a Bool saying whether this view controller's view is about to appear (true) or disappear (false)
- endAppearanceTransition

Here's what to do if you've implemented shouldAutomaticallyForwardAppearance-Methods to return false. There are two main occasions on which your custom container view controller must forward appear and disappear events to a child.

First, what happens when your custom container view controller's own view itself appears or disappears? If it has a child view controller's view within its own view, it must implement and forward all four appear and disappear events to that child. You'll need an implementation along these lines, for each of the four events:

```
override func viewWillAppear(_ animated: Bool) {
    super.viewWillAppear(animated)
    let child = // whatever
    if child.isViewLoaded && child.view.superview != nil {
        child.beginAppearanceTransition(true, animated: true)
    }
}
override func viewDidAppear(_ animated: Bool) {
    super.viewDidAppear(animated)
    let child = // whatever
    if child.isViewLoaded && child.view.superview != nil {
        child.endAppearanceTransition()
    }
}
```

(The implementations for viewDidAppear(_:) and viewDidDisappear(_:) are similar, except that the first argument for beginAppearanceTransition is false.)

Second, what happens when you swap one view controller's child for another in your interface? Apple warns that you should *not* call the UIViewController method transition(from:...); instead, you perform the transition animation directly, calling beginAppearanceTransition(_:animated:) and endAppearanceTransition yourself.

A minimal correct implementation might involve the UIView transition class method (see Chapter 4). Here's an example of a parent view controller swapping one child view controller and its view for another, while taking charge of notifying the child view controllers of the appearance and disappearance of their views. I've put asterisks to call attention to the additional method calls that forward the appear and disappear events to the children (fromvc and tovc):

```
    self.addChildViewController(tovc) // "will" called for us
    fromvc.willMove(toParentViewController: nil)
    fromvc.beginAppearanceTransition(false, animated:true) // *
    tovc.beginAppearanceTransition(true, animated:true) // *
    UIView.transition(
        from:fromvc.view, to:tovc.view,
        duration:0.4, options:.transitionFlipFromLeft) {_ in
            tovc.endAppearanceTransition() // *
            fromvc.endAppearanceTransition() // *
            tovc.didMove(toParentViewController: self)
            fromvc.removeFromParentViewController()
    }
}
```

View Controller Memory Management

Memory is at a premium on a mobile device. Thus you want to minimize your app's use of memory. Your motivations are partly altruistic and partly selfish. While your app is running, other apps are suspended in the background; you want to keep your memory usage as low as possible so that those other apps have room to remain suspended and the user can readily switch to them from your app. You also want to prevent your own app from being terminated! If your app is backgrounded and suspended while using a lot of memory, it may be terminated in the background when memory runs short. If your app uses an inordinate amount of memory while in the foreground, it may be summarily killed before the user's very eyes.

One strategy for avoiding using too much memory is to release any memory-hogging objects you're retaining if they are not needed at this moment. Because a view controller is the basis of so much of your application's architecture, it is likely to be a place where you'll concern yourself with releasing unneeded memory.

One of your view controller's most memory-intensive objects is its view. Fortunately, the iOS runtime manages a view controller's view's memory for you. If a view controller's view is not in the interface, it can be temporarily dispensed with. In such a situation, if memory is getting tight, then even though the view controller itself persists, and even though it retains its actual view, the runtime may release its view's backing store (the cached bitmap representing the view's drawn contents). The view will then be redrawn when and if it is to be shown again later.

In addition, if memory runs low, your view controller may be sent this message:

didReceiveMemoryWarning
    Sent to a view controller to advise it of a low-memory situation. It is preceded by
    a call to the app delegate's applicationDidReceiveMemoryWarning, together with
    a .UIApplicationDidReceiveMemoryWarning notification posted to any regis-
    tered objects. You are invited to respond by releasing any data that you can do

without. Do not release data that you can't readily and quickly recreate! The documentation advises that you should call super.

Lazy Loading

If you're going to release data in didReceiveMemoryWarning, you must concern yourself with how you're going to get it back. A simple and reliable mechanism is *lazy loading* — a getter that reconstructs or fetches the data if it is nil.

For example, suppose we have a property myBigData which might be a big piece of data. We make this a calculated property, storing the real data in a private property (I'll call it _myBigData). Our calculated property's setter simply writes through to the private property. In didReceiveMemoryWarning, we write myBigData out as a file (Chapter 22) and set myBigData to nil — thus setting _myBigData to nil as well, and releasing the big data from memory. The getter for myBigData implements lazy loading: if we try to get myBigData when _myBigData is nil, we attempt to fetch the data from the file — and if we succeed, we delete the file (to prevent stale data):

```
private let fnam = "myBigData"
private var _myBigData : Data! = nil
var myBigData : Data! {
    set (newdata) { self._myBigData = newdata }
    get {
        if _myBigData == nil {
            let fm = FileManager.default
            let f = fm.temporaryDirectory.appendingPathComponent(self.fnam)
            if let d = try? Data(contentsOf:f) {
                self._myBigData = d
                do {
                    try fm.removeItem(at:f)
                } catch {
                    print("Couldn't remove temp file")
                }
            }
        }
        return self._myBigData
    }
}
func saveAndReleaseMyBigData() {
    if let myBigData = self.myBigData {
        let fm = FileManager.default
        let f = fm.temporaryDirectory.appendingPathComponent(self.fnam)
        if let _ = try? myBigData.write(to:f) {
            self.myBigData = nil
        }
    }
}
```

```
override func didReceiveMemoryWarning() {
    super.didReceiveMemoryWarning()
    self.saveAndReleaseMyBigData()
}
```

NSCache, NSPurgeableData, and Memory-Mapping

When your big data can be reconstructed from scratch on demand, you can take advantage of the built-in NSCache class, which is like a dictionary with the ability to clear out its own entries automatically under memory pressure. As in the previous example, a calculated property can be used as a façade:

```
private let _cache = NSCache<NSString, NSData>()
var cachedData : Data {
    let key = "somekey" as NSString
    if let olddata = self._cache.object(forKey:key) {
        return olddata as Data
    }
    let newdata = // recreated data
    self._cache.setObject(newdata as NSData, forKey: key)
    return newdata
}
```

Another built-in class that knows how to clear itself out is NSPurgeableData. It is a subclass of NSMutableData. To signal that the data should be discarded, send your object discardContentIfPossible. Wrap any access to data in calls to beginContent-Access and endContentAccess; the former returns a Bool to indicate whether the data was accessible. The tricky part is getting those access calls right; when you create an NSPurgeableData, you must send it an unbalanced endContentAccess to make its content discardable:

```
private var _purgeable = NSPurgeableData()
var purgeabledata : Data {
    if self._purgeable.beginContentAccess() && self._purgeable.length > 0 {
        let result = self._purgeable.copy() as! Data
        self._purgeable.endContentAccess()
        return result
    } else {
        let data = // ... recreate data ...
        self._purgeable = NSPurgeableData(data:data)
        self._purgeable.endContentAccess()
        return data
    }
}
```

(For more about NSCache and NSPurgeableData, see the "Caching and Purgeable Memory" chapter of Apple's *Memory Usage Performance Guidelines*.)

At an even lower level, you can store your data as a file (in some reasonable location such the Caches directory) and read it using the Data initializer init(contentsOf-

URL:options:) with an `options:` argument `.alwaysMapped`. This creates a memory-mapped data object, which has the remarkable feature that it isn't considered to belong to your memory at all; the system has no hesitation in clearing it from RAM, because it is backed through the virtual memory system by the file, and will be read back into memory automatically when you next access it. This is suitable only for large immutable data, because small data runs the risk of fragmenting a virtual memory page.

Background Memory Usage

You will also wish to concern yourself with releasing memory when your app is about to be suspended. If your app has been backgrounded and suspended and the system later discovers it is running short of memory, it will go hunting through the suspended apps, looking for memory hogs that it can kill in order to free up that memory. If the system decides that your suspended app is a memory hog, it isn't politely going to wake your app and send it a memory warning; it's just going to terminate your app in its sleep. The time to be concerned about releasing memory, therefore, is *before* the app is suspended. You'll probably want your view controller to be registered with the shared application to receive `.UIApplicationDidEnterBackground`. The arrival of this notification is an opportunity to release any easily restored memory-hogging objects, such as `myBigData` in the previous example:

```
override func viewDidLoad() {
    super.viewDidLoad()
    NotificationCenter.default.addObserver(self,
        selector: #selector(backgrounding),
        name: .UIApplicationDidEnterBackground,
        object: nil)
}
func backgrounding(_ n:Notification) {
    self.saveAndReleaseMyBigData()
}
```

 A very nice feature of NSCache is that it evicts its objects automatically when your app goes into the background.

Testing Memory Usage

To test low-memory circumstances artificially, run your app in the Simulator and choose Hardware → Simulate Memory Warning. I don't believe this has any actual effect on memory, but a memory warning of sufficient severity is sent to your app, so you can see the results of triggering your low-memory response code, including the app delegate's `applicationDidReceiveMemoryWarning` and your view controller's `didReceiveMemoryWarning`.

Another approach, which works also on a device, is to call an undocumented method. First, define a dummy protocol to make the selector legal:

```
@objc protocol Dummy {
    func _performMemoryWarning()
}
```

Now you can send that selector to the shared application:

```
UIApplication.shared.perform(#selector(Dummy._performMemoryWarning))
```

(Be sure to remove that code when it is no longer needed for testing, as the App Store won't accept it.)

Testing how your app's memory behaves in the background isn't easy. In a WWDC 2011 video, an interesting technique is demonstrated. The app is run under Instruments on a device, using the virtual memory instrument, and is then backgrounded by pressing the Home button, thus revealing how much memory it voluntarily relinquishes at that time. Then a special memory-hogging app is launched on the device: it loads a very large image and displays it in a UIImageView. Even though your app is backgrounded and suspended, the virtual memory instrument continues to track its memory usage, and you can see whether further memory is reclaimed under pressure from the demands of the memory-hogging app in the foreground.

State Restoration

When the user leaves your app and then later returns to it, one of two things might have happened in the meantime:

Your app was suspended
> Your app was suspended in the background, and remained suspended while the user did something else. When the user returns to your app, the system simply unfreezes your app, and there it is, looking just as it did when the user left it.

Your app was terminated
> Your app was suspended in the background, and then, as the user worked with other apps, a moment came where the system decided it needed the resources (such as memory) being held by your suspended app. Therefore, it terminated your app. When the user returns to your app, the app launches from scratch.

The user, however, doesn't know the difference between those two things, so why should the app behave differently some of the time? Ideally, your app, when it comes to the foreground, should *always* appear looking as it did when the user left it, even if in fact it was terminated while suspended in the background. Otherwise, as the WWDC 2013 video on this topic puts it, the user will feel that the app has "lost my place."

That's where *state restoration* comes in. Your app has a state at every moment: some view controller's view is occupying the screen, and views within it are displaying certain values (for example, a certain switch is set to On, or a certain table view is scrolled to a certain position). The idea of state restoration is to save that information when the app goes into the background, and use it to make all those things true again if the app is subsequently launched from scratch.

iOS provides a general solution to the problem of state restoration. This solution is centered around view controllers, which makes sense, since view controllers are the heart of the problem. What is the user's "place" in the app, which we don't want to "lose"? It's the chain of view controllers that got us to where we were when the app was backgrounded, along with the configuration of each one. The goal of state restoration must therefore be to *reconstruct all existing view controllers*, initializing each one into the state it previously had.

Note that *state*, in this sense, is neither user defaults nor data. If something is a preference, store it in UserDefaults. If something is data, keep it in a file (Chapter 22). Don't misuse the state saving and restoration mechanism for such things. The reason for this is not only conceptual; it's also because *saved state can be lost*. (For example, saved state is deleted if the user flicks your app's snapshot out of the app switcher, or if your app crashes.) You don't want to commit anything to the state restoration mechanism if it would be a disaster to have lost it the next time the app launches.

How to Test State Restoration

To test whether your app is saving and restoring state as you expect:

1. Run the app from Xcode as usual, in the Simulator or on a device.
2. At some point, in the Simulator or on the device, click the Home button (Hardware → Home in the Simulator). This causes the app to be suspended in good order, and state is saved.
3. Now, back in Xcode, stop the running project and run it again. If there is saved state, it is restored.

(To test the app's behavior from a truly cold start, delete it from the Simulator or device. You might need to do this, for example, after you've changed something about the underlying save-and-restore model.)

Apple also provides some debugging tools (search for "restorationArchiveTool for iOS" at *https://developer.apple.com/download/more/*):

restorationArchiveTool
 A command-line tool letting you examine a saved state archive in textual format. The archive is in a folder called Saved Application State in your app's sandboxed

Library. See Chapter 22 for more about the app's sandbox, and how to copy it to your computer from a device.

StateRestorationDebugLogging.mobileconfig
A configuration profile. When installed on a device, it causes the console to dump information as state saving and restoration proceeds.

StateRestorationDeveloperMode.mobileconfig
A configuration profile. When installed on a device, it prevents the state archive from being jettisoned after unexpected termination of the app (a crash, or manual termination through the app switcher interface). This can allow you to test state restoration a bit more conveniently.

To install a *.mobileconfig* file on a device, the simplest approach is to email it to yourself on the device and tap the file in the Mail message. You can subsequently delete the file, if desired, through the Settings app.

Participating in State Restoration

Built-in state restoration is an opt-in technology: it operates only if you explicitly tell the system that you want to participate in it. To do so, you do three things:

Implement app delegate methods
The app delegate must implement these methods to return `true`:

- `application(_:shouldSaveApplicationState:)`
- `application(_:shouldRestoreApplicationState:)`

(Naturally, your code can instead return `false` to prevent state from being saved or restored on some particular occasion.)

Implement `application(_:willFinishLaunchingWithOptions:)`
Although it is very early, `application(_:didFinishLaunchingWithOptions:)` is too late for state restoration. Your app needs its basic interface *before* state restoration begins. The solution is to use a different app delegate method, `application(_:willFinishLaunchingWithOptions:)`.

Your implementation *must* call `makeKeyAndVisible` explicitly on the window! Otherwise, the interface doesn't come into existence soon enough for restoration to happen during launch. Apart from that, you can typically just reuse your existing `application(_:didFinishLaunchingWithOptions:)` implementation, by changing `did` to `will` in its name.

Provide restoration IDs
Both UIViewController and UIView have a `restorationIdentifier` property, which is a string. Setting this string to a non-`nil` value is your signal to the

system that you want this view controller (or view) to participate in state restoration. If a view controller's `restorationIdentifier` is `nil`, neither it nor any subsequent view controllers down the chain will be saved or restored. (A nice feature of this architecture is that it lets you participate *partially* in state restoration, omitting some view controllers by not assigning them a restoration identifier.)

You can set the `restorationIdentifier` manually, in code; typically you'll do that early in a view controller's lifetime. If a view controller or view is instantiated from a nib, you'll want to set the restoration identifier in the nib editor; the Identity inspector has a Restoration ID field for this purpose. If you're using a storyboard, it's a good idea, in general, to make a view controller's restoration ID in the storyboard the same as its storyboard ID — such a good idea, in fact, that the storyboard editor provides a checkbox, "Use Storyboard ID," that equates the two values automatically.

(In your `application(_:willFinishLaunchingWithOptions:)` implementation, before calling `makeKeyAndVisible`, it may also be useful to assign the window itself a restoration identifier. This might not make any detectable difference, but in some cases it can help restore size class information.)

In the case of a simple storyboard-based app, where each needed view controller instance can be reconstructed directly from the storyboard, those steps alone can be sufficient to bring state restoration to life, operating correctly at the view controller level. Let's test it! Start with a storyboard-based app with the following architecture (Figure 6-11):

- A navigation controller.
- Its root view controller, connected by a relationship from the navigation controller. Call its class RootViewController.
  - A presented view controller, connected by a modal segue from a Present button in RootViewController's view. Call its class PresentedViewController. Its view contains a Dismiss button.
- A second view controller, connected by a push segue from a Push button in RootViewController's view. Call its class SecondViewController.
  - The very same presented view controller (PresentedViewController), also connected by a modal segue from a Present button in the second view controller's view.

This storyboard-based app runs perfectly with just about no code at all; all we need is an empty implementation of an unwind method in RootViewController and SecondViewController so that we can create an unwind segue from the PresentedViewController's Dismiss button.

Figure 6-11. Architecture of an app for testing state restoration

We will now make this app implement state restoration:

1. In the app delegate, change the name of `application(_:didFinishLaunching-WithOptions:)` to `application(_:willFinishLaunchingWithOptions:)`, and insert this line of code:

   ```
   self.window?.makeKeyAndVisible()
   ```

2. In the app delegate, implement these two methods to return `true`:

- application(_:shouldSaveApplicationState:)
- application(_:shouldRestoreApplicationState:)

3. In the storyboard, give restoration IDs to all four view controller instances: let's call them "nav", "root", "second", and "presented".

The app now saves and restores state! When we run the app, navigate to any view controller, quit, and later relaunch, the app appears in the same view controller it was in when we quit.

Restoration ID, Identifier Path, and Restoration Class

Having everything done for us by the storyboard reveals nothing about what's really happening. To learn more, let's rewrite the example without using the storyboard. Suppose we implement the same architecture using code alone:

```
// AppDelegate.swift:
func application(_ application: UIApplication,
    didFinishLaunchingWithOptions launchOptions:
    [UIApplicationLaunchOptionsKey : Any]?) -> Bool {
        self.window = self.window ?? UIWindow()
        let rvc = RootViewController()
        let nav = UINavigationController(rootViewController:rvc)
        self.window!.rootViewController = nav
        self.window!.backgroundColor = .white
        self.window!.makeKeyAndVisible()
        return true
}

// RootViewController.swift:
override func viewDidLoad() {
    super.viewDidLoad()
    // ... color view background, create buttons ...
}
func doPresent(_ sender: Any?) {
    let pvc = PresentedViewController()
    self.present(pvc, animated:true)
}
func doPush(_ sender: Any?) {
    let svc = SecondViewController()
    self.navigationController!.pushViewController(svc, animated:true)
}

// SecondViewController.swift:
override func viewDidLoad() {
    super.viewDidLoad()
    // ... color view background, create button ...
}
func doPresent(_ sender: Any?) {
    let pvc = PresentedViewController()
```

```
        self.present(pvc, animated:true)
    }

    // PresentedViewController.m:
    override func viewDidLoad() {
        super.viewDidLoad()
        // ... color view background, create button ...
    }
    func doDismiss(_ sender: Any?) {
        self.presentingViewController?.dismiss(animated:true)
    }
```

That's a working app. Now let's start adding state restoration, just as before:

1. In the app delegate, change the name of `application(_:didFinishLaunching-WithOptions:)` to `application(_:willFinishLaunchingWithOptions:)`.

2. In the app delegate, implement these two methods to return `true`:

   • `application(_:shouldSaveApplicationState:)`

   • `application(_:shouldRestoreApplicationState:)`

3. Give all four view controller instances restoration IDs *in code*. Again, let's call them `"nav"`, `"root"`, `"second"`, and `"presented"`. We're creating each view controller instance manually, so we may as well assign its `restorationIdentifier` in the next line, like this:

   ```
   let rvc = RootViewController()
   rvc.restorationIdentifier = "root"
   let nav = UINavigationController(rootViewController:rvc)
   nav.restorationIdentifier = "nav"
   ```

   And so on.

Run the app. Oops! We are *not* getting state restoration. Why not?

The reason is that the `restorationIdentifier` alone is not sufficient to tell the state restoration mechanism what to do as the app launches. The restoration mechanism knows the chain of view controller *classes* that needs to be generated, but it is up to us to generate the *instances* of those classes. Our storyboard-based example didn't exhibit this problem, because the storyboard itself was the source of the instances. To make our code-based example work, we need to know about the *identifier path* and the *restoration class*.

Identifier path

Any particular view controller instance, given its position in the view controller hierarchy, is uniquely identified by the sequence of `restorationIdentifier` values of *all* the view controllers (including itself) in the chain that leads to it. Those `restoration-`

`Identifier` values, taken together in sequence, constitute the *identifier path* for any given view controller instance. A view controller's identifier path is like a trail of breadcrumbs that you left behind as you created it while the app was running, and that will now be used to identify it again as the app launches.

There's nothing mysterious about an identifier path; it's just an array of strings. For example, if we launch the app and press the Push button and then the Present button, then all four view controllers have been instantiated; those instances are identified as:

- The navigation controller: `["nav"]`
- The RootViewController: `["nav", "root"]`
- The SecondViewController: `["nav", "second"]`
- The PresentedViewController: `["nav", "presented"]` (because the navigation controller is the actual presenting view controller)

Observe that a view controller's identifier path is not a record of the full story of how we got here. It's just an identifier! The state-saving mechanism uses those identifiers to save a relational tree, which *does* tell the full story. For example, if the app is suspended in the current situation, then the state-saving mechanism will record the true state of affairs, namely that the root view controller (`["nav"]`) has two children (`["nav", "root"]` and `["nav", "second"]`) and a presented view controller (`["nav", "presented"]`).

Now consider what the state restoration mechanism needs to do when the app has been suspended and killed, and comes back to life, from the situation I just described. We need to restore four view controllers; we know their identifiers and mutual relationships. State restoration doesn't start until *after* `application(_:willFinish-LaunchingWithOptions:)`. So when the state restoration mechanism starts examining the situation, it discovers that the `["nav"]` and `["nav", "root"]` view controller instances have already been created! However, the view controller instances for `["nav", "second"]` and `["nav", "presented"]` must also be created now. The state restoration mechanism doesn't know how to do that — so it's going to ask your code for the instances.

Restoration class

The state restoration mechanism needs to ask your code for the view controller instances that haven't been created already. But *what* code should it ask? There are two ways to specify this. One way is for you to provide a *restoration class* for each view controller instance that is *not* restored by the time `application(_:willFinish-LaunchingWithOptions:)` returns. Here's how you do that:

1. Give the view controller a `restorationClass`. Typically, this will be the view controller's own class, or the class of the view controller responsible for creating this view controller instance. You will need to specify formally that a class to be designated as a `restorationClass` adopts the UIViewControllerRestoration protocol.

2. Implement the class method `viewController(withRestorationIdentifier-Path:coder:)` on the class named by each view controller's `restorationClass` property, returning a view controller instance as specified by the identifier path. Very often, the implementation will be to instantiate the view controller directly and return that instance.

Let's make our PresentedViewController and SecondViewController instances restorable. I'll start with PresentedViewController. Our app can have *two* PresentedViewController instances (though not simultaneously) — the one created by RootViewController, and the one created by SecondViewController. Let's start with the one created by RootViewController.

Since RootViewController creates and configures a PresentedViewController instance, it can reasonably act also as the restoration class for that instance. In its implementation of `viewController(withRestorationIdentifierPath:coder:)`, RootViewController should then create and configure a PresentedViewController instance *exactly* as it was doing before we added state restoration to our app — except for putting it into the view controller hierarchy! The state restoration mechanism itself, remember, is responsible for assembling the view controller hierarchy; our job is merely to supply any needed view controller instances.

So RootViewController now must adopt UIViewControllerRestoration, and will contain this code:

```
func doPresent(_ sender: Any?) {
    let pvc = PresentedViewController()
    pvc.restorationIdentifier = "presented"
    pvc.restorationClass = type(of:self) // *
    self.present(pvc, animated:true)
}
class func viewController(withRestorationIdentifierPath ip: [Any],
    coder: NSCoder) -> UIViewController? {
        var vc : UIViewController? = nil
        let last = ip.last as! String
        switch last {
        case "presented":
            let pvc = PresentedViewController()
            pvc.restorationIdentifier = "presented"
            pvc.restorationClass = self
            vc = pvc
```

```
        default: break
        }
        return vc
    }
```

You can see what I mean when I say that the restoration class must do exactly what it was doing before state restoration was added. Clearly this situation has led to some annoying code duplication, so let's factor out the common code. In doing so, we must bear in mind that doPresent is an instance method, whereas viewController(with-RestorationIdentifierPath:coder:) is a class method; our factored-out code must therefore be a class method, so that they can both call it:

```
class func makePresentedViewController () -> UIViewController {
    let pvc = PresentedViewController()
    pvc.restorationIdentifier = "presented"
    pvc.restorationClass = self
    return pvc
}
func doPresent(_ sender: Any?) {
    let pvc = type(of:self).makePresentedViewController()
    self.present(pvc, animated:true)
}
class func viewController (withRestorationIdentifierPath ip: [Any],
    coder: NSCoder) -> UIViewController? {
        var vc : UIViewController? = nil
        let last = ip.last as! String
        switch last {
        case "presented":
            vc = self.makePresentedViewController()
        default: break
        }
        return vc
    }
```

The structure of our viewController(withRestorationIdentifierPath:coder:) is typical. We test the identifier path — usually, it's sufficient to examine its last element — and return the corresponding view controller; ultimately, we are also prepared to return nil, in case we are called with an identifier path we can't interpret. We can also return nil deliberately, to tell the restoration mechanism, "Go no further; don't restore the view controller you're asking for here, or any view controller further down the same path."

Continuing in the same vein, we expand RootViewController still further to make it also the restoration class for SecondViewController, and SecondViewController can make itself the restoration class for the PresentedViewController instance that it creates. There's no conflict in the notion that both RootViewController and Second-ViewController can fulfill the role of PresentedViewController restoration class, as we're talking about two different PresentedViewController instances. (The details are left as an exercise for the reader.)

The app now performs state saving and restoration correctly!

App delegate instead of restoration class

I said earlier that the state restoration mechanism can ask your code for needed instances in two ways. The second way is that you implement this method in your app delegate:

- `application(_:viewControllerWithRestorationIdentifierPath:coder:)`

If you implement that method, it will be called for *every* view controller that doesn't have a restoration class. Your job is to create the requested view controller based on its path and return it, or return `nil` to prevent restoration of that view controller. Be prepared to receive identifier paths for an existing view controller! If that happens, *don't* make a new one and *don't* return `nil` — *return the existing view controller.*

 The same method works in a storyboard-based app as well, and thus gives you a chance to intervene and prevent the restoration of a particular view controller on a particular occasion by returning `nil`.

Restoring View Controller State

I have explained how the state restoration mechanism creates a view controller and places it into the view controller hierarchy. But at that point, the work of restoration is only half done. What about the *state* of that view controller?

A newly restored view controller probably won't have the data and property values it was holding at the time the app was terminated. The history of the configuration of this view controller throughout the time the app was previously running is *not* magically recapitulated during restoration. It is up to each view controller to *restore its own state* when it itself is restored. And in order to do that, it must previously *save its own state* when the app is backgrounded.

The state saving and restoration mechanism provides a way of helping your view controllers do this, through the use of a *coder* (an NSCoder object). Think of the coder as a box in which the view controller is invited to place its valuables for safekeeping, and from which it can retrieve them later. Each of these valuables needs to be identified, so it is tagged with a key (an arbitrary string) when it is placed into the box, and is then later retrieved by using the same key, much as in a dictionary.

Anyone who has anything to save at the time it is handed a coder can do so by calling `encode(_:forKey:)`, provided the object to be encoded conforms to NSCoding. (I'll talk in Chapter 22 about how to encode other sorts of object.) Views and view controllers can be safely encoded, because they are treated as references. Whatever was saved in the coder can later be extracted using the same key. You can call `decode-`

`Object(forKey:)` and cast down as needed, or you can call a specialized method corresponding to the expected type, such as `decodeFloat(forKey:)`.

The keys do not have to be unique across the entire app; they only need to be unique for a particular view controller. Each object that is handed a coder is handed *its own personal coder*. It is handed this coder at state saving time, and it is handed the same coder (that is, a coder with the same archived objects and keys) at state restoration time.

Here's the sequence of events involving coders:

Saving state

When it's time to *save* state (as the app is about to be backgrounded), the state saving mechanism provides coders as follows:

1. The app delegate is sent `application(_:shouldSaveApplicationState:)`. The coder is the second parameter.

2. The app delegate is sent `application(_:willEncodeRestorableState-With:)`. The coder is the second parameter, and is the same coder as in the previous step.

3. Each view controller down the chain, starting at the root view controller, is sent `encodeRestorableState(with:)`. The coder is the parameter. The implementation should call `super`. Each view controller gets its own coder.

Restoring state

When it's time to *restore* state (as the app is launched), the state restoration mechanism provides coders as follows:

1. The app delegate is sent `application(_:shouldRestoreApplication-State:)`. The coder is the second parameter.

2. As each view controller down the chain is to be created, one of these methods is called (as I've already explained); the coder is the one appropriate to the view controller that's to be created:

   • The restoration class's `viewController(withRestorationIdentifier-Path:coder:)`, if the view controller has a restoration class.

   • Otherwise, the app delegate's `application(_:viewControllerWith-RestorationIdentifierPath:coder:)`.

3. Each view controller down the chain, starting at the root view controller, is sent `decodeRestorableState(with:)`. The coder appropriate to that view controller is the parameter. The implementation should call `super`.

4. The app delegate is sent `application(_:didDecodeRestorableStateWith:)`. The coder is the second parameter, and is the same one as in the first step.

The *UIStateRestoration.h* header file describes five built-in keys that are available from every coder during restoration:

`UIStateRestorationViewControllerStoryboardKey`
A reference to the storyboard from which this view controller came, if any.

`UIApplicationStateRestorationBundleVersionKey`
Your *Info.plist* `CFBundleVersion` string at the time of state saving.

`UIApplicationStateRestorationUserInterfaceIdiomKey`
An NSNumber wrapping a UIUserInterfaceIdiom value, either `.phone` or `.pad`, telling what kind of device we were running on when state saving happened. You can extract this information as follows:

```
let key = UIApplicationStateRestorationUserInterfaceIdiomKey
if let idiomraw = coder.decodeObject(forKey: key) as? Int {
    if let idiom = UIUserInterfaceIdiom(rawValue:idiomraw) {
        if idiom == .phone {
            // ...
        }
    }
}
```

`UIApplicationStateRestorationTimestampKey`
A Date telling when state saving happened.

`UIApplicationStateRestorationSystemVersionKey`
A string telling the system version under which state saving happened.

One purpose of these keys is to allow your app to opt out of state restoration, wholly or in part, because the archive is too old, was saved on the wrong kind of device (and presumably migrated to this one by backup and restore), and so forth.

A typical implementation of `encodeRestorableState(with:)` and `decode-RestorableState(with:)` will concern itself with properties and interface views. `decodeRestorableState(with:)` is guaranteed to be called *after* `viewDidLoad`, so you know that `viewDidLoad` won't overwrite any direct changes to the interface performed in `decodeRestorableState(with:)`.

To illustrate, I'll add state saving and restoration to my earlier UIPageViewController example, the one that displays a Pep Boy on each page. Recall how that example is architected. The project has no storyboard. The code defines just two classes, the app delegate and the Pep view controller. The app delegate creates a UIPageView-Controller and makes it the window's root view controller, and makes itself the page view controller's data source; its `self.pep` instance property holds the data model, which is just an array of string Pep Boy names. The page view controller's data source methods, `pageViewController(_:viewControllerAfter:)` and `pageView-Controller(_:viewControllerBefore:)`, create and supply an appropriate Pep instance whenever an adjacent page is needed for the page view controller, based on the index of the current Pep page's boy property in `self.pep`.

The challenge is to restore the Pep object displayed in the page view controller as the app launches. One solution involves recognizing that a Pep object is completely configured once created, and it is created just by handing it the name of a Pep Boy in its designated initializer, which becomes its boy property. Thus we can mediate between a Pep object and a mere string, and all we really need to save and restore is that string.

All the additional work, therefore, can be performed in the app delegate. We save and restore the current Pep Boy name in the app delegate's encode and decode methods:

```
func application(_ application: UIApplication,
    willEncodeRestorableStateWith coder: NSCoder) {
        let pvc = self.window!.rootViewController as! UIPageViewController
        let boy = (pvc.viewControllers![0] as! Pep).boy
        coder.encode(boy, forKey:"boy")
}
func application(_ application: UIApplication,
    didDecodeRestorableStateWith coder: NSCoder) {
        let boyMaybe = coder.decodeObject(forKey:"boy")
        guard let boy = boyMaybe as? String else {return}
        let pvc = self.window!.rootViewController as! UIPageViewController
        let pep = Pep(pepBoy: boy)
        pvc.setViewControllers([pep], direction: .forward, animated: false)
}
```

A second, more general solution is to make our Pep view controller class itself capable of saving and restoration. This means that every view controller down the chain from the root view controller to our Pep view controller must have a restoration identifier. In our simple app, there's just one such view controller, the UIPageView-Controller; the app delegate can assign it a restoration ID when it creates it:

```
let pvc = UIPageViewController(
    transitionStyle: .scroll, navigationOrientation: .horizontal)
pvc.restorationIdentifier = "pvc" // *
```

We'll have a Pep object assign itself a restoration ID in its own designated initializer. The Pep object will also need a restoration class; as I said earlier, this can perfectly well be the Pep class itself, and that seems most appropriate here:

```
    required init(pepBoy boy:String) { // *
        self.boy = boy
        super.init(nibName: nil, bundle: nil)
        self.restorationIdentifier = "pep" // *
        self.restorationClass = type(of:self) // *
    }
```

The only state that a Pep object needs to save is its boy string, so we implement
encodeRestorableState to do that. We don't need to implement decodeRestorable-
State, because the coder that will come back to us in viewController(with-
RestorationIdentifierPath:coder:) contains the boy string, and once we use it to
create the Pep instance, the Pep instance is completely configured. This is a class
method, and it can't call an initializer on self unless that initializer is marked as
required; we *did* mark it required (in the previous code):

```
    override func encodeRestorableState(with coder: NSCoder) {
        super.encodeRestorableState(with:coder)
        coder.encode(self.boy, forKey:"boy")
    }
    class func viewController(withRestorationIdentifierPath ip: [Any],
        coder: NSCoder) -> UIViewController? {
            let boy = coder.decodeObject(forKey:"boy") as! String
            return self.init(pepBoy: boy)
    }
```

Now comes a surprise. We run the app and test it, and we find that we're *not* getting
saving and restoration of our Pep object. It isn't being archived; its encodeRestorable-
State(with:) isn't even being called! The reason is that the state saving mechanism
doesn't work automatically for a UIPageViewController and its children (or for a custom container view controller and *its* children, for that matter). It is up to us to see to
it that the current Pep object is archived.

To do so, we can archive and unarchive the current Pep object in an implementation
of encodeRestorableState(with:) and decodeRestorableState(with:) that *is*
being called. For our app, that would have to be in the app delegate. The code we've
written so far has all been necessary to make the current Pep object archivable and
restorable; now the app delegate will make sure that it *is* archived and restored:

```
    func application(_ application: UIApplication,
        willEncodeRestorableStateWith coder: NSCoder) {
            let pvc = self.window!.rootViewController as! UIPageViewController
            let pep = pvc.viewControllers![0] as! Pep
            coder.encode(pep, forKey:"pep")
    }
    func application(_ application: UIApplication,
        didDecodeRestorableStateWith coder: NSCoder) {
            let pepMaybe = coder.decodeObject(forKey:"pep")
```

```
            guard let pep = pepMaybe as? Pep else {return}
            let pvc = self.window!.rootViewController as! UIPageViewController
            pvc.setViewControllers([pep], direction: .forward, animated: false)
    }
```

This solution may seem rather heavyweight, but it isn't. We're not really archiving an entire Pep instance; it's just a reference. The Pep instance that arrives in `application(_:didDecodeRestorableStateWith:)` was never in the archive; it's just a pointer to the instance created by Pep's implementation of `viewController(withRestorationIdentifierPath:coder:)`.

Restoration Order of Operations

When you implement state saving and restoration for a view controller, the view controller ends up with two different ways of being configured. One way involves the view controller lifetime events I discussed earlier ("View Controller Lifetime Events" on page 394). The other involves the state restoration events I've been discussing here. You want your view controller to be correctly configured regardless of whether this view controller is undergoing state restoration or not.

To help you with this, there's another view controller event I haven't mentioned yet: `applicationFinishedRestoringState`. If you implement this method in a view controller subclass, it will be called if and only if we're doing state restoration, at a time when *all* view controllers have already been sent `decodeRestorableState(with:)`.

Thus, the known order of events during state restoration is like this:

1. `application(_:shouldRestoreApplicationState:)`

2. `application(_:viewControllerWithRestorationIdentifierPath:coder:)`

3. `viewController(withRestorationIdentifierPath:coder:)`, in order down the chain

4. `viewDidLoad`, in order down the chain, possibly interleaved with the foregoing

5. `decodeRestorableState(with:)`, in order down the chain

6. `application(_:didDecodeRestorableStateWith:)`

7. `applicationFinishedRestoringState`, in order down the chain

Observe that I've said nothing about when `viewWillAppear(_:)` and `viewDidAppear(_:)` will arrive. You can't be sure about this, or even whether `viewDidAppear(_:)` will arrive at all. That's another of those view controller lifetime event incoherencies I complained about earlier. But in `applicationFinishedRestoringState` you can reliably finish configuring your view controller and your interface.

A typical situation is that you will want to update your interface after all properties have been set. So you'll factor out your interface-updating code into a single method. Now there are two possibilities, and they are both handled coherently:

We're not restoring state

Properties will be set through initialization and configuration, and then you'll call your interface-updating method. All this could happen as soon as the end of viewDidLoad.

We are restoring state

Properties will be set by decodeRestorableState(with:), and then application-FinishedRestoringState calls your interface-updating method.

There is still some indeterminacy as to what's going to happen, but the interface-updating method can mediate that indeterminacy by checking for two things that can go wrong:

It is called too soon

The interface-updating method should check to see that the properties have in fact been set; if not, it should just return. It will be called again when the properties *have* been set.

It is called unnecessarily

The interface-updating method might run twice in quick succession with the same set of properties. This is not a disaster, but if you don't like it, you can prevent it by comparing the properties to the interface and return if the interface has already been configured with these properties.

In this simple example, our view controller has a boy property, and its interface configuration consists of displaying the corresponding Pep boy's image in an image view. So we factor out the construction of the initial interface into a method, finishInterface, which starts by checking whether boy has been set:

```
var boy : String?
func finishInterface() {
    if let boy = self.boy {
        let im = UIImageView(image: UIImage(named:boy.lowercased()))
        self.view.addSubview(im)
        // ...
    }
}
```

If we are launched without state restoration, boy is set by whoever creates this view controller, *before* viewDidLoad. Thus, when we call finishInterface from viewDidLoad, self.boy has been set and the image view is created:

```
override func viewDidLoad() {
    super.viewDidLoad()
    self.finishInterface()
}
```

But if we are launched with state restoration, boy is not set when viewDidLoad runs, and the call to finishInterface does nothing, because self.boy is nil. Now restoration continues:

```
override func decodeRestorableState(with coder: NSCoder) {
    if let boy = coder.decodeObject(forKey: "boy") as? String {
        self.boy = boy
    }
}
override func encodeRestorableState(with coder: NSCoder) {
    coder.encode(self.boy, forKey: "boy")
}
override func applicationFinishedRestoringState() {
    self.finishInterface()
}
```

Our applicationFinishedRestoringState implementation calls finishInterface *again*. But this time, decodeRestorableState has been called, and self.boy has been set — so now finishInterface finishes the interface by creating the image view. In this way, the image view is added to the interface just once, no matter what.

If your app has additional state restoration work to do on a background thread (Chapter 24), the documentation says you should call UIApplication's extendStateRestoration as you begin and completeStateRestoration when you've finished. The idea is that if you *don't* call completeStateRestoration, the system can assume that something has gone wrong and will throw away the saved state information in case it is faulty.

Restoration of Other Objects

A view will participate in automatic saving and restoration of state if its view controller does, and if it itself has a restoration identifier. Some built-in UIView subclasses have built-in restoration abilities. For example, a scroll view that participates in state saving and restoration will automatically return to the point to which it was scrolled previously. You should consult the documentation on each UIView subclass to see whether it participates usefully in state saving and restoration, and I'll mention a few significant cases when we come to discuss those views in later chapters.

In addition, an arbitrary object can be made to participate in automatic saving and restoration of state. There are three requirements for such an object:

- The object's class must be an NSObject subclass adopting the UIStateRestoring protocol. This protocol declares three optional methods:

- encodeRestorableState(with:)

- decodeRestorableState(with:)

- applicationFinishedRestoringState

- When the object is created, someone must register it with the runtime by calling this UIApplication class method:

  - registerObject(forStateRestoration:restorationIdentifier:)

- Someone who participates in state saving and restoration, such as a view controller, must make the archive aware of this object by storing a reference to it in the archive (typically in encodeRestorableState(with:)) — much as we did with the Pep object earlier.

So, for example, here's an NSObject subclass Thing with a word property, that participates in state saving and restoration:

```
class Thing : NSObject, UIStateRestoring {
    var word = ""
    func encodeRestorableState(with coder: NSCoder) {
        coder.encode(self.word, forKey:"word")
    }
    func decodeRestorableState(with coder: NSCoder) {
        self.word = coder.decodeObject(forKey:"word") as! String
    }
    func applicationFinishedRestoringState() {
        // not used
    }
}
```

And here's a view controller with an Optional Thing property (self.thing):

```
class func makeThing () -> Thing {
    let thing = Thing()
    UIApplication.registerObject(
        forStateRestoration: thing, restorationIdentifier: "thing")
    return thing
}
override func awakeFromNib() {
    super.awakeFromNib()
    self.thing = type(of:self).makeThing()
}
override func encodeRestorableState(with coder: NSCoder) {
    super.encodeRestorableState(with:coder)
    coder.encode(self.thing, forKey: "mything") // *
}
```

The starred line is crucial; it introduces our Thing object to the archive and brings its UIStateRestoring methods to life. The result is that if we background the app while an instance of this view controller exists, and if state restoration is performed on the next launch, the view controller's Thing has the same word that it had before; the Thing has participated in state saving and restoration along with the view controller that owns it.

There is an optional `objectRestorationClass` property of the restorable object, and an `object(withRestorationIdentifierPath:coder:)` class method that the designated class must implement. The class in question should formally adopt UIObjectRestoration. Its `object(withRestorationIdentifierPath:coder:)` should return the restorable object, by creating it or pointing to it; alternatively, it can return `nil` to prevent restoration. If you want to assign an `objectRestorationClass`, you'll have to declare the property:

```
var objectRestorationClass: UIObjectRestoration.Type?
```

However, our Thing object was restorable even without an `objectRestorationClass`; presumably, just calling `registerObject` sufficiently identifies this object to the runtime.

Another optional property of the restorable object is `restorationParent`. Again, if you want to assign to it, you'll have to declare it:

```
var restorationParent: UIStateRestoring?
```

The purpose of the restoration parent is to give the restorable object an identifier path. For example, if we have a chain of view controllers with a path `["nav", "second"]`, then if that last view controller is the `restorationParent` of our Thing object, the Thing object's identifier path in `object(withRestorationIdentifierPath:coder:)` will be `["nav", "second", "thing"]`, rather than simply `["thing"]`. This is useful if we are worried that `["thing"]` alone will not uniquely identify this object.

CHAPTER 7

Scroll Views

A scroll view (UIScrollView) is a view whose content is larger than its bounds. To reveal a desired area, the *user* can scroll the content by dragging, or *you* can reposition the content in code.

A scroll view isn't magic; it takes advantage of ordinary UIView features (Chapter 1). The content is simply the scroll view's subviews. When the scroll view scrolls, what's really changing is the scroll view's own bounds origin; the subviews are positioned with respect to the bounds origin, so they move with it. The scroll view's clipsTo-Bounds is usually true, so any content positioned within the scroll view is visible and any content positioned outside it is not. A scroll view thus functions as a limited window on a larger world of content.

A scroll view has the following specialized abilities:

- It knows how to shift its bounds origin in response to the user's gestures.
- It provides scroll indicators whose size and position give the user a clue as to the content's size and position.
- It can enforce paging, whereby the user can scroll only by a fixed amount.
- It supports zooming, so that the user can resize the content with a pinch gesture.
- It provides a plethora of delegate methods, so that your code knows exactly how the user is scrolling and zooming.

Content Size

How *far* should a scroll view scroll? Clearly, that depends on how much content it has.

The scroll view already knows how far it should be allowed to slide its subviews downward and rightward — in general, the limit is reached when the scroll view's bounds origin is CGPoint.zero. What the scroll view *needs* to know is how far it should be allowed to slide its subviews upward and leftward. That is the scroll view's *content size* — its contentSize property.

The scroll view uses its contentSize, in combination with its own bounds size, to set the limits on how large its bounds origin can become. It may be helpful to think of the scroll view's scrollable content as the rectangle defined by CGRect(origin:.zero, size:contentSize); this is the rectangle that the user can inspect by scrolling.

If a dimension of the contentSize isn't larger than the same dimension of the scroll view's own bounds, the content won't be scrollable in that dimension: there is nothing to scroll, as the entire scrollable content is already showing. The default is that the contentSize is .zero — meaning that the scroll view *isn't scrollable*. To get a working scroll view, therefore, it will be crucial to set its contentSize correctly. You can do this directly, in code; or, if you're using autolayout (Chapter 1), the contentSize can be calculated for you based on the constraints of the scroll view's subviews. I'll demonstrate both approaches.

Creating a Scroll View in Code

I'll start by creating a scroll view, providing it with subviews, and making those subviews viewable by scrolling, entirely in code.

Manual Content Size

In the first instance, let's not use autolayout. Our project is based on the Single View app template, with a single view controller class, ViewController. In ViewController's viewDidLoad, I'll create the scroll view to fill the main view, and populate it with a vertical column of 30 UILabels whose text contains a sequential number so that we can see where we are when we scroll:

```
let sv = UIScrollView(frame: self.view.bounds)
sv.autoresizingMask = [.flexibleWidth, .flexibleHeight]
self.view.addSubview(sv)
sv.backgroundColor = .white
var y : CGFloat = 10
for i in 0 ..< 30 {
    let lab = UILabel()
    lab.text = "This is label \(i+1)"
    lab.sizeToFit()
    lab.frame.origin = CGPoint(10,y)
    sv.addSubview(lab)
    y += lab.bounds.size.height + 10
```

```
    }
var sz = sv.bounds.size
sz.height = y
sv.contentSize = sz // *
```

The crucial move is the last line, where we tell the scroll view how large its content is to be. If we omit this step, the scroll view won't be scrollable; the window will appear to consist of a static column of labels.

There is no rule about the order in which you perform the two operations of setting the contentSize and populating the scroll view with subviews. In that example, we set the contentSize afterward because it is more convenient to track the heights of the subviews as we add them than to calculate their total height in advance. You can alter a scroll view's content (subviews) or contentSize, or both, dynamically as the app runs.

The contentSize does not change just because the scroll view's bounds change; if you want the contentSize to change in response to rotation, you will need to change it manually, in code. Conversely, resizing the contentSize has no effect on the size of the scroll view's subviews; it merely determines the scrolling limit.

Automatic Content Size with Autolayout

With autolayout, things are different. Under autolayout, a scroll view interprets the constraints of its immediate subviews in a special way. Constraints between a scroll view and its direct subviews are *not* a way of positioning the subviews relative to the scroll view (as they would be if the superview were an ordinary UIView). Rather, they are a way of describing the scroll view's contentSize *from the inside out*.

To see this, let's rewrite the preceding example to use autolayout. The scroll view and its subviews have their translatesAutoresizingMaskIntoConstraints set to false, and we're giving them explicit constraints:

```
let sv = UIScrollView()
sv.backgroundColor = .white
sv.translatesAutoresizingMaskIntoConstraints = false
self.view.addSubview(sv)
NSLayoutConstraint.activate([
    sv.topAnchor.constraint(equalTo:self.view.topAnchor),
    sv.bottomAnchor.constraint(equalTo:self.view.bottomAnchor),
    sv.leadingAnchor.constraint(equalTo:self.view.leadingAnchor),
    sv.trailingAnchor.constraint(equalTo:self.view.trailingAnchor),
])
var previousLab : UILabel? = nil
for i in 0 ..< 30 {
    let lab = UILabel()
    // lab.backgroundColor = .red
    lab.translatesAutoresizingMaskIntoConstraints = false
    lab.text = "This is label \(i+1)"
```

```
        sv.addSubview(lab)
        lab.leadingAnchor.constraint(
            equalTo: sv.leadingAnchor, constant: 10).isActive = true
        lab.topAnchor.constraint(
            // first one, pin to top; all others, pin to previous
            equalTo: previousLab?.bottomAnchor ?? sv.topAnchor,
            constant: 10).isActive = true
        previousLab = lab
    }
```

The labels are correctly positioned relative to one another, but the scroll view isn't scrollable. Moreover, setting the `contentSize` manually doesn't help; it has no effect!

Why is that? It's because we're using autolayout, so we must generate the `contentSize` by means of constraints between the scroll view and its immediate subviews. We've almost done that, but not quite. We are *missing a constraint*. We have to add one more constraint, showing the scroll view what the height of its `contentSize` should be:

```
sv.bottomAnchor.constraint(
    equalTo: previousLab!.bottomAnchor, constant: 10).isActive = true
```

The constraints of the scroll view's subviews now describe the `contentSize` height: the top label is pinned to the top of the scroll view, the next one is pinned to the one above it, and so on — *and the bottom one is pinned to the bottom of the scroll view*. Consequently, the runtime calculates the `contentSize` height from the inside out, as it were, as the sum of all the vertical constraints (including the intrinsic heights of the labels), and the scroll view is vertically scrollable to show all the labels.

We should also provide a `contentSize` width; here, I'll add a trailing constraint from the bottom label, which will surely be narrower than the scroll view, so we won't actually scroll horizontally:

```
previousLab!.trailingAnchor.constraint(
    equalTo:sv.trailingAnchor).isActive = true
```

Scroll View Layout Guides

New in iOS 11, there's another way to do everything we did in the previous example. A UIScrollView in iOS 11 has a `contentLayoutGuide` that we can pin its immediate subviews to, instead of pinning them to the scroll view itself, in order to determine the `contentSize` from the inside out. I'll rewrite the entire previous example to use the `contentLayoutGuide`:

```
let sv = UIScrollView()
sv.backgroundColor = .white
sv.translatesAutoresizingMaskIntoConstraints = false
self.view.addSubview(sv)
NSLayoutConstraint.activate([
    sv.topAnchor.constraint(equalTo:self.view.topAnchor),
    sv.bottomAnchor.constraint(equalTo:self.view.bottomAnchor),
```

```
        sv.leadingAnchor.constraint(equalTo:self.view.leadingAnchor),
        sv.trailingAnchor.constraint(equalTo:self.view.trailingAnchor),
    ])
    let svclg = sv.contentLayoutGuide
    var previousLab : UILabel? = nil
    for i in 0 ..< 30 {
        let lab = UILabel()
        // lab.backgroundColor = .red
        lab.translatesAutoresizingMaskIntoConstraints = false
        lab.text = "This is label \(i+1)"
        sv.addSubview(lab)
        lab.leadingAnchor.constraint(
            equalTo: svclg.leadingAnchor,
            constant: 10).isActive = true
        lab.topAnchor.constraint(
            // first one, pin to top; all others, pin to previous
            equalTo: previousLab?.bottomAnchor ?? svclg.topAnchor,
            constant: 10).isActive = true
        previousLab = lab
    }
    svclg.bottomAnchor.constraint(
        equalTo: previousLab!.bottomAnchor, constant: 10).isActive = true
    svclg.widthAnchor.constraint(equalToConstant:0).isActive = true // *
```

The last line of that example demonstrates one advantage of using the content layout guide: we can set its height or width constraint *directly* to determine that dimension of the content size. Thus, I'm able to set the content size width directly to zero, which states precisely what I mean: don't scroll horizontally.

Also new in iOS 11 is a second UIScrollView property, its frameLayoutGuide, which is pinned to the scroll view's frame. This gives us another way to state that the scroll view should not scroll horizontally, by making the content layout guide width the same as the frame layout guide width:

```
    let svflg = sv.frameLayoutGuide
    svclg.widthAnchor.constraint(equalTo:svflg.widthAnchor).isActive = true
```

Using a Content View

A commonly used arrangement is to give a scroll view just *one* immediate subview; all other views inside the scroll view are subviews of this single immediate subview of the scroll view, which is often called the *content view*. The content view is usually a generic UIView; the user won't even know it's there. It has no purpose other than to contain the other subviews — and to help determine the scroll view's content size.

If we're using a content view, then, under autolayout, we have two choices for setting the scroll view's contentSize:

• Set the content view's translatesAutoresizingMaskIntoConstraints to true, and set the scroll view's contentSize manually to the size of the content view.

- Set the content view's `translatesAutoresizingMaskIntoConstraints` to `false`, set its size with constraints, and pin its edges with constraints to the scroll view (or, under iOS 11, to the scroll view's content layout guide). Usually, all four of those edge constraints will have a `constant` of `0`, thus making the scroll view's `contentSize` the same as the size of the content view.

A convenient consequence of this arrangement is that it works independently of whether the content view's own subviews are positioned explicitly by their frames or using constraints. There are thus four possible combinations:

No constraints
> The content view is sized by its frame, its contents are positioned by their frames, and the scroll view's `contentSize` is set explicitly.

Content view constraints
> The content view is sized by *its own height and width constraints*, and its edges are pinned to the scroll view (or its content layout guide) to set the scroll view's content size.

Content view and content constraints
> The content view is sized from the inside out *by the constraints of its subviews*, and its edges are pinned to the scroll view (or its content layout guide) to set the scroll view's content size.

Content constraints only
> The content view is sized by its frame, and the scroll view's `contentSize` is set explicitly; but the content view's subviews are positioned using constraints.

I'll illustrate by rewriting the previous example to use a content view in each of those ways. All four possible combinations start the same way:

```
let sv = UIScrollView()
sv.backgroundColor = .white
sv.translatesAutoresizingMaskIntoConstraints = false
self.view.addSubview(sv)
NSLayoutConstraint.activate([
    sv.topAnchor.constraint(equalTo:self.view.topAnchor),
    sv.bottomAnchor.constraint(equalTo:self.view.bottomAnchor),
    sv.leadingAnchor.constraint(equalTo:self.view.leadingAnchor),
    sv.trailingAnchor.constraint(equalTo:self.view.trailingAnchor),
])
let v = UIView() // content view
sv.addSubview(v)
```

The differences lie in what happens next. The first combination is that no constraints are used, and the scroll view's content size is set explicitly. It's very like the first example in the chapter, except that the labels are added to the content view, not to the scroll view. The content view's height is a little taller than the bottom of the lowest label; its width is a little wider than the widest label. Thus, it neatly contains all the labels:

```
var y : CGFloat = 10
var maxw : CGFloat = 0
for i in 0 ..< 30 {
    let lab = UILabel()
    lab.text = "This is label \(i+1)"
    lab.sizeToFit()
    lab.frame.origin = CGPoint(10,y)
    v.addSubview(lab)
    y += lab.bounds.size.height + 10
    maxw = max(maxw, lab.frame.maxX + 10)
}
// set content view frame and content size explicitly
v.frame = CGRect(0,0,maxw,y)
sv.contentSize = v.frame.size
```

The second combination is that the content view is sized by width and height constraints and its edges are pinned by constraints to the scroll view's content layout guide to give the scroll view a content size. It's just like the preceding code, except that we set the content view's constraints rather than the scroll view's content size:

```
var y : CGFloat = 10
var maxw : CGFloat = 0
for i in 0 ..< 30 {
    let lab = UILabel()
    lab.text = "This is label \(i+1)"
    lab.sizeToFit()
    lab.frame.origin = CGPoint(10,y)
    v.addSubview(lab)
    y += lab.bounds.size.height + 10
    maxw = max(maxw, lab.frame.maxX + 10)
}
// set content view width, height, and edge constraints
// content size is calculated for us
v.translatesAutoresizingMaskIntoConstraints = false
let svclg = sv.contentLayoutGuide
NSLayoutConstraint.activate([
    v.widthAnchor.constraint(equalToConstant:maxw),
    v.heightAnchor.constraint(equalToConstant:y),
    svclg.topAnchor.constraint(equalTo:v.topAnchor),
    svclg.bottomAnchor.constraint(equalTo:v.bottomAnchor),
    svclg.leadingAnchor.constraint(equalTo:v.leadingAnchor),
    svclg.trailingAnchor.constraint(equalTo:v.trailingAnchor),
])
```

The third combination is that explicit constraints are used throughout. The labels are positioned within the content view by constraints; the content view's edges are pinned by constraints to the scroll view. In a very real sense, the scroll view gets its content size *from the labels*. This is similar to the second example in the chapter, except that the labels are added to the content view:

```swift
var previousLab : UILabel? = nil
for i in 0 ..< 30 {
    let lab = UILabel()
    // lab.backgroundColor = .red
    lab.translatesAutoresizingMaskIntoConstraints = false
    lab.text = "This is label \(i+1)"
    v.addSubview(lab)
    lab.leadingAnchor.constraint(
        equalTo: v.leadingAnchor,
        constant: 10).isActive = true
    lab.topAnchor.constraint(
        // first one, pin to top; all others, pin to previous
        equalTo: previousLab?.bottomAnchor ?? v.topAnchor,
        constant: 10).isActive = true
    previousLab = lab
}
// last one, pin to bottom, this dictates content size height
v.bottomAnchor.constraint(
    equalTo: previousLab!.bottomAnchor, constant: 10).isActive = true
// need to do something about width
v.trailingAnchor.constraint(
    equalTo: previousLab!.trailingAnchor, constant: 10).isActive = true
// pin content view to scroll view, sized by its subview constraints
// content size is calculated for us
v.translatesAutoresizingMaskIntoConstraints = false
let svclg = sv.contentLayoutGuide
NSLayoutConstraint.activate([
    svclg.topAnchor.constraint(equalTo:v.topAnchor),
    svclg.bottomAnchor.constraint(equalTo:v.bottomAnchor),
    svclg.leadingAnchor.constraint(equalTo:v.leadingAnchor),
    svclg.trailingAnchor.constraint(equalTo:v.trailingAnchor),
])
```

The fourth combination is that the content view's subviews are positioned using constraints, but we set the content view's frame and the scroll view's content size explicitly. But how can we find out the final content view size based on its subviews' constraints? Fortunately, `systemLayoutSizeFitting(_:)` tells us:

```swift
var previousLab : UILabel? = nil
for i in 0 ..< 30 {
    let lab = UILabel()
    // lab.backgroundColor = .red
    lab.translatesAutoresizingMaskIntoConstraints = false
    lab.text = "This is label \(i+1)"
    v.addSubview(lab)
    lab.leadingAnchor.constraint(
        equalTo: v.leadingAnchor,
        constant: 10).isActive = true
    lab.topAnchor.constraint(
```

```
            // first one, pin to top; all others, pin to previous
            equalTo: previousLab?.bottomAnchor ?? v.topAnchor,
            constant: 10).isActive = true
        previousLab = lab
    }
    // last one, pin to bottom, this dictates content size height!
    v.bottomAnchor.constraint(
        equalTo: previousLab!.bottomAnchor, constant: 10).isActive = true
    // need to do something about width
    v.trailingAnchor.constraint(
        equalTo: previousLab!.trailingAnchor, constant: 10).isActive = true
    // autolayout helps us learn the consequences of those constraints
    let minsz = v.systemLayoutSizeFitting(UILayoutFittingCompressedSize)
    // set content view frame and content size explicitly
    v.frame = CGRect(origin:.zero, size:minsz)
    sv.contentSize = minsz
```

Scroll View in a Nib

A UIScrollView object is available in the nib editor's Object library, so you can drag it into a view in the canvas and give it subviews. Alternatively, you can wrap existing views in the canvas in a UIScrollView as an afterthought: to do so, select the views and choose Editor → Embed In → Scroll View.

The scroll view can't be scrolled in the nib editor, so to design its subviews, you make the scroll view large enough to accommodate them; if this makes the scroll view too large, you can resize the actual scroll view instance later, in code or by means of autolayout, after the nib loads. You may have to make the view controller's main view too large as well, in order to see and work with the full scroll view and its contents (Figure 7-1). To do so, set the view controller's Simulated Size pop-up menu in its Size inspector to Freeform; now you can change the main view's size.

No Internal Autolayout

If you're not using autolayout inside the scroll view, judicious use of autoresizing settings in the nib editor can be a big help. In Figure 7-1, the scroll view is pinned to its superview, the view controller's main view. Thus, when the app runs and the main view is resized (as I discussed in Chapter 6), the scroll view will be resized too, to fit the main view. The content view, on the other hand, doesn't use autolayout. It must not be resized vertically, so its height is not flexible (it's a strut, not a spring). Horizontally, it has structs externally and a spring internally, to keep it centered within the scroll view.

But although everything is correctly sized at runtime, the scroll view doesn't scroll. That's because we have failed to set the scroll view's contentSize. Unfortunately, the nib editor provides no way to do that! Thus, we'll have to do it in code.

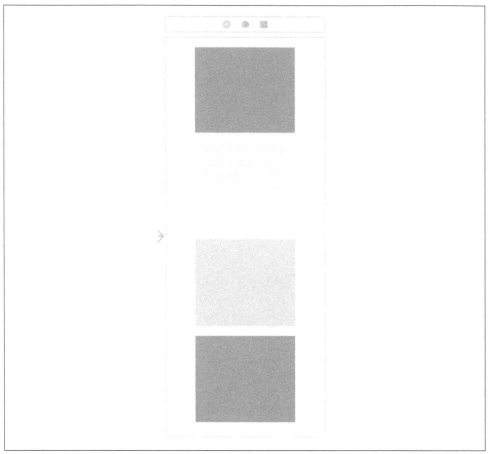

Figure 7-1. A scroll view in the nib editor

But what should the content size be? It should be the size of the content view! The content view is the correct size in the nib, and it won't be resized through autoresizing, so at runtime, when the nib loads, its size will be the desired `contentSize`. I have an outlet to the scroll view (`self.sv`) and an outlet to the content view (`self.cv`), and I set the scroll view's `contentSize` to the content view's size in `viewDidLayout-Subviews`:

```
var didSetup = false
override func viewDidLayoutSubviews() {
    if !self.didSetup {
        self.didSetup = true
        self.sv.contentSize = self.cv.bounds.size
    }
}
```

Internal Autolayout

If you're using autolayout inside the scroll view, there is no need for any code to set the scroll view's `contentSize` (and such code wouldn't work in any case). The content view's edges are pinned to those of its superview, the scroll view. If the `constant` of each edge constraint between the content view and the scroll view is `0`, then that tells the scroll view: "Your `contentSize` is the size of the content view."

The question is how you'd like to dictate the content view's size. You have two choices, corresponding to the second and third combinations in the preceding section: you can set the content view's width and height constraints explicitly, or you can let the content view's width and height be completely determined by the constraints of its subviews. Do whichever feels suitable. The nib editor understands this aspect of scroll view configuration, and will alert you with a warning (about the "scrollable content size") until you've provided enough constraints to determine unambiguously the scroll view's `contentSize`.

Content Inset

The content inset of a scroll view is a margin space around its content. In effect, it changes where the content stops when it is scrolled all the way to its extreme limit.

To see why this is important, consider the app with 30 labels that we created at the start of this chapter. The scroll view occupies the entirety of the view controller's main view. But the view controller's main view underlaps the status bar. And that means that the top of the scroll view underlaps the status bar. And *that* means that at launch time, and whenever the scroll view's content is scrolled all the way down, the first label, which is now as far down as it can go, is still partly hidden by the text of the status bar.

One solution, obviously, would be to pin the top of the scroll view to the bottom of the status bar, instead of to the top of the main view. But that isn't necessarily what we want. When we scroll the scroll view's content upward, we may want the content to be visible passing behind the status bar. So what we want to adjust is not where the top of the scroll view is, but where the top of its content is considered to be. When the content is being moved upward, it's fine for it to pass behind the status bar; therefore, the top of the scroll view has to be at the *top* of the status bar. But when the content is moved downward as far as it can go, it shouldn't stop at the top of the scroll view; the stopping point should be further down, at the *bottom* of the status bar.

In iOS 10 and earlier, the stopping point was set by setting the scroll view's `content-Inset` property. This is a UIEdgeInsets struct consisting of four CGFloats — `top`, `left`, `bottom`, and `right` — specifying an extra distance inward from the edge of the scroll view, where the content is to reach its extreme limit. So we would have code like this (or we could make the same specification in the nib editor):

```
sv.contentInset = UIEdgeInsetsMake(20, 0, 0, 0)
```

To set the `contentInset` alone is rare; typically, the scroll view's `scrollIndicatorInsets` property would be changed to match it. This, too, is a UIEdgeInsets struct; it specifies a shift in the position of the scroll indicators. Consider again the scroll view whose `contentInset` we have just set. When the content is scrolled all the way down, there is now a nice gap between the bottom of the status bar and the top of the first label; but the top of the scroll indicator is still up behind the status bar. This would be prevented by setting the `scrollIndicatorInsets` to the same value as the `contentInset`:

```
sv.contentInset = UIEdgeInsetsMake(20, 0, 0, 0)
sv.scrollIndicatorInsets = sv.contentInset
```

However, there's an obvious problem with this entire approach: the status bar can come and go. If we're going to set the `contentInset` and the `scrollIndicatorInsets` to have a `top` of `20` when there's a status bar, as on an iPhone in portrait orientation, then, if the app is permitted to perform compensatory rotation, we're going to have to set them both to have a `top` of `0` when there's *no* status bar, as on an iPhone in landscape orientation.

Moreover, the status bar isn't the only kind of top bar; there's also the navigation bar, which can change its height. And there are bottom bars, which can change *their* heights. As I mentioned in Chapter 6, top bars and bottom bars are likely to be translucent, and the runtime would like to make your view underlap them. With a scroll view, this looks cool, because the scroll view's contents are visible in a blurry way through the translucent bar; but clearly the content inset and the scroll indicator insets need to be adjusted so that the scrolling limits stay between the top bar and the bottom bar, even as these can come and go and change their heights.

The obvious solution in iOS 10 and before was to implement some appropriate event, such as `viewWillLayoutSubviews`, to adjust the scroll view's content inset; but this was a lot of work, and it wasn't always easy to get right. To help out, a UIViewController had a property of its own, `automaticallyAdjustsScrollViewInsets`; if `true`, the view controller would adjust a scroll view's content insets automatically as the top and bottom bars changed. The problem with that was that it worked inconsistently: it was difficult to know whether it would apply to any particular scroll view and, if so, whether it would do the right thing.

In iOS 11, there's a completely new solution to the whole problem. `automaticallyAdjustsScrollViewInsets` is deprecated; `contentInset` and `scrollIndicatorInsets` still exist, but you probably won't need to set them. Instead, the power of responding to the position of the top and bottom bars is vested in each individual scroll view. The scroll view knows where the top and bottom bars are because of the safe area, which propagates down the entire view hierarchy. The only thing you'll have to do is tell the scroll view whether you want it to adjust its content inset to respond to the safe area. To do that, you set its `contentInsetAdjustmentBehavior` property to one of the following (UIScrollViewContentInsetAdjustmentBehavior):

`.always`
> The content is inset to match the safe area.

`.never`
> The content is not inset to match the safe area.

`.scrollableAxes`
> The content is inset to match the safe area only for a dimension in which the scroll view is scrollable.

`.automatic`
> Similar to `scrollableAxes`, but can also respond to the view controller's `automaticallyAdjustsScrollViewInsets`, for backward compatibility. This is the default.

In iOS 11, the `contentInset` and `scrollIndicatorInsets` are *unaffected* by this automatic adjustment. Instead, what changes is a new property, the scroll view's `adjustedContentInset`. Thus, for example, suppose we're in a navigation interface without a large title in the navigation bar, and suppose that the scroll view coincides with the view controller's main view and underlaps the top bars. The status bar and the navigation bar add 64 points to the top of the safe area, so if the scroll view's content inset adjustment behavior is `.always`, its `contentInset` and `scrollIndicator-Insets` are both `.zero`, but its `adjustedContentInset` is {64,0,0,0}.

If you *do* set the `contentInset` for some reason, that value is applied additively to increase the `adjustedContentInset`. For example, in the navigation interface scenario from the preceding paragraph, if we also set the scroll view's `contentInset` to `UIEdgeInsetsMake(30,0,0,0)`, then the `adjustedContentInset` will have a top value of 94 (and there will be an additional 30-point gap between the top of the content and the bottom of the navigation bar when the content is scrolled all the way down).

 When your scroll view first appears, it might not be scrolled all the way down in accordance with the `adjustedContentInset`. For example, in our navigation interface scenario, the scroll view might appear initially with the top of its content behind the navigation bar. I regard this as a bug. A possible workaround is to set the scroll view's `alwaysBounceVertical` property to `true`; this probably gives the runtime an earlier hint that we consider ourselves vertically scrollable.

Scrolling

For the most part, the purpose of a scroll view will be to let the user scroll. Here are some scroll view properties that affect the user experience with regard to scrolling:

isScrollEnabled
> If false, the user can't scroll, but you can still scroll in code (as explained later in this section). You could put a UIScrollView to various creative purposes other than letting the user scroll; for example, scrolling in code to a different region of the content might be a way of replacing one piece of interface by another, possibly with animation.

scrollsToTop
> If true (the default), and assuming scrolling is enabled, the user can tap on the status bar as a way of making the scroll view scroll its content to the top (that is, the content moves all the way down). You can override this setting dynamically through the scroll view's delegate, discussed later in this chapter.

bounces
> If true (the default), then when the user scrolls to a limit of the content, it is possible to scroll somewhat further (possibly revealing the scroll view's background-Color behind the content, if a subview was covering it); the content then snaps back into place when the user releases it. Otherwise, the user experiences the limit as a sudden inability to scroll further in that direction.

alwaysBounceVertical
alwaysBounceHorizontal
> If true, and assuming that bounces is true, then even if the contentSize in the given dimension isn't larger than the scroll view (so that no scrolling is actually possible in that dimension), this axis is treated as scrollable: the user can scroll somewhat and the content then snaps back into place when the user releases it. Otherwise, the user experiences a simple inability to scroll in this dimension.

isDirectionalLockEnabled
> If true, and if scrolling is possible in both dimensions (even if only because the appropriate alwaysBounce... is true), then the user, having begun to scroll in one dimension, can't scroll in the other dimension without ending the gesture and starting over. In other words, the user is constrained to scroll vertically or horizontally but not both at once.

decelerationRate
> The rate at which scrolling is damped out, and the content comes to a stop, after the user's gesture ends. As convenient examples, standard constants are provided:
>
> - UIScrollViewDecelerationRateNormal (0.998)

- UIScrollViewDecelerationRateFast (0.99)

Lower values mean faster damping; experimentation suggests that values lower than 0.5 are viable but barely distinguishable from one another. You can effectively override this value dynamically through the scroll view's delegate, discussed later in this chapter.

showsHorizontalScrollIndicator
showsVerticalScrollIndicator

The scroll indicators are bars that appear only while the user is scrolling in a scrollable dimension (where the content is larger than the scroll view), and serve to indicate both the size of the content in that dimension relative to the scroll view and the user's position within it. The default is true for both.

Because the user cannot see the scroll indicators except when actively scrolling, there is normally no indication that the view is scrollable. I regard this as somewhat unfortunate, because it makes the possibility of scrolling less discoverable; I'd prefer an option to make the scroll indicators constantly visible. Apple suggests that you call flashScrollIndicators when the scroll view appears, to make the scroll indicators visible momentarily.

indicatorStyle

The way the scroll indicators are drawn. Your choices (UIScrollViewIndicatorStyle) are .black, .white, and .default (black with a white border).

 The scroll indicators are subviews of the scroll view (they are actually UIImageViews). Do not assume that the subviews you add to a UIScrollView are its only subviews!

You can scroll in code, and you can do so even if the user can't scroll. The content moves to the position you specify, with no bouncing and no exposure of the scroll indicators. You can specify the new position in two ways:

contentOffset

The point (CGPoint) of the content that is located at the scroll view's top left (effectively the same thing as the scroll view's bounds origin). You can get this property to learn the current scroll position, and set it to change the current scroll position. The values normally go up from (0.0,0.0) until the limit dictated by the contentSize and the scroll view's own bounds size is reached. Call setContentOffset(_:animated:) to set the contentOffset with animation.

scrollRectToVisible(_:animated:)

Adjusts the content so that the specified CGRect of the content is within the scroll view's bounds. This is less precise than setting the contentOffset, because you're not saying exactly what the resulting scroll position will be, but sometimes guaranteeing the visibility of a certain portion of the content is exactly what you're after.

The `adjustedContentInset` (discussed in the previous section) can affect the meaning of the `contentOffset`. For example, recall the scenario where the scroll view underlaps the status bar and a navigation bar and acquires an `adjustedContentInset` with a `top` of 64. Then when the scroll view is scrolled all the way to the top — that is, the content is scrolled all the way down — the `contentOffset` is not (0.0,0.0) but (0.0,-64.0). The (0.0,0.0) point is the top of the content rect, which is located at the bottom of the navigation bar; the point at the top left of the scroll view itself is 64 points above that.

If a scroll view participates in state restoration (Chapter 6), its `contentOffset` is saved and restored, so when the app is relaunched, the scroll view will reappear scrolled to the same position as before.

Paging

If its `isPagingEnabled` property is `true`, the scroll view doesn't let the user scroll freely; instead, the content is considered to consist of equal-sized sections. The user can scroll only in such a way as to move to a different section. The size of a section is set automatically to the size of the scroll view's bounds. The sections are the scroll view's *pages*.

When the user stops dragging, a paging scroll view gently snaps automatically to the nearest whole page. For example, let's say that the scroll view scrolls only horizontally, and that its subviews are image views showing photos, sized to match the scroll view's bounds. If the user drags horizontally to the left to a point where *less* than half of the next photo to the right is visible, and raises the dragging finger, the paging scroll view snaps its content back to the right until the entire first photo is visible again. If the user drags horizontally to the left to a point where *more* than half of the next photo to the right is visible, and raises the dragging finger, the paging scroll view snaps its content further to the left until the entire second photo is visible.

The usual arrangement is that a paging scroll view is as large, or nearly as large, in its scrollable dimension, as the screen. Under this arrangement, it is impossible for the user to move the content more than a single page in any direction with a single gesture; the size of the page is the size of the scroll view's bounds, so the user will run out of surface area to drag on before being able to move the content the distance of a page and a half, which is what would be needed to make the scroll view snap to a page not adjacent to the page we started on.

Sometimes, indeed, the paging scroll view will be slightly *larger* than the window in its scrollable dimension. This allows each page's content to fill the scroll view while also providing gaps between the pages, visible when the user starts to scroll. The user is still able to move from page to page, because it is still possible to drag more than half a new page into view (and the scroll view will then snap the rest of the way when the user raises the dragging finger).

When the user raises the dragging finger, the scroll view's action in adjusting its content is considered to be *decelerating*, and the scroll view's delegate (discussed in more detail later in this chapter) will receive scrollViewWillBeginDecelerating(_:), followed by scrollViewDidEndDecelerating(_:) when the scroll view's content has stopped moving and a full page is showing. Thus, these messages can be used to detect efficiently that the page may have changed.

You can take advantage of this, for example, to coordinate a paging scroll view with a UIPageControl (Chapter 12). In this example, a page control (self.pager) is updated whenever the user causes a horizontally scrollable scroll view (self.sv) to display a different page:

```
func scrollViewDidEndDecelerating(_ scrollView: UIScrollView) {
    let x = self.sv.contentOffset.x
    let w = self.sv.bounds.size.width
    self.pager.currentPage = Int(x/w)
}
```

Conversely, we can scroll the scroll view to a new page manually when the user taps the page control; we have to calculate the page boundaries ourselves:

```
@IBAction func userDidPage(_ sender: Any?) {
    let p = self.pager.currentPage
    let w = self.sv.bounds.size.width
    self.sv.setContentOffset(CGPoint(CGFloat(p)*w,0), animated:true)
}
```

A useful interface is a paging scroll view where you supply pages dynamically as the user scrolls. In this way, you can display a huge number of pages without having to put them all into the scroll view at once. In fact, a scrolling UIPageViewController (Chapter 6) implements exactly that interface! Its UIPageViewControllerOption-InterPageSpacingKey even provides the gap between pages that I mentioned earlier.

A compromise between a UIPageViewController and a completely preconfigured paging scroll view is a scroll view whose contentSize can accommodate all pages, but whose actual page content is supplied lazily. The only pages that have to be present at all times are the page visible to the user and the two pages adjacent to it on either side, so that there is no delay in displaying a new page's content when the user starts to scroll. (This approach is exemplified by Apple's PageControl sample code; unfortunately, that example does not also remove page content that is no longer needed, so there is ultimately no conservation of memory.)

There are times when a scroll view, even one requiring a good deal of dynamic configuration, is better than a scrolling UIPageViewController, because the scroll view provides full information to its delegate about the user's scrolling activity (as described later in this chapter). For example, if you wanted to respond to the user's scrolling one area of the interface by programmatically scrolling another area of the interface in a coordinated fashion, you might want what the user is scrolling to be a scroll view, because it tells you what the user is up to at every moment.

Tiling

Suppose we have some finite but really big content that we want to display in a scroll view, such as a very large image that the user can inspect, piecemeal, by scrolling. To hold the entire image in memory may be onerous or impossible.

Tiling is one solution to this kind of problem. It takes advantage of the insight that there's really no need to hold the entire image in memory; all we need at any given moment is the part of the image visible to the user right now. Mentally, divide the content rectangle into a matrix of rectangles; these rectangles are the tiles. In reality, divide the huge image into corresponding rectangles. Then whenever the user scrolls, we look to see whether part of any empty tile has become visible, and if so, we supply its content. At the same time, we can release the content of all tiles that are completely offscreen. Thus, at any given moment, only the tiles that are showing have content. There is some latency associated with this approach (the user scrolls, then any newly visible empty tiles are filled in), but we will have to live with that.

There is actually a built-in CALayer subclass for helping us implement tiling — CATiledLayer. Its `tileSize` property sets the dimensions of a tile. The usual approach to using CATiledLayer is to implement `draw(_:)` in a UIView whose underlying layer is the CATiledLayer; under that arrangement, the host view's `draw(_:)` is called every time a new tile is needed, and its parameter is the rect of the tile we are to draw.

The `tileSize` may need to be adjusted for the screen resolution. On a double-resolution device, for example, the CATiledLayer's `contentsScale` will be doubled, and the tiles will be half the size that we ask for. If that isn't acceptable, we can double the `tileSize` dimensions.

To illustrate, I'll use as my tiles a few of the "CuriousFrog" images already created for us as part of Apple's own PhotoScroller sample code. The images all have names of the form *CuriousFrog_500_x_y.png*, where *x* and *y* are integers corresponding to the picture's position within the matrix. The images are 256×256 pixels (except for the ones on the extreme right and bottom edges of the matrix, which are shorter in one dimension, but I won't be using those in this example); I've selected a 3×3 matrix of images.

We will give our scroll view (`self.sv`) one subview, a TiledView, a UIView subclass that exists purely to give our CATiledLayer a place to live. `TILESIZE` is defined as 256, to match the image dimensions:

```
override func viewDidLoad() {
    let f = CGRect(0,0,3*TILESIZE,3*TILESIZE)
    let content = TiledView(frame:f)
    let tsz = TILESIZE * content.layer.contentsScale
    (content.layer as! CATiledLayer).tileSize = CGSize(tsz, tsz)
    self.sv.addSubview(content)
    self.sv.contentSize = f.size
    self.content = content
}
```

Here's the code for TiledView. As Apple's sample code points out, we must fetch images with `init(contentsOfFile:)` in order to avoid the automatic caching behavior of `init(named:)` — after all, we're going to all this trouble exactly to avoid using more memory than we have to:

```
override class var layerClass : AnyClass {
    return CATiledLayer.self
}
override func draw(_ r: CGRect) {
    let tile = r
    let x = Int(tile.origin.x/TILESIZE)
    let y = Int(tile.origin.y/TILESIZE)
    let tileName = String(format:"CuriousFrog_500_\(x+3)_\(y)")
    let path = Bundle.main.path(forResource: tileName, ofType:"png")!
    let image = UIImage(contentsOfFile:path)!
    image.draw(at:CGPoint(CGFloat(x)*TILESIZE,CGFloat(y)*TILESIZE))
}
```

In this configuration, our TiledView's `drawRect` is called *on a background thread*. This is unusual, but it shouldn't cause any trouble as long as you confine yourself to standard thread-safe activities. Fortunately, fetching the image and drawing it *are* thread-safe.

 You may encounter a nasty issue where a CATiledLayer's host view's `draw(_:)` is called simultaneously on *multiple* background threads. It isn't clear to me whether this problem is confined to the Simulator or whether it can also occur on a device. The workaround is to wrap the whole interior of `draw(_:)` in a call to a serial DispatchQueue's `sync` (see Chapter 24).

There is no special call for invalidating an offscreen tile. You can call `setNeedsDisplay` on the TiledView, but this doesn't erase offscreen tiles. You're just supposed to trust that the CATiledLayer will eventually clear offscreen tiles if needed to conserve memory.

CATiledLayer has a class method `fadeDuration` that dictates the duration of the animation that fades a new tile into view. You can create a CATiledLayer subclass and override this method to return a value different from the default (`0.25`), but this is probably not worth doing, as the default value is a good one. Returning a smaller value won't make tiles appear faster; it just replaces the nice fade-in with an annoying flash.

Zooming

To implement zooming of a scroll view's content, you set the scroll view's `minimum-ZoomScale` and `maximumZoomScale` so that at least one of them isn't 1 (the default). You also implement `viewForZooming(in:)` in the scroll view's delegate to tell the scroll view which of its subviews is to be the scalable view. The scroll view then zooms by applying a scale transform (Chapter 1) to this subview. The amount of that transform is the scroll view's `zoomScale` property.

Typically, you'll want the scroll view's entire content to be scalable, so you'll have one direct subview of the scroll view that acts as the scalable view, and anything else inside the scroll view will be a subview of the scalable view, so as to be scaled together with it. This is another reason for arranging your scroll view's subviews inside a single content view, as I suggested earlier.

To illustrate, we can start with any of the four content view–based versions of our scroll view containing 30 labels from earlier in this chapter ("Using a Content View" on page 429). I called the content view v. Now we add these lines:

```
v.tag = 999
sv.minimumZoomScale = 1.0
sv.maximumZoomScale = 2.0
sv.delegate = self
```

We have assigned a tag to the view that is to be scaled, so that we can refer to it later. We have set the scale limits for the scroll view. And we have made ourselves the scroll view's delegate. Now all we have to do is implement `viewForZooming(in:)` to return the scalable view:

```
func viewForZooming(in scrollView: UIScrollView) -> UIView? {
    return scrollView.viewWithTag(999)
}
```

This works: the scroll view now responds to pinch gestures by scaling appropriately! Recall that in our 30 labels example, the scroll view is not scrollable horizontally. Nevertheless, in this scenario, the width of the content view matters, because when it is scaled up, including while zooming, the user will be able to scroll to see any part of it. Thus the content view should embrace its content quite tightly.

The user can actually scale considerably beyond the limits we set in both directions; in that case, when the gesture ends, the scale snaps back to the limit value. If we wish to confine scaling strictly to our defined limits, we can set the scroll view's `bounces-Zoom` to `false`; when the user reaches a limit, scaling will simply stop.

The actual amount of zoom is reflected as the scroll view's current zoomScale. If a scroll view participates in state restoration, its zoomScale is saved and restored, so when the app is relaunched, the scroll view will reappear zoomed by the same amount as before.

If the minimumZoomScale is less than 1, then when the scalable view becomes smaller than the scroll view, it is pinned to the scroll view's top left. If you don't like this, you can change it by subclassing UIScrollView and overriding layoutSubviews, or by implementing the scroll view delegate method scrollViewDidZoom(_:). Here's a simple example (drawn from a WWDC 2010 video) demonstrating an override of layoutSubviews that keeps the scalable view centered in either dimension whenever it is smaller than the scroll view in that dimension:

```
override func layoutSubviews() {
    super.layoutSubviews()
    if let v = self.delegate?.viewForZooming?(in:self) {
        let svw = self.bounds.width
        let svh = self.bounds.height
        let vw = v.frame.width
        let vh = v.frame.height
        var f = v.frame
        if vw < svw {
            f.origin.x = (svw - vw) / 2.0
        } else {
            f.origin.x = 0
        }
        if vh < svh {
            f.origin.y = (svh - vh) / 2.0
        } else {
            f.origin.y = 0
        }
        v.frame = f
    }
}
```

 One of the WWDC 2017 videos claims that the problem of zooming while keeping the scalable view centered can be solved by pinning it to the center of the contentLayoutGuide, but my experimentation does not confirm that claim.

Earlier, I said that the scroll view zooms by applying a scale transform to the scalable view. This has two important secondary consequences that can surprise you if you're unprepared:

- *The frame of the scalable view* is scaled to match the current zoomScale. This follows as a natural consequence of applying a scale transform to the scalable view.

- The scroll view is concerned to make scrolling continue to work correctly: the limits as the user scrolls should continue to match the limits of the content, and commands like scrollRectToVisible(_:animated:) should continue to work the same way for the same values. Therefore, the scroll view automatically scales *its own* `contentSize` to match the current `zoomScale`.

Zooming Programmatically

To zoom programmatically, you have two choices:

`setZoomScale(_:animated:)`
> Zooms in terms of scale value. The `contentOffset` is automatically adjusted to keep the current center centered and the content occupying the entire scroll view.

`zoomTo(_:animated:)`
> Zooms so that the given rectangle of the content occupies as much as possible of the scroll view's bounds. The `contentOffset` is automatically adjusted to keep the content occupying the entire scroll view.

In this example, I implement double tapping as a zoom gesture. In my action method for the double tap UITapGestureRecognizer attached to the scalable view, a double tap means to zoom to maximum scale, minimum scale, or actual size, depending on the current scale value:

```
@IBAction func tapped(_ tap : UIGestureRecognizer) {
    let v = tap.view!
    let sv = v.superview as! UIScrollView
    if sv.zoomScale < 1 {
        sv.setZoomScale(1, animated:true)
        let pt = CGPoint((v.bounds.width - sv.bounds.width)/2.0,0)
        sv.setContentOffset(pt, animated:false)
    }
    else if sv.zoomScale < sv.maximumZoomScale {
        sv.setZoomScale(sv.maximumZoomScale, animated:true)
    }
    else {
        sv.setZoomScale(sv.minimumZoomScale, animated:true)
    }
}
```

Zooming with Detail

By default, when a scroll view zooms, it merely applies a scale transform to the scaled view. The scaled view's drawing is cached beforehand into its layer, so when we zoom in, the bits of the resulting bitmap are drawn larger. This means that a zoomed-in scroll view's content may be fuzzy (pixellated). In some cases this might be acceptable, but in others you might like the content to be redrawn more sharply at its new size.

(On a high-resolution device, this might not be such an issue. For example, if the user is allowed to zoom only up to double scale, you can draw at double scale right from the start; the results will look good at single scale, because the screen has high resolution, as well as at double scale, because that's the scale you drew at.)

One solution is to take advantage of a CATiledLayer feature that I didn't mention earlier. It turns out that CATiledLayer is aware not only of scrolling but also of scaling: you can configure it to ask for tiles to be drawn when the layer is scaled to a new order of magnitude. When your drawing routine is called, the graphics context itself has already been scaled appropriately by a transform.

In the case of an image into which the user is to be permitted to zoom deeply, you would be forearmed with multiple tile sets constituting the image, each set having double the tile size of the previous set (as in Apple's PhotoScroller example). In other cases, you may not need tiles at all; you'll just draw again, at the new resolution.

Besides its `tileSize`, you'll need to set two additional CATiledLayer properties:

`levelsOfDetail`
    The number of different resolutions at which you want to redraw, where each level has twice the resolution of the previous level. So, for example, with two levels of detail we can ask to redraw when zooming to double size (2x) and when zooming back to single size (1x).

`levelsOfDetailBias`
    The number of levels of detail that are *larger* than single size (1x). For example, if `levelsOfDetail` is 2, then if we want to redraw when zooming to 2x and when zooming back to 1x, the `levelsOfDetailBias` needs to be 1, because one of those levels is larger than 1x. (If we were to leave `levelsOfDetailBias` at 0, the default, we would be saying we want to redraw when zooming to 0.5x and back to 1x — we have two levels of detail but neither is larger than 1x, so one must be smaller than 1x.)

The CATiledLayer will ask for a redraw at a higher resolution as soon as the view's size becomes larger than the previous resolution. In other words, if there are two levels of detail with a bias of 1, the layer will be redrawn at 2x as soon as it is zoomed even a little bit larger than 1x. This is an excellent approach, because although a level of detail would look blurry if scaled up, it looks pretty good scaled down.

For example, let's say I have a TiledView that hosts a CATiledLayer, in which I intend to draw an image. I haven't broken the image into tiles, because the maximum size at which the user can view it isn't prohibitively large; the original image happens to be 838×958, and can be held in memory easily. Rather, I'm using a CATiledLayer in order to take advantage of its ability to change resolutions automatically. The image will be displayed initially at less than quarter-size (namely 208×238), and if the user never zooms in to view it larger, we will be saving memory by drawing only a quarter-size version of the image.

The CATiledLayer is configured like this:

```
let scale = lay.contentsScale
lay.tileSize = CGSize(208*scale,238*scale)
lay.levelsOfDetail = 3
lay.levelsOfDetailBias = 2
```

The `tileSize` has been adjusted for screen resolution, so the result is as follows:

- As originally displayed at 208×238, there is one tile and we can draw our image at quarter size.

- If the user zooms in, to show the image larger than its originally displayed size, there will be 4 tiles and we can draw our image at half size.

- If the user zooms in still further, to show the image larger than double its originally displayed size (416×476), there will be 16 tiles and we can draw our image at full size, which will continue to look good as the user zooms all the way in to the full size of the original image.

We don't need to draw each tile individually. Each time we're called upon to draw a tile, we'll draw the entire image into the TiledView's bounds; whatever falls outside the requested tile will be clipped out and won't be drawn.

Here's my TiledView's `draw(_:)` implementation. I have an Optional UIImage property `currentImage`, initialized to `nil`, and a CGSize property `currentSize` initialized to `.zero`. Each time `draw(_:)` is called, I compare the tile size (the incoming `rect` parameter's size) to `currentSize`. If it's different, I know that we've changed by one level of detail and we need a new version of `currentImage`, so I create the new version of `currentImage` at a scale appropriate to this level of detail. Finally, I draw `currentImage` into the TiledView's bounds:

```
override func drawRect(rect: CGRect) {
    let (lay, bounds) = DispatchQueue.main.sync {
        return (self.layer as! CATiledLayer, self.bounds)
    }
    let oldSize = self.currentSize
    if !oldSize.equalTo(rect.size) {
        // make a new size
        self.currentSize = rect.size
        // make a new image
        let tr = UIGraphicsGetCurrentContext()!.ctm
        let sc = tr.a/lay.contentsScale
        let scale = sc/4.0
        let path = Bundle.main.path(
            forResource: "earthFromSaturn", ofType:"png")!
        let im = UIImage(contentsOfFile:path)!
        let sz = CGSize(im.size.width * scale, im.size.height * scale)
        let f = UIGraphicsImageRendererFormat.default()
        f.opaque = true; f.scale = 1 // *
```

```
        let r = UIGraphicsImageRenderer(size: sz, format: f)
        self.currentImage = r.image { _ in
            im.draw(in:CGRect(origin:.zero, size:sz))
        }
    }
}
self.currentImage?.draw(in:bounds)
}
```

(The `DispatchQueue.main.sync` call at the start initializes my local variables `lay` and `bounds` on the main thread, even though `drawRect` is called on a background thread; see Chapter 24.)

An alternative and much simpler approach (from a WWDC 2011 video) is to make yourself the scroll view's delegate so that you get an event when the zoom ends, and then change the scalable view's `contentScaleFactor` to match the current zoom scale, compensating for the high-resolution screen at the same time:

```
func scrollViewDidEndZooming(_ scrollView: UIScrollView,
    with view: UIView?, atScale scale: CGFloat) {
        scrollView.bounces = self.oldBounces
        view.contentScaleFactor = scale * UIScreen.main.scale // *
    }
}
```

In response, the scalable view's `draw(_:)` will be called, and its `rect` parameter will be the CGRect to draw into. Thus, the view may appear fuzzy for a while as the user zooms in, but when the user stops zooming, the view is redrawn sharply. That approach comes with a caveat, however: you mustn't overdo it. If the zoom scale, screen resolution, and scalable view size are high, you will be asking for a very large graphics context, which could cause your app to use too much memory.

For more about displaying a large image in a zoomable scroll view, see Apple's Large Image Downsizing example.

Scroll View Delegate

The scroll view's delegate (adopting the UIScrollViewDelegate protocol) receives lots of messages that can help you track, in great detail, just what the scroll view is up to:

scrollViewDidScroll(_:)
> If you scroll in code without animation, you will receive this message *once* afterward. If the user scrolls, either by dragging or with the scroll-to-top feature, or if you scroll in code with animation, you will receive this message *repeatedly* throughout the scroll, including during the time the scroll view is decelerating after the user's finger has lifted; there are other delegate messages that tell you, in those cases, when the scroll has finally ended.

`scrollViewDidEndScrollingAnimation(_:)`

If you scroll in code with animation, you will receive this message afterward, when the animation ends.

`scrollViewWillBeginDragging(_:)`
`scrollViewWillEndDragging(_:withVelocity:targetContentOffset:)`
`scrollViewDidEndDragging(_:willDecelerate:)`

If the user scrolls by dragging, you will receive these messages at the start and end of the user's finger movement. If the user brings the scroll view to a stop before lifting the finger, `willDecelerate` is `false` and the scroll is over. If the user lets go of the scroll view while the finger is moving, or when paging is turned on, `willDecelerate` is `true` and we proceed to the delegate messages reporting deceleration.

The purpose of `scrollViewWillEndDragging` is to let you customize the outcome of the content's deceleration. The third argument is a pointer to a CGPoint; you can use it to set a different CGPoint, specifying the `contentOffset` value the scroll view should have when the deceleration is over. By taking the `velocity:` into account, you can allow the user to "fling" the scroll view with momentum before it comes to a halt.

`scrollViewWillBeginDecelerating(_:)`
`scrollViewDidEndDecelerating(_:)`

Sent once each after `scrollViewDidEndDragging(_:willDecelerate:)` arrives with a value of `true`. When `scrollViewDidEndDecelerating(_:)` arrives, the scroll is over.

`scrollViewShouldScrollToTop(_:)`
`scrollViewDidScrollToTop(_:)`

These have to do with the feature where the user can tap the status bar to scroll the scroll view's content to its top. You won't get either of them if `scrollsToTop` is `false`, because the scroll-to-top feature is turned off in that case. The first lets you prevent the user from scrolling to the top on this occasion even if `scrollsToTop` is `true`. The second tells you that the user has employed this feature and the scroll is over.

So, if you wanted to do something after a scroll ends completely regardless of how the scroll was performed, you'd need to implement multiple delegate methods:

- `scrollViewDidEndDragging(_:willDecelerate:)` in case the user drags and stops (`willDecelerate` is `false`).

- `scrollViewDidEndDecelerating(_:)` in case the user drags and the scroll continues afterward.

- `scrollViewDidScrollToTop(_:)` in case the user uses the scroll-to-top feature.
- `scrollViewDidEndScrollingAnimation(_:)` in case you scroll with animation.

(You don't need a delegate method to tell you when the scroll is over after you scroll in code *without* animation: it's over immediately, so if you have work to do after the scroll ends, you can do it in the next line of code.)

In addition, the scroll view has read-only properties reporting its state:

`isTracking`
> The user has touched the scroll view, but the scroll view hasn't decided whether this is a scroll or some kind of tap.

`isDragging`
> The user is dragging to scroll.

`isDecelerating`
> The user has scrolled and has lifted the finger, and the scroll is continuing.

There are also three delegate messages that report zooming:

`scrollViewWillBeginZooming(_:with:)`
> If the user zooms or you zoom in code, you will receive this message as the zoom begins.

`scrollViewDidZoom(_:)`
> If you zoom in code, even with animation, you will receive this message *once*. If the user zooms, you will receive this message *repeatedly* as the zoom proceeds. (You will probably also receive `scrollViewDidScroll(_:)`, possibly many times, as the zoom proceeds.)

`scrollViewDidEndZooming(_:with:atScale:)`
> If the user zooms or you zoom in code, you will receive this message after the last `scrollViewDidZoom(_:)`.

In addition, the scroll view has read-only properties reporting its state during a zoom:

`isZooming`
> The scroll view is zooming. It is possible for `isDragging` to be true at the same time.

`isZoomBouncing`
> The scroll view is returning automatically from having been zoomed outside its minimum or maximum limit. As far as I can tell, you'll get only one `scrollView-DidZoom(_:)` while the scroll view is in this state.

New in iOS 11, the delegate also receives `scrollViewDidChangeAdjustedContent-Inset(_:)` when the adjusted content inset changes. This is matched by a method `adjustedContentInsetDidChange` that can be overridden in a UIScrollView subclass.

Scroll View Touches

Since the early days of iOS, improvements in UIScrollView's internal implementation have eliminated most of the worry once associated with scroll view touches. A scroll view will interpret a drag or a pinch as a command to scroll or zoom, and any other gesture will fall through to the subviews; thus buttons and similar interface objects inside a scroll view work just fine.

You can even put a scroll view inside a scroll view, and this can be quite a useful thing to do, in contexts where you might not think of it at first. Apple's PhotoScroller example, based on principles discussed in a delightful WWDC 2010 video, is an app where a single photo fills the screen: you can page-scroll from one photo to the next, and you can zoom into the current photo with a pinch gesture. This is implemented as a scroll view inside a scroll view: the outer scroll view is for paging between images, and the inner scroll view contains the current image and is for zooming (and for scrolling to different parts of the zoomed-in image). Similarly, a WWDC 2013 video deconstructs the iOS 7 lock screen in terms of scroll views embedded in scroll views.

Gesture recognizers (Chapter 5) have also greatly simplified the task of adding custom gestures to a scroll view. For instance, some older code in Apple's documentation, showing how to implement a double tap to zoom in and a two-finger tap to zoom out, uses old-fashioned touch handling, but this is no longer necessary. Simply attach to your scroll view's scalable subview any gesture recognizers for these sorts of gesture, and they will mediate automatically among the possibilities.

In the past, making something inside a scroll view draggable required setting the scroll view's `canCancelContentTouches` property to `false`. (The reason for the name is that the scroll view, when it realizes that a gesture is a drag or pinch gesture, normally sends `touchesCancelled(_:with:)` to a subview tracking touches, so that the scroll view and not the subview will be affected.) However, unless you're implementing old-fashioned direct touch handling, you probably won't have to concern yourself with this. Regardless of how `canCancelContentTouches` is set, a draggable control, such as a UISlider, remains draggable inside a scroll view.

Here's an example of a draggable object inside a scroll view implemented through a gesture recognizer. Suppose we have an image of a map, larger than the screen, and we want the user to be able to scroll it in the normal way to see any part of the map, but we also want the user to be able to drag a flag into a new location on the map. We'll put the map image in an image view and wrap the image view in a scroll view, with the scroll view's `contentSize` the same as the map image view's size. The flag is a

Figure 7-2. A scrollable map with a draggable flag

small image view; it's another subview of the scroll view, and it has a UIPanGesture-Recognizer. The gesture recognizer's action method allows the flag to be dragged, exactly as described in Chapter 5:

```
@IBAction func dragging (_ p: UIPanGestureRecognizer) {
    let v = p.view!
    switch p.state {
    case .began, .changed:
        let delta = p.translation(in:v.superview!)
        v.center.x += delta.x
        v.center.y += delta.y
        p.setTranslation(.zero, in: v.superview)
    default: break
    }
}
```

The user can now drag the map or the flag (Figure 7-2). Dragging the map brings the flag along with it, but dragging the flag doesn't move the map.

An interesting addition to that example would be to implement *autoscrolling*, meaning that the scroll view scrolls itself when the user drags the flag close to its edge. This, too, is greatly simplified by gesture recognizers; in fact, we can add autoscrolling code directly to the dragging(_:) action method:

```swift
@IBAction func dragging (_ p: UIPanGestureRecognizer) {
    let v = p.view!
    switch p.state {
    case .began, .changed:
        let delta = p.translation(in:v.superview!)
        v.center.x += delta.x
        v.center.y += delta.y
        p.setTranslation(.zero, in: v.superview)
        // autoscroll
        let sv = self.sv!
        let loc = p.location(in:sv)
        let f = sv.bounds
        var off = sv.contentOffset
        let sz = sv.contentSize
        var c = v.center
        // to the right
        if loc.x > f.maxX - 30 {
            let margin = sz.width - sv.bounds.maxX
            if margin > 6 {
                off.x += 5
                sv.contentOffset = off
                c.x += 5
                v.center = c
                self.keepDragging(p)
            }
        }
        // to the left
        if loc.x < f.origin.x + 30 {
            let margin = off.x
            if margin > 6 {
                // ...
            }
        }
        // to the bottom
        if loc.y > f.maxY - 30 {
            let margin = sz.height - sv.bounds.maxY
            if margin > 6 {
                // ...
            }
        }
        // to the top
        if loc.y < f.origin.y + 30 {
            let margin = off.y
            if margin > 6 {
                // ...
            }
        }
    default: break
    }
}
func keepDragging (_ p: UIPanGestureRecognizer) {
    let del = 0.1
```

```
        delay(del) {
            self.dragging(p)
        }
    }
```

The `delay` in `keepDragging` (see Appendix B), combined with the change in offset, determines the speed of autoscrolling. The material omitted in the second, third, and fourth cases is obviously parallel to the first case, and is left as an exercise for the reader.

A scroll view's touch handling is itself based on gesture recognizers attached to the scroll view, and these are available to your code through the scroll view's `panGesture-Recognizer` and `pinchGestureRecognizer` properties. This means that if you want to customize a scroll view's touch handling, it's easy to add more gesture recognizers and have them interact with those already attached to the scroll view.

To illustrate, I'll build on the previous example. Suppose we want the flag to start out offscreen, and we'd like the user to be able to summon it with a rightward swipe. We can attach a UISwipeGestureRecognizer to our scroll view, but it will never recognize its gesture because the scroll view's own pan gesture recognizer will recognize first. But we have access to the scroll view's pan gesture recognizer, so we can compel it to yield to our swipe gesture recognizer by sending it `require(toFail:)`:

```
    self.sv.panGestureRecognizer.require(toFail:self.swipe)
```

The UISwipeGestureRecognizer can now recognize a rightward swipe. The flag has been waiting invisibly offscreen; in the gesture recognizer's action method, we position the flag just off to the top left of the scroll view's visible content and animate it onto the screen:

```
@IBAction func swiped (_ g: UISwipeGestureRecognizer) {
    let sv = self.sv!
    let p = sv.contentOffset
    self.flag.frame.origin = p
    self.flag.frame.origin.x -= self.flag.bounds.width
    self.flag.isHidden = false
    UIView.animate(withDuration:0.25) {
        self.flag.frame.origin.x = p.x
        // thanks for the flag, now stop operating altogether
        g.isEnabled = false
    }
}
```

Floating Scroll View Subviews

A scroll view's subview will appear to "float" over the scroll view if it remains stationary while the rest of the scroll view's content is being scrolled.

Before autolayout, this sort of thing was rather tricky to arrange; you had to use a delegate event to respond to every change in the scroll view's bounds origin by shifting the "floating" view's position to compensate, so as to appear to remain fixed. With autolayout, in iOS 10 and before, the solution was to set up constraints pinning the subview to something *outside* the scroll view.

New in iOS 11, there's an even better solution. Recall that the scroll view itself provides a `frameLayoutGuide`; pin a subview to it to make that subview stand still while the scroll view scrolls. Here's an example:

```
let iv = UIImageView(image:UIImage(named:"smiley"))
iv.translatesAutoresizingMaskIntoConstraints = false
self.sv.addSubview(iv)
let svflg = self.sv.frameLayoutGuide
NSLayoutConstraint.activate([
    iv.rightAnchor.constraint(equalTo:svflg.rightAnchor, constant: -5),
    iv.topAnchor.constraint(equalTo:svflg.topAnchor, constant: 25)
])
```

Scroll View Performance

At several points in earlier chapters I've mentioned performance problems and ways to increase drawing efficiency. Nowhere are you so likely to need these as in connection with a scroll view. As a scroll view scrolls, views must be drawn very rapidly as they appear on the screen. If the drawing system can't keep up with the speed of the scroll, the scrolling will visibly stutter.

Performance testing and optimization is a big subject, so I can't tell you exactly what to do if you encounter stuttering while scrolling. But certain general suggestions, mostly extracted from a really great WWDC 2010 video, should come in handy (and see also "Layer Efficiency" on page 147, some of which I'm repeating here):

- Everything that can be opaque should be opaque: don't force the drawing system to composite transparency, and remember to tell it that an opaque view or layer *is* opaque by setting its `isOpaque` property to `true`. If you really must composite transparency, keep the size of the nonopaque regions to a minimum; for example, if a large layer is transparent at its edges, break it into five layers — the large central layer, which is opaque, and the four edges, which are not.

- If you're drawing shadows, don't make the drawing system calculate the shadow shape for a layer: supply a `shadowPath`, or use Core Graphics to create the shadow with a drawing. Similarly, avoid making the drawing system composite the shadow as a transparency against another layer; for example, if the background layer is white, your opaque drawing can itself include a shadow already drawn on a white background.

- Don't make the drawing system scale images for you; supply the images at the target size for the correct resolution.

- In a pinch, you can just eliminate massive swatches of the rendering operation by setting a layer's `shouldRasterize` to `true`. You could, for example, do this when scrolling starts and then set it back to `false` when scrolling ends.

Apple's documentation also says that setting a view's `clearsContextBeforeDrawing` to `false` may make a difference. I can't confirm or deny this; it may be true, but I haven't encountered a case that positively proves it.

Xcode provides tools that will help you detect inefficiencies in the drawing system. In the Simulator, the Debug menu shows you blended layers (where transparency is being composited) and images that are being copied, misaligned, or rendered off-screen. On a device, the Core Animation module of Instruments provides the same functionality, plus it tracks the frame rate for you, allowing you to scroll and measure performance objectively.

CHAPTER 8

Table Views and Collection Views

I'm gonna ask you the three big questions. — Go ahead. — Who made you? — You did. — Who owns the biggest piece of you? — You do. — What would happen if I dropped you? — I'd go right down the drain.
—Dialogue by Garson Kanin
and Ruth Gordon,
Pat and Mike

A table view (UITableView) is a vertically scrolling UIScrollView (Chapter 7) containing a single column of rectangular cells. Each cell is a UITableViewCell, a UIView subclass. A table view has three main purposes:

Information

The cells constitute a list, which will often be text. The cells are usually quite small, in order to maximize the quantity appearing on the screen at once, so the information may be condensed, truncated, or summarized.

Choice

The cells may represent choices. The user chooses by tapping a cell, which selects the cell; the app responds appropriately to that choice.

Navigation

The response to the user's choosing a cell might be navigation to another interface.

An extremely common configuration is a *master–detail interface*, a navigation interface where the master view is a table view (Chapter 6): the user taps a table view cell to navigate to the details about that cell. This is one reason why the information in a table view cell can be a summary: to see the full information, the user can ask for the detail view.

In addition to its column of cells, a table view can have a number of other features:

- A table can include a header view at the top and a footer view at the bottom.

- The cells can be clumped into sections. Each section can have a header and a footer, which explain the section and tell the user where we are within the table.

- If the table has sections, a section index can also be provided as an overlay column of abbreviated section titles, which the user can tap or drag to jump to the start of a section; this makes a long table tractable.

- Tables can be editable: the user can be permitted to insert, delete, and reorder cells, and to edit information within a cell.

- Cells can have actions: the user can swipe a cell sideways to reveal buttons that act in relation to that cell.

- Cells can have menus: the user can long press a cell to pop up a menu with tappable menu items.

- A table can have a grouped format, where the cells are embedded into a common background that includes the section header and footer information. This format is often used for clumping small numbers of related cells, with explanations provided by the headers and footers.

Table view cells themselves can be extremely flexible. Some basic cell formats are provided, such as a text label along with a small image view, but you are free to design your own cell as you would any other view. There are also some standard interface items that are commonly used in a cell, such as a checkmark to indicate selection, or a right-pointing chevron to indicate that tapping the cell navigates to a detail view.

Figure 8-1 shows a familiar table view: Apple's Music app. Each table cell displays a song's name and artist, in truncated form; the user can tap to play the song. The table is divided into sections; as the user scrolls, the current section header stays pinned to the top of the table view, and the table can also be navigated using the section index at the right.

Figure 8-2 shows a familiar grouped table: Apple's Settings app. It's a master–detail interface. The master view has sections, but they aren't labeled: they merely clump related topics. The detail view sometimes has just a single cell per section, using section headers and footers to explain what that cell does.

It would be difficult to overstate the importance of table views. An iOS app without a table view somewhere in its interface would be a rare thing, especially on the small iPhone screen. Indeed, table views are key to the small screen's viability. I've written apps consisting almost entirely of table views.

It is not uncommon to use a table view even in situations that have nothing particularly table-like about them, simply because it is so convenient. For example, in one of my apps I want the user to be able to choose between three levels of difficulty and two

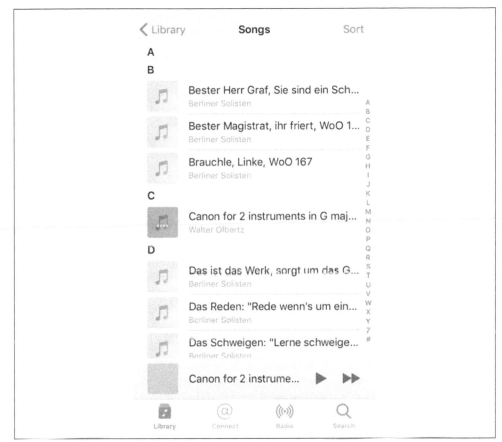

Figure 8-1. A familiar table view

sets of images. In a desktop application I'd probably use radio buttons; but there are no radio buttons among the standard iOS interface objects. Instead, I use a grouped table view so small that it doesn't even scroll. This gives me section headers, tappable cells, and a checkmark indicating the current choice (Figure 8-3).

Table View Controller

In the examples throughout this chapter, I'll use a table view controller in conjunction with a table view. This is a built-in view controller subclass, UITableViewController, whose main view is a table view. You're not obliged to use a UITableViewController with every table view — it doesn't do anything that you couldn't do yourself by other means — but it is certainly convenient. Here are some features of a table view controller:

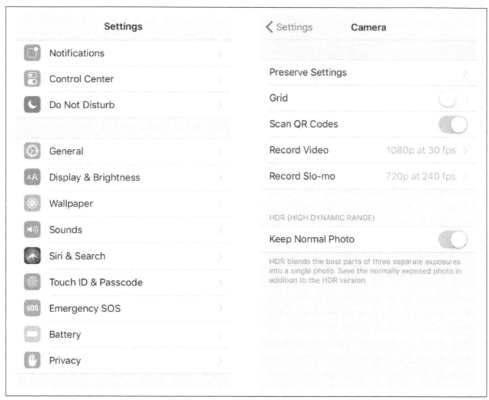

Figure 8-2. A familiar grouped table

Figure 8-3. A grouped table view as an interface for choosing options

- UITableViewController's `init(style:)` initializer creates the table view with a plain or grouped format.
- Every table view needs a data source and a delegate (as I'll explain later); a table view controller is its table view's data source and delegate by default.
- The table view is the table view controller's `tableView`. It is also the table view controller's `view`, but the `tableView` property is typed as a UITableView, so you can send table view messages to it without casting.
- A table view controller lets you configure the layout and content of an entire table in a storyboard (a static table).
- A table view controller provides interface for automatic toggling of its table view's edit mode.

A table view controller is so convenient, in fact, that if a table view is to be a small subview of some view controller's main view, it is often best to make the view controller a custom container view controller with a table view controller as its child ("Container View Controllers" on page 368), rather than trying to implement a "loose" table view.

Table View Cells

A table view's structure and contents are generally not configured in advance. Rather, you supply the table view with a data source and a delegate (which will often be the same object), and the table view turns to these in real time, as the app runs, whenever it needs a piece of information about its own structure and contents.

This architecture may be surprising, especially to beginners, but in fact it is part of a brilliant strategy to conserve resources. Imagine a long table consisting of thousands of rows. It must appear to consist of thousands of cells as the user scrolls. But a cell is a UIView and is memory-intensive; to maintain thousands of cells internally would put a terrible strain on memory. Therefore, the table typically maintains only as many cells as are showing simultaneously at any one moment (about twelve, let's say). As the user scrolls to reveal new cells, those cells are created on the spot; meanwhile, the cells that have been scrolled out of view are permitted to die.

That's ingenious, but wouldn't it be even cleverer if, instead of letting a cell die as it scrolls *out* of view, we whisked it around to the other end and reused it as one of the cells being scrolled *into* view? Yes, and in fact that's exactly what you're supposed to do. You do it by assigning each cell a *reuse identifier*.

As cells with a given reuse identifier are scrolled out of view, the table view maintains a bunch of them in a pile. As a cell is about to be scrolled into view, you ask the table view for a cell from that pile, specifying the pile by means of the reuse identifier. The table view hands an old used cell back to you, and now you can configure it as the cell that is about to be scrolled into view. Cells are thus reused to minimize not only the number of actual cells in existence at any one moment, but the number of actual cells *ever created*. A table of 1000 rows might very well never need to create more than about a dozen cells *over the entire lifetime of the app!*

To facilitate this architecture, your code must be prepared, on demand, to supply the table with pieces of requested data. Of these, the most important is the cell to be slotted into a given position. A position in the table is specified by means of an index path (IndexPath), used here to combine a section number with a row number; it is often referred to as a *row* of the table. Your data source object may at any moment be sent the message `tableView(_:cellForRowAt:)`, and you must respond by returning the UITableViewCell to be displayed at that row of the table. And you must return it *fast*: the user is scrolling *now*, so the table needs that cell *now*.

In this section, I'll discuss *what* you're going to be supplying — the table view cell. After that, I'll talk about *how* you supply it.

Built-In Cell Styles

The simplest way to obtain a table view cell is to start with one of the four built-in table view cell styles. To create a cell using a built-in style, call `init(style:reuse-Identifier:)`. The `reuseIdentifier:` is what allows cells previously assigned to rows that are no longer showing to be reused for cells that are; it will usually be the same for all cells in a table. Your choices of cell style (UITableViewCellStyle) are:

`.default`
> The cell has a UILabel (its `textLabel`), with an optional UIImageView (its `image-View`) at the left. If there is no image, the label occupies the entire width of the cell.

`.value1`
> The cell has two UILabels (its `textLabel` and its `detailTextLabel`) side by side, with an optional UIImageView (its `imageView`) at the left. The first label is left-aligned; the second label is right-aligned. If the first label's text is too long, the second label won't appear.

`.value2`
> The cell has two UILabels (its `textLabel` and its `detailTextLabel`) side by side. No UIImageView will appear. The first label is right-aligned; the second label is left-aligned. The label sizes are fixed, and the text of either will be truncated if it's too long.

Hello there! 1

Hello there! 2

Hello there! 3

Hello there! 4

Figure 8-4. The world's simplest table

`.subtitle`

> The cell has two UILabels (its `textLabel` and its `detailTextLabel`), one above the other, with an optional UIImageView (its `imageView`) at the left.

To experiment with the built-in cell styles, do this:

1. Start with the Single View app template.

2. We're going to ignore the storyboard (as in the examples at the start of Chapter 6). So we need a class to serve as our root view controller. Choose File → New › File and specify iOS → Source → Cocoa Touch Class. Click Next.

3. Make this class a UITableViewController subclass called RootViewController. The XIB checkbox should be *checked*; Xcode will create an eponymous *.xib* file containing a table view, correctly configured with its File's Owner as our Root-ViewController class. Click Next.

4. Make sure you're saving into the correct folder and group, and that the app target is checked. Click Create.

5. Rewrite AppDelegate's `application(_:didFinishLaunchingWithOptions:)` to make our RootViewController the window's `rootViewController`:

```
self.window = self.window ?? UIWindow()
self.window!.rootViewController = RootViewController() // *
self.window!.backgroundColor = .white
self.window!.makeKeyAndVisible()
return true
```

6. Now modify the RootViewController class (which comes with a lot of templated code), as in Example 8-1.

Run the app to see the world's simplest table (Figure 8-4).

Example 8-1. Basic table data source schema

```
let cellID = "Cell"
override func numberOfSections(in tableView: UITableView) {
    -> Int {
        return 1 ❶
}
override func tableView(_ tableView: UITableView,
    numberOfRowsInSection section: Int) -> Int {
        return 20 ❷
}
override func tableView(_ tableView: UITableView,
    cellForRowAt indexPath: IndexPath) -> UITableViewCell {
        var cell : UITableViewCell! = tableView.dequeueReusableCell(
            withIdentifier: self.cellID) ❸
        if cell == nil {
            cell = UITableViewCell(style:.default,
                reuseIdentifier: self.cellID) ❹
            cell.textLabel!.textColor = .red ❺
        }
        cell.textLabel!.text = "Hello there! \(indexPath.row)" ❻
        return cell
}
```

The key parts of the code are:

❶ Our table will have one section.

❷ Our table will consist of 20 rows. Having multiple rows will give us a sense of how our cell looks when placed next to other cells.

❸ In `tableView(_:cellForRowAt:)`, you should *always* start by asking the table view for a reusable cell. Here, we will receive either an already existing reused cell or `nil`; in the latter case, we must create the cell from scratch, ourselves.

❹ If we did receive `nil`, we do create the cell. This is where you specify the built-in table view cell style you want to experiment with.

❺ At this point in the code you can modify characteristics of the cell (`cell`) that are to be the same for *every* cell of the table. For the moment, I've symbolized this by assuming that every cell's text is to be the same color.

❻ We now have the cell to be used for *this* row of the table, so at this point in the code you can modify features of the cell (`cell`) that are unique to this row. I've symbolized this by appending the row number to the text of each row. (Of course, in real life the different cells would reflect meaningful data. I'll talk about that later in this chapter.)

Now you can experiment with your cell's appearance by tweaking the code and running the app. Feel free to try different built-in cell styles in the place where we are now specifying .default. Further flexibility within each built-in style comes from the flexibility of a UILabel. Not everything can be customized, because after you return the cell some further configuration takes place, which may override your settings; for example, the size and position of the cell's subviews are not up to you. (I'll explain, a little later, how to get around that.) But you get a remarkable degree of freedom. Here are a few basic UILabel properties for you to play with now (by customizing cell.textLabel), and I'll talk much more about UILabels in Chapter 10:

text
> The string shown in the label.

textColor, highlightedTextColor
> The color of the text. The highlightedTextColor applies when the cell is highlighted or selected (tap on a cell to select it).

textAlignment
> How the text is aligned; some possible choices (NSTextAlignment) are .left, .center, and .right.

numberOfLines
> The maximum number of lines of text to appear in the label. Text that is long but permitted to wrap, or that contains explicit linefeed characters, can appear completely in the label if the label is tall enough and the number of permitted lines is sufficient. 0 means there's no maximum; the default is 1.

font
> The label's font. You could reduce the font size as a way of fitting more text into the label. A font name includes its style. For example:
>
>   cell.textLabel!.font = UIFont(name:"Helvetica-Bold", size:12.0)

shadowColor, shadowOffset
> The text shadow. Adding a little shadow can increase clarity and emphasis for large text.

You can also assign the image view (cell.imageView) an image. The frame of the image view can't be changed, but you can inset its apparent size by supplying a smaller image and setting the image view's contentMode to .center. It's probably a good idea in any case, for performance reasons, to supply images at their drawn size and resolution rather than making the drawing system scale them down for you (see the last section of Chapter 7). For example:

```
let im = UIImage(named:"moi")!
let r = UIGraphicsImageRenderer(size:CGSize(36,36))
let im2 = r.image { _ in
    im.draw(in:CGRect(0,0,36,36))
}
cell.imageView!.image = im2
cell.imageView!.contentMode = .center
```

The cell itself also has some properties you can play with:

accessoryType

A built-in type (UITableViewCellAccessoryType) of accessory view, which appears at the cell's right end. For example:

```
cell.accessoryType = .disclosureIndicator
```

accessoryView

Your own UIView, which appears at the cell's right end (overriding the accessory-Type). For example:

```
let b = UIButton(type:.system)
b.setTitle("Tap Me", for:.normal)
b.sizeToFit()
// ... add action and target here ...
cell.accessoryView = b
```

indentationLevel, indentationWidth

These properties give the cell a left margin, useful for suggesting a hierarchy among cells. You can also set a cell's indentation level in real time, with respect to the table row into which it is slotted, by implementing the delegate's table-View(_:indentationLevelForRowAt:) method.

separatorInset

A UIEdgeInsets. Only the left and right insets matter. The default is a left inset of 15, but the built-in table view cell styles may shift it to match the left layout margin of the root view (so, 16 or 20). This property affects both the drawing of the separator between cells and the indentation of content of the built-in cell styles. If you don't like the default, you can take control of the inset by setting the separatorInset yourself. (New in iOS 11, this actually works as expected; I'll talk more about it in a moment, in connection with the table view's separator-Inset property.)

selectionStyle

How the background looks when the cell is selected (UITableViewCellSelection-Style). The default is solid gray (.default), or you can choose .none.

Figure 8-5. A cell with an image background

backgroundColor
backgroundView
selectedBackgroundView

> What's behind everything else drawn in the cell. The selectedBackgroundView is drawn in front of the backgroundView (if any) when the cell is selected, and will appear instead of whatever the selectionStyle dictates. The backgroundColor is behind the backgroundView. There is no need to set the frame of the backgroundView and selectedBackgroundView; they will be resized automatically to fit the cell.

multipleSelectionBackgroundView

> If defined (not nil), and if the table's allowsMultipleSelection (or, if editing, allowsMultipleSelectionDuringEditing) is true, used instead of the selected-BackgroundView when the cell is selected.

In this example, we set the cell's backgroundView to display an image with some transparency at the outside edges, so that the backgroundColor shows behind it, and we set the selectedBackgroundView to an almost transparent blue rectangle, to darken that image when the cell is selected (Figure 8-5):

```
cell.textLabel!.textColor = .white
let v = UIImageView() // no need to set frame
v.contentMode = .scaleToFill
v.image = UIImage(named:"linen")
cell.backgroundView = v
let v2 = UIView() // no need to set frame
v2.backgroundColor = UIColor.blue.withAlphaComponent(0.2)
cell.selectedBackgroundView = v2
cell.backgroundColor = .red
```

If those features are to be true of every cell ever displayed in the table, then that code should go in the spot numbered 5 in Example 8-1; it would be wasteful to do the same thing all over again when an existing cell is reused.

Finally, here are a few properties of the table view itself worth playing with:

`rowHeight`

The height of every cell. Taller cells may accommodate more information. You can also change this value in the nib editor; the table view's row height appears in the Size inspector. With a built-in cell style, the cell's subviews have their autoresizing set so as to compensate correctly. You can also set a cell's height in real time by implementing the delegate's `tableView(_:heightForRowAt:)` method; thus a table's cells may differ from one another in height (more about that later in this chapter).

`separatorStyle, separatorColor`

These can also be set in the nib. Separator styles (UITableViewCellSeparatorStyle) are `.none` and `.singleLine`.

`separatorInset, separatorInsetReference`

These can also be set in the nib. The table view's `separatorInset` is adopted by individual cells that don't have their own explicit `separatorInset`; to put it another way, the table view's `separatorInset` is the default, but a cell can override it.

The `separatorInsetReference` is new in iOS 11; it determines how the separator inset is understood, either `.fromCellEdges` or `.fromAutomaticReference` (meaning from the margins). This puts an end to a long-standing problem in iOS 10 and before, where it used to be difficult to get the separator to adopt a zero left inset, because it wanted to interpret that as meaning zero relative to the margin; in iOS 11, the default is `.fromCellEdges` and zero means zero.

`backgroundColor, backgroundView`

What's behind all the cells of the table; this may be seen if the cells have transparency, or if the user scrolls the cells beyond their limit. The `backgroundView` is drawn on top of the `backgroundColor`.

`tableHeaderView, tableFooterView`

Views to be shown before the first row and after the last row, respectively, as part of the table's scrolling content. Their background color is, by default, the background color of the table, but you can change that. You must dictate their heights explicitly, by setting their frame or bounds height; their widths will be dynamically resized to fit the table. You can allow the user to interact with these views (and their subviews); for example, a view can be (or can contain) a UIButton.

You can alter a table header or footer view dynamically during the lifetime of the app; if you change its height, you must set the corresponding table view property afresh to notify the table view of what has happened.

`insetsContentViewsToSafeArea`

> New in iOS 11; can also be set in the nib. The cell's contents, such as its `text-Label`, are inside an unseen view called the `contentView`; those contents are thus positioned with respect to the content view's bounds. If this property is `true` (the default), the safe area insets will inset the frame of the content view; that's significant on an iPhone without a bezel, such as the iPhone X.

`cellLayoutMarginsFollowReadableWidth`

> If this property is `true` and the `separatorInsetReference` is `.fromAutomatic-Reference`, the content view margins will be inset on a wide screen (such as an iPad in landscape) to prevent text content from becoming overly wide.

Registering a Cell Class

In Example 8-1, I used this method to obtain the reusable cell:

- `dequeueReusableCell(withIdentifier:)`

However, there's another way:

- `dequeueReusableCell(withIdentifier:for:)`

The *outward* difference is that the second method has a second parameter — an IndexPath. This should in fact always be the index path you received to begin with as the last parameter of `tableView(_:cellForRowAt:)`. The *functional* difference is very dramatic. The second method has three advantages:

The result is never `nil`

> Unlike `dequeueReusableCell(withIdentifier:)`, the value returned by `dequeue-ReusableCell(withIdentifier:for:)` is never `nil` (in Swift, it isn't an Optional). If there is a free reusable cell with the given identifier, it is returned. If there isn't, a new one is created for you, automatically. Step 4 of Example 8-1 can thus be eliminated!

The cell size is known earlier

> Unlike `dequeueReusableCell(withIdentifier:)`, the cell returned by `dequeue-ReusableCell(withIdentifier:for:)` has its final bounds. That's possible because you've passed the index path as an argument, so the runtime knows this cell's ultimate destination within the table, and has already consulted the table's `rowHeight` or the delegate's `tableView(_:heightForRowAt:)`. This can make laying out the cell's contents much easier.

The identifier is consistent

A danger with `dequeueReusableCell(withIdentifier:)` is that you may accidentally pass an incorrect reuse identifier, and end up not reusing cells. With `dequeueReusableCell(withIdentifier:for:)`, that can't happen (for reasons that I will now explain).

Let's go back to the first advantage of `dequeueReusableCell(withIdentifier:for:)` — if there isn't a reusable cell with the given identifier, the table view will create the cell *for you*, so that you never have to instantiate the cell yourself. How does it know how to do that? You have to tell it, associating the reuse identifier with the correct means of instantiation. There are three possibilities:

Provide a class

You *register* a class with the table view, associating that class with the reuse identifier. The table view will instantiate that class.

Provide a nib

You *register* a *.xib* file with the table view, associating that nib with the reuse identifier. The table view will load the nib to instantiate the cell.

Provide a storyboard

If you're getting the cell from a storyboard, you *enter* the reuse identifier as the Identifier for the cell in the storyboard. The table view will instantiate that cell from the storyboard.

In my examples so far, we're not using a storyboard (I'll discuss that approach later). So let's use the first approach: we'll *register a class* with the table view. To do so, before we call `dequeueReusableCell(withIdentifier:for:)` for the first time, we call `register(_:forCellReuseIdentifier:)`, where the first parameter is UITableViewCell or a subclass thereof. That will associate this class with our reuse identifier. It will also add a measure of safety, because henceforth if we pass a bad identifier into `dequeueReusableCell(withIdentifier:for:)`, the app will crash (with a helpful log message); we are forcing ourselves to reuse cells properly.

This is a very elegant mechanism. It also raises some new questions:

When should I register with the table view?

Do it early, before the table view starts generating cells; `viewDidLoad` is a good place:

```
override func viewDidLoad() {
    super.viewDidLoad()
    self.tableView.register(
        UITableViewCell.self, forCellReuseIdentifier: self.cellID)
}
```

How do I specify a built-in table view cell style?

We are no longer calling `init(style:reuseIdentifier:)`, so where do we make our choice of built-in cell style? The default cell style is `.default`, so if that's what you wanted, the problem is solved. Otherwise, subclass UITableViewCell and register the subclass; in the subclass, override `init(style:reuseIdentifier:)` to substitute the cell style you're after (passing along the reuse identifier you were handed).

For example, suppose we want the `.subtitle` style. Let's call our UITableView-Cell subclass MyCell. So we now specify `MyCell.self` in our call to `register(_:forCellReuseIdentifier:)`. MyCell's initializer looks like this:

```
override init(style: UITableViewCellStyle, reuseIdentifier: String?) {
    super.init(style:.subtitle, reuseIdentifier: reuseIdentifier)
}
```

How do I know whether the returned cell is new or reused?

Good question! `dequeueReusableCell(withIdentifier:for:)` never returns `nil`, so we need some *other* way to distinguish between configurations that are to apply once and for all to a *new cell* (step 5 of Example 8-1) and configurations that differ for *each row* (step 6). It's now up to you, when performing one-time configuration on a cell, to give that cell some distinguishing mark that you can look for later to determine whether a cell requires one-time configuration.

For example, if every cell is to have a two-line text label, there is no point configuring the text label of *every* cell returned by `dequeueReusableCell(withIdentifier:for:)`; the reused cells have already been configured. But how will we know which cells need their text label to be configured? It's easy: they are the ones whose text label *hasn't* been configured:

```
override func tableView(_ tableView: UITableView,
    cellForRowAt indexPath: IndexPath) -> UITableViewCell {
        let cell = tableView.dequeueReusableCell(
            withIdentifier: self.cellID, for: indexPath) as! MyCell
        if cell.textLabel!.numberOfLines != 2 { // cell not configured!
            cell.textLabel!.numberOfLines = 2
            // other one-time configurations here ...
        }
        cell.textLabel!.text = // ...
        // other individual configurations here ...
        return cell
}
```

Based on our new understanding of `dequeueReusableCell(withIdentifier:for:)`, let's rewrite Example 8-1 to use it. The result is Example 8-2, which represents the schema that I use in real life (and that I'll be using throughout the rest of this book).

Example 8-2. Basic table data source schema, revised

```
let cellID = "Cell"
override func viewDidLoad() {
    super.viewDidLoad()
    self.tableView.register(
        UITableViewCell.self, forCellReuseIdentifier: self.cellID) ❶
}
override func numberOfSections(in tableView: UITableView) {
    -> Int {
        return 1 ❷
}
override func tableView(_ tableView: UITableView,
    numberOfRowsInSection section: Int) -> Int {
        return 20 ❸
}
override func tableView(_ tableView: UITableView,
    cellForRowAt indexPath: IndexPath) -> UITableViewCell {
        let cell = tableView.dequeueReusableCell(
            withIdentifier: self.cellID, for: indexPath) ❹
        if cell.textLabel!.numberOfLines != 2 { ❺
            cell.textLabel!.numberOfLines = 2
            // ... other universal configurations here ...
        }
        cell.textLabel!.text = "Hello there! \(indexPath.row)" ❻
        // ... other individual configurations here ...
        return cell
}
```

❶ Register the cell identifier with the table view. No law requires that this be done in `viewDidLoad`, but it's a good place because it's called once, early. But this step *must be omitted* if the cell is to come from a storyboard, as I'll explain later.

❷ Give the number of sections our table is to have.

❸ Give the number of rows each section is to have.

❹ Call `dequeueReusableCell(withIdentifier:for:)` to obtain a cell for this reuse identifier, passing along the incoming index path. (If the registered cell class is a UITableViewCell subclass, you'll probably need to cast down here.)

❺ If there are configurations to be performed that are the same for *every* cell, look to see whether *this* cell has already been configured. If not, configure it.

❻ Modify features of the cell that are *unique to this row*, and return the cell.

Custom Cells

The built-in cell styles give the beginner a leg up in getting started with table views, but there is nothing sacred about them, and soon you'll probably want to transcend them, putting yourself in charge of how a table's cells look and what subviews they contain. You are perfectly free to do this. The thing to remember is that the cell has a contentView property, which is one of its subviews; things like the accessoryView are outside the contentView. All *your* custom subviews must be subviews of the contentView; this allows the cell to continue working correctly.

I'll illustrate four possible approaches to customizing the contents of a cell:

- Start with a built-in cell style, but supply a UITableViewCell subclass and override layoutSubviews to alter the frames of the built-in subviews.
- In tableView(_:cellForRowAt:), add subviews to each cell's contentView as the cell is created.
- Design the cell in a nib, and load that nib in tableView(_:cellForRowAt:) each time a cell needs to be created.
- Design the cell in a storyboard.

 As long as you never speak of the cell's textLabel, detailTextLabel, or imageView, they are never created or inserted into the cell. Thus, you don't need to remove them if you don't want to use them.

Overriding a cell's subview layout

You can't directly change the frame of a built-in cell style subview in tableView(_:cellForRowAt:), because the cell's layoutSubviews comes along later and overrides your changes. The workaround is to override the cell's layoutSubviews! This is a straightforward solution if your main objection to a built-in style is the frame of an existing subview.

To illustrate, let's modify a .default cell so that the image is at the right end instead of the left end (Figure 8-6). We'll make a UITableViewCell subclass; here is MyCell's layoutSubviews:

```
override func layoutSubviews() {
    super.layoutSubviews()
    let cvb = self.contentView.bounds
    let imf = self.imageView!.frame
    self.imageView!.frame.origin.x = cvb.size.width - imf.size.width - 15
    self.textLabel!.frame.origin.x = 15
}
```

We must also make sure to *use* MyCell as our cell type. For example:

The author of this book, who would rather be out dirt biking	

Figure 8-6. A cell with its label and image view swapped

```
self.tableView.register(MyCell.self, forCellReuseIdentifier: self.cellID)
```

Adding subviews in code

Instead of modifying the existing default subviews, you can add completely new views to each UITableViewCell's content view. The best place to do this in code is `tableView(_:cellForRowAt:)`. Here are some things to keep in mind:

- The new views must be added when we configure a brand new cell — but not when we reuse a cell, because a reused cell already has them. (Adding multiple copies of the same subview repeatedly, as the cell is reused, is a common beginner mistake.)

- We must never send `addSubview(_:)` to the cell itself — only to its `contentView` (or some subview thereof).

- We should assign the new views an appropriate `autoresizingMask` or constraints, because the cell's content view might be resized.

- Each new view needs a way to be identified and referred to elsewhere. A `tag` is a simple solution.

I'll rewrite the previous example (Figure 8-6) to use this technique. We don't need a UITableViewCell subclass; the registered cell class can be UITableViewCell itself. If this is a new cell, we add the subviews, position them with autolayout, and assign them tags. If this is a reused cell, we *don't* add the subviews — the cell already has them! Either way, we then use the tags to refer to the subviews:

```
override func tableView(_ tableView: UITableView,
    cellForRowAt indexPath: IndexPath) -> UITableViewCell {
        let cell = tableView.dequeueReusableCell(
            withIdentifier: self.cellID, for: indexPath)
        if cell.viewWithTag(1) == nil { // no subviews! add them
            let iv = UIImageView(); iv.tag = 1
            cell.contentView.addSubview(iv)
            let lab = UILabel(); lab.tag = 2
            cell.contentView.addSubview(lab)
            // autolayout
            let d = ["iv":iv, "lab":lab]
            iv.translatesAutoresizingMaskIntoConstraints = false
            lab.translatesAutoresizingMaskIntoConstraints = false
            var con = [NSLayoutConstraint]()
            con.append(iv.centerYAnchor.constraint(
                equalTo:cell.contentView.centerYAnchor))
```

```
            con.append(iv.widthAnchor.constraint(
                equalTo:iv.heightAnchor))
            con.append(contentsOf:
                NSLayoutConstraint.constraints(
                    withVisualFormat:"V:|[lab]|",
                    metrics:nil, views:d))
            // horizontal margins
            con.append(contentsOf:
                NSLayoutConstraint.constraints(
                    withVisualFormat:"H:|-15-[lab]-15-[iv]-15-|",
                    metrics:nil, views:d))
            NSLayoutConstraint.activate(con)
            // ...
        }
        // can refer to subviews by their tags
        let lab = cell.viewWithTag(2) as! UILabel
        let iv = cell.viewWithTag(1) as! UIImageView
        // ...
        return cell
    }
```

Designing a cell in a nib

We can avoid the verbosity of the previous code by designing the cell in a nib. We start by creating a *.xib* file that will consist, in effect, solely of this one cell; then we design the cell:

1. In Xcode, create the *.xib* file by specifying iOS → User Interface → View. Let's call it *MyCell.xib*.

2. Edit *MyCell.xib*. In the nib editor, delete the existing View and replace it with a Table View Cell from the Object library.

   The cell's design window shows a standard-sized cell; you can resize it as desired, but the actual size of the cell in the interface will be dictated by the table view's width and its rowHeight (or the delegate's response to tableView(_:heightFor-RowAt:)). The cell already has a contentView, and any subviews you add will be inside that; do not subvert that arrangement.

3. You can choose a built-in table view cell style in the Style pop-up menu of the Attributes inspector, and this gives you the default subviews, locked in their standard positions; for example, if you choose Basic, the textLabel appears, and if you specify an image, the imageView appears. If you set the Style pop-up menu to Custom, you start with a blank slate. Let's do that.

4. Design the cell! For example, let's implement, from scratch, the same subviews we've already implemented in the preceding two examples: a UILabel on the left side of the cell, and a UIImageView on the right side. Just as when adding subviews in code, we should set each subview's autoresizing behavior or constraints,

and *give each subview a tag*, so that later, in tableView(_:cellForRowAt:), we'll be able to refer to the label and the image view using viewWithTag(_:), exactly as in the previous example.

The only remaining question is how to load the cell from the nib. It's simple! When we register with the table view, which we're currently doing in viewDidLoad, when we call register(_:forCellReuseIdentifier:), we supply a nib instead of a class. To specify the nib, call UINib's initializer init(nibName:bundle:), like this:

```
self.tableView.register(
    UINib(nibName:"MyCell", bundle:nil), forCellReuseIdentifier:self.cellID)
```

That's all there is to it. In tableView(_:cellForRowAt:), when we call dequeue-ReusableCell(withIdentifier:for:), if the table has no free reusable cell already in existence, the nib will automatically be loaded and the cell will be instantiated from it and returned to us.

You may wonder how that's possible, when we haven't specified a File's Owner class or added an outlet from the File's Owner to the cell in the nib. The answer is that the nib conforms to a specific format. The UINib instance method instantiate(with-Owner:options:) can load a nib with a nil owner, and it returns an array of the nib's instantiated top-level objects. A nib registered with the table view is expected to have exactly one top-level object, and that top-level object is expected to be a UITable-ViewCell; that being so, the cell can easily be extracted from the resulting array, as it is the array's only element. Our nib meets those expectations!

 The nib *must* conform to this format: it must have *exactly* one top-level object, a UITableViewCell. Unfortunately, this means that some configurations are difficult or impossible in the nib. For example, a cell's backgroundView cannot be configured in the nib, because this would require the presence of a second top-level nib object. The simplest workaround is to add the backgroundView in code.

The advantages of this approach should be immediately obvious. The subviews can now be designed in the nib editor, and code that was creating and configuring each subview can be deleted. All the autolayout code from the previous example can be removed; we can specify the constraints in the nib editor. If we were configuring the label — assigning it a font, a line break mode, a numberOfLines — all of that code can be removed; we can specify those things in the nib editor.

But we can go further. In tableView(_:cellForRowAt:), we are still referring to the cell's subviews by way of viewWithTag(_:). There's nothing wrong with that, but perhaps you'd prefer to use names. Now that we're designing the cell in a nib, that's easy. Provide a UITableViewCell subclass with outlet properties, and configure the nib file accordingly:

1. Create a UITableViewCell subclass — let's call it MyCell — and declare two outlet properties:

```
class MyCell : UITableViewCell {
    @IBOutlet var theLabel : UILabel!
    @IBOutlet var theImageView : UIImageView!
}
```

   That is the *entirety* of MyCell's code; it exists solely so that we can create these outlets.

2. Edit the table view cell nib *MyCell.xib*. Change the class of the cell (in the Identity inspector) to MyCell, and connect the outlets from the cell to the respective subviews.

The result is that in our implementation of `tableView(_:cellForRowAt:)`, once we've typed the cell as a MyCell, the compiler will let us use the property names to access the subviews:

```
let cell = tableView.dequeueReusableCell(
    withIdentifier: self.cellID, for: indexPath) as! MyCell // *
let lab = cell.theLabel! // *
let iv = cell.theImageView! // *
// ... configure lab and iv ...
```

Designing a cell in a storyboard

If your table view is instantiated from a storyboard, then, in addition to all the ways of obtaining and designing its cells that I've already described, there is an additional option. You can have the table view obtain its cells *from the storyboard itself*. This means you can also *design* the cell in the storyboard.

Let's experiment with this way of obtaining and designing a cell:

1. Start with a project based on the Single View app template.

2. In the storyboard, delete the View Controller scene.

3. In the project, create a file for a UITableViewController subclass called Root-ViewController, *without* a corresponding *.xib* file.

4. In the storyboard, drag a Table View Controller into the empty canvas, and set its class to RootViewController. Make sure it's the initial view controller.

5. The table view controller in the storyboard comes with a table view. In the storyboard, select that table view, and, in the Attributes inspector, set the Content pop-up menu to Dynamic Prototypes, and set the number of Prototype Cells to 1 (these are the defaults).

The table view in the storyboard now contains a single table view cell with a content view. You can do in this cell exactly what we were doing before when designing a table view cell in a *.xib* file! So, let's do that. I like being able to refer to my custom cell subviews with property names. Our procedure is just like what we did in the previous example:

1. In code, declare a UITableViewCell subclass — let's call it MyCell — with two outlet properties:

   ```
   class MyCell : UITableViewCell {
       @IBOutlet var theLabel : UILabel!
       @IBOutlet var theImageView : UIImageView!
   }
   ```

2. In the storyboard, select the table view's prototype cell and change its class in the Identity inspector to MyCell.

3. Drag a label and an image view into the prototype cell, position and configure them as desired, and connect the cell's outlets to them appropriately.

So far, so good; but there is one crucial question I have not yet answered: how will your code tell the table view to get its cells from the storyboard? The answer is: by *not* calling `register(_:forCellReuseIdentifier:)`! Instead, when you call `dequeue-ReusableCell(withIdentifier:for:)`, you supply an identifier that matches the *prototype cell's identifier* in the storyboard. So:

1. If you are calling `register(_:forCellReuseIdentifier:)` in RootViewController's code, *delete that line.*

2. In the storyboard, select the prototype cell. In the Attributes inspector, enter `Cell` (the string value of `self.cellID`) in the Identifier field.

Now RootViewController's `tableView(_:cellForRowAt:)` works exactly as it did in the previous example; our `cellID` is `"Cell"`, and this matches the `Cell` we entered as the prototype cell's Identifier in the storyboard:

```
let cell = tableView.dequeueReusableCell(
    withIdentifier: self.cellID, for: indexPath) as! MyCell
let lab = cell.theLabel!
let iv = cell.theImageView!
```

When your UITableViewController is to get its cells from the UITableViewController scene in the storyboard, there are several ways to go wrong. These are all common beginner mistakes:

Wrong view controller class

In the storyboard, make sure that your UITableViewController's class, in the Identity inspector, matches the class of your UITableViewController subclass in code. If you get this wrong, none of your table view controller code will run.

Wrong cell identifier

In the storyboard, make sure that the prototype cell identifier matches the reuse identifier in your code's `dequeueReusableCell(withIdentifier:for:)` call. If you get this wrong, your app will crash (with a helpful message in the console).

Wrong cell class

In the storyboard, make sure that your prototype cell's class, in the Identity inspector, is the class you expect to receive from `dequeueReusableCell(withIdentifier:for:)`. If you get this wrong, your app will crash when the cell can't be cast down.

Wrong registration

In your table view controller code, make sure you do *not* call `register(_:forCellReuseIdentifier:)`. If you do call it, you will be telling the runtime *not* to get the cell from the storyboard. If you get this wrong by registering a nib, then (if you're lucky) your app will crash (with a helpful message in the console). If you get it wrong by registering a class, your cell might be blank, or your app might crash in some other way (for example, when you access outlets that have never been connected).

Table View Data

The structure and content of the actual data portrayed in a table view comes from the *data source*, an object pointed to by the table view's dataSource property and adopting the UITableViewDataSource protocol. The data source is thus the heart and soul of the table. What surprises beginners is that the data source operates not by *setting* the table view's structure and content, but by *responding on demand*. The data source, *qua* data source, consists of a set of methods that the table view will call when it needs information; in effect, the table view will ask your data source some questions. This architecture has important consequences for how you write your code, which can be summarized by these simple guidelines:

Be ready

Your data source cannot know *when* or *how often* any of these methods will be called, so it must be prepared to answer *any question at any time*.

Be fast

The table view is asking for data in real time; the user is probably scrolling through the table *right now*. So you mustn't gum up the works; you must be ready to supply responses just as fast as you possibly can. (If you can't supply a piece of data fast enough, you may have to skip it, supply a placeholder, and insert the data into the table later. This may involve you in threading issues that I don't want to get into here. I'll give an example in Chapter 23.)

Be consistent

There are multiple data source methods, and you cannot know *which* one will be called at a given moment. So you must make sure your responses are mutually consistent at *any* moment. For example, a common beginner error is forgetting to take into account, in your data source methods, the possibility that the data might not yet be ready.

This may sound daunting, but you'll be fine as long as you maintain an unswerving adherence to the principles of model–view–controller. How and when you accumulate the actual data, and how that data is structured, is a *model* concern. Acting as a data source is a *controller* concern. So you can acquire and arrange your data whenever and however you like, just so long as, when the table view actually turns to you and asks what to do, you can lay your hands on the relevant data rapidly and consistently. You'll want to design the model in such a way that the controller can access any desired piece of data more or less instantly.

Another source of confusion for beginners is that methods are rather oddly distributed between the data source and the *delegate*, an object pointed to by the table view's `delegate` property and adopting the UITableViewDelegate protocol; in some cases, one may seem to be doing the job of the other. This is not usually a cause of any real difficulty, because the object serving as data source will probably also be the object serving as delegate. Nevertheless, it is rather inconvenient when you're consulting the documentation; you'll probably want to keep the data source and delegate documentation pages open simultaneously as you work.

 When you're using a table view controller with a corresponding table view in the storyboard (or in a *.xib* file created at the same time), the table view controller comes to you already configured as both the table view's data source and the table view's delegate. Creating a table view in some other way, and then forgetting to set its `dataSource` and `delegate`, is a common beginner mistake.

The Three Big Questions

Pretend now that you are the data source. Like Katherine Hepburn in *Pat and Mike*, the basis of your success is your ability, at any time, to answer the Three Big Questions. The questions the table view will ask you are a little different from the questions Mike asks Pat, but the principle is the same: know the answers, and be able to recite them at any moment. Here they are:

How many sections does this table have?

The table will call `numberOfSections(in:)`; respond with an integer. In theory you can sometimes omit this method, as the default response is 1, which is often correct. However, I never omit it; for one thing, returning 0 is a good way to say that you've no data yet, and will prevent the table view from asking any other questions.

How many rows does this section have?

The table will call `tableView(_:numberOfRowsInSection:)`. The table supplies a section number — the first section is numbered 0 — and you respond with an integer. In a table with only one section, of course, there is probably no need to examine the incoming section number.

What cell goes in this row of this section?

The table will call `tableView(_:cellForRowAt:)`. The index path is expressed as an IndexPath; UITableView extends IndexPath to add two read-only properties — `section` and `row`. Using these, you extract the requested section number and row number, and return a fully configured UITableViewCell, ready for display in the table view. The first row of a section is numbered 0. I have already explained how to obtain the cell in the first place, by calling `dequeueReusableCell(with-Identifier:for:)` (see Example 8-2).

I have nothing particular to say about precisely how you're going to fulfill these obligations. It all depends on your data model and what your table is trying to portray. The important thing is to remember that you're going to be receiving an IndexPath specifying a section and a row, and you need to be able to lay your hands on the data corresponding to that slot *now* and configure the cell *now*. So construct your model, and your algorithm for consulting it in the Three Big Questions, and your way of configuring the cell, in accordance with that necessity.

For example, suppose our table is to list the names of the Pep Boys. Our data model might be an array of string names (`self.pep`). Our table has only one section. We're using a UITableViewController, and it is the table view's data source. So our code might look like this:

```
let pep = ["Manny", "Moe", "Jack"]
override func numberOfSections(in tableView: UITableView) -> Int {
    return 1
}
override func tableView(_ tableView: UITableView,
    numberOfRowsInSection section: Int) -> Int {
        return self.pep.count
}
override func tableView(_ tableView: UITableView,
    cellForRowAt indexPath: IndexPath) -> UITableViewCell {
        let cell = tableView.dequeueReusableCell(
```

```
                  withIdentifier: self.cellID, for: indexPath)
            cell.textLabel!.text = pep[indexPath.row]
            return cell
    }
```

At this point you may be feeling some exasperation. You want to object: "But that's trivial!" Exactly so! Your access to the data model *should* be trivial. That's the sign of a data model that's well designed for access by your table view's data source. Your implementation of `tableView(_:cellForRowAt:)` might have some interesting work to do in order to configure the *form* of the cell, but accessing the actual *data* should be simple and boring.

 If a table view's contents are known beforehand, you can alternatively design the entire table, *including the contents of individual cells*, in a storyboard as a static table. I'll give an example later in this chapter.

Reusing Cells

Another important goal of `tableView(_:cellForRowAt:)` should be to conserve resources by reusing cells. As I've already explained, once a cell's row is no longer visible on the screen, that cell can be slotted into a row that *is* visible — with its portrayed data appropriately modified, of course! — so that only a few more than the number of simultaneously visible cells will ever need to be instantiated.

A table view is ready to implement this strategy for you; all you have to do is call `dequeueReusableCell(withIdentifier:for:)`. For any given identifier, you'll be handed either a newly minted cell or a reused cell that previously appeared in the table view but is now no longer needed because it has scrolled out of view.

The table view can maintain more than one cache of reusable cells; this could be useful if your table view contains more than one type of cell (where the meaning of the concept "type of cell" is pretty much up to you). This is why you must *name* each cache, by attaching an identifier string to any cell that can be reused. All the examples in this chapter (and in this book, and in fact in every UITableView I've ever created) use just one cache and just one identifier, but there can be more than one. If you're using a storyboard as a source of cells, there would then need to be more than one prototype cell.

To prove to yourself the efficiency of the cell-caching architecture, do something to differentiate newly instantiated cells from reused cells, and count the newly instantiated cells, like this:

```
override func numberOfSections(in tableView: UITableView) -> Int {
    return 1
}
override func tableView(_ tableView: UITableView,
    numberOfRowsInSection section: Int) -> Int {
```

```
            return 1000 // make a lot of rows this time!
    }
    var cells = 0
    override func tableView(_ tableView: UITableView,
        cellForRowAt indexPath: IndexPath) -> UITableViewCell {
        let cell = tableView.dequeueReusableCell(
            withIdentifier: self.cellID, for: indexPath) as! MyCell
        let lab = cell.theLabel!
        lab.text = "Row \(indexPath.row) of section \(indexPath.section)"
        if lab.tag != 999 {
            lab.tag = 999
            self.cells += 1; print("New cell \(self.cells)")
        }
        return cell
    }
```

When we run this code and scroll through the table, every cell is numbered correctly, so there appear to be 1000 cells. But the console messages show that only about a dozen distinct cells are ever actually created.

Be certain that *your* table view code passes that test, and that you are truly reusing cells! Fortunately, one of the benefits of calling dequeueReusableCell(withIdentifier:for:) is that it forces you to use a valid reuse identifier.

 A common beginner error is to obtain a cell in some other way, such as instantiating it directly every time tableView(_:cellForRowAt:) is called. I have even seen beginners call dequeueReusableCell(withIdentifier:for:), only to instantiate a fresh cell manually in the *next* line. Don't do that. Don't subvert the architecture of cell reuse!

When your tableView(_:cellForRowAt:) implementation configures *individual* cells (step 6 in Example 8-2), the cell might be new or reused; at this point in your code, you don't know or care which. Therefore, you should always configure *everything* about the cell that might need configuring. If you fail to do this, and if the cell is reused, you might be surprised when some aspect of the cell is left over from its previous use; similarly, if you fail to do this, and if the cell is new, you might be surprised when some aspect of the cell isn't configured at all.

As usual, I learned that lesson the hard way. In the TidBITS News app, there is a little loudspeaker icon that should appear in a given cell in the master view's table view only if there is a recording associated with this article. So I initially wrote this code:

```
if item.enclosures != nil && item.enclosures.count > 0 {
    cell.speaker.isHidden = false
}
```

That turned out to be a mistake, because the cell might be reused. Every reused cell *always* had a visible loudspeaker icon if, in a previous usage, that cell had *ever* had a visible loudspeaker icon! The solution was to rewrite the logic to cover all possibilities completely, like this:

```
cell.speaker.isHidden =
    !(item.enclosures != nil && item.enclosures.count > 0)
```

You do get a sort of second bite of the cherry: there's a delegate method, `table-View(_:willDisplay:forRowAt:)`, that is called for every cell just before it appears in the table. This is absolutely the last minute to configure a cell. But don't misuse this method. You're functioning as the delegate here, not the data source; you may set the final details of the cell's appearance, but you shouldn't be consulting the data model at this point. It is of great importance that you not do anything even slightly time-consuming in `tableView(_:willDisplay:forRowAt:)`; the cell is literally just milliseconds away from appearing in the interface.

An additional delegate method is `tableView(_:didEndDisplaying:forRowAt:)`. This tells you that the cell no longer appears in the interface and has become free for reuse. You could take advantage of this to tear down any resource-heavy customization of the cell or simply to prepare it somehow for subsequent future reuse.

Table View Sections

Your table data may be clumped into sections. You might clump your data into sections for various reasons (and doubtless there are other reasons beyond these):

- You want to clump the table cells into sections in the table view.
- You want to supply section headers (or footers, or both) in the table view.
- You want to make navigation of the table view easier by supplying an index down the right side. You can't have an index without sections.
- You want to facilitate programmatic rearrangement of the table view's contents. For example, it's possible to hide or move an entire section at once, optionally with animation.

Section Headers and Footers

A section header or footer appears between the cells, before the first row of a section or after the last row of a section, respectively. In a nongrouped table, a section header or footer detaches itself while the user scrolls the table, pinning itself to the top or bottom of the table view and floating over the scrolled rows, giving the user a clue, at every moment, as to where we are within the table. Also, a section header or footer can contain custom views, so it's a place where you might put additional information, or even functional interface, such as a button the user can tap.

Don't confuse the section headers and footers with the header and footer of the table as a whole. The latter are properties of the table view itself, its `tableHeader-View` and `tableFooterView`, discussed earlier in this chapter. The table header view appears only when the table is scrolled all the way down; the table footer view appears only when the table is scrolled all the way up.

The number of sections is determined by your reply to the first Big Question, `number-OfSections(in:)`. For each section, the table view will consult your data source and delegate to learn whether this section has a header or a footer, or both, or neither (the default).

A section header or footer in the table view will usually be a UITableViewHeaderFooterView. This is a UIView subclass intended specifically for this purpose; much like a table view cell, it is reusable. It has the following properties:

`textLabel`
A label (UILabel) for displaying the text of the header or footer.

`detailTextLabel`
This label, if you set its text, appears only in a grouped style table.

`contentView`
A subview of the header or footer, to which you can add custom subviews.

`backgroundView`
Any view you want to assign. The `contentView` is in front of the `background-View`. The `contentView` has a clear background by default, so the `background-View` shows through. An opaque `contentView.backgroundColor` would completely obscure the `backgroundView`.

If the `backgroundView` is `nil` (the default), the header or footer view will supply its own background view whose `backgroundColor` is derived (in some unspecified way) from the table's `backgroundColor`.

 Don't set a UITableViewHeaderFooterView's `backgroundColor`; instead, give it a `backgroundView` and set that view's `backgroundColor`.

There are two ways in which you can supply a header or footer. You can use both, but it will be less confusing if you pick just one:

Header or footer title string
You implement the data source method `tableView(_:titleForHeaderIn-Section:)` or `tableView(_:titleForFooterInSection:)` (or both). Return `nil` to indicate that the given section has no header (or footer). The header or footer

view itself is a UITableViewHeaderFooterView, and is reused automatically. The string you supply becomes the view's `textLabel.text`.

(In a grouped style table, the string's capitalization may be changed. To avoid that, use the second way of supplying the header or footer.)

Header or footer view

You implement the delegate method `tableView(_:viewForHeaderInSection:)` or `tableView(_:viewForFooterInSection:)` (or both). The view you supply is used as the entire header or footer and is automatically resized to the table's width and the section header or footer height (I'll discuss how the height is determined in a moment).

You are not required to return a UITableViewHeaderFooterView, but you should do so. The procedure is much like making a cell reusable. You register beforehand with the table view by calling `register(_:forHeaderFooterViewReuse-Identifier:)` with the UITableViewHeaderFooterView class or a subclass. To obtain the reusable view, call `dequeueReusableHeaderFooterView(with-Identifier:)` on the table view; the result will be either a newly instantiated view or a reused view.

You can then configure this view as desired. For example, you can set its `text-Label.text`, or you can give its `contentView` custom subviews. In the latter case, use autoresizing or constraints to ensure that the subviews will be positioned and sized appropriately when the view itself is resized.

 The documentation says that you can call `register(_:forHeaderFooterView-ReuseIdentifier:)` to register a nib instead of a class. But the nib editor's Object library doesn't include a UITableViewHeaderFooterView! So this approach is useless.

In addition, these delegate methods permit you to perform final configurations on your header or footer views:

`tableView(_:willDisplayHeaderView:forSection:)`
`tableView(_:willDisplayFooterView:forSection:)`

You can perform further configurations here, if desired. A useful possibility is to generate the default UITableViewHeaderFooterView by implementing `title-For...` and then tweak its form slightly here. These delegate methods are matched by `didEndDisplaying` methods.

The runtime resizes your header or footer before displaying it. Its width will be the table view's width; its height will be the table view's `sectionHeaderHeight` or `section-FooterHeight` unless you implement one of these delegate methods to say otherwise:

```
tableView(_:heightForHeaderInSection:)
tableView(_:heightForFooterInSection:)
```
Returning 0 (or failing to dictate the height at all) hides the header or footer. Returning UITableViewAutomaticDimension means 0 if titleFor... returns nil or the empty string (or isn't implemented); otherwise, it means the table view's sectionHeaderHeight or sectionFooterHeight.

 New in iOS 11, you can size a section header or footer from the inside out, using autolayout constraints. I'll talk about that later in the chapter.

A header or footer view in a nongrouped table is in front of the table's cells, and you can take advantage of this to create some nice effects. For example, a header with transparency, when pinned to the top of the table view, shows the cells as they scroll behind it; a header with a shadow casts that shadow on the adjacent cell.

When a header or footer view is not pinned to the top or bottom of the table view, there is a transparent gap behind it. If the header or footer view has some transparency, the table view's background is visible through this gap. You'll want to take this into account when planning your color scheme.

Section Data

A table that is to have sections may require some planning in the construction and architecture of its data model. The row data must somehow be clumped into sections, because you're going to be asked for a row *with respect to its section*. And, just as with a cell, a section title must be readily available so that it can be supplied quickly in real time.

A minimal solution is a custom struct that does no more than pair the section title with the row data:

```
struct Section {
    var sectionName : String
    var rowData : [ /* ... */ ]
}
```

The data model itself will then be an array of our custom struct. The type of the row-Data array elements will depend on the nature of the data; it might be another custom struct.

To illustrate, suppose we intend to display the names of all 50 U.S. states in alphabetical order as the rows of a table view, and that we wish to divide the table into sections according to the first letter of each state's name. Let's say I have the alphabetized list as a text file, which starts like this:

```
Alabama
Alaska
Arizona
Arkansas
California
Colorado
Connecticut
Delaware
...
```

If the only thing we intend to display in our table view cells is the name of the state, the row data for each cell is a String:

```
struct Section {
    var sectionName : String
    var rowData : [String]
}
var sections : [Section]! // data model
```

I'll prepare the data model by loading the text file and parsing it into a Section array:

```
override func viewDidLoad() {
    super.viewDidLoad()
    let s = try! String(
        contentsOfFile: Bundle.main.path(
            forResource: "states", ofType: "txt")!)
    let states = s.components(separatedBy:"\n")
    let d = Dictionary(grouping: states) {String($0.prefix(1))}
    self.sections = Array(d).sorted{$0.key < $1.key}.map {
        Section(sectionName: $0.key, rowData: $0.value)
    }
    // ...
}
```

The value of this preparatory dance is evident when we are bombarded with questions from the table view about cells and headers; supplying the answers is trivial, just as it should be:

```
override func numberOfSections(in tableView: UITableView) -> Int {
    return self.sections.count
}
override func tableView(_ tableView: UITableView,
    numberOfRowsInSection section: Int) -> Int {
        return self.sections[section].rowData.count
}
override func tableView(_ tableView: UITableView,
    cellForRowAt indexPath: IndexPath) -> UITableViewCell {
        let cell = tableView.dequeueReusableCell(
            withIdentifier: self.cellID, for: indexPath)
        let s = self.sections[indexPath.section].rowData[indexPath.row]
        cell.textLabel!.text = s
        return cell
}
```

```
override func tableView(_ tableView: UITableView,
    titleForHeaderInSection section: Int) -> String? {
        return self.sections[section].sectionName
}
```

Let's modify that example to illustrate customization of a header view. I register my header identifier in `viewDidLoad`:

```
let headerID = "Header"
override func viewDidLoad() {
    super.viewDidLoad()
    // ...
    self.tableView.register(UITableViewHeaderFooterView.self,
        forHeaderFooterViewReuseIdentifier: self.headerID)
}
```

I'll implement `tableView(_:viewForHeaderInSection:)`, because it's more interesting than `tableView(_:titleForHeaderInSection:)`. For completely new views, I'll place my own label inside the `contentView` and give it some basic configuration; then I'll perform individual configuration on all views, new or reused:

```
override func tableView(_ tableView: UITableView,
    viewForHeaderInSection section: Int) -> UIView? {
        let h = tableView.dequeueReusableHeaderFooterView(
            withIdentifier: self.headerID)!
        if h.viewWithTag(1) == nil {
            h.backgroundView = UIView()
            h.backgroundView?.backgroundColor = .black
            let lab = UILabel()
            lab.tag = 1
            lab.font = UIFont(name:"Georgia-Bold", size:22)
            lab.textColor = .green
            lab.backgroundColor = .clear
            h.contentView.addSubview(lab)
            // ... add constraints ...
        }
        let lab = h.contentView.viewWithTag(1) as! UILabel
        lab.text = self.sections[section].sectionName
        return h
}
```

Section Index

If your table view has the plain style, you can add an index down the right side of the table, where the user can tap or drag to jump to the start of a section — helpful for navigating long tables. To generate the index, implement the data source method `sectionIndexTitles(for:)`, returning an array of string titles to appear as entries in the index. For our list of state names, that's trivial once again, just as it should be:

```
override func sectionIndexTitles(for tv: UITableView) -> [String]? {
    return self.sections.map{$0.sectionName}
}
```

The index can appear even if there are no section headers. It will appear only if the number of rows exceeds the table view's `sectionIndexMinimumDisplayRowCount` property value; the default is 0, so the index is always displayed by default. You will want the index entries to be short — preferably just one character — because each cell's content view will shrink to compensate, so you're sacrificing some cell real estate.

You can modify three properties that affect the index's appearance:

`sectionIndexColor`
The index text color.

`sectionIndexBackgroundColor`
The index background color. I advise giving the index some background color, even if it is `clearColor`, because otherwise the index distorts the colors of what's behind it in a distracting way.

`sectionIndexTrackingBackgroundColor`
The index background color while the user's finger is sliding over it. By default, it's the same as the `sectionIndexBackgroundColor`.

Normally, there will be a one-to-one correspondence between the index entries and the sections; when the user taps an index entry, the table jumps to the start of the corresponding section. However, under certain circumstances you may want to customize this correspondence.

For example, suppose there are 100 sections, but there isn't room to display 100 index entries comfortably on the iPhone. The index will automatically curtail itself, omitting some index entries and inserting bullets to suggest the omission, but you might prefer to take charge of the situation.

To do so, supply a shorter index, and implement the data source method `tableView(_:sectionForSectionIndexTitle:at:)`, returning the number of the section to jump to. You are told both the title and the index number of the section index listing that the user chose, so you can use whichever is convenient.

 If the table view has a section index, its scroll indicators will never appear.

Refreshing a Table View

A table view has no direct connection to its underlying data. If you want the table view display to change because the underlying data have changed, you have to cause the table view to refresh itself; basically, you're requesting that the Big Questions be asked all over again. At first blush, this seems inefficient ("regenerate *all* the data?"); but it isn't. Remember, in a table that caches reusable cells, there are no cells of interest other than those actually showing in the table at this moment. Thus, having worked out the layout of the table through the section header and footer heights and row heights, the table has to regenerate only those cells that are actually visible.

You can cause the table data to be refreshed using any of several methods:

reloadData
> The table view will ask the Three Big Questions all over again, including heights of rows and section headers and footers, and the index, exactly as it does when the table view first appears.

reloadRows(at:with:)
> The table view will ask the Three Big Questions all over again, including heights, but not index entries. Cells are requested only for visible cells among those you specify. The first parameter is an array of index paths; to form an index path, use the initializer init(row:section:).

reloadSections(_:with:)
> The table view will ask the Three Big Questions all over again, including heights of rows and section headers and footers, and the index. Cells, headers, and footers are requested only for visible elements of the sections you specify. The first parameter is an IndexSet.

The latter two methods can perform animations that cue the user as to what's changing. For the with: argument, you'll specify what animation you want by passing one of the following (UITableViewRowAnimation):

.fade
> The old fades into the new.

.right, .left, .top, .bottom
> The old slides out in the stated direction, and is replaced from the opposite direction.

.middle
> Hard to describe; it's a sort of venetian blind effect on each cell individually.

`.automatic`

The table view just "does the right thing." This is especially useful for grouped style tables, because if you pick the wrong animation, the display can look very funny as it proceeds.

`.none`

No animation.

If all you need is to refresh the index, call `reloadSectionIndexTitles`; this calls the data source's `sectionIndexTitles(for:)`.

Direct Access to Cells

It is also possible to access and alter a table's individual cells directly. This can be a lightweight approach to refreshing the table, plus you can supply your own animation within the cell as it alters its appearance. It is important to bear in mind, however, that the cells are not the data (view is not model). If you change the content of a cell manually, make sure that you have also changed the model corresponding to it, so that the row will appear correctly if its data is reloaded later.

 Do *not* change the display of a table cell directly *without* also changing the underlying data! It's your job to design your data model and your implementation of `tableView(_:cellForRowAt:)` to accommodate any real-time changes you'll need to make.

When accessing a cell directly, you'll probably want to make sure the cell is visible within the table view's bounds; nonvisible cells don't really exist (except as potential cells waiting in the reuse cache), and there's no point changing them manually, as they'll be changed when they are scrolled into view, through the usual call to `tableView(_:cellForRowAt:)`.

Here are some UITableView properties and methods that mediate between cells, rows, and visibility:

`visibleCells`

An array of the cells actually showing within the table's bounds.

`indexPathsForVisibleRows`

An array of the rows actually showing within the table's bounds.

`cellForRow(at:)`

Returns a UITableViewCell if the table is maintaining a cell for the given row (typically because this is a visible row); otherwise, returns `nil`.

`indexPath(for:)`

Given a cell obtained from the table view, returns the row into which it is slotted.

By the same token, you can get access to the views constituting headers and footers, by calling headerView(forSection:) or footerView(forSection:). Thus you could modify a view directly. You should assume that if a section is returned by indexPaths-ForVisibleRows, its header or footer might be visible.

Refresh Control

If you want to grant the user some interface for requesting that a table view be refreshed, you might like to use a UIRefreshControl. You aren't required to use this; it's just Apple's attempt to provide a standard interface.

To give a table view a refresh control, assign a UIRefreshControl to the table view's refreshControl property; this property is actually inherited from UIScrollView. You can also configure this in the nib editor through a table view controller's Refreshing pop-up menu.

To request a refresh, the user scrolls the table view downward to display the refresh control and holds long enough to indicate that this scrolling is deliberate. The refresh control then acknowledges visually that it is refreshing, and remains visible until refreshing is complete.

The refresh control is normally displayed at the top of the scrolling part of the table view. New in iOS 11, however, if we're in a navigation interface (UINavigation-Controller) with a navigation bar that displays large titles, the refresh control appears *in the navigation bar*, which stretches to accommodate it when visible; for this to work, it is *crucial* that the table view should underlap the navigation bar.

A refresh control is a control (UIControl, Chapter 12), and you will want to hook its Value Changed event to an action method; you can do that in the nib editor by making an action connection, or you can do it in code. Here's an example of creating and configuring a refresh control entirely in code:

```
self.tableView!.refreshControl = UIRefreshControl()
self.tableView!.refreshControl!.addTarget(
    self, action: #selector(doRefresh), for: .valueChanged)
```

Once a refresh control's action message has fired, the control remains visible and indicates by animation (similar to an activity indicator) that it is refreshing, until you send it the endRefreshing message:

```
@IBAction func doRefresh(_ sender: Any) {
    // ...
    (sender as! UIRefreshControl).endRefreshing()
}
```

You can initiate a refresh animation in code with beginRefreshing, but this does not fire the action message. It also doesn't display the refresh control; to display it, scroll the table view:

```
self.refreshControl!.sizeToFit()
let top = self.tableView.adjustedContentInset.top
let y = self.refreshControl!.frame.maxY + top
self.tableView.setContentOffset(CGPoint(0, -y), animated:true)
self.refreshControl!.beginRefreshing()
self.doRefresh(self.refreshControl!)
```

A refresh control also has these properties:

isRefreshing *(read-only)*
> Whether the refresh control is refreshing.

tintColor
> The refresh control's color. It is *not* inherited from the view hierarchy (I regard this as a bug).

attributedTitle
> Styled text displayed below the refresh control's activity indicator. On attributed strings, see Chapter 10.

backgroundColor *(inherited from UIView)*
> If you give a table view controller's refreshControl a background color, that color completely covers the table view's own background color when the refresh control is revealed. For some reason, I find the drawing of the attributedTitle more reliable if the refresh control has a background color.

Variable Row Heights

Most tables have rows that are all the same height, as set by the table view's row-Height. However, it's possible for different rows to have different heights. You can see an example in the TidBITS News app (Figure 6-1).

Back when I first wrote my TidBITS News and Albumen apps for iOS 4, variable row heights were possible but virtually unheard-of; I knew of no other app that was using them, and Apple provided no guidance, so I had to invent my own technique by trial and error. There were three main challenges:

Measurement
> *What* should the height of a given row be?

Timing
> *When* should the determination of each row's height be made?

Layout
> How should the *subviews* of each cell be configured for its individual height?

Over the years since then, implementing variable row heights has become considerably easier. In iOS 6, with the advent of autolayout, both measurement and layout became much simpler. In iOS 7, new table view properties made it possible to improve the timing. Then iOS 8 permitted variable row heights to be implemented *automatically*, without your having to worry about any of these problems. New in iOS 11, section header and footer heights can be implemented automatically as well.

I will briefly describe, in historical order, four different techniques that I have used over the years in my own apps. Perhaps you won't use any of the first three, because the automatic variable row heights feature makes them unnecessary; nevertheless, a basic understanding of them will give you an appreciation of what the fourth approach is doing for you. Besides, in my experience, the automatic variable row heights feature can be slow; for efficiency and speed, you might want to revert to one of the earlier techniques.

Manual Row Height Measurement

In its earliest incarnation, my variable row heights technique depends on the delegate's `tableView(_:heightForRowAt:)`. Whatever height I return for a given row, that's the height that the cell at that row will be given.

The timing is interesting. It turns out that the runtime wants to know the heights of *everything* in the table at the outset, before it starts asking for *any* cells. Thus, before our `tableView(_:cellForRowAt:)` is called for even *one* row, we are sent `tableView(_:heightForRowAt:)` for *every* row.

In preparation for this situation, I start with an array of Optional CGFloats stored in a property, `self.rowHeights`. (Assume, for simplicity, that the table has just one section; the row number can thus serve directly as an index into the array.) Initially, all the values in the array are `nil`. Once the real values have been filled in, the array can be used to supply a requested height instantly.

To calculate the cell heights, I have a utility method, `setUpCell(_:for:)`, that lays out a cell for a given row, using the actual data for that row. It takes a cell and an index path, lays out the cell, and returns the cell's resulting height as a CGFloat. Before the days of autolayout, doing the actual work of measurement in `setUpCell(_:for:)` is laborious; I have to lay out the cell manually, assigning a frame to each subview, one by one. The main challenge is dealing with labels whose text, and therefore height, could vary from row to row.

The strategy is now clear. When the delegate's `tableView(_:heightForRowAt:)` is called, either this is the very first time it's been called or it isn't. Thus, either we've already constructed `self.rowHeights` or we haven't. If we haven't, we construct it now, by immediately calling the `setUpCell(_:for:)` utility method for *every row* and storing each resulting height in `self.rowHeights`. The cell that I'm passing to `setUpCell(_:for:)` isn't going into the table; it's just a dummy copy of the cell, to give me something to configure and work out the resulting cell height.

For now on, I'm ready to answer `tableView(_:heightForRowAt:)` for *any* row, *imme-diately* — all I have to do is return the appropriate value from the `self.rowHeights` array! At this point, calls to `tableView(_:cellForRowAt:)` start to come in; I simply call my `setUpCell(_:for:)` utility method *again* — but this time, I'm laying out the *real* cell (and ignoring the returned height value).

Measurement and Layout with Constraints

With autolayout in the picture, constraints are of great assistance. They obviously perform layout of each cell for us, because that's what constraints do. But they can also perform measurement of the height of each cell. If constraints ultimately pin every subview to the `contentView` in such a way as to size the `contentView` height unambiguously *from the inside out*, then we simply call `systemLayoutSize-Fitting(_:)` to learn the resulting height of the cell.

My `setUpCell(_:for:)` thus no longer needs to return a value; I hand it a reference to a cell, it puts the data into the cell, and now I can do whatever I like with that cell. If this is the model cell being used for measurement in `tableView(_:heightForRow-At:)`, I call `systemLayoutSizeFitting(_:)` to get the height; if it's the real cell gener-ated by dequeuing in `tableView(_:cellForRowAt:)`, I return it.

The overall strategy is similar to the previous approach. My implemention of `table-View(_:heightForRowAt:)`: is called repeatedly before the table is displayed; the first time it is called, I calculate all the row height values and store them in `self.row-Heights` (this is actual code from my Albumen app):

```
override func tableView(_ tableView: UITableView,
    heightForRowAt indexPath: IndexPath) -> CGFloat {
        let ix = indexPath.row
        if self.rowHeights[ix] == nil {
            let objects = UINib(nibName: "TrackCell2", bundle: nil)
                .instantiate(withOwner: nil)
            let cell = objects.first as! UITableViewCell
            for ix in 0..<self.rowHeights.count {
                let indexPath = IndexPath(row: ix, section: 0)
                self.setUpCell(cell, for: indexPath)
                let v = cell.contentView
                let sz = v.systemLayoutSizeFitting(
                    UILayoutFittingCompressedSize)
                self.rowHeights[ix] = sz.height
            }
        }
        return self.rowHeights[ix]!
}
```

My `tableView(_:cellForRowAt:)` implementation is trivial, because `setUp-Cell(_:for:)` does all the real work of putting the data into the cell:

```swift
override func tableView(_ tableView: UITableView,
    cellForRowAt indexPath: IndexPath) -> UITableViewCell {
        let cell = tableView.dequeueReusableCell(
            withIdentifier: "TrackCell", for: indexPath)
        self.setUpCell(cell, for:indexPath)
        return cell
}
```

The one danger to watch out for here is that a `.singleLine` separator eats into the cell height. This can cause the height of the cell in the table to differ very slightly from its height as calculated by `systemLayoutSizeFitting(_:)`. If you've overdetermined the cell's subview constraints, this can result in a conflict among constraints. Careful use of lowered constraint priorities can solve this problem nicely if it arises (though it is simpler, in practice, to set the cell separator to `.none`).

Estimated Height

In iOS 7, three new table view properties were introduced:

- `estimatedRowHeight`
- `estimatedSectionHeaderHeight`
- `estimatedSectionFooterHeight`

To accompany those, there are also three table view delegate methods:

- `tableView(_:estimatedHeightForRowAt:)`
- `tableView(_:estimatedHeightForHeaderInSection:)`
- `tableView(_:estimatedHeightForFooterInSection:)`

The idea here is to reduce the amount of time spent calculating row heights at the outset. If you supply an estimated row height, then when `tableView(_:heightFor-RowAt:)` is called repeatedly before the table is displayed, it is called *only for the visible cells* of the table; for the remaining cells, the *estimated* height is used. The runtime thus obtains enough information to lay out the entire table very quickly: the only real heights you have to provide up front are those of the initially visible rows. The downside is that this layout is only an approximation, and will have to be corrected later: as new rows are scrolled into view, `tableView(_:heightForRowAt:)` will be called for those new rows, and the layout of the whole table will be revised accordingly.

To illustrate, I'll revise the previous example to use estimated heights. The estimated height is set in `viewDidLoad` (it can alternatively be set in the nib editor):

```swift
self.tableView.estimatedRowHeight = 75
```

Now in my tableView(_:heightForRowAt:) implementation, when I find that a requested height value in self.rowHeights is nil, I don't fill in *all* the values of self.rowHeights — I fill in *just that one height*. It's simply a matter of removing the for loop:

```
override func tableView(_ tableView: UITableView,
    heightForRowAt indexPath: IndexPath) -> CGFloat {
        let ix = indexPath.row
        if self.rowHeights[ix] == nil {
            let objects = UINib(nibName: "TrackCell2", bundle: nil)
                .instantiate(withOwner: nil)
            let cell = objects.first as! UITableViewCell
            let indexPath = IndexPath(row: ix, section: 0)
            self.setUpCell(cell, for: indexPath)
            let v = cell.contentView
            let sz = v.systemLayoutSizeFitting(
                UILayoutFittingCompressedSize)
            self.rowHeights[ix] = sz.height
        }
        return self.rowHeights[ix]!
}
```

Automatic Row Height

In iOS 8, a completely automatic calculation of variable row heights was introduced. This, in effect, does behind the scenes what I'm doing in tableView(_:heightForRow-At:) in the preceding code: it relies upon autolayout for the calculation of each row's height, and it calculates and caches a row's height the first time it is needed, as it is about to appear on the screen.

To use this mechanism, first configure your cell using autolayout to determine the size of the contentView from the inside out. Now all you have to do is to set the table view's estimatedRowHeight — and *don't* implement tableView(_:heightForRowAt:) at all! In some cases, it may be necessary to set the table view's row height to UITable-ViewAutomaticDimension as well (again, this can be configured in the nib editor instead):

```
self.tableView.rowHeight = UITableViewAutomaticDimension
self.tableView.estimatedRowHeight = 75
```

Once I've done that, all I have to do in order to adopt this approach in my app is to delete my tableView(_:heightForRowAt:) implementation entirely.

New in iOS 11, you don't even have to supply an estimatedRowHeight; it can be UITableViewAutomaticDimension as well:

```
self.tableView.rowHeight = UITableViewAutomaticDimension
self.tableView.estimatedRowHeight = UITableViewAutomaticDimension
```

Basically, the rule in iOS 11 is this: if the `rowHeight` is `UITableViewAutomatic-Dimension`, then as long as the `estimatedRowHeight` isn't 0, you'll get variable row heights, with determination of the `contentView` height using autolayout constraints from the inside out.

Also new in iOS 11, section headers and footers participate in the same variable height mechanism. For example, if the table view's `sectionHeaderHeight` and `estimatedSectionHeaderHeight` are both `UITableViewAutomaticDimension`, the headers will have their heights determined by autolayout from the inside out.

Keep in mind that, whatever your table view's `height` settings may be, you can override it for individual rows, headers, or footers by implementing a `height` delegate method. For example:

- If `tableView(_:heightForRowAt:)` returns `UITableViewAutomaticDimension`, you'll get automatic determination of row heights, even if the table view's `rowHeight` is absolute.
- If `tableView(_:heightForRowAt:)` returns an absolute height, that height will be used, even if the table view's `rowHeight` is `UITableViewAutomaticDimension`.

 In iOS 11, you still have to provide an absolute height for the table view's `table-HeaderView` and `tableFooterView`, by setting its bounds or frame height; its height cannot be determined by internal constraints alone. I regard this as a bug.

The automatic row height mechanism is particularly well suited to cells containing UILabels whose height will depend upon their text contents, because the label provides that height in its `intrinsicContentSize`. If you want to use the automatic row height mechanism in conjunction with a custom UIView subclass whose height you intend to set in `tableView(_:cellForRowAt:)`, you should make your view behave like a label. Don't set your view's height constraint directly; instead, have your UIView subclass override `intrinsicContentSize`, and set some property on which that override depends. For example:

```
class MyView : UIView {
    var h : CGFloat = 200 {
        didSet {
            self.invalidateIntrinsicContentSize()
        }
    }
    override var intrinsicContentSize: CGSize {
        return CGSize(width:300, height:self.h)
    }
}
```

Obviously, taking advantage of the automatic row height mechanism is very easy: but easy does not necessarily mean best. There is also a question of performance. The four techniques I've outlined here run not only from oldest to newest but also from fastest to slowest. Manual layout is faster than calling `systemLayoutSize-Fitting(_:)`, and calculating the heights of all rows up front, though it may cause a longer pause initially, makes scrolling faster for the user because no row heights have to be calculated while scrolling. You will have to measure and decide which approach is most suitable.

And there's one more thing to watch out for. I said earlier that the cell returned to you from `dequeueReusableCell(withIdentifier:for:)` in your implementation of `tableView(_:cellForRowAt:)` already has its final size. But if you use automatic variable row heights, that's not true, because automatic calculation of a cell's height can't take place until after the cell exists! Any code that relies on the cell having its final size in `tableView(_:cellForRowAt:)` will break when you switch to automatic variable row heights. You can probably work around this by moving that code to `table-View(_:willDisplay:forRowAt:)`, where the final cell size has definitely been achieved.

Table View Cell Selection

A table view cell has a normal state, a highlighted state (according to its `isHighlighted` property), and a selected state (according to its `isSelected` property). It is possible to change these states directly, optionally with animation, by calling `setHighlighted(_:animated:)` or `setSelected(_:animated:)` on the cell. But you don't want to act behind the table's back, so you are more likely to manage selection through the table view, letting the table view manage and track the state of its cells.

Selection implies highlighting. When a cell is selected, it propagates the highlighted state down through its subviews by setting each subview's `isHighlighted` property if it has one. That is why a UILabel's `highlightedTextColor` applies when the cell is selected. Similarly, a UIImageView (such as the cell's `imageView`) can have a `highlightedImage` that is shown when the cell is selected, and a UIControl (such as a UIButton) takes on its `.highlighted` state when the cell is selected.

One of the chief purposes of your table view is likely to be to let the user select a cell. This will be possible, provided you have not set the value of the table view's `allows-Selection` property to `false`. The user taps a cell, and the cell switches to its selected state. You can also permit the user to select multiple cells simultaneously; to do so, set the table view's `allowsMultipleSelection` property to `true`. If the user taps an already selected cell, by default it stays selected if the table doesn't allow multiple selection, but it is deselected if the table does allow multiple selection.

By default, being selected will mean that the cell is redrawn with a gray background view, but you can change this at the individual cell level, as I've already explained: you can change the cell's `selectionStyle` or, for full customization, set its `selected-BackgroundView` (or `multipleSelectionBackgroundView`).

Managing Cell Selection

Your code can learn and manage the selection through these UITableView properties and instance methods:

`indexPathForSelectedRow`
`indexPathsForSelectedRows`

These read-only properties report the currently selected row(s), or `nil` if there is no selection.

Don't accidentally examine the wrong property! For example, asking for `index-PathForSelectedRow` when the table view allows multiple selection gives a result that will have you scratching your head in confusion. (As usual, I speak from experience.)

`selectRow(at:animated:scrollPosition:)`

The animation involves fading in the selection, but the user may not see this unless the selected row is already visible.

The last parameter dictates whether and how the table view should scroll to reveal the newly selected row; your choices (UITableViewScrollPosition) are `.top`, `.middle`, `.bottom`, and `.none`. For the first three options, the table view scrolls (with animation, if the second parameter is `true`) so that the selected row is at the specified position among the visible cells. For `.none`, the table view does not scroll; if the selected row is not already visible, it does not become visible.

`deselectRow(at:animated:)`

Deselects the given row (if it is selected); the optional animation involves fading out the selection. No automatic scrolling takes place.

To deselect *all* currently selected rows, call `selectRow(at:...)` with a `nil` index path.

Selection is preserved when a selected cell is scrolled off the screen; the row is still reported as selected, and the cell will still appear selected when it is scrolled back on screen. Calling a `reload` method, however, deselects any affected cells; calling `reload-Data` deselects *all* selected cells. (Calling `reloadData`, and then calling `indexPathFor-SelectedRow` and wondering what happened to the selection, is a common beginner mistake.)

Responding to Cell Selection

Response to user selection is through the table view's delegate:

- `tableView(_:shouldHighlightRowAt:)`
- `tableView(_:didHighlightRowAt:)`
- `tableView(_:didUnhighlightRowAt:)`
- `tableView(_:willSelectRowAt:)`
- `tableView(_:didSelectRowAt:)`
- `tableView(_:willDeselectRowAt:)`
- `tableView(_:didDeselectRowAt:)`

Despite their names, the two `will` methods are actually `should` methods and expect a return value:

- Return `nil` to prevent the selection (or deselection) from taking place.
- Return the index path handed in as argument to permit the selection (or deselection), or a different index path to cause a different cell to be selected (or deselected).

The `highlight` methods are more sensibly named, and they arrive first, so you can return `false` from `tableView(_:shouldHighlightRowAt:)` to prevent a cell from being selected.

Let's focus in more detail on the relationship between a cell's highlighted state and its selected state. They are, in fact, two different states. When the user touches a cell, the cell passes through a complete highlight cycle. Then, if the touch turns out to be the beginning of a scroll motion, the cell is unhighlighted immediately, and the cell is not selected. Otherwise, the cell is unhighlighted and selected.

But the user doesn't know the difference between these two states: whether the cell is highlighted or selected, the cell's subviews are highlighted, and the `selectedBackgroundView` appears. Here's what actually happens and what the user sees:

The user touches and scrolls
The cell is highlighted; the user sees the flash of the `selectedBackgroundView` and the highlighted subviews, until the table begins to scroll and the cell returns to normal.

The user touches and lifts the finger
The cell is highlighted, then selected; the user sees the `selectedBackgroundView` and highlighted subviews appear and remain. There is actually a moment in the sequence where the cell has been highlighted and then unhighlighted and not yet selected, but the user doesn't see any momentary unhighlighting of the cell, because no redraw moment occurs (see Chapter 4).

Here's the sequence in detail:

1. The user's finger goes down. If `shouldHighlight` permits, the cell highlights, which propagates to its subviews. Then `didHighlight` arrives.

2. There is a redraw moment. Thus, the user will *see* the cell as highlighted (including the appearance of the `selectedBackgroundView`), regardless of what happens next.

3. The user either starts scrolling or lifts the finger. The cell unhighlights, which also propagates to its subviews, and `didUnhighlight` arrives.

   - If the user starts scrolling, there is a redraw moment, so the user now sees the cell unhighlighted. The sequence ends.

   - If the user merely lifts the finger, there is no redraw moment, so the cell keeps its highlighted appearance. The sequence continues.

4. If `willSelect` permits, the cell is selected, and `didSelect` arrives. The cell is *not* highlighted, but highlighting is propagated to its subviews.

5. There's another redraw moment. The user still sees the cell as highlighted (including the appearance of the `selectedBackgroundView`).

When `willSelect` is called because the user taps a cell, and if this table view permits only single cell selection, `willDeselect` will be called subsequently for any previously selected cells.

Here's an example of implementing `tableView(_:willSelectRowAt:)`. When `allows-Selection` is true and `allowsMultipleSelection` is not, the default behavior is that if the user taps an already selected row, the selection does not change. We can alter this so that tapping a selected row deselects it:

```
override func tableView(_ tableView: UITableView,
    willSelectRowAt indexPath: IndexPath) -> IndexPath? {
        if tableView.indexPathForSelectedRow == indexPath {
            tableView.deselectRow(at:indexPath, animated:false)
            return nil
        }
        return indexPath
}
```

Navigation from a Table View

An extremely common response to user selection is navigation. A master–detail architecture is typical: the table view lists things the user can see in more detail, and a tap displays the detailed view of the tapped thing. On the iPhone, very often the table view will be in a navigation interface, and you will respond to user selection by creating the detail view and pushing it onto the navigation controller's stack.

For example, here's the code from my Albumen app that navigates from the list of albums to the list of songs in the album that the user has tapped:

```
override func tableView(_ tableView: UITableView,
    didSelectRowAt indexPath: IndexPath) {
        let t = TracksViewController(
            mediaItemCollection: self.albums[indexPath.row])
        self.navigationController!.pushViewController(t, animated: true)
}
```

In a storyboard, when you draw a segue from a UITableViewCell, you are given a choice of two segue triggers: Selection Segue and Accessory Action. If you create a Selection Segue, the segue will be triggered when the user selects a cell. Thus you can readily push or present another view controller in response to cell selection.

If you're using a UITableViewController, then by default, whenever the table view appears, the selection is cleared automatically in viewWillAppear(_:), and the scroll indicators are flashed in viewDidAppear(_:). You can prevent the automatic clearing of the selection by setting the table view controller's clearsSelectionOnViewWill-Appear to false. If you do that, and implement deselection in viewDidAppear(_:) instead, the effect is that when the user returns to the table, the row remains momentarily selected before it deselects itself.

By convention, if selecting a table view cell causes navigation, the cell should be given an accessoryType (UITableViewCellAccessory) of .disclosureIndicator. This is a plain gray right-pointing chevron at the right end of the cell. The chevron itself doesn't respond to user interaction; it is not a button, but just a visual cue that the user can tap the cell to learn more.

Two additional accessoryType settings *are* buttons:

.detailButton
> Drawn as a letter "i" in a circle.

.detailDisclosureButton
> Drawn like .detailButton, along with a disclosure indicator chevron to its right.

To respond to the tapping of an accessory button, implement the table view delegate's tableView(_:accessoryButtonTappedForRowWith:). In a storyboard, you can Control-drag a connection from a cell and choose an Accessory Action segue.

A common convention is that selecting the cell as a whole does one thing and tapping the detail button does something else. For example, in Apple's Phone app, tapping a contact's listing in the Recents table places a call to that contact, but tapping the detail button navigates to that contact's detail view.

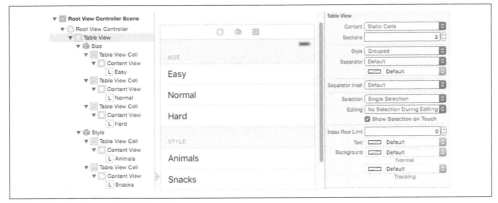

Figure 8-7. Designing a static table in the storyboard editor

Cell Choice and Static Tables

Another use of cell selection is to implement a choice among cells, where a section of a table effectively functions as an iOS alternative to macOS radio buttons. The table view usually has the grouped format. An `accessoryType` of `.checkmark` is typically used to indicate the current choice. Implementing radio button behavior is up to you.

As an example, I'll implement the interface shown in Figure 8-3. The table view has the grouped style, with two sections. The first section, with a "Size" header, has three mutually exclusive choices: "Easy," "Normal," or "Hard." The second section, with a "Style" header, has two choices: "Animals" or "Snacks."

This is a *static table*; its contents are known beforehand and won't change. In a case like this, if we're using a UITableViewController subclass instantiated from a storyboard, the nib editor lets us design the entire table, including the headers and the cells *and their content*, directly in the storyboard. Select the table and set its Content pop-up menu in the Attributes inspector to Static Cells to make the table editable in this way (Figure 8-7).

When you're using a static table, you are still free to implement table view data source and delegate methods, provided you cooperate with what the static table is already doing for you. This is useful when you'll have relevant information at runtime that you don't have while designing the storyboard. For example, you can implement `tableView(_:cellForRowAt:)`, but your implementation must not dequeue a cell explicitly; instead, obtain the cell by calling `super`. Now you can add your own modifications to the cell.

To illustrate, I'll add the checkmarks to our static table by implementing `table-View(_:cellForRowAt:)` to set the cell's `accessoryType`. Note the call to `super`, as well as the call to `tableView(_:titleForHeaderInSection:)` to learn the title of the current section. The user defaults will store the current choice in each of the two categories; in both cases, the key is the section title and the value is the label text of the chosen cell:

```
override func tableView(_ tv: UITableView,
    cellForRowAt ix: IndexPath) -> UITableViewCell {
        let cell = super.tableView(tv, cellForRowAt:ix)
        let ud = UserDefaults.standard
        cell.accessoryType = .none
        if let title = self.tableView(
            tv, titleForHeaderInSection:ix.section) {
                if let label = ud.object(forKey:title) as? String {
                    if label == cell.textLabel!.text {
                        cell.accessoryType = .checkmark
                    }
                }
        }
        return cell
}
```

When the user taps a cell, the cell is selected. I want the user to see that selection momentarily, as feedback, but then I want to deselect, adjusting the checkmarks so that that cell is the only one checked in its section. In `tableView(_:didSelectRow-At:)`, I set the user defaults, and then I reload the table view's data. This removes the selection and causes `tableView(_:cellForRowAt:)` to be called to adjust the checkmarks:

```
override func tableView(_ tv: UITableView, didSelectRowAt ix: IndexPath) {
    let ud = UserDefaults.standard
    let setting = tv.cellForRow(at:ix)!.textLabel!.text
    let header = self.tableView(tv, titleForHeaderInSection:ix.section)!
    ud.setValue(setting, forKey:header)
    tv.reloadData()
}
```

Table View Scrolling and Layout

A UITableView is a UIScrollView, so everything you already know about scroll views is applicable (Chapter 7). In addition, a table view supplies two convenience methods for scrolling in code:

- `scrollToRow(at:at:animated:)`
- `scrollToNearestSelectedRow(at:animated:)`

One of the parameters is a scroll position, like the `scrollPosition` parameter for `selectRow`, discussed earlier in this chapter.

The following UITableView methods mediate between the table's bounds coordinates on the one hand and table structure on the other:

- `indexPathForRow(at:)`
- `indexPathsForRows(in:)`
- `rect(forSection:)`
- `rectForRow(at:)`
- `rectForFooter(inSection:)`
- `rectForHeader(inSection:)`

The table view's own header view and footer view are its direct subviews, so their positions within the table's bounds are given by their frames.

Table View State Restoration

If a UITableView participates in state saving and restoration (Chapter 6), the restoration mechanism would like to restore the selection and the scroll position. This behavior is automatic; the restoration mechanism knows both what cells should be visible and what cells should be selected, in terms of their index paths. If that's satisfactory, you've no further work to do.

In some apps, however, there is a possibility that when the app is relaunched, the underlying data may have been rearranged somehow. Perhaps what's meaningful in dictating what the user should see in such a case is not the previous *rows* but the previous *data*. The state saving and restoration mechanism doesn't know anything about the relationship between the cells and the underlying data. If you'd like to tell it, adopt the UIDataSourceModelAssociation protocol and implement two methods:

`modelIdentifierForElement(at:in:)`
> Based on an index path, you return some string that you will *later* be able to use to identify uniquely this bit of model data.

`indexPathForElement(withModelIdentifier:in:)`
> Based on the unique identifier you provided earlier, you return the index path at which this bit of model data is displayed in the table *now*.

Devising a system of unique identification and incorporating it into your data model is up to you.

Table View Searching

A common need is to make a table view searchable, typically through a search field (a UISearchBar; see Chapter 12). A typical interface for listing the results of such a search is itself a table view. The interface should respond to what the user types in the search field by changing what appears in the list of results. Such an interface is managed through a UIViewController subclass, UISearchController.

UISearchController has nothing to do, *per se*, with table views! UISearchController itself is completely agnostic about what is being searched and about the form in which the results are presented. However, using a table view to present the results of searching a table view is a common interface. So this is a good place to introduce UISearchController.

Configuring a Search Controller

A UISearchController is a view controller; it provides an interface containing a search bar and the results of the search. The search controller vends its search bar, and you'll put that search bar into your initial interface. When the user taps in the search bar to begin searching, the search controller will take over the screen. And that's basically *all* the search controller does. It knows nothing about doing any actual searching or about showing the user the results of the search. All of that is up to you. You provide two things:

Search results controller
> The search results controller is your view controller that shows the user the results of the search. The UISearchController will display the search results controller's view, but what happens in that view is completely up to you.

Search results updater
> The search results updater is the search controller's conduit to you; basically, it's a kind of delegate. The search results controller will be repeatedly informing you that the user has edited the text in the search field; in response, you'll perform the actual search and update the results.

Here's what's going to happen:

- When the time comes to display search results (because the user has tapped inside the search bar in your initial interface), the search controller will present itself as a presented view controller, displaying the same search bar, with the search results controller's view embedded inside its own view.

- When the user edits in the search bar, the search controller will notify the search results updater.

- When the user taps the search bar's Cancel button, the search controller will dismiss itself.

The minimalistic nature of the search controller's behavior is exactly the source of its power and flexibility, because it leaves you free to manage the details: what searching means, and what displaying search results means, is up to you.

Here are the general steps for configuring a UISearchController (and I'll talk about exceptions in subsequent sections):

1. Instantiate a view controller whose job will be to display the results of the search. This is the search results controller. (In this discussion, the search results controller will be a UITableViewController, but as I've just said, no law requires this.)

2. Instantiate UISearchController, calling the designated initializer, `init(search-ResultsController:)`, with the search results controller as argument. *Retain the search controller.* The search controller will retain the search results controller as a child view controller.

3. Assign to the search controller's `searchResultsUpdater` an object to be notified when the search results change. This is the search results updater. It must be an object adopting the UISearchResultsUpdating protocol, which means that it implements one method: `updateSearchResults(for:)`. Typically, the search results updater will be the search results controller, but no law requires this.

4. Acquire the search controller's `searchBar` and put it into the interface.

A UISearchController has just a few other properties you might want to configure:

`obscuresBackgroundDuringPresentation`
Whether a "dimming view" should appear behind the search controller's own view. Defaults to `true`, but I'll give an example later where it needs to be set to `false`.

`hidesNavigationBarDuringPresentation`
Whether a navigation bar, if present, should be hidden. Defaults to `true`, but I'll give an example later where it needs to be set to `false`.

A UISearchController can also be assigned a real delegate (UISearchControllerDelegate), which is notified before and after presentation and dismissal. The delegate works in one of two ways:

`presentSearchController(_:)`
If you implement this method, then you are expected to present the search controller yourself, by calling `present(_:animated:completion:)`. In that case, the other delegate methods are *not* called.

`willPresentSearchController(_:)`
`didPresentSearchController(_:)`
`willDismissSearchController(_:)`
`didDismissSearchController(_:)`
Called only if you didn't implement `presentSearchController(_:)`.

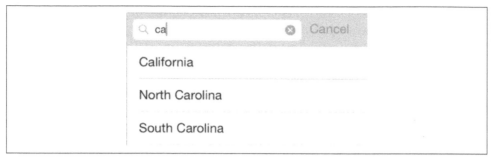

Figure 8-8. Searching a table

Using a Search Controller

I'll demonstrate several variations on the theme of using a search controller to make a table view searchable. In these examples, the searchable table view will be the list of U.S. states, with sections and an index, developed earlier in this chapter. Searching will mean finding the search text within the text of the single label displayed in the table view's cells — that is, we will search the state names.

Minimal search results table

Let's start with the simplest possible case. We will have two table view controllers — one managing the original table view, the other managing the search results table view. I propose to make the search results table view as minimal as possible, a rock-bottom table view with `.default` style cells, where each search result will be the `text` of a cell's `textLabel` (Figure 8-8).

In the original table's UITableViewController, I configure the UISearchController as I described earlier. I have a property, `self.searcher`, waiting to retain the search controller. I also have a second UITableViewController subclass, boringly named Search-ResultsController, whose job will be to obtain and present the search results. In `viewDidLoad`, I instantiate SearchResultsController, create the UISearchController, and put the search controller's search bar into the interface as the table view's header view (and scroll to hide that search bar initially, a common convention):

```
let src = SearchResultsController(data: self.sections)
let searcher = UISearchController(searchResultsController: src)
self.searcher = searcher
searcher.searchResultsUpdater = src
let b = searcher.searchBar
b.sizeToFit() // crucial, trust me on this one
b.autocapitalizationType = .none
self.tableView.tableHeaderView = b
self.tableView.reloadData()
self.tableView.scrollToRow(
    at:IndexPath(row: 0, section: 0), at:.top, animated:false)
```

Adding the search bar as the table view's header view has an odd side effect: it causes the table view's background color to be covered by an ugly gray color, visible above the search bar when the user scrolls down. The official workaround is to assign the table view a backgroundView with the desired color.

Now we turn to SearchResultsController. As a table view controller, it is completely simple. I'm not using sections in the SearchResultsController's table, so as I receive the searchable data, I flatten it to a simple array:

```
var originalData : [String]
var filteredData = [String]()
init(data:[RootViewController.Section]) {
    self.originalData = data.map{$0.rowData}.flatMap{$0}
    super.init(nibName: nil, bundle: nil)
}
required init(coder: NSCoder) {
    fatalError("NSCoding not supported")
}
```

What I display in the table view is not self.originalData but a *different* array, self.filteredData. This is initially empty, because there are no search results until the user starts typing in the search field. The table display code is trivial boilerplate:

```
let cellID = "Cell"
override func viewDidLoad() {
    super.viewDidLoad()
    self.tableView.register(UITableViewCell.self,
        forCellReuseIdentifier: self.cellID)
}
override func numberOfSections(in tableView: UITableView) -> Int {
    return 1
}
override func tableView(_ tableView: UITableView,
    numberOfRowsInSection section: Int) -> Int {
        return self.filteredData.count
}
override func tableView(_ tableView: UITableView,
    cellForRowAt indexPath: IndexPath) -> UITableViewCell {
        let cell = tableView.dequeueReusableCell(
            withIdentifier: self.cellID, for: indexPath)
        cell.textLabel!.text = self.filteredData[indexPath.row]
        return cell
}
```

But how does our search results table go from being empty to displaying any search results? SearchResultsController is the searchResultsUpdater of our UISearchController. It adopts UISearchResultsUpdating, so it implements updateSearchResults(for:), which will be called each time the user changes the text of the search bar. This method simply uses the current text of the search controller's searchBar to filter self.originalData into self.filteredData, and reloads the table view:

```
func updateSearchResults(for searchController: UISearchController) {
    let sb = searchController.searchBar
    let target = sb.text!
    self.filteredData = self.originalData.filter { s in
        let found = s.range(of:target, options: .caseInsensitive)
        return (found != nil)
    }
    self.tableView.reloadData()
}
```

That's all! Of course, it's an artificially simple example; in real life you would presumably want to allow the user to *do* something with the search results, perhaps by tapping on a cell in the search results table.

When the user taps in the search field and the UISearchController interface appears, the results view is not visible; it appears only after the user enters at least one character in the search field, and vanishes again if the user empties the search field. I find that interface ugly and annoying. Fortunately, there's an easy trick to make the results view appear all the time in the UISearchController interface:

```
override func viewWillAppear(_ animated: Bool) {
    super.viewWillAppear(animated)
    self.view.isHidden = false // *
}
func updateSearchResults(for searchController: UISearchController) {
    self.view.isHidden = false // *
    // ...
}
```

Scope buttons

A search bar can have scope buttons, but it's hard to make a search bar with scope buttons work properly in a UISearchController interface. A simple workaround is to use a UISegmentedControl elsewhere in the interface. That's how Apple's Mail app behaves in iOS 11: in the UISearchController interface, the results table view has a UISegmentedControl in its `tableHeaderView`.

Let's extend the preceding example to behave like that. Our segmented control will allow the user to distinguish between a Contains search and a Starts With search.

We're going to need access to the search bar from inside the search results controller, so we'll give it a weak `searchBar` instance property which must be set when the search controller and search results controller are initially configured in the main view controller's `viewDidLoad`:

```
    let src = SearchResultsController(data: self.sections)
    let searcher = UISearchController(searchResultsController: src)
    self.searcher = searcher
    searcher.searchResultsUpdater = src
    let b = searcher.searchBar
    src.searchBar = b // *
    // ...
```

In SearchResultsController, we create the segmented control and put it into the table
view:

```
lazy var seg : UISegmentedControl = {
    let seg = UISegmentedControl(items: ["Contains", "Starts With"])
    seg.sizeToFit()
    seg.selectedSegmentIndex = 0
    seg.addTarget(self, action: #selector(scopeChanged),
        for: .primaryActionTriggered)
    return seg
}()
override func viewDidLoad() {
    super.viewDidLoad()
    self.tableView.register(UITableViewCell.self,
        forCellReuseIdentifier: self.cellID)
    self.tableView.tableHeaderView = self.seg // *
}
override func viewWillAppear(_ animated: Bool) {
    super.viewWillAppear(animated)
    self.view.isHidden = false
}
```

We need to revise the results table view not only whenever the user edits in the search
bar but also when the user changes the segmented control's selection. Therefore, the
segmented control's action method shares its functionality with our updateSearch-
Results(for:) method. We use the current text of the search bar to filter
self.originalData into self.filteredData, as before, but we take into account the
segmented control's selection:

```
func doUpdate() {
    let target = self.searchBar.text!
    self.filteredData = self.originalData.filter { s in
        var options = String.CompareOptions.caseInsensitive
        if self.seg.selectedSegmentIndex == 1 {
            options.insert(.anchored)
        }
        let found = s.range(of:target, options: options)
        return (found != nil)
    }
    self.tableView.reloadData()
}
func updateSearchResults(for searchController: UISearchController) {
    self.view.isHidden = false
    self.doUpdate()
```

```
    }
    @objc func scopeChanged(_ sender : UISegmentedControl) {
        self.doUpdate()
    }
```

Search bar in navigation bar

In a navigation interface, you can put the UISearchController's search bar into the navigation bar. In iOS 11, that interface seems to be preferred over putting it into the table view's header view, and a new iOS 11 property facilitates it: instead of trying to find a place for the search bar in the navigation bar yourself — as its `titleView`, for instance — you use the `navigationItem` of your view controller, setting its `search-Controller` directly to your UISearchController instance. This means that you do *not* need to retain the search controller; the navigation item will retain it for you. It is also crucial to set the search controller's `hidesNavigationBarDuringPresentation` to `true`:

```
let src = SearchResultsController(data: self.sections)
let searcher = MySearchController(searchResultsController: src)
searcher.searchResultsUpdater = src
self.navigationItem.searchController = searcher // *
searcher.hidesNavigationBarDuringPresentation = true // *
```

Nothing else needs to change; our search results controller just keeps right on working.

The consequences of this arrangement are simply stunning:

- The navigation bar stretches to accommodate the search bar, which appears *below* everything else; thus the search bar makes no inroads on the space used by the title and the bar button items.

- If the navigation bar's `prefersLargeTitles` is `true`, the interface still works just fine, with the search bar displayed below the large title if there is one.

- If the navigation item's `hidesSearchBarWhenScrolling` property (also new in iOS 11) is `true`, the navigation bar expands and contracts to reveal or hide the search bar as the user scrolls down or up.

- The search bar can have scope buttons! Set the search bar's `scopeButtonTitles` as desired, and set its `showsScopeBar` to `false`; the scope buttons will appear in the navigation bar when the search controller presents its view.

No search results controller

You can also use a search controller *without* a search results controller. Instead, you can present the search results *in the original table view*.

To configure our search controller, we pass `nil` as its `searchResultsController` and set the original table view controller as the `searchResultsUpdater`. We must also set the search controller's `obscuresBackgroundDuringPresentation` to `false`; this allows the original table view to remain *visible and touchable* behind the search controller's view:

```
let searcher = UISearchController(searchResultsController:nil)
self.searcher = searcher
searcher.obscuresBackgroundDuringPresentation = false
searcher.searchResultsUpdater = self
searcher.delegate = self
```

Observe that we have also made ourselves the search controller's delegate. That's because we might need to distinguish whether we're in the middle of a search or not. We have a Bool property, `self.searching`, that acts as a flag; we raise and lower the flag when searching begins and ends. We also create a copy of our data model whenever we're about to start searching; the reason for that will be clear in a moment:

```
func willPresentSearchController(_ searchController: UISearchController) {
    self.originalSections = self.sections // keep copy of the original data
    self.searching = true
}
func willDismissSearchController(_ searchController: UISearchController) {
    self.searching = false
}
```

Our table view data source and delegate methods don't need to change unless there's a difference in the interface depending on whether or not we're searching. For example, let's say we want to remove the index while searching is in progress:

```
override func sectionIndexTitlesForTableView(tableView: UITableView)
    -> [String]? {
        return self.searching ? nil : self.sections.map{$0.sectionName}
}
```

All that remains is to implement `updateSearchResults(for:)`. Just as in our search results controller, whenever we're doing a search we're going to filter `self.original-Sections` into `self.sections` based on the search bar text:

```
func updateSearchResults(for searchController: UISearchController) {
    let sb = searchController.searchBar
    let target = sb.text!
    if target == "" {
        self.sections = self.originalSections
    } else {
        self.sections = self.originalSections.reduce(into:[]) {acc, sec in
            let rowData = sec.rowData.filter {
                $0.range(of:target, options: .caseInsensitive) != nil
            }
            if rowData.count > 0 {
                acc.append(Section(
```

```
                         sectionName: sec.sectionName, rowData: rowData))
            }
        }
    }
    self.tableView.reloadData()
}
```

Table View Editing

A table view cell has a normal state and an editing state, according to its `isEditing` property. The editing state (or *edit mode*) is typically indicated visually by one or more of the following:

Editing controls
> At least one editing control will usually appear, such as a Minus button (for deletion) at the left side.

Shrinkage
> The content of the cell will usually shrink to allow room for an editing control. If there is no editing control, you can prevent a cell shifting its left end rightward in edit mode with the delegate's `tableView(_:shouldIndentWhileEditingRowAt:)`.

Changing accessory view
> The cell's accessory view will change automatically in accordance with its `editingAccessoryType` or `editingAccessoryView`. If you assign neither, so that they are `nil`, the cell's existing accessory view will vanish when in edit mode.

As with selection, you could set a cell's `isEditing` property directly, but you are more likely to let the table view manage editability. Table view editability is controlled through the table view's `isEditing` property, usually by sending the table the `setEditing(_:animated:)` message. The table responds by changing the edit mode of its cells.

A cell in edit mode can be selected by the user if the table view's `allowsSelectionDuringEditing` or `allowsMultipleSelectionDuringEditing` is `true`. The default is `false`.

Putting the table into edit mode is usually left up to the user. A typical interface would be an Edit button that the user can tap. In a navigation interface, we might have our view controller supply the button as a bar button item in the navigation bar:

```
let b = UIBarButtonItem(barButtonSystemItem: .edit,
    target: self, action: #selector(doEdit))
self.navigationItem.rightBarButtonItem = b
```

Our action method will be responsible for putting the table into edit mode, so in its simplest form it might look like this:

```
@objc func doEdit(_ sender: Any?) {
    self.tableView.setEditing(true, animated:true)
}
```

But now we face the problem of getting *out* of edit mode. The standard interface is that the Edit button replaces itself with a Done button:

```
@objc func doEdit(_ sender: Any?) {
    var which : UIBarButtonSystemItem
    if !self.tableView.isEditing {
        self.tableView.setEditing(true, animated:true)
        which = .done
    } else {
        self.tableView.setEditing(false, animated:true)
        which = .edit
    }
    let b = UIBarButtonItem(barButtonSystemItem: which,
        target: self, action: #selector(doEdit))
    self.navigationItem.rightBarButtonItem = b
}
```

However, it turns out that all of that is completely unnecessary; if we want standard behavior, it's already implemented for us! A UIViewController has an editButton-Item property, which vends a bar button item that does precisely what we need:

- It calls the UIViewController's setEditing(_:animated:) when tapped.
- It tracks the UIViewController's isEditing property, and changes its own title accordingly (Edit or Done).

Moreover, UITableViewController's implementation of setEditing(_:animated:) is to call setEditing(_:animated:) on its table view. Thus, if we're using a UITable-ViewController, we get all of the desired behavior for free, just by retrieving the edit-ButtonItem and inserting the resulting button into our interface:

```
self.navigationItem.rightBarButtonItem = self.editButtonItem
```

When the table view enters edit mode, it consults its data source and delegate about the editability of individual rows:

tableView(_:canEditRowAt:) *to the data source*
The default is true. The data source can return false to prevent the given row from entering edit mode.

tableView(_:editingStyleForRowAt:) *to the delegate*
Each standard editing style corresponds to a control that will appear in the cell. The choices (UITableViewCellEditingStyle) are:

`.delete`

> The cell shows a Minus button at its left end. The user can tap this to summon a Delete button, which the user can then tap to confirm the deletion. This is the default.

`.insert`

> The cell shows a Plus button at its left end; this is usually taken to be an insert button.

`.none`

> No editing control appears.

If the user taps an insert button (the Plus button) or a delete button (the Delete button that appears after the user taps the Minus button), the data source is sent the `tableView(_:commit:forRowAt:)` message. This is where the actual insertion or deletion needs to happen. In addition to altering the data model, you will probably want to alter the structure of the table, and UITableView methods for doing this are provided:

- `insertRows(at:with:)`
- `deleteRows(at:with:)`
- `insertSections(_:with:)`
- `deleteSections(_:with:)`
- `moveSection(_:toSection:)`
- `moveRow(at:to:)`

The `with:` parameters are row animations that are effectively the same ones discussed earlier in connection with refreshing table data; `.left` for an insertion means to slide in from the left, and for a deletion it means to slide out to the left, and so on. The two "move" methods provide animation with no provision for customizing it.

If you're issuing more than one of these commands, you can express them as a single batch operation, combining not only the animations but also the structural changes. For example, if you were to delete row 1 of a certain section and then row 2 of the same section, you might reasonably worry that the notion "row 2" would have changed its meaning after row 1 is removed, so that you might need to delete row 1 twice, or change the order of your deletions. But with a batch operation, you just say what you mean, in any order: you delete row 1 and row 2 as part of the same batch, expressing yourself in terms of the state of the table *before* the deletions, and the right thing happens. If you perform insertions and deletions together in one batch, the deletions are performed first, regardless of the order of your commands, and the insertion commands refer to the state of the table *after* the deletions.

In iOS 10 and before, a batch operation is expressed by surrounding your commands with `beginUpdates` and `endUpdates`. New in iOS 11, this imperative mode of expression is superseded by a new command, `performBatchUpdates(_:completion:)`, which takes two functions (similar to an animation).

 A batch operation can include `reloadRows` and `reloadSections` commands — but not `reloadData`.

If you rearrange the table with these commands, you *must* also change the data model *beforehand*, so that when the table rearrangements are over, the table can coherently refresh itself from the data model. For example, if you delete a row, you *must* remove from the model the datum that it represents, and you must do it *before* you delete the row. The runtime will try to help you with error messages if you forget to do this.

Deleting Cells

Deletion of cells is the default, so it's easy to implement. If you don't implement `tableView(_:editingStyleForRowAt:)`, the default for all rows is `.delete`. If you don't implement `tableView(_:canEditRowAt:)`, the default for all rows is that they are editable. Therefore, you get two features automatically:

Minus button and Delete button
> If the table view is placed in edit mode, all editable cells get a Minus button at the left end; if the user taps it, the cell displays a Delete button at the right end. If the user taps the Delete button, `tableView(_:commit:forRowAt:)` is called with the `.delete` action.

Swipe-to-delete
> If you have implemented `tableView(_:commit:forRowAt:)`, all editable cells permit swipe-to-delete. The user can swipe left on a cell and the Delete button appears; if the user taps the Delete button, or if the user keeps swiping left, `tableView(_:commit:forRowAt:)` is called with the `.delete` action.

You can customize the Delete button's title with the table view delegate method `tableView(_:titleForDeleteConfirmationButtonForRowAt:)`.

Let's modify our table of state names so that the user can delete any cell. All we have to do is implement `tableView(_:commit:forRowAt:)` to get swipe-to-delete. In that implementation, we proceed in two stages. First, we remove the deleted row — from the data and then from the table. Second, if the deletion of that row emptied a section, we remove the deleted section — from the data and then from the table:

```
override func tableView(_ tableView: UITableView,
    commit editingStyle: UITableViewCellEditingStyle,
    forRowAt ip: IndexPath) {
        switch editingStyle {
        case .delete:
            self.sections[ip.section].rowData.remove(at:ip.row)
            tableView.performBatchUpdates({
                tableView.deleteRows(at:[ip], with: .automatic)
            }) {_ in
                if self.sections[ip.section].rowData.count == 0 {
                    self.sections.remove(at:ip.section)
                    tableView.performBatchUpdates ({
                        tableView.deleteSections(
                            IndexSet(integer: ip.section), with:.fade)
                    })
                }
            }
        default: break
        }
}
```

We can also allow the user to delete a row when the table view is in edit mode. All we have to do is provide the user with a way to get the table view into edit mode! But we already solved that problem in the preceding section. When the table view is managed by a table view controller in a navigation interface, we can simply say this:

```
self.navigationItem.rightBarButtonItem = self.editButtonItem
```

The user can now put the table view into edit mode, tap a row's Minus button to reveal the Delete button, and tap the Delete button to delete the row.

An interesting problem is how to turn swipe-to-delete *off* while still allowing the user to delete rows when the table view is in edit mode. We get swipe-to-delete "for free" by virtue of our having supplied an implementation of `tableView(_:commit:forRowAt:)`, and we cannot remove that implementation — we need it so that when the user taps the Minus button and the Delete button in edit mode, deletion actually occurs. One solution is to make all rows noneditable unless the table view is already in edit mode:

```
override func tableView(_ tableView: UITableView,
    editingStyleForRowAt indexPath: IndexPath)
    -> UITableViewCellEditingStyle {
        return tableView.isEditing ? .delete : .none
}
```

Custom Action Buttons

Instead of disabling swipe-to-delete, you might choose to extend it, introducing additional buttons that the user can reveal by swiping a cell sideways. That's how Apple's

---

Mail app works: the user can swipe a message listing left to reveal three buttons, or right to reveal one button, and can tap a button to take action on that message.

In iOS 10 and before, a version of this functionality was implemented through the delegate method `tableView(_:editActionsForRowAt:)`. But its powers were very limited in comparison to the behavior of the Mail app: the user could swipe left but not right; a button could have only a title, not an image; the buttons couldn't stretch to allow the user to perform an action by swiping alone.

New in iOS 11, Apple provides an API that allows your app to have the same kind of interface as the Mail app. You provide a cell with *swipe actions;* these are buttons that can appear at the right or left (leading or trailing) end of the cell when the user swipes sideways, and so there are two delegate methods you can implement:

- `tableView(_:leadingSwipeActionsConfigurationForRowAt:)`
- `tableView(_:trailingSwipeActionsConfigurationForRowAt:)`

Your job here is to return a UISwipeActionsConfiguration object (or `nil`), which wraps an array of UIContextualAction objects; a UIContextualAction is a button, initialized with a style (`.normal` or `.destructive`), a title, and an action function that will be called when the action is to be executed. The title can be `nil`, because you might set the UIContextualAction's `image` instead. Here's a simple example, where we implement a Delete button with a trash-can icon, along with a blue Mark button; the user can swipe left to see them:

```
override func tableView(_ tableView: UITableView,
    trailingSwipeActionsConfigurationForRowAt ip: IndexPath)
    -> UISwipeActionsConfiguration? {
        let d = UIContextualAction(style: .destructive, title: nil) {
            action, view, completion in
            // ... exactly as before ...
            completion(true)
        }
        d.image = UIGraphicsImageRenderer(size:CGSize(30,30)).image { _ in
            UIImage(named:"trash")?.draw(in: CGRect(0,0,30,30))
        }
        let m = UIContextualAction(style: .normal, title: "Mark") {
            action, view, completion in
            print("Mark") // in real life, do something here
            completion(true)
        }
        m.backgroundColor = .blue
        let config = UISwipeActionsConfiguration(actions: [d,m])
        return config
}
```

The omitted code (where my comment says "exactly as before") comes directly from the `.delete` case of the `tableView(_:commit:forRowAt:)` implementation developed

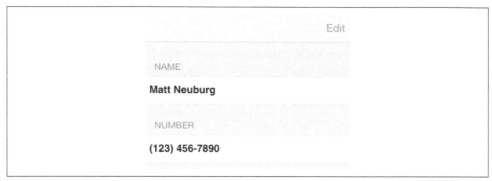

Figure 8-9. A simple phone directory app

in the preceding section; indeed, it is quite possible that if you use swipe actions, you won't implement `tableView(_:commit:forRowAt:)` at all. The index path of the affected row was handed to us as the second parameter of `tableView(_:trailing-SwipeActionsConfigurationForRowAt:)`.

The action function receives as its parameters the UIContextualAction itself, the view (which you probably won't need), and a completion function. You *must* call this completion function, with a Bool argument, to signal that the action is over and the swiped cell should slide back into place.

The `actions` for the UISwipeActionsConfiguration object are supplied in order, starting at the far end of the cell. A UISwipeActionsConfiguration object has one additional property, a Bool called `performsFirstActionWithFullSwipe`. If this is `true`, the user can keep swiping to perform the first action; if `false`, the user must swipe to reveal the button and then tap the button. The default is `true` for trailing actions, `false` for leading actions.

Editable Content in Cells

A cell might have content that the user can edit directly, such as a UISwitch that the user can switch on or off (Chapter 12), or a UITextField where the user can change the text (Chapter 10). This situation is effectively the inverse of our implementation of row deletion: the user is making changes in the view, and you must update the model accordingly. The challenge, in general, is twofold:

- You need to *hear* that the user has made a change in the view.
- You need to determine *what row* the user has changed.

Imagine an app that maintains a list of names and phone numbers. The data are displayed as a grouped style table, and they become editable when the user taps the Edit button (Figure 8-9).

The table displays just one name but can display multiple phone numbers, so my data model looks like this:

```
var name = ""
var numbers = [String]()
```

We don't need a button at the left end of the cell when it's being edited:

```
override func tableView(_ tableView: UITableView,
    editingStyleForRowAt indexPath: IndexPath)
    -> UITableViewCellEditingStyle {
        return .none
}
```

A UITextField is editable if its isEnabled is true. To tie this to the cell's isEditing state, I'll use a custom UITableViewCell class called MyCell with a single UITextField connected to an outlet property called textField:

```
class MyCell : UITableViewCell {
    @IBOutlet weak var textField : UITextField!
    override func didTransition(to state: UITableViewCellStateMask) {
        self.textField.isEnabled = state.contains(.showingEditControlMask)
        super.didTransition(to:state)
    }
}
```

Now we're ready to face the two challenges I mentioned a moment ago. How will we hear that the user is editing a text field? One obvious way is to be the text field's delegate. We can conveniently set that up when we configure the cell:

```
override func tableView(_ tableView: UITableView,
    cellForRowAt indexPath: IndexPath) -> UITableViewCell {
        let cell = tableView.dequeueReusableCell(
            withIdentifier: self.cellID, for: indexPath) as! MyCell
        switch indexPath.section {
        case 0:
            cell.textField.text = self.name
        case 1:
            cell.textField.text = self.numbers[indexPath.row]
            cell.textField.keyboardType = .numbersAndPunctuation
        default: break
        }
        cell.textField.delegate = self // *
        return cell
}
```

Acting as the text field's delegate, we are responsible for implementing the Return button in the keyboard to dismiss the keyboard; we can do that by implementing textFieldShouldReturn(_:) (I'll talk more about this in Chapter 10):

```
func textFieldShouldReturn(_ textField: UITextField) -> Bool {
    textField.endEditing(true)
    return false
}
```

Still acting as the text field's delegate, we can hear that the user has changed the text field's text, by implementing `textFieldDidEndEditing(_:)`. And here comes the second challenge — working out which row the edited text field belongs to. I like to do that by walking up the view hierarchy until I come to the table view cell and asking the table view for the index path of the row that it occupies. It is then trivial to update the model:

```
func textFieldDidEndEditing(_ textField: UITextField) {
    // some cell's text field has finished editing; which cell?
    var v : UIView = textField
    repeat { v = v.superview! } while !(v is UITableViewCell)
    let cell = v as! MyCell
    // what row is that?
    let ip = self.tableView.indexPath(for:cell)!
    // update data model to match
    if ip.section == 1 {
        self.numbers[ip.row] = cell.textField.text!
    } else if ip.section == 0 {
        self.name = cell.textField.text!
    }
}
```

Inserting Cells

I'll continue with the name-and-phone-number example from the previous section, to illustrate insertion of cells. We'll let the user switch the table into edit mode to reveal a Plus (insert) button at the left of a phone number cell. You are unlikely to attach a Plus button to *every* row. More likely, every row will have a Minus button except the last row, which has a Plus button; this shows the user that a new row can be appended at the end of the list (Figure 8-10).

It's easy to make the buttons accord with that specification:

```
override func tableView(_ tableView: UITableView,
    editingStyleForRowAt indexPath: IndexPath)
    -> UITableViewCellEditingStyle {
        if indexPath.section == 1 {
            let ct = self.tableView(
                tableView, numberOfRowsInSection:indexPath.section)
            if ct-1 == indexPath.row {
                return .insert
            }
            return .delete;
        }
        return .none
}
```

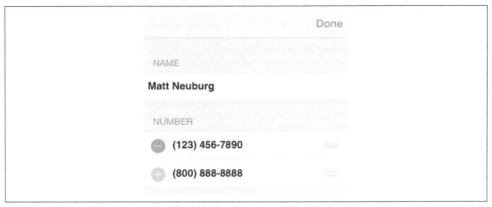

Figure 8-10. Phone directory app in edit mode

The person's name has no editing control (a person must have exactly one name), so we'll also prevent it from indenting in edit mode:

```
override func tableView(_ tableView: UITableView,
    shouldIndentWhileEditingRowAt indexPath: IndexPath) -> Bool {
        if indexPath.section == 1 {
            return true
        }
        return false
}
```

Now we're ready to implement a response to the editing control button:

```
override func tableView(_ tv: UITableView,
    commit editingStyle: UITableViewCellEditingStyle,
    forRowAt ip: IndexPath) {
        tv.endEditing(true) ❶
        // so we must force saving to the model
        if editingStyle == .insert {
            self.numbers += [""] ❷
            let ct = self.numbers.count
            tv.performBatchUpdates({
                tv.insertRows(at: ❸
                    [IndexPath(row:ct-1, section:1)], with:.automatic)
                tv.reloadRows(at: ❹
                    [IndexPath(row:ct-2, section:1)], with:.automatic)
            }) { _ in
                let cell = self.tableView.cellForRow(at:
                    IndexPath(row:ct-1, section:1))
                (cell as! MyCell).textField.becomeFirstResponder() ❺
            }
        }
        if editingStyle == .delete { ❻
            self.numbers.remove(at:ip.row)
            tv.performBatchUpdates({
                tv.deleteRows(at:[ip], with:.automatic)
```

```
                    tv.reloadSections(IndexSet(integer:1), with:.automatic)
                })
            }
        }
```

❶ First, we force our text fields to cease editing. This is effectively a way of causing our `textFieldDidEndEditing` to be called; the user may have tapped the button while editing, and we want our model to contain the very latest changes.

❷ When the tapped control is an insert button, the new row will be empty, and it will be at the end of the table, so we append an empty string to the `self.numbers` model array.

❸ We also insert a corresponding row at the end of the table view.

❹ Now two successive rows have a Plus button; the way to fix that is to reload the first of those rows.

❺ Finally, we show the keyboard for the new empty phone number, so that the user can start editing it immediately.

❻ We already know what to do when the tapped control is a delete button, so let's consider that a previously solved problem.

Rearranging Cells

You can permit the user to rearrange rows of a table. If the data source implements `tableView(_:moveRowAt:to:)`, the table displays a reordering control at the right end of each row in edit mode (Figure 8-10), and the user can drag it to rearrange cells. The reordering control can be suppressed for individual cells by implementing `tableView(_:canMoveRowAt:)`.

The user is free to move rows that display a reordering control, but the delegate can limit where a row can be moved to by implementing `tableView(_:targetIndexPathForMoveFromRowAt:toProposedIndexPath:)`.

To illustrate, we'll add to our name-and-phone-number app the ability to rearrange phone numbers. There must be multiple phone numbers to rearrange:

```
override func tableView(_ tableView: UITableView,
    canMoveRowAt indexPath: IndexPath) -> Bool {
        if indexPath.section == 1 && self.numbers.count > 1 {
            return true
        }
        return false
}
```

A phone number must not be moved out of its section, so we implement the delegate method to prevent this. We also take this opportunity to dismiss the keyboard if it is showing:

```
override func tableView(_ tableView: UITableView,
    targetIndexPathForMoveFromRowAt sourceIndexPath: IndexPath,
    toProposedIndexPath proposedDestinationIndexPath: IndexPath)
    -> IndexPath {
        tableView.endEditing(true)
        if proposedDestinationIndexPath.section == 0 {
            return IndexPath(row:0, section:1)
        }
        return proposedDestinationIndexPath
}
```

After the user moves an item, `tableView(_:moveRowAt:to:)` is called, and we trivially update the model to match. We also reload the table, to fix the editing controls:

```
override func tableView(_ tableView: UITableView,
    moveRowAt fromIndexPath: IndexPath,
    to toIndexPath: IndexPath) {
        let s = self.numbers[fromIndexPath.row]
        self.numbers.remove(at:fromIndexPath.row)
        self.numbers.insert(s, at:toIndexPath.row)
        tableView.reloadData()
}
```

Dynamic Cells

By rearranging a table in code, you can obtain some very effective dynamic interfaces. For example, let's permit the user to double tap on a section header as a way of collapsing or expanding the section. (This idea is shamelessly stolen from a WWDC 2010 video.)

In reality, we'll suppress or permit the display of the rows of the section, with a nice animation as the change takes place. We'll use our table of U.S. states, whose data model is `self.sections`, an array of Section. We'll also maintain a Set (of Int), `self.hiddenSections`, listing the sections that aren't displaying their rows. A section is to show all of its rows or none of them, depending on whether it's included in `self.hiddenSections`:

```
override func tableView(_ tableView: UITableView,
    numberOfRowsInSection section: Int) -> Int {
        if self.hiddenSections.contains(section) { // *
            return 0
        }
        return self.sections[section].rowData.count
}
```

Curiously, UITableView provides no correspondence between a section header and the number of its section. My solution is to subclass UITableViewHeaderFooterView and give my subclass a `section` property:

```
class MyHeaderView : UITableViewHeaderFooterView {
    var section = 0
}
```

Whenever `tableView(_:viewForHeaderInSection:)` is called, I make sure the header has a double tap gesture recognizer, and I set the header view's `section` property:

```
override func tableView(_ tableView: UITableView,
    viewForHeaderInSection section: Int) -> UIView? {
        let h = tableView.dequeueReusableHeaderFooterView(
            withIdentifier: self.headerID) as! MyHeaderView
        if h.gestureRecognizers == nil {
            let tap = UITapGestureRecognizer(
                target: self, action: #selector(tapped))
            tap.numberOfTapsRequired = 2
            h.addGestureRecognizer(tap) // *
            // ...
        }
        // ...
        h.section = section // *
        return h
}
```

When the user double taps a section header, we learn from the header what section this is, we find out from the model how many rows this section has, and we derive the index paths of the rows we're about to insert or remove. Now we look for the section number in our `hiddenSections` set. If it's there, we're about to display the rows, so we *remove* that section number from `hiddenSections`, and we *insert* the rows. If it's *not* there, we're about to hide the rows, so we *insert* that section number into `hidden-Sections`, and we *delete* the rows:

```
@objc func tapped (_ g : UIGestureRecognizer) {
    let v = g.view as! MyHeaderView
    let sec = v.section
    let ct = self.sections[sec].rowData.count
    let arr = (0..<ct).map {IndexPath(row:$0, section:sec)}
    if self.hiddenSections.contains(sec) {
        self.hiddenSections.remove(sec)
        self.tableView.performBatchUpdates({
            self.tableView.insertRows(at:arr, with:.automatic)
        }) { _ in
            self.tableView.scrollToRow(at:arr[0], at:.none, animated:true)
        }
    } else {
        self.hiddenSections.insert(sec)
        self.tableView.performBatchUpdates({
```

```
                self.tableView.deleteRows(at:arr, with:.automatic)
        }) { _ in
            let rect = self.tableView.rect(forSection: sec)
            self.tableView.scrollRectToVisible(rect, animated: true)
        }
    }
}
```

Another useful device is to animate a change in the height of one or more cells. The trick here is to use an empty batch operation:

```
self.tableView.performBatchUpdates(nil)
```

This causes the section and row structure of the table to be asked for, along with calculation of all heights, but no cells, headers or footers are requested; the table view is laid out freshly without reloading any cells. If any heights have changed since the last time the table view was laid out, *the change in height is animated.*

Apple's Calendar app is an example. When you're editing an event and you tap on the Starts or Ends date, a space opens up just below that row of the table, revealing a date picker. In reality, the date picker is in its own table view cell. It was there all along, but you couldn't see it because the cell had zero height and its clipsToBounds is true. When you tap on the Starts or Ends date, performBatchUpdates is called. This causes tableView(_:heightForRowAt:) to be called, and a different answer is given for the height of this cell. The cell thus opens up to reveal the date picker.

We can get the same effect using code along these lines:

```
var showDatePicker = false
func toggleDatePickerCell() {
    self.showDatePicker = !self.showDatePicker
    self.tableView.performBatchUpdates(nil)
}
func tableView(_ tableView: UITableView,
    heightForRowAt indexPath: IndexPath) -> CGFloat {
        if indexPath == datePickerPath {
            return self.showDatePicker ? 200 : 0
        }
        return tableView.rowHeight
}
```

Table View Menus

A menu, in iOS, is a sort of balloon containing tappable menu items such as Copy, Cut, and Paste. You can permit the user to summon a menu by performing a long press on a table view cell. The long press followed by display of the menu gives the cell a selected appearance, which goes away when the menu is dismissed.

To allow the user to summon a menu from a table view's cells, you implement three delegate methods:

`tableView(_:shouldShowMenuForRowAt:)`

> Return `true` if the user is to be permitted to summon a menu by performing a long press on this cell.

`tableView(_:canPerformAction:forRowAt:withSender:)`

> You'll be called repeatedly with selectors for various actions that the system knows about. Returning `true`, regardless, causes the Copy, Cut, and Paste menu items to appear in the menu, corresponding to the UIResponderStandardEdit-Actions `copy`, `cut`, and `paste`; return `false` to prevent the menu item for an action from appearing. The menu itself will appear unless you return `false` to all three actions. The `sender` is the shared UIMenuController.

`tableView(_:performAction:forRowAt:withSender:)`

> The user has tapped one of the menu items; your job is to respond to it somehow.

Here's an example where the user can summon a Copy menu from any cell (Figure 8-11):

```
let copy = #selector(UIResponderStandardEditActions.copy)
override func tableView(_ tableView: UITableView,
    shouldShowMenuForRowAt indexPath: IndexPath) -> Bool {
        return true
}
override func tableView(_ tableView: UITableView,
    canPerformAction action: Selector,
    forRowAt indexPath: IndexPath,
    withSender sender: Any?) -> Bool {
        return action == copy
}
override func tableView(_ tableView: UITableView,
    performAction action: Selector,
    forRowAt indexPath: IndexPath,
    withSender sender: Any?) {
        if action == copy {
            // ... do whatever copying consists of ...
        }
}
```

To add a custom menu item to the menu is a little more work. Using our table of U.S. states, imagine that one can copy a state's two-letter abbreviation to the clipboard. We want to give the menu an additional menu item whose title is Abbrev. The trick is that this menu item's action must correspond to a method in the *cell*. We will therefore need our table to use a custom UITableViewCell subclass; we'll call it MyCell:

```
class MyCell : UITableViewCell {
    @objc func abbrev(_ sender: Any?) {
        // ...
    }
}
```

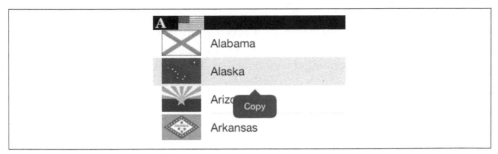

Figure 8-11. A table view cell with a menu

We must tell the shared UIMenuController to append the menu item to the global menu; the `tableView(_:shouldShowMenuForRowAt:)` delegate method is a good place to do this:

```
let copy = #selector(UIResponderStandardEditActions.copy)
let abbrev = #selector(MyCell.abbrev)
override func tableView(_ tableView: UITableView,
    shouldShowMenuForRowAt indexPath: IndexPath) -> Bool {
        let mi = UIMenuItem(title: "Abbrev", action: abbrev)
        UIMenuController.shared.menuItems = [mi]
        return true
}
```

If we want this menu item to appear in the menu, and if we want to respond to it when the user taps it, we must add its action selector to the two `performAction:` delegate methods:

```
override func tableView(_ tableView: UITableView,
    canPerformAction action: Selector,
    forRowAt indexPath: IndexPath,
    withSender sender: Any?) -> Bool {
        return action == copy || action == abbrev
}
override func tableView(_ tableView: UITableView,
    performAction action: Selector,
    forRowAt indexPath: IndexPath,
    withSender sender: Any?) {
        if action == copy {
            // ... do whatever copying consists of ...
        }
        if action == abbrev {
            // ... do whatever abbreviating consists of ...
        }
}
```

The Abbrev menu item now appears when the user long presses a cell of our table, and the cell's `abbrev` method is called when the user taps that menu item. Now we'll implement that method. We could make the cell itself respond to the tap by doing whatever abbreviating consists of; but we have already configured the table view delegate to respond to the abbrev action, so it makes more sense to forward the message to the table view delegate. We simply have to work out what row this is and who the table view's delegate is; once we get a reference to the containing table view, it will tell us both of those things:

```
func abbrev(_ sender: Any?) {
    // find my table view
    var v : UIView = self
    repeat {v = v.superview!} while !(v is UITableView)
    let tv = v as! UITableView
    // ask it what index path we are
    let ip = tv.indexPath(for: self)!
    // talk to its delegate
    tv.delegate?.tableView?(tv,
        performAction:#selector(abbrev), forRowAt:ip, withSender:sender)
}
```

Collection Views

A collection view (UICollectionView) is a UIScrollView that *generalizes* the notion of a table view. Indeed, knowing about table views, you know a great deal about collection views already. Where a table view has *rows*, a collection view has *items*. (UICollectionView extends IndexPath so that you can refer to its item property instead of its row property, though in fact they are interchangeable.) Otherwise, collection views and table views are extremely similar; here are some facts about collection views:

- The items are portrayed by reusable cells. These are UICollectionViewCell instances. If the collection view is instantiated from a storyboard, you can get reusable cells from the storyboard; otherwise, you'll register a class or nib with the collection view.

- A collection view can clump its items into sections, identified by section number.

- A collection view has a data source (UICollectionViewDataSource) and a delegate (UICollectionViewDelegate), and it's going to ask the data source Three Big Questions:

  - numberOfSections(in:)

  - collectionView(_:numberOfItemsInSection:)

  - collectionView(_:cellForItemAt:)

- To answer the third Big Question, your data source will obtain a reusable cell by calling:

  - dequeueReusableCell(withReuseIdentifier:for:)

- A collection view allows the user to select a cell, or multiple cells. The delegate is notified of highlighting and selection.

- Your code can rearrange the cells, inserting, moving, and deleting cells or entire sections, with animation.

- If the delegate permits, the user can long press a cell to produce a menu, or rearrange the cells by dragging.

- A collection view can have a refresh control.

- You can manage your UICollectionView through a UICollectionViewController.

A collection view section can have a header and footer, but the collection view itself does not call them that; instead, it generalizes its subview types into cells, on the one hand, and *supplementary views*, on the other. A supplementary view is just a UICollectionReusableView, which is UICollectionViewCell's superclass. A supplementary view is associated with a *kind*, which is just a string identifying its type; thus you can have a header as one kind, a footer as another kind, and anything else you can imagine. A supplementary view in a collection view is then similar to a section header or footer view in a table view:

- Supplementary views are reusable

- The data source method where you are asked for a supplementary view will be:

  - `collectionView(_:viewForSupplementaryElementOfKind:at:)`

- In that method, your data source will obtain a reusable supplementary view by calling:

  - `dequeueReusableSupplementaryView(ofKind:withReuseIdentifier:for:)`

Here are some small differences between a table view and a collection view:

- A collection view has no edit mode (nor has a collection view cell).

- A collection view has no section index.

The big difference between a table view and a collection view is how the collection view lays out its elements (cells and supplementary views). A table view lays out its cells in just one way: a vertically scrolling column, where the cells' widths are the width of the table view, their heights are dictated by the table view or the delegate, and the cells are touching one another. A collection view has no such rules. In fact, a collection view doesn't lay out its elements at all! That job is left to another object, a *collection view layout*.

A collection view layout is an instance of a UICollectionViewLayout subclass. It is responsible for the overall layout of the collection view that owns it. It does this by answering some Big Questions of its own, posed by the collection view; the most important are these:

`collectionViewContentSize`
How big is the entire content? The collection view needs to know this, because it is a scroll view (Chapter 7), and this will be the content size of the scrollable material that it will display.

`layoutAttributesForElements(in:)`
Where are the elements to be positioned within the content rectangle? The layout attributes, as I'll explain in more detail in a moment, are bundles of positional information.

To answer these questions, the collection view layout needs to ask the collection view some questions as well. It will want to know the collection view's bounds; also, it will probably call such methods as `numberOfSections` and `numberOfItems(inSection:)`, and the collection view, in turn, will get the answers to those questions from its data source.

The collection view layout can thus assign the elements any positions it likes, and the collection view will faithfully draw them in those positions within its content rectangle. That seems very open-ended, and indeed it is. To get you started, there's one built-in UICollectionViewLayout subclass — UICollectionViewFlowLayout.

UICollectionViewFlowLayout arranges its cells in something like a grid. The grid can be scrolled either horizontally or vertically, but not both, so it's a series of rows or columns. Through properties and a delegate protocol of its own (UICollectionViewDelegateFlowLayout), the UICollectionViewFlowLayout instance lets you provide instructions about how big the cells are and how they should be spaced. It defines two supplementary view types to let you give each section a header and a footer.

Figure 8-12 shows a collection view, laid out with a flow layout, from my Latin flashcard app. This interface lists the chapters and lessons into which the flashcards themselves are divided, and allows the user to jump to a desired lesson by tapping it. Previously, I was using a table view to present this list; when collection views were introduced (in iOS 6), I adopted one for this interface, and you can see why. Instead of a lesson item like "1a" occupying an entire row that stretches the whole width of a table, it's just a little rectangle; in landscape orientation, the flow layout fits five of these rectangles onto a line for me (and on a bigger phone, it might be seven or eight). So a collection view is a much more compact and appropriate way to present this interface than a table view.

If UICollectionViewFlowLayout doesn't quite meet your needs, you can subclass it, or you can subclass UICollectionViewLayout itself. (I'll talk more about that later on.) A familiar example of a collection view interface is Apple's Photos app; it probably uses a UICollectionViewFlowLayout subclass.

Figure 8-12. A collection view in my Latin flashcard app

Collection View Classes

Here are the main classes associated with UICollectionView. This is just a conceptual overview; I don't recite all the properties and methods of each class, which you can gather from the documentation:

UICollectionViewController
A UIViewController subclass. Like a table view controller, UICollectionView-Controller is convenient if a UICollectionView is to be a view controller's view, but using it is not required. It is the delegate and data source of its collection-View by default. The designated initializer requires you to supply a collection view layout instance, which will be its collectionViewLayout. In the nib editor, there is a Collection View Controller nib object, which comes with a collection view.

UICollectionView
A UIScrollView subclass. Its capabilities are parallel to those of a UITableView, as I outlined in the preceding section. It has a backgroundColor (because it's a view) and optionally a backgroundView in front of that. Its designated initializer requires you to supply a collection view layout instance, which will be its collectionViewLayout. In the nib editor, there is a Collection View nib object, which comes with a Collection View Flow Layout by default; you can change the collection view layout class with the Layout pop-up menu in the Attributes inspector.

UICollectionViewLayoutAttributes
A value class (a bunch of properties), tying together an element's indexPath with the specifications for how and where it should be drawn. These specifications are

reminiscent of view or layer properties, with names like `frame`, `center`, `size`, `transform`, and so forth. Layout attributes objects function as the mediators between the collection view layout and the collection view; they are what the collection view layout passes to the collection view to tell it where all the elements of the view should go.

UICollectionViewCell

An extremely minimal view class. It has an `isHighlighted` property and an `isSelected` property. It has a `contentView`, a `selectedBackgroundView`, a `backgroundView`, and of course (since it's a view) a `backgroundColor`, layered in that order, just like a table view cell; everything else is up to you. If you start with a collection view in a storyboard, you get prototype cells, which you obtain by dequeuing. Otherwise, you obtain cells through registration and dequeuing.

UICollectionReusableView

The superclass of UICollectionViewCell — so it is even more minimal! This is the class of supplementary views such as headers and footers. If you're using a flow layout in a storyboard, you are given header and footer prototype views, which you obtain by dequeuing; otherwise, you obtain reusable views through registration and dequeuing.

UICollectionViewLayout

The layout workhorse class for a collection view. A collection view cannot exist without a collection view layout instance! As I've already said, the collection view layout knows how much room all the subviews occupy, and supplies the `collectionViewContentSize` that sets the `contentSize` of the collection view, *qua* scroll view. In addition, the collection view layout must answer questions from the collection view, by supplying a UICollectionViewLayoutAttributes object, or an array of such objects, saying where and how elements should be drawn. These questions come in two categories:

Static attributes

The collection view wants to know the layout attributes of an item or supplementary view, specified by index path, or of all elements within a given rect.

Dynamic attributes

The collection view is inserting or removing elements. It asks for the layout attributes that an element, specified by index path, should have as insertion begins or removal ends. The collection view can animate between the element's static attributes and these dynamic attributes. For example, if an element's layout attributes `alpha` is 0 as removal ends, the element will appear to fade away as it is removed.

The collection view also notifies the collection view layout of pending changes through some methods whose names start with `prepare` and `finalize`. This is another way for the collection view layout to participate in animations, or to per-form other kinds of preparation and cleanup.

UICollectionViewLayout is an abstract class; to use it, you must subclass it, or start with the built-in subclass, UICollectionViewFlowLayout.

UICollectionViewFlowLayout

A concrete subclass of UICollectionViewLayout; you can use it as is, or you can subclass it. It lays out items in a grid that can be scrolled either horizontally or vertically, and it defines two supplementary element types to serve as the header and footer of a section. A collection view in the nib editor has a Layout pop-up menu that lets you choose a Flow layout, and you can configure the flow layout in the Size inspector; in a storyboard, you can even add and design a header and a footer.

A flow layout has the following configurable properties:

- `scrollDirection`, either `.vertical` or `.horizontal`
- `sectionInset` (the margins for a section); new in iOS 11, the `sectionInset-Reference` property lets you specify the reference for this inset (`.from-ContentInset`, `.fromLayoutMargins`, or `.fromSafeArea`)
- `itemSize`, along with a `minimumInteritemSpacing` and `minimumLineSpacing`
- `headerReferenceSize` and `footerReferenceSize`
- `sectionHeadersPinToVisibleBounds` and `sectionFootersPinToVisible-Bounds`; if `true`, they cause the headers and footers to behave like table view section headers and footers when the user scrolls

At a minimum, if you want to see any section headers, you must assign the flow layout a header ReferenceSize, because the default is `.zero`. Otherwise, you get initial defaults that will at least allow you to see something immediately, such as an `itemSize` of `(50.0,50.0)` along with reasonable default spacing between items and rows (or columns).

UICollectionViewFlowLayout also defines a delegate protocol of its own, UICollectionViewDelegateFlowLayout. The flow layout automatically treats the collection view's delegate as its own delegate. The section margins, item size, item spacing, line spacing, and header and footer size can be set for individual sec-tions, cells, and supplementary views through this delegate.

Using a Collection View

Here's how the view shown in Figure 8-12 is created. I have a UICollectionViewCon-troller subclass, LessonListController. Every collection view must have a collection view layout, so LessonListController's designated initializer initializes itself with a UICollectionViewFlowLayout:

```
init(terms data:[Term]) {
    // ... other self-initializations here ...
    let layout = UICollectionViewFlowLayout()
    super.init(collectionViewLayout:layout)
}
```

In `viewDidLoad`, we give the flow layout its hints about the sizes of the margins, cells, and headers, as well as registering for cell and header reusability:

```
let headerID = "LessonHeader"
let cellID = "LessonCell"
override func viewDidLoad() {
    super.viewDidLoad()
    let layout = self.collectionView!.collectionViewLayout
        as! UICollectionViewFlowLayout
    layout.sectionInset = UIEdgeInsetsMake(10,20,10,20)
    layout.headerReferenceSize = CGSize(0,40)
    layout.itemSize = CGSize(70,45)
    self.collectionView!.register(
        UINib(nibName: self.cellID, bundle: nil),
        forCellWithReuseIdentifier: self.cellID)
    self.collectionView!.register(
        UICollectionReusableView.self,
        forSupplementaryViewOfKind: UICollectionElementKindSectionHeader,
        withReuseIdentifier: self.headerID)
    self.collectionView!.backgroundColor = .myGolden
}
```

My data model is just like the model for the table of U.S. states I've been using throughout this chapter. (What are the chances of *that?*) The difference is that my `row-Data`, instead of being an array of Strings, is an array of Terms. (Term is basically a custom value class.) The first two of the Three Big Questions to the data source are extremely familiar:

```
override func numberOfSections(
    in collectionView: UICollectionView) -> Int {
        return self.sections.count
}
override func collectionView(_ collectionView: UICollectionView,
    numberOfItemsInSection section: Int) -> Int {
        return self.sections[section].rowData.count
}
```

The third of the Three Big Questions to the data source creates and configures the cells. In a *.xib* file, I've designed the cell with a single subview, a UILabel with tag 1; if the text of that label is still `"Label"`, the cell has come freshly minted from the nib and needs further initial configuration. Among other things, I assign each new cell a selectedBackgroundView and give the label a highlightedTextColor, to get an automatic indication of selection:

```
override func collectionView(_ collectionView: UICollectionView,
    cellForItemAt indexPath: IndexPath) -> UICollectionViewCell {
        let cell = collectionView.dequeueReusableCell(
            withReuseIdentifier: self.cellID, for: indexPath)
        let lab = cell.viewWithTag(1) as! UILabel
        if lab.text == "Label" {
            lab.highlightedTextColor = .white
            cell.backgroundColor = .myPaler
            cell.layer.borderColor = UIColor.brown.cgColor
            cell.layer.borderWidth = 5
            cell.layer.cornerRadius = 5
            let v = UIView()
            v.backgroundColor = UIColor.blue.withAlphaComponent(0.8)
            cell.selectedBackgroundView = v
        }
        let term = self.sections[indexPath.section].rowData[indexPath.item]
        lab.text = term.lesson + term.sectionFirstWord
        return cell
}
```

The data source is also asked for the supplementary element views; in my case, these are the section headers. I configure the header entirely in code. Again I distinguish between newly minted views and reused views; the latter will already have a single subview, a UILabel:

```
override func collectionView(_ collectionView: UICollectionView,
    viewForSupplementaryElementOfKind kind: String,
    at indexPath: IndexPath) -> UICollectionReusableView {
        let v = collectionView.dequeueReusableSupplementaryView(
            ofKind: UICollectionElementKindSectionHeader,
            withReuseIdentifier: self.headerID, for: indexPath)
        if v.subviews.count == 0 {
            let lab = UILabel(frame:CGRect(10,0,100,40))
            lab.font = UIFont(name:"GillSans-Bold", size:20)
            lab.backgroundColor = .clear
            v.addSubview(lab)
            v.backgroundColor = .black
            lab.textColor = .myPaler
        }
        let lab = v.subviews[0] as! UILabel
        lab.text = self.sections[indexPath.section].sectionName
        return v
}
```

As you can see from Figure 8-12, the first section is treated specially — it has no header, and its cell is wider. I take care of that with two UICollectionViewDelegate-FlowLayout methods:

```
func collectionView(_ collectionView: UICollectionView,
    layout lay: UICollectionViewLayout,
    sizeForItemAt indexPath: IndexPath) -> CGSize {
        var sz = (lay as! UICollectionViewFlowLayout).itemSize
        if indexPath.section == 0 {
            sz.width = 150
        }
        return sz
}
func collectionView(_ collectionView: UICollectionView,
    layout lay: UICollectionViewLayout,
    referenceSizeForHeaderInSection section: Int) -> CGSize {
        var sz = (lay as! UICollectionViewFlowLayout).headerReferenceSize
        if section == 0 {
            sz.height = 0
        }
        return sz
}
```

When the user taps a cell, I hear about it through the delegate method `collection-View(_:didSelectItemAt:)` and respond accordingly. And that's the entire code for managing this collection view!

Deleting Cells

Unlike table views, collection views don't provide any standard interface for allowing the user to delete cells. You are free to display a UICollectionViewController's `edit-ButtonItem`, and when the user taps it, the collection view controller's `set-Editing(_:animated:)` is called; but the interface does not automatically change in response, and neither a collection view nor a collection view cell has an `isEditing` property. Providing interface that lets the user express a desire to delete a cell, such as a Delete button that appears in every cell when the view controller's `isEditing` is `true`, is left completely up to you.

Actually deleting cells is straightforward. Here's an example. Assume that the cells to be deleted have been selected, with multiple selection being possible. The user now taps a button asking to delete the selected cells. If there are selected cells, I obtain them as an array of IndexPaths. My data model is once again the usual Section array. I delete each `rowData` entry (in reverse order), keeping track of any sections that end up empty; then I delete the corresponding items from the collection view. Finally, I do the same for the sections, deleting first the empty Section objects from my model, then the corresponding sections from the collection view (for the `remove(at:)` utility, see Appendix B):

```
@IBAction func doDelete(_ sender: Any) { // button, delete selected cells
    guard var arr =
        self.collectionView!.indexPathsForSelectedItems,
        arr.count > 0 else {return}
```

```
        arr.sort()
        var empties : Set<Int> = []
        for ip in arr.reversed() {
            self.sections[ip.section].rowData.remove(at:ip.item)
            if self.sections[ip.section].rowData.count == 0 {
                empties.insert(ip.section)
            }
        }
        self.collectionView!.performBatchUpdates({
            self.collectionView!.deleteItems(at:arr)
            if empties.count > 0 {
                self.sections.remove(at:empties)
                self.collectionView!.deleteSections(IndexSet(empties))
            }
        })
    }
```

Rearranging Cells

You can permit the user to rearrange cells by dragging them. If you're using a collection view controller, it supplies a gesture recognizer ready to respond to the user's long press gesture followed by a drag.

To permit the drag to proceed, you implement two data source methods:

collectionView(_:canMoveItemAt:)
:   Return true to allow this item to be moved.

collectionView(_:moveItemAt:to:)
:   The item has been moved to a new index path. Update the data model, and reload cells as needed.

You can also limit where the user can drag with this delegate method:

collectionView(_:targetIndexPathForMoveFromItemAt:toProposedIndexPath:)
:   Return either the proposed index path or some other index path. To prevent the drag entirely, return the original index path (the second parameter).

To illustrate, I'll continue with my example where the data model consists of an array of Sections. Things get very complex very fast if dragging beyond the current section is permitted, so I'll forbid that with the delegate method:

```
override func collectionView(_ collectionView: UICollectionView,
    canMoveItemAt indexPath: IndexPath) -> Bool {
        return true // allow dragging
}
override func collectionView(_ collectionView: UICollectionView,
    targetIndexPathForMoveFromItemAt orig: IndexPath,
    toProposedIndexPath prop: IndexPath) -> IndexPath {
        if orig.section != prop.section {
            return orig // prevent dragging outside section
```

```
        }
        return prop
    }
    override func collectionView(_ cv: UICollectionView,
        moveItemAt source: IndexPath, to dest: IndexPath) {
        // drag is over; rearrange model
        if source.section == dest.section { // exclusive access!
            self.sections[source.section].rowData.swapAt(
                source.item, dest.item)
        } else {
            swap(
                &self.sections[source.section].rowData[source.item],
                &self.sections[dest.section].rowData[dest.item]
            )
        }
        // reload
        cv.reloadSections(IndexSet(integer:source.section))
    }
```

If you prefer to provide your own gesture recognizer, then if you're using a collection view controller, set its `installsStandardGestureForInteractiveMovement` to `false`. Your gesture recognizer action method will need to call these collection view methods to keep the collection view apprised of what's happening (and the data source and delegate methods will then be called appropriately):

- `beginInteractiveMovementForItem(at:)`
- `updateInteractiveMovementTargetPosition(_:)`
- `endInteractiveMovement`
- `cancelInteractiveMovement`

Custom Collection View Layouts

A UICollectionViewFlowLayout is a great way to get started with UICollectionView, and will probably meet your basic needs at the outset. To unlock the real power of collection views, however, you'll write your own layout class. The topic is a very large one, but getting started is not difficult; this section explores the basics.

Flow Layout Subclass

UICollectionViewFlowLayout is a powerful starting point, so let's introduce a simple modification of it. By default, the flow layout wants to full-justify every row of cells horizontally, spacing the cells evenly between the left and right margins, except for the last row, which is left-aligned. Let's say that this isn't what you want — you'd rather that *every* row be left-aligned, with every cell as far to the left as possible given the size of the preceding cell and the minimum spacing between cells.

To achieve this, we can subclass UICollectionViewFlowLayout and override two methods, layoutAttributesForElements(in:) and layoutAttributesForItem(at:). The default implementations almost give the desired answer, so we can call super and make modifications as necessary.

The really important method here is layoutAttributesForItem(at:), which takes an index path and returns a single UICollectionViewLayoutAttributes object. If the index path's item is 0, we have a degenerate case: the answer we got from super is right. Alternatively, if this cell is at the start of a row — we can find this out by asking whether the left edge of its frame is close to the margin — we have another degenerate case: the answer we got from super is right. Otherwise, where this cell goes depends on where the previous cell goes, so we obtain the frame of the previous cell recursively. We wish to position our left edge a minimal spacing amount from the right edge of the previous cell. We do that by copying the layout attributes object that we got from super; we change the frame of that copy and return it:

```
override func layoutAttributesForItem(at indexPath: IndexPath)
    -> UICollectionViewLayoutAttributes? {
        var atts = super.layoutAttributesForItem(at:indexPath)!
        if indexPath.item == 0 {
            return atts // degenerate case 1
        }
        if atts.frame.origin.x - 1 <= self.sectionInset.left {
            return atts // degenerate case 2
        }
        let ipPv =
            IndexPath(item:indexPath.row-1, section:indexPath.section)
        let fPv =
            self.layoutAttributesForItem(at:ipPv)!.frame
        let rightPv =
            fPv.origin.x + fPv.size.width + self.minimumInteritemSpacing
        atts = atts.copy() as! UICollectionViewLayoutAttributes
        atts.frame.origin.x = rightPv
        return atts
}
```

The other method, layoutAttributesForElements(in:), takes a CGRect and returns an array of UICollectionViewLayoutAttributes objects for all the cells and supplementary views in that rect. Again we call super and modify the resulting array so that if an element is a cell, its UICollectionViewLayoutAttributes is the result of our layoutAttributesForItem(at:):

```
override func layoutAttributesForElements(in rect: CGRect)
    -> [UICollectionViewLayoutAttributes]? {
        let arr = super.layoutAttributesForElements(in: rect)!
        return arr.map { atts in
            var atts = atts
            if atts.representedElementCategory == .cell {
                let ip = atts.indexPath
```

```
                atts = self.layoutAttributesForItem(at:ip)!
            }
            return atts
        }
    }
```

Apple supplies some further interesting examples of subclassing UICollectionView-
FlowLayout. For instance, the LineLayout example, accompanying the WWDC 2012
videos, implements a single row of horizontally scrolling cells, where a cell grows as it
approaches the center of the screen and shrinks as it moves away (sometimes called a
carousel). To do this, it first of all overrides a UICollectionViewLayout method I
didn't mention earlier, shouldInvalidateLayout(forBoundsChange:); this causes
layout to happen repeatedly while the collection view is scrolled. It then overrides
layoutAttributesForElements(in:) to do the same sort of thing I did a moment
ago: it calls super and then modifies, as needed, the transform3D property of the
UICollectionViewLayoutAttributes for the onscreen cells.

Collection View Layout Subclass

For total freedom, you can subclass UICollectionViewLayout itself. The WWDC 2012
videos demonstrate a UICollectionViewLayout subclass that arranges its cells in a circle; the WWDC 2013 videos demonstrate a UICollectionViewLayout subclass that
piles its cells into a single stack in the center of the collection view, like a deck of cards
seen from above. For my example, I'll write a simple collection view layout that
ignores sections and presents all cells as a plain grid of squares.

In my UICollectionViewLayout subclass, called MyLayout, the really big questions I
need to answer are collectionViewContentSize and layoutAttributesFor-
Elements(in:). To answer them, I'll calculate the entire layout of my grid beforehand. The prepareLayout method is the perfect place to do this; it is called every
time something about the collection view or its data changes. I'll calculate the grid of
cells and express their positions as an array of UICollectionViewLayoutAttributes
objects; I'll store that information in a property self.atts, which is a dictionary
keyed by index path so that I can retrieve a given layout attributes object by its index
path quickly. I'll also store the size of the grid in a property self.sz:

```
override func prepare() {
    let sections = self.collectionView!.numberOfSections
    // work out cell size based on bounds size
    let sz = self.collectionView!.bounds.size
    let width = sz.width
    let shortside = (width/50.0).rounded(.down)
    let side = width/shortside
    // generate attributes for all cells
    var (x,y) = (0,0)
    var atts = [UICollectionViewLayoutAttributes]()
    for i in 0 ..< sections {
```

```
                let jj = self.collectionView!.numberOfItems(inSection:i)
                for j in 0 ..< jj {
                    let att = UICollectionViewLayoutAttributes(
                        forCellWith: IndexPath(item:j, section:i))
                    att.frame = CGRect(CGFloat(x)*side,CGFloat(y)*side,side,side)
                    atts += [att]
                    x += 1
                    if CGFloat(x) >= shortside {
                        x = 0; y += 1
                    }
                }
            }
            for att in atts {
                self.atts[att.indexPath] = att
            }
            let fluff = (x == 0) ? 0 : 1
            self.sz = CGSize(width, CGFloat(y+fluff) * side)
        }
```

It is now trivial to implement collectionViewContentSize, layoutAttributesFor-
Elements(in:), and layoutAttributesForItem(at:). I'll just fetch the requested
information from the sz or atts property:

```
        override var collectionViewContentSize : CGSize {
            return self.sz
        }
        override func layoutAttributesForElements(in rect: CGRect)
            -> [UICollectionViewLayoutAttributes]? {
                return Array(self.atts.values)
        }
        override func layoutAttributesForItem(at indexPath: IndexPath)
            -> UICollectionViewLayoutAttributes? {
                return self.atts[indexPath]
        }
```

Finally, I want to implement shouldInvalidateLayout(forBoundsChange:) to
return true, so that if the interface is rotated, my prepareLayout will be called again
to recalculate the grid. There's a potential source of inefficiency here, though: the user
scrolling the collection view counts as a bounds change as well. Therefore, I return
false unless the bounds width has changed:

```
        override func shouldInvalidateLayout(forBoundsChange newBounds: CGRect)
            -> Bool {
                return newBounds.size.width != self.sz.width
        }
```

Decoration Views

A *decoration view* is a third type of collection view item, on a par with cells and supplementary views. The difference is that it is implemented entirely by the collection
view layout. A collection view will faithfully draw a decoration view imposed by the

collection view layout, but none of the methods and properties of a collection view, its data source, or its delegate involve decoration views; for example, there is no support for letting the user select a decoration view or reposition a decoration view, or even for finding out what decoration views exist or where they are located. To supply any decoration views, you will need to write your own UICollectionViewLayout subclass; you are free to define any desired mechanism for allowing a user of this collection view layout to customize your decoration views.

To illustrate, I'll subclass UICollectionViewFlowLayout to impose a title label at the top of the collection view's content rectangle — the collection view equivalent of a table view's `tableHeaderView`. For simplicity, I'll start by hard-coding the whole thing, giving the client no ability to customize any aspect of this view. Then I'll show how to add that ability.

There are four steps to implementing a decoration view in a UICollectionViewLayout subclass:

1. Define a UICollectionReusableView subclass.

2. Register the UICollectionReusableView subclass with the collection view layout (*not* the collection view), by calling `register(_:forDecorationViewOfKind:)`. The collection view layout's initializer is a good place to do this.

3. Implement `layoutAttributesForDecorationView(ofKind:at:)` to return layout attributes that position the UICollectionReusableView. To construct the layout attributes, call `init(forDecorationViewOfKind:with:)` and configure the attributes.

4. Override `layoutAttributesForElements(in:)` so that the result of `layout-AttributesForDecorationView(ofKind:at:)` is included in the returned array.

The last step is what causes the decoration view to appear in the collection view. When the collection view calls `layoutAttributesForElements(in:)`, it finds that the resulting array includes layout attributes for a decoration view of a specified kind. The collection view knows nothing about decoration views, so it comes back to the collection view layout, asking for an actual instance of this kind of decoration view. You've registered this kind of decoration view to correspond to your UICollection-ReusableView subclass, so your UICollectionReusableView subclass is instantiated and that instance is returned, and the collection view positions it in accordance with the layout attributes.

So let's follow the steps. Define the UICollectionReusableView subclass, named MyTitleView:

```
class MyTitleView : UICollectionReusableView {
    weak var lab : UILabel!
    override init(frame: CGRect) {
        super.init(frame:frame)
        let lab = UILabel(frame:self.bounds)
        self.addSubview(lab)
        lab.autoresizingMask = [.flexibleWidth, .flexibleHeight]
        lab.font = UIFont(name: "GillSans-Bold", size: 40)
        lab.text = "Testing"
        self.lab = lab
    }
    required init?(coder aDecoder: NSCoder) {
        fatalError("init(coder:) has not been implemented")
    }
}
```

Now we turn to our UICollectionViewLayout subclass, which I'll call MyFlowLayout
(because it's a UICollectionViewFlowLayout subclass). We register MyTitleView in
the collection view layout's initializer; I've also defined some private properties that
I'll need for the remaining steps:

```
private let titleKind = "title"
private let titleHeight : CGFloat = 50
private var titleRect : CGRect {
    return CGRect(10,0,200,self.titleHeight)
}
override init() {
    super.init()
    self.register(MyTitleView.self, forDecorationViewOfKind:self.titleKind)
}
```

Implement layoutAttributesForDecorationView(ofKind:at:):

```
override func layoutAttributesForDecorationView(
    ofKind elementKind: String, at indexPath: IndexPath)
    -> UICollectionViewLayoutAttributes? {
        if elementKind == self.titleKind {
            let atts = UICollectionViewLayoutAttributes(
                forDecorationViewOfKind:self.titleKind, with:indexPath)
            atts.frame = self.titleRect
            return atts
        }
        return nil
}
```

Override layoutAttributesForElements(in:); the index path here is arbitrary (I
ignored it in the preceding code):

```
override func layoutAttributesForElements(in rect: CGRect)
    -> [UICollectionViewLayoutAttributes]? {
        var arr = super.layoutAttributesForElements(in: rect)!
        if let decatts = self.layoutAttributesForDecorationView(
            ofKind:self.titleKind, at: IndexPath(item: 0, section: 0)) {
```

```
                    if rect.contains(decatts.frame) {
                        arr.append(decatts)
                    }
            }
            return arr
    }
```

This works! A title label reading "Testing" appears at the top of the collection view.

Now I'll show how to make the label customizable. Instead of hard-coding the title "Testing," we'll allow the client to set a property that determines the title. I'll give my collection view layout a public `title` property:

```
class MyFlowLayout : UICollectionViewFlowLayout {
    var title = ""
    // ...
}
```

Whoever uses this collection view layout should set this property. For example, suppose this collection view is displaying the 50 U.S. states:

```
func setUpFlowLayout(_ flow:UICollectionViewFlowLayout) {
    flow.headerReferenceSize = CGSize(50,50)
    flow.sectionInset = UIEdgeInsetsMake(0, 10, 10, 10)
    (flow as? MyFlowLayout)?.title = "States" // *
}
```

We now come to a curious puzzle. Our collection view layout has a `title` property, the value of which needs to be communicated somehow to our MyTitleView instance. But when can that possibly happen? We are not in charge of instantiating MyTitle-View; it happens automatically, when the collection view asks for the instance behind the scenes. There is no moment when the MyFlowLayout instance and the MyTitle-View instance meet.

The solution is to *use the layout attributes* as a messenger. MyFlowLayout never meets MyTitleView, but it does create the layout attributes object that gets passed to the collection view to configure MyFlowLayout. So the layout attributes object is like an envelope. By subclassing UICollectionViewLayoutAttributes, we can include in that envelope any information we like — such as a title:

```
class MyTitleViewLayoutAttributes : UICollectionViewLayoutAttributes {
    var title = ""
}
```

There's our envelope! Now we rewrite our implementation of `layoutAttributesFor-DecorationView`. When we instantiate the layout attributes object, we instantiate our subclass and set its `title` property:

```
override func layoutAttributesForDecorationView(
    ofKind elementKind: String, at indexPath: IndexPath) ->
    UICollectionViewLayoutAttributes? {
        if elementKind == self.titleKind {
            let atts = MyTitleViewLayoutAttributes( // *
                forDecorationViewOfKind:self.titleKind, with:indexPath)
            atts.title = self.title // *
            atts.frame = self.titleRect
            return atts
        }
        return nil
}
```

Finally, in MyTitleView, we implement the apply(_:) method. This will be called when the collection view configures the decoration view — with the layout attributes object as its parameter! So we pull out the title and use it as the text of our label:

```
class MyTitleView : UICollectionReusableView {
    weak var lab : UILabel!
    // ... the rest as before ...
    override func apply(_ atts: UICollectionViewLayoutAttributes) {
        if let atts = atts as? MyTitleViewLayoutAttributes {
            self.lab.text = atts.title
        }
    }
}
```

It's easy to see how you might extend the example to make such label features as font and height customizable. Since we are subclassing UICollectionViewFlowLayout, some further modifications might also be needed to make room for the decoration view by pushing down the other elements. All of that is left as an exercise for the reader.

Switching Layouts

An astonishing feature of a collection view is that its collection view layout object can be swapped out on the fly. You can substitute one collection view layout for another, by calling setCollectionViewLayout(_:animated:completion:). The data hasn't changed, and the collection view can identify each element uniquely and persistently, so it responds by moving every element from its position according to the old layout to its position according to the new layout — and, if the animated: argument is true, it does this *with animation!* Thus the elements are seen to rearrange themselves, as if by magic.

This animated change of layout can even be driven interactively (in response, for example, to a user gesture; compare Chapter 6 on interactive transitions). You call startInteractiveTransition(to:completion:) on the collection view, and a special layout object is returned — a UICollectionViewTransitionLayout instance (or a

subclass thereof; to make it a subclass, you need to have implemented `collection-`
`View(_:transitionLayoutForOldLayout:newLayout:)` in your collection view delegate). This transition layout is temporarily made the collection view's layout, and
your job is then to keep it apprised of the transition's progress (through its
`transitionProgress` property) and ultimately to call `finishInteractive-`
`Transition` or `cancelInteractiveTransition` on the collection view.

Furthermore, when one collection view controller is pushed on top of another in a
navigation interface, the runtime will do exactly the same thing for you, as a custom
view controller transition. To arrange this, the first collection view controller's `use-`
`LayoutToLayoutNavigationTransitions` property must be `false` and the second
collection view controller's `useLayoutToLayoutNavigationTransitions` property
must be `true`. The result is that when the second collection view controller is pushed
onto the navigation controller, *the collection view remains in place*, and the collection
view layout specified by the second collection view controller is substituted for the
collection view's existing collection view layout, with animation of the elements as
they adopt their new positions.

During the transition, as the second collection view controller is pushed onto the
navigation stack, the two collection view controllers share the same collection view,
and the collection view's data source and delegate remain the first view controller.
After the transition is complete, however, the collection view's delegate becomes the
second view controller, even though its data source is still the *first* view controller. I
find this profoundly weird; why does the runtime change who the delegate is, and
why would I want the delegate to be different from the data source? I solve the problem by resetting the delegate in the second view controller, like this:

```
override func viewDidAppear(_ animated: Bool) {
    super.viewDidAppear(animated)
    let oldDelegate = self.collectionView!.delegate
    DispatchQueue.main.async {
        self.collectionView!.delegate = oldDelegate
    }
}
```

Collection Views and UIKit Dynamics

The UICollectionViewLayoutAttributes class adopts the UIDynamicItem protocol
(see Chapter 4). Thus, collection view elements can be animated under UIKit dynamics. The world of the animator here is not a superview but the collection view layout
itself; instead of `init(referenceView:)`, you'll create the UIDynamicAnimator by
calling `init(collectionViewLayout:)`. The collection view layout's `collectionView-`
`ContentSize` determines the bounds of this world.

To see any animation, you'll need a custom collection view layout subclass. On every frame of its animation, the UIDynamicAnimator is going to change the layout attributes of some items, but the collection view knows nothing of that; it is still going to draw those items in accordance with the collection view layout's `layout-AttributesForElements(in:)`. The simplest solution, therefore, is to override `layoutAttributesForElements(in:)` so as to obtain those layout attributes from the UIDynamicAnimator. (This cooperation will be easiest if the collection view layout itself owns and configures the animator.) There are UIDynamicAnimator convenience methods to help you:

```
layoutAttributesForCell(at:)
layoutAttributesForSupplementaryView(ofKind:at:)
```
> The layout attributes for the requested item, in accordance with where the animator wants to put them — or `nil` if the specified item is not being animated.

In this example, we're in a UICollectionViewLayout subclass, setting up the animation. We have a property to hold the animator, as well as a Bool property to signal when an animation is in progress:

```
let visworld = self.collectionView!.bounds
let anim = MyDynamicAnimator(collectionViewLayout:self)
self.animator = anim
self.animating = true
// ... configure rest of animation
```

Our implementation of `layoutAttributesForElements(in:)`, if we are animating, substitutes the layout attributes that come from the animator for those we would normally return. In this particular example, both cells and supplementary items can be animated, so the two cases have to be distinguished:

```
override func layoutAttributesForElements(in rect: CGRect)
    -> [UICollectionViewLayoutAttributes]? {
        let arr = super.layoutAttributesForElements(in: rect)!
        if self.animating {
            return arr.map { atts in
                let path = atts.indexPath
                switch atts.representedElementCategory {
                case .cell:
                    if let atts2 = self.animator?
                        .layoutAttributesForCell(at: path) {
                            return atts2
                    }
                case .supplementaryView:
                    if let kind = atts.representedElementKind {
                        if let atts2 = self.animator?
                            .layoutAttributesForSupplementaryView(
                                ofKind: kind, at:path) {
                                    return atts2
                        }
                    }
```

```
                }
            default: break
            }
            return atts
        }
    }
    return arr
}
```

iPad Interface

This chapter discusses some iOS interface features that differ between the iPad and the iPhone:

Popovers and split views

Popovers and split views are forms of interface designed originally for the iPad alone. Starting in iOS 8, both became available also on the iPhone, where they typically adapt, appearing in an altered form more appropriate to the smaller screen.

iPad multitasking

iPad multitasking, introduced in iOS 9, is an interface confined to a subset of iPad models, where two apps can occupy the screen simultaneously.

Drag and drop

Drag and drop was introduced in iOS 11 primarily to allow the user to drag from one app to another — for example, in an iPad multitasking interface. It can also be used within a single app, even on the iPhone.

Popovers

A *popover* is a temporary view layered in front of the main interface. It is usually associated, through a sort of arrow, with a view in the main interface, such as the button that the user tapped to summon the popover. It might be effectively modal, preventing the user from working in the rest of the interface; alternatively, it might vanish if the user taps outside it.

Popovers bring to the larger iPad the smaller, more lightweight flavor of the iPhone. For example, in my LinkSame app, both the settings view (where the user configures the game) and the help view (which describes how to play the game) are popovers

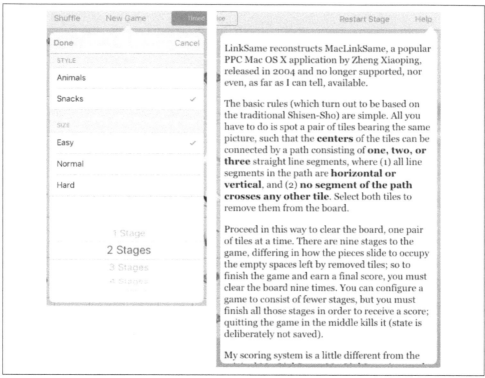

Figure 9-1. Two popovers

(Figure 9-1). On the iPhone, such a view would occupy the entire screen; we'd navigate to it, and the user would later have to navigate back to the main interface. But with the larger iPad screen, neither view is large enough, or important enough, to occupy the entire screen exclusively. A popover is the perfect solution. Our view is small and secondary; the user summons it temporarily, works with it, and then dismisses it, while the main interface continues to occupy the rest of the screen.

A popover is actually a form of presented view controller — a presented view controller with a `modalPresentationStyle` of `.popover` (which I didn't tell you about in Chapter 6). There's a guideline that a maximum of one popover at a time should be shown; a view controller can't have more than one presented view controller at a time, so the guideline is enforced automatically.

Like a `.formSheet` presented view controller, a popover can adapt, depending on the size class environment. The default adaptation is that a `.popover` presented view controller is treated as `.fullScreen` on the iPhone. But you don't have to accept the default; it is legal for a popover to appear on the iPhone as a popover, and I'll explain later how to make it do that.

A view controller presented as a popover has a .compact horizontal size class, even on an iPad.

To display a popover, you're going to present a view controller. Before that presentation takes place, you'll turn this into a popover presentation by setting the view controller's modalPresentationStyle to .popover:

```
let vc = MyViewController()
vc.modalPresentationStyle = .popover
self.present(vc, animated: true)
```

It turns out, however, that that code is insufficient. In fact, it will crash at runtime when the popover is presented! The reason is that some further *configuration* of the popover is required before it appears.

To configure a popover, you'll talk to its *presentation controller*. Setting the view controller's modalPresentationStyle to .popover, as in the preceding code, causes its presentationController to become a UIPopoverPresentationController (a UIPresentationController subclass); that is the object you need to talk to. The popover view controller's popoverPresentationController property points to that UIPopoverPresentationController (or to nil).

In general, it is permissible to perform your configurations just *after* telling your view controller to present the popover, because even though you have ordered the presentation, it hasn't actually started yet. This is a common pattern:

```
let vc = MyViewController()
vc.modalPresentationStyle = .popover
self.present(vc, animated: true)
if let pop = vc.popoverPresentationController {
    // ... configure pop here ...
}
```

I'll talk next about some of the configurations you'll perform on the popover presentation controller.

Arrow Source and Direction

At a minimum, the popover presentation controller needs to know where its arrow should point. You'll specify this by setting one of the following:

barButtonItem
> A bar button item in the interface, with which the popover should be associated. The popover's arrow will point to this bar button item. Typically, this will be the bar button item that was tapped in order to summon the popover (as in Figure 9-1).

sourceView, sourceRect

A UIView in the interface, along with a CGRect *in that view's coordinate system*, with which the popover should be associated. The popover's arrow will point to this rect. Typically, the sourceView will be the view that was tapped in order to summon the popover, and the sourceRect will be its bounds.

Here's a minimal popover presentation that works without crashing; the popover is summoned by tapping a UIButton in the interface, and this is that button's action method:

```
@IBAction func doButton(_ sender: Any) {
    let vc = MyViewController()
    vc.modalPresentationStyle = .popover
    self.present(vc, animated: true)
    if let pop = vc.popoverPresentationController {
        let v = sender as! UIView
        pop.sourceView = v
        pop.sourceRect = v.bounds
    }
}
```

In addition to the arrow source, you can set the desired arrow direction, as the popover presentation controller's permittedArrowDirections. This is a bitmask with possible values .up, .down, .left, and .right. The default is .any, comprising all four bitmask values; this will usually be what you want.

Popover Size

You can specify the desired size of the popover view. This information is provided through the presented view controller's preferredContentSize. Recall (from Chapter 6) that a view controller can use its preferredContentSize to communicate to its container view controller the size that it would like to be. The popover presentation controller is a presentation controller (UIPresentationController), which is also a UIContentContainer; it will consult the presented view controller's preferred-ContentSize and will try, within limits, to respect it.

The presentation of the popover won't fail if you don't supply a size for the popover, but you probably will want to supply one, as the default is unlikely to be desirable.

Who will set the presented view controller's preferredContentSize, and when? It's up to you. The presented view controller might set its own preferredContentSize; its viewDidLoad is a reasonable place, or, if the view controller is instantiated from a nib, the nib editor provides Content Size fields in the Attributes inspector. Alternatively, you can set the presented view controller's preferredContentSize when you configure the popover presentation controller:

```
if let pop = vc.popoverPresentationController {
    let v = sender as! UIView
    pop.sourceView = v
    pop.sourceRect = v.bounds
    vc.preferredContentSize = CGSize(200,500)
}
```

It is possible to change the presented view controller's `preferredContentSize` while the popover is showing. The popover presentation controller will hear about this (through the `preferredContentSizeDidChange` mechanism discussed in Chapter 6), and may respond by changing the popover's size, with animation.

If the popover is a navigation controller, the navigation controller will look at its current view controller's `preferredContentSize`, adjust for the presence of the navigation bar, and set its own `preferredContentSize` appropriately. Subsequently pushing or popping a view controller with a *different* `preferredContentSize` may not work as you expect — to be precise, the popover's *width* will change to match the new preferred width, but the popover's *height* will change only if the new preferred height is *taller*. I regard this as a bug; it is possible to work around it by nudging the navigation controller's `preferredContentSize` in a navigation controller delegate method:

```
extension ViewController : UINavigationControllerDelegate {
    func navigationController(_ nc: UINavigationController,
        didShow vc: UIViewController, animated: Bool) {
            nc.preferredContentSize = vc.preferredContentSize
    }
}
```

The popover presentation controller's `canOverlapSourceViewRect` can be set to `true` to permit the popover to cover the source view if space becomes tight while attempting to comply with the `preferredContentSize`. The default is `false`.

 The documentation claims that you can set the popover presentation controller's `popoverLayoutMargins` as a way of encouraging the popover to keep a certain distance from the edges of the presenting view controller's view. But my experience is that this setting is ignored.

Popover Appearance

By default, a popover presentation controller takes charge of the background color of the presented view controller's view, including the arrow. If the resulting color isn't to your taste, you can set the popover presentation controller's `backgroundColor`; this sets the arrow color as well.

For more control, you can customize the entire outside of the popover — that is, the "frame" surrounding the content, *including* the arrow. To do so, you set the UIPopoverPresentationController's `popoverBackgroundViewClass` to your own sub-

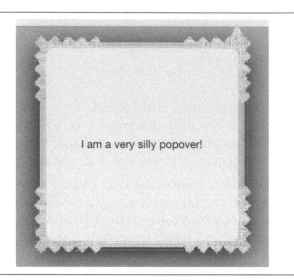

Figure 9-2. A very silly popover

class of UIPopoverBackgroundView (a UIView subclass). You then implement the UIPopoverBackgroundView's draw(_:) method to draw the arrow and the frame. The size of the arrow is dictated by your implementation of the arrowHeight property. The thickness of the frame is dictated by your implementation of the content-ViewInsets property.

A very silly example is shown in Figure 9-2. Here's how that result was achieved. I start by implementing five inherited members that we are required to override, along with our initializer:

```
class MyPopoverBackgroundView : UIPopoverBackgroundView {
    override class func arrowBase() -> CGFloat { return 20 }
    override class func arrowHeight() -> CGFloat { return 20 }
    override class func contentViewInsets() -> UIEdgeInsets {
        return UIEdgeInsetsMake(20,20,20,20)
    }
    // we are required to implement these, even trivially
    var arrOff : CGFloat
    var arrDir : UIPopoverArrowDirection
    override var arrowDirection : UIPopoverArrowDirection {
        get { return self.arrDir }
        set { self.arrDir = newValue }
    }
    override var arrowOffset : CGFloat {
        get { return self.arrOff }
        set { self.arrOff = newValue }
    }
    override init(frame:CGRect) {
        self.arrOff = 0
```

```
            self.arrDir = .any
            super.init(frame:frame)
            self.isOpaque = false
        }
        // ...
    }
```

Now I'll implement draw(_:). Its job is to draw the frame and the arrow. This can be a bit tricky, because we need to draw differently depending on the arrow direction (which we can learn from the UIPopoverBackgroundView's arrowDirection property). I'll simplify by assuming that the arrow direction will always be .up.

I'll start with the frame. I divide the view's overall rect into two areas, the arrow area on top and the frame area on the bottom, and I draw the frame into the bottom area as a resizable image (Chapter 2):

```
    override func draw(_ rect: CGRect) {
        let linOrig = UIImage(named: "linen.png")!
        let capw = linOrig.size.width / 2.0 - 1
        let caph = linOrig.size.height / 2.0 - 1
        let lin = linOrig.resizableImage(
            withCapInsets:UIEdgeInsetsMake(caph, capw, caph, capw),
            resizingMode:.tile)
            let klass = type(of:self)
        let arrowHeight = klass.arrowHeight()
        let arrowBase = klass.arrowBase()
        // ... draw arrow here ...
        let (_,body) = rect.divided(atDistance: arrowHeight, from: .minYEdge)
        lin.draw(in:body)
    }
```

Our next task is to fill in the blank left by the "draw arrow here" comment in the preceding code. We don't actually have to do that; we could quite legally stop at this point. Our popover would then have no arrow, but that's no disaster; many developers dislike the arrow and seek a way to remove it, and this constitutes a legal way. However, let's continue by drawing the arrow.

My arrow will consist simply of a texture-filled isosceles triangle, with an excess base rectangle joining it to the frame. The runtime has set the arrowOffset property to tell us where to draw the arrow: this offset measures the positive distance between the center of the view's edge and the center of the arrow. However, the runtime will have no hesitation in setting the arrowOffset all the way at the edge of the view, or even beyond its bounds (in which case it won't be drawn); to prevent this, I provide a maximum offset limit:

```
    let con = UIGraphicsGetCurrentContext()!
    con.saveGState()
    // clamp offset
    var propX = self.arrowOffset
    let limit : CGFloat = 22.0
```

```
let maxX = rect.size.width/2.0 - limit
propX = min(max(propX, limit), maxX)
// draw!
con.translateBy(x: rect.size.width/2.0 + propX - arrowBase/2.0, y: 0)
con.move(to:CGPoint(0, arrowHeight))
con.addLine(to:CGPoint(arrowBase / 2.0, 0))
con.addLine(to:CGPoint(arrowBase, arrowHeight))
con.closePath()
con.addRect(CGRect(0,arrowHeight,arrowBase,15))
con.clip()
lin.draw(at:CGPoint(-40,-40))
con.restoreGState()
```

Passthrough Views

When you're configuring your popover, you'll want to plan ahead for how the popover is to be dismissed. The default is that the user can tap anywhere *outside* the popover to dismiss it, and this will often be what you want. You can, however, modify this behavior in two ways:

UIPopoverPresentationController's `passthroughViews` *property*
An array of views in the interface behind the popover; the user can interact normally with these views while the popover is showing, and the popover will *not* be dismissed.

UIViewController's `isModalInPopover` *property*
If this is `true` for the presented view controller (or for its current child view controller, as in a tab bar interface or navigation interface), then if the user taps outside the popover, the popover is *not* dismissed. The default is `false`.

 The claim made by the documentation that `isModalInPopover` prevents *all* user interaction outside a popover is wrong. The user can still interact with a view listed in the `passthroughViews`, even if `isModalInPopover` is `true`.

If you've set the presented view controller's `isModalInPopover` to `true`, you've removed the user's ability to dismiss the popover by tapping outside it. You would then presumably provide some other way of letting the user dismiss the popover — typically, a button *inside* the popover which the user can tap in order to call `dismiss(animated:completion:)`.

Surprisingly, if a popover is summoned by the user tapping a UIBarButton item in a toolbar, other UIBarButtonItems in that toolbar are automatically turned into passthrough views! This means that, while the popover is showing, the user can tap any other button in the toolbar. Preventing this unwanted behavior is remarkably difficult. If you set the popover presentation controller's `passthroughViews` too soon, your setting is overridden by the runtime. The best place is the presentation's completion function:

```
    self.present(vc, animated: true) {
        vc.popoverPresentationController?.passthroughViews = nil
    }
```

Popover Presentation, Dismissal, and Delegate

A popover is a form of presented view controller. To show a popover, you'll call present(_:animated:completion:). If you want to dismiss a popover in code, rather than letting the user dismiss it by tapping outside it, you'll call dismiss(animated:completion:).

Messages to the popover presentation controller's delegate (UIPopoverPresentation-ControllerDelegate) provide further information and control. Typically, you'll set the delegate in the same place you're performing the other configurations:

```
    if let pop = vc.popoverPresentationController {
        // ... other configurations go here ...
        pop.delegate = self
    }
```

The three most commonly used delegate methods are:

prepareForPopoverPresentation(_:)
> The popover is being presented. This is another opportunity to perform initial configurations, such as what interface object the arrow points to. (But this method is still called too early for you to work around the passthroughViews issue I discussed a moment ago.)

popoverPresentationControllerShouldDismissPopover(_:)
> The user is dismissing the popover by tapping outside it. Return false to prevent dismissal. *Not* called when you dismiss the popover in code.

popoverPresentationControllerDidDismissPopover(_:)
> The user has dismissed the popover by tapping outside it. The popover is gone from the screen and dismissal is complete, even though the popover presentation controller still exists. *Not* called when you dismiss the popover in code.

popoverPresentationController(_:willRepositionPopoverTo:in:)
> The popover's sourceView is involved in new layout activity. This might be because the interface is rotating. The to: and in: parameters are mutable pointers to the popover's sourceRect and sourceView respectively, so you can change them through their pointee properties, thus changing the attachment of the arrow.

The delegate methods provide the popover presentation controller as parameter, and if necessary you can use it to identify the popover more precisely; for example, you can learn what view controller is being presented by examining the popover presentation controller's `presentedViewController`. The delegate `dismiss` methods make up for the fact that, when the user dismisses the popover, you don't have the sort of direct information and control that you would get if *you* had dismissed the popover by calling `dismiss(animated:completion:)` with a completion function.

If the user can dismiss the popover *either* by tapping outside the popover *or* by tapping an interface item that calls `dismiss(animated:completion:)`, you may have to duplicate some code in order to cover all cases. For example, consider the first popover shown in Figure 9-1. It has a Done button and a Cancel button; the idea here is that the user sets up a desired game configuration and then, while dismissing the popover, either saves it (Done) or doesn't (Cancel). But what if the user taps outside the popover? I interpret that as cancellation. Thus, if the Cancel button's action function does any work besides dismissing the popover, my `popoverPresentation-ControllerDidDismissPopover(_:)` implementation will have to do the same thing.

Adaptive Popovers

A popover is a presented view controller, so it's *adaptive*. By default, in a horizontally compact environment (such as an iPhone), the `.popover` modal presentation style will adapt as `.fullScreen`; what appears as a popover on the iPad will appear as a fullscreen presented view on the iPhone, completely replacing the interface. Thus, with no extra code, you'll get something eminently sensible on both types of device.

Sometimes, however, the default is not quite what you want. A case in point appears in Figure 9-1. The popover on the right, containing our help info, has no internal button for dismissal. It doesn't need one on the iPad, because the user can dismiss the popover by tapping outside it. But this is a universal app. Unless we take precautions, the same help info will appear on the iPhone as a fullscreen presented view, *and the user will have no way to dismiss it.* Clearly, we need a Done button that appears inside the presented view controller's view — but only on the iPhone.

To achieve this, we can take advantage of UIPresentationController delegate methods. A UIPopoverPresentationController is also a UIPresentationController, and you can set its delegate (UIAdaptivePresentationControllerDelegate). The adaptive presentation delegate methods thus spring to life, allowing you to tweak how the popover adapts (see "Adaptive Presentation" on page 324). The trick is that you must set the presentation controller's delegate *before* calling `present(_:animated:completion:)`; otherwise, the adaptive presentation delegate methods won't be called:

```
let vc = MyViewController()
vc.modalPresentationStyle = .popover
if let pop = vc.popoverPresentationController {
    pop.delegate = self // *
}
self.present(vc, animated: true)
```

We'll implement the delegate method `presentationController(_:viewController-ForAdaptivePresentationStyle:)` to substitute a different view controller. The substitute view controller can be the old view controller wrapped in a UINavigationController! If we also give our old view controller a `navigationItem` with a working Done button, the problem is solved:

```
func presentationController(_ controller: UIPresentationController,
    viewControllerForAdaptivePresentationStyle
    style: UIModalPresentationStyle) -> UIViewController? {
        if style != .popover {
            let vc = controller.presentedViewController
            let nav = UINavigationController(rootViewController: vc)
            let b = UIBarButtonItem(barButtonSystemItem: .done,
                target: self, action: #selector(dismissHelp))
            vc.navigationItem.rightBarButtonItem = b
            return nav
        }
        return nil
    }
@objc func dismissHelp(_ sender: Any) {
    self.dismiss(animated:true)
}
```

The outcome is that in a `.regular` horizontal size class environment we get a popover that can be dismissed by tapping outside it; otherwise, we get a fullscreen presented view controller that can be dismissed with a Done button in a navigation bar at the top of the interface.

You can also implement the delegate method `adaptivePresentationStyle(for:traitCollection:)` to return something other than `.fullScreen` in a `.compact` horizontal size class environment. One possibility is to return `.none`, in which case the presented view controller will be a popover *even on iPhone*:

```
func adaptivePresentationStyle(for controller: UIPresentationController,
    traitCollection: UITraitCollection) -> UIModalPresentationStyle {
        return .none
}
```

Popover Segues

If you're using a storyboard with Use Trait Variations checked, you can configure a popover presentation with little or no code. Draw (Control-drag) a segue from a button or view controller that is to *summon* the popover to a view controller that is to *be* the popover, and specify Present As Popover as the segue type. The result is a *popover segue*.

The segue, as it is triggered, configures the presentation just as you would configure it in code. It instantiates and initializes the presented view controller, sets its modal presentation style to `.popover`, and presents it. There is no need to set the `sourceView`, `barButtonItem`, or `permittedArrowDirections` in code; those properties can be set in the nib editor, in the segue's Attributes inspector. You can also set the passthrough views in the nib editor — but not in such a way as to override the unwanted default bar button item behavior I discussed earlier.

To perform additional configurations in code, implement `prepare(for:sender:):`. Here you can obtain the segue's `destination`, get a reference to its `popoverPresentationController`, and configure it. At the time `prepare(for:sender:)` is called, the presentation has not yet begun, so you can successfully set the popover presentation controller's delegate here if desired:

```
override func prepare(for segue: UIStoryboardSegue, sender: Any?) {
    if segue.identifier == "MyPopover" {
        let dest = segue.destination
        if let pop = dest.popoverPresentationController {
            pop.delegate = self
        }
    }
}
```

The popover version of an unwind segue is dismissal of the popover. Thus, both presentation and dismissal can be managed through the storyboard. A further possibility is to specify a custom segue class (as I explained in Chapter 6).

 A popover triggered through a popover segue doesn't point its arrow correctly at its source view. I regard this as a major bug. I recommend avoiding popover segues altogether.

Popover Presenting a View Controller

A popover can present a view controller internally; you'll specify a `modalPresentationStyle` of `.currentContext` or `.overCurrentContext`, because otherwise the presented view will be fullscreen by default (see Chapter 6).

What happens when the user taps *outside* a popover that is currently *presenting* a view controller's view internally? Unfortunately, different systems behave differently. Here's a sample:

iOS 7 and before
    Nothing happens; `isModalInPopover` is `true`.

iOS 8.1
    The entire popover, including the internal presented view controller, is dismissed.

iOS 8.3
    The internal presented view controller is dismissed, while the popover remains.

iOS 9 and later
    Like iOS 8.1.

In my opinion, the iOS 7 behavior was correct. Presented view controllers are supposed to be modal. They don't spontaneously dismiss themselves because the user taps elsewhere; there has to be some internal interface, such as a Done button or a Cancel button, that the user must tap in order to dismiss the view controller and proceed. You can restore the iOS 7 behavior by implementing the delegate method `popoverPresentationControllerShouldDismissPopover(_:)` to prevent dismissal if the popover is itself presenting a view controller:

```
func popoverPresentationControllerShouldDismissPopover(
    _ pop: UIPopoverPresentationController) -> Bool {
        return pop.presentedViewController.presentedViewController == nil
}
```

Split Views

A *split view* involves two views belonging to two view controllers. The view controllers are the children of a parent view controller, a *split view controller* (UISplitViewController). The child view controllers are the split view controller's viewControllers. A UIViewController that is a child, at any depth, of a UISplitViewController has a reference to the UISplitViewController through its `splitViewController` property.

The chief purpose of a split view controller is to implement a *master–detail architecture*. The first view is the *master* view, and is typically a list — that is, a table view. The user taps an item of that list to specify what should appear in the second view, which is the *detail* view. We may thus speak of the two children of the split view controller as the *master view controller* and the *detail view controller*. Officially, they are the *primary* and *secondary* view controllers.

The split view controller is *adaptive*, meaning that, by default, the implementation appears differently depending on whether we're running on an iPad or an iPhone:

Split view on the iPhone
    The master–detail architecture is expressed as a navigation interface. The user sees one view at a time. The master view occupies the screen; the user taps an item in the master view; the detail view replaces the master view.

Split view on the iPad
    Both views are displayed simultaneously. Usually, the master view is narrower, roughly the width of a typical iPhone. The user taps an item in the master view; the detail view responds by changing its contents.

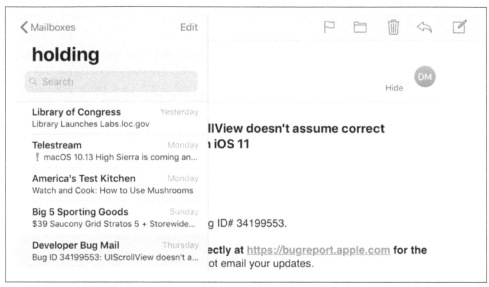

Figure 9-3. A familiar split view interface

In landscape orientation, the master view and the detail view appear side by side. In portrait orientation, there are two possible arrangements:

Side by side
> The two views appear side by side, just as in landscape orientation. Apple's Settings app is an example.

Overlay
> The detail view appears alone, with an option to summon the master view from the side as an overlay, either by tapping a bar button item or by swiping from the edge of the screen. Apple's Mail app is an example (Figure 9-3).

If a split view controller is the top-level view controller, it determines your app's compensatory rotation behavior. To take a hand in that determination without having to subclass UISplitViewController, make one of your objects the split view controller's delegate (UISplitViewControllerDelegate) and implement these methods, as needed:

- `splitViewControllerSupportedInterfaceOrientations(_:)`
- `splitViewControllerPreferredInterfaceOrientationForPresentation(_:)`

A split view controller does not relegate decisions about the status bar appearance to its children. To hide the status bar when a split view controller is the root view controller, you might have to subclass UISplitViewController; alternatively, you could wrap the split view controller in a custom container view controller, as I describe later in this chapter.

Xcode's Master–Detail app template will give you an adaptive UISplitViewController instantiated from the storyboard, with no work on your part. For pedagogical purposes, however, I'll begin by constructing and configuring a split view controller entirely in code. We'll get it working on the iPad before proceeding to the iPhone version. Then we'll return to the Master–Detail app template and examine how it works.

Expanded Split View Controller (iPad)

For reasons that will be clear later, a split view controller on the iPad is called an *expanded* split view controller. An expanded split view controller has two child view controllers simultaneously.

In this example, our master view (owned by MasterViewController) will be a table view listing the names of the three Pep Boys. Our detail view (owned by DetailViewController) will contain a single label displaying the name of the Pep Boy selected in the master view.

Our first cut at writing MasterViewController simply displays the table view:

```
class MasterViewController: UITableViewController {
    let model = ["Manny", "Moe", "Jack"]
    let cellID = "Cell"
    override func viewDidLoad() {
        super.viewDidLoad()
        self.tableView.register(UITableViewCell.self,
            forCellReuseIdentifier: self.cellID)
    }
    override func numberOfSections(in tableView: UITableView) -> Int {
        return 1
    }
    override func tableView(_ tableView: UITableView,
        numberOfRowsInSection section: Int) -> Int {
            return model.count
    }
    override func tableView(_ tableView: UITableView,
        cellForRowAt indexPath: IndexPath) -> UITableViewCell {
            let cell = tableView.dequeueReusableCell(
                withIdentifier: self.cellID, for: indexPath)
            cell.textLabel!.text = model[indexPath.row]
            return cell
    }
}
```

DetailViewController, in its viewDidLoad implementation, puts the label (self.lab) into the interface; it also has a public boy string property whose value appears in the label. We are deliberately agnostic about the order of events; our interface works correctly regardless of whether boy is set before or after viewDidLoad is called:

```
class DetailViewController: UIViewController {
    var lab : UILabel!
    var boy : String = "" {
        didSet {
            if self.lab != nil {
                self.lab.text = self.boy
            }
        }
    }
    override func viewDidLoad() {
        super.viewDidLoad()
        self.view.backgroundColor = .white
        let lab = UILabel()
        lab.translatesAutoresizingMaskIntoConstraints = false
        self.view.addSubview(lab)
        NSLayoutConstraint.activate([
            lab.topAnchor.constraint(
                equalTo: self.view.safeAreaLayoutGuide.topAnchor,
                constant: 100),
            lab.centerXAnchor.constraint(
                equalTo: self.view.centerXAnchor)
        ])
        self.lab = lab
        self.lab.text = self.boy
    }
}
```

Our app delegate constructs the interface by creating a UISplitViewController, giving it its two initial children, and putting its view into the window:

```
func application(_ application: UIApplication,
    didFinishLaunchingWithOptions launchOptions:
    [UIApplicationLaunchOptionsKey : Any]?) -> Bool {
        self.window = self.window ?? UIWindow()
        let svc = UISplitViewController()
        svc.viewControllers =
            [MasterViewController(style:.plain), DetailViewController()]
        self.window!.rootViewController = svc
        self.window!.backgroundColor = .white
        self.window!.makeKeyAndVisible()
        return true
}
```

The result certainly *looks* like a split view interface. In landscape orientation, the two views appear side by side; in portrait orientation, the detail view appears alone, but the master view can be summoned by swiping from the edge of the screen, and it can be dismissed by tapping outside it.

However, the app doesn't *do* anything! In particular, when we tap on a Pep Boy's name in the master view, the detail view doesn't change. Let's add that code (to MasterViewController):

```
override func tableView(_ tableView: UITableView,
    didSelectRowAt indexPath: IndexPath) {
        let detail = DetailViewController()
        detail.boy = model[indexPath.row]
        self.showDetailViewController(detail, sender: self) // *
}
```

The starred line is the key to the entire implementation of the master–detail architecture. Despite being sent to self, the call to showDetailViewController(_:sender:) actually walks up the view controller hierarchy until it arrives at the split view controller. (The mechanism of this walk is quite interesting of itself; I'll discuss it later.) The split view controller responds by making the detail view controller its second child, replacing the existing detail view and causing the selected Pep Boy's name to appear in the interface.

Things are going very well, but our app still doesn't quite look like a standard master–detail view interface. The usual thing is for both the master view and the detail view to contain a navigation bar. The detail view in portrait orientation can then display in its navigation bar a left button that summons the master view, so that the user doesn't have to know about the swipe gesture. This button is vended by the UISplitViewController, through its displayModeButtonItem property. Thus, to construct the interface properly, we need to change our app delegate code as follows:

```
let svc = UISplitViewController()
let master = MasterViewController(style:.plain)
master.title = "Pep" // *
let nav1 = UINavigationController(rootViewController:master) // *
let detail = DetailViewController()
let nav2 = UINavigationController(rootViewController:detail) // *
svc.viewControllers = [nav1, nav2]
self.window!.rootViewController = svc
let b = svc.displayModeButtonItem // *
detail.navigationItem.leftBarButtonItem = b // *
detail.navigationItem.leftItemsSupplementBackButton = true // *
```

Having made that adjustment, we must also adjust our MasterViewController code. Consider what will happen when the user taps a Pep Boy name in the master view. At the moment, we are making a new DetailViewController and making it the split view controller's second child. That is now wrong; we must make a new UINavigationController instead, with a new DetailViewController as its child. And this new DetailViewController doesn't have the displayModeButtonItem as its leftBarButtonItem, so we have to set it:

```
override func tableView(_ tableView: UITableView,
    didSelectRowAt indexPath: IndexPath) {
        let detail = DetailViewController()
        detail.boy = model[indexPath.row]
        let b = self.splitViewController?.displayModeButtonItem
        detail.navigationItem.leftBarButtonItem = b // *
```

```
        detail.navigationItem.leftItemsSupplementBackButton = true // *
        let nav = UINavigationController(rootViewController: detail) // *
        self.showDetailViewController(nav, sender: self)
    }
```

When the app is in portrait orientation, showing just the detail view, the `displayMode-ButtonItem` summons the master view. When the app is in landscape orientation with the two views displayed side by side, the `displayModeButtonItem` automatically hides itself. Our iPad split view implementation is complete!

Collapsed Split View Controller (iPhone)

As I've already said, a split view controller is adaptive. We can see this if we now launch our existing app on the iPhone: astoundingly, it works almost perfectly. There's a navigation interface. Tapping a Pep Boy's name in the master view pushes the new detail view controller onto the navigation stack, with its view displaying that name. The detail view's navigation bar has a back button that pops the detail view controller and returns us to the master view.

The only thing that isn't quite right is that the app launches with the detail view showing, rather than the master view. To fix that, we first add a line to our app delegate's `application(_:didFinishLaunchingWithOptions:)` to assign a delegate to the UISplitViewController:

```
let svc = UISplitViewController()
svc.delegate = self // *
```

We then implement one delegate method:

```
extension AppDelegate : UISplitViewControllerDelegate {
    func splitViewController(_ svc: UISplitViewController,
        collapseSecondary vc2: UIViewController,
        onto vc1: UIViewController) -> Bool {
            return true
    }
}
```

That's all; on the iPhone, the app now behaves correctly!

To understand what that delegate method does, you need to know more about how the split view controller works. It adopts one of two states: it is either collapsed or expanded, in accordance with its `isCollapsed` property. This distinction corresponds to whether or not the environment's trait collection has a `.compact` horizontal size class: if so, the split view controller collapses. Thus, the split view controller collapses as it launches on an iPhone.

An expanded split view controller has *two* child view controllers simultaneously. But a collapsed split view controller has only *one* child view controller. Thus, as the app launches on the iPhone, and the split view controller collapses, it must remove one child view controller. But which one? To find out, the split view controller *asks its delegate* how to proceed. In particular, it calls these delegate methods:

`primaryViewController(forCollapsing:)`
> The collapsed split view controller will have only one child view controller. *What* view controller should this be? By default, it will be the current *first* view controller, but you can implement this method to return a different answer.

`splitViewController(_:collapseSecondary:onto:)`
> The collapsing split view controller is going to remove its *second* view controller, leaving its *first* view controller as its only child view controller. Return `true` to permit this to happen.
>
> If this method returns `false` (the default), the split view controller sends `collapseSecondaryViewController(_:for:)` to the *first* view controller. What happens to the second view controller is now up to the first view controller.

Our first view controller is a UINavigationController, which has a built in response to `collapseSecondaryViewController(_:for:)` — namely, it pushes the specified secondary view controller onto its own stack. If it does that, we end up launching with the detail view showing on the iPhone, as we've already seen. Therefore, we implement `splitViewController(_:collapseSecondary:onto:)` to return `true`. That permits the split view controller to remove its second view controller, and we end up launching with the master view showing on the iPhone.

As on the iPad, the call to `showDetailViewController(_:sender:)`, when the user taps a row of the master table view, is the heart of the interface's functionality. The key here is that the interface responds in two different ways, depending on whether the split view controller is expanded or collapsed. On the iPad (expanded), the new view controller becomes the split view controller's second (detail) view controller, and the detail view, already visible in the interface, is replaced. On the iPhone (collapsed), there is just one child view controller; it is a navigation controller, and the new view controller is pushed onto its stack.

 In a standard split view controller architecture, the second view controller is a UINavigationController. On an iPhone, therefore, we are pushing a UINavigationController onto a UINavigationController's stack. This is an odd thing to do, but thanks to some internal voodoo, the parent UINavigationController will do the right thing: in displaying this child's view, it turns to the child UINavigationController's `topViewController` and displays *its* view (and its `navigationItem`), and the child UINavigationController's navigation bar never gets into the interface. Do not imitate this architecture in any other context!

Expanding Split View Controller (iPhone 6/7/8 Plus)

The iPhone 6/7/8 Plus is a hybrid: it's horizontally compact in portrait orientation, but *not* in landscape orientation. Thus, in effect, the split view controller thinks it's on an iPhone when the app is in portrait, but it thinks it has been magically moved over to an iPad when the app rotates to landscape. Thus, the split view controller *alternates* between `isCollapsed` being `true` and `false` on a single device. In portrait, the split view displays a single navigation interface, with the master view controller at its root, like an iPhone. In landscape, the master and detail views are displayed side by side, like an iPad.

When the app, running on the iPhone 6/7/8 Plus, rotates to portrait, or if it launches into portrait, the split view controller collapses, going through the very same procedure I just described for an iPhone. When it rotates to landscape, it performs the opposite of collapsing — namely, *expanding*. As the split view controller expands, it has the inverse of the problem it has when it collapses. A collapsed split view controller has just *one* child view controller, but an expanded split view controller has *two* child view controllers. Where will this second child view controller come from, and how should it be incorporated? To find out, the split view controller *asks its delegate* how to proceed:

`primaryViewController(forExpanding:)`
> The collapsed split view controller has just one child. The expanded split view controller will have two children. What view controller should be its *first* child view controller? By default, it will be the *current* child view controller, but you can implement this method to return a different answer.

`splitViewController(_:separateSecondaryFrom:)`
> What view controller should be the expanded split view controller's *second* child view controller? Implement this method to return that view controller.
>
> If you don't implement this method, or if you return `nil`, the split view controller sends `separateSecondaryViewController(for:)` to the *first* view controller. This method returns a view controller, or `nil`. If it returns a view controller, the split view controller makes that view controller its second view controller. The default response of a plain vanilla UIViewController to `separateSecondaryViewController(for:)` is to return `nil`. But a UINavigationController, if it has two children (a root view controller and a pushed view controller), pops its `topViewController` off the navigation stack and returns the popped view controller.

Thus, when our app is rotated from portrait to landscape, exactly the right thing happens, with no further coding on our part: if the navigation controller has pushed a DetailViewController onto its stack, it now pops it and hands it to the split view controller, which displays its view as the detail view!

On the iPhone 6/7/8 Plus in landscape, the displayModeButtonItem is present (whereas it disappears automatically on an iPad in landscape). Instead of appearing as a "back" chevron, it's an "expand" symbol (two arrows pointing away from each other). When the user taps it, the master view is hidden and the detail view occupies the entire screen — and the displayModeButtonItem changes to a chevron. Tapping the chevron toggles back the other way: the master view is shown again.

So, is our split view interface finished? Not quite! There is one remaining problem. Suppose we're in landscape (.regular horizontal size class) and the user is looking at the *detail* view controller. Now the user rotates to portrait (.compact horizontal size class). The split view controller collapses. Without extra precautions, we'll end up displaying the *master* view controller — because we went to the trouble of arranging that, back when we thought the only way to collapse was to *launch* into a .compact horizontal size class:

```
func splitViewController(_ svc: UISplitViewController,
    collapseSecondary vc2: UIViewController,
    onto vc1: UIViewController) -> Bool {
        return true
}
```

The result is that the user's place in the application has been lost. I think we can solve this satisfactorily simply by having the split view controller's delegate keep track of whether the user has ever chosen a detail view. I'll use an instance property, self.did-ChooseDetail:

```
class AppDelegate : UIResponder, UIApplicationDelegate {
    var window : UIWindow?
    var didChooseDetail = false
    // ...
}
```

When the user taps a row of the master view list to navigate to the detail view, we set that instance property to true:

```
override func tableView(_ tableView: UITableView,
    didSelectRowAt indexPath: IndexPath) {
        // ... as before ...
        if let del = self.splitViewController?.delegate as? AppDelegate {
            del.didChooseDetail = true
        }
}
```

When the split view controller collapses, the split view controller's delegate uses that instance property to decide what to do — that is, whether to display the master view controller or the detail view controller:

```
func splitViewController(_ svc: UISplitViewController,
    collapseSecondary vc2: UIViewController,
    onto vc1: UIViewController) -> Bool {
        if let nav = vc2 as? UINavigationController,
            nav.topViewController is DetailViewController,
            self.didChooseDetail {
                return false
        }
        return true
}
```

Customizing a Split View Controller

Here are some properties of a UISplitViewController that allow it to be customized:

primaryEdge
> New in iOS 11, you can determine which side the primary view appears on. Your choices (UISplitViewControllerPrimaryEdge) are .leading and .trailing.

presentsWithGesture
> A Bool. If false, the screen edge swipe gesture that shows the master view in portrait orientation on an iPad is disabled. The default is true.

preferredDisplayMode
> The display mode describes how an expanded split view controller's primary view is displayed. Set this property to change the current display mode of an expanded split view controller programmatically, or set it to .automatic to allow the display mode to adopt its default value. To learn the actual display mode being used, ask for the current displayMode.

> An expanded split view controller has three possible display modes (UISplit-ViewControllerDisplayMode):

.allVisible
> The two views are shown side by side.

.primaryHidden
> The primary view is not present.

.primaryOverlay
> The primary view is shown as a temporary overlay in front of the secondary view.

The default automatic behaviors are:

iPad in landscape
> The displayModeButtonItem is hidden, and the display mode is .allVisible.

---

iPad in portrait

> The `displayModeButtonItem` is shown, and the display mode toggles between `.primaryHidden` and `.primaryOverlay`.

iPhone 6/7/8 Plus in landscape

> The `displayModeButtonItem` is shown, and the display mode toggles between `.primaryHidden` and `.allVisible`.

`preferredPrimaryColumnWidthFraction`

> Sets the master view width in `.allVisible` and `.primaryOverlay` display modes, as a percentage of the whole split view (between 0 and 1). Your setting may have no effect unless you also constrain the width limits absolutely through the `minimumPrimaryColumnWidth` and `maximumPrimaryColumnWidth` properties. To specify the default width, use `UISplitViewControllerAutomaticDimension`. To learn the actual width being used, ask for the current `primaryColumnWidth`.

You can also track and govern the display mode with these delegate methods:

`splitViewController(_:willChangeTo:)`

> The `displayMode` of an expanded split view controller is about to change, meaning that its first view controller's view will be shown or hidden. You might want to alter the interface somehow in response.

`targetDisplayModeForAction(in:)`

> Called whenever something happens that might affect the display mode, such as:
>
> * The split view controller is showing for the first time.
> * The interface is rotating.
> * The user summons or dismisses the primary view.
>
> Return a display mode to specify what the user's tapping the `displayModeButton-Item` should subsequently do (and, by extension, how the button is portrayed), or `.automatic` to accept what the split view controller would normally do.

After collapsing or expanding, a UISplitViewController emits the `.UIView-ControllerShowDetailTargetDidChange` notification.

Split View Controller in a Storyboard

To see how to configure a split view controller in a storyboard, make a new project from the Master–Detail app template and study the storyboard that it provides. The storyboard starts with a split view controller, configured in essentially the same way as the split view controller that I created in code earlier (Figure 9-4):

- The split view controller has two relationships, "master view controller" and "detail view controller," specifying its two children. Those two children are both navigation controllers.

- The first navigation controller has a "root view controller" relationship to a MasterViewController, which is a UITableViewController.

- The second navigation controller has a "root view controller" relationship to a DetailViewController.

- The prototype table view cell in the master table view has an action segue — a Show Detail segue whose destination is the detail navigation controller. A Show Detail segue, when triggered, calls `showDetailViewController(_:sender:)` — and you already know what *that* does.

Unfortunately, that's not the end of the initial configuration required to get this split view controller to work. The `displayModeButtonItem` has to be added. That's done *in code*, in the app delegate's implementation of `application(_:didFinishLaunching-WithOptions:)`. The code obtains a reference to the split view controller and to the detail view controller, and creates and configures the `displayModeButtonItem`:

```
let splitViewController =
    window!.rootViewController as! UISplitViewController
let navigationController =
    splitViewController
        .viewControllers[splitViewController.viewControllers.count-1]
        as! UINavigationController
navigationController.topViewController!.navigationItem.leftBarButtonItem =
    splitViewController.displayModeButtonItem
```

The `displayModeButtonItem` must also be managed when the Show Detail segue is triggered. Again, that's done *in code*, in the master view controller:

```
override func prepare(for segue: UIStoryboardSegue, sender: Any?) {
    if segue.identifier == "showDetail" {
        if let indexPath = tableView.indexPathForSelectedRow {
            let controller =
                (segue.destination as! UINavigationController)
                    .topViewController as! DetailViewController
            controller.navigationItem.leftBarButtonItem =
                splitViewController?.displayModeButtonItem
            controller.navigationItem.leftItemsSupplementBackButton = true
            // ... also pass data to controller ...
        }
    }
}
```

In addition, the template code sets the app delegate as the split view controller's delegate, and implements `splitViewController(_:collapseSecondary:onto:)`, as we did earlier. Moreover, the split view controller in the storyboard has no configurable

Figure 9-4. How the storyboard configures a split view interface

properties in the Attributes inspector; if you want to set its `preferredPrimaryColumn-WidthFraction`, for example, you must do *that* in code as well.

The upshot is that the Master–Detail app template, even though it instantiates the view controllers from the storyboard, *still* ends up doing in code almost everything we did when we created the view controllers in code. One is therefore naturally led to ask what advantage there is to instantiating the split view controller and its child view controllers from the storyboard, as opposed to creating them in code. In my opinion, there is *no* such advantage. In fact, the Master–Detail app template is arguably *worse* than the code we wrote to start with; the template code is verbose and opaque. That's because the architecture has been constructed automatically, behind the code's back, and the code must now scramble just to get references to the various view controllers.

Setting the Collapsed State

Suppose you want side-by-side display of the two child view controllers' views in landscape *even on an iPhone*. How would you arrange that? The problem here is that we need to control the value of the split view controller's `isCollapsed` property — but we can't just set it directly, because this property is read-only.

The solution is to realize that the split view controller decides its own expanded or collapsed state depending on the environment — in particular, on whether the current trait collection's horizontal size class is `.compact`. We need, therefore, to *lie to the split view controller* about its trait collection environment, effectively making it believe that it's on an iPad even though it's really on an iPhone.

We can do that by interposing our own custom container view controller above the split view controller in the view controller hierarchy — typically, as the split view controller's direct parent. We can then send this container view controller the `setOverrideTraitCollection(_:forChildViewController:)` message, causing it to pass the trait collection of our choosing down the view controller hierarchy to the split view controller.

In this example, our container view controller is the app's root view controller; its child is a split view controller. The split view controller's view completely occupies the container view controller's view. In other words, the container's own view is never seen independently; the container view controller exists *solely* in order to manage the split view controller. Early in the life of the app, the container view controller configures the split view controller and lies to it about the environment:

```
var didInitialSetup = false
override func viewWillLayoutSubviews() {
    if !self.didInitialSetup {
        self.didInitialSetup = true
        let svc = self.childViewControllers[0] as! UISplitViewController
        svc.preferredDisplayMode = .allVisible
        svc.preferredPrimaryColumnWidthFraction = 0.5
        svc.maximumPrimaryColumnWidth = 500
        let traits = UITraitCollection(traitsFrom: [
            UITraitCollection(horizontalSizeClass: .regular)
        ])
        self.setOverrideTraitCollection(traits,
            forChildViewController: svc)
    }
}
```

The result is that the split view controller displays both its children's views side by side, both in portrait and landscape, like the Settings app on the iPad, *even on the iPhone.*

Another use of this same trick, based on Apple's AdaptivePhotos sample code, is to make the iPhone behave more like an iPhone 6/7/8 Plus, with a `.regular` horizontal size class in landscape (the split view controller expands) but a `.compact` horizontal size class in portrait (the split view controller collapses):

```
override func viewWillTransition(to size: CGSize,
    with coordinator: UIViewControllerTransitionCoordinator) {
        let svc = self.childViewControllers[0] as! UISplitViewController
        if size.width > size.height {
            let traits = UITraitCollection(traitsFrom: [
                UITraitCollection(horizontalSizeClass: .regular)
            ])
            self.setOverrideTraitCollection(traits,
                forChildViewController: svc)
        } else {
            self.setOverrideTraitCollection(nil,
                forChildViewController: svc)
        }
        super.viewWillTransition(to: size, with: coordinator)
}
```

View Controller Message Percolation

The `showDetailViewController(_:sender:)` method, which lies at the heart of the split view controller master–detail architecture, works in an interesting way. As I mentioned earlier, my code sends this message to `self` (the master view controller), but it is actually the split view controller that responds. How is that possible? The answer is that this message *percolates up* the view controller hierarchy to the split view controller.

Just two built-in UIViewController methods are implemented to behave in this way: `show(_:sender:)` and `showDetailViewController(_:sender:)`. Underlying this behavior is a *general* architecture for percolating a message up the view controller hierarchy, which I will now describe.

The heart of the message-percolation architecture is the method `targetViewController(forAction:sender:)`, where the `action:` parameter is the selector for the method we're inquiring about. This method, using some deep introspective voodoo, looks to see whether the view controller to which the message was sent *overrides the UIViewController implementation* of the method in question. If so, it returns `self`; if not, it effectively recurses *up* the view controller hierarchy, returning the result of calling the same method with the same parameters on its parent view controller or presenting view controller — or `nil` if no view controller is ultimately returned to it.

(A view controller subclass that *does* override the method in question but does *not* want to be the target view controller can implement the UIResponder method can-PerformAction(_:withSender:) to return false.)

So show(_:sender:) and showDetailViewController(_:sender:) are implemented to call targetViewController(forAction:sender:). If this call returns a target, they send themselves to that target. If it *doesn't* return a target, they call present(_:animated:completion:) as a kind of fallback.

Here's what actually happens when the master view controller sends showDetailView-Controller(_:sender:) to self:

1. The master view controller doesn't implement any override of showDetailView-Controller(_:sender:); it inherits the UIViewController implementation, which is called.

2. The showDetailViewController(_:sender:) implementation inherited from UIViewController calls targetViewController(forAction:sender:) on self (here, the master view controller).

3. targetViewController(forAction:sender:) sees that the method in question, namely showDetailViewController(_:sender:), is *not* overridden by this view controller (the master view controller); so it calls targetViewController(for-Action:sender:) on the *parent* view controller, which is a UINavigation-Controller.

4. Now we're looking at the UINavigationController. targetViewController(for-Action:sender:) sees that the method in question, namely showDetailView-Controller(_:sender:), is not overridden by *this* view controller either. So it calls targetViewController(forAction:sender:) on *its* parent view controller, which is a UISplitViewController.

5. Now we're looking at the UISplitViewController. It turns out that UISplitView-Controller *does* override the UIViewController implementation of showDetail-ViewController(_:sender:)!

   Thus, targetViewController(forAction:sender:) in the split view controller returns self, and *all* the nested calls to targetViewController(for-Action:sender:) return, with the split view controller as the result.

6. We are now back in showDetailViewController(_:sender:), originally sent to the master view controller. From its call to targetViewController(for-Action:sender:), it has acquired a target — the split view controller. So it finishes by sending showDetailViewController(_:sender:) to the split view controller.

The reason for the percolation architecture is that it allows show(_:sender:) and showDetailViewController(_:sender:) to work *differently* depending on how the view controller to which they are originally sent is situated in the view controller hierarchy. Two built-in UIViewController subclasses, UINavigationController and UISplitViewController, override one or both of these methods, and thus, if they are *further up the view controller hierarchy* than the view controller on which these methods are called, they will take charge of what happens:

UINavigationController show(_:sender:)
> UINavigationController implements show(_:sender:) to call pushViewController(_:animated:). That explains the dual behavior of show(_:sender:) — everything depends on whether or not we're in a navigation interface:

> *In a navigation interface*
>> If you send show(_:sender:) to a view controller whose parent is a UINavigationController, it is the navigation controller's implementation that will be called, meaning that the parameter view controller is *pushed* onto the stack.

> *Not in a navigation interface*
>> If you send show(_:sender:) to a view controller *without* a parent that overrides this method, it can't find a target, so it executes its fallback, meaning that the parameter view controller is *presented*.

UISplitViewController showDetailViewController(_:sender:)
> UISplitViewController implements showDetailViewController(_:sender:) as follows. First, it calls the delegate method splitViewController(_:showDetail:sender:); if the delegate returns true, UISplitViewController does nothing (and in that case, *you* would be responsible for getting the parameter view controller's view into the interface). Otherwise:

> *If the split view controller is expanded*
>> The split view controller replaces its second child view controller with the parameter view controller.

> *If the split view controller is collapsed*
>> If the split view controller's first (and only) child view controller is a UINavigationController, it sends show(_:sender:) to it — and the navigation controller responds by pushing the parameter view controller onto its own stack.

>> If not, the split view controller calls present(_:animated:completion:).

UISplitViewController show(_:sender:)

UISplitViewController implements show(_:sender:) as follows. First, it calls the delegate method splitViewController(_:show:sender:); if the delegate returns true, UISplitViewController does nothing (and that case, *you* would be responsible for getting the parameter view controller's view into the interface). Otherwise:

If the split view controller is expanded

If the sender: is the split view controller's first view controller, the split view controller replaces the *first* view controller with the parameter view controller.

If not, it replaces its *second* view controller with the parameter view controller.

If the split view controller is collapsed

The split view controller calls present(_:animated:completion:).

Now that you understand the percolation mechanism, perhaps you'd like to know whether your own custom methods can participate in it. They can! Extend UIView-Controller to implement your method such that it calls targetViewController(for-Action:sender:) on self and sends the action method to the target if there is one. For example:

```
extension UIViewController {
    @objc func showHide(_ sender: Any?) {
        if let target = self.targetViewController(
            forAction:#selector(showHide), sender: sender) {
                target.showHide(self)
        }
    }
}
```

In that example, I don't know what any particular UIViewController subclass's override of showHide(_:) may do, and I don't care! What matters is that if showHide(_:) is sent to a view controller that *doesn't* override it, it will percolate up the view controller hierarchy until we find a view controller that *does* override it, and it is *that override* that will be called.

iPad Multitasking

Starting in iOS 9, certain models of iPad can perform a kind of multitasking where the windows of *two different apps* can appear *simultaneously*. There are two multitasking modes (Figure 9-5):

Figure 9-5. Slideover multitasking mode and splitscreen multitasking mode

Slideover

> One app appears in a narrow format in front of the other, occupying roughly one-third of the screen's width. The rear app continues to occupy the full width of the screen; in iOS 9 and 10 it is deactivated and covered by a dimming view, but in iOS 11 it remains active.

Splitscreen

> The two apps appear side by side; they are both active simultaneously. In landscape orientation, the apps can divide the screen's width equally, or one of them can occupy roughly one-third of the screen's width. Splitscreen multitasking mode is available on a narrower range of iPad models than slideover mode.

Your iPad or Universal app, by default, will participate in iPad multitasking if it is built against iOS 9 or later, permits all four orientations, and uses a launch screen storyboard or *.xib*. If your app does all those things, but you would like it to opt out of participation in iPad multitasking, set the *Info.plist* key `UIRequiresFullScreen` to YES. An app that doesn't participate in iPad multitasking can occupy the screen while another app appears in front of it in slideover mode, but it cannot itself appear as the front app in slideover mode, and it cannot be involved in splitscreen mode at all.

If your app participates in iPad multitasking, it can appear at a size that's different from the device's screen size. This, in turn, may be accompanied by a change in the trait collection. Your app, even though it's on an iPad, can be launched or summoned into a `.compact` horizontal size class situation, and it can be toggled between a `.compact` horizontal size class and a `.regular` horizontal size class. In particular, if your app appears in narrow format (because it is occupying roughly one-third of the screen, in slideover or splitscreen mode), it *will* have a `.compact` horizontal size class; and if your app occupies half the screen in splitscreen mode, it *might* have a `.compact` horizontal size class, depending on how large this iPad's screen is and what orientation the iPad is in.

When your app changes size because of multitasking, your view controller will receive `viewWillTransition(to:with:)` to report the *size* change. It may receive this event more than once, and it will receive it while the app is inactive. If the size change *also* involves a transition from one horizontal size class to another, then your view controller will also receive `willTransition(to:with:)` and `traitCollectionDidChange(_:)` to report the *trait collection* change, also while the app is inactive.

The good news is that, if your app is a universal app, it is probably prepared *already* to respond coherently to these events, and might well be able to participate in iPad multitasking with no significant change. You can't assume that a `.compact` horizontal size class means you're on an iPhone, but you probably weren't thinking in those terms anyway — and even if you were, you can still detect what kind of device you are *really* on, if you have to, by looking at the trait collection's `userInterfaceIdiom`.

If a view controller is a *presented* view controller, then if the size transition involves a trait collection transition, the view controller will adapt. For example, a `.formSheet` or `.popover` presented view controller will, by default, turn into a `.fullScreen` presented view controller as the app transitions from a `.regular` horizontal size class to `.compact` — and will then change back again as the app transitions back to `.regular`. You can take a hand in how the presented view controller adapts by functioning as the presentation controller's delegate.

Similarly, in a split view controller interface, the split view controller will collapse and expand as the app transitions from a `.regular` horizontal size class to `.compact` and back again. This is no different from the ability of a split view controller to collapse and expand when an iPhone 6/7/8 Plus is rotated, and the same precautions will take care of it satisfactorily.

The large variety of absolute sizes that your app's interface might assume under iPad multitasking is unlikely to be of much interest. Again, if this is a universal app, then you are *already* taking care of a wide range of possible sizes through size classes and autolayout, and you probably won't have to do anything new to cover these new sizes. More striking, and possibly more daunting, is the possible range of *ratios* between the longer and shorter dimensions of your app's size. For example, on the large iPad Pro, your app can go from a roughly square `1.04` height to width ratio all the way up to a very tall and narrow `3.6`. Designing an interface that looks decent and can be operated correctly under such widely variable size ratios can be something of a challenge.

What actually changes when your app's size is changed is the size of its *window*. Thus, under iPad multitasking, your app's window bounds can be different from screen bounds. Moreover, if your app appears on the right, its window origin is shifted to the right; this changes the relationship between a view's position in window coordinates and its position in screen coordinates. However, it is unlikely that any of that will make a difference to your code.

Another major challenge introduced by iPad multitasking is the possibility that your app will effectively be frontmost *at the same time* as some other app. This means that the other app can be using both the processor (especially the main thread) and memory at a time when your app is not suspended. For this to work, all apps participating in iPad multitasking need to be on their best behavior, adhering to best practices with regard to threading (see Chapter 24) and memory usage (see "View Controller Memory Management" on page 400).

Drag and Drop

Drag and drop, new in iOS 11, allows the user to drag something from one app into another; it can also be used within a single app. What the user appears to drag is a view, but what is actually communicated to the target app is data. Thus, drag and drop is effectively a visual form of copy and paste — with this important difference:

Copy and paste uses a clipboard
Typically, copy and paste starts by copying the actual data to be communicated onto a clipboard. The data sits in the clipboard, ready to paste anywhere. The data in the clipboard can be pasted multiple times in multiple places.

Drag and drop uses a promise
With drag and drop between apps, no actual data is carried around during the drag. The data might be large; it might take time to acquire. What's carried is effectively a promise to supply a certain type of data on request; that promise isn't fulfilled until the drop takes place. Only the drop target can receive the data.

Drag and Drop Architecture

From an app's point of view, drag and drop operates at the level of individual views. The user performs a set sequence of actions:

1. The user long presses on a view; if this is a view from which dragging is possible (a *drag source*), a visible avatar — a *preview* — appears under the user's finger.

2. The user may then start dragging the preview.

3. The user drags the preview over some other view, possibly in a different app; if this is a view on which dropping is possible (a *drop destination*), the preview is badged to indicate this.

4. If the user releases the preview over a drop destination, the preview disappears, and the actual data is communicated from the source to the destination. (If the user releases the preview when it is *not* badged, the drag and drop is cancelled and no data is communicated.)

To prepare for drag and drop, therefore, your app will need either a drag source view or a drop destination view (or both):

Configuring a drag source view
> To configure a view so that dragging from it is possible, you create a UIDragInteraction object and attach it to that view. You don't subclass UIDragInteraction; rather, you give it a *delegate* (adopting the UIDragInteractionDelegate protocol). From your app's standpoint, it is this delegate that does all the work if the user actually tries to perform a drag from the source view.

Configuring a drop destination view
> To configure a view so that dropping onto it is possible, you create a UIDropInteraction object and attach it to that view. You don't subclass UIDropInteraction; rather, you give it a *delegate* (adopting the UIDropInteractionDelegate protocol). From your app's standpoint, it is this delegate that does all the work if the user actually tries to drop onto the destination view.

Drag and drop needs to operate between apps and outside of any app; it is a system-level technology. Between the start of the drag and the ultimate drop, the user, moving the preview, is interacting with the runtime — not the source app or the destination app. The preview being dragged doesn't belong to either app. In a sense, while dragging, the user isn't "in" any app at all; by the same token, while dragging, the user is not prevented from interacting with your app.

The runtime sends messages to the drag interaction delegate or the drop interaction delegate, as appropriate, at the start and end of the drag and drop. In those messages, the runtime presents two different faces:

- To the drag interaction delegate, it presents a UIDragSession object (a UIDragDropSession subclass).
- To the drop interaction delegate, it presents a UIDropSession object (another UIDragDropSession subclass).

More than one piece of data can be supplied through a single drag and drop session. The data itself is accessed through a nest of envelopes. Here's how the session is initially configured by the drag interaction delegate:

1. At the heart of each envelope is a single NSItemProvider representing a single piece of data.

---

2. Each item provider is wrapped in a UIDragItem.

3. The drag items are attached to the drag session.

At the other end of the process, the drop interaction delegate reverses the procedure:

1. The drop session contains drag items.

2. Each drag item contains a single NSItemProvider.

3. Each item provider is the conduit for fetching the corresponding piece of data.

Basic Drag and Drop

You now know enough for an example! I'll talk through a basic drag and drop operation. In my example, the source view will be a simple color swatch; it vends a color. The destination view will receive that color as the session's data. The source view and the destination view could be in two different apps, but the architecture is completely general, so they could be in the same app — it makes no difference.

The drag source view

The drag source view (which I'm calling dragview) can be configured like this:

```
@IBOutlet weak var dragView: UIView!
override func viewDidLoad() {
    super.viewDidLoad()
    let dragger = UIDragInteraction(delegate: self)
    self.dragView.addInteraction(dragger)
}
```

The user long presses on the source view, and the UIDragInteraction detects this. (If you think this makes a UIDragInteraction rather like a gesture recognizer, you're exactly right; in fact, adding a drag interaction to a view installs *four* gesture recognizers on that view.) The drag interaction turns to its delegate (UIDragInteractionDelegate) to find out what to do. A UIDragInteractionDelegate has just one required method, and this is it:

```
func dragInteraction(_ interaction: UIDragInteraction,
    itemsForBeginning session: UIDragSession) -> [UIDragItem] {
        let ip = NSItemProvider(object:UIColor.red)
        let di = UIDragItem(itemProvider: ip)
        return [di]
}
```

The drag delegate's dragInteraction(_:itemsForBeginning:) must return an array of drag items. If the array is empty, that's the end of the story; there will be no drag. In our case, we want to permit the drag. Our data is very simple, so we just package it up inside an item provider, pop the item provider into a drag item, and return an array consisting of that drag item.

The user now sees the preview and can drag it. The source effectively retires from the story. So much for the source view!

You may be wondering: where did the preview come from? We didn't supply a custom preview, so the system takes a snapshot of the drag source view, enlarges it a little, makes it slightly transparent, and uses that as the draggable preview. For our color swatch example, that might be perfectly acceptable.

The drop destination view

The drop destination view (which I'm calling `dropView`) can be configured in a manner remarkably similar to how we configured the source view:

```
@IBOutlet weak var dropView: UIView!
override func viewDidLoad() {
    super.viewDidLoad()
    let dropper = UIDropInteraction(delegate: self)
    self.dropView.addInteraction(dropper)
}
```

A drop interaction delegate has no required methods, but nothing is going to happen unless we implement this method:

```
func dropInteraction(_ interaction: UIDropInteraction,
    sessionDidUpdate session: UIDropSession) -> UIDropProposal {
        return UIDropProposal(operation: .copy)
}
```

In `dropInteraction(_:sessionDidUpdate:)`, our job is to return a UIDropProposal. This will be initialized with a UIDropOperation that will usually be `.cancel` or `.copy`. If it's `.cancel`, the user won't see any feedback while dragging over this view, and if the user drops onto this view, nothing will happen (the entire operation will be cancelled). If it's `.copy`, the preview is badged with a Plus sign while the user is dragging over this view, and if the user drops onto this view, we can be notified of this and can proceed to ask for the data.

In our implementation of `dropInteraction(_:sessionDidUpdate:)`, we have expressed a willingness to accept a drop regardless of what sort of data is associated with this session. Let's refine that. If what we accept is a color, we should base our response on whether any of the session's item providers promise us color data. We can query the item providers individually, or we can ask the session itself:

```
func dropInteraction(_ interaction: UIDropInteraction,
    sessionDidUpdate session: UIDropSession) -> UIDropProposal {
        let op : UIDropOperation =
            session.canLoadObjects(ofClass: UIColor.self) ? .copy : .cancel
        return UIDropProposal(operation:op)
}
```

Finally, let's say the drop actually occurs on the destination view. The drop interaction delegate's opportunity to obtain the data is its implementation of drop-Interaction(_:performDrop:). There are two ways to ask for the data. The simple way is to ask the session itself:

```
func dropInteraction(_ interaction: UIDropInteraction,
    performDrop session: UIDropSession) {
        session.loadObjects(ofClass: UIColor.self) { colors in
            if let color = colors[0] as? UIColor {
                // do something with color here
            }
        }
}
```

The more elaborate way is to get a reference to an item provider and ask the item provider to load the data:

```
func dropInteraction(_ interaction: UIDropInteraction,
    performDrop session: UIDropSession) {
        for item in session.items {
            let ip = item.itemProvider
            ip.loadObject(ofClass: UIColor.self) { (color, error) in
                if let color = color as? UIColor {
                    // do something with color here
                }
            }
        }
}
```

There's an important difference between those two approaches:

loadObjects(ofClass:)
> When calling the session's loadObjects(ofClass:), the completion function is called on the *main* thread.

loadObject(ofClass:)
> When calling an item provider's loadObject(ofClass:), the completion function is called on a *background* thread.

If you use the second way and you intend to update or otherwise communicate with the interface, you'll need to step out to the main thread (see Chapter 24); I'll show an example later in this chapter.

Item Providers

It's no coincidence that my color swatch example in the preceding section uses a UIColor as the data passed through the drag and drop session. UIColor implements two key protocols, NSItemProviderWriting and NSItemProviderReading. That's why my code was able to make two important method calls:

The drag source
> At the drag source end of things, I was able to construct my item provider by calling NSItemProvider's initializer `init(object:)`. That's because UIColor adopts the NSItemProviderWriting protocol; the class of the parameter of `init(object:)` must be an NSItemProviderWriting adopter.

The drop destination
> At the drop destination end of things, I was able to get the data from my item provider by calling `loadObject(ofClass:)`. That's because UIColor adopts the NSItemProviderReading protocol; the parameter of `loadObject(ofClass:)` must be an NSItemProviderReading adopter.

Other common classes that adopt these protocols include NSString, UIImage, NSURL, MKMapItem, and CNContact. But what if your data's class isn't one of those? Then adopt those protocols in *your* class!

To illustrate, I'll create a Person class and then configure it so that Person data can be passed through drag and drop. Here's the basic Person class:

```
final class Person : NSObject, Codable {
    let firstName: String
    let lastName: String
    init(firstName:String, lastName:String) {
        self.firstName = firstName
        self.lastName = lastName
        super.init()
    }
    override var description : String {
        return self.firstName + " " + self.lastName
    }
    enum MyError : Error { case oops }
    static let personUTI = "neuburg.matt.person"
}
```

It turns out that the only kind of data that can actually pass through a drag and drop session is a Data object. Therefore, I'm going to need a way to serialize a Person as Data to pass it from the source to the destination. That's why my Person class adopts the Codable protocol, which makes serialization trivial (Chapter 22). I also supply a simple Error type, to use as a signal if things go wrong. Finally, there is no standard UTI (universal type identifier) for my Person type, so I've made one up.

NSItemProviderWriting

Now I'll make it possible to call NSItemProvider's init(object:) when the object: is a Person. To do so, I adopt NSItemProviderWriting, which has two required members:

```
extension Person : NSItemProviderWriting {
    static var writableTypeIdentifiersForItemProvider = [personUTI] ❶
    func loadData(withTypeIdentifier typeid: String,
        forItemProviderCompletionHandler
        ch: @escaping (Data?, Error?) -> Void) -> Progress? { ❷
            switch typeid {
            case type(of:self).personUTI:
                do {
                    ch(try PropertyListEncoder().encode(self), nil)
                } catch {
                    ch(nil, error)
                }
            default: ch(nil, MyError.oops)
            }
            return nil
    }
}
```

❶ The writableTypeIdentifiersForItemProvider property lists type identifiers for the various representations in which we are willing to supply our data. At the moment, I'm willing to supply a Person only as a Person.

❷ The loadData(withTypeIdentifier:forItemProviderCompletionHandler:) method will be called when a drop destination asks for our data. The drop has occurred, and our Person object, originally passed into NSItemProvider's init(object:), is going to package itself up as a Data object. That's easy, because Person is Codable. There are no existing conventions for the format in which a Person is coded as Data, so I use a property list. Whatever happens, I make sure to *call the completion function* — either I pass in a Data object as the first parameter, or I pass in an Error object as the second parameter. That's crucial!

Our data doesn't take any time to generate, so I'm returning nil from the loadData method. If our data were time-consuming to supply, we might wish to return a Progress object with the fetching of our data tied to the updating of that object. I'll talk more about the purpose of the Progress object later.

NSItemProviderReading

Next I'll make it possible to call NSItemProvider's loadObject(ofClass:) when the class: is Person.self. To do so, I adopt NSItemProviderReading, which has two required members:

```
extension Person : NSItemProviderReading {
    static var readableTypeIdentifiersForItemProvider = [personUTI] ❶
    static func object(withItemProviderData data: Data,
        typeIdentifier typeid: String) throws -> Self { ❷
            switch typeid {
            case personUTI:
                do {
                    let p = try PropertyListDecoder().decode(self, from: data)
                    return p
                } catch {
                    throw error
                }
            default: throw MyError.oops
            }
    }
}
```

Everything I'm doing to implement NSItemProviderReading complements what I did
to implement NSItemProviderWriting:

❶ The `readableTypeIdentifiersForItemProvider` property lists type identifiers
    for any representations that we know how to transform into a Person. At the
    moment, we do this only for an actual Person.

❷ When `object(withItemProviderData:typeIdentifier:)` is called with the Per-
    son type identifier, this means that a Person object is arriving at the destination,
    packaged up as a Data object. Our job is to extract it and return it. Well, we know
    how it must be encoded; it's a property list! So we decode it and return it. If any-
    thing goes wrong, we throw an error instead.

The upshot is that drag and drop of a Person object now works perfectly within our
app, if we drop on a view whose UIDropInteractionDelegate expects a Person object.

Vending additional representations

What if we want a Person to be draggable from our app to some other app? It's
unlikely that another app will know about our Person class. Or what if we want a Person to be draggable within our app to a view that expects some other kind of data?

So far, our `writableTypeIdentifiersForItemProvider` property declares just one
UTI, signifying that we dispense a Person object. But we can add other UTIs, signifying that we provide alternate representations of a Person. For example, let's decide to
vend a Person as text:

```
static var writableTypeIdentifiersForItemProvider =
    [personUTI, kUTTypeUTF8PlainText as String]
```

(The constant `kUTTypeUTF8PlainText`, along with other UTI names, can be found in
the MobileCoreServices framework, which you'll need to import.)

Now we need to supplement our implementation of loadData(withType-Identifier:forItemProviderCompletionHandler:) to take account of the possibility that we may be called by someone who is expecting a String instead of a Person. What string shall we provide? How about a string rendering of the Person's name? It happens that our description property is ready and willing to provide that. And there's a simple standard way to wrap a UTF8 string as Data: just call data(using: .utf8). So all we have to do is add this case to our switch statement:

```
case kUTTypeUTF8PlainText as NSString as String:
    ch(self.description.data(using: .utf8)!, nil)
```

The result is that if a Person is dragged and dropped onto a view that expects a string to be dropped on it, the Person's name is provided as the data. A text field is such a view; if a Person is dragged and dropped onto a text field, the Person's name is inserted into the text field!

Receiving additional representations

We can also extend our implementation of the NSItemProviderReading protocol in a similar way. Here, our app contains a view that expects a Person to be dropped onto it, and we want it to have the ability to accept data of some other kind. For example, suppose the user drags a String and drops it onto our view. A String is not a Person, but perhaps this String is in fact a person's name. We could make a Person from that String.

To make that possible, we add a UTI to our readableTypeIdentifiersForItem-Provider property, signifying that we can derive a Person from text:

```
static var readableTypeIdentifiersForItemProvider =
    [personUTI, kUTTypeUTF8PlainText as String]
```

To go with that, we add a case to the switch statement in our object(withItem-ProviderData:typeIdentifier:) implementation. We pull the String out of the Data object, parse it in a crude way into a first and last name, and create a Person object:

```
case kUTTypeUTF8PlainText as NSString as String:
    if let s = String(data: data, encoding: .utf8) {
        let arr = s.split(separator:" ")
        let first = arr.dropLast().joined(separator: " ")
        let last = arr.last ?? ""
        return self.init(firstName: first, lastName: String(last))
    }
    throw MyError.oops
```

The result is that if the string "Matt Neuburg" is dragged onto a view that expects a Person object, the drop is accepted, because our Person type has signified that it knows how to turn a string into a Person, and the result of the drop is a Person with first name "Matt" and last name "Neuburg".

Similarly, we might want to permit a drag of a vCard to be dropped where a Person is expected. (For example, that's what we might get if the user were to drag a listing from the Contacts app onto our destination view.) Our readableTypeIdentifiers-ForItemProvider now needs yet another UTI:

```
static var readableTypeIdentifiersForItemProvider =
    [personUTI, kUTTypeVCard as String, kUTTypeUTF8PlainText as String]
```

We also add yet another case to our switch statement; the Contacts framework (Chapter 18) provides a standard way to decode a vCard from Data, along with straightforward extraction of the first and last names:

```
case kUTTypeVCard as NSString as String:
    do {
        let con = try CNContactVCardSerialization.contacts(with: data)[0]
        if con.givenName.isEmpty && con.familyName.isEmpty {
            throw MyError.oops
        }
        return self.init(firstName:con.givenName, lastName:con.familyName)
    } catch {
        throw MyError.oops
    }
```

(My implementation is not very sophisticated: if the vCard has no first or last name, we just give up instead of trying to handle the situation gracefully. But at least this way I won't end up with a nameless Person.)

Slow Data Delivery

Pretend that you are the drop interaction delegate, and you are now asking for the data in your implementation of dropInteraction(_:performDrop:). Whether you call the session's loadObjects(ofClass:) or an item provider's loadObject(of-Class:), your completion function is called *asynchronously* when the data arrives. This could take some considerable time, depending on the circumstances. (See Appendix C for more about what "asynchronous" means.)

Therefore, by default, if things take too long, the runtime puts up a dialog tracking the overall progress of data delivery and allowing the user to cancel it. If you like, you can replace the runtime's dialog with your own progress interface. (If you intend to do that, set the drop session's progressIndicatorStyle to .none, to suppress the default dialog — and be sure that your interface gives the user a way to cancel.)

You can stay informed about the supplying of the data through a Progress object (Chapter 12). A Progress object has fractionCompleted and isFinished properties that you can track through key–value observing in order to update your interface;

you can also cancel the loading process by telling the Progress object to cancel. There are two ways to get such an object:

- The session vends an overall Progress object as its progress property.
- An individual item provider's loadObject method can return a Progress object tracking the delivery of its own data.

Even if you rely on the runtime's default progress dialog, there can be a disconcerting effect of blankness when all the apparent action comes to an end without any data to display. You can discover this situation by implementing your drop interaction delegate's dropInteraction(_:concludeDrop:) method. When that method is called, all visible activity in the interface has stopped. If you discover here that the drop session's progress.isFinished is false, then depending on the nature of your interface, you might need to provide some sort of temporary view, to show the user that something has happened, until the actual data arrives.

Additional Delegate Methods

Additional UIDragInteractionDelegate and UIDropInteractionDelegate methods allow the delegate to dress up the drag or drop process in more detail.

Drag interaction delegate
> Drag interaction delegate methods let the delegate supply drag items, provide a preview, restrict the type of drag permitted, animate along with the start of the drag, and hear about each stage of the entire session.

Drop interaction delegate
> Drop interaction delegate methods let the delegate signify willingness to accept the drop, track the user's finger dragging over the view, and, when an actual drop takes place, provide a preview, perform an animation, and request the associated data.

Here are some examples; for full details, consult the documentation.

Custom drag preview

The drag interaction delegate can supply a preview to replace the snapshot of its view. Let's modify our earlier color swatch example to illustrate. Our color swatch is red; it will create a label containing the word "RED" and provide that as the preview.

The trick is that we have to say where this label should initially appear. To do that, we create a UIDragPreviewTarget, which specifies a container view in the interface to which our preview will be added as a subview, along with a center for the preview in that view's coordinate system. (The preview view will be snapshotted by the runtime. It will be removed from the container when the user either fails to initiate the drag or does in fact start dragging; in the latter case, it will be replaced by the snapshot.) Then we combine our preview with that target as a UITargetedDragPreview. In this case, we want the center of the label under the user's finger; we can find out from the session where the user's finger is:

```
func dragInteraction(_ interaction: UIDragInteraction,
    previewForLifting item: UIDragItem, session: UIDragSession)
    -> UITargetedDragPreview? {
        let lab = UILabel()
        lab.text = "RED"
        lab.textAlignment = .center
        lab.textColor = .red
        lab.layer.borderWidth = 1
        lab.layer.cornerRadius = 10
        lab.sizeToFit()
        lab.frame = lab.frame.insetBy(dx: -10, dy: -10)
        let v = interaction.view!
        let ptrLoc = session.location(in: v)
        let targ = UIDragPreviewTarget(container: v, center: ptrLoc)
        let params = UIDragPreviewParameters()
        params.backgroundColor = .white
        return UITargetedDragPreview(view: lab,
            parameters: params, target: targ)
}
```

In addition to a view and a target, a UITargetedDragPreview is initialized with a UIDragPreviewParameters object. In the preceding code, I used the UIDragPreview-Parameters object to make the preview's background white, just to give it a role in the example. Another useful possibility is to set the UIDragPreviewParameters visible-Path property, supplying a clipping path; for example, you might want the preview to be a snapshot of a certain subregion of the source view.

The drag interaction delegate can also *change* the preview in the course of the drag. To do so, it will set the drag item's previewProvider to a function returning a UIDragPreview (which has no target, because it has no relationship to the app's interface). If the drag interaction delegate does this in, say, dragInteraction(_:itemsFor-Beginning:), the previewProvider function won't be called until the drag begins, so the user will see the lifting preview first, and will see the previewProvider preview after the drag starts. Another strategy is to implement dragInteraction(_:session-DidMove:) and set the previewProvider there; the preview will change at that moment. But dragInteraction(_:sessionDidMove:) is called repeatedly, so be careful not to set the same drag item's previewProvider to the same function over and over.

In addition, the drag interaction delegate can set a cancelling preview, with drag-Interaction(_:previewForCancelling:withDefault:). This is used if the user begins to drag the preview but then releases it while not over a drop destination. A nice effect is to keep the existing drag preview (accessible through the third parameter) but retarget it to say where it should fall to as it vanishes; and in fact UITargeted-DragPreview has a `retargetedPreview(with:)` method for this very purpose. Furthermore, the UIDragPreviewTarget initializer lets you supply a `transform:` parameter that will be applied over the course of the animation as the preview falls.

The drop interaction delegate, too, can provide a preview to replace the dragged preview when the drop animation occurs; it works just like the cancelling preview.

Additional animation

Another drag interaction delegate possibility is to make the source view perform some sort of animation along with the runtime's initial animated display of the preview. In this example, I'll fade the color swatch slightly:

```
func dragInteraction(_ interaction: UIDragInteraction,
    willAnimateLiftWith anim: UIDragAnimating, session: UIDragSession) {
        if let v = interaction.view {
            anim.addAnimations {
                v.alpha = 0.5
            }
        }
}
```

I could have supplied a completion function by calling `addCompletion`, but I didn't, so the color swatch stays faded throughout the drag. Clearly, I don't want it to stay faded forever; when the drag ends, I'll be called back again, and I'll restore the swatch's alpha then:

```
func dragInteraction(_ interaction: UIDragInteraction,
    session: UIDragSession, willEndWith operation: UIDropOperation) {
        if let v = interaction.view {
            UIView.animate(withDuration:0.3) {
                v.alpha = 1
            }
        }
}
```

 The animations you pass with `addAnimations` are applied *before* the runtime takes its snapshot to form the default preview. Therefore, the results of those animations appear *in* the default preview. To avoid that, supply your own preview.

The drop interaction delegate gets a corresponding message, `drop-Interaction(_:item:willAnimateDropWith:)`. By retargeting the drop preview and performing its own animations alongside the drop, the drop interaction delegate can create some vivid effects.

Flocking

If a source view's drag interaction delegate implements `dragInteraction(_:items-ForAddingTo:withTouchAt:)`, and if that implementation returns a nonempty array of drag items, the user can tap on this source view *while already dragging a preview*, as a way of adding *more* drag items to the existing session. Apple calls this *flocking*.

If you permit flocking, be careful of unintended consequences. For example, if the user can tap a source view to get flocking *once* during a drag, the user can tap the *same* source view to get flocking *again* during that drag. This will result in the session effectively carrying multiple copies of the same data, which is probably not what you want. You can solve this problem by examining the session's current drag items to make sure you're not adding another drag item whose item provider refers to the same data.

Table Views and Collection Views

Table views and collection views get a special implementation of drag and drop, focusing on their cells. There is no need to supply a UIDragInteraction or UIDrop-Interaction; instead, simply give the table view or collection view an appropriate delegate:

- UITableViewDragDelegate
- UITableViewDropDelegate
- UICollectionViewDragDelegate
- UICollectionViewDropDelegate

The methods of these delegates are generally analogous to, but simpler than, those of UIDragInteractionDelegate and UIDropInteractionDelegate. I'll discuss some table view drag and drop delegate methods; collection views work very similarly.

To illustrate dragging, let's return to the table of U.S. states developed in Chapter 8, and make it possible to drag a cell and drop it on a view that expects text. Our text will be, appropriately enough, the name of the state. The implementation is trivial. First, in some early event such as `viewDidLoad`, we give our table view a drag delegate:

```
self.tableView.dragDelegate = self
```

Then, acting as drag delegate, we implement the only required method, `tableView(_:itemsForBeginning:at:)`. There's nothing new or surprising about our implementation:

```
func tableView(_ tableView: UITableView,
    itemsForBeginning session: UIDragSession,
    at indexPath: IndexPath) -> [UIDragItem] {
        let s = self.sections[indexPath.section].rowData[indexPath.row]
```

```
        let ip = NSItemProvider(object:s as NSString)
        let di = UIDragItem(itemProvider: ip)
        return [di]
    }
```

That's all we have to do! It is now possible to long press on a cell to get a drag preview snapshotting the cell, and that preview can be dropped on any drop target that expects text.

Now let's do the converse: we'll make it possible to drop on a table. Imagine that I have a table of person names, whose underlying model is an array containing a single Section whose rowData is an array of Person. I want the user to be able to drop a Person onto the table view; in response, I'll insert that person into the data, and I'll insert a cell representing that person into the table. We give our table view a drop delegate:

```
    self.tableView.dropDelegate = self
```

Acting as the drop delegate, I implement two delegate methods. First, I implement tableView(_:dropSessionDidUpdate:withDestinationIndexPath:) to determine, as the user's finger passes over the table view, whether the drop should be possible. The destination index path might be nil, indicating that the user's finger is not over a row of the table. Also, the dragged data might not be something that can generate a Person. In either case, I return the .cancel operation. Otherwise, I return the .copy operation to badge the dragged preview and permit the drop:

```
    func tableView(_ tableView: UITableView,
        dropSessionDidUpdate session: UIDropSession,
        withDestinationIndexPath ip: IndexPath?) -> UITableViewDropProposal {
            if ip == nil {
                return UITableViewDropProposal(operation: .cancel)
            }
            if !session.canLoadObjects(ofClass: Person.self) {
                return UITableViewDropProposal(operation: .cancel)
            }
            return UITableViewDropProposal(operation: .copy,
                intent: .insertAtDestinationIndexPath)
    }
```

Note the use of the UITableViewDropProposal initializer init(operation:intent:); the intent: argument (UITableViewDropIntent) tells the table view how to animate as the user's finger hovers over it:

.insertAtDestinationIndexPath
   For when the drop would insert rows; the table view opens a gap between rows under the user's finger.

`.insertIntoDestinationIndexPath`
> For when the drop would not insert rows; the row under the user's finger high-lights, suggesting that the dropped material will be incorporated into that row in some way.

`.automatic`
> A combination of the previous two, depending on precisely where the user's finger is.

`.unspecified`
> The table doesn't respond while the user's finger is over it.

Next, I implement the required `tableView(_:performDropWith:)` method. The drop is now happening; we need to retrieve the incoming data and update the table. The second parameter is a UITableViewDropCoordinator; everything we need to know about what's happening, such as the index path and the session, is available through the coordinator:

```
func tableView(_ tableView: UITableView,
    performDropWith coord: UITableViewDropCoordinator) {
        if let ip = coord.destinationIndexPath {
            coord.session.loadObjects(ofClass: Person.self) { persons in
                for person in (persons as! [Person]).reversed() {
                    tableView.performBatchUpdates({
                        self.sections[ip.section].rowData.insert(
                            person, at: ip.row)
                        tableView.insertRows(at: [ip], with: .none)
                    })
                }
            }
        }
    }
```

That works, but we are not updating the table until the data arrives. We are thus skirting the issue of what will happen if the data takes time to arrive. The drop happens, and we should insert a row *right now* — that is, *before* asking for the data. But at that moment, we obviously don't yet have the data! So either we must freeze the interface while we wait for the data to arrive, which sounds like very bad interface, or we must update the table with data that we don't yet have, which sounds like a metaphysical impossibility.

The solution is to use a *placeholder cell* for each new row while we wait for its data. The technique is best understood through an example. I'll use the item provider to fetch the data this time:

```
func tableView(_ tableView: UITableView,
    performDropWith coord: UITableViewDropCoordinator) {
        guard let ip = coord.destinationIndexPath else {return}
        for item in coord.items {
```

```
            let item = item.dragItem
            guard item.itemProvider.canLoadObject(ofClass: Person.self)
                else {continue}
            let ph = UITableViewDropPlaceholder( ❶
                insertionIndexPath: ip,
                reuseIdentifier: self.cellID,
                rowHeight: self.tableView.rowHeight)
            ph.cellUpdateHandler = { cell in ❷
                cell.textLabel?.text = ""
            }
            let con = coord.drop(item, to: ph) ❸
            item.itemProvider.loadObject(ofClass: Person.self) { p, e in ❹
                DispatchQueue.main.async { ❺
                    guard let p = p as? Person else { ❻
                        con.deletePlaceholder(); return
                    }
                    con.commitInsertion(dataSourceUpdates: {ip in ❼
                        tableView.performBatchUpdates({
                            self.sections[ip.section].rowData.insert(
                                p, at: ip.row)
                        })
                    })
                }
            }
        }
    }

    }
```

For each drag item capable of providing a Person object, this is what we do:

❶ We make a UITableViewDropPlaceholder, supplying our cell's reuseIdentifier
so that the table view can dequeue a cell for us to use as a placeholder cell.

❷ We set the placeholder's cellUpdateHandler to a function that will be called to
configure the placeholder cell. In my simple table, we're using a basic default cell
with a textLabel that normally displays the full name of a Person; for the place‐
holder cell, the textLabel should be blank.

❸ We call the coordinator's drop(_:to:) with the placeholder, to perform the drop
animation and create the placeholder cell; a context object (UITableViewDrop‐
PlaceholderContext) is returned. The placeholder cell is now visible in the table.
The important thing is, however, that the table view knows that this is not a real
cell! For purposes of all data source and delegate methods, it will behave as if the
cell didn't exist. In particular, it won't call tableView(_:cellForRowAt:) for this
cell; the cell is static and is already completely configured by the cellUpdate‐
Handler function we supplied earlier.

❹ Now, at long last, we call loadObject(ofClass:) to ask for the actual data!

⑤ Eventually, we are called with the data on a background thread. We step out to the main thread, because we're about to talk to the interface.

⑥ If we didn't get the expected data, the placeholder cell is no longer needed, and we remove it by calling the context object's `deletePlaceholder`.

⑦ If we reach this point, we've got data! We call the context object's `commit-Insertion(dataSourceUpdates:)` with a function that updates *the model only*. As a result, `tableView(_:cellForRowAt:)` is called to supply the real cell, which quietly replaces the placeholder cell in good order.

While your table view contains placeholders, the table view's `hasUncommitted-Updates` is `true`. Use that property as a flag to prevent your other code from calling `reloadData` on the table view, which would cause the placeholders to be lost and the entire table view update process to get out of whack.

In step 3 of the preceding example, we gave the UITableViewDropCoordinator a drop animation command to create the placeholder cell. This command must be given outside of the `loadObject` completion function, because the drop is about to happen *now*, so the animation must replace the default drop animation *now*, not at some asynchronous future time. The drop coordinator obeys three additional drop animation commands that work similarly:

`drop(_:intoRowAt:rect:)`
Animates the drop preview into the cell at the specified row, to the frame specified in that cell's bounds coordinates.

`drop(_:to:)`
Animates the drop preview *anywhere*. The second parameter is a UIDragPreview-Target combining a container and a center in the container's bounds coordinates.

`drop(_:toRowAt:)`
Snapshots the cell at the given row, replaces the drop preview with that snapshot, and animates the snapshot to fit the cell. This is useful under a very limited set of circumstances:

- You want to give the impression that the drop *replaces* the contents of a cell.
- The drag and drop must be *local* (see later in this chapter), so that the model can be updated with the new data and the row can be reloaded *before* the snapshot is taken.

Spring Loading

Spring loading is an effect similar to what happens on an iOS device's home screen when the user goes into "jiggly mode" and then drags an app's icon over a folder: the folder highlights, then flashes several times, then opens. In this way, the user can open the folder as part of the drag, and can then continue the drag, dropping the icon inside the opened folder.

You can use spring loading in an analogous way. For example, suppose there's a button in your interface that the user can tap to transition to a presented view controller. You can make that button be spring loaded, so that the user, in the middle of a drag, can hover over that button to make it perform that transition — and can then drop on something inside the newly presented view.

To make a button be spring loaded, set its `isSpringLoaded` property to `true`, and call its `addInteraction(_:)` method with a UISpringLoadedInteraction object. That object's initializer takes a function to be performed when the spring loaded interaction actually fires. (The button's normal control event action function, which fires in response to the button being tapped, does *not* fire as a result of spring loading, though of course you can make the spring loaded interaction function fire it.) For example:

```
self.button.isSpringLoaded = true
self.button.addInteraction(UISpringLoadedInteraction() { int, con in
    let vc = // some view controller
    // ... other preparations ,,,
    self.present(vc, animated: true)
})
```

In the spring loaded interaction function, the second parameter (con in the preceding code) is a UISpringLoadedInteractionContext object providing information about the interaction. For example, it reports the location of the drag, and it has a `state` describing how the view is currently responding. The first parameter (int) is the UISpringLoadedInteraction itself.

A fuller form of initializer lets you give the UISpringLoadedInteraction object two further properties:

An interaction behavior
> A UISpringLoadedInteractionBehavior, to which you can attach two functions — one to be called when the interaction wants permission to proceed, the other to be called when the interaction has finished.

An interaction effect
> A UISpringLoadedInteractionEffect, to which you can attach a function to be called every time the interaction's state changes.

Spring loading is available for buttons and button-like interface objects such as bar button items and tab bar items, as well as for UIAlertController (Chapter 13), where the spring loading is applied to the alert's buttons. It is also supported by table views and collection views, where it applies to the cells; if turned on, it can be turned off for individual cells by delegate methods:

- `tableView(_:shouldSpringLoadRowAt:with:)`
- `collectionView(_:shouldSpringLoadItemAt:with:)`

iPhone and Local Drag and Drop

By default, a UIDragInteraction comes into existence with its `isEnabled` property set to `false` on an iPhone. To bring dragging to life on an iPhone, set that property to `true`. Similarly, table views and collection views have a `dragInteractionEnabled` property that you'll need to set explicitly to `true` on an iPhone if you want dragging to work.

There's no iPad multitasking interface on the iPhone, so the only drag and drop your app will be capable of will be *local* drag and drop, within the app itself.

On an iPad, local drag and drop is always *possible*, of course, but you can also *restrict* a drag originating in your app to remain local to the app by implementing the drag interaction delegate method `dragInteraction(_:sessionIsRestrictedToDragging-Application:)` to return `true`. That situation can subsequently be detected by reading the session's `isRestrictedToDraggingApplication` property.

A drag that is dropped within the same app can provide the drop destination with more information, and more directly, than the same drag can provide to another app. We no longer have to pipe the data asynchronously through the session by means of a Data object; instead (or in addition), we can use these properties:

UIDragItem `localObject`
> The drag item can carry actual data with it, or a reference to an object that can provide the data, in its `localObject` property, and the drop interaction delegate can read this value directly, in real time, on the main thread — but only in the same app. If you try to read the `localObject` in an app different from the one where the drag originated, it will be `nil`.

UIDragSession `localContext`
> The drag session can maintain state, in its `localContext` property, and the drop interaction delegate can read this value directly, in real time, on the main thread, by way of the drop session's `localDragSession` — but only in the same app. If you try to read the `localDragSession` in an app different from the one where the drag originated, it will be `nil`.

Table and collection view `sourceIndexPath`

If drag and drop takes place within a table view or collection view, the UITable-ViewDropItem or UICollectionViewDropItem has a `sourceIndexPath` revealing where the drag started. If you try to read the `sourceIndexPath` in an app different from the one where the drag originated, it will be `nil`.

CHAPTER 10

Text

Drawing text into your app's interface is one of the most complex and powerful things that iOS does for you. Fortunately, iOS also shields you from much of that complexity. All you need is some text to draw, and possibly an interface object to draw it for you.

Text to appear in your app's interface will be an NSString (bridged from Swift String) or an NSAttributedString. NSAttributedString adds text styling to an NSString, including runs of different character styles, along with paragraph-level features such as alignment, line spacing, and margins.

To make your NSString or NSAttributedString appear in the interface, you can draw it into a graphics context, or hand it to an interface object that knows how to draw it:

Self-drawing text

Both NSString and NSAttributedString have methods for drawing themselves into any graphics context.

Text-drawing interface objects

Interface objects that know how to draw an NSString or NSAttributedString are:

UILabel

Displays text, possibly consisting of multiple lines; neither scrollable nor editable.

UITextField

Displays a single line of user-editable text; may have a border, a background image, and overlay views at its right and left end.

UITextView

Displays scrollable multiline text, possibly user-editable.

Deep under the hood, all text drawing is performed through a low-level technology with a C API called Core Text. At a higher level, iOS provides Text Kit, a middle-level technology lying on top of Core Text. UITextView is largely just a lightweight wrapper around Text Kit, and Text Kit can also draw directly into a graphics context. By working with Text Kit, you can readily do all sorts of useful text-drawing tricks without having to sweat your way through Core Text.

(Another way of drawing text is to use a web view, a scrollable view displaying rendered HTML. A web view can also display various additional document types, such as PDF, RTF, and *.doc*. Web views draw their text using a somewhat different technology, and are discussed in Chapter 11.)

Fonts and Font Descriptors

There are two ways of describing a font: as a UIFont (suitable for use with an NSString or a UIKit interface object) or as a CTFont (suitable for Core Text). Most font transformations can be performed through UIFontDescriptor, and if you need to convert between UIFont and CTFont, you can easily do so by passing through CTFontDescriptor, which is toll-free bridged to UIFontDescriptor so that you can cast between them.

Fonts

A font (UIFont) is an extremely simple object. You specify a font by its name and size by calling the UIFont initializer `init(name:size:)`, and you can also transform a font to the same font in a different size by calling the `withSize(_:)` instance method. UIFont also provides some properties for learning a font's various metrics, such as its `lineHeight` and `capHeight`.

To ask for a font by name, you have to *know* the font's name. Every font variant (bold, italic, and so on) counts as a different font, and font variants are clumped into families. UIFont has class methods that tell you the names of the families and the names of the fonts within them. To learn, in the console, the name of every installed font, you would say:

```
UIFont.familyNames.forEach {
    UIFont.fontNames(forFamilyName:$0).forEach {print($0)}}
```

When calling `init(name:size:)`, you can specify a font by its family name or by its font name (technically, its PostScript name). For example, `"Avenir"` is a family name; the plain font within that family is `"Avenir-Book"`. Either is legal as the `name:` argument. The initializer is failable, so you'll know if you've specified the font incorrectly — you'll get `nil`.

System font

The system font (used, for example, by default in a UIButton) can be obtained by call-ing `systemFont(ofSize:weight:)`. A UIFont class property such as `buttonFontSize` will give you the standard size. Possible weights, expressed as constant names of CGFloats, in order from lightest to heaviest, are:

- `UIFontWeightUltraLight`
- `UIFontWeightThin`
- `UIFontWeightLight`
- `UIFontWeightRegular`
- `UIFontWeightMedium`
- `UIFontWeightSemibold`
- `UIFontWeightBold`
- `UIFontWeightHeavy`
- `UIFontWeightBlack`

Starting in iOS 9, the system font (which was formerly Helvetica) is San Francisco, and comes in all of those weights, except at sizes smaller than 20 points, where the extreme ultralight, thin, and black are missing. A variety of the system font whose digits are monospaced can be obtained by calling `monospacedDigitSystemFont(ofSize:weight:)`. I'll talk later about how to obtain additional variants.

Dynamic type

If you have text for the user to read or edit — in a UILabel, a UITextField, or a UITextView (all discussed later in this chapter) — you are encouraged to take advan-tage of dynamic type. If a font is linked to dynamic type, then:

Text size is up to the user

The user specifies a dynamic type size using a slider in the Settings app, under Display & Brightness → Text Size. Additional sizes may be enabled under General → Accessibility → Larger Text. Possible sizes (UIContentSizeCategory) are:

- `.unspecified`
- `.extraSmall`
- `.small`
- `.medium`
- `.large`
- `.extraLarge`
- `.extraExtraLarge`
- `.extraExtraExtraLarge`
- `.accessibilityMedium`
- `.accessibilityLarge`
- `.accessibilityExtraLarge`
- `.accessibilityExtraExtraLarge`
- `.accessibilityExtraExtraExtraLarge`

You specify a role

You specify a dynamic type font in terms of the *role* it is to play in your layout. The size and weight are determined for you by the system, based on the user's text size preference. Possible roles that you can specify (UIFontTextStyle) are:

- `.largeTitle`
- `.title1`
- `.title2`
- `.title3`
- `.headline`
- `.subheadline`
- `.body`
- `.callout`
- `.footnote`
- `.caption1`
- `.caption2`

You'll probably want to experiment with specifying various roles for your individual pieces of text, to see which looks appropriate in context. (In Figure 6-1, the headlines are `.subheadline` and the blurbs are `.caption1`.)

One way to participate in dynamic type is to specify a dynamic type font supplied by the system. You can do so in the nib editor or in code. In the nib editor, set the font to one of the text styles. In code, call the UIFont class method `preferredFont(forText-Style:)`. For example:

```
self.label.font = UIFont.preferredFont(forTextStyle: .headline)
```

The font, in that case, is effectively the system font in another guise. But you might prefer to use some other font. New in iOS 11, there's an easy way to do that: instantiate a UIFontMetrics object by calling `init(forTextStyle: UIFontTextStyle)` (or use the `default` class property, which corresponds to the `.body` text style); then call `scaledFont(for:)` with your base font. In this example, I convert an existing label to adopt a dynamic type size:

```
let f = self.label2.font
self.label2.font = UIFontMetrics(forTextStyle: .caption1).scaledFont(for: f)
```

When dynamic type was first introduced, in iOS 7, it wasn't actually dynamic. The user could change the preferred text size, but responding to that change, by refreshing the fonts of your interface objects, was completely up to you. Starting in iOS 10, however, dynamic type can be genuinely dynamic. Set the `adjustsFontForContent-SizeCategory` property of your UILabel, UITextField, or UITextView to `true`; if this interface object uses dynamic type, then it will respond automatically if the user changes the Text Size preference in the Settings app.

New in iOS 11, you can set the `adjustsFontForContentSizeCategory` property in the nib editor: check Automatically Adjusts Font in the Attributes inspector. What you *can't* do in the nib editor is access UIFontMetrics. For example, if your label's font in the nib editor is Georgia, checking Automatically Adjusts Font won't make it dynamic; to do that, you have to use UIFontMetrics in code (as in the preceding example).

Adoption of dynamic type means that your interface must now respond to the possibility that text will grow and shrink, with interface objects changing size in response. Obviously, autolayout can be a big help here (Chapter 1). New in iOS 11, a standard vertical spacing constraint between labels, from the upper label's last baseline to the lower label's first baseline, will respond to dynamic type size changes. You can configure this in the nib editor, or in code with `constraintEqualToSystemSpacing-Below(_:multiplier:)`. If the distance you want is not identically the standard system spacing, adjust the constraint's `multiplier`.

Figure 10-1. Embedding a font in an app bundle

Sometimes, more radical adjustments of the overall layout may be needed, especially when we get into the five very large `.accessibility` text sizes. You'll have to respond to text size changes in code in order to make those adjustments. To do so, implement `traitCollectionDidChange(_:)`. The text size preference is reported through the trait collection's `preferredContentSizeCategory`. New in iOS 11, UIContentSize-Category overloads the comparison operators so that you can determine easily whether one size is larger than another; also, the `isAccessibilityCategory` property tells you whether this size is one of the `.accessibility` text sizes. To help you scale actual numeric values, the UIFontMetrics instance method `scaledValue(for:)` adjusts a CGFloat with respect to the user's current text size preferences.

Adding fonts

You are not limited to the fonts installed by default as part of the system. There are two ways to obtain additional fonts:

Include a font in your app bundle
A font included at the top level of your app bundle will be loaded at launch time if your *Info.plist* lists it under the "Fonts provided by application" key (`UIApp-Fonts`).

Download a font in real time
All macOS fonts are available for download from Apple's servers; you can obtain and install one while your app is running.

Figure 10-1 shows a font included in the app bundle, along with the *Info.plist* entry that lists it. Observe that what you're listing here is the name of the font *file*.

To download a font in real time, you'll have to specify the font as a font descriptor (discussed in the next section) and drop down to the level of Core Text (`import Core-Text`) to call `CTFontDescriptorMatchFontDescriptorsWithProgressHandler`. It takes a function which is called repeatedly at every stage of the download process; it will be called on a background thread, so if you want to use the downloaded font immediately in the interface, you must step out to the main thread (see Chapter 24).

In this example, I'll attempt to use Nanum Brush Script as my UILabel's font; if it isn't installed, I'll attempt to download it and *then* use it as my UILabel's font. I've inserted a lot of unnecessary logging to mark the stages of the download process (using `NSLog` because `print` isn't thread-safe):

```
let name = "NanumBrush"
let size : CGFloat = 24
let f : UIFont! = UIFont(name:name, size:size)
if f != nil {
    self.lab.font = f
    print("already installed")
    return
}
print("attempting to download font")
let desc = UIFontDescriptor(name:name, size:size)
CTFontDescriptorMatchFontDescriptorsWithProgressHandler(
    [desc] as CFArray, nil, { state, prog in
        switch state {
        case .didBegin:
            NSLog("%@", "matching did begin")
        case .willBeginDownloading:
            NSLog("%@", "downloading will begin")
        case .downloading:
            let d = prog as NSDictionary
            let key = kCTFontDescriptorMatchingPercentage
            let cur = d[key]
            if let cur = cur as? NSNumber {
                NSLog("progress: %@%%", cur)
            }
        case .didFinishDownloading:
            NSLog("%@", "downloading did finish")
        case .didFailWithError:
            NSLog("%@", "downloading failed")
        case .didFinish:
            NSLog("%@", "matching did finish")
            DispatchQueue.main.async {
                let f : UIFont! = UIFont(name:name, size:size)
                if f != nil {
                    NSLog("%@", "got the font!")
                    self.lab.font = f
                }
            }
        default:break
        }
        return true
})
```

Font Descriptors

A font descriptor (UIFontDescriptor, toll-free bridged to Core Text's CTFont-Descriptor) describes a font in terms of its *features*. You can then use those features to convert between font descriptors, and ultimately to derive a new font. For example,

> A *wild* and crazy label

Figure 10-2. A dynamic type font with an italic variant

given a font descriptor `desc`, you can ask for a corresponding italic font descriptor like this:

```
let desc2 = desc.withSymbolicTraits(.traitItalic)
```

If `desc` was originally a descriptor for Avenir-Book 15, `desc2` is now a descriptor for Avenir-BookOblique 15. However, it is not the *font* Avenir-BookOblique 15; a font descriptor is not a font.

The question, therefore, is how to get from a font to a corresponding font descriptor, and *vice versa:*

- To convert from a font to a font descriptor, ask for the font's `fontDescriptor` property. Alternatively, you can obtain a font descriptor directly just as you would obtain a font, by calling its initializer `init(name:size:)` or its class method `preferredFontDescriptor(withTextStyle:)`.

- To convert from a font descriptor to a font, call the UIFont initializer `init(descriptor:size:)`, typically supplying a size of `0` to signify that the size should not change.

Thus, this will be a common pattern in your code, as you convert from font to font descriptor to perform some transformation, and then back to font:

```
let f = UIFont(name: "Avenir", size: 15)!
let desc = f.fontDescriptor
let desc2 = desc.withSymbolicTraits(.traitItalic)
let f2 = UIFont(descriptor: desc2!, size: 0) // Avenir-BookOblique 15
```

The same technique is useful for obtaining styled variants of the dynamic type fonts. In this example, I prepare to form an NSAttributedString whose font is mostly `UIFontTextStyle.body`, but with one italicized word (Figure 10-2):

```
let body = UIFontDescriptor.preferredFontDescriptor(withTextStyle:.body)
let emphasis = body.withSymbolicTraits(.traitItalic)!
fbody = UIFont(descriptor: body, size: 0)
femphasis = UIFont(descriptor: emphasis, size: 0)
```

You can explore a font's features by way of a UIFontDescriptor. Some features are available directly as properties, such as `postscriptName` and `symbolicTraits`. The `symbolicTraits` is expressed as a bitmask:

Figure 10-3. A small caps font variant

```
let f = UIFont(name: "GillSans-BoldItalic", size: 20)!
let d = f.fontDescriptor
let traits = d.symbolicTraits
let isItalic = traits.contains(.traitItalic) // true
let isBold = traits.contains(.traitBold) // true
```

For other types of information, start with the name of an attribute whose value you want, as a `UIFontDescriptor.AttributeName`, and call `object(forKey:)`. For example:

```
let f = UIFont(name: "GillSans-BoldItalic", size: 20)!
let d = f.fontDescriptor
let vis = d.object(forKey:.visibleName)!
// Gill Sans Bold Italic
```

Another use of font descriptors is to access hidden built-in typographical features of individual fonts. To do so, you construct a dictionary whose keys (`UIFont-Descriptor.FeatureKey`) specify two pieces of information: the feature type (`.featureIdentifier`) and the feature selector (`.typeIdentifer`). In this example, I'll obtain a variant of the Didot font that draws its minuscules as small caps (Figure 10-3):

```
let desc = UIFontDescriptor(name:"Didot", size:18)
let d = [
    UIFontDescriptor.FeatureKey.featureIdentifier: kLowerCaseType,
    UIFontDescriptor.FeatureKey.typeIdentifier: kLowerCaseSmallCapsSelector
]
let desc2 = desc.addingAttributes([.featureSettings:[d]])
)
let f = UIFont(descriptor: desc2, size: 0)
```

The system (and dynamic type) font can also portray small caps; in fact, it can do this in two different ways: in addition to `kLowerCaseType` and `kLowerCaseSmallCaps-Selector`, where lowercase characters are shown as small caps, it implements `kUpper-CaseType` and `kUpperCaseSmallCapsSelector`, where uppercase characters are shown as small caps.

Another system (and dynamic type) font feature is an alternative set of glyph forms designed for legibility, with a type of `kStylisticAlternativesType`. If the selector is `kStylisticAltOneOnSelector`, the 6 and 9 glyphs have straight tails. If the selector is `kStylisticAltSixOnSelector`, certain letters also have special distinguishing shapes; for example, the lowercase "l" (ell) has a curved bottom, to distinguish it from capital "I" which has a top and bottom bar.

Typographical feature identifier constants such as `kLowerCaseSmallCapsSelector` come from the Core Text header *SFNTLayoutTypes.h*. What isn't so clear is how you're supposed to discover what features a particular font supports. The simple answer is that you have to drop down to the level of Core Text. For example:

```
let desc = UIFontDescriptor(name: "Didot", size: 20) as CTFontDescriptor
let f = CTFontCreateWithFontDescriptor(desc,0,nil)
let arr = CTFontCopyFeatures(f)
```

The resulting array of dictionaries includes entries [`CTFeatureTypeIdentifier`:37], which is `kLowerCaseType`, and [`CTFeatureSelectorIdentifier`:1], which is `kLower‐CaseSmallCapsSelector`. A more practical (and fun) approach to exploring a font's features is to obtain a copy of the font on the desktop, install it, launch TextEdit, choose Format → Font → Show Fonts, select the font, and open the Typography panel, thus exposing the font's various features. Now you can experiment on selected text.

Attributed Strings

Styled text — that is, text consisting of multiple style runs, with different font, size, color, and other text features in different parts of the text — is expressed as an *attributed string* (NSAttributedString and its mutable subclass, NSMutableAttributed‐String). An NSAttributedString consists of an NSString (its `string`) plus the attributes, applied in ranges.

For example, if the string "one red word" is blue except for the word "red" which is red, and if these are the only changes over the course of the string, then there are three distinct style runs — everything before the word "red," the word "red" itself, and everything after the word "red." However, we can apply the attributes in two steps, first making the whole string blue, and then making the word "red" red, just as you would expect.

Attributed String Attributes

The attributes applied to a range of an attributed string are described in dictionaries. Each possible attribute has a predefined name, used as a key in these dictionaries; here are some of the most important attributes names (NSAttributedStringKey) and their value types:

`.font`
   A UIFont. The default is Helvetica 12 (not San Francisco, the system font).

`.foregroundColor`
   The text color, a UIColor.

`.backgroundColor`
> The color *behind* the text, a UIColor. You could use this to highlight a word, for example.

`.ligature`
> An NSNumber wrapping 0 or 1, expressing whether or not you want ligatures used. Some fonts, such as Didot, have ligatures that are on by default.

`.kern`
> An NSNumber wrapping the floating-point amount of kerning. A negative value brings a glyph closer to the following glyph; a positive value adds space between them.

`.strikethroughStyle`
`.underlineStyle`
> An NSNumber wrapping one of these values (NSUnderlineStyle) describing the line weight:
>
> * `.styleNone`
> * `.styleSingle`
> * `.styleDouble`
> * `.styleThick`
>
> Optionally, you may include a specification of the line pattern, with names like `.patternDot`, `.patternDash`, and so on.
>
> Optionally, you may include `.byWord`; if you do not, then if the underline or strikethrough range spans multiple words, the whitespace between the words will be underlined or struck through.

 Unfortunately, Swift sees NSUnderlineStyle as an enum, not an option set, even though it is in fact a bitmask. Therefore, to use it, you'll have to take its raw value, and to specify multiple options, you'll have to use bitwise-or to combine their raw values. I regard this as a bug.

`.strikethroughColor`
`.underlineColor`
> A UIColor. If not defined, the foreground color is used.

`.strokeWidth`
> An NSNumber wrapping a Float. The stroke width is peculiarly coded. If it's positive, then the text glyphs are stroked but not filled, giving an outline effect, and the foreground color is used unless a separate stroke color is defined. If it's negative, then its absolute value is the width of the stroke, and the glyphs are both filled (with the foreground color) and stroked (with the stroke color).

`.strokeColor`

> The stroke color, a UIColor.

`.shadow`

> An NSShadow object. An NSShadow is just a value class, combining a `shadow‐Offset`, `shadowColor`, and `shadowBlurRadius`.

`.textEffect`

> An `NSAttributedString.TextEffectStyle`. The only text effect style you can specify is `.letterpressStyle`.

`.attachment`

> An NSTextAttachment object. A text attachment is basically an inline image. I'll discuss text attachments later on.

`.link`

> A URL. This may give the style range a default appearance, such as color and underlining, but you can override this by adding attributes to the same style range. In a noneditable, selectable UITextView, the link is tappable to go to the URL (as I'll explain later in this chapter).

`.baselineOffset`
`.obliqueness`
`.expansion`

> An NSNumber wrapping a Float.

`.paragraphStyle`

> An NSParagraphStyle object. This is basically just a value class, assembling text features that apply properly to paragraphs as a whole, not merely to characters, even if your string consists only of a single paragraph. Here are its most important properties:
>
> - `alignment` (NSTextAlignment)
>   - `.left`
>   - `.center`
>   - `.right`
>   - `.justified`
>   - `.natural` (left-aligned or right-aligned depending on the writing direction)
> - `lineBreakMode` (NSLineBreakMode)
>   - `.byWordWrapping`
>   - `.byCharWrapping`

- .byClipping
- .byTruncatingHead
- .byTruncatingTail
- .byTruncatingMiddle

- `firstLineHeadIndent`, `headIndent` (left margin), `tailIndent` (right margin)
- `lineHeightMultiple`, `maximumLineHeight`, `minimumLineHeight`
- `lineSpacing`
- `paragraphSpacing`, `paragraphSpacingBefore`
- `hyphenationFactor` (0 or 1)
- `defaultTabInterval`, `tabStops` (the tab stops are an array of NSTextTab objects; I'll give an example in a moment)
- `allowsDefaultTighteningForTruncation` (if `true`, permits some negative kerning to be applied automatically to a `truncating` paragraph if this would prevent truncation)

To construct an NSAttributedString, you can call `init(string:attributes:)` if the entire string has the same attributes; otherwise, you'll use its mutable subclass NSMutableAttributedString, which lets you set attributes over a range.

To construct an NSParagraphStyle, you'll use its mutable subclass NSMutableParagraphStyle. It is sufficient to apply a paragraph style to the first character of a paragraph; to put it another way, the paragraph style of the first character of a paragraph dictates how the whole paragraph is rendered.

Both NSAttributedString and NSParagraphStyle come with default values for all attributes, so you only have to set the attributes you care about. However, Apple says that supplying a font, foreground color, and paragraph style makes attributed strings more efficient.

Making an Attributed String

We now know enough for an example! I'll draw my attributed strings in a disabled (noninteractive) UITextView; its background is white, but its superview's background is gray, so you can see the text view's bounds relative to the text. (Ignore the text's vertical positioning, which is configured independently as a feature of the text view itself.)

First, two words of my attributed string are made extra-bold by stroking in a different color. I start by dictating the entire string and the overall style of the text; then I apply the special style to the two stroked words (Figure 10-4):

Figure 10-4. An attributed string

```
let s1 = """
    The Gettysburg Address, as delivered on a certain occasion \
    (namely Thursday, November 19, 1863) by A. Lincoln
    """
let content = NSMutableAttributedString(string:s1, attributes:[
    .font: UIFont(name:"Arial-BoldMT", size:15)!,
    .foregroundColor: UIColor(red:0.251, green:0.000, blue:0.502, alpha:1)
])
let r = (content.string as NSString).range(of:"Gettysburg Address")
content.addAttributes([
    .strokeColor: UIColor.red,
    .strokeWidth: -2.0
], range: r)
self.tv.attributedText = content
```

Carrying on from the previous example, I'll also make the whole paragraph centered and indented from the edges of the text view. To do so, I create a paragraph style and apply it to the first character. Note how the margins are dictated: the `tailIndent` is negative, to bring the right margin leftward, and the `firstLineHeadIndent` must be set separately, as the `headIndent` does not automatically apply to the first line (Figure 10-5):

```
let para = NSMutableParagraphStyle()
para.headIndent = 10
para.firstLineHeadIndent = 10
para.tailIndent = -10
para.lineBreakMode = .byWordWrapping
para.alignment = .center
para.paragraphSpacing = 15
content.addAttribute(
    .paragraphStyle,
    value:para, range:NSMakeRange(0,1))
self.tv.attributedText = content
```

The Gettysburg Address, as
delivered on a certain occasion
(namely Thursday, November 19,
1863) by A. Lincoln

Figure 10-5. An attributed string with a paragraph style

Fourscore and seven years ago,
our fathers brought forth upon
this continent a new nation,
conceived in liberty and dedicated
to the proposition that all men are
created equal.

Figure 10-6. An attributed string with an expanded first character

> When working temporarily with a value class such as NSMutableParagraphStyle, it feels clunky to be forced to instantiate the class and configure the instance *before* using it for the one and only time. So I've written a little Swift generic function, lend (see Appendix B), that lets me do all that in an anonymous function at the point where the value class is used.

In this next example, I'll enlarge the first character of a paragraph. I assign the first character a larger font size, I expand its width slightly, and I reduce its kerning (Figure 10-6):

```
let s2 = """
    Fourscore and seven years ago, our fathers brought forth \
    upon this continent a new nation, conceived in liberty and \
    dedicated to the proposition that all men are created equal.
    """
content2 = NSMutableAttributedString(string:s2, attributes: [
    .font: UIFont(name:"HoeflerText-Black", size:16)!
])
content2.addAttributes([
    .font: UIFont(name:"HoeflerText-Black", size:24)!,
    .expansion: 0.3,
    .kern: -4
], range:NSMakeRange(0,1))
self.tv.attributedText = content2
```

Carrying on from the previous example, I'll once again construct a paragraph style and add it to the first character. My paragraph style (applied using the lend function

Figure 10-7. An attributed string with justification and autohyphenation

Figure 10-8. A single attributed string comprising differently styled paragraphs

from Appendix B) illustrates full justification and automatic hyphenation (Figure 10-7):

```
content2.addAttribute(.paragraphStyle,
    value:lend { (para:NSMutableParagraphStyle) in
        para.headIndent = 10
        para.firstLineHeadIndent = 10
        para.tailIndent = -10
        para.lineBreakMode = .byWordWrapping
        para.alignment = .justified
        para.lineHeightMultiple = 1.2
        para.hyphenationFactor = 1.0
    }, range:NSMakeRange(0,1))
self.tv.attributedText = content2
```

Now we come to the Really Amazing Part. I can make a *single* attributed string consisting of *both* paragraphs, and a single text view can portray it (Figure 10-8):

```
let end = content.length
content.replaceCharacters(in:NSMakeRange(end, 0), with:"\n")
content.append(content2)
self.tv.attributedText = content
```

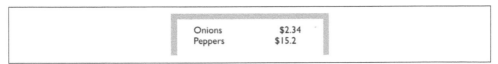

Figure 10-9. Tab stops in an attributed string

Tab stops

A tab stop is an NSTextTab, a value class whose initializer lets you set its location (points from the left edge) and alignment.

The initializer also lets you include an options: dictionary whose key (NSText-Tab.OptionKey) is .columnTerminators, as a way of setting the tab stop's column terminator characters. A common use is to create a decimal tab stop, for aligning currency values at their decimal point. You can obtain a value appropriate to a given locale by calling NSTextTab's class method columnTerminators(for:).

Here's an example (Figure 10-9); I have deliberately omitted the last digit from the second currency value, to prove that the tab stop really is aligning the numbers at their decimal points:

```
let s = "Onions\t$2.34\nPeppers\t$15.2\n"
let mas = NSMutableAttributedString(string:s, attributes:[
    .font:UIFont(name:"GillSans", size:15)!,
    .paragraphStyle:lend { (p:NSMutableParagraphStyle) in
        let terms = NSTextTab.columnTerminators(for:Locale.current)
        let tab = NSTextTab(textAlignment:.right, location:170,
            options:[.columnTerminators:terms])
        p.tabStops = [tab]
        p.firstLineHeadIndent = 20
    }
])
self.tv.attributedText = mas
```

The tabStops array can also be modified by calling addTabStop(_:) or removeTab-Stop(_:) on the paragraph style. Note that a paragraph style comes with default tab stops.

Text attachments

A text attachment is basically an inline image. To make one, you need an instance of NSTextAttachment initialized with image data; the easiest way is to start with a UIImage and assign it directly to the NSTextAttachment's image property. You must also give the NSTextAttachment a nonzero bounds; the image will be scaled to the size of the bounds you provide, and a .zero origin places the image on the text baseline.

A text attachment is attached to an NSAttributedString using the .attachment key; the text attachment itself is the value. The range of the string that has this attribute

Figure 10-10. Text attachments in an attributed string

must be a special nonprinting character whose codepoint is `NSAttachmentCharacter` (`0xFFFC`). The simplest way to arrange that is to call the NSAttributedString initializer `init(attachment:)`; you hand it an NSTextAttachment and it hands you an attributed string consisting of the `NSAttachmentCharacter` with the `.attachment` attribute set to that text attachment. You can then insert this attributed string into your own attributed string at the point where you want the image to appear.

To illustrate, I'll add an image of onions and an image of peppers just after the words "Onions" and "Peppers" in the attributed string (`mas`) that I created in the previous example (Figure 10-10):

```
let onions = // ... get image ...
let peppers = // ... get image ...
let onionatt = NSTextAttachment()
onionatt.image = onions
onionatt.bounds = CGRect(0,-5,onions.size.width,onions.size.height)
let onionattchar = NSAttributedString(attachment:onionatt)
let pepperatt = NSTextAttachment()
pepperatt.image = peppers
pepperatt.bounds = CGRect(0,-1,peppers.size.width,peppers.size.height)
let pepperattchar = NSAttributedString(attachment:pepperatt)
let r = (mas.string as NSString).range(of:"Onions")
mas.insert(onionattchar, at:(r.location + r.length))
let r2 = (mas.string as NSString).range(of:"Peppers")
mas.insert(pepperattchar, at:(r2.location + r2.length))
self.tv.attributedText = mas
```

Other ways to create an attributed string

The nib editor provides an ingenious interface for letting you construct attributed strings wherever built-in interface objects (such as UILabel or UITextView) accept them as a property; it's not perfect, however, and isn't suitable for lengthy or complex text.

It is possible to import an attributed string from text in some other standard format, such as HTML or RTF. (There are also corresponding export methods.) To import, get the target text into a Data object and call `init(data:options:document-Attributes:)`; alternatively, start with a file and call `init(url:options:document-Attributes:)`. The `options:` allow you to specify the target text's format. For example, here we read an RTF file from the app bundle as an attributed string and show it in a UITextView (`self.tv`):

```
let url = Bundle.main.url(forResource: "test", withExtension: "rtf")!
let opts : [NSAttributedString.DocumentReadingOptionKey : Any] =
    [.documentType : NSAttributedString.DocumentType.rtf]
var d : NSDictionary? = nil
let s = try! NSAttributedString(
    url: url, options: opts, documentAttributes: &d)
self.tv.attributedText = s
```

Modifying and Querying an Attributed String

We can coherently modify just the character content of a mutable attributed string by calling `replaceCharacters(in:with:)`, which takes an NSRange and a substitute string. If the range has zero length, we're inserting characters; if the range has non-zero length, we're replacing characters. The question is then what attributes will be applied to the new characters. The rule is:

- If we *replace* characters, the replacement characters all take on the attributes of the *first replaced* character.
- If we *insert* characters, the inserted characters all take on the attributes of the character *preceding* the insertion — except that, if we insert at the *start*, there is no preceding character, so the inserted characters take on the attributes of the character *following* the insertion.

You can query an attributed string about the attributes applied to a single character, asking either about all attributes at once with `attributes(at:effectiveRange:)`, or about a particular attribute by name with `attribute(_:at:effectiveRange:)`. The `effectiveRange:` argument is a pointer to an NSRange variable, which will be set by indirection to the range over which the same attribute value, or set of attribute values, applies.

In this example, we ask about the last character of our content attributed string:

```
var range : NSRange = NSMakeRange(0,0)
let d = content.attributes(at:content.length-1, effectiveRange:&range)
```

From that code we learn (in d), that the last character's `.font` attribute is Hoefler Text 16, and (in `range`) that that attribute is applied over a stretch of 175 characters starting at character 111.

Because style runs are something of an artifice, the `effectiveRange` might not be what you would think of as the *entire* style run. The methods with `longestEffective-Range:` parameters do (at the cost of some efficiency) work out the entire style run range for you; in practice, however, you typically don't need that, because you're cycling through ranges, and speed, even at the cost of *more* iterations, matters more than getting the longest effective range on *every* iteration.

In this example, I start with the content attributed string and change all the size 15 material to Arial Bold 20. I don't care whether I'm handed longest effective ranges (and my code explicitly says so); I just want to cycle efficiently:

```
content.enumerateAttribute(.font,
    in:NSMakeRange(0,content.length),
    options:.longestEffectiveRangeNotRequired) { value, range, stop in
        let font = value as! UIFont
        if font.pointSize == 15 {
            content.addAttribute(.font,
                value:UIFont(name: "Arial-BoldMT", size:20)!,
                range:range)
        }
    }
```

Custom Attributes

You are permitted to apply your own custom attributes to a stretch of text in an attributed string. Your attributes won't directly affect how the string is drawn, because the text engine doesn't know what to make of them; but it doesn't object to them either. In this way, you can mark a stretch of text invisibly for your own future use.

In this example, I have a UILabel whose text includes a date. Every so often, I want to replace the date by the current date. The problem is that when the moment comes to replace the date, I don't know where it is: I know neither its length nor the length of the text that precedes it. The solution is to use an attributed string where the date part is marked with a custom attribute.

My custom attribute is defined by extending NSAttributedStringKey:

```
extension NSAttributedStringKey {
    static let myDate = NSAttributedStringKey(rawValue:"myDate")
}
```

I've applied this attribute to the date part of my label's attributed text, with an arbitrary value of 1. Now I can readily find the date again later, because the text engine will tell me where it is:

```
let mas = NSMutableAttributedString(
    attributedString: self.lab.attributedText!)
mas.enumerateAttribute(.myDate, in: NSMakeRange(0, mas.length)) {
    value, r, stop in
    if let value = value as? Int, value == 1 {
        mas.replaceCharacters(in: r, with: Date().description)
        stop.pointee = true
    }
}
self.lab.attributedText = mas
```

Drawing and Measuring an Attributed String

You can draw an attributed string yourself, rather than having a built-in text display interface object do it for you; and sometimes this will prove to be the most reliable approach. An NSString can be drawn into a rect with `draw(in:withAttributes:)` and related methods; an NSAttributedString can be drawn with `draw(at:)`, `draw(in:)`, and `draw(with:options:context:)`.

Here, I draw an attributed string (content) into an image graphics context and extract the image, which might then be displayed by an image view:

```
let rect = CGRect(0,0,280,250)
let r = UIGraphicsImageRenderer(size:rect.size)
let im = r.image { ctx in
    UIColor.white.setFill()
    ctx.cgContext.fill(rect)
    content.draw(in:rect)
}
```

Similarly, you can draw an attributed string directly in a UIView's `draw(_:)` override. For example, imagine that we have a UIView subclass called StringDrawer that has an `attributedText` property. The idea is that we just assign an attributed string to that property and the StringDrawer redraws itself:

```
self.drawer.attributedText = content
```

And here's StringDrawer:

```
class StringDrawer : UIView {
    @NSCopying var attributedText : NSAttributedString! {
        didSet {
            self.setNeedsDisplay()
        }
    }
    override func draw(_ rect: CGRect) {
        let r = rect.offsetBy(dx: 0, dy: 2)
        let opts : NSStringDrawingOptions = .usesLineFragmentOrigin
        self.attributedText.draw(with:r, options: opts, context: context)
    }
}
```

The `.usesLineFragmentOrigin` option is crucial here. Without it, the string is drawn with its *baseline* at the rect origin (so that it appears *above* that rect), and it doesn't wrap. The rule is that `.usesLineFragmentOrigin` is the implicit default for simple `draw(in:)`, but with `draw(with:options:context:)` you must specify it explicitly.

NSAttributedString also provides methods to *measure* an attributed string, such as `boundingRect(with:options:context:)`. Again, the `.usesLineFragmentOrigin` option is crucial; without it, the measured text doesn't wrap and the returned height will be very small. The documentation warns that the returned height can be fractional and that you should round up to an integer if the height of a view is going to depend on this result.

The `context:` parameter of methods such as `draw(with:options:context:)` lets you attach an instance of NSStringDrawingContext, a simple value class whose `total-Bounds` property tells you where you just drew.

 Other features of NSStringDrawingContext, such as its `minimumScaleFactor`, appear to be nonfunctional.

Labels

A label (UILabel) is a simple built-in interface object for displaying text. I listed some of its chief properties in Chapter 8 ("Built-In Cell Styles" on page 464).

If you're displaying a plain NSString in a label, by way of the label's `text` property, then you are likely also to set its `font`, `textColor`, and `textAlignment` properties, and possibly its `shadowColor` and `shadowOffset` properties. The label's text can have an alternate `highlightedTextColor`, to be used when its `isHighlighted` property is `true` — as happens, for example, when the label is in a selected cell of a table view.

On the other hand, if you're using an NSAttributedString, then you'll set just the label's `attributedText` property and let the attributes dictate things like color, alignment, and shadow. In general, if your intention is to display text in a single font, size, color, and alignment, you probably won't bother with `attributedText`; but if you *do* set the `attributedText`, you should let it do *all* the work of dictating text style features. Those other UILabel properties do mostly still work, but they're going to change the attributes of your *entire* attributed string, in ways that you might not intend. Setting the `text` of a UILabel that has `attributedText` will effectively override the attributes.

 The `highlightedTextColor` property affects the `attributedText` only if the latter is the same color as the `textColor`.

Number of Lines

A UILabel's `numberOfLines` property is extremely important. Together with the label's line breaking behavior and resizing behavior, it determines how much of the text will appear. The default is `1` — a single line — which can come as a surprise. To make a label display more than one line of text, you must explicitly set its `numberOfLines` to a value greater than 1, or to `0` to indicate that there is to be no maximum.

Line break characters in a label's text are honored. Thus, for example, in a single-line label, you won't see whatever follows the first line break character.

Wrapping and Truncation

UILabel line breaking (wrapping) and truncation behavior, which applies to both single-line and multiline labels, is determined by the `lineBreakMode` (of the label or the attributed string). The options (NSLineBreakMode) are those that I listed earlier in discussing NSParagraphStyle, but their *behavior* within a label needs to be described:

`.byClipping`
> Lines break at word-end, but the *last* line can continue past its boundary, even if this leaves a character showing only partially.

`.byWordWrapping`
> Lines break at word-end, but if this is a single-line label, indistinguishable from `.byClipping`.

`.byCharWrapping`
> Lines break in midword in order to maximize the number of characters in each line.

`.byTruncatingHead`
`.byTruncatingMiddle`
`.byTruncatingTail`
> Lines break at word-end; if the text is too long for the label, then the *last* line displays an ellipsis at the start, middle, or end of the line respectively, and text is omitted at the point of the ellipsis.

Starting in iOS 9, `allowsDefaultTighteningForTruncation`, if `true`, permits some negative kerning to be applied automatically to a `truncating` label if this would prevent truncation.

A UILabel's line break behavior is *not the same* as what happens when an NSAttributedString draws itself into a graphics context. The default line break mode for a new label is `.byTruncatingTail`, but the default line break mode for an NSAttributedString's NSParagraphStyle is `.byWordWrapping`. More significantly, an NSAttributedString whose NSParagraphStyle's `lineBreakMode` doesn't have `wrapping` in its name *doesn't wrap* when it draws itself (it consists of a single line), but a multiline UILabel *always* wraps, regardless of its line break mode.

Resizing a Label to Fit Its Text

If a label is too small for its text, the entire text won't show. If a label is too big for its text, the text is vertically centered in the label, with space above and below. Either of those might be undesirable; you might prefer the label to fit its text.

If you're not using autolayout, in most simple cases `sizeToFit` will do the right thing; I believe that behind the scenes it is calling `boundingRect(with:options:context:)`.

If you're using autolayout, a label will correctly configure its own `intrinsicContent-Size` automatically, based on its contents — and therefore, all other things being equal, will size itself to fit its contents *with no code at all*. Every time you reconfigure the label in a way that affects its contents (setting its text, changing its font, setting its attributed text, and so forth), the label automatically invalidates and recalculates its intrinsic content size. There are two general cases to consider:

Short single-line label
> You might give the label no width or height constraints; you'll constrain its position, but you'll let the label's `intrinsicContentSize` provide both the label's width and its height.

Multiline label
> Most likely, you'll want to dictate the label's width, while letting the label's height change automatically to accommodate its contents. There are two ways to do this:

> *Set the label's width constraint*
>> This is appropriate particularly when the label's width is to remain fixed ever after.

> *Set the label's `preferredMaxLayoutWidth`*
>> This property is a hint to help the label's calculation of its `intrinsicContent-Size`. It is the width at which the label, as its contents increase, will stop growing horizontally to accommodate those contents, and start growing vertically instead.

Consider a label whose top, left, and right edges are pinned to its superview, while its height is free to change based on its `intrinsicContentSize`. Presume also that the superview's width can change, possibly due to rotation, thus changing the width of the label. Then the label's height will always perfectly fit its contents, provided that, after every such change, the label's `preferredMaxLayoutWidth` is adjusted *to match its actual width*.

To ensure that that happens, simply set the label's `preferredMaxLayoutWidth` to 0. That's a signal that the label should change its `preferredMaxLayoutWidth` to match its width *automatically* whenever its width changes. Moreover, that happens to be the default `preferredMaxLayoutWidth` value! Thus, by default, such a label will *always* fit its contents, with no effort on your part.

You can perform this same configuration in the nib editor: at the top of the Size inspector, uncheck the Explicit checkbox (if it is checked). The Preferred Width field says "Automatic," meaning that the `preferredMaxLayoutWidth` will change automatically to match the label's actual width as dictated by its constraints.

Instead of letting a label grow, you can permit its text font size to shrink if this would allow more of the text to fit. How the text is repositioned when the font size shrinks is determined by the label's `baselineAdjustment` property. For this feature to operate, *all* of the following conditions must be the case:

- The label's `adjustsFontSizeToFitWidth` property must be `true`.
- The label's `minimumScaleFactor` must be less than `1.0`.
- The label's size must be limited.
- *Either* this must be a single-line label (`numberOfLines` is 1) *or* the line break mode (of the label or the attributed string) must *not* have `wrapping` in its name.

Customized Label Drawing

Methods that you can override in a subclass to modify a label's drawing are `drawText(in:)` and `textRect(forBounds:limitedToNumberOfLines:)`.

For example, this is the code for a UILabel subclass that outlines the label with a black rectangle and puts a five-point margin around the label's contents:

```
class BoundedLabel: UILabel {
    override func awakeFromNib() {
        super.awakeFromNib()
        self.layer.borderWidth = 2.0
        self.layer.cornerRadius = 3.0
    }
    override func drawText(in rect: CGRect) {
        super.drawText(in: rect.insetBy(dx: 5, dy: 5).integral)
    }
}
```

 A CATextLayer (Chapter 3) is like a lightweight, layer-level version of a UILabel. If the width of the layer is insufficient to display the entire string, we can get truncation behavior with the `truncationMode` property. If the `isWrapped` property is set to `true`, the string will wrap. We can also set the alignment with the `alignmentMode` property. And its `string` property can be an NSAttributedString.

Text Fields

A text field (UITextField) is for brief user text entry. It portrays just a single line of text; any line break characters in its text are treated as spaces. It has many of the same properties as a label. You can provide it with a plain NSString, setting its `text`, `font`, `textColor`, and `textAlignment`, or provide it with an attributed string, setting its `attributedText`.

You can learn (and set) a text field's overall text attributes as an attributes dictionary through its `defaultTextAttributes` property. However, this dictionary takes String keys, not NSAttributedStringKey keys; I regard that as a bug. (The String corresponding to an NSAttributedStringKey is its `rawValue`.)

UITextField adopts the UITextInput protocol, which itself adopts the UIKeyInput protocol. These protocols endow a text field with important and often overlooked methods for such things as obtaining the text field's current selection and inserting text at the current selection. I'll give examples later in this section.

Under autolayout, a text field's `intrinsicContentSize` will attempt to set its width to fit its contents; if its width is fixed, you can set its `adjustsFontSizeToFitWidth` and `minimumFontSize` properties to allow the text size to shrink somewhat.

Text that is too long for the text field is displayed with an ellipsis at the end. A text field has no `lineBreakMode`, but you can change the position of the ellipsis by assigning the text field an attributed string with different truncation behavior, such as `.byTruncatingHead`. When long text is being edited, the ellipsis (if any) is removed, and the text shifts horizontally to show the insertion point.

Regardless of whether you originally supplied a plain string or an attributed string, if the text field's `allowsEditingTextAttributes` property is `true`, the user, when editing in the text field, can summon a menu toggling the selected text's bold, italics, or underline features.

A text field has a `placeholder` property, which is the text that appears faded within the text field when it has no text (its `text` or `attributedText` has been set to `nil`, or the user has removed all the text); the idea is that you can use this to suggest to the user what the text field is for. It has a styled text alternative, `attributedPlaceholder`.

If a text field's `clearsOnBeginEditing` property is `true`, it automatically deletes its existing text (and displays the placeholder) when editing begins within it. If a text field's `clearsOnInsertion` property is `true`, then when editing begins within it, the text remains, but is invisibly selected, and will be replaced by the user's typing.

A text field's border drawing is determined by its `borderStyle` property. Your options (UITextFieldBorderStyle) are:

`.none`
>   No border.

`.line`
>   A plain black rectangle.

`.bezel`
>   A gray rectangle, where the top and left sides have a very slight, thin shadow.

`.roundedRect`
>   A larger rectangle with slightly rounded corners and a flat, faded gray color.

You can supply a background image (`background`); if you combine this with a `border-Style` of `.none`, or if the image has no transparency, you get to supply your own border — unless the `borderStyle` is `.roundedRect`, in which case the `background` is ignored. The image is automatically resized as needed (and you will probably supply a resizable image). A second image (`disabledBackground`) can be displayed when the text field's `isEnabled` property, inherited from UIControl, is `false`. The user can't interact with a disabled text field, but without a `disabledBackground` image, the user may lack any visual clue to this fact (though a `.line` or `.roundedRect` disabled text field is subtly different from an enabled one). You can't set the `disabledBackground` unless you have also set the `background`.

A text field may contain one or two ancillary overlay views, its `leftView` and `right-View`, and possibly a Clear button (a gray circle with a white X). The automatic visibility of each of these is determined by the `leftViewMode`, `rightViewMode`, and `clearButtonMode`, respectively. The view mode values (UITextFieldViewMode) are:

`.never`
>   The view never appears.

`.whileEditing`
>   A Clear button appears if there is text in the field and the user is editing. A left or right view appears if there is *no* text in the field and the user is editing.

`.unlessEditing`
>   A Clear button appears if there is text in the field and the user is not editing. A left or right view appears if the user is not editing, or if the user is editing but there is no text in the field.

`.always`
>   A Clear button appears if there is text in the field. A left or right view always appears.

Depending on what sort of view you use, your `leftView` and `rightView` may have to be sized manually so as not to overwhelm the text view contents. If a right view and a

Clear button appear at the same time, the right view may cover the Clear button unless you reposition it.

The positions and sizes of *any* of the components of the text field can be set in relation to the text field's bounds by overriding the appropriate method in a subclass:

- `clearButtonRect(forBounds:)`
- `leftViewRect(forBounds:)`
- `rightViewRect(forBounds:)`
- `borderRect(forBounds:)`
- `textRect(forBounds:)`
- `placeholderRect(forBounds:)`
- `editingRect(forBounds:)`

 You should make no assumptions about when or how frequently these methods will be called; the same method might be called several times in quick succession. Also, these methods should all be called with a parameter that is the bounds of the text field, but some are sometimes called with a 100×100 bounds; this feels like a bug.

You can also override in a subclass the methods `drawText(in:)` and `drawPlaceholder(in:)`. You should either draw the specified text or call `super` to draw it; if you do neither, the text won't appear. Both these methods are called with a parameter whose size is the dimensions of the text field's text area, but whose origin is `.zero`. In effect what you've got is a graphics context for just the text area; any drawing you do outside the given rectangle will be clipped.

Summoning and Dismissing the Keyboard

The presence or absence of the onscreen simulated keyboard is intimately tied to a text field's editing state. They both have to do with the text field's status as the *first responder*:

- When a text field is first responder, it is being edited and the keyboard is present.
- When a text field is no longer first responder, it is no longer being edited, and if no other text field (or text view) becomes first responder, the keyboard is not present. The keyboard is not dismissed if one text field takes over first responder status from another.

When the user taps in a text field, by default it *is* first responder, and so the keyboard appears *automatically* if it was not already present. You can also control the presence or absence of the keyboard *in code*, together with a text field's editing state, by way of the text field's first responder status:

Becoming first responder

To make the insertion point appear within a text field and to cause the keyboard to appear, you send `becomeFirstResponder` to that text field. An example appeared in Chapter 8 ("Inserting Cells" on page 526).

Resigning first responder

To make a text field stop being edited and to cause the keyboard to disappear, you send `resignFirstResponder` to that text field. (Actually, `resignFirstResponder` returns a Bool, because a responder might return `false` to indicate that for some reason it refuses to obey this command.)

Alternatively, call the UIView `endEditing(_:)` method on the first responder *or any superview* (including the window) to ask or compel the first responder to resign first responder status.

The `endEditing(_:)` method is useful particularly because there may be times when you want to dismiss the keyboard without knowing who the first responder is. You can't send `resignFirstResponder` if you don't know who to send it to. And, amazingly, there is no simple way to learn what view is first responder!

 In a view presented in the `.formSheet` modal presentation style on the iPad (Chapter 6), the keyboard, by default, does *not* disappear when a text field resigns first responder status. This is presumably because a form sheet is intended primarily for text input, so the keyboard is felt as accompanying the form as a whole, not individual text fields. Optionally, you can prevent this exceptional behavior: in your UIViewController subclass, override `disablesAutomatic-KeyboardDismissal` to return `false`.

Once the user has tapped in a text field and the keyboard has automatically appeared, how is the user supposed to get rid of it? On the iPad, the keyboard may contain a button that dismisses the keyboard. Otherwise, this is an oddly tricky issue. You would think that the Return key in the keyboard would dismiss the keyboard, since you can't enter a Return character in a text field; but, of itself, it doesn't.

One solution is to be the text field's delegate and to implement a text field delegate method, `textFieldShouldReturn(_:)`. When the user taps the Return key in the keyboard, we hear about it through this method, and we receive a reference to the text field; we can respond by telling the text field to resign its first responder status, which dismisses the keyboard:

```
func textFieldShouldReturn(_ tf: UITextField) -> Bool {
    tf.resignFirstResponder()
    return true
}
```

Certain keyboards lack even a Return key. In that case, you'll need some other way to allow the user to dismiss the keyboard. I'll be returning to this issue in the course of the discussion.

Keyboard Covers Text Field

The keyboard, having appeared from offscreen, occupies a position "docked" at the bottom of the screen. This may cover the text field in which the user wants to type, even if it is first responder. You'll typically want to do something to reveal the text field.

To help with this, you can register for keyboard-related notifications:

- `.UIKeyboardWillShow`
- `.UIKeyboardDidShow`
- `.UIKeyboardWillHide`
- `.UIKeyboardDidHide`

Those notifications all have to do with the docked position of the keyboard. On the iPhone, keyboard docking and keyboard visibility are equivalent: the keyboard is visible if and only if it is docked. On the iPad, where the user can undock the keyboard and slide it up and down the screen, the keyboard is said to show if it is being docked, whether that's because it is appearing from offscreen or because the user is docking it, and it is said to hide if it is being undocked, whether that's because it is moving offscreen or because the user is undocking it.

Two additional notifications are sent *both* when the keyboard enters and leaves the screen *and* (on the iPad) when the user drags it, splits or unsplits it, and docks or undocks it:

- `.UIKeyboardWillChangeFrame`
- `.UIKeyboardDidChangeFrame`

The most important situations to respond to are those corresponding to `.UIKeyboardWillShow` and `.UIKeyboardWillHide`, when the keyboard is attaining or leaving its docked position at the bottom of the screen. You might think that it would be necessary to handle `.UIKeyboardWillChangeFrame` too, in case the keyboard changes its height — as can happen, for example, if user switches from the text keyboard to the emoji keyboard on the iPhone. But in fact `.UIKeyboardWillShow` is sent in that situation as well.

Each notification's `userInfo` dictionary contains information describing what the keyboard will do or has done, under these keys:

- `UIKeyboardFrameBeginUserInfoKey`

- `UIKeyboardFrameEndUserInfoKey`

- `UIKeyboardAnimationDurationUserInfoKey`

- `UIKeyboardAnimationCurveUserInfoKey`

In `.UIKeyboardWillShow`, by looking at the `UIKeyboardFrameEndUserInfoKey`, you know what position the keyboard is moving to. It is an NSValue wrapping a CGRect in screen coordinates. By converting the coordinate system as appropriate, you can compare the keyboard's new frame with the frame of your interface items. For example, if the keyboard's new frame intersects a text field's frame (in the same coordinates), the keyboard is going to cover that text field.

A natural-looking response, in that case, is to slide the entire interface upward as the keyboard appears, just enough to expose the text field being edited above the top of the keyboard. The simplest way to do that is for the entire interface to be inside a scroll view (Chapter 7), which is, after all, a view that knows how to slide its contents.

This scroll view need not be ordinarily scrollable by the user, who may be completely unaware of its existence. But *after* the keyboard appears, the scroll view *should* be scrollable by the user, so that the user can inspect the entire interface at will, even while the keyboard is covering part of it. We can ensure that by adjusting the scroll view's `contentInset`.

This behavior is in fact implemented automatically by a UITableViewController. When a text field inside a table cell is first responder, the table view controller adjusts the table view's `contentInset` and `scrollIndicatorInsets` to compensate for the keyboard. The result is that the entire table view content is available within the space between the top of the table view and the top of the keyboard.

Moreover, a scroll view has two additional bits of built-in behavior that will help us:

- It scrolls automatically to reveal the first responder. This will make it easy for us to expose the text field being edited.

- It has a `keyboardDismissMode`, governing what will happen to the keyboard when the user scrolls. This can give us an additional way to allow the user to dismiss the keyboard.

Let's imitate UITableViewController's behavior with a scroll view containing text fields. In particular, our interface consists of a scroll view containing a content view; the content view contains several text fields.

In `viewDidLoad`, we register for keyboard notifications:

```
NotificationCenter.default.addObserver(self,
    selector: #selector(keyboardShow),
    name: .UIKeyboardWillShow, object: nil)
NotificationCenter.default.addObserver(self,
    selector: #selector(keyboardHide),
    name: .UIKeyboardWillHide, object: nil)
```

We are the delegate of any text fields, so that we can hear about it when the user taps the Return key in the keyboard. We use that as a signal to dismiss the keyboard, as I suggested earlier:

```
func textFieldShouldReturn(_ tf: UITextField) -> Bool {
    tf.resignFirstResponder()
    return true
}
```

To implement the notification methods keyboardShow and keyboardHide, it will help to have on hand a utility function that works out the geometry based on the notification's userInfo dictionary and the bounds of the view we're concerned with (which will be the scroll view). If the keyboard wasn't within the view's bounds and now it will be, it is entering; if it was within the view's bounds and now it won't be, it is exiting. We return that information, along with the keyboard's frame in the view's bounds coordinates:

```
enum KeyboardState {
    case unknown
    case entering
    case exiting
}
func keyboardState(for d:[AnyHashable:Any], in v:UIView?)
    -> (KeyboardState, CGRect?) {
        var rold = d[UIKeyboardFrameBeginUserInfoKey] as! CGRect
        var rnew = d[UIKeyboardFrameEndUserInfoKey] as! CGRect
        var ks : KeyboardState = .unknown
        var newRect : CGRect? = nil
        if let v = v {
            let co = UIScreen.main.coordinateSpace
            rold = co.convert(rold, to:v)
            rnew = co.convert(rnew, to:v)
            newRect = rnew
            if !rold.intersects(v.bounds) && rnew.intersects(v.bounds) {
                ks = .entering
            }
            if rold.intersects(v.bounds) && !rnew.intersects(v.bounds) {
                ks = .exiting
            }
        }
        return (ks, newRect)
}
```

When the keyboard shows, we check whether it is initially appearing on the screen; if so, we store the current content offset, content inset, and scroll indicator insets. Then we alter the scroll view's insets appropriately, allowing the scroll view itself to scroll the first responder into view if needed:

```
@objc func keyboardShow(_ n:Notification) {
    let d = n.userInfo!
    let (state, rnew) = keyboardState(for:d, in:self.scrollView)
    if state == .entering {
        self.oldContentInset = self.scrollView.contentInset
        self.oldIndicatorInset = self.scrollView.scrollIndicatorInsets
        self.oldOffset = self.scrollView.contentOffset
    }
    if let rnew = rnew {
        let h = rnew.intersection(self.scrollView.bounds).height
        self.scrollView.contentInset.bottom = h
        self.scrollView.scrollIndicatorInsets.bottom = h
    }
}
```

When the keyboard hides, we reverse the process, restoring the saved values:

```
@objc func keyboardHide(_ n:Notification) {
    let d = n.userInfo!
    let (state, _) = keyboardState(for:d, in:self.scrollView)
    if state == .exiting {
        self.scrollView.contentOffset = self.oldOffset
        self.scrollView.scrollIndicatorInsets = self.oldIndicatorInset
        self.scrollView.contentInset = self.oldContentInset
    }
}
```

Behind the scenes, we are inside an animations function at the time that our notifications arrive. This means that our changes to the scroll view's offset and insets are nicely animated in coordination with the keyboard appearing and disappearing.

A UIScrollView's keyboardDismissMode provides ways of letting the user dismiss the keyboard. The options (UIScrollViewKeyboardDismissMode) are:

.none
> The default; if the keyboard doesn't contain a button that lets the user dismiss it, we must use code to dismiss it.

.interactive
> The user can dismiss the keyboard by dragging it down. (This is the option I like to use in this situation.)

.onDrag
> The keyboard dismisses itself if the user scrolls the scroll view.

A scroll view with a keyboardDismissMode that isn't .none also calls resignFirst-Responder on the text field when it dismisses the keyboard.

Under iPad multitasking (Chapter 9), your app can receive keyboard show and hide notifications if *another* app summons or dismisses the keyboard. This makes sense because the keyboard is, after all, covering your app. You can distinguish whether your app was responsible for summoning the keyboard by examining the show notification userInfo dictionary's UIKeyboardIsLocalUserInfoKey; but in general you won't have to. If you were handling keyboard notifications coherently before iPad multitasking came along, you are probably still handling them coherently.

Keyboard and Input Configuration

There are various ways to configure the keyboard that appears when a text field becomes first responder. This configuration is performed through properties, not of the keyboard, but of the text field.

Text input traits

A UITextField adopts the UITextInputTraits protocol. This protocol's properties customize physical features and behaviors of the keyboard, as well as the text field's response to input. (These properties can also be set in the nib editor.) For example:

- Set the keyboardType to choose one of many alternate built-in keyboard layouts. For example, set it to .phonePad to make the keyboard for this text field consist of digits. (This does *not* prevent a user with a hardware keyboard from entering nondigits in this text field. To do that, you'd use a delegate method, as I'll explain later.)

- Set the returnKeyType to determine the text of the Return key (if the keyboard is of a type that has one).

- Give the keyboard a dark or light shade (keyboardAppearance).

- Turn off autocapitalization or autocorrection (autocapitalizationType, autocorrectionType).

- New in iOS 11, use or don't use smart quotes, smart dashes, and smart spaces during insertion and deletion (smartQuotesType, smartDashesType, smartInsertDeleteType).

- Make the Return key disable itself if the text field has no content (enablesReturnKeyAutomatically).

- Make the text field a password field (secureTextEntry).

- Set the `textContentType` to assist the system in making appropriate spelling and autofill suggestions.

 Some alternate built-in keyboard layouts (`keyboardType`) have no Return key, so you can't misuse it as a way of letting the user dismiss the keyboard. You might use a Done button in an accessory view instead (I'll discuss accessory views in a moment). Alternatively, you might have a Done button elsewhere in the interface. A scroll view's `keyboardDismissMode` can help solve the problem too.

Accessory view

You can attach an accessory view to the top of the keyboard by setting the text field's `inputAccessoryView`. For instance, an accessory view containing a button can serve as a way to let the user dismiss keyboards whose type has no Return key, such as `.numberPad`, `.phonePad`, and `.decimalPad`.

In this example, the accessory view contains a button that lets the user navigate to the next text field. My accessory view is retained in a property, `self.accessoryView`; acting as the text field's delegate, when editing starts on the text field, I configure the keyboard and store a reference to the current text field in a property (`self.currentField`):

```
func textFieldDidBeginEditing(_ tf: UITextField) {
    self.currentField = tf // keep track of first responder
    tf.inputAccessoryView = self.accessoryView
}
```

I also have an array property (`self.textFields`) populated with references to all the text fields in the interface. The accessory view contains a Next button; the button's action method moves editing to the next text field:

```
@objc func doNextButton(_ sender: Any) {
    var ix = self.textFields.index(of:self.currentField)!
    ix = (ix + 1) % self.textFields.count
    let v = self.textFields[ix]
    v.becomeFirstResponder()
}
```

Input view

Going even further, you can replace the system keyboard entirely with a view of your own creation. This is done by setting the text field's `inputView`. For best results, the custom view should be a UIInputView, and in particular, for maximum power, it should be the `inputView` of a UIInputViewController (which is also the input view controller's `view`). The input view controller needs to be retained, but not as a child view controller in the view controller hierarchy; the keyboard is not one of your app's views, but is layered by the system in front of your app.

The input view's contents might imitate a standard system keyboard, or they may consist of any interface you like. To illustrate, I'll implement the standard beginner example: I'll replace a text field's keyboard with a UIPickerView.

Here's the input view controller, MyPickerViewController. Its `viewDidLoad` puts the UIPickerView into the `inputView` and positions it with autolayout constraints:

```
class MyPickerViewController : UIInputViewController {
    override func viewDidLoad() {
        let iv = self.inputView!
        iv.translatesAutoresizingMaskIntoConstraints = false
        let p = UIPickerView()
        p.delegate = self
        p.dataSource = self
        iv.addSubview(p)
        p.translatesAutoresizingMaskIntoConstraints = false
        NSLayoutConstraint.activate([
            p.topAnchor.constraint(equalTo: iv.topAnchor),
            p.bottomAnchor.constraint(equalTo: iv.bottomAnchor),
            p.leadingAnchor.constraint(equalTo: iv.leadingAnchor),
            p.trailingAnchor.constraint(equalTo: iv.trailingAnchor),
        ])
    }
}
extension MyPickerViewController : UIPickerViewDelegate,
                                   UIPickerViewDataSource {
    // ...
}
```

The text field itself is configured in our main view controller:

```
class ViewController: UIViewController {
    @IBOutlet weak var tf: UITextField!
    let pvc = MyPickerViewController()
    override func viewDidLoad() {
        super.viewDidLoad()
        self.tf.inputView = self.pvc.inputView
    }
}
```

The input view controller has indirect access to the text field being edited, by way of its `textDocumentProxy` property. This is a UITextDocumentProxy instance that provides a limited window on the text field: basically, it forces you to see the text field as a keyboard would see it. You can learn the selected text, as well as the text before and after the selection; you can insert text; and you can backspace to delete text. But in our example we are not limited in this way; the input view controller can be put into communication with our main view controller, and our main view controller can operate on the text field as a text field.

An input view controller, used in this way, is also the key to supplying *other* apps with a keyboard. See the "Custom Keyboard" chapter of Apple's *App Extension Programming Guide.*

It is also possible to use an input view controller to manage a text field's input-AccessoryView. To do that, you set the text field's inputAccessoryViewController instead of its inputAccessoryView. To do *that*, you have to subclass UITextField to give it a writable inputAccessoryViewController (because this property, as inherited from UIResponder, is read-only):

```
class MyTextField : UITextField {
    var _iavc : UIInputViewController?
    override var inputAccessoryViewController: UIInputViewController? {
        get {
            return self._iavc
        }
        set {
            self._iavc = newValue
        }
    }
}
```

How, for example, are we going to dismiss the "keyboard" consisting entirely of a UIPickerView? One way would be to attach a Done button as the text field's accessory input view. I'll configure the button much as I configured the picker view, by putting it into an input view controller's inputView:

```
class MyDoneButtonViewController : UIInputViewController {
    override func viewDidLoad() {
        let iv = self.inputView!
        iv.translatesAutoresizingMaskIntoConstraints = false
        iv.allowsSelfSizing = true // crucial
        let b = UIButton(type: .system)
        b.tintColor = .black
        b.setTitle("Done", for: .normal)
        b.sizeToFit()
        b.addTarget(self, action: #selector(doDone), for: .touchUpInside)
        b.backgroundColor = UIColor.lightGray
        iv.addSubview(b)
        b.translatesAutoresizingMaskIntoConstraints = false
        NSLayoutConstraint.activate([
            b.topAnchor.constraint(equalTo: iv.topAnchor),
            b.bottomAnchor.constraint(equalTo: iv.bottomAnchor),
            b.leadingAnchor.constraint(equalTo: iv.leadingAnchor),
            b.trailingAnchor.constraint(equalTo: iv.trailingAnchor),
        ])
    }
}
```

Now our main view controller configures the text field like this:

```
class ViewController: UIViewController {
    @IBOutlet weak var tf: UITextField!
    let pvc = MyPickerViewController()
    let mdbvc = MyDoneButtonViewController()
    override func viewDidLoad() {
        super.viewDidLoad()
        self.tf.inputView = self.pvc.inputView
        (self.tf as! MyTextField).inputAccessoryViewController = self.mdbvc
    }
}
```

An important advantage of using an input view controller is that it is a view controller. Despite not being part of the app's view controller hierarchy, it is sent standard view controller messages such as `viewDidLayoutSubviews` and `traitCollectionDidChange`, allowing you to respond coherently to rotation and other size changes.

Input view without a text field

With only a slight modification, you can use the techniques described in the preceding section to present a custom input view to the user *without* the user editing any text field. For example, suppose we have a label in our interface; we can allow the user to tap a button to summon our custom input view and use that input to change the text of the label (Figure 10-11).

The trick here is that the relevant UITextField properties and methods are all inherited from UIResponder — and a UIViewController is a UIResponder. All we have to do is override our view controller's `canBecomeFirstResponder` to return `true`, and then call its `becomeFirstResponder` — just like a text field. If the view controller has overridden `inputView`, our custom input view will appear as the onscreen keyboard. If the view controller has overridden `inputAccessoryView` or `inputAccessoryViewController`, the accessory view will be attached to that keyboard.

Here's an implementation of that scenario. Normally, our view controller's `canBecomeFirstResponder` returns `false`, so that the input view won't appear. But when the user taps the button in our interface, we switch to returning `true` and call `becomeFirstResponder`. Presto, the input view appears along with the accessory view, because we've also overridden `inputView` and `inputAccessoryViewController`. When the user taps the Done button in the accessory view, we update the label and dismiss the keyboard:

```
class ViewController: UIViewController {
    @IBOutlet weak var lab: UILabel!
    let pvc = MyPickerViewController()
    let mdbvc = MyDoneButtonViewController()
    override func viewDidLoad() {
        super.viewDidLoad()
        self.mdbvc.delegate = self // for dismissal
    }
```

Figure 10-11. Editing a label with a custom input view

```
var showKeyboard = false
override var canBecomeFirstResponder: Bool {
    return showKeyboard
}
override var inputView: UIView? {
    return self.pvc.inputView
}
override var inputAccessoryViewController: UIInputViewController? {
    return self.mdbvc
}
@IBAction func doPickBoy(_ sender: Any) { // button in the interface
    self.showKeyboard = true
    self.becomeFirstResponder()
}
@objc func doDone() { // user tapped Done button in accessory view
    self.lab.text = pvc.currentPep // update label
    self.resignFirstResponder() // dismiss keyboard
    self.showKeyboard = false
}
}
```

Shortcuts bar

On the iPad, the shortcuts bar appears along with spelling suggestions at the top of the keyboard. You can customize it by adding bar button items.

The shortcuts bar is the text field's inputAssistantItem (inherited from UIResponder), and it has leadingBarButtonGroups and trailingBarButtonGroups. A button group is a UIBarButtonItemGroup, an array of UIBarButtonItems along with an optional representativeItem to be shown if there isn't room for the whole array; if the representative item has no target–action pair, tapping it will summon a popover containing the actual group.

In this example, we add a Camera bar button item to the right (trailing) side of the shortcuts bar for our text field (`self.tf`):

```
let bbi = UIBarButtonItem(
    barButtonSystemItem: .camera, target: self, action: #selector(doCamera))
let group = UIBarButtonItemGroup(
    barButtonItems: [bbi], representativeItem: nil)
let shortcuts = self.tf.inputAssistantItem
shortcuts.trailingBarButtonGroups.append(group)
```

Keyboard language

Suppose your app performs a Russian dictionary lookup. It would be nice to be able to force the keyboard to appear as Russian in conjunction with your text field. But you can't. You can't access the Russian keyboard unless the user has explicitly enabled it; and even if the user *has* explicitly enabled it, your text field can only express a preference as to the language in which the keyboard initially appears. To do so, override your view controller's `textInputMode` property along these lines:

```
override var textInputMode: UITextInputMode? {
    for tim in UITextInputMode.activeInputModes {
        if tim.primaryLanguage == "ru-RU" {
            return tim
        }
    }
    return super.textInputMode
}
```

Another keyboard language–related property is `textInputContextIdentifier`. You can use this to ensure that the runtime remembers the language to which the keyboard was set the last time each text field was edited. To do so, override `textInputContextIdentifier` in your view controller as a computed variable whose getter fetches the value of a stored variable, and set that stored variable to some appropriate unique value whenever the editing context changes, whatever that may mean for your app.

Text Field Delegate and Control Event Messages

As editing begins and proceeds in a text field, various messages are sent to the text field's delegate, adopting the UITextFieldDelegate protocol. Some of these messages are also available as notifications. Using them, you can customize the text field's behavior during editing:

`textFieldShouldBeginEditing(_:)`
    Return `false` to prevent the text field from becoming first responder.

`textFieldDidBeginEditing(_:)`
`.UITextFieldTextDidBeginEditing`
> The text field has become first responder.

`textFieldShouldClear(_:)`
> Return `false` to prevent the operation of the Clear button or of automatic clearing on entry (`clearsOnBeginEditing`). This event is *not* sent when the text is cleared because `clearsOnInsertion` is `true`, because the user is not clearing the text but rather changing it.

`textFieldShouldReturn(_:)`
> The user has tapped the Return button in the keyboard. We have already seen that this can be misused as a signal to dismiss the keyboard.

`textField(_:shouldChangeCharactersIn:replacementString:)`
`.UITextFieldTextDidChange`
> The notification is just a signal that the user has edited the text, but the delegate method is your chance to *interfere* with the user's editing *before* it takes effect. You can return `false` to prevent the proposed change; if you're going to do that, you can replace the user's edit with your own by changing the text field's text directly (there is no circularity, as this delegate method is not called when you do that).
>
> In this example, the user can enter only lowercase characters (the `insertText` method comes from the UIKeyInput protocol, which UITextField adopts):
>
> ```
> func textField(_ textField: UITextField,
>     shouldChangeCharactersIn range: NSRange,
>     replacementString string: String) -> Bool {
>         // backspace
>         if string.isEmpty {
>             return true
>         }
>         let lc = string.lowercased()
>         textField.insertText(lc)
>         return false
> }
> ```
>
> As the example shows, you can distinguish whether the user is typing or pasting, on the one hand, or backspacing or cutting, on the other; in the latter case, the replacement string will be empty. You are *not* notified when the user changes text styling through the Bold, Italics, or Underline menu items.

`textFieldShouldEndEditing(_:)`
> Return `false` to prevent the text field from resigning first responder (even if you just sent `resignFirstResponder` to it). You might do this, for example, because the text is invalid or unacceptable in some way. The user will not know why the

text field is refusing to end editing, so the usual thing is to put up an alert (Chapter 13) explaining the problem.

`textFieldDidEndEditing(_:)`
`.UITextFieldTextDidEndEditing`
> The text field has resigned first responder. See Chapter 8 ("Editable Content in Cells" on page 524) for an example of using the delegate method to fetch the text field's current text and store it in the model.

A text field is also a control (UIControl; see also Chapter 12). That means you can attach a target–action pair to any of the events that it reports in order to receive a message when that event occurs. Of the various control event messages emitted by a text field, the two most useful (in my experience) are:

Editing Changed (`.editingChanged`*)*
> Sent after the user performs any editing. If your goal is to respond to changes, rather than to forestall them, this is a better way than the delegate method `text-Field(_:shouldChangeCharactersIn:replacementString:)`, because it arrives at the right moment, namely *after* the change has occurred, and because it can detect attributes changes, which the delegate method can't do.

Did End on Exit (`editingDidEndOnExit`*)*
> Provides a clean alternative way to dismiss the keyboard when the user taps a text field keyboard's Return button. If there is a Did End on Exit target–action pair for this text field, then (assuming the text field's delegate does not return `false` from `textFieldShouldReturn(_:)`) the keyboard will be dismissed *automatically* when the user taps the Return key.

> For this trick to work, the action method for Did End on Exit doesn't actually have to *do* anything. In fact, it doesn't even have to exist; the action can be `nil`-targeted. There is no penalty for implementing a `nil`-targeted action that walks up the responder chain without finding a method that handles it.

In this example, I create a UITextField subclass that automatically dismisses itself when the user taps Return:

```
@objc protocol Dummy {
    func dummy(_ sender: Any?)
}
class MyTextField: UITextField {
    required init?(coder aDecoder: NSCoder) {
        super.init(coder:aDecoder)
        self.addTarget(nil,
            action:#selector(Dummy.dummy), for:.editingDidEndOnExit)
    }
}
```

Alternatively, you can configure the same thing in the nib editor. Edit the First Responder proxy object in the Attributes inspector, adding a new First Responder Action; call it dummy:. Now hook the Did End on Exit event of the text field to the dummy: action of the First Responder proxy object.

Text Field Menu

When the user double taps or long presses in a text field, the menu appears. It contains menu items such as Select, Select All, Paste, Copy, Cut, and Replace; which menu items appear depends on the circumstances. Many of the selectors for these standard menu items are listed in the UIResponderStandardEditActions protocol. Commonly used standard actions are:

- cut(_:)
- copy(_:)
- select(_:)
- selectAll(_:)
- paste(_:)
- delete(_:)
- toggleBoldface(_:)
- toggleItalics(_:)
- toggleUnderline(_:)

Some other menu items are known only through their Objective-C selectors:

- _promptForReplace:
- _define:
- _showTextStyleOptions:

The menu can be customized; just as with a table view cell's menus (Chapter 8), this involves setting the shared UIMenuController object's menuItems property to an array of UIMenuItem instances representing the menu items that may appear in addition to those that the system puts there.

Actions for menu items are nil-targeted, so they percolate up the responder chain. You can thus implement a menu item's action anywhere up the responder chain; if you do this for a standard menu item at a point in the responder chain before the system receives it, you can interfere with and customize what it does. You govern the presence or absence of a menu item by implementing the UIResponder method canPerformAction(_:withSender:) in the responder chain.

As an example, we'll devise a text field whose menu includes our own menu item, Expand. I'm imagining a text field where the user can select a U.S. state two-letter abbreviation (such as "CA") and can then summon the menu and tap Expand to replace it with the state's full name (such as "California").

I'll implement this in a UITextField subclass called MyTextField, in order to guarantee that the Expand menu item will be available when an instance of this subclass is first responder, but at no other time.

At some moment before the user taps in an instance of MyTextField (such as our view controller's `viewDidLoad`), we modify the global menu:

```
let mi = UIMenuItem(title:"Expand", action:#selector(MyTextField.expand))
let mc = UIMenuController.shared
mc.menuItems = [mi]
```

Now we turn to the text field subclass. It has a property, `self.list`, which has been set to a dictionary whose keys are state name abbreviations and whose values are the corresponding state names. A utility function looks up an abbreviation in the dictionary:

```
func state(for abbrev:String) -> String? {
    return self.list[abbrev.uppercased()]
}
```

We implement `canPerformAction(_:withSender:)` to govern the contents of the menu. Let's presume that we want our Expand menu item to be present only if the selection consists of a two-letter state abbreviation. UITextField itself provides no way to learn the selected text, but it conforms to the UITextInput protocol, which does:

```
override func canPerformAction(_ action: Selector,
    withSender sender: Any?) -> Bool {
        if action == #selector(expand) {
            if let r = self.selectedTextRange, let s = self.text(in:r) {
                return (s.count == 2 && self.state(for:s) != nil)
            }
        }
        return super.canPerformAction(action, withSender:sender)
}
```

When the user chooses the Expand menu item, the `expand` message is sent up the responder chain. We catch it in our UITextField subclass and obey it by replacing the selected text with the corresponding state name:

```
@objc func expand(_ sender: Any?) {
    if let r = self.selectedTextRange, let s = self.text(in:r) {
        if let ss = self.state(for:s) {
            self.replace(r, withText:ss)
        }
    }
}
```

We can also implement the selector for, and thus modify the behavior of, any of the standard menu items. For example, I'll implement copy(_:) and modify its behavior. First we call super to get standard copying behavior; then we modify what's now on the pasteboard:

```
override func copy(_ sender:Any?) {
    super.copy(sender)
    let pb = UIPasteboard.general
    if let s = pb.string {
        let ss = // ... alter s here ...
        pb.string = ss
    }
}
```

Drag and Drop

A text field implements drag and drop (Chapter 9) by way of the UITextDraggable and UITextDroppable protocols. By default a text field's text is draggable on an iPad and not draggable on an iPhone, but you can set the isEnabled property of its text-DragInteraction to change that. If a text field's text is draggable, then by default its dragged text can be dropped within the same text field.

To customize a text field's drag and drop behavior, provide a textDragDelegate (UITextDragDelegate) or textDropDelegate (UITextDropDelegate) and implement any of their various methods. For example, you can change the drag preview, change the drag items, and so forth. To turn a text field's droppability on or off depending on some condition, give it a textDropDelegate and implement textDroppable-View(_:proposalForDrop:) to return an appropriate UITextDropProposal. Consult the documentation for further details.

Text Views

A text view (UITextView) is a scroll view subclass (UIScrollView); it is *not* a control. It displays multiline text, possibly scrollable, possibly user-editable. Many of its properties are similar to those of a text field:

- A text view has text, font, textColor, and textAlignment properties.
- A text view has attributedText, allowsEditingTextAttributes, and typing-Attributes properties, as well as clearsOnInsertion.
- An editable text view governs its keyboard just as a text field does: when it is first responder, it is being edited and shows the keyboard, and it adopts the UIText-Input protocol and has inputView and inputAccessoryView properties.
- A text view's menu works the same way as a text field's.

- A text view implements drag and drop similarly to a text field.

A text view can be user-editable or not, according to its `isEditable` property. You can do things with a noneditable text view that you can't do otherwise, as I'll explain later. The user can still interact with a noneditable text view's text, provided its `isSelectable` property is `true`; for example, in a selectable noneditable text view, the user can select text and copy it.

A text view is a scroll view, so everything you know about scroll views applies (see Chapter 7). It can be user-scrollable or not. Its `contentSize` is maintained for you automatically as the text changes, so as to contain the text exactly; thus, if the text view is scrollable, the user can see any of its text.

A text view provides information about, and control of, its selection: it has a `selectedRange` property which you can get and set, along with a `scrollRangeTo-Visible(_:)` method so that you can scroll in terms of a range of its text.

A text view's delegate messages (UITextViewDelegate protocol) and notifications, too, are similar to those of a text field. The following delegate methods and notifications should have a familiar ring:

- `textViewShouldBeginEditing(_:)`
- `textViewDidBeginEditing(_:)` and `.UITextViewTextDidBeginEditing`
- `textViewShouldEndEditing(_:)`
- `textViewDidEndEditing(_:)` and `.UITextViewTextDidEndEditing`
- `textView(_:shouldChangeTextIn:replacementText:)`

Some differences are:

`textViewDidChange(_:)`
`.UITextViewTextDidChange`
> Sent when the user changes text or attributes. A text field has no corresponding delegate method, though the Editing Changed control event is similar.

`textViewDidChangeSelection(_:)`
> Sent when the user changes the selection. In contrast, a text field is officially uninformative about the selection (though you can learn about and manipulate a UITextField's selection by way of the UITextInput protocol).

Links, Text Attachments, and Data

The default appearance of links in a text view is determined by the text view's `link-TextAttributes`. By default, this is a bluish color with no underline, but you can change it. (The `linkTextAttributes` dictionary keys are Strings, not NSAttribute-

StringKeys; I regard this as a bug.) Alternatively, you can apply any desired attributes to the individual links in the attributed string that you set as the text view's `attributedText`; in that case, set the `linkTextAttributes` to an empty dictionary to prevent it from overriding the individual link attributes.

A text view's delegate can decide how to respond when the user taps on a text attachment or a link. The text view must have its `isSelectable` property set to `true`, and its `isEditable` property set to `false`:

`textView(_:shouldInteractWith:in:interaction:)`
> The third parameter is a range. The last parameter tells you what the user is doing (UITextItemInteraction): `.invokeDefaultAction` means tap, `.present-Actions` means long press, `.preview` means 3D touch. Comes in two forms:

> *The second parameter is a URL*
>> The user is interacting with a link. The default is `true`. Default responses are:
>>
>> - `.invokeDefaultAction`: the URL is opened in Safari.
>> - `.presentActions`: an action sheet is presented, with menu items Open, Add to Reading List, Copy, and Share.
>> - `.preview`: a peek and pop preview of the web page is presented, along with menu items Open Link, Add to Reading List, and Copy.

> *The second parameter is an NSTextAttachment*
>> The user is interacting with an inline image. The default is `false`. Default responses are:
>>
>> - `.invokeDefaultAction`: nothing happens.
>> - `.presentActions`: an action sheet is presented, with menu items Copy Image and Save to Camera Roll.
>> - `.preview`: nothing happens; my experience is that you should return `false` or the app may crash.

> Return `true` for the default response. By returning `false`, you can substitute your own response, effectively treating the link or image as a button.

A text view also has a `dataDetectorTypes` property; this, too, if the text view is selectable but not editable, allows text of certain types, specified as a bitmask (and presumably located using NSDataDetector), to be treated as tappable links.

`textView(_:shouldInteractWith:in:interaction:)` will catch these taps as well; the second parameter will be a URL, but it won't necessarily be much use to you. You can distinguish a phone number through the URL's `scheme` (it will be `"tel"`), and the rest of the URL is the phone number; but other types will be more or less opaque (the scheme is "x-apple-data-detectors"). However, you have the range, so you can obtain the tapped text. Again, you can return false and substitute your own response, or return true for the default responses.

In addition to .link, some common UIDataDetectorTypes are:

.phoneNumber
Default responses are:

- .invokeDefaultAction: an alert is presented, with an option to call the number.

- .presentActions: an action sheet is presented, with menu items Call, Face-Time, Send Message, Add to Contacts, and Copy.

- .preview: a preview is presented, looking up the phone number in the user's Contacts database, along with menu items Call, Message, Add to Existing Contact, and Create New Contact.

.address
Default responses are:

- .invokeDefaultAction: the address is looked up in the Maps app.

- .presentActions: an action sheet is presented, with menu items Get Directions, Open in Maps, Add to Contacts, and Copy.

- .preview: a preview is presented, combining the preceding two.

.calendarEvent
Default responses are:

- .invokeDefaultAction: an action sheet is presented, with menu items Create Event, Show in Calendar, and Copy.

- .presentActions: same as the preceding.

- .preview: a preview is presented, displaying the relevant time from the user's Calendar, along with the same menu items.

Starting in iOS 10, there are three more data detector types: shipmentTracking-Number, flightNumber, and lookupSuggestion.

 In my tests, if the interaction type is .preview, then if the user cancels (releasing the press), the delegate method is called again with interaction .presentActions. I regard this as a bug.

Self-Sizing Text View

On some occasions, you may want a *self-sizing* text view — that is, a text view that adjusts its height automatically to embrace the amount of text it contains.

The simplest approach, under autolayout, is to prevent the text view from scrolling, by setting its isScrollEnabled to false. The text view now has an intrinsic content size and will behave just like a label ("Resizing a Label to Fit Its Text" on page 632). Pin the top and sides of the text view, and the bottom will shift automatically to accomodate the content as the user types. In effect, you've made a cross between a label (the height adjusts to fit the text) and a text field (the user can edit).

To put a limit on how tall a self-sizing text view can grow, keep track of the height of its contentSize and, if it gets too big, set the text view's isScrollEnabled to true and constrain its height.

Text View and Keyboard

The fact that a text view is a scroll view comes in handy when the keyboard partially covers a text view. The text view quite often dominates the screen, and you can respond to the keyboard partially covering it by adjusting the text view's content-Inset and scrollIndicatorInsets, exactly as we did earlier in this chapter with a scroll view containing a text field ("Keyboard Covers Text Field" on page 638). There is no need to worry about the text view's contentOffset: the text view will scroll as needed to reveal the insertion point as the keyboard shows, and will scroll itself correctly as the keyboard hides.

Now let's talk about how the keyboard is to be dismissed. The Return key is meaningful for character entry, so you won't want to misuse it to dismiss the keyboard. On the iPad, there is usually a separate button in the keyboard that dismisses the keyboard, thus solving the problem. On the iPhone, however, there might be no such button.

On the iPhone, the interface might well consist of a text view and the keyboard, which is *always* showing: instead of dismissing the keyboard, the user dismisses the entire interface. For example, in Apple's Mail app on the iPhone, when the user is composing a message, the keyboard is present; if the user taps Cancel or Send, the mail composition interface is dismissed and so is the keyboard.

Alternatively, you can provide interface for dismissing the keyboard explicitly. For example, in Apple's Notes app, when a note is being edited, the keyboard is present and a Done button appears; the user taps the Done button to dismiss the keyboard. If there's no good place to put a Done button in the interface, you could attach an accessory view to the keyboard itself, as I did in an earlier example.

Finally, being a scroll view, a text view has a `keyboardDismissMode`. Thus, by making text view's keyboard dismiss mode `.interactive`, you can permit the user to hide the keyboard by dragging it. Apple's Notes app is a case in point.

Text Kit

Text Kit comes originally from macOS, where you may already be more familiar with it than you realize. (For example, much of the text-editing "magic" of Xcode itself is due to Text Kit.) Text Kit comprises a small group of classes that are responsible for drawing text; simply put, they turn an NSAttributedString into graphics. You can take advantage of Text Kit to modify text drawing in ways that were once possible only by dipping down to the low-level C-based world of Core Text.

Text Kit has three chief classes: NSTextStorage, NSLayoutManager, and NSTextContainer. Instances of these three classes join to form a "stack" of objects that allow Text Kit to operate. In the minimal and most common case, a text storage has a layout manager, and a layout manager has a text container, thus forming the "stack."

Here's what the three chief Text Kit classes do:

NSTextStorage
  A subclass of NSMutableAttributedString. It is, or holds, the underlying text. It has one or more layout managers, and notifies them when the text changes. By subclassing and delegation (NSTextStorageDelegate), its behavior can be modified so that it applies attributes in a custom fashion.

NSLayoutManager
  This is the master text drawing class. It has one or more text containers, and is owned by a text storage. It draws the text storage's text into the boundaries defined by the text container(s).

  A layout manager can have a delegate (NSLayoutManagerDelegate), and can be subclassed. This, as you may well imagine, is a powerful and sophisticated class.

NSTextContainer
  It is owned by a layout manager, and helps that layout manager by defining the region in which the text is to be laid out. It does this in three primary ways:

Size
  The text container's top left is the origin for the text layout coordinate system, and the text will be laid out within the text container's rectangle.

Exclusion paths
  The `exclusionPaths` property consists of UIBezierPath objects within which no text is to be drawn.

Subclassing

By subclassing, you can place each chunk of text drawing anywhere at all (except inside an exclusion path).

Text View and Text Kit

A UITextView provides direct access to the underlying Text Kit engine. It has the following Text Kit–related properties:

textContainer

The text view's text container (an NSTextContainer instance). UITextView's designated initializer is init(frame:textContainer:); the textContainer: can be nil to get a default text container, or you can supply your own custom text container.

textContainerInset

The margins of the text container, designating the area within the contentSize rectangle in which the text as a whole is drawn. Changing this value changes the margins immediately, causing the text to be freshly laid out. The default is a top and bottom of 8.

layoutManager

The text view's layout manager (an NSLayoutManager instance).

textStorage

The text view's text storage (an NSTextStorage instance).

When you initialize a text view with a custom text container, you hand it the entire "stack" of Text Kit instances, the stack is retained, and the text view is operative. Thus, the simplest case might look like this:

```
let r = // ... frame for the new text view
let lm = NSLayoutManager()
let ts = NSTextStorage()
ts.addLayoutManager(lm)
let tc = NSTextContainer(size:CGSize(r.width, .greatestFiniteMagnitude))
lm.addTextContainer(tc)
let tv = UITextView(frame:r, textContainer:tc)
```

Text Container

An NSTextContainer has a size, within which the text will be drawn.

By default, a text view's text container's width is the width of the text view, while its height is effectively infinite, allowing the drawing of the text to grow vertically but not horizontally beyond the bounds of the text view, and making it possible to scroll the text vertically.

Figure 10-12. A text view with an exclusion path

NSTextContainer also has `heightTracksTextView` and `widthTracksTextView` properties, causing the text container to be resized to match changes in the size of the text view — for example, if the text view is resized because of interface rotation. By default, as you might expect, `widthTracksTextView` is `true` (the documentation is wrong about this), while `heightTracksTextView` is `false`: the text fills the width of the text view, and is laid out freshly if the text view's width changes, but its height remains effectively infinite. The text view itself configures its own `contentSize` so that the user can scroll just to the bottom of the existing text.

When you change a text view's `textContainerInset`, it modifies its text container's size as necessary. In the default configuration, this means that it modifies the text container's width; the top and bottom insets are implemented through the text container's position within the content rect. Within the text container, additional side margins correspond to the text container's `lineFragmentPadding`; the default is 5, but you can change it.

If the text view's `isScrollEnabled` is `false`, then by default its text container's `heightTracksTextView` and `widthTracksTextView` are both `true`, and the text container size is adjusted so that the text fills the text view. In that case, you can also set the text container's `lineBreakMode`. This works like the line break mode of a UILabel. For example, if the line break mode is `.byTruncatingTail`, then the last line has an ellipsis at the end (if the text is too long for the text view). You can also set the text container's `maximumNumberOfLines`, which is like a UILabel's `numberOfLines`. In effect, you've turned the text view into a label!

But a nonscrolling text view isn't *just* a label, because you've got access to the Text Kit stack that backs it. For example, you can apply exclusion paths to the text container. Figure 10-12 shows a case in point. The text wraps in longer and longer lines, and then in shorter and shorter lines, because there's an exclusion path on the right side of the text container that's a rectangle with a large V-shaped indentation.

Figure 10-13. A text view with a subclassed text container

In Figure 10-12, the text view (`self.tv`) is initially configured in the view controller's `viewDidLoad`:

```
self.tv.attributedText = // ...
self.tv.textContainerInset = UIEdgeInsetsMake(20, 20, 20, 0)
self.tv.isScrollEnabled = false
```

The exclusion path is then drawn and applied in `viewDidLayoutSubviews`:

```
override func viewDidLayoutSubviews() {
    let sz = self.tv.textContainer.size
    let p = UIBezierPath()
    p.move(to: CGPoint(sz.width/4.0,0))
    p.addLine(to: CGPoint(sz.width,0))
    p.addLine(to: CGPoint(sz.width,sz.height))
    p.addLine(to: CGPoint(sz.width/4.0,sz.height))
    p.addLine(to: CGPoint(sz.width,sz.height/2.0))
    p.close()
    self.tv.textContainer.exclusionPaths = [p]
}
```

Instead of (or in addition to) an exclusion path, you can subclass NSTextContainer to modify the rectangle in which the layout manager wants to position a piece of text. (Each piece of text is actually a line fragment; I'll explain in the next section what a line fragment is.) In Figure 10-13, the text is inside a circle.

To achieve the layout shown in Figure 10-13, I set the attributed string's line break mode to `.byCharWrapping` (to bring the right edge of each line as close as possible to the circular shape), and construct the Text Kit stack by hand to include an instance of my NSTextContainer subclass:

```
let r = self.tv.frame
let lm = NSLayoutManager()
let ts = NSTextStorage()
ts.addLayoutManager(lm)
let tc = MyTextContainer(size:CGSize(r.width, r.height))
lm.addTextContainer(tc)
let tv = UITextView(frame:r, textContainer:tc)
```

Here's my NSTextContainer subclass; it overrides just one property and one method, to dictate the rect of each line fragment:

```
class MyTextContainer : NSTextContainer {
    override var isSimpleRectangularTextContainer : Bool { return false }
    override func lineFragmentRect(forProposedRect proposedRect: CGRect,
        at characterIndex: Int,
        writingDirection baseWritingDirection: NSWritingDirection,
        remaining remainingRect: UnsafeMutablePointer<CGRect>?) -> CGRect {
            var result = super.lineFragmentRect(
                forProposedRect:proposedRect, at:characterIndex,
                writingDirection:baseWritingDirection,
                remaining:remainingRect)
            let r = self.size.height / 2.0
            // convert initial y so that circle is centered at origin
            let y = r - result.origin.y
            let theta = asin(y/r)
            let x = r * cos(theta)
            // convert resulting x from circle centered at origin
            let offset = self.size.width / 2.0 - r
            result.origin.x = r-x+offset
            result.size.width = 2*x
            return result
    }
}
```

Alternative Text Kit Stack Architectures

The default Text Kit stack is one text storage, which has one layout manager, which has one text container. But a text storage can have multiple layout managers, and a layout manager can have multiple text containers. What's that all about?

If one layout manager has multiple text containers, the overflow from each text container is drawn in the next one. For example, in Figure 10-14, there are two text views; the text has filled the first text view, and has then continued by flowing into and filling the second text view. As far as I can tell, the text views can't be made editable in this configuration; but clearly this is a way to achieve a multicolumn or multipage layout, or you could use text views of different sizes for a magazine-style layout.

It is possible to achieve that arrangement by disconnecting the layout managers of existing text views from their text containers and rebuilding the stack from below. In this example, though, I'll build the entire stack by hand:

Figure 10-14. A layout manager with two text containers

Figure 10-15. A text storage with two layout managers

```
let r = // frame
let r2 = // frame
let mas = // content
let ts1 = NSTextStorage(attributedString:mas)
let lm1 = NSLayoutManager()
ts1.addLayoutManager(lm1)
let tc1 = NSTextContainer(size:r.size)
lm1.addTextContainer(tc1)
let tv = UITextView(frame:r, textContainer:tc1)
let tc2 = NSTextContainer(size:r2.size)
lm1.addTextContainer(tc2)
let tv2 = UITextView(frame:r2, textContainer:tc2)
```

If one text storage has multiple layout managers, then each layout manager is laying out the same text. For example, in Figure 10-15, there are two text views displaying the same text. The remarkable thing is that if you edit one text view, the other changes to match. (That's how Xcode lets you edit the same code file in different windows, tabs, or panes.)

Again, this arrangement is probably best achieved by building the entire text stack by hand:

```
let r = // frame
let r2 = // frame
let mas = // content
let ts1 = NSTextStorage(attributedString:mas)
let lm1 = NSLayoutManager()
ts1.addLayoutManager(lm1)
let lm2 = NSLayoutManager()
ts1.addLayoutManager(lm2)
let tc1 = NSTextContainer(size:r.size)
let tc2 = NSTextContainer(size:r2.size)
lm1.addTextContainer(tc1)
lm2.addTextContainer(tc2)
let tv = UITextView(frame:r, textContainer:tc1)
let tv2 = UITextView(frame:r2, textContainer:tc2)
```

Layout Manager

The first thing to know about a layout manager is the geometry in which it thinks. To envision a layout manager's geometrical world, think in terms of glyphs and line fragments:

Glyph

The drawn analog of a character. The layout manager's primary job is to get glyphs from a font and draw them.

Line fragment

A rectangle in which glyphs are drawn, one after another. (The reason it's a line *fragment*, and not just a line, is that a line might be interrupted by the text container's exclusion paths.)

A glyph has a location in terms of the line fragment into which it is drawn. A line fragment's coordinates are in terms of the text container. The layout manager can convert between these coordinate systems, and between text and glyphs. Given a range of text in the text storage, it knows where the corresponding glyphs are drawn in the text container. Conversely, given a location in the text container, it knows what glyph is drawn there and what range of text in the text storage that glyph represents.

What's missing from that geometry is what, if anything, the text container corresponds to in the real world. A text container is not, itself, a real rectangle in the real world; it's just a class that tells the layout manager a size to draw into. Making that rectangle meaningful for drawing purposes is up to some other class outside the Text Kit stack. A UITextView, for example, has a text container, which it shares with a layout manager. The text view knows how its own content is scrolled and how the rectangle represented by its text container is inset within that scrolling content. The layout manager, however, doesn't know anything about that; it sees the text container as a purely theoretical rectangular boundary. Only when the layout manager actually draws does it make contact with the real world of some graphics context — and it must be told, on those occasions, how the text container's rectangle is offset within that graphics context.

To illustrate, consider a text view scrolled so as to place some word at the top left of its visible bounds. I'll use the layout manager to learn what word it is.

I can ask the layout manager what character or glyph corresponds to a certain point in the text container, but what point should I ask about? Translating from the real world to text container coordinates is up to me; I must take into account both the scroll position of the text view's content and the inset of the text container within that content:

```
let off = self.tv.contentOffset
let top = self.tv.textContainerInset.top
let left = self.tv.textContainerInset.left
var tctopleft = CGPoint(off.x - left, off.y - top)
```

Now I'm speaking in text container coordinates, which are layout manager coordinates. One possibility is then to ask directly for the index (in the text storage's string) of the corresponding character:

```
let ixx = self.tv.layoutManager.characterIndex(for:tctopleft,
    in:self.tv.textContainer,
    fractionOfDistanceBetweenInsertionPoints:nil)
```

That, however, does not give quite the results one might intuitively expect. If *any* of a word is poking down from above into the visible area of the text view, that is the word whose first character is returned. I think we intuitively expect, if a word isn't fully visible, that the answer should be the word that starts the *next* line, which *is* fully visible. So I'll modify that code in a simpleminded way. I'll obtain the index of the *glyph* at my initial point; from this, I can derive the rect of the line fragment containing it. If that line fragment is not at least three-quarters visible, I'll add one line fragment height to the starting point and derive the glyph index again. Then I'll convert the glyph index to a character index:

```
var ix = self.tv.layoutManager.glyphIndex(for:tctopleft,
    in:self.tv.textContainer, fractionOfDistanceThroughGlyph:nil)
let frag = self.tv.layoutManager.lineFragmentRect(
    forGlyphAt:ix, effectiveRange:nil)
if tctopleft.y > frag.origin.y + 0.5*frag.size.height {
    tctopleft.y += frag.size.height
    ix = self.tv.layoutManager.glyphIndex(for:tctopleft,
        in:self.tv.textContainer, fractionOfDistanceThroughGlyph:nil)
}
let charRange = self.tv.layoutManager.characterRange(
    forGlyphRange: NSMakeRange(ix,0), actualGlyphRange:nil)
ix = charRange.location
```

Finally, I'll use NSLinguisticTagger to get the range of the entire word to which this character belongs:

```
let sch = NSLinguisticTagScheme.tokenType
let t = NSLinguisticTagger(tagSchemes:[sch], options:0)
t.string = self.tv.text
var r : NSRange = NSMakeRange(0,0)
let tag = t.tag(at:ix, scheme:sch, tokenRange:&r, sentenceRange:nil)
if tag == .word {
    if let s = self.tv.text {
        if let range = Range(r, in: s) {
            let word = s[range]
            print(word)
        }
    }
}
```

Clearly, the same sort of technique could be used to formulate a custom response to a tap — answering the question, "What word did the user just tap on?"

By subclassing NSLayoutManager (and by implementing its delegate), many powerful effects can be achieved. As a simple example, I'll carry on from the preceding code by drawing a rectangular outline around the word we just located. To make this possible, I have an NSLayoutManager subclass, MyLayoutManager, an instance of which is built into the Text Kit stack for this text view. MyLayoutManager has a public NSRange property, wordRange. Having worked out what word I want to outline, I set the layout manager's wordRange and invalidate its drawing of that word, to force a redraw:

```
let lm = self.tv.layoutManager as! MyLayoutManager
lm.wordRange = r
lm.invalidateDisplay(forCharacterRange:r)
```

In MyLayoutManager, I've overridden the method that draws the background behind glyphs, drawBackground(forGlyphRange:at:). At the moment this method is called, there is already a graphics context, so all we have to do is draw.

First, I call super. Then, if the range of glyphs to be drawn includes the glyphs for the range of characters in self.wordRange, I ask for the rect of the bounding box of those glyphs, and stroke it to form the rectangle. As I mentioned earlier, the bounding box is in text container coordinates, but now we're drawing in the real world, so I have to compensate by offsetting the drawn rectangle by the same amount that the text container is supposed to be offset in the real world; fortunately, the text view tells us (through the origin: parameter) what that offset is:

```
override func drawBackground(forGlyphRange glyphsToShow: NSRange,
    at origin: CGPoint) {
        super.drawBackground(forGlyphRange:glyphsToShow, at:origin)
        if self.wordRange.length == 0 {
            return
```

```
    }
    var range = self.glyphRange(forCharacterRange:self.wordRange,
        actualCharacterRange:nil)
    range = NSIntersectionRange(glyphsToShow, range)
    if range.length == 0 {
        return
    }
    if let tc = self.textContainer(forGlyphAt:range.location,
        effectiveRange:nil, withoutAdditionalLayout:true) {
            var r = self.boundingRect(forGlyphRange:range, in:tc)
            r.origin.x += origin.x
            r.origin.y += origin.y
            let c = UIGraphicsGetCurrentContext()!
            c.saveGState()
            c.setStrokeColor(UIColor.black.cgColor)
            c.setLineWidth(1.0)
            c.stroke(r)
            c.restoreGState()
    }
}
```

Text Kit Without a Text View

UITextView is the only built-in iOS class that has a Text Kit stack to which you are
given programmatic access. But that doesn't mean it's the only place where you can
draw with Text Kit! You can draw with Text Kit *anywhere you can draw* — that is, in
any graphics context (Chapter 2). When you do so, you should always call both draw-
Background(forGlyphRange:at:) (the method I overrode in the previous example)
and drawGlyphs(forGlyphRange:at:), in that order. The at: argument is the point
where you consider the text container's origin to be within the current graphics
context.

To illustrate, I'll change the implementation of the StringDrawer class that I described
earlier in this chapter. Previously, StringDrawer's draw(_:) implementation told the
attributed string (self.attributedText) to draw itself:

```
override func draw(_ rect: CGRect) {
    let r = rect.offsetBy(dx: 0, dy: 2)
    let opts : NSStringDrawingOptions = .usesLineFragmentOrigin
    self.attributedText.draw(with:r, options: opts, context: context)
}
```

Instead, I'll construct the Text Kit stack and tell its layout manager to draw the text:

```
override func draw(_ rect: CGRect) {
    let lm = NSLayoutManager()
    let ts = NSTextStorage(attributedString:self.attributedText)
    ts.addLayoutManager(lm)
    let tc = NSTextContainer(size:rect.size)
    lm.addTextContainer(tc)
    tc.lineFragmentPadding = 0
```

ALABAMA	MONTANA
ALASKA	NEBRASKA
ARIZONA	NEVADA
ARKANSAS	NEW HAMPSHIRE
CALIFORNIA	NEW JERSEY
COLORADO	NEW MEXICO
CONNECTICUT	NEW YORK
DELAWARE	NORTH CAROLINA
FLORIDA	NORTH DAKOTA
GEORGIA	OHIO
HAWAII	OKLAHOMA
IDAHO	OREGON
ILLINOIS	PENNSYLVANIA
INDIANA	RHODE ISLAND
IOWA	SOUTH CAROLINA
KANSAS	SOUTH DAKOTA
KENTUCKY	TENNESSEE
LOUISIANA	TEXAS
MAINE	UTAH
MARYLAND	VERMONT
MASSACHUSETTS	VIRGINIA
MICHIGAN	WASHINGTON
MINNESOTA	WEST VIRGINIA
MISSISSIPPI	WISCONSIN
MISSOURI	WYOMING

Figure 10-16. Two-column text in small caps

```
    let r = lm.glyphRange(for:tc)
    lm.drawBackground(forGlyphRange:r, at:CGPoint(0,2))
    lm.drawGlyphs(forGlyphRange: r, at:CGPoint(0,2))
}
```

Building the entire Text Kit stack by hand may seem like overkill for that simple example, but imagine what *else* I could do now that I have access to the entire Text Kit stack! I can use properties, subclassing, delegation, and alternative stack architectures to achieve customizations and effects that, before Text Kit was migrated to iOS, were difficult or impossible to achieve without dipping down to the level of Core Text.

For example, the two-column display of U.S. state names on the iPad shown in Figure 10-16 was a Core Text example in early editions of this book, requiring 50 or 60 lines of elaborate C code, complicated by the necessity of flipping the context to prevent the text from being drawn upside-down. Nowadays, it can be achieved easily through Text Kit — effectively just by reusing code from earlier examples in this chapter.

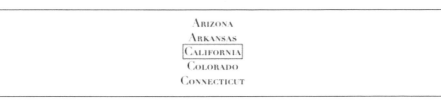

Figure 10-17. The user has tapped on California

Furthermore, the example from previous editions went on to describe how to make the display of state names interactive, with the name of the tapped state briefly outlined with a rectangle (Figure 10-17). With Core Text, this was almost insanely difficult, not least because we had to keep track of all the line fragment rectangles ourselves. But it's easy with Text Kit, because the layout manager knows all the answers.

We have a UIView subclass, StyledText. In its layoutSubviews, it creates the Text Kit stack — a layout manager with two text containers, to achieve the two-column layout — and stores the whole stack, along with the rects at which the two text containers are to be drawn, in properties:

```swift
override func layoutSubviews() {
    super.layoutSubviews()
    var r1 = self.bounds
    r1.origin.y += 2 // a little top space
    r1.size.width /= 2.0 // column 1
    var r2 = r1
    r2.origin.x += r2.size.width // column 2
    let lm = MyLayoutManager()
    let ts = NSTextStorage(attributedString:self.text)
    ts.addLayoutManager(lm)
    let tc = NSTextContainer(size:r1.size)
    lm.addTextContainer(tc)
    let tc2 = NSTextContainer(size:r2.size)
    lm.addTextContainer(tc2)
    self.lm = lm; self.ts = ts; self.tc = tc; self.tc2 = tc2
    self.r1 = r1; self.r2 = r2
}
```

Our draw(_:) is just like the previous example, except that we have two text containers to draw:

```swift
override func draw(_ rect: CGRect) {
    let range1 = self.lm.glyphRange(for:self.tc)
    self.lm.drawBackground(forGlyphRange:range1, at: self.r1.origin)
    self.lm.drawGlyphs(forGlyphRange:range1, at: self.r1.origin)
    let range2 = self.lm.glyphRange(for:self.tc2)
    self.lm.drawBackground(forGlyphRange:range2, at: self.r2.origin)
    self.lm.drawGlyphs(forGlyphRange:range2, at: self.r2.origin)
}
```

So much for drawing the text! We now have Figure 10-16.

On to Figure 10-17. When the user taps on our view, a tap gesture recognizer's action method is called. We are using the same layout manager subclass developed in the preceding section of this chapter: it draws a rectangle around the glyphs corresponding to the characters of its wordRange property. Thus, all we have to do in order to make the flashing rectangle around the tapped word is work out what that range is, set our layout manager's wordRange property and redraw ourselves, and then (after a short delay) set the wordRange property back to a zero range and redraw ourselves again to remove the rectangle.

We start by working out which column the user tapped in; this tells us which text container it is, and what the tapped point is in text container coordinates (g is the tap gesture recognizer):

```
var p = g.location(in:self)
var tc = self.tc!
if !self.r1.contains(p) {
    tc = self.tc2!
    p.x -= self.r1.size.width
}
```

Now we can ask the layout manager what glyph the user tapped on, and hence the whole range of glyphs within the line fragment the user tapped in. If the user tapped to the left of the first glyph or to the right of the last glyph, no word was tapped, and we return:

```
var f : CGFloat = 0
let ix =
    self.lm.glyphIndex(for:p, in:tc, fractionOfDistanceThroughGlyph:&f)
var glyphRange : NSRange = NSMakeRange(0,0)
self.lm.lineFragmentRect(forGlyphAt:ix, effectiveRange:&glyphRange)
if ix == glyphRange.location && f == 0.0 {
    return
}
if ix == glyphRange.location + glyphRange.length - 1 && f == 1.0 {
    return
}
```

If the last glyph of the line fragment is a whitespace glyph, we don't want to include it in our rectangle, so we subtract it from the end of our range. Then we're ready to convert to a character range, and thus we can learn the name of the state that the user tapped on:

```
func lastCharIsControl () -> Bool {
    let lastCharRange = glyphRange.location + glyphRange.length - 1
    let property = self.lm.propertyForGlyph(at:lastCharRange)
    let mask1 = property.rawValue
    let mask2 = NSLayoutManager.GlyphProperty.controlCharacter.rawValue
    return mask1 & mask2 != 0
```

```
    }
    while lastCharIsControl() {
        glyphRange.length -= 1
    }
    let characterRange =
        self.lm.characterRange(forGlyphRange:glyphRange, actualGlyphRange:nil)
    let s = self.text.string
    if let r = Range(characterRange, in:s) {
        let stateName = s[r]
        print("you tapped \(stateName)")
    }
```

Finally, we flash the rectangle around the state name by setting and resetting the word-Range property of the subclassed layout manager:

```
let lm = self.lm as! MyLayoutManager
lm.wordRange = characterRange
self.setNeedsDisplay()
delay(0.3) {
    lm.wordRange = NSMakeRange(0, 0)
    self.setNeedsDisplay()
}
```

CHAPTER 11

Web Views

A web view is a web browser, which is a powerful thing: it knows how to fetch resources through the Internet, and it can render HTML and CSS, and can respond to JavaScript. Thus it is a network communication device, as well as an interactive layout, animation, and media display engine.

In a web view, links and other ancillary resources work automatically. If your web view's HTML refers to an image, the web view will fetch it and display it. If the user taps on a link, the web view will fetch that content and display it; if the link is to some sort of media (a sound or video file), the web view will allow the user to play it.

A web view can also display some other types of content commonly encountered as Internet resources. For example, it can display PDF files, as well as documents in such formats as *.rtf*, Microsoft Word (*.doc* and *.docx*), and Pages.

 A Pages file that is actually a bundle must be compressed to form a single *.pages.zip* resource. A web view should also be able to display *.rtfd* files, but this feature is not working properly; Apple suggests that you convert to an attributed string as I described in Chapter 10 (specifying a document type of NSRTFDTextDocumentType), or use a QLPreviewController (Chapter 22).

The loading and rendering of a web view's content takes time, and may involve networking. Your app's interface, however, is not blocked or frozen while the content is loading. On the contrary, your interface remains accessible and operative. The web view, in fetching and rendering a web page and its linked components, is doing something quite complex, involving both threading and network interaction — I'll have a lot more to say about this in Chapters 23 and 24 — but it shields you from this complexity, and it operates *asynchronously* (in the background, off the main thread). Your own interaction with the web view stays on the main thread and is straightforward.

You ask the web view to load some content; then you sit back and let it worry about the details.

There are actually *three* web view objects:

UIWebView

UIWebView, a UIView subclass, has been around since the earliest days of iOS. Apple would like you to move away from use of UIWebView, though as far as I can tell it has not been formally deprecated.

WKWebView

WKWebView, a UIView subclass, appeared in iOS 8. The "WK" stands for Web-Kit.

SFSafariViewController

SFSafariViewController, a UIViewController subclass, was introduced in iOS 9, as part of the Safari Services framework. It is a full-fledged browser, in effect embedding Mobile Safari in your app as a separate process.

I'll describe WKWebView and SFSafariViewController. For a discussion of UIWeb-View, consult an earlier edition of this book.

 iOS 9 introduced App Transport Security. Your app, by default, cannot load external URLs that are not secure (`https:`). You can turn off this restriction completely or in part in your *Info.plist*. See Chapter 23 for details.

WKWebView

WKWebView is part of the WebKit framework; to use it, you'll need to `import` Web-Kit. New in Xcode 9, the nib editor's Object library contains a WKWebView object that you can drag into your interface as you design it.

The designated initializer is `init(frame:configuration:)`. The second parameter, `configuration:`, is a WKWebViewConfiguration. You can create a configuration beforehand:

```
let config = WKWebViewConfiguration()
// ... configure config here ...
let wv = WKWebView(frame: rect, configuration:config)
```

Alternatively, you can initialize your web view with `init(frame:)` to get a default configuration and modify it through the web view's `configuration` property later:

```
let wv = WKWebView(frame: rect)
let config = wv.configuration
// ... configure config here ...
```

Either way, you'll probably want to perform configurations before the web view has a chance to load any content, because some settings will affect *how* it loads or renders that content.

Here are some of the more important WKWebViewConfiguration properties:

suppressesIncrementalRendering
> If true, the web view's visible content doesn't change until all linked renderable resources (such as images) have finished loading. The default is false. Can be set in the nib editor.

allowsInlineMediaPlayback
> If true, linked media are played inside the web page. The default is false (the fullscreen player is used). Can be set in the nib editor.

mediaTypesRequiringUserActionForPlayback
> Types of media that won't start playing without a user gesture. A bitmask (WKAudiovisualMediaTypes) with possible values .audio, .video, and .all. Can be set in the nib editor.

allowsPictureInPictureMediaPlayback
> See Chapter 15 for a discussion of picture-in-picture playback. Can be set in the nib editor.

dataDetectorTypes
> Types of content that may be transformed automatically into tappable links. Similar to a text view's data detectors (Chapter 10). Can be set in the nib editor.

websiteDataStore
> A WKWebsiteDataStore. By supplying a data store, you get control over stored resources. New in iOS 11, its httpCookieStore is a WKHTTPCookieStore where you can examine, add, and remove cookies.

preferences
> A WKPreferences object. Can be configured in the nib editor. This is a value class embodying three properties:
>
> - minimumFontSize
> - javaScriptEnabled
> - javaScriptCanOpenWindowsAutomatically

userContentController
> A WKUserContentController object. This is how you can inject JavaScript into a web page and communicate between your code and the web page's content. I'll

give an example later. Also, new in iOS 11, you can give the `userContent-Controller` a rule list (WKContentRuleList) that filters the web view's content.

A WKWebView is not a scroll view, but it *has* a scroll view (`scrollView`). You can use this to scroll the web view's content programatically; you can also get references to its gesture recognizers, and add gesture recognizers of your own (see Chapter 7).

New in iOS 11, you can take a snapshot of a web view's content with `take-Snapshot(with:completionHandler:)`. The snapshot image is passed into the completion function as a UIImage.

Web View Content

You can supply a web view with content using one of four methods, depending on the type of your content. All four methods return a WKNavigation object, an opaque object that can be used to identify an individual page-loading operation, but you will usually ignore it. The content types and methods are:

A URLRequest
> Form a URLRequest from a URL and call `load(_:)`. The URLRequest initializer is `init(url:cachePolicy:timeoutInterval:)`, but the second and third parameters are optional and will often be omitted. Additional configuration includes such properties as `allowsCellularAccess`. For example:

```
let url = URL(string: "https://www.apple.com")!
let req = URLRequest(url: url)
self.wv.load(req)
```

A local file
> Obtain a local file URL and call `loadFileURL(_:allowingReadAccessTo:)`. The second parameter effectively sandboxes the web view into a single file or directory. In this example from one of my apps, the HTML refers to images in the same directory as itself:

```
let url = Bundle.main.url(
    forResource: "zotzhelp", withExtension: "html")!
view.loadFileURL(url, allowingReadAccessTo: url)
```

An HTML string
> Prepare a string consisting of valid HTML, and call `loadHTMLString(_:base-URL:)`. The `baseURL:` specifies how partial URLs in your HTML are to be resolved; for example, the HTML might refer to resources in your app bundle.

> Starting with an HTML string is useful particularly when you want to construct your HTML programmatically or make changes to it before handing it to the web view. In this example from the TidBITS News app, my HTML consists of two strings: a wrapper with the usual <html> tags, and the body content derived from

an RSS feed. I assemble them and hand the resulting string to my web view for display:

```
let templatepath = Bundle.main.path(
    forResource: "htmlTemplate", ofType:"txt")!
let base = URL(fileURLWithPath:templatepath)
var s = try! String(contentsOfFile:templatepath)
let ss = // actual body content for this page
s = s.replacingOccurrences(of:"<content>", with:ss)
self.wv.loadHTMLString(s, baseURL:base)
```

A Data object

Call `load(_:MIMEType:characterEncodingName:baseURL:)`. This is useful particularly when the content has itself arrived from the network, as the parameters correspond to the properties of a URLResponse. This example will be more meaningful to you after you've read Chapter 23:

```
let sess = URLSession.shared
let url = URL(string:"https://www.someplace.net/someImage.jpg")!
let task = sess.dataTask(with: url) { data, response, err in
    if let response = response,
        let mime = response.mimeType,
        let enc = response.textEncodingName,
        let data = data {
            self.wv.load(data, mimeType: mime,
                characterEncodingName: enc, baseURL: url)
    }
}
```

 In iOS 11, internal links (where the `href` value starts with "#") don't work unless the web view content was supplied as a URLRequest or a file URL. I regard this as a bug.

Tracking Changes in a Web View

A WKWebView has properties that can be tracked with key–value observing, such as:

- `loading`
- `estimatedProgress`
- `url`
- `title`

You can observe these properties to be notified as a web page loads or changes.

For example, as preparation to give the user feedback while a page is loading, I'll put an activity indicator (Chapter 12) in the center of my web view and keep a reference to it:

```
let act = UIActivityIndicatorView(activityIndicatorStyle:.whiteLarge)
act.backgroundColor = UIColor(white:0.1, alpha:0.5)
self.wv.addSubview(act)
act.translatesAutoresizingMaskIntoConstraints = false
NSLayoutConstraint.activate([
    act.centerXAnchor.constraint(equalTo:wv.centerXAnchor),
    act.centerYAnchor.constraint(equalTo:wv.centerYAnchor)
])
self.activity = act
```

Now I observe the web view's `loading` property (`self.obs` is a Set instance property). When the web view starts loading or stops loading, I'm notified, so I can show or hide the activity view:

```
obs.insert(self.wv.observe(\.loading, options:.new) {[unowned self] wv,ch in
    if let val = ch.newValue {
        if val {
            self.activity.startAnimating()
        } else {
            self.activity.stopAnimating()
        }
    }
})
```

Web View Navigation

A WKWebView maintains a back and forward list of the URLs to which the user has navigated. The list is its `backForwardList`, a WKBackForwardList, which is a collection of read-only properties (and one method) such as:

- `currentItem`
- `backItem`
- `forwardItem`
- `item(at:)`

Each item in the list is a WKBackForwardItem, a simple value class basically consisting of a `url` and a `title`.

The WKWebView itself responds to `goBack`, `goForward` and `go(to:)`, so you can tell it in code to navigate the list. Its properties `canGoBack` and `canGoForward` are key-value observable; typically you would use that fact to enable or disable a Back and Forward button in your interface in response to the list changing.

A WKWebView also has a settable property, `allowsBackForwardNavigation-Gestures`. The default is `false`; if `true`, the user can swipe sideways to go back and forward in the list. This property can also be set in the nib editor.

To prevent or reroute navigation that the user tries to perform by tapping links, set yourself as the WKWebView's navigationDelegate (WKNavigationDelegate) and implement webView(_:decidePolicyFor:decisionHandler:). You are handed a decisionHandler function which you *must* call, handing it a WKNavigationAction-Policy — either .cancel or .allow. The for: parameter is a WKNavigationAction that you can examine to help make your decision; it has a request which is the URL-Request we are proposing to perform — look at its url to see where we are proposing to go — along with a navigationType, which will be one of the following (WKNavigationType):

- .linkActivated
- .backForward
- .reload
- .formSubmitted
- .formResubmitted
- .other

In this example, I permit navigation in the most general case — otherwise nothing would ever appear in my web view! — but if the user taps a link, I forbid it and show that URL in Mobile Safari instead:

```swift
func webView(_ webView: WKWebView,
    decidePolicyFor navigationAction: WKNavigationAction,
    decisionHandler: @escaping (WKNavigationActionPolicy) -> Swift.Void) {
        if navigationAction.navigationType == .linkActivated {
            if let url = navigationAction.request.url {
                UIApplication.shared.open(url)
                decisionHandler(.cancel)
                return
            }
        }
        decisionHandler(.allow)
}
```

Several other WKNavigationDelegate methods can notify you as a page loads (or fails to load). Under normal circumstances, you'll receive them in this order:

- webView(_:didStartProvisionalNavigation:)
- webView(_:didCommit:)
- webView(_:didFinish:)

Those delegate methods, and all navigation commands, like the four ways of loading your web view with initial content, supply a WKNavigation object. This object is opaque, but you can use it in an equality comparison to determine whether the navigations referred to in different methods are the same navigation (roughly speaking, the same page-loading operation).

Communicating with a Web Page

Your code can pass JavaScript messages into and out of a WKWebView's web page, thus allowing you to change the page's contents or respond to changes within it, even while it is being displayed.

Communicating into a web page

To send a message into an already loaded WKWebView web page, call `evaluateJava-Script(_:completionHandler:)`. Your JavaScript runs within the context of the web page.

In this example, the user is able to decrease the size of the text in the web page. We have prepared some JavaScript that generates a `<style>` element containing CSS that sets the `font-size` for the page's `<body>` in accordance with a property, `self.fontsize`:

```
var fontsize = 18
var cssrule : String {
    return """
    var s = document.createElement('style');
    s.textContent = 'body { font-size: \(self.fontsize)px; }';
    document.documentElement.appendChild(s);
    """
}
```

When the user taps a button, we decrement `self.fontsize`, construct that JavaScript, and send it to the web page:

```
func doDecreaseSize (_ sender: Any) {
    self.fontsize -= 1
    if self.fontsize < 10 {
        self.fontsize = 20
    }
    let s = self.cssrule
    self.wv.evaluateJavaScript(s)
}
```

That's clever, but we have not done anything about setting the web page's *initial* `font-size`. Let's fix that.

A WKWebView allows us to inject JavaScript into the web page at the time it is loaded. To do so, we use the `userContentController` of the WKWebView's `configuration`. We create a WKUserScript, specifying the JavaScript it contains, along with an `injectionTime` which can be either before (`.documentStart`) or after

(.documentEnd) a page's content has loaded. In this case, we want it to be before; otherwise, the user will see the font size change suddenly:

```
let script = WKUserScript(source: self.cssrule,
    injectionTime: .atDocumentStart, forMainFrameOnly: true)
let config = self.wv.configuration
config.userContentController.addUserScript(script)
```

Communicating out of a web page

To communicate out of a web page, you need first to install a message handler to receive the communication. Again, this involves the userContentController. You call add(_:name:), where the first argument is an object that must implement the WKScriptMessageHandler protocol, so that its userContentController(_:did-Receive:) method can be called later:

```
let config = self.wv.configuration
config.userContentController.add(self, name: "playbutton")
```

We have just installed a playbutton message handler. This means that the DOM for our web page now contains an element, among its window.webkit.messageHandlers, called playbutton. A message handler sends its message when it receives a post-Message() function call. Thus, the WKScriptMessageHandler (self in this example) will get a call to its userContentController(_:didReceive:) method if JavaScript inside the web page sends postMessage() to the window.webkit.message-Handlers.playbutton object.

To make that actually happen, I've put an <img> tag into my web page's HTML, specifying an image that will act as a tappable button:

```
<img src=\"listen.png\"
    onclick=\"window.webkit.messageHandlers.playbutton.postMessage('play')\">
```

When the user taps that image, the message is posted, and so my code runs and I can respond:

```
func userContentController(_ userContentController: WKUserContentController,
    didReceive message: WKScriptMessage) {
        if message.name == "playbutton" {
            if let body = message.body as? String {
                if body == "play" {
                    // ... do stuff here ...
                }
            }
        }
}
```

There's just one little problem: that code causes a retain cycle. The reason is that a WKUserContentController leaks, and it retains the WKScriptMessageHandler, which in this case is self — and so self will never be deallocated. But self is the view controller, so that's very bad. My solution is to create an intermediate trampoline object that can be harmlessly retained, and that has a weak reference to `self`:

```
class MyMessageHandler : NSObject, WKScriptMessageHandler {
    weak var delegate : WKScriptMessageHandler?
    init(delegate:WKScriptMessageHandler) {
        self.delegate = delegate
        super.init()
    }
    func userContentController(_ ucc: WKUserContentController,
        didReceive message: WKScriptMessage) {
            self.delegate?.userContentController(ucc, didReceive: message)
    }
}
```

Now when I add myself as a script message handler, I do it by way of the trampoline object:

```
let config = self.wv.configuration
let handler = MyMessageHandler(delegate:self)
config.userContentController.add(handler, name: "playbutton")
```

Now that I've broken the retain cycle, my own `deinit` is called, and I can release the offending objects:

```
deinit {
    let ucc = self.wv.configuration.userContentController
    ucc.removeAllUserScripts()
    ucc.removeScriptMessageHandler(forName:"playbutton")
}
```

JavaScript alerts

If a web page might put up a JavaScript alert, nothing will happen in your app unless you assign the WKWebView a `uiDelegate`, an object adopting the WKUIDelegate protocol, and implement these methods:

`webView(_:runJavaScriptAlertPanelWithMessage:initiatedByFrame:completion-Handler:)`

    Called by JavaScript `alert`.

`webView(_:runJavaScriptConfirmPanelWithMessage:initiatedBy-Frame:completionHandler:)`

    Called by JavaScript `confirm`.

`webView(_:runJavaScriptTextInputPanelWithPrompt:defaultText:initiatedBy-Frame:completionHandler:)`

    Called by JavaScript `prompt`.

Your implementation should put up an appropriate alert (UIAlertController, see Chapter 13) and call the completion function when it is dismissed. Here's a minimal implementation for the `alert` method:

```
func webView(_ webView: WKWebView,
    runJavaScriptAlertPanelWithMessage message: String,
    initiatedByFrame frame: WKFrameInfo,
    completionHandler: @escaping () -> Void) {
        let host = frame.request.url?.host
        let alert = UIAlertController(title: host, message: message,
            preferredStyle: .alert)
        alert.addAction(UIAlertAction(title: "OK", style: .default) { _ in
            completionHandler()
        })
        self.present(alert, animated:true)
}
```

Similarly, if a web page's JavaScript might call `window.open`, implement this method:

- `webView(_:createWebViewWith:for:windowFeatures:`

Your implementation can return `nil`, or else create a new WKWebView, get it into the interface, and return it.

Custom Schemes

New in iOS 11, you can pass custom data into a web page by implementing a custom URL scheme. When the web page asks for the data by way of the scheme, the WKWebView turns to your code to supply the data.

For example, let's say I have an MP3 file called "theme" in my app's asset catalog, and I want the user to be able to play it through an <audio> tag in my web page. I've invented a unique custom scheme that signals to my app that we want this audio data, and my web page's <source> tag asks for its data using that scheme:

```
weak var wv: WKWebView!
let sch = "neuburg-custom-scheme-demo-audio"
override func viewDidLoad() {
    super.viewDidLoad()
    // ... configure the web view ...
    let s = """
    <!DOCTYPE html><html><head>
    <meta name="viewport" content="initial-scale=1.0, user-scalable=no" />
    </head><body>
    <p>Here you go:</p>
    <audio controls>
    <source src="\(sch)://theme" />
    </audio>
```

```
        </body></html>
        """
        self.wv.loadHTMLString(s, baseURL: nil)
    }
```

Now let's fill in the missing code, where we configure the web view to accept sch as a custom scheme. Unfortunately, this works only if we create the web view ourselves, in code, using the init(frame:configuration:) initializer, with the WKWebViewConfiguration object prepared beforehand (I regard this limitation as a bug):

```
let config = WKWebViewConfiguration()
let sh = SchemeHandler()
sh.sch = self.sch
config.setURLSchemeHandler(sh, forURLScheme: self.sch)
let wv = WKWebView(frame: CGRect(30,30,200,300), configuration: config)
self.view.addSubview(wv)
```

The call to setURLSchemeHandler requires that we provide an object that adopts the WKURLSchemeHandler protocol. That object cannot be self, or we'll get ourselves into a retain cycle (similar to the problem we had with WKScriptMessageHandler earlier); so I'm configuring and passing a custom SchemeHandler helper object instead.

The WKURLSchemeHandler protocol methods are where the action is. When the web page wants data with our custom scheme, it calls our SchemeHandler's web-View(_:start:) method. The second parameter is a WKURLSchemeTask that operates as our gateway back to the web view. Its request property contains the URLRequest from the web page. We must call the WKURLSchemeTask's methods, first supplying a URLResponse, then handing it the data, then telling it that we've finished:

```
class SchemeHandler : NSObject, WKURLSchemeHandler {
    var sch : String?
    func webView(_ webView: WKWebView, start task: WKURLSchemeTask) {
        if let url = task.request.url,
            let sch = self.sch,
            url.scheme == sch,
            let host = url.host,
            let theme = NSDataAsset(name:host) {
                let data = theme.data
                let resp = URLResponse(url: url, mimeType: "audio/mpeg",
                    expectedContentLength: data.count,
                    textEncodingName: nil)
                task.didReceive(resp)
                task.didReceive(data)
                task.didFinish()
        } else {
            task.didFailWithError(NSError(domain: "oops", code: 0))
        }
    }
}
```

```
        func webView(_ webView: WKWebView, stop task: WKURLSchemeTask) {
            print("stop")
        }
    }
```

The outcome is that the audio controls appear in our web page, and when the user taps the Play button, what plays is the MP3 file from the app's asset catalog.

Web View Peek and Pop

If a WKWebView's `allowsLinkPreview` property is `true`, the user can employ 3D touch on a link to peek at the linked page. This property can be set in the nib editor.

The default pop response, if the user peeks and then continues pressing harder, is to open the link in Safari. This mechanism does *not* pass through your navigation delegate's implementation of `webView(_:decidePolicyFor:decisionHandler:)`. Instead, if you wish to customize your app's response to the user previewing links, implement these methods in your web view's `uiDelegate`:

`webView(_:shouldPreviewElement:)`
> Return `false` to suppress peek and pop on this link even if it is enabled for the web view as a whole. The second parameter is a WKPreviewElementInfo object whose `linkURL` you can examine.

`webView(_:previewingViewControllerForElement:defaultActions:)`
> Your job is to supply a view controller that can display the preview.

`webView(_:commitPreviewingViewController:)`
> Your job is to navigate to the view controller that can display the preview.

The second and third methods are similar to UIViewControllerPreviewingDelegate methods (see Chapter 6). I'll give an example later in this chapter.

Web View State Saving and Restoration

WKWebView, as far as I can tell, does not automatically participate in any way in the iOS view controller state saving and restoration mechanism (Chapter 6). This, if true, would be a major flaw in WKWebView.

A UIWebView, if it has an actual URL request as the source of its content at the time the user leaves the app, has that URL request archived by the state saving mechanism, along with the UIWebView's Back and Forward lists and the content offset of its scroll view. If state restoration takes place, the UIWebView's `request` property, and its Back and Forward lists, and its scroll view's content offset, including the offsets of all previously viewed pages, are restored automatically; all you have to do is load the restored request, which you can easily do in `applicationFinishedRestoringState`, like this:

```
override func applicationFinishedRestoringState() {
    if self.wv.request != nil { // self.wv is a UIWebView
        self.wv.reload()
    }
}
```

But you can't do anything like that with a WKWebView. It has no `request` property. It has a `url` property, but that property is not saved and restored. Moreover, a WKWebView's `backForwardList` is not writable. Thus, it appears that there is no way to save and restore a WKWebView's state as a web browser.

Safari View Controller

A Safari view controller (SFSafariViewController, introduced in iOS 9) embeds the Mobile Safari interface in a separate process inside your app. It provides the user with a browser interface familiar from Mobile Safari itself. In a toolbar, which can be shown or hidden by scrolling, there are Back and Forward buttons, a Share button including standard Safari features such as Add Bookmark and Add to Reading List, and a Safari button that lets the user load the same page in the real Safari app. In a navigation bar, which can be shrunk or grown by scrolling, are a read-only URL field with a Reader button (if this page has a Reader mode available) and a Refresh button, and a Done button. The user has access to autofill and to Safari cookies with no intervention by your app.

The idea, according to Apple, is that when you want to present internal HTML content, such as an HTML string, you'll use a WKWebView, but when you really want to allow the user to access the web, you'll use a Safari view controller. In this way, you are saved from the trouble of trying to build a full-fledged web browser yourself.

To use a Safari view controller, you'll need to `import SafariServices`. Create the SFSafariViewController, initialize it with a URL, and present it:

```
let svc = SFSafariViewController(url: url)
self.present(svc, animated: true)
```

In this example, we interfere (as a WKWebView's `navigationDelegate`) with the user tapping on a link in our web view, so that the linked page is displayed in an SFSafariViewController within our app:

```
func webView(_ webView: WKWebView,
    decidePolicyFor navigationAction: WKNavigationAction,
    decisionHandler: @escaping (WKNavigationActionPolicy) -> Swift.Void) {
        if navigationAction.navigationType == .linkActivated {
            if let url = navigationAction.request.url {
                let svc = SFSafariViewController(url: url)
                self.present(svc, animated: true)
                decisionHandler(.cancel)
                return
```

```
        }
    }
    decisionHandler(.allow)
}
```

In this example, we interfere (as a WKWebView's uiDelegate) with the user using 3D touch to preview a link in our web view, so that popping displays the linked page in an SFSafariViewController within our app:

```
func webView(_ webView: WKWebView,
    previewingViewControllerForElement elementInfo: WKPreviewElementInfo,
    defaultActions acts: [WKPreviewActionItem]) -> UIViewController? {
        if let url = elementInfo.linkURL {
            let sf = SFSafariViewController(url: url)
            return sf
        }
        return nil
}
func webView(_ webView: WKWebView,
    commitPreviewingViewController pvc: UIViewController) {
        self.present(pvc, animated:true)
}
```

When the user taps the Done button in the navigation bar, the Safari view controller is dismissed. New in iOS 11, you can change the title of the Done button. To do so, set the Safari view controller's dismissButtonStyle to .done, .close, or .cancel.

You can set the color of the Safari view controller's navigation bar (preferredBarTint-Color) and bar button items (preferredControlTintColor). This allows the look of the view to harmonize with the rest of your app.

New in iOS 11, you can configure a Safari view controller by creating an SFSafari-ViewController.Configuration object and passing it to the Safari view controller through its initializer init(url:configuration:). Using the configuration object, you can prevent the Safari view controller's top and bottom bars from collapsing when the user scrolls; to do so, set its barCollapsingEnabled property to false. You can set the entersReaderIfAvailable property to make the Safari view controller switch to Reader mode automatically, if possible, as it appears.

You can make yourself the Safari view controller's delegate (SFSafariViewController-Delegate) and implement any of these methods:

safariViewController(_:didCompleteInitialLoad:)
safariViewControllerDidFinish(_:)
> Called on presentation and dismissal of the Safari view controller, respectively.

func safariViewController(_:initialLoadDidRedirectTo:)
> Reports that the Safari view controller's initial web page differs from the URL you originally provided, because redirection occurred.

```
safariViewController(_:activityItemsFor:title:)
```
Allows you to supply your own Share button items; I'll explain what activity items are in Chapter 13.

```
safariViewController(_:excludedActivityTypesFor:title:)
```
New in iOS 11. In a sense, the converse of the preceding: allows you to eliminate unwanted activity types from the Share button.

I have not found any way in which a Safari view controller participates in view controller state saving and restoration. Needless to say, I regard this as a bug.

Developing Web View Content

Before designing the HTML to be displayed in a web view, you might want to read up on the brand of HTML native to the mobile WebKit rendering engine. There are certain limitations; for example, mobile WebKit doesn't use plug-ins such as Flash, and it imposes limits on the size of resources (such as images) that it can display. On the plus side, WebKit is in the vanguard of the march toward HTML5 and CSS3, and has many special capabilities suited for display on a mobile device. For documentation and other resources, see Apple's Safari Dev Center.

A good place to start is the *Safari Web Content Guide*. It contains links to other relevant documentation, such as the *Safari CSS Visual Effects Guide*, which describes some things you can do with WebKit's implementation of CSS3 (like animations), and the *Safari HTML5 Audio and Video Guide*, which describes WebKit's audio and video player support.

If nothing else, you'll want to be aware of one important aspect of web page content — the *viewport*. This is typically set through a `<meta>` tag in the `<head>` area. For example:

```
<meta name="viewport" content="initial-scale=1.0, user-scalable=no">
```

Without that line, or something similar, a web page may be laid out incorrectly when it is rendered. Without a viewport, your content may appear tiny (because it is being rendered as if the screen were large), or it may be too wide for the view, forcing the user to scroll horizontally to read it. See the *Safari Web Content Guide* for details. The viewport's `user-scalable` attribute can be treated as `yes` by setting the WKWebView-Configuration's `ignoresViewportScaleLimits` to `true`.

Another important section of the *Safari Web Content Guide* describes how you can use a `media` attribute in the `<link>` tag that loads your CSS to load *different* CSS depending on what kind of device your app is running on. For example, you might have one CSS file that lays out your web view's content on an iPhone, and another that lays it out on an iPad.

Figure 11-1. The Web Inspector inspects a running app

Inspecting, debugging, and experimenting with web view content is greatly eased by the Web Inspector, built into Safari on the desktop. It can see a web view in your app running on a device or the Simulator, and lets you analyze every aspect of how it works. For example, in Figure 11-1, I'm examining an image to understand how it is sized and scaled.

You can hover the mouse over a web page element in the Web Inspector to highlight the rendering of that element in the running app. Moreover, the Web Inspector lets you change your web view's content in real time, with many helpful features such as CSS autocompletion.

JavaScript and the document object model (*DOM*) are also extremely powerful. Event listeners allow JavaScript code to respond directly to touch and gesture events, so that the user can interact with elements of a web page much as if they were iOS-native touchable views; it can also take advantage of Core Location and Core Motion facilities to respond to where the user is on earth and how the device is positioned (Chapter 21). Additional helpful documentation includes Apple's *WebKit DOM Programming Topics* and the WebKit JS framework reference page.

CHAPTER 12

Controls and Other Views

This chapter discusses all UIView subclasses provided by UIKit that haven't been discussed already. It's remarkable how few of them there are; UIKit exhibits a notable economy of means in this regard.

Additional UIView subclasses, as well as UIViewController subclasses that create interface, are provided by other frameworks. There will be examples in Part III.

UIActivityIndicatorView

An activity indicator (UIActivityIndicatorView) appears as the spokes of a small wheel. You set the spokes spinning with startAnimating, giving the user a sense that some time-consuming process is taking place. You stop the spinning with stopAnimating. If the activity indicator's hidesWhenStopped is true (the default), it is visible only while spinning.

An activity indicator comes in a style, its activityIndicatorViewStyle; if it is created in code, you'll set its style with init(activityIndicatorStyle:). Your choices (UIActivityIndicatorViewStyle) are:

- .whiteLarge
- .white
- .gray

An activity indicator has a standard size, which depends on its style. Changing its size in code changes the size of the view, but not the size of the spokes. For bigger spokes, you can resort to a scale transform.

Figure 12-1. A large activity indicator

You can assign an activity indicator a `color`; this overrides the color of the spokes assigned through the style. An activity indicator is a UIView, so you can also set its `backgroundColor`; a nice effect is to give an activity indicator a contrasting background color and to round its corners by way of the view's layer (Figure 12-1).

Here's some code from a UITableViewCell subclass in one of my apps. In this app, it takes some time, after the user taps a cell to select it, for me to construct the next view and navigate to it; to cover the delay, I show a spinning activity indicator in the center of the cell while it's selected:

```
override func setSelected(_ selected: Bool, animated: Bool) {
    if selected {
        let v = UIActivityIndicatorView(activityIndicatorStyle: .whiteLarge)
        v.color = .yellow
        DispatchQueue.main.async {
            v.backgroundColor = UIColor(white:0.2, alpha:0.6)
        }
        v.layer.cornerRadius = 10
        v.frame = v.frame.insetBy(dx: -10, dy: -10)
        let cf = self.contentView.convert(self.bounds, from:self)
        v.center = CGPoint(cf.midX, cf.midY);
        v.tag = 1001
        self.contentView.addSubview(v)
        v.startAnimating()
    } else {
        if let v = self.viewWithTag(1001) {
            v.removeFromSuperview()
        }
    }
    super.setSelected(selected, animated: animated)
}
```

If activity involves the network, you might want to set the UIApplication's `isNetwork-ActivityIndicatorVisible` to `true`. This displays a small spinning activity indicator in the status bar. The indicator is not reflecting actual network activity; if it's visible, it's spinning. Be sure to set it back to `false` when the activity is over.

An activity indicator is simple and standard, but you can't change the way it's drawn. One obvious alternative would be a UIImageView with an animated image, as described in Chapter 4. Another solution is a CAReplicatorLayer, a layer that makes multiple copies of its sublayer; by animating the sublayer, you animate the copies.

Figure 12-2. A custom activity indicator

This is a very common approach (in fact, it wouldn't surprise me to learn that UIActivityIndicatorView is implemented using CAReplicatorLayer). For example:

```
let lay = CAReplicatorLayer()
lay.frame = CGRect(0,0,100,20)
let bar = CALayer()
bar.frame = CGRect(0,0,10,20)
bar.backgroundColor = UIColor.red.cgColor
lay.addSublayer(bar)
lay.instanceCount = 5
lay.instanceTransform = CATransform3DMakeTranslation(20, 0, 0)
let anim = CABasicAnimation(keyPath: #keyPath(CALayer.opacity))
anim.fromValue = 1.0
anim.toValue = 0.2
anim.duration = 1
anim.repeatCount = .infinity
bar.add(anim, forKey: nil)
lay.instanceDelay = anim.duration / Double(lay.instanceCount)
self.view.layer.addSublayer(lay)
lay.position = CGPoint(
    self.view.layer.bounds.midX, self.view.layer.bounds.midY)
```

Our single red vertical bar (bar) is replicated to make five red vertical bars. We repeatedly fade the bar from opaque to transparent, but because we've set the replicator layer's instanceDelay, the replicated bars fade in sequence, so that the darkest bar appears to be marching repeatedly to the right (Figure 12-2).

UIProgressView

A progress view (UIProgressView) is a "thermometer," graphically displaying a percentage. This may be a static percentage, or it might represent a time-consuming process whose percentage of completion is known (if the percentage of completion is unknown, you're more likely to use an activity indicator). In one of my apps I use a progress view to show how many cards are left in the deck; in another app I use a progress view to show the current position within the song being played by the built-in music player.

A progress view comes in a style, its progressViewStyle; if the progress view is created in code, you'll set its style with init(progressViewStyle:). Your choices (UIProgressViewStyle) are:

Figure 12-3. A progress view

Figure 12-4. A thicker progress view using a custom progress image

- .default
- .bar

A .bar progress view is intended for use in a UIBarButtonItem, as the title view of a navigation item, and so on. Both styles by default draw the thermometer extremely thin — just 2 pixels and 3 pixels, respectively. (Figure 12-3 shows a .default progress view.) Changing a progress view's frame height directly has no visible effect on how the thermometer is drawn. Under autolayout, to make a thicker thermometer, supply a height constraint with a larger value (thus overriding the intrinsic content height). Alternatively, subclass UIProgressView and override sizeThatFits(_:).

The fullness of the thermometer is the progress view's progress property. This is a value between 0 and 1, inclusive; you'll usually need to do some elementary arithmetic to convert from the actual value you're reflecting to a value within that range. (It is also a Float; in Swift, you may have to coerce explicitly.) A change in progress value can be animated by calling setProgress(_:animated:). For example, to reflect the number of cards remaining in a deck of 52 cards:

```
let r = self.deck.cards.count
self.prog.setProgress(Float(r)/52, animated: true)
```

The default color of the filled portion of a progress view is the tintColor (which may be inherited from higher up the view hierarchy). The default color for the unfilled portion is gray for a .default progress view and transparent for a .bar progress view. You can customize the colors; set the progress view's progressTintColor and track-TintColor, respectively. This can also be done in the nib editor.

Alternatively, you can customize the image used to draw the filled portion of the progress view, its progressImage, along with the image used to draw the unfilled portion, the trackImage. This can also be done in the nib editor. Each image must be stretched to the length of the filled or unfilled area, so you'll want to use a resizable image.

Here's a simple example from one of my apps (Figure 12-4):

Figure 12-5. A custom progress view

```
self.prog.trackTintColor = .black
let r = UIGraphicsImageRenderer(size:CGSize(10,10))
let im = r.image { ctx in
    let con = ctx.cgContext
    con.setFillColor(UIColor.yellow.cgColor)
    con.fill(CGRect(0, 0, 10, 10))
    let r = con.boundingBoxOfClipPath.insetBy(dx: 1,dy: 1)
    con.setLineWidth(2)
    con.setStrokeColor(UIColor.black.cgColor)
    con.stroke(r)
    con.strokeEllipse(in: r)
}.resizableImage(withCapInsets:UIEdgeInsetsMake(4, 4, 4, 4),
    resizingMode:.stretch)
self.prog.progressImage = im
```

Progress View Alternatives

For maximum flexibility, you can design your own UIView subclass that draws something similar to a thermometer. Figure 12-5 shows a simple custom thermometer view; it has a value property, and you set this to something between 0 and 1 and call setNeedsDisplay to make the view redraw itself. Here's its draw(_:) code:

```
override func draw(_ rect: CGRect) {
    let c = UIGraphicsGetCurrentContext()!
    UIColor.white.set()
    let ins : CGFloat = 2
    let r = self.bounds.insetBy(dx: ins, dy: ins)
    let radius : CGFloat = r.size.height / 2
    let d90 = CGFloat.pi/2
    let path = CGMutablePath()
    path.move(to:CGPoint(r.maxX - radius, ins))
    path.addArc(center:CGPoint(radius+ins, radius+ins),
        radius: radius, startAngle: -d90, endAngle: d90, clockwise: true)
    path.addArc(center:CGPoint(r.maxX - radius, radius+ins),
        radius: radius, startAngle: d90, endAngle: -d90, clockwise: true)
    path.closeSubpath()
    c.addPath(path)
    c.setLineWidth(2)
    c.strokePath()
    c.addPath(path)
    c.clip()
    c.fill(CGRect(r.origin.x, r.origin.y, r.width * self.value, r.height))
}
```

Your custom progress view doesn't have to look like a thermometer. For instance, Apple's Music app, in some iOS versions, shows the current playing position within

Figure 12-6. A circular custom progress view

an album's song by drawing the arc of a circle (Figure 12-6). This effect is easily achieved by setting the strokeEnd of a CAShapeLayer with a circular path (and possibly a rotation transform, to start the circle at the top).

The Progress Class

A progress view has an observedProgress property which you can set to a Progress object. Progress is a Foundation class that abstracts the notion of task progress: it has a totalUnitCount property and a completedUnitCount property, and their ratio generates its fractionCompleted, which is read-only and observable with KVO. If you assign a Progress object to a progress view's observedProgress property and configure and update it, the progress view will automatically use the changes in the Progress object's fractionCompleted to update its own progress. That's useful because you might already have a time-consuming process that maintains and vends its own Progress object. (For a case in point, see "Slow Data Delivery" on page 596.) Thus, you can use a progress view to reflect the time-consuming process's progress.

In extremely simple cases, you might set your progress view's observedProgress *directly* to the time-consuming process's Progress object. Alternatively, you can configure your progress view's observedProgress as the *parent* of the process's Progress object. When Progress objects stand in a parent–child relationship, the progress of an operation reported to the child automatically forms an appropriate fraction of the progress reported by the parent; this allows a single Progress object, acting as the ultimate parent, to conglomerate the progress of numerous individual operations.

There are two ways to put two Progress objects into a parent–child relationship:

Explicit parent

   Call the parent's addChild(_:withPendingUnitCount:) method. Alternatively, create the child by initializing it with reference to the parent, by calling init(totalUnitCount:parent:pendingUnitCount:).

Implicit parent

   This approach uses the notion of the *current* Progress object. The rule is that while a Progress object is current, any new Progress objects will become its child automatically. The whole procedure thus comes down to doing things in the right order:

1. Tell the prospective parent Progress object to `becomeCurrent(withPendingUnitCount:)`.

2. Create the child Progress object without an explicit parent, by calling `init(totalUnitCount:)`. As if by magic, it becomes the other Progress object's child (because the other Progress object is current).

3. Tell the parent to `resignCurrent`. This balances the earlier `becomeCurrent(withPendingUnitCount:)` and completes the configuration.

UIPickerView

A picker view (UIPickerView) displays selectable choices using a rotating drum metaphor. Its default height is adaptive — 162 in an environment with a `.compact` vertical size class (an iPhone in landscape orientation) and 216 otherwise — but you are free to set its height to something else. Its width is generally up to you.

Each drum, or column, is called a *component*. Your code configures the UIPickerView's content through its data source (UIPickerViewDataSource) and delegate (UIPickerViewDelegate), which are usually the same object. Your data source and delegate must answer some Big Questions similar to those posed by a UITableView (Chapter 8):

`numberOfComponents(in:)`
> How many components (drums) does this picker view have?

`pickerView(_:numberOfRowsInComponent:)`
> How many rows does this component have? The first component is numbered 0.

`pickerView(_:titleForRow:forComponent:)`
`pickerView(_:attributedTitleForRow:forComponent:)`
`pickerView(_:viewForRow:forComponent:reusing:)`
> What should this row of this component display? The first row is numbered 0. You can supply a simple string, an attributed string (Chapter 10), or an entire view such as a UILabel; but you should supply every row of every component the same way.
>
> The `reusing:` parameter, if not `nil`, is supposed to be a view that you supplied for a row now no longer visible, giving you a chance to reuse it, much as cells are reused in a table view. In actual fact, the `reusing:` parameter is *always* `nil`. Views don't leak — they go out of existence in good order when they are no longer visible — but they aren't reused. I regard this as a bug.

Figure 12-7. A picker view

Here's the code for a UIPickerView (Figure 12-7) that displays the names of the 50 U.S. states, stored in an array (`self.states`). We implement `pickerView(_:view-ForRow:forComponent:reusing:)` just because it's the most interesting case; as our views, we supply UILabel instances. The state names appear centered because the labels are centered within the picker view:

```
func numberOfComponents(in pickerView: UIPickerView) -> Int {
    return 1
}
func pickerView(_ pickerView: UIPickerView,
    numberOfRowsInComponent component: Int) -> Int {
        return self.states.count
}
func pickerView(_ pickerView: UIPickerView,
    viewForRow row: Int,
    forComponent component: Int,
    reusing view: UIView?) -> UIView {
        let lab = UILabel() // reusable view is always nil
        lab.text = self.states[row]
        lab.backgroundColor = .clear
        lab.sizeToFit()
        return lab
}
```

The delegate may further configure the UIPickerView's physical appearance by means of these methods:

- `pickerView(_:rowHeightForComponent:)`
- `pickerView(_:widthForComponent:)`

The delegate may implement `pickerView(_:didSelectRow:inComponent:)`, so as to be notified each time the user spins a drum to a new position. You can also query the picker view directly by sending it `selectedRow(inComponent:)`.

You can set the value to which any drum is turned using `selectRow(_:in-Component:animated:)`. Other handy picker view methods allow you to request that the data be reloaded, and there are properties and methods to query the picker view's structure:

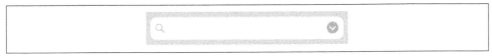

Figure 12-8. A search bar with a search results button

- `reloadComponent(_:)`
- `reloadAllComponents`
- `numberOfComponents`
- `numberOfRows(inComponent:)`
- `view(forRow:forComponent:)`

By implementing `pickerView(_:didSelectRow:inComponent:)` and calling `reload-Component(_:)`, you can make a picker view where the values displayed by one drum depend dynamically on what is selected in another. For example, one can imagine extending our U.S. states example to include a second drum listing major cities in each state; when the user switches to a different state in the first drum, a different set of major cities appears in the second drum.

UISearchBar

A search bar (UISearchBar) is essentially a wrapper for a text field; it has a text field as one of its subviews, though there is no official access to it. It is displayed by default as a rounded rectangle containing a magnifying glass icon, where the user can enter text (Figure 12-8). It does not, of itself, do any searching or display the results of a search; a common interface involves displaying the results of a search in a table view, and the UISearchController class makes this easy to do (see Chapter 8).

A search bar's current text is its `text` property. It can have a `placeholder`, which appears when there is no text. A `prompt` can be displayed above the search bar to explain its purpose. Delegate methods (UISearchBarDelegate) notify you of editing events; for their use, compare the text field and text view delegate methods discussed in Chapter 10:

- `searchBarShouldBeginEditing(_:)`
- `searchBarTextDidBeginEditing(_:)`
- `searchBar(_:textDidChange:)`
- `searchBar(_:shouldChangeTextIn:replacementText:)`
- `searchBarShouldEndEditing(_:)`

- `searchBarTextDidEndEditing(_:)`

A search bar has a `barStyle` (UIBarStyle):

- `.default`, a flat light gray background and a white search field
- `.black`, a black background and a black search field

In addition, there's a `searchBarStyle` property (UISearchBarStyle):

- `.default`, as already described
- `.prominent`, identical to `.default`
- `.minimal`, transparent background and dark transparent search field

Alternatively, you can set a search bar's `barTintColor` to change its background color; if the bar style is `.black`, the `barTintColor` will also tint the search field itself. The `tintColor` property, meanwhile, whose value may be inherited from higher up the view hierarchy, governs the color of search bar components such as the Cancel button title and the flashing insertion cursor.

A search bar can also have a custom `backgroundImage`; this will be treated as a resizable image. The full setter method is `setBackgroundImage(_:for:barMetrics:)`; I'll talk later about what the parameters mean. The `backgroundImage` overrides all other ways of determining the background, and the search bar's `backgroundColor`, if any, appears behind it — though under some circumstances, if the search bar's `isTranslucent` is `false`, the `barTintColor` may appear behind it instead.

The search field area where the user enters text can be offset with respect to its background, using the `searchFieldBackgroundPositionAdjustment` property; you might do this, for example, if you had enlarged the search bar's height and wanted to position the search field within that height. The text can be offset within the search field with the `searchTextPositionAdjustment` property.

You can also replace the image of the search field itself; this is the image that is normally a rounded rectangle. To do so, call `setSearchFieldBackgroundImage(_:for:)`; the second parameter is a UIControlState (even though a search bar is not a control). According to the documentation, the possible states are `.normal` and `.disabled`; but the API provides no way to disable a search field, so what does Apple have in mind here? The only way I've found is to cycle through the search bar's subviews, find the text field, and disable that:

```
    for v in self.sb.subviews[0].subviews {
        if let tf = v as? UITextField {
            tf.isEnabled = false
            break
        }
    }
```

The search field image will be drawn vertically centered in front of the background and behind the contents of the search field (such as the text); its width will be adjusted for you, but it is up to you choose an appropriate height, and to ensure an appropriate background color so that the user can read the text.

A search bar displays an internal cancel button automatically (normally an X in a circle) if there is text in the search field. Internally, at its right end, a search bar may display a search results button (showsSearchResultsButton), which may be selected or not (isSearchResultsButtonSelected), or a bookmark button (showsBookmark-Button); if you ask to display both, you'll get the search results button. These buttons vanish if text is entered in the search bar so that the cancel button can be displayed. There is also an option to display a Cancel button externally (showsCancelButton, or call setShowsCancelButton(_:animated:)). The internal cancel button works automatically to remove whatever text is in the field; the other buttons do nothing, but delegate methods notify you when they are tapped:

- searchBarResultsListButtonClicked(_:)
- searchBarBookmarkButtonClicked(_:)
- searchBarCancelButtonClicked(_:)

You can customize the images used for the search icon (a magnifying glass, by default) and any of the internal right icons (the internal cancel button, the search results button, and the bookmark button) with setImage(_:for:state:). The images will be resized for you, except for the internal cancel button, for which about 20×20 seems to be a good size. The icon in question (the for: parameter) is specified as follows (UISearchBarIcon):

- .search
- .clear (the internal cancel button)
- .bookmark
- .resultsList

The documentation says that the possible state: values are .normal and .disabled, but this is wrong; the choices are .normal and .highlighted. The highlighted image appears while the user taps on the icon (except for the search icon, which isn't a button). If you don't supply a normal image, the default image is used; if you supply a normal image but no highlighted image, the normal image is used for both. Setting isSearchResultsButtonSelected to true reverses the search results button's behavior: it displays the highlighted image, but when the user taps it, it displays the normal image. To change an icon's location, call setPositionAdjustment(_:for:).

A search bar may also display scope buttons. These are intended to let the user alter the meaning of the search; precisely how you use them is up to you. To make the scope buttons appear, use the showsScopeBar property; the button titles are the scope-ButtonTitles property, and the currently selected scope button is the selectedScope-ButtonIndex property. The delegate is notified when the user taps a different scope button:

- searchBar(_:selectedScopeButtonIndexDidChange:)

The overall look of the scope bar can be heavily customized. Its background is the scopeBarBackgroundImage, which will be stretched or tiled as needed. To set the background of the smaller area constituting the actual buttons, call setScopeBar-ButtonBackgroundImage(_:for:); the states (the for: parameter) are .normal and .selected. If you don't supply a separate .selected image, a darkened version of the .normal image is used. If you don't supply a resizable image, the image will be made resizable for you; the runtime decides what region of the image will be stretched behind each button.

The dividers between the buttons are normally vertical lines, but you can customize them as well: call setScopeBarButtonDividerImage(_:forLeftSegmentState:right-SegmentState:). A full complement of dividers consists of three images, one when the buttons on both sides of the divider are normal (unselected) and one each when a button on one side or the other is selected; if you supply an image for just one state combination, it is used for the other two state combinations. The height of the divider image is adjusted for you, but the width is not; you'll normally use an image just a few pixels wide.

The text attributes of the titles of the scope buttons can customized by calling set-ScopeBarButtonTitleTextAttributes(_:for:). The attributes are specified like the attributes dictionary of an NSAttributedString (Chapter 10), but the dictionary keys are typed as String, not as NSAttributedStringKey (I regard that as a bug), so you have to take their raw values.

 It may appear that there is no way to customize the external Cancel button, but in fact, although you've no official direct access to it through the search bar, the Cancel button is a UIBarButtonItem and you can customize it using the UIBar-ButtonItem appearance proxy, discussed later in this chapter.

Figure 12-9. A horrible search bar

By combining the various customization possibilities, a completely unrecognizable search bar of inconceivable ugliness can easily be achieved (Figure 12-9). Let's be careful out there.

The problem of allowing the keyboard to appear without covering the search bar is exactly as for a text field (Chapter 10). Text input properties of the search bar configure its keyboard and typing behavior like a text field as well.

When the user taps the Search key in the keyboard, the delegate is notified, and it is then up to you to dismiss the keyboard (resignFirstResponder) and perform the search:

- searchBarSearchButtonClicked(_:)

A search bar can be embedded in a toolbar or navigation bar as a bar button item's custom view, or in a navigation bar as a titleView. See also the discussion of the new iOS 11 UINavigationItem searchController property in Chapter 8. When used in this way, you may encounter some limitations on the extent to which the search bar's appearance can be customized. Alternatively, a UISearchBar can *itself* function as a top bar, without being inside any other bar. If you use a search bar in this way, you'll want its height to be extended automatically under the status bar; I'll explain later in this chapter how to arrange that.

UIControl

UIControl is a subclass of UIView whose chief purpose is to be the superclass of several further built-in classes (controls) and to endow them with common behavior.

The most important thing that controls have in common is that they automatically track and analyze touch events (Chapter 5) and report them to your code as significant control events by way of action messages. Each control implements some subset of the possible control events. The control events (UIControlEvents) are:

- .touchDown
- .touchDownRepeat

- `.touchDragInside`
- `.touchDragOutside`
- `.touchDragEnter`
- `.touchDragExit`
- `.touchUpInside`
- `.touchUpOutside`
- `.touchCancel`
- `.valueChanged`
- `.editingDidBegin`
- `.editingChanged`
- `.editingDidEnd`
- `.editingDidEndOnExit`
- `.allTouchEvents`
- `.allEditingEvents`
- `.allEvents`

The control events also have informal names that are visible in the Connections inspector when you're editing a nib. I'll mostly use the informal names in the next couple of paragraphs.

Control events fall roughly into three groups: the user has touched the screen (Touch Down, Touch Drag Inside, Touch Up Inside, etc.), edited text (Editing Did Begin, Editing Changed, etc.), or changed the control's value (Value Changed).

Apple's documentation is rather coy about which controls normally emit actions for which control events, so here's a list obtained through experimentation:

UIButton
    All Touch events.

UIDatePicker
    Value Changed.

UIPageControl
    All Touch events, Value Changed.

UIRefreshControl
    Value Changed.

UISegmentedControl
    Value Changed.

Touch Inside and Touch Outside

There is no explicit Touch Down Inside event, because *any* sequence of Touch events begins with Touch Down, which *must* be inside the control. If it weren't, this sequence of touches would not belong to this control, and there would be no control events at all!

When the user taps within a control and starts dragging, the Inside events are triggered even after the drag moves outside the control's bounds. But after a certain distance from the control is exceeded, an invisible boundary is crossed, Touch Drag Exit is triggered, and now Outside events are reported until the drag crosses back within the invisible boundary, at which point Touch Drag Enter is triggered and the Inside events are reported again. In the case of a UIButton, the crossing of this invisible boundary is exactly when the button automatically unhighlights (as the drag exits). Thus, to catch a legitimate button press, you probably want to consider only Touch Up Inside.

For other controls, there may be some slight complications. For example, a UISwitch will unhighlight when a drag reaches a certain distance from it, but the touch is still considered legitimate and can still change the UISwitch's value; therefore, when the user's finger leaves the screen, the UISwitch reports a Touch Up Inside event, even while reporting Touch Drag Outside events.

UISlider
> All Touch events, Value Changed.

UISwitch
> All Touch events, Value Changed.

UIStepper
> All Touch events, Value Changed.

UITextField
> All Touch events except the Up events, and all Editing events (see Chapter 10 for details).

UIControl (generic)
> All Touch events.

A control also has a *primary* control event, a UIControlEvent called `.primaryAction-Triggered`, presumably to save you from having to remember what the primary control event is. The primary control event is Value Changed for all controls except for UIButton, where it is Touch Up Inside, and UITextField, where it is Did End On Exit.

For each control event that you want to hear about, you attach to the control one or more target–action pairs. You can do this in the nib editor or in code.

For any given control, each control event and its target–action pairs form a dispatch table. The following methods and properties permit you to manipulate and query the dispatch table:

- `addTarget(_:action:for:)`
- `removeTarget(_:action:for:)`
- `actions(forTarget:forControlEvent:)`
- `allTargets`
- `allControlEvents` (a bitmask of control events with at least one target–action pair attached)

An action method (the method that will be called on the target when the control event occurs) may adopt any of three signatures, whose parameters are:

- The control and the UIEvent
- The control only
- No parameters

The second signature is by far the most common. It's unlikely that you'd want to dispense altogether with the parameter telling you which control sent the control event. It's equally unlikely that you'd want to examine the original UIEvent that triggered this control event, since control events deliberately shield you from dealing with the nitty-gritty of touches. (I suppose you might, on rare occasions, have some reason to examine the UIEvent's `timestamp`.)

When a control event occurs, the control consults its dispatch table, finds all the target–action pairs associated with that control event, and reports the control event by sending each action message to the corresponding target.

 The action messaging mechanism is actually more complex than I've just stated. The UIControl does not really send the action message directly; rather, it tells the shared application to send it. When a control wants to send an action message reporting a control event, it calls its own `sendAction(_:to:for:)` method. This in turn calls the shared application instance's `sendAction(_:to:from:for:)`, which actually sends the specified action message to the specified target. In theory, you could call or override either of these methods to customize this aspect of the message-sending architecture, but it is extremely unlikely that you would do so.

To make a control emit its action message(s) corresponding to a particular control event right now, in code, call its `sendActions(for:)` method (which is never called automatically by the runtime). For example, suppose you tell a UISwitch programmatically to change its setting from Off to On. This doesn't cause the switch to report a control event, as it would if the *user* had slid the switch from Off to On; if you wanted it to do so, you could use `sendActions(for:)`, like this:

```
self.sw.setOn(true, animated: true)
self.sw.sendActions(for: .valueChanged)
```

You might also use `sendActions(for:)` in a subclass to customize the circumstances under which a control reports control events. I'll give an example later in this chapter.

A control has `isEnabled`, `isSelected`, and `isHighlighted` properties; any of these can be `true` or `false` independently of the others. Together, they correspond to the control's `state`, which is reported as a bitmask of three possible values (UIControl-State):

- `.highlighted`
- `.disabled`
- `.selected`

A fourth state, `.normal`, corresponds to a zero `state` bitmask, and means that `isEnabled` is `true`, and `isSelected` and `isHighlighted` are both `false`.

A control that is not enabled does not respond to user interaction. Whether the control also portrays itself differently, to cue the user to this fact, depends upon the control. For example, a disabled UISwitch is faded; but a rounded rect text field, by default, gives the user no cue that it is disabled. The visual nature of control selection and highlighting, too, depends on the control. Neither highlighting nor selection make any difference to the appearance of a UISwitch, but a highlighted UIButton usually looks quite different from a nonhighlighted UIButton.

A control has `contentHorizontalAlignment` and `contentVerticalAlignment` properties. These matter only if the control has content that can be aligned. You are most likely to use them in connection with a UIButton to position its title and internal image (I'll say more about that later in this chapter).

A text field (UITextField) is a control; see Chapter 10. A refresh control (UIRefresh-Control) is a control; see Chapter 8. The remaining controls are covered here, and then I'll give a simple example of writing your own custom control.

UISwitch

A switch (UISwitch, Figure 12-10) portrays a Bool value: it looks like a sliding switch, and its `isOn` property is either `true` or `false`. The user can slide or tap to toggle the switch's setting. When the user changes the switch's setting, the switch reports a Value Changed control event. To change the `isOn` property's value with accompanying animation, call `setOn(_:animated:)`.

Figure 12-10. A switch

Figure 12-11. A stepper

A switch has only one size; any attempt to set its size will be ignored.

You can customize a switch's appearance by setting these properties:

onTintColor
> The color of the track when the switch is at the On setting.

thumbTintColor
> The color of the slidable button.

tintColor
> The color of the outline when the switch is at the Off setting.

A switch's track when the switch is at the Off setting is transparent, and can't be customized. I regard this as a bug. (Changing the switch's backgroundColor is not a successful workaround, because the background color shows outside the switch's outline.)

> The UISwitch properties onImage and offImage, added in iOS 6 after much clamoring (and hacking) by developers, have no effect in iOS 7 and later.

UIStepper

A stepper (UIStepper, Figure 12-11) lets the user increase or decrease a numeric value: it looks like two buttons side by side, one labeled (by default) with a minus sign, the other with a plus sign. The user can tap or hold a button, and can slide a finger from one button to the other as part of the same interaction with the stepper. It has only one size; any attempt to set its size will be ignored. It maintains a numeric value, which is its value. Each time the user increments or decrements the value, it changes by the stepper's stepValue. If the minimumValue or maximumValue is reached, the user can go no further in that direction, and to show this, the corresponding button is disabled — unless the stepper's wraps property is true, in which case the value goes beyond the maximum by starting again at the minimum, and *vice versa*.

As the user changes the stepper's `value`, a Value Changed control event is reported. Portraying the numeric value itself is up to you; you might, for example, use a label or (as here) a progress view:

```
@IBAction func doStep(_ sender: Any) {
    let step = sender as! UIStepper
    self.prog.setProgress(
        Float(step.value / (step.maximumValue - step.minimumValue)),
        animated:true)
}
```

If a stepper's `isContinuous` is `true` (the default), a long touch on one of the buttons will update the value repeatedly; the updates start slowly and get faster. If the stepper's `autorepeat` is `false`, the updated value is not reported as a Value Changed control event until the entire interaction with the stepper ends; the default is `true`.

The appearance of a stepper can be customized. The color of the outline and the button captions is the stepper's `tintColor`, which may be inherited from further up the view hierarchy. You can also dictate the images that constitute the stepper's structure with these methods:

- `setDecrementImage(_:for:)`
- `setIncrementImage(_:for:)`
- `setDividerImage(_:forLeftSegmentState:rightSegmentState:)`
- `setBackgroundImage(_:for:)`

The images work similarly to a search bar's scope bar (described earlier in this chapter). The background images should probably be resizable. They are stretched behind both buttons, half the image being seen as the background of each button. If the button is disabled (because we've reached the value's limit in that direction), it displays the `.disabled` background image; otherwise, it displays the `.normal` background image, except that it displays the `.highlighted` background image while the user is tapping it. You'll probably want to provide all three background images if you're going to provide any; the default is used if a state's background image is `nil`. You'll probably want to provide three divider images as well, to cover the three combinations of one or neither segment being highlighted. The increment and decrement images, replacing the default minus and plus signs, are composited on top of the background image; they are treated as template images, colored by the `tintColor`, unless you explicitly provide an `.alwaysOriginal` image. If you provide only a `.normal` image, it will be adjusted automatically for the other two states. Figure 12-11 shows a customized stepper.

Figure 12-12. A customized stepper

UIPageControl

A page control (UIPageControl) is a row of dots; each dot is called a *page*, because it is intended to be used in conjunction with some other interface that portrays something analogous to pages, such as a UIScrollView with its `isPagingEnabled` set to `true`. Coordinating the page control with this other interface is usually up to you; see Chapter 7 for an example. A UIPageViewController in scroll style can optionally display a page control that's automatically coordinated with its content (Chapter 6).

The number of dots is the page control's `numberOfPages`. To learn the minimum bounds size required to accommodate a given number of dots, call `size(forNumberOfPages:)`. You can make the page control wider than the dots to increase the target region on which the user can tap. The user can tap to one side or the other of the current page's dot to increment or decrement the current page; the page control then reports a Value Changed control event.

The dot colors differentiate the current page, the page control's `currentPage`, from the others; by default, the current page is portrayed as a solid dot, while the others are slightly transparent. You can customize a page control's `pageIndicatorTintColor` (the color of the dots in general) and `currentPageIndicatorTintColor` (the color of the current page's dot); you will almost certainly want to do this, as the default dot color is white, which under normal circumstances may be hard to see.

It is possible to set a page control's `backgroundColor`; you might do this to show the user the tappable area, or to make the dots more clearly visible by contrast.

If a page control's `hidesForSinglePage` is `true`, the page control becomes invisible when its `numberOfPages` changes to 1.

If a page control's `defersCurrentPageDisplay` is `true`, then when the user taps to increment or decrement the page control's value, the display of the current page is not changed. A Value Changed control event is reported, but it is up to your code to handle this action and call `updateCurrentPageDisplay`. A case in point might be if the user's changing the current page triggers an animation, and you don't want the current page dot to change until the animation ends.

UIDatePicker

A date picker (UIDatePicker) looks like a UIPickerView (discussed earlier in this chapter), but it is not a UIPickerView subclass; it uses a UIPickerView to draw itself, but it provides no official access to that picker view. Its purpose is to express the notion of a date and time, taking care of the calendrical and numerical complexities so that you don't have to. When the user changes its setting, the date picker reports a Value Changed control event.

A UIDatePicker has one of four modes (`datePickerMode`), determining how it is drawn (UIDatePickerMode):

`.time`
> The date picker displays a time; for example, it has an hour component and a minutes component.

`.date`
> The date picker displays a date; for example, it has a month component, a day component, and a year component.

`.dateAndTime`
> The date picker displays a date and time; for example, it has a component showing day of the week, month, and day, plus an hour component and a minutes component.

`.countDownTimer`
> The date picker displays a number of hours and minutes; for example, it has an hours component and a minutes component.

Exactly what components a date picker displays, and what values they contain, depends by default upon the user's preferences in the Settings app (General → Language & Region → Region). For example, a U.S. time displays an hour numbered 1 through 12 plus minutes and AM or PM, but a British time displays an hour numbered 1 through 24 plus minutes. If the user changes the region format in the Settings app, the date picker's display will change immediately.

A date picker has `calendar` and `timeZone` properties, respectively a Calendar and a TimeZone; these are `nil` by default, meaning that the date picker responds to the user's system-level settings. You can also change these values manually; for example, if you live in California and you set a date picker's `timeZone` to GMT, the displayed time is shifted forward by 8 hours, so that 11 AM is displayed as 7 PM (if it is winter).

 Don't change the `timeZone` of a `.countDownTimer` date picker; if you do, the displayed value will be shifted, and you will confuse the heck out of yourself (and your users).

The minutes component, if there is one, defaults to showing every minute, but you can change this with the `minuteInterval` property. The maximum value is 30, in which case the minutes component values are 0 and 30. An attempt to set the `minuteInterval` to a value that doesn't divide evenly into 60 will be silently ignored.

The date represented by a date picker (unless its mode is `.countDownTimer`) is its `date` property, a Date. The default date is now, at the time the date picker is instantiated. For a `.date` date picker, the time by default is 12 AM (midnight), local time; for a `.time` date picker, the date by default is today. The internal value is reckoned in the local time zone, so it may be different from the displayed value, if you have changed the date picker's `timeZone`.

The maximum and minimum values enabled in the date picker are determined by its `maximumDate` and `minimumDate` properties. Values outside this range may appear disabled. There isn't really any practical limit on the range that a date picker can display, because the "drums" representing its components are not physical, and values are added dynamically as the user spins them. In this example, we set the initial minimum and maximum dates of a date picker (dp) to the beginning and end of 1954. We also set the actual `date`, so that the date picker will be set initially to a value within the minimum–maximum range:

```
dp.datePickerMode = .date
var dc = DateComponents(year:1954, month:1, day:1)
let c = Calendar(identifier:.gregorian)
let d1 = c.date(from: dc)!
dp.minimumDate = d1
dp.date = d1
dc.year = 1955
let d2 = c.date(from: dc)!
dp.maximumDate = d2
```

 Don't set the `maximumDate` and `minimumDate` properties values for a `.countDown-Timer` date picker; if you do, you might cause a crash with an out-of-range exception.

To convert between a Date and a string, you'll need a DateFormatter (see Apple's *Date and Time Programming Guide*):

```
@IBAction func dateChanged(_ sender: Any) {
    let dp = sender as! UIDatePicker
    let d = dp.date
    let df = DateFormatter()
    df.timeStyle = .full
    df.dateStyle = .full
    print(df.string(from: d))
    // Tuesday, August 10, 1954 at 3:16:00 AM GMT-07:00
}
```

The value displayed in a `.countDownTimer` date picker is its `countDownDuration`; this is a TimeInterval, which is a Double representing a number of seconds, even though the minimum interval displayed is a minute. A `.countDownTimer` date picker does not actually do any counting down! You are expected to count down in some other way, and to use some other interface to display the countdown. The Timer tab of Apple's

---

Clock app shows a typical interface; the user configures a picker view to set the count-DownDuration initially, but once the counting starts, the picker view is hidden and a label displays the remaining time.

 A nasty bug makes the Value Changed event from a .countDownTimer date picker unreliable (especially just after the app launches, and whenever the user has tried to set the timer to zero). The workaround is not to rely on the Value Changed event; for example, provide a button in the interface that the user can tap to make your code read the date picker's countDownDuration.

UISlider

A slider (UISlider) is an expression of a continuously settable value (its value, a Float) between some minimum and maximum (its minimumValue and maximumValue; they are 0 and 1 by default). It is portrayed as an object, the *thumb*, positioned along a *track*. As the user changes the thumb's position, the slider reports a Value Changed control event; it may do this continuously as the user presses and drags the thumb (if the slider's isContinuous is true, the default) or only when the user releases the thumb (if isContinuous is false). While the user is pressing on the thumb, the slider is in the .highlighted state. To change a slider's value with animation of the thumb, call setValue(_:animated:) *in an animations function*; I'll show an example in a moment.

A commonly expressed desire is to modify a slider's behavior so that if the user taps on its track, the slider moves to the spot where the user tapped. Unfortunately, a slider does not, of itself, respond to taps on its track; no control event is reported. However, with a gesture recognizer, most things are possible; here's the action method for a UITapGestureRecognizer attached to a UISlider:

```
@objc func tapped(_ g:UIGestureRecognizer) {
    let s = g.view as! UISlider
    if s.isHighlighted {
        return // tap on thumb, let slider deal with it
    }
    let pt = g.location(in:s)
    let track = s.trackRect(forBounds: s.bounds)
    if !track.insetBy(dx: 0, dy: -10).contains(pt) {
        return // not on track, forget it
    }
    let percentage = pt.x / s.bounds.size.width
    let delta = Float(percentage) * (s.maximumValue - s.minimumValue)
    let value = s.minimumValue + delta
    delay(0.1) {
        UIView.animate(withDuration: 0.15) {
```

Figure 12-13. Repositioning a slider's images and track

```
                s.setValue(value, animated:true) // animate sliding the thumb
        }
    }
}
```

A slider's `tintColor` (which may be inherited from further up the view hierarchy) determines the color of the track to the left of the thumb. You can change the color of the thumb with the `thumbTintColor` property. You can change the color of the two parts of the track with the `minimumTrackTintColor` and `maximumTrackTintColor` properties.

The images at the ends of the track are the slider's `minimumValueImage` and `maximumValueImage`, and they are `nil` by default. If you set them to actual images (which can also be done in the nib editor), the slider will attempt to position them within its own bounds, shrinking the drawing of the track to compensate. You can change that behavior by overriding these methods in a subclass:

- `minimumValueImageRect(forBounds:)`
- `maximumValueImageRect(forBounds:)`
- `trackRect(forBounds:)`

The bounds passed in are the slider's bounds. In this example (Figure 12-13), we expand the track width to the full width of the slider, and draw the images outside the slider's bounds. The images are still visible, because the slider does not clip its subviews to its bounds. In the figure, I've given the slider a background color so you can see how the track and images are related to its bounds:

```
override func maximumValueImageRect(forBounds bounds: CGRect) -> CGRect {
    return super.maximumValueImageRect(
        forBounds:bounds).offsetBy(dx: 31, dy: 0)
}
override func minimumValueImageRect(forBounds bounds: CGRect) -> CGRect {
    return super.minimumValueImageRect(
        forBounds: bounds).offsetBy(dx: -31, dy: 0)
}
override func trackRect(forBounds bounds: CGRect) -> CGRect {
    var result = super.trackRect(forBounds: bounds)
    result.origin.x = 0
    result.size.width = bounds.size.width
    return result
}
```

Figure 12-14. Replacing a slider's thumb

The thumb is also an image, and you set it with setThumbImage(_:for:). There are two chiefly relevant states, .normal and .highlighted. If you supply images for both, the thumb will change automatically while the user is dragging it. By default, the image will be centered in the track at the point represented by the slider's current value; you can shift this position by overriding thumbRect(forBounds:track-Rect:value:) in a subclass. In this example, the image is repositioned slightly upward (Figure 12-14):

```
override func thumbRect(forBounds bounds: CGRect,
    trackRect rect: CGRect, value: Float) -> CGRect {
        return super.thumbRect(forBounds: bounds,
            trackRect: rect, value: value).offsetBy(dx: 0, dy: -7)
}
```

Enlarging or offsetting a slider's thumb can mislead the user as to the area on which it can be touched to drag it. The slider, not the thumb, is the touchable UIControl; only the part of the thumb that intersects the slider's bounds will be draggable. The user may try to drag the part of the thumb that is drawn outside the slider's bounds, and will fail (and be confused). One solution is to increase the slider's height; if you're using autolayout, you can add an explicit height constraint in the nib editor, or override intrinsicContentSize in code (Chapter 1). Another solution is to subclass and use hit-test munging (Chapter 5):

```
override func hitTest(_ point: CGPoint, with e: UIEvent?) -> UIView? {
    let tr = self.trackRect(forBounds: self.bounds)
    if tr.contains(point) { return self }
    let r = self.thumbRect(
        forBounds: self.bounds, trackRect: tr, value: self.value)
    if r.contains(point) { return self }
    return nil
}
```

The track is two images, one appearing to the left of the thumb, the other to its right. They are set with setMinimumTrackImage(_:for:) and setMaximumTrack-Image(_:for:). If you supply images both for .normal state and for .highlighted state, the images will change while the user is dragging the thumb. The images should be resizable, because that's how the slider cleverly makes it look like the user is dragging the thumb along a single static track. In reality, there are two images; as the user drags the thumb, one image grows horizontally and the other shrinks horizontally. For the left track image, the right end cap inset will be partially or entirely hidden under the thumb; for the right track image, the left end cap inset will be partially or

Figure 12-15. Replacing a slider's track

Figure 12-16. A segmented control

entirely hidden under the thumb. Figure 12-15 shows a track derived from a single 15×15 image of a circular object (a coin):

```
let coinEnd = UIImage(named:"coin")!.resizableImage(withCapInsets:
    UIEdgeInsetsMake(0,7,0,7), resizingMode: .stretch)
self.setMinimumTrackImage(coinEnd, for:.normal)
self.setMaximumTrackImage(coinEnd, for:.normal)
```

UISegmentedControl

A segmented control (UISegmentedControl, Figure 12-16) is a row of tappable segments; a segment is rather like a button. The user taps a segment to choose among options. By default (`isMomentary` is `false`), the most recently tapped segment remains selected. Alternatively (`isMomentary` is `true`), the tapped segment is shown as highlighted momentarily (by default, highlighted is indistinguishable from selected, but you can change that); afterward, no segment selection is displayed, though internally the tapped segment remains the selected segment.

The selected segment can be set and retrieved with the `selectedSegmentIndex` property; when you set it in code, the selected segment remains visibly selected, even for an `isMomentary` segmented control. A `selectedSegmentIndex` value of `UISegmentedControlNoSegment` means no segment is selected. When the user taps a segment that isn't already visibly selected, the segmented control reports a Value Changed event.

A segmented control's change of selection is animatable; change the selection *in an animations function*, like this:

```
UIView.animateWithDuration(0.4, animations: {
    self.seg.selectedSegmentIndex = 1
})
```

To animate the change more slowly when the user taps on a segment, set the segmented control's layer's `speed` to a fractional value.

A segment can be separately enabled or disabled with `setEnabled(_:forSegment-At:)`, and its enabled state can be retrieved with `isEnabledForSegment(at:)`. A disabled segment, by default, is drawn faded; the user can't tap it, but it can still be selected in code.

The color of a segmented control's outline and selection are dictated by its `tintColor`, which may be inherited from further up the view hierarchy.

A segment has either a title or an image; when one is set, the other becomes `nil`. An image is treated as a template image, colored by the `tintColor`, unless you explicitly provide an `.alwaysOriginal` image. The title is colored by the `tintColor` unless you set its attributes to include a different color (as I'll explain later). The methods for setting and fetching the title and image for existing segments are:

- `setTitle(_:forSegmentAt:)`, `titleForSegment(at:)`
- `setImage(_:forSegmentAt:)`, `imageForSegment(at:)`

If you're creating the segmented control in code, configure the segments with `init(items:)`, which takes an array, each item being either a string or an image:

```
let seg = UISegmentedControl(items:
    [UIImage(named:"one")!.withRenderingMode(.alwaysOriginal), "Two"])
seg.frame.origin = CGPoint(30,30)
self.view.addSubview(seg)
```

Methods for managing segments dynamically are:

- `insertSegment(withTitle:at:animated:)`
- `insertSegment(with:at:animated:)` (the parameter is a UIImage)
- `removeSegment(at:animated:)`
- `removeAllSegments`

The number of segments can be retrieved with the read-only `numberOfSegments` property.

If the segmented control's `apportionsSegmentWidthsByContent` property is `false`, segment sizes will be made equal to one another; if it is `true`, each segment's width will be sized individually to fit its content. Alternatively, you can set a segment's width explicitly with `setWidth(_:forSegmentAt:)` (and retrieve it with `widthFor-Segment(at:)`); setting a segment's width to 0 means that this segment is to be sized automatically.

A segmented control has a standard height; if you're using autolayout, you can change the height through constraints or by overriding `intrinsicContentSize` — or by setting its background image, as I'll describe in a moment. A segmented control's height does *not* automatically increase to accommodate a segment image that's too tall; instead, the image's height is squashed to fit the segmented control's height.

Figure 12-17. A segmented control, customized

To change the position of the content (title or image) within a segment, call `set-ContentOffset(_:forSegmentAt:)` (and retrieve it with `contentOffsetFor-Segment(at:)`).

Further methods for customizing a segmented control's appearance are parallel to those for setting the look of a stepper or the scope bar portion of a search bar, both described earlier in this chapter. You can set the overall background, the divider image, the text attributes for the segment titles, and the position of segment contents:

- `setBackgroundImage(_:for:barMetrics:)`
- `setDividerImage(_:forLeftSegmentState:rightSegmentState:barMetrics:)`
- `setTitleTextAttributes(_:for:)`
- `setContentPositionAdjustment(_:forSegmentType:barMetrics:)`

You don't have to customize for every state, as the segmented control will use the `.normal` state setting for the states you don't specify. As I mentioned a moment ago, setting a background image changes the segmented control's height. In the last method, the `segmentType:` parameter is needed because, by default, the segments at the two extremes have rounded ends (and, if a segment is the lone segment, both its ends are rounded); the argument (UISegmentedControlSegment) allows you distinguish between the various possibilities:

- `.any`
- `.left`
- `.center`
- `.right`
- `.alone`

Figure 12-17 shows a heavily customized segmented control.

UIButton

A button (UIButton) is a fundamental tappable control, which may contain a title, an image, and a background image (and may have a `backgroundColor`). A button has a type, and the initializer is `init(type:)`. The types (UIButtonType) are:

`.system`

The title text appears in the button's `tintColor`, which may be inherited from further up the view hierarchy; when the button is tapped, the title text color momentarily changes to a color derived from what's behind it (which might be the button's `backgroundColor`). The image is treated as a template image, colored by the `tintColor`, unless you explicitly provide an `.alwaysOriginal` image; when the button is tapped, the image (even if it isn't a template image) is momentarily tinted to a color derived from what's behind it.

`.detailDisclosure, .infoLight, .infoDark, .contactAdd`

Basically, these are all `.system` buttons whose image is set automatically to a standard image. The first three are an "i" in a circle, and the last is a Plus in a circle; the two `info` types are identical, and they differ from `.detailDisclosure` only in that their `showsTouchWhenHighlighted` is `true` by default.

`.custom`

There's no automatic coloring of the title or image, and the image is a normal image by default.

There is no built-in button type with an outline (border), comparable to the Rounded Rect style of iOS 6 and before. You can provide an outline by using a background color or a background image, along with some manipulation of the button's layer, as in Figure 12-20.

A button has a title, a title color, and a title shadow color — or you can supply an attributed title, thus dictating these features and more in a single value through an NSAttributedString (Chapter 10).

Distinguish a button's image, which is an internal image, from its background image. The background image, if any, is stretched, if necessary, to fill the button's bounds (technically, its `backgroundRect(forBounds:)`). The internal image, on the other hand, if smaller than the button, is not resized. The button can have both a title and an image, provided the image is small enough, in which case the image is shown to the left of the title by default; if the image is too large, the title won't appear.

These six features — title, title color, title shadow color, attributed title, image, and background image — can all be made to vary depending on the button's current state: `.highlighted`, `.selected`, `.disabled`, and `.normal`. The button can be in more than one state at once, except for `.normal` which means "none of the other states." A state change, whether automatic (the button is highlighted while the user is tapping it) or programmatically imposed, will thus in and of itself alter a button's appearance. The methods for setting these button features, therefore, all involve specifying a corresponding state — or multiple states, using a bitmask:

- `setTitle(_:for:)`

- setTitleColor(_:for:)
- setTitleShadowColor(_:for:)
- setAttributedTitle(_:for:)
- setImage(_:for:)
- setBackgroundImage(_:for:)

Similarly, when getting these button features, you must either specify a single state you're interested in or ask about the feature as currently displayed:

- title(for:), currentTitle
- titleColor(for:), currentTitleColor
- titleShadowColor(for:), currentTitleShadowColor
- attributedTitle(for:), currentAttributedTitle
- image(for:), currentImage
- backgroundImage(for:), currentBackgroundImage

If you don't specify a feature for a particular state, or if the button adopts more than one state at once, an internal heuristic is used to determine what to display. I can't describe all possible combinations, but here are some general observations:

- If you specify a feature for a particular state (highlighted, selected, or disabled), and the button is in *only* that state, that feature will be used.
- If you *don't* specify a feature for a particular state (highlighted, selected, or disabled), and the button is in *only* that state, the normal version of that feature will be used as fallback. (That's why many examples earlier in this book have assigned a title for .normal only; that's sufficient to give the button a title in every state.)
- Combinations of states often cause the button to fall back on the feature for normal state. For example, if a button is both highlighted and selected, the button will display its normal title, even if it has a highlighted title, a selected title, or both.

A .system button with an attributed normal title will tint the title to the tintColor if you don't give the attributed string a color, and will tint the title while highlighted to the color derived from what's behind the button if you haven't supplied a highlighted title with its own color. But a .custom button will not do any of that; it leaves control of the title color for each state completely up to you.

In addition, a UIButton has some properties determining how it draws itself in various states, which can save you the trouble of specifying different images for different states:

showsTouchWhenHighlighted

If `true`, then the button projects a circular white glow when highlighted. If the button has an internal image, the glow is centered behind it. Thus, this feature is suitable particularly if the button image is small and circular; for example, it's the default behavior for an `.infoLight` or `.infoDark` button. If the button has no internal image, the glow is centered at the button's center. The glow is drawn on top of the background image or color, if any.

adjustsImageWhenHighlighted

In a `.custom` button, if this property is `true` (the default), then if there is no separate highlighted image (and if `showsTouchWhenHighlighted` is `false`), the normal image is darkened when the button is highlighted. This applies equally to the internal image and the background image. (A `.system` button is already tinting its highlighted image, so this property doesn't apply.)

adjustsImageWhenDisabled

If `true`, then if there is no separate disabled image, the normal image is shaded when the button is disabled. This applies equally to the internal image and the background image. The default is `true` for a `.custom` button and `false` for a `.system` button.

A button has a natural size in relation to its contents. If you're using autolayout, the button can adopt that size automatically as its `intrinsicContentSize`, and you can modify the way it does this by overriding `intrinsicContentSize` in a subclass or by applying explicit constraints. If you're not using autolayout and you create a button in code, send it `sizeToFit` or give it an explicit size; otherwise, the button may have size `.zero`. Creating a zero-size button and then wondering why the button isn't visible in the interface is a common beginner mistake.

The title is displayed in a UILabel (Chapter 10), and the label features of the title can be accessed through the button's `titleLabel`. For example, beginners often wonder how to make a button's title consist of more than one line; the answer is obvious, once you remember that the title is displayed in a label: set the button's `title-Label.numberOfLines`. In general, the label's properties may be set, provided they do not conflict with existing UIButton features. For example, you can use the label to set the title's `font` and `shadowOffset`; but the title's text, color, and shadow color should be set using the appropriate button methods specifying a button state. If the title is given a shadow in this way, then the button's `reversesTitleShadowWhenHighlighted` property also applies: if `true`, the `shadowOffset` values are replaced with their additive inverses when the button is highlighted. The modern way, however, is to do that sort of thing through the button's attributed title.

The internal image is drawn by a UIImageView (Chapter 2), whose features can be accessed through the button's `imageView`. Thus, for example, you can change the internal image view's `alpha` to make the image more transparent.

The internal position of the image and title as a whole are governed by the button's `contentVerticalAlignment` and `contentHorizontalAlignment` (inherited from UIControl). You can also tweak the position of the image and title, together or separately, by setting the button's `contentEdgeInsets`, `titleEdgeInsets`, or `imageEdgeInsets`. Increasing an inset component increases that margin; thus, for example, a positive `top` component makes the distance between that object and the top of the button larger than normal (where "normal" is where the object would be according to the alignment settings). The `titleEdgeInsets` or `imageEdgeInsets` values are added to the overall `contentEdgeInsets` values. So, for example, if you really wanted to, you could make the internal image appear to the right of the title by decreasing the left `titleEdgeInsets` and increasing the left `imageEdgeInsets`.

Four methods also provide access to the button's positioning of its elements:

- `titleRect(forContentRect:)`
- `imageRect(forContentRect:)`
- `contentRect(forBounds:)`
- `backgroundRect(forBounds:)`

These methods are called whenever the button is redrawn, including every time it changes state. The content rect is the area in which the title and image are placed. By default, the content rect and the background rect are the same. You can override these methods in a subclass to change the way the button's elements are positioned.

Here's an example of a customized button (Figure 12-18). In a UIButton subclass, we increase the button's `intrinsicContentSize` to give it larger margins around its content, and we configure the background rect to shrink the button slightly when highlighted as a way of providing feedback (for `sizeByDelta`, see Appendix B):

```
override func backgroundRect(forBounds bounds: CGRect) -> CGRect {
    var result = super.backgroundRect(forBounds:bounds)
    if self.isHighlighted {
        result = result.insetBy(dx: 3, dy: 3)
    }
    return result
}
override var intrinsicContentSize : CGSize {
    return super.intrinsicContentSize.sizeByDelta(dw:25, dh: 20)
}
```

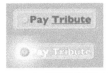

Figure 12-18. A custom button

The button, which is a `.custom` button, is assigned an internal image and a background image from the same resizable image, along with attributed titles for the `.normal` and `.highlighted` states. The internal image glows when highlighted, thanks to `adjustsImageWhenHighlighted`.

Custom Controls

If you create your own UIControl subclass, you automatically get the built-in Touch events; in addition, there are several methods that you can override in order to customize touch tracking, along with properties that tell you whether touch tracking is going on:

- `beginTracking(_:with:)`
- `continueTracking(_:with:)`
- `endTracking(_:with:)`
- `cancelTracking(with:)`
- `isTracking`
- `isTouchInside`

The main reason for using a custom UIControl subclass — rather than, say, a UIView subclass and gesture recognizers — would probably be to obtain the convenience of control events. Also, the touch-tracking methods, though not as high-level as gesture recognizers, are at least a level up from the UIResponder touch methods (Chapter 5): they track a single touch, and both `beginTracking` and `continueTracking` return a Bool, giving you a chance to stop tracking the current touch.

Here's a simple example. We'll build a simplified knob control (Figure 12-19). The control starts life at its minimum position, with an internal angle value of 0; it can be rotated clockwise with a single finger as far as its maximum position, with an internal angle value of 5 (radians). To keep things simple, the words "Min" and "Max" appearing in the interface are actually labels; the control just draws the knob, and to rotate it we'll apply a rotation transform.

Our control is a UIControl subclass, MyKnob. It has a public CGFloat `angle` property, and a private CGFloat property `self.initialAngle` that we'll use internally

Figure 12-19. A custom control

during rotation. Because a UIControl is a UIView, it can draw itself, which it does with an image file included in our app bundle:

```
override func draw(_ rect: CGRect) {
    UIImage(named:"knob")!.draw(in: rect)
}
```

We'll need a utility function for transforming a touch's Cartesian coordinates into polar coordinates, giving us the angle to be applied as a rotation to the view:

```
func pToA (_ t:UITouch) -> CGFloat {
    let loc = t.location(in: self)
    let c = CGPoint(self.bounds.midX, self.bounds.midY)
    return atan2(loc.y - c.y, loc.x - c.x)
}
```

Now we're ready to override the tracking methods. beginTracking simply notes down the angle of the initial touch location. continueTracking uses the difference between the current touch location's angle and the initial touch location's angle to apply a transform to the view, and updates the angle property. endTracking triggers the Value Changed control event. So our first draft looks like this:

```
override func beginTracking(_ t: UITouch, with _: UIEvent?) -> Bool {
    self.initialAngle = pToA(t)
    return true
}
override func continueTracking(_ t: UITouch, with _: UIEvent?) -> Bool {
    let ang = pToA(t) - self.initialAngle
    let absoluteAngle = self.angle + ang
    self.transform = self.transform.rotated(by: ang)
    self.angle = absoluteAngle
    return true
}
override func endTracking(_: UITouch?, with _: UIEvent?) {
    self.sendActions(for: .valueChanged)
}
```

This works: we can put a MyKnob into the interface and hook up its Value Changed control event (this can be done in the nib editor), and sure enough, when we run the

---

app, we can rotate the knob and, when our finger lifts from the knob, the Value Changed action method is called.

However, our class needs modification. When the `angle` is set programmatically, we should respond by rotating the knob; at the same time, we need to clamp the incoming value to the allowable minimum or maximum:

```
var angle : CGFloat = 0 {
    didSet {
        self.angle = min(max(self.angle, 0), 5) // clamp
        self.transform = CGAffineTransform(rotationAngle: self.angle)
    }
}
```

Now we should revise `continueTracking`. We no longer need to perform the rotation, since setting the angle will do that for us. On the other hand, we do need to clamp the gesture when the minimum or maximum rotation is exceeded. My solution is simply to stop tracking; in that case, `endTracking` will never be called, so we also need to trigger the Value Changed control event. Also, it might be nice to give the programmer the option to have the Value Changed control event reported continuously as `continueTracking` is called repeatedly; so we'll add a public `isContinuous` Bool property and obey it:

```
override func continueTracking(_ t: UITouch, with _: UIEvent?) -> Bool {
    let ang = pToA(t) - self.initialAngle
    let absoluteAngle = self.angle + ang
    switch absoluteAngle {
    case -CGFloat.infinity...0:
        self.angle = 0
        self.sendActions(for: .valueChanged)
        return false
    case 5...CGFloat.infinity:
        self.angle = 5
        self.sendActions(for: .valueChanged)
        return false
    default:
        self.angle = absoluteAngle
        if self.isContinuous {
            self.sendActions(for: .valueChanged)
        }
        return true
    }
}
```

Bars

There are three bar types: navigation bar (UINavigationBar), toolbar (UIToolbar), and tab bar (UITabBar). They can be used independently, but are often used in conjunction with a built-in view controller (Chapter 6):

UINavigationBar

> A navigation bar should appear only at the top of the screen. It is usually used in conjunction with a UINavigationController.

UIToolbar

> A toolbar may appear at the bottom or at the top of the screen, though the bottom is more common. It is usually used in conjunction with a UINavigation-Controller, where it appears at the bottom.

UITabBar

> A tab bar should appear only at the bottom of the screen. It is usually used in conjunction with a UITabBarController.

This section summarizes the facts about the three bar types — along with UISearch-Bar, which can act independently as a top bar — and about the items that populate them.

Bar Position and Bar Metrics

If a bar is to occupy the top of the screen, its apparent height should be increased to underlap the transparent status bar. This is taken care of for you in the case of a UINavigationBar owned by a UINavigationController; otherwise, it's up to you. To make this possible, iOS provides the notion of a *bar position*. The UIBarPositioning protocol, adopted by UINavigationBar, UIToolbar, and UISearchBar (the bars that can go at the top of the screen), defines one property, `barPosition`, whose possible values (UIBarPosition) are:

- `.any`
- `.bottom`
- `.top`
- `.topAttached`

But `barPosition` is read-only, so how are you supposed to set it? Use the bar's delegate! The delegate protocols UINavigationBarDelegate, UIToolbarDelegate, and UISearchBarDelegate all conform to UIBarPositioningDelegate, which defines one method, `position(for:)`. This provides a way for a bar's delegate to dictate the bar's `barPosition`:

```
class ViewController: UIViewController, UINavigationBarDelegate {
    @IBOutlet weak var navbar: UINavigationBar!
    override func viewDidLoad() {
        super.viewDidLoad()
        self.navbar.delegate = self
    }
```

```
func position(for bar: UIBarPositioning) -> UIBarPosition {
    return .topAttached
}
}
```

The bar's apparent height will be extended upward so as to underlap the status bar if the bar's delegate returns `.topAttached` from its implementation of `position(for:)`. To get the final position right, the bar's top should also have a zero-length constraint to the safe area layout guide's top.

By the same token, new in iOS 11, a toolbar or tab bar whose bottom has a zero-length constraint to the safe area layout guide bottom will have its apparent height extended downward behind the home indicator on the iPhone X.

 I say that a bar's *apparent* height is extended, because in fact its height remains untouched. It is *drawn* extended, and this drawing is visible because the bar's `clipsToBounds` is `false`. For this reason (and others), you should not set a bar's `clipsToBounds` to `true`.

A bar's height is reflected also by its *bar metrics*. This refers to a change in the standard height of the bar in response to a change in the orientation of the app. This change is *not* a behavior of the bar itself; rather, it is performed automatically by a parent view controller in a `.compact` horizontal size class environment:

UINavigationController
A UINavigationController adjusts the heights of its navigation bar and toolbar to be 44 (`.regular` vertical size class) or 32 (`.compact` vertical size class).

UITabBarController
New in iOS 11, a UITabBarController adjusts the height of its tab bar to be 49 (`.regular` vertical size class) or 32 (`.compact` vertical size class).

Possible bar metrics values are (UIBarMetrics):

- `.default`
- `.compact`
- `.defaultPrompt`
- `.compactPrompt`

The `compact` metrics apply in a `.compact` vertical size class environment. The `prompt` metrics apply to a bar whose height is extended downward to accommodate prompt text (and to a search bar whose scope buttons are showing).

When you're customizing a feature of a bar (or a bar button item), you may find yourself calling a method that takes a bar metrics parameter, and possibly a bar position parameter as well. The idea is that you can customize that feature differently depending on the bar position and the bar metrics. But you don't have to set that value for *every* possible combination of bar position and bar metrics; in general (though, unfortunately, the details are a little inconsistent), `UIBarPosition.any` and `UIBarMetrics.default` are treated as defaults that encompass any positions and metrics you don't specify.

Bar Appearance

A bar can be styled at three levels:

`barStyle, isTranslucent`
> The `barStyle` options are (UIBarStyle):
>
> - `.default` (flat white)
> - `.black` (flat black)
>
> The `isTranslucent` property turns on or off the characteristic blurry translucency.

`barTintColor`
> This property tints the bar with a solid color.

`backgroundImage`
> The background image is set with `setBackgroundImage(_:for:barMetrics:)`. If the image is too large, it is sized down to fit; if it is too small, it is tiled by default, but you can change that behavior by supplying a resizable image. If a bar's `isTranslucent` is `false`, then the `barTintColor` may appear behind the background image, but if its `isTranslucent` is `true`, the bar is transparent behind the image.

The degree of translucency and the interpretation of the bar tint color may vary from system to system and even from device to device, so the color you specify might not be quite the color you see. An opaque background image, however, is a reliable way to color a bar.

A UINavigationController uses the navigation bar's `barStyle` in its implementation of `preferredStatusBarStyle`. A `barStyle` of `.default` results in a status bar style of `.default` (dark text); a `barStyle` of `.black` results in a status bar style of `.lightContent` (light text). Even if you are setting the navigation bar's appearance in some other way, you might want to set its bar style as a way of setting the status bar's text color.

If you assign a bar a background image, you can also customize its shadow, which is cast from the bottom of the bar (if the bar is at the top) or the top of the bar (if the bar is at the bottom) on whatever is behind it. To do so, set the `shadowImage` property

---

— except that a toolbar can be either at the top or the bottom, so its setter is set-ShadowImage(_:forToolbarPosition:), and the UIBarPosition determines whether the shadow should appear at the top or the bottom of the toolbar.

You'll want a shadow image to be very small and very transparent; the image will be tiled horizontally. You won't see the shadow if the bar's clipsToBounds is true. Here's an example for a navigation bar:

```
do { // must set the background image if you want a shadow image
    let sz = CGSize(20,20)
    let r = UIGraphicsImageRenderer(size:sz)
    self.navbar.setBackgroundImage( r.image { ctx in
        UIColor(white:0.95, alpha:0.85).setFill()
        ctx.fill(CGRect(0,0,20,20))
    }, for:.any, barMetrics: .default)
}
do { // now we can set the shadow image
    let sz = CGSize(4,4)
    let r = UIGraphicsImageRenderer(size:sz)
    self.navbar.shadowImage = r.image { ctx in
        UIColor.gray.withAlphaComponent(0.3).setFill()
        ctx.fill(CGRect(0,0,4,2))
        UIColor.gray.withAlphaComponent(0.15).setFill()
        ctx.fill(CGRect(0,2,4,2))
    }
}
```

UIBarButtonItem

You don't add subviews to a bar; instead, you populate the bar with *bar items*. For a toolbar or navigation bar, these will be bar button items (UIBarButtonItem, a subclass of UIBarItem). A bar button item is not a UIView, but you can still put an arbitrary view into a bar, because a bar button item can contain a custom view.

A bar button item may be instantiated with any of five methods:

- init(barButtonSystemItem:target:action:)
- init(title:style:target:action:)
- init(image:style:target:action:)
- init(image:landscapeImagePhone:style:target:action:)
- init(customView:)

The style: options (UIBarButtonItemStyle) are .plain and .done; the only difference is that .done title text is bold.

A bar button item's image is treated by default as a template image, unless you explicitly provide an .alwaysOriginal image.

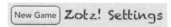

Figure 12-20. A bar button item with a border

Many aspects of a bar button item can be made dependent upon the bar metrics of the containing bar. For example, you can initialize a bar button item with both an image and a landscapeImagePhone, the latter to be used when the bar metrics has compact in its name. A bar button item inherits from UIBarItem the ability to adjust the image position with imageInsets (and landscapeImagePhoneInsets), plus the isEnabled and tag properties.

You can set a bar button item's width property; new in iOS 11, if a bar button item has a custom view, you can size the view from the inside out using constraints.

A bar button item's tintColor property tints the title text or template image of the button; it is inherited from the tintColor of the bar, or you can override it for an individual bar button item.

You can apply an attributes dictionary to a bar button item's title, and you can give a bar button item a background image:

- setTitleTextAttributes(_:for:) (inherited from UIBarItem)
- setTitlePositionAdjustment(_:for:)
- setBackgroundImage(_:for:barMetrics:)
- setBackgroundImage(_:for:style:barMetrics:)
- setBackgroundVerticalPositionAdjustment(_:for:)

In addition, these methods apply only if the bar button item is being used as a back button item in a navigation bar (as I'll describe in the next section):

- setBackButtonTitlePositionAdjustment(_:for:)
- setBackButtonBackgroundImage(_:for:barMetrics:)
- setBackButtonBackgroundVerticalPositionAdjustment(_:for:)

No bar button item style supplies an outline (border). (The .bordered style is deprecated, and its appearance is identical to .plain.) If you want an outline, you have to supply it yourself. For the left bar button item in the settings view of my Zotz! app (Figure 12-20), I use a custom view that's a UIButton with a background image.

UINavigationBar

A navigation bar (UINavigationBar) is populated by navigation items (UINavigation-Item). The UINavigationBar maintains a stack; UINavigationItems are pushed onto and popped off of this stack. Whatever UINavigationItem is currently topmost in the stack (the UINavigationBar's `topItem`), in combination with the UINavigationItem just beneath it in the stack (the UINavigationBar's `backItem`), determines what appears in the navigation bar:

`title`, `titleView`

> The `title` (string) or `titleView` (UIView) of the `topItem` appears in the center of the navigation bar. New in iOS 11, you can size the `titleView` from the inside out using constraints.

`prefersLargeTitles`

> New in iOS 11, allows the `title` to appear by itself at the bottom of the navigation bar, which will appear extended downward to accommodate it. In that case, both the `title` and the `titleView` can appear simultaneously. Whether the title will in fact be displayed in this way depends upon the navigation item's `large-TitleDisplayMode` — `.always`, `.never`, or `.automatic` (inherited from further down the stack).

`prompt`

> The `prompt` (string) appears at the top of the navigation bar, whose height increases to accommodate it.

`rightBarButtonItem`, `rightBarButtonItems`
`leftBarButtonItem`, `leftBarButtonItems`

> The `rightBarButtonItem` and `leftBarButtonItem` appear at the right and left ends of the navigation bar. A UINavigationItem can have multiple right bar button items and multiple left bar button items; its `rightBarButtonItems` and `left-BarButtonItems` properties are arrays (of bar button items). The bar button items are displayed from the outside in: that is, the first item in the `leftBar-ButtonItems` is leftmost, while the first item in the `rightBarButtonItems` is rightmost. If there are multiple buttons on a side, the `rightBarButtonItem` is the first item of the `rightBarButtonItems` array, and the `leftBarButtonItem` is the first item of the `leftBarButtonItems` array.

`backBarButtonItem`

> The `backBarButtonItem` *of the backItem* appears at the left end of the navigation bar. It is automatically configured so that, when tapped, the `topItem` is popped off the stack. If the `backItem` has no `backBarButtonItem`, then there is *still* a back button at the left end of the navigation bar, taking its title from the `title` of the `backItem`. However, if the `topItem` has its `hidesBackButton` set to `true`, the back

Figure 12-21. A back button animating to the left

button is suppressed. Also, unless the `topItem` has its `leftItemsSupplementBack-Button` set to `true`, the back button is suppressed if the `topItem` has a `leftBar-ButtonItem`.

The indication that the back button *is* a back button is supplied by the navigation bar's `backIndicatorImage`, which by default is a left-pointing chevron appearing to the left of the back button. You can customize this image; the image that you supply is treated as a template image by default. If you set the `backIndicatorImage`, you must also supply a `backIndicatorTransitionMaskImage`. The purpose of the mask image is to indicate the region where the back button should disappear as it slides out to the left when a new navigation item is pushed onto the stack. For example, in Figure 12-21, the back button title, which is sliding out to the left, is visible to the right of the chevron but not to the left of the chevron; that's because on the left side of the chevron it is masked out.

In this example, I replace the chevron with a vertical bar. The vertical bar is not the entire image; the image is actually a wider rectangle, with the vertical bar *at its right side*. The mask is the entire wider rectangle, and is completely transparent; thus, the back button disappears as it passes behind the bar and stays invisible as it continues on to the left:

```
let sz = CGSize(10,20)
self.navbar.backIndicatorImage =
    UIGraphicsImageRenderer(size:sz).image { ctx in
        ctx.fill(CGRect(6,0,4,20))
    }
self.navbar.backIndicatorTransitionMaskImage =
    UIGraphicsImageRenderer(size:sz).image {_ in}
```

Changes to the navigation bar's buttons can be animated by sending its `topItem` any of these messages:

- `setRightBarButton(_:animated:)`
- `setLeftBarButton(_:animated:)`
- `setRightBarButtonItems(_:animated:)`
- `setLeftBarButtonItems(_:animated:)`
- `setHidesBackButton(_:animated:)`

Figure 12-22. A navigation bar

UINavigationItems are pushed and popped with `pushItem(_:animated:)` and `pop-ItemAnimated(_:)`, or you can call `setItems(_:animated:)` to set all items on the stack at once.

You can determine the attributes dictionary for the title by setting the navigation bar's `titleTextAttributes`, and you can shift the title's vertical position by calling `setTitleVerticalPositionAdjustment(for:)`. New in iOS 11, you can determine the large title's attributes dictionary by setting the navigation bar's `largeTitleTextAttributes`.

When you use a UINavigationBar implicitly as part of a UINavigationController interface, the navigation controller is the navigation bar's delegate. If you were to use a UINavigationBar on its own, you might want to supply your own delegate. The delegate methods are:

- `navigationBar(_:shouldPush:)`
- `navigationBar(_:didPush:)`
- `navigationBar(_:shouldPop:)`
- `navigationBar(_:didPop:)`

This simple (and silly) example of a standalone UINavigationBar implements the legendary baseball combination trio of Tinker to Evers to Chance; see the relevant Wikipedia article if you don't know about them (Figure 12-22, which also shows the custom back indicator and the custom shadow I described earlier):

```
override func viewDidLoad() {
    super.viewDidLoad()
    let ni = UINavigationItem(title: "Tinker")
    let b = UIBarButtonItem(title: "Evers", style: .plain,
        target: self, action: #selector(pushNext))
    ni.rightBarButtonItem = b
    self.navbar.items = [ni]
}
@objc func pushNext(_ sender: Any) {
    let oldb = sender as! UIBarButtonItem
    let s = oldb.title!
    let ni = UINavigationItem(title:s)
    if s == "Evers" {
        let b = UIBarButtonItem(title:"Chance", style: .plain,
            target:self, action:#selector(pushNext))
```

Figure 12-23. A toolbar

```
        ni.rightBarButtonItem = b
    }
    self.navbar.pushItem(ni, animated:true)
}
```

UIToolbar

A toolbar (UIToolbar, Figure 12-23) displays a row of UIBarButtonItems, which are its items. The items are displayed from left to right in the order in which they appear in the items array. You can set the items with animation by calling set-Items(_:animated:). The items within the toolbar are positioned automatically; you can intervene in this positioning by using the system bar button items .flexible-Space and .fixedSpace, along with the UIBarButtonItem width property.

UITabBar

A tab bar (UITabBar) displays tab bar items (UITabBarItem), its items, each consisting of an image and a name. New in iOS 11, the title is displayed next to the image, except on an iPhone in portrait orientation, where it is displayed below the image. To change the items with animation, call setItems(_:animated:).

The tab bar maintains a current selection among its items, its selectedItem, which is a UITabBarItem, not an index number; you can set it in code, or the user can set it by tapping on a tab bar item. To hear about the user changing the selection, implement tabBar(_:didSelect:) in the delegate (UITabBarDelegate).

You get some control over how the tab bar items are laid out:

itemPositioning
> There are three possible values (UITabBarItemPositioning):
>
> .centered
>> The items are crowded together at the center.
>
> .fill
>> The items are spaced out evenly.
>
> .automatic
>> On the iPad, the same as .centered; on the iPhone, the same as .fill.

`itemSpacing`

> The space between items, if the positioning is `.centered`. For the default space, specify 0.

`itemWidth`

> The width of the items, if the positioning is `.centered`. For the default width, specify 0.

You can set an image to be drawn behind the selected tab bar item to indicate that it's selected; it is the tab bar's `selectionIndicatorImage`.

A UITabBarItem is created with one of these methods:

- `init(tabBarSystemItem:tag:)`
- `init(title:image:tag:)`
- `init(title:image:selectedImage:)`

UITabBarItem is a subclass of UIBarItem, so in addition to its `title` and `image` it inherits the ability to adjust the image position with `imageInsets`, plus the `isEnabled` and `tag` properties. The UITabBarItem itself adds the `selectedImage` property; this image replaces the image when this item is selected.

New in iOS 11, you can assign a tab bar item an alternate `landscapeImagePhone` (inherited from UIBarItem) to be used on the iPhone in landscape orientation. However, doing so disables the `selectedImage`; I regard that as a bug.

A tab bar item's images are treated, by default, as template images. Its title text and template image are tinted with the tab bar's `tintColor` when selected and with its `unselectedItemTintColor` otherwise. To get full control of the title color (and other text attributes), call `setTitleTextAttributes(_:for:)`, inherited from UIBarItem; if you set a color for `.normal` and a color for `.selected`, the `.normal` color will be used when the item is deselected (unless you have set the tab bar's `unselectedItemTint-Color`). You can also adjust the title's position with the `titlePositionAdjustment` property. To get full control of the image's color, supply an `.alwaysOriginal` image for both the `image` and `selectedImage`.

Figure 12-24 is an example of a customized tab bar; I've set the tab bar's selection indicator image (the checkmark) and tint color (golden) of the tab bar, and the text attributes (including the green color, when selected) of the tab bar items.

The user can be permitted to alter the contents of the tab bar, setting its tab bar items from among a larger repertoire of tab bar items. To summon the interface that lets the user do this, call `beginCustomizingItems(_:)`, passing an array of UITabBarItems that may or may not appear in the tab bar. (To prevent the user from removing an

Figure 12-24. A tab bar

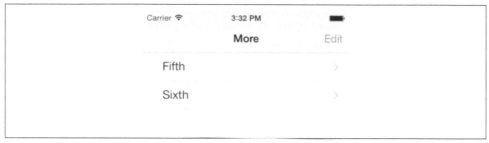

Figure 12-25. Automatically generated More list

item from the tab bar, include it in the tab bar's `items` and *don't* include it in the argument passed to `beginCustomizingItems(_:)`.) A presented view with a Done button appears, behind the tab bar but in front of everything else, displaying the customizable items. The user can then drag an item into the tab bar, replacing an item that's already there. To hear about the customizing view appearing and disappearing, implement delegate methods:

- `tabBar(_:willBeginCustomizing:)`
- `tabBar(_:didBeginCustomizing:)`
- `tabBar(_:willEndCustomizing:changed:)`
- `tabBar(_:didEndCustomizing:changed:)`

When used in conjunction with a UITabBarController, the customization interface is provided automatically, in an elaborate way. If there are a lot of items, a More item is present as the last item in the tab bar; the user can tap this to access the remaining items through a table view. In this table view, the user can select any of the excess items, navigating to the corresponding view; or the user can switch to the customization interface by tapping the Edit button. Figure 12-25 shows how a More list looks by default.

The way this works is that the automatically provided More item corresponds to a UINavigationController with a root view controller (UIMoreListController) whose `view` is a UITableView. Thus, a navigation interface containing this UITableView appears through the tabbed interface when the user taps the More button. When the user selects an item in the table, the corresponding UIViewController is pushed onto the UINavigationController's stack.

You can access this UINavigationController: it is the UITabBarController's more-NavigationController. Through it, you can access the root view controller: it is the first item in the UINavigationController's viewControllers array. And through that, you can access the table view: it is the root view controller's view. This means you can customize what appears when the user taps the More button! For example, let's make the navigation bar red with white button titles, and let's remove the word More from its title:

```
let more = self.tabBarController.moreNavigationController
let list = more.viewControllers[0]
list.title = ""
let b = UIBarButtonItem()
b.title = "Back"
list.navigationItem.backBarButtonItem = b
more.navigationBar.barTintColor = .red
more.navigationBar.tintColor = .white
```

We can go even further by supplementing the table view's data source with a data source of our own and proceeding to customize the table itself. This is tricky because we have no internal access to the actual data source, and we mustn't accidentally disable it from populating the table. Still, it can be done. I'll continue from the previous example by replacing the table view's data source with an instance of my own MyDataSource, initializing it with a reference to the *original* data source object:

```
let tv = list.view as! UITableView
let mds = MyDataSource(originalDataSource: tv.dataSource!)
self.myDataSource = mds
tv.dataSource = mds
```

In MyDataSource, I'll use message forwarding (see Apple's *Objective-C Runtime Programming Guide*) so that MyDataSource acts as a front end for the original data source. MyDataSource will thus magically appear to respond to any message that the original data source responds to, with any message that that MyDataSource can't handle being forwarded to the original data source:

```
unowned let orig : UITableViewDataSource
init(originalDataSource:UITableViewDataSource) {
    self.orig = originalDataSource
}
override func forwardingTarget(for aSelector: Selector) -> Any? {
    if self.orig.responds(to:aSelector) {
        return self.orig
    }
    return super.forwardingTarget(for:aSelector)
}
```

Finally, we'll implement the two Big Questions required by the UITableViewDataSource protocol, to quiet the compiler. In both cases, we first pass the message along to the original data source (analogous to calling super); then we add our own

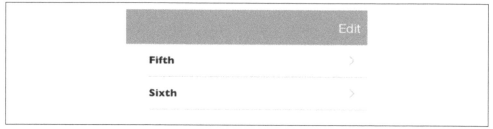

Figure 12-26. Customized More list

customizations as desired. Here, as a proof of concept, I'll change each cell's text font (Figure 12-26):

```
func tableView(_ tv: UITableView, numberOfRowsInSection sec: Int) -> Int {
    return self.orig.tableView(tv, numberOfRowsInSection: sec)
}
func tableView(_ tableView: UITableView,
    cellForRowAt indexPath: IndexPath) -> UITableViewCell {
        let cell = self.orig.tableView(tableView, cellForRowAt: indexPath)
        cell.textLabel!.font = UIFont(name: "GillSans-Bold", size: 14)!
        return cell
}
```

Tint Color

Both UIView and UIBarButtonItem have a `tintColor` property. This property has a remarkable built-in feature: its value, if not set explicitly (or if set to `nil`), is inherited from its superview. (UIBarButtonItems don't have a superview, because they aren't views; but for purposes of this feature, pretend that they are views, and that the containing bar is their superview.)

The idea is to simplify the task of giving your app a consistent overall appearance. Many built-in interface objects use the `tintColor` for some aspect of their appearance, as I've already described. For example, if a `.system` button's `tintColor` is red, either because you've set it directly or because it has inherited that color from higher up the view hierarchy, it will have red title text by default. If the highest superview in your view hierarchy — the window — has a red `tintColor`, then unless you do something to prevent it, *all* your buttons will have red title text.

The inheritance architecture works exactly the way you would expect:

Views and subviews

When you set the `tintColor` of a view, that value is inherited by all subviews of that view. The ultimate superview is the window; thus, you can set the `tintColor` of your UIWindow instance, and its value will be inherited by *every* view that ever appears in your interface.

Overriding

The inherited `tintColor` can be overridden by setting a view's `tintColor` explicitly. Thus, you can set the `tintColor` of a view partway down the view hierarchy so that it and all its subviews have a different `tintColor` from the rest of the interface. In this way, you might subtly suggest that the user has entered a different world.

Propagation

If you change the `tintColor` of a view, the change immediately propagates down the hierarchy of its subviews — except, of course, that a view whose `tintColor` has been explicitly set to a color of its own is unaffected, along with its subviews.

Whenever a view's `tintColor` changes, including when its `tintColor` is initially set at launch time, and including when *you* set it in code, *this view and all its affected subviews* are sent the `tintColorDidChange` message. A subview whose `tintColor` has been explicitly set to a color of its own is *not* sent the `tintColorDidChange` message merely because its superview's `tintColor` changes; that's because the subview's own `tintColor` *didn't* change.

When you ask a view for its `tintColor`, what you get is the `tintColor` of the view itself, if its own `tintColor` has been explicitly set to a color, or else the `tintColor` inherited from higher up the view hierarchy. In this way, you can always learn what the *effective* tint color of a view is.

A UIView also has a `tintAdjustmentMode`. Under certain circumstances, such as the summoning of an alert (Chapter 13) or a popover (Chapter 9), the system will set the `tintAdjustmentMode` of the view at the top of the view hierarchy to `.dimmed`. This causes the `tintColor` to change to a variety of gray. The idea is that the tinting of the background should become monochrome, thus emphasizing the primacy of the view that occupies the foreground (the alert or popover). See "Custom Presented View Controller Transition" on page 354 for an example of my own code making this change.

By default, a change in the `tintAdjustmentMode` propagates all the way down the view hierarchy, changing *all* `tintAdjustmentMode` values and *all* `tintColor` values — and sending *all* subviews the `tintColorDidChange` message. When the foreground view goes away, the system will set the topmost view's `tintAdjustmentMode` to `.normal`, and that change, too, will propagate down the hierarchy.

This propagation behavior is governed by the `tintAdjustmentMode` of the subviews. The default `tintAdjustmentMode` value is `.automatic`, meaning that you want this view's `tintAdjustmentMode` to adopt its superview's `tintAdjustmentMode` automatically. When you ask for such a view's `tintAdjustmentMode`, what you get is just like what you get for `tintColor` — you're told the *effective* tint adjustment mode (`.normal` or `.dimmed`) inherited from up the view hierarchy.

If, on the other hand, you set a view's `tintAdjustmentMode` *explicitly* to `.normal` or `.dimmed`, this tells the system that you want to be left in charge of the `tintAdjustmentMode` for this part of the hierarchy; the automatic propagation of the `tintAdjustmentMode` down the view hierarchy is prevented. To turn automatic propagation back on, set the `tintAdjustmentMode` back to `.automatic`.

Appearance Proxy

When you want to customize the look of an interface object, instead of sending a message to the object itself, you can send that message to an *appearance proxy* for that object's class. The appearance proxy then passes that same message along to the actual *future* instances of that class. You'll usually configure your appearance proxies once very early in the lifetime of the app, and never again. The app delegate's `application(_:didFinishLaunchingWithOptions:)`, before the app's window has been displayed, is the obvious place to do this.

This architecture, like the `tintColor` that I discussed in the previous section, helps you give your app a consistent appearance, as well as saving you from having to write a lot of code. For example, instead of having to send `setTitleTextAttributes(_:for:)` to *every* UITabBarItem your app *ever* instantiates, you send it *once* to the appearance proxy, and it is sent to all future UITabBarItems for you:

```
UITabBarItem.appearance().setTitleTextAttributes([
    .font:UIFont(name:"Avenir-Heavy", size:14)!
], for:.normal)
```

Also, the appearance proxy sometimes provides access to interface objects that might otherwise be difficult to refer to. For example, you don't get direct access to a search bar's external Cancel button, but it is a UIBarButtonItem and you can customize it through the UIBarButtonItem appearance proxy.

There are four class methods for obtaining an appearance proxy:

`appearance`
> Returns a general appearance proxy for the receiver class. The method you call on the appearance proxy will be applied generally to future instances of this class.

`appearance(for:)`
> The parameter is a *trait collection*. The method you call on the appearance proxy will be applied to future instances of the receiver class when the environment matches the specified trait collection.

appearance(whenContainedInInstancesOf:)

> The argument is an *array of classes*, arranged in order of containment from inner to outer. The method you call on the appearance proxy will be applied only to instances of the receiver class that are actually contained in the way you describe. The notion of what "contained" means is deliberately left vague; basically, it works the way you intuitively expect it to work.

appearance(for:whenContainedInInstancesOf:)

> A combination of the preceding two.

When configuring appearance proxy objects, *specificity trumps generality*. Thus, you could call appearance to say what should happen for *most* instances of some class, and call the other methods to say what should happen instead for *certain* instances of that class. Similarly, longer whenContainedInInstancesOf: chains are more specific than shorter ones.

For example, here's some code from my Latin flashcard app (myGolden and myPaler are class properties defined by an extension on UIColor):

```
UIBarButtonItem.appearance().tintColor = .myGolden ❶
UIBarButtonItem.appearance(
    whenContainedInInstancesOf: [UIToolbar.self])
        .tintColor = .myPaler ❷
UIBarButtonItem.appearance(
    whenContainedInInstancesOf: [UIToolbar.self, DrillViewController.self])
        .tintColor = .myGolden ❸
```

That means:

❶ In general, bar button items should be tinted golden.

❷ But bar button items in a toolbar are an exception: they should be tinted paler.

❸ But bar button items in a toolbar in DrillViewController's view are an exception to the exception: they should be tinted golden.

Sometimes, in order to express sufficient specificity, I find myself defining subclasses for no other purpose than to refer to them when obtaining an appearance proxy. For example, here's some more code from my Latin flashcard app:

```
UINavigationBar.appearance().setBackgroundImage(marble, for:.default)
// counteract the above for the black navigation bar
BlackNavigationBar.appearance().setBackgroundImage(nil, for:.default)
```

In that code, BlackNavigationBar is a UINavigationBar subclass that does nothing whatever. Its sole purpose is to tag one navigation bar in my interface so that I can refer to it in that code! Thus, I'm able to say, in effect, "All navigation bars in this app should have marble as their background image, unless they are instances of Black-NavigationBar."

The ultimate in specificity is to customize the look of an instance directly. Thus, for example, if you set one particular UIBarButtonItem's `tintColor` property, then setting the tint color by way of a UIBarButtonItem appearance proxy will have no effect on that particular bar button item.

Not every message that can be sent to an instance of a class can be sent to that class's appearance proxy. Unfortunately, the compiler can't help you here; illegal code like this will compile, but will probably crash at runtime:

```
UIBarButtonItem.appearance().action = #selector(configureAppearance)
```

The problem is not that UIBarButtonItem has no `action` property; in the contrary, that code compiles because it *does* have an `action` property! But that property is not one that you can set by way of the appearance proxy, and the mistake isn't caught until that line executes and the runtime tries to configure an actual UIBarButtonItem.

When in doubt, look at the class documentation; there should be a section that lists the properties and methods applicable to the appearance proxy for this class. For example, the UINavigationBar class documentation has a section called "Customizing the Bar Appearance," the UIBarButtonItem class documentation has a section called "Customizing Appearance," and so forth.

 To define your own appearance-compliant property, declare that property `@objc dynamic` in your UIView subclass.

CHAPTER 13

Modal Dialogs

A modal dialog demands attention; while it is present, the user can do nothing other than work within it or dismiss it. This chapter discusses various forms of modal dialog:

- Within your app, you might want to interrupt to give the user some information or to ask the user how to proceed. For this purpose, iOS provides two types of rudimentary modal dialog — alerts and action sheets. An *alert* is basically a message, possibly with an opportunity for text entry, and some buttons. An *action sheet* is effectively a column of buttons.

- You can provide a sort of action sheet even when your app is not frontmost (or even running) by allowing the user to summon *quick actions* — also known as *shortcut items* — by pressing with 3D touch on your app's icon in the home screen.

- A *local notification* is an alert that the system presents on your app's behalf, even when your app isn't frontmost.

- A *today widget* is interface that appears in the screen that the user sees by swiping sideways in the lock screen or home screen. Your app can provide a today widget by means of a today extension. Your today widget can also appear as a quick action.

- An *activity view* is a modal dialog displaying icons representing activities. Activities are possible courses of external and internal action, such as handing off data to Mail or Messages, or processing it internally. Your app can present an activity view; you can also provide your own activities, either privately within your app or publicly to other apps as an action extension or share extension.

Alerts and Action Sheets

Alerts and action sheets are both forms of presented view controller (Chapter 6). They are managed through the UIAlertController class, a UIViewController subclass. To show an alert or an action sheet is a three-step process:

1. Instantiate UIAlertController with `init(title:message:preferredStyle:)`. The `title:` and `message:` are large and small descriptive text to appear at the top of the dialog. The `preferredStyle:` argument (UIAlertControllerStyle) will be either `.alert` or `.actionSheet`.

2. Configure the dialog by calling `addAction(_:)` on the UIAlertController as many times as needed. An action is a UIAlertAction, which basically means it's a button to appear in the dialog, along with a function to be executed when the button is tapped; to create one, call `init(title:style:handler:)`. Possible `style:` values are (UIAlertActionStyle):

   - `.default`
   - `.cancel`
   - `.destructive`

   An alert may also have text fields (I'll talk about that in a moment).

3. Call `present(_:animated:completion:)` to present the UIAlertController.

The dialog is automatically dismissed when the user taps any button.

Alerts

An alert (UIAlertController style `.alert`) pops up unexpectedly in the middle of the screen, with an elaborate animation, and may be thought of as an attention-getting interruption. It contains a title, a message, and some number of buttons, one of which may be the cancel button, meaning that it does nothing but dismiss the alert. In addition, an alert may contain one or two text fields.

Alerts are minimal, and intentionally so: they are meant for simple, quick interactions or display of information. Often there is only a cancel button, the primary purpose of the alert being to show the user the message ("You won the game"); additional buttons may be used to give the user a choice of how to proceed ("You won the game; would you like to play another?" "Cancel," "Play Another," "Replay").

Figure 13-1 shows a basic alert, illustrating the title, the message, and the three button styles: `.destructive`, `.default`, and `.cancel` respectively. Here's the code that generated it:

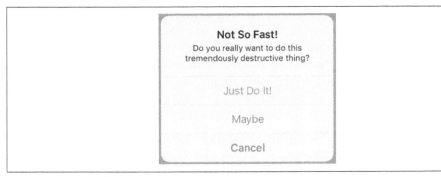

Figure 13-1. An alert

```
let alert = UIAlertController(title: "Not So Fast!",
    message: """
    Do you really want to do this \
    tremendously destructive thing?
    """,
    preferredStyle: .alert)
func handler(_ act:UIAlertAction!) {
    print("User tapped \(act.title as Any)")
}
alert.addAction(UIAlertAction(title: "Cancel",
    style: .cancel, handler: handler))
alert.addAction(UIAlertAction(title: "Just Do It!",
    style: .destructive, handler: handler))
alert.addAction(UIAlertAction(title: "Maybe",
    style: .default, handler: handler))
self.present(alert, animated: true)
```

In Figure 13-1, observe that the `.destructive` button appears first and the `.cancel` button appears last, without regard to the order in which they are defined. The `.default` button order of definition, on the other hand, will be the order of the buttons themselves. If no `.cancel` button is defined, the last `.default` button will be displayed as a `.cancel` button.

You can also designate an action as the alert's `preferredAction`. This appears to bol-dify the title of that button. For example, suppose I append this to the preceding code:

```
alert.preferredAction = alert.actions[2]
```

The order of the `actions` array is the order in which we added actions; thus, the pre-ferred action is now the Maybe button. The order isn't changed — the Maybe button still appears second — but the bold styling is removed from the Cancel button and placed on the Maybe button instead.

As I've already mentioned, the dialog is dismissed automatically when the user taps a button. If you don't want to respond to the tap of a particular button, you can supply `nil` as the `handler:` argument (or omit it altogether). In the preceding code, I've provided a minimal `handler:` function for each button, just to show what one looks like. As the example demonstrates, the function receives the original UIAlertAction as a parameter, and can examine it as desired. The function can also access the alert controller itself, provided the alert controller is in scope at the point where the `handler:` function is defined (which will usually be the case). My example code assigns the same function to all three buttons, but more often you'll give each button its own individual `handler:` function, probably as a trailing closure.

Now let's talk about adding text fields to an alert. Because space is limited on the smaller iPhone screen, especially when the keyboard is present, an alert that is to contain a text field should probably should have at most two buttons, with short titles such as "OK" and "Cancel," and at most two text fields. To add a text field to an alert, call `addTextField(configurationHandler:)`. The `handler:` function will receive the text field as a parameter; it is called before the alert appears, and can be used to configure the text field. Other `handler:` functions can access the text field through the alert's `textFields` property, which is an array. In this example, the user is invited to enter a number in the text field; if the alert is dismissed with the OK button, its `handler:` function reads the text from the text field:

```
let alert = UIAlertController(title: "Enter a number:",
    message: nil, preferredStyle: .alert)
alert.addTextField { tf in
    tf.keyboardType = .numberPad
}
func handler(_ act:UIAlertAction) {
    let tf = alert.textFields![0]
    // ... can read tf.text here ...
}
alert.addAction(UIAlertAction(title: "Cancel", style: .cancel))
alert.addAction(UIAlertAction(title: "OK",
    style: .default, handler: handler))
self.present(alert, animated: true)
```

A puzzle arises as to how to prevent the user from dismissing the alert if the text fields are not acceptably filled in. The alert will be dismissed if the user taps a button, and no button `handler:` function can prevent this. The solution is to *disable* the relevant buttons until the text fields are satisfactory. A UIAlertAction has an `isEnabled` property for this very purpose. I'll modify the preceding example so that the OK button is disabled initially:

```
alert.addAction(UIAlertAction(title: "Cancel", style: .cancel))
alert.addAction(UIAlertAction(title: "OK",
    style: .default, handler: handler))
alert.actions[1].isEnabled = false
self.present(alert, animated: true)
```

But this raises a new puzzle: how will the OK button ever be enabled? The text field can have a delegate or a control event target–action pair (Chapter 10), and so we can hear about the user typing in it. I'll modify the example again so that I'm notified as the user edits in the text field:

```
alert.addTextField { tf in
    tf.keyboardType = .numberPad
    tf.addTarget(self,
        action: #selector(self.textChanged), for: .editingChanged)
}
```

Our `textChanged` method will now be called when the user edits, but this raises one final puzzle: how will this method, which receives a reference to the text field, get a reference to the OK button in the alert in order to enable it? My approach is to work my way up the responder chain from the text field to the alert controller. Here, I enable the OK button if and only if the text field contains some text:

```
@objc func textChanged(_ sender: Any) {
    let tf = sender as! UITextField
    var resp : UIResponder! = tf
    while !(resp is UIAlertController) { resp = resp.next }
    let alert = resp as! UIAlertController
    alert.actions[1].isEnabled = (tf.text != "")
}
```

Action Sheets

An action sheet (UIAlertController style `.actionSheet`) may be considered the iOS equivalent of a menu; it consists primarily of buttons. On the iPhone, it slides up from the bottom of the screen; on the iPad, it appears as a popover.

Where an alert is an interruption, an action sheet is a logical branching of what the user is already doing: it typically divides a single piece of interface into multiple possible courses of action. For example, in Apple's Mail app, a single Action button summons an action sheet that lets the user reply to the current message, forward it, or print it (or cancel and do nothing).

Figure 13-2 shows a basic action sheet on the iPhone. Here's the code that constructed it:

```
let action = UIAlertController(
    title: "Choose New Layout", message: nil, preferredStyle: .actionSheet)
action.addAction(UIAlertAction(title: "Cancel", style: .cancel))
func handler(_ act:UIAlertAction) {
    // ... do something here with act.title ...
}
for s in ["3 by 3", "4 by 3", "4 by 4", "5 by 4", "5 by 5"] {
    action.addAction(UIAlertAction(title: s,
        style: .default, handler: handler))
}
self.present(action, animated: true)
```

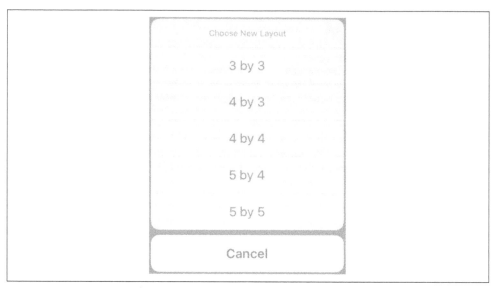

Figure 13-2. An action sheet on the iPhone

On the iPad, an action sheet wants to be a popover. This means that a UIPopover-PresentationController will take charge of it. It will thus be incumbent upon you to provide something for the popover's arrow to point to (as explained in Chapter 9). Be sure to do that; otherwise, you'll crash at runtime. For example:

```
self.present(action, animated: true)
if let pop = action.popoverPresentationController {
    let v = sender as! UIView
    pop.sourceView = v
    pop.sourceRect = v.bounds
}
```

The cancel button for a popover action sheet on the iPad is suppressed, because the user can dismiss the popover by tapping outside it. On the iPhone, too, where the cancel button is displayed, the user can *still* dismiss the action sheet by tapping outside it. When the user does that, the cancel button's handler: function will be called, just as if the user had tapped the cancel button — even if the cancel button is not displayed.

An action sheet can also be presented *inside* a popover. In that case, the containing popover is treated as an iPhone: the action sheet slides up from the bottom of the popover, and the cancel button is *not* suppressed. The action sheet's modal presentation style defaults to .overCurrentContext, which is exactly what we want, so there is no need to set it. You are then presenting a view controller inside a popover; see "Popover Presenting a View Controller" on page 566 for the considerations that apply.

Figure 13-3. A presented view behaving like an alert

Dialog Alternatives

Alerts and action sheets are limited, inflexible, and inappropriate to any but the simplest cases. Their interface can contain title text, buttons, and (for an alert) one or two text fields, and that's all. What if you wanted more interface than that?

Some developers have hacked into their alerts or action sheets in an attempt to force them to be more customizable. *This is wrong*, and in any case there is no need for such extremes. These are just presented view controllers, and if you don't like what they contain, you can make your own presented view controller with its own customized view. If you also want that view to look and behave like an alert or an action sheet, then make it so!

As I have shown ("Custom Presented View Controller Transition" on page 354), it is easy to create a small presented view that looks and behaves quite like an alert or action sheet, floating in front of the main interface and darkening everything behind it — the difference being that this is an ordinary view controller's view, belonging entirely to you, and capable of being populated with any interface you like (Figure 13-3). You can even add a UIMotionEffect to your presented view, giving it the same parallax as a real alert.

Often, however, there will no need for such elaborate measures. Consider some alternatives:

A popover

A popover is virtually a secondary window, and can be truly modal. The popovers in Figure 9-1, for example, are effectively modal dialogs. A popover can internally display a secondary presented view or even an action sheet, as we've already seen.

A form sheet

A presented view can use the .formSheet presentation style, which is effectively a dialog window smaller than the screen.

Figure 13-4. A presented view functioning as a modal dialog

A fullscreen presented view controller

On the iPhone, *any* presented view is essentially a modal dialog. The color picker in my Zotz! app (Figure 13-4) is a case in point. It occupies the entire screen, and is modal for that very reason; and it has the same lightweight, temporary quality that an alert offers.

Quick Actions

Quick actions are essentially a column of buttons summoned outside of your app when the user employs 3D touch on your app's icon in the home screen. (If the user's device lacks 3D touch, quick actions won't be available.) They should represent convenient ways of accessing functionality that the user could equally have performed from within your app.

Quick actions are of two kinds:

Static quick actions

Static quick actions are described in your app's *Info.plist*. The system can present them even if your app isn't running — indeed, even if your app has *never* run — because it can read your app's *Info.plist*.

Dynamic quick actions

Dynamic quick actions are configured in code. This means that they are not available until your app's code has actually run. Your code can alter and remove dynamic quick actions, but it cannot affect your app's static quick actions.

When the user taps a quick action, your app is brought to the front (launching it if necessary) and your app delegate's `application(_:performActionFor:completion-Handler:)` is called. The second parameter is a UIApplicationShortcutItem describing the button the user tapped. You can now respond as appropriate. You must then call the `completionHandler`, passing a Bool to indicate success or failure (though in fact I see no difference in behavior regardless of whether you pass `true` or `false`, or even if you omit to call the `completionHandler` entirely).

A UIApplicationShortcutItem is just a value class, embodying five properties describing the button that will appear in the interface. In order for static quick actions to work, those five properties all have analogs in the *Info.plist*. The *Info.plist* entry that generates your static quick actions is an array called `UIApplicationShortcutItems`. This array's items are dictionaries, one for each quick action, containing the properties and values you wish to set. The UIApplicationShortcutItem properties and corresponding *Info.plist* keys are:

`type`
`UIApplicationShortcutItemType`

An arbitrary string. You'll use this string in your implementation of `application(_:performActionFor:completionHandler:)` to identify the button that was tapped. Required.

`localizedTitle`
`UIApplicationShortcutItemTitle`

The button title; a string. Required.

`localizedSubtitle`
`UIApplicationShortcutItemSubtitle`

The button subtitle; a string. Optional.

`icon`
`UIApplicationShortcutItemIconType`
`UIApplicationShortcutItemIconFile`

An icon to appear in the button. Optional, but it's good to supply some icon, because if you don't, you'll get an ugly filled circle by default. When forming a UIApplicationShortcutItem in code, you'll supply a UIApplicationShortcutIcon object as its `icon` property. UIApplicationShortcutIcon has three initializers:

Figure 13-5. Quick actions

`init(type:)`

> A UIApplicationShortcutIconType. This is an enum of about 30 cases, each representing a built-in standard image, such as `.time` (a clock icon).

`init(templateImageName:)`

> Works like UIImage's `init(named:)`. The image will be treated as a template image. Apple says that the image should be 35x35, though a larger image will be scaled down appropriately.

`init(contact:)`

> A CNContact (see Chapter 18). The icon will be based on the contact's picture or initials.

> In the *Info.plist*, you may use either the `IconType` key or the `IconFile` key. The value for the `IconType` key is the Objective-C name of a UIApplicationShortcut-IconType case — for example, `UIApplicationShortcutIconTypeTime`. The value for the `IconFile` key is the name of an image file in your app, suitable for use with `UIImage(named:)`.

`userInfo`
`UIApplicationShortcutItemUserInfo`

> An optional dictionary of additional information, whose usage in your `application(_:performActionFor:completionHandler:)` is completely up to you.

Imagine, for example, that our app's purpose is to remind the user periodically to go get a cup of coffee. Figure 13-5 shows a quick actions menu of three items generated when the user uses 3D touch to press our app's icon. The first two items are static items, generated by our settings in the *Info.plist*, which is shown in Figure 13-6.

The third quick action item in Figure 13-5 is a dynamic item. The idea is that the user, employing our app to configure a reminder, also gets to set a time interval as a favorite default interval. We cannot know what this favorite interval will be until the app runs and the user sets it; that's why this item is dynamic. Here's the code that

Figure 13-6. Static quick actions in the Info.plist

generates it; all we have to do is set our shared UIApplication object's `shortcutItems` property:

```
// ... assume we have worked out the subtitle and time ...
let item = UIApplicationShortcutItem(type: "coffee.schedule",
    localizedTitle: "Coffee Reminder", localizedSubtitle: subtitle,
    icon: UIApplicationShortcutIcon(templateImageName: "cup"),
    userInfo: ["time":time])
UIApplication.shared.shortcutItems = [item]
```

When the user taps a quick action button, our app delegate's `application(_:perform-ActionFor:completionHandler:)` is called. Here you can see my purpose in setting the `userInfo` (and `UIApplicationShortcutItemUserInfo`) of these shortcut items; to learn what time interval the user wants to use for this reminder, we just look at the `"time"` key:

```
func application(_ application: UIApplication,
    performActionFor shortcutItem: UIApplicationShortcutItem,
    completionHandler: @escaping (Bool) -> ()) {
        if shortcutItem.type == "coffee.schedule" {
            if let d = shortcutItem.userInfo {
                if let time = d["time"] as? Int {
                    // ... do something with time ...
                    completionHandler(true)
                }
            }
        }
        completionHandler(false)
}
```

Figure 13-7. A local notification alert

Local Notifications

A local notification is an alert to the user that can appear even if your app is not running. Where it may appear depends upon the user's preferences in the Settings app, either under Notifications or under your app's own listing:

- On the lock screen
- In the notification history; this is the interface that appears when the user swipes down from the top screen edge (formerly called the notification center)
- As a banner at the top of the screen

In iOS 11, the Settings app distinguishes between a *temporary* banner, which vanishes spontaneously after displaying itself briefly, and a *persistent* banner, which remains until the user dismisses it. (In earlier systems, the distinction was between a banner and an alert.)

Figure 13-7 shows a local notification alert appearing in the user's notification history.

Your app does not present a local notification; the system does. You hand the system instructions for when the local notification is to *fire*, and then you just stand back and let the system deal with it. That's why the local notification can appear even if your app isn't frontmost or isn't even running. Starting in iOS 10, the local notification alert can appear even when your app *is* frontmost; but even then it is the system that is presenting it on your behalf.

The user, in the Settings app, can veto any of the interface options for your app's local notifications, or turn them off entirely. Thus, your local notifications can be effectively suppressed; in that case, you can still create a local notification, but when it fires, only your app will hear about it, and only if it is frontmost. Moreover, the system itself will suppress your app's local notifications entirely unless the user first explicitly approves; thus, the user must deliberately opt in if your notifications are ever to appear in any form. Figure 13-8 shows the alert that the system will show your user, once, offering the initial opportunity to opt in to your local notifications.

Figure 13-8. The user will see this only once

A local notification alert is also a way for the user to summon your app, bringing it to the front if it is backgrounded, and launching it if it isn't running. This response to the alert is the *default action* when the user taps the alert.

You can add further *custom actions*, in the form of buttons. The user must manipulate the alert in order to reveal the buttons. For example, on a device with 3D touch, the user presses with force touch to summon the buttons; on a device without 3D touch, the user drags downward on the alert, or slides the alert sideways to reveal the View button and taps the View button. The custom action buttons then appear. Let's call this the alert's *secondary interface*. An action button can communicate with your app without bringing it to the front — though it can alternatively be told to bring your app to the front as well.

A local notification can carry an *attachment*, which may be an image, a sound file, or a video. If it's an image, the image is previewed with a small thumbnail in the alert itself. But the real way the user gets to see the attachment is in the alert's secondary interface. If the attachment is an image, the image is shown; if the attachment is audio or video, interface is provided for playing it.

In Figure 13-7, the little image at the right of the alert is the thumbnail of an image attachment. In Figure 13-9, the user has summoned the alert's secondary interface, displaying the image as well as two custom action buttons.

You can modify the secondary interface by writing a notification *content extension*. Figure 13-10 shows an example; I've replaced the default title and body with a caption in my own font, and I've shown the attachment image in a smaller size.

Use of a local notification involves several steps:

1. Your app must *request authorization* for notifications. This ensures that the user has seen the opt-in dialog (Figure 13-8).

2. If your notification is to have custom actions or a custom secondary interface, you must register a notification *category*, including the custom actions.

3. Your app creates and *schedules* the local notification itself.

Figure 13-9. Local notification secondary interface with custom actions

Figure 13-10. Local notification with custom secondary interface

4. Your app is prepared to hear about the user *responding* to the notification alert.

I'll describe this sequence one step at a time, and then talk about writing a notification content extension to customize the secondary interface.

You'll need to import the User Notifications framework (`import User-Notifications`). Most of your activity will ultimately involve the user notification center, a singleton UNUserNotificationCenter instance available by calling `UNUser-NotificationCenter.current()`.

Authorizing for Local Notifications

The first step in requesting authorization for local notifications is to find out whether we are already authorized. To do so, call `getNotificationSettings` on the user notification center, which returns a UNNotificationSettings object asynchronously. You'll examine this property of the settings object:

`authorizationStatus`
> A UNAuthorizationStatus: `.authorized`, `.denied`, or `.notDetermined`.

If the status is `.notDetermined`, the user has never seen the authorization request dialog, and you'll present it by sending `requestAuthorization(options:)` to the user notification center. A Bool is returned asynchronously, telling you whether authorization was granted. The `options:` (UNAuthorizationOptions) are modes in which you'd like to affect the user interface:

`.badge`
> You want to be allowed to badge your app's icon with a number. Apple's Phone and Mail apps are familiar examples.

`.sound`
> You want to play a sound when your notification fires.

`.alert`
> You want to present a notification alert when your notification fires.

If the status is `.authorized`, there's no point requesting authorization; you already have it. If the status is `.denied`, there's no point requesting authorization, and there's probably no point scheduling any local notifications, as the user will likely never receive them.

The thing to watch out for is that both `getNotificationSettings` and `requestAuthorization(options:)` return their results *asynchronously*. This means that you cannot simply follow a call to `getNotificationSettings` with a call to `requestAuthorization(options:)`; if you do, `requestAuthorization(options:)` will run before `getNotificationSettings` has a chance to return its UNNotificationSettings object (see Appendix C). Instead, you must *nest* the calls by means of their completion functions, like this:

```
let center = UNUserNotificationCenter.current()
center.getNotificationSettings { settings in
    switch settings.authorizationStatus {
    case .notDetermined:
        center.requestAuthorization(options:[.alert, .sound]) { ok, err in
```

```
                if let err = err {
                    print(err); return
                }
                if ok {
                    // authorized; could proceed to schedule a notification
                }
            }
        case .denied: break
        case .authorized: break // or proceed to schedule a notification
        }
    }
```

You might also wish to call getNotificationSettings again later, perhaps just before configuring and scheduling a local notification. You can obtain full information on how the user has configured the relevant settings through the properties of the UNNotificationSettings object:

soundSetting
badgeSetting
alertSetting
notificationCenterSetting
lockScreenSetting
> A UNNotificationSetting: .enabled, .disabled, or .notSupported.

alertStyle
> A UNAlertStyle: .banner, .alert, or .none.

New in iOS 11, there is also a showPreviewsSetting; this is a UNShowPreviews-Setting, .always, .whenAuthenticated, or .never, and corresponds to the Show Previews setting in Settings → Notifications. I'll discuss the implications of this setting in a moment.

Notification Category

If your local notification alert is to have a secondary interface that displays custom action buttons or a custom interface, you'll need to register a notification category. You do this before creating the notification. When you create the notification itself, you match it with a previously registered category by an arbitrary string identifier; that tells the user notification center that this notification should be accompanied by this set of action buttons.

An action button is a UNNotificationAction, a value class whose initializer is:

- init(identifier:title:options:)

The identifier is arbitrary; you'll use it to identify the button when it is tapped. The title is the text to appear in the button. The `options:` are a UNNotificationAction-Options bitmask:

`.foreground`

Tapping this button summons your app to the foreground. If not present, this button will call your app in the background; your app, if suspended, will be awakened just long enough to respond.

`.destructive`

This button will be marked in the interface as dangerous (by being displayed in red).

`.authenticationRequired`

If this option is present, and if this is not a `.foreground` button, then if the user's device requires a passcode to go beyond the lock screen, tapping this button in the lock screen will also require a passcode. The idea is to prevent performance of this action without authentication directly from the lock screen.

An action, instead of being a button, can be a text field where the user can type and then tap a button to send the text to your app. This is a UNTextInputNotification-Action, and its initializer is:

- `init(identifier:title:options:textInputButtonTitle:textInput-Placeholder:)`

To configure a category, create your UNNotificationActions and call the UNNotificationCategory initializer:

- `init(identifier:actions:intentIdentifiers:options:)`

This `identifier` is how a subsequent notification will be matched to this category. The most important `options:` value (UNNotificationCategoryOptions) is `.custom-DismissAction`; if you don't set this, your code won't get any event if the user dismisses your notification alert without tapping it to summon your app — the default action — and without tapping a custom action button.

Having created all your categories, you then call `setNotificationCategories` on the user notification center.

Here's an example of the entire process:

```
let action1 = UNNotificationAction(identifier: "snooze", title: "Snooze")
let action2 = UNNotificationAction(identifier: "reconfigure",
    title: "Reconfigure", options: [.foreground])
let cat = UNNotificationCategory(identifier: self.categoryIdentifier,
```

```
        actions: [action1, action2], intentIdentifiers: [],
        options: [.customDismissAction])
    let center = UNUserNotificationCenter.current()
    center.setNotificationCategories([cat])
```

Scheduling a Local Notification

A local notification is scheduled to fire with respect to a *trigger*. The trigger is how the system knows when it's time to fire. This will be expressed as a subclass of UNNotificationTrigger:

UNTimeIntervalNotificationTrigger
> Fires starting a certain number of seconds from now, possibly repeating every time that number of seconds elapses. The initializer is:
>
> • init(timeInterval:repeats:)

UNCalendarNotificationTrigger
> Fires at a certain date-time, expressed using DateComponents, possibly repeating when the same DateComponents occurs again. For example, you might use the DateComponents to express nine o'clock in the morning, without regard to date; the trigger, if repeating, would then be nine o'clock *every* morning. The initializer is:
>
> • init(dateMatching:repeats:)

UNLocationNotificationTrigger
> Fires when the user enters or leaves a certain geographical region. I'll discuss this further in Chapter 21.

The payload of the notification is expressed as a UNMutableNotificationContent object. Its properties are:

title, subtitle, body
> Text visible in the notification alert.

attachments
> UNNotificationAttachment objects. In the simplest case, attachments work best if there is just one, as the secondary interface may not give the user a way to access them all; however, if you are supplying a custom secondary interface, you might be able to retrieve and display multiple attachments. Attachment objects must be fairly small, because the system, in order to present them on your behalf whenever this notification fires, is going to *copy* them off to a private secure area of its own.

sound
> A sound (UNNotificationSound) to be played when the notification fires. You can specify a sound file in your app bundle by name, or call `default` to specify the default sound.

badge
> A number to appear on your app's icon after this notification fires. Specify 0 to remove an existing badge. (You can also set or remove your app's icon badge at any time by means of the shared application's `applicationIconBadgeNumber`.)

categoryIdentifier
> The identifier string of a previously registered category. This is how your local notification will be associated at presentation time with custom action buttons or a custom secondary interface.

userInfo
> An arbitrary dictionary, to carry extra information you'll retrieve later.

threadIdentifier
> A string; notification alerts with the same thread identifier are clumped together physically.

launchImageName
> Your app might be launched from scratch by the user tapping this notification's alert. Suppose that when this happens, you're going to configure your app so that it appears differently from how it normally launches. You might want the momentary launch screen, shown while your app starts up, to correspond to that different interface. This is how you specify the alternative launch image to be used in that situation.

Having constructed your notification's trigger and content, you package them up with an arbitrary identifier into a UNNotificationRequest by calling its initializer:

• `init(identifier:content:trigger:)`

You then tell the user notification center to add this notification to its internal list of scheduled notifications.

As an example, here's the code that generated Figure 13-7:

```
let interval = // ... whatever ...
let trigger = UNTimeIntervalNotificationTrigger(
    timeInterval: interval, repeats: false)
let content = UNMutableNotificationContent()
content.title = "Caffeine!"
content.body = "Time for another cup of coffee!"
content.sound = UNNotificationSound.default()
```

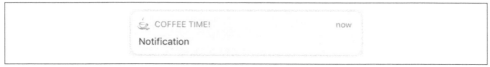

Figure 13-11. Local notification with preview suppressed

```
content.categoryIdentifier = self.categoryIdentifier
let url = Bundle.main.url(forResource: "cup2", withExtension: "jpg")!
if let att = try? UNNotificationAttachment(
    identifier: "cup", url: url, options:nil) {
        content.attachments = [att]
}
let req = UNNotificationRequest(
    identifier: "coffeeNotification", content: content, trigger: trigger)
let center = UNUserNotificationCenter.current()
center.add(req)
```

Preview Suppression

New in iOS 11, the user has the option, in Settings, to turn off previews for your app's notifications. This means that, by default, a notification's alerts will have their `title`, `subtitle`, and body suppressed and replaced by placeholder text, such as "Notification" (Figure 13-11). The idea is to allow the user to prevent possibly sensitive details from popping up on the screen spontaneously. (The secondary interface is unaffected.)

To cope with this possibility, you can supply your own placeholder. To do so, when you register your notification category, call this UNNotificationCategory initializer:

- `init(identifier:actions:intentIdentifiers:hiddenPreviewsBody-Placeholder:options:)`

The `placeholder:` is a format string to appear when previews are turned off. You can also add `options:` values `.hiddenPreviewsShowTitle` and `.hiddenPreviewsShow-Subtitle` if your title and subtitle contain no sensitive information, causing them to appear even if previews are turned off.

Hearing About a Local Notification

In order to hear about your scheduled local notification after it fires, you need to configure some object to be the user notification center's `delegate`, adopting the UNUser-NotificationCenterDelegate protocol. You'll want to do this very early your app's lifetime, because you might need to be sent a delegate message immediately upon launching; thus, `application(_:didFinishLaunchingWithOptions:)` is a good place:

```
func application(_ application: UIApplication,
    didFinishLaunchingWithOptions launchOptions:
    [UIApplicationLaunchOptionsKey : Any]?) -> Bool {
        let center = UNUserNotificationCenter.current()
        center.delegate = self // or whatever
        return true
}
```

The UNUserNotificationCenterDelegate protocol consists of just two optional methods:

userNotificationCenter(_:willPresent:withCompletionHandler:)

You can ask that the system present the local notification alert and play the sound and badge the icon even if the notification fires when your app is frontmost, and this is how you do so. (If your app is *not* frontmost when the notification fires, this method won't be called.)

The second parameter is a UNNotification object containing the fire date and your original request (UNNotificationRequest). Thus, you can identify the local notification if desired, and can respond accordingly; you can also extract information from it, such as an attachment or the userInfo dictionary.

You are handed a completion function; you must call it with some combination of (UNNotificationPresentationOptions) .alert, .sound, and .badge — or nothing, if you want to suppress the alert completely.

userNotificationCenter(_:didReceive:withCompletionHandler:)

Called when the user interacts with your local notification alert. The second parameter is a UNNotificationResponse, consisting of two properties. One, the notification, is the same UNNotification object that I described for the previous method; again, you can use it to identify and extract information from this local notification. The other, the actionIdentifier, is a string telling you what the user did. There are three possibilities:

UNNotificationDefaultActionIdentifier

The user performed the default action, tapping the alert to summon your app.

UNNotificationDismissActionIdentifier

The user dismissed the local notification alert. You won't hear about this (and this method won't be called) unless you specified the .customDismiss-Action option for this notification's category.

A custom action identifier string

The user tapped a custom action button, and this is its identifier.

You are handed a completion function, which you must call when you're done. You must be quick, because it may be that you are being awakened momentarily in the background.

Here's an example of implementing the first delegate method, telling the runtime to present the local notification alert within our app:

```
func userNotificationCenter(_ center: UNUserNotificationCenter,
    willPresent notification: UNNotification,
    withCompletionHandler completionHandler:
    @escaping (UNNotificationPresentationOptions) -> ()) {
        completionHandler([.sound, .alert])
}
```

Here's an example of implementing the second delegate method, responding to the user tapping a custom action button; I use my `delay` utility (Appendix B) so as to return immediately before proceeding to obey the button:

```
func userNotificationCenter(_ center: UNUserNotificationCenter,
    didReceive response: UNNotificationResponse,
    withCompletionHandler completionHandler: @escaping () -> ()) {
        let id = response.actionIdentifier
        if id == "snooze" {
            delay(0.1) {
                self.rescheduleNotification(response.notification)
            }
        }
        // ... other tests might go here ...
        completionHandler()
}
```

If the custom action was a text input action, then this UNNotificationResponse will be a subclass, UNTextInputNotificationResponse, which has an additional `userText` property. Thus, to learn whether this was a text input action, you simply test its class with `is` or `as?`, and then retrieve its `userText`:

```
if let textresponse = response as? UNTextInputNotificationResponse {
    let text = textresponse.userText
    // ...
}
```

Managing Scheduled Notifications

The user notification center is introspectable. You can examine the list of scheduled notifications; UNUserNotificationCenter methods for managing scheduled notifications are:

- `getPendingNotificationRequests(completionHandler:)`
- `removePendingNotificationRequests(withIdentifiers:)`

- removeAllPendingNotificationRequests

You can learn when each notification is scheduled to fire; if a notification has an interval trigger or a calendar trigger, you can ask for its nextTriggerDate. You can remove a notification from the list, thus canceling it. You can effectively reschedule a notification by removing it, copying it with any desired alterations, and adding the resulting notification.

You can also examine the list of notifications that have already fired but have not yet been removed from the user's notification history; UNUserNotificationCenter methods for managing delivered notifications are:

- getDeliveredNotifications(completionHandler:)
- removeDeliveredNotifications(withIdentifiers:)
- removeAllDeliveredNotifications

By judicious removal of notifications, you can keep the user's notification history trimmed; for example, you might prefer that only your most recently delivered notification should appear in the notification history. You can even modify the text of a delivered notification, so that the notification will be up-to-date when the user gets around to dealing with it; to do so, you add a notification whose identifier is the same as that of an existing notification.

 Canceling a repeating local notification is up to your code; if you don't provide the user with a way of doing that, then if the user wants to prevent the notification from recurring, the only recourse may be to delete your app.

Notification Content Extensions

If your local notification has a category, you can customize what appears in its secondary interface. To do so, you write a *notification content extension*. This is a target, separate from your app target, because the system needs to access it outside your app, and even if your app isn't running.

To add a notification content extension to your app, create a new target and specify iOS → Application Extension → Notification Content. The template gives you a good start on your extension. You have a storyboard with a single scene, and the code for a corresponding view controller that imports both the User Notifications framework and the User Notifications UI framework, as well as adopting the UNNotification-ContentExtension protocol.

The view controller code contains a stub implementation of the didReceive(_:) method, which is the only required method. (Other methods are optional and have mostly to do with playback of media attached to your local notification.) The parameter is a UNNotification containing your original UNNotificationRequest; you can examine this and extract information from it. The idea is that you might use this information to configure your interface. If you want to extract an attachment, you will have to wrap your access in calls to the URL methods `startAccessingSecurity-ScopedResource` and `stopAccessingSecurityScopedResource`.

The only other thing your view controller really needs to do is to set its own `preferredContentSize` to the desired dimensions of the custom interface. Alternatively, you can use autolayout to size the interface from the inside out, like a table view cell (Chapter 8).

For example, here's how the custom interface in Figure 13-10 was attained. The interface consists of a label and an image view. The image view is to contain the image attachment from the local notification, so I extract the image from the attachment and set it as the image view's image; I find that the interface doesn't reliably appear unless we also call `setNeedsLayout` at the end:

```
override func viewDidLoad() {
    super.viewDidLoad()
    self.preferredContentSize = CGSize(320, 80)
}
func didReceive(_ notification: UNNotification) {
    let req = notification.request
    let content = req.content
    let atts = content.attachments
    if let att = atts.first, att.identifier == "cup" {
        if att.url.startAccessingSecurityScopedResource() {
            if let data = try? Data(contentsOf: att.url) {
                self.imageView.image = UIImage(data: data)
            }
            att.url.stopAccessingSecurityScopedResource()
        }
    }
    self.view.setNeedsLayout()
}
```

The template also includes an *Info.plist* for your extension. You will need to modify it by configuring these keys:

UNNotificationExtensionCategory
:   A string corresponding to the `categoryIdentifier` of the local notification(s) to which this custom secondary interface is to be applied.

UNNotificationExtensionInitialContentSizeRatio
:   A number representing the width of your custom interface divided by its height. This doesn't have to be perfect — and indeed it probably can't be, since you don't know the actual width of the screen on which this interface will be displayed —

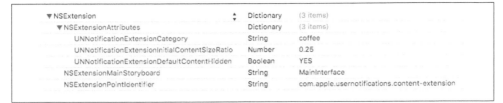

▼ NSExtension		Dictionary	(3 items)
▼ NSExtensionAttributes		Dictionary	(3 items)
UNNotificationExtensionCategory		String	coffee
UNNotificationExtensionInitialContentSizeRatio		Number	0.25
UNNotificationExtensionDefaultContentHidden		Boolean	YES
NSExtensionMainStoryboard		String	MainInterface
NSExtensionPointIdentifier		String	com.apple.usernotifications.content-extension

Figure 13-12. A content extension's Info.plist

but the idea is to give the system a rough idea of the size as it prepares to display the custom interface.

UNNotificationExtensionDefaultContentHidden
> Optional. A Boolean. Set to YES if you want to eliminate the default display of the local notification's title, subtitle, and body from the custom interface.

UNNotificationExtensionOverridesDefaultTitle
> Optional. A Boolean. Set to YES if you want to replace the default display of your app's name at the top of the interface (where it says "Coffee Time!" in Figure 13-10) with a title of your own choosing. To determine that title, set your view controller's title property in your didReceive(_:) implementation.

Figure 13-12 shows the relevant part of the *Info.plist* for my content extension.

Your custom interface (the view controller's main view) is *not interactive*. There is no point putting a UIButton into the interface, for example, as the user cannot tap it. But this is not quite as harsh a restriction as you might suppose, because the interface has these features:

Play/pause button
> If you like, the runtime can add a tappable play/pause button for you. This is useful if your custom interface contains video or audio material. Three UNNotificationContentExtension properties can be overridden to dictate that the play/pause button should appear and where it should go, and two methods can be implemented to hear when the user taps the button.

Custom action buttons
> The user can tap your custom action buttons. You can hear about such a tap in your content extension's view controller by implementing didReceive(_:completionHandler:).

Custom input view
> As I described in Chapter 10 ("Input view without a text field" on page 646), your view controller can summon a custom input view, to appear where the keyboard would be. This is a custom view, so it can contain live interface.

Figure 13-13. A built-in today extension

In your implementation of didReceive(_:completionHandler:), or in your response to the user tapping in your custom input view, *you can change the interface.* Thus your user *feels* that the interface is alive and responsive, even though the main view itself is not interactive.

Here's some more about didReceive(_:completionHandler:). By implementing this method, you have effectively put yourself in front of your user notification center delegate's userNotificationCenter(_:didReceive:withCompletionHandler:); the user's tap on a custom action button will be routed initially to the content extension's view controller instead. The runtime now needs to know precisely how to proceed; you tell it by calling the completion function with one of these responses (UNNotificationContentExtensionResponseOption):

.doNotDismiss
: The local notification alert remains in place, still displaying the custom secondary interface.

.dismiss
: The alert is dismissed.

.dismissAndForwardAction
: The alert is dismissed and the action is passed along to your user notification center delegate's userNotificationCenter(_:didReceive:withCompletionHandler:).

Even if you tell the completion function to dismiss the alert, you can *still* modify the custom interface, delaying the call to the completion function so that the user has time to see the change.

Today Extensions

The interface that appears when the user swipes sideways in the lock screen or the home screen is the today list. Here, apps can contribute *today widgets* — informative bits of interface. For example, Apple's Weather app posts the local temperature here, in a widget that the user can tap to open the Weather app itself (Figure 13-13).

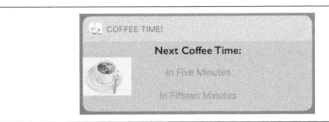

Figure 13-14. A custom today extension

Your app, too, can provide a widget to appear here. To make that happen, you give your app a *today extension*. Your app vends the extension, and the user has the option of adding it to the today list (Figure 13-14).

To add a today extension to your app, create a new target and specify iOS → Application Extension → Today Extension. The template gives you a good start on your extension. You have a storyboard with a single scene, and the code for a corresponding view controller that adopts the NCWidgetProviding protocol. You might need to edit the extension's *Info.plist* to set the "Bundle display name" entry — this is the title that will appear above your extension.

 The today extension target will be explicitly linked to the Notification Center framework (import NotificationCenter). Do not meddle with this linkage. This framework is crucial; without it, your today extension target may compile, but the today extension itself will crash.

Design your extension's interface in the storyboard provided. To size your extension's height, provide sufficient constraints to determine the full height of the interface from the inside out, or set your view controller's preferredContentSize.

Each time your today extension's interface is about to appear, your code is given an opportunity to update its interface, through its implementation of the NCWidget-Providing method widgetPerformUpdate(completionHandler:). Be sure to finish up by calling the completionHandler, handing it an NCUpdateResult, which will be .newData, .noData, or .failed. Time-consuming work should be performed off the main thread (see Chapter 24):

```
func widgetPerformUpdate(completionHandler:
    @escaping (NCUpdateResult) -> ()) {
        // ... do stuff quickly ...
        completionHandler(.newData)
}
```

Communication back to your app can be a little tricky. In Figure 13-14, two buttons invite the user to set up a reminder notification; I've implemented these to open our CoffeeTime app by calling open(_:completionHandler:) — a method of the auto-

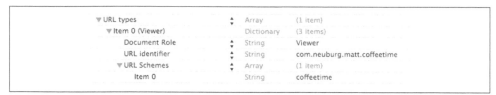

▼ URL types		Array	(1 item)
▼ Item 0 (Viewer)		Dictionary	(3 items)
Document Role		String	Viewer
URL identifier		String	com.neuburg.matt.coffeetime
▼ URL Schemes		Array	(1 item)
Item 0		String	coffeetime

Figure 13-15. A custom URL declaration

matically provided `extensionContext`, not the shared application, which is not available from here:

```
@IBAction func doButton(_ sender: Any) {
    let v = sender as! UIView
    var comp = URLComponents()
    comp.scheme = "coffeetime"
    comp.host = String(v.tag) // button's tag is number of minutes
    if let url = comp.url {
        self.extensionContext?.open(url)
    }
}
```

The CoffeeTime app receives this message because I've given it two things:

A custom URL scheme

The `coffeetime` scheme is declared in the app's *Info.plist* (Figure 13-15).

An implementation of `application(_:open:options:)`

In the app delegate, I've implemented `application(_:open:options:)` to analyze the URL when it arrives. I've coded the original URL so that the "host" is actually the number of minutes announced in the tapped button; thus, I can respond appropriately (presumably by scheduling a local notification for that number of minutes from now):

```
func application(_ app: UIApplication, open url: URL,
    options: [UIApplicationOpenURLOptionsKey : Any]) -> Bool {
        let scheme = url.scheme
        let host = url.host
        if scheme == "coffeetime" {
            if let host = host, let min = Int(host) {
                // ... do something here ...
                return true
            }
        }
        return false
}
```

A today extension's widget interface can have two heights: compact and expanded. If you take advantage of this feature, your widget will have a Show More or Show Less button (similar to the Weather app's widget). To do so:

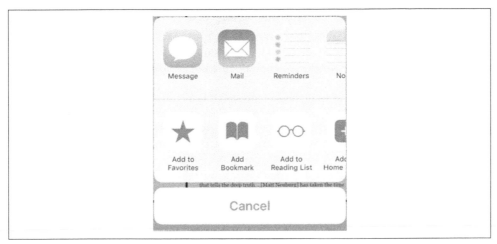

Figure 13-16. An activity view

1. Run this code early in the life of your view controller, probably in its viewDid-
   Load:

   ```
   self.extensionContext?.widgetLargestAvailableDisplayMode = .expanded
   ```

2. Implement `widgetActiveDisplayModeDidChange(_:withMaximumSize:)`. The
   first parameter is an NCWidgetDisplayMode, either `.compact` or `.expanded`. The
   idea is that you would respond by changing your view controller's `preferred-
   ContentSize` to the smaller or larger size, respectively.

If your app has a today extension, the today extension widget is displayed *automatically* when the user performs the 3D touch gesture that summons quick actions. Since
our widget is interactive, we actually don't need the static quick action buttons shown
in Figure 13-5!

Activity Views

An activity view is the view belonging to a UIActivityViewController, typically
appearing when the user taps a Share button. To display it, you start with one or more
pieces of data, such as a string or an image, that you want the user to have the option
of sharing or working with. The activity view, when it appears, will then contain an
icon for every activity (UIActivity) that can work with this type of data. The user may
tap an icon in the activity view, and is then perhaps shown additional interface,
belonging to the provider of the chosen activity. Figure 13-16 shows an example,
from Mobile Safari.

In Figure 13-16, the top row of the activity view lists some applicable built-in system-
wide activities; the bottom row shows some activities provided internally by Safari

itself. When you present an activity view within your app, your app can add to the lower row additional activities that are available only within your app. Moreover, your app can provide system-wide activities that are available when *any* app presents an activity view; such system-wide activities come in two forms:

Share extensions
> A *share extension* is shown in the *upper* row of an activity view. Share extensions are for apps that can accept information into themselves, either for storage, such as Notes and Reminders, or for sending out to a server, such as Twitter and Facebook.

Action extensions
> An *action extension* is shown in the *lower* row of an activity view. Action extensions offer to perform some kind of manipulation on the data provided by the host app, and can hand back the resulting data in reply.

I'll describe how to present an activity view and how to construct an activity that's private to your app. Then I'll give an example of writing an action extension, and finally an example of writing a share extension.

Presenting an Activity View

You will typically want to present an activity view in response to the user tapping a Share button in your app. To do so:

1. Instantiate UIActivityViewController. The initializer you'll be calling is `init(activityItems:applicationActivities:)`, where the first argument is an array of objects to be shared or operated on, such as string or image objects. Presumably these are objects associated somehow with the interface the user is looking at right now.

2. Set the activity view controller's `completionWithItemsHandler` property to a function that will be called when the user's interaction with the activity interface ends.

3. Present the activity view controller, as a presented view controller; on the iPad, it will be a popover, so you'll also configure the popover presentation controller. The presented view or popover will be dismissed automatically when the user cancels or chooses an activity.

So, for example:

```
let url = Bundle.main.url(forResource:"sunglasses", withExtension:"png")!
let things : [Any] = ["This is a cool picture", url]
let avc = UIActivityViewController(
    activityItems:things, applicationActivities:nil)
avc.completionWithItemsHandler = { type, ok, items, err in
```

```
        // ...
    }
    self.present(avc, animated:true)
    if let pop = avc.popoverPresentationController {
        let v = sender as! UIView
        pop.sourceView = v
        pop.sourceRect = v.bounds
    }
```

There is no cancel button in the popover presentation of the activity view; the user cancels by tapping outside the popover. Actually, the user can cancel by tapping outside the activity view even on the iPhone.

The activity view is populated automatically with known system-wide activities that can handle any of the types of data you provided as the `activityItems:` argument. These activities represent UIActivity types, and are designated by UIActivityType constants:

- `.postToFacebook`
- `.postToTwitter`
- `.postToWeibo`
- `.message`
- `.mail`
- `.print`
- `.copyToPasteboard`
- `.assignToContact`
- `.saveToCameraRoll`
- `.addToReadingList`
- `.postToFlickr`
- `.postToVimeo`
- `.postToTencentWeibo`
- `.airDrop`
- `.openInIBooks`
- `.markupAsPDF`

Consult the UIActivity class documentation to learn what types of activity item each of these activities can handle. For example, the `.mail` activity will accept a string, an image, or a file (such as an image file) designated by a URL; it will present a mail composition interface with the activity item(s) in the body. Figure 13-17 shows what appears if the user taps the Mail icon in our activity view.

Figure 13-17. Mail accepts text and an image URL

Since the default is to include all the system-wide activities that can handle the provided data, if you *don't* want a certain system-wide activity included in the activity view, you must exclude it explicitly. You do this by setting the UIActivityViewController's `excludedActivityTypes` property to an array of activity type constants.

 The Notes and Reminders activities have no corresponding UIActivity, because they are implemented as share extensions; it is up to the *user* to exclude them if desired.

In the UIActivityViewController initializer `init(activityItems:application-Activities:)`, if you would prefer that an element of the `activityItems:` array should be an object that will supply the data instead of the data itself, make it an object that adopts the UIActivityItemSource protocol. Typically, this object will be `self` (the view controller in charge of all this code). Here's a minimal, artificial example:

```
extension ViewController : UIActivityItemSource {
    func activityViewControllerPlaceholderItem(
        _ activityViewController: UIActivityViewController) -> Any {
            return ""
    }
    func activityViewController(
        _ activityViewController: UIActivityViewController,
        itemForActivityType activityType: UIActivityType?) -> Any? {
            return "Coolness"
    }
}
```

The first method provides a placeholder that exemplifies the type of data that will be returned; the second method returns the actual data. The second method can return different data depending on the activity type that the user chose; for example, you could provide one string to Notes and another string to Mail.

The UIActivitySource protocol also answers a commonly asked question about how to get the Mail activity to populate the mail composition form with a default subject:

```
extension ViewController : UIActivityItemSource {
    // ...
    func activityViewController(
        _ activityViewController: UIActivityViewController,
        subjectForActivityType activityType: UIActivityType?) -> String {
            return "This is cool"
    }
}
```

If your `activityItems:` data is time-consuming to provide, substitute an instance of a `UIActivityItemProvider` subclass:

```
let avc = UIActivityViewController(
    activityItems:[MyProvider(placeholderItem: "")],
    applicationActivities:nil)
```

The `placeholderItem:` in the initializer signals the type of data that this UIActivityItemProvider object will actually provide. Your UIActivityItemProvider subclass should override the `item` property to return the actual object. This property will be consulted on a background thread, and UIActivityItemProvider is itself an Operation subclass (see Chapter 24).

Custom Activities

The purpose of the `applicationActivities:` parameter of `init(activity Items:applicationActivities:)` is for you to list any additional activities implemented internally by your own app. Their icons will then appear as choices in the lower row when your app presents an activity view. Each activity will be an instance of one of your own UIActivity subclasses.

To illustrate, I'll create a minimal (and nonsensical) activity called Be Cool that accepts string activity items. It is a UIActivity subclass called MyCoolActivity. So, to include Be Cool among the choices presented to the user by a UIActivityViewController, I'd say:

```
let things : [Any] = ["This is a cool picture", url]
let avc = UIActivityViewController(
    activityItems:things, applicationActivities:[MyCoolActivity()])
```

Now let's implement MyCoolActivity. It has an array property called `items`, for reasons that will be apparent in a moment. We need to arm ourselves with an image to represent this activity in the activity view; this will be treated as a template image. It should be no larger than 60×60 (76×76 on iPad); it can be smaller, and looks better if it is, because the system will draw a rounded rectangle around it, and the image should be somewhat inset from this. It needn't be square, as it will be centered in the rounded rectangle automatically.

Here's the preparatory part of the implementation of MyCoolActivity:

```
var items : [Any]?
var image : UIImage
override init() {
    // ... construct self.image ...
    super.init()
}
override class var activityCategory : UIActivityCategory {
    return .action // the default
}
override var activityType : UIActivityType {
    return UIActivityType("com.neuburg.matt.coolActivity")
}
override var activityTitle : String? {
    return "Be Cool"
}
override var activityImage : UIImage? {
    return self.image
}
override func canPerform(withActivityItems activityItems: [Any]) -> Bool {
    for obj in activityItems {
        if obj is String {
            return true
        }
    }
    return false
}
override func prepare(withActivityItems activityItems: [Any]) {
    self.items = activityItems
}
```

If we return `true` from `canPerform(withActivityItems:)`, then an icon for this activity, labeled Be Cool and displaying our `activityImage`, will appear in the activity view (Figure 13-18).

If the user taps our icon, `prepare(withActivityItems:)` will be called. We retain the `activityItems` into our `items` property, because they won't be arriving again when we are actually told to perform the activity. The next step is that we will be called upon to perform the activity. To do so, we implement one of these:

perform *method*
    We immediately perform the activity directly, using the activity items we've already retained. If the activity is time-consuming, the activity should be

Figure 13-18. Our activity's icon appears in our activity view

performed on a background thread (Chapter 24) so that we can return immediately; the activity view interface will be taken down and the user will be able to go on interacting with the app.

activityViewController *property*

We have further interface that we'd like to show the user as part of the activity, so we provide an instance of a UIViewController subclass. The activity view mechanism will present this view controller for us; it is not our job to present or dismiss it. (We may, however, present or dismiss dependent interface. For example, if our view controller is a navigation controller with a custom root view controller, we might push another view controller onto its stack while the user is interacting with the activity.)

No matter which of these two methods we implement, we *must* eventually call this activity instance's activityDidFinish(_:). This is the signal to the activity view mechanism that the activity is over. If the activity view mechanism is still presenting any interface, it will be taken down, and the argument we supply here, a Bool signifying whether the activity completed successfully, will be passed into the function we supplied earlier as the activity view controller's completionWithItemsHandler. So, for example:

```
override func perform() {
    // ... do something with self.items here ...
    self.activityDidFinish(true)
}
```

If your UIActivity is providing a view controller as its activityViewController, it will want to hand that view controller a reference to self beforehand, so that the view controller can call its activityDidFinish(_:) when the time comes.

For example, suppose our activity involves letting the user draw a mustache on a photo of someone. Our view controller will provide interface for doing that, including some way of letting the user signal completion, such as a Cancel button and a

Done button. When the user taps either of those, we'll do whatever else is necessary (such as saving the altered photo somewhere if the user tapped Done) and then call activityDidFinish(_:). Thus, we could implement the activityViewController property like this:

```
override var activityViewController : UIViewController? {
    let mvc = MustacheViewController(activity: self, items: self.items!)
    return mvc
}
```

And then MustacheViewController would have code like this:

```
weak var activity : UIActivity?
var items: [Any]
init(activity:UIActivity, items:[Any]) {
    self.activity = activity
    self.items = items
    super.init(nibName: "MustacheViewController", bundle: nil)
}
// ... other stuff ...
@IBAction func doCancel(_ sender: Any) {
    self.activity?.activityDidFinish(false)
}
@IBAction func doDone(_ sender: Any) {
    self.activity?.activityDidFinish(true)
}
```

Note that MustacheViewController's reference to the UIActivity (self.activity) is weak; otherwise, a retain cycle ensues.

 The purpose of the SFSafariViewController delegate method safariView-Controller(_:activityItemsFor:title:) (Chapter 11) is now clear. This view controller's view appears inside your app, but it isn't your view controller, its Share button is not your button, and the activity view that it presents is not your activity view. Therefore, you need some other way to add custom UIActivity items to that activity view; to do so, implement this method.

Action Extensions

To provide a system-wide activity — one that appears when some *other* app puts up an activity view — you can write a share extension (to appear in the upper row) or an action extension (to appear in the lower row). Your app can provide just one share extension, but can provide multiple action extensions. I'll describe first the basics of writing an action extension.

Start with the appropriate target template, iOS → Application Extension → Action Extension. There are two kinds of action extension, with or without an interface; you'll make your choice in the second pane as you create the target.

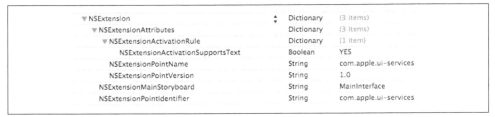

Figure 13-19. An action extension Info.plist

In the *Info.plist*, in addition to setting the bundle name, which will appear below the activity's icon in the activity view, you'll need to specify what types of data this activity accepts as its operands. In the `NSExtensionActivationRule` dictionary, you'll provide one or more keys, such as:

- `NSExtensionActivationSupportsFileWithMaxCount`

- `NSExtensionActivationSupportsImageWithMaxCount`

- `NSExtensionActivationSupportsMovieWithMaxCount`

- `NSExtensionActivationSupportsText`

- `NSExtensionActivationSupportsWebURLWithMaxCount`

For the full list, see the "Action Extension Keys" section of Apple's *Information Property List Key Reference*. It is also possible to declare in a more sophisticated way what types of data your activity accepts, by writing an NSPredicate string as the value of the `NSExtensionActivationRule` key. Figure 13-19 shows the relevant part of the *Info.plist* for an action extension that accepts one text object.

When your action extension appears in an activity view within some other app that provides the appropriate type(s) of data, it will be represented by an icon which you need to specify in your action extension target. This icon is the same size as an app icon, and can conveniently come from an asset catalog; it will be treated as a template image.

There is one big difference between an action extension and a custom UIActivity: an action extension can return data to the calling app. The transport mechanism for this data involves the use of NSItemProviders, already familiar from drag and drop (Chapter 9).

Action extension without an interface

I'll start by giving an example of an action extension that has no interface. Our code goes into the class provided by the template, ActionRequestHandler, an NSObject subclass.

Our example extension takes a string object and returns a string. In particular, it accepts a string that might be the two-letter abbreviation of one of the U.S. states, and if it is, it returns the name of the actual state. To prepare, we provide some properties:

```
var extensionContext: NSExtensionContext?
let desiredType = kUTTypePlainText as String
let list : [String:String] = { /* ... */ }()
```

`self.extensionContext` is a place to store the NSExtensionContext that will be provided to us. `self.desiredType` is just a convenient constant expressing the acceptable data type. In addition, we have a property `self.list` which, as in Chapter 10, is a dictionary whose keys are state name abbreviations and whose values are the corresponding state names.

There is just one entry point into our extension's code — `beginRequest(with:)`. Here we must store a reference to the NSExtensionContext provided as the parameter, retrieve the data, process the data, and return the result. You will probably want to factor the processing of the data out into a separate function; I've called mine `process(item:)`. Here's a sketch of my `beginRequest(with:)` implementation; as it shows, my plan is to make one of two possible calls to `self.process(item:)`, either passing the string retrieved from `items`, or else passing `nil` to signify that there was no data:

```
func beginRequest(with context: NSExtensionContext) {
    self.extensionContext = context
    let items = self.extensionContext!.inputItems
    // ... if there is no data, call self.process(item:) with nil
    // ... if there is data, call self.process(item:) with the data
}
```

Now let's implement the retrieval of the data. Think of this as a nest of envelopes that we must examine and open:

- What arrives from the NSExtensionContext's `inputItems` is an array of NSExtensionItem objects.

- An NSExtensionItem has an `attachments` array of NSItemProvider objects.

- An NSItemProvider vends items, each of which represents the data in a particular format. In particular:

  - We can *ask* whether an NSItemProvider has an item of a particular type, by calling `hasItemConformingToTypeIdentifier(_:)`.

  - We can *retrieve* the item of a particular type, by calling `loadItem(forTypeIdentifier:options:completionHandler:)`. The item may be vended lazily, and can thus take time to prepare and provide; so we proceed in the `completionHandler:` function to receive the item and do something with it.

We are expecting only one item, so it will be provided by the first NSItemProvider inside the first NSExtensionItem. Here, then, is the code that I omitted from begin-RequestWithExtensionContext:

```
guard let extensionItem = items[0] as? NSExtensionItem,
    let provider = extensionItem.attachments?[0] as? NSItemProvider,
    provider.hasItemConformingToTypeIdentifier(self.desiredType)
    else {
        self.process(item:nil)
        return
    }
provider.loadItem(forTypeIdentifier: self.desiredType) { item, err in
    DispatchQueue.main.async {
        self.process(item: item as? String)
    }
}
```

Now we have the data, and we're ready to do something with it. In my code, that happens in the method that I've named process(item:). This method must do two things:

1. Call the NSExtensionContext's completeRequest(returningItems:completion-Handler:) to hand back the data.

2. Release the NSExtensionContext by setting our retaining property to nil.

I'll start with the simplest case: we didn't get any data. In that case, the returned value is nil:

```
func process(item:String?) {
    var result : [NSExtensionItem]? = nil
    // ... what goes here? ...
    self.extensionContext?.completeRequest(returningItems: result)
    self.extensionContext = nil
}
```

That was easy, because we cleverly omitted the only case where we have any work to do. Now let's implement that case. We have received a string in the item parameter. The first question is: is it the abbreviation of a state? To answer that question, I've implemented a utility function:

```
func state(for abbrev:String) -> String? {
    return self.list[abbrev.uppercased()]
}
```

If we call that method with our item string and the answer comes back nil, we simply proceed just as before — we return nil:

```
func process(item:String?) {
    var result : [NSExtensionItem]? = nil
    if let item = item,
        let state = self.state(for:item) {
            // ... what goes *here*? ...
    }
    self.extensionContext?.completeRequest(returningItems: result)
    self.extensionContext = nil
}
```

We come at last to the dreaded moment that I have been postponing all this time:
what if we get an abbreviation? In that case, we must reverse the earlier process of
opening envelopes: we must put envelopes within envelopes and hand back an array
of NSExtensionItems. We have only one result, so this will be an array of one
NSExtensionItem, whose `attachments` is an array of one NSItemProvider, whose
`item` is the string and whose `typeIdentifier` is the type of that string. Confused? I've
written a little utility function that should clarify:

```
func stuffThatEnvelope(_ item:String) -> [NSExtensionItem] {
    let extensionItem = NSExtensionItem()
    let itemProvider = NSItemProvider(
        item: item as NSString, typeIdentifier: desiredType)
    extensionItem.attachments = [itemProvider]
    return [extensionItem]
}
```

We can now write the full implementation of `process(item:)`, and our action extension is finished:

```
func process(item:String?) {
    var result : [NSExtensionItem]? = nil
    if let item = item,
        let state = self.state(for:item) {
            result = self.stuffThatEnvelope(state)
    }
    self.extensionContext?.completeRequest(returningItems: result)
    self.extensionContext = nil
}
```

Action extension with an interface

If an action extension has an interface, then the template provides a storyboard with
one scene, along with the code for a corresponding UIViewController class. The code
is actually simpler, because:

- A view controller already has an `extensionContext` property, and it is automatically set for us.

- There are no special entry points to our code. This is a UIViewController, and
  everything happens just as you would expect.

So, in my implementation, I use `viewDidLoad` to open the data envelope from `self.extensionContext`, get the abbreviation if there is one, get the expansion if there is one (storing it in a property, `self.expansion`), *and stop*. I've equipped my interface with a Done button and a Cancel button. The action methods for those buttons are where I hand the result back to the `extensionContext`:

```
@IBAction func cancel(_ sender: Any) {
    self.extensionContext?.completeRequest(returningItems: nil)
}
@IBAction func done(_ sender: Any) {
    self.extensionContext?.completeRequest(
        returningItems: self.stuffThatEnvelope(self.expansion!))
}
```

The runtime responds by dismissing the interface in good order.

Receiving data from an action extension

Now switch roles and pretend that your app is presenting a UIActivityViewController. We now know that this activity view might contain action extension icons. If the user taps one, how will your code retrieve the result? In my earlier implementation, I avoided this issue by pretending that action extensions didn't exist. Here's a more complete sketch:

```
let avc = UIActivityViewController(
    activityItems:[things], applicationActivities:nil)
avc.completionWithItemsHandler = { type, ok, items, err in
    if ok {
        guard let items = items, items.count > 0 else { return }
        // ... open the envelopes! ...
    }
}
self.present(avc, animated:true)
```

If what the user interacted with in the activity view is one of the built-in UIActivity types, no data has been returned. But if the user interacted with an action extension, then there may be data inside the `items` envelopes, and it is up to us to retrieve it.

The structure here is exactly the same as the `items` of an NSExtensionContext: `items` is an array, each element of which is presumably an NSExtensionItem, whose `attachments` is presumably an array of NSItemProvider objects, each of which can be queried for its data. In the case where we are prepared to receive a string, therefore, the code is effectively just the same as the envelope-opening code we've already written:

```
guard let items = items, items.count > 0 else { return }
guard let extensionItem = items[0] as? NSExtensionItem,
    let provider = extensionItem.attachments?[0] as? NSItemProvider,
    provider.hasItemConformingToTypeIdentifier(self.desiredType)
    else { return }
```

```
provider.loadItem(forTypeIdentifier: self.desiredType) { item, err in
    DispatchQueue.main.async {
        if let s = item as? String {
            // ... do something with s ...
        }
    }
}
```

Share Extensions

Your app can appear in the top row of an activity view if it provides a share extension. A share extension is similar to an action extension, but simpler: it accepts some data and returns nothing. The idea is that it will then do something with that data, such as storing it or posting it to a server.

The user, after tapping an app's icon in the activity view, is given an opportunity to interact further with the data, possibly modifying it or canceling the share operation. To make this possible, the Share Extension template, when you create the target (iOS → Application Extension → Share Extension), will give you a storyboard and a view controller. This view controller can be one of two types:

An SLComposeServiceViewController
> The SLComposeServiceViewController provides a standard interface for display-ing editable text in a UITextView along with a possible preview, plus user-configurable option buttons, along with a Cancel button and a Post button.

A plain view controller subclass
> If you opt for a plain view controller subclass, then designing its interface, including providing a way to dismiss it, will be up to you.

Whichever form of interface you elect to use, your way of dismissing it will be this familiar-looking incantation:

```
self.extensionContext?.completeRequestReturningItems([])
```

A custom view controller is easy to implement, so I won't bother to discuss it. Instead, I'll describe briefly some of the basics of working with an SLComposeServiceView-Controller. Its view is displayed with a text view already populated with the text passed along from the host app, so there's very little more for you to do; you can add a preview view and option buttons, and that's just about all. I'll concentrate on option buttons.

An option button displays a title string and a value string. When tapped, it will typi-cally summon interface where the user can change the value string. In Figure 13-20, I've created a single option button — a Size button, whose value can be Large, Medium, or Small. (I have no idea what this choice is supposed to signify for my app; it's only an example!)

Figure 13-20. A share extension

To create the configuration option, I override the SLComposeServiceViewController configurationItems method to return an array of one SLComposeSheetConfigurationItem. Its title and value are displayed in the button. Its tapHandler will be called when the button is tapped. Typically, you'll create a view controller and push it into the interface with pushConfigurationViewController:

```
weak var config : SLComposeSheetConfigurationItem?
var selectedText = "Large" {
    didset {
        self.config?.value = self.selectedText
    }
}
override func configurationItems() -> [Any]! {
    let c = SLComposeSheetConfigurationItem()!
    c.title = "Size"
    c.value = self.selectedText
    c.tapHandler = { [unowned self] in
        let tvc = TableViewController(style: .grouped)
        tvc.selectedSize = self.selectedText
        tvc.delegate = self
        self.pushConfigurationViewController(tvc)
    }
    self.config = c
    return [c]
}
```

My TableViewController is a UITableViewController subclass. Its table view displays three rows whose cells are labeled Large, Medium, and Small, along with a checkmark (compare the table view described in "Cell Choice and Static Tables" on page 507). The tricky part is that I need a way to communicate with this table view controller: I need to tell it what the configuration item's value is now, and I need to hear from it what the user chooses in the table view. So I've given the table view controller a property (selectedSize) where I can deposit the configuration item's value, and I've declared a delegate protocol so that the table view controller can set a property of mine (selectedText). This is the relevant portion of my TableViewController class:

```
protocol SizeDelegate : class {
    var selectedText : String {get set}
}
class TableViewController: UITableViewController {
    var selectedSize : String?
    weak var delegate : SizeDelegate?
    override func tableView(_ tableView: UITableView,
        didSelectRowAt indexPath: IndexPath) {
            let cell = tableView.cellForRow(at:indexPath)!
            let s = cell.textLabel!.text!
            self.selectedSize = s
            self.delegate?.selectedText = s
            tableView.reloadData()
    }
    // ...
}
```

The navigation interface is provided for me, so I don't have to do anything about popping the table view controller: the user will do that by tapping the Back button after choosing a size. In my `configurationItems` implementation, I cleverly kept a reference to my configuration item as `self.config`. When the user chooses from the table view, its `tableView(_:didSelectRowAt:)` sets my `selectedText`, and my `selectedText` setter observer promptly changes the `value` of the configuration item to whatever the user chose.

The user, when finished interacting with the share extension interface, will tap one of the provided buttons, either Cancel or Post. The Cancel button is handled automatically: the interface is dismissed. The Post button is hooked automatically to my `didSelectPost` implementation, where I fetch the text from my own `contentText` property, do something with it, and dismiss the interface:

```
override func didSelectPost() {
    let s = self.contentText
    // ... do something with it ...
    self.extensionContext?.completeRequest(returningItems:[])
}
```

If the material provided from the host app were more elaborate, I would pull it out of `self.extensionContext` in the same way as for an action extension. If there were networking to do at this point, I would initiate a background URLSession (as explained in Chapter 23).

There is no official way, as far as I can tell, to change the title or appearance of the Cancel and Post buttons. Apps that show different buttons, such as Reminders and Notes, are either not using SLComposeServiceViewController or are using a technique available only to Apple. I was able to change my Post button to a Save button like this:

```
override func viewDidLayoutSubviews() {
    super.viewDidLayoutSubviews()
    self.navigationController?.navigationBar.topItem?
        .rightBarButtonItem?.title = "Save"
}
```

But whether that's legal, and whether it will keep working on future systems, is anybody's guess.

PART III

Some Frameworks

This part of the book gets you started on some of Cocoa's specialized frameworks.

- Chapter 14 talks about playing sound.
- Chapter 15 talks about playing video and introduces the powerful AV Foundation framework.
- Chapter 16 is about how to access the user's music library.
- Chapter 17 is about how to access the user's photo library, and discusses using the device's camera.
- Chapter 18 is about how to access the user's contacts.
- Chapter 19 is about how to access the user's calendars and reminders.
- Chapter 20 explains how to display and customize a map, how to show the user's current location, and how to convert between a location and an address.
- Chapter 21 is about the device sensors that tell your app where the device is located and how it is oriented.

CHAPTER 14

Audio

iOS provides various technologies that allow your app to produce, record, and process sound. The topic is a large one, so this chapter can only introduce it; I'll concentrate on basic sound production. You'll want to read Apple's *Media Playback Programming Guide* and *Core Audio Overview*.

None of the classes discussed in this chapter provides any interface within your app for allowing the user to stop and start playback of sound (transport control). If you want transport interface, here are some options:

- You can create your own interface.
- You can associate the built-in "remote control" buttons with your application, as I'll explain in this chapter.
- A web view (Chapter 11) supports the IITML5 `<audio>` tag; this can be a simple, lightweight way to play audio and to allow the user to control playback (including use of AirPlay).
- You could treat the sound as a movie and use the interface-providing classes that I'll discuss in Chapter 15; this can also be a good way to play a sound file located remotely over the Internet.

System Sounds

The simplest form of sound is *system sound*, which is the iOS equivalent of the basic computer "beep." This is implemented through System Sound Services, part of the Audio Toolbox framework; you'll need to `import AudioToolbox`. The API for playing a system sound comes in two forms — the old form and the new form (introduced in

iOS 9). I'll show you the old form first (it still works, and has not yet been deprecated); then I'll demonstrate the new form.

The old form involves calling one of two C functions, which behave very similarly to
one another:

AudioServicesPlayAlertSound
On an iPhone, may also vibrate the device, depending on the user's settings.

AudioServicesPlaySystemSound
On an iPhone, there won't be an accompanying vibration, but you can specifi-
cally elect to have this "sound" *be* a device vibration (by passing kSystemSound-
ID_Vibrate as the name of the "sound").

The sound file to be played needs to be an uncompressed AIFF or WAV file (or an
Apple CAF file wrapping one of those). To hand the sound to these functions, you'll
need a SystemSoundID, which you obtain by calling AudioServicesCreateSystem-
SoundID with a URL that points to a sound file. In this example, the sound file is in
our app bundle:

```
let sndurl = Bundle.main.url(forResource:"test", withExtension: "aif")!
var snd : SystemSoundID = 0
AudioServicesCreateSystemSoundID(sndurl as CFURL, &snd)
AudioServicesPlaySystemSound(snd)
```

That code works — we hear the sound — but there's a problem: we have failed to
exercise proper memory management. We need to call AudioServicesDispose-
SystemSoundID to release our SystemSoundID. But when shall we do this? Audio-
ServicesPlaySystemSound executes *asynchronously*. So the solution can't be to call
AudioServicesDisposeSystemSoundID in the next line of the same snippet, because
this would release our sound just as it is about to start playing, resulting in silence.

The solution is to implement a *sound completion function* to be called when the sound
has finished playing. The sound completion function is specified by calling Audio-
ServicesAddSystemSoundCompletion. It must be supplied as a C pointer-to-function,
but Swift lets you pass a global or local Swift function (including an anonymous function) where a C pointer-to-function is expected. So our code now looks like this:

```
let sndurl = Bundle.main.url(forResource:"test", withExtension: "aif")!
var snd : SystemSoundID = 0
AudioServicesCreateSystemSoundID(sndurl as CFURL, &snd)
AudioServicesAddSystemSoundCompletion(snd, nil, nil, { sound, context in
    AudioServicesRemoveSystemSoundCompletion(sound)
    AudioServicesDisposeSystemSoundID(sound)
}, nil)
AudioServicesPlaySystemSound(snd)
```

Note that when we are about to release the sound, we first release the sound completion function itself.

Now for the new form. The new calls take *two* parameters: a SystemSoundID and a completion function. The completion function takes no parameters; we can still refer to the SystemSoundID in order to dispose of its memory, because it is in scope. Here, we'll call `AudioServicesPlaySystemSoundWithCompletion` instead of `AudioServices-PlaySystemSound`; we no longer need to call `AudioServicesRemoveSystemSound-Completion`, because we never called `AudioServicesAddSystemSoundCompletion`:

```
let sndurl = Bundle.main.url(forResource:"test", withExtension: "aif")!
var snd : SystemSoundID = 0
AudioServicesCreateSystemSoundID(sndurl as CFURL, &snd)
AudioServicesPlaySystemSoundWithCompletion(snd) {
    AudioServicesDisposeSystemSoundID(snd)
}
```

Audio Session

Audio on the device — *all* audio belonging to *all* apps and processes — is controlled and mediated by the *media services daemon*. This daemon must juggle many demands; your app is just one of many clamoring for its attention and cooperation. As a result, your app's audio can be affected and even overruled by other apps and external factors.

Your communication with the audio services daemon is conducted through an *audio session*, which is a singleton AVAudioSession instance created automatically as your app launches. This is part of the AV Foundation framework; you'll need to `import` `AVFoundation`. You'll refer to your app's AVAudioSession by way of the class method `sharedInstance`.

Category

Your app, if it is going to be producing sound, needs to specify a *policy* regarding that sound and tell the media services daemon about it. This policy will answer such questions as:

- Should your app's sound be stopped when the screen is locked?
- If other sound is being produced (for example, if the Music app is playing a song in the background), should your app stop it or be layered on top of it?

To declare your audio session's policy, you'll set its *category* by calling `set-Category(_:mode:options:)`. I'll explain later about the `mode:` and `options:`; if you have no mode or options, you can omit both parameters, and if you have options but no mode, you can use a mode of `AVAudioSessionModeDefault`. Your app needn't set just one category for all time; different activities or moments in the lifetime of your app might require that the category should change.

The basic policies for audio playback are:

Ambient (`AVAudioSessionCategoryAmbient`*)*
 Your app's audio plays even while another app is playing audio, and is stopped by the phone's Silent switch and screen locking.

Solo Ambient (`AVAudioSessionCategorySoloAmbient`*, the default)*
 Your app stops any audio being played by other apps, and is stopped by the phone's Silent switch and screen locking.

Playback (`AVAudioSessionCategoryPlayback`*)*
 Your app stops any audio being played by other apps, and is *not* stopped by the Silent switch. It is stopped by screen locking, unless it is also configured to play in the background (as explained later in this chapter).

Audio session category options (the `options:` parameter) allow you to modify the playback policies (AVAudioSessionCategoryOptions). For example:

Mixable audio (`.mixWithOthers`*)*
 You can override the Playback policy so as to allow other apps to continue playing audio. Your sound is then said to be *mixable*. Mixability can also affect you in the other direction: another app's mixable audio can continue to play even when your app's Playback policy is *not* mixable.

Mixable except for speech (`.interruptSpokenAudioAndMixWithOthers`*)*
 Similar to `.mixWithOthers`, but although you are willing to mix with background music, you are electing to stop speech audio. An app's audio is marked as speech by setting the audio session mode to `AVAudioSessionModeSpokenAudio`.

Ducking audio (`.duckOthers`*)*
 You can override a policy that allows other audio to play, so as to *duck* (diminish the volume of) that other audio. Ducking is thus a form of mixing.

Activation and Deactivation

Your audio session policy is not in effect unless your audio session is also *active*. By default, it isn't. Thus, asserting your audio session policy is done by a combination of configuring the audio session and activating the audio session. To activate (or deactivate) your audio session, you call `setActive(true)`.

The question is *when* to call `setActive(true)`. This depends on whether you need your audio session to be active all the time, or only when you are producing sound. In many cases, it will be best not to activate your audio session until just before you really need it, that is, when you are starting to produce sound. However, let's take a very simple case where our sounds are always occasional, intermittent, and nonessential. So we want sound from other apps, such as the Music app, to be allowed to continue playing when the user launches or switches to our app. That's the Ambient policy. Our policy will never vary, and it doesn't stop other audio, so we might as well set our app's category and activate it at launch time:

```
func application(_ application: UIApplication,
    didFinishLaunchingWithOptions launchOptions:
    [UIApplicationLaunchOptionsKey : Any]?) -> Bool {
        let sess = AVAudioSession.sharedInstance()
        try? sess.setCategory(AVAudioSessionCategoryAmbient)
        try? sess.setActive(true)
        return true
}
```

It is also possible to call `setActive(false)`, thus deactivating your audio session. There are various reasons why you might deactivate (and perhaps reactivate) your audio session over the lifetime of your app.

One possible reason is that you want to *change* something about your audio session policy. Certain changes in your audio session category and options don't take effect unless you deactivate the existing policy and activate the new policy. Ducking is a good example; I'll demonstrate in the next section.

Another reason for deactivating your audio session is that you have stopped playing sound; you no longer need to hog the device's audio, and you want to yield to other apps that were stopped by your audio session policy, so that they can resume playing. You can even send a message to other apps as you do this:

```
let sess = AVAudioSession.sharedInstance()
try? sess.setActive(false, with: .notifyOthersOnDeactivation)
```

 Apple suggests that you might want to register for the `.AVAudioSessionMedia-ServicesWereReset` notification. If this notification arrives, the media services daemon was somehow hosed. In this situation, you should basically start from scratch, configuring your category and activating your audio session, as well as resetting and recreating any audio-related objects.

Ducking

As an example of deactivating and activating your audio session, I'll describe how to implement ducking.

Presume that we have configured and activated an Ambient category audio session, as described in the preceding sections. This category permits other audio to continue playing. Now let's say we do sometimes play a sound, but it's brief and doesn't require other sound to stop entirely — but we'd like other audio to be quieter momentarily while we're playing our sound. That's ducking!

Background sound is not ducked automatically just because we play a sound of our own. It is up to *us* to duck the background sound as we start to play our sound, and to stop ducking when our sound ends. We do this by changing our Ambient category to use, or not to use, the `.duckOthers` option. To make such a change, the most reliable approach is three steps:

1. Deactivate our audio session.
2. Reconfigure our audio session category with a changed set of options.
3. Activate our audio session.

So, just before we play our sound, we duck any other sound by adding `.duckOthers` to the options on our Ambient category:

```
let sess = AVAudioSession.sharedInstance()
try? sess.setActive(false)
let opts = sess.categoryOptions.union(.duckOthers)
try? sess.setCategory(sess.category, mode: sess.mode, options: opts)
try? sess.setActive(true)
```

When our sound finishes playing, we unduck any other sound by removing `.duckOthers` from the options on our category:

```
let sess = AVAudioSession.sharedInstance()
try? sess.setActive(false)
let opts = sess.categoryOptions.subtracting(.duckOthers)
try? sess.setCategory(sess.category, mode: sess.mode, options:opts)
try? sess.setActive(true)
```

Interruptions

Management of your audio session is complicated by the fact that it can be *interrupted*. For example, on an iPhone a phone call can arrive or an alarm can go off. Or another app might assert its audio session over yours, possibly because your app went into the background and the other app came into the foreground. Under certain circumstances, merely going into the background will interrupt your audio session.

When your audio session is interrupted, *it is deactivated*. That means you need to know when the interruption ends, so that you can reactivate your audio session. In order to know that, you will need to register for the `.AVAudioSessionInterruption` notification. You should do this as early as possible, perhaps at launch time.

The `.AVAudioSessionInterruption` notification can arrive either because an interruption begins or because it ends. To learn whether the interruption began or ended, examine the `AVAudioSessionInterruptionTypeKey` entry in the notification's `userInfo` dictionary; this will be a UInt encoding an AVAudioSessionInterruptionType, either `.began` or `.ended`. So, for example:

```
NotificationCenter.default.addObserver(forName:
    .AVAudioSessionInterruption, object: nil, queue: nil) { n in
        let why = n.userInfo![AVAudioSessionInterruptionTypeKey] as! UInt
        let type = AVAudioSessionInterruptionType(rawValue: why)!
        switch type {
        case .began:
            // update interface if needed
        case .ended:
            try? AVAudioSession.sharedInstance().setActive(true)
            // update interface if needed
            // resume playback?
        }
}
```

When an interruption to your audio session begins, your audio has already paused and your audio session has been deactivated. If your app contains interface for playing and pausing, you might change a Pause button to a Play button. But apart from this there's no particular work for you to do. When the interruption ends, on the other hand, activating your audio session and possibly resuming playback of your audio might be up to you.

The notification telling you that the interruption is over can include a message from some other app that interrupted you and has now deactivated its audio session. The other app sends that message by deactivating its audio session along with the .notify-OthersOnDeactivation option. You'll receive the message in the userInfo dictionary's AVAudioSessionInterruptionOptionKey entry; its value will be a UInt encoding an AVAudioSessionInterruptionOptions, which might be .shouldResume:

```
guard let opt = n.userInfo![AVAudioSessionInterruptionOptionKey] as? UInt
    else {return}
if AVAudioSessionInterruptionOptions(rawValue:opt).contains(.shouldResume) {
    // resume playback
}
```

Secondary Audio

When your app is frontmost and the user brings up the control center and uses the Play button to resume, say, the current Music app song, there may be no interruption of your audio session, because your app never went into the background. Instead, what you might get, if you've registered for it, is a notification of a different kind, namely .AVAudioSessionSilenceSecondaryAudioHint. You'll receive this notification only while your app is in the foreground.

This notification, corresponding to the AVAudioSession Bool property secondary-AudioShouldBeSilencedHint, expresses a fine-grained distinction between primary and secondary audio. Apple's example is a game app, where intermittent sound effects are the primary audio, while an ongoing underlying soundtrack is the secondary audio. The idea is that the user might start playing a song from the Music app, and that your app would therefore pause its secondary audio while continuing to produce its primary audio — because the user's chosen Music track will do just as well as a background soundtrack behind your game's sound effects.

To respond to this notification, examine the `AVAudioSessionSilenceSecondary-AudioHintTypeKey` entry in the notification's `userInfo` dictionary; this will be a UInt equating to an AVAudioSessionSilenceSecondaryAudioHintType, either `.begin` or `.end`. So, for example:

```
NotificationCenter.default.addObserver(forName:
    .AVAudioSessionSilenceSecondaryAudioHint, object: nil, queue: nil) { n in
        let why = n.userInfo![AVAudioSessionSilenceSecondaryAudioHintTypeKey]
            as! UInt
        let type = AVAudioSessionSilenceSecondaryAudioHintType(rawValue: why)!
        switch type {
        case .begin:
            // pause secondary audio
        case .end:
            // resume secondary audio
        }
}
```

Routing Changes

Your audio is routed through a particular output (and input). External events, such a phone call arriving, can cause a change in audio routing, and the user can also make changes in audio routing — for example, by plugging headphones into the device, which causes sound to stop coming out of the speaker and to come out of the headphones instead. You can and should register for the `.AVAudioSessionRouteChange` notification to hear about routing changes and respond to them.

The notification's `userInfo` dictionary is chock full of useful information about what just happened. Here's the console log of the dictionary that results when I detach headphones from the device:

```
AVAudioSessionRouteChangeReasonKey = 2;
AVAudioSessionRouteChangePreviousRouteKey =
    <AVAudioSessionRouteDescription: 0x174019ee0,
        inputs = (null);
        outputs = (
            <AVAudioSessionPortDescription: 0x174019f00,
                type = Headphones;
                name = Headphones;
                UID = Wired Headphones;
                selectedDataSource = (null)>
        )>;
```

Upon receipt of this notification, I can find out what the audio route is now, by calling AVAudioSession's `currentRoute` method; here's the result logged to the console:

```
<AVAudioSessionRouteDescription: 0x174019fc0,
    inputs = (null);
    outputs = (
        <AVAudioSessionPortDescription: 0x17401a000,
            type = Speaker;
            name = Speaker;
            UID = Speaker;
            selectedDataSource = (null)>
    )>
```

The classes mentioned here — AVAudioSessionRouteDescription and AVAudio-SessionPortDescription — are value classes. The `AVAudioSessionRouteChangeReason-Key` refers to an AVAudioSessionRouteChangeReason; the value here, 2, is `.oldDeviceUnavailable` — we stopped using the headphones and started using the speaker, because there are no headphones any longer.

A routing change may not of itself interrupt your sound, but Apple suggests that in this particular situation you might like to respond by stopping your audio deliberately, because otherwise sound may now suddenly be coming out of the speaker in a public place.

Audio Player

The easiest way to play sounds is to use an *audio player* (AVAudioPlayer). AVAudio-Player is part of the AV Foundation framework; you'll need to `import AVFoundation`.

An audio player is initialized with its sound, using a local file URL or Data; optionally, the initializer can also state the expected sound file format. A wide range of sound types is acceptable, including MP3, AAC, and ALAC, as well as AIFF and WAV. New in iOS 11, FLAC is an acceptable format, as well as Opus (a lossy compression codec commonly used for streaming and VoIP). A single audio player can possess and play only one sound; but you can have multiple audio players, they can play separately or simultaneously, and you can synchronize them. You can set a sound's volume and stereo pan features, loop a sound, change the playing rate, and set playback to begin somewhere in the middle of a sound. You can even execute a fade in or fade out over time.

Having created and initialized an audio player, you must *retain it*, typically by assigning it to an instance property. Assigning an audio player to a local variable and telling it to play, and hearing nothing — because the player has gone out of existence immediately, before it has a chance even to start playing — is a common beginner mistake.

To play the sound, first make sure your audio session is configured correctly. Now tell the audio player to `prepareToPlay`, causing it to load buffers and initialize hardware; then tell it to `play`. The audio player's delegate (AVAudioPlayerDelegate) is notified when the sound has finished playing, through a call to `audioPlayerDidFinish-`

Playing(_:successfully:); do *not* repeatedly check the audio player's isPlaying property to learn its state. Other useful methods include pause and stop; the chief difference between them is that pause doesn't release the buffers and hardware set up by prepareToPlay, but stop does, so you'd want to call prepareToPlay again before resuming play. Neither pause nor stop changes the playhead position, the point in the sound where playback will start if play is sent again; for that, use the currentTime property.

Devising a strategy for instantiating, retaining, and releasing your audio players is up to you. In one of my apps, I define a class called Player, which implements a play-File(atPath:) method expecting a string path to a sound file. This method creates a new AVAudioPlayer, stores it as a property, and tells it to play the sound file; it also sets itself as that audio player's delegate, and notifies its own delegate when the sound finishes playing (by way of a PlayerDelegate protocol that I also define). In this way, by maintaining a single Player instance, I can play different sounds in succession:

```
protocol PlayerDelegate : class {
    func soundFinished(_ sender: Any)
}
class Player : NSObject, AVAudioPlayerDelegate {
    var player : AVAudioPlayer!
    weak var delegate : PlayerDelegate?
    func playFile(atPath path:String) {
        self.player?.delegate = nil
        self.player?.stop()
        let fileURL = URL(fileURLWithPath: path)
        guard let p = try? AVAudioPlayer(contentsOf:fileURL) else {return}
        self.player = p
        self.player.prepareToPlay()
        self.player.delegate = self
        self.player.play()
    }
    func audioPlayerDidFinishPlaying(_ player: AVAudioPlayer,
        successfully flag: Bool) {
            self.delegate?.soundFinished(self)
}
```

Here are some useful AVAudioPlayer properties:

pan, volume
> Stereo positioning and loudness, respectively.

numberOfLoops
> How many times the sound should repeat after it finishes playing; 0 (the default) means it doesn't repeat. A negative value causes the sound to repeat indefinitely (until told to stop).

duration
> The length of the sound (read-only).

currentTime
> The playhead position within the sound. If the sound is paused or stopped, play will start at the currentTime. You can set this property in order to "seek" to a playback position within the sound.

enableRate, rate
> These properties allow the sound to be played at anywhere from half speed (0.5) to double speed (2.0). Set enableRate to true *before* calling prepareToPlay; you are then free to set the rate.

isMeteringEnabled
> If true (the default is false), you can call updateMeters followed by average-Power(forChannel:) and/or peakPower(forChannel:) periodically to track how loud the sound is. Presumably this would be so you could provide some sort of graphical representation of this value in your interface.

settings
> A read-only dictionary describing features of the sound, such as its bit rate (AVEncoderBitRateKey), its sample rate (AVSampleRateKey), and its data format (AVFormatIDKey). You can alternatively learn the sound's data format from the format property.

The playAtTime(_:) method allows playing to be scheduled to start at a certain time. The time should be described in terms of the audio player's deviceCurrentTime property.

An audio player handles certain types of interruption seamlessly; in particular, if your sound was forced to stop playing when your app was moved to the background, then when your app comes to front, the audio player reactivates your audio session and resumes playing — and you won't get any interruption notifications. But resumption of play is not automatic for every kind of interruption, so you may still need to register for interruption notifications.

Remote Control of Your Sound

Various sorts of signal constitute *remote control*. There is hardware remote control: for example, the user might be using earbuds with buttons. There is also software remote control — the playback controls that you see in the control center (Figure 14-1) and in the lock screen (Figure 14-2).

Your app can arrange to be targeted by *remote control events* reporting that the user has tapped a remote control. Your sound-playing app can respond to the remote play/

Figure 14-1. The software remote controls in the control center

Figure 14-2. The software remote controls on the lock screen

pause button, for example, by playing or pausing its sound. For this to work, your app's audio session category must be Solo Ambient or Playback, and your app must actually produce some sound; this causes your app's sound to become the device's *now playing* sound. The rule is that the running app that is capable of receiving remote control events and that last actually produced sound is the target of remote control events. The remote control event target defaults to the Music app if no other app takes precedence by this rule.

To configure your app to receive remote control events, use the Media Player framework (import MediaPlayer). You talk to the *remote command center*, through the shared command center that you get from the MPRemoteCommandCenter shared class method, and configure its commands to send you messages, to which you then respond as appropriate. There are two ways to perform such configuration: you can give a command a target–action pair, or you can hand it a function directly (similar to the two choices when you register with the NotificationCenter for a Notification).

For example, let's say that our app plays audio, and we want to respond to remote commands to pause or resume this audio. We will need to configure the play command and the pause command, because they are triggered by the software play/pause button, as well as the play/pause commmand, because it is triggered by an earbud button. I'll demonstrate the target–action style of configuration. This code could appear in our view controller's `viewDidLoad`:

```
let scc = MPRemoteCommandCenter.shared()
scc.playCommand.addTarget(self, action:#selector(doPlay))
scc.pauseCommand.addTarget(self, action:#selector(doPause))
scc.togglePlayPauseCommand.addTarget(self, action: #selector(doPlayPause))
```

Obviously, that code won't compile unless we also have doPlay, doPause, and doPlayPause methods. Each of these methods will be sent the appropriate remote command event (MPRemoteCommandEvent). Assuming that `self.player` is an AVAudioPlayer, our implementations might look like this:

```
@objc func doPlayPause(_ event:MPRemoteCommandEvent) {
    let p = self.player
    if p.isPlaying { p.pause() } else { p.play() }
}
@objc func doPlay(_ event:MPRemoteCommandEvent) {
    let p = self.player
    p.play()
}
@objc func doPause(_ event:MPRemoteCommandEvent) {
    let p = self.player
    p.pause()
}
```

This works! Once our app is playing a sound, that sound can be paused and resumed using the control center or an earbud switch. (It can also be paused and resumed using the lock screen, but only if our app is capable of playing sound in the background; I'll explain in the next section how to arrange that.)

However, we are not quite finished. Having registered a target with the remote command center, we must remember to unregister when that target is about to go out of existence; otherwise, there is a danger that the remote command center will attempt to send a remote command event to a nonexistent target, resulting in a crash. If we registered in our view controller's `viewDidLoad`, we can conveniently unregister in its `deinit`:

```
deinit {
    let scc = MPRemoteCommandCenter.shared()
    scc.togglePlayPauseCommand.removeTarget(self)
    scc.playCommand.removeTarget(self)
    scc.pauseCommand.removeTarget(self)
}
```

Having formed the connection between our app and the software remote control interface, we can proceed to refine that interface. For example, we can influence what information the user will see, in the remote control interface, about what's being played. For that, we use the MPNowPlayingInfoCenter. Call the class method `default` and set the resulting instance's `nowPlayingInfo` property to a dictionary. The relevant keys are listed in the class documentation; many of these are actually MPMediaItem properties, and will make more sense after you've read Chapter 16. For example, we can make the command center show the title and artist of the sound file our app is playing:

```
let mpic = MPNowPlayingInfoCenter.default()
mpic.nowPlayingInfo = [
    MPMediaItemPropertyArtist: "Matt Neuburg",
    MPMediaItemPropertyTitle: "About Tiagol",
]
```

To make the progress view appear in the software remote control interface, displaying our sound's duration and the current play position within it, we need to tell the MPNowPlayingInfoCenter what that duration is. If we also tell it that we are actively playing, it will automatically increment its display of the current play position as the time goes by. So, when we start playing, we would say something like this:

```
let mpic = MPNowPlayingInfoCenter.default()
mpic.nowPlayingInfo = [
    MPMediaItemPropertyArtist: "Matt Neuburg",
    MPMediaItemPropertyTitle: "About Tiagol",
    MPMediaItemPropertyPlaybackDuration: self.player.duration,
    MPNowPlayingInfoPropertyElapsedPlaybackTime: 0,
    MPNowPlayingInfoPropertyPlaybackRate: 1
]
```

The MPNowPlayingInfoCenter is not actually watching our sound play; it just blindly advances the current play position display. Therefore, if our sound pauses or resumes, we need to keep the MPNowPlayingInfoCenter updated. When the sound pauses, we need to tell it not only that we have paused, but also what the current play position is; otherwise, it will assume we have stopped and that the play position is zero:

Figure 14-3. Using Capabilities to enable background audio

```
let p = self.player
let mpic = MPNowPlayingInfoCenter.default()
if var d = mpic.nowPlayingInfo {
    d[MPNowPlayingInfoPropertyPlaybackRate] = 0
    d[MPNowPlayingInfoPropertyElapsedPlaybackTime] = p.currentTime
    mpic.nowPlayingInfo = d
}
```

If we don't want the user to be able to slide the slider that would tell our app to change the current play position, we must use the MPRemoteCommandCenter to disable it:

```
let scc = MPRemoteCommandCenter.shared()
scc.changePlaybackPositionCommand.isEnabled = false
```

The MPRemoteCommandCenter offers many other commands you can configure. When you do so, the appropriate software remote control interface springs to life. For example, if you assign a target–action pair to the likeCommand, a menu button appears in the control center; the user taps this button to see an action sheet that includes your like command button.

Playing Sound in the Background

When the user switches away from your app to another app, by default, your app is suspended and stops producing sound. But if the business of your app is to play sound, you might like your app to continue playing sound in the background. To play sound in the background, your app must do these things:

- In your *Info.plist*, you must include the "Required background modes" key (UIBackgroundModes) with a value that includes "App plays audio or streams audio/video using AirPlay" (audio). The simplest way to arrange that is through the Background Modes checkbox in the Capabilities tab of the target editor (Figure 14-3).

- Your audio session's policy must be active and must be Playback.

If those things are true, then the sound that your app is playing will go right on playing when the user clicks the Home button and dismisses your app, or when the user switches to another app, or when the screen is locked. Your app is now running in the background for the purpose of playing sound.

Your app, playing in the background, may be interrupted by the foreground app's audio session policy. However, having registered for the `.AVAudioSession-Interruption` notification, your app may receive this notification in the background, and, if the AVAudioSessionInterruptionType is `.ended`, may be able to resume playing — still in the background.

Remote control events continue to work when your app is in the background. In fact, even if your app was *not* actively playing at the time it was put into the background, it may nevertheless be the remote control target (because it *was* playing sound earlier, as explained in the preceding section). In that case, if the user causes a remote control event to be sent, your app, if suspended in the background, will be woken up (still in the background) in order to receive the remote control event, and can then begin playing sound. Your app may also be able to start playing in the background if it is mixable (`.mixWithOthers`, see earlier in this chapter), even if it was not playing previously.

When your app is capable of playing sound in the background, there's an interesting byproduct: while it *is* playing sound, a Timer can fire in the background. The timer must have been created and scheduled in the foreground, but after that, it will fire even while your app is in the background, unless your app is currently not playing any sound. This is remarkable, because many other sorts of activity are forbidden when your app is running in the background.

Another byproduct of your app playing sound in the background has to do with app delegate events (see Appendix A). Typically, your app delegate will probably never receive the `applicationWillTerminate(_:)` message, because by the time the app terminates, it will already have been suspended and incapable of receiving any events. However, an app that is playing sound in the background is obviously *not* suspended, even though it is in the background. If it is terminated while playing sound in the background, it *will* receive `applicationWillTerminate(_:)`.

AVAudioEngine

AVAudioEngine is modeled after a mixer board. You can construct and manipulate a graph of sound-producing objects in real time, varying their relative volumes and other attributes, mixing them down to a single sound. This is a deep topic; I'll just provide an introductory overview.

The key classes are:

AVAudioEngine
> The overall engine object, representing the world in which everything else happens. You'll probably make and retain just one at a time; it is perfectly reasonable to replace your engine with a new one, as a way of starting over with a clean slate. Its chief jobs are:

- To connect and disconnect *nodes* (AVAudioNode), analogous to patch cords on a mixer board. The engine itself has three built-in nodes — its `inputNode`, its `mixerNode`, and its `outputNode` — and you can add others.

- To start and stop the production of sound. The engine must be running if any sound is to be produced.

AVAudioNode

An abstract class embracing the various types of object for producing, processing, mixing, and receiving sound. An audio node is useful only when it has been attached to the audio engine. An audio node has inputs and outputs, and the audio engine can connect the output of one node to the input of another. It is also possible to put a *tap* on a node, copying the node's sound data off into a buffer as it passes through the node, for analysis or monitoring, or to save it off into a file. Some subclasses are:

AVAudioMixerNode

A node with an output volume; it mixes its inputs down to a single output. The AVAudioEngine's built-in `mixerNode` is an AVAudioMixerNode.

AVAudioIONode

A node that patches through to the system's (device's) own input (AVAudioInputNode) or output (AVAudioOutputNode). The AVAudioEngine's built-in `inputNode` and `outputNode` are AVAudioIONodes.

AVAudioPlayerNode

A node that produces sound, analogous to an AVAudioPlayer. It can play from a file or from a buffer.

AVAudioEnvironmentNode

Gives three-dimensional spatial control over sound sources (suitable for games). With it, a bunch of additional AVAudioNode properties spring to life.

AVAudioUnit

A node that processes its input with special effects before passing it to the output. Built-in subclasses include:

AVAudioUnitTimePitch

Independently changes the pitch and rate of the input.

AVAudioUnitVarispeed

Changes the pitch and rate of the input together.

AVAudioUnitDelay

Adds to the input a delayed version of itself.

AVAudioUnitDistortion
Adds distortion to the input.

AVAudioUnitEQ
Constructs an equalizer, for processing different frequency bands separately.

AVAudioUnitReverb
Adds a reverb effect to the input.

To give an idea of what working with AVAudioEngine looks like, I'll start by simply playing a file. Our AVAudioEngine has already been instantiated and assigned to an instance property, `self.engine`, so that it will persist for the duration of the exercise. We will need an AVAudioPlayerNode and an AVAudioFile. We attach the AVAudio-PlayerNode to the engine and patch it to the engine's built-in mixer node. (In this simple case, we could have patched the player node to the engine's output node; but the engine's mixer node is already patched to the output node, so it makes no difference.) We associate the file with the player node, supplying a completion function that stops the engine so as not to waste resources after the file finishes playing. Finally, we start the engine running and tell the player node to play:

```
let player = AVAudioPlayerNode()
let url = Bundle.main.url(forResource:"aboutTiagol", withExtension:"m4a")!
let f = try! AVAudioFile(forReading: url)
let mixer = self.engine.mainMixerNode
self.engine.attach(player)
self.engine.connect(player, to: mixer, format: f.processingFormat)
player.scheduleFile(f, at: nil) { [unowned self] in
    delay(0.1) {
        if self.engine.isRunning {
            self.engine.stop()
        }
    }
}
self.engine.prepare()
try! self.engine.start()
player.play()
```

 New in iOS 11, instead of stopping the engine in our player node's completion function, we can configure the engine to stop automatically by setting its `isAuto-ShutdownEnabled` property to `true`.

So far, we've done nothing that we couldn't have done with an AVAudioPlayer. But now let's start patching some more nodes into the graph. I'll play two sounds simultaneously, the first one directly from a file, the second one through a buffer — which will allow me to loop the second sound. I'll pass the first sound through a time-pitch effect node and then through a reverb effect node. And I'll set the volumes and pan positions of the two sounds:

```swift
// first sound
let player = AVAudioPlayerNode()
let url = Bundle.main.url(forResource:"aboutTiagol", withExtension:"m4a")!
let f = try! AVAudioFile(forReading: url)
self.engine.attach(player)
// add some effect nodes to the chain
let effect = AVAudioUnitTimePitch()
effect.rate = 0.9
effect.pitch = -300
self.engine.attach(effect)
self.engine.connect(player, to: effect, format: f.processingFormat)
let effect2 = AVAudioUnitReverb()
effect2.loadFactoryPreset(.cathedral)
effect2.wetDryMix = 40
self.engine.attach(effect2)
self.engine.connect(effect, to: effect2, format: f.processingFormat)
// patch last node into engine mixer and start playing first sound
let mixer = self.engine.mainMixerNode
self.engine.connect(effect2, to: mixer, format: f.processingFormat)
player.scheduleFile(f, at: nil) {
    delay(0.1) {
        if self.engine.isRunning {
            self.engine.stop()
        }
    }
}
self.engine.prepare()
try! self.engine.start()
player.play()
// second sound; loop it
let url2 = Bundle.main.url(forResource:"Hooded", withExtension: "mp3")!
let f2 = try! AVAudioFile(forReading: url2)
let buffer = AVAudioPCMBuffer(
    pcmFormat: f2.processingFormat, frameCapacity: UInt32(f2.length))
try! f2.read(into:buffer!)
let player2 = AVAudioPlayerNode()
self.engine.attach(player2)
self.engine.connect(player2, to: mixer, format: f2.processingFormat)
player2.scheduleBuffer(buffer!, at: nil, options: .loops)
// mix down a little, start playing second sound
player.pan = -0.5
player2.volume = 0.5
player2.pan = 0.5
player2.play()
```

You can split a node's output between multiple nodes. Instead of calling connect(_:to:format:), you call connect(_:to:fromBus:format:), where the second argument is an array of AVAudioConnectionPoint objects, each of which is simply a node and a bus. In this example, I'll split my player's output three ways: I'll connect it simultaneously to a delay effect and a reverb effect, both of which are connected to the output mixer, and I'll connect the player itself directly to the output mixer as well:

```
let effect = AVAudioUnitDelay()
effect.delayTime = 0.4
effect.feedback = 0
self.engine.attach(effect)
let effect2 = AVAudioUnitReverb()
effect2.loadFactoryPreset(.cathedral)
effect2.wetDryMix = 40
self.engine.attach(effect2)
let mixer = self.engine.mainMixerNode
// patch player node to _both_ effect nodes _and_ the mixer
let cons = [
    AVAudioConnectionPoint(node: effect, bus: 0),
    AVAudioConnectionPoint(node: effect2, bus: 0),
    AVAudioConnectionPoint(node: mixer, bus: 1),
]
self.engine.connect(player, to: cons,
    fromBus: 0, format: f.processingFormat)
// patch both effect nodes into the mixer
self.engine.connect(effect, to: mixer, format: f.processingFormat)
self.engine.connect(effect2, to: mixer, format: f.processingFormat)
```

Finally, I'll demonstrate how to process sound into a file. When I first wrote this example, I was hoping that the processing might be done rapidly in the background, but that turned out to be impossible; you had to play the sound in real time, by installing a tap on a node to collect its sound into a buffer and writing the buffer into a file. New in iOS 11, however, rapid offline rendering through AVAudioEngine *is* possible.

To demonstrate, I'll pass a sound file through a reverb effect and save the output into a new file. Initial configuration is much as you would expect:

```
let url = Bundle.main.url(forResource:"Hooded", withExtension: "mp3")!
let f = try! AVAudioFile(forReading: url)
let player = AVAudioPlayerNode()
self.engine.attach(player)
// patch the player into the effect
let effect = AVAudioUnitReverb()
effect.loadFactoryPreset(.cathedral)
effect.wetDryMix = 40
self.engine.attach(effect)
self.engine.connect(player, to: effect, format: f.processingFormat)
let mixer = self.engine.mainMixerNode
self.engine.connect(effect, to: mixer, format: f.processingFormat)
```

We create an output file with an appropriate format:

```
let fm = FileManager.default
let doc = try! fm.url(for:.documentDirectory, in: .userDomainMask,
    appropriateFor: nil, create: true)
let outurl = doc.appendingPathComponent("myfile.aac", isDirectory:false)
```

```
let outfile = try! AVAudioFile(forWriting: outurl, settings: [
    AVFormatIDKey : kAudioFormatMPEG4AAC,
    AVNumberOfChannelsKey : 1,
    AVSampleRateKey : 22050,
])
```

Now comes the interesting part. Before we start playing through the audio engine, we configure it for offline rendering:

```
var done = false
player.scheduleFile(f, at: nil)
let sz : UInt32 = 4096
try! self.engine.enableManualRenderingMode(.offline,
    format: f.processingFormat, maximumFrameCount: sz)
self.engine.prepare()
try! self.engine.start()
player.play()
```

We have told the engine to start and the player to play, but nothing happens. That's because it's up to us to *pull* the sound data through the engine into a buffer one chunk at a time, and write the buffer into a file. I create the buffer, and then loop repeatedly until all the sound data has been read:

```
let outbuf = AVAudioPCMBuffer(
    pcmFormat: f.processingFormat, frameCapacity: sz)!
var rest : Int64 { return f.length - self.engine.manualRenderingSampleTime }
while rest > 0 {
    let ct = min(outbuf.frameCapacity, UInt32(rest))
    let stat = try! self.engine.renderOffline(ct, to: outbuf)
    if stat == .success {
        try! outfile.write(from: outbuf)
    }
}
```

The result is that the input file is processed very quickly into the output file. I have one quibble with the result: our reverb effect is not given a chance to fade away at the end of the output, because we stop writing to the output file as soon as the input file is exhausted. One solution might be to add a couple of seconds arbitrarily onto the size of rest; another might be to examine the contents of outbuf and keep looping after reading the input file until the amplitude of the sound data falls below some threshold of quiet.

MIDI Playback

iOS allows communication with MIDI devices through the CoreMIDI framework, which I'm not going to discuss here. But playing a MIDI file is another matter; it's just as simple as playing an audio file. In this example, I'm already armed with a MIDI file, which provides the music, and a SoundFont file, which provides the instrument that will play it; self.player will be an AVMIDIPlayer:

```
let midurl = Bundle.main.url(forResource: "presto", withExtension: "mid")!
let sndurl = Bundle.main.url(forResource: "Piano", withExtension: "sf2")!
self.player = try! AVMIDIPlayer(contentsOf: midurl, soundBankURL: sndurl)
self.player.prepareToPlay()
self.player.play()
```

Starting in iOS 9, a MIDI player can also act as a source in an AVAudioEngine. In this case, you'll want an AVAudioUnitSampler as your starting AVAudioUnit. The MIDI file will be parsed by an AVAudioSequencer; this is not part of the audio engine node structure, but rather it *has* the audio engine as a property, so you'll need to retain it in a property (`self.seq` in this example):

```
let midurl = Bundle.main.url(forResource: "presto", withExtension: "mid")!
let sndurl = Bundle.main.url(forResource: "Piano", withExtension: "sf2")!
let unit = AVAudioUnitSampler()
self.engine.attach(unit)
let mixer = self.engine.outputNode
self.engine.connect(unit, to: mixer, format: mixer.outputFormat(forBus:0))
try! unit.loadInstrument(at:sndurl)
self.seq = AVAudioSequencer(audioEngine: self.engine)
try! self.seq.load(from:midurl)
self.engine.prepare()
try! engine.start()
try! self.seq.start()
```

That code is rather mysterious: where's the connection between the AVAudio-Sequencer and the AVAudioUnitSampler? The answer is that the sequencer just finds the first AVAudioUnitSampler in the audio engine graph and proceeds to drive it. If that isn't what you want, get the AVAudioSequencer's `tracks` property, which is an array of AVMusicTrack; now you can set each track's `destinationAudioUnit` explicitly.

Text to Speech

Text can be transformed into synthesized speech using the AVSpeechUtterance and AVSpeechSynthesizer classes. As with an AVAudioPlayer, you'll need to retain the AVSpeechSynthesizer (`self.talker` in my example); here, I also use the AVSpeech-SynthesisVoice class to make sure the device speaks the text in English, regardless of the user's language settings:

```
let utter = AVSpeechUtterance(string:"Polly, want a cracker?")
if let v = AVSpeechSynthesisVoice(language: "en-US") {
    utter.voice = v
    self.talker.delegate = self
    self.talker.speak(utter)
}
```

You can also set the utterance's speech rate. The delegate (AVSpeechSynthesizerDelegate) is told when the speech starts, when it comes to a new range of text (usually a word), and when it finishes.

To get the user's current language, call the AVSpeechSynthesisVoice class method `currentLanguageCode`. Instead of specifying a voice by language, you can use the system's `identifier`. To get a list of all voices, call the class method `speechVoices`.

If a word within your AVSpeechUtterance needs extra pronunciation guidance, you can write it out using the International Phonetic Alphabet (IPA; see *https://www.internationalphoneticassociation.org/content/ipa-chart*). Form an NSMutableAttributedString from your overall phrase; then call `addAttribute(_:value:range:)`, where the first parameter is `NSAttributedStringKey(rawValue: AVSpeechSynthesisIPANotationAttribute)` and the second parameter is the IPA notation to be substituted at the range of that word. Now form the speech utterance from the attributed string with the initializer `init(attributedString:)`.

Speech to Text

Your app can participate in the same speech recognition engine used by Siri and by the Dictate button in the onscreen keyboard. In this way, you can transcribe speech to text. To do so, you'll use the Speech framework (`import Speech`).

Use of the speech recognition engine requires authorization from the user. You'll need to have an entry in your *Info.plist* under the "Privacy — Speech Recognition Usage Description" key (`NSSpeechRecognitionUsageDescription`) explaining to the user why you want to do speech recognition. In your code, check the value of `SFSpeechRecognizer.authorizationStatus()` If it is `.notDetermined`, request authorization by calling `SFSpeechRecognizer.requestAuthorization`. The system will put up an alert containing both its own explanation of what speech recognition entails and your entry from the *Info.plist* (Figure 14-4). A user who denies your app speech recognition authorization may grant it later in Settings. (In Chapter 16, I'll discuss in more detail the business of coherently getting user authorization and proceeding only when you have it; see "Checking for Authorization" on page 841.)

Once you have authorization, the basic procedure is simple. You form a speech recognition request and hand it off to an SFSpeechRecognizer. Recognition can be performed in various languages, which are expressed as locales; to learn what these are, call the `supportedLocales` class method. The device's current locale is used by default, or you can specify a locale when you initialize the SFSpeechRecognizer.

There are two kinds of speech recognition: transcription of an existing file, and transcription of live speech. For transcription of a file, your speech recognition request will be an SFSpeechURLRecognitionRequest initialized with the file URL. In this

Figure 14-4. The user is asked to authorize speech recognition

example, I have a recording of myself saying "This is a test." I speak American English, so just to be on the safe side, I initialize my SFSpeechRecognizer with the "en-US" locale. Interestingly, none of the objects needs to be retained in an instance property:

```
let f = Bundle.main.url(forResource: "test", withExtension: "aif")!
let req = SFSpeechURLRecognitionRequest(url: f)
let loc = Locale(identifier: "en-US")
guard let rec = SFSpeechRecognizer(locale:loc)
    else {return} // no recognizer
rec.recognitionTask(with: req) { result, err in
    if let result = result {
        let trans = result.bestTranscription
        let s = trans.formattedString
        print(s)
        if result.isFinal {
            print("finished!")
        }
    } else {
        print(err!)
    }
}
```

In that code, we're calling recognitionTask(with:resultHandler:) with an anonymous function. The function is called several times, passing us an SFSpeechRecognitionResult containing possible transcriptions (an array of SFTranscription). We ignore these, asking instead for the bestTranscription and extracting its formattedString. We know when we've been called for the last time because the recognition result's isFinal is true. In real life, it might be sufficient to extract the transcription only on the final pass, but for the purposes of this demonstration, I've logged every call to the function; the resulting console log looks like this:

```
This
This is
This is
This is
This is a test
This is a test
finished!
```

For transcription of live speech, your app is going to be using the device's microphone. This requires an additional authorization from the user. You'll need to have an entry in your *Info.plist* under the "Privacy — Microphone Usage Description" key (NSMicrophoneUsageDescription) explaining to the user why you want to use the microphone. You don't have to request authorization explicitly; the system will put up the authorization request dialog on your behalf as soon as you try to use microphone. If you do want to request authorization explicitly, call your AVAudioSession's record-Permission to learn whether we have authorization, and call its requestRecord-Permission, if necessary, to request authorization.

Once you have authorization for both speech recognition and microphone usage, the procedure is almost exactly the same as before — except that the speech recognition request will be an SFSpeechAudioBufferRecognitionRequest, and we need a way to pass the microphone input to it. A buffer recognition request has an append method whose parameter is an AVAudioPCMBuffer. To obtain an AVAudioPCMBuffer, we can use AVAudioEngine and put a tap on a node. Here, that node will be the audio engine's inputNode, representing the device's microphone:

```
let engine = AVAudioEngine()
let req = SFSpeechAudioBufferRecognitionRequest()
func doLive() {
    let loc = Locale(identifier: "en-US")
    guard let rec = SFSpeechRecognizer(locale:loc)
        else {return} // no recognizer
    let input = self.engine.inputNode
    input.installTap(onBus: 0, bufferSize: 4096,
        format: input.outputFormat(forBus: 0)) { buffer, time in
            self.req.append(buffer)
    }
    self.engine.prepare()
    try! self.engine.start()
    // provide the user with "recording" feedback
    rec.recognitionTask(with: self.req) { result, err in
        // ... and the rest is as before ...
    }
}
```

You must provide the user with a clear indication in the interface that the microphone is now live and the speech recognition engine is listening. You must also provide a way for the user to *stop* recognition, signaling that the speech is over (like the Done button in the dictation interface). That's why our buffer recognition request is an instance property (`self.req`): the buffer recognition request has an `endAudio` instance method, which we need to able to call when the user taps our Done button. I also stop the audio engine and remove the tap from its input node, so as to be ready if the user wants to do more speech recognition later:

```
@IBAction func endLive(_ sender: Any) {
    self.engine.stop()
    self.engine.inputNode.removeTap(onBus: 0)
    self.req.endAudio()
    // take down "recording" feedback
}
```

Instead of calling `recognitionTask(with:resultHandler:)`, you can call `recognitionTask(with:delegate:)`, providing an adopter of the SFSpeechRecognitionTaskDelegate protocol. Here you can implement any of half a dozen optional methods, called at various stages of the recognition process, to allow your response to be more fine-grained. You can also assist the recognition request with hints, retrieve confidence levels and alternatives from the segments of a transcription, and move the task messages onto a background queue.

Speech recognition is a resource-heavy operation. It may require an Internet connection, with the work being done by Apple's servers; be prepared for the connection to fail. Apple warns that recognized snippets must be short, and that excessive use of the server may result in access being throttled.

Further Topics in Sound

iOS is a powerful milieu for production and processing of sound; its sound-related technologies are extensive. This is a big topic, and an entire book could be written about it (in fact, such books do exist). I'll talk in Chapter 16 about accessing sound files in the user's music library. Here are some further topics that there is no room to discuss here:

Other audio session policies
> If your app accepts sound input or does audio processing, you'll want to look into some audio session policies that I didn't talk about earlier — Record, Play and Record, and Audio Processing. In addition, if you're using Record or Play and Record, there are modes — voice chat, video recording, and measurement (of the sound being input) — that optimize how sound is routed (for example, what microphone is used) and how it is modified. Note that your app must obtain the user's permission to use the microphone, as I explained in the previous section.

Recording sound
> To record sound simply, use AVAudioRecorder. Your audio session will need to adopt a Record policy before recording begins.

Audio queues

Audio queues — Audio Queue Services, part of the Audio Toolbox framework — implement sound playing and recording through a C API with more granularity than the Objective-C AVAudioPlayer and AVAudioRecorder (though it is still regarded as a high-level API), giving you access to the buffers used to move chunks of sound data between a storage format (a sound file) and sound hardware.

Extended Audio File Services

A C API for reading and writing sound files in chunks. It is useful in connection with technologies such as audio queues.

Audio Converter Services

Originally, a C API for converting sound files between formats. Starting in iOS 9, the AVAudioConverter class (along with AVAudioCompressedBuffer) gives this API an object-oriented structure.

Streaming audio

Audio streamed in real time over the network, such as an Internet radio station, can be played with Audio File Stream Services, in connection with audio queues.

Audio units

Plug-ins that generate sound or modify sound as it passes through them. Starting in iOS 9, the API was migrated from C into Objective-C and given a modern object-oriented structure; audio units can vend interface (AUViewController); and an audio unit from one app can be hosted inside another (audio unit extensions).

CHAPTER 15

Video

Video playback is performed using classes such as AVPlayer provided by the AV Foundation framework (`import AVFoundation`). An AVPlayer is not a view; rather, an AVPlayer's content is made visible through a CALayer subclass, AVPlayerLayer, which can be added to your app's interface.

An AV Foundation video playback interface can be wrapped in a simple view controller, AVPlayerViewController: you provide an AVPlayer, and the AVPlayerViewController *automatically* hosts an associated AVPlayerLayer in its own main view, providing standard playback transport controls so that the user can start and stop play, seek to a different frame, and so forth. AVPlayerViewController is provided by the AVKit framework; you'll need to `import AVKit`.

A simple interface for letting the user trim video (UIVideoEditorController) is also supplied. Sophisticated video editing can be performed through the AV Foundation framework, as I'll demonstrate later in this chapter.

If an AVPlayer produces sound, you may need to concern yourself with your application's audio session; see Chapter 14. AVPlayer deals gracefully with the app being sent into the background: it will pause when your app is backgrounded and resume when your app returns to the foreground.

A movie file can be in a standard movie format, such as *.mov* or *.mp4*, but it can also be a sound file. An AVPlayerViewController is thus an easy way to play a sound file, including a sound file obtained in real time over the Internet, along with standard controls for pausing the sound and moving the playhead — unlike AVAudioPlayer, which, as I pointed out in Chapter 14, lacks a user interface.

A web view (Chapter 11) supports the HTML5 <video> tag. This can be a simple lightweight way to present video and to allow the user to control playback. Both web view video and AVPlayer support AirPlay.

AVPlayerViewController

An AVPlayerViewController is a view controller whose view contains an AVPlayer-Layer and transport controls. It must be assigned a `player`, which is an AVPlayer. An AVPlayer can be initialized directly from the URL of the video it is to play, with `init(url:)`. Thus, you'll instantiate AVPlayerViewController, create and set its AVPlayer, and get the AVPlayerViewController into the view controller hierarchy. You can instantiate an AVPlayerViewController in code or from a storyboard; look for the AVKit Player View Controller object in the Object library.

The simplest approach is to use an AVPlayerViewController as a presented view controller. In this example, I present a video from the app bundle:

```
let av = AVPlayerViewController()
let url = Bundle.main.url(forResource:"ElMirage", withExtension: "mp4")!
let player = AVPlayer(url: url)
av.player = player
self.present(av, animated: true)
```

The AVPlayerViewController knows that it's being shown as a fullscreen presented view controller, so it provides fullscreen video controls, including a Done button which automatically dismisses the presented view controller. Thus, there is literally no further work for you to do.

Figure 15-1 shows a fullscreen presented AVPlayerViewController. Exactly what controls you'll see depends on the circumstances; in my case, at the top there's the Done button (which appears as an X in iOS 11) and a volume control, and at the bottom are transport controls including the current playhead position slider. The user can hide or show the controls by tapping the video.

If the AVPlayer's file is in fact a sound file, the central region is replaced by a Quick-Time symbol (Figure 15-2), and the controls can't be hidden.

If you want the convenience and the control interface that come from using an AVPlayerViewController, while displaying its view as a subview of your own view controller's view, make your view controller a parent view controller with the AVPlayerViewController as its child, adding the AVPlayerViewController's view in good order (see "Container View Controllers" on page 368):

```
let url = Bundle.main.url(forResource:"ElMirage", withExtension:"mp4")!
let player = AVPlayer(url:url)
let av = AVPlayerViewController()
av.player = player
av.view.frame = CGRect(10,10,300,200)
self.addChildViewController(av)
self.view.addSubview(av.view)
av.didMove(toParentViewController:self)
```

Figure 15-1. A presented AVPlayerViewController

Figure 15-2. The QuickTime symbol

Once again, the AVPlayerViewController behaves intelligently, reducing its controls to a minimum to adapt to the reduced size of its view. On my device, at the given view size, there is room for a fullscreen button, a volume button, a play button, a playhead position slider, and nothing else (Figure 15-3). However, the user can enter fullscreen mode, either by tapping the fullscreen button or by pinching outward on the video view, and now the full complement of controls is present (exactly as in Figure 15-1).

New in iOS 11, you can also configure the video view to switch to and from fullscreen mode automatically when play begins and ends. To do so, set the AVPlayerView-Controller properties `entersFullScreenWhenPlaybackBegins` and `exitsFullScreen-WhenPlaybackEnds` to `true`.

Other AVPlayerViewController Properties

An AVPlayerViewController has very few properties:

Figure 15-3. An embedded AVPlayerViewController's view

player

> The view controller's AVPlayer, whose AVPlayerLayer will be hosted in the view controller's view. You can set the player while the view is visible, to change what video it displays (though you are more likely to keep the player and tell *it* to change the video). It is legal to assign an AVQueuePlayer, an AVPlayer subclass; an AVQueuePlayer has multiple items, and the AVPlayerViewController will treat these as chapters of the video. An AVPlayerLooper object can be used in conjunction with an AVQueuePlayer to repeat play automatically. (I'll give an AVQueuePlayer example in Chapter 16, and an AVPlayerLooper example in Chapter 17.)

showsPlaybackControls

> If false, the controls are hidden. This could be useful, for example, if you want to display a video for decorative purposes, or if you are substituting your own controls.

contentOverlayView

> A UIView to which you are free to add subviews. These subviews will appear overlaid in front of the video but behind the playback controls. This is a great way to cover that dreadful QuickTime symbol (Figure 15-2). New in iOS 11, the content overlay is sized to fit its contents, or you can give it constraints to size it as you prefer.

videoGravity

> How the video should be positioned within the view. Possible values are (AVLayerVideoGravity):
>
> - .resizeAspect (the default)
> - .resizeAspectFill
> - .resize (fills the view, possibly distorting the video)

Unfortunately, the AVPlayerViewController `videoGravity` property itself is typed as a String, not as an AVLayerVideoGravity struct, so you have to take the struct's `rawValue` in order to assign it.

`videoBounds`
`isReadyForDisplay`

The video position within the view, and the ability of the video to display its first frame and start playing, respectively. If the video is not ready for display, we probably don't yet know its bounds either. In any case, `isReadyForDisplay` will initially be `false` and the `videoBounds` will initially be reported as `.zero`. This is because, with video, things take time to prepare. I'll explain in detail later in this chapter.

`updatesNowPlayingInfoCenter`

If `true` (the default), the AVPlayerViewController keeps the MPNowPlayingInfoCenter (Chapter 14) apprised of the movie's duration and current playhead position.

If `false`, it doesn't do that, leaving your code in charge of managing the MPNowPlayingInfoCenter.

Everything else there is to know about an AVPlayerViewController comes from its `player`, an AVPlayer. I'll discuss AVPlayer in more detail in a moment.

Picture-in-Picture

An iPad that supports iPad multitasking (Chapter 9) also supports picture-in-picture video playback (unless the user turns it off in the Settings app: General → Multitasking & Dock → Persistent Video Overlay). This means that the user can move your video into a small system window that floats in front of everything else on the screen. This floating window persists if your app is put into the background.

Your iPad app will support picture-in-picture if it supports background audio, as I described in Chapter 14: you check the checkbox in the Capabilities tab of the target editor (Figure 14-3), and your audio session's policy must be active and must be Playback. If you want to do those things *without* having your app be forced to support picture-in-picture, set the AVPlayerViewController's `allowsPictureInPicturePlayback` to `false`.

If picture-in-picture is supported, an extra button appears among the upper set of playback controls (Figure 15-4). When the user taps this button, the video is moved into the system window (and the AVPlayerViewController's view displays a placeholder). The user is now free to leave your app while continuing to see and hear the video. Moreover, if the video is being played fullscreen when the user leaves your app, the video is moved into the picture-in-picture system window *automatically*.

Figure 15-4. The picture-in-picture button appears

The user can move the system window to any corner. Buttons in the system window, which can be shown or hidden by tapping, allow the user to play and pause the video or to dismiss the system window. There's also a button to dismiss the system window plus return to your app; if the user taps it while the video is playing, the video goes right on playing as it moves back into place within your app.

If your AVPlayerViewController is being presented fullscreen when the video is taken into picture-in-picture mode, then the presented view controller, by default, *is dismissed*. If the user tries to return to your app from the system picture-in-picture window, the video has no place to return to. To handle this situation, give the AVPlayerViewController a `delegate` (AVPlayerViewControllerDelegate) and deal with it in a delegate method. You have two choices:

Don't dismiss the presented view controller
> Implement `playerViewControllerShouldAutomaticallyDismissAtPictureInPictureStart(_:)` to return `false`. Now the presented view controller remains, and the video has a place in your app to which it can be restored.

Recreate the presented view controller
> Implement `playerViewController(_:restoreUserInterfaceForPictureInPictureStopWithCompletionHandler:)`. Do what the name tells you: restore the user interface! The first parameter is your original AVPlayerViewController; all you have to do is get it back into the view controller hierarchy. At the end of the process, *call the completion function.*

I'll demonstrate the second approach:

```
func playerViewController(_ pvc: AVPlayerViewController,
    restoreUserInterfaceForPictureInPictureStopWithCompletionHandler
    ch: @escaping (Bool) -> ()) {
        self.present(pvc, animated:true) {
            ch(true)
        }
}
```

Other delegate methods inform you of various stages as picture-in-picture mode begins and ends. Thus you could respond by rearranging the interface. One good reason for being conscious that you've entered picture-in-picture mode is that at that point you are effectively a background app, and you should reduce resources and activity so that playing the video is *all* you're doing until picture-in-picture mode ends.

Introducing AV Foundation

The video display performed by AVPlayerViewController is supplied by classes from the AV Foundation framework. This is a big framework with a lot of classes, but there's a good reason for that: video has a lot of structure and can be manipulated in many ways, and AV Foundation very carefully and correctly draws all the distinctions needed for good object-oriented encapsulation.

AV Foundation is very big, so I'll merely introduce it here. I'll point out some of the principal classes, features, and techniques associated with video. Further AV Foundation examples will appear in Chapters 16 and 17.

Some AV Foundation Classes

The heart of AV Foundation video playback is AVPlayer. AVPlayer is not a UIView, but rather is the locus of video transport; the actual video, if shown, appears in an AVPlayerLayer associated with the AVPlayer. For example, AVPlayerViewController provides a play button, but what if you wanted to start video playback in code? You'd tell the AVPlayerViewController's `player` (an AVPlayer) to `play` or set its `rate` to 1.

An AVPlayer's video is its `currentItem`, an AVPlayerItem. In the examples earlier in this chapter we initialized an AVPlayer directly from a URL, with no reference to any AVPlayerItem; that, however, was just a shortcut. AVPlayer's *real* initializer is `init(playerItem:)`; when we called `init(url:)`, the AVPlayerItem was created for us.

An AVPlayerItem, too, can be initialized from a URL with `init(url:)`, but again, this is just a shortcut. AVPlayerItem's *real* initalizer is `init(asset:)`, which takes an AVAsset. An AVAsset is an actual video resource, and comes in one of two subclasses:

AVURLAsset
> An asset specified through a URL.

AVComposition
> An asset constructed by editing video in code. I'll give an example later in this chapter.

Thus, to configure an AVPlayer using the complete "stack" of objects that constitute it, you could say something like this:

```
let url = Bundle.main.url(forResource:"ElMirage", withExtension:"mp4")!
let asset = AVURLAsset(url:url)
let item = AVPlayerItem(asset:asset)
let player = AVPlayer(playerItem:item)
```

Once an AVPlayer exists and has an AVPlayerItem, that player item's tracks, as seen from the player's perspective, are AVPlayerItemTrack objects, which can be individually enabled or disabled. That's different from an AVAssetTrack, which is a fact about an AVAsset. This distinction is a good example of what I said earlier about how AV Foundation encapsulates its objects correctly: an AVAssetTrack is a hard and fast reality, but an AVPlayerItemTrack lets a track be manipulated for purposes of playback on a particular occasion.

Things Take Time

Working with video is time-consuming. Just because you give an AVPlayer a command or set a property doesn't mean that it obeys immediately. All sorts of operations, from reading a video file and learning its metadata to transcoding and saving a video file, take a significant amount of time. The user interface must not freeze while a video task is in progress, so AV Foundation relies heavily on threading (Chapter 24). In this way, AV Foundation covers the complex and time-consuming nature of its operations; but your code must cooperate. You'll frequently use key–value observing and callbacks to run your code at the right moment.

Here's an example; it's slightly artificial, but it illustrates the principles and techniques you need to know about. There's an elementary interface flaw when we create an embedded AVPlayerViewController:

```
let url = Bundle.main.url(forResource:"ElMirage", withExtension:"mp4")!
let asset = AVURLAsset(url:url)
let item = AVPlayerItem(asset:asset)
let player = AVPlayer(playerItem:item)
let av = AVPlayerViewController()
av.view.frame = CGRect(10,10,300,200)
av.player = player
self.addChildViewController(av)
self.view.addSubview(av.view)
av.didMove(toParentViewController: self)
```

There are two issues here:

- The AVPlayerViewController's view is initially appearing empty in the interface, because the video is not yet ready for display. Then there's a visible flash when the video appears, because now it *is* ready for display.

- The proposed frame of the AVPlayerViewController's view doesn't fit the actual aspect ratio of the video, which results in the video being letterboxed within that frame (visible in Figure 15-3).

To prevent the flash, we can start out with the AVPlayerViewController's view hidden, and not show it until isReadyForDisplay is true. But how will we know when that is? *Not* by repeatedly polling the isReadyForDisplay property! That sort of behavior is absolutely wrong. Rather, we should use KVO to register as an observer of this property. Sooner or later, isReadyForDisplay will become true, and we'll be notified. Now we can unregister from KVO and show the AVPlayerViewController's view:

```
av.view.isHidden = true
var ob : NSKeyValueObservation!
ob = av.observe(\.isReadyForDisplay, options: .new) { vc, ch in
    guard let ok = ch.newValue, ok else {return}
    self.obs.remove(ob)
    DispatchQueue.main.async {
        vc.view.isHidden = false
    }
}
self.obs.insert(ob) // obs is a Set<NSKeyValueObservation>
```

Note that, in that code, I make no assumptions about what thread KVO calls me back on: I intend to operate on the interface, so I step out to the main thread.

Next, let's talk about setting the AVPlayerViewController's view.frame in accordance with the video's aspect ratio. An AVAsset has tracks (AVAssetTrack); in particular, an AVAsset representing a video has a video track. A video track has a naturalSize, which will give me the aspect ratio I need.

However, it turns out that, for the sake of efficiency, these properties, like many AV Foundation object properties, are not even evaluated unless you specifically ask for them — and evaluating them takes time. AV Foundation objects that behave this way conform to the AVAsynchronousKeyValueLoading protocol. You call loadValues-Asynchronously(forKeys:completionHandler:) ahead of time, for any properties you're going to be interested in. When your completion function is called, you check the status of a key and, if its status is .loaded, you are now free to access it.

In order to obtain the video's aspect ratio, then, I'm going to need to do that, first for the AVAsset's tracks property in order to get the video track, and then for the video track's naturalSize property. Let's go all the way back to the beginning. I'll start by creating the AVAsset *and then stop*, waiting to hear in the completion function that the AVAsset's tracks property is ready:

```
let url = Bundle.main.url(forResource:"ElMirage", withExtension:"mp4")!
let asset = AVURLAsset(url:url)
let track = #keyPath(AVURLAsset.tracks)
asset.loadValuesAsynchronously(forKeys:[track]) {
    let status = asset.statusOfValue(forKey:track, error: nil)
    if status == .loaded {
        DispatchQueue.main.async {
            self.getVideoTrack(asset)
        }
    }
}
```

When the `tracks` property is ready, my completion function is called, and I call my `getVideoTrack` method. Here, I obtain the video track *and then stop* once again, waiting to hear in the completion function that the video track's `naturalSize` property is ready:

```
func getVideoTrack(_ asset:AVAsset) {
    let visual = AVMediaCharacteristic.visual
    let vtrack = asset.tracks(withMediaCharacteristic: visual)[0]
    let size = #keyPath(AVAssetTrack.naturalSize)
    vtrack.loadValuesAsynchronously(forKeys: [size]) {
        let status = vtrack.statusOfValue(forKey: size, error: nil)
        if status == .loaded {
            DispatchQueue.main.async {
                self.getNaturalSize(vtrack, asset)
            }
        }
    }
}
```

When the video track's `naturalSize` property is ready, my completion function is called, and I call my `getNaturalSize` method. Here, I get the natural size and use it to finish constructing the AVPlayer and to set AVPlayerController's frame:

```
func getNaturalSize(_ vtrack:AVAssetTrack, _ asset:AVAsset) {
    let sz = vtrack.naturalSize
    let item = AVPlayerItem(asset:asset)
    let player = AVPlayer(playerItem:item)
    let av = AVPlayerViewController()
    av.view.frame = AVMakeRect(
        aspectRatio: sz, insideRect: CGRect(10,10,300,200))
    av.player = player
    // ... and the rest is as before ...
}
```

AVPlayerItem provides another way of loading an asset's properties: initialize it with `init(asset:automaticallyLoadedAssetKeys:)` and observe its `status` using KVO. When that `status` is `.readyToPlay`, you are guaranteed that the player item's `asset` has attempted to load those keys, and you can query them just as you would in `loadValuesAsynchronously`.

Time is Measured Oddly

Another peculiarity of AV Foundation is that time is measured in an unfamiliar way. This is necessary because calculations using an ordinary built-in numeric class such as CGFloat will always have slight rounding errors that quickly begin to matter when you're trying to specify a time within a large piece of media.

Therefore, the Core Media framework provides the CMTime class, which under the hood is a pair of integers; they are called the `value` and the `timescale`, but they are

An AVURLAsset's URL doesn't have to be a local file URL; it can point to a resource located across the Internet. Management of such an asset, however, is tricky, because now things *really* take time: the asset has to arrive by way of the network, which may be slow, interrupted, or missing in action. There's a buffer, and if it isn't sufficiently full of your AVAsset's data, playback will stutter or stop.

In the past, management of such an asset could be tricky. You had to use your AVPlayer's AVPlayerItem as the locus of information about the arrival and playback of your AVAsset from across the network, keeping track of properties such as `playbackLikelyToKeepUp` and the `accessLog`, along with notifications such as `AVPlayerItemPlaybackStalled`, to keep abreast of any issues, pausing and resuming to optimize the user experience.

Starting in iOS 10, Apple has made this entire procedure much easier: just tell the AVPlayer to play and stand back! Play won't start until the buffer has filled to the point where the whole video can play without stalling, and if it *does* stall, it will resume automatically. To learn what's happening, check the AVPlayer's `timeControl-Status`; if it is `.waitingToPlayAtSpecifiedRate`, check the AVPlayer's `reasonFor-WaitingToPlay`. To learn the actual current play rate, call `CMTimebaseGetRate` on the AVPlayerItem's `timebase`.

simply the numerator and denominator of a rational number. When you call the CMTime initializer `init(value:timescale:)` (equivalent to C `CMTimeMake`), that's what you're providing. The denominator represents the degree of granularity; a typical value is 600, sufficient to specify individual frames in common video formats.

In the convenience initializer `init(seconds:preferredTimescale:)` (equivalent to C `CMTimeMakeWithSeconds`), the two arguments are *not* the numerator and denominator; they are the time's equivalent in seconds and the denominator. For example, `CMTime(seconds:2.5, preferredTimescale:600)` yields the CMTime `(1500,600)`.

Constructing Media

AV Foundation allows you to construct your own media asset in code as an AVComposition, an AVAsset subclass, using *its* subclass, AVMutableComposition. An AVMutableComposition is an AVAsset, so given an AVMutableComposition, we could make an AVPlayerItem from it (by calling `init(asset:)`) and hand it over to an AVPlayerViewController's player; we will thus be creating and displaying our own movie.

Let's try it! In this example, I start with an AVAsset (`asset1`, a video file) and assemble its first 5 seconds of video and its last 5 seconds of video into an AVMutableComposition (`comp`):

```
let type = AVMediaType.video
let arr = asset1.tracks(withMediaType: type)
let track = arr.last!
let duration : CMTime = track.timeRange.duration
let comp = AVMutableComposition()
let comptrack = comp.addMutableTrack(withMediaType: type,
    preferredTrackID: Int32(kCMPersistentTrackID_Invalid))!
try! comptrack.insertTimeRange(CMTimeRange(
    start: CMTime(seconds:0, preferredTimescale:600),
    duration: CMTime(seconds:5, preferredTimescale:600)),
    of:track, at:CMTime(seconds:0, preferredTimescale:600))
try! comptrack.insertTimeRange(CMTimeRange(
    start: CMTimeSubtract(duration,
        CMTime(seconds:5, preferredTimescale:600)),
    duration: CMTime(seconds:5, preferredTimescale:600)),
    of:track, at:CMTime(seconds:5, preferredTimescale:600))
```

This works perfectly. We are not very good video editors, however, as we have forgotten the corresponding soundtrack from `asset1`. Let's go back and get it and add it to our AVMutableComposition (`comp`):

```
let type2 = AVMediaType.audio
let arr2 = asset1.tracks(withMediaType: type2)
let track2 = arr2.last!
let comptrack2 = comp.addMutableTrack(withMediaType: type2,
    preferredTrackID:Int32(kCMPersistentTrackID_Invalid))!
try! comptrack2.insertTimeRange(CMTimeRange(
    start: CMTime(seconds:0, preferredTimescale:600),
    duration: CMTime(seconds:5, preferredTimescale:600)),
    of:track2, at:CMTime(seconds:0, preferredTimescale:600))
try! comptrack2.insertTimeRange(CMTimeRange(
    start: CMTimeSubtract(duration,
        CMTime(seconds:5, preferredTimescale:600)),
    duration: CMTime(seconds:5, preferredTimescale:600)),
    of:track2, at:CMTime(seconds:5, preferredTimescale:600))
```

But wait! Now let's overlay *another* audio track from *another* asset; this might be, for example, some additional narration:

```
let type3 = AVMediaType.audio
let s = Bundle.main.url(forResource:"aboutTiagol", withExtension:"m4a")!
let asset2 = AVURLAsset(url:s)
let arr3 = asset2.tracks(withMediaType: type3)
let track3 = arr3.last!
let comptrack3 = comp.addMutableTrack(withMediaType: type3,
    preferredTrackID:Int32(kCMPersistentTrackID_Invalid))!
```

```
try! comptrack3.insertTimeRange(CMTimeRange(
    start: CMTime(seconds:0, preferredTimescale:600),
    duration: CMTime(seconds:10, preferredTimescale:600)),
    of:track3, at:CMTime(seconds:0, preferredTimescale:600))
```

You can also apply audio volume changes, and video opacity and transform changes, to the playback of individual tracks. I'll continue from the previous example, applying a fadeout to the last three seconds of the narration track (comptrack3) by creating an AVAudioMix:

```
let params = AVMutableAudioMixInputParameters(track:comptrack3)
params.setVolume(1, at:CMTime(seconds:0, preferredTimescale:600))
params.setVolumeRamp(fromStartVolume: 1, toEndVolume:0,
    timeRange:CMTimeRange(
        start: CMTime(seconds:7, preferredTimescale:600),
        duration: CMTime(seconds:3, preferredTimescale:600)))
let mix = AVMutableAudioMix()
mix.inputParameters = [params]
```

The audio mix must be applied to a playback milieu, such as an AVPlayerItem. So when we make an AVPlayerItem out of our AVComposition, we can set its audioMix property to mix:

```
let item = AVPlayerItem(asset:comp)
item.audioMix = mix
```

Similar to AVAudioMix, you can use AVVideoComposition to dictate how video tracks are to be composited. You can even add a CIFilter (Chapter 2) to be applied to your video.

Synchronizing Animation with Video

An intriguing feature of AV Foundation is AVSynchronizedLayer, a CALayer subclass that effectively crosses the bridge between video time (the CMTime within the progress of a movie) and Core Animation time (the time within the progress of an animation). This means that you can coordinate animation in your interface (Chapter 4) with the playback of a movie. You attach an animation to a layer in more or less the usual way, but the animation takes place in movie playback time: if the movie is stopped, the animation is stopped; if the movie is run at double rate, the animation runs at double rate; and the current "frame" of the animation always corresponds to the current frame of the video within its overall duration.

The synchronization is performed with respect to an AVPlayer's AVPlayerItem. To demonstrate, I'll draw a long thin gray rectangle containing a little black square; the horizontal position of the black square within the gray rectangle will be synchronized to the movie playhead position:

Figure 15-5. The black square's position is synchronized to the movie

```
let vc = self.childViewControllers[0] as! AVPlayerViewController
let p = vc.player!
// create synch layer, put it in the interface
let item = p.currentItem!
let syncLayer = AVSynchronizedLayer(playerItem:item)
syncLayer.frame = CGRect(10,220,300,10)
syncLayer.backgroundColor = UIColor.lightGray.cgColor
self.view.layer.addSublayer(syncLayer)
// give synch layer a sublayer
let subLayer = CALayer()
subLayer.backgroundColor = UIColor.black.cgColor
subLayer.frame = CGRect(0,0,10,10)
syncLayer.addSublayer(subLayer)
// animate the sublayer
let anim = CABasicAnimation(keyPath:#keyPath(CALayer.position))
anim.fromValue = subLayer.position
anim.toValue = CGPoint(295,5)
anim.isRemovedOnCompletion = false
anim.beginTime = AVCoreAnimationBeginTimeAtZero // important trick
anim.duration = CMTimeGetSeconds(item.asset.duration)
subLayer.add(anim, forKey:nil)
```

The result is shown in Figure 15-5. The gray rectangle is the AVSynchronizedLayer, tied to our movie. The little black square inside it is its sublayer; when we animate the black square, that animation will be synchronized to the movie, changing its position from the left end of the gray rectangle to the right end, starting at the beginning of the movie and with the same duration as the movie. Thus, although we attach this animation to the black square layer in the usual way, that animation is frozen: the black square *doesn't move* until we start the movie playing. Moreover, if we pause the movie, the black square stops. The black square is thus *automatically* representing the current play position within the movie. This may seem a silly example, but if you were to suppress the video controls it could prove downright useful.

AVPlayerLayer

An AVPlayer is not an interface object. The corresponding interface object — an AVPlayer made visible, as it were — is an AVPlayerLayer (a CALayer subclass). It has no controls for letting the user play and pause a movie and visualize its progress; it just shows the movie, acting as a bridge between the AV Foundation world of media and the CALayer world of things the user can see.

An AVPlayerViewController's view hosts an AVPlayerLayer for you automatically; otherwise you would not see any video in the AVPlayerViewController's view. But there may be situations where you find AVPlayerViewController too heavyweight, where you don't need the standard transport controls, where you don't want the video to be expandable or to have a fullscreen mode — you just want the simple direct power that can be obtained only by putting an AVPlayerLayer into the interface yourself. And you are free to do so!

Here, I'll display the same movie as before, but without an AVPlayerViewController:

```
let m = Bundle.main.url(forResource:"ElMirage", withExtension:"mp4")!
let asset = AVURLAsset(url:m)
let item = AVPlayerItem(asset:asset)
let p = AVPlayer(playerItem:item)
self.player = p // might need a reference later
let lay = AVPlayerLayer(player:p)
lay.frame = CGRect(10,10,300,200)
self.playerLayer = lay // might need a reference later
self.view.layer.addSublayer(lay)
```

As before, if we want to prevent a flash when the video becomes ready for display, we can postpone adding the AVPlayerLayer to our interface until its isReadyForDisplay property becomes true — which we can learn through KVO.

In a WWDC 2016 video, Apple suggests an interesting twist on the preceding code: create the AVPlayer *without* an AVPlayerItem, create the AVPlayerLayer, and *then* assign the AVPlayerItem to AVPlayer, like this:

```
let m = Bundle.main.url(forResource:"ElMirage", withExtension:"mp4")!
let asset = AVURLAsset(url:m)
let item = AVPlayerItem(asset:asset)
let p = AVPlayer() // *
self.player = p
let lay = AVPlayerLayer(player:p)
lay.frame = CGRect(10,10,300,200)
self.playerLayer = lay
p.replaceCurrentItem(with: item) // *
self.view.layer.addSublayer(lay)
```

Apparently, there is some increase in efficiency if you do things in that order. The reason, it turns out, is that when an AVPlayerItem is assigned to an AVPlayer that doesn't have an associated AVPlayerLayer, the AVPlayer assumes that only the audio track of the AVAsset is important — and then, when an AVPlayerLayer *is* assigned to it, the AVPlayer must scramble to pick up the video track as well.

The movie is now visible in the interface, but it isn't doing anything. We haven't told our AVPlayer to play, and there are no transport controls, so the user can't tell the video to play either. That's why I kept a reference to the AVPlayer in a property! We can start play either by calling `play` or by setting the AVPlayer's `rate`. Here, I imagine that we've provided a simple play/pause button that toggles the playing status of the movie by changing its rate:

```
@IBAction func doButton (_ sender: Any) {
    let rate = self.player.rate
    self.player.rate = rate < 0.01 ? 1 : 0
}
```

Without trying to replicate the full transport controls, we might also like to give the user a way to jump the playhead back to the start of the movie. The playhead position is a feature of an AVPlayerItem:

```
@IBAction func restart (_ sender: Any) {
    let item = self.player.currentItem!
    item.seek(to:CMTime(seconds:0, preferredTimescale:600))
}
```

If we want our AVPlayerLayer to support picture-in-picture, then (in addition to making the app itself support picture-in-picture, as I've already described) we need to call upon AVKit to supply us with an AVPictureInPictureController. This is *not* a view controller; it merely endows our AVPlayerLayer with picture-in-picture behavior. You create the AVPictureInPictureController (checking first to see whether the environment supports picture-in-picture in the first place), initialize it with the AVPlayerLayer, *and retain it*:

```
if AVPictureInPictureController.isPictureInPictureSupported() {
    let pic = AVPictureInPictureController(playerLayer: self.playerLayer)
    self.pic = pic
}
```

There are no transport controls, so there is no picture-in-picture button. Supplying one is up to you. Don't forget to hide the button if picture-in-picture isn't supported! When the button is tapped, tell the AVPictureInPictureController to `startPictureInPicture`:

```
@IBAction func doPicInPic(_ sender: Any) {
    if self.pic.isPictureInPicturePossible {
        self.pic.startPictureInPicture()
    }
}
```

You might also want to set yourself as the AVPictureInPictureController's `delegate` (AVPictureInPictureControllerDelegate). As with the AVPlayerViewController delegate, you are informed of stages in the life of the picture-in-picture window so that you can adjust your interface accordingly. When the user taps the button that dismisses the system window and returns to your app, then if the AVPlayerLayer is still sitting in your interface, there may be no work to do. If you removed the AVPlayerLayer from your interface, and you now want to restore it, implement this delegate method:

`picture(_:restoreUserInterfaceForPictureInPictureStopWithCompletion-Handler:)`

> Configure your interface so that the AVPlayerLayer is present. Make sure that the AVPlayerLayer that you now put into your interface is *the same one* that was removed earlier; in other words, your player layer must continue to be the same as the AVPictureInPictureController's `playerLayer`.

Further Exploration of AV Foundation

Here are some other things you can do with AV Foundation:

- Extract single images ("thumbnails") from a movie (AVAssetImageGenerator).
- Export a movie in a different format (AVAssetExportSession), or read/write raw uncompressed data through a buffer to or from a track (AVAssetReader, AVAssetReaderOutput, AVAssetWriter, AVAssetWriterInput, and so on).
- Capture audio, video, and stills through the device's hardware (AVCaptureSession and so on). I'll say more about that in Chapter 17.
- Tap into video and audio being captured or played, including capturing video frames as still images (AVPlayerItemVideoOutput, AVCaptureVideoDataOutput, and so on; and see Apple's *Technical Q&A QA1702*).

UIVideoEditorController

UIVideoEditorController is a view controller that presents an interface where the user can trim video. Its view and internal behavior are outside your control, and you're not supposed to subclass it. You are expected to treat the view controller as a presented view controller on the iPhone or as a popover on the iPad, and respond by way of its delegate.

 UIVideoEditorController is one of the creakiest pieces of interface in iOS. It dates back to iOS 3.1, and hasn't been revised since its inception — and it looks and feels like it. It has *never* worked properly on the iPad, and still doesn't. I'm going to show how to use it, but I'm not going to explore its bugginess or we'd be here all day.

Before summoning a UIVideoEditorController, be sure to call its class method can-EditVideo(atPath:). (This call can take some noticeable time to return.) If it returns false, don't instantiate UIVideoEditorController to edit the given file. Not every video format is editable, and not every device supports video editing. You must also set the UIVideoEditorController instance's delegate and videoPath before presenting it; the delegate should adopt both UINavigationControllerDelegate and UIVideoEditorControllerDelegate. You must manually set the video editor controller's modalPresentationStyle to .popover on the iPad (a good instance of the creakiness I was just referring to):

```
let path = Bundle.main.path(forResource:"ElMirage", ofType: "mp4")!
let can = UIVideoEditorController.canEditVideo(atPath:path)
if !can {
    print("can't edit this video")
    return
}
let vc = UIVideoEditorController()
vc.delegate = self
vc.videoPath = path
if UIDevice.current.userInterfaceIdiom == .pad {
    vc.modalPresentationStyle = .popover
}
self.present(vc, animated: true)
if let pop = vc.popoverPresentationController {
    let v = sender as! UIView
    pop.sourceView = v
    pop.sourceRect = v.bounds
    pop.delegate = self
}
```

The view's interface (on the iPhone) contains Cancel and Save buttons, a trimming box displaying thumbnails from the movie, a play/pause button, and the movie itself. The user slides the ends of the trimming box to set the beginning and end of the saved movie. The Cancel and Save buttons do *not* dismiss the presented view; you must do that in your implementation of the delegate methods. There are three of them, and you should implement all three and dismiss the presented view in all of them:

- videoEditorController(_:didSaveEditedVideoToPath:)
- videoEditorControllerDidCancel(_:)
- videoEditorController(_:didFailWithError:)

Implementing the second two delegate methods is straightforward:

```
func videoEditorControllerDidCancel(_ editor: UIVideoEditorController) {
    self.dismiss(animated:true)
}
func videoEditorController(_ editor: UIVideoEditorController,
    didFailWithError error: Error) {
        self.dismiss(animated:true)
}
```

Saving the trimmed video is more involved. Like everything else about a movie, it takes time. When the user taps Save, there's a progress view while the video is trimmed and compressed. By the time the delegate method `videoEditor-Controller(_:didSaveEditedVideoToPath:)` is called, the trimmed video has *already* been saved to a file in your app's temporary directory.

Doing something useful with the saved file at this point is up to you; if you merely leave it in the temporary directory, you can't rely on it to persist. In this example, I copy the edited movie into the Camera Roll album of the user's photo library, by calling `UISaveVideoAtPathToSavedPhotosAlbum`. For this to work, our app's *Info.plist* must have a "Privacy - Photo Library Additions Usage Description" entry (`NSPhoto-LibraryAddUsageDescription`) so that the runtime can ask for the user's permission on our behalf (that requirement is new in iOS 11):

```
func videoEditorController(_ editor: UIVideoEditorController,
    didSaveEditedVideoToPath path: String) {
        self.dismiss(animated:true)
        if UIVideoAtPathIsCompatibleWithSavedPhotosAlbum(path) {
            UISaveVideoAtPathToSavedPhotosAlbum(path, self,
                #selector(savedVideo), nil)
        } else {
            // can't save to photo album, try something else
        }
}
```

The function reference `#selector(savedVideo)` in that code refers to a callback method that must take three parameters: a String (the `path`), an Optional wrapping an Error, and an UnsafeMutableRawPointer. It's important to check for errors, because things can still go wrong. In particular, the user could deny us access to the photo library (see Chapter 17 for more about that). If that's the case, we'll get an Error whose domain is `ALAssetsLibraryErrorDomain`:

```
@objc func savedVideo(at path:String, withError error:Error?,
    ci:UnsafeMutableRawPointer) {
        if let error = error {
            print("error: \(error)")
        }
}
```

CHAPTER 16

Music Library

An iOS device can be used for the same purpose as the original iPod — to hold and play music, podcasts, and audiobooks. These items constitute the device's *music library*. iOS provides the programmer with various forms of access to the device's music library; you can:

- Explore the music library.
- Play an item from the music library.
- Control the Music app's music player.
- Present a standard interface where the user can select a music library item.

These features are all provided by the Media Player framework; you'll need to `import MediaPlayer`.

This chapter assumes that the user's music library consists of sound files that are actually present on the device. However, the user might be using the iCloud Music Library (iTunes Match); and, new in iOS 11, MusicKit allows your app to interface on the user's behalf with the cloud-based Apple Music service. MusicKit is beyond the scope of this book; see the *Apple Music API Reference* for information about it.

Music Library Authorization

Access to the music library requires authorization from the user. You'll need to include in your *Info.plist* an entry under the "Privacy — Media Library Usage Description" key (`NSAppleMusicUsageDescription`) justifying to the user your desire for access. This will be used in the alert that will be presented to the user on your behalf by the system (Figure 16-1).

Figure 16-1. The system prompts for music library access

The system will present the authorization alert once, automatically, the first time your app attempts to access the music library. Instead of letting that happen, you will probably want to take control by checking for authorization yourself and requesting it if necessary. To learn whether you already have authorization, call the MPMediaLibrary `authorizationStatus` class method. The result is an MPMediaLibraryAuthorizationStatus. Here are the status cases and what they mean for how you might proceed:

`.notDetermined`
> Authorization has never been requested. In that case, you'll want to request authorization, causing the system's authorization alert to appear.

`.authorized`
> We're already authorized. Go ahead and access the music library.

`.denied`
> We have been refused authorization. It is possible to do nothing, but if your app depends upon music library access, it is also reasonable to put up an alert begging for authorization. Your alert can even take the user directly to the spot in the Settings app where the user can provide authorization:
> ```
> let url = URL(string:UIApplicationOpenSettingsURLString)!
> UIApplication.shared.open(url)
> ```

`.restricted`
> We have been refused authorization and the user may not have the power to authorize us. There's no point harassing the user about this, so it is best to do nothing.

If the authorization status is `.notDetermined`, and you want to request authorization, call the MPMediaLibrary class method `requestAuthorization`. This method executes asynchronously. To hear about the user's response to the alert, you pass a completion function as parameter; it will be called, possibly on a background thread, when the user dismisses the alert, with an MPMediaLibraryAuthorizationStatus parameter. If the status is now `.authorized`, you can proceed to access the music library.

Checking for Authorization

The user can switch to the Settings app and change your authorization status at any time. Thus you'll probably need to check for authorization whenever your app is activated. An even better strategy might be to wait until just before performing any action that actually requires authorization; if you have authorization, or can get it, you'll proceed to perform that action.

Taking the MPMediaLibrary as an example, we can construct a general strategy for performing an action if and only if we have or can obtain authorization. We must proceed to our action by two different paths — either because we already have authorization, or because we request authorization and receive it. On the one hand, learning our authorization status is immediate, and if we are authorized, we can take our action directly; on the other hand, requesting authorization proceeds *asynchronously*, meaning that the reply to our request arrives in the completion function (see Appendix C).

Since the same "next action" appears in two places, we can encapsulate our strategy neatly into a general authorization function that takes the "next action" as a function parameter:

```swift
func checkForMusicLibraryAccess(andThen f:(()->())? = nil) {
    let status = MPMediaLibrary.authorizationStatus()
    switch status {
    case .authorized: f?()
    case .notDetermined:
        MPMediaLibrary.requestAuthorization() { status in
            if status == .authorized {
                DispatchQueue.main.async {
                    f?()
                }
            }
        }
    case .restricted: break // do nothing
    case .denied: break // do nothing, or beg for authorization in Settings
    }
}
```

I've made the function parameter an Optional in case there is no immediate "next action." That way, our utility is useful even if we just want to check for authorization in general.

To retest the system authorization request alert and other access-related behaviors, go to the Settings app and choose General → Reset → Reset Location & Privacy.

Exploring the Music Library

Everything in the user's music library, as seen by your code, is an MPMediaEntity. This is an abstract class. It has two concrete subclasses:

MPMediaItem
> An MPMediaItem is a single item (a "song").

MPMediaCollection
> An MPMediaCollection is an ordered list of MPMediaItems, rather like an array; it has a `count`, and its `items` property *is* an array.

MPMediaEntity endows its subclasses with the ability to describe themselves through key–value pairs called *properties*. The property keys have names like `MPMediaItemPropertyTitle`. To fetch a property's value, call `value(forProperty:)` with its key. You can fetch multiple properties with `enumerateValues(forProperties:using:)`. As a convenience, MPMediaEntity and its subclasses also have instance properties whose names correspond to the property key names. Thus, for example, with an MPMediaItem you can say either `myItem.value(forProperty:MPMediaItemPropertyTitle)` or `myItem.title`, and in most cases you will surely prefer the latter. But you'll still need the full property key name if you're going to form an MPMediaPropertyPredicate, as I'll demonstrate later.

An MPMediaItem has a type (`mediaType`, or `MPMediaItemPropertyMediaType`); it might, for example, be music, a podcast, or an audiobook. Different types of item have slightly different properties; these will be intuitively familiar from your use of iTunes. For example, a song (music) has a title, an album title, a track number, an artist, a composer, and so on; a podcast, in addition to its normal title, has a podcast title.

A playlist is an MPMediaPlaylist, a subclass of MPMediaCollection. Its properties include a title, a flag indicating whether it is a "smart" playlist, and so on.

An item's artwork image is available through an instance of the MPMediaItemArtwork class. From this, you are supposed to be able to get the image itself scaled to a specified size by calling `image(at:)`. My experience, however, is that in reality you'll receive an image of any old size the system cares to give you, so you may have to scale it further yourself.

Querying the Music Library

Obtaining actual information from the music library involves a *query*, an MPMediaQuery. First, you *form* the query. There are three main ways to do this:

Without limits

Create a simple MPMediaQuery by calling `init` (that is, `MPMediaQuery()`). The result is an unlimited query; it asks for everything in the music library.

With a convenience constructor

MPMediaQuery provides several class methods that form a query asking the music library for a limited subset of its contents — all of its songs, or all of its podcasts, and so on. Here's the complete list:

- `songs`
- `podcasts`
- `audiobooks`
- `playlists`
- `albums`
- `artists`
- `composers`
- `genres`
- `compilations`

With filter predicates

You can limit a query more precisely by attaching to it one or more MPMedia-PropertyPredicate instances. These predicates filter the music library according to criteria you specify; to be included in the result, a media item must successfully pass through all the filters (in other words, the predicates are combined using logical-and). A predicate is a simple comparison. It has three aspects:

A property

The key name of the property you want to compare against. Not every property can be used in a filter predicate; the documentation makes the distinction clear (and you can get additional help from an MPMediaEntity class method, `canFilter(byProperty:)`).

A value

The value that the property must have in order to pass through the filter.

A comparison type (optional)

An MPMediaPredicateComparison. In order to pass through the filter, a media item's property value can either *match* the value you provide (`.equal-To`, the default) or *contain* the value you provide (`.contains`).

The two ways of forming a limited query are actually the same; a convenience constructor is just a quick way of obtaining a query already endowed with a filter predicate.

A query also *groups* its results, according to its groupingType (MPMediaGrouping). Your choices are:

- .title
- .album
- .artist
- .albumArtist
- .composer
- .genre
- .playlist
- .podcastTitle

The query convenience constructors all supply a groupingType in addition to a filter predicate. Indeed, the grouping is often the salient aspect of the query. For example, an albums query is in fact merely a songs query with the added feature that its results are grouped by album.

After you form the query, you *perform* the query. You do this simply by asking for the query's properties. You can ask for its items, an array of MPMediaItems, if you don't care about the groups returned from the query. Alternatively, you can ask for its collections, an array of MPMediaItemCollections each of which represents one group.

An MPMediaItemCollection has a representativeItem property that can come in handy when it is obtained from a grouped query. It gives you just one item from the collection, and the reason you need it is that properties of a group collection are often embodied in its items rather than in the collection itself. For example, an album has no title; rather, its items have album titles that are all the same. So to learn the title of an album, you ask for the album title of a representative item.

Here, as an example, I'll discover the titles of all the albums:

```
let query = MPMediaQuery.albums()
guard let result = query.collections else {return}
// prove we've performed the query, by logging the album titles
for album in result {
    print(album.representativeItem!.albumTitle!)
}
/*
Bach, CPE, Symphonies
```

```
Beethoven Canons
Beethoven Dances
Scarlatti Continuo
*/
```

Now let's make our query more elaborate; we'll get the titles of all the albums whose name contains "Beethoven." We simply add a filter predicate to the previous query:

```
let query = MPMediaQuery.albums()
let hasBeethoven = MPMediaPropertyPredicate(value:"Beethoven",
    forProperty:MPMediaItemPropertyAlbumTitle,
    comparisonType:.contains)
query.addFilterPredicate(hasBeethoven)
guard let result = query.collections else {return}
for album in result {
    print(album.representativeItem!.albumTitle!)
}
/*
Beethoven Canons
Beethoven Dances
*/
```

Similarly, we can get the titles of all the albums containing any songs whose name contains "Sonata." This is like the previous example, but here we are concerned with the song's own title rather than its album title:

```
let query = MPMediaQuery.albums()
let hasSonata = MPMediaPropertyPredicate(value:"Sonata",
    forProperty:MPMediaItemPropertyTitle,
    comparisonType:.contains)
query.addFilterPredicate(hasSonata)
guard let result = query.collections else {return}
for album in result {
    print(album.representativeItem!.albumTitle!)
}
/*
Scarlatti Continuo
*/
```

An album is a collection of songs (MPMediaItems). Let's modify the output from our previous query to print the titles of all the matching songs in the first album returned. We don't have to change our query, so I'll start at the point where we perform it; result is the array of collections returned from our query, so result[0] is an MPMediaItemCollection holding the filtered songs of one album:

```
// ... same as before ...
let album = result[0]
for song in album.items {
    print(song.title!)
}
/*
Sonata in E minor Kk 81 - I Grave
```

```
Sonata in E minor Kk 81 - II Allegro
Sonata in E minor Kk 81 - III Grave
Sonata in E minor Kk 81 - IV Allegro
Sonata in G minor Kk 88 - I Grave
... and so on ...
*/
```

Persistence and Change in the Music Library

One of the properties of an MPMediaEntity is its persistentID, which uniquely identifies it. All sorts of things have persistent IDs — entities in general, songs (media items), albums, artists, composers, and more. Two songs or two playlists can have the same title, but a persistent ID is unique. It is also persistent: using the persistent ID, you can retrieve again at a later time the same song or playlist you retrieved earlier, even across launches of your app.

While you are maintaining the results of a search, the contents of the music library may themselves change. For example, the user might connect the device to a computer and add or delete music with iTunes. This can put your results out of date. For this reason, the library's own modified date is available through the MPMediaLibrary class. Call the class method default to get the actual library instance; now you can ask for its lastModifiedDate.

You can also register to receive a notification, .MPMediaLibraryDidChange, when the music library is modified. This notification is not emitted unless you first call the MPMediaLibrary instance method beginGeneratingLibraryChangeNotifications; you should eventually balance this with endGeneratingLibraryChange-Notifications.

Music Player

The Media Player framework class for playing an MPMediaItem is MPMusicPlayer-Controller. It comes in two flavors, depending on which class property you use to get an instance:

systemMusicPlayer
> The very same player used by the Music app. This might already be playing an item, or it might be paused with a current item, at any time while your app runs; you can learn or change what item this is. The system music player continues playing independently of the state of your app; the user, by way of the Music app, can at any time alter what it is doing.

applicationQueuePlayer
> New in iOS 11; supersedes the applicationMusicPlayer. What you do with this music player doesn't affect, and is not affected by, what the Music app does; the

song it is playing can be different from the Music app's current song. Neverthe-less, it isn't really inside your app. For example, it has its own audio session; tell-ing the player to play interrupts your audio session. If your app's *Info.plist* includes the "Required background modes" key with the audio mode (Chap-ter 14), the player will keep playing when your app is backgrounded, even if your app's audio session category is not Playback.

The application queue player has no user interface; the remote playback controls (Figure 14-1) do not automatically work on it (despite claims to the contrary, both in the documentation and in a WWDC 2017 video), and if you want the user to have controls for playing and stopping a song, you'll have to create them yourself. The sys-tem music player, on the other hand, has a complete user interface — not only the remote playback controls, but the entire Music app.

A music player doesn't merely play an item; it plays from a *queue* of items. This behavior is familiar from iTunes and the Music app. For example, in the Music app, when you tap the first song of a playlist to start playing it, when the end of that song is reached, we proceed by default to the next song in the playlist. That's because tap-ping the first song of a playlist causes the queue to be the totality of songs in the play-list. The music player behaves the same way: when it reaches the end of a song, it proceeds to the next song in its queue.

Your methods for controlling playback also reflect this queue-based orientation. In addition to the expected play, pause, and stop commands, there's a skipToNextItem and skipToPreviousItem command. Anyone who has ever used iTunes or the Music app (or, for that matter, an old-fashioned iPod) will have an intuitive grasp of this and everything else a music player does. You can even set a music player's repeatMode and shuffleMode, just as in iTunes.

You provide a music player with its queue by calling setQueue(_:), where the param-eter is one of the following:

A query
> You hand the music player an MPMediaQuery. The query's items are the items of the queue.

A collection
> You hand the music player an MPMediaItemCollection. This might be obtained from a query you performed, but you can also assemble your own collection of MPMediaItems in any way you like, putting them into an array and calling MPMediaItemCollection's init(items:).

My experience is that the player can behave in unexpected ways if you don't ask it to play, or at least prepareToPlay, immediately after setting the queue. Apparently the queue does not actually take effect until you do that. Stopping the player empties its queue; pausing it does not.

In this example, we collect all songs actually present in the library that are shorter than 30 seconds, and set them playing in random order using the application queue player. Observe that I explicitly stop the player before setting its queue; I have found that this is the most reliable approach:

```
let query = MPMediaQuery.songs()
let isPresent = MPMediaPropertyPredicate(value:false,
    forProperty:MPMediaItemPropertyIsCloudItem,
    comparisonType:.equalTo)
query.addFilterPredicate(isPresent)
guard let items = query.items else {return}
let shorties = items.filter {
    let dur = $0.playbackDuration
    return dur < 30
}
guard shorties.count > 0 else {
    print("no songs that short!")
    return
}
let queue = MPMediaItemCollection(items:shorties)
let player = MPMusicPlayerController.applicationQueuePlayer
player.stop()
player.setQueue(with:queue)
player.shuffleMode = .songs
player.play()
```

You can ask a music player for its `nowPlayingItem`, and since this is an MPMedia-Item, you can learn all about it through its properties. You can ask a music player which song within the queue is currently playing (`indexOfNowPlayingItem`). Unfortunately, you can't ask the system music player for its actual queue. You can, however, obtain the application queue player's current queue, in rather a roundabout way — by calling `perform(queueTransaction:completionHandler:)`, whose real purpose I'll discuss in a moment.

Modification of the queue is new in iOS 11 (actually, it was quietly introduced in iOS 10.3). There are two distinct approaches:

Play next and play later
> For either the system music player or the application queue player, you can call `prepend(_:)` or `append(_:)`. Apple characterizes these as equivalent to Play Next and Play Later functionality; `prepend(_:)` inserts into the queue just after the currently playing item, while `append(_:)` inserts at the end of the queue. The parameter is an MPMusicPlayerQueueDescriptor, an abstract class whose subclasses are:
>
> - MPMusicPlayerPlayParametersQueueDescriptor

- MPMusicPlayerStoreQueueDescriptor
- MPMusicPlayerMediaItemQueueDescriptor

The first two have to do with Apple Music. The third, MPMusicPlayerMediaItem-QueueDescriptor, allows you to supply a list of MPMediaItems directly. It has two initializers, `init(itemCollection:)` and `init(query:)` — but unfortunately, as of this writing, `init(itemCollection:)` seems to be completely broken (a queue descriptor formed with an MPMediaItemCollection has no effect on the behavior of the music player), so you have to start with an MPMediaQuery and call `init(query:)`.

Insert and remove

For the application queue player, you can call `perform(queue-Transaction:completionHandler:)` and, in the `queueTransaction` function, call `insert(_:after:)` or `remove(_:)` on the MPMusicPlayerControllerMutable-Queue object that you get as the parameter.

Like `prepend(_:)` and `append(_:)`, you'll need an MPMusicPlayerQueue-Descriptor in order to call `insert(_:after:)`.

MPMusicPlayerControllerMutableQueue is a subclass of MPMusicPlayer-ControllerQueue, which has an `items` property that you can use to examine the queue. The completion function receives an MPMusicPlayerControllerQueue and an Optional Error as parameters.

A music player has a `playbackState` that you can query to learn what it's doing (whether it is playing, paused, stopped, or seeking). It also emits notifications informing you of changes in its state:

- `.MPMusicPlayerControllerPlaybackStateDidChange`
- `.MPMusicPlayerControllerNowPlayingItemDidChange`
- `.MPMusicPlayerControllerVolumeDidChange`

These notifications are not emitted until you tell the music player to `begin-GeneratingPlaybackNotifications`. (You should eventually balance this call with `endGeneratingPlaybackNotifications`.) This is an instance method, so you can arrange to receive notifications from either of the two music players. If you are receiving notifications from both, you can distinguish them by examining the Notification's `object` and comparing it to each player.

To illustrate, I'll extend the previous example to set the text of a UILabel in our interface (`self.label`) every time a different song starts playing. Before we start the player playing, we insert these lines to generate the notifications:

```
player.beginGeneratingPlaybackNotifications()
NotificationCenter.default.addObserver(self,
    selector: #selector(self.changed),
    name: .MPMusicPlayerControllerNowPlayingItemDidChange,
    object: player)
```

And here's how we respond to those notifications:

```
@objc func changed(_ n:Notification) {
    self.label.text = ""
    let player = MPMusicPlayerController.applicationQueuePlayer
    guard let obj = n.object, obj as AnyObject === player else { return }
    guard let title = player.nowPlayingItem?.title else {return}
    let ix = player.indexOfNowPlayingItem
    guard ix != NSNotFound else {return}
    player.perform(queueTransaction: { _ in }) { q,_ in
        self.label.text = "\(ix+1) of \(q.items.count): \(title)"
    }
}
```

There's no periodic notification as a song plays and the current playhead position advances. To get this information, you'll have to resort to polling. This is not objectionable as long as your polling interval is reasonably sparse; your display may occasionally fall a little behind reality, but that won't usually matter. To illustrate, let's add to our existing example a UIProgressView (`self.prog`) showing the current percentage of the current song being played by the music player. I'll use a Timer to poll the state of the player every second:

```
self.timer = Timer.scheduledTimer(timeInterval:1,
    target: self, selector: #selector(self.timerFired),
    userInfo: nil, repeats: true)
self.timer.tolerance = 0.1
```

When the timer fires, the progress view displays the state of the currently playing item:

```
@objc func timerFired(_: Any) {
    let player = MPMusicPlayerController.applicationQueuePlayer
    guard let item = player.nowPlayingItem,
        player.playbackState != .stopped else {
            self.prog.isHidden = true
            return
    }
    self.prog.isHidden = false
    let current = player.currentPlaybackTime
    let total = item.playbackDuration
    self.prog.progress = Float(current / total)
}
```

MPVolumeView

The Media Player framework offers a slider for letting the user set the system output volume, along with an AirPlay route button if appropriate; this is an MPVolumeView. It is customizable similarly to a UISlider (Chapter 12); you can set the images for the two halves of the track, the thumb, and even the AirPlay route button, for both the normal and the highlighted state (while the user is touching the thumb).

For further customization, you can subclass MPVolumeView and override `volume-SliderRect(forBounds:)`. (An additional overridable method is documented, `volumeThumbRect(forBounds:volumeSliderRect:value:)`, but in my testing it is never called; I regard this as a bug.)

The MPVolumeView automatically updates itself to reflect changes in the system output volume. You can also register for notifications when a wireless route (Bluetooth or AirPlay) appears or disappears, and when a wireless route becomes active or inactive:

- `.MPVolumeViewWirelessRoutesAvailableDidChange`
- `.MPVolumeViewWirelessRouteActiveDidChange`

Playing Songs with AV Foundation

MPMusicPlayerController is convenient and simple, but it's also simpleminded. Its audio session isn't your audio session; the music player doesn't really belong to you. So what else can you use to play an MPMediaItem? The answer lies in the fact that an MPMediaItem representing a file in the user's music library has an `assetURL` property whose value is a file URL. Now you have a general reference to the music file — and everything from Chapters 14 and 15 comes into play.

So, for example, having obtained an MPMediaItem's asset URL, you could use that URL to initialize an AVAudioPlayer, an AVAsset, or an AVPlayer. Each of these ways of accessing an MPMediaItem has its advantages:

- An AVAudioPlayer is easy to use, and lets you loop a sound, poll the power value of its channels, and so forth.
- An AVAsset gives you the full power of the AV Foundation framework, letting you edit the sound, assemble multiple sounds, perform a fadeout effect, and even attach the sound to a video (and then play it with an AVPlayer).
- An AVPlayer can be assigned to an AVPlayerViewController, which gives you a built-in play/pause button and playhead slider. Another major advantage of an AVPlayerViewController is that it automatically manages the software remote

control interface for you (unless you set its `updatesNowPlayingInfoCenter` property to `false`).

In this example, I'll use an AVQueuePlayer (an AVPlayer subclass) to play a sequence of MPMediaItems, just as an MPMusicPlayerController does. We might be tempted to treat the AVQueuePlayer as a playlist, handing it the entire array of songs to be played:

```
let arr = // array of MPMediaItem
let items = arr.map {
    let url = $0.assetURL!
    let asset = AVAsset(url:url)
    return AVPlayerItem(asset: asset)
}
self.qp = AVQueuePlayer(items:items)
self.qp.play()
```

Instead of adding a whole batch of AVPlayerItems to an AVQueuePlayer all at once, however, we should add just a few AVPlayerItems to start with, and then append each additional AVPlayerItem when an item finishes playing. So I'll start out by adding just three AVPlayerItems, and use key–value observing to watch for changes in the AVQueuePlayer's `currentItem`:

```
let arr = // array of MPMediaItem
self.items = arr.map {
    let url = $0.assetURL!
    let asset = AVAsset(url:url)
    return AVPlayerItem(asset: asset)
}
let seed = min(3,self.items.count)
self.qp = AVQueuePlayer(items:Array(self.items.prefix(upTo:seed)))
self.items = Array(self.items.suffix(from:seed))
// use .initial option so that we get an observation for the first item
let ob = qp.observe(\.currentItem, options: .initial) { _,_ in
    self.changed()
}
self.obs.insert(ob)
self.qp.play()
```

In our `changed` method, we pull an AVPlayerItem off the front of our `items` array and add it to the end of the AVQueuePlayer's queue. The AVQueuePlayer itself deletes an item from the start of its queue after playing it, so in this way the queue never exceeds three items in length:

```
guard let item = self.qp.currentItem else {return}
guard self.items.count > 0 else {return}
let newItem = self.items.removeFirst()
self.qp.insert(newItem, after:nil) // means "at end"
```

Since we're already being notified each time a new song starts playing, we can insert some code to update a label's text with the title of each successive song. This will demonstrate how to extract metadata from an AVAsset by way of an AVMetadata-Item; here, we fetch the AVMetadata.commonKeyTitle and get its value property:

```
var arr = item.asset.commonMetadata
arr = AVMetadataItem.metadataItems(from:arr,
    withKey:AVMetadataKey.commonKeyTitle,
    keySpace:.common)
let met = arr[0]
let value = #keyPath(AVMetadataItem.value)
met.loadValuesAsynchronously(forKeys:[value]) {
    if met.statusOfValue(forKey:value, error:nil) == .loaded {
        guard let title = met.value as? String else {return}
        DispatchQueue.main.async {
            self.label.text = "\(title)"
        }
    }
}
```

We can also update a progress view to reflect the current item's current time and duration. Unlike an MPMusicPlayerController, we don't need to poll with a Timer; we can install a *time observer* on our AVQueuePlayer:

```
self.timeObserver = self.qp.addPeriodicTimeObserver(
    forInterval: CMTime(seconds:0.5, preferredTimescale:600),
    queue: nil) { [unowned self] t in
        self.timerFired(time:t)
}
```

To get our AVPlayerItems to load their duration property, we'll need to go back and modify the code we used to initialize them:

```
let url = $0.assetURL!
let asset = AVAsset(url:url)
return AVPlayerItem(asset: asset,
    automaticallyLoadedAssetKeys: [#keyPath(AVAsset.duration)])
```

Our time observer now causes our timerFired method to be called periodically, reporting the current time of the current player item; we obtain the current item's duration and configure our progress view (self.prog):

```
func timerFired(time:CMTime) {
    if let item = self.qp.currentItem {
        let asset = item.asset
        let dur = #keyPath(AVAsset.duration)
        if asset.statusOfValue(forKey:dur, error: nil) == .loaded {
            let dur = asset.duration
            self.prog.setProgress(Float(time.seconds/dur.seconds),
                animated: false)
        }
    }
}
```

Media Picker

The media picker (MPMediaPickerController), supplied by the Media Player framework, is a view controller whose view is a self-contained navigation interface in which the user can select a media item from the music library, similar to the Music app. You are expected to treat the picker as a presented view controller.

As with any access to the music library, the media picker requires user authorization. If you present the media picker without authorization, there is no penalty, but nothing will appear to happen (and the picker will report that the user cancelled).

You can use the initializer, `init(mediaTypes:)`, to limit the type of media items displayed. You can make a prompt appear at the top of the navigation bar (`prompt`). You can govern whether the user can choose multiple media items or just one, with the `allowsPickingMultipleItems` property. You can filter out items stored in the cloud by setting `showsCloudItems` to `false`.

 Starting in iOS 9, the `mediaTypes:` values `.podcast` and `.audioBook` don't work. I believe that this is because podcasts are considered to be the purview of the Podcasts app, and audiobooks are considered to be the purview of iBooks — not the Music app. You can see podcasts and audiobooks as MPMediaEntity objects in the user's music library, but *not* by way of an MPMediaPickerController.

While the media picker controller's view is showing, you learn what the user is doing through two delegate methods (MPMediaPickerControllerDelegate); the presented view controller is not automatically dismissed, so it is up to you dismiss it in these delegate methods:

- `mediaPicker(_:didPickMediaItems:)`
- `mediaPickerDidCancel(_:)`

The behavior of the delegate methods depends on the value of the controller's `allowsPickingMultipleItems`:

The controller's `allowsPickingMultipleItems` *is* `false` *(the default)*
There's a Cancel button. When the user taps a media item, your `mediaPicker(_:didPickMediaItems:)` is called, handing you an MPMediaItemCollection consisting of that item; you are likely to dismiss the presented view controller at this point. When the user taps Cancel, your `mediaPickerDidCancel(_:)` is called.

The controller's `allowsPickingMultipleItems` *is* `true`
There's a Done button. Every time the user taps a media item, it is checked to indicate that it has been selected. When the user taps Done, your `mediaPicker(_:didPickMediaItems:)` is called, handing you an MPMediaItem-

Collection consisting of all items the user tapped — unless the user tapped no items, in which case your mediaPickerDidCancel(_:) is called.

In this example, we put up the media picker; we then play the user's chosen media item(s) with the application queue player. The example works equally well whether allowsPickingMultipleItems is true or false:

```
func presentPicker (_ sender: Any) {
    checkForMusicLibraryAccess {
        let picker = MPMediaPickerController(mediaTypes:.music)
        picker.delegate = self
        self.present(picker, animated: true)
    }
}
func mediaPicker(_ mediaPicker: MPMediaPickerController,
    didPickMediaItems mediaItemCollection: MPMediaItemCollection) {
        let player = MPMusicPlayerController.applicationQueuePlayer
        player.setQueue(with:mediaItemCollection)
        player.play()
        self.dismiss(animated:true)
}
func mediaPickerDidCancel(_ mediaPicker: MPMediaPickerController) {
    self.dismiss(animated:true)
}
```

On the iPad, the media picker can be displayed as a fullscreen presented view, but it also works reasonably well in a popover, especially if we increase its preferred-ContentSize. This code presents as fullscreen on an iPhone and as a reasonably-sized popover on an iPad:

```
let picker = MPMediaPickerController(mediaTypes:.music)
picker.delegate = self
picker.modalPresentationStyle = .popover
picker.preferredContentSize = CGSize(500,600)
self.present(picker, animated: true)
if let pop = picker.popoverPresentationController {
    if let b = sender as? UIBarButtonItem {
        pop.barButtonItem = b
    }
}
```

CHAPTER 17

Photo Library and Camera

The stored photos and videos accessed by the user through the Photos app constitute the device's photo library.

Your app can give the user an interface for exploring the photo library through the UIImagePickerController class. In addition, the Photos framework, also known as PhotoKit, lets you access the photo library and its contents programmatically — including the ability to modify a photo's image. You'll need to `import Photos`.

The UIImagePickerController class can also be used to give the user an interface similar to the Camera app, letting the user capture photos and videos. Having allowed the user to capture an image, you can store it in the photo library, just as the Camera app does.

At a deeper level, the AV Foundation framework (Chapter 15) provides direct control over the camera hardware. You'll need to `import AVFoundation`.

Constants such as `kUTTypeImage`, referred to in this chapter, are provided by the Mobile Core Services framework; you'll need to `import MobileCoreServices`.

Browsing with UIImagePickerController

UIImagePickerController is a view controller providing an interface in which the user can choose an item from the photo library, similar to the Photos app. You are expected to treat the UIImagePickerController as a presented view controller. You can use a popover on the iPad, but it also looks good as a fullscreen presented view. (The documentation claims that a fullscreen presented view is forbidden on the iPad, but that is not true.)

Image Picker Controller Presentation

To let the user choose an item from the photo library, instantiate UIImagePicker-Controller and assign its `sourceType` one of these values (UIImagePickerController-SourceType):

`.photoLibrary`
> The user is shown a table of all albums, and can navigate into any of them.

`.savedPhotosAlbum`
> In theory, the user is supposed to be confined to the contents of the Camera Roll album. Instead, ever since iOS 8, the user sees the Moments interface and all photos are shown; I regard this as a bug.

You should call the class method `isSourceTypeAvailable(_:)` beforehand; if it doesn't return `true`, don't present the picker with that source type.

You'll probably want to specify an array of `mediaTypes` you're interested in. This array will usually contain `kUTTypeImage`, `kUTTypeMovie`, or both; or you can specify all available types by calling the class method `availableMediaTypes(for:)`.

There is an additional type that you might want to include in the `mediaTypes` array — `kUTTypeLivePhoto`. This signifies your willingness to receive a live photo as a live photo. The rule is that UIImagePickerController can return a live photo as a live photo if the following two conditions are met:

- The picker's `mediaTypes` includes both `kUTTypeLivePhoto` and `kUTTypeImage`.
- The picker's `allowsEditing` property is `false` (the default).

I'll talk later about how to display a live photo as a live photo. If you fail to include `kUTTypeLivePhoto` in the `mediaTypes` array, then if the user chooses a live photo, you'll receive it as an ordinary still image.

 The results from `availableMediaTypes(for:)` do *not* include `kUTTypeLive-Photo`; you have to add it explicitly.

New in iOS 11, the `videoExportPreset` property lets you set the transcoding format to be used if the user chooses a video. Preset names are listed at the end of the AVAssetExportSession class documentation page.

Optionally, you can set the picker's `allowsEditing` property to `true`. In the case of an image, the interface then allows the user to scale the image up and to move it so as to be cropped by a preset rectangle; in the case of a movie, the user can trim the movie as with a UIVideoEditorController (Chapter 15).

After configuring the picker as desired, and having supplied a delegate (adopting UIImagePickerControllerDelegate and UINavigationControllerDelegate), present the picker:

```
let src = UIImagePickerControllerSourceType.photoLibrary
guard UIImagePickerController.isSourceTypeAvailable(src)
    else {return}
guard let arr UIImagePickerController.availableMediaTypes(for:src)
    else {return}
let picker = UIImagePickerController()
picker.sourceType = src
picker.mediaTypes = arr
picker.delegate = self
picker.videoExportPreset = AVAssetExportPreset640x480 // for example
self.present(picker, animated: true)
```

Image Picker Controller Delegate

When the user has finished working with the image picker controller, the delegate will receive one of these messages.

imagePickerController(_:didFinishPickingMediaWithInfo:)
: The user selected an item from the photo library. The info: parameter describes it; I'll give details in a moment.

imagePickerControllerDidCancel(_:)
: The user tapped Cancel.

If a UIImagePickerControllerDelegate method is not implemented, the view controller is dismissed automatically at the point where that method would be called; but rather than relying on this, you should probably implement both delegate methods and dismiss the view controller yourself in each.

The info in the first delegate method is a dictionary of information about the chosen item. The keys in this dictionary depend on the media type:

An image
: The UIImagePickerControllerMediaType key's value will be kUTTypeImage. The other keys are:

UIImagePickerControllerPHAsset
: A PHAsset representing the image in the photo library; I'll discuss how to access PHAsset information later in this chapter. (New in iOS 11; supersedes the UIImagePickerControllerReferenceURL key.)

UIImagePickerControllerOriginalImage
: A UIImage.

UIImagePickerControllerImageURL
> A file URL to a copy of the image data saved into a temporary directory. (New in iOS 11.)

If the picker's `allowsEditing` was `true`, these further keys may be present:

UIImagePickerControllerCropRect
> An NSValue wrapping a CGRect.

UIImagePickerControllerEditedImage
> A UIImage. This becomes the image you are expected to use.

A live photo
> The `UIImagePickerControllerMediaType` key's value will be `kUTTypeLivePhoto`. In addition to the image keys, there's a further key:

UIImagePickerControllerLivePhoto
> A PHLivePhoto (a type supplied by the Photos framework).

A movie
> The `UIImagePickerControllerMediaType` key's value will be `kUTTypeMovie`. The other keys are:

UIImagePickerControllerPHAsset
> A PHAsset representing the video in the photo library; I'll discuss how to access PHAsset information later in this chapter. (New in iOS 11; supersedes the `UIImagePickerControllerReferenceURL` key.)

UIImagePickerControllerMediaURL
> A file URL to a copy of the movie data saved into a temporary directory.

Here's an implementation of the first delegate method that picks up all the needed keys; the idea is that we immediately dismiss the picker and then proceed to deal with the chosen item in the completion function:

```
func imagePickerController(_ picker: UIImagePickerController,
    didFinishPickingMediaWithInfo info: [String : Any]) {
        let asset = info[UIImagePickerControllerPHAsset] as? PHAsset
        let url = info[UIImagePickerControllerMediaURL] as? URL
        var im = info[UIImagePickerControllerOriginalImage] as? UIImage
        if let ed = info[UIImagePickerControllerEditedImage] as? UIImage {
            im = ed
        }
        let live = info[UIImagePickerControllerLivePhoto] as? PHLivePhoto
        let imurl = info[UIImagePickerControllerImageURL] as? URL
        self.dismiss(animated:true) {
            // do something with the chosen item here
        }
}
```

Presenting an image picker controller does *not* require user authorization to access the photo library, presumably because an image is just an image. But getting the full repertoire of information in the delegate method *does* require user authorization; without it, you'll get the image and the media URL but that's all. Obtaining user authorization to access the photo library is discussed later in this chapter.

Dealing with Image Picker Controller Results

What should happen in the preceding code's completion function? If you're going to display the user's chosen item in your interface, you'll want to deal differently with each possible type that the user can choose.

You might suppose that the info dictionary's UIImagePickerControllerMediaType would sufficiently distinguish the possible types — kUTTypeImage, kUTTypeLive-Photo, or kUTTypeMovie. Indeed, that was true up through iOS 10. But iOS 11 introduces two new possible image types that might be present in the photo library, so the UIImagePickerControllerMediaType turns out to be insufficiently fine-grained. Instead, use the PHAsset returned by the UIImagePickerControllerPHAsset key, and examine its playbackStyle. There are five possible values (PHAsset.Playback-Style):

.image
> You have received (im) a UIImage, suitable for display in a UIImageView. The image may be very large; to save memory, you should redraw the image at the largest size and resolution needed for actual display in the interface (see Chapter 2).

.imageAnimated
> You have received an animated GIF. The ability to store an animated GIF in the photo library is new in iOS 11. However, as I mentioned in Chapter 4, iOS 11 doesn't include any native ability to display an animated GIF as animated in your interface. You can display as a still image the UIImage you have already received (im), or you can use the image URL (imurl) to load the GIF data and convert it yourself into a sequence of images for display.

.livePhoto
> You have received (live) a PHLivePhoto. To display it in your interface, use a PHLivePhotoView (supplied by the Photos UI framework; import PhotosUI). This view has many powerful properties and delegate methods, but you don't need any of them just to display the live photo; the live photo is treated as a live photo automatically, meaning that the user can use force touch on it (or long press on a device without 3D touch) to show the accompanying movie. The only

properties you really need to set are the PHLivePhotoView's `frame` and its `contentMode` (similar to a UIImageView).

`.video`

You have received (`url`) the file URL of the exported video in the temporary directory, suitable for display with AVPlayer and other AVFoundation and AVKit classes discussed in Chapter 15.

`.videoLooping`

You have received a live photo to which the Loop or Bounce effect has been applied (new in iOS 11). It comes to you as a video file URL (`url`), but implementing the looping is up to you. You can do this easily using an AVPlayerLooper object (mentioned in Chapter 15). Start with an AVQueuePlayer rather than an AVPlayer, configure the AVPlayerLooper and retain it in an instance property, and use the AVQueuePlayer to show the video. For example:

```
let av = AVPlayerViewController()
let player = AVQueuePlayer(url:url)
av.player = player
self.looper = AVPlayerLooper(
    player: player, templateItem: player.currentItem!)
// ... and so on ...
```

Still image metadata can be obtained from the image data stored at the `UIImage-PickerControllerImageURL`, using the Image I/O framework to extract the metadata as a dictionary (`import ImageIO`, and see Chapter 22):

```
guard let src = CGImageSourceCreateWithURL(imurl! as CFURL, nil)
    else {return}
let result = CGImageSourceCopyPropertiesAtIndex(src,0,nil)! as NSDictionary
```

Photos Framework

The Photos framework (`import Photos`), also known as PhotoKit, does for the photo library roughly what the Media Player framework does for the music library (Chapter 16), letting your code explore the library's contents — and then some. You can manipulate albums, add photos, and even perform edits on the user's photos.

The photo library itself is represented by the PHPhotoLibrary class, and by its shared instance, which you can obtain through the `shared` method. You do not need to retain the shared photo library instance. Then there are the classes representing the kinds of things that inhabit the library (the *photo entities*):

PHAsset

A single photo or video file.

PHCollection
> An abstract class representing collections of all kinds. Its concrete subclasses are:

> *PHAssetCollection*
>> A collection of photos. For example, albums and moments are PHAssetCollections.

> *PHCollectionList*
>> A collection of asset collections. For example, a folder of albums is a collection list; a year of moments is a collection list.

Finer typological distinctions are drawn, not through subclasses, but through a system of types and subtypes, which are properties:

- A PHAsset has `mediaType` and `mediaSubtypes` properties.
- A PHAssetCollection has `assetCollectionType` and `assetCollectionSubtype` properties.
- A PHCollectionList has `collectionListType` and `collectionListSubtype` properties.

For example, a PHAsset might have a type of `.image` and a subtype of `.photoPanorama`; a PHAssetCollection might have a type of `.album` and a subtype of `.albumRegular`; and so on. Smart albums on the user's device help draw further distinctions for you; for example, a PHAssetCollection with a type of `.smartAlbum` and a subtype of `.smartAlbumPanoramas` contains all the user's panorama photos.

New in iOS 11, a PHAsset's `playbackStyle` (discussed earlier in this chapter) draws the distinction between a true image and an animated GIF, and between a video and a looped or bounced live photo.

The photo entity classes are actually all subclasses of PHObject, an abstract class that endows them with a `localIdentifier` property that functions as a persistent unique identifier.

Access to the photo library requires user authorization. You'll use the PHPhotoLibrary class for this. To learn what the current authorization status is, call the class method `authorizationStatus`. To ask the system to put up the authorization request alert if the status is `.notDetermined`, call the class method `requestAuthorization(_:)`. The *Info.plist* must contain some text that the system authorization request alert can use to explain why your app wants access. For the photo library, the relevant key is "Privacy — Photo Library Usage Description" (`NSPhotoLibraryUsageDescription`). See "Checking for Authorization" on page 841 for detailed consideration of authorization strategy and testing.

Querying the Photo Library

When you want to know what's in the photo library, start with one of the photo entity classes — the one that represents the type of entity you want to know about. The photo entity class will supply class methods whose names begin with `fetch`; you'll pick the class method that expresses the kind of criteria you're starting with.

For example, to fetch one or more PHAssets, you'll call a PHAsset `fetch` method; you can fetch by local identifier, by media type, or by containing asset collection. Similarly, you can fetch PHAssetCollections by identifier, by type and subtype, by URL, or by whether they contain a given PHAsset. You can fetch PHCollectionLists by identifier, or by whether they contain a given PHAssetCollection. And so on.

In addition to the various `fetch` method parameters, you can supply a PHFetch-Options object letting you refine the results even further. You can set its `predicate` to limit your request results, and its `sortDescriptors` to determine the results order. Its `fetchLimit` can limit the number of results returned, and its `includeAssetSource-Types` can specify where the results should come from, such as eliminating cloud items.

What you get back from a `fetch` method query is not images or videos but *information*. A `fetch` method returns a collection of PHObjects of the type to which you sent the `fetch` method originally; these *refer* to entities in the photo library, rather than handing you an entire file (which would be huge and might take considerable time). The collection itself is expressed as a PHFetchResult, which behaves very like an array: you can ask for its `count`, obtain the object at a given index (possibly by subscripting), look for an object within the collection, and enumerate the collection with an `enumerate` method.

 You cannot enumerate a PHFetchResult with `for...in` in Swift, even though you can do so in Objective-C. I regard this as a bug (caused by the fact that PHFetch-Result is a generic).

For example, let's say we want to know how moments are divided into years. A clump of moments grouped by year is a PHCollectionList, so the relevant class is PHCollectionList. This code is a fairly standard template for fetching any sort of information from the photo library:

```
let opts = PHFetchOptions()
let desc = NSSortDescriptor(key: "startDate", ascending: true)
opts.sortDescriptors = [desc]
let result = PHCollectionList.fetchCollectionLists(with: .momentList,
    subtype: .momentListYear, options: opts)
for ix in 0..<result.count {
    let list = result[ix]
    let f = DateFormatter()
    f.dateFormat = "yyyy"
```

```
        print(f.string(from:list.startDate!))
    }
    /*
    1987
    1988
    1989
    1990
    ...
    */
```

Each resulting `list` object in the preceding code is a PHCollectionList comprising a list of moments. Let's dive into that object to see how those moments are clumped into clusters. A cluster of moments is a PHAssetCollection, so the relevant class is PHAssetCollection:

```
let result = PHAssetCollection.fetchMoments(inMomentList:list, options:nil)
for ix in 0 ..< result.count {
    let coll = result[ix]
    if ix == 0 {
        print("======= \(result.count) clusters")
    }
    f.dateFormat = ("yyyy-MM-dd")
    print("""
        starting \(f.string(from:coll.startDate!)): \
        \(coll.estimatedAssetCount)
        """)
}
/*
======= 12 clusters
starting 1987-05-15: 2
starting 1987-05-16: 6
starting 1987-05-17: 2
starting 1987-05-20: 4
....
*/
```

Observe that in that code we can learn how many moments are in each cluster only as its `estimatedAssetCount`. This is probably the right answer, but to obtain the real count, we'd have to dive one level deeper and fetch the cluster's actual moments.

Next, let's list all albums that have been synced onto the device from iPhoto. An album is a PHAssetCollection, so the relevant class is PHAssetCollection:

```
let result = PHAssetCollection.fetchAssetCollections(with: .album,
    subtype: .albumSyncedAlbum, options: nil)
for ix in 0 ..< result.count {
    let album = result[ix]
    print("""
        \(album.localizedTitle as Any): \
        approximately \(album.estimatedAssetCount) photos
        """)
}
```

Again, let's dive further: given an `album`, let's list its contents. An album's contents are its assets (photos and videos), so the relevant class is PHAsset:

```
let result = PHAsset.fetchAssets(in:album, options: nil)
for ix in 0 ..< result.count {
    let asset = result[ix]
    print(asset.localIdentifier)
}
```

If the `fetch` method you need seems not to exist, don't forget about PHFetchOptions. For example, there is no PHAsset `fetch` method for fetching from a certain collection all assets of a certain type — for example, to specify that you want all photos (but no videos) from the user's Camera Roll. But you can perform such a fetch by forming an NSPredicate and setting a PHFetchOptions object's `predicate` property. In this example, I'll fetch ten photos (not videos) from the user's Camera Roll — but no HDR photos, please:

```
let recentAlbums = PHAssetCollection.fetchAssetCollections(with:
    .smartAlbum, subtype: .smartAlbumUserLibrary, options: nil)
guard let rec = recentAlbums.firstObject else {return}
let options = PHFetchOptions() // photos only, please, no HDRs
options.fetchLimit = 10 // let's not take all day about it
let pred = NSPredicate(
    format: "mediaType == %d && !((mediaSubtype & %d) == %d)",
    PHAssetMediaType.image.rawValue,
    PHAssetMediaSubtype.photoHDR.rawValue,
    PHAssetMediaSubtype.photoHDR.rawValue)
options.predicate = pred
self.photos = PHAsset.fetchAssets(in:rec, options: options)
```

Modifying the Library

Structural modifications to the photo library are performed through a *change request class* corresponding to the class of photo entity we wish to modify. The name of the change request class is the name of a photo entity class followed by "ChangeRequest." Thus, for PHAsset, there's the PHAssetChangeRequest class — and so on.

A change request is usable only by calling a `performChanges` method on the shared photo library. Typically, the method you'll call will be `performChanges(_:completion-Handler:)`, which takes two functions. The first function, the *changes function*, is where you describe the changes you want performed; the second function, the *completion function*, is called back after the changes have been performed. The reason for this peculiar structure is that the photo library is a live database. While we are working, the photo library can change. Therefore, the changes function is used to batch our desired changes and send them off as a single transaction to the photo library, which responds by calling the completion function when the outcome of the entire batch is known.

Each change request class comes with methods that ask for a change of some particular type. Here are some examples:

PHAssetChangeRequest
> Class methods include `deleteAssets(_:)`, `creationRequestForAssetFrom-Image(atFileURL:)`, and so on. By default, creating a PHAsset puts it into the user's Camera Roll album immediately. If you're creating an asset and what you're starting with is raw data, use the PHAssetCreationRequest class; it's a subclass of PHAssetChangeRequest that provides instance methods such as `add-Resource(with:data:options:)`.

PHAssetCollectionChangeRequest
> Class methods include `deleteAssetCollections(_:)` and `creationRequestFor-AssetCollection(withTitle:)`. In addition, there are initializers like `init(for:)`, which takes an asset collection, along with instance methods `add-Assets(_:)`, `removeAssets(_:)`, and so on.

A `creationRequest` class method also returns an instance of the change request class. You can throw this away if you don't need it for anything. Its value is that it lets you perform further changes as part of the same batch. For example, once you have a PHAssetChangeRequest instance, you can use its properties to set the asset's features, such as its creation date or its associated geographical location, which would be read-only if accessed through the PHAsset.

To illustrate, let's create an album called "Test Album." An album is a PHAsset-Collection, so we start with the PHAssetCollectionChangeRequest class and call its `creationRequestForAssetCollection(withTitle:)` class method in the `perform-Changes` function. This method returns a PHAssetCollectionChangeRequest instance, but we don't need that instance for anything, so we simply throw it away:

```
PHPhotoLibrary.shared().performChanges({
    let t = "TestAlbum"
    typealias Req = PHAssetCollectionChangeRequest
    Req.creationRequestForAssetCollection(withTitle:t)
})
```

(The class name PHAssetCollectionChangeRequest is very long, so purely as a matter of style and presentation I've shortened it with a type alias.)

It may appear, in that code, that we didn't actually do anything — we asked for a creation request, but we didn't tell it to do any creating. Nevertheless, that code is sufficient; generating the creation request for a new asset collection in the `performChanges` function constitutes an instruction to create an asset collection.

That code, however, is rather silly. The album was created asynchronously, so to use it, we need a completion function (see Appendix C). Moreover, we're left with no reference to the album we created. For that, we need a PHObjectPlaceholder. This minimal PHObject subclass has just one property — `localIdentifier`, which it inherits from PHObject. But this is enough to permit a reference to the created object to survive into the completion function, where we can do something useful with it, such as saving it off to an instance property:

```
var ph : PHObjectPlaceholder?
PHPhotoLibrary.shared().performChanges({
    let t = "TestAlbum"
    typealias Req = PHAssetCollectionChangeRequest
    let cr = Req.creationRequestForAssetCollection(withTitle:t)
    ph = cr.placeholderForCreatedAssetCollection
}) { ok, err in
    if ok, let ph = ph {
        self.newAlbumId = ph.localIdentifier
    }
}
```

Now suppose we subsequently want to populate our newly created album. For example, let's say we want to make the first asset in the user's Recently Added smart album a member of our new album as well. No problem! First, we need a reference to the Recently Added album; then we need a reference to its first asset; and finally, we need a reference to our newly created album (whose identifier we've already captured as `self.newAlbumId`). Those are all basic fetch requests, which we can perform in succession — and we then use their results to form the change request:

```
// find Recently Added smart album
let result = PHAssetCollection.fetchAssetCollections(with: .smartAlbum,
    subtype: .smartAlbumRecentlyAdded, options: nil)
guard let rec = result.firstObject else { return }
// find its first asset
let result2 = PHAsset.fetchAssets(in:rec, options: nil)
guard let asset1 = result2.firstObject else { return }
// find our newly created album by its local id
let result3 = PHAssetCollection.fetchAssetCollections(
    withLocalIdentifiers: [self.newAlbumId], options: nil)
guard let alb2 = result3.firstObject else { return }
// ready to perform the change request
PHPhotoLibrary.shared().performChanges({
    typealias Req = PHAssetCollectionChangeRequest
    let cr = Req(for: alb2)
    cr?.addAssets([asset1] as NSArray)
})
```

A PHObjectPlaceholder has a further use. To see what it is, think about this problem: What if we created, say, an asset collection and wanted to add *it* to something (presumably to a PHCollectionList), all in one batch request? Requesting the creation of an asset collection gives us a PHAssetCollectionChangeRequest instance; you can't add *that* to a collection. And the requested PHAssetCollection itself hasn't been created yet! The solution is to obtain a PHObjectPlaceholder. Because it is a PHObject, it can be used as the argument of change request methods such as `addChild-Collections(_:)`.

Being Notified of Changes

When the library is modified, whether by your code or by some other means while your app is running, any information you've collected about the library — information which you may even be displaying in your interface at that very moment — may become out of date. To cope with this possibility, you should, perhaps very early in the life of your app, register a change observer (adopting the PHPhotoLibraryChange-Observer protocol) with the photo library:

```
PHPhotoLibrary.shared().register(self)
```

The outcome is that, whenever the library changes, the observer's `photoLibraryDid-Change(_:)` method is called, with a PHChange object encapsulating a description of the change. The observer can then probe the PHChange object by calling `change-Details(for:)`. The parameter can be one of two types:

A PHObject

> The parameter is a single PHAsset, PHAssetCollection, or PHCollectionList you're interested in. The result is a PHObjectChangeDetails object, with properties like `objectBeforeChanges`, `objectAfterChanges`, and `objectWasDeleted`.

A PHFetchResult

> The result is a PHFetchResultChangeDetails object, with properties like `fetch-ResultBeforeChanges`, `fetchResultAfterChanges`, `removedObjects`, `inserted-Objects`, and so on.

The idea is that if you're hanging on to information in an instance property, you can use what the PHChange object tells you to modify that information (and possibly your interface).

For example, suppose my interface is displaying a list of album names, which I obtained originally through a PHAssetCollection fetch request. And suppose that, at the time that I performed the fetch request, I also *retained* as an instance property (self.albums) the PHFetchResult that it returned. Then if my `photoLibraryDid-Change(_:)` method is called, I can update the fetch result and change my interface accordingly:

```
func photoLibraryDidChange(_ changeInfo: PHChange) {
    if self.albums !== nil {
        let details = changeInfo.changeDetails(for:self.albums)
        if details !== nil {
            self.albums = details!.fetchResultAfterChanges
```

```
            // ... and adjust interface if needed ...
        }
    }
}
```

Fetching Images

Sooner or later, you'll probably want to go beyond information about the structure of the photo library and fetch an actual photo or video for display in your app. This is surprisingly tricky, because the process of obtaining an image can be time-consuming: not only may the image data may be large, but also it may be stored in the cloud. Thus, you supply a completion function which can be called back *asynchronously* with the data (see Appendix C).

To obtain an image, you'll need an *image manager*, which you'll get by calling the PHImageManager default class method. You then call a method whose name starts with request, supplying a completion function. For an image, you can ask for a UIImage or the original Data; for a video, you can ask for an AVPlayerItem, an AVAsset, or an AVAssetExportSession suitable for exporting the video file to a new location (see Chapter 15). The result comes back to you as a parameter passed into your completion function.

If you're asking for a UIImage, information about the image may increase in accuracy and detail in the course of time — with the curious consequence that your completion function may be called multiple times. The idea is to give you *some* image to display as fast as possible, with better versions of the image arriving later. If you would rather receive just *one* version of the image, you can specify that through a PHImageRequestOptions object (as I'll explain in a moment).

The various request methods take parameters letting you refine the details of the data-retrieval process. For example, when asking for a UIImage, you supply these parameters:

targetSize:
> The size of the desired image. It is a waste of memory to ask for an image larger than you need for actual display, and a larger image may take longer to supply (and a photo, remember, is a *very* large image). The image retrieval process performs the desired downsizing so that you don't have to. For the largest possible size, pass PHImageManagerMaximumSize.

contentMode:
> A PHImageContentMode, either .aspectFit or .aspectFill, with respect to your targetSize. With .aspectFill, the image retrieval process does any needed cropping so that you don't have to.

`options:`

A PHImageRequestOptions object. This is a value class representing a grab-bag of additional tweaks, such as:

- Do you want the original image or the edited image?
- Do you want one call to your completion function or many, and if one, do you want a degraded thumbnail (which will arrive quickly) or the best possible quality (which may take some considerable time)?
- Do you want custom cropping?
- Do you want the image fetched over the network if necessary, and if so, do you want to install a progress callback function?
- Do you want the image fetched synchronously? If you do, you will get only *one* call to your completion function — but then you *must* make your call *on a background thread,* and the image will arrive on that same background thread (see Chapter 24).

In this simple example, I have a view controller called DataViewController, good for displaying one photo in an image view (`self.iv`). It has a PHAsset property, `self.asset`, which is assumed to have been set when this view controller instance was created. In `viewDidLoad`, I call my `setUpInterface` utility method to populate the interface:

```
func setUpInterface() {
    guard let asset = self.asset else { return }
    PHImageManager.default().requestImage(for: asset,
        targetSize: CGSize(300,300), contentMode: .aspectFit,
        options: nil) { im, info in
            if let im = im {
                self.iv.image = im
            }
    }
}
```

This may result in the image view's `image` being set multiple times as the requested image is supplied repeated with its quality improving each time, but there is nothing wrong with that. Using this technique with a UIPageViewController, you can easily write an app that allows the user to browse photos one at a time.

The second parameter in an image request's completion function is a dictionary whose elements may be useful in a variety of circumstances. Among the keys are:

`PHImageResultRequestIDKey`

Uniquely identifies a single image request for which this result function is being called multiple times. This value is also *returned* by the original request method call (I didn't bother to capture it in the previous example). You can also use this identifier to call `cancelImageRequest(_:)` if it turns out that you don't need this image after all.

`PHImageCancelledKey`

Reports that an attempt to cancel an image request with `cancelImage-Request(_:)` succeeded.

`PHImageResultIsInCloudKey`

Warns that the image is in the cloud and that your request must be resubmitted with the `PHImageRequestOptions` `isNetworkAccessAllowed` property set to `true`.

If you imagine that your interface is a table view or collection view, you can see why the asynchronous, time-consuming nature of image fetching can be significant. As the user scrolls, a cell comes into view and you request the corresponding image. But as the user keeps scrolling, that cell goes out of view, and now the requested image, if it hasn't arrived, is no longer needed, so you cancel the request. (I'll tackle the same sort of problem with regard to Internet-based images in a table view in Chapter 23.)

There is also a PHImageManager subclass, PHCachingImageManager, that can help do the opposite: you can prefetch some images *before* the user scrolls to view them, thus improving response time. For an example that displays photos in a UICollection-View, look at Apple's SamplePhotosApp sample code (also called "Example app using Photos framework"). It uses the PHImageManager class to fetch individual photos; but for the UICollectionViewCell thumbnails, it uses PHCachingImageManager.

If a PHAsset represents a live photo, you can call the PHImageManager `requestLive-Photo` method, parallel to `requestImage`; what you get in the completion function is a PHLivePhoto (and see earlier in this chapter on how to display it in your interface).

Fetching a video resource is far simpler, and there's little to say about it. In this example, I fetch a reference to the first video in the user's photo library and display it in the interface (using an AVPlayerViewController); unlike an image, I am not guaranteed that the result will arrive on the main thread, so I must step out to the main thread before interacting with the app's user interface:

```
func fetchMovie() {
    let opts = PHFetchOptions()
    opts.fetchLimit = 1
    let result = PHAsset.fetchAssets(with: .video, options: opts)
    guard result.count > 0 else {return}
    let asset = result[0]
    PHImageManager.default().requestPlayerItem(
        forVideo: asset, options: nil) { item, info in
        if let item = item {
            DispatchQueue.main.async {
                self.display(item:item)
            }
```

```
        }
    }
}
func display(item:AVPlayerItem) {
    let player = AVPlayer(playerItem: item)
    let vc = AVPlayerViewController()
    vc.player = player
    vc.view.frame = self.v.bounds
    self.addChildViewController(vc)
    self.v.addSubview(vc.view)
    vc.didMove(toParentViewController: self)
}
```

You can also access an asset's various kinds of data directly through the PHAsset-ResourceManager class. The `request` method takes a PHAssetResource object based on a PHAsset or PHLivePhoto. For example, you can retrieve an image's RAW and JPEG data separately. For a list of the data types we're talking about here, see the documentation on the PHAssetResourceType enum.

Editing Images

Astonishingly, PhotoKit allows you to *change* an image in the user's photo library. Why is this even legal? There are two reasons:

- The user will have to give permission every time your app proposes to modify a photo in the library (and will be shown the proposed modification).

- Changes to library photos are undoable, because the original image remains in the database along with the changed image that the user sees (and the user can revert to that original at any time).

How to change a photo image

To change a photo image is a three-step process:

1. You send a PHAsset the `requestContentEditingInput(with:completion-Handler:)` message. Your completion function is called, and is handed a PHContentEditingInput object. This object wraps some image data which you can display to the user (`displaySizeImage`), along with a pointer to the real image data as a file (`fullSizeImageURL`).

2. You create a PHContentEditingOutput object by calling `init(contentEditing-Input:)`, handing it the PHContentEditingInput object. This PHContentEditing-Output object has a `renderedContentURL` property, representing a file URL. Your mission is to *write the edited photo image data to that URL*. Thus, what you'll typically do is:

a. Fetch the image data from the PHContentEditingInput object's `fullSize-ImageURL`.

b. Process the image.

c. Write the resulting image data to the PHContentEditingOutput object's `renderedContentURL`.

3. You notify the photo library that it should pick up the edited version of the photo. To do so, you call `performChanges(_:completionHandler:)` and, inside the changes function, create a PHAssetChangeRequest and set its `content-EditingOutput` property to the PHContentEditingOutput object. This is when the user will be shown the alert requesting permission to modify this photo; your completion function is then called, with a first parameter of `false` if the user refuses (or if anything else goes wrong).

Handling the adjustment data

So far, so good. However, if you do *only* what I have just described, your attempt to modify the photo will fail. The reason is that I have omitted something: before the third step, you *must* set the PHContentEditingOutput object's `adjustmentData` property to a newly instantiated PHAdjustmentData object. The initializer is `init(format-Identifier:formatVersion:data:)`. What goes into these parameters is completely up to you, but the goal is to store with the photo a message to your future self in case you are called upon to edit the *same* photo again on some *later* occasion. In that message, you describe to yourself how you edited the photo on *this* occasion.

Your handling of the adjustment data works in three steps, interwoven with the three steps I already outlined. As you start to edit the photo, first you say whether you *can* read its existing PHAdjustmentData, and then you *do* read its existing PHAdjustmentData and use it as part of your editing. When you have finished editing the photo, you make a *new* PHAdjustmentData, ready for the *next* time you edit this same photo. Here are the details:

1. When you call the `requestContentEditingInput(with:completionHandler:)` method, the `with:` argument should be a PHContentEditingInputRequest-Options object. You are to create this object and set its `canHandleAdjustment-Data` property to a function that takes a PHAdjustmentData and returns a Bool. This Bool will be based mostly on whether you recognize this photo's PHAdjustmentData as yours — typically because you recognize its `format-Identifier`. That determines what image you'll get when you receive your PHContentEditingInput object:

Your `canHandleAdjustmentData` *function returns* `false`
The image you'll be editing is the edited image displayed in the Photos app.

Your `canHandleAdjustmentData` *function returns* `true`

> The image you'll be editing is the *original* image, stripped of your edits. This is because, by returning `true`, you are asserting that you can reconstruct your edits based on what's in the PHAdjustmentData's `data`.

2. When your completion function is called and you receive your PHContent-EditingInput object, it has (you guessed it) an `adjustmentData` property, which is an Optional wrapping a PHAdjustmentData object. If this isn't `nil`, and if you edited this image previously, its `data` is the `data` you put in the last time you edited this image, and you are expected to extract it and use it to recreate the edited state of the image.

3. After editing the image, when you prepare the PHContentEditingOutput object, you give it a *new* PHAdjustmentData object whose `data` summarizes the *new* edited state of the photo from your point of view — and so the whole cycle can start again if the same photo is to be edited again later.

Example: Before editing

An actual implementation is quite straightforward and almost pure boilerplate. The details will vary only in regard to the actual editing of the photo and the particular form of the `data` by which you'll summarize that editing — so, in constructing an example, I'll keep that part very simple. Recall, from Chapter 2 ("CIFilter and CIImage" on page 97), my example of a custom "vignette" CIFilter called MyVignette-Filter. I'll provide an interface whereby the user can apply that filter to a photo. My interface will include a slider that allows the user to set the *degree* of vignetting that should be applied (MyVignetteFilter's `inputPercentage`). Moreover, my interface will include a button that lets the user remove *all* vignetting from the photo, even if that vignetting was applied in a previous editing session.

First, I'll plan the structure of the PHAdjustmentData:

`formatIdentifier`
> This can be any unique string; I'll use `"com.neuburg.matt.PhotoKit-Images.vignette"`, a constant that I'll store in a property (`self.myidentifier`).

`formatVersion`
> This is likewise arbitrary; I'll use `"1.0"`.

`data`
> This will express the only thing about my editing that is adjustable — the `input-Percentage`. The `data` will wrap an NSNumber which itself wraps a Double whose value is the `inputPercentage`.

As editing begins, I construct the PHContentEditingInputRequestOptions object that expresses whether a photo's most recent editing belongs to me. Then, starting with the photo that is to be edited (a PHAsset), I ask for the PHContentEditingInput object:

```
let options = PHContentEditingInputRequestOptions()
options.canHandleAdjustmentData = { adjustmentData in
    return adjustmentData.formatIdentifier == self.myidentifier
}
var id : PHContentEditingInputRequestID = 0
id = self.asset.requestContentEditingInput(with: options) { input, info in
    // ...
}
```

In the completion function, I receive my PHContentEditingInput object as a parameter (input). I'm going to need this object later when editing ends, so I immediately store it in a property. I then unwrap its `adjustmentData`, extract the `data`, and construct the editing interface; in this case, that happens to be a presented view controller, but the details are irrelevant and are omitted here:

```
guard let input = input else {
    self.asset.cancelContentEditingInputRequest(id)
    return
}
self.input = input
let im = input.displaySizeImage! // show this to user during editing
if let adj = input.adjustmentData,
    adj.formatIdentifier == self.myidentifier {
        if let vigAmount =
            NSKeyedUnarchiver.unarchiveObject(with: adj.data) as? Double {
                // ... store vigAmount ...
        }
}
// ... present editing interface, passing it the vigAmount ...
```

The important thing about that code is how we deal with the `adjustmentData` and its `data`. The question is whether we *have* data, and whether we recognize this as *our* data from some previous edit on this image. This will affect how our editing interface needs to behave. There are two possibilities:

It's our data

    If we were able to extract a `vigAmount` from the `adjustmentData`, then the `displaySizeImage` is the *original, unvignetted image*. Therefore, our editing interface initially applies the `vigAmount` of vignetting to this image — thus *reconstructing the vignetted state of the photo* as shown in the Photos app, while allowing the user to *change* the amount of vignetting, or even to remove all vignetting entirely.

It's not our data

On the other hand, if we *weren't* able to extract a vigAmount from the adjustment-Data, then there is nothing to reconstruct; the displaySizeImage is the actual photo image from the Photos app, and our editing interface will apply vignetting to it directly.

Example: After editing

Let's skip ahead now to the point where the user's interaction with our editing interface comes to an end. If the user cancelled, that's all; the user doesn't want to modify the photo after all. Otherwise, the user either asked to apply a certain amount of vignetting (vignette) or asked to remove all vignetting; in the latter case, I use an arbitrary vignette value of -1 as a signal.

Up to now, our editing interface has been using the displaySizeImage to show the user a *preview* of what the edited photo would look like. Now, however, the time has come to perform the vignetting that the user is asking us to perform — that is, we must apply this amount of vignetting to the *real* photo image, which has been sitting waiting for us all this time, untouched, at the PHContentEditingInput's fullSize-ImageURL. This is a big image, which will take significant time to load, to alter, and to save (which is why we haven't been working with it in the editing interface).

So, depending on the value of vignette requested by the user, I either pass the input image from the fullSizeImageURL through my vignette filter or I don't; either way, I must write a JPEG to the PHContentEditingOutput's renderedContentURL:

```
let inurl = self.input.fullSizeImageURL!
let inorient = self.input.fullSizeImageOrientation
let output = PHContentEditingOutput(contentEditingInput:self.input)
let outurl = output.renderedContentURL
var ci = CIImage(contentsOf:inurl)!.oriented(forExifOrientation:inorient)
let space = ci.colorSpace!
if vignette >= 0.0 {
    let vig = MyVignetteFilter()
    vig.setValue(ci, forKey: "inputImage")
    vig.setValue(vignette, forKey: "inputPercentage")
    ci = vig.outputImage!
}
try! CIContext().writeJPEGRepresentation(
    of: ci, to: outurl, colorSpace: space)
```

(The CIContext method called in the last line is time-consuming. The preceding code should therefore probably be called on background thread, with a UIActivity-IndicatorView or similar to let the user know that work is being done.)

We are still not quite done. Don't forget about setting the PHContentEditingOutput's adjustmentData! My goal here is to send a message to myself, in case I am asked later to edit this same image again, stating what amount of vignetting is already applied to the image. That amount is represented by `vignette` — so that's the value I store in the adjustmentData:

```
let data = NSKeyedArchiver.archivedData(withRootObject: vignette)
output.adjustmentData = PHAdjustmentData(
    formatIdentifier: self.myidentifier, formatVersion: "1.0", data: data)
```

We conclude by telling the photo library to retrieve the edited image. This will cause the alert to appear, asking the user whether to allow us to modify this photo. If the user taps Modify, the modification is made, and if we are displaying the image, we should get onto the main thread and redisplay it:

```
PHPhotoLibrary.shared().performChanges({
    typealias Req = PHAssetChangeRequest
    let req = Req(for: self.asset)
    req.contentEditingOutput = output // triggers alert
}) { ok, err in
    if ok {
        // if we are displaying image, redisplay it - on main thread
    } else {
        // user refused to allow modification, do nothing
    }
}
```

You can also edit a live photo, using a PHLivePhotoEditingContext: you are handed each frame of the video as a CIImage, making it easy, for example, to apply a CIFilter. For a demonstration, see Apple's Photo Edit sample app (also known as Sample Photo Editing Extension).

Photo Editing Extension

A photo editing extension is photo-modifying code supplied by your app that is effectively injected into the Photos app. When the user edits a photo from within the Photos app, your extension appears as an option and can modify the photo being edited.

To make a photo editing extension, create a new target in your app, specifying iOS → Application Extension → Photo Editing Extension. The template supplies a storyboard containing one scene, along with the code file for a corresponding UIViewController subclass. This file imports not only the Photos framework but also the Photos UI framework, which supplies the PHContentEditingController protocol, to which the view controller conforms. This protocol specifies the methods through which the runtime will communicate with your extension's code.

A photo editing extension works almost exactly the same way as modifying photo library assets in general, as I described in the preceding section. The chief differences are:

- You don't put a Done or a Cancel button into your editing interface. The Photos app will wrap your editing interface in its own interface, providing those buttons when it presents your view.

- You must situate the pieces of your code so as to respond to the calls that will come through the PHContentEditingController methods.

The PHContentEditingController methods are as follows:

canHandle(_:)
:   You will not be instantiating PHContentEditingInput; the runtime will do it for you. Therefore, instead of configuring a PHContentEditingInputRequestOptions object and setting its canHandleAdjustmentData, you implement this method; you'll receive the PHAdjustmentData and return a Bool.

startContentEditing(with:placeholderImage:)
:   The runtime has obtained the PHContentEditingInput object for you. Now it supplies that object to you, along with a very temporary initial version of the image to be displayed in your interface; you are expected to replace this with the PHContentEditingInput object's displaySizeImage. Just as in the previous section's code, you should retain the PHContentEditingInput object in a property, as you will need it again later.

cancelContentEditing
:   The user tapped Cancel. You may well have nothing to do here.

finishContentEditing(completionHandler:)
:   The user tapped Done. In your implementation, you get onto a background thread (the template configures this for you) and do *exactly* the same thing you would do if this were not a photo editing extension — get the PHContentEditing Output object and set its adjustmentData; get the photo from the PHContent-EditingInput object's fullSizeImageURL, modify it, and save the modified image as a full-quality JPEG at the PHContentEditingOutput object's renderedContent-URL. When you're done, *don't* notify the PHPhotoLibrary; instead, call the completionHandler that arrived as a parameter, handing it the PHContent-EditingOutput object.

    During the time-consuming part of this method, the Photos app puts up a UIActivityIndicatorView, just as I suggested you might want to do in your own app. When you call the completionHandler, there is no alert asking the user to confirm the modification of the photo; the user is already *in* the Photos app and has explicitly asked to edit the photo, so no confirmation is needed — and moreover, the user will have one more chance to remove all changes made in the editing interface.

Using the Camera

Use of the camera requires user authorization. You'll use the AVCaptureDevice class for this (part of the AV Foundation framework; import AVFoundation). To learn what the current authorization status is, call the class method authorization-Status(forMediaType:). To ask the system to put up the authorization request alert if the status is .notDetermined, call the class method requestAccess(forMedia-Type:completionHandler:). The media type (AVMediaType) will be .video; this embraces both stills and movies. Your app's *Info.plist* must contain some text that the system authorization request alert can use to explain why your app wants camera use; the relevant key is "Privacy — Camera Usage Description" (NSCameraUsage-Description).

If your app will let the user capture movies (as opposed to stills), you will also need to obtain permission from the user to access the microphone. The same methods apply, but with argument .audio. Your app's *Info.plist* must contain some explanatory text under the "Privacy — Microphone Usage Description" key (NSMicrophoneUsage-Description).

See "Checking for Authorization" on page 841 for detailed consideration of authorization strategy and testing.

 Use of the camera is greatly curtailed, and is interruptible, under iPad multitasking. Watch WWDC 2015 video 211 for details.

Capture with UIImagePickerController

The simplest way to prompt the user to take a photo or video is to use the same UIImagePickerController class discussed earlier in this chapter. It provides an interface that is effectively a limited subset of the Camera app.

The procedure is similar to what you do when you use UIImagePickerController to browse the photo library. First, check isSourceTypeAvailable(_:) for .camera; it will be false if the user's device has no camera or the camera is unavailable. If it is true, call availableMediaTypes(for:.camera) to learn whether the user can take a still photo (kUTTypeImage), a video (kUTTypeMovie), or both. Now instantiate UIImagePickerController, set its source type to .camera, and set its mediaTypes in accordance with which types you just learned are available; if your setting is an array of both kUTTypeImage and kUTTypeMovie, the user will see a Camera-like interface allowing a choice of either one. Finally, set a delegate (adopting UINavigation-ControllerDelegate and UIImagePickerControllerDelegate), and present the picker:

```
let src = UIImagePickerControllerSourceType.camera
guard UIImagePickerController.isSourceTypeAvailable(src)
    else {return}
guard = UIImagePickerController.availableMediaTypes(for:src) != nil
    else {return}
let picker = UIImagePickerController()
picker.sourceType = src
picker.mediaTypes = arr
picker.delegate = self
self.present(picker, animated: true)
```

For video, you can also specify the `videoQuality` and `videoMaximumDuration`. Moreover, these additional properties and class methods allow you to discover the camera capabilities:

`isCameraDeviceAvailable:`
  Checks to see whether the front or rear camera is available, using one of these values as argument (UIImagePickerControllerCameraDevice):

  - `.front`
  - `.rear`

`cameraDevice`
  Lets you learn and set which camera is being used.

`availableCaptureModes(for:)`
  Checks whether the given camera can capture still images, video, or both. You specify the front or rear camera; returns an array of integers. Possible modes are (UIImagePickerControllerCameraCaptureMode):

  - `.photo`
  - `.video`

`cameraCaptureMode`
  Lets you learn and set the capture mode (still or video).

`isFlashAvailable(for:)`
  Checks whether flash is available.

`cameraFlashMode`
  Lets you learn and set the flash mode (or, for a movie, toggles the LED "torch"). Your choices are (UIImagePickerControllerCameraFlashMode):

  - `.off`
  - `.auto`
  - `.on`

When the view controller's view appears, the user will see the interface for taking a picture, familiar from the Camera app, possibly including flash options, camera selection button, photo/video option (if your `mediaTypes` setting allows both), and Cancel and shutter buttons. If the user takes a picture, the presented view offers an opportunity to use the picture or to retake it.

Allowing the user to edit the captured image or movie (`allowsEditing`), and handling the outcome with the delegate messages, is the same as I described earlier for dealing with an image or movie selected from the photo library, with these additional points regarding the `info` dictionary delivered to the delegate:

- There won't be any `UIImagePickerControllerPHAsset` key, because the image isn't in the photo library.
- There won't be any `UIImagePickerControllerImageURL` key; if the user takes a still image, no copy is saved as a file.
- There won't be any `UIImagePickerControllerLivePhoto` key; the user can't capture a live photo with the UIImagePickerController camera interface.
- A still image might be accompanied by a `UIImagePickerControllerMedia-Metadata` key containing the metadata for the photo.

The photo library was not involved in the process of media capture, so no user permission to access the photo library is needed; of course, if you *now* propose to save the media into the photo library, you *will* need permission. Suppose, for example, that the user takes a still image, and you now want to save it into the user's Camera Roll album. Creating the PHAsset is sufficient:

```
func imagePickerController(_ picker: UIImagePickerController,
    didFinishPickingMediaWithInfo info: [String : Any]) {
        var im = info[UIImagePickerControllerOriginalImage] as? UIImage
        if let ed = info[UIImagePickerControllerEditedImage] as? UIImage {
            im = ed
        }
        let m = info[UIImagePickerControllerMediaMetadata] as? NSDictionary
        self.dismiss(animated:true) {
            let mediatype = info[UIImagePickerControllerMediaType]
            guard let type = mediatype as? NSString else {return}
            switch type as CFString {
            case kUTTypeImage:
                if im != nil {
                    let lib = PHPhotoLibrary.shared()
                    lib.performChanges({
                        typealias Req = PHAssetChangeRequest
                        Req.creationRequestForAsset(from: im!)
                    })
                }
```

```
            default:break
            }
        }
    }
```

In that code, the metadata associated with the photo is received (m), but nothing is done with it, and it is not folded into the PHAsset created from the image (im). To attach the metadata to the photo, use the Image I/O framework (import ImageIO) to make a copy of the image data along with the metadata. Now you can use a PHAsset-CreationRequest to make the PHAsset from the data:

```
let jpeg = UIImageJPEGRepresentation(im!, 1)!
let src = CGImageSourceCreateWithData(jpeg as CFData, nil)!
let data = NSMutableData()
let uti = CGImageSourceGetType(src)!
let dest = CGImageDestinationCreateWithData(
    data as CFMutableData, uti, 1, nil)!
CGImageDestinationAddImageFromSource(dest, src, 0, m)
CGImageDestinationFinalize(dest)
let lib = PHPhotoLibrary.shared()
lib.performChanges({
    let req = PHAssetCreationRequest.forAsset()
    req.addResource(with: .photo, data: data as Data, options: nil)
})
```

You can customize the UIImagePickerController image capture interface. If you need to do that, you should probably consider dispensing entirely with UIImagePicker-Controller and instead designing your own image capture interface from scratch, based around AV Foundation and AVCaptureSession, which I'll introduce in the next section. Still, it may be that a modified UIImagePickerController is all you need.

In the image capture interface, you can hide the standard controls by setting shows-CameraControls to false, replacing them with your own overlay view, which you supply as the value of the cameraOverlayView. That removes the shutter button, so you're probably going to want to provide some new means of allowing the user to take a picture! You can do that through these methods:

- takePicture
- startVideoCapture
- stopVideoCapture

The UIImagePickerController is a UINavigationController, so if you need additional interface — for example, to let the user vet the captured picture before dismissing the picker — you can push it onto the navigation interface.

Capture with AV Foundation

Instead of using UIImagePickerController, you can control the camera and capture images directly using the AV Foundation framework (Chapter 15). You get no help with interface, but you get vastly more detailed control than UIImagePicker-Controller can give you. For example, for stills, you can control focus and exposure directly and independently, and for video, you can determine the quality, size, and frame rate of the resulting movie.

To understand how AV Foundation classes are used for image capture, imagine how the Camera app works. When you are running the Camera app, you have, at all times, a "window on the world" — the screen is showing you what the camera sees. At some point, you might tap the button to take a still image or start taking a video; now what the camera sees goes into a file.

Think of all that as being controlled by an engine. This engine, the heart of all AV Foundation capture operations, is an AVCaptureSession object. It has inputs (such as a camera) and outputs (such as a file). It also has an associated layer in your interface. When you start the engine running, by calling `startRunning`, data flows from the input through the engine; that is how you get your "window on the world," displaying on the screen what the camera sees.

As a rock-bottom example, let's start by implementing just the "window on the world" part of the engine. Our AVCaptureSession is retained in an instance property (`self.sess`). We also need a special CALayer that will display what the camera is seeing — namely, an AVCaptureVideoPreviewLayer. This layer is not really an AVCaptureSession output; rather, the layer receives its imagery by association with the AVCaptureSession. Our capture session's input is the default camera. We have no intention, as yet, of capturing anything to a file, so no output is needed:

```
self.sess = AVCaptureSession()
guard let cam = AVCaptureDevice.default(for: .video),
    let input = try? AVCaptureDeviceInput(device:cam)
    else {return}
self.sess.addInput(input)
let lay = AVCaptureVideoPreviewLayer(session:self.sess)
lay.frame = // ... some reasonable frame ...
self.view.layer.addSublayer(lay)
self.sess.startRunning()
```

Presto! Our interface now displays a "window on the world," showing what the camera sees.

Suppose now that our intention is that, while the engine is running and the "window on the world" is showing, the user is to be allowed to tap a button that will capture a still photo. Now we *do* need an output for our AVCaptureSession. This will be an AVCapturePhotoOutput instance. We should also configure the session with a preset

---

(AVCaptureSession.Preset) to match our intended use of it; in this case, the preset will be .photo.

So let's modify the preceding code to give the session an output and a preset. We can do this directly before we start the session running. We can also do it while the session is already running (and in general, if you want to reconfigure a running session, doing so while it is running is far more efficient than stopping the session and starting it again), but then we must wrap our configuration changes in begin-Configuration and commitConfiguration:

```
self.sess.beginConfiguration()
guard self.sess.canSetSessionPreset(self.sess.sessionPreset)
    else {return}
self.sess.sessionPreset = .photo
let output = AVCapturePhotoOutput()
guard self.sess.canAddOutput(output)
    else {return}
self.sess.addOutput(output)
self.sess.commitConfiguration()
```

The session is now running and is ready to capture a photo. The user taps the button that asks to capture a photo, and we respond by telling the session's photo output to capturePhoto(with:delegate:). The first parameter is an AVCapturePhotoSettings object. It happens that for a standard JPEG photo a default instance will do, but to make things more interesting I'll specify explicitly that I want the camera to use automatic flash and automatic image stabilization:

```
let settings = AVCapturePhotoSettings()
settings.flashMode = .auto
settings.isAutoStillImageStabilizationEnabled = true
```

If we intend to display the user's captured photo in our interface, we should request a preview image explicitly as part of our configuration of the AVCapturePhotoSettings object. It's a lot more efficient for AV Foundation to create an uncompressed preview image of the correct size than for us to try to display or downsize a huge photo image. Here's how we might ask for the preview image:

```
let pbpf = settings.availablePreviewPhotoPixelFormatTypes[0]
let len = // desired maximum dimension
settings.previewPhotoFormat = [
    kCVPixelBufferPixelFormatTypeKey as String : pbpf,
    kCVPixelBufferWidthKey as String : len,
    kCVPixelBufferHeightKey as String : len
]
```

Another good idea, when configuring the AVCapturePhotoSettings object, is to ask for a thumbnail image (new in iOS 11). This is different from the preview image: the preview image is for you to display in your interface, but the thumbnail image is stored with the photo and is suitable for rapid display by other applications. Here's how to request a thumbnail image at a standard size (160×120):

```
settings.embeddedThumbnailPhotoFormat = [
    AVVideoCodecKey : AVVideoCodecType.jpeg
]
```

When the AVCapturePhotoSettings object is fully configured, we're ready to call capturePhoto(with:delegate:), like this:

```
guard let output = self.sess.outputs[0] as? AVCapturePhotoOutput
    else {return}
output.capturePhoto(with: settings, delegate: self)
```

In that code, I specified self as the delegate (an AVCapturePhotoCaptureDelegate adopter). Functioning as the delegate, we will now receive a sequence of events. The exact sequence depends on what sort of capture we're doing; in this case, it will be:

1. photoOutput(_:willBeginCaptureFor:)

2. photoOutput(_:willCapturePhotoFor:)

3. photoOutput(_:didCapturePhotoFor:)

4. photoOutput(_:didFinishProcessingPhoto:error:)

5. photoOutput(_:didFinishCaptureFor:)

The for: parameter throughout is an AVCaptureResolvedSettings object, embodying the settings actually used during the capture; for example, we could use it to find out whether flash was actually used.

 The delegate method names are all new in iOS 11.

The delegate event of interest to our example is obviously the fourth one. This is where we receive the photo! It will arrive in the second parameter as an AVCapturePhoto object (new in iOS 11) containing a lot of information, including the resolvedSettings, a pixelBuffer holding the image data, and a previewPixelBuffer with data for the preview image if we requested one in our AVCapturePhotoSettings.

We can extract the image data from the AVCapturePhoto by calling its fileDataRepresentation method. This is a powerful method that (among other things) embeds into the data the capture metadata. (There is also a longer form of the same method, allowing you do to do such things as *modify* the metadata.)

In this example, we implement the fourth delegate method to save the actual image as a PHAsset in the user's photo library, while we also store the preview image as a property, for subsequent display in our interface:

```
func photoOutput(_ output: AVCapturePhotoOutput,
    didFinishProcessingPhoto photo:
    AVCapturePhoto, error: Error?) {
        if let cgim =
            photo.previewCGImageRepresentation()?.takeUnretainedValue() {
                let orient = // work out desired UIImageOrientation
                self.previewImage = UIImage(
                    cgImage: cgim, scale: 1, orientation: orient)
        }
        if let data = photo.fileDataRepresentation() {
            let lib = PHPhotoLibrary.shared()
            lib.performChanges({
                let req = PHAssetCreationRequest.forAsset()
                req.addResource(with: .photo, data: data, options: nil)
            })
        }
    }
}
```

Image capture with AV Foundation is a huge subject, and our example of a simple photo capture has barely scratched the surface. AVCaptureVideoPreviewLayer provides methods for converting between layer coordinates and capture device coordinates; without such methods, this can be a very difficult problem to solve. You can scan bar codes, shoot video at 60 frames per second (on some devices), and more. You can turn on the LED "torch" by setting the back camera's torchMode to AVCaptureTorchModeOn, even if no AVCaptureSession is running. You get direct hardware-level control over the camera focus, manual exposure, and white balance. You can capture bracketed images; starting in iOS 10, you can capture live images on some devices, and you can capture RAW images on some devices; and iOS 11 introduces yet another raft of new features such as depth-based image capture. There are very good WWDC videos about all this, stretching back over the past several years, and the AVCam iOS and AVCamManual sample code examples are absolutely superb, demonstrating how to deal with tricky issues such as orientation that would otherwise be very difficult to figure out.

CHAPTER 18

Contacts

The user's contacts, which the user sees through the Contacts app, constitute a database that your code can access programmatically through the Contacts framework. You'll need to import Contacts.

An interface for letting the user interact with the contacts database from within your app is provided by the Contacts UI framework. You'll need to import ContactsUI.

Access to the contacts database requires user authorization. You'll use the CNContactStore class for this. To learn what the current authorization status is, call the class method authorizationStatus(for:) with a CNEntityType of .contacts. To ask the system to put up the authorization request alert if the status is .notDetermined, call the instance method requestAccess(for:completionHandler:). The *Info.plist* must contain some text that the system authorization request alert can use to explain why your app wants access. The relevant key is "Privacy — Contacts Usage Description" (NSContactsUsageDescription). See "Checking for Authorization" on page 841 for detailed consideration of authorization strategy and testing.

Contact Classes

Here are the chief object types you'll be concerned with when you work with the user's contacts:

CNContactStore
> The user's database of contacts is accessed through an instance of the CNContactStore class. You do not need to keep a reference to an instance of this class. When you want to fetch a contact from the database, or when you want to save a created or modified contact into the database, instantiate CNContactStore, do your fetching or saving, and let the CNContactStore instance vanish.

CNContactStore instance methods for fetching and saving information can take time. Therefore, they should be called on a background thread; for example, you might call `DispatchQueue.global(qos:.userInitiated).async`. For details about what that means, see Chapter 24.

CNContact

An individual contact is an instance of the CNContact class. Its properties correspond to the fields displayed in the Contacts app. In addition, it has an `identifier` which is unique and persistent. A CNContact that comes from the CNContactStore has no connection with the database; it is safe to preserve it and to pass it around between objects and between threads. It is also immutable by default (its properties are read-only). To create your own CNContact, start with its mutable subclass, CNMutableContact; to modify an existing CNContact, call `mutableCopy` to make it a CNMutableContact.

The properties of a CNContact are matched by constant key names designating those properties. For example, a CNContact has a `familyName` property, and there is also a `CNContactFamilyNameKey`. This should remind you of MPMedia-Item (Chapter 16), and indeed the purpose is similar: the key names allow you, when you fetch a CNContact from the CNContactStore, to state which properties of the CNContact you want populated. By limiting the properties to be fetched, you fetch more efficiently and quickly.

Most properties of a CNContact have familiar types such as String or an enum. However, the Contacts framework defines a number of specialized types as well; for example, a phone number is a CNPhoneNumber, and a postal address is a CNPostalAddress. Such types tend to be wrapped up in a generic CNLabeled-Value, whose purpose I'll explain later. Dates, such as a birthday, are not Date objects but rather DateComponents; this is because they do not necessarily require full date information (for example, I know when someone's birthday is without knowing the year they were born).

CNContactFormatter, CNPostalAddressFormatter

A formatter is an engine for displaying aspects of a CNContact as a string. For example, a CNContactFormatter whose `style` is `.fullName` assembles the name-related properties of a CNContact into a name string. Moreover, a formatter will hand you the key names of the properties that it needs in order to form its string, so that you can easily include them among the contact properties that you fetch initially from the store.

The user's contacts database can change while your app is running. To detect this, register for the `.CNContactStoreDidChange` notification. The arrival of this notification means that any contacts-related objects that you are retaining, such as CNContact instances, may be outdated.

Fetching Contact Information

You now know enough to get started! Let's put it all together and *fetch* some contacts. When we perform a fetch, there are two parameters to provide in order to limit the information to be returned to us:

A predicate
> An NSPredicate. CNContact provides class methods that will generate the predicates you're allowed to use; you are most likely to call `predicateForContacts(matchingName:)` or `predicateForContacts(withIdentifiers:)`.

Keys
> An array of objects adopting the CNKeyDescriptor protocol; such an object will be either a string key name such as `CNContactFamilyNameKey` or a descriptor provided by a formatter such as CNContactFormatter.

Fetching a Contact

I'll start by finding the contact in my contacts database that represents me. To do so, I'll first fetch all contacts whose name is Matt. I'll call the CNContactStore instance method `unifiedContacts(matching:keysToFetch:)`. To determine which resulting Matt is me, I don't need more than the first name and the last name of those contacts, so those are the keys I'll ask for. I'll cycle through the resulting array of contacts in an attempt to find one whose last name is Neuburg. There are some parts of the process that I'm not bothering to show: we are using a CNContactStore fetch method, so everything should be done on a background thread, and the fetch should be wrapped in a `do...catch` construct because it can throw:

```
let pred = CNContact.predicateForContacts(matchingName: "Matt")
var matts = try CNContactStore().unifiedContacts(matching: pred,
    keysToFetch: [
        CNContactFamilyNameKey as CNKeyDescriptor,
        CNContactGivenNameKey as CNKeyDescriptor
])
matts = matts.filter{$0.familyName == "Neuburg"}
guard let moi = matts.first else {
    print("couldn't find myself")
    return
}
```

Alternatively, since I intend to cycle through the fetched contacts, I could call `enumerateContacts(with:usingBlock:)`, which hands me contacts one at a time. The parameter is a CNContactFetchRequest, a simple value class; in addition to `keysToFetch` and `predicate`, it has some powerful properties allowing me to retrieve CNMutableContacts instead of CNContacts, to dictate the sort order, and to suppress the unification of linked contacts (I'll talk later about what that means). Thus, one should perhaps regard enumerateContacts(with:usingBlock:) as the *primary* way to fetch contacts. I don't need those extra features here, however. Again, assume we're in a background thread and inside a do...catch construct:

```
let pred = CNContact.predicateForContacts(matchingName:"Matt")
let req = CNContactFetchRequest(
    keysToFetch: [
        CNContactFamilyNameKey as CNKeyDescriptor,
        CNContactGivenNameKey as CNKeyDescriptor
])
req.predicate = pred
var matt : CNContact? = nil
try CNContactStore().enumerateContacts(with:req) { con, stop in
    if con.familyName == "Neuburg" {
        matt = con
        stop.pointee = true
    }
}
guard let moi = matt else {
    print("couldn't find myself")
    return
}
```

 A commonly asked question is: where's the predicate for fetching information about *all* contacts? There isn't one. Simply call enumerateContacts(with:using-Block:) without a predicate.

Repopulating a Contact

The contact that I fetched in the preceding examples is only partially populated. That means I can't use it to obtain any further contact property information. To illustrate, let's say that I now want to access my own email addresses. If I were to carry on directly from the preceding code by reading the emailAddresses property of moi, I'd crash because that property isn't populated:

```
let emails = moi.emailAddresses // crash
```

If I'm unsure what properties of a particular contact are populated, I can test for safety beforehand with the isKeyAvailable(_:) method:

```
if moi.isKeyAvailable(CNContactEmailAddressesKey) {
    let emails = moi.emailAddresses
}
```

But even though I'm not crashing any more, I still want those email addresses. One solution, obviously, would have been to plan ahead and include CNContactEmail-AddressesKey in the list of properties to be fetched. Unfortunately, I failed to do that. Luckily, there's another way; I can go back to the store and *repopulate* this contact, based on its identifier:

```
let moi2 = try CNContactStore().unifiedContact(withIdentifier: moi.identifier,
    keysToFetch: [
        CNContactFamilyNameKey as CNKeyDescriptor,
        CNContactGivenNameKey as CNKeyDescriptor,
        CNContactEmailAddressesKey as CNKeyDescriptor
])
let emails = moi2.emailAddresses
```

Labeled Values

Now let's talk about the structure of the thing I've just obtained — the value of the emailAddresses property. It's an array of CNLabeledValue objects.

A CNLabeledValue has a label and a value (and an identifier). This class handles the fact that some contact attributes can have more than one value, each intended for a specific purpose (which is described by the label). For example, I might have a home email address and a work email address. These addresses are not keyed by their labels — we cannot, for example, use a dictionary here — because I can have, say, *two* work email addresses. Rather, the label is simply another piece of information accompanying the value. You can make up your own labels, or you can use the built-in labels; the latter are very strange-looking strings like "_$!<Work>!$_", but there are also some constants that you can use instead, such as CNLabelWork.

Carrying on from the previous example, I'll look for all my work email addresses:

```
let workemails = emails.filter{ $0.label == CNLabelWork }.map{ $0.value }
```

Postal addresses are similar, except that their value is a CNPostalAddress. (Recall that there's a CNPostalAddressFormatter, to be used when presenting an address as a string.) Phone number values are CNPhoneNumber objects. And so on.

Contact Formatters

To illustrate the point about formatters and keys, let's say that now I want to present the full name and work email of this contact to the user, as a string. I should not assume either that the full name is to be constructed as givenName followed by familyName nor that those are the only two pieces that constitute it. Rather, I should rely on the intelligence of a CNContactFormatter:

```
let full = CNContactFormatterStyle.fullName
let keys = CNContactFormatter.descriptorForRequiredKeys(for:full)
let moi3 = try CNContactStore().unifiedContact(withIdentifier: moi.identifier,
    keysToFetch: [
        keys,
        CNContactEmailAddressesKey as CNKeyDescriptor
])
if let name = CNContactFormatter.string(from: moi3, style: full) {
    print("\(name): \(workemails[0])") // Matt Neuburg: matt@tidbits.com
}
```

Figure 18-1. A contact created programmatically

Saving Contact Information

All saving of information into the user's contacts database involves a CNSaveRequest object. You describe to this object your proposed changes by calling instance methods such as add(_:toContainerWithIdentifier:), update(_:), and delete(_:). The CNSaveRequest object batches those proposed changes. Then you hand the CNSave-Request object over to the CNContactStore with execute(_:), and the changes are performed in a single transaction.

In this example, I'll create a contact for Snidely Whiplash with a Home email snidely@villains.com and add him to the contacts database. Yet again, assume we're in a background thread and inside a do...catch construct:

```
let snidely = CNMutableContact()
snidely.givenName = "Snidely"
snidely.familyName = "Whiplash"
let email = CNLabeledValue(label: CNLabelHome,
    value: "snidely@villains.com" as NSString)
snidely.emailAddresses.append(email)
snidely.imageData = UIImagePNGRepresentation(UIImage(named:"snidely")!)
let save = CNSaveRequest()
save.add(snidely, toContainerWithIdentifier: nil)
try CNContactStore().execute(save)
```

Sure enough, if we then check the state of the database through the Contacts app, our Snidely contact exists (Figure 18-1).

Contact Sorting, Groups, and Containers

Contacts are naturally *sorted* either by family name or by given name, and the user can choose between them (in the Settings app) in arranging the list of contacts to be displayed by the Contacts app and other apps that display the same list. The CNContact class provides a comparator, through the `comparator(forNameSortOrder:)` class method, suitable for use with NSArray methods such as `sortedArray(comparator:)`. To make sure your CNContact is populated with the properties needed for sorting, call the class method `descriptorForAllComparatorKeys`. Your sort order choices (CNContactSortOrder) are:

- `.givenName`
- `.familyName`
- `.userDefault`

Contacts can belong to *groups*, and the Contacts application in macOS provides an interface for manipulating contact groups — though the Contacts app on an iOS device does not. (The Contacts app on an iOS device allows contacts to be filtered by group, but does not permit editing of groups — creation of groups, addition of contacts to groups, and so on. It's a curious omission, and I don't know the reason for it.) A group in the Contacts framework is a CNGroup; its mutable subclass, CNMutableGroup, allows you to create a group and set its name. All manipulation of contacts and groups — creating, renaming, or deleting a group, adding a contact to a group or removing a contact from a group — is performed through CNSaveRequest instance methods.

Contacts come from *sources*. A contact or group might be on the device or might come from an Exchange server or a CardDAV server. The source really does, in a sense, own the group or contact; a contact can't belong to two sources. A complicating factor, however, is that the same real person might be listed in two different sources as two different contacts; to deal with this, it is possible for multiple contacts to be linked, indicating that they are the same person. That's why the methods that fetch contacts from the database describe the resulting contacts as "unified" — the linkage between linked contacts from different sources has already been used to consolidate the information before you receive them as a single contact. In the Contacts framework, a source is a CNContainer. When I called the CNSaveRequest instance method `add(_:toContainerWithIdentifier:)` earlier, I supplied a container identifier of `nil`, signifying the user's default container.

 In the rare event that you *don't* want unification of linked contacts across sources as you fetch contacts, call `enumerateContacts(with:usingBlock:)` with a CNContactFetchRequest whose `unifyResults` property is `false`.

Contacts Interface

The Contacts UI framework endows your app with an interface, similar to the Contacts app, that lets the user perform common tasks involving the listing, display, and editing of contacts in the database. This is a great help, because designing your own interface to do the same thing would be tedious and involved. The framework provides two UIViewController subclasses:

CNContactPickerViewController
> Presents a navigation interface, effectively the same as the Contacts app but without an Edit button: it lists the contacts in the database and allows the user to pick one and view the details.

CNContactViewController
> Presents an interface showing the properties of a specific contact. It comes in three variants:

> *Existing contact*
>> Displays the details, possibly editable, of an existing contact fetched from the database.

> *New contact*
>> Displays editable properties of a new contact, allowing the user to save the edited contact into the database.

> *Unknown contact*
>> Displays a proposed contact with a partial set of properties, for editing and saving or merging into an existing contact in the database.

Some of the Contacts UI framework view controllers allow the user to select (tap) a property of a contact in the interface. Therefore, they need a way to package up the information about that property so as to communicate to your code *what* property this is — for example, Matt Neuburg's work email, whose value is matt@tidbits.com. For this purpose, the Contacts framework provides the CNContactProperty class. This a value class, consisting of a key (effectively the name of the property), a value, a label (in case the property comes from a CNLabeledValue), a contact, and an identifier. The contact arrives fully populated, so we can access all its properties from here without returning to the CNContactStore.

 You do *not* need user authorization to use these view controllers, and in the case of an editable CNContactViewController you *cannot* prevent the user from saving the edited contact into the database.

CNContactPickerViewController

A CNContactPickerViewController is a UINavigationController. With it, the user can see a list of all contacts in the database, and can filter that list by group.

To use CNContactPickerViewController, instantiate it, assign it a delegate (CNContactPickerDelegate), and present it as a presented view controller:

```
let picker = CNContactPickerViewController()
picker.delegate = self
self.present(picker, animated:true)
```

That code works — the picker appears, and there's a Cancel button so the user can dismiss it. When the user taps a contact, that contact's details are pushed onto the navigation controller. And when the user taps a piece of information among the details, some default action is performed: for a postal address, it is displayed in the Maps app; for an email address, it becomes the addressee of a new message in the Mail app; for a phone number, the number is dialed; and so on.

However, we have so far provided no way for any information to travel from the picker to *our app*. For that, we need to implement the delegate method `contactPicker(_:didSelect:)`. This method comes in two basic forms:

The second parameter is a CNContact
> When the user taps a contact name, the contact's details are *not* pushed onto the navigation controller. Instead, the delegate method is called, the tapped contact is passed to us, and the picker is dismissed.

The second parameter is a CNContactProperty
> When the user taps a contact name, the contact's details *are* pushed onto the navigation controller. If the user now taps a piece of information among the details, the delegate method is called, the tapped property is passed to us, and the picker is dismissed.

(If we implement both forms of this method, it is as if we had implemented only the first form. However, it's possible to change that, using the `predicateForSelectionOfContact` property, as I'm about to explain.)

You can perform additional configuration of what information appears in the picker and what happens when it is tapped, by setting properties of the picker before you present it. These properties are all NSPredicates:

`predicateForEnablingContact`
> The predicate describes the contact. A contact will be enabled in the picker only if the predicate evaluates to `true`. A disabled contact cannot be tapped, so it can't be selected and its details can't be displayed.

predicateForSelectionOfContact

> The predicate describes the contact. If the predicate evaluates to `true`, tapping the contact calls the *first* delegate method (the parameter is the contact). Otherwise, tapping the contact displays the contact details.

predicateForSelectionOfProperty

> The predicate describes the property (in the detail view). If the predicate evaluates to `true`, tapping the property calls the *second* delegate method (the parameter is a CNContactProperty). Otherwise, tapping the property performs the default action.

You can also determine *what* properties appear in the detail view, by setting the `displayedPropertyKeys` property.

For example, let's say we want the user to pass us an email address, and that's the only reason we're displaying the picker. Then a reasonable configuration would be:

```
picker.displayedPropertyKeys =
    [CNContactEmailAddressesKey]
picker.predicateForEnablingContact =
    NSPredicate(format: "emailAddresses.@count > 0")
```

We would then implement only the second form of the delegate method (the parameter is a CNContactProperty). Our code, in combination with the delegate method implementation and the property defaults that we have not set, effectively says: "Only enable contacts that have email addresses. When the user taps an enabled contact, show the details. In the details view, show only email addresses. When the user taps an email address, report it to the delegate method and dismiss the picker."

It is also possible to enable multiple selection. To do so, we implement a different pair of delegate methods:

contactPicker(_:didSelect:)

> The second parameter is an array of CNContact.

contactPicker(_:didSelectContactProperties:)

> The second parameter is an array of CNContactProperty.

This causes a Done button to appear in the interface, and our delegate method is called when the user taps it.

 The interface for letting the user select multiple properties, if incorrectly configured, can be clumsy and confusing, and can even send your app into limbo. Experiment carefully before deciding to use it.

CNContactViewController

A CNContactViewController is a UIViewController. It comes, as I've already said, in three flavors, depending on how you instantiate it:

- Existing contact: `init(for:)`
- New contact: `init(forNewContact:)`
- Unknown contact: `init(forUnknownContact:)`

The first and third flavors display a contact initially, with an option to show a secondary editing interface. The second flavor consists *solely* of the editing interface.

You can configure the initial display of the contact in the first and third flavors, by means of these properties:

`allowsActions`
> Refers to extra buttons that can appear in the interface if it is `true` — things like Share Contact, Add to Favorites, and Share My Location. Exactly what buttons appear depends on what categories of information are displayed.

`displayedPropertyKeys`
> Limits the properties shown for this contact.

`message`
> A string displayed beneath the contact's name.

There are two delegate methods (CNContactViewControllerDelegate):

`contactViewController(_:shouldPerformDefaultActionFor:)`
> Used by the first and third flavors, in the initial display of the contact. This is like a live version of the picker `predicateForSelectionOfProperty`, except that the meaning is reversed: returning `true` means that the tapped property should proceed to trigger the Mail app or the Maps app or whatever is appropriate. This includes the message and mail buttons at the top of the interface. You are handed the CNContactProperty, so you know what was tapped and can take action yourself if you return `false`.

`contactViewController(_:didCompleteWith:)`
> Used by all three flavors. Called when the user dismisses *the editing interface*. If the user taps Done in the editing interface, you receive the edited contact, *which has already been saved into the database*. (If the user cancels out of the editing interface, then if this delegate method is called, the received contact will be `nil`.)

Existing contact

To display an existing contact in a CNContactViewController, call `init(for:)` with a CNContact that has *already* been populated with all the information needed to display it in this view controller. For this purpose, CNContactViewController supplies a class method `descriptorForRequiredKeys`, and you will want to call it to set the keys when you fetch your contact from the store, prior to using it with a CNContactViewController. Here's an example:

```
let pred = CNContact.predicateForContacts(matchingName: "Snidely")
let keys = CNContactViewController.descriptorForRequiredKeys()
let snides = try CNContactStore().unifiedContacts(matching: pred,
    keysToFetch: [keys])
guard let snide = snides.first else {
    print("no snidely")
    return
}
```

We now have a sufficiently populated contact, `snide`, and can use it in a subsequent call to CNContactViewController's `init(for:)`.

 Handing an insufficiently populated contact to CNContactViewController's `init(for:)` will crash your app.

Having instantiated CNContactViewController, you set its delegate (CNContactViewControllerDelegate) and *push* the view controller onto an existing UINavigationController's stack.

An Edit button appears at the top right, and the user can tap it to edit this contact in a presented view controller — unless you have set the view controller's `allowsEditing` property to `false`, in which case the Edit button is suppressed.

Here's a minimal working example; I'll display the Snidely Whiplash contact that I obtained earlier. Note that, even if we were in a background thread earlier when we fetched `snide` from the database, we need to be on the main thread now:

```
let vc = CNContactViewController(for:snide)
vc.delegate = self
vc.message = "Nyah ah ahhh"
self.navigationController?.pushViewController(vc, animated: true)
```

New contact

To use a CNContactViewController to allow the user to create a new contact, instantiate it with `init(forNewContact:)`. The parameter can be `nil`, or it can be a CNMutableContact that you've created and partially populated; but your properties will be only suggestions, because the user is going to be shown the contact editing interface and can change anything you've put.

Having set the view controller's delegate, you then do a little dance: you instantiate a UINavigationController with the CNContactViewController as its root view controller, and *present the navigation controller*. Thus, this is a minimal implementation:

```
let con = CNMutableContact()
con.givenName = "Dudley"
con.familyName = "Doright"
let npvc = CNContactViewController(forNewContact: con)
npvc.delegate = self
self.present(UINavigationController(rootViewController: npvc),
    animated:true)
```

 You must dismiss the presented navigation controller yourself in your implementation of contactViewController(_:didCompleteWith:).

Unknown contact

To use a CNContactViewController to allow the user to edit an unknown contact, instantiate it with init(forUnknownContact:). You must provide a CNContact parameter, which you may have made up from scratch using a CNMutableContact. You must set the view controller's contactStore to a CNContactStore instance; if you don't, it's not an error, but the view controller is then useless. You then set a delegate and *push* the view controller onto an existing navigation controller:

```
let con = CNMutableContact()
con.givenName = "Johnny"
con.familyName = "Appleseed"
con.phoneNumbers.append(CNLabeledValue(label: "woods",
    value: CNPhoneNumber(stringValue: "555-123-4567")))
let unkvc = CNContactViewController(forUnknownContact: con)
unkvc.message = "He knows his trees"
unkvc.contactStore = CNContactStore()
unkvc.delegate = self
unkvc.allowsActions = false
self.navigationController?.pushViewController(unkvc, animated: true)
```

The interface contains these two buttons (among others):

Create New Contact
    The editing interface is presented, with a Cancel button and a Done button.

Add to Existing Contact
    The contact picker is presented. The user can tap Cancel or tap an existing contact. If the user taps an existing contact, that contact is presented for editing, with fields from the partial contact merged in, along with a Cancel button and an Update button.

If the framework thinks that this partial contact is the same as an existing contact, there will be a third button offering explicitly to update that particular contact. The result is as if the user had tapped Add to Existing Contact and picked this existing contact: the editing interface for that contact appears, with the fields from the partial contact merged in, along with Cancel and Update buttons.

In the editing interface, if the user taps Cancel, you'll never hear about it; `contactViewController(_:didCompleteWith:)` won't even be called.

CHAPTER 19

Calendar

The user's calendar information, which the user sees through the Calendar app, is effectively a database of calendar events. The calendar database also includes reminders, which the user sees through the Reminders app. This database can be accessed directly through the EventKit framework. You'll need to `import EventKit`.

An interface for allowing the user to interact with the calendar from within your app is also provided, through the EventKit UI framework. You'll need to `import EventKitUI`.

The calendar database is accessed as an instance of the EKEventStore class. This instance is expensive to obtain but lightweight to maintain, so your usual strategy will be to instantiate and retain one EKEventStore instance. There is no harm in initializing a property or global as an EKEventStore instance and keeping that reference for the rest of the app's lifetime:

```
let database = EKEventStore()
```

In the examples in this chapter, my EKEventStore instance is called `self.database` throughout.

Access to the calendar database requires user authorization. You'll use the EKEventStore class for this. Although there is one database, access to calendar events and access to reminders are considered two separate forms of access and require separate authorizations. To learn what the current authorization status is, call the class method `authorizationStatus(for:)` with an EKEntityType, either `.event` (for access to calendar events) or `.reminder` (for access to reminders). To ask the system to put up the authorization request alert if the status is `.notDetermined`, call the instance method `requestAccess(to:completion:)`. The *Info.plist* must contain some text that the system authorization request alert can use to explain why your app wants access. The relevant key is either "Privacy — Calendars Usage Description" (NSCalendarsUsage-

Description) or "Privacy — Reminders Usage Description" (NSRemindersUsage-Description). See "Checking for Authorization" on page 841 for detailed consideration of authorization strategy and testing.

Calendar Database Contents

Starting with an EKEventStore instance, you can obtain two kinds of object — a calendar or a calendar item.

Calendars

A calendar represents a named (title) collection of calendar items, meaning events or reminders. It is an instance of EKCalendar. Curiously, however, an EKCalendar instance doesn't contain or link to its calendar items; to obtain and create calendar items, you work directly with the EKEventStore itself. A calendar's allowedEntity-Types, despite the plural, will probably return just one entity type; you can't create a calendar that allows both.

Calendars themselves come in various types (type, an EKCalendarType), reflecting the nature of their origin: a calendar can be created and maintained by the user locally (.local), but it might also live remotely on the network (.cal-DAV, .exchange); the Birthday calendar (.birthday) is generated automatically from information in the address book; and so on.

The type is supplemented and embraced by the calendar's source, an EKSource whose sourceType (EKSourceType) can be .local, .exchange, .calDAV (which includes iCloud), and so forth; a source can also have a title, and it has a unique identifier (sourceIdentifier). You can get an array of all sources known to the EKEventStore, or specify a source by its identifier. You'll probably use the source exclusively and ignore the calendar's type property.

There are three ways of requesting a calendar:

All calendars
> Fetch all calendars permitting a particular calendar item type (.event or .reminder), by calling calendars(for:). You can send this message either to the EKEventStore or to an EKSource.

Particular calendar
> Fetch an individual calendar from the EKEventStore by means of a previously obtained calendarIdentifier, by calling calendar(withIdentifier:).

Default calendar
> Fetch the default calendar for a particular calendar item type, by asking for the EKEventStore's defaultCalendarForNewEvents or defaultCalendarForNew-

`Reminders`; this is appropriate particularly if your intention is to create a new calendar item.

You can also create a calendar, by means of the initializer `init(for:eventStore:)`. At that point, you can specify the source to which the calendar belongs. I'll give an example later.

Depending on the source, a calendar will be modifiable in various ways. The calendar's `isSubscribed` might be `true`. If the calendar's `isImmutable` is `true`, you can't delete the calendar or change its attributes; but its `allowsContentModifications` might still be `true`, in which case you can add, remove, and alter its events.

Calendar Items

A calendar item (EKCalendarItem) is either a calendar event (EKEvent) or a reminder (EKReminder). Think of it as a memorandum describing when something happens. As I mentioned a moment ago, you don't get calendar items from a calendar; rather, a calendar item *has* a `calendar`, but you get it from the EKEventStore as a whole. There are two chief ways of doing so:

By predicate
Fetch all events or reminders according to a predicate (NSPredicate):

- `events(matching:)`
- `enumerateEvents(matching:using:)`
- `fetchReminders(matching:completion:)`

EKEventStore methods starting with `predicateFor` supply the needed predicate.

By identifier
Fetch an individual calendar item by means of a previously obtained `calendarItemIdentifier`, by calling `calendarItem(withIdentifier:)`.

Calendar Database Changes

Changes to the database can be atomic. There are two prongs to the implementation of this feature:

- The EKEventStore methods for saving and removing calendar items and calendars have a `commit:` parameter. If you pass `false` as the argument, the changes that you're ordering are batched without performing them; later, you can call `commit` (or `reset` if you change your mind). If you pass `false` and fail to call `commit` later, your changes will never happen.

- An abstract class, EKObject, functions as the superclass for all the other persistent object types, such as EKCalendar, EKCalendarItem, EKSource, and so on. It endows those classes with methods `refresh`, `rollback`, and `reset`, along with read-only properties `isNew` and `hasChanges`.

A calendar can change while your app is running (the user might sync, or the user might edit with the Calendar app), which can put your information out of date. You can register for a single EKEventStore notification, `.EKEventStoreChanged`; if you receive it, you should assume that any calendar-related instances you're holding are invalid. This situation is made relatively painless by the fact that every calendar-related instance can be refreshed with `refresh`. Keep in mind that `refresh` returns a Boolean; if it returns `false`, this object is *really* invalid and you should stop working with it entirely (it may have been deleted from the database).

Creating Calendars and Events

You now know enough for an example! Let's start by creating an events calendar. We need to assign a source type (EKSourceType); we'll choose `.local`, meaning that the calendar will be created on the device itself. We can't ask the database for the local source directly, so we have to cycle through all sources looking for it. When we find it, we make a new calendar called "CoolCal" (saving into the database can fail, so assume we're running inside a `do...catch` construct):

```
let locals = self.database.sources.filter {$0.sourceType == .local}
guard let src = locals.first else {
    print("failed to find local source")
    return
}
let cal = EKCalendar(for:.event, eventStore:self.database)
cal.source = src
cal.title = "CoolCal"
try self.database.saveCalendar(cal, commit:true)
```

 On a device where the calendar is subscribed to a remote source (such as iCloud), `.local` calendars are inaccessible. The examples in this chapter use a local calendar, because I don't want to risk damaging your online calendars; to test them, you'll need to turn off iCloud for your Calendar app temporarily.

Now let's create an event. EKEvent is a subclass of EKCalendarItem, from which it inherits some of its important properties. If you've ever used the Calendar app in iOS or macOS, you already have a sense for how an EKEvent can be configured. It has a `title` and optional `notes`. It is associated with a `calendar`, as I've already said. It can have one or more alarms and one or more recurrence rules; I'll talk about each of those in a moment.

All of that is inherited from EKCalendarItem. EKEvent itself adds the all-important startDate and endDate properties; these are Dates and involve both date and time. If the event's isAllDay property is true, the time aspect of its dates is ignored; the event is associated with a day or a stretch of days as a whole. If the event's isAllDay property is false, the time aspect of its dates matters; an event will then typically be bounded by two times on the same day.

Making an event is simple, if tedious. You *must* provide a startDate and an endDate! The simplest way to construct dates, and to do the date math that you'll often need in order to derive one date from another, is with DateComponents. I'll create an event and add it to our new calendar. First, I need a way to locate the new calendar. I'll locate it by its title. I really should be using the calendarIdentifier; the title isn't reliable, since the user might change it, and since multiple calendars can have the same title. However, it's only an example:

```
func calendar(name:String ) -> EKCalendar? {
    let cals = self.database.calendars(for:.event)
    return cals.filter {$0.title == name}.first
}
```

Now I'll create an event, configure it, and add it to our CoolCal calendar:

```
guard let cal = self.calendar(name:"CoolCal") else {
    print("failed to find calendar")
    return
}
// form the start and end dates
let greg = Calendar(identifier:.gregorian)
var comp = DateComponents(year:2017, month:8, day:10, hour:15)
let d1 = greg.date(from:comp)!
comp.hour = comp.hour! + 1
let d2 = greg.date(from:comp)!
// form the event
let ev = EKEvent(eventStore:self.database)
ev.title = "Take a nap"
ev.notes = "You deserve it!"
ev.calendar = cal
(ev.startDate, ev.endDate) = (d1,d2)
// save it
try self.database.save(ev, span:.thisEvent, commit:true)
```

An alarm is an EKAlarm, a very simple class; it can be set to fire either at an absolute date or at a relative offset from the event time. On an iOS device, an alarm fires through a local notification (Chapter 13). We could easily have added an alarm to our event as we were configuring it:

```
let alarm = EKAlarm(relativeOffset:-3600) // one hour before
ev.addAlarm(alarm)
```

Figure 19-1. A programmatically created event

Switching to the Calendar app, it's easy to see that our event has been successfully created (Figure 19-1).

Recurrence

Recurrence is embodied in a recurrence rule (EKRecurrenceRule); a calendar item can have multiple recurrence rules, which you manipulate through its `recurrence-Rules` property, along with methods `addRecurrenceRule(_:)` and `removeRecurrence-Rule(_:)`. A simple EKRecurrenceRule is described by three properties:

Frequency
> By day, by week, by month, or by year.

Interval
> Fine-tunes the notion "by" in the frequency. A value of 1 means "every." A value of 2 means "every other." And so on.

End
> Optional, because the event might recur forever. It is an EKRecurrenceEnd instance, describing the limit of the event's recurrence either as an end date or as a maximum number of occurrences.

The options for describing a more complex EKRecurrenceRule are best summarized by its initializer:

```
init(recurrenceWith type: EKRecurrenceFrequency,
             interval: Int,
        daysOfTheWeek: [EKRecurrenceDayOfWeek]?,
       daysOfTheMonth: [NSNumber]?,
      monthsOfTheYear: [NSNumber]?,
       weeksOfTheYear: [NSNumber]?,
        daysOfTheYear: [NSNumber]?,
         setPositions: [NSNumber]?,
                  end: EKRecurrenceEnd?)
```

The meanings of all those parameters are mostly obvious from their names and types. The EKRecurrenceDayOfWeek class allows specification of a week number as well as a day number so that you can say things like "the fourth Thursday of the month." Many of the numeric values can be negative to indicate counting backward from the last one. Numbers are all 1-based, not 0-based. The setPositions: parameter is an array of numbers filtering the occurrences defined by the rest of the specification against the interval; for example, if daysOfTheWeek is Sunday, -1 means the final Sunday.

An EKRecurrenceRule is intended to embody the RRULE event component in the iCalendar standard specification (*http://datatracker.ietf.org/doc/rfc5545*); in fact, the documentation tells you how each EKRecurrenceRule property corresponds to an RRULE attribute, and if you log an EKRecurrenceRule, what you're shown *is* the underlying RRULE. RRULE can describe some amazingly sophisticated recurrence rules, such as this one:

```
RRULE:FREQ=YEARLY;INTERVAL=2;BYMONTH=1;BYDAY=SU
```

That means: "Every Sunday in January, every other year." Let's form this rule. Observe that we should attach it to an event whose startDate and endDate actually obey the rule — that is, the event should fall on a Sunday in January. Fortunately, DateComponents makes that easy:

```
let everySunday = EKRecurrenceDayOfWeek(.sunday)
let january = 1 as NSNumber
let recur = EKRecurrenceRule(
    recurrenceWith:.yearly, // every year
    interval:2, // no, every *two* years
    daysOfTheWeek:[everySunday],
    daysOfTheMonth:nil,
    monthsOfTheYear:[january],
    weeksOfTheYear:nil,
    daysOfTheYear:nil,
    setPositions: nil,
    end:nil)
let ev = EKEvent(eventStore:self.database)
ev.title = "Mysterious biennial Sunday-in-January morning ritual"
```

Figure 19-2. The user specifies a span

```
ev.addRecurrenceRule(recur)
ev.calendar = cal // assume we have our calendar
// need a start date and end date
let greg = Calendar(identifier:.gregorian)
var comp = DateComponents(year:2017, month:1, hour:10)
comp.weekday = 1 // Sunday
comp.weekdayOrdinal = 1 // *first* Sunday
ev.startDate = greg.date(from:comp)!
comp.hour = 11
ev.endDate = greg.date(from:comp)!
try self.database.save(ev, span:.futureEvents, commit:true)
```

In that code, the event we save into the database is a recurring event. When we save or delete a recurring event, we must specify a `span:` argument (EKSpan). This is either `.thisEvent` or `.futureEvents`, and corresponds to the two buttons the user sees in the Calendar interface when saving or deleting a recurring event (Figure 19-2). The buttons and the span types reflect their meaning exactly: the change affects either this event alone, or this event plus all *future* (not past) recurrences. This choice determines not only how this and future recurrences of the event are affected now, but also how they relate to one another from now on.

Fetching Events

Now let's talk about how to extract an event from the database. One way, as I mentioned earlier, is by its identifier (`calendarItemIdentifier`). Not only is this identifier a fast and unique way to obtain an event, but also it's just a string, which means that it persists even if the EKEventStore subsequently goes out of existence, whereas an actual EKEvent drawn from the database loses its meaning and its usability if the EKEventStore instance is destroyed.

You can also extract events from the database by matching a predicate (NSPredicate). To form this predicate, you specify a start and end date and an array of eligible calendars, and call this EKEventStore method:

- `predicateForEvents(withStart:end:calendars:)`

That's the only kind of predicate you can use, so any further filtering of events is then up to you. In this example, I'll look through the events of our CoolCal calendar to find the nap event I created earlier; because I have to specify a date range, I ask for events occurring over a two-year span. Because `enumerateEvents(matching:using:)` can be time-consuming, it's best to run it on a background thread (Chapter 24):

```
let greg = Calendar(identifier:.gregorian)
let d = Date() // today
let d1 = greg.date(byAdding:DateComponents(year:-1), to:d)!
let d2 = greg.date(byAdding:DateComponents(year:2), to:d)!
let pred = self.database.predicateForEvents(withStart:
    d1, end:d2, calendars:[cal]) // assume we have our calendar
DispatchQueue.global(qos:.default).async {
    self.database.enumerateEvents(matching:pred) { ev, stop in
        if ev.title.range(of:"nap") != nil {
            self.napid = ev.calendarItemIdentifier
            stop.pointee = true
        }
    }
}
```

When you fetch events from the database, they are provided in no particular order; the convenience method `compareStartDate(with:)` is provided as a sort selector to put them in order by start date. For example:

```
events.sort { $0.compareStartDate(with:$1) == .orderedAscending }
```

When you extract events from the database, event recurrences are treated as separate events. Recurrences of the same event will have different start and end dates but the same `calendarItemIdentifier`. When you fetch an event by identifier, you get the *earliest* event with that identifier. This makes sense, because if you're going to make a change affecting this and future recurrences of the event, you need the option to start with the earliest possible recurrence (so that "future" means "all").

Reminders

A reminder (EKReminder) is very parallel to an event (EKEvent); the chief difference is that EKReminder was invented some years after EKEvent and so its API is a little more modern. They both inherit from EKCalendarItem, so a reminder has a calendar (which the Reminders app refers to as a "list"), a title, notes, alarms, and recurrence rules. Instead of a start date and an end date, it has a start date, a due date, a completion date, and an `isCompleted` property. The start date and due date are expressed directly as DateComponents, so you can supply any desired degree of detail: if you don't include any time components, it's an all-day reminder.

To illustrate, I'll make an all-day reminder for today:

```
let cal = self.database.defaultCalendarForNewReminders()
let rem = EKReminder(eventStore:self.database)
rem.title = "Get bread"
rem.calendar = cal
let today = Date()
let greg = Calendar(identifier:.gregorian)
let comps : Set<Calendar.Component> = [.year, .month, .day]
rem.dueDateComponents = greg.dateComponents(comps, from:today)
try self.database.save(rem, commit:true)
```

When you call `fetchReminders(matching:completion:)`, the possible predicates let you fetch all reminders in given calendars, incomplete reminders, or completed reminders. You don't have to call it on a background thread, because it calls your completion function asynchronously.

Proximity Alarms

A proximity alarm is triggered by the user's approaching or leaving a certain location (also known as *geofencing*). This is appropriate particularly for reminders: one might wish to be reminded of some task when approaching the place where that task can be accomplished. To form the location, you'll need to use the CLLocation class (see Chapter 21). Here, I'll attach a proximity alarm to a reminder (`rem`); the alarm will fire when I'm near my local Trader Joe's:

```
let alarm = EKAlarm()
let loc = EKStructuredLocation(title:"Trader Joe's")
loc.geoLocation = CLLocation(latitude:34.271848, longitude:-119.247714)
loc.radius = 10*1000 // meters
alarm.structuredLocation = loc
alarm.proximity = .enter // "geofence": we alarm when *arriving*
rem.addAlarm(alarm)
```

Use of a proximity alarm requires Location Services authorization, but that's of no concern here, because the app that needs this authorization is not our app but the Reminders app! Now that we've placed a reminder with a proximity alarm into the database, the Reminders app will request authorization, if needed, the next time the user brings it frontmost. If you add a proximity alarm to the event database and the Reminders app can't perform background geofencing, the alarm will not fire (unless the Reminders app is frontmost).

 You can also construct a local notification based on geofencing without involving reminders or the Reminders app. See Chapter 21.

Calendar Interface

The EventKit UI framework provides three view controller classes that manage views for letting the user work with events and calendars:

EKEventViewController
>   Shows the description of a single event, possibly editable.

EKEventEditViewController
>   Allows the user to create or edit an event.

EKCalendarChooser
>   Allows the user to pick a calendar.

These view controllers automatically listen for changes in the database and, if needed, will automatically call `refresh` on the information being edited, updating their display to match. If a view controller is displaying an event in the database and the event is deleted while the user is viewing it, the delegate will get the same notification as if the user had deleted it.

EKEventViewController

EKEventViewController shows the event display, listing the event's title, date and time, calendar, alert, and notes, familiar from the Calendar app (Figure 19-3; observe the resemblance to Figure 19-1). To use EKEventViewController, instantiate it, give it an event from the database, assign it a delegate (EKEventViewDelegate), and *push* it onto an existing navigation controller:

```
let ev = self.database.calendarItem(withIdentifier:self.napid) as! EKEvent
let evc = EKEventViewController()
evc.event = ev
evc.delegate = self
self.navigationController?.pushViewController(evc, animated: true)
```

 Do *not* use EKEventViewController for an event that isn't in the database, or at a time when the database isn't open! It won't function correctly if you do.

If `allowsEditing` is `true`, an Edit button appears in the navigation bar, and by tapping this, the user can edit the various aspects of an event in the same interface as the Calendar app, including the Delete button at the bottom. If the user ultimately deletes the event, or edits it and taps Done, the change is saved into the database.

If the user deletes the event, you will be notified in the delegate method, `eventViewController(_:didCompleteWith:)`. The second parameter is an EKEventViewAction, which will be `.deleted`; it is then up to you to pop the navigation controller:

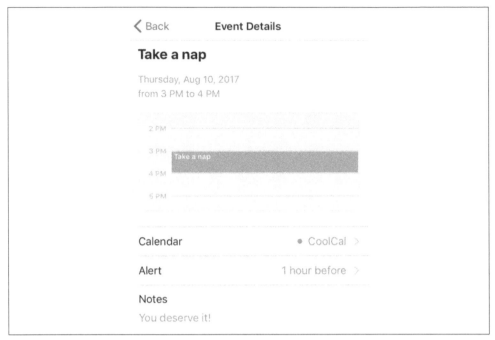

Figure 19-3. *The event interface*

```
func eventViewController(_ controller: EKEventViewController,
    didCompleteWith action: EKEventViewAction) {
        if action == .deleted {
            self.navigationController?.popViewController(animated:true)
        }
}
```

 Even if allowsEditing is false (the default), the user can change what calendar this event belongs to, can change an alert's firing time if there is one, and can delete the event. I regard this as a bug.

EKEventEditViewController

EKEventEditViewController (a UINavigationController) presents the interface for editing an event. To use it, set its eventStore and editViewDelegate (EKEventEdit-ViewDelegate, *not* delegate), and optionally its event, and *present* it as a presented view controller (which looks best on the iPad as a popover). The event can be nil for a completely empty new event; it can be an event you've just created (and possibly partially configured) and not stored in the database; or it can be an existing event from the database.

The delegate method eventEditViewControllerDefaultCalendar(forNewEvents:) may be implemented to specify what calendar a completely new event should be assigned to. If you're partially constructing a new event, you can assign it a calendar then, and of course an event from the database already has a calendar.

You must implement the delegate method `eventEditViewController(_:did-CompleteWith:)` so that you can dismiss the presented view controller. The second parameter is an EKEventEditViewAction telling you what the user did; possible actions are that the user cancelled (`.canceled`), saved the edited event into the database (`.saved`), or deleted an already existing event from the database (`.deleted`). You can get a reference to the edited event as the view controller's `event`.

EKCalendarChooser

EKCalendarChooser displays a list of calendars, choosable by tapping; a chosen calendar displays a checkmark. To use it, instantiate it with `init(selectionStyle:displayStyle:entityType:eventStore:)`, set a `delegate` (adopting the EKCalendarChooserDelegate protocol), and then do a little dance: make it the *root view controller* of a UINavigationController and *present* the navigation controller as a presented view controller (which looks best as a popover on the iPad). The `selectionStyle` dictates whether the user can pick one or multiple calendars; the `displayStyle` states whether all calendars or only writable calendars will be displayed.

Two properties, `showsCancelButton` and `showsDoneButton`, determine whether these buttons will appear in the navigation bar. You can perform additional customizations through the view controller's `navigationItem`.

There are three delegate methods, the first two being required:

- `calendarChooserDidFinish(_:)` (the user tapped Done)
- `calendarChooserDidCancel(_:)`
- `calendarChooserSelectionDidChange(_:)`

In the `finish` and `cancel` methods, you should dismiss the presented view controller.

In this example, we offer to delete the selected calendar. Because this is potentially destructive, we pass through an action sheet for confirmation:

```
@IBAction func deleteCalendar (_ sender: Any) {
    let choo = EKCalendarChooser(
        selectionStyle:.single, displayStyle:.allCalendars,
        entityType:.event, eventStore:self.database)
    choo.showsDoneButton = true
    choo.showsCancelButton = true
    choo.delegate = self
    choo.navigationItem.prompt = "Pick a calendar to delete:"
    let nav = UINavigationController(rootViewController: choo)
    self.present(nav, animated: true)
```

```
    }
    func calendarChooserDidCancel(_ choo: EKCalendarChooser) {
        self.dismiss(animated:true)
    }
    func calendarChooserDidFinish(_ choo: EKCalendarChooser) {
        let cals = choo.selectedCalendars
        guard cals.count > 0 else { self.dismiss(animated:true); return }
        let calsToDelete = cals.map {$0.calendarIdentifier}
        let alert = UIAlertController(title:"Delete selected calendar?",
            message:nil, preferredStyle:.actionSheet)
        alert.addAction(UIAlertAction(title:"Cancel", style:.cancel))
        alert.addAction(UIAlertAction(title:"Delete", style:.destructive) {_ in
            for id in calsToDelete {
                if let cal = self.database.calendar(withIdentifier:id) {
                    try? self.database.removeCalendar(cal, commit: true)
                }
            }
            self.dismiss(animated:true) // dismiss *everything*
        })
        choo.present(alert, animated: true)
    }
```

CHAPTER 20

Maps

Your app can imitate the Maps app, displaying a map interface and placing annotations and overlays on the map. The relevant classes are provided by the Map Kit framework. You'll need to import MapKit. The classes used to describe locations in terms of latitude and longitude, whose names start with "CL," come from the Core Location framework, but you won't need to import it explicitly if you're already importing the Map Kit framework.

Displaying a Map

A map is displayed through a UIView subclass, an MKMapView. You can instantiate an MKMapView from a nib or create one in code. A map has a type, which is usually one of the following (MKMapType):

- .standard
- .satellite
- .hybrid

(New in iOS 11, a further MKMapType, .mutedStandard, dims the map elements so that your additions to the map view stand out.)

The area displayed on the map is its region, an MKCoordinateRegion. This is a struct comprising two things:

center
    A CLLocationCoordinate2D. The latitude and longitude of the point at the center of the region.

Figure 20-1. A map view showing a happy place

span

> An MKCoordinateSpan. The quantity of latitude and longitude embraced by the region (and hence the scale of the map).

Convenience functions help you construct an MKCoordinateRegion.

In this example, I'll initialize the display of an MKMapView (`self.map`) to show a place where I like to go dirt biking (Figure 20-1):

```
let loc = CLLocationCoordinate2DMake(34.927752,-120.217608)
let span = MKCoordinateSpanMake(0.015, 0.015)
let reg = MKCoordinateRegionMake(loc, span)
self.map.region = reg
```

An MKCoordinateSpan is described in degrees of latitude and longitude. It may be, however, that what you know is the region's proposed dimensions in meters. To convert, call `MKCoordinateRegionMakeWithDistance`. The ability to perform this conversion is important, because an MKMapView shows the world through a Mercator projection, where longitude lines are parallel and equidistant, and scale increases at higher latitudes.

I happen to know that the area I want to display is about 1200 meters on a side. Hence, this is yet another way of displaying roughly the same region:

```
let loc = CLLocationCoordinate2DMake(34.927752,-120.217608)
let reg = MKCoordinateRegionMakeWithDistance(loc, 1200, 1200)
self.map.region = reg
```

Yet another way of describing a map region is with an MKMapRect, a struct built up from MKMapPoint and MKMapSize. The earth has already been projected onto the map for us, and now we are describing a rectangle of that map, in terms of the units in which the map is drawn. The exact relationship between an MKMapPoint and the corresponding location coordinate is arbitrary and of no interest; what matters is that you can ask for the conversion, along with the ratio of points to meters (which will vary with latitude):

- MKMapPointForCoordinate
- MKCoordinateForMapPoint
- MKMetersPerMapPointAtLatitude
- MKMapPointsPerMeterAtLatitude
- MKMetersBetweenMapPoints

To determine what the map view is showing in MKMapRect terms, use its `visible-MapRect` property. Thus, this is another way of displaying approximately the same region:

```
let loc = CLLocationCoordinate2DMake(34.927752,-120.217608)
let pt = MKMapPointForCoordinate(loc)
let w = MKMapPointsPerMeterAtLatitude(loc.latitude) * 1200
self.map.visibleMapRect = MKMapRectMake(pt.x - w/2.0, pt.y - w/2.0, w, w)
```

In none of those examples did I bother with the question of the actual dimensions of the map view itself. I simply threw a proposed region at the map view, and it decided how best to portray the corresponding area. Values you assign to the map views's `region` and `visibleMapRect` are unlikely to be the exact values it adopts, because the map view will optimize for display without distorting the map's scale. You can perform this same optimization in code by calling these methods:

- regionThatFits(_:)
- mapRectThatFits(_:)
- mapRectThatFits(_:edgePadding:)

By default, the user can zoom and scroll the map with the usual gestures; you can turn this off by setting the map view's `isZoomEnabled` and `isScrollEnabled` to `false`. Usually you will set them both to `true` or both to `false`. For further customization of an MKMapView's response to touches, use a UIGestureRecognizer (Chapter 5).

You can change programmatically the region displayed, optionally with animation, by calling these methods:

- setRegion(_:animated:)
- setCenter(_:animated:)
- setVisibleMapRect(_:animated:)

- setVisibleMapRect(_:edgePadding:animated:)

The map view's delegate (MKMapViewDelegate) is notified as the map loads and as the region changes (including changes triggered programmatically):

- mapViewWillStartLoadingMap(_:)
- mapViewDidFinishLoadingMap(_:)
- mapViewDidFailLoadingMap(_:withError:)
- mapView(_:regionWillChangeAnimated:)
- mapView(_:regionDidChangeAnimated:)

An MKMapView has Bool properties such as showsCompass, showsScale, and shows-Traffic; set these to dictate whether the corresponding map components should be displayed. New in iOS 11, the compass and the scale legend can be displayed as independent views, an MKCompassButton and an MKScaleView; if you use these, you'll probably want to set the corresponding Bool property to false so as not to get two compasses or scales. Both views are initialized with the map view as parameter, so that their display will reflect the rotation and zoom of the map. The MKCompass-Button, like the internal compass, is a button; if the user taps it, the map is reoriented with north at the top. The visibility of these views is governed by properties (compass-Visibility and scaleVisibility) whose value is one of these (MKFeature-Visibility):

- .hidden
- .visible
- .adaptive

The .adaptive behavior (the default) is that the compass is visible only if the map is rotated, and the scale legend is visible only if the map is zoomed.

 There may be an annoying flash as the compass or scale view first appears. I regard this as a bug. The workaround is to set the view's isHidden to true before adding it as a subview to the interface; the compassVisibility or scale-Visibility behavior will subsequently take over, and the view will be shown correctly.

You can also enable 3D viewing of the map (pitchEnabled), and there's a large and powerful API putting control of 3D viewing in your hands. Discussion of 3D map viewing is beyond the scope of this chapter; an excellent WWDC 2013 video surveys the topic. Starting in iOS 9, there are 3D flyover map types .satelliteFlyover and .hybridFlyover; a WWDC 2015 video explains about these.

Annotations

An *annotation* is a marker associated with a location on a map. To make an annotation appear on a map, two objects are needed:

The object attached to the MKMapView

> The annotation itself is attached to the MKMapView. It is an instance of any class that adopts the MKAnnotation protocol, which specifies a `coordinate`, a `title`, and a `subtitle` for the annotation. You might have reason to define your own class to handle this task, or you can use the simple built-in MKPointAnnotation class. The annotation's coordinate is crucial; it says where on earth the annotation should be drawn. The title and subtitle are optional.

The object that draws the annotation

> An annotation is drawn by an MKAnnotationView, a UIView subclass. This can be extremely simple. In fact, even a `nil` MKAnnotationView might be perfectly satisfactory, because the runtime will then supply a view for you. In iOS 10 and before, this was a realistic rendering of a physical pin, red by default but configurable to any color, supplied by the built-in MKPinAnnotationView class. New in iOS 11, it is an MKMarkerAnnotationView, by default portraying a pin schematically in a circular red "balloon."

Not only does an annotation require two distinct objects, but in fact those two objects do not initially exist together. An annotation object has no pointer to the annotation view object that will draw it. Rather, it is up to you to supply the annotation view object in real time, on demand. This architecture may sound confusing, but in fact it's a very clever way of reducing the amount of resources needed at any given moment. An annotation itself is merely a lightweight object that a map can always possess; the corresponding annotation view is a heavyweight object that is needed only so long as that annotation's coordinates are within the visible portion of the map.

Let's add the simplest possible annotation to our map. The point where the annotation is to go has been stored in an instance property (`self.annloc`):

```
let annloc = CLLocationCoordinate2DMake(34.923964,-120.219558)
```

We create the annotation, configure it, and add it to the MKMapView:

```
let ann = MKPointAnnotation()
ann.coordinate = self.annloc
ann.title = "Park here"
ann.subtitle = "Fun awaits down the road!"
self.map.addAnnotation(ann)
```

That code is sufficient to produce Figure 20-2. I didn't take any steps to supply an MKAnnotationView, so the MKAnnotationView is `nil`. But a `nil` MKAnnotation-

Figure 20-2. A simple annotation

View, as I've already said, means an MKMarkerAnnotationView that produces a drawing of a pin in a red balloon.

By default, an MKMarkerAnnotationView displays its `title` below the annotation. This differs markedly from an MKPinAnnotationView, whose `title` and `subtitle` are displayed in a separate *callout* view that appears above the annotation view only when the annotation is *selected* (because the user taps it, or because you set the MKAnnotationView's `isSelected` to `true`). A selected MKMarkerAnnotationView is drawn larger and displays the `subtitle` in addition to the `title`.

Customizing an MKMarkerAnnotationView

MKMarkerAnnotationView has many customizable properties affecting its display. You can set the balloon color, as the view's `markerTintColor`. You can set the color used to tint the glyph portrayed inside the balloon, as the `glyphTintColor`.

You can also change the balloon contents, overriding the default drawing of a pin. To do so, set either the `glyphText` (this should be at most one or two characters) or the `glyphImage`; in the latter case, use a 40×40 image, which will be sized down automatically to 20×20 when the view is not selected, or supply both a larger and a smaller image, the `selectedGlyphImage` and `glyphImage` respectively. The image is treated as a template image; setting the rendering mode to `.alwaysOriginal` has no effect.

In addition, you can govern the visibility of the title and subtitle, through the `titleVisibility` and `subtitleVisibility` properties. These are MKFeatureVisibility enums, where `.adaptive` is the default behavior that I've already described.

 I find that the `glyphTintColor` has no effect on the default pin image, and that the `subtitleVisibility` has no effect unless you also set the `titleVisibility`. You may need to experiment to get the best results.

Doubtless you are now thinking: that's all very well, but *what* MKMarkerAnnotationView are we talking about? No such view appears in our code, so there is no object whose properties we can set! One way to access the annotation view is to give the map view a `delegate` and implement the MKMapViewDelegate method `mapView(_:view-`

For:). The second parameter is the MKAnnotation for which we are to supply a view. In our implementation of this method, we can *dequeue* an annotation view from the map view, passing in a string reuse identifier, similar to dequeuing a table cell from a table view (Chapter 8). As we have taken no steps to the contrary, this will give us the default view, which in this case is an MKMarkerAnnotationView.

The notion of view reuse here is similar to the reuse of table view cells. The map may have a huge number of annotations, but it needs to display annotation views for only those annotations that are within its current region. Any extra annotation views that have been scrolled out of view can thus be reused and are held for us by the map view in a cache for exactly this purpose.

The key to writing a minimal implementation of mapView(_:viewFor:) is to call this method:

dequeueReusableAnnotationView(withIdentifier:for:)
New in iOS 11. In the minimal case, pass as the identifier: the constant MKMap-ViewDefaultAnnotationViewReuseIdentifier. The second argument should be the annotation that arrived as the second parameter of the delegate method. This method will return an MKAnnotationView — the result is never nil as could happen in iOS 10 and before.

In this example, I check to see that my MKAnnotationView is indeed an MKMarker-AnnotationView, as expected. I also attempt to distinguish this particular annotation by looking at its title; that's not a very good way to distinguish annotation types, but I'll postpone further discussion of the matter until later:

```
func mapView(_ mapView: MKMapView,
    viewFor annotation: MKAnnotation) -> MKAnnotationView? {
        let id = MKMapViewDefaultAnnotationViewReuseIdentifier
        if let v = mapView.dequeueReusableAnnotationView(
            withIdentifier: id, for: annotation) as? MKMarkerAnnotationView {
                if let t = annotation.title, t == "Park here" {
                    v.titleVisibility = .visible
                    v.subtitleVisibility = .visible
                    v.markerTintColor = .green
                    v.glyphText = "!"
                    v.glyphTintColor = .black
                    return v
                }
        }
        return nil
}
```

The result is shown in Figure 20-3.

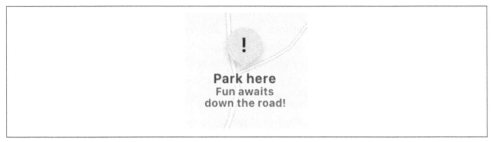

Figure 20-3. Customizing a marker annotation view

Changing the Annotation View Class

Instead of accepting the default MKMarkerAnnotationView as the class of our annotation view, we can substitute a different MKAnnotationView subclass. This might be our own MKMarkerAnnotationView subclass, or some other MKAnnotationView subclass, or MKAnnotationView itself. The way to do that in iOS 11 is to *register* our class with the map view, associating it with the reuse identifier, by calling `register(_:forAnnotationViewWithReuseIdentifier:)` beforehand.

To illustrate, I'll use MKAnnotationView itself as our annotation view class. We won't get the default drawing of a balloon and a pin, because we're not using MKMarkerAnnotationView any longer; instead, I'll set the MKAnnotationView's `image` property directly. We also won't get the title and subtitle drawn beneath the image; instead, I'll set the annotation view's `canShowCallout` to `true`, and the title and subtitle will appear in the callout when the annotation view is selected.

So, assume that I have an identifier declared as an instance property:

```
let bikeid = "bike"
```

And assume that I've registered MKAnnotationView as the class that goes with that identifier:

```
self.map.register(MKAnnotationView.self,
    forAnnotationViewWithReuseIdentifier: self.bikeid)
```

Then my implementation of `mapView(_:viewFor:)` might look like this:

```
func mapView(_ mapView: MKMapView,
    viewFor annotation: MKAnnotation) -> MKAnnotationView? {
        let v = mapView.dequeueReusableAnnotationView(
            withIdentifier: self.bikeid, for: annotation)
        if let t = annotation.title, t == "Park here" {
            v.image = UIImage(named:"clipartdirtbike.gif")
            v.bounds.size.height /= 3.0
            v.bounds.size.width /= 3.0
            v.centerOffset = CGPoint(0,-20)
            v.canShowCallout = true
```

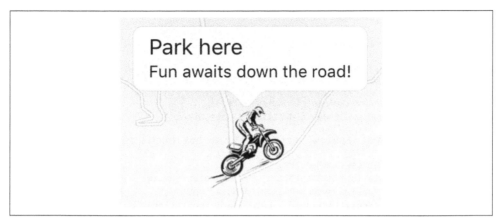

Figure 20-4. A custom annotation image

```
            return v
        }
        return nil
    }
}
```

The dirt bike image is too large, so I shrink the view's bounds before returning it; I also move the view up a bit, so that the bottom of the image is at the coordinates on the map. The result is shown in Figure 20-4.

Custom Annotation View Class

A better way to write the preceding example might be for us to create our own MKAnnotationView subclass and endow it with the ability to draw itself. This will allow us to move the code that configures the image and the callout out of the delegate method and into the subclass itself, where it more properly belongs.

A minimal implementation of an MKAnnotationView subclass should override the annotation property with a setter observer, so that every time the view is reused and a new annotation value is assigned, the view is reconfigured. It might also override the designated initializer, init(annotation:reuseIdentifier:), and possibly declare some additional instance variables; but for purposes of this example, I'll simply move what I was previously doing in the delegate method directly into my annotation setter observer:

```
class MyBikeAnnotationView : MKAnnotationView {
    override var annotation: MKAnnotation? {
        willSet {
            self.image = UIImage(named:"clipartdirtbike.gif")
            self.bounds.size.height /= 3.0
            self.bounds.size.width /= 3.0
            self.centerOffset = CGPoint(0,-20)
```

```
                self.canShowCallout = true
            }
        }
    }
```

We register our custom annotation view class to associate it with our identifier:

```
self.map.register(MyBikeAnnotationView.self,
    forAnnotationViewWithReuseIdentifier: self.bikeid)
```

Our implementation of `mapView(_:viewFor:)` now has much less work to do:

```
func mapView(_ mapView: MKMapView,
    viewFor annotation: MKAnnotation) -> MKAnnotationView? {
        let v = mapView.dequeueReusableAnnotationView(
            withIdentifier: self.bikeid, for: annotation)
        if let t = annotation.title, t == "Park here" {
            // nothing else to do!
            return v
        }
        return nil
}
```

If, in fact, MyBikeAnnotationView is the *only* annotation view type we will *ever* use, we can go even further: we can register MyBikeAnnotationView *as the default*:

```
self.map.register(MyBikeAnnotationView.self,
    forAnnotationViewWithReuseIdentifier:
        MKMapViewDefaultAnnotationViewReuseIdentifier)
```

At that point, we can delete our implementation of `mapView(_:viewFor:)` entirely! It has no work to do, because it has no choices to make; our MKBikeAnnotationView, which configures itself, will be the annotation view class automatically.

Custom Annotation Class

Let's suppose precisely the opposite of what I just said — namely, that our implementation of `mapView(_:viewFor:)` *does* have choices to make. Depending on the nature of the annotation, it must configure our annotation view class differently, or even pick a different annotation view class. For example, some annotations might show a dirt bike, but other annotations might show a different image.

The difference in question will need to be expressed somehow as part of *the annotation itself*. Different annotation types must therefore be somehow distinguishable from one another. So far, I've been avoiding that issue entirely by having my `mapView(_:viewFor:)` implementation examine the incoming annotation's `title`; but that is obviously a fragile and inappropriate solution. The proper way is to use one or more *custom annotation classes* that allow the desired distinction to be drawn.

A minimal custom annotation class will look like this:

```
class MyBikeAnnotation : NSObject, MKAnnotation {
    dynamic var coordinate : CLLocationCoordinate2D
    var title: String?
    var subtitle: String?
    init(location coord:CLLocationCoordinate2D) {
        self.coordinate = coord
        super.init()
    }
}
```

Now when we create our annotation and add it to the map, our code looks like this:

```
let ann = MyBikeAnnotation(location:self.annloc)
ann.title = "Park here"
ann.subtitle = "Fun awaits down the road!"
self.map.addAnnotation(ann)
```

In `mapView(_:viewFor:)`, we can now decide what to do just by looking at the class of the incoming annotation:

```
if annotation is MyBikeAnnotation {
    let v = mapView.dequeueReusableAnnotationView(
        withIdentifier: self.bikeid, for: annotation)
    // ...
    return v
}
return nil
```

You can readily see how this architecture gives our implementation room to grow. For example, at the moment, every MyBikeAnnotation is drawn the same way, but we could now add another property to MyBikeAnnotation that tells us what drawing to use. We could also give MyBikeAnnotation further properties saying such things as which way the bike should face, what angle it should be drawn at, and so on. Each MyBikeAnnotationView instance will end up with a reference to the corresponding MyBikeAnnotation instance (as its `annotation` property), so it will be able to read those MyBikeAnnotation properties and configure the drawing of its own image appropriately.

Annotation View Hiding and Clustering

Annotation views don't change size as the map is zoomed in and out, so if there are several annotations and they are brought close together by the user zooming out, the display can become crowded. Moreover, if too many annotation views are being drawn simultaneously in a map view, scroll and zoom performance can degrade.

In the past, the only way to prevent this has been to respond to changes in the map's visible region — for example, in the delegate method `mapView(_:regionDidChange-Animated:)` — by removing and adding annotations dynamically. MKMapView has extensive support for adding and removing annotations, and its `annotations(in:)`

method efficiently lists the annotations within a given MKMapRect. Also, given a bunch of annotations, you can ask your MKMapView to zoom in such a way that all of them are showing (`showAnnotations(_:animated:)`). Nevertheless, the problem has always been a tricky one; deciding which annotations to eliminate or restore, and when, has always been up to you.

New in iOS 11, the entire problem is solved for you. Annotation views can *automatically* show and hide themselves as the display becomes crowded. And the built-in solution goes even further: if annotations are hidden, they can be replaced by a special *cluster annotation* so that the user *knows* there are hidden annotations. MKAnnotationView has properties that allow you to customize what happens:

displayPriority

> An MKFeatureDisplayPriority struct, which works rather like a layout constraint priority: a value of `.required`, corresponding to `1000`, means that the view shouldn't be hidden, and values `defaultHigh` and `defaultLow`, corresponding to `750` and `250`, give some alternative priorities, but you can set any value you like through the struct's `init(rawValue:)` initializer. If all your annotation views have a `displayPriority` of `.required` (the default), your map view will not participate at all in iOS 11's automatic annotation view hiding feature.

clusteringIdentifier

> A string. The idea is that birds of a feather should flock together: if two annotation views have the same clustering identifier, then the same cluster annotation can be used to represent them when they are hidden. This will in fact happen only if the runtime judges that they are sufficiently close to one another when they are hidden. If you don't set an annotation view's `clusteringIdentifier`, it won't participate in clustering. Giving all annotation views the same `clusteringIdentifier` gives the runtime permission to cluster them however it sees fit.

collisionMode

> An MKAnnotationViewCollisionMode. Two annotation views with the same `clusteringIdentifier` will be replaced by a cluster annotation if the map is zoomed out so far that they collide. But what constitutes a collision between two annotation views? To know that, we need a collision edge. It might be:

> .rectangle
>> The edge is the view's frame.

> .circle
>> The edge is the largest circle inscribable in and centered within the view's frame.

> If you need to offset or resize the boundary of the rectangle or circle that describes the collision edge, use the annotation view's `alignmentRectInsets`.

A minimal approach to make your annotation views opt in to both hiding and clustering would thus be to set the displayPriority of all your annotation views to .defaultHigh and the clusteringIdentifier of all your annotation views to some single string.

A cluster annotation is a real annotation — an MKClusterAnnotation. Its member-Annotations are the annotations whose views have been hidden and subsumed into this cluster. It has a title and subtitle; by default, these are based on the member-Annotations, but you can customize them.

A cluster annotation's view is a real annotation view. It has, itself, a displayPriority and a collisionMode. (The displayPriority is, by default, the highest display-Priority among the annotation views it replaces.) If an annotation view has been hidden and replaced by a cluster annotation view, its cluster property points to the cluster annotation view. The default cluster annotation view corresponds to a reuse identifier MKMapViewDefaultClusterAnnotationViewReuseIdentifier.

You can thus customize a cluster annotation view as you would any other annotation view. You can substitute your own MKAnnotationView subclass by registering or dequeuing it, exactly as in the earlier examples. Your mapView(_:viewFor:) will know that this annotation is a cluster annotation because it will be an MKCluster-Annotation. Or you can register your custom cluster annotation view as the class for MKMapViewDefaultClusterAnnotationViewReuseIdentifier, in which case you might not need an implementation of mapView(_:viewFor:) at all.

Other Annotation Features

When an MKPinAnnotationView initially appears on the map, if its animatesDrop property is true, it seems to drop into place from above. When an MKMarkerAnnotationView initially appears on the map, if its animatesWhenAdded property is true, it grows slightly into place.

In like fashion, we can add our own animation to an annotation view as it initially appears on the map. To do so, we implement the map view delegate method mapView(_:didAdd:), which hands us an array of MKAnnotationViews. When this method is called, the annotation views have been added but the redraw moment has not yet arrived (Chapter 4); so if we animate a view, that animation will be performed as the view appears onscreen. Here, I'll animate the opacity of our annotation view so that it fades in, while growing the view from a point to its full size; I identify the view type through its reuseIdentifier:

```
func mapView(_ mapView: MKMapView, didAdd views: [MKAnnotationView]) {
    for aView in views {
        if aView.reuseIdentifier == self.bikeid {
            aView.transform = CGAffineTransform(scaleX: 0, y: 0)
```

```
            aView.alpha = 0
            UIView.animate(withDuration:0.8) {
                aView.alpha = 1
                aView.transform = .identity
            }
        }
    }
}
```

Certain annotation properties and annotation view properties are automatically animatable through view animation, provided you've implemented them in a KVO compliant way. In MyBikeAnnotation, for example, the `coordinate` property *is* KVO compliant (because we declared it `dynamic`); therefore, we are able to animate shifting the annotation's position:

```
UIView.animate(withDuration:0.25) {
    var loc = ann.coordinate
    loc.latitude = loc.latitude + 0.0005
    loc.longitude = loc.longitude + 0.001
    ann.coordinate = loc
}
```

MKMapView has methods allowing annotations to be selected or deselected programmatically, doing in code the same thing that happens when the user taps. The delegate has methods notifying you when the user selects or deselects an annotation, and you are free to override your custom MKAnnotationView's `set-Selected(_:animated:)` if you want to change what happens when the user taps an annotation. For example, you could show and hide a custom view instead of, or in addition to, the built-in callout.

A callout can contain left and right accessory views; these are the MKAnnotation-View's `leftCalloutAccessoryView` and `rightCalloutAccessoryView`. They are UIViews, and should be small (less than 32 pixels in height). There is also a `detail-CalloutAccessoryView` which replaces the subtitle; for example, you could supply a multiline label with smaller text. The map view's `tintColor` (see Chapter 12) affects such accessory view elements as template images and button titles. You can respond to taps on these views as you would any view or control.

An MKAnnotationView can optionally be draggable by the user; set its `draggable` property to `true`. If you're using a custom annotation class, its `coordinate` property must also be settable. In our custom annotation class, MyBikeAnnotation, the `coordinate` property *is* settable; it is explicitly declared as a read-write property (`var`), as opposed to the `coordinate` property in the MKAnnotation protocol which is read-only. You can also customize changes to the appearance of the view as it is dragged, by implementing your annotation view class's `setDragState(_:animated:)` method.

Figure 20-5. An overlay

Overlays

An *overlay* differs from an annotation in being drawn entirely with respect to points on the surface of the earth. Thus, whereas an annotation's size is always the same, an overlay's size is tied to the zoom of the map view.

Overlays are implemented much like annotations. You provide an object that adopts the MKOverlay protocol (which itself conforms to the MKAnnotation protocol) and add it to the map view. When the map view delegate method `mapView(_:renderer-For:)` is called, you provide an MKOverlayRenderer and hand it the overlay object; the overlay renderer then draws the overlay on demand. As with annotations, this architecture means that the overlay itself is a lightweight object, and the overlay is drawn only if the part of the earth that the overlay covers is actually being displayed in the map view. An MKOverlayRenderer has no reuse identifier; it isn't a view, but rather a drawing engine that draws into a CGContext supplied by the map view.

Some built-in MKShape subclasses adopt the MKOverlay protocol: MKCircle, MKPolygon, and MKPolyline. In parallel to those, MKOverlayRenderer has built-in subclasses MKCircleRenderer, MKPolygonRenderer, and MKPolylineRenderer, ready to draw the corresponding shapes. Thus, as with annotations, you can base your overlay entirely on the power of existing classes.

In this example, I'll use MKPolygonRenderer to draw an overlay triangle pointing up the road from the parking place annotated in our earlier examples (Figure 20-5). We add the MKPolygon as an overlay to our map view, and supply its corresponding MKPolygonRenderer in our implementation of `mapView(_:rendererFor:)`. First, the MKPolygon overlay:

```
let lat = self.annloc.latitude
let metersPerPoint = MKMetersPerMapPointAtLatitude(lat)
var c = MKMapPointForCoordinate(self.annloc)
c.x += 150/metersPerPoint
c.y -= 50/metersPerPoint
var p1 = MKMapPointMake(c.x, c.y)
```

```
    p1.y -= 100/metersPerPoint
    var p2 = MKMapPointMake(c.x, c.y)
    p2.x += 100/metersPerPoint
    var p3 = MKMapPointMake(c.x, c.y)
    p3.x += 300/metersPerPoint
    p3.y -= 400/metersPerPoint
    var points = [p1, p2, p3]
    let tri = MKPolygon(points:&points, count:3)
    self.map.add(tri)
```

Second, the delegate method, where we provide the MKPolygonRenderer:

```
func mapView(_ mapView: MKMapView,
    rendererFor overlay: MKOverlay) -> MKOverlayRenderer {
        if let overlay = overlay as? MKPolygon {
            let r = MKPolygonRenderer(polygon:overlay)
            r.fillColor = UIColor.red.withAlphaComponent(0.1)
            r.strokeColor = UIColor.red.withAlphaComponent(0.8)
            r.lineWidth = 2
            return r
        }
        return MKOverlayRenderer()
}
```

Custom Overlay Class

The triangle in Figure 20-5 is rather crude; I could draw a better arrow shape using a
CGPath (Chapter 2). The built-in MKOverlayRenderer subclass that lets me do that is
MKOverlayPathRenderer. To structure things similarly to the preceding example, I'd
like to supply the CGPath when I add the overlay instance to the map view. No built-
in class lets me do that, so I'll use a custom class, MyPathOverlay, that adopts the
MKOverlay protocol.

A minimal overlay class looks like this:

```
class MyPathOverlay : NSObject, MKOverlay {
    var coordinate : CLLocationCoordinate2D {
        get {
            let pt = MKMapPointMake(
                MKMapRectGetMidX(self.boundingMapRect),
                MKMapRectGetMidY(self.boundingMapRect))
            return MKCoordinateForMapPoint(pt)
        }
    }
    var boundingMapRect : MKMapRect
    init(rect:MKMapRect) {
        self.boundingMapRect = rect
        super.init()
    }
}
```

Our actual MyPathOverlay class will also have a `path` property; this will be a UIBezierPath that holds our CGPath and supplies it to the MKOverlayPathRenderer.

Just as the `coordinate` property of an annotation tells the map view where on earth the annotation is to be drawn, the `boundingMapRect` property of an overlay tells the map view where on earth the overlay is to be drawn. Whenever any part of the `boundingMapRect` is displayed within the map view's bounds, the map view will have to concern itself with drawing the overlay. With MKPolygon, we supplied the points of the polygon in earth coordinates and the `boundingMapRect` was calculated for us. With our custom overlay class, we must supply or calculate it ourselves.

At first it may appear that there is a typological impedance mismatch: the `bounding-MapRect` is an MKMapRect, whereas a CGPath is defined by CGPoints. However, it turns out that these units are interchangeable: the CGPoints of our CGPath will be translated for us directly into MKMapPoints on the same scale — that is, the *distance* between any two CGPoints will be the distance between the two corresponding MKMapPoints. However, the *origins* are different: the CGPath must be described relative to the top-left corner of the `boundingMapRect`. To put it another way, the `boundingMapRect` is described in earth coordinates, but the top-left corner of the `boundingMapRect` is `.zero` as far as the CGPath is concerned. (You might think of this difference as analogous to the difference between a UIView's frame and its bounds.)

To make life simple, I'll think in meters; actually, I'll think in chunks of 75 meters, because this turns out to be a good unit for positioning and laying out this particular arrow. Thus, a line one unit long would in fact be 75 meters long if I were to arrive at this actual spot on the earth and discover the overlay literally drawn on the ground. Having derived this chunk (unit), I use it to lay out the `boundingMapRect`, four units on a side and positioned slightly east and north of the annotation point (because that's where the road is). Then I simply construct the arrow shape within the 4×4-unit square, rotating it so that it points in roughly the same direction as the road:

```
// start with our position and derive a nice unit for drawing
let lat = self.annloc.latitude
let metersPerPoint = MKMetersPerMapPointAtLatitude(lat)
let c = MKMapPointForCoordinate(self.annloc)
let unit = CGFloat(75.0/metersPerPoint)
// size and position the overlay bounds on the earth
let sz = CGSize(4*unit, 4*unit)
let mr = MKMapRectMake(
    c.x + 2*Double(unit), c.y - 4.5*Double(unit),
    Double(sz.width), Double(sz.height))
// describe the arrow as a CGPath
let p = CGMutablePath()
let start = CGPoint(0, unit*1.5)
let p1 = CGPoint(start.x+2*unit, start.y)
let p2 = CGPoint(p1.x, p1.y-unit)
let p3 = CGPoint(p2.x+unit*2, p2.y+unit*1.5)
```

Figure 20-6. A nicer overlay

```
let p4 = CGPoint(p2.x, p2.y+unit*3)
let p5 = CGPoint(p4.x, p4.y-unit)
let p6 = CGPoint(p5.x-2*unit, p5.y)
let points = [start, p1, p2, p3, p4, p5, p6]
// rotate the arrow around its center
let t1 = CGAffineTransform(translationX: unit*2, y: unit*2)
let t2 = t1.rotated(by:-.pi/3.5)
let t3 = t2.translatedBy(x: -unit*2, y: -unit*2)
p.addLines(between: points, transform: t3)
p.closeSubpath()
// create the overlay and give it the path
let over = MyPathOverlay(rect:mr)
over.path = UIBezierPath(cgPath:p)
// add the overlay to the map
self.map.add(over)
```

The delegate method, where we provide the MKOverlayPathRenderer, is simple. We pull the CGPath out of the MyPathOverlay instance and hand it to the MKOverlay-PathRenderer, also telling the MKOverlayPathRenderer how to stroke and fill that path:

```
func mapView(_ mapView: MKMapView,
    rendererFor overlay: MKOverlay) -> MKOverlayRenderer {
        if let overlay = overlay as? MyPathOverlay {
            let r = MKOverlayPathRenderer(overlay:overlay)
            r.path = overlay.path.cgPath
            r.fillColor = UIColor.red.withAlphaComponent(0.2)
            r.strokeColor = .black
            r.lineWidth = 2
            return r
        }
        return MKOverlayRenderer()
}
```

The result is a much nicer arrow (Figure 20-6), and of course this technique can be generalized to draw an overlay from any CGPath we like.

Custom Overlay Renderer

For full generality, you could define your own MKOverlayRenderer subclass; your subclass must override and implement draw(_:zoomScale:in:). The first parameter is an MKMapRect describing a tile of the visible map (not the size and position of the overlay); the third parameter is the CGContext into which you are to draw. Your implementation may be called several times simultaneously on different background threads, one for each tile, so be sure to draw in a thread-safe way. The overlay itself is available through the inherited overlay property, and MKOverlayRenderer instance methods such as rect(for:) are provided for converting between the map's MKMapRect coordinates and the overlay renderer's graphics context coordinates. The graphics context arrives already configured such that our drawing will be clipped to the current tile. (All this should remind you of CATiledLayer, Chapter 7.)

In our example, we can move the entire functionality for drawing the arrow into an MKOverlayRenderer subclass, which I'll call MyPathOverlayRenderer. Its initializer takes an angle: parameter, with which I'll set its angle property; now our arrow can point in any direction. Another nice benefit of this architectural change is that we can use the zoomScale: parameter to determine the stroke width. For simplicity, my implementation of draw(_:zoomScale:in:) ignores the incoming MKMapRect value and just draws the entire arrow every time it is called.

```
var angle : CGFloat = 0
init(overlay:MKOverlay, angle:CGFloat) {
    self.angle = angle
    super.init(overlay:overlay)
}
override func draw(_ mapRect: MKMapRect,
    zoomScale: MKZoomScale, in con: CGContext) {
        con.setStrokeColor(UIColor.black.cgColor)
        con.setFillColor(UIColor.red.withAlphaComponent(0.2).cgColor)
        con.setLineWidth(1.2/zoomScale)
        let unit =
            CGFloat(MKMapRectGetWidth(self.overlay.boundingMapRect)/4.0)
        let p = CGMutablePath()
        let start = CGPoint(0, unit*1.5)
        let p1 = CGPoint(start.x+2*unit, start.y)
        let p2 = CGPoint(p1.x, p1.y-unit)
        let p3 = CGPoint(p2.x+unit*2, p2.y+unit*1.5)
        let p4 = CGPoint(p2.x, p2.y+unit*3)
        let p5 = CGPoint(p4.x, p4.y-unit)
        let p6 = CGPoint(p5.x-2*unit, p5.y)
        let points = [start, p1, p2, p3, p4, p5, p6]
        let t1 = CGAffineTransform(translationX: unit*2, y: unit*2)
        let t2 = t1.rotated(by:self.angle)
        let t3 = t2.translatedBy(x: -unit*2, y: -unit*2)
        p.addLines(between: points, transform: t3)
```

```
        p.closeSubpath()
        con.addPath(p)
        con.drawPath(using: .fillStroke)
    }
```

To add the overlay to our map, we still must determine its MKMapRect:

```
let lat = self.annloc.latitude
let metersPerPoint = MKMetersPerMapPointAtLatitude(lat)
let c = MKMapPointForCoordinate(self.annloc)
let unit = 75.0/metersPerPoint
// size and position the overlay bounds on the earth
let sz = CGSize(4*CGFloat(unit), 4*CGFloat(unit))
let mr = MKMapRectMake(
    c.x + 2*unit, c.y - 4.5*unit,
    Double(sz.width), Double(sz.height))
let over = MyPathOverlay(rect:mr)
self.map.add(over, level:.aboveRoads)
```

The delegate method, providing the overlay renderer, now has very little work to do; in our implementation, it merely supplies an angle for the arrow:

```
func mapView(_ mapView: MKMapView,
    rendererFor overlay: MKOverlay) -> MKOverlayRenderer {
        if overlay is MyPathOverlay {
            let r = MyPathOverlayRenderer(overlay:overlay, angle: -.pi/3.5)
            return r
        }
        return MKOverlayRenderer()
}
```

Other Overlay Features

Our MyPathOverlay class, adopting the MKOverlay protocol, also implements the coordinate property by means of a getter method to return the center of the boundingMapRect. This is crude, but it's a good minimal implementation. The purpose of this property is to specify the position where you would add an annotation describing the overlay. For example:

```
// ... create overlay and assign it a path as before ...
self.map.add(over, level:.aboveRoads)
let annot = MKPointAnnotation()
annot.coordinate = over.coordinate
annot.title = "This way!"
self.map.addAnnotation(annot)
```

The MKOverlay protocol also lets you provide an implementation of intersects(_:) to refine your overlay's definition of what constitutes an intersection with itself; the default is to use the boundingMapRect, but if your overlay is drawn in some nonrectangular shape, you might want to use its actual shape as the basis for determining intersection.

Overlays are maintained by the map view as an array and are drawn from back to front starting at the beginning of the array. MKMapView has extensive support for adding and removing overlays, and for managing their layering order. When you add the overlay to the map, you can say where you want it drawn among the map view's sublayers. This is also why methods for adding and inserting overlays have a `level:` parameter. The levels are (MKOverlayLevel):

- `.aboveRoads` (and below labels)
- `.aboveLabels`

The MKTileOverlay class, adopting the MKOverlay protocol, lets you superimpose, or even substitute (`canReplaceMapContent`), a map view's drawing of the map itself. You provide a set of tiles at multiple sizes to match multiple zoom levels, and the map view fetches and draws the tiles needed for the current `region` and degree of zoom. In this way, for example, you could integrate your own topo map into an MKMapView's display. It takes a lot of tiles to draw an area of any size, so MKTileOverlay is initialized with a URL, which can be a remote URL for tiles to be fetched across the Internet.

Map Kit and Current Location

A device may have sensors that can report its current location. Map Kit provides simple integration with these facilities. Keep in mind that the user can turn off these sensors or can refuse your app access to them (in the Settings app, under Privacy → Location Services), so trying to use these features may fail. Also, determining the device's location can take time.

The real work here is being done by a CLLocationManager instance, which needs to be created and retained; the usual thing is to initialize a view controller instance property by assigning a new CLLocationManager instance to it:

```
let locman = CLLocationManager()
```

Moreover, you must obtain user authorization, and your *Info.plist* must state the reason why you want it (as I'll explain in more detail in Chapter 21):

```
self.locman.requestWhenInUseAuthorization()
```

You can then ask an MKMapView in your app to display the device's location just by setting its `showsUserLocation` property to `true`; the map will automatically put an annotation at that location. This will be an MKUserLocation, adopting the MKAnnotation protocol. (The map view's `userLocation` property will also point to this annotation.) If your map view delegate's implementation of `mapView(_:viewFor:)` returns `nil` for this annotation, or if there is no such implementation, you'll get the default user location annotation view; you are free to substitute your own annotation view.

An MKUserLocation has a `location` property, a CLLocation, whose `coordinate` is a CLLocationCoordinate2D; if the map view's `showsUserLocation` is `true` and the map view has actually worked out the user's location, the `coordinate` describes that location. It also has `title` and `subtitle` properties, which appear in a callout if the annotation view is selected; plus you can check whether it currently `isUpdating`.

MKMapViewDelegate methods keep you informed of the map's attempts to locate the user:

- `mapViewWillStartLocatingUser(_:)`
- `mapViewDidStopLocatingUser(_:)`
- `mapView(_:didUpdate:)` (provides the new MKUserLocation)
- `mapView(_:didFailToLocateUserWithError:)`

In this cheeky example, I use `mapView(_:viewFor:)` to substitute my own title (though if that's all I want to do, it might be simpler to implement `mapView(_:didUpdate:)` instead):

```
func mapView(_ mapView: MKMapView,
    viewFor annotation: MKAnnotation) -> MKAnnotationView? {
        if let annotation = annotation as? MKUserLocation {
            annotation.title = "You are here, stupid!"
            return nil // or could substitute my own MKAnnotationView
        }
        return nil
}
```

You can ask the map view whether the user's location, if known, is in the visible region of the map (`isUserLocationVisible`). But what if it isn't? Displaying the appropriate region of the map — that is, actually *showing* the part of the world where the user is located — is a separate task. The simplest way is to take advantage of the MKMapView's `userTrackingMode` property, which determines how the user's real-world location should be tracked *automatically* by the map display; your options are (MKUserTrackingMode):

`.none`

If `showsUserLocation` is `true`, the map gets an annotation at the user's location, but that's all; the map's `region` is unchanged. You could set it manually in `mapView(_:didUpdate:)`.

`.follow`

Setting this mode sets `showsUserLocation` to `true`. The map automatically centers the user's location and scales appropriately. When the map is in this mode, you should *not* set the map's `region` manually, as you'll be struggling against the tracking mode's attempts to do the same thing.

`.followWithHeading`

Like `.follow`, but the map is also rotated so that the direction the user is facing is up. In this case, the `userLocation` annotation also has a `heading` property, a CLHeading; I'll talk more about headings in Chapter 21.

Thus, this code turns out to be sufficient to start displaying the user's location:

```
self.map.userTrackingMode = .follow
```

When the `userTrackingMode` is one of the `.follow` modes, if the user is left free to zoom and scroll the map, the `userTrackingMode` may be automatically changed back to `.none` (and the user location annotation may be removed). You'll probably want to provide a way to let the user turn tracking back on again, or to toggle among the three tracking modes.

One way to do that is with an MKUserTrackingBarButtonItem, a UIBarButtonItem subclass. You initialize MKUserTrackingBarButtonItem with a map view, and its behavior is automatic from then on: when the user taps it, it switches the map view to the next tracking mode, and its icon reflects the current tracking mode. A map view delegate method tells you when the MKUserTrackingMode changes:

- `mapView(_:didChange:animated:)`

New in iOS 11, you can instead use an MKUserTrackingButton; like an MKScaleView or MKCompassButton, it has the advantage that it can be used anywhere (not just in a toolbar or navigation bar).

Communicating with the Maps App

Your app can communicate with the Maps app. For example, instead of displaying a point of interest in a map view in our own app, we can ask the Maps app to display it. The user could then bookmark or share the location. The channel of communication between your app and the Maps app is the MKMapItem class.

Here, I'll ask the Maps app to display the same point marked by the annotation in our earlier examples, on a standard map portraying the same region of the earth that our map view is currently displaying (Figure 20-7):

```
let p = MKPlacemark(coordinate:self.annloc, addressDictionary:nil)
let mi = MKMapItem(placemark: p)
mi.name = "A Great Place to Dirt Bike" // label to appear in Maps app
mi.openInMaps(launchOptions:[
    MKLaunchOptionsMapTypeKey: MKMapType.standard.rawValue,
    MKLaunchOptionsMapCenterKey: self.map.region.center,
    MKLaunchOptionsMapSpanKey: self.map.region.span
])
```

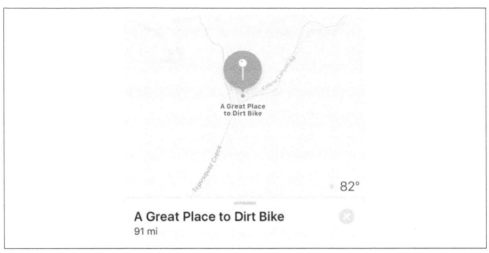

Figure 20-7. The Maps app displays our point of interest

If you start with an MKMapItem returned by the class method `mapItemForCurrent-Location`, you're asking the Maps app to display the device's current location. This call doesn't attempt to determine the device's location, nor does it contain any location information; it merely generates an MKMapItem which, when sent to the Maps app, will cause *it* to attempt to determine (and display) the device's location:

```
let mi = MKMapItem.forCurrentLocation()
mi.openInMaps(launchOptions:[
    MKLaunchOptionsMapTypeKey: MKMapType.standard.rawValue
])
```

Geocoding, Searching, and Directions

Map Kit provides your app with three services that involve performing queries over the network. These services take time and might not succeed at all, as they depend upon network and server availability; moreover, results may be more or less uncertain. Therefore, they involve a completion function that is called back asynchronously (see Appendix C) on the main thread. The three services are:

Geocoding
> Translation of a street address to a coordinate and *vice versa*. For example, what address am I at right now? Or conversely, what are the coordinates of my home address?

Searching
> Lookup of possible matches for a natural language search. For example, what are some Thai restaurants near me?

Directions

Lookup of turn-by-turn instructions and route mapping from a source location to a destination location.

The completion function is called with a single response object plus an Error, each wrapped in an Optional. If the response object is nil, the Error tells you what the problem was.

Geocoding

Geocoding functionality is encapsulated in the CLGeocoder class. You call geocode-AddressString(_:completionHandler:) or, new in iOS 11, geocodePostal-Address(_:completionHandler:); the latter takes a CNPostalAddress, from the Contacts framework, so you'll need to import Contacts (see Chapter 18). The response, if things went well, is an array of CLPlacemark objects, a series of guesses from best to worst; if things went *really* well, the array will contain exactly one CLPlacemark.

A CLPlacemark can be used to initialize an MKPlacemark, a CLPlacemark subclass that adopts the MKAnnotation protocol, and is therefore suitable to be handed directly over to an MKMapView for display.

Here is an (unbelievably simpleminded) example that allows the user to enter an address in a UISearchBar (Chapter 12) to be displayed in an MKMapView:

```
guard let s = searchBar.text else { return }
let geo = CLGeocoder()
geo.geocodeAddressString(s) { placemarks, error in
    guard let placemarks = placemarks else { return }
    let p = placemarks[0]
    let mp = MKPlacemark(placemark:p)
    self.map.addAnnotation(mp)
    self.map.setRegion(
        MKCoordinateRegionMakeWithDistance(mp.coordinate, 1000, 1000),
        animated: true)
}
```

By default, the resulting annotation's callout title contains a nicely formatted string describing the address.

The converse operation is *reverse geocoding*: you start with a coordinate — actually a CLLocation, which you'll obtain from elsewhere, or construct from a coordinate using init(latitude:longitude:) — and then, in order to obtain the corresponding address, you call reverseGeocodeLocation(_:completionHandler:).

The address is expressed through the CLPlacemark postalAddress CNPostalAddress property (new in iOS 11; be sure to import Contacts). You can then use a CNPostal-AddressFormatter to format the address nicely. Alternatively, you can consult directly such CLPlacemark properties as subthoroughfare (a house number), thoroughfare (a street name), locality (a town), and administrativeArea (a state).

In this example of reverse geocoding, we have an MKMapView that is already tracking the user, and so we have the user's location as the map's userLocation; we ask for the corresponding address:

```
guard let loc = self.map.userLocation.location else { return }
let geo = CLGeocoder()
geo.reverseGeocodeLocation(loc) { placemarks, error in
    guard let ps = placemarks, ps.count > 0 else {return}
    let p = ps[0]
    if let addy = p.postalAddress {
        let f = CNPostalAddressFormatter()
        print(f.string(from: addy))
    }
}
```

Searching

The MKLocalSearch class, along with MKLocalSearchRequest and MKLocalSearch-Response, lets you ask the server to perform a natural language search for you. This is less formal than forward geocoding, described in the previous section; instead of searching for an address, you can search for a point of interest by name or description. It can be useful, for some types of search, to constrain the area of interest by setting the MKLocalSearchRequest's region.

In this example, I'll do a natural language search for a Thai restaurant near the user location currently displayed in the map, and I'll display it with an annotation in our map view:

```
guard let loc = self.map.userLocation.location else { return }
let req = MKLocalSearchRequest()
req.naturalLanguageQuery = "Thai restaurant"
req.region = MKCoordinateRegionMake(loc.coordinate, MKCoordinateSpanMake(1,1))
let search = MKLocalSearch(request:req)
search.start { response, error in
    guard let response = response else { print(error); return }
    self.map.showsUserLocation = false
    let mi = response.mapItems[0] // I'm feeling lucky
    let place = mi.placemark
    let loc = place.location!.coordinate
    let reg = MKCoordinateRegionMakeWithDistance(loc, 1200, 1200)
    self.map.setRegion(reg, animated:true)
    let ann = MKPointAnnotation()
    ann.title = mi.name
    ann.subtitle = mi.phoneNumber
    ann.coordinate = loc
    self.map.addAnnotation(ann)
}
```

MKLocalSearchCompleter lets you use the MKLocalSearch remote database to suggest completions as the user types a search query.

Directions

The MKDirections class, along with MKDirectionsRequest and MKDirections-Response, looks up walking or driving directions between two locations expressed as MKMapItem objects. The resulting MKDirectionsResponse includes an array of MKRoute objects; each MKRoute includes an MKPolyline suitable for display as an overlay in your map, as well as an array of MKRouteStep objects, each of which provides its own MKPolyline plus instructions and distances. The MKDirections-Response also has its own `source` and `destination` MKMapItems, which may be different from what we started with.

To illustrate, I'll continue from the Thai food example in the previous section, starting at the point where we obtained the Thai restaurant's MKMapItem:

```
// ... same as before up to this point ...
let mi = response.mapItems[0] // I'm still feeling lucky
let req = MKDirectionsRequest()
req.source = MKMapItem.forCurrentLocation()
req.destination = mi
let dir = MKDirections(request:req)
dir.calculate { response, error in
    guard let response = response else { print(error); return }
    let route = response.routes[0] // I'm feeling insanely lucky
    let poly = route.polyline
    self.map.add(poly)
    for step in route.steps {
        print("After \(step.distance) meters: \(step.instructions)")
    }
}
```

The step-by-step instructions appear in the console; in real life, of course, we would presumably display these in our app's interface. The route is drawn in our map view, provided we have an appropriate implementation of `mapView(_:rendererFor:)`, such as this:

```
func mapView(_ mapView: MKMapView,
    rendererFor overlay: MKOverlay) -> MKOverlayRenderer {
        if let overlay = overlay as? MKPolyline {
            let r = MKPolylineRenderer(polyline:overlay)
            r.strokeColor = UIColor.blue.withAlphaComponent(0.8)
            r.lineWidth = 2
            return r
        }
        return MKOverlayRenderer()
}
```

You can also ask MKDirections to estimate the time of arrival, by calling `calculate-ETA(completionHandler:)`, and iOS 9 introduced arrival time estimation for some public transit systems (and you can tell the Maps app to display a transit directions map).

 Instead of your app providing geocoding, searching, or directions, you can ask the Maps app to provide them: form a URL and call UIApplication's `open(_:options:completionHandler:)`. For the structure of this URL, see the "Map Links" chapter of Apple's *Apple URL Scheme Reference*. You can also use this technique to ask the Maps app to display a point of interest, as discussed in the previous section.

CHAPTER 21

Sensors

A device may contain hardware for sensing the world around itself — where it is located, how it is oriented, how it is moving.

Information about the device's current location and how that location is changing over time, using its Wi-Fi, cellular networking, and GPS capabilities, along with information about the device's orientation relative to north, using its magnetometer, is provided through the Core Location framework.

Information about the device's change in speed and attitude using its accelerometer is provided through the UIEvent class (for device shake) and the Core Motion framework, which provides increased accuracy by incorporating the device's gyroscope, if it has one, as well as the magnetometer. In addition, the device may have an extra chip that analyzes and records the user's activity, such as walking or running, and even a barometer that reports changes in altitude; the Core Motion framework provides access to this information as well.

One of the major challenges associated with writing code that takes advantage of the sensors is that different devices have different hardware. If you don't want to impose stringent restrictions on what devices your app will run on in the first place (UIRequiredDeviceCapabilities in the *Info.plist*), your code must be prepared to fail gracefully, perhaps providing a subset of your app's full capabilities, when it turns out that the current device lacks certain features.

Moreover, certain sensors may experience momentary inadequacy; for example, Core Location might not be able to get a fix on the device's position because it can't see cell towers, GPS satellites, or both. And some sensors take time to "warm up," so that the values you'll get from them initially will be invalid. You'll want to respond to such changes in the external circumstances, in order to give the user a decent experience of your application regardless.

One final consideration: all sensor usage means battery usage, to a lesser or a greater degree — sometimes to a *considerably* greater degree. There's a compromise to be made here: you want to please the user with your app's convenience and usefulness, without disagreeably surprising and annoying the user through rapid depletion of the device's battery charge.

Core Location

The Core Location framework (`import CoreLocation`) provides facilities for the device to determine and report its location (*location services*). It takes advantage of three sensors:

Wi-Fi

The device, if Wi-Fi is turned on, may scan for nearby Wi-Fi networks and compare these against an online database.

Cell

The device, if it has cell capabilities and they are not turned off, may detect nearby telephone cell towers and compare them against an online database.

GPS

The device's GPS, if it has one, may be able to obtain a position fix from GPS satellites. The GPS is obviously the most accurate location sensor, but it takes the longest to get a fix, and in some situations it will fail — indoors, for example, or in a city of tall buildings, where the device can't "see" enough of the sky.

Core Location will automatically use whatever facilities the device has available; all *you* have to do is ask for the device's location. Core Location allows you to specify how accurate a position fix you want; more accurate fixes may require more time.

To help you test code that depends on where the device is, Xcode lets you pretend that the device is at a particular location on earth. The Simulator's Debug → Location menu lets you enter a location; the Scheme editor lets you set a default location (under Options); and the Debug → Simulate Location menu lets you switch among locations. You can set a built-in location or supply a standard GPX file containing a waypoint. You can also set the location to None; it's important to test for what happens when no location information is available.

Location Manager, Delegate, and Authorization

Use of Core Location requires a *location manager* object, an instance of CLLocation-Manager. This object needs to be created on the main thread and retained thereafter. A standard strategy is to pick an instance that persists throughout the life of your app — your app delegate, or your root view controller, for example — and initialize an instance property with a location manager:

```
let locman = CLLocationManager()
```

Your location manager will generally be useless without a *delegate* (CLLocation-ManagerDelegate). You don't want to change a location manager's delegate, so you'll want to set it once, early in the life of the location manager. This delegate will need to be an instance that persists together with the location manager. For example, if locman is a constant property of our root view controller, then we can set the root view controller as its delegate. It's a good idea to do this as early as possible — for example, in the root view controller's initializer:

```
required init?(coder aDecoder: NSCoder) {
    super.init(coder:aDecoder)
    self.locman.delegate = self
}
```

You must also explicitly request authorization from the user when you first start tracking the device's location. There are two types of authorization:

When In Use

When In Use authorization allows your app to perform basic location determination when the app is running.

Always

Always authorization gives your app use of all Core Location modes and features, including those that operate even if the app is not running. (I'll describe later what these are.)

If you request Always authorization, you're asking the user to enable extra capabilities for which a compelling case needs to be made, especially because granting such authorization implies that the user's location may be tracked, along with some depletion of the device's battery, without the user's being aware of it. New in iOS 11, therefore, you *cannot* get Always authorization without *also* letting the user opt for the lesser When In Use authorization instead; an authorization request alert asking for Always authorization also contains a button allowing the user to pick When In Use authorization (Figure 21-1). An app that will want Always authorization should therefore be prepared to operate satisfactorily with only When In Use authorization.

Keep in mind, too, that the user can change your app's authorization at any time. The Settings app lets the user turn on and off location access for your app; new in iOS 11, if your app has ever requested Always authorization, the user will have three choices — Never, While Using the App, and Always — and can switch freely among them (Figure 21-2).

Figure 21-1. The Weather app requests authorization

Figure 21-2. Settings choices for the Weather app

 If you're going to request Always authorization, Apple would like you first to request When In Use authorization separately; if the user grants you When In Use authorization and you subsequently request Always authorization, a special "transition" authorization request alert will be presented on your behalf. However, Apple's own apps do not necessarily obey this protocol, as Figure 21-1 shows.

A further complication is that the user can turn off location services as a whole. If location services are off, and if you proceed to try to use Core Location anyway, the system may put up an alert on your behalf offering to switch to the Settings app so that the user can turn location services on. The CLLocationManager class method `locationServicesEnabled` reports whether location services as a whole are switched off. If so, a possible strategy is to call `startUpdatingLocation` on your location manager anyway. The attempt to learn the device's location will fail, but this failure may also cause the user to see the system alert:

```
if !CLLocationManager.locationServicesEnabled() {
    self.locman.startUpdatingLocation()
    return
}
```

Once location services are enabled, you'll call the CLLocationManager class method `authorizationStatus` to learn your app's actual authorization status. There are two types of authorization, so there are two status cases reporting that you have authorization: `.authorizedWhenInUse` and `.authorizedAlways`. If the status is `.notDetermined`, you can request that the system put up the authorization request alert on your behalf by calling one of two instance methods, either `requestWhenInUseAuthorization` or `requestAlwaysAuthorization`. You must also have a corresponding entry in your app's *Info.plist* providing the body of the authorization request alert; in iOS 11, these are "Privacy — Location When In Use Description" (`NSLocationWhenInUseUsageDescription`) and "Privacy — Location Always and When In Use Usage Description" (`NSLocationAlwaysAndWhenInUseUsageDescription`).

 The pre–iOS 11 "Privacy — Location Always Usage Description" (`NSLocationAlwaysUsageDescription`) is not used in iOS 11, though you will need it if your app is to be backward-compatible to iOS 10 or earlier.

Oddly, neither `requestWhenInUseAuthorization` nor `requestAlwaysAuthorization` takes a completion function. Your code just continues blithely on. If you call `requestWhenInUseAuthorization` and then attempt to track the device's location by calling `startUpdatingLocation`, you might succeed if the user grants authorization, but you might fail. The Core Location API provides no simple way for you to proceed only when you know the outcome of the authorization request.

On the other hand, whenever the user changes your authorization status — either granting authorization in the authorization request alert, or switching to the Settings app and providing authorization there — your location manager delegate's `locationManager(_:didChangeAuthorization:)` is called. Thus, if you were to *store* whatever action you want to perform *before* obtaining authorization, you could *perform* that action *after* obtaining authorization.

Here's a strategy for doing that. Instead of making our CLLocationManager a property of the root view controller, we have a utility class, ManagerHolder; it creates and retains the location manager, asks for authorization if needed, and stores the function we want to call when we have authorization:

```
class ManagerHolder {
    let locman = CLLocationManager()
    var doThisWhenAuthorized : (() -> ())?
    func checkForLocationAccess(always:Bool = false,
        andThen f: (()->())? = nil) {
            // no services? try to get alert
            guard CLLocationManager.locationServicesEnabled() else {
```

```
            self.locman.startUpdatingLocation()
            return
        }
        let status = CLLocationManager.authorizationStatus()
        switch status {
        case .authorizedWhenInUse:
            if always { // try to step up
                self.doThisWhenAuthorized = f
                self.locman.requestAlwaysAuthorization()
            } else {
                f?()
            }
        case .authorizedAlways:
            f?()
        case .notDetermined:
            self.doThisWhenAuthorized = f
            always ?
                self.locman.requestAlwaysAuthorization() :
                self.locman.requestWhenInUseAuthorization()
        case .restricted:
            // do nothing
            break
        case .denied:
            // do nothing, or beg the user to authorize us in Settings
            break
        }
    }
}
```

Our utility class encapsulates management and authorization of the location manager. (For the structure of checkForLocationAccess, compare the discussion under "Checking for Authorization" on page 841.) This gives us flexibility. With my utility class, I can instantiate a location manager *anywhere* and it will be managed correctly. My current plan is to attach a ManagerHolder instance to the root view controller; but it would be trivial to attach a ManagerHolder to the app delegate instead, or to both.

So now I *do* attach a ManagerHolder instance to the root view controller. The root view controller initializes and stores a ManagerHolder instance as an instance property, thus bringing the location manager to life as early as possible. For convenience, I'll still give our root view controller a locman property, but this will be a computed property that bounces to the ManagerHolder's location manager instance:

```
class ViewController: UIViewController, CLLocationManagerDelegate {
    let managerHolder = ManagerHolder()
    var locman : CLLocationManager {
        return self.managerHolder.locman
    }
    required init?(coder aDecoder: NSCoder) {
        super.init(coder:aDecoder)
```

```
            self.locman.delegate = self
        }
        // ...
    }
```

Acting as the location manager delegate, the root view controller can now implement `locationManager(_:didChangeAuthorizationStatus:)` to call the function stored in the ManagerHolder:

```
func locationManager(_ manager: CLLocationManager,
    didChangeAuthorization status: CLAuthorizationStatus) {
        switch status {
        case .authorizedAlways, .authorizedWhenInUse:
            self.managerHolder.doThisWhenAuthorized?()
            self.managerHolder.doThisWhenAuthorized = nil
        default: break
        }
}
```

If we now call our ManagerHolder's `checkForLocationAccess` before tracking location, everything will work correctly. If we pass a completion function in our call to `checkForLocationAccess`, then if we already have authorization, that function will be called immediately, but if our status is `.notDetermined` and the authorization request alert is presented, that function will be called as soon as the user grants us authorization.

Location Tracking

To use the location manager to track the user's location, make sure the location manager has a delegate, configure the location manager further as needed (I'll go into more detail in a moment), and then tell the location manager to `startUpdatingLocation`. The location manager will begin calling the delegate's `locationManager(_:didUpdateLocations:)` delegate method repeatedly. The delegate will deal with each such call as it arrives. In this way, you will be kept more or less continuously informed of where the device is. This will go on until you call `stopUpdatingLocation`; don't forget to call it when you no longer need location tracking!

The pattern here is common to virtually *all* uses of the location manager. The location manager can do various kinds of tracking, but they all work the same way: you'll tell it to start, a corresponding delegate method will be called repeatedly, and ultimately you'll tell it to stop. Your delegate should also implement `locationManager(_:didFailWithError:)` to receive error messages.

Here are some location manager configuration properties that are useful to set *before* you start location tracking:

desiredAccuracy
  Your choices are:

- kCLLocationAccuracyBestForNavigation

- kCLLocationAccuracyBest

- kCLLocationAccuracyNearestTenMeters

- kCLLocationAccuracyHundredMeters

- kCLLocationAccuracyKilometer

- kCLLocationAccuracyThreeKilometers

It might be sufficient for your purposes to know very quickly but very roughly the device's location; in that case, use kCLLocationAccuracyKilometer or kCLLocationAccuracyThreeKilometers. At the other end of the scale, highest accuracy may cause the highest battery drain; indeed, kCLLocationAccuracyBest-ForNavigation is supposed to be used only when the device is connected to external power. The accuracy setting is not a filter: the location manager will send you whatever location information it has, even if it isn't as accurate as you asked for, and checking a location's horizontalAccuracy to see if it's good enough is then up to you.

distanceFilter
Perhaps you don't need a location report unless the device has moved a certain distance since the previous report. This property can help keep you from being bombarded with events you don't need. The distance is measured in meters. To turn off the distance filter entirely, set this property to kCLDistanceFilterNone (the default).

pausesLocationUpdatesAutomatically
A Bool. The default, true, means that your setting for the location manager's activityType is significant. Your activityType choices are (CLActivityType):

- .fitness

- .automotiveNavigation

- .otherNavigation

- .other (the default)

Think of these as an autopause setting, based on the movement of the device; if we don't seem to be moving sufficiently to warrant updates based on the activity type, updates can pause and we'll conserve power. The idea here is that the user may have stopped working out, driving, or whatever, but has forgotten to turn off your app's location tracking. A paused location manager does *not* automatically resume updates; it's up to you to implement the delegate method location-ManagerDidPauseLocationUpdates(_:) and configure updates to resume when appropriate. Apple suggests that, as an alternative, you might save power by setting `pausesLocationUpdatesAutomatically` to `false` but accepting the broadest `desiredAccuracy` (namely `kCLLocationAccuracyThreeKilometers`), which will probably mean that the GPS isn't used.

Here's a basic example, taking advantage of the authorization strategy described in the previous section. Our goal here is quite extreme — we want to get a very accurate location as soon as possible and keep tracking the user's location until we say to stop:

```
self.managerHolder.checkForLocationAccess {
    self.locman.desiredAccuracy = kCLLocationAccuracyBest
    self.locman.distanceFilter = kCLDistanceFilterNone
    self.locman.activityType = .other
    self.locman.pausesLocationUpdatesAutomatically = false
    self.locman.startUpdatingLocation()
}
```

We have a location manager, we are set as the location manager's delegate, we have requested authorization if needed, and if we have or can get authorization, we have configured the location manager and started tracking location. All we have to do now is sit back and wait for our implementation of `locationManager(_:didUpdate-Locations:)` to be called. The second parameter is an array of CLLocation, a value class that encapsulates the notion of a location. Its properties include:

`coordinate`
A CLLocationCoordinate2D, a struct consisting of two Doubles representing latitude and longitude.

`altitude`
A CLLocationDistance, which is a Double representing a number of meters.

`speed`
A CLLocationSpeed, which is a Double representing meters per second.

`course`
A CLLocationDirection, which is a Double representing degrees (*not* radians) clockwise from north.

`horizontalAccuracy`
A CLLocationAccuracy, which is a Double representing meters.

`timestamp`
A Date.

In this situation, the array that we receive is likely to contain just one CLLocation — and even if it contains more than one, the *last* CLLocation in the array is guaranteed to be the newest. Thus, it is sufficient for our `locationManager(_:didUpdate-Locations:)` implementation to extract the last element of the array:

```
let REQ_ACC : CLLocationAccuracy = 10
func locationManager(_ manager: CLLocationManager,
    didUpdateLocations locations: [CLLocation]) {
        let loc = locations.last!
        let acc = loc.horizontalAccuracy
        print(acc)
        if acc < 0 || acc > REQ_ACC {
            return // wait for the next one
        }
        let coord = loc.coordinate
        print("You are at \(coord.latitude) \(coord.longitude)")
}
```

It's instructive to see, from the console logs, how the accuracy improves as the sensors warm up and the GPS obtains a fix:

```
1285.19869645162
1285.19869645172
1285.19869645173
65.0
65.0
30.0
30.0
30.0
10.0
You are at ...
```

Where Am I?

A common desire is, rather than tracking location continuously, to get *one* location *once*. To do that, a common beginner mistake is to call startUpdatingLocation and implement locationManager(_:didUpdateLocations:) to stop updating as soon as it is called:

```
func locationManager(_ manager: CLLocationManager,
    didUpdateLocations locations: [CLLocation]) {
        let loc = locations.last!
        let coord = loc.coordinate
        print("You are at \(coord.latitude) \(coord.longitude)")
        manager.stopUpdatingLocation() // this won't work!
}
```

That's unlikely to work. As I demonstrated in the preceding section, the sensors take time to warm up, and many calls to locationManager(_:didUpdateLocations:) may be made before a reasonably accurate CLLocation arrives. The correct strategy would be to do just what I did in the preceding section, and then call stopUpdating-Location at the very end, when a sufficiently accurate location has in fact been received. That's a lot of work to get just one reading, however — and there's a simpler way. Instead of calling startUpdatingLocation, you should call requestLocation:

```
self.locman.desiredAccuracy = kCLLocationAccuracyBest
self.locman.requestLocation()
```

Your `locationManager(_:didUpdateLocations:)` will be called *once* with a good location, based on the `desiredAccuracy` you've already set:

```
func locationManager(manager: CLLocationManager,
    didUpdateLocations locations: [CLLocation]) {
        let loc = locations.last!
        let coord = loc.coordinate
        print("You are at \(coord.latitude) \(coord.longitude)")
}
```

Keep in mind, however, that calling `requestLocation` will *not* magically cause an accurate location to arrive any faster! It's a great convenience that `location-Manager(_:didUpdateLocations:)` will be called just once, but some considerable time may elapse before that call arrives.

You do not have to call `stopUpdatingLocation`, though you can do so if you change your mind and decide before the location arrives that it is no longer needed.

 If you call `requestLocation` soon after calling it previously, you may get a cached value rather than a new position fix.

Background Location

You can use Core Location when your app is not in the foreground. There are two quite different ways to do this:

Continuous background location
> This is an extension of basic location tracking. You tell the location manager to `startUpdatingLocation`, and updates are permitted to continue even if the app goes into the background. Your app runs in the background in order to receive these updates.

Location monitoring
> Your app does *not* run in the background! Rather, the system monitors location for you. If a significant location event occurs, your app may be awakened in the background (or launched in the background, if it is not running) and notified.

Continuous background location

Use of Core Location to perform continuous background updates is parallel to production of sound in the background (Chapter 14):

- In your app's *Info.plist*, the "Required background modes" key (`UIBackground-Modes`) should include `location`; you can set this up easily by checking "Location updates" under Background Modes in the Capabilities tab when editing the target.

- You must also set your location manager's `allowsBackgroundLocationUpdates` to `true`. You should do this only at moments when you actually need to start allowing background location updates, and set it back to `false` as soon as you no longer need to allow background updates.

The result is that if you have a location manager to which you have sent `start-UpdatingLocation` and the user sends your app into the background, your app is not suspended: the use of location services continues, and your delegate keeps receiving location updates. You cannot *start* tracking locations when your app is *already* in the background (well, you can try, but in all probability your app will be suspended and location tracking will cease).

What the user sees when you're tracking location in the background depends on what type of authorization you have:

When In Use
The device will make the user aware that your app is doing background location tracking, through a blue double-height status bar. The user can tap this to summon your app to the front. (If you see the blue bar *momentarily* as your app goes into the background, that's because you didn't do what I said a moment ago: set `allowsBackgroundLocationUpdates` to `true` only when you really are going to track location in the background.)

Always
When you track location in the background, the blue double-height status bar doesn't appear by default (and the system may present the authorization dialog every few days). However, new in iOS 11, if you set the location manager's `shows-BackgroundLocationIndicator` to `true`, the blue status bar *does* appear when your app tracks location in the background. Apple suggests that you'll want opt in to that behavior, because the blue bar makes clearer to the user what's happening, increases the user's trust in your app, and gives the user a quick way to summon your app.

Background use of location services can cause a power drain, but if you want your app to function as a positional data logger, it may be the only way. You can help conserve power, however, by making judicious choices, such as:

- By setting a coarse `distanceFilter` value.
- By not requiring overly high accuracy.
- By being correct about the `activityType` and allowing updates to pause.

- By operating in *deferred mode*.

What is deferred mode? It's an arrangement whereby your app, which is already receiving updates because you've called startUpdatingLocation, states that it doesn't need to receive updates until the user has moved a specified amount or until a fixed time interval has elapsed. This can make sense if your app runs in the background; you don't need to update your interface constantly because there isn't any interface to update. Instead, you're willing to accept updates in occasional batches and plot or record them whenever they happen to arrive. In this way, you conserve the device's power, for two reasons: the device may be able to power down some of its sensors temporarily, and your app can be suspended in the background between updates.

Deferred mode is dependent on hardware capabilities; use it only if this class method returns true:

- deferredLocationUpdatesAvailable

For this feature to work, the location manager's desiredAccuracy must be kCLLocationAccuracyBest or kCLLocationAccuracyBestForNavigation, and its distanceFilter must be kCLDistanceFilterNone; basically you're telling the GPS to run, but you're also telling it to accumulate readings rather than constantly reporting them to you.

To use deferred mode, call this method:

- allowDeferredLocationUpdates(untilTraveled:timeout:)

It is reasonable to specify a very large distance or time; in fact, constants are provided for this very purpose — CLLocationDistanceMax and CLTimeIntervalMax. The reason is that, when your app is brought to the foreground, all accumulated updates are then delivered, so that your app can update its interface.

You'll need to implement these delegate methods:

locationManager(_:didFinishDeferredUpdatesWithError:)
When this method is called, deferred mode ends; if your app is still in the background, and you want another round of deferred mode, call allowDeferred-LocationUpdates again.

(It is an error to call allowDeferredLocationUpdates after calling it previously but before locationManager(_:didFinishDeferredUpdatesWithError:) is called; that's why you want to call it again *in* this method.)

locationManager(_:didUpdateLocations:)
The locations: parameter in this situation may be an array containing multiple locations; these will be the accumulated updates.

Location monitoring

Location monitoring is not something your app does; it's something the system does on your behalf. Thus, it *doesn't* require your app to run continuously in the background, and you do *not* have to set the UIBackgroundModes of your *Info.plist*. Your app still requires a location manager with a delegate, however, and it needs appropriate user authorization; in general, this will be Always authorization.

Location monitoring is less battery-intensive than full-fledged location tracking. That's because it relies on cell tower positions to estimate the device's location. Since the cell is probably operating anyway — for example, the device is a phone, so the cell is always on and is always concerned with what cell towers are available — little or no additional power is required. Apple says that the system will also take advantage of other clues (requiring no extra battery drain) to decide that there may have been a change in location: for example, the device may observe a change in the available Wi-Fi networks, strongly suggesting that the device has moved.

Nevertheless, location monitoring does use the battery, and over the course of time the user will notice this. Therefore, you should use it only during periods when you need it. Every startMonitoring method has a corresponding stopMonitoring method. Don't forget to call that method when location monitoring is no longer needed! The system is performing this work on your behalf, and it will continue to do so until you tell it not to.

 It is *crucial* that you remember to stop location monitoring. A failure to do this will drain the battery significantly. The user can figure out, by looking at the Battery screen in Settings, that your app is responsible, and if you have provided no other way to turn location monitoring off, the user will have no choice but to delete your app.

If your app isn't in the foreground at the time the system wants to send your location manager delegate a location monitoring event, there are two possible states in which your app might find itself:

Your app is suspended in the background
> Your app is woken up (remaining in the background) long enough to receive the delegate event and do something with it.

Your app is not running at all
> Your app is relaunched (remaining in the background), and your app delegate will be sent application(_:didFinishLaunchingWithOptions:) with the options: dictionary containing UIApplicationLaunchOptionsLocationKey, thus allowing you to discern the special nature of the situation.

> At this point you probably have no location manager — your app has just launched from scratch. You need one, and you need it to have a delegate, so that

you can receive the appropriate delegate events. This is another reason why you should create a location manager and assign it a delegate *early* in the lifetime of the app.

There are four distinct forms of location monitoring:

Significant location change monitoring
Check this class method:

- significantLocationChangeMonitoringAvailable

If it returns true, you can call this method:

- startMonitoringSignificantLocationChanges

Implement this delegate method:

locationManager(_:didUpdateLocations:)
Called whenever the device's location has changed significantly.

Visit monitoring
By tracking significant changes in your location along with the *pauses* between those changes, the system decides that the user is visiting a spot. Visit monitoring is basically a form of significant location change monitoring, but requires even less power and notifies you less often, because locations that don't involve pauses are filtered out.

Check this class method:

- significantLocationChangeMonitoringAvailable

If it returns true, you can call this method:

- startMonitoringVisits

Implement this delegate method:

locationManager(_:didVisit:)
Called whenever the user's location pauses in a way that suggests a visit is beginning, and again whenever a visit ends. The second parameter is a CLVisit, a simple value class wrapping visit data; in addition to coordinate and horizontalAccuracy, you get an arrivalDate and departureDate. If this is an arrival, the departureDate will be Date.distantFuture. If this is a departure and we were not monitoring visits when the user arrived, the arrivalDate will be Date.distantPast.

Region monitoring
Region monitoring depends upon your defining one more *regions*. A region is a CLRegion, which basically expresses a *geofence*, an area that triggers an event

when the user enters or leaves it (or both). This class is divided into two sub-classes, CLBeaconRegion and CLCircularRegion. CLBeaconRegion is used in connection with iBeacon monitoring; I'm not going to discuss iBeacon in this book, so that leaves us with CLCircularRegion. Its initializer is `init(center:radius:identifier:)`; the `center:` parameter is a CLLocation-Coordinate2D, and the `identifier:` serves as a unique key. The region's `notify-OnEntry` and `notifyOnExit` properties are both `true` by default; set one to `false` if you're interested in only the other type of event.

Check this class method:

- `isMonitoringAvailable(for:)`
  with an argument of `CLCircularRegion.self`

If it returns `true`, then you can call this method:

- `startMonitoring(for:)`

Call that method for each region in which you are interested. Regions being monitored are maintained as a set, which is the location manager's `monitored-Regions`. A region's `identifier` serves as a unique key, so that if you start monitoring for a region whose identifier matches that of a region already in the `monitoredRegions` set, the latter will be ejected from the set. Implement these delegate methods:

- `locationManager(_:didEnterRegion:)`
- `locationManager(_:didExitRegion:)`
- `locationManager(_:monitoringDidFailFor:withError:)`

Geofenced local notifications

This is a special case of region monitoring where everything is handled through the local notification mechanism (Chapter 13); therefore, you only need When In Use authorization, you don't start monitoring or stop monitoring, and you don't implement any delegate methods.

You configure a local notification (UNNotification) using a request whose trigger is a UNLocationNotificationTrigger initialized with `init(region:repeats:)` — and thus you can supply a CLRegion. If `repeats:` is `true`, the notification won't be unscheduled after it fires; rather, it will fire again whenever the user crosses the region boundary in the specified direction again (depending on the CLRegion's `notifyOnEntry` and `notifyOnExit` settings).

Heading

For appropriately equipped devices, Core Location supports use of the magnetometer to determine which way the device is facing (its *heading*). Although this information is accessed through a location manager, you do *not* need location services to be turned on merely to use the magnetometer to report the device's orientation with respect to *magnetic* north; you *do* need location services to be turned on in order to report *true* north, as this depends on the device's location.

As with location, you'll first check that the desired feature is available (heading-Available); then you'll configure the location manager, and call startUpdating-Heading. The delegate will be sent locationManager(_:didUpdateHeading:) repeatedly until you call stopUpdatingHeading (or else locationManager(_:didFail-WithError:) will be called).

A heading object is a CLHeading instance; its magneticHeading and trueHeading properties are CLLocationDirection values, which report degrees (*not* radians) clockwise from the reference direction (magnetic or true north, respectively). If the true-Heading is not available, it will be reported as -1. The trueHeading will *not* be available unless both of the following are true in the Settings app:

- Location services are turned on (Privacy → Location Services).
- Compass calibration is turned on (Privacy → Location Services → System Services).

Beyond that, explicit user authorization is *not* needed in order to get the device's heading with respect to true north.

Implement the delegate method locationManagerShouldDisplayHeading-Calibration(_:) to return true if you want the system's compass calibration dialog to be permitted to appear if needed.

In this example, I'll use the device as a compass. The headingFilter setting is to prevent us from being bombarded constantly with readings. For best results, the device should probably be held level (like a tabletop, or a compass); we are setting the headingOrientation so that the reported heading will be the direction in which the top of the device (the end away from the Home button) is pointing:

```
guard CLLocationManager.headingAvailable() else {return} // no hardware
self.locman.headingFilter = 5
self.locman.headingOrientation = .portrait
self.locman.startUpdatingHeading()
```

In the delegate, I'll display our heading as a rough cardinal direction in a label in the interface (self.lab). If we have a trueHeading, I'll use it; otherwise I'll use the magneticHeading:

```
func locationManager(_ manager: CLLocationManager,
    didUpdateHeading newHeading: CLHeading) {
        var h = newHeading.magneticHeading
        let h2 = newHeading.trueHeading // -1 if no location info
        if h2 >= 0 {
            h = h2
        }
        let cards = ["N", "NE", "E", "SE", "S", "SW", "W", "NW"]
        var dir = "N"
        for (ix, card) in cards.enumerated() {
            if h < 45.0/2.0 + 45.0*Double(ix) {
                dir = card
                break
            }
        }
        if self.lab.text != dir {
            self.lab.text = dir
        }
}
```

Heading is not the same as course. For example, a boat may be *facing* north (its heading) but *moving* northeast (its course). There are times, however, when what you are interested in really is course. For example, in a moving automobile, how the user is holding the device is probably unimportant to you: what you want to know when you ask for heading is probably which way the car is moving. If the runtime concludes, from the nature of the device's motion, that when you ask for heading you probably want course, it will provide the course as the heading. New in iOS 11, if that's not what you want, then instead of using Core Location to determine heading, you can use Core Motion (discussed in the next section) to obtain the device's orientation in space as a CMDeviceMotion object's heading property.

Acceleration, Attitude, and Activity

Acceleration results from the application of a force to the device, and is detected through the device's accelerometer, supplemented by the gyroscope if the device has one. Gravity is a force, so the accelerometer always has something to measure, even if the user isn't consciously applying a force to the device; thus the device can use acceleration detection to report its attitude relative to the vertical.

Acceleration information can arrive in two ways:

As a prepackaged UIEvent
    You can receive a UIEvent notifying you of a predefined gesture performed by accelerating the device. At present, the only such gesture is the user shaking the device.

With the Core Motion framework
> You instantiate CMMotionManager and then obtain information of a desired type. You can ask for accelerometer information, gyroscope information, or device motion information (and you can also use Core Motion to get magneto-meter and heading information); device motion combines the gyroscope data with data from the other sensors to give you the best possible description of the device's attitude in space.

Shake Events

A shake event is a UIEvent (Chapter 5). Receiving shake events involves the notion of the first responder. To receive shake events, your app must contain a UIResponder which:

- Returns `true` from `canBecomeFirstResponder`
- Is in fact first responder

This responder, or a UIResponder further up the responder chain, should implement some or all of these methods:

`motionBegan(_:with:)`
> Something has started to happen that might or might not turn out to be a shake.

`motionEnded(_:with:)`
> The motion reported in `motionBegan` is over and has turned out to be a shake.

`motionCancelled(_:with:)`
> The motion reported in `motionBegan` wasn't a shake after all.

It might be sufficient to implement `motionEnded(_:with:)`, because this arrives if and only if the user performs a shake gesture. The first parameter will be the event subtype, but at present this is guaranteed to be `.motionShake`, so testing it is pointless.

The view controller in charge of the current view is a good candidate to receive shake events. Thus, a minimal implementation might look like this:

```
override var canBecomeFirstResponder : Bool {
    return true
}
override func viewDidAppear(_ animated: Bool) {
    super.viewDidAppear(animated)
    self.becomeFirstResponder()
}
override func motionEnded(_ motion: UIEventSubtype, with e: UIEvent?) {
    print("hey, you shook me!")
}
```

By default, if some other object is first responder, and is of a type that supports undo (such as a UITextField), and if `motionBegan(_:with:)` is sent up the responder chain, and if you have not set the shared UIApplication's `applicationSupportsShakeToEdit` property to `false`, a shake will be handled through an Undo or Redo alert. Your view controller might not want to rob any responders in its view of this capability. A simple way to avoid doing so is to test whether the view controller is itself the first responder; if it isn't, we call `super` to pass the event on up the responder chain:

```swift
override func motionEnded(_ motion: UIEventSubtype, with e: UIEvent?) {
    if self.isFirstResponder {
        print("hey, you shook me!")
    } else {
        super.motionEnded(motion, with: e)
    }
}
```

Using Core Motion

The standard pattern for using the Core Motion framework (`import CoreMotion`) to read the accelerometer, magnetometer, gyroscope, and combined device motion is in some ways similar to how you use Core Location:

1. You start by instantiating CMMotionManager; retain the instance somewhere, typically as an instance property. There is no reason not to initialize the property directly:

   ```swift
   let motman = CMMotionManager()
   ```

2. Confirm that the desired hardware is available by checking the appropriate instance property, such as `isAccelerometerAvailable`.

3. Set the interval at which you wish the motion manager to update itself with new sensor readings by setting the appropriate property, such as `accelerometerUpdateInterval`.

4. Call the appropriate `start` method, such as `startAccelerometerUpdates`.

5. You probably expect me to say now that the motion manager will call into a delegate. Surprise! A motion manager has no delegate. You have two choices:

   Pull
   > Poll the motion manager whenever you want data, asking for the appropriate `data` property. The polling interval doesn't have to be the same as the motion manager's update interval; when you poll, you'll obtain the motion manager's *current* data — that is, the data generated by its most recent update, whenever that was.

Push

If your purpose is to collect *all* the data, then instead of calling a simple `start` method, you can call a related method that takes a function that will be called back, preferably on a background thread managed by an OperationQueue (Chapter 24). This method will have the form `start...Updates(to:withHandler:)`. For example, for accelerometer updates, instead of `startAccelerometerUpdates`, you would call `start-AccelerometerUpdates(to:withHandler:)`.

6. Don't forget to call the corresponding `stop` method, such as `stopAccelerometer-Updates`, when you no longer need data.

So there are two ways to get motion manager data — pull and push. Which approach should you use? It depends on what you're trying to accomplish. Polling (pull) is a good way to learn the device's instantaneous state at some significant moment. A stream of callbacks (push) is a good way to detect a gesture, typically by recording the most recent data into a circular buffer. It's perfectly possible to use *both* methods; having configured push, you can perform an occasional pull.

Raw Acceleration

If the device has an accelerometer but no gyroscope, you can learn about the forces being applied to it, but some compromises will be necessary. The chief problem is that, even if the device is completely motionless, its acceleration values will constitute a normalized vector pointing toward the center of the earth, popularly known as *gravity*. The accelerometer is thus constantly reporting a combination of gravity and user-induced acceleration. This is good and bad. It's good because it means that, with certain restrictions, you can use the accelerometer to detect the device's attitude in space. It's bad because gravity values and user-induced acceleration values are mixed together. Fortunately, there are ways to separate these values mathematically:

With a low-pass filter
A low-pass filter will damp out user acceleration so as to report gravity only.

With a high-pass filter
A high-pass filter will damp out the effect of gravity so as to detect user acceleration only, reporting a motionless device as having zero acceleration.

In some situations, it is desirable to apply both a low-pass filter and a high-pass filter, so as to learn both the gravity values and the user acceleration values. A common additional technique is to run the output of the high-pass filter itself through a low-pass filter to reduce noise and small twitches. Apple provides some nice sample code for implementing a low-pass or a high-pass filter; see especially the Accelerometer-

Graph example, which is also very helpful for exploring how the accelerometer behaves.

The technique of applying filters to the accelerometer output has some serious downsides, which are inevitable in a device that lacks a gyroscope:

- It's up to you to apply the filters; you have to implement boilerplate code and hope that you don't make a mistake.
- Filters mean *latency*. Your response to the accelerometer values will lag behind what the device is actually doing; this lag may be noticeable.

In this example, I will simply report whether the device is lying flat on its back. I start by configuring my motion manager; then I launch a repeating timer to trigger polling:

```
guard self.motman.isAccelerometerAvailable else { return }
self.motman.accelerometerUpdateInterval = 1.0 / 30.0
self.motman.startAccelerometerUpdates()
self.timer = Timer.scheduledTimer(
    timeInterval:self.motman.accelerometerUpdateInterval,
    target: self, selector: #selector(pollAccel),
    userInfo: nil, repeats: true)
```

My `pollAccel` method is now being called repeatedly. In it, I ask the motion manager for its accelerometer data. This arrives as a CMAccelerometerData object, which is a timestamp plus a CMAcceleration; a CMAcceleration is simply a struct of three values, one for each axis of the device, measured in Gs. The positive x-axis points to the right of the device. The positive y-axis points toward the top of the device, away from the Home button. The positive z-axis points out the front of the screen.

The two axes orthogonal to gravity, which are the x- and y-axes when the device is lying more or less on its back, are much more accurate and sensitive to small variation than the axis pointing toward or away from gravity. So our approach is to ask first whether the x and y values are close to zero; only then do we use the z value to learn whether the device is on its back or on its face. To keep from updating our interface constantly, we implement a crude state machine; the state property (`self.state`) starts out at `.unknown`, and then switches between `.lyingDown` (device on its back) and `.notLyingDown` (device not on its back), and we update the interface only when there is a state change:

```
guard let data = self.motman.accelerometerData else {return}
let acc = data.acceleration
let x = acc.x
let y = acc.y
let z = acc.z
let accu = 0.08
if abs(x) < accu && abs(y) < accu && z < -0.5 {
    if self.state == .unknown || self.state == .notLyingDown {
```

```
        self.state = .lyingDown
        self.label.text = "I'm lying on my back... ahhh..."
    }
} else {
    if self.state == .unknown || self.state == .lyingDown {
        self.state = .notLyingDown
        self.label.text = "Hey, put me back down on the table!"
    }
}
```

This works, but it's sensitive to small motions of the device on the table. To damp this sensitivity, we can run our input through a low-pass filter. The low-pass filter code comes straight from Apple's own examples, and involves maintaining the previously filtered reading as a set of properties:

```
func add(acceleration accel:CMAcceleration) {
    let alpha = 0.1
    self.oldX = accel.x * alpha + self.oldX * (1.0 - alpha)
    self.oldY = accel.y * alpha + self.oldY * (1.0 - alpha)
    self.oldZ = accel.z * alpha + self.oldZ * (1.0 - alpha)
}
```

Our polling code now starts out by passing the data through the filter:

```
guard let data = self.motman.accelerometerData else {return}
self.add(acceleration: data.acceleration)
let x = self.oldX
let y = self.oldY
let z = self.oldZ
// ... and the rest is as before ...
```

As I mentioned earlier, instead of polling (pull), you can receive callbacks to a function (push). This approach is useful particularly if your goal is to collect updates or to receive updates on a background thread (or both). To illustrate, I'll rewrite the previous example to use this technique; to keep things simple, I'll ask for my callbacks on the main thread (the documentation advises against this, but Apple's own sample code does it). We now start our accelerometer updates like this:

```
self.motman.startAccelerometerUpdates(to: .main) { data, err in
    guard let data = data else {
        print(err)
        self.stopAccelerometer()
        return
    }
    self.receive(acceleration:data)
}
```

`receive(acceleration:)` is just like our earlier `pollAccel`, except that we already have the accelerometer data:

```
func receive(acceleration data:CMAccelerometerData) {
    self.add(acceleration: data.acceleration)
    let x = self.oldX
    let y = self.oldY
    let z = self.oldZ
    // ... and the rest is as before ...
}
```

In this next example, the user is allowed to slap the side of the device into an open
hand — perhaps as a way of telling it to go to the next or previous image or whatever
it is we're displaying. We pass the acceleration input through a high-pass filter to
eliminate gravity (again, the filter code comes straight from Apple's examples):

```
func add(acceleration accel:CMAcceleration) {
    let alpha = 0.1
    self.oldX = accel.x - ((accel.x * alpha) + (self.oldX * (1.0 - alpha)))
    self.oldY = accel.y - ((accel.y * alpha) + (self.oldY * (1.0 - alpha)))
    self.oldZ = accel.z - ((accel.z * alpha) + (self.oldZ * (1.0 - alpha)))
}
```

What we're looking for, in our polling routine, is a high positive or negative x value. A
single slap is likely to consist of several consecutive readings above our threshold, but
we want to report each slap only once, so we take advantage of the timestamp
attached to a CMAccelerometerData, maintaining the timestamp of our previous
high reading as a property and ignoring readings that are too close to one another in
time. Another problem is that a sudden jerk involves both an acceleration (as the user
starts the device moving) and a deceleration (as the device stops moving); thus a left
slap might be preceded by a high value in the opposite direction, which we might
interpret wrongly as a right slap. We can compensate crudely, at the expense of some
latency, with delayed performance:

```
@objc func pollAccel(_: Any) {
    guard let data = self.motman.accelerometerData else {return}
    self.add(acceleration: data.acceleration)
    let x = self.oldX
    let thresh = 1.0
    if x < -thresh {
        if data.timestamp - self.oldTime > 0.5 || self.lastSlap == .right {
            self.oldTime = data.timestamp
            self.lastSlap = .left
            self.canceltimer?.invalidate()
            self.canceltimer = .scheduledTimer(
                withTimeInterval:0.5, repeats: false) { _ in
                    print("left")
            }
        }
    } else if x > thresh {
        if data.timestamp - self.oldTime > 0.5 || self.lastSlap == .left {
            self.oldTime = data.timestamp
            self.lastSlap = .right
            self.canceltimer?.invalidate()
```

```
                self.canceltimer = .scheduledTimer(
                    withTimeInterval:0.5, repeats: false) { _ in
                        print("right")
                }
            }
        }
    }
```

The gesture we're detecting is a little tricky to make: the user must slap the device into an open hand *and hold it there*; if the device jumps out of the open hand, that movement may be detected as the last in the series, resulting in the wrong report (left instead of right, or *vice versa*). And the latency of our gesture detection is very high.

Of course we might try tweaking some of the magic numbers in this code to improve accuracy and performance, but a more sophisticated analysis would probably involve storing a stream of all the most recent CMAccelerometerData objects in a circular buffer and studying the buffer contents to work out the overall trend.

Gyroscope

The inclusion of an electronic gyroscope in the panoply of onboard hardware in some devices makes a huge difference in the accuracy and speed of gravity and attitude reporting. A gyroscope has the property that its attitude in space remains constant; thus it can detect any change in the attitude of the containing device. This has two important consequences for accelerometer measurements:

- The accelerometer can be supplemented by the gyroscope to detect quickly the difference between gravity and user-induced acceleration.

- The gyroscope can observe pure rotation, where little or no acceleration is involved and so the accelerometer would not have been helpful. The extreme case is constant attitudinal rotation around the gravity axis, which the accelerometer alone would be completely unable to detect (because there is no user-induced force, and gravity remains constant).

It is possible to track the raw gyroscope data: make sure the device has a gyroscope (isGyroAvailable), and then call startGyroUpdates. What we get from the motion manager is a CMGyroData object, which combines a timestamp with a CMRotation-Rate that reports the *rate of rotation* around each axis, measured in radians per second, where a positive value is *counterclockwise* as seen by someone whose eye is pointed to by the positive axis. (This is the opposite of the direction graphed in Figure 3-9.) The problem, however, is that the gyroscope values are *scaled* and *biased*. This means that the values are based on an arbitrary scale and are gradually increasing (or decreasing) over time at a roughly constant rate. Thus there is very little merit in the exercise of dealing with the raw gyroscope data.

What you are likely to be interested in is a combination of at least the gyroscope and the accelerometer. The mathematics required to combine the data from these sensors can be daunting. Fortunately, there's no need to know anything about that. Core Motion will happily package up the calculated combination of data as a device motion instance (CMDeviceMotion), with the effects of the sensors' internal bias and scaling already factored out.

CMDeviceMotion consists of the following properties, all of which provide a triple of values corresponding to the device's natural 3D frame (x increasing to the right, y increasing to the top, z increasing out the front):

gravity
A CMAcceleration expressing a vector with value 1 pointing to the center of the earth, measured in Gs.

userAcceleration
A CMAcceleration describing user-induced acceleration, with no gravity component, measured in Gs.

rotationRate
A CMRotationRate describing how the device is rotating around its own center. This is essentially the CMGyroData rotationRate with scale and bias accounted for.

magneticField
A CMCalibratedMagneticField describing (in its field, a CMMagneticField) the magnetic forces acting on the device, measured in microteslas. The sensor's internal bias has already been factored out. The accuracy is one of the following (CMMagneticFieldCalibrationAccuracy):

- .uncalibrated
- .low
- .medium
- .high

attitude
A CMAttitude, descriptive of the device's instantaneous attitude in space. The attitude is measured against a reference frame (CMAttitudeReferenceFrame) which you specify when you ask the motion manager to start generating updates, having first called the class method availableAttitudeReferenceFrames to ascertain that the desired reference frame is available on this device. In every case, the negative z-axis points at the center of the earth; what varies between reference frames is where the x-axis is (and the y-axis is then orthogonal to the other two):

`.xArbitraryZVertical`
> The x-axis could be pointing anywhere.

`.xArbitraryCorrectedZVertical`
> The same as in the previous option, but the magnetometer is used to maintain accuracy (preventing drift of the reference frame over time).

`.xMagneticNorthZVertical`
> The x-axis points toward magnetic north.

`.xTrueNorthZVertical`
> The x-axis points toward true north. This value will be inaccurate unless you are also using Core Location to obtain the device's location.

The `attitude` value's numbers can be accessed through various CMAttitude properties corresponding to three different systems, each being convenient for a different purpose:

`pitch, roll, yaw`
> The device's angle of offset from the reference frame, in radians, around the device's natural x-axis, y-axis, and z-axis respectively (also known as Euler angles).

`rotationMatrix`
> A CMRotationMatrix struct embodying a 3×3 matrix expressing a rotation in the reference frame.

`quaternion`
> A CMQuaternion describing an attitude. (Quaternions are commonly used in OpenGL.)

`heading`
> New in iOS 11; a Double giving the device's orientation as a number of degrees (*not* radians) clockwise from north, in accordance with the reference frame which must be `.xMagneticNorthZVertical` or `.xTrueNorthZVertical` (otherwise, you'll get a value of `-1`). Unlike a Core Location CLHeading, it is a pure orientation reading, without the course folded into it. Not only the magnetometer but also the accelerometer and gyroscope are used, thus helping to eliminate errors caused by local magnetic anomalies.

In this example, we turn the device into a simple compass/clinometer, merely by asking for its `attitude` with reference to magnetic north and taking its `pitch`, `roll`, and `yaw`. We begin by making the usual preparations; notice the use of the `showsDeviceMovementDisplay` property, intended to allow the runtime to prompt the user if the magnetometer needs calibration:

```
guard self.motman.isDeviceMotionAvailable else { return }
let r = CMAttitudeReferenceFrame.xMagneticNorthZVertical
guard CMMotionManager.availableAttitudeReferenceFrames().contains(r) else {
    return
}
self.motman.showsDeviceMovementDisplay = true
self.motman.deviceMotionUpdateInterval = 1.0 / 30.0
self.motman.startDeviceMotionUpdates(using: r)
let t = self.motman.deviceMotionUpdateInterval * 10
self.timer = Timer.scheduledTimer(timeInterval:t,
    target:self, selector:#selector(pollAttitude),
    userInfo:nil, repeats:true)
```

In `pollAttitude`, we wait until the magnetometer is ready, and then we start taking attitude readings (converted to degrees):

```
guard let mot = self.motman.deviceMotion else {return}
let acc = mot.magneticField.accuracy.rawValue
if acc <= CMMagneticFieldCalibrationAccuracy.low.rawValue {
    return // not ready yet
}
let att = mot.attitude
let to_deg = 180.0 / .pi
print("\(att.pitch * to_deg), \(att.roll * to_deg), \(att.yaw * to_deg)")
```

The values are all close to zero when the device is level (flat on its back) with its x-axis (right edge) pointing to magnetic north, and each value increases as the device is rotated *counterclockwise* with respect to an eye that has the corresponding positive axis pointing at it. So, for example, a device held upright (top pointing at the sky) has a `pitch` approaching 90; a device lying on its right edge has a `roll` approaching 90; and a device lying on its back with its top pointing north has a `yaw` approaching -90.

There are some quirks in the way Euler angles operate mathematically:

- `roll` and `yaw` increase with counterclockwise rotation from 0 to π (180 degrees) and then jump to -π (-180 degrees) and continue to increase to 0 as the rotation completes a circle; but `pitch` increases to $\pi/2$ (90 degrees) and then decreases to 0, then decreases to -$\pi/2$ (-90 degrees) and increases to 0. This means that attitude alone, if we are exploring it through `pitch`, `roll`, and `yaw`, is insufficient to describe the device's attitude, since a `pitch` value of, say, $\pi/4$ (45 degrees) could mean two different things. To distinguish those two things, we can supplement `attitude` with the z-component of `gravity`:

  ```
  let g = mot.gravity
  let whichway = g.z > 0 ? "forward" : "back"
  print("pitch is tilted \(whichway)")
  ```

- Values become inaccurate in certain orientations. In particular, when `pitch` approaches ±90 degrees (the device is upright or inverted), `roll` and `yaw` become erratic. (You may see this effect referred to as "the singularity" or as "gimbal lock.") I believe that, depending on what you are trying to accomplish, you can solve this by using a different expression of the attitude, such as the `rotation-Matrix`, which does not suffer from this limitation.

This next (simple and very silly) example illustrates a use of CMAttitude's `rotation-Matrix` property. Our goal is to make a CALayer rotate in response to the current attitude of the device. We start as before, except that our reference frame is `.xArbitraryZVertical`; we are interested in how the device moves from its initial attitude, without reference to any particular fixed external direction such as magnetic north. In `pollAttitude`, our first step is to store the device's current attitude in a CMAttitude property, `self.ref`:

```
guard let mot = self.motman.deviceMotion else {return}
let att = mot.attitude
if self.ref == nil {
    self.ref = att
    return
}
```

That code works correctly because on the first few polls, as the attitude-detection hardware warms up, `att` is `nil`, so we don't get past the `return` call until we have a valid initial attitude. Our next step is highly characteristic of how CMAttitude is used: we call the CMAttitude instance method `multiply(byInverseOf:)`, which transforms our attitude so that it is relative *to the stored initial attitude*:

```
att.multiply(byInverseOf: self.ref)
```

Finally, we apply the attitude's rotation matrix directly to a layer in our interface as a transform. Well, not quite directly: a rotation matrix is a 3×3 matrix, whereas a CATransform3D, which is what we need in order to set a layer's `transform`, is a 4×4 matrix. However, it happens that the top left nine entries in a CATransform3D matrix constitute its rotation component, so we start with an identity matrix and set those entries directly:

```
let r = att.rotationMatrix
var t = CATransform3DIdentity
t.m11 = CGFloat(r.m11)
t.m12 = CGFloat(r.m12)
t.m13 = CGFloat(r.m13)
t.m21 = CGFloat(r.m21)
t.m22 = CGFloat(r.m22)
t.m23 = CGFloat(r.m23)
t.m31 = CGFloat(r.m31)
t.m32 = CGFloat(r.m32)
t.m33 = CGFloat(r.m33)
let lay = // whatever
CATransaction.setAnimationDuration(1.0/10.0)
lay.transform = t
```

The result is that the layer apparently tries to hold itself still as the device rotates. The example is rather crude because we aren't using OpenGL to draw a three-dimensional object, but it illustrates the principle well enough.

There is a quirk to be aware of in this case as well: over time, the transform has a tendency to drift. Thus, even if we leave the device stationary, the layer will gradually rotate. That is the sort of effect that .xArbitraryCorrectedZVertical is designed to help mitigate, at the expense of some CPU and battery usage, by bringing the magnetometer into play.

Here are some additional considerations to be aware of when using Core Motion:

- Your app should create only one CMMotionManager instance.
- Use of Core Motion is legal while your app is running in the background. To take advantage of this, however, your app would need to be running in the background for some *other* reason; there is no Core Motion UIBackgroundModes setting in an *Info.plist*. For example, you might run in the background because you're using Core Location, and take advantage of this to employ Core Motion as well.
- Core Motion requires that various sensors be turned on, such as the magnetometer and the gyroscope. This can result in some increased battery drain, so try not to use any sensors you don't have to, and remember to stop generating updates as soon as you no longer need them.
- If your app will *not* be running in the background, then you should tell the motion manager explicitly to stop generating updates when your app goes into the background.

Other Core Motion Data

In addition to CMDeviceMotion, the Core Motion framework lets you obtain four other types of data:

CMMotionActivityManager
Some devices have a motion coprocessor chip with the ability to detect, analyze, and keep a record of device motion even while the device is asleep and with very little drain on power. This is *not*, in and of itself, a form of location determination; it is an analysis of the device's physical motion and attitude in order to draw conclusions about what the user has been doing while carrying or wearing the device. You can learn that the user is walking, or walked for an hour, but not where the user was walking.

Start by maintaining a CMMotionActivityManager instance, typically as an instance property. To find out whether the device has a motion coprocessor, call the CMMotionActivityManager class method `isActivityAvailable`. There are two ways to query the motion activity manager:

Real-time updates
> This is similar to getting motion manager updates with a callback function. You call this method:
>
> - `startActivityUpdates(to:withHandler:)`
>
> Your callback function is called periodically. When you no longer need updates, call `stopActivityUpdates`.

Historical data
> The motion coprocessor records about a week's-worth of data. You ask for a chunk of that recorded data by calling this method:
>
> - `queryActivityStarting(from:to:withHandler:)`
>
> It's fine to query the historical data while the motion activity manager is already delivering updates.

CMPedometer
> The pedometer is a step counter, deducing steps from the back and forth motion of the device; it can also be used to receive events alerting you to the fact that user has started or stopped activity. The pedometer may work reliably under circumstances where Core Location doesn't.
>
> Start by maintaining a CMPedometer instance, typically as an instance property. Before using the pedometer, check the `isStepCountingAvailable` class method. Different devices add further capabilities. Some devices can deduce the size of the user's stride and compute distance (`isDistanceAvailable`); some devices can use barometric data to estimate whether the user mounted a flight of stairs (`isFloorCountingAvailable`). You can also ask for instantaneous cadence (`isCadenceAvailable`) and pace (`isPaceAvailable`).
>
> Pedometer data is queried just like motion activity data:

Real-time updates
> You can ask for constant updates with this method:
>
> - `startUpdates(from:withHandler:)`

Historical data
> You can ask for the stored history with this method:
>
> - `queryPedometerData(from:to:withHandler:)`

Each bit of data arrives as a CMPedometerData object.

To be notified of changes in the user's motion, call `startEvent-`
`Updates(handler:)`; the `handler:` function receives a CMPedometerEvent
whose `type` (CMPedometerEventType) is `.pause` or `.resume`.

CMAltimeter

Some devices have an altimeter — in essence, a barometer. The idea here is not so
much to tell you the user's absolute altitude, since atmospheric pressure can very
considerably at a fixed altitude, but to alert you to changes in the user's relative
altitude during activity.

Start by maintaining a CMAltimeter instance, typically as an instance property.
Before using the altimeter, check the `isRelativeAltitudeAvailable` class
method. Then call `startRelativeAltitudeUpdates(to:withHandler:)` to start
delivery of CMAltitudeData objects; the key metric is the `relativeAltitude`
property, an NSNumber wrapping a Double representing meters. It starts life at 0,
and subsequent CMAltitudeData objects provide a measurement relative to that
initial base.

CMSensorRecorder

Some devices can record the output of the accelerometer over time in the background. Before using the recorder, check the `isAccelerometerRecording-`
`Available`. Then instantiate CMSensorRecorder (you do *not* need to retain the
instance) and call `recordAccelerometer(forDuration:)`. Recording is done by
the system, 50 times per second, on your behalf, regardless of whether your app
is in the foreground or even whether it is running, and stops automatically when
the `duration` is over.

To retrieve the data, instantiate CMSensorRecorder again, and call
`accelerometerData(from:to:)`. You are given a CMSensorDataList, which
unfortunately is rather tricky to deal with. First, you'll need to make CMSensor-
DataList conform to Sequence by means of an extension:

```
extension CMSensorDataList: Sequence {
    public typealias Iterator = NSFastEnumerationIterator
    public func makeIterator() -> NSFastEnumerationIterator {
        return NSFastEnumerationIterator(self)
    }
}
```

Now you can iterate over CMSensorDataList to obtain CMRecordedAccelerome-
terData instances, each consisting of a `timestamp` and an `acceleration` (a
CMAcceleration, discussed earlier in this chapter):

```
let rec = CMSensorRecorder() // and d1 and d2 are Dates
if let list = rec.accelerometerData(from: d1, to: d2) {
    for datum in list {
        if let accdatum = datum as? CMRecordedAccelerometerData {
```

```
                    let accel = accdatum.acceleration
                    let t = accdatum.timestamp
                    // do something with data here
                }
            }
        }
```

All four types of data have in common that you need user authorization to obtain them (and even if you obtain such authorization, the user can later use the Settings app to withdraw it). Your *Info.plist* must contain an entry under the "Privacy - Motion Usage Description" key (`NSMotionUsageDescription`) explaining your purpose. Oddly, there is no `requestAuthorization` method. In the past, there wasn't even any easy way to learn in advance whether we had authorization; the technique was to "tickle" the appropriate class by trying to query it for data and see if you got an error. In this example, I have a Bool property, `self.authorized`, which I set based on the outcome of trying to query the motion activity manager:

```
guard CMMotionActivityManager.isActivityAvailable() else { return }
let now = Date()
self.actman.queryActivityStarting(from:now, to:now, to:.main) { arr, err in
    let notauth = Int(CMErrorMotionActivityNotAuthorized.rawValue)
    if err != nil && (err! as NSError).code == notauth {
        self.isAuthorized = false
    } else {
        self.isAuthorized = true
    }
}
```

On the first run of that code, the system puts up the authorization request alert if necessary. The completion function is not called until the user deals with the alert, so the outcome tells you what the user decided. On subsequent runs, that same code reports the current authorization status.

New in iOS 11, however, there's an easier way: you can simply ask the class in question for its `authorizationStatus`. This returns a status enum with the usual four cases. You *still* need to "tickle" the class to summon the authorization dialog if the status is `.notDetermined`. This allows us to use a strategy similar to the one devised earlier ("Checking for Authorization" on page 841). I assume here that `self.actman` is a CMMotionActivityManager instance:

```
func checkAuthorization(andThen f:(()->())? = nil) {
    let status = CMMotionActivityManager.authorizationStatus()
    switch status {
    case .notDetermined: // bring up dialog
        let now = Date()
        self.actman.queryActivityStarting(from: now, to:now, to:.main) {
            _,err in
            print("asked for authorization")
            if err == nil {
```

```
            f?()
        }
    }
case .authorized: f?()
case .restricted: break // do nothing
case .denied: break // could beg for authorization here
}
}
```

As an example, I'll illustrate querying for historical motion activity manager data by fetching the data for the past 24 hours. I have prepared an OperationQueue property, `self.queue`:

```
let now = Date()
let yester = now - (60*60*24)
self.actman.queryActivityStarting(
    from: yester, to: now, to: self.queue) { arr, err in
        guard var acts = arr else {return}
        // ...
}
```

We now have an array of CMMotionActivity objects representing every *change* in the device's activity status. This is a value class. It has a `startDate`, a `confidence` (a CMMotionActivityConfidence, `.low`, `.medium`, or `.high`) ranking the activity manager's faith in its own categorization of what the user was doing, and a bunch of Bool properties actually categorizing the activity:

- `stationary`
- `walking`
- `running`
- `automotive`
- `cycling`
- `unknown`

A common first response to the flood of data is to pare it down (sometimes referred to as *smoothing* or *decimating*). To help with this, I've extended CMMotionActivity with a utility method that summarizes its Bool properties as a string:

```
extension CMMotionActivity {
    private func tf(_ b:Bool) -> String {
        return b ? "t" : "f"
    }
    func overallAct() -> String {
        let s = tf(self.stationary)
        let w = tf(self.walking)
        let r = tf(self.running)
        let a = tf(self.automotive)
        let c = tf(self.cycling)
```

```
        let u = tf(self.unknown)
        return "\(s) \(w) \(r) \(a) \(c) \(u)"
    }
}
```

So, as a straightforward way of paring down the data, I remove every CMMotion-Activity with no definite activity, with a low degree of confidence, or whose activity is the same as its predecessor. Then I set an instance property with my data, ready for use:

```
let blank = "f f f f f f"
acts = acts.filter {act in act.overallAct() != blank}
acts = acts.filter {act in act.confidence == .high}
for i in (1..<acts.count).reversed() {
    if acts[i].overallAct() == acts[i-1].overallAct() {
        acts.remove(at:i)
    }
}
DispatchQueue.main.async {
    self.data = acts
}
```

PART IV

Final Topics

This part of the book is a miscellany of topics.

- Chapter 22 is about files and how your app can store data persistently. It also discusses sharing files with the user and with other apps, plus the document architecture and iCloud, and surveys some common file formats.

- Chapter 23 introduces networking, with an emphasis on downloading of data, along with some specialized forms of networking such as on-demand resources and in-app purchases.

- Chapter 24 is about making your code multithreaded.

- Chapter 25 describes how to support undo in your app.

- Appendix A discusses the lifetime event messages sent to your app delegate.

- Appendix B is a catalog of some useful Swift utility functions that I've written.

- Appendix C is an excursus on asynchronous code execution.

CHAPTER 22

Persistent Storage

Your app can save data into files that persist on the device when your app isn't running and even when the device is powered down. This chapter is about how and where files are saved and retrieved. It also talks about some of the additional ways in which files can be manipulated: for example, apps can define document types in which they specialize and can hand such documents to one another, and can share documents into the cloud (iCloud), so that multiple copies of the same app can retrieve them on different devices.

The chapter also explains how user preferences are maintained in UserDefaults, and describes some specialized file formats and ways of working with their data, such as XML, JSON, SQLite, Core Data, PDF, and images.

The Sandbox

The device's contents as a whole are not open to your app's view. Instead, a limited region of the device's persistent storage is dedicated to your app alone: this is your app's *sandbox*. The idea is that every app, seeing only its own sandbox, is hindered from spying or impinging on the files belonging to other apps, and in turn is protected from having its own files spied or impinged on by other apps. Your app's sandbox is thus a safe place for you to store your data. Your sandbox, and hence your data, will be deleted if the user deletes your app; otherwise, it should reliably persist.

Standard Directories

The preferred way to refer to a file or directory is with a *file URL*. The other possible way is with a file path, or *pathname*, which is a string; if necessary, you can convert from a file URL to a file path as the URL's `path`, or from a pathname to a file URL with the URL initializer `init(fileURLWithPath:)`. But on the whole, you should try to stick with URL objects.

The sandbox contains some standard directories, and there are built-in methods for referring to them. You can obtain a URL for a standard directory by starting with a FileManager instance, which will usually be `FileManager.default`, and calling `url(for:in:appropriateFor:create:)`, like this:

```
do {
    let fm = FileManager.default
    let docsurl = try fm.url(for:.documentDirectory,
        in: .userDomainMask, appropriateFor: nil, create: false)
    // use docsurl here
} catch {
    // deal with error here
}
```

A question that will immediately occur to you is: where should I put files and folders that I want to save now and read later? The Documents directory can be a good place. But if your app supports file sharing (discussed later in this chapter), the user can see and modify your app's Documents directory through iTunes, so you might not want to put things there that the user isn't supposed to see and change. A good alternative is the Application Support directory. In iOS, each app gets a private Application Support directory in its own sandbox, so you can safely put files directly into it. This directory may not exist initially, but you can obtain it and create it at the same time:

```
do {
    let fm = FileManager.default
    let suppurl = try fm.url(for:.applicationSupportDirectory,
        in: .userDomainMask, appropriateFor: nil, create: true)
    // use suppurl here
} catch {
    // deal with error here
}
```

Temporary files, whose loss you are willing to accept (because their contents can be recreated), can be written into the Caches directory (`.cachesDirectory`) or the Temporary directory (the FileManager's `temporaryDirectory`). You can write temporary files into the Application Support folder, but by default this means they can be backed up by the user through iTunes or iCloud; to prevent that, exclude such a file from backup by way of its attributes:

```
var myFileURL = // file URL
var rv = URLResourceValues()
rv.isExcludedFromBackup = true
try myFileURL.setResourceValues(rv)
```

Figure 22-1. An app's sandbox in the Simulator

Inspecting the Sandbox

The Simulator's sandbox is a folder on your Mac that you can, with some difficulty, inspect visually. In your user *~/Library/Developer/CoreSimulator/Devices* folder, you'll find mysteriously named folders representing the different simulators. The *device.plist* file inside each folder can help you identify which simulator a folder represents; so can `xcrun simctl list` at the command line. Inside a simulator's *data/Containers/Data/Application* folder are some additional mysteriously named folders representing apps on that simulator. I don't know how to identify the different apps, but one of them is the app you're interested in, and inside it is that app's sandbox.

In Figure 22-1, I've drilled down from my user *Library* to an app that I've run in the Simulator. My app's Documents folder is visible, and I've opened it to show a folder and a couple of files that I've created programmatically (the code that created them will appear later in this chapter).

You can also view the file structure of your app's sandbox on a device. When the device is connected, choose Window → Devices and Simulators, and switch to the Devices tab. Select your device on the left; on the right, under Installed Apps, select your app. Click the Gear icon and choose Show Container to view your app's sandbox hierarchy in a modal sheet (Figure 22-2). Alternatively, choose Download Container to copy your app's sandbox to your computer; the sandbox arrives on your computer as an *.xcappdata* package, and you can open it in the Finder with Show Package Contents.

Figure 22-2. Summoning and displaying an app's sandbox on a device

Basic File Operations

Let's say we intend to create a folder *MyFolder* inside the Documents directory. We already know how to use a FileManager instance to get a URL pointing at the Documents directory. We can then generate a reference to the *MyFolder* folder, from which we can ask our FileManager instance to create the folder if it doesn't exist already:

```
let foldername = "MyFolder"
let fm = FileManager.default
let docsurl = try fm.url(for:.documentDirectory,
    in: .userDomainMask, appropriateFor: nil, create: false)
let myfolder = docsurl.appendingPathComponent(foldername)
try fm.createDirectory(at:myfolder, withIntermediateDirectories: true)
```

To learn what files and folders exist within a directory, you can ask for an array of the directory's contents:

```
let fm = FileManager.default
let docsurl = try fm.url(for:.documentDirectory,
    in: .userDomainMask, appropriateFor: nil, create: false)
let arr = try fm.contentsOfDirectory(at:docsurl,
    includingPropertiesForKeys: nil)
arr.forEach{ print($0.lastPathComponent) } // MyFolder
```

The array resulting from `contentsOfDirectory` lists full URLs of the directory's immediate contents; it is *shallow*. For a *deep* traversal of a directory's contents, you can enumerate it by means of a directory enumerator (`FileManager.Directory-Enumerator`); this is efficient with regards to memory, because you are handed just one file reference at a time. In this example, *MyFolder* is in the Documents directory, and I am looking for two *.txt* files that I have saved into *MyFolder* (as explained in the next section); I find them by doing a deep traversal of the Documents directory:

```
let fm = FileManager.default
let docsurl = try fm.url(for:.documentDirectory,
    in: .userDomainMask, appropriateFor: nil, create: false)
let dir = fm.enumerator(at:docsurl, includingPropertiesForKeys: nil)!
for case let f as URL in dir where f.pathExtension == "txt" {
    print(f.lastPathComponent) // file1.txt, file2.txt
}
```

A directory enumerator also permits you to decline to dive into a particular subdirectory (`skipDescendants`), so you can make your traversal even more efficient.

Consult the FileManager class documentation for more about what you can do with files, and see also Apple's *File System Programming Guide*.

Saving and Reading Files

Certain Cocoa classes endow their instances with the ability to write themselves out as a file and read themselves back in again later. If you can couch your data as an instance of one of these classes, persistent storage and retrieval is straightforward. The classes are NSString, NSData, NSArray, and NSDictionary. They provide methods `write(to:)` for writing and `init(contentsOf:)` for reading:

NSString and NSData

NSString and NSData objects map directly between their own contents and the contents of the file. Here, I'll generate a text file in *MyFolder* directly from a string:

```
try "howdy".write(to: myfolder.appendingPathComponent("file1.txt"),
    atomically: true, encoding:.utf8)
```

(You can also read and write an attributed string using a file in a standard format, as I mentioned in Chapter 10.)

NSArray and NSDictionary

NSArray and NSDictionary files are actually *property lists*, and require all the contents of the array or dictionary to be *property list types*. Those types are NSString, NSData, NSDate, NSNumber, NSArray, and NSDictionary. As long as you can reduce your data to an array or dictionary containing only those types, you can write it out directly to a file with `write(to:)`. Here, I create an array of strings and write it out as a property list file (the error-throwing version of `write` is new in iOS 11):

```
let arr = ["Manny", "Moe", "Jack"]
let temp = FileManager.default.temporaryDirectory
let f = temp.appendingPathComponent("pep.plist")
try (arr as NSArray).write(to: f)
```

So how do you save to a file an object of some *other* type? The strategy is to *serialize* it to an NSData object (Swift Data) — which, as we already know, can be saved directly to a file, or can be part of an array or dictionary to be saved to a file, and so the problem is solved. Serializing means that we describe the object in terms of the values of its properties. There are two approaches to serializing an object as Data — the older Cocoa way (NSCoding) and the new Swift way (Codable).

NSCoding

The Cocoa Foundation provides that if an object's class adopts the NSCoding protocol, you can convert it to an NSData and back again using the NSCoder subclasses NSKeyedArchiver and NSKeyedUnarchiver.

Many built-in Cocoa classes adopt NSCoding — and you can make your own class adopt NSCoding as well. This can become somewhat complicated because an object can refer (through a property) to another object, which may also adopt the NSCoding protocol, and thus you can end up saving an entire graph of interconnected objects if you wish. However, I'll confine myself to illustrating a simple case (and you can read Apple's *Archives and Serializations Programming Guide* for more information).

Let's say, then, that we have a simple Person class with a `firstName` property and a `lastName` property. We'll declare that it adopts the NSCoding protocol:

```
class Person: NSObject, NSCoding {
    var firstName : String
    var lastName : String
    override var description : String {
        return self.firstName + " " + self.lastName
    }
    init(firstName:String, lastName:String) {
        self.firstName = firstName
        self.lastName = lastName
        super.init()
    }
    // ... does not yet conform to NSCoding ...
}
```

To make this class actually conform to NSCoding, we must implement
encode(with:) to archive the object, and init(coder:) to unarchive the object.

In encode(with:), we must first call super if the superclass adopts NSCoding — in
this case, it doesn't — and then call the encode method for each property we want
preserved:

```
func encode(with coder: NSCoder) {
    // do not call super in this case
    coder.encode(self.lastName, forKey: "last")
    coder.encode(self.firstName, forKey: "first")
}
```

In init(coder:), we call a decode method for each property stored earlier, thus
restoring the state of our object. We must also call super, using either init(coder:) if
the superclass adopts the NSCoding protocol or the designated initializer if not:

```
required init(coder: NSCoder) {
    self.lastName = coder.decodeObject(forKey:"last") as! String
    self.firstName = coder.decodeObject(forKey:"first") as! String
    // do not call super init(coder:) in this case
    super.init()
}
```

We can test our code by creating, configuring, and saving a Person instance as a file:

```
let fm = FileManager.default
let docsurl = try fm.url(for:.documentDirectory,
    in: .userDomainMask, appropriateFor: nil, create: false)
let moi = Person(firstName: "Matt", lastName: "Neuburg")
let moidata = NSKeyedArchiver.archivedData(withRootObject: moi)
let moifile = docsurl.appendingPathComponent("moi.txt")
try moidata.write(to: moifile, options: .atomic)
```

We can retrieve the saved Person at a later time:

```
let fm = FileManager.default
let docsurl = try fm.url(for:.documentDirectory,
    in: .userDomainMask, appropriateFor: nil, create: false)
let moifile = docsurl.appendingPathComponent("moi.txt")
let persondata = try Data(contentsOf: moifile)
let person = NSKeyedUnarchiver.unarchiveObject(with: persondata) as! Person
print(person) // "Matt Neuburg"
```

If the Data object is itself the entire content of the file, as here, then instead of using archivedData(withRootObject:) and unarchiveObject(with:), you can skip the intermediate Data object and use archiveRootObject(_:toFile:) and unarchive-Object(withFile:).

Archiving a single Person may seem like overkill; why didn't we just make a text file consisting of the first and last names? But imagine that a Person has a lot more properties, or that we have an array of hundreds of Persons, or an array of hundreds of dictionaries where one value in each dictionary is a Person; now the power of an archivable Person is evident.

Even though Person now adopts the NSCoding protocol, an NSArray containing a Person object still cannot be written to a file using NSArray's write(to:), because Person is still not a property list type. But the array can be archived with NSKeyed-Archiver and the resulting Data object *can* be written to a file with write(to:). That's because NSArray conforms to NSCoding and, if its elements are Person objects, all its elements conform to NSCoding as well.

Codable

New in Swift 4, an object can be serialized (archived) as long as it conforms to the Encodable protocol, and can be restored from serial form (unarchived) as long as it conforms to the Decodable protocol. Most commonly, an object will conform to both, and this will be expressed by having it adopt the Codable protocol. There are three modes of serialization:

Property list
   Use PropertyListEncoder encode(_:) to encode and PropertyListDecoder decode(_:from:) to decode.

JSON
   Use JSONEncoder encode(_:) to encode and JSONDecoder decode(_:from:) to decode.

NSCoder
   Use NSKeyedArchiver encodeEncodable(_:forKey:) to encode and NSKeyed-Unarchiver decodeDecodable(_:forKey:) to decode.

You'll probably prefer to use Swift Codable rather than Cocoa NSCoding wherever possible. It has three broad advantages:

- Not only a class instance but also a struct instance can be encoded; you can even encode an enum instance, provided the enum is RawRepresentable (that is, it has a raw value). Most built-in Swift types are Codable right out of the box.

- The result of decoding is strongly typed (as opposed to NSCoding which yields an Any that has to be cast down).

- In the vast majority of cases, your object type will be able to adopt Codable without any further code. There are encode(to:) and init(from:) methods, similar to NSCoding encode(with:) and init(coder:), but you usually won't need to implement them because the default methods, inherited through a protocol extension, will be sufficient.

To illustrate, I'll rewrite my Person class to adopt Codable instead of NSCoding:

```
class Person: NSObject, Codable {
    var firstName : String
    var lastName : String
    override var description : String {
        return self.firstName + " " + self.lastName
    }
    init(firstName:String, lastName:String) {
        self.firstName = firstName
        self.lastName = lastName
        super.init()
    }
}
```

That's all! Person conforms to Codable with no further effort on our part. The primary reason is that our properties are Strings, and String is itself Codable. To save a Person to a file, we just have to pick an encoding format. I recommend using a property list unless there is some reason not to; it is simplest, and is closest to what NSKeyedArchiver does under the hood:

```
let fm = FileManager.default
let docsurl = try fm.url(for:.documentDirectory,
    in: .userDomainMask, appropriateFor: nil, create: false)
let moi = Person(firstName: "Matt", lastName: "Neuburg")
let moidata = try PropertyListEncoder().encode(moi)
let moifile = docsurl.appendingPathComponent("moi.txt")
try moidata.write(to: moifile, options: .atomic)
```

And here's how to retrieve our saved Person later:

```
let fm = FileManager.default
let docsurl = try fm.url(for:.documentDirectory,
    in: .userDomainMask, appropriateFor: nil, create: false)
let moifile = docsurl.appendingPathComponent("moi.txt")
let persondata = try Data(contentsOf: moifile)
let person = try PropertyListDecoder().decode(Person.self, from: persondata)
print(person) // "Matt Neuburg"
```

To save an array of Codable Person objects, do exactly the same thing: Array conforms to Codable, so use PropertyListEncoder to encode the array directly into a Data object and call `write(to:options:)`, precisely as we did for a single Person object. To retrieve the array, read the data from the file as a Data object and use a PropertyListDecoder to call `decode([Person].self, from:data)`.

When your goal is to serialize your own object type to a file, there usually won't be any more to it than that. Your Codable implementation may be more elaborate when the format of the encoded data is out of your hands, such as when you are communicating with a server through a JSON API dictated by the server. I'll illustrate later in this chapter.

The existence of Codable does not mean that you'll never need to use NSCoding. Cocoa is written in Objective-C; its encodable object types adopt NSCoding, not Codable. And the vast majority of your objects will be Cocoa objects. For example, if you want to turn a UIColor into a Data object, you'll use an NSKeyedArchiver, not a PropertyListEncoder; UIColor adopts NSCoding, not Codable.

You can, however, combine Swift Codable with Cocoa NSCoding, thanks to the NSCoder subclass methods `encodeEncodable(_:forKey:)` and `decodeDecodable(_:forKey:)`. For example, suppose you have a view controller that is to participate in view controller state saving and restoration (Chapter 6). You implement `encodeRestorableState(with:)` to store your view controller's property values in the coder:

```
class Pep: UIViewController {
    let boy : String
    // ...
    override func encodeRestorableState(with coder: NSCoder) {
        super.encodeRestorableState(with:coder)
        coder.encode(self.boy, forKey:"boy")
    }
}
```

That example works because `self.boy` is a String, String is bridged to NSString, and NSString adopts NSCoding. But now suppose that our view controller class, Pep, also has a property `prop` whose type is a struct MyStruct. In the past you couldn't have archived a MyStruct directly into the coder, but with Swift 4 you can, because MyStruct can adopt Codable. `coder` is typed as an NSCoder, but in reality it is an NSKeyedArchiver; cast it down and call `encodeEncodable(_:forKey:)`, like this:

```
class Pep: UIViewController {
    let boy : String
    let prop : MyStruct // adopts Codable
    // ...
    override func encodeRestorableState(with coder: NSCoder) {
        super.encodeRestorableState(with:coder)
        coder.encode(self.boy, forKey: "boy")
        let arch = coder as! NSKeyedArchiver
        try! arch.encodeEncodable(self.prop, forKey: "prop")
    }
}
```

The complementary implementation of decodeRestorableState(with:) is parallel: cast the coder down to an NSKeyedUnarchiver and call decodeDecodable(_:for-Key:) to extract the encoded struct.

User Defaults

User defaults (UserDefaults) act as persistent storage of the user's preferences. They are little more, really, than a special case of an NSDictionary property list file. You talk to the UserDefaults standard object much as if it were a dictionary; it has keys and values.

Because user defaults is actually a property list file, the only legal values that can be stored in it are property list values. Therefore, everything I said in the preceding section about saving objects applies. If an object type is not a property list type, you'll have to archive it to a Data object if you want to store it in user defaults. If the object type is a class that belongs to Cocoa and adopts NSCoding, you'll archive it through an NSKeyedArchiver. If the object type belongs to you, you might prefer to make it adopt Codable and archive it through a PropertyListEncoder.

The user defaults dictionary is saved for you automatically as a property list file — but you don't know where or when, and you don't care. You simply set or retrieve values from the dictionary by way of their keys, secure in the knowledge that the file is being read into memory or saved as a file as needed. Your chief concern is to make sure that you've written everything needful into user defaults before your app terminates; this will usually mean when the app delegate receives applicationDidEnter-Background(_:) at the latest (see Appendix A). If you're worried that your app might crash, you can tell the standard object to synchronize as a way of forcing it to save right now, but this is rarely necessary.

To provide the value for a key before the user has had a chance to do so — the default default, as it were — use register(defaults:). What you're supplying here is a transient dictionary whose key–value pairs will be held in memory but not saved; a pair will be used only if there is no pair with the same key already stored in the user defaults dictionary. For example:

Figure 22-3. An app's preferences interface

```
UserDefaults.standard.register(defaults: [
    Default.HazyStripy : HazyStripy.hazy.rawValue,
    Default.Color1 : NSKeyedArchiver.archivedData(
        withRootObject: UIColor.blue),
    Default.Color2 : NSKeyedArchiver.archivedData(
        withRootObject: UIColor.red),
    Default.Color3 : NSKeyedArchiver.archivedData(
        withRootObject: UIColor.green),
        Default.CardMatrixRows : 4,
    Default.CardMatrixColumns : 3,
])
```

The idea is that we call `register(defaults:)` extremely early as the app launches. Either the app has run at some time previously and the user has set these preferences, in which case this call has no effect and does no harm, or not, in which case we now have initial values for these preferences with which to get started. In the game app from which that code comes, we start out with a 4×3 game layout, but the user can change this at any time.

You will probably want to offer your user a way to interact explicitly with the defaults. One possibility is that your app provides some kind of interface. For example, the game app from which the previous code comes has a tab bar interface; in the second tab, the user explicitly sets the very preferences whose default values are configured in that code (Figure 22-3).

Alternatively, you can provide a *settings bundle*, consisting mostly of one or more property list files describing an interface and the corresponding user default keys and their initial values; the Settings app is then responsible for translating your instructions into an actual interface, and for presenting it to the user. Writing a settings bundle is described in Apple's *Preferences and Settings Programming Guide*.

Using a settings bundle means that the user has to leave your app to access preferences, and you don't get the kind of control over the interface that you have within your own app. Also, the user can set your preferences while your app is backgrounded or not running; you'll need to register for `UserDefaults.didChangeNotification` in order to hear about this. Still, a settings bundle has some clear advantages. Keeping the preferences interface out of your app can make your app's own interface cleaner and simpler. You don't have to write any of the "glue" code that coordinates the preferences interface with the user default values. And it may be appropriate for the user to be able to set at least certain preferences for your app when your app isn't running. Moreover, you can transport your user directly from your app to your app's preferences in the Settings app, and a Back button then appears in the status bar, making it easy for the user to return from Settings to your app:

```
let url = URL(string:UIApplicationOpenSettingsURLString)!
UIApplication.shared.open(url)
```

It is common practice to misuse UserDefaults ever so slightly for various purposes. For example, every method in your app can access the `UserDefaults.standard` object, so it often serves as a global "drop" where one instance can deposit a piece of information for another instance to pick up later, when those two instances might not have ready communication with one another or might not even exist simultaneously.

UserDefaults is also a lightweight alternative to the built-in view controller–based state saving and restoration mechanism discussed in Chapter 6. My Zotz! app (Figure 22-3) is a case in point. In addition to using the user defaults to store the user's explicit preferences, it also misuses them to store state information: it records the state of the game board and the card deck into user defaults every time these change, so that if the app is terminated and then launched again later, we can restore the game as it was when the user left off. One might argue that the contents of the card deck are not a user preference, so I am misusing the user defaults to store data. However, while purists may grumble, it's a very small amount of data and I don't think the distinction is terribly significant in this case.

Yet another use of UserDefaults is as a way to communicate data between your app and an extension provided by your app. For example, let's say you've written a today extension (Chapter 13) whose interface details depend upon some data belonging to your app. After configuring your extension and your app to constitute an app group, both the extension and the app can access the UserDefaults associated with the app group (call `init(suiteName:)` instead of `standard`). For more information, see the "Handling Common Scenarios" chapter of Apple's *App Extension Programming Guide*.

Figure 22-4. The iTunes file sharing interface

Simple Sharing and Previewing of Files

iOS provides some simple and safe passageways by which a file can pass in and out of your sandbox. File sharing lets the user manipulate the contents of your app's Documents directory. UIDocumentInteractionController allows the user to tell another app to hand your app a copy of a document, or to tell your app to hand a copy of a document to another app. UIDocumentInteractionController also permits previewing a document, provided it is compatible with Quick Look.

File Sharing

File sharing means that an app's Documents directory becomes accessible to the user through iTunes (Figure 22-4). The user can add files to your app's Documents directory, and can save files and folders from your app's Documents directory to the computer, as well as renaming and deleting files and folders. This could be appropriate, for example, if your app works with common types of file that the user might obtain elsewhere, such as PDFs or JPEGs.

To support file sharing, set the *Info.plist* key "Application supports iTunes file sharing" (`UIFileSharingEnabled`) to YES.

Once your entire Documents directory is exposed to the user this way, you are unlikely to use the Documents directory to store private files. As I mentioned earlier, I like to use the Application Support directory instead.

Your app doesn't get any automatic notification when the user has altered the contents of the Documents directory. Noticing that the situation has changed and responding appropriately is entirely up to you; Apple's DocInteraction sample code demonstrates one approach using the kernel-level `kqueue` mechanism.

Document Types and Receiving a Document

Your app can declare itself willing to open documents of a certain type. In this way, if another app obtains a document of this type, it can propose to hand a copy of the document over to your app. For example, the user might download the document

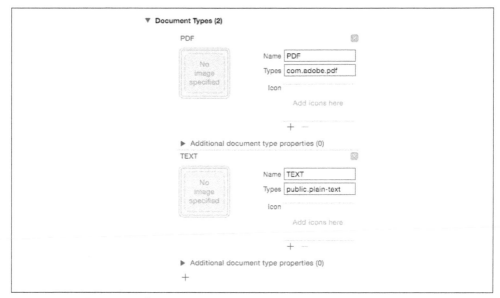

Figure 22-5. Creating a document type

with Mobile Safari, or receive it in a mail message with the Mail app; now we need a way to get it from Safari or Mail to you.

To let the system know that your app is a candidate for receiving a certain kind of document, you will configure the "Document types" (`CFBundleDocumentTypes`) key in your *Info.plist*. This is an array, where each entry will be a dictionary specifying a document type by using keys such as "Document Content Type UTIs" (`LSItem-ContentTypes`), "Document Type Name" (`CFBundleTypeName`), `CFBundleTypeIcon-Files`, and `LSHandlerRank`.

The simplest method for configuring the *Info.plist* is through the interface available in the Info tab when you edit the target. For example, suppose I want to declare that my app opens PDFs and text files. In my target's Info tab in Xcode, I would edit the Document Types section to look like Figure 22-5.

Now suppose the user receives a PDF in an email message. The Mail app can display this PDF, but the user can also bring up an activity view offering, among other things, to copy the file to some other app. The interface will resemble Figure 22-6; various apps that can deal with a PDF are listed here, and my app (MyCoolApp) is among them.

So far, so good. But what if the user actually *taps* the button that sends the PDF over to my app? Then my app delegate's `application(_:open:options:)` is called. When that happens, my app has been brought to the front, either by launching it from scratch or by reviving it from background suspension; its job is now to handle the

Figure 22-6. The Mail app offers to hand off a PDF

opening of the document whose URL has arrived as the second parameter. The system has already copied the document into an *Inbox* folder which it has created in my Documents directory for exactly this purpose.

 If your app implements file sharing, the user can see the *Inbox* folder using iTunes; you may wish to delete the *Inbox* folder, therefore, as soon as you're done retrieving files from it.

In this simple example, my app has just one view controller, which has an outlet to a web view where we will display any PDFs that arrive in this fashion. So my app delegate contains this code:

```
func application(_ app: UIApplication, open url: URL,
    options: [UIApplicationOpenURLOptionsKey : Any]) -> Bool {
        let vc = self.window!.rootViewController as! ViewController
        vc.displayDoc(url: url)
        return true
}
```

And my view controller contains this code:

```
func displayDoc (url:URL) {
    let req = URLRequest(url: url)
    self.wv.loadRequest(req)
}
```

In real life, things might be more complicated. Our implementation of `application(_:open:options:)` might check to see whether this really *is* a PDF, and return `false` if it isn't. Also, our app might be in the middle of something else, possibly displaying a completely different view controller's view; realizing that `application(_:open:options:)` can arrive at any time, we may have to be prepared to drop whatever we were doing and display the incoming document instead.

If our app is launched from scratch by the arrival of this URL, `application(_:did-FinishLaunchingWithOptions:)` will be sent to our app delegate as usual. The `options:` dictionary will contain the `UIApplicationLaunchOptionsURLKey`, and we can take into account, if we like, the fact that we are being launched specifically to open a document. If we return `true` as usual, `application(_:open:options:)` will arrive in good order after our interface has been set up; but if we have dealt completely with the URL in `application(_:didFinishLaunchingWithOptions:)`, we can return `false` to prevent `application(_:open:options:)` from being called.

The example I've been discussing assumes that the UTI for the document type is standard and well-known. It is also possible that your app will operate on a new document type, that is, a type of document that the app itself defines. In that case, you'll also want to add this UTI to your app's list of Exported UTIs in the *Info.plist*. I'll give an example later in this chapter.

Handing Over a Document

The converse of the situation discussed in the previous section is this: your app has somehow acquired a document and wants to let the user hand over a copy of it to some other app to deal with it. This is done through the UIDocumentInteraction-Controller class. This class operates asynchronously, so retaining an instance of it is up to you; typically, you'll store it in a property, and there is no reason not to initialize this property directly:

```
let dic = UIDocumentInteractionController()
```

For example, assuming we have a file URL `url` pointing to a stored document file, presenting the interface for handing the document over to some other application could be as simple as this (`sender` is a button that the user has just tapped):

```
self.dic.url = url
let v = sender as! UIView
self.dic.presentOpenInMenu(from:v.bounds, in: v, animated: true)
```

The interface is an activity view (Figure 22-7; see Chapter 13). There are actually two activity views available, each of which is summoned by either of two methods (the first method of each pair expects a CGRect and a UIView, while the second expects a UIBarButtonItem):

```
presentOpenInMenu(from:in:animated:)
presentOpenInMenu(from:animated:)
```
Presents an activity view listing apps to which the document can be copied.

Figure 22-7. The document Open In activity view

```
presentOptionsMenu(from:in:animated:)
presentOptionsMenu(from:animated:)
```
> Presents an activity view listing apps to which the document can be copied, along with other possible actions, such as Message, Mail, Copy, and Print.

Previewing a Document

A UIDocumentInteractionController can be used for an entirely different purpose: it can present a preview of the document, if the document is of a type for which preview is enabled, by calling `presentPreview(animated:)`. You must give the UIDocument-InteractionController a delegate (UIDocumentInteractionControllerDelegate), and the delegate must implement `documentInteractionControllerViewControllerFor-Preview(_:)`, returning an existing view controller that will contain the preview's view controller. So, here we ask for the preview:

```
self.dic.url = url
self.dic.delegate = self
self.dic.presentPreview(animated:true)
```

In the delegate, we supply the view controller; it happens that, in my code, this delegate *is* a view controller, so it simply returns `self`:

```
func documentInteractionControllerViewControllerForPreview(
    _ controller: UIDocumentInteractionController) -> UIViewController {
        return self
}
```

If the view controller returned were a UINavigationController, the preview's view controller would be pushed onto it; in this case it isn't, so the preview's view controller is a presented view controller with a Done button. The preview interface also contains a Share button that lets the user summon the Options activity view (Figure 22-8).

Figure 22-8. The preview interface

 There is another way for the user to reach this interface. If you call `present-OptionsMenu` on your UIDocumentInteractionController, and if its delegate implements `documentInteractionControllerViewControllerForPreview(_:)`, then the activity view will contain a Quick Look icon that the user can tap to summon the preview interface.

Additional delegate methods allow you to track what's happening in the interface presented by the UIDocumentInteractionController. Probably most important are those that inform you that key stages of the interaction are ending:

- `documentInteractionControllerDidDismissOptionsMenu(_:)`
- `documentInteractionControllerDidDismissOpenInMenu(_:)`
- `documentInteractionControllerDidEndPreview(_:)`
- `documentInteractionController(_:didEndSendingToApplication:)`

Quick Look Previews

Previews are actually provided through the Quick Look framework. You can skip the UIDocumentInteractionController and present the preview yourself through a QLPreviewController; you'll need to `import QuickLook`. It's a view controller, so to display the preview you show it as a presented view controller or push it onto a navigation controller's stack, just as UIDocumentInteractionController would have done.

A nice feature of QLPreviewController is that you can give it more than one document to preview; the user can move between these, within the preview, by paging sideways or using a table of contents summoned by a button at the bottom of the interface. Apart from this, the interface looks like the interface presented by the UIDocumentInteractionController.

In this example, I may have somewhere in my Documents directory one or more PDF or text documents. I acquire a list of their URLs and present a preview for them (`self.exts` has been initialized to a set consisting of [`"pdf"`, `"txt"`]):

```
self.docs = [URL]()
do {
    let fm = FileManager.default
    let docsurl = try fm.url(for:.documentDirectory,
        in: .userDomainMask, appropriateFor: nil, create: false)
    let dir = fm.enumerator(at: docsurl, includingPropertiesForKeys: nil)!
    for case let f as URL in dir {
        if self.exts.contains(f.pathExtension) {
            if QLPreviewController.canPreview(f as QLPreviewItem) {
                self.docs!.append(f)
            }
        }
    }
    guard self.docs!.count > 0 else { return }
    let preview = QLPreviewController()
    preview.dataSource = self
    preview.currentPreviewItemIndex = 0
    self.present(preview, animated: true)
} catch {
    print(error)
}
```

You'll notice that I haven't told the QLPreviewController what documents to preview. That is the job of QLPreviewController's data source. In my code, I (`self`) am also the data source. I simply fetch the requested information from the list of URLs, which I previously saved into `self.docs`:

```
func numberOfPreviewItems(in controller: QLPreviewController) -> Int {
    return self.docs!.count
}
func previewController(_ controller: QLPreviewController,
    previewItemAt index: Int) -> QLPreviewItem {
        return self.docs![index] as QLPreviewItem
}
```

The second data source method requires us to return an object that adopts the QLPreviewItem protocol. By a wildly improbable coincidence, URL *does* adopt this protocol, so the example works.

 New in iOS 11, you can supply your own Quick Look preview for document types that you own. I'll discuss that later in this chapter.

Document Architecture

A *document* is a file of a specific type. If your app's basic operation depends on opening, saving, and maintaining documents of a type particular to itself, you may want to take advantage of the *document architecture*. At its simplest, this architecture revolves around the UIDocument class. Think of a UIDocument instance as managing the relationship between your app's internal model data and a document file storing that data.

Interacting with a stored document file involves a number of pesky issues. The good news is that UIDocument handles all of them seamlessly:

- Reading or writing your data might take some time, so UIDocument does those things on a background thread.

- A document owned by your app may be exposed to reading and writing by other apps, so your app must read and write to that document coherently without interference from other apps. The solution is to use an NSFileCoordinator. UIDocument does that for you.

- Your document data needs to be synchronized to the document file. UIDocument provides autosaving behavior, so that your data is written out automatically whenever it changes.

- Information about a document can become stale while the document is open. To prevent this, the NSFilePresenter protocol notifies editors that a document has changed. UIDocument participates in this system.

- With iCloud, your app's documents on one of the user's devices can automatically be mirrored onto another of the user's devices. UIDocument is the simplest gateway for allowing your documents to participate in iCloud.

Getting started with UIDocument is not difficult. You'll declare a UIDocument subclass, and you'll override two methods:

load(fromContents:ofType:)
: Called when it's time to open a document from its file. You are expected to convert the contents value into a model object that your app can use, and to store that model object, probably in an instance property.

contents(forType:)
: Called when it's time to save a document to its file. You are expected to convert the app's model object into a Data instance (or, if your document is a package, a FileWrapper) and return it.

To instantiate a UIDocument, call its designated initializer, init(fileURL:). This sets the UIDocument's fileURL property, and associates the UIDocument with the file at this URL; typically, this association will remain constant for the rest of the document's lifetime. You will then probably store the UIDocument instance in an instance property, and use it to create (if necessary), open, save, and close the document file:

Make a new document

> Having initialized the UIDocument with a `fileURL:` pointing to a nonexistent file, send it `save(to:for:completionHandler:)`; the first argument will be the UIDocument's own `fileURL`, and the second argument (a UIDocumentSave-Operation) will be `.forCreating`.
>
> This, in turn, causes `contents(forType:)` to be called, and the contents of an empty document will saved out to a file. Your UIDocument subclass will need to supply some default value representing the model data when there is no data.

Open an existing document

> Send the UIDocument instance `open(completionHandler:)`.
>
> This, in turn, causes `load(fromContents:ofType:)` to be called.

Save an existing document

> There are two approaches to saving an existing document:
>
> *Autosave*
>
> > Usually, you'll simply mark the document as "dirty" by calling `updateChange-Count(_:)`. From time to time, the UIDocument will notice this situation and will save the document to its file for you, calling `contents(forType:)` as it does so.
>
> *Manual save*
>
> > On certain occasions, waiting for autosave won't be appropriate. We've already seen one such occasion — when the document file needs to be created on the spot. Another case is that the app is going into the background; we will want to preserve our document there and then, in case the app is terminated. To force the document to be saved right now, call `save(to:for:completionHandler:)`; the second argument will be `.forOverwriting`.
> >
> > Alternatively, if you know you're finished with the document (perhaps the interface displaying the document is about to be torn down), you can call `close(completionHandler:)`.

The `open`, `close`, and `save` methods take a `completionHandler:` function. This is UIDocument's solution to the fact that reading and saving may take time. The file operations themselves take place on a background thread; your completion function is then called on the main thread.

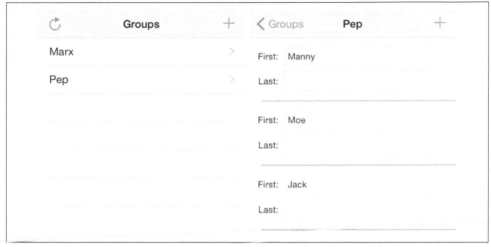

Figure 22-9. The People Groups interface

A Basic Document Example

We now know enough for an example! I'll reuse my Person class from earlier in this chapter. Imagine a document effectively consisting of multiple Person instances; I'll call each such document a *people group*. Our app, People Groups, will list all people group documents in the user's Documents folder; the user can then select any people group document and our app will open that document and display its contents, allowing the user to create a new Person and to edit any existing Person's firstName or lastName (Figure 22-9).

My first step is to edit my project and use the Info tab to define a custom UTI in my app's *Info.plist,* associating a file type com.neuburg.pplgrp with a file extension "pplgrp"; I also define a document type corresponding to this UTI (Figure 22-10).

Now let's write our UIDocument subclass, which I'll call PeopleDocument. A document consists of multiple Persons, so a natural model implementation is a Person array. PeopleDocument therefore has a public people property, initialized to an empty Person array; this will not only hold the model data when we have it, but will also give us something to save into a new empty document. Since Person implements Codable, a Person array can be archived directly into a Data object, and our implementation of the loading and saving methods is straightforward:

```
class PeopleDocument: UIDocument {
    var people = [Person]()
    override func load(fromContents contents: Any,
        ofType typeName: String?) throws {
            if let contents = contents as? Data {
                if let arr = try? PropertyListDecoder().decode(
                    [Person].self, from: contents) {
```

Figure 22-10. Defining a custom UTI

```
                        self.people = arr
                        return
                }
        }
        // if we get here, there was some kind of problem
        throw NSError(domain: "NoDataDomain", code: -1, userInfo: nil)
    }

    override func contents(forType typeName: String) throws -> Any {
        if let data = try? PropertyListEncoder().encode(self.people) {
            return data
        }
        // if we get here, there was some kind of problem
        throw NSError(domain: "NoDataDomain", code: -2, userInfo: nil)
    }
}
```

The first view controller, GroupLister, is a master table view (its view appears on the left in Figure 22-9). It merely looks in the Documents directory for people group documents and lists them by name; it also provides an interface for letting the user ask to create a new people group. None of that is challenging, so I won't discuss it further.

The second view controller, PeopleLister, is the detail view; it is also a table view (its view appears on the right in Figure 22-9). It displays the first and last names of the people in the currently open people group document. This is the only place where we actually work with PeopleDocument, so let's focus our attention on that.

PeopleLister's designated initializer demands a `fileURL:` parameter pointing to a people group document, and uses it to set the `self.fileURL` property. From this, we instantiate a PeopleDocument, keeping a reference to it in the `self.doc` property. PeopleLister's own `people` property, acting as the data model for its table view, is nothing but a pointer to this PeopleDocument's `people` property.

As PeopleLister comes into existence, the document file pointed to by `self.fileURL` need not yet exist. If it doesn't, we create it; if it does, we open it. In both cases, our `people` data are now ready for display, so the completion function reloads the table view:

```
let fileURL : URL
var doc : PeopleDocument!
var people : [Person] { // point to the document's model object
    get { return self.doc.people }
    set { self.doc.people = newValue }
}
init(fileURL:URL) {
    self.fileURL = fileURL
    super.init(nibName: "PeopleLister", bundle: nil)
}
required init(coder: NSCoder) {
    fatalError("NSCoding not supported")
}
override func viewDidLoad() {
    super.viewDidLoad()
    self.title = (self.fileURL.lastPathComponent as NSString)
        .deletingPathExtension
    // ... interface configuration goes here ...
    let fm = FileManager.default
    self.doc = PeopleDocument(fileURL:self.fileURL)
    func listPeople(_ success:Bool) {
        if success {
            self.tableView.reloadData()
        }
    }
    if let _ = try? self.fileURL.checkResourceIsReachable() {
        self.doc.open(completionHandler: listPeople)
    } else {
        self.doc.save(to:self.doc.fileURL,
            for: .forCreating, completionHandler: listPeople)
    }
}
```

Displaying people, creating a new person, and allowing the user to edit a person's first and last names, are all trivial uses of a table view (Chapter 8). Let's proceed to the only other aspect of PeopleLister that involves working with PeopleDocument, namely saving.

When the user performs a significant editing maneuver, such as creating or deleting a person or editing a person's first or last name, PeopleLister tells its PeopleDocument that the document is dirty, and allows autosaving to take it from there:

```
self.doc.updateChangeCount(.done)
```

When the app is about to go into the background, or when PeopleLister's own view is disappearing, PeopleLister forces PeopleDocument to save immediately:

```
func forceSave(_: Any?) {
    self.tableView.endEditing(true)
    self.doc.save(to:self.doc.fileURL, for:.forOverwriting)
}
```

That's all it takes! Adding UIDocument support to your app is easy, because UIDocument is merely acting as a supplier and preserver of your app's data model object. The UIDocument class documentation may give the impression that this is a large and complex class, but that's chiefly because it is so heavily customizable both at high and low levels; for the most part, you won't need any such customization. You might work with your UIDocument's undo manager to give it a more sophisticated understanding of what constitutes a significant change in your data; I'll talk about undo managers in Chapter 25. For further details, see Apple's *Document-based App Programming Guide for iOS*.

New in iOS 11, if your app supports iTunes file sharing, and if the *Info.plist* key "Supports opening documents in place" (LSSupportsOpeningDocumentsInPlace) is also set to YES, files in your app's Documents directory will be visible in the Files app, and the user can tap one to call your app delegate's application(_:open:options:), as described earlier in this chapter. That's safe only if your document access uses NSFile-Presenter and NSFileCoordinator; but if you're using UIDocument, it does.

iCloud

Once your app is operating through UIDocument, basic iCloud compatibility effectively falls right into your lap. You have just two steps to perform:

Obtain iCloud entitlements

> Edit the target and, in the Capabilities tab, set the iCloud switch to On. This causes a transaction to take place between Xcode and the Member Center; automatically, your app gets a ubiquity container, and an appropriately configured entitlements file is added to the project (Figure 22-11).

Figure 22-11. Turning on iCloud support

Obtain an iCloud-compatible directory

Early in your app's lifetime, call FileManager's `url(forUbiquityContainer-Identifier:)` (typically passing `nil` as the argument), on a background thread, to obtain the URL of the cloud-shared directory. Any documents your app puts here by way of your UIDocument subclass will be automatically shared into the cloud.

Thus, having thrown the switch in the Capabilities tab, I can make my People Groups example app iCloud-compatible with just two code changes. In the app delegate, as my app launches, I step out to a background thread (Chapter 24), obtain the cloud-shared directory's URL, and then step back to the main thread and retain the URL through a property, `self.ubiq`:

```
DispatchQueue.global(qos:.default).async {
    let fm = FileManager.default
    let ubiq = fm.url(forUbiquityContainerIdentifier:nil)
    DispatchQueue.main.async {
        self.ubiq = ubiq
    }
}
```

When I determine where to seek and save people groups, I specify `ubiq` — unless it is `nil`, implying that iCloud is not enabled, in which case I specify the user's Documents folder:

```
var docsurl : URL {
    let del = UIApplication.shared.delegate
    if let ubiq = (del as! AppDelegate).ubiq {
        return ubiq
    } else {
        do {
            let fm = FileManager.default
            return try fm.url(for:.documentDirectory, in: .userDomainMask,
                appropriateFor: nil, create: false)
        } catch {
            print(error)
```

```
            }
        }
        return NSURL() as URL // shouldn't happen
    }
```

To test, iCloud Drive must be turned on under iCloud in my device's Settings. I run the app and create a people group with some people in it. I then switch to a different device and run the app there, and tap the Refresh button. This is a very crude implementation, purely for testing purposes; it looks through the docsurl directory, first for cloud items to download, and then for pplgrp files:

```
do {
    let fm = FileManager.default
    self.files = try fm.contentsOfDirectory(at: self.docsurl,
        includingPropertiesForKeys: nil).filter {
            if fm.isUbiquitousItem(at:$0) {
                try fm.startDownloadingUbiquitousItem(at:$0)
            }
            return $0.pathExtension == "pplgrp"
    }
    self.tableView.reloadData()
} catch {
    print(error)
}
```

Presto, the app on this device now displays my people group documents created on a different device! It's quite thrilling.

My Refresh button approach, although it works (possibly after a couple of tries), is decidedly crude. My UIDocument works with iCloud, but my app is not a good iCloud citizen. The truth is that I should not be using FileManager like this; instead, I should be running an NSMetadataQuery. The usual strategy is:

1. Instantiate NSMetadataQuery and retain the instance.

2. Configure the search. This means giving the metadata query a search scope of NSMetadataQueryUbiquitousDocumentsScope, and supplying a serial queue (OperationQueue, see Chapter 24) for it to run on.

3. Register for notifications such as .NSMetadataQueryDidFinishGathering and .NSMetadataQueryDidUpdate.

4. Start the search by calling start. The NSMetadataQuery instance then remains in place, with the search continuing to run more or less constantly, for the entire lifetime of the app.

5. When a notification arrives, check the NSMetadataQuery's results. These will be NSMetadataItem objects, whose value(forAttribute:NSMetadataItem-URLKey) is the document file URL.

Similarly, in my earlier code I called `checkResourceIsReachable`, but for a cloud item I should be calling `checkPromisedItemIsReachable` instead.

Further iCloud details are outside the scope of this discussion; see Apple's *iCloud Design Guide*. Getting started is easy; making your app a good iCloud citizen, capable of dealing with the complexities that iCloud may entail, is not. What if the currently open document changes because someone edited it on another device? What if that change is in conflict with changes I've made on *this* device? What if the availability of iCloud changes while the app is open — for example, the user switches it on, or switches it off? Apple's sample code has a bad habit of skirting these knotty issues.

Document Browser

An iOS device has no universal file browser interface parallel to the Mac desktop's Finder. So if your app maintains document files, it must also implement the nitty-gritty details of file management, allowing the user not only to see a list of the documents but also to delete them, rename them, move them, and so forth. This is a heavy responsibility, and matters are not helped by the fact that every app must provide its own independent implementation of all this functionality.

New in iOS 11, the UIDocumentBrowserViewController class lifts that responsibility from your app by providing a standard interface where the user can manage your app's documents — plus the documents of every other app that maintains its documents in a compatible way. In effect, it puts the Files app interface inside your app, along with all its file management facilities, as well as exposing your app's documents to the Files app itself.

If we incorporate UIDocumentBrowserViewController into our People Groups app, we can eliminate the GroupLister view controller class that has been acting as a master view controller to list our documents (left side in Figure 22-9). We can also ignore everything I said in the preceding section about how to make our app participate in iCloud; with UIDocumentBrowserViewController, our app participates in iCloud *automatically*, with no need for any code or entitlements.

Let's try it. The easiest way to get started is from the template provided by Apple; choose File → New → Project and choose iOS → Application → Document Based App. The template provides three important features:

Info.plist configuration
> The template gives us a start on the configuration of our *Info.plist*. In particular, it includes the "Supports Document Browser" key (`UISupportsDocumentBrowser`) with its value set to YES.

Classes and storyboard

The template provides a basic set of classes: in addition to a UIDocumentBrowserViewController subclass (DocumentBrowserViewController), it gives us a UIDocument subclass called Document, along with a DocumentViewController intended for display of documents of that class, parallel to our PeopleDocument and PeopleLister, and puts instances of the two view controllers into the storyboard.

Structure

The template makes the UIDocumentBrowserViewController instance our app's *root view controller*. This is absolutely essential. The entire remainder of our app's interface, such as when the user is viewing the contents of a document, must be displayed through a fullscreen presented view controller.

The first step is to complete the configuration of the *Info.plist*. As before, we must declare and export our document type; I'll give it a file type `com.neuburg.pplgrp2` with a file extension `"pplgrp2"`, to distinguish it from the document type owned by the previous example app. Apple says that our UTI must also conform to `public.data` and `public.content`, and that our document type must declare a role of Editor and a rank of Owner (Figure 22-12).

Now we customize DocumentBrowserViewController. The template gets us started, setting this class as its own delegate (UIDocumentBrowserViewControllerDelegate) and allowing document creation and single selection:

```
override func viewDidLoad() {
    super.viewDidLoad()
    self.delegate = self
    self.allowsDocumentCreation = true
    self.allowsPickingMultipleItems = false
}
```

The template also implements delegate methods for when the user selects an existing document in our app's ubiquity container or imports a document into our app's ubiquity container from elsewhere; both call a custom method, `presentDocument(at:)`, for which the template provides a stub implementation:

```
func documentBrowser(_ controller: UIDocumentBrowserViewController,
    didPickDocumentURLs documentURLs: [URL]) {
        guard let sourceURL = documentURLs.first else { return }
        self.presentDocument(at: sourceURL)
}
func documentBrowser(_ controller: UIDocumentBrowserViewController,
    didImportDocumentAt sourceURL: URL,
    toDestinationURL destinationURL: URL) {
        self.presentDocument(at: destinationURL)
}
```

Figure 22-12. Configuring a document browser app's document type

Providing a real implementation of `presentDocument(at:)` is up to us. I've replaced the template's Document and DocumentViewController classes with People-Document and PeopleLister from the previous People Groups example. We are no longer in a master–detail navigation interface, but PeopleLister expects one; so when I instantiate PeopleLister, I wrap it in a navigation controller and present that navigation controller:

```
func presentDocument(at documentURL: URL) {
    let lister = PeopleLister(fileURL: documentURL)
    let nav = UINavigationController(rootViewController: lister)
    self.present(nav, animated: true)
}
```

Finally, we come to the really interesting case: the user asks the document browser to create a People Groups document. This causes the delegate's `documentBrowser(_:did-RequestDocumentCreationWithHandler:)` to be called. Our job is to provide the URL of *an existing empty document file* and call the `handler:` function with that URL. But where are we going to get a document file? Well, we already know how to create an empty document; we proved that in our earlier example. So I'll create that document in the Temporary directory and feed the `handler:` function its URL. This is exactly the strategy advised by the documentation on this delegate method, and my code is adapted directly from the example code there.

I'm a little unclear about what we're intended to do about the *name* of the new file. In the past, Apple's advice was not to worry about this; any unique name would do. But that was before the user could *see* file names in a standard interface. My solution is an adaptation of what I was already doing in the People Groups app's GroupLister when the user asked to create a new people group: I present a UIAlertController where the user can enter the new document's name, and proceed to create the new document in its OK button's action function. Observe that I call the `importHandler` function under every circumstance; if the user cancels or if something else goes wrong, I call it with a nil URL:

```swift
func documentBrowser(_ controller: UIDocumentBrowserViewController,
    didRequestDocumentCreationWithHandler importHandler:
    @escaping (URL?, UIDocumentBrowserViewController.ImportMode) -> Void) {
        var docname = "People"
        let alert = UIAlertController(
            title: "Name for new people group:",
            message: nil, preferredStyle: .alert)
        alert.addTextField { tf in
            tf.autocapitalizationType = .words
        }
        alert.addAction(UIAlertAction(title: "Cancel", style: .cancel) {_ in
            importHandler(nil, .none)
        })
        alert.addAction(UIAlertAction(title: "OK", style: .default) {_ in
            if let proposal = alert.textFields?[0].text {
                if !proposal.trimmingCharacters(in: .whitespaces).isEmpty {
                    docname = proposal
                }
            }
            let fm = FileManager.default
            let temp = fm.temporaryDirectory
            let fileURL = temp.appendingPathComponent(docname + ".pplgrp2")
            let newdoc = PeopleDocument(fileURL: fileURL)
            newdoc.save(to: fileURL, for: .forOverwriting) { ok in
                guard ok else { importHandler(nil, .none); return }
                newdoc.close() { ok in
                    guard ok else { importHandler(nil, .none); return }
                    importHandler(fileURL, .move)
                }
            }
        })
        self.present(alert, animated: true)
}
```

Exactly one path of execution calls `importHandler` with an actual file URL. If that happens, our delegate method `documentBrowser(_:didImportDocumentAt:to-`

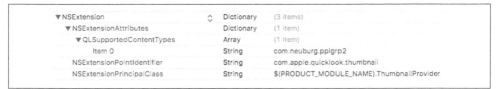

▼ NSExtension	⇕	Dictionary	(3 items)
▼ NSExtensionAttributes		Dictionary	(1 item)
▼ QLSupportedContentTypes		Array	(1 item)
Item 0		String	com.neuburg.pplgrp2
NSExtensionPointIdentifier		String	com.apple.quicklook.thumbnail
NSExtensionPrincipalClass		String	$(PRODUCT_MODULE_NAME).ThumbnailProvider

Figure 22-13. Configuring a thumbnail extension

DestinationURL:) is called — and so our PeopleLister view controller is presented, displaying the new empty document.

Custom Thumbnails

Once the user can see our document files represented in the file browser, both in the Files app and in any apps based around UIDocumentBrowserViewController, we will probably want to give some attention to their icons. New in iOS 11, we can use a *thumbnail extension* to supply a custom thumbnail icon representing our document file. Let's do that.

Make a new target and choose iOS → Application Extension → Thumbnail Extension. As usual, we must configure the *Info.plist* to specify the UTI for the document type whose thumbnail we will be providing (Figure 22-13).

Now we customize the ThumbnailProvider class given to us by the template. In particular, we implement provideThumbnail(for:_:). Its parameters are a QLFileThumbnailRequest and a completion function. Our job is to examine the incoming QLFileThumbnailRequest, construct a QLThumbnailReply, and call the completion function, handing it the QLThumbnailReply.

There are three ways to make a QLThumbnailReply:

init(imageFileURL:)
> We might use this initializer if our extension bundle contains an image file that we always want to use as a document icon.

init(contextSize:currentContextDrawing:)
> A graphics context is going to be prepared for us and made the current context. We supply a function that draws the thumbnail in real time into the current context.

init(contextSize:drawing:)
> A graphics context is supplied as the second parameter. We supply a function that draws into that context. But beware: this graphics context is *flipped* with respect to the usual iOS coordinate system — its origin is at the lower left and the y-axis increases upward. For this reason, you'll probably find it simpler to use the preceding initializer.

Figure 22-14. Documents with custom thumbnails

To illustrate, I'll use the second initializer. My thumbnail will be extremely silly; I'll draw a smiley face from an image file, and write the name of the file over it. Still, this is a good demonstration, because it proves that we are supplying the thumbnail individually for each document file, and also because it shows how to size the graphics context:

```
override func provideThumbnail(for request: QLFileThumbnailRequest,
    _ handler: @escaping (QLThumbnailReply?, Error?) -> Void) {
        let furl = request.fileURL
        let name = furl.deletingPathExtension().lastPathComponent
        let im = UIImage(named:"smiley.jpg")!
        let maxsz = request.maximumSize
        let r = AVMakeRect(aspectRatio: im.size,
            insideRect: CGRect(origin:.zero, size:maxsz))
        let att = NSAttributedString(string:name, attributes:[
            .font:UIFont(name:"Georgia", size:14)!
        ])
        let attsz = att.size()
        func draw() -> Bool {
            im.draw(in: CGRect(origin:.zero, size:r.size))
            att.draw(at: CGPoint(
                (r.width-attsz.width)/2, (r.height-attsz.height)/2))
            return true
        }
        let reply = QLThumbnailReply(
            contextSize: r.size, currentContextDrawing: draw)
        handler(reply, nil)
}
```

The result is that our app's document browser and the Files app display our files with their custom thumbnails (Figure 22-14).

Custom Previews

New in iOS 11, your app can supply a Quick Look preview for a custom document type that it exports, suitable for display in a UIDocumentInteractionController or QLPreviewController (discussed earlier in this chapter). For example, suppose someone emails your user a People Group document. In the mail app, the user opens the

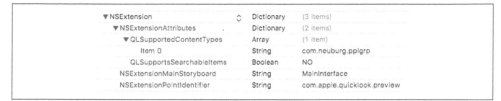

▼ NSExtension	⌃	Dictionary	(3 items)
▼ NSExtensionAttributes	.	Dictionary	(2 items)
▼ QLSupportedContentTypes		Array	(1 item)
Item 0		String	com.neuburg.pplgrp
QLSupportsSearchableItems		Boolean	NO
NSExtensionMainStoryboard		String	MainInterface
NSExtensionPointIdentifier		String	com.apple.quicklook.preview

Figure 22-15. Defining a preview extension's document type

message, sees the document icon, and presses it to preview its contents. That works for a standard document type such as a PDF or text file, but not for our custom People Group document type. Let's fix that.

To do so, we'll add a *Quick Look preview extension* to our People Groups app. Add a target; choose iOS → Application Extension → Quick Look Preview Extension. The template provides a view controller class, PreviewViewController, and a storyboard containing a PreviewViewController instance and its main view. When the user tries to preview a document of our custom type, this view controller will be instantiated and its main view will be displayed in the Quick Look preview interface (just like the PDF displayed in Figure 22-8).

For this to work, our extension's *Info.plist* must declare, in the QLSupportedContent-Types array, the UTI of the document type for which it provides a preview (Figure 22-15). I've also turned off the `QLSupportsSearchableItems` setting (it's for Spotlight searches, with which we're not concerned here).

We must now implement `preparePreviewOfFile(at:completionHandler:)` in our PreviewViewController. We are handed a file URL pointing to a document file. Our job is to examine that file, configure our view controller and its view, and call the `completionHandler:` function with a parameter of `nil` (or with an Error object if there was an error).

I'll configure PreviewViewController as a reduced version of PeopleLister. Similar to the right side of Figure 22-9, it will be a UITableViewController whose table shows the first and last names of the people in this group; but the text fields will be disabled — we don't want the user trying to edit in a preview — and there is no need to implement document saving, or even to maintain a reference to a PeopleDocument. Instead, we merely use a PeopleDocument temporarily as a conduit to construct the `people` array from the document file, storing the array in an instance property so that our table view data source methods can access it. I tried to write this code by calling UIDocument's open method, but that failed, so I use an NSFileCoordinator and call `load(fromContents:ofType:)` manually:

```
func preparePreviewOfFile(at url: URL,
    completionHandler handler: @escaping (Error?) -> Void) {
        let fc = NSFileCoordinator()
        let intent = NSFileAccessIntent.readingIntent(with: url)
        let queue = OperationQueue()
        fc.coordinate(with: [intent], queue: queue) { err in
            do {
                let data = try Data(contentsOf: intent.url)
                let doc = PeopleDocument(fileURL: url)
                try doc.load(fromContents: data, ofType: nil)
                self.people = doc.people
                DispatchQueue.main.async {
                    self.tableView.register(
                        UINib(nibName: "PersonCell", bundle: nil),
                        forCellReuseIdentifier: "Person")
                    self.tableView.reloadData()
                }
                handler(nil)
            } catch {
                handler(error)
            }
        }
}
```

XML

XML is a highly flexible and widely used general-purpose text file format for storage and retrieval of structured data. You might use it yourself to store data that you'll need to retrieve later, or you could encounter it when obtaining information from elsewhere, such as the Internet.

On macOS, Cocoa provides a set of classes (XMLDocument and so forth) for reading, parsing, maintaining, searching, and modifying XML data in a completely general way; but iOS does *not* include these. I think the reason must be that their tree-based approach is too memory-intensive. Instead, iOS provides XMLParser, a much simpler class that walks through an XML document, sending delegate messages as it encounters elements. With this, you can parse an XML document once, but what you do with the pieces as you encounter them is up to you. The general assumption here is that you know in advance the structure of the particular XML data you intend to read and that you have provided classes for representation of the same data in object form and for transforming the XML pieces into that representation.

To illustrate, let's return once more to our Person class with a firstName and a lastName property. Imagine that as our app starts up, we would like to populate it with Person objects, and that we've stored the data describing these objects as an XML file in our app bundle, like this:

```
<?xml version="1.0" encoding="utf-8"?>
<people>
    <person>
        <firstName>Matt</firstName>
        <lastName>Neuburg</lastName>
    </person>
    <person>
        <firstName>Snidely</firstName>
        <lastName>Whiplash</lastName>
    </person>
    <person>
        <firstName>Dudley</firstName>
        <lastName>Doright</lastName>
    </person>
</people>
```

This data could be mapped to an array of Person objects, each with its firstName and lastName properties appropriately set. (This is a deliberately easy example, of course; not all XML is so readily expressed as objects.) Let's consider how we might do that.

Using XMLParser is not difficult in theory. You create the XMLParser, handing it the URL of a local XML file (or a Data object, perhaps downloaded from the Internet), set its delegate, and tell it to parse. The delegate starts receiving delegate messages. For simple XML like ours, there are only three delegate messages of interest:

parser(_:didStartElement:namespaceURI:qualifiedName:attributes:)
   The parser has encountered an opening element tag. In our document, this would be <people>, <person>, <firstName>, or <lastName>.

parser(_:didEndElement:namespaceURI:qualifiedName:)
   The parser has encountered the corresponding closing element tag. In our document this would be </people>, </person>, </firstName>, or </lastName>.

parser(_:foundCharacters:)
   The parser has encountered some text between the starting and closing tags for the current element. In our document this would be, for example, "Matt" or "Neuburg" and so on.

In practice, responding to these delegate messages poses challenges of maintaining state. If there is just one delegate, it will have to bear in mind at every moment what element it is currently encountering; this could make for a lot of properties and a lot of if-statements in the implementation of the delegate methods. To aggravate the issue, parser(_:foundCharacters:) can arrive multiple times for a single stretch of text; that is, the text may arrive in pieces, which we must accumulate into a property.

An elegant way to meet these challenges is by resetting the XMLParser's delegate to different objects at different stages of the parsing process. We make each delegate responsible for parsing one type of element; when a child of that element is encountered, we make a new object and make *it* the delegate. The child element delegate is then responsible for making the parent the delegate once again when it finishes parsing its own element. This is slightly counterintuitive because it means `parser(_:didStartElement:...)` and `parser(_:didEndElement:...)` for the same element are arriving at *two different objects*.

To see what I mean, think about how we could implement this in our example. We are going to need a PeopleParser that handles the `<people>` element, and a PersonParser that handles the `<person>` elements. Now imagine how PeopleParser will operate when it is the XMLParser's delegate:

1. When `parser(_:didStartElement:...)` arrives, the PeopleParser looks to see if this is a `<person>`. If so, it creates a PersonParser, handing to it (the PersonParser) a reference to itself (the PeopleParser) — and makes the PersonParser the XMLParser's delegate.

2. Delegate messages now arrive at this newly created PersonParser. We can assume that `<firstName>` and `<lastName>` are simple enough that the PersonParser can maintain state as it encounters them. When text is encountered, `parser(_:foundCharacters:)` will be called, and the text must be accumulated into an appropriate property.

3. Eventually, `parser(_:didEndElement:...)` arrives. The PersonParser now uses its reference to make the PeopleParser the XMLParser's delegate once again. The PeopleParser, having received from the PersonParser any data it may have collected, is now ready in case another `<person>` element is encountered (and the old PersonParser might now go quietly out of existence).

An obvious way to assemble the data is that the PersonParser should create a fully configured Person object and hand it up to the PeopleParser. The PeopleParser's job is thus simply to accumulate such Person objects into an array.

This approach may seem like a lot of work to configure, but in fact it is neatly object-oriented, with classes corresponding to the elements of the XML. Moreover, those classes have a great deal in common, which can be readily factored out and encapsulated into a superclass.

JSON

JSON (*http://www.json.org*) is very often used as a universal lightweight structured data format for server communication. In the past, parsing JSON with the JSONSerialization class was not difficult, but it was rather annoying because each piece of data arrived typed as Any and had to be cast down — a clumsy and error-prone procedure. This is one of the main problems solved by the Swift 4 Decodable protocol. You know in advance what the format of your JSON will be, so you devise a struct — possibly a nest of structs — into which it can be parsed directly. The JSONDecoder class comes with properties that allow you to specify how certain specially formatted values should be handled, such as dates and floating-point numbers. You are not in control of the JSON structure, however, so that might not be enough; you may also have to implement the mapping between the JSON structure and your struct explicitly, by supplying a CodingKey adopter and an implementation of init(from:).

As an example, here's a piece of real-life JSON:

```
[
    {
        "categoryName": "Trending",
        "Trending": [
            {
                "category": "Trending",
                "price": 20.5,
                "isFavourite": true,
                "isWatchlist": null
            }
        ]
    },
    {
        "categoryName": "Comedy",
        "Comedy": [
            {
                "category": "Comedy",
                "price": 24.32,
                "isFavourite": null,
                "isWatchlist": false
            }
        ]
    }
]
```

Suppose we have received that JSON over the Internet, wrapped up in a Data object, and now we want to parse it. It's an array of dictionaries, where each dictionary has a "categoryName" key along with one other key, whose name varies (in our example, it might be "Trending" or "Comedy") but whose value is an array of dictionaries with four keys — "category", "price", "isFavourite", and "isWatchlist".

Let's start with the inner dictionary. That's easy to parse; we can map it directly to a struct, with no additional code:

```
struct Inner : Decodable {
    let category : String
    let price : Double
    let isFavourite : Bool?
    let isWatchlist : Bool?
}
```

The outer dictionary, however, is trickier. Clearly it has a "categoryName" key, but the name of the second key won't be known until we actually encounter the JSON and read the "categoryName" key's *value*. So I'll call the corresponding struct property unknown:

```
struct Outer : Decodable {
    let categoryName : String
    let unknown : [Inner]
    // ...
}
```

That won't work without some further code, because the JSON won't have any "unknown" key. So what do we do? We're going to have to write our own implementation of init(from:), to explore the dictionary key by key:

```
init(from decoder: Decoder) throws {
    let con = try! decoder.container(keyedBy: /* ... */)
    // ...
}
```

Before we can get started with that, however, we need something to act as the keyed-By: argument. This has to be a CodingKey adopter.

Now, the usual reason for supplying a CodingKey adopter is to rectify a mismatch between the name of a key in the JSON and the name of the corresponding property in your struct. Here's a typical example:

```
struct Person: Decodable {
    var firstName: String
    var lastName: String
    enum CodingKeys: String, CodingKey {
        case firstName = "first_name"
        case lastName = "last_name"
    }
}
```

The idea here is that our JSON will have keys "first_name" and "last_name", but we prefer our struct to use property names firstName and lastName. The CodingKeys enum, which is a CodingKey adopter, solves that problem. This Person struct is a complete Decodable implementation, because the default implementation of init(from:) will automatically use an enum called CodingKeys, if there is one, to tell it how to perform the mapping.

That, however, is *not* the situation in which we find ourselves. We don't want to do *any* automatic mapping between keys and property names; we want to perform the mapping manually, ourselves, in our init(from:) implementation. Our CodingKey adopter thus needs to be nothing but a bare minimum self-contained object that implements the four instance members required by the CodingKey protocol:

```
var stringValue: String {get}
init?(stringValue: String)
var intValue: Int? {get}
init?(intValue: Int)
```

We don't expect to encounter any Int values, so all we really have to do is implement `init?(stringValue:)` to initialize `stringValue`, allowing `init?(intValue)` to fail:

```
struct CK : CodingKey {
    var stringValue: String
    init?(stringValue: String) {
        self.stringValue = stringValue
    }
    var intValue: Int?
    init?(intValue: Int) {
        return nil
    }
}
```

Now we're ready to write `init(from:)`, because we've got something to pass as the `keyedBy:` argument in the first line:

```
init(from decoder: Decoder) throws {
    let con = try! decoder.container(keyedBy: CK.self)
    // ...
}
```

To complete our implementation, we simply fetch the two keys, one at a time. First we fetch the `"categoryName"` key, and set our `categoryName` property to its value. But that value is also the name of the second key! We fetch the value of *that* key, and set our `unknown` property to *its* value:

```
init(from decoder: Decoder) throws {
    let con = try! decoder.container(keyedBy: CK.self)
    self.categoryName = try! con.decode(
        String.self, forKey:CK(stringValue:"categoryName")!)
    self.unknown = try! con.decode(
        [Inner].self, forKey: CK(stringValue:self.categoryName)!)
}
```

Now we're ready to parse our JSON data! Here we go:

```
let myjson = try! JSONDecoder().decode([Outer].self, from: jsondata)
```

The outcome is that `myjson` is an array of Outer objects, each of which has an `unknown` property whose value is an array of Inner objects — the exact object-oriented analog of the original JSON data:

```
[
    Outer(categoryName: "Trending",
            unknown:
                [Inner(category: "Trending",
                    price: 20.5,
```

```
                            isFavourite: Optional(true),
                            isWatchlist: nil)
                    ]),
        Outer(categoryName: "Comedy",
                unknown:
                    [Inner(category: "Comedy",
                        price: 24.32,
                        isFavourite: nil,
                        isWatchlist: Optional(false))
                    ])
    ]
```

SQLite

SQLite (*http://www.sqlite.org/docs.html*) is a lightweight, full-featured relational data-base that you can talk to using SQL, the universal language of databases. This can be an appropriate storage format when your data comes in rows and columns (records and fields) and needs to be rapidly searchable. Also, the database as a whole is never loaded into memory; the data is accessed only as needed. This is valuable in an environment like an iOS device, where memory is at a premium.

To use SQLite, say `import SQLite3`. Talking to SQLite involves an elaborate C interface which may prove annoying; there are, however, a number of lightweight front ends. I like to use `fmdb` (*https://github.com/ccgus/fmdb*); it's Swift-friendly, but it's written in Objective-C, so we'll need a bridging header in which we `#import "FMDB.h"`.

To illustrate, I'll create a database and add a `people` table consisting of `lastname` and `firstname` columns:

```
let db = FMDatabase(path:self.dbpath)
db.open()
do {
    db.beginTransaction()
    try db.executeUpdate(
        "create table people (lastname text, firstname text)",
        values:nil)
    try db.executeUpdate(
        "insert into people (firstname, lastname) values (?,?)",
        values:["Matt", "Neuburg"])
    try db.executeUpdate(
        "insert into people (firstname, lastname) values (?,?)",
        values:["Snidely", "Whiplash"])
    try db.executeUpdate(
        "insert into people (firstname, lastname) values (?,?)",
        values:["Dudley", "Doright"])
    db.commit()
} catch {
    db.rollback()
}
```

At some later time, I come along and read the data from that database:

```
let db = FMDatabase(path:self.dbpath)
db.open()
if let rs = try? db.executeQuery("select * from people", values:nil) {
    while rs.next() {
        if let firstname = rs["firstname"], let lastname = rs["lastname"] {
            print(firstname, lastname)
        }
    }
}
db.close()
/*
Matt Neuburg
Snidely Whiplash
Dudley Doright
*/
```

You can include a previously constructed SQLite file in your app bundle, but you can't write to it there; the solution is to copy it from your app bundle into another location, such as the Documents directory, before you start working with it.

Core Data

The Core Data framework (`import CoreData`) provides a generalized way of expressing objects and properties that form a relational graph; moreover, it has built-in facilities for maintaining those objects in persistent storage — typically using SQLite as a file format — and reading them from storage only when they are needed, thus making efficient use of memory. For example, a person might have not only multiple addresses but also multiple friends who are also persons; expressing persons and addresses as explicit object types, working out how to link them and how to translate between objects in memory and data in storage, and tracking the effects of changes, such as when a person is deleted, can be tedious. Core Data can help.

It is important to stress, however, that Core Data is *not* a beginner-level technology. It is difficult to use and extremely difficult to debug. It expresses itself in a highly verbose, rigid, arcane way. It has its own elaborate way of doing things — everything you already know about how to create, access, alter, or delete an object within an object collection becomes completely irrelevant! — and trying to bend it to your particular needs can be tricky and can have unintended side effects. Nor should Core Data be seen as a substitute for a true relational database.

A full explanation of Core Data would require an entire book; indeed, such books exist, and if Core Data interests you, you should read some of them. See also Apple's *Core Data Programming Guide* and the other resources referred to there. Here, I'll just illustrate what it's like to work with Core Data.

I will rewrite the People Groups example from earlier in this chapter as a Core Data app. This will still be a master–detail interface consisting of two table view controllers, GroupLister and PeopleLister, just as in Figure 22-9. But we will no longer have multiple documents, each representing a single group of people; instead, we will now have a single document, maintained for us by Core Data, containing all of our groups and all of their people.

To construct a Core Data project from scratch, it is simplest to specify the Master–Detail app template (or the Single View app template) and check Use Core Data in the second screen. Among other things, this gives you template code in the app delegate class for constructing the Core Data *persistence stack*, a set of objects that work together to fetch and save your data; in most cases there will no reason to alter this template code significantly.

The persistence stack consists of three objects:

- A *managed object model* (NSManagedObjectModel) describing the structure of the data
- A *managed object context* (NSManagedObjectContext) for communicating with the data
- A *persistent store coordinator* (NSPersistentStoreCoordinator) for dealing with actual storage of the data as a file

Starting in iOS 10, this entire stack is created for us by an NSPersistentContainer object. The template code provides a lazy initializer for this object:

```
lazy var persistentContainer: NSPersistentContainer = {
    let con = NSPersistentContainer(name: "PeopleGroupsCoreData")
    con.loadPersistentStores { desc, err in
        if let err = err {
            fatalError("Unresolved error \(err)")
        }
    }
    return con
}()
```

The managed object context is the persistent container's viewContext. This will be our point of contact with Core Data. The managed object context is the world in which your data objects live and move and have their being: to obtain an object, you fetch it from the managed object context; to create an object, you insert it into the managed object context; to save your data, you save the managed object context.

To provide the rest of the app with easy access to the managed object context, our root view controller has a managedObjectContext property, and the app delegate's application(_:didFinishLaunchingWithOptions:) configures it to point back at the persistent container's viewContext:

Figure 22-16. The Core Data model for the People Groups app

```
let nav = self.window!.rootViewController as! UINavigationController
let tvc = nav.topViewController as! GroupLister
tvc.managedObjectContext = self.persistentContainer.viewContext
```

To describe the structure and relationships of the objects constituting your data model (the managed object model), you design an object graph in a data model document. Our object graph is very simple: a Group can have multiple Persons (Figure 22-16). The attributes, analogous to object properties, are all strings, except for the timestamps which are dates, and the Group UUID which is a UUID. (The timestamps will be used for determining the sort order in which groups and people will be displayed in the interface.)

Group and Person are not classes; they are *entity* names. And their attributes, such as name and firstName, are not properties. All Core Data model objects are instances of NSManagedObject, which has no firstName property and so on. Instead, Core Data model objects make themselves dynamically KVC compliant for attribute names. For example, Core Data knows, thanks to our object graph, that a Person entity is to have a firstName attribute, so if an NSManagedObject represents a Person entity, you can set its firstName attribute by calling setValue(_:forKey:) and retrieve its first-Name attribute by calling value(forKey:), using a key "firstName".

Management of entities, and talking to them with KVC, is maddening, to say the least. Fortunately, there's a simple solution: you configure your entities, in the Data Model inspector, to perform *code generation* of class definitions (Figure 22-17). The result is that, when we compile our project, class files will be created for our entities (here, Group and Person) as NSManagedObject subclasses. These classes are endowed with properties corresponding to the entity attributes. Thus, Person now *is* a class, and it *does* have a firstName property. Code generation, in short, allows us to treat entity types as classes, and managed objects as instances of those classes.

Now let's talk about the first view controller, GroupLister. Its job is to list groups and to allow the user to create a new group (Figure 22-9). How will GroupLister get a list of groups? The way you ask Core Data for a model object is with a fetch request; and in iOS, where Core Data model objects are often (as here) the model data for a UITableView, fetch requests are conveniently managed through an NSFetchedResults-

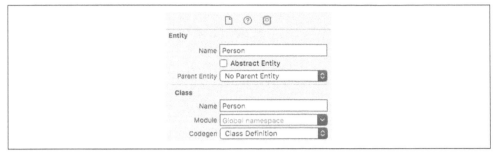

Figure 22-17. Configuring code generation

Controller. Once again, the template sets us up just as we would wish. It provides a fetched results controller stored in a property, ready to perform the fetch request and to supply our table view's data source with the actual data. My code essentially copies the template code; the first two lines demonstrate not only that Group is a class with a fetchRequest method, but also that both NSFetchedResultsController and NSFetchRequest are generics:

```
lazy var frc: NSFetchedResultsController<Group> = {
    let req: NSFetchRequest<Group> = Group.fetchRequest()
    req.fetchBatchSize = 20
    let sortDescriptor = NSSortDescriptor(key:"timestamp", ascending:true)
    req.sortDescriptors = [sortDescriptor]
    let frc = NSFetchedResultsController(
        fetchRequest:req,
        managedObjectContext:self.managedObjectContext,
        sectionNameKeyPath:nil, cacheName:nil)
    frc.delegate = self
    do {
        try frc.performFetch()
    } catch {
        fatalError("Aborting with unresolved error")
    }
    return frc
}()
```

The table view's data source treats self.frc, the NSFetchedResultsController, as the model data, consisting of Group objects; observe how, in the starred line, we are able to retrieve an actual Group instance from the NSFetchedResultsController (because the latter is a generic):

```
override func numberOfSections(in tableView: UITableView) -> Int {
    return self.frc.sections!.count
}
override func tableView(_ tableView: UITableView,
    numberOfRowsInSection section: Int) -> Int {
        let sectionInfo = self.frc.sections![section]
        return sectionInfo.numberOfObjects
}
```

```
override func tableView(_ tableView: UITableView,
    cellForRowAt indexPath: IndexPath) -> UITableViewCell {
        let cell = tableView.dequeueReusableCell(
            withIdentifier: self.cellID, for: indexPath)
        cell.accessoryType = .disclosureIndicator
        let group = self.frc.object(at:indexPath) // *
        cell.textLabel!.text = group.name
        return cell
}
```

GroupLister's table is initially empty because our app starts life with no data. When the user asks to create a group, I put up an alert asking for the name of the new group. In the handler: function for its OK button, I create a new Group object, save it into the managed object context, and navigate to the detail view, PeopleLister. Again, my code is drawn largely from the template code:

```
let context = self.frc.managedObjectContext
let group = Group(context: context)
group.name = av.textFields![0].text!
group.uuid = UUID()
group.timestamp = Date()
do {
    try context.save()
} catch {
    return
}
let pl = PeopleLister(group: group)
self.navigationController!.pushViewController(pl, animated: true)
```

The detail view controller class is PeopleLister. It lists all the people in a particular Group, so I don't want PeopleLister to be instantiated without a Group; therefore, its designated initializer is init(group:). As the preceding code shows, when I want to navigate from the GroupLister view to the PeopleLister view, I instantiate People-Lister and push it onto the navigation controller's stack. I do the same sort of thing when the user taps an existing Group name in the GroupLister table view:

```
override func tableView(_ tableView: UITableView,
    didSelectRowAt indexPath: IndexPath) {
        let pl = PeopleLister(group: self.frc.object(at:indexPath))
        self.navigationController!.pushViewController(pl, animated: true)
}
```

PeopleLister, too, has an frc property that's an NSFetchedResultsController. However, a PeopleLister instance should list only the People belonging to *one particular group*, which has been stored as its group property. So PeopleLister's implementation of the frc initializer contains these lines (req is the fetch request we're configuring):

```
let pred = NSPredicate(format:"group = %@", self.group)
req.predicate = pred
```

As shown in Figure 22-9, the PeopleLister interface consists of a table of text fields. Populating the table is similar to what GroupLister did; in particular, in my `table-View(_:cellForRowAt:)` implementation, `self.frc.object(at:indexPath)` is a Person object, so I can use its `firstName` and `lastName` to set the `text` of the text fields.

When the user edits a text field to change the first or last name of a Person, I hear about it as the text field's delegate. I update the data model and save the managed object context (the first part of this code should be familiar from Chapter 8):

```
func textFieldDidEndEditing(_ textField: UITextField) {
    var v : UIView = textField
    repeat { v = v.superview! } while !(v is UITableViewCell)
    let cell = v as! UITableViewCell
    let ip = self.tableView.indexPath(for:cell)!
    let object = self.frc.object(at:ip)
    object.setValue(textField.text!, forKey: (
        (textField.tag == 1) ? "firstName" : "lastName"))
    do {
        try object.managedObjectContext!.save()
    } catch {
        return
    }
}
```

The trickiest part is what happens when the user asks to make a new Person. It starts out analogously to making a new Group; I make a new Person object, configure its attributes with an empty first name and last name, and save it into the context:

```
@objc func doAdd(_:AnyObject) {
    self.tableView.endEditing(true)
    let context = self.frc.managedObjectContext
    let person = Person(context:context)
    person.group = self.group
    person.lastName = ""
    person.firstName = ""
    person.timestamp = NSDate()
    do {
        try context.save()
    } catch {
        return
    }
}
```

But we must also make this empty Person appear in the table! Once again, the template code shows us the way. We act as the NSFetchedResultsController's delegate (NSFetchedResultsControllerDelegate); the delegate methods are triggered by the call to `context.save()` in the preceding code:

```
func controllerWillChangeContent(
    _ controller: NSFetchedResultsController<NSFetchRequestResult>) {
        self.tableView.beginUpdates()
}
func controllerDidChangeContent(
    _ controller: NSFetchedResultsController<NSFetchRequestResult>) {
        self.tableView.endUpdates()
}
func controller(
    _ controller: NSFetchedResultsController<NSFetchRequestResult>,
    didChange anObject: Any,
    at indexPath: IndexPath?,
    for type: NSFetchedResultsChangeType,
    newIndexPath: IndexPath?) {
        if type == .insert {
            self.tableView.insertRows(at:[newIndexPath!], with: .automatic)
            DispatchQueue.main.async {
                let cell = self.tableView.cellForRow(at:newIndexPath!)!
                let tf = cell.viewWithTag(1) as! UITextField
                tf.becomeFirstResponder()
            }
        }
    }
}
```

Core Data files are not suitable for use as iCloud documents. If you want to reflect structured data into the cloud, a better alternative is the CloudKit framework. In effect, this allows you to maintain a database online, and to synchronize changed data up to and down from that database. You might, for example, use Core Data as a form of *local* storage, but use CloudKit to communicate the data between the user's devices. For more information, see Apple's *CloudKit Quick Start* guide.

PDFs

Earlier in this chapter, I displayed the contents of a PDF file by means of a web view, or in a Quick Look preview. In the past, other ways of showing a PDF existed, but they were complicated. New in iOS 11 is PDF Kit (import PDFKit), brought over at long last from macOS. It provides a native UIView subclass, PDFView, whose job is to display a PDF nicely.

Basic use of a PDFView is simple. Initialize a PDFDocument, either from data or from a file URL, and assign it as the PDFView's document:

```
let v = PDFView(frame:self.view.bounds)
self.view.addSubview(v)
let url = Bundle.main.url(forResource: "notes", withExtension: "pdf")!
let doc = PDFDocument(url: url)
v.document = doc
```

There are many other configurable aspects of a PDFView. A particularly nice touch is that a PDFView can embed a UIPageViewController for layout and navigation of the PDF's individual pages:

```
v.usePageViewController(true)
```

A PDFDocument consists of pages, represented by PDFPage objects. You can manipulate those pages — for example, you can add and remove pages from the document. You can even draw a PDFPage's contents yourself, meaning that you can, in effect, create a PDF document from scratch. Again, this was possible but complicated previously; in iOS 11, it's easy.

As a demonstration, I'll create a PDF document consisting of one page with the words "Hello, world!" in the center. I start with a PDFPage subclass, MyPage, where I override the draw(with:to:) method. The parameters are a PDFDisplayBox that tells me the page size, along with a CGContext to draw into. There's just one thing to watch out for: a PDF graphics context is flipped with respect to the normal iOS coordinate system. So I apply a transform to the context before I draw into it:

```
override func draw(with box: PDFDisplayBox, to context: CGContext) {
    UIGraphicsPushContext(context)
    context.saveGState()
    let r = self.bounds(for: box)
    let s = NSAttributedString(string: "Hello, world!", attributes: [
        .font : UIFont(name: "Georgia", size: 80)!
    ])
    let sz = s.boundingRect(with: CGSize(10000,10000),
        options: .usesLineFragmentOrigin, context: nil)
    context.translateBy(x: 0, y: r.height)
    context.scaleBy(x: 1, y: -1)
    s.draw(at: CGPoint(
        (r.maxX - r.minX) / 2 - sz.width / 2,
        (r.maxY - r.minY) / 2 - sz.height / 2
    ))
    context.restoreGState()
    UIGraphicsPopContext()
}
```

To create and display my PDFPage in a PDFView (v) is simple:

```
let doc = PDFDocument()
v.document = doc
doc.insert(MyPage(), at: 0)
```

If my document consisted of more than one MyPage, they would all draw the same thing. If that's not what I want, my draw(with:to:) code can ask what page of the document this is:

```
let pagenum = self.document?.index(for: self)
```

In addition, a host of ancillary PDF Kit classes allow you to manipulate page thumbnails, selection, annotations, and more.

Image Files

The Image I/O framework provides a simple, unified way to open image files, to save image files, to convert between image file formats, and to read metadata from standard image file formats, including EXIF and GPS information from a digital camera. You'll need to `import ImageIO`. The Image I/O API is written in C, not Objective-C, and it uses CFTypeRefs, not objects. Unlike Core Graphics, there is no Swift "renamification" overlay that represents the API as object-oriented; you have to call the framework's global C functions directly, casting between the CFTypeRefs and their Foundation counterparts. However, that's not hard to do.

Use of the Image I/O framework starts with the notion of an *image source* (CGImage-Source). This can be created from the URL of a file (actually CFURL, to which URL is toll-free bridged) or from a Data object (actually CFData, to which Data is toll-free bridged).

For example, here we obtain the metadata from a photo file in our app bundle:

```
let url = Bundle.main.url(forResource:"colson", withExtension: "jpg")!
let src = CGImageSourceCreateWithURL(url as CFURL, nil)!
let result = CGImageSourceCopyPropertiesAtIndex(src,0,nil)!
let d = result as! [AnyHashable:Any]
```

Without having opened the image file as an image, we now have a dictionary full of information about it, including its pixel dimensions (`kCGImagePropertyPixelWidth` and `kCGImagePropertyPixelHeight`), its resolution, its color model, its color depth, and its orientation — plus, because this picture originally comes from a digital camera, the EXIF data such as the aperture and exposure at which it was taken, plus the make and model of the camera.

To obtain the image as a CGImage, we can call `CGImageSourceCreateImageAtIndex`. Alternatively, we can request a *thumbnail* of the image. This is a very useful thing to do, and the name "thumbnail" doesn't really do justice to its importance and power. If your purpose in opening this image is to display it in your interface, you don't care about the original image data; a thumbnail is *precisely* what you want, especially because you can specify any size for this "thumbnail" all the way up to the original size of the image! This is tremendously convenient, because to assign a large image to a small image view wastes all the memory reflected by the size difference.

To generate a thumbnail at a given size, you start with a dictionary specifying the size along with other instructions, and pass that, together with the image source, to `CGImageSourceCreateThumbnailAtIndex`. The only pitfall is that, because we are working with a CGImage and specifying actual pixels, we must remember to take account of the scale of our device's screen. So, for example, let's say we want to scale our image so that its largest dimension is no larger than the width of the UIImage-View (`self.iv`) into which we intend to place it:

```
let url = Bundle.main.url(forResource:"colson", withExtension: "jpg")!
let src = CGImageSourceCreateWithURL(url as CFURL, nil)!
let scale = UIScreen.main.scale
let w = self.iv.bounds.width * scale
let d : [AnyHashable:Any] = [
    kCGImageSourceShouldAllowFloat : true ,
    kCGImageSourceCreateThumbnailWithTransform : true ,
    kCGImageSourceCreateThumbnailFromImageAlways : true ,
    kCGImageSourceThumbnailMaxPixelSize : w
]
let imref = CGImageSourceCreateThumbnailAtIndex(src, 0, d as CFDictionary)!
let im = UIImage(cgImage: imref, scale: scale, orientation: .up)
self.iv.image = im
```

To save an image using a specified file format, we need an *image destination*. As a final example, I'll show how to save our image as a TIFF. We never open the image as an image! We save directly from the image source to the image destination:

```
let url = Bundle.main.url(forResource:"colson", withExtension: "jpg")!
let src = CGImageSourceCreateWithURL(url as CFURL, nil)!
let fm = FileManager.default
let suppurl = try! fm.url(for:.applicationSupportDirectory,
    in: .userDomainMask, appropriateFor: nil, create: true)
let tiff = suppurl.appendingPathComponent("mytiff.tiff")
let dest =
    CGImageDestinationCreateWithURL(tiff as CFURL, kUTTypeTIFF, 1, nil)!
CGImageDestinationAddImageFromSource(dest, src, 0, nil)
let ok = CGImageDestinationFinalize(dest)
```

CHAPTER 23

Basic Networking

Networking is difficult and complicated, not least because it's ultimately out of your control. You can ask for a resource from across the network, but at that point anything can happen: the resource might not be found, it might take a while to arrive, it might never arrive, the server or the network might be unavailable, or even worse, might vanish after the resource has partially arrived. There are numerous technicalities to deal with, not to mention the need for extensive background threading so that nothing interferes with the operation of your app's interface (Chapter 24).

iOS, however, handles all of that behind the scenes, and makes basic networking extremely easy. To go further into networking than this chapter takes you, start with Apple's *URL Session Programming Guide*. Apple also provides a generous amount of sample code.

Many earlier chapters have described interface and frameworks that network for you automatically. Put a web view in your interface (Chapter 11) and poof, you're networking; the web view does all the grunt work, and it does it a lot better than you'd be likely to do it from scratch. The same is true of AVPlayer (Chapter 15), MKMapView (Chapter 20), and so on.

Ever since iOS 9, App Transport Security has been enforced, meaning that HTTP requests must be HTTPS requests and that the server must be using TLS 1.2 or higher. To tweak the behavior of App Transport Security, you must make an entry in your app's *Info.plist*, in the "App Transport Security Settings" dictionary (NSApp-TransportSecurity). For example, to allow HTTP requests in general, the dictionary's "Allow Arbitrary Loads" key (NSAllowsArbitraryLoads) must be YES. See the "App Transport Security" section in Apple's *Information Property List Key Reference*.

A device used for development has a Network Link Conditioner switch in Settings (under Developer). Use it to impose different networking situations to stress-test your networking code.

HTTP Requests

An HTTP request is made through a URLSession object. A URLSession is a kind of grand overarching environment in which network-related tasks are to take place.

Obtaining a Session

There are three chief ways to obtain a URLSession:

The shared session
> The URLSession class vends a singleton shared session object through its `shared` class property. This object is supplied and configured by the runtime, so it is good primarily for very simple, occasional use, where you don't need authentication, dedicated cookie storage, delegate messages, and so forth.

Session without a delegate
> You create the URLSession by calling `init(configuration:)`. You'll hand the session a URLSessionConfiguration object describing the desired environment. This means that you can configure the URLSession, but you still can't interact with it while it's performing a networking task for you, because you have no delegate. All you can do is order some task to be performed and then stand back and wait for it to finish.

Session with a delegate
> You create the URLSession by calling `init(configuration:delegate:delegateQueue:)`. Like the preceding initializer, you'll hand the session a URLSessionConfiguration object. But now you also have a delegate, which can receive various callbacks during the course of a networking task (and you even get to say whether those callbacks should occur on the main thread or in the background). Clearly, this is the most powerful approach; it is also more complicated than the others, but that complexity can be worthwhile.

The shared session is owned by the runtime, so there's no need to retain it; you simply access it and tell it what you want it to do. But if you create a URLSession by calling an initializer, you'll probably want it to persist. Your app will typically need to create only one URLSession object; it is reasonable to store it in a global variable, or in an instance property of some object that will persist throughout your app's lifetime, such as the app delegate or the root view controller.

Session Configuration

The URLSession initializers require a URLSessionConfiguration object dictating various options to be applied to the session. Thus, to initialize a URLSession, you'll start by creating the URLSessionConfiguration and setting its properties; then you'll create the URLSession and hand it the URLSessionConfiguration. A legitimate reason for creating multiple URLSession objects might be that you need them to have different configurations.

There are three URLSessionConfiguration class members that you can use to obtain a URLSessionConfiguration instance:

default *class property*
: A basic vanilla URLSessionConfiguration. This is what you'll use most of the time.

ephemeral *class property*
: Configures a URLSession whose cookies and caches are maintained in memory only; they are never saved. You can actually configure a default URLSession-Configuration to give the same behavior, so this is purely a convenience.

background(withIdentifier:) *class method*
: Configures a URLSession that will proceed with its networking tasks independently of your app at some future time. I'll discuss background sessions later.

Here are some of the basic URLSessionConfiguration properties:

allowsCellularAccess
: Whether to permit cell data use or to require Wi-Fi.

waitsForConnectivity
: New in iOS 11. Determines how to deal with reachability issues: if true, the session will try again later if the network is unavailable initially. Apple says that it is better to use this property, and let the URLSession do the work, than to try to determine reachability for yourself (using, for example, SCNetworkReachability).

httpMaximumConnectionsPerHost
: The maximum number of simultaneous connections to the remote server.

Timeout values
: There are two of them:

timeoutIntervalForRequest
: The maximum time you're willing to wait *between* pieces of data. The timer starts when the connection succeeds, and then again each time a piece of data is received. For example, a download will time out because things stalled

for longer than this interval. If this is not a background session, the timeout will trigger failure of the download. The default is one minute.

timeoutIntervalForResource

The maximum time for the *entire* download to arrive. The timer starts when the networking task is told to start, and just keeps ticking until completion. This is appropriate for limiting the request's overall time-to-live. Failure to complete in the required time will always trigger failure of the download. The default is seven days.

There are also numerous cookie, caching, credential, proxy, and protocol properties. Consult the class documentation.

Session Tasks

To use the URLSession object to perform a networking task, you need a URLSession-Task object, representing one upload or download process. You do not instantiate URLSessionTask yourself; rather, you ask the URLSession for a task of the desired type.

The session task types are all subclasses:

URLSessionDataTask

A URLSessionTask subclass. With a data task, the data is provided incrementally to your app as it arrives across the network. You should not use a data task for a large hunk of data, because the data is accumulating in memory throughout the download.

URLSessionDownloadTask

A URLSessionTask subclass. With a download task, the data never passes through your app's memory; instead, it is accumulated into a file, and the saved file URL is handed to you at the end of the process. The file is outside your sandbox and will be destroyed, so preserving it (or its contents) is up to you.

URLSessionUploadTask

A URLSessionDataTask subclass. With an upload task, you can provide a file to be uploaded and stand back, though you can also hear about the upload progress if you wish.

URLSessionStreamTask

A URLSessionTask subclass. This type of task makes it possible to deal conveniently with streams.

The URLSessionTask class itself is an abstract superclass, embodying various properties common to all types of task, such as:

- A `taskDescription` and `taskIdentifier`; the former is up to you, while the latter is a unique identifier within the URLSession
- The `originalRequest` and `currentRequest` (the request can change because there might be a redirect)
- The `priority`; a Float between 0 and 1, used as a hint to help rank the relative importance of your tasks. For convenience, URLSessionTask dispenses three constant class properties:
  - `URLSessionTask.lowPriority` (0.25)
  - `URLSessionTask.defaultPriority` (0.5)
  - `URLSessionTask.highPriority` (0.75)
- An initial `response` from the server
- Various `countOfBytes...` properties allowing you to track progress
- A `progress` property that vends a Progress object; this is new in iOS 11, and is probably a better way to track progress than the `countOfBytes...` properties
- A `state`, which might be:
  - `.running`
  - `.suspended`
  - `.canceling`
  - `.completed`
- An `error` if the task failed

You can tell a task to `resume`, `suspend`, or `cancel`. A task is *born suspended*; it does *not* start until it is told to `resume` for the first time. Typically you'll obtain the task, configure it, and then tell it to `resume` to start it. The Progress object vended by a task's `progress` property is a second gateway to these methods; telling the Progress object to `resume`, `pause`, or `cancel` is the same as telling the task to `resume`, `suspend`, or `cancel` respectively.

Once you've obtained a new session task from the URLSession, the session retains it; you can keep a reference to the task if you wish, but you don't have to. The session will provide you with a list of its tasks in progress; call `getAllTasks(completionHandler:)` to receive the existing tasks in the completion function. The session releases a task after the task is cancelled or completed; thus, if a URLSession has no running or suspended tasks, it has no tasks at all.

There are two ways to ask your URLSession for a new URLSessionTask. Which one you use depends on how you obtained the URLSession; in turn, they entail two different ways of working with the task (and later in this chapter, I'll demonstrate both):

With a completion function

> This is the approach to use if you are using the `shared` session or a session created without a delegate by calling `init(configuration:)`. You'll call a convenience method that takes a `completionHandler:` parameter, such as `downloadTask(with:completionHandler:)`. You supply a completion function, typically an anonymous function, to be called when the task process ends. This approach is simple, but it generates no delegate callbacks.

Without a completion function

> This is the approach to use if you gave the URLSession a delegate when you created it by calling `init(configuration:delegate:delegateQueue:)`. You'll call a method without a `completionHandler:` parameter, such as `downloadTask(with:)`. The delegate is called back at various stages of the task's progress.

For a data task or a download task, the `with:` parameter can be either a URL or a URLRequest. A URL is simpler, but a URLRequest allows you more power to perform additional configuration.

Session Delegate

If the session is created by calling `init(configuration:delegate:delegateQueue:)`, you'll specify a delegate, as well as specifying the queue (roughly, the thread — see Chapter 24) on which the delegate methods are to be called. For each type of session task, there's a delegate protocol, which is itself often a composite of multiple protocols.

For example, for a data task, we would want a data delegate — an object conforming to the URLSessionDataDelegate protocol, which itself conforms to the URLSessionTaskDelegate protocol, which in turn conforms to the URLSessionDelegate protocol, resulting in about a dozen delegate methods we could implement, though only a few are crucial:

`URLSession(_:dataTask:didReceive:)`

> Some data has arrived, as a Data object (the third parameter). The data will arrive piecemeal, so this method may be called many times during the download process, supplying new data each time. Our job is to accumulate all those chunks of data; this involves maintaining state between calls.

`URLSession(_:task:didCompleteWithError:)`

> If there is an error, we'll find out about it here. If there's no error, this is our signal that the download is over; we can now do something with the accumulated data.

Similarly, for a download task, we need a download delegate, conforming to the URLSessionDownloadDelegate protocol, which conforms to the URLSessionTask-Delegate protocol, which conforms to the URLSessionDelegate protocol. Here are some useful delegate methods:

URLSession(_:downloadTask:didResumeAtOffset:expectedTotalBytes:)
: This method is of interest only in the case of a resumable download that has been paused and resumed.

URLSession(_:downloadTask:didWriteData:totalBytesWritten:totalBytes-ExpectedToWrite:)
: Called periodically, to keep us apprised of the download's progress. It might be more convenient to keep a reference to the task's Progress object (new in iOS 11).

URLSession(_:downloadTask:didFinishDownloadingTo:)
: Called at the end of the process. The last parameter is a file URL; we must grab the downloaded file immediately from there, as it will be destroyed. This is the only required delegate method.

URLSession(_:task:didCompleteWithError:)
: Unlike with a data task, this delegate method is not crucial for a download task. Still, if there was a communication problem, this is where you'd hear about it.

Some delegate methods provide a completionHandler: parameter. These are delegate methods that require a response from you. For example, in the case of a data task, URLSession(_:dataTask:didReceive:completionHandler:) arrives when we first connect to the server. The third parameter is the response (URLResponse), and we could now check its status code. We must also return a response of our own, saying whether or not to proceed (or whether to convert the data task to a download task, which could certainly come in handy). But because of the multithreaded, asynchronous nature of networking (see Appendix C), we do this, not by returning a value directly, but by *calling the completion function* and passing our response into it.

New in iOS 11, the various delegate protocols also inherit this method from the URLSessionTaskDelegate protocol:

urlSession(_:taskIsWaitingForConnectivity:)
: Called only if the session configuration has its waitsForConnectivity set to true. The task has tried to start and has failed; instead of giving up with an error (as it would have done if waitsForConnectivity were false), it will wait and try again later. You might respond by updating your interface somehow.

HTTP Request with Task Completion Function

At long last, we are ready for some examples! I'll start by illustrating the utmost in simplicity. This is the absolute minimum approach to downloading a file:

- We use the shared URLSession, which requires (and accepts) no configuration.
- We obtain a download task, handing it a remote URL and a completion function. When the download is complete, the completion function will be called with a file URL; we retrieve the data from that URL and do something with it.
- Having obtained the session and the task, don't forget to call `resume` to start the download!

Our overall code looks like this:

```
let s = "https://www.someserver.com/somefolder/someimage.jpg"
let url = URL(string:s)!
let session = URLSession.shared
let task = session.downloadTask(with:url) { loc, resp, err in
    // ... completion function body goes here ...
}
task.resume()
```

All that remains for us is to write the body of the completion function. The downloaded data (here, an image file) is stored temporarily; if we want to do something with it, we must retrieve it right now. We must make no assumptions about what thread the completion function will be called on; indeed, unless we take steps to the contrary, it will be a background thread. In this particular example, the URL is that of an image that I intend to display in my interface; therefore, I step out to the main thread (Chapter 24) in order to talk to the interface:

```
let task = session.downloadTask(with:url) { fileURL, resp, err in
    if let url = fileURL, let d = try? Data(contentsOf:url) {
        let im = UIImage(data:d)
        DispatchQueue.main.async {
            self.iv.image = im
        }
    }
}
```

That's all there is to it! If there's an error or a negative response from the server (such as "File not found"), `url` will be `nil` and we'll do nothing. Optionally, you might like to have the completion function report those conditions:

```
guard err == nil else { print(err); return }
let status = (resp as! HTTPURLResponse).statusCode
guard status == 200 else { print(status); return }
```

A data task is similar, except that the data itself arrives as the first parameter of the completion function:

```
let task = session.dataTask(with:url) { data, resp, err in
    if let d = data {
        let im = UIImage(data:d) // ... and so on
```

New in iOS 11, a session task vends a Progress object. This means that we can track the progress of our task without using a session delegate (as described in the next section). If we have a UIProgressView (`self.prog`) in our interface, displaying the task's progress to the user could be as simple as this:

```
self.prog.observedProgress = task.progress
```

Recall, too, that one Progress object can act as the parent of other Progress objects (Chapter 12). If we are going to perform multiple tasks simultaneously, our UIProgressView's observedProgress can be configured to show the *overall* progress of those tasks.

HTTP Request with Session Delegate

Now let's go to the other extreme and be very formal and complete:

- We'll start by creating and configuring a URLSessionConfiguration object.
- We'll create and retain our own URLSession.
- We'll give the session a delegate, implementing delegate methods to deal with the session task as it proceeds.
- When we request our session task, instead of a mere URL, we'll start with a URL-Request.

We are now creating our own URLSession, rather than borrowing the system's shared session. Since one URLSession can perform multiple tasks, there will typically be just one URLSession; so I'll make a lazy initializer that creates and configures it, supplying a URLSessionConfiguration and setting the delegate:

```
lazy var session : URLSession = {
    let config = URLSessionConfiguration.ephemeral
    config.allowsCellularAccess = false
    let session = URLSession(configuration: config, delegate: self,
        delegateQueue: .main)
    return session
}()
```

I've specified, for purposes of the example, that no caching is to take place and that data downloading via cell is forbidden; you could configure things much more heavily and meaningfully, of course. I have specified `self` as the delegate, and I have requested delegate callbacks on the main thread.

When I ask for the session task, I'll supply a URLRequest instead of a URL:

```
let url = URL(string:s)!
let req = URLRequest(url:url)
// ask for the task
```

In my examples in this section, there is very little merit in using a URLRequest instead of a URL to form our task. Still, a URLRequest can come in handy, and an upload task requires one; this is where you configure such things as the HTTP request method, body, and header fields.

 Do *not* use the URLRequest to configure properties of the request that are configurable through the URLSessionConfiguration. Those properties are left over from the era before URLSession existed. For example, there is no point setting the URLRequest's timeoutInterval, as it is the URLSessionConfiguration's timeout properties that are significant.

Download task

Here is my recasting of the same image file download task as in the previous example. I blank out the image view, to make the progress of the task more obvious for test purposes, and I create and start the download task:

```
self.iv.image = nil
let s = "https://www.someserver.com/somefolder/someimage.jpg"
let url = URL(string:s)!
let req = URLRequest(url:url)
let task = self.session.downloadTask(with:req)
task.resume()
```

Here are some delegate methods for responding to the download:

```
func urlSession(_ session: URLSession,
    downloadTask: URLSessionDownloadTask,
    didWriteData bytesWritten: Int64,
    totalBytesWritten writ: Int64,
    totalBytesExpectedToWrite exp: Int64) {
        print("downloaded \(100*writ/exp)%")
}
func urlSession(_ session: URLSession,
    task: URLSessionTask,
    didCompleteWithError error: Error?) {
        print("completed: error: \(error)")
}
func urlSession(_ session: URLSession,
    downloadTask: URLSessionDownloadTask,
    didFinishDownloadingTo fileURL: URL) {
        if let d = try? Data(contentsOf:fileURL) {
            let im = UIImage(data:d)
            DispatchQueue.main.async {
                self.iv.image = im
            }
        }
}
```

```
}
/*
downloaded 23%
downloaded 47%
downloaded 71%
downloaded 100%
completed: error: nil
*/
```

New in iOS 11, as I've already mentioned, we would probably forgo the use of `URLSession(_:downloadTask:didWriteData:totalBytesWritten:totalBytes-ExpectedToWrite:)` and instead use the task's `progress` object to track its progress.

Data task

A data task leaves it up to you to accumulate the data as it arrives in chunks. For this purpose, you'll clearly want to keep a mutable Data object on hand; I'll use an instance property (`self.data`):

```
var data = Data()
```

To get started, I prepare `self.data` by giving it a zero count, and then I create and start the data task:

```
self.iv.image = nil
self.data.count = 0 // *
let s = "https://www.someserver.com/somefolder/someimage.jpg"
let url = URL(string:s)!
let req = URLRequest(url:url)
let task = self.session.dataTask(with:req) // *
task.resume()
```

As the chunks of data arrive, I keep appending them to `self.data`. When all the data has arrived, it is ready for use:

```
func urlSession(_ session: URLSession,
    dataTask: URLSessionDataTask,
    didReceive data: Data) {
        self.data.append(data)
        print("\(data.count) bytes of data; total \(self.data.count)")
}
func urlSession(_ session: URLSession,
    task: URLSessionTask,
    didCompleteWithError error: Error?) {
        if error == nil {
            DispatchQueue.main.async {
                self.iv.image = UIImage(data:self.data)
            }
        }
}
/*
received 16384 bytes of data; total 16384
```

```
received 16384 bytes of data; total 32768
received 16384 bytes of data; total 49152
received 16384 bytes of data; total 65536
received 2876 bytes of data; total 68412
*/
```

One Session, One Delegate

The URLSession delegate architecture dictates that the delegate belongs to the *session as a whole*, not to each task individually. Because of this architecture, the preceding data task code is broken. To see why, ask yourself: What happens if our session is asked to perform another data task while this data task is still in progress? Our one session delegate is accumulating the chunks of data into a single Data property, self.data, without regard to what data task this chunk of data comes from. Clearly this is a potential train wreck: we're going to interleave the data from two different tasks, ending up with nonsense.

Let's revise the data task code to fix the problem. We need a way to *separate* the data streams belonging to the different tasks. Fortunately, a session task has a unique identifier — its taskIdentifier, which is an Int. So instead of a single Data property, we can maintain a dictionary keyed by each data task's taskIdentifier, where the corresponding value is a Data object:

```
var data = [Int:Data]()
```

Our code for obtaining and starting a new data task now adds an entry to the data dictionary, like this:

```
let task = self.session.dataTask(with:req)
self.data[task.taskIdentifier] = Data() // *
task.resume()
```

As a chunk of data arrives, we append it to the correct entry in the dictionary:

```
func urlSession(_ session: URLSession,
    dataTask: URLSessionDataTask,
    didReceive data: Data) {
        self.data[dataTask.taskIdentifier]!.append(data)
}
```

When a task's full data has arrived, we pluck it out of the dictionary and remove that dictionary entry (so that data from stale tasks doesn't accumulate) before using the data:

```
func urlSession(_ session: URLSession,
    task: URLSessionTask,
    didCompleteWithError error: Error?) {
        let d = self.data[task.taskIdentifier]!
        self.data[task.taskIdentifier] = nil
        if error == nil {
            DispatchQueue.main.async {
```

```
                    self.iv.image = UIImage(data:d)
                }
            }
        }
    }
```

Delegate Memory Management

A URLSession does an unusual thing: it *retains its delegate*. This is understandable, as it would be disastrous if the delegate could simply vanish in the middle of an asynchronous time-consuming process; but it requires special measures on our part. In all the preceding delegate examples, we have a retain cycle! That's because we (the view controller) have a URLSession instance property self.session, but that URLSession is retaining us (self) as its delegate.

The way to break the cycle is to *invalidate* the URLSession at some appropriate moment. There are two ways to do this:

finishTasksAndInvalidate

Allows any existing tasks to run to completion. Afterward, the URLSession *releases* the delegate and cannot be used for anything further.

invalidateAndCancel

Interrupts any existing tasks immediately. The URLSession *releases* the delegate and cannot be used for anything further.

If the delegate caught in this retain cycle is a view controller, then viewWill-Disappear(_:) could be a good place to invalidate the URLSession. (We cannot use deinit, because deinit won't be called until *after* we have invalidated the URLSession; that's what it means to have a retain cycle.) So, for example:

```
override func viewWillDisappear(_ animated: Bool) {
    super.viewWillDisappear(animated)
    self.session.finishTasksAndInvalidate()
}
```

A more elaborate solution is to encapsulate:

- Start with an instance of some *separate* class whose job is to hold the URLSession in a property.
- Make the URLSession's delegate an instance of yet *another* class — an instance that is not retained by any object other than the URLSession (so, not a view controller).

Now our memory management problems are over. The URLSession retains its delegate, so there is no need for any *other* object to retain the delegate. The delegate does not retain the session or the instance that holds the session, so there is no retain cycle. And there is no entanglement with the memory management of a view controller.

Our URLSession-holding instance can live anywhere; if it is being retained by a view controller, then it will go out of existence in good order if the view controller goes out of existence.

To illustrate, I'll design a class Downloader, which holds a URLSession and creates its delegate. I imagine that our view controller will create and maintain an instance of Downloader early in its lifetime, as an instance property:

```
let downloader : Downloader = {
    // ...
    return Downloader( /* ... */ )
}()
```

In that code, I omitted the initialization of Downloader. How should this work? The Downloader object will create its own URLSession, but I think the client should be allowed to configure the session. So let's posit that Downloader's initializer takes a URLSessionConfiguration parameter:

```
let downloader : Downloader = {
    let config = URLSessionConfiguration.ephemeral
    config.allowsCellularAccess = false
    return Downloader(configuration:config)
}()
```

Now let's design Downloader itself. It creates and retains the URLSession, handing it as delegate an instance of a private class, DownloaderDelegate — an instance which the URLSession itself will retain. Since there is no retain cycle, Downloader can cancel its own session when it goes out of existence:

```
class Downloader: NSObject {
    let config : URLSessionConfiguration
    lazy var session : URLSession = {
        return URLSession(configuration:self.config,
            delegate:DownloaderDelegate(), delegateQueue:.main)
    }()
    init(configuration config:URLSessionConfiguration) {
        self.config = config
        super.init()
    }
    // ...
    deinit {
        self.session.invalidateAndCancel()
    }
}
```

Next, let's decide how a client will communicate with a Downloader object. The client will presumably hand a URL to the Downloader instance; the Downloader will obtain the URLSessionDownloadTask and start it. The DownloaderDelegate will be told when the download is over. At that point, the DownloaderDelegate has a file URL for the downloaded object, which it needs to hand back to the client immediately.

The way to arrange this is that the client, when it hands the Downloader object a URL to initiate a download, should also supply a *completion function* (see Appendix C). In that way, we deal with the asynchronous nature of networking, as well as keeping Downloader independent and agnostic about who the caller is. To return the file URL at the end of a download, the DownloaderDelegate *calls* the completion function, passing it the file URL as a parameter. I can even define a type alias naming my completion function type:

```
typealias DownloaderCH = (URL?) -> ()
```

From the client's point of view, then, the process will look something like this:

```
let s = "https://www.someserver.com/somefolder/someimage.jpg"
let url = URL(string:s)!
self.downloader.download(url:url) { url in
    if let url = url, let d = try? Data(contentsOf: url) {
        let im = UIImage(data:d)
        self.iv.image = im // assume we're called back on main thread
    }
}
```

Now let's implement this architecture within Downloader. We have posited a method download(url:completionHandler:). When that method is called, Downloader stores the completion function; it then asks for a new download task and sets it going:

```
@discardableResult
func download(url:URL,
    completionHandler ch : @escaping DownloaderCH) -> URLSessionTask {
        let task = self.session.downloadTask(with:url)
        // ... store the completion function somehow ...
        task.resume()
        return task
}
```

(I return to the client a reference to the task, so that the client can subsequently cancel the task if need be.)

When the download finishes, the DownloaderDelegate calls the completion function:

```
func urlSession(_ session: URLSession,
    downloadTask: URLSessionDownloadTask,
    didFinishDownloadingTo url: URL) {
        let ch = // ... retrieve the completion function somehow ...
        ch(url)
}
```

In my carefree speculative coding design, I have left a blank — the storage and retrieval of the completion function corresponding to each download task. Let's use the same technique I used earlier for accumulating the data of multiple data tasks, namely a dictionary keyed by the task's taskIdentifier. This will be a private property of DownloaderDelegate, along with a public method:

```
private var handlers = [Int:DownloaderCH]()
func appendHandler(_ ch:@escaping DownloaderCH, task:URLSessionTask {
    self.handlers[task.taskIdentifier] = ch
}
```

We are now ready to fill in the blank in Downloader's `download(url:completion-Handler:)` method. By the time this method is called by the client, the delegate has already been created and handed to the session, and only the session has a reference to it; so we obtain the delegate from the session and call the `append-Handler(_:task:)` method that we gave it for this purpose:

```
func download(url:URL,
    completionHandler ch : @escaping DownloaderCH) -> URLSessionTask {
        let task = self.session.downloadTask(with:url)
        let del = self.session.delegate as! DownloaderDelegate
        del.appendHandler(ch, task: task)
        task.resume()
        return task
}
```

All that remains is to write the delegate methods for DownloaderDelegate. There are two of them that we need to implement. When the download arrives, we find the completion function corresponding to this download task and call it, handing it the file URL where the downloaded data has been stored:

```
func urlSession(_ session: URLSession,
    downloadTask: URLSessionDownloadTask,
    didFinishDownloadingTo url: URL) {
        let ch = self.handlers[downloadTask.taskIdentifier]
        ch?(url)
}
```

When the task completes, whether successfully or not, we purge the completion function from the dictionary:

```
func urlSession(_ session: URLSession,
    task: URLSessionTask,
    didCompleteWithError error: Error?) {
        self.handlers[task.taskIdentifier] = nil
}
```

 As written, DownloaderDelegate's delegate methods are being called on the main thread. That's not necessarily a bad thing, but it may be preferable to run that code on a background thread. I'll describe in Chapter 24 how to do that.

Downloading Table View Data

To exercise Downloader, I'll show how to solve a pesky problem that arises quite often in real life: we have a UITableView where each cell displays text and a picture, and the picture needs to be downloaded from the Internet. We'll supply each picture lazily, when that cell might become visible. That way, if a cell never becomes visible, we might never have to download its picture.

What will our implementation of `tableView(_:cellForRowAt:)` do? It must *not* try to network synchronously — that is, it mustn't wait around for the picture to arrive before returning the cell. We must not gum up the works; this method needs to return a cell *immediately*. The correct strategy, if we don't have the image yet, is to put a placeholder (or no image at all) in the cell, and *then* see about downloading it.

The model object for a table row will be an instance of a dedicated Model class, which is nothing but a bundle of properties:

```
class Model {
    var text : String! // text for the cell's text label
    var im : UIImage! // image for the cell's image view; initially nil
    var picurl : String! // url for downloading the image
    var task : URLSessionTask! // current download task, if any
}
```

Presume, for simplicity, that we have only one section. Then our table view model is an array of Model. When the table turns to the data source for a cell in `table-View(_:cellForRowAt:)`, the data source will turn to the model and consult the Model object corresponding to the requested row, asking for its `im` property, which is supposed to be its image. Initially, this will be `nil`. In that case, the data source will display no image in this cell, and will immediately return a cell without an image.

We also want to request that the image be downloaded from this Model object's `picurl`. Later, when the image arrives and this Model object's `im` is no longer `nil`, we can *reload* the row, and this time `tableView(_:cellForRowAt:)` will find that image and display it in the cell.

This is an opportunity to exercise a feature of UITableView (and UICollectionView) that I didn't mention in Chapter 8 — *prefetching*. If we assign to our table view's `prefetchDataSource` property some object adopting the UITableViewDataSource-Prefetching protocol, the runtime will call that object's delegate method `table-View(_:prefetchRowsAt:)` *before* calling `tableView(_:cellForRowAt:)` — not only when the user *is* scrolling a cell onto the screen, but when the user *might* scroll a cell onto the screen.

This architecture allows us to separate provision of the *data* from provision of the *cell*. For example, let's say that initially the first 12 rows of the table are displayed. Then the runtime will call `tableView(_:prefetchRowsAt:)` for the *next* 12 rows — because if the user scrolls at all, those are the rows that will come into view.

Presume, then, that we (`self`, the view controller) adopt UITableViewDataSourcePre-fetching, and that we have configured the table view accordingly in our `viewDidLoad`:

```
override func viewDidLoad() {
    super.viewDidLoad()
    self.tableView.prefetchDataSource = self // turn on prefetching
}
```

Our implementation of `tableView(_:cellForRowAt:)` is trivial, just as it should be; everything we need to know is right there in the Model object for this row. The image displayed in the image view will be a downloaded UIImage or `nil`, depending on whether the Model has acquired the image for this row:

```
override func tableView(_ tableView: UITableView,
    cellForRowAt indexPath: IndexPath) -> UITableViewCell {
        let cell = tableView.dequeueReusableCell(
            withIdentifier: self.cellID, for: indexPath)
        let m = self.model[indexPath.row]
        cell.textLabel!.text = m.text
        cell.imageView!.image = m.im // picture or nil
        return cell
}
```

Meanwhile, the runtime is busy calling `tableView(_:prefetchRowsAt:)` for us. In this method we deal directly with the model data. We examine the Model for the given row; if it already has an image, obviously the image was *already* downloaded, so there's nothing more to do. We also examine the Model's `task`; if it is not `nil`, that's a marker that this image is *currently* being downloaded, so there's nothing more to do. Otherwise, we start the download, storing the download task in the Model's `task` as a sign that the download for this row has been requested:

```
func tableView(_ tableView: UITableView,
    prefetchRowsAt indexPaths: [IndexPath]) {
        for ip in indexPaths {
            let m = self.model[ip.row]
            guard m.im == nil else { return } // we have a picture already
            guard m.task == nil else { return } // already downloading
            let url = URL(string:m.picurl)!
            m.task = self.downloader.download(url:url) { url in
                // ...
            }
        }
}
```

When the download finishes, our completion function is called. We reset the Model's `task` to `nil`, because we are no longer downloading. If the image data has been successfully downloaded, we store it in the Model. Now we call `reloadRows` for this row. There's no telling when this will happen; remember, the completion function is being called asynchronously. But that doesn't matter. If the row is visible on the screen, `tableView(_:cellForRowAt:)` will be called for this row, and the image will be displayed now; if the row is no longer visible on the screen, there are no ill effects, and the image is still stored, ready for the *next* time the row becomes visible:

```
m.task = self.downloader.download(url:url) { url in
    m.task = nil
    if let url = url, let data = try? Data(contentsOf: url) {
        m.im = UIImage(data:data)
        tableView.reloadRows(at:[ip], with: .none)
    }
}
}
```

But there's a problem. When the table view *initially* appears, the images are all missing from the visible rows. That's because the runtime calls tableView(_:prefetchRowsAt:) for the *next* 12 rows, but *not* for the 12 rows that are initially visible! (I regard that as a bug in the table view architecture.) However, it's easy to deal with that; at the end of tableView(_:cellForRowAt:), I call tableView(_:prefetchRowsAt:) myself:

```
// ... same as before ...
cell.imageView!.image = m.im // picture or nil
if m.task == nil && m.im == nil {
    self.tableView(tableView, prefetchRowsAt:[indexPath])
}
return cell
```

Our table view is now working perfectly!

Further details are merely a matter of progressive refinement. For example, if these are large images, we could end up retaining many large images in the model array, which might cause us to run out of memory. There are lots of ways to deal with that. We might start by reducing each image, as it arrives, to the size needed for display. If that's still too much memory, we can implement tableView(_:didEndDisplaying:forRowAt:) to expunge each image from its Model (by setting the Model object's im to nil) when the cell scrolls out of sight; if the cell comes back into view, we would then automatically download the image again. Or, as we expunge the image from the Model, we might save it to disk and substitute the file URL as its picurl (with appropriate adjustments in the rest of the code).

Background Session

If your app goes into the background while in the middle of a normal networking task, the task might not be completed. However, iOS provides a way to request that a download or upload task be carried out regardless, even if your app isn't frontmost — indeed, even if your app isn't running. That way is to make the URLSession a *background session*. To do that, assign it a URLSessionConfiguration created with the class method background(withIdentifier:).

A background session hands the work of downloading over to the system. Your app can be suspended or terminated and the download will still be taken care of. As with location monitoring (Chapter 21), your app does not formally run in the background just because you have a background session with tasks, so you do *not* have to set the UIBackgroundModes of your *Info.plist*. But the session still serves as a gateway for putting your app in touch with the networking task as it proceeds; in particular, you need to provide the URLSession with a delegate so that you can receive messages informing you of how things are going.

The argument that you pass to `background(withIdentifier:)` is a string identifier intended to distinguish your background session from all the other background sessions that other apps have requested from the system. It should be unique; a good approach is to use your app's bundle ID as its basis.

You may want to set the URLSessionConfiguration's `isDiscretionary` to `true`. This will permit the system to postpone network communications to some moment that will conserve bandwidth and battery — for example, when Wi-Fi is available, and the device is plugged into a power socket. Of course, that might be days from now! But this is part of the beauty of background downloads.

There is no need to set a background session's `waitsForConnectivity`; it is `true` automatically, and cannot be changed. Similarly, a task does not fail if a background session's `timeoutIntervalForRequest` arrives; the background session will simply try again. However, a task is abandoned if the `timeoutIntervalForResource` arrives.

New in iOS 11, you can also set your URLSessionTask's `earliestBeginDate`. This is a date in the future; the start of the networking task is delayed until after that date. You can also implement this delegate method:

`urlSession(_:task:willBeginDelayedRequest:completionHandler:)`
New in iOS 11; optional. If implemented, called only if your URLSessionTask's `earliestBeginDate` was set. The begin date has arrived, and the system is thinking of starting the networking task. The purpose of this method is to give your app a chance to change its mind about this task, possibly canceling it or even substituting a different request. The completion function takes two parameters; your job is to call it, passing as its first argument a `URLSession.DelayedRequest-Disposition` stating your decision:

- `.cancel` (the second completion function argument will be `nil`)

- `.continueLoading` (the second completion function argument will be `nil`)

- `.useNewRequest` (the second completion function argument will be the new URLRequest)

Once the background session is configured and the task is told to `resume`, the system is going to have to get back in touch with your code somehow when it has a delegate message to send you. How it does this depends on what state your app is in at that moment:

Your app is frontmost and still running

Your app may have gone into the background one or more times, but it was never terminated, and it is frontmost now. In that case, your background URLSession still exists and is still hooked to its delegate, and the delegate messages are simply sent as usual.

Your app is not frontmost or was terminated

Your app is in the background or not running, or it is frontmost but it was terminated since the time you told your task to resume. Now the system needs to perform a handshake with your URLSession in order to get in touch with it. To make that handshake possible, you must implement these two methods:

```
application(_:handleEventsForBackgroundURLSession:completion-
Handler:)
```

This message is sent *to the app delegate*. The session: parameter is the string identifier you handed earlier to the configuration object; you might use this to identify the session, or to create and configure the session if you haven't done so already. You do *not* call the completion function now! Instead, you must *store* it, because it will be needed later.

```
urlSessionDidFinishEvents(forBackgroundURLSession:)
```

This message is sent *to the session delegate*. This is the moment when you must *call* the previously stored completion function.

When the system wants to send you a delegate message, if your app is not frontmost, it is awakened in the background and remains in the background. If it is not running, it is launched in the background and remains in the background. In the latter case, you should immediately create a URLSession, giving it a URLSessionConfiguration initialized by calling background(withIdentifier:) with the *same identifier* as before, and assigning a session delegate, which will then be able to receive delegate messages.

This is all much easier if the app delegate and the session delegate are one and the same object. In this example, the app delegate holds the URLSession property, which is created lazily; it also provides storage for the completion function:

```
lazy var session : URLSession = {
    let id = "com.neuburg.matt.backgroundDownload"
    let config = URLSessionConfiguration.background(withIdentifier: id)
    config.allowsCellularAccess = false
    // could set config.isDiscretionary here
    let sess = URLSession(
        configuration: config, delegate: self, delegateQueue: .main)
    return sess
}()
var ch : (() -> ())!
```

The URLSessionDownloadDelegate methods are as before, plus we have the two required handshake methods in case the system needs to get back in touch with us:

```
func application(_ application: UIApplication,
    handleEventsForBackgroundURLSession identifier: String,
    completionHandler: @escaping () -> ()) {
        self.ch = completionHandler
        _ = self.session // *
}
func urlSessionDidFinishEvents(forBackgroundURLSession session: URLSession) {
    self.ch?()
}
```

The starred line will "tickle" the `session` lazy initializer and bring the background session to life if needed.

 If the user kills your app in the background by way of the app switcher interface, pending background downloads will *not* be completed. The system assumes that the user doesn't want your app coming magically back to life in the background.

On-Demand Resources

Your app can store resources, such as images and sound files, on Apple's server instead of including them in the app bundle that the user initially installs on the device. Your app can then download those resources as needed when the app runs. Such resources are *on-demand resources*.

To designate a resource as being an on-demand resource in Xcode, you assign it one or more *tags* (arbitrary strings); you can do this in many places in the Xcode interface. A tag may be assigned to an individual resource or to a folder. Any resources to which you have assigned tags are *not* copied into the app when you build it; you have to obtain them as on-demand resources, in code, when your app runs.

Your on-demand resource configuration is summarized and managed in the Resource Tags pane of the target editor. Figure 23-1 shows the Resource Tags pane displaying the `"pix"` tag, which has been attached to a folder called *images* in my app bundle.

How do you obtain an on-demand resource? In code, you instantiate an NSBundle-ResourceRequest, handing it the tags of the resources you want to use. Let's call this the *request object*. You will probably want to retain the request object, probably in an instance property (I'll talk more about that in a moment). You then toggle access to the resource associated with those tags by sending the request object these messages:

beginAccessingResources(completionHandler:)
　　Your completion function is called when the resources are available (which could be immediately if they have already been downloaded). *Do not assume that the*

Figure 23-1. An on-demand resource

completion function runs on the main thread. The parameter is an Optional Error. If it is nil, you can now use the resources.

If your call causes the resources to be downloaded, you can track the download progress using the NSBundleResourceRequest's progress property, which is a Progress object. This might be desirable if the download causes a perceptible delay in your app's action and you need to let the user know what's happening. Optimally, you might use a more proactive strategy to prefetch the resources so that they are present by the time the user needs them.

endAccessingResources

Lets the runtime know that you are no longer actively using these resources. You are expected to call this method eventually. After that, you can no longer access these resources. This doesn't mean that the resources will be deleted — but they might be.

Having called endAccessingResources, you should now abandon use of this NSBundleResourceRequest instance; its life cycle is over. If you need to access the same resources again, start over by creating a new NSBundleResourceRequest and calling beginAccessingResources again.

If your app is terminated before you call endAccessingResources, then on relaunch you obviously have no NSBundleResourceRequest instance. But that doesn't matter, because you just keep following the same rules about how to access the resources. When you need access to them, you create an NSBundleResourceRequest and call beginAccessingResources; your resources might still be present, in which case you will get access immediately.

A request object, as I've already suggested, will probably need to persist, most likely as an instance property of a view controller. Indeed, because an individual NSBundle-ResourceRequest instance is tied to a specific set of tags, and hence to a specific bunch of resources, you might need to keep multiple request objects stored simultaneously. One reasonable strategy might be to declare each instance property as an Optional of type NSBundleResourceRequest?. That way, you can set the property to nil when you're done with that request instance, so that you won't accidentally use it again. A more sophisticated approach might be to maintain a single mutable dictionary of type [Set<String>:NSBundleResourceRequest], keyed by the request object's tags.

Your code that actually accesses on-demand resources does so in the normal way. For example, if the resource is an image, you can access it using UIImage's init(named:). If it's a data set in the asset catalog, you can access it using NSDataAsset's init(name:). If it is a resource at the top level of the main bundle, you can get its URL by calling url(forResource:withExtension:) on the bundle. And so forth.

What makes an on-demand resource special, from your code's point of view, is merely that your attempt to access it in this way will fail in good order — you'll get nil — until you have successfully called beginAccessingResources. After a call to begin-AccessingResources and a signal of success in its completion function, the resources spring to life and you can access them. After calling endAccessingResources, these values will all be nil again, even if the resources have not been deleted.

How on earth does this architecture work? Is it a violation of the rule that your app bundle can't be modified? No; it's all an ingenious illusion. In actual fact, your on-demand resources are kept in your app's *OnDemandResources* directory, outside the app bundle — and the methods that access resources are rejiggered so as to point to them, or to return nil, as appropriate.

There are two special categories of on-demand resource tags (visible in Figure 23-1) — *initial install* tags and *prefetch* tags:

Initial install tags
Resources with initial install tags are downloaded *at the same time* the app is installed; in effect, they appear to be part of the app.

Prefetch tags
Resources with prefetch tags are downloaded automatically by the system *after* the app is installed.

Neither of these special categories relieves you of the responsibility to call begin-Accessing before you actually use a tagged resource, nor does it prevent the resources from being deleted if you are not accessing them. The difference is that the desired resources will probably be already present when you call beginAccessing early in the lifetime of the app.

 Amazingly, you can test on-demand resources directly by running your app from Xcode. Also, you can check the status of your on-demand resources in the Disk gauge of the Debug navigator.

In-App Purchases

An in-app purchase is a specialized form of network communication: your app communicates with the App Store to permit the user to buy something there, or to confirm that something has already been bought there. This is a way to make your app itself inexpensive or free to download, while providing an optional increased price in exchange for increased functionality later. In-app purchases are made possible through the Store Kit framework; you'll need to `import StoreKit`.

There are various kinds of in-app purchase — consumables, nonconsumables, and subscriptions. You'll want to read the relevant discussion in Apple's *In-App Purchase Configuration Guide for iTunes Connect* and *In-App Purchase Programming Guide*.

To configure an in-app purchase, you need first to use iTunes Connect to create, in connection with your app, something that the user can purchase; this is easiest to do if your app is already available through the App Store. For a simple nonconsumable purchase, you are associating your app's bundle ID with a name and arbitrary product ID representing your in-app purchase, along with a price.

In order to test your app's in-app purchase interface and functionality, you will want to create a special Apple ID, called a *sandbox* ID, for testing purposes; you *cannot* test your in-app purchase interface without one. Sandbox IDs are created and managed in the Users and Roles section of iTunes Connect.

To test, you'll need to do these things:

- Test on a device. In-app purchases don't work properly in the simulator (in my experience).
- On the device, sign out of your normal Apple ID.
- Build and run directly from Xcode to the device. The development profile embedded in the app is what tells the system that App Store communication should remain inside the testing sandbox.

Now exercise your app. When the purchase dialog asks you for an Apple ID, use the sandbox ID and password. As you test repeatedly, you will probably need to delete the app from the device and sign out from the sandbox ID before building and running afresh.

 If you accidentally perform the in-app purchase later when logged into the App Store with your *real* Apple ID, you'll be charged for the purchase and you won't be able to get your money back. Can you guess how I know that?

Here's an example from an actual game app of mine, which offers a single nonconsumable purchase: it unlocks functionality allowing users to involve their own photos in the game by tapping the Choose button. When a user taps the Choose button, if

Figure 23-2. Interface for an in-app purchase

the in-app purchase has *not* been made, a pair of dialogs will appear, offering and describing the purchase (Figure 23-2); if the in-app purchase *has* been made, a UIImagePickerController's view appears instead (Chapter 17).

For a nonconsumable in-app purchase, the app must provide the following interface (all of which is visible in Figure 23-2):

- A place where the in-app purchase is described. You do not hard-code the description into your app; rather, it is downloaded in real time from the App Store, using the Display Name and Description (and price) that you entered at iTunes Connect.

- A button that launches the purchase process.

- A button that *restores* an existing purchase. The idea here is that the user has performed the purchase, but is now on a different device or has deleted and reinstalled your app, so that the UserDefaults entry stating that the purchase has been performed is missing. The user needs to be able to contact the App Store to get your app to recognize that the purchase has been performed and turn on the purchased functionality.

Both the actual purchase process and the actual restore process are performed through dialogs presented by the system; the purpose of the interface shown in Figure 23-2 is to give the user a way to initiate those processes.

In my app, the purchase process proceeds in two stages. When the user taps the Learn More button (on the left in Figure 23-2), I first confirm that the user has not been restricted from making purchases; then I create an SKProductsRequest, which will attempt to download an SKProductsResponse object embodying the details about the in-app purchase corresponding to my single product ID:

```
if !SKPaymentQueue.canMakePayments() {
    // ... put up alert saying we can't do it ...
    return
}
let req = SKProductsRequest(productIdentifiers: ["DiabelliChoose"])
req.delegate = self
req.start()
```

This kicks off some network activity, and eventually the delegate of this SKProducts-
Request, namely `self` (conforming to SKProductsRequestDelegate), is called back
with one of two delegate messages. If we get `request(_:didFailWithError:)`, I put
up an apologetic alert, and that's the end. But if we get `productsRequest(_:did-`
`Receive:)`, the request has succeeded, and we can proceed to the second stage.

In `productsRequest(_:didReceive:)`, the response from the App Store arrives as the
second parameter. It is an SKProductsResponse object containing an SKProduct representing the proposed purchase. I create the second view controller, give it a reference to the SKProduct, and present it:

```
func productsRequest(_ request: SKProductsRequest,
    didReceive response: SKProductsResponse) {
        let p = response.products[0]
        let s = StoreViewController2(product:p)
        // and on to the next view controller
        if let presenter = self.presentingViewController {
            self.dismiss(animated: true} {
                presenter.present(s, animated: true)
            }
        }
}
```

My second view controller is now being presented (on the right in Figure 23-2). This
view controller has a `product` property that was set in its initializer. In its `viewDid-`
`Load`, it populates its interface based on the information that the product contains
(for my `lend` utility, see Appendix B):

```
self.titleLabel.text = self.product.localizedTitle
self.descriptionLabel.text = self.product.localizedDescription
self.priceLabel.text = lend { (nf : NumberFormatter) in
    nf.formatterBehavior = .behavior 10_4
    nf.numberStyle = .currency
    nf.locale = self.product.priceLocale
}.string(from: self.product.price)
```

If the user taps the Purchase button, I dismiss the presented view controller, load the
SKProduct into the default SKPaymentQueue, and stand back:

```
self.dismiss(animated: true) {
    let p = SKPayment(product:self.product)
    SKPaymentQueue.default().add(p)
}
```

The system is now in charge of presenting a sequence of dialogs, confirming the purchase, asking for the user's App Store password, and so forth. My app knows nothing about that. If the user performs the purchase, however, the runtime will call `payment-Queue(_:updatedTransactions:)` on my *transaction observer*, which is an object adopting the SKPaymentTransactionObserver protocol whose job it will be to receive messages from the payment queue. But how does the runtime know who that is? When my app launches, it must *register* the transaction observer:

```
func application(application: UIApplication,
    didFinishLaunchingWithOptions launchOptions:
    [UIApplicationLaunchOptionsKey : Any]?) -> Bool {
        SKPaymentQueue.default().add(
            self.window!.rootViewController
                as! SKPaymentTransactionObserver)
        return true
}
```

As you can see, I've made my root view controller the transaction observer. It adopts the SKPaymentTransactionObserver protocol. There is only one required method — `paymentQueue(_:updatedTransactions:)`. It is called with a reference to the payment queue and an array of SKPaymentTransaction objects. My job is to cycle through these transactions and, for each one, do whatever it requires, and then, if there was an actual transaction (or an error), send `finishTransaction(_:)` to the payment queue, to clear the queue.

My implementation is extremely simple, because I have only one purchasable product, and because I'm not maintaining any separate record of receipts. For each transaction, I check its `transactionState` (SKPaymentTransactionState). If its state is `.purchased`, I pull out its `payment`, confirm that the payment's `productIdentifier` is my product identifier (it had darned well better be, since I have only the one product), and, if so, I throw the UserDefaults switch that indicates to my app that the user has performed the purchase:

```
func paymentQueue(_ queue: SKPaymentQueue,
    updatedTransactions transactions: [SKPaymentTransaction]) {
        for t in transactions {
            switch t.transactionState {
            case .purchasing, .deferred: break // do nothing
            case .purchased, .restored:
                let p = t.payment
                if p.productIdentifier == "DiabelliChoose" {
                    UserDefaults.standard.set(true, forKey: CHOOSE)
                    // ... put up an alert thanking the user ...
                    queue.finishTransaction(t)
                }
            case .failed:
```

```
                        queue.finishTransaction(t)
                }
        }
    }
```

Finally, let's talk about what happens when the user taps the Restore button (on the left in Figure 23-2). It's very simple; I just tell the default SKPaymentQueue to restore any existing purchases:

```
self.dismiss(animated: true) {
    SKPaymentQueue.default().restoreCompletedTransactions()
}
```

Again, what happens now in the interface is out of my hands; the system will present the necessary dialogs. If the purchase is restored, however, my transaction observer will be sent paymentQueue(_:updatedTransactions:) with a transactionState of .restored. We pass through exactly the same case in my switch as if the user had freshly purchased the app; as before, I throw the UserDefaults switch indicating that the user has performed the purchase.

There remains one piece of the puzzle: what if the user taps the Restore button and the purchase is *not* restored? This can happen, for example, because the user is lying or mistaken about having previously made this purchase. In that case, payment-Queue(_:updatedTransactions:) is *not* called. I regard this as a bug in the store architecture; in my view, we should be called with a .failed transaction state, so that I can learn what just happened.

As a workaround, I also implement the SKPaymentTransactionObserver method paymentQueueRestoreCompletedTransactionsFinished(_:). It is called after any restoration attempt where communication with the store was successful. This method still gives us no way to learn definitively what happened, but if payment-Queue(_:updatedTransactions:) is called, it is called *first*, so if the UserDefaults switch has *not* been thrown, we can guess that restoration failed because the user has never made the purchase in the first place.

CHAPTER 24

Threads

A *thread* is a subprocess of your app that can execute even while other subprocesses are also executing. Such simultaneous execution is called *concurrency*. The iOS frameworks use threads all the time; if they didn't, your app would be less responsive to the user — perhaps even completely unresponsive. For the most part, however, the iOS frameworks use threads behind the scenes on your behalf; you don't have to worry about threads because the frameworks are worrying about them for you.

For example, suppose your app is downloading something from the network (Chapter 23). This download doesn't happen all by itself; somewhere, someone is running code that interacts with the network and obtains data. Yet none of that interferes with your code, or prevents the user from tapping and swiping things in your interface. The networking code runs "in the background." That's concurrency in action.

This chapter discusses concurrency that involves *your* code in the use of background threads. It would have been nice to dispense with this topic altogether. Background threads can be tricky and are always potentially dangerous, and should be avoided if possible. However, sometimes you *can't* avoid them. So this chapter introduces threads. But beware: background threads entail complications and subtle pitfalls, and can make your code hard to debug. There is much more to threads, and especially to making your threaded code safe, than this chapter can possibly touch on. For detailed information about the topics introduced in this chapter, read Apple's *Concurrency Programming Guide* and *Threading Programming Guide*.

Main Thread

Distinguish between the *main* thread and all other threads. There is only one main thread; other threads are background threads. All your code must run on some thread, but you are not usually conscious of this fact, because that thread is usually

Figure 24-1. The Main Thread Checker is watching you

the main thread. The reason your code runs on the main thread is that the Cocoa frameworks ensure that this is so. How? Well, the only reason your code *ever* runs is that Cocoa calls it. When Cocoa does this, it is generally careful to call your code from the main thread. Whenever code calls a function, that function runs on the same thread as the code that called it. Thus, your code runs on the main thread.

The main thread is the interface thread. This means that the main thread is the meeting-place between you and your user. When the user interacts with the interface, those interactions are reported as events *on the main thread*. When your code interacts with the interface, it must do so *on the main thread*. Of course that will usually happen automatically, because your code normally runs on the main thread. But when you are involved with background threads, you must be careful.

So pretend now that I'm banging the table and shouting: If your code touches the interface, it *must* do so *on the main thread*. Don't *fetch* any interface-related values on a background thread. Don't *set* any interface-related values on a background thread. Whenever you use background threads, there is a chance you might touch the interface on a background thread. *Don't!*

Unfortunately, touching the interface on a background thread is a very common beginner mistake. A typical sign of trouble in this regard is an unaccountable delay of several seconds. In some cases, the console will also help with a warning. But in other, less fortunate cases, you might touch the interface on a background thread and never know it. New in Xcode 9, the Main Thread Checker will automatically report runtime violations, where your code touches the interface on a background thread; the Main Thread Checker is a diagnostic in your scheme's Run and Test actions, and is turned on by default (and I strongly recommend that you leave it turned on; Figure 24-1).

Since you and the user are both using the main thread, the main thread is a very busy place. Imagine how things proceed in your app:

1. An event arrives — on the main thread. The user has tapped a button, for example, and this is reported to your app as a UIEvent, which passes to the button through the touch delivery mechanism (Chapter 5) — on the main thread.

2. The button emits a control event that causes your code (the button's action method) to be called — on the main thread. Your code now runs — on the main thread. *While your code runs, nothing else can happen on the main thread.* Your code might perform some changes in the interface; this is safe, because your code is running on the main thread.

3. Your code finishes. The main thread's run loop is now free to report more events, and the user is free to interact with the interface once again.

The bottleneck here is obviously step 2, the running of your code. Your code runs on the main thread. That means the main thread can't do anything else while your code is running. No events can arrive while your code is running. The user can't interact with the interface while your code is running. Main thread code *blocks* the main thread — two things can't happen on the main thread at the same time — and therefore *blocks* the interface. But this is usually no problem, because:

Your code is fast
Your code executes really fast. It's true that the user can't interact with the interface while your code runs, but this is such a tiny interval of time that the user will probably never even notice.

Blocking briefly is good
Your code, as it runs, blocks the user from interacting with the interface. As long as your code finishes quickly, that's actually a good thing. Your code, in response to what the user does, might update the interface; it would be insane if the user could do something else in the interface while you're in the middle of updating it.

The iOS frameworks frequently operate on background threads. This usually doesn't affect you, because the frameworks usually talk to *your* code on the *main* thread. You have seen many examples of this in the preceding chapters:

- During an animation (Chapter 4), the interface remains responsive to the user, and it is possible for your code to run. The Core Animation framework is running the animation and updating the presentation layer on a background thread. But your delegate methods and completion functions are called on the main thread.

- A web view's fetching and loading of its content is asynchronous (Chapter 11); that means the work is done in a background thread. But your delegate methods are called on the main thread.

- Sounds are played asynchronously (Chapters 14 and 16). But your delegate methods are called on the main thread. Similarly, loading, preparation, and playing of movies happens asynchronously (Chapter 15). But your delegate methods are called on the main thread.

- Saving a movie file takes time (Chapters 15 and 17). So the saving takes place on a background thread. Similarly, UIDocument saves and reads on a background thread (Chapter 22). But your delegate methods and completion functions are called on the main thread.

Thus, you can (and should) usually ignore the existence of background threads and just keep plugging away on the main thread.

Nevertheless, there are two kinds of situation in which your code will need to be explicitly aware of background threads:

Your code is called back, but not on the main thread

Some frameworks explicitly inform you in their documentation that callbacks are not guaranteed to take place on the main thread. For example, the documentation on CATiledLayer (Chapter 7) warns that draw(_:in:) is called on a background thread. By implication, our draw(_:) code, triggered by CATiledLayer to update tiles, is running on a background thread. (Fortunately, drawing into the current graphics context is thread-safe.)

Similarly, the documentation on AV Foundation (Chapters 15 and 17) warns that its completion functions and notifications can arrive on a background thread. So if you intend to update the user interface, or use a value that might also be used by your main-thread code, you'll need to be thread-conscious.

Your code takes significant time

If your code takes significant time to run, you might need to run that code on a background thread, rather than letting it block the main thread and prevent anything else from happening there:

During launch and other app state transitions

For example, in Chapter 22, I called URL(forUbiquityContainer-Identifier:) during app launch. The documentation told me to call this method on a background thread, because it can take some time to return; we don't want to block the main thread waiting for it, because the app is trying to launch on the main thread, and the user won't see our interface until the launch process is over. Similarly, when your app is in the process of being suspended into the background, or resumed from the background, your app should not occupy the main thread; it must act quickly and get out of the way.

When the user can see or interact with the app

For example, in Chapter 19, I called enumerateEvents(matching:using:) on a background thread, because it can take some time to run. If I were to call this method on the main thread, then when the user taps the button that triggers this call, the button might stay highlighted for a significant amount of time, during which the interface will be completely frozen. I would be perceptibly blocking the main thread. Similarly, in a table view data source (Chapter 8), `tableView(_:cellForRowAt:)` needs to be fast. Otherwise, the user won't be able to scroll the table view; you'll be freezing the interface because you are blocking the main thread.

 Moving time-consuming code off the main thread, so that the main thread is not blocked, isn't just a matter of aesthetics or politeness: the system "watchdog" will summarily *kill your app* if it discovers that the main thread is blocked for too long.

Why Threading Is Hard

The one certain thing about computer code is that it just clunks along the path of execution, one statement at a time. Successive lines of code, in effect, are performed in the order in which they appear, and nothing else happens between them. With threading, that certainty goes right out the window.

If you have code that can be performed on a background thread, then *you don't know* when your code will be performed. Your code is now *concurrent*. This means that any line of your background-thread code could be *interleaved* between any two lines of your main-thread code. Indeed, under certain circumstances, your background-thread code can be called multiple times on multiple background threads, meaning that any line of your background-thread code could be interleaved between any two lines of *itself*.

The reason this can be problematic is because of *shared data*. There are variables in your app, such as instance properties, that persist and can be accessed from multiple places. Background threads mean that such variables can be accessed at unexpected moments. That is a really scary thought. Suppose, while one thread is in the middle of using a variable, another thread changes it. Who knows what horrors might result?

This problem cannot be solved by simple logic. For example, suppose you try to make access to a variable safe with a condition, as in this pseudocode:

```
if no other thread is touching this variable {
    ... do something to the variable ...
}
```

Such logic is specious. Suppose the condition succeeds: no other thread is touching this variable. But between the time when that condition is evaluated and the time when the next line executes and you start to do something to the variable, another thread can still come along and start touching the variable!

It is possible to request assistance at a deeper level to ensure that a section of code is not run by two threads simultaneously. For example, you can implement a *lock* around a section of code. But locks generate an entirely new level of potential pitfalls. In general, a lock is an invitation to forget to use the lock, or to forget to remove the lock after you've set it. And threads can end up contending for a lock in a way that permits neither thread to proceed.

Another problem has to do with thread *lifetimes*. The lifetime of a thread is independent of the lifetimes of other objects in your app. When an object is about to go out of existence and its `deinit` has been called and executed, you are supposed to be guaranteed that none of your code in that object will ever run again. But a thread might still be running, and might try to talk to your object, even after your object has supposedly gone out of existence. This can result in a crash, if you're lucky; if you're not lucky, your object might become a kind of zombie.

Not only is threaded code hard to get right; it's also hard to test and hard to debug. It introduces indeterminacy, so you can easily make a mistake that never appears in your testing, but that does appear for some user. The real danger is that the user's experience will consist only of distant consequences of your mistake, long after the point where you made it, making the true cause of the problem extraordinarily difficult to track down.

Perhaps you think I'm trying to scare you away from using threads. You're right! For an excellent (and suitably frightening) account of some of the dangers and considerations that threading involves, see Apple's technical note *Simple and Reliable Threading with NSOperation*. If terms like *race condition* and *deadlock* don't strike fear into your veins, look them up on Wikipedia.

Naturally, Xcode provides lots of aids to assist you in studying your app's use of threads. The Debug navigator distinguishes threads; you can even see pending calls and learn when a call was enqueued. When you call `NSLog`, the output in the console displays a number (in square brackets, after the colon) identifying the thread on which it was called. In Instruments, the Time Profiler records activity on different threads. And the Thread Sanitizer (visible in Figure 24-1) can help catch threading violations that would otherwise be difficult to track down.

Blocking the Main Thread

To illustrate making your code multithreaded, I need some code that is worth making multithreaded. I'll use as my example an app that draws the Mandelbrot set. (This code is adapted from a small open source project found on the Internet.) All it does is draw the basic Mandelbrot set in black and white, but that's a sufficiently elaborate calculation to introduce a significant delay, especially on an older, slower device. The idea is then to see how we can safely get that delay off the main thread.

The app contains a UIView subclass, MyMandelbrotView, which has one property, a CGContext called `bitmapContext`. Here's MyMandelbrotView:

```
let MANDELBROT_STEPS = 1000 // determines how long the calculation takes
var bitmapContext: CGContext!
// jumping-off point: draw the Mandelbrot set
func drawThatPuppy () {
    self.makeBitmapContext(size: self.bounds.size)
    let center = CGPoint(self.bounds.midX, self.bounds.midY)
    self.draw(center: center, bounds: self.bounds, zoom: 1)
    self.setNeedsDisplay()
}
// create bitmap context
func makeBitmapContext(size:CGSize) {
    var bitmapBytesPerRow = Int(size.width * 4)
    bitmapBytesPerRow += (16 - (bitmapBytesPerRow % 16)) % 16
    let colorSpace = CGColorSpaceCreateDeviceRGB()
    let prem = CGImageAlphaInfo.premultipliedLast.rawValue
    let context = CGContext(data: nil,
        width: Int(size.width), height: Int(size.height),
        bitsPerComponent: 8, bytesPerRow: bitmapBytesPerRow,
        space: colorSpace, bitmapInfo: prem)
    self.bitmapContext = context
}
// draw pixels of bitmap context
func draw(center:CGPoint, bounds:CGRect, zoom:CGFloat) {
    func isInMandelbrotSet(_ re:Float, _ im:Float) -> Bool {
        var fl = true
        var (x, y, nx, ny) : (Float, Float, Float, Float) = (0,0,0,0)
        for _ in 0 ..< MANDELBROT_STEPS {
            nx = x*x - y*y + re
            ny = 2*x*y + im
            if nx*nx + ny*ny > 4 {
                fl = false
                break
            }
            x = nx
            y = ny
        }
        return fl
    }
    self.bitmapContext.setAllowsAntialiasing(false)
    self.bitmapContext.setFillColor(red: 0, green: 0, blue: 0, alpha: 1)
    var re : CGFloat
    var im : CGFloat
    let maxi = Int(bounds.size.width)
    let maxj = Int(bounds.size.height)
    for i in 0 ..< maxi {
        for j in 0 ..< maxj {
            re = (CGFloat(i) - 1.33 * center.x) / 160
            im = (CGFloat(j) - 1.0 * center.y) / 160
            re /= zoom
```

```
            im /= zoom
            if (isInMandelbrotSet(Float(re), Float(im))) {
                self.bitmapContext.fill(
                    CGRect(CGFloat(i), CGFloat(j), 1.0, 1.0))
            }
        }
    }
}
// turn pixels of bitmap context into CGImage, draw into ourselves
override func draw(_ rect: CGRect) {
    if self.bitmapContext != nil {
        let context = UIGraphicsGetCurrentContext()!
        let im = self.bitmapContext.makeImage()
        context.draw(im!, in: self.bounds)
    }
}
```

The `draw(center:bounds:zoom:)` method, which calculates the pixels of `self.bitmapContext`, is time-consuming, and we can see this by running the app on a device. If the entire process is kicked off by tapping a button whose action method calls `drawThatPuppy`, there is a significant delay before the Mandelbrot graphic appears in the interface, during which time *the button remains highlighted*. This is a sure sign that we are blocking the main thread.

We need to move the calculation-intensive part of this code onto a background thread, so that the main thread is not blocked by the calculation. In doing so, we have two chief concerns:

Synchronization of threads

> The button is tapped, and `drawThatPuppy` is called, on the main thread. `setNeeds-Display` is thus also called on the main thread — and rightly so, since this affects the interface — and so `draw(_:)` is rightly called on the main thread as well. In between, however, the calculation-intensive `draw(center:bounds:zoom:)` is to be called on a background thread. Yet these three methods must still run *in order*: `drawThatPuppy` on the main thread, then `draw(center:bounds:zoom:)` on a background thread, then `draw(_:)` on the main thread. But threads are concurrent, so how will we ensure this?

Shared data

> The property `self.bitmapContext` is referred to in three different methods — in `makeBitmapContext(size:)`, and in `draw(center:bounds:zoom:)`, and in `draw(_:)`. But we have just said that those three methods involve two different threads; they must not be permitted to touch the same property in a way that might conflict or clash. Indeed, because `draw(center:bounds:zoom:)` runs on a background thread, it might run on multiple background threads simultaneously; the access to `self.bitmapContext` by `draw(center:bounds:zoom:)` must not be permitted to conflict or clash *with itself*. How will we ensure this?

Manual Threading

A naïve way of dealing with our time-consuming code would involve spawning off a background thread as we reach the calculation-intensive part of the procedure, by calling performSelector(inBackground:with:). This is a very bad idea, and you should *not* imitate the code in this section. I'm showing it to you only to demonstrate how horrible it is.

Adapting your code to use performSelector(inBackground:with:) is not at all simple. There is additional work to do:

Pack the arguments
> The method designated by the selector in performSelector(in-Background:with:) can take only one parameter, whose value you supply as the second argument. So if you want to pass more than one piece of information into the thread, you'll need to pack it into a single object. Typically, this will be a dictionary.

Set up an autorelease pool
> Background threads don't participate in the global autorelease pool. So the first thing you must do in your threaded code is to wrap everything in an autorelease pool. Otherwise, you'll probably leak memory as autoreleased objects are created behind the scenes and are never released.

We'll rewrite MyMandelbrotView to use manual threading. Because our draw(center:bounds:zoom:) method takes three parameters, the argument that we pass into the thread will have to pack that information into a dictionary. Once inside the thread, we'll set up our autorelease pool and unpack the dictionary. This will all be much easier if we interpose a trampoline method between drawThatPuppy and draw(center:bounds:zoom:). So our implementation now starts like this:

```
func drawThatPuppy () {
    self.makeBitmapContext(size:self.bounds.size)
    let center = CGPoint(self.bounds.midX, self.bounds.midY)
    let d : [AnyHashable:Any] =
        ["center":center, "bounds":self.bounds, "zoom":CGFloat(1)]
    self.performSelector(inBackground: #selector(reallyDraw), with: d)
}
// trampoline, background thread entry point
@objc func reallyDraw(_ d: [AnyHashable:Any]) {
    autoreleasepool {
        self.draw(center: d["center"] as! CGPoint,
            bounds: d["bounds"] as! CGRect,
            zoom: d["zoom"] as! CGFloat)
        // ...
    }
}
```

The comment with the ellipsis indicates a missing piece of functionality: we have yet to call setNeedsDisplay, which will cause the actual drawing to take place. This call used to be in drawThatPuppy, but that is now too soon; the call to perform-Selector(inBackground:with:) launches the thread and returns immediately, so our bitmapContext property isn't ready yet. Clearly, we need to call setNeedsDisplay *after* draw(center:bounds:zoom:) has *finished* generating the pixels of the graphics context. We can do this at the end of our trampoline method reallyDraw(_:).

But then we must remember that reallyDraw(_:) runs in a background thread. Because setNeedsDisplay is a form of communication with the interface, we should call it on the main thread, with performSelector(onMainThread:with:waitUntil-Done:). For maximum flexibility, it will probably be best to implement a second trampoline method:

```
// trampoline, background thread entry point
func reallyDraw(_ d: [AnyHashable:Any]) {
    autoreleasepool {
        self.draw(center: d["center"] as! CGPoint,
            bounds: d["bounds"] as! CGRect,
            zoom: d["zoom"] as! CGFloat)
        self.performSelector(onMainThread: #selector(allDone), with: nil,
            waitUntilDone: false)
    }
}
// called on main thread! background thread exit point
@objc func allDone() {
    self.setNeedsDisplay()
}
```

This works, in the sense that when we tap the button, it is highlighted momentarily and then immediately unhighlighted; the time-consuming calculation is taking place on a background thread. But the seeds of nightmare are already sown:

- We now have a single object, MyMandelbrotView, some of whose methods are to be called on the main thread and some on a background thread; this invites us to become confused at some later time.

- The main thread and the background thread are constantly sharing a piece of data, the instance property self.bitmapContext; this is messy and fragile. And what's to stop some other code from coming along and triggering draw(_:) while draw(center:bounds:zoom:) is in the middle of manipulating the bitmap context that draw(_:) draws?

To solve these problems, we might need to use locks, and we would probably have to manage the thread more explicitly. Such code can become quite elaborate and difficult to understand; guaranteeing its integrity is even more difficult. There are much better ways, and I will now demonstrate two of them.

Operation

An excellent strategy is to turn to a brilliant pair of classes, Operation and Operation-Queue. The essence of Operation is that it encapsulates a task, not a thread. You don't concern yourself with threads directly; the threading is determined for you by an OperationQueue. You describe the task as an Operation, and add it to an Operation-Queue to set it going. You arrange to be notified when the task ends, typically by the Operation posting a notification. (You can also safely query both the queue and its operations from outside with regard to their state.)

We'll rewrite MyMandelbrotView to use Operation and OperationQueue. We need an OperationQueue property; we'll call it `queue`, and we'll create the OperationQueue and configure it in the property's initializer:

```
let queue : OperationQueue = {
    let q = OperationQueue()
    // ... further configurations can go here ...
    return q
}()
```

We also have a new class, MyMandelbrotOperation, an Operation subclass. (It is possible to take advantage of a built-in Operation subclass such as BlockOperation, but I'm deliberately illustrating the more general case by subclassing Operation itself.) Our implementation of `drawThatPuppy` creates an instance of MyMandelbrot-Operation, configures it, registers for its notification, and adds it to the queue:

```
func drawThatPuppy () {
    let center = CGPoint(self.bounds.midX, self.bounds.midY)
    let op = MyMandelbrotOperation(
        center: center, bounds: self.bounds, zoom: 1)
    NotificationCenter.default.addObserver(self,
        selector: #selector(operationFinished),
        name: .mandelOpFinished, object: op)
    self.queue.addOperation(op)
}
```

Our time-consuming calculations will be performed by MyMandelbrotOperation. An Operation subclass, such as MyMandelbrotOperation, will typically have at least two methods:

A designated initializer
> The Operation may need some configuration data. Once the Operation is added to a queue, it's too late to talk to it, so you'll usually hand it this configuration data as you create it, in its designated initializer.

A main method
> This method will be called automatically by the OperationQueue when it's time for the Operation to start.

MyMandelbrotOperation has three private properties center, bounds, and zoom, to be set in its initializer; it must be told MyMandelbrotView's geometry explicitly because it is completely separate from MyMandelbrotView. MyMandelbrotOperation also has its own CGContext property, bitmapContext; it must be publicly gettable so that MyMandelbrotView can retrieve the finished graphics context. Note that this is different from MyMandelbrotView's bitmapContext, thus helping to solve the problem of sharing data promiscuously between threads:

```
private let center : CGPoint
private let bounds : CGRect
private let zoom : CGFloat
private(set) var bitmapContext : CGContext! = nil
init(center c:CGPoint, bounds b:CGRect, zoom z:CGFloat) {
    self.center = c
    self.bounds = b
    self.zoom = z
    super.init()
}
```

makeBitmapContext(size:) and draw(center:bounds:zoom:), the methods that perform the time-consuming calculation, have been transferred from MyMandelbrotView to MyMandelbrotOperation unchanged; the only difference is that when these methods refer to self.bitmapContext, that now means MyMandelbrotOperation's bitmapContext property:

```
let MANDELBROT_STEPS = 1000
func makeBitmapContext(size:CGSize) {
    // ... same as before
}
func draw(center:CGPoint, bounds:CGRect, zoom:CGFloat) {
    // ... same as before
}
```

Finally, we come to MyMandelbrotOperation's main method. First, we check the Operation isCancelled property to make sure we haven't been cancelled while sitting in the queue; this is good practice. Then, we do exactly what drawThatPuppy used to do, initializing our graphics context and drawing into its pixels. At that point, the calculation is over and it's time for MyMandelbrotView to come and fetch our data. There are two ways in which MyMandelbrotView can learn this; either main can post a notification through the NotificationCenter, or MyMandelbrotView can use key-value observing to be notified when our isFinished property changes. We've chosen the former approach; observe that we check one more time to make sure we haven't been cancelled:

```
override func main() {
    guard !self.isCancelled else {return}
    self.makeBitmapContext(size: self.bounds.size)
    self.draw(center: self.center, bounds: self.bounds, zoom: self.zoom)
    if !self.isCancelled {
```

```
            NotificationCenter.default.post(
                name: .mandelOpFinished, object: self)
        }
    }
```

Now we are back in MyMandelbrotView, hearing through the notification that MyMandelbrotOperation has finished. We must immediately pick up any required data, because the OperationQueue is about to release this Operation. However, we must be careful; the notification may have been posted on a background thread, in which case our method for responding to it will also be called on a background thread. We are about to set our own graphics context and tell ourselves to redraw; those are things we want to do on the main thread. So we immediately step out to the main thread (using Grand Central Dispatch, described more fully in the next section). We remove ourselves as notification observer for this operation instance, copy the operation's bitmapContext into our own bitmapContext, and we're ready to redraw:

```
// warning! called on background thread
@objc func operationFinished(_ n:Notification) {
    if let op = n.object as? MyMandelbrotOperation {
        DispatchQueue.main.async {
            NotificationCenter.default.removeObserver(self,
                name: .mandelOpFinished, object: op)
            self.bitmapContext = op.bitmapContext
            self.setNeedsDisplay()
        }
    }
}
```

Adapting our code to use Operation has involved some work, but the result has many advantages that help to ensure that our use of multiple threads is coherent and safe:

The background task is encapsulated

Because MyMandelbrotOperation is an object, we've been able to move all the code having to do with drawing the pixels of the Mandelbrot set into it. The *only* MyMandelbrotView method that can be called in the background is operation-Finished(_:), and that's a method we'd never call explicitly ourselves, so we won't misuse it accidentally — and it immediately steps out to the main thread in any case.

The data sharing is rationalized

Because MyMandelbrotOperation is an object, it has its own bitmapContext property. The only moment of data sharing comes in operationFinished(_:), when we must set MyMandelbrotView's bitmapContext to MyMandelbrotOperation's bitmapContext — and that happens on the main thread, so there's no danger. Even if multiple MyMandelbrotOperation objects are added to the queue, they are separate objects with separate `bitmapContext` properties, which MyMandelbrotView retrieves only on the main thread, so there is no conflict.

The threads are synchronized

The calculation-intensive operation doesn't start until MyMandelbrotView tells it to start (`self.queue.addOperation(op)`). MyMandelbrotView then takes its hands off the steering wheel and makes *no* attempt to draw itself. If `draw(_:)` is unexpectedly called by the runtime, `self.bitmapContext` will be `nil` or will contain the results of an earlier calculation operation, and no harm done. Nothing else happens until the operation ends and the notification arrives (`operationFinished(_:)`); then and only then does MyMandelbrotView update the interface — on the main thread.

If we are concerned with the possibility that more than one instance of MyMandelbrotOperation might be added to the queue and executed concurrently, we have a further line of defense — we can set the OperationQueue's maximum concurrency level to 1:

```
let q = OperationQueue()
q.maxConcurrentOperationCount = 1
```

This turns the OperationQueue into a *serial* queue: every operation on the queue must be completely executed before the next can begin. This might cause an operation added to the queue to take longer to execute, if it must wait for another operation to finish before it can even get started; however, this delay might not be important. What *is* important is that by executing the operations on this queue separately from one another, we guarantee that only one operation at a time can do any data sharing. A serial queue is thus implicitly a safe and reliable form of data locking.

Because MyMandelbrotView can be destroyed (if, for example, its view controller is destroyed), there is still a risk that it will create an operation that will outlive it and will try to access it after it has been destroyed. We can reduce that risk by canceling all operations in our queue as MyMandelbrotView goes out of existence:

```
deinit {
    self.queue.cancelAllOperations()
}
```

There is more to know about Operation; it's a powerful tool. One Operation can have another Operation as a *dependency*, meaning that the former cannot start until the latter has finished, even if they are in different OperationQueues. Moreover, the behavior of an Operation can be customized; for example, an Operation subclass can redefine what `isReady` means and thus can control when it is capable of execution. Thus, Operations can be combined to express your app's logic, guaranteeing that one thing happens before another (cogently argued in a brilliant WWDC 2015 video).

Grand Central Dispatch

Grand Central Dispatch, or *GCD*, is a sort of low-level analogue to Operation and OperationQueue; in fact, OperationQueue uses GCD under the hood. When I say GCD is low-level, I'm not kidding; it is effectively baked into the operating system kernel. Thus it can be used by any code whatsoever and is tremendously efficient.

GCD is like OperationQueue in that it uses queues: you express a task and add it to a queue, and the task is executed on a thread as needed. A GCD queue is represented by a *dispatch queue* (DispatchQueue), a lightweight opaque pseudo-object consisting essentially of a list of functions to be executed. You can use a built-in system queue or you can make your own; if you make your own, your queue by default is a *serial* queue, with each task on that queue finishing before the next is started, which, as I've already said, is a form of data locking.

We'll rewrite MyMandelbrotView to use GCD. We start by creating a queue and storing it in an instance property:

```
let MANDELBROT_STEPS = 1000
var bitmapContext: CGContext!
let draw_queue = DispatchQueue(label: "com.neuburg.mandeldraw")
```

Our goal is to eliminate data sharing, so our `makeBitmapContext(size:)` method now returns a graphics context rather than setting a property directly:

```
func makeBitmapContext(size:CGSize) -> CGContext {
    // ... as before ...
    let context = CGContext(data: nil,
        width: Int(size.width), height: Int(size.height),
        bitsPerComponent: 8, bytesPerRow: bitmapBytesPerRow,
        space: colorSpace, bitmapInfo: prem)
    return context!
}
```

For the same reason, our `draw(center:bounds:zoom:)` method now takes an additional `context:` parameter, the graphics context to draw into, and operates on that context without ever referring to `self.bitmapContext`:

```
func draw(center:CGPoint, bounds:CGRect, zoom:CGFloat, context:CGContext) {
    // ... as before, but we refer to local context, not self.bitmapContext
}
```

Now for the implementation of `drawThatPuppy`. This is where all the action is:

```
func drawThatPuppy () {
    let center = CGPoint(self.bounds.midX, self.bounds.midY)
    let bounds = self.bounds ❶
    self.draw_queue.async { ❷
        let bitmap = self.makeBitmapContext(size: bounds.size) ❸
        self.draw(center: center, bounds: bounds, zoom: 1, context: bitmap)
        DispatchQueue.main.async { ❹
```

```
            self.bitmapContext = bitmap ❺
            self.setNeedsDisplay()
        }
    }
}
```

That's all there is to it: *all* our app's multithreading is concentrated in those few lines! There are no notifications; there is no sharing of data between threads; and the synchronization of our threads is expressed directly through the sequential order of the code.

Our code makes two calls to the DispatchQueue `async` method, which takes as its parameter a function — usually, an anonymous function — expressing what we want done asynchronously on this queue. This is the GCD method you'll use most, because asynchronous execution will be your primary reason for using GCD in the first place. It has several optional parameters, but we don't need any of them here; we simply supply an anonymous function.

Our two calls to `async` are *nested* — the first call takes an anonymous function, which contains the second call, which takes another anonymous function. This nesting is crucial, because trailing anonymous functions are closures that can see the higher surrounding scope. As a result, we don't need to use any passing of parameters from an outer scope to an inner scope. The local variables `center` and `bounds` simply "fall" into the anonymous function of the first call to `async`, and the local variable `bitmap` simply "falls" into the anonymous function of the second call to `async`. Thus there is no data sharing, because values cascade sequentially from one scope into the next.

Here's how `drawThatPuppy` works:

❶ We begin by calculating our `center` and `bounds`. These local variables will be visible within the subsequent anonymous functions, because a function body's code can see its surrounding context and capture it.

❷ Now comes our task to be performed in a separate background thread on our queue, `self.draw_queue`. We specify this task with the `async` method. We describe what we want to do on the background thread in an anonymous function.

❸ In the anonymous function, we begin by declaring `bitmap` as a *local* variable. This is our graphics context. We call `makeBitmapContext(size:)` to create it, and then call `draw(center:bounds:zoom:context:)` to set its pixels. Those calls are made on a *background* thread, because `self.draw_queue` is a background queue.

❹ Now we need to step back out to the *main* thread. How do we do that? With the `async` method again! This time, we specify the main queue (which is effectively the main thread), whose name is `DispatchQueue.main`. We describe what we want to do on the main queue in *another* anonymous function.

❺ Here we are in the second anonymous function. Because the first function is part of the second function's surrounding context, the second function can see the first function's local `bitmap` variable. Using it, we set our `bitmapContext` property and call `setNeedsDisplay` — on the main thread! — and we're done.

The benefits and elegance of GCD as a form of concurrency management are simply stunning:

No data sharing
> The only time we ever refer to a property of `self` is at the start (`self.bounds`) and at the end (`self.bitmapContext`), when we are *on the main thread*. The bitmap context where all the drawing action takes place is a *local* variable, `bitmap`, confined to each individual call to `drawThatPuppy`. Moreover, that drawing action is performed on a serial queue, so no two drawing actions can ever overlap.

Transparent synchronization of threads
> The threads are correctly synchronized, and this is *obvious*, because the nested anonymous functions are executed *in succession*, so any instance of `bitmap` must be completely filled with pixels before being used to set the `bitmapContext` property.

Maintainability
> Our code is highly maintainable, because the entire task on all threads is expressed within the single `drawThatPuppy` method; indeed, the code is modified only very slightly from the original nonthreaded version

You might object that we still have the methods `makeBitmapContext(size:)` and `draw(center:bounds:zoom:context:)` hanging around MyMandelbrotView, and that we must therefore still be careful not to call them on the main thread, or indeed from anywhere except from within `drawThatPuppy`. If that were true, we could at this point destroy both methods and move their functionality completely into `drawThatPuppy`. But we don't have to, because these methods are now *thread-safe*: they are self-contained utilities that touch no properties or persistent objects, so it doesn't matter what thread they are called on. Still, I'll demonstrate later how we can intercept an accidental attempt to call a method on the wrong thread.

Commonly Used GCD Methods

The most important DispatchQueue methods are:

`async(execute:)`

Push a function onto the end of a queue for later execution, and *proceed immediately* with the next line of our own code. The function will execute whenever the queue determines, and meanwhile we can finish our own execution without waiting for that to happen. Commonly, however, there is *no* next line of our own code; an `async` call is typically the last statement (as was the case for both `async` calls in the preceding example).

You might use `async` to execute code in a background thread or, conversely, from *within* a background thread as a way of stepping back onto the main thread in order to talk to the interface. Also, it can be useful to call `async` to step out to the main thread even though you're *already* on the main thread, as a minimal form of delayed performance, a way of waiting for the run loop to complete and for the interface to settle down; examples have appeared throughout this book.

`asyncAfter(deadline:execute:)`

Similar to `async`, but the function is executed only after a certain amount of time has been permitted to elapse following the call (*delayed performance*). Many examples in this book have made use of it through my `delay` utility function (see Appendix B).

`sync(execute:)`

Push a function onto the end of a queue for later execution, and *wait* until the function has executed before proceeding with our own code. You should do this only in special circumstances, typically where you need the queue as a lock, mediating access to a shared resource, but you also need to *use a result* that the function is to provide.

The use of `sync` is sufficiently unusual that it deserves an example. Let's say we'd like to revise the Downloader class from Chapter 23 so that the delegate methods are run on a background thread, thus taking some strain off the main thread (and hence the user interface) while these messages are flying around behind the scenes. This looks like a reasonable and safe thing to do, because the URLSession and its delegate are packaged inside the Downloader object, isolated from our view controller.

To begin with, we'll need our own background OperationQueue, which we can maintain as a property:

```
let queue = OperationQueue()
```

Our session is now configured and created using this background queue:

```
lazy var session : URLSession = {
    return URLSession(configuration:self.config,
        delegate:DownloaderDelegate(), delegateQueue:self.queue)
}()
```

This means that `urlSession(_:downloadTask:didFinishDownloadingTo:)` will be called on our background queue. So what will happen when we call back into the client through the completion function that the client handed us at the outset? My feeling is that there is no need to involve the client in threading issues; so I want to step out to the main thread as I call the completion function. But we cannot do this by calling `async`:

```
let ch = self.handlers[downloadTask.taskIdentifier]
DispatchQueue.main.async { // bad idea!
    ch?(url)
}
```

The reason is that the downloaded file is slated to be *destroyed* as soon as we return from `urlSession(_:downloadTask:didFinishDownloadingTo:)` — and if we call `async`, we will return *immediately*, the downloaded file *will* be destroyed, and `url` will end up pointing at nothing by the time the client receives it! The solution is to use `sync` instead:

```
let ch = self.handlers[downloadTask.taskIdentifier]
DispatchQueue.main.sync {
    ch?(url)
}
```

That code steps out to the main thread and also postpones returning from `url-Session(_:downloadTask:didFinishDownloadingTo:)` until the client has had an opportunity to do something with the file pointed to by `url`. In this way we lock down the shared data (the downloaded file). We are blocking our background OperationQueue, but this is legal, and in any case we're blocking very briefly and in a coherent manner.

Another useful GCD feature to know about is *dispatch groups*. A dispatch group effectively combines independent tasks into a single task; we proceed only when *all* of them have completed. Its usage is structured as in Example 24-1.

Example 24-1. Dispatch group usage

```
let group = DispatchGroup()
// here we go...
group.enter()
queue1.async {
    // ... do task here ...
    group.leave()
}
group.enter()
queue2.async {
    // ... do task here ...
    group.leave()
}
group.enter()
```

```
queue3.async {
    // ... do task here ...
    group.leave()
}
// ... more as needed ...
group.notify(queue: DispatchQueue.main) {
    // finished!
}
```

In Example 24-1, each task to be performed asynchronously is preceded by a call to our dispatch group's enter and is followed by a call to our dispatch group's leave. The queues on which the tasks are performed do not have to be different queues; the point is that it doesn't matter if they are. Only when every enter has been balanced by a leave will the completion function in our dispatch group's notify be called. Thus, this is effectively a way of *waiting* until all the tasks have completed independently, before proceeding with whatever the notify completion function says to do.

Concurrent Queues

Besides serial dispatch queues, there are also *concurrent* dispatch queues. A concurrent queue's functions are started in the order in which they were submitted to the queue, but a function is allowed to start while another function is still executing. Obviously, you wouldn't want to submit to a concurrent queue a task that touches a shared resource! The advantage of concurrent queues is a possible speed boost when you don't care about the order in which multiple tasks are finished — for example, when you want to do something with regard to every element of an array.

The built-in global queues, available by calling DispatchQueue.global(qos:), are concurrent. You specify *which* built-in global queue you want by means of the qos: argument; this is a DispatchQoS.QoSClass value (QoS is an acronym for "quality of service"), which can be:

- .userInteractive
- .userInitiated
- .default
- .utility
- .background

You can also create a concurrent queue yourself by calling the DispatchQueue initializer init(label:attributes:) with a .concurrent attribute.

Ensuring One-time Calls Without GCD

Sometimes, you need a thread-safe way of ensuring that code is run only once; this is often used, for example, to help vend a singleton. In Objective-C, you'd use dispatch_once, which is part of GCD; in Swift, however, dispatch_once is unavailable (because it can't be implemented in a thread-safe way).

The workaround is *not* to use GCD, but rather to take advantage of the built-in lazy initialization feature of global and static variables.

In this example, my view controller has a constant property oncer whose value is an instance of a struct Oncer that has a doThisOnce method; the actual functionality of that method is embedded in the initializer of a private static property once. The result is that, no matter how many times we call self.oncer.doThisOnce() in the course of this view controller's lifetime, that functionality will be performed only once:

```
class ViewController: UIViewController {
    struct Oncer {
        private static var once : Void = {
            print("I did it!")
        }()
        func doThisOnce() {
            _ = Oncer.once
        }
    }
    let oncer = Oncer()
    override func viewDidLoad() {
        super.viewDidLoad()
        self.oncer.doThisOnce() // I did it!
        self.oncer.doThisOnce() // nothing
    }
}
```

To change the temporal scope of the "onceness," change the semantic scope of oncer. If oncer is defined at the top level of a file, its once functionality can be performed only once in the entire lifetime of the app.

Checking the Queue

A question that sometimes arises is how to make certain that a method is called only on the correct queue. Recall that in our Mandelbrot drawing example, we may be concerned that a method such as makeBitmapContext(size:) might be called on some other queue than the background queue that we created for this purpose. This sort of problem can be solved quite elegantly by calling the dispatchPrecondition(condition:) global function. It takes a DispatchPredicate enum, whose cases are:

- `.onQueue`
- `.onQueueAsBarrier`
- `.notOnQueue`

These cases each take an associated value which is a DispatchQueue. (I told you it was elegant!) Thus, to assert that we are on our `draw_queue` queue, we would say:

```
dispatchPrecondition(condition: .onQueue(self.draw_queue))
```

The outcome is similar to Swift's native `precondition` function: if our assertion is false, we'll crash.

Threads and App Backgrounding

A problem arises if your app is backgrounded and suspended while your code is running. The system doesn't want to stop your code while it's executing; on the other hand, some other app may need to be given the bulk of the device's resources now. So as your app goes into the background, the system waits a very short time for your app to finish doing whatever it may be doing, and it then suspends your app.

This shouldn't be a problem from your main thread's point of view, because your app shouldn't have any time-consuming code on the main thread in the first place; you now know that you can avoid this by using a background thread. On the other hand, it could be a problem for lengthy background tasks, including asynchronous tasks performed by the frameworks.

To solve that kind of issue, you can *request extra time* to complete a lengthy task (or at to least abort it yourself, coherently) in case your app is backgrounded, by wrapping it in calls to UIApplication's `beginBackgroundTask(expirationHandler:)` and `endBackgroundTask(_:)`. Here's how you do it:

1. You call `beginBackgroundTask(expirationHandler:)` to announce that a lengthy task is beginning; it returns an identification number. This tells the system that if your app is backgrounded, you'd like to be woken from suspension in the background now and then in order to complete the task.

2. At the end of your lengthy task, you call `endBackgroundTask(_:)`, passing in the same identification number that you got from your call to `beginBackgroundTask(expirationHandler:)`. This tells the system that your lengthy task is over and that there is no need to grant you any more background time.

The function that you pass as the argument to `beginBackgroundTask(expirationHandler:)` does *not* express the lengthy task. It expresses what you will do *if your extra time expires* before you finish your lengthy task. This is a chance for you to

---

clean up. At the very least, your expiration function must call endBackground-Task(_:)! Otherwise, the runtime won't know that you've run your expiration function, and your app may be killed as a punishment for trying to use too much background time. If your expiration function *is* called, you should make no assumptions about what thread it is running on.

Let's use MyMandelbrotView as an example. Let's say that if drawThatPuppy is started, we'd like it to be allowed to finish, even if the app is suspended in the middle of it, so that our bitmapContext property is updated as requested. To try to ensure this, we call beginBackgroundTask(expirationHandler:) before doing anything else; our hope is that if our app is backgrounded while drawThatPuppy is in progress, it will be given enough background time to run so that it can eventually proceed all the way to the end:

```
func drawThatPuppy () {
    // prepare for background task
    var bti : UIBackgroundTaskIdentifier = UIBackgroundTaskInvalid
    bti = UIApplication.shared.beginBackgroundTask {
        UIApplication.shared.endBackgroundTask(bti) // expiration
    }
    guard bti != UIBackgroundTaskInvalid else { return }
    // now do our task as before
    let center = CGPoint(self.bounds.midX, self.bounds.midY)
    let bounds = self.bounds
    self.draw_queue.async {
        let bitmap = self.makeBitmapContext(size: bounds.size)
        self.draw(center: center, bounds: bounds, zoom: 1, context: bitmap)
        DispatchQueue.main.async {
            self.bitmapContext = bitmap
            self.setNeedsDisplay()
            UIApplication.shared.endBackgroundTask(bti) // completion
        }
    }
}
```

Observe that there are two routes by which endBackgroundTask(_:) might be called:

We are not given enough time

Our expiration function is called. There is no cleanup to do, so we just call end-BackgroundTask(_:).

We are given enough time

Our entire drawThatPuppy runs from start to finish; thus, self.bitmapContext will be updated, and setNeedsDisplay will be called, while we are still in the background, and we signal completion by calling endBackgroundTask(_:). Our draw(_:) will not be called until our app is brought back to the front, but there's nothing wrong with that.

CHAPTER 25

Undo

The ability to undo the most recent action is familiar from macOS. The idea is that, provided the user realizes soon enough that a mistake has been made, that mistake can be reversed. Typically, a Mac application will maintain an internal stack of undoable actions; choosing Edit → Undo or pressing Command-Z will reverse the action at the top of the stack, and will also make that action available for redo.

Some iOS apps may benefit from an undo facility. Certain built-in views — in particular, those that involve text entry, namely UITextField and UITextView (Chapter 10) — implement undo already. And you can add it in other areas of your app.

Undo is provided through an instance of UndoManager, which basically just maintains a stack of undoable actions, along with a secondary stack of redoable actions. The goal in general is to work with the UndoManager so as to handle both undo and redo in the standard manner: when the user chooses to undo the most recent action, the action at the top of the undo stack is popped off and reversed and is pushed onto the top of the redo stack.

In this chapter, I'll illustrate an UndoManager for a simple app that has just one kind of undoable action. More complicated apps, obviously, will be more complicated; on the other hand, iOS apps, unlike macOS apps, do not generally need deep or pervasive undo functionality. For more about the UndoManager class and how to use it, read Apple's *Undo Architecture* and the class documentation.

 UIDocument (see Chapter 22) has an undo manager (its undoManager property), which appropriately updates the document's "dirty" state for you automatically.

Undo Manager

In our artificially simple app, the user can drag a small square around the screen. We'll start with an instance of a UIView subclass, MyView, to which has been attached a UIPanGestureRecognizer to make it draggable, as described in Chapter 5. The gesture recognizer's action target is the MyView instance itself, and its action method is called `dragging(_:)`:

```
@objc func dragging (_ p : UIPanGestureRecognizer) {
    switch p.state {
    case .began, .changed:
    let delta = p.translation(in:self.superview!)
        var c = self.center
        c.x += delta.x; c.y += delta.y
        self.center = c
        p.setTranslation(.zero, in: self.superview!)
    default:break
    }
}
```

Our goal is to make dragging of this view undoable. We will need an UndoManager instance. Let's store this in a property of MyView itself, `self.undoer`:

```
let undoer = UndoManager()
```

Now we need to use the undo manager to *register* the drag action as undoable. I'll show two ways of doing that.

Target–Action Undo

I'll start with this UndoManager method:

- `registerUndo(withTarget:selector:object:)`

This method uses a target–action architecture: you provide a target, a selector for a method that takes one parameter, and the object value to be passed as argument when the method is called. Later, if the UndoManager is sent the `undo` message, it simply sends that action to that target with that argument. The job of the action method is to undo whatever it is that needs undoing.

What we want to undo here is the setting of our `center` property — this line in the earlier code:

```
self.center = c
```

We need to express this as a method taking one parameter, so that the undo manager can call it (the `selector:`). So, in our `dragging(_:)` method, instead of setting `self.center` to c directly, we now call a secondary method:

```
var c = self.center
c.x += delta.x; c.y += delta.y
self.setCenterUndoably(c) // *
```

We have posited a method setCenterUndoably(_:). Now let's write it. What should it do? At a minimum, it should do the job that setting self.center used to do. At the same time, we want the undo manager to be able to call this method. The undo manager doesn't know the *type* of the parameter that it will be passing to us, so its object: parameter is typed as Any. Therefore, the parameter of this method also needs to be typed as Any:

```
func setCenterUndoably (_ newCenter:Any) {
    self.center = newCenter as! CGPoint
}
```

This works, in the sense that the view is draggable exactly as before; but we have not yet made this action undoable. To do so, we must ask ourselves what message the UndoManager would need to send in order to undo the action we are about to perform. We would want the UndoManager to set self.center back to the value it has *now*, before we change it as we are about to do. And what method would the Undo-Manager call in order to do that? It would call setCenterUndoably(_:), the very method we are implementing! So now we have this:

```
@objc func setCenterUndoably (_ newCenter:Any) {
    self.undoer.registerUndo(withTarget: self,
        selector: #selector(setCenterUndoably),
        object: self.center)
    self.center = newCenter as! CGPoint
}
```

That code works; it makes our action undoable. And it also has an astonishing secondary effect: it makes our action redoable as well! How can this be? Well, it turns out that UndoManager has an internal state, and responds differently to register-Undo(withTarget:selector:object:) depending on that state. If the UndoManager is sent registerUndo(withTarget:selector:object:) *while it is undoing*, it puts the target–action information on the redo stack instead of the undo stack (because redo *is* the undo of an undo, if you see what I mean).

Confused? Here's how our code works to undo and then redo an action:

1. We set self.center by way of setCenterUndoably(_:), which calls register-Undo(withTarget:selector:object:) with the *old* value of self.center. The UndoManager adds this to its *undo* stack.

2. Now suppose we want to undo that action. We send undo to the UndoManager.

3. The UndoManager calls setCenterUndoably(_:) with the *old* value that we passed it in step 1. Thus, we are going to set the center back to that old value. But before we do that, we send registerUndo(withTarget:selector:object:) to

the UndoManager with the *current* value of `self.center`. The UndoManager knows that it is currently undoing, so it understands this registration as something to be added to its *redo* stack.

4. Now suppose we want to redo that undo. We send `redo` to the UndoManager, and sure enough, the UndoManager calls `setCenterUndoably(_:)` with the value that we previously undid. And, once again, we call `registerUndo(withTarget:selector:object:)` with an action that goes onto the UndoManager's *undo* stack.

Undo Grouping

So far, so good. But our implementation of undo is very annoying, because we are adding a single object to the undo stack every time `dragging(_:)` is called — and it is called *many times* during the course of a single drag! Thus, undoing merely undoes the tiny increment corresponding to one individual `dragging(_:)` call. What we'd like is for undoing to undo an *entire* dragging gesture. We can implement this through *undo grouping*. As the gesture begins, we start a group; when the gesture ends, we end the group:

```
func dragging (_ p : UIPanGestureRecognizer) {
    switch p.state {
    case .began:
        self.undoer.beginUndoGrouping() // *
        fallthrough
    case .changed:
        let delta = p.translation(in:self.superview!)
        var c = self.center
        c.x += delta.x; c.y += delta.y
        self.setCenterUndoably(c)
        p.setTranslation(.zero, in: self.superview!)
    case .ended, .cancelled:
        self.undoer.endUndoGrouping() // *
    default:break
    }
}
```

This works: each complete gesture of dragging MyView, from the time the user's finger contacts the view to the time it leaves, is now undoable (and redoable) as a single unit.

A further refinement would be to animate the "drag" that the UndoManager performs when it undoes or redoes a user drag gesture. To do so, we take advantage of the fact that we, too, can examine the UndoManager's state by way of its `isUndoing` and `isRedoing` properties; we animate the `center` change when the UndoManager is "dragging," but not when the user is dragging:

```
@objc func setCenterUndoably (_ newCenter:Any) {
    self.undoer.registerUndo(withTarget: self,
        selector: #selector(setCenterUndoably),
        object: self.center)
    if self.undoer.isUndoing || self.undoer.isRedoing {
        UIView.animate(withDuration:0.4, delay: 0.1, animations: {
            self.center = newCenter as! CGPoint
        })
    } else { // just do it
        self.center = newCenter as! CGPoint
    }
}
```

Functional Undo

Starting in iOS 9, there's a more modern way to register an action as undoable:

- `registerUndo(withTarget:handler:)`

The `handler:` is a function that will take one parameter, namely whatever you pass as the `target:` argument, and will be called when undoing (or, if we register while undoing, when redoing). This gives us a far more idiomatic way to express registration of an action. In addition, `setCenterUndoably(_:)` no longer needs to take an Any as its parameter; it can take a CGPoint, because instead of asking Objective-C to call it for us, we are calling it directly:

```
func setCenterUndoably (_ newCenter:CGPoint) {
    self.undoer.registerUndo(withTarget: self) {
        [oldCenter = self.center] myself in
        myself.setCenterUndoably(oldCenter)
    }
    if self.undoer.isUndoing || self.undoer.isRedoing {
        UIView.animate(withDuration:0.4, delay: 0.1, animations: {
            self.center = newCenter
        })
    } else { // just do it
        self.center = newCenter
    }
}
```

The example shows what the `target:` parameter is for — it's to avoid retain cycles. By passing `self` as the `target:` argument, I can retrieve it as the parameter, which I've called `myself`, in the `handler:` function. Thus, in the body of the `handler:` function, I never have to refer to `self` and there is no retain cycle.

I've also taken advantage of a little-known feature of Swift anonymous functions allowing me to capture the value of `self.center` as it is *now*, as a local value `old-Center`. The reason is that if the anonymous function were to call `setCenter-`

Undoably(myself.center), we'd be using the value that myself.center will have *at undo time*, and would thus be pointlessly setting the center to itself.

Our code works perfectly, but we can go further. So far, we are failing to take full advantage of the fact that we now have the ability to register with the undo manager a full-fledged function body rather than a mere function call. This means that the handler: function can contain *everything* that should happen when undoing, including the animation:

```
self.undoer.registerUndo(withTarget: self) {
    [oldCenter = self.center] myself in
    UIView.animate(withDuration:0.4, delay: 0.1, animations: {
        myself.center = oldCenter
    })
    myself.setCenterUndoably(oldCenter)
}
```

But we can go further still. Let's ask ourselves: Why are we setting self.center here at all? We can do it back in the gesture recognizer's dragging(_:) action method, just as we were doing before we added undo to this app! And in *that* case, why do we need a separate setCenterUndoably method at all? True, we still need *some* function that calls registerUndo with a call to itself, because that's how we get redo registration during undo; but this can be a *local* function inside the dragging(_:) method.

Our dragging(_:) method can thus provide a complete undo implementation *internally*, resulting in a far more legible and encapsulated architecture:

```
@objc func dragging (_ p : UIPanGestureRecognizer) {
    switch p.state {
    case .began:
        self.undoer.beginUndoGrouping()
        fallthrough
    case .began, .changed:
        let delta = p.translation(in:self.superview!)
        var c = self.center
        c.x += delta.x; c.y += delta.y
        func registerForUndo() {
            self.undoer.registerUndo(withTarget: self) {
                [oldCenter = self.center] myself in
                UIView.animate(withDuration:0.4, delay: 0.1, animations: {
                    myself.center = oldCenter
                })
                registerForUndo()
            }
        }
        registerForUndo() // *
        self.center = c // *
        p.setTranslation(.zero, in: self.superview!)
    case .ended, .cancelled:
```

```
                self.undoer.endUndoGrouping()
        default: break
        }
    }
```

Undo Interface

We must also decide how to let the user *request* undo and redo. While I was developing the code from the preceding section, I used two buttons: an Undo button that sent undo to the UndoManager, and a Redo button that sent redo to the UndoManager. This can be a perfectly reasonable interface, but let's talk about some others.

Shake-To-Edit

By default, your app supports *shake-to-edit*. This means that the user can shake the device to bring up an undo/redo interface. We discussed this briefly in Chapter 21. If you don't turn off this feature by setting the shared UIApplication's application-SupportsShakeToEdit property to false, then when the user shakes the device, the runtime walks up the responder chain, starting with the first responder, looking for a responder whose inherited undoManager property returns an actual UndoManager instance. If it finds one, it puts up an alert with an Undo button, a Redo button, or both; if the user taps a button, the runtime communicates directly with that Undo-Manager, calling its undo or redo method.

You will recall what it takes for a UIResponder to be first responder in this sense: it must return true from canBecomeFirstResponder, and it must actually be made first responder through a call to becomeFirstResponder. Let's have MyView satisfy these requirements. For example, we might call becomeFirstResponder at the end of dragging(_:), like this:

```
override var canBecomeFirstResponder : Bool {
    return true
}
@objc func dragging (_ p : UIPanGestureRecognizer) {
    switch p.state {
    // ... the rest as before ...
    case .ended, .cancelled:
        self.undoer.endUndoGrouping()
        self.becomeFirstResponder()
    default: break
    }
}
```

Then, to make shake-to-edit work, we have only to provide a getter for the undo-Manager property that returns our undo manager, self.undoer:

Figure 25-1. The shake-to-edit undo/redo alert

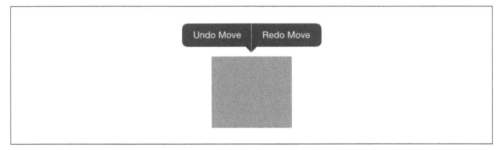

Figure 25-2. The shared menu as an undo/redo interface

```
let undoer = UndoManager()
override var undoManager : UndoManager? {
    return self.undoer
}
```

This works: shaking the device now brings up the undo/redo alert, and its buttons work correctly. However, I don't like the way the buttons are labeled; they just say Undo and Redo. To make this interface more expressive, we should provide a string describing each undoable action. We do that by calling setActionName(_:); we can call it at the same time that we register our undo action:

```
self.undoer.setActionName("Move")
```

Now the undo/redo alert has more informative labels, as shown in Figure 25-1.

Undo Menu

Another possible undo/redo interface is through a menu (Figure 25-2). Personally, I prefer this approach, as I am not fond of shake-to-edit (it seems both violent and unreliable). This is the same menu used by a UITextField or UITextView for displaying the Copy and Paste menu items (Chapter 10). The requirements for summoning this menu are effectively the same as those for shake-to-edit: we need a responder chain with a first responder at the bottom of it. So the code we've just supplied for making MyView first responder remains applicable.

Let's cause the menu to appear in response to a long press on our MyView instance. We'll attach another gesture recognizer to MyView. This will be a UILongPress-GestureRecognizer, whose action method is called longPress(_:). Recall from Chapter 10 how to implement the menu: we get the singleton global UIMenuController object and specify an array of custom UIMenuItems as its menuItems property. We can make the menu appear by sending the UIMenuController the setMenu-Visible(_:animated:) message. But a particular menu item will appear in the menu only if we also return true from canPerformAction(_:withSender:) for that menu item's action. Delightfully, the UndoManager's canUndo and canRedo properties tell us what value canPerformAction(_:withSender:) should return. We can also get the titles for our custom menu items from the UndoManager itself, through its undoMenu-ItemTitle and redoMenuItemTitle properties:

```
@objc func longPress (_ g : UIGestureRecognizer) {
    if g.state == .began {
        let m = UIMenuController.shared
        m.setTargetRect(self.bounds, in: self)
        let mi1 = UIMenuItem(title: self.undoer.undoMenuItemTitle,
            action: #selector(undo))
        let mi2 = UIMenuItem(title: self.undoer.redoMenuItemTitle,
            action: #selector(redo))
        m.menuItems = [mi1, mi2]
        m.setMenuVisible(true, animated:true)
    }
}
override func canPerformAction(_ action: Selector,
    withSender sender: Any?) -> Bool {
        if action == #selector(undo) {
            return self.undoer.canUndo
        }
        if action == #selector(redo) {
            return self.undoer.canRedo
        }
        return super.canPerformAction(action, withSender: sender)
}
@objc func undo(_: Any?) {
    self.undoer.undo()
}
@objc func redo(_: Any?) {
    self.undoer.redo()
}
```

Application Lifetime Events

When your app launches, the UIApplicationMain function creates its one and only UIApplication instance as the shared application object, along with the app delegate, adopting the UIApplicationDelegate protocol (see "How an App Launches" on page 4). The application then proceeds to report *lifetime events* to its delegate through calls to protocol-defined methods; other objects can also register to receive most of these events as notifications.

These fundamental events, notifying you of stages in the lifetime of your app as a whole and giving your code an opportunity to run in response, are extraordinarily important. This appendix is devoted to a survey of them, along with some typical scenarios in which they will arrive.

Application States

In the early days of iOS — before iOS 4 — the lifetime of an app was extremely simple: either it was running or it wasn't. The user tapped your app's icon in the home screen, and your app was launched and began to run. The user used your app for a while. Eventually, the user pressed the Home button (the physical button next to the screen) and your app was terminated — it was no longer running. The user had *quit* your app. Launch, run, quit: that was the entire life cycle of an app. If the user decided to use your app again, the whole cycle started over.

The reason for this simplicity was that, before iOS 4, an iOS device, with its slow processor and its almost brutal paucity of memory and other resources, compensated for its own shortcomings by a simple rule: it could run *only one app at a time*. While your app was running, it occupied not only the entire screen but the vast majority of the device's resources, leaving room only for the system and some hidden built-in processes to support it; it had, in effect, sole and complete control of the device.

Starting in iOS 4, that changed. Apple devised an ingenious architecture whereby, despite the device's limited resources, more than one app could run simultaneously — sort of. The Home button changed its meaning and its effect upon your app: contrary to the naïve perception of some users, the Home button was no longer a Quit button. Nowadays, when the user presses the Home button to leave your app, your app does not die; technically, the Home button does not terminate your app. When your app occupies the entire screen, it is *in the foreground* (or *frontmost*); when some other app proceeds to occupy the entire screen, your app is *backgrounded and suspended*.

Suspension means that your app is essentially freeze-dried; its process still exists, but it isn't actively running, and it isn't getting any events — though notifications can be stored by the system for later delivery in case your app comes to the front once again. And because it isn't running, it isn't using very much of the device's precious resources. Later, when the user returns to your app after having left it to use some other app for a while, your app is found in the *very same state* as when the user left it. The app was not terminated; it simply stopped and froze, and waited in suspended animation. Returning to your app no longer means that your app is *launched*, but merely that it is *resumed*.

All of this is not to say, however, that your app *can't* be terminated. It can be — though not by the user pressing the Home button. For example, the user might switch off the device; *that* will certainly terminate your app. And a savvy user might force-terminate your app from the app switcher. The most common scenario, however, is that the system quietly kills your app while it is suspended. This undermines the app's ability to resume; when the user returns to your app, it *will* have to launch from scratch, just as in the pre–iOS 4 days. The death of your app under these circumstances is rather like that of the scientists killed by HAL 9000 in *2001: A Space Odyssey* — they went to sleep expecting to wake up later, but instead their life-support systems were turned off while they slept. The iOS system's reasons for killing your app are not quite as paranoid as HAL's, but they do have a certain Darwinian ruthlessness: your app, while suspended, continues to occupy a chunk of the device's memory, and the system needs to reclaim that memory so some *other* app can use it.

After the user leaves your app, therefore, one of two things might happen later when the user returns to it. It could be woken and resumed from suspended animation, in the very state that it was in when the user left it, or it could be launched from scratch because it was terminated in the background. It is this bifurcation of your app's possible fates that state saving and restoration, discussed at the end of Chapter 6, is intended to cope with. The idea, in theory, is that your app should behave the same way when it comes to the front, regardless of whether it was terminated or merely suspended. We all know from experience, however, that this goal is difficult to achieve, and Apple's own apps are noteworthy for failing to achieve it; for example, when Apple's iBooks app comes to the front, it is perfectly obvious from its behavior and appearance whether it was terminated or merely suspended in the background.

Over time, successive iOS systems have complicated the picture. A modern iPad that does iPad multitasking (Chapter 9) is capable of running two apps at once: they are both in the foreground at the same time. This seems oddly incoherent; even on the macOS desktop, which has *true* multitasking, usually just one application at a time is in the foreground.

A further complication is that your app can be backgrounded without being suspended. This is a special privilege, accorded in order that your app may perform a limited range of highly focused activities. For example, an app that is playing music or tracking the device's location when it goes into the background may be permitted to continue doing so in the background. In addition, an app that has been suspended can be woken briefly, *remaining in the background*, in order to receive and respond to a message — in order to be told, for example, that the user has crossed a geofence, or that a background download has completed. (See Chapters 14, 21, and 23.)

There is also an intermediate state in which your app can find itself, where it is neither frontmost nor backgrounded. This happens, for example, when the user summons the control center or notification history in front of your app. In such situations, your app may be *inactive* without actually being backgrounded.

Your app's code can thus, in fact, be running even though the app is not frontmost. If your code needs to know the app's state in this regard, it can ask the shared UIApplication object for its `applicationState` (UIApplicationState), which will be one of these:

- `.active`
- `.inactive`
- `.background`

 Your app can opt out of background suspension: you set the "Application does not run in background" key (`UIApplicationExitsOnSuspend`) to YES in your *Info.plist*, and now the Home button *does* terminate your app, just as in the pre–iOS 4 days. It's improbable that you would want to do this, but it could make sense for some apps.

App Delegate Events

The suite of basic application lifetime events that may be sent to your app delegate is surprisingly limited and considerably less informative than one might have hoped. The events are as follows:

`application(_:didFinishLaunchingWithOptions:)`
   The app has started up from scratch. You'll typically perform initializations here. If an app doesn't have a main storyboard, or is ignoring the main storyboard at

launch time, this code must also ensure that the app has a window, set its root view controller, and show the window (see Appendix B).

(Another event, `application(_:willFinishLaunchingWithOptions:)`, arrives even earlier. Its purpose is to allow your app to participate in the state saving and restoration mechanism discussed in Chapter 6.)

`applicationDidBecomeActive(_:)`

The app is now well and truly frontmost. Received after `application(_:did-FinishLaunchingWithOptions:)`. Also received after the end of any situation that caused the app delegate to receive `applicationWillResignActive(_:)`.

`applicationWillResignActive(_:)`

The app is entering a situation where it is neither frontmost nor backgrounded; it will be *inactive*. Perhaps something has blocked the app's interface — for example, the screen has been locked, or the user has summoned the notification history. A local notification alert or an incoming phone call could also cause this event. Whatever the cause, the app delegate will receive `applicationDidBecomeActive(_:)` when this situation ends.

Alternatively, the app may be about to go into the background (and will then probably be suspended); in that case, the next event will be `applicationDidEnterBackground(_:)`.

`applicationDidEnterBackground(_:)`

The application has been backgrounded. Always preceded by `applicationWillResignActive(_:)`.

Your app will then probably be suspended; before that happens, you have a little time to finish up last-minute tasks, such as relinquishing unneeded memory (see Chapter 6), and if you need more time for a lengthy task, you can ask for it (see Chapter 24).

`applicationWillEnterForeground(_:)`

The application was backgrounded, and is now coming back to the front. Always followed by `applicationDidBecomeActive(_:)`. Note that this message is *not* sent on launch, because the app wasn't previously in the background.

`applicationWillTerminate(_:)`

The application is about to be killed dead. Surprisingly, even though every running app will eventually be terminated, it is extremely unlikely that your app will *ever* receive this event (unless it has opted out of background suspension, as I explained earlier). The reason is that, by the time your app is terminated by the system, it is usually already suspended and incapable of receiving events. (I'll mention some exceptional cases in the next section, and see Chapter 14 for another.)

App Lifetime Scenarios

A glance at some typical scenarios will demonstrate the chief ways in which your app delegate will receive app lifetime events. I find it helpful to group these scenarios according to the general behavior of the events.

Major State Changes

During very significant state changes, such as the app launching, being backgrounded, or coming back to the front, the app delegate receives a sequence of events:

The app launches from scratch
Your app delegate receives these messages:

- `application(_:didFinishLaunchingWithOptions:)`
- `applicationDidBecomeActive(_:)`

The user clicks the Home button
If your app was frontmost, your app delegate receives these messages:

- `applicationWillResignActive(_:)`
- `applicationDidEnterBackground(_:)`

The user summons your backgrounded app to the front
Your app delegate receives these messages:

- `applicationWillEnterForeground(_:)`
- `applicationDidBecomeActive(_:)`

If the user summons your backgrounded app to the front indirectly, another delegate message may be sent between these two calls. For example, if the user asks another app to hand a file over to your app (Chapter 22), your app delegate receives the `application(_:open:options:)` call between `applicationWillEnterForeground(_:)` and `applicationDidBecomeActive(_:)`.

The screen is locked
If your app is frontmost, your app delegate receives these messages:

- `applicationWillResignActive(_:)`
- `applicationDidEnterBackground(_:)`

The screen is unlocked
If your app is frontmost, your app delegate receives these messages:

- `applicationWillEnterForeground(_:)`
- `applicationDidBecomeActive(_:)`

Paused Inactivity

Certain user actions effectively pause the foreground-to-background sequence in the middle, leaving the app inactive and capable of being either backgrounded or foregrounded, depending on what the user does next. Thus, when the app becomes active again, it might or might not be coming from a backgrounded state. For example:

The user double-clicks the Home button
> The user can now work in the app switcher interface. If your app is frontmost, your app delegate receives this message:
>
> - `applicationWillResignActive(_:)`

The user, in the app switcher, chooses another app
> If your app was frontmost, your app delegate receives this message:
>
> - `applicationDidEnterBackground(_:)`

The user, in the app switcher, chooses your app
> If your app was the most recently frontmost app, then it was never backgrounded, so your app delegate receives this message:
>
> - `applicationDidBecomeActive(_:)`

The user, in the app switcher, terminates your app
> If your app was the most recently frontmost app, your app delegate receives these messages:
>
> - `applicationDidEnterBackground(_:)`
> - `applicationWillTerminate(_:)`
>
> This is one of the few extraordinary circumstances under which your app can receive `applicationWillTerminate(_:)`, perhaps because it was never backgrounded long enough to be suspended.

The user summons the control center or notification history
> If your app is frontmost, your app delegate receives this message:
>
> - `applicationWillResignActive(_:)`

The user dismisses the control center or notification history
> If your app was frontmost, your app delegate receives this message:
>
> - `applicationDidBecomeActive(_:)`

But if the user has summoned the notification history, there's another possibility: the user might tap a notification alert or a today widget to switch to that app. In that case, your app will continue on to the background, and your app delegate will receive this message:

- `applicationDidEnterBackground(_:)`

The user holds down the screen-lock button
The device offers to shut itself off. If your app is frontmost, your app delegate receives this message:

- `applicationWillResignActive(_:)`

The user, as the device offers to shut itself off, cancels
If your app was frontmost, your app delegate receives this message:

- `applicationDidBecomeActive(_:)`

The user, as the device offers to shut itself off, accepts
If your app was frontmost, the app delegate receives these messages:

- `applicationDidEnterBackground(_:)`
- `applicationWillTerminate(_:)`

Transient Inactivity

There are certain circumstances where your app may become inactive and then active again in quick succession. These have mostly to do with multitasking on the iPad. If this happens, your app delegate may receive these messages:

- `applicationWillResignActive(_:)`
- `applicationDidBecomeActive(_:)`

Here are some examples:

The user summons the dock
The dock is new in iOS 11. The results in my testing are inconsistent. Sometimes the app delegate indicates that we pass through transient inactivity; most of the time, nothing happens. Either way, your app ultimately remains active while the dock is present.

The user drags an app from the dock into slideover or splitscreen position
The results in my testing are similar to the previous case: sometimes there is transient inactivity, sometimes nothing happens, but either way, the app ultimately remains active. That behavior is new in iOS 11. On earlier systems, in slideover mode your app delegate's `applicationWillResignActive(_:)` would

have been called and your app would have remained inactive, and to reach splitscreen mode, the user would have had to pass through slideover mode, causing your app to receive `applicationWillResignActive(_:)` and `application-DidBecomeActive(_:)`.

The user toggles between split sizes
> The app undergoes transient inactivity. As I mentioned in Chapter 9, if your view controller is notified of a change of size and possibly trait collection, this will happen *during* the period of transient inactivity.

Lifetime Event Timing

The app delegate messages may well be interwoven in unexpected ways with the lifetime events received by other objects. View controller lifetime events ("View Controller Lifetime Events" on page 394) are the most notable case in point.

For example, there are circumstances where the root view controller may receive its initial lifetime events, such as `viewDidLoad:` and `viewWillAppear(_:)`, before `application(_:didFinishLaunchingWithOptions:)` has even finished running, which may come as a surprise.

Different systems can also introduce changes in timing. For example, when I started programming iOS, back in the days of iOS 3.2, I noted the opening sequence of events involving the app delegate and the root view controller; they arrived in this order:

1. `application(_:didFinishLaunchingWithOptions:)`

2. `viewDidLoad`

3. `viewWillAppear(_:)`

4. `applicationDidBecomeActive(_:)`

5. `viewDidAppear(_:)`

Relying on that order, I would typically use the root view controller's `viewDid-Appear(_:)` to register for `.UIApplicationDidBecomeActive` in order to be notified of *subsequent* activations of the app.

That worked fine for some years. However, iOS 8 brought with it a momentous change: the app delegate now received `applicationDidBecomeActive(_:)` *after* the root view controller received `viewDidAppear(_:)`, like this:

1. `application(_:didFinishLaunchingWithOptions:)`

2. `viewDidLoad`

3. `viewWillAppear(_:)`

4. `viewDidAppear(_:)`

5. `applicationDidBecomeActive(_:)`

This was a disaster for many of my apps, because the notification I just registered for in `viewDidAppear(_:)` arrived *immediately*.

Then, in iOS 9, the order returned to what it was in iOS 7 and before — knocking my apps into confusion once again.

And *now*, in iOS 11, the order is back to what it was in iOS 8!

Such capricious changes from one system version to the next are likely to pose challenges for the longevity and backward compatibility of your app. The moral is that you should not, as I did, rely upon the timing relationship between lifetime events of different objects.

Some Useful Utility Functions

As you work with iOS and Swift, you'll doubtless develop a personal library of frequently used convenience functions. Here are some of mine. Each of them has come in handy in my own life; I keep them available as user snippets in Xcode so that I can paste them into any project.

Launch Without Main Storyboard

As I explained in Chapter 1, if an app lacks a main storyboard, or if you want to ignore the main storyboard and generate the app's initial interface yourself, configuring the window and supplying the root view controller is up to you. A minimal app delegate class would look something like this:

```
@UIApplicationMain
class AppDelegate : UIResponder, UIApplicationDelegate {
    var window : UIWindow?
    func application(_ application: UIApplication,
        didFinishLaunchingWithOptions launchOptions:
        [UIApplicationLaunchOptionsKey : Any]?) -> Bool {
            self.window = self.window ?? UIWindow()
            self.window!.backgroundColor = .white
            self.window!.rootViewController = ViewController()
            self.window!.makeKeyAndVisible()
            return true
    }
}
```

Core Graphics Initializers

The Core Graphics CGRectMake function needs no argument labels when you call it. Swift cuts off access to this function, leaving only the various CGRect initializers, all of which *do* need argument labels. That's infuriating. We know what each argument signifies, so why clutter the call with labels? The solution is *another* CGRect initializer, *without* labels:

```
extension CGRect {
    init(_ x:CGFloat, _ y:CGFloat, _ w:CGFloat, _ h:CGFloat) {
        self.init(x:x, y:y, width:w, height:h)
    }
}
```

As long as we're doing that, we may as well supply label-free initializers for the three other common Core Graphics structs:

```
extension CGSize {
    init(_ width:CGFloat, _ height:CGFloat) {
        self.init(width:width, height:height)
    }
}
extension CGPoint {
    init(_ x:CGFloat, _ y:CGFloat) {
        self.init(x:x, y:y)
    }
}
extension CGVector {
    init (_ dx:CGFloat, _ dy:CGFloat) {
        self.init(dx:dx, dy:dy)
    }
}
```

Center of a CGRect

One so frequently wants the center point of a CGRect that even the shorthand `CGPoint(rect.midX, rect.midY)` becomes tedious. You can extend CGRect to do the work for you:

```
extension CGRect {
    var center : CGPoint {
        return CGPoint(self.midX, self.midY)
    }
}
```

Adjust a CGSize

There's a CGRect method `insetBy(dx:dy:)`, but there's no comparable method for changing an existing CGSize by a width delta and a height delta. Let's make one:

```
extension CGSize {
    func sizeByDelta(dw:CGFloat, dh:CGFloat) -> CGSize {
        return CGSize(self.width + dw, self.height + dh)
    }
}
```

String Range

String ranges are hard to construct, because they are a range of `String.Index` rather than Int. Let's write a String extension that takes a Character index and count as integers and converts them into either a Swift Range or a Cocoa NSRange. While we're up, let's permit a negative index, something that most modern languages allow:

```
func range(_ start:Int, _ count:Int) -> Range<String.Index> {
    let i = self.index(start >= 0 ?
        self.startIndex :
        self.endIndex, offsetBy: start)
    let j = self.index(i, offsetBy: count)
    return i..<j
}
func nsRange(_ start:Int, _ count:Int) -> NSRange {
    return NSRange(self.range(start,count), in:self)
}
```

Here's some sample input and output:

```
let s = "abcdefg"
let r1 = s.range(2,2)
let r2 = s.range(-3,2)
let r3 = s.nsRange(2,2)
let r4 = s.nsRange(-3,2)

print(s[r1]) // cd
print(s[r2]) // ef
print((s as NSString).substring(with:r3)) // cd
print((s as NSString).substring(with:r4)) // ef
```

Delayed Performance

Delayed performance is of paramount importance in iOS programming, where the interface often needs a moment to settle down before we proceed to the next command. Calling `asyncAfter` is not difficult (Chapter 24), but we can simplify with a utility function:

```
func delay(_ delay:Double, closure: @escaping ()->()) {
    let when = DispatchTime.now() + delay
    DispatchQueue.main.asyncAfter(deadline: when, execute: closure)
}
```

Call it like this:

```
delay(0.4) {
    // do something here
}
```

Dictionary of Views

When you generate constraints from a visual format string by calling NSLayout-Constraint's `constraints(withVisualFormat:options:metrics:views:)`, you need a dictionary of string names and view references as the last argument (Chapter 1). Forming this dictionary is tedious. Let's make it easier.

There are no Swift macros (because there's no Swift preprocessor), so you can't write the equivalent of Objective-C's `NSDictionaryOfVariableBindings`, which forms the dictionary from a literal list of view names. You can, however, generate a dictionary with *fixed* string names, like this:

```
func dictionaryOfNames(_ arr:UIView...) -> [String:UIView] {
    var d = [String:UIView]()
    for (ix,v) in arr.enumerated() {
        d["v\(ix+1)"] = v
    }
    return d
}
```

That utility function takes a list of views and simply makes up new string names for them, of the form `"v1"`, `"v2"`, and so on, in order. Knowing the rule by which the string names are generated, you then use those string names in your visual format strings.

For example, if you generate the dictionary by calling `dictionaryOf-Names(mainview, myLabel)`, then in any visual format string that uses this dictionary as its `views:` dictionary, you will refer to `mainview` by the name `v1` and to `myLabel` by the name `v2`.

Constraint Priority Arithmetic

It is often desired to increment or decrement a constraint's priority in order to prevent layout ambiguity. That used to be easy, because a priority was just a number, but in iOS 11, a constraint priority became a UILayoutPriority struct (Chapter 1). This extension allows a number to be added to a UILayoutPriority struct:

```
extension UILayoutPriority {
    static func +(lhs: UILayoutPriority, rhs: Float) -> UILayoutPriority {
        let raw = lhs.rawValue + rhs
        return UILayoutPriority(rawValue:raw)
    }
}
```

Constraint Issues

These are NSLayoutConstraint class methods aimed at helping to detect and analyze constraint issues (referred to in Chapter 1):

```
extension NSLayoutConstraint {
    class func reportAmbiguity (_ v:UIView?) {
        var v = v
        if v == nil {
            v = UIApplication.shared.keyWindow
        }
        for vv in v!.subviews {
            print("\(vv) \(vv.hasAmbiguousLayout)")
            if vv.subviews.count > 0 {
                self.reportAmbiguity(vv)
            }
        }
    }
    class func listConstraints (_ v:UIView?) {
        var v = v
        if v == nil {
            v = UIApplication.shared.keyWindow
        }
        for vv in v!.subviews {
            let arr1 = vv.constraintsAffectingLayout(for: .horizontal)
            let arr2 = vv.constraintsAffectingLayout(for:.vertical)
            NSLog("\n\n%@\nH: %@\nV:%@", vv, arr1, arr2);
            if vv.subviews.count > 0 {
                self.listConstraints(vv)
            }
        }
    }
}
```

Configure a Value Class at Point of Use

A recurring pattern in Cocoa is that a value class instance is created and configured beforehand for one-time use. Here's a case in point:

```
let para = NSMutableParagraphStyle()
para.headIndent = 10
para.firstLineHeadIndent = 10
para.tailIndent = -10
para.lineBreakMode = .byWordWrapping
para.alignment = .center
para.paragraphSpacing = 15
content.addAttribute(
    .paragraphStyle,
    value:para, range:NSMakeRange(0,1))
```

That feels clunky, procedural, and wasteful. First we create the NSMutableParagraph-Style; then we set its properties; then we use it once; then we throw it away.

It would be clearer and more functional, as well as reflecting the natural order of thought, if the creation and configuration of `para` could happen just at the actual moment when we *need* this object, namely when we supply the `value:` argument. Here's a generic function that permits us to do that:

```
func lend<T> (_ closure: (T)->()) -> T where T:NSObject {
    let orig = T()
    closure(orig)
    return orig
}
```

Now we can express ourselves like this:

```
content.addAttribute(.paragraphStyle,
    value:lend { (para:NSMutableParagraphStyle) in
        para.headIndent = 10
        para.firstLineHeadIndent = 10
        para.tailIndent = -10
        para.lineBreakMode = .byWordWrapping
        para.alignment = .center
        para.paragraphSpacing = 15
    }, range:NSMakeRange(0,1))
```

Drawing Into an Image Context

My original goal was to encapsulate the clunky, boilerplate, imperative-programming dance of drawing into an image graphics context (Chapter 2): begin an image graphics context; draw into it; extract the image; end the context. In its place, I wrote a utility function that did everything but the drawing, which would be provided as a function parameter.

Then iOS 10 introduced UIGraphicsImageRenderer, which works in exactly that way. But now there's a new problem: what if you want backward compatibility? So now my utility function combines the old implementation with the new one:

```
func imageOfSize(_ size:CGSize, opaque:Bool = false,
    closure: () -> ()) -> UIImage {
        if #available(iOS 10.0, *) {
            let f = UIGraphicsImageRendererFormat.default()
            f.opaque = opaque
            let r = UIGraphicsImageRenderer(size: size, format: f)
            return r.image {_ in closure()}
        } else {
            UIGraphicsBeginImageContextWithOptions(size, opaque, 0)
            closure()
            let result = UIGraphicsGetImageFromCurrentImageContext()!
```

```
                UIGraphicsEndImageContext()
                return result
            }
    }
```

You call it like this (using my label-free Core Graphics initializers, of course):

```
let im = imageOfSize(CGSize(100,100)) {
    let con = UIGraphicsGetCurrentContext()!
    con.addEllipse(in: CGRect(0,0,100,100))
    con.setFillColor(UIColor.blue.cgColor)
    con.fillPath()
}
```

Finite Repetition of an Animation

This is a solution to the problem of how to repeat a view animation a fixed number of times without using begin-and-commit syntax (Chapter 4). My approach is to employ tail recursion and a counter to chain the individual animations. The delay call unwinds the call stack and works around possible drawing glitches:

```
extension UIView {
    class func animate(times:Int,
        duration dur: TimeInterval,
        delay del: TimeInterval,
        options opts: UIViewAnimationOptions,
        animations anim: @escaping () -> (),
        completion comp: ((Bool) -> ())?) {
            func helper(_ t:Int,
                _ dur: TimeInterval,
                _ del: TimeInterval,
                _ opt: UIViewAnimationOptions,
                _ anim: @escaping () -> (),
                _ com: ((Bool) -> ())?) {
                    UIView.animate(withDuration: dur,
                        delay: del, options: opt,
                        animations: anim, completion: { done in
                            if com != nil {
                                com!(done)
                            }
                            if t > 0 {
                                delay(0) {
                                    helper(t-1, dur, del, opt, anim, com)
                                }
                            }
                    })
            }
            helper(times-1, dur, del, opts, anim, comp)
    }
}
```

The calling syntax is exactly like ordering a UIView animation in its full form, except that there's an initial `times` parameter:

```swift
let opts = UIViewAnimationOptions.autoreverse
let xorig = self.v.center.x
UIView.animate(times:3, duration:1, delay:0, options:opts, animations:{
    self.v.center.x += 100
    }, completion:{ _ in
        self.v.center.x = xorig
})
```

Remove Multiple Indexes From Array

It is often convenient to collect the indexes of items to be deleted from an array, and then to delete those items. We must be careful to sort the indexes in decreasing numeric order first, because array indexes will be off by one after an item at a lower index is removed:

```swift
extension Array {
    mutating func remove(at ixs:Set<Int>) -> () {
        for i in Array<Int>(ixs).sorted(by:>) {
            self.remove(at:i)
        }
    }
}
```

How Asynchronous Works

Beginners sometimes don't quite understand what it means for code to run *asynchronously*. Asynchronous code runs at an *indefinite time*. It runs *out of order* with respect to the surrounding code.

Consider the following (and see Chapter 23):

```
func doSomeNetworking() {
    // ... prepare url ...
    let session = URLSession.shared ❶
    let task = session.downloadTask(with:url) { loc, resp, err in ❷
        // ... completion function body goes here ... ❹
    }
    task.resume() ❸
}
```

The method downloadTask(with:completionHandler:) calls its completion function asynchronously. It calls it when the networking finishes — and networking takes time. The order in which the chunks of code run is the numerical order of the numbered lines:

❶ The code before the call.

❷ The call itself.

❸ The code after the call, including the return from the surrounding function doSomeNetworking. Your code has now come to a complete stop!

❹ The code inside the completion function. This is the asynchronous code. It runs later — possibly *much* later, and certainly well after the surrounding function doSomeNetworking has returned.

This means that the surrounding function *cannot return a value from the asynchronous code*. Beginners might try to write this sort thing:

```
func doSomeNetworking() -> UIImage? { // vain attempt to return an image
    // ... prepare url ...
    var image : UIImage? = nil
    let session = URLSession.shared
    let task = session.downloadTask(with:url) { loc, resp, err in
        if let loc = loc, let d = try? Data(contentsOf:loc) {
            let im = UIImage(data:d)
            image = im // too late!
        }
    }
    task.resume()
    return image // can only be nil!
}
```

The author of that code seems to be hoping that the data will be downloaded and turned into an image, and that image will be *returned* from the surrounding function doSomeNetworking. But that can never work, because the last line, return image, will execute *before* the line image = im has ever had a chance to execute. Thus, the returned UIImage is useless: it will always be nil.

Beginners might then think: So maybe I can *wait* until my asynchronous code has finished. That is *wrong!* Asynchronous means you *don't* wait. When you obtain a value in some asynchronous code and you want to do something with it, do it *in* the asynchronous code.

Here, for example, our goal is to update the interface with the downloaded image:

```
func doSomeNetworking() {
    // ... prepare url ...
    let session = URLSession.shared
    let task = session.downloadTask(with:url) { loc, resp, err in
        if let loc = loc, let d = try? Data(contentsOf:loc) {
            let im = UIImage(data:d)
            DispatchQueue.main.async {
                self.iv.image = im // update the interface _here_
            }
        }
    }
    task.resume()
}
```

That's an excellent solution. But now let's say you really do want to *hand back* a value from the asynchronous code to *whoever called the surrounding method* in the first place, leaving it up to the *caller* what to do with it. We've already established that you can't *return* the value. But you can *call back* to whoever called the surrounding method in order to hand them the value. That is the strategy used throughout Cocoa; it *propagates asynchronousness*.

A typical architecture is that you allow the caller to hand you *a completion function*. Inside your asynchronous code, you *call* the caller's completion function — like this:

```
func doSomeNetworking(callBackWithImage: @escaping (UIImage?) -> ()) {
    let s = "https://www.apeth.net/matt/images/phoenixnewest.jpg"
    let url = URL(string:s)!
    let session = URLSession.shared
    let task = session.downloadTask(with:url) { loc, resp, err in
        if let loc = loc, let d = try? Data(contentsOf:loc) {
            let im = UIImage(data:d)
            callBackWithImage(im) // call the caller's completion function
        }
    }
    task.resume()
}
```

Let's look at the example from the caller's point of view. The caller of doSome-Networking(callBackWithImage:) passes in a completion function that does whatever the caller ultimately wants done. Here, once again, our goal is to update the interface with the downloaded image:

```
doSomeNetworking { im in // completion function
    DispatchQueue.main.async {
        self.iv.image = im
    }
}
```

That completion function, too, is asynchronous! The caller doesn't know when or whether this completion function will be called back; perhaps there aren't even any rules about what thread it will be called back on. But when and if it *is* called back, the image will arrive as its parameter — and now the caller can dispose of it as desired.

Index

R

range, string, 1111
reachability, 1037
reading a file, 987
rectangle, rounded, 145
redraw moment, 152, 183
redrawing with animation, 179
reference, storyboard, 387
refresh control, 495
relationship (see segue)
reminders (see calendar)
Reminders app, 903
removeAtIndexes, 1116
resizable image, 81
resizing interface, responding to, 300, 586
resolution, 77, 94, 133
resources
    depending on size class, 78
    differing on iPad, 77
    in app bundle, 76
    network-based, 673, 1035
    on-demand, 1056
responder chain, xx
    gesture recognizers, 245
    nil-targeted actions, 651
    shake events, 963
    undo, 1095
    view controllers, 276, 283
    views, 3
    walking, 747
restoration identifier, 406
restoration identifier path, 411
restoration of state, 404
retain cycle, xx, 219, 379, 398, 682, 684, 778, 1047, 1093
Retina display (see screen, high-resolution)
root view, 5
root view controller, 277
rotation, 22, 302, 306
    (see also orientation)
    bar height, 727
    compensatory, 303
    drawing, 116
    forced, 303, 326
    interface, 302-312, 326
    layer, 139
    presented view controllers, 326
    responding to, 300, 309
    view, 19

rounded rectangle, 145
route, 943
row of a table, 464
RTF files, 626, 673

S

Safari view controller, 686
safe area, 42, 298
sandbox, 983
saving data (see files)
saving state, 404, 995
scene, 294, 379
screen coordinates, 17
screen, high-resolution, 77, 94, 133
screen, user locks or unlocks, 1103
screens, multiple, 4
scroll indicators, 439
scroll views, 425-457
    autolayout, 427
    content inset, 435
    content layout guide, 428
    content size, 426
    content view, 429
    delegate, 449
    floating subviews, 455
    gesture recognizers, 455
    inset, 437
    keyboard dismissal, 641
    nib-instantiated, 433
    paging, 440
    scrolling, 438
    stuttering, 456
    tiling, 442
    touches, 452
    underlapping bars, 436
    zooming, 444
scrolling in response to keyboard, 638
search bar, 699
    in navigation bar, 516
    in table view, 512
    scope buttons, 514, 702
    top bar, 726
search field (see search bar)
searching, interface for, 510
secondary view controller, 567
section data model, 489
segmented control, 716
segue, 295, 382-394
    action, 382, 384

About the Author

Matt Neuburg started programming computers in 1968, when he was 14 years old, as a member of a literally underground high school club, which met once a week to do timesharing on a bank of PDP-10s by way of primitive teletype machines. He also occasionally used Princeton University's IBM-360/67, but gave it up in frustration when one day he dropped his punch cards. He majored in Greek at Swarthmore College, and received his PhD from Cornell University in 1981, writing his doctoral dissertation (about Aeschylus) on a mainframe. He proceeded to teach Classical languages, literature, and culture at many well-known institutions of higher learning, most of which now disavow knowledge of his existence, and to publish numerous scholarly articles unlikely to interest anyone. Meanwhile he obtained an Apple IIc and became hopelessly hooked on computers again, migrating to a Macintosh in 1990. He wrote some educational and utility freeware, became an early regular contributor to the online journal *TidBITS*, and in 1995 left academe to edit *MacTech* magazine. In August 1996 he became a freelancer, which means he has been looking for work ever since. He is the author of *Frontier: The Definitive Guide*, *REALbasic: The Definitive Guide*, and *AppleScript: The Definitive Guide*.

Colophon

The animal on the cover of *Programming iOS 11* is a kingbird, one of the 13 species of North American songbirds making up the genus *Tyrannus*. A group of kingbirds is called a "coronation," a "court," or a "tyranny."

Kingbirds eat insects, which they often catch in flight, swooping from a perch to grab the insect midair. They may also supplement their diets with berries and fruits. They have long, pointed wings, and males perform elaborate aerial courtship displays.

Both the genus name (meaning "tyrant" or "despot") and the common name ("kingbird") refer to these birds' aggressive defense of their territories, breeding areas, and mates. They have been documented attacking red-tailed hawks (which are more than twenty times their size), knocking bluejays out of trees, and driving away crows and ravens. (For its habit of standing up to much larger birds, the gray kingbird has been adopted as a Puerto Rican nationalist symbol.)

"Kingbird" most often refers to the Eastern kingbird (*T. tyrannus*), an average-size kingbird (7.5–9 inches long, wingspan 13–15 inches) found all across North America. This common and widespread bird has a dark head and back, with a white throat, chest, and belly. Its red crown patch is rarely seen. Its high-pitched, buzzing, stuttering sounds have been described as resembling "sparks jumping between wires" or an electric fence.

The cover image is from *Cassell's Natural History*. The cover fonts are URW Typewriter and Guardian Sans. The text font is Adobe Minion Pro; the heading font is Adobe Myriad Condensed; and the code font is Dalton Maag's Ubuntu Mono.

Learn from experts.
Find the answers you need.

Sign up for a **10-day free trial** to get **unlimited access** to all of the content on Safari, including Learning Paths, interactive tutorials, and curated playlists that draw from thousands of ebooks and training videos on a wide range of topics, including data, design, DevOps, management, business—and much more.

Start your free trial at:
oreilly.com/safari

(No credit card required.)

1-19-18

$69.99

CPSIA information can be obtaine
at www.ICGtesting.com
Printed in the USA
BVHW02s0824151217
502502BV00001B/1

781491 999226